African Development
Indicators

United Nations
Development Programme
New York, N.Y.

●

The World Bank
Washington, D.C.

This volume was prepared by the Economics and Finance Division,
Africa Technical Department, of the World Bank

The complete backlist of publications from the World Bank is shown in the annual *Index of Publications*, which contains an alphabetical title list and indexes of subjects, authors, and countries and regions; it is of value principally to libraries and institutional purchasers. The latest edition is available free of charge from the Publications Distribution Unit, The World Bank, 1818 H Street, N.W., Washington, D.C. 20433, U.S.A., or from Publications, The World Bank, 66, avenue d'Iena, 75116 Paris, France

Library of Congress Cataloging-in-Publication Data

African development indicators.
     p.   cm.
    "Builds upon the work undertaken in preparing African economic and financial data by extending coverage by three years and by including many more variablesk"-- Pref.
    Includes bibliographical references (p.   ).
    ISBN 0-8213-2044-0
    1. Economic indicators--Africa. 2. Africa--Economic conditions--1960— --Statistics. 3. Social indicators--Africa.
4. Africa--Social conditions--1960— --Statistics. I. United Nations Development Programme. II. International Bank for Reconstruction and Development.
HC800.A5653 1992
330.96--dc20

92-3997
CIP

Contents

Part II: Social and Environmental Data

Attribution

This book has been prepared by a team led by Mark Gallagher and Gilbert Uwujaren, and comprising Marcelo Baptista, Yonas Biru, Marian Mabel, Philemon Oyewole, and Cliff Papik, under the general guidance of Luis Ernesto Derbez. Alicia Hetzer and Virginia Hitchcock provided assistance in editing and formatting. Mavita Gomes provided secretarial support.

Members of an advisory group reviewed an early draft of the book. A subgroup of the advisory group met for two days to discuss the technical and presentational aspects of the project. Those participating in the two-day conference included Sam Adamu, Biyi Afonja, Robert Allison, Morton Brown, Ramesh Chander, J.O. Iyaniwura, and Robert Tendere; Graham Eele and John Mason provided input but were unable to attend the conference.

This project has also benefited from comments provided by Stephen Adei, Charles Becker, Magnus Blomstrom, Henry Bruton, Mark Gersovitz, Michael Hurd, Phillip LeBel, Robert Lipsey, Malcolm McPherson, Mohammed Shibli, Johnathan Skinner, Christopher Udry, and Jennifer Widner.

In addition, several World Bank staff have provided information on their countries of specialization or economic sector work. Other staff have aided in the design of this volume, data definitions, table formatting, and general planning.

Data for this book were collected under a UNDP project to monitor development programs and aid flows in Africa, executed by the World Bank. This project was implemented in the Economics and Finance Division of the Africa Technical Department, with ongoing support from the International Economics Department.

Preface

In June 1986 the United Nations General Assembly, in a Special Session, adopted a Program of Action for African Economic Recovery and Development. This action taken by the General Assembly was in response to the situation in Africa, widely perceived in and out of Africa as a deepening crisis. The program called on Africans and the international community to take measures to improve opportunities and prospects for economic growth and social development. Since then, there has been a keen interest in monitoring the implementation of this UN program.

In 1989 the United Nations Development Programme and the World Bank jointly published *African Economic and Financial Data*, which was a provisional data book intended to provide Africans and those interested in Africa with a consistent and convenient set of data to monitor development programs and aid flows in the region. It was published to broaden access to information and as a step in improving the quality and availability of the data.

African Development Indicators builds upon the work undertaken in preparing the previous volume by extending coverage by three years and by including many more variables. In particular, *African Development Indicators* not only extends coverage of basic national accounts information and other economic and financial data, but also includes social statistics (namely, education, health and demographics) as well as statistics on the environment and natural resources and on labor markets.

This data book contains data that are in the first instance collected by national statistical services in Africa. Additionally, many international agencies collect or compile data on African countries. This data book draws heavily from such sources. However, flaws in those data, missing data and inconsistent reporting have, in many instances, led to supplementing such data by drawing upon other means of estimations. Some of the methods used in this volume differ from methods used in other sources. Throughout the book, in introductions to chapters or in technical notes, such differences in methodologies are discussed. Users are then free to chose the data sources and methods they feel are most appropriate.

It is intended that this data book serve as a prime source of information on Africa and that its wide dissemination to African and non-African analysts and policymakers will help set Africa on a path of sustainable economic development and rising welfare.

Acronyms and Abbreviations

BIS Bank for International Settlements
CFA Communauté financière Africaine (franc zone)
c.i.f. Cost, insurance, freight
CMEA Council for Mutual Economic Assistance
CPI Consumer price index
DAC Development Assistance Committee of the OECD
DOD Debt outstanding and disbursed
DOU Debt outstanding, including undisbursed
DRS Debtor reporting system
ECA Economic Commission for Africa
FAO U.N. Food and Agriculture Organization
f.o.b. Free on board
GDI Gross domestic investment
GDP Gross domestic product
GDS Gross domestic savings
GFS *Government Finance Statistics*
GNFS Goods and nonfactor services
GNP Gross national product
GNS Gross national savings
IBRD International Bank for Reconstruction and Development
ICP U.N. International Comparison Project
IDA International Development Association
IECDI Debt and International Finance Division in the International Economics Department of the World Bank

IFAD International Fund for Agricultural Development
IFS *International Financial Statistics*
IMF International Monetary Fund
LIBOR London interbank offered rate
ODA Official development assistance
OECD Organisation for Economic Co-operation and Development
OPEC Organization of Petroleum Exporting Countries
PE Public enterprise
PPP Purchasing power parity
SAF Structural adjustment facility
SNA System of National Accounts
SDR Special drawing right
TDS Total debt service
UNCTAD United Nations Conference on Trade and Development
UNESCO United Nations Educational, Scientific and Cultural Organization
UNICEF United Nations Children's Fund
UNDP United Nations Development Programme
UNPAAERD United Nations Programme of Action for African Economic Recovery and Development
XGS Exports of goods and services

Introduction

The task of monitoring Africa's development progress and aid flows requires basic empirical data that can be readily used by analysts. This volume consolidates relevant data for 1980-90, and, in a few cases, for years before 1980. The data in this document are grouped into two parts—economic and financial data and social and environmental data—and 14 chapters: background data, national accounts; prices and exchange rates, money and banking, external sector; external debt and related flows, government finance, agriculture, industry, public enterprises, labor force and employment, aid flows, social indicators, and environmental indicators. Part II -- social and environment indicators -- is new. Part I contains several indicators that were not included in the first data volume published in 1989. Each chapter begins with a brief introduction on the nature of the data and their limitations, followed by a set of statistical tables and by technical notes that define the indicators and identify specific sources.

A companion set of diskettes (expected to be available later through the World Bank) will extend many of the time series back to the 1970s and, in some cases, the 1960s. These longer series will provide analysts with data needed to help place the 1980s and especially the most recent years in an historical context.

This issue includes data on social and environmental indicators, unlike the previous edition. Throughout this volume the symbol ".." indicates that data are not available or not applicable. A zero indicates either zero value or an insignificant value, that is, less than one half of the smallest unit shown.

Many of the numbers that were published in the *African Economic and Financial Data (AEFD)* differ from the numbers published here. There are several reasons for this. First, updating economic and financial data never entails solely adding new data to old series. Instead, new estimates and revisions are the normal course to follow. As was stated in *AEFD*, many estimates had to be considered preliminary. Much effort has been made to improve these estimates. Second, the World Bank's basic data base, the Bank Economic and Social Data base (BESD), has been rescaled so that all economic data are now based on 1987 exchange rates and prices. *AEFD* was based on 1980 exchange rates and prices. This rescaling causes changes not just in the levels of economic variables but also in calculations of growth rates, since rescaling alters calculations of the foreign sectors, as well as other sectors, in national GDPs.

Many international data bases provide economic and financial data based on 1980, 1985, or even 1990 exchange rates and prices. Indeed, there are even some World Bank puiblications based on 1985 prevailing rates. The World Bank has, however, standardized its economic and financial data on 1987 rates since it has been decided that 1985, due to radical swings in exchange rates and commodity prices, was a year of great distortion and disequilibium in international financial and commodity markets. It is believed that 1987 prevailing rates provide a more realistic basis for making international comparisons of economic and financial statistics.

Considerable effort has been made to standardize the data and to harmonize related data sets drawn from diverse sources. Because statistical methods, coverage, practices, and definitions differ widely, full comparability cannot be assured, and the indicators must be interpreted with care. In addition, the statistical systems in many developing economies are still weak, and this affects the availability and reliability of their data. Moreover, intercountry and intertemporal comparisons always involve complex technical problems, which have no full and unequivocal solution.

The data are drawn from sources thought to be the most authoritative, but many of them are subject to considerable margins of error. To provide reasonably timely data required for meaningful monitoring the World Bank, the International Monetary Fund (IMF) and other agencies sometimes make estimates on the basis of available secondary information to fill critical gaps in national reporting, especially for the most recent years when data cannot be readily produced by national statistical sources. Nonetheless, data gaps exist for many indicators, and some (mainly small) countries are covered only sporadically.

In several instances the staff preparing this volume have been able to estimate values based upon other available data, consultation with experts on the particular item, accounting procedures, or by interpolation. These estimated values are given given in *italic* type.

Readers are urged to take these limitations into account in using the data and interpreting the indicators, particularly when making comparisons across economies. Weaknesses in the data point to the need for strengthened statistical systems throughout the region.

The data are arranged by indicator to facilitate cross-country comparisons. For country-specific work, data can be arranged to show all indicators

together for each country. Other sources of data, drawn on for this volume, that arrange data in this way include the *World Tables*, published by the World Bank.

The statistical tables are usually arranged as time series, by country and by country groups. The largest country group is All Africa, consisting of two subgroups: North Africa and Sub-Saharan Africa. In the AFED the Sub-Saharan countries were grouped into low-income countries (defined here as countries eligible for credits from the International Development Association [IDA] but not for loans from the International Bank for Reconstruction and Development [IBRD]). All other Sub-Saharan countries are defined as middle-income, either oil importers or oil exporters. Oil-exporting countries were shown separately because the large swings in the price of oil have a strong impact on their terms of trade, total output, and income levels. In the durrent book, the groupings have been simplified by eliminating the IDA eligible category as well as the middle income (oil exporter or importer) categproes. Data for South Africa are not included in the table but are shown separately below the All Africa group.

The country groups as defined here are considered useful analytically and reflect, in part, a widely used classification. Other groups, based, for example, on geographical location or on other measures of income and development, are often used by other agencies. Countries were classified according to figures from early 1991, when preparation of this volume began. This classification will not consistently reflect the gross national product (GNP) per capita figures in the first table, which is based on the most recent (early 1991) estimates available.

Annual data shown for country groups are totals or averages for the countries included in the group. Most averages are weighted according to the relative importance of the countries in the group total for that indicator, based on simple addition across countries when the indicator is expressed in reasonably comparable units. Group averages for analytical ratios (like imports to gross domestic product [GDP]) are usually calculated from the group totals for both the numerator and the denominator, which is analytically equivalent to calculating weighted averages, where the weight for each country is its share in the group total for the denominator. (Alternatively, other weighted averages of analytical ratios for country groups could be calculated from the country ratios, which may give different results, sometimes significantly so, depending on what variable is used to assign country weights.) A few averages are arithmetic, that is, each country is assigned equal weight, when it is appropriate to treat the experiences of different countries equally in determining a representative value for the group.

Summary statistics calculated from time series data for both countries and country groups are either average annual growth rates in real terms or, when annual data are expressed as ratios, simple (unweighted) multiyear averages. Summary statistics are often shown for 1980-85 because this period covers the first half of the 1980s, immediately before the United Nations adopted its program of action for Africa, and 1986-90 (or most recent date for which data is available) to coincide with the United Nations Programme of Action for African Economic Recovery and Development (UNPAAERD) period. Single-year growth rates are percentage changes in constant price series. Average annual growth rates for periods longer than one year are calculated from constant price series using the least-squares method. The leastsquares growth rate, r, is estimated by fitting a least-squares linear regression trend line to the logarithmic annual values of the variable in the relevant period. More specifically, the regression equation takes the form: $\log X_t = a + bt + e_t$, where this is equivalent to the logarithmic transformation of the compound growth rate equation, $X_t = X_o(1 + r)^t$. In these equations X is the variable, t is time, and $a = \log X_o$ and $b = \log (1 + r)$ are the parameters to be estimated; e is the error term. If b^* is the least squares estimate of b, then the annual average growth rate, r, is obtained as [antilog (b^*)] - 1 and multiplied by 100 to express it in percentage terms. The least-squares growth rate dampens the influence of exceptional values, particularly at the end points. Other methods could be used to compute growth rates, including simple averages of annual percentage changes or

annual average compound growth rates between the beginning and end of the series.

When values are missing for a country or a year, estimates are made for calculating the group total or average to maintain the same country composition of the groups through time. (But the estimated values are not shown separately in the tables for the countries with missing data.) These estimates are made, and the group statistics shown, only if the countries for which data are available for a given year account for at least two-thirds of the full group, as defined by benchmarks in 1987. (These benchmarks are either the indicator being aggregated or, if data for it are unavailable for all countries in 1987, GNP as a proxy). Procedurally, the method estimates values for a country in years with missing data from actual values in other years on the basis of the annual trends for all other countries in the group that have available data. Other methods may give somewhat different results. This procedure, which was used only for country groups for the national accounts and the balance of payments, is a relatively straight forward approach, which is useful in summarizing data files covering several countries and years. It is standard for many World Bank statistical publications.

Estimating missing country data is necessary to compute averages or totals for groups that are comparable across years despite myriad problems with country data. But the estimating process has limitations. Nothing meaningful can be deduced about actual behavior in countries with missing data by working back from group indicators that include estimates for the missing data. The weighting process may result in discrepancies between overall totals shown for country groups and the summation of available data shown for countries in the respective groups. National accounting identities may not be maintained for group totals because the estimates of missing data for each component of national accounts are made independently. The method used here assumes that countries without current or full historical data series experience, for years when their data are missing, the same trends as other countries in the group for which data are available; but this may not always be the case. The greater the length of time between the current and the base year, the less the benchmark weights are likely to be representative of the current year, which could affect both the quality of the actual estimates and whether or not they are made.

The data must be qualified in other respects. Indicators in this volume generally follow standard definitions, but some differ in exact definition, coverage, and scope. The data presented here may differ from those found in other sources depending on when the data were compiled. The data in this volume generally reflect the information available in late 1990 to early 1991, depending on the chapter. Because data are continually updated, the statistics here may be different from those in other publications. In general, data series for national accounts, debt, and some trade data were generated at the end of 1990; balance of payments and other data were generated in early or mid-1991. However, for any individual country, the data series may still include earlier estimates.

To facilitate cross-country comparisons, values of many national series have been converted from the national currencies to U.S. dollars. Except for GNP per capita, these conversions reflect average annual official exchange rates (or, in a few cases where the exchange rate is egregiously out of line, an alternative conversion factor, as discussed in Chapter 2). The dollar values will be biased upward—in an economic sense — to the extent that domestic currencies are overvalued relative to the dollar.

The use of official exchange rates to convert national currency figures to the U.S. dollar does not attempt to measure the relative domestic purchasing powers of currencies. The U.N. International Comparison Program (ICP) has developed measures of real GDP on an internationally comparable scale using purchasing power parities (PPPS) instead of exchange rates as conversion factors. The ICP has now covered more than 70 countries in five phases at five-year intervals, including 23 in Africa in 1985. However, exchange rates remain the only generally available means of converting GNP and other national economic indicators from national currencies to U.S. dollars.

The chapter introductions and technical notes give details on when the data were compiled and other specific data limitations. Further

information is also available from the data sources and through the references listed at the end of the volume.

The rebasing of the national accounts to 1987 from the previous 1980 base year will affect computation of growth rates and may somewhat reduce comparability with the previous volume for indicators involving real GDP.

This database was originally designed to meet the monitoring needs of the United Nations Secretary General, who was required to report on the implementation and results of the UN Program of Action for African Economic Recovery and Development (UNPAAERD). Reporting on the UNPAAERD has been on a "pan-African" basis, with the experiences of African countries aggregated into a single analytical unit. While such pan-African analysis has met the general requirements of the UN General Assembly, data users are cautioned about the pitfalls they are likely to encounter in such analyses. These pitfalls fall into three broad categories: aggregation procedures, cross-country comparisons, and mathematical aspects of aggregations.

Aggregation procedures that treat Africa as a single economy or ignore the range and great variance in individual economies can lead to inappropriate and incorrect conclusions. The primary difficulty is that it makes little sense to consider these individual countries collectively as a single unit. Each country has its own set of institutions and policies. Each country has its own government, which sets policies on government spending, taxation, external borrowing, and foreign exchange relations (not withstanding the CFA countries). In addition, each government poses differing restriction on private economic activities. Some countries, such as Mauritius, allow the private sector to flourish and serve as the country's primary engine of economic growth. This can be compared with Ethiopia, where the private sector has been tightly controlled, and often discouraged, by deliberate government policies.

Ignoring the very wide range of experiences in Africa can lead to inappropriate or statistically insupportable conclusions. For instance, while the international terms of trade for African countries during the UNPAAERD program (1986-90) experienced some deterioration, when one considers the international terms of trade for Sub-Saharan countries excluding Nigeria, we see the terms of trade actually improved by about 4 percent a year. Because of the great weight of Nigeria in African statistics, events affecting Nigeria tend to overshadow events in much of the rest of the continent. In addition, the great range in economic variables across countries also makes broad statements misleading and less than useful. For instance, although on average GDP growth during 1986-90 was somewhat slower than population growth, in 1990 GDP grew at 7.8 percent in Lesotho compared with a decline of 6.1 percent in the Cote d' Ivoire. Such wide ranges in economic performance and terms of trade suggest that serious investigation into the relationships between economic performance, policy reform, and the external environment should be conducted country by country or variable by variable, that is, we can relate changes in a variable in a particular country with other changes in that country. At a minimum, the divergent experiences and the wide range of experiences of African economies must be taken into account.

Cross-country comparison among African countries remains difficult even when the ranges and varying experiences mentioned above are taken into account. For instance, a study of the education systems in five African countries (Ogbu and Gallagher 1991) indicates the varying degree to which countries rely upon private schools and community inputs to provide primary schooling to their children. Simple comparisons of education spending levels, or even the rate of change in these spending levels, can cause the unwary to arrive at faulty conclusions about the state of educational systems in Africa. Other institutional differences exist for other sectors. For instance, in Ethiopia most modern medical care is provided by government hospitals and clinics, whereas in Senegal Catholic health facilities provide the greatest access to medical care for the country's poor. Thus, deterioration of medical spending by government in Ethiopia can be expected to have more immediate impact on the welfare of the poor than reduced spending on health by the government of Senegal.

A number of mathematical issues arise in pan-African analysis. It is not at all clear how to best average growth rates in different variables for several countries over time. In this volume indicators of welfare, such as GDP growth, are averaged according to each country's relative weight. At the same time, policy-related indicators, such as the share of government spending in the economy, are unweighted. Deciding which procedure to use is not always straightforward. However, even when we are sure whether to treat an indicator of welfare or policy, it becomes less clear what should be the best procedure for grouping averages. Should numbers be indexed and averaged, before growth rates are calculated? Or should growth rates be calculated for each country and then averaged? The estimate arrived at will very much depend upon the choice of method, yet we are left without guidelines as to the optimal choice. The problems are illustrated in the table below.

Country	1981	1982	1983	1984	1985	1986	Average growth	A,B, C average
A	8	12	13	14	15	16	12.8	
B	12	11	12	15	11	15	3.9	
C	55	50	56	55	50	45	-2.9	4.6
Average	25	24	27	28	25	25	0.6	
Index nos	1981	1982	1983	1984	1985	1986		
A	100	150	163	175	188	200	12.8	
B	100	92	100	125	92	125	3.9	
C	100	91	102	100	91	82	-2.9	4.6
Average	100	111	121	133	123	136	5.7	

Clearly the choice of aggregation greatly affects the resulting calculation of average growth. Calculating a period growth rate for the raw data series in the top half of the table and then averaging these growth rates yields an average growth rate for all the series of 4.6 percent. Yet, if the average value for these series are taken annually and then the average growth rate for the entire period is taken (as is done for many of the policy indicators), then the average growth rate is 0.6 percent. Yet more ways exist to calculate the average growth rate for these three series. If the observations are indexed, as found in the second half of the table, the indexing does not affect growth rate calculations for any single series, but taking the average value of the series each year and then calculating the average growth rate for this average index series results in a growth rate calculation of 5.7 percent. There is no clear-cut answer as to which aggregation method is best, but these four different methods arrive at answers

ranging from 0.6 to 6.5 percent. Obviously, if such aggregate growth rates must be calculated extreme care must be taken in explaining the choice of method.

In short, this database provides a useful starting place for monitoring African economic development, growth, foreign aid, and international balances. Yet, to adequately analyze African economic performance, considerable investigation into the specific details and developments of Africa's economies is necessary for the analysis to be meaningful. Africa should not be treated as a single, homogenous entity. To do so would obfuscate the great diversity of the continent. Issues related to institutional differences are extremely important and complicate any sort of pan-African analysis.

This data volume is meant to provide a starting point for rigorous analysis of African economies and the monitoring of their progress.

Part I

Economic and Financial Data

1

___

Selected Background Data

The first two tables of the volume provide selected indicators, including a series on population, as background to the data in the rest of the volume. Table 1-1 provides a comparative view, across indicators, of some of the more important indicators for all countries in the most recent year for which relatively complete information is available.

1–1. Basic indicators

	Population mid–1990 (millions)	Area (thousands of square km.)	GNP per capita Atlas dollars 1989	GNP per capita Av. annual percentage growth 1965–90	Life expectancy at birth (years) 1990	School enrollment Primary 1965	School enrollment Primary 1989	School enrollment Secondary 1965	School enrollment Secondary 1989	Total net ODA per capita 1989
SUB-SAHARAN AFRICA	479.8	23,064	339	0.3	..	41	65	4	..	30
excluding Nigeria	366.1	22,140	367	0.3	..	43	65	4	..	38
Angola	9.7	1,247	624	..	46	..	..	..	..	16
Benin	4.6	113	394	-0.1	51	34	63	3	..	56
Botswana	1.2	582	1,655	8.5	68	65	116	3	33	135
Burkina Faso	8.8	274	329	1.4	48	12	31	1	6	33
Burundi	5.3	28	223	3.6	50	26	70	1	..	38
Cameroon	11.6	475	1,028	3.2	57	94	111	5	27	42
Cape Verde	0.4	4	801	5.9	67	..	109	..	16	213
Central African Republic	3.0	623	398	-0.5	51	56	67	2	11	67
Chad	5.5	1,284	192	-1.2	47	34	51	1	6	45
Comoros	0.5	2	473	0.5	55	..	80	..	..	101
Congo, People's Republic of the	2.2	342	974	3.3	54	114	..	10	..	41
Cote d'Ivoire	11.7	323	827	0.8	53	60	..	6	19	37
Djibouti	0.4	23	..	..	49	..	46	..	15	191
Equatorial Guinea	0.4	28	341	..	47	..	..	..	..	105
Ethiopia	49.5	1,222	126	-0.1	48	11	36	2	15	16
Gabon	1.1	268	3,040	0.9	54	134	..	11	..	123
Gambia, The	0.8	11	245	0.7	44	..	61	..	16	113
Ghana	14.4	239	398	-1.5	55	69	73	13	39	40
Guinea	5.6	246	439	..	43	..	30	..	9	64
Guinea-Bissau	1.0	36	184	-1.1	40	..	53	..	6	109
Kenya	23.5	580	378	2.0	60	54	93	4	23	43
Lesotho	1.7	30	486	5.0	57	94	112	4	25	76
Liberia	2.5	111	..	-1.6	54	41	..	5	..	25
Madagascar	11.3	587	233	-1.9	51	65	97	8	19	30
Malawi	8.2	119	183	1.0	48	44	72	2	4	50
Mali	8.2	1,240	275	1.7	48	24	23	4	6	57
Mauritania	1.9	1,026	519	-0.5	47	13	52	1	16	131
Mauritius	1.1	2	2,010	3.0	70	101	105	26	53	56
Mozambique	15.3	802	83	..	49	37	68	3	5	51
Namibia	1.7	824	1,060	..	58	..	..	1	..	35
Niger	7.4	1,267	301	-2.4	46	11	30	1	7	41
Nigeria	113.8	924	257	0.2	52	32	62	5	16	3
Rwanda	6.9	26	327	1.2	49	53	64	2	6	35
Sao Tome & Principe	0.1	1	353	-0.3	66	..	138	..	..	285
Senegal	7.2	197	675	-0.7	49	40	59	7	16	93
Seychelles	0.1	0	4,254	3.2	71	..	..	..	..	293
Sierra Leone	4.0	72	225	0.2	42	29	53	5	18	26
Somalia	6.1	638	..	0.3	48	10	..	2	..	71
Sudan	24.5	2,506	483	-0.1	51	29	..	4	..	32
Swaziland	0.8	17	929	2.1	57	..	105	..	44	41
Tanzania	23.8	945	133	-0.1	50	32	66	2	4	40
Togo	3.5	57	408	0.0	54	55	101	5	24	54
Uganda	16.8	236	..	-2.8	49	67	77	4	8	25
Zaire	34.5	2,345	265	-2.0	53	70	76	5	22	19
Zambia	7.8	753	407	-2.0	54	53	..	7	..	52
Zimbabwe	9.6	391	670	1.2	64	110	128	6	51	29
NORTH AFRICA	112.3	5,753	1,299	1.9	..	72	88	18	58	22
Algeria	24.4	2,382	2,314	2.3	65	68	96	7	62	6
Egypt, Arab Republic of	51.0	1,001	653	4.2	60	75	90	26	69	31
Libya	4.4	1,760	5,495	-3.0	62	78	..	14	..	2
Morocco	24.5	447	899	2.3	62	57	67	11	36	19
Tunisia	8.0	164	1,290	3.3	67	91	116	16	44	31
ALL AFRICA	592.1	28,817	533	1.0	..	47	72	7	23	28
South Africa	35.0	1,221	..	0.8	62	..	..	..	..	..

Notes: School enrollment figures for the most recent year are for 1988 instead of 1989.

1-2. Population

	1980	1981	1982	1983	1984	1985	1986	1987	1988	1989	1990	75-79	80-85	86-MR
	Millions of people											Average annual percentage growth		
SUB-SAHARAN AFRICA	352.78	363.04	373.86	385.25	397.21	409.73	422.75	436.28	450.31	464.83	479.83	2.8	3.1	3.2
excluding Nigeria	270.39	278.31	286.56	295.11	304.02	313.34	323.09	333.23	343.78	354.73	366.08	2.9	3.0	3.2
Angola	7.49	7.72	7.94	8.15	8.36	8.56	8.75	8.96	9.18	9.42	9.69	2.6	2.6	2.6
Benin	3.37	3.46	3.57	3.68	3.80	3.92	4.04	4.17	4.31	4.45	4.59	2.7	3.1	3.2
Botswana	0.87	0.90	0.93	0.97	1.00	1.04	1.07	1.11	1.14	1.18	1.22	3.4	3.5	3.3
Burkina Faso	6.80	6.96	7.13	7.31	7.49	7.68	7.88	8.09	8.31	8.53	8.77	2.3	2.5	2.7
Burundi	4.02	4.11	4.21	4.32	4.44	4.56	4.70	4.84	4.99	5.14	5.31	2.0	2.6	3.1
Cameroon	8.43	8.70	8.98	9.26	9.55	9.85	10.17	10.49	10.84	11.19	11.56	3.5	3.2	3.3
Cape Verde	0.29	0.29	0.29	0.30	0.31	0.32	0.32	0.33	0.34	0.35	0.36	0.0	2.2	2.7
Central African Republic	2.26	2.32	2.38	2.45	2.51	2.58	2.65	2.72	2.79	2.87	2.95	2.7	2.7	2.8
Chad	4.38	4.48	4.58	4.68	4.79	4.90	5.02	5.14	5.27	5.40	5.54	2.1	2.3	2.5
Comoros	0.32	0.33	0.34	0.36	0.37	0.38	0.40	0.41	0.43	0.44	0.46	2.0	3.4	3.8
Congo, People's Republic of	1.58	1.63	1.69	1.75	1.81	1.87	1.94	2.00	2.07	2.14	2.21	3.2	3.5	3.3
Cote d'Ivoire	7.89	8.19	8.51	8.84	9.18	9.54	9.93	10.35	10.79	11.25	11.73	3.8	3.9	4.3
Djibouti	0.29	0.30	0.31	0.32	0.33	0.34	0.35	0.37	0.38	0.40	0.41	4.6	3.1	3.8
Equatorial Guinea	0.34	0.34	0.35	0.35	0.36	0.37	0.37	0.38	0.39	0.40	0.41	1.6	1.8	2.2
Ethiopia	36.72	37.72	38.74	39.79	40.89	42.06	43.35	44.74	46.22	47.79	49.45	2.7	2.8	3.3
Gabon	0.76	0.80	0.84	0.88	0.92	0.96	1.00	1.02	1.05	1.08	1.11	3.3	4.6	2.6
Gambia, The	0.61	0.63	0.66	0.68	0.70	0.72	0.75	0.77	0.80	0.82	0.85	3.6	3.4	3.2
Ghana	10.50	10.74	11.03	11.37	11.75	12.17	12.62	13.07	13.53	13.98	14.43	1.6	3.1	3.4
Guinea	4.39	4.46	4.55	4.64	4.75	4.86	4.99	5.12	5.26	5.41	5.56	1.4	2.2	2.8
Guinea-Bissau	0.78	0.81	0.82	0.84	0.85	0.87	0.89	0.90	0.92	0.94	0.96	5.6	2.0	2.0
Kenya	16.00	16.63	17.30	18.00	18.72	19.47	20.24	21.03	21.84	22.66	23.51	3.9	4.0	3.8
Lesotho	1.32	1.36	1.39	1.43	1.47	1.50	1.55	1.59	1.63	1.68	1.72	2.7	2.7	2.8
Liberia	1.82	1.88	1.94	2.00	2.07	2.13	2.20	2.27	2.34	2.41	2.48	3.1	3.2	3.1
Madagascar	8.48	8.71	8.95	9.19	9.44	9.71	9.99	10.28	10.59	10.92	11.26	2.8	2.7	3.1
Malawi	5.90	6.09	6.29	6.50	6.72	6.95	7.19	7.43	7.70	7.96	8.23	3.0	3.3	3.5
Mali	6.45	6.59	6.74	6.89	7.04	7.21	7.39	7.58	7.78	7.99	8.22	2.3	2.3	2.7
Mauritania	1.52	1.55	1.59	1.62	1.65	1.69	1.73	1.77	1.82	1.87	1.92	2.6	2.2	2.6
Mauritius	0.95	0.97	0.98	1.00	1.01	1.01	1.02	1.03	1.04	1.05	1.06	4.0	1.2	0.9
Mozambique	11.79	12.10	12.43	12.75	13.09	13.44	13.79	14.16	14.54	14.94	15.35	2.7	2.6	2.7
Namibia	1.27	1.31	1.34	1.39	1.43	1.47	1.52	1.57	1.62	1.67	1.72	2.7	3.0	3.2
Niger	5.33	5.52	5.71	5.92	6.13	6.35	6.56	6.78	7.00	7.22	7.44	2.7	3.5	3.2
Nigeria	82.39	84.73	87.31	90.14	93.20	96.39	99.67	103.05	106.52	110.10	113.76	4.4	3.2	3.4
Rwanda	4.99	5.16	5.34	5.53	5.72	5.91	6.10	6.29	6.48	6.68	6.89	3.2	3.4	3.1
Sao Tome & Principe	0.09	0.09	0.10	0.10	0.10	0.10	0.11	0.11	0.11	0.12	0.12	3.3	2.6	2.9
Senegal	5.38	5.54	5.70	5.86	6.03	6.21	6.40	6.59	6.79	6.99	7.21	0.0	2.9	3.0
Seychelles	0.06	0.06	0.06	0.06	0.06	0.07	0.07	0.07	0.07	0.07	0.07	1.9	0.7	0.8
Sierra Leone	3.18	3.26	3.33	3.41	3.49	3.57	3.65	3.74	3.84	3.93	4.03	2.9	2.3	2.5
Somalia	4.55	4.67	4.80	4.94	5.08	5.23	5.38	5.55	5.72	5.90	6.09	2.2	2.8	3.1
Sudan	18.62	19.15	19.69	20.23	20.77	21.35	21.93	22.54	23.17	23.82	24.49	2.6	2.8	2.8
Swaziland	0.55	0.56	0.58	0.60	0.62	0.64	0.66	0.69	0.71	0.74	0.76	0.0	3.3	3.5
Tanzania	17.52	18.10	18.69	19.30	19.91	20.53	21.16	21.80	22.46	23.13	23.82	3.0	3.2	3.0
Togo	2.51	2.58	2.66	2.74	2.83	2.93	3.04	3.15	3.26	3.38	3.51	3.3	3.3	3.7
Uganda	12.30	12.64	13.00	13.38	13.79	14.22	14.68	15.16	15.67	16.21	16.77	2.4	3.0	3.4
Zaire	25.48	26.23	27.00	27.79	28.62	29.49	30.40	31.35	32.35	33.39	34.46	2.6	3.0	3.2
Zambia	5.47	5.65	5.84	6.05	6.28	6.51	6.75	7.01	7.27	7.55	7.83	2.9	3.6	3.8
Zimbabwe	6.80	7.01	7.26	7.52	7.80	8.10	8.41	8.71	9.02	9.30	9.57	3.4	3.6	3.3
NORTH AFRICA	86.01	88.35	90.80	93.34	95.98	98.71	101.47	104.25	107.02	109.67	112.30	2.4	2.8	2.6
Algeria	18.11	18.67	19.25	19.86	20.50	21.17	21.85	22.50	23.12	23.75	24.40	2.5	3.2	2.8
Egypt, Arab Republic of	39.85	40.88	41.94	43.05	44.19	45.34	46.51	47.66	48.80	49.91	51.00	3.1	2.6	2.3
Libya	2.91	3.04	3.18	3.33	3.48	3.63	3.79	3.94	4.10	4.25	4.40	2.4	4.5	3.8
Morocco	18.93	19.38	19.87	20.38	20.92	21.48	22.06	22.71	23.38	23.96	24.52	4.4	2.6	2.7
Tunisia	6.22	6.38	6.56	6.73	6.91	7.08	7.26	7.44	7.62	7.80	7.99	2.3	2.6	2.4
ALL AFRICA	438.79	451.40	464.66	478.60	493.19	508.43	524.22	540.53	557.32	574.50	592.13	2.6	3.0	3.1
South Africa	27.66	28.27	28.88	29.50	30.14	30.83	31.57	32.36	33.20	34.08	34.98	2.3	2.2	2.6

Technical Notes

Table 1-1. Basic indicators

The data for the 1-1 table, **basic indicators**, are from the World Bank's *World Development Report 1989*, and the Bank's Economic and Social Database (BESD), except for the growth rates for GNP per capita for country groups and all growth rates for official development assistance (ODA) per capita, which are explained below. Summary measures for GNP per capita, life expectancy, and education are weighted by population. The indicators are explained below.

- **Population** estimates are mid-year estimates from the U.N. Population Division or from World Bank sources and include refugee populations living abroad if they are not permanently settled in the country of asylum. In many cases, the data take into account the results of recent population censuses. Other figures are from projections and estimates, and some of them are neither very recent nor very accurate. (See also the notes to Tables 13-1 to 13-3 below). Earlier figures are used in some tables showing per capita indicators, and these exceptions are pointed out in the technical notes for these tables.

- **Area** refers to the total area of a country, which generally includes major rivers and lakes. The data are from the *FAO Production Yearbook*, which obtains them from the U.N. Statistical Office.

- **GNP per capita** is calculated according to the *World Bank Atlas* method, which uses a three-year average of conversion factors to convert GNP data, expressed in different national currencies, to a common denomination, conventionally U.S. dollars. The Atlas conversion factor for any year is the average of the official exchange rate (or alternative conversion factor) for that year and the exchange rates for the two preceding years, after adjusting them for differences in relative inflation

between the country and the United States. This three-year average smooths annual fluctuations in prices and exchange rates for each country. The resulting GNP in U.S. dollars is divided by the midyear population of the latest of the three years to derive GNP per capita.

The following formulas describe the procedures for computing the conversion factor for year *t*:

$$[e^{*}_{t-2,t} = \frac{1}{3}[e_{t-2}(\frac{P_t}{P_{t-2}} | \frac{P_t^\$}{P_{t-2}^\$}) + e_{t-1}(\frac{P_t}{P_{t-1}} | \frac{P_t^\$}{P_{t-1}^\$}) + e_t]$$

and for calculating GNP per capita in U.S. dollars for year t:

$$Y_t^\$ = (Y_t/N_t + e^{*}_t - 2,t)$$

where
Y_t = current GNP (national currency) for year *t*,
P_t = GNP deflator for year *t*, e_t = annual average official exchange rate or alternative conversion factor (national currency/US dollar) for year *t*, and
N_t = midyear population for year *t*.

$$P_t^\$ = U.S. GNP.$$

The levels and ranking of GNP per capita estimates have sometimes changed in ways not necessarily related to the relative domestic growth of the economies considered. Terms of trade changes affect relative income levels as do currency fluctuations, which have been sharp during the past decade.

Growth rates of GNP per capita are calculated by the least-squares metod using the real GNP percapita series in constant 1987 prices, expressed in national currency (see also technical notes for Table 2-17), which do not reflect changes in the terms of trade.

GNP is the total domestic and foreign value-added claimed by residents and is calculated without deducting for depreciation. It comprises GDP (defined in the notes to Table 2-1) plus net factor income from abroad, which is the income residents receive from abroad for factor services (labor and capital) less similar payments made to nonresidents who contributed to the domestic economy, including interest payments on external debt. Figures are in current U.S. dollars, converted from national currency series using single-year official exchange rates or alternative conversion factors (as explained in the notes to Table 3-6).

• **Life expectancy at birth** is the number of years a newborn infant would live if patterns of mortality for all people at the time of its birth were to remain the same throughout its life. Data are from the U.N. Population Division, supplemented by World Bank estimates.

• **Primary school enrollment** is the ratio of children of all ages enrolled in primary school to he population of children of primary school age. While many countries consider the primary school age to be 6 to 11 years, others do not. These different country practices are also reflected in the ratios. Data are mostly from Unesco and refer to a variety of years but generally are not more than two years distant from the exact years specified. Wherever gross enrollment ratios exceed 100 percent, enrollment figures include pupils that are younger or older than the country's standard primary school age. In addition, in practice, enrollment does not necessarily equal attendance, nor does enrollment remain constant throughout the year.

• **Secondary school enrollment** is the ratio of children of all ages enrolled in secondary school to the population of children of secondary school age, generally between 12 to 17 years old, although the definition of secondary school age differs among countries. Data are from Unesco, as described above.

• **Total net ODA per capita** consists of net disbursements of loans and grants from all official sources on concessional financial terms to promote economic development and welfare, divided by the midyear population for the corresponding year. The technical notes to Chapter 12 give sources and other information. Statistical background for the population estimates is available in the U.N.'s Population and Vital Statistics Report and the World Bank's World Population Projections.

2

National Accounts

National accounts data provide the broadest picture of a nation's economic performance. National accounts provide information on the structure of production in the form of gross domestic product (GDP) and its components by industrial origin, GDP and its components by expenditure, and information on a nation's economic relations with the outside world. These are the key statistics for assessing a nation's economic condition at a given point in time and/or the trends in a nation's economic performance over time. Moreover, national accounts data provide a quantitative basis for forecasting and policymaking and as such are used widely both by analysts and policy makers.

GDP and its components by industrial origin are compiled following the widely used System of National Accounts (SNA). The SNA methodology accounts for virtually all activities pertinent to the production of goods and the provisions of services in an economy, by residents and nonresidents, regardless of the allocation to domestic and foreign claims. GDP does not account for the depreciation of fixed capital. There are three methods of compiling GDP figures: income, expenditure, and production methods. Because of technical and resource constraints, the income method is not used in most developing countries. In this volume, GDP and its components by industrial origin are compiled using the production method. The three components of GDP by industrial origin

are value added in agriculture, value added in industry, and value added in services. (See the technical notes at the end of this chapter).

The national accounts are constructed in national currencies and in current prices. Figures reported in this chapter are, however, in US dollars, usually converted from national currency series at the official exchange rate. If the official exchange rate is significantly different from the prevailing market rate or shows extreme volatility, the conversion of local currency into US dollars is done by using an alternative conversion factors. The conversion factors used for this purpose are presented in Table 3-6. Reporting currencies in a common denominator facilitates cross-country comparisons, and aggregations in country groups.

In addition, estimates of GDP and its components by industrial origin are converted into constant prices. Reporting figures in constant prices is essential for monitoring real changes in the structure of production and for analyzing relationships between prices, production, employment, and so forth.

Constant price series in U.S. dollars use a 1987 base year and are converted from national currency series using 1987 exchange rates. To establish a common base year for all countries, national accounts in national currencies at constant prices based on years other than 1987 have been

14

partially rebased to 1987 by rescaling constant price series of components of GDP.

Using a single base year raises problems when there are profound structural changes or significant changes in relative prices. For example, values expressed in constant U.S. dollars necessarily reflect the exchange rates prevailing during the base year. Where subsequent exchange rate changes have been substantial, as they have for many African countries since 1980, comparisons among countries and aggregate trends will be affected. For this reason alone, the data should be used with considerable caution.

Monitoring resource allocations across sectors in any given point in time requires the use of current prices. Accordingly, in addition to GDP in constant prices, GDP in current prices is provided. Following GDP in current prices are components of GDP by expenditure. Data on consumption, investment, and savings are constructed using SNA's convention. Conceptually, all income is either consumed or saved, and as such the sum of total consumption and gross domestic saving equals GDP.

When viewed from production point of view, by definition, saving equals investment. Investment measures additions to fixed assets of an economy, whether it represents additions to the stock of capital or merely replenishes depreciated capital stock, plus net changes in the level of inventories. It is financed either through domestic saving or by drawing on the savings of foreigners. Data on gross domestic investment and gross domestic saving thus shed light not only on the nature of the domestic intertemporal resource allocation but also on the size of the resource gap. Gross national saving, however, indicates the amount of saving generated by the residents of a nation.

Although this volume includes a chapter on international trade, the fact that balance of payments is an integral part of the national

accounts warrants the inclusion of resource balance and its components in this chapter. Moreover, a closer examination of the fourth edition of the IMF's *Balance of Payments Manual* reflects differences in concepts, definitions, and classifications from the UN's SNA guidelines. For instance, in SNA, factor services rendered by residents of another country are excluded from goods and services, but this practice is not universally followed. The tables on resource balance, and on values of exports (f.o.b.) and imports (c.i.f.) of goods and nonfactor services in current U.S. dollars provide a comprehensive and systematic framework for macroeconomic analysis in general. Those interested in a more specialized and rigorous study of international trade transaction should use the data provided in Chapter 5.

The rate of growth of real domestic product is an important indicator of economic progress and as such is widely monitored. Because these growth rates are calculated from national series, they are suitable for both cross-country comparisons and trend analysis for individual countries. Aggregate values and trends, however, reflect the choice of the base year, as explained above.

Gross national income per capita, which is GDP per capita adjusted for changes in international terms of trade and to include net factor income from abroad, and total consumption per capita are also widely monitored indicators of economic progress. When expressed in current U.S. dollars to facilitate comparison and aggregation, however, the values for these indicators necessarily reflect exchange rate fluctuations as well as underlying economic and demographic changes. These indicators may be used with caution for cross-country comparison during any single year. They require special attention when used for trend analysis.

2-1. Gross domestic product

	Millions of U.S. dollars, constant 1987 prices and exchange rates											Average annual percentage growth		
	1980	*1981*	*1982*	*1983*	*1984*	*1985*	*1986*	*1987*	*1988*	*1989*	*1990*	*75–80*	*80–85*	*86–MR*
SUB-SAHARAN AFRICA	123,757	125,793	129,121	129,245	127,818	132,642	138,768	138,316	141,476	145,862	148,244	2.7	1.1	1.9
excluding Nigeria	95,505	99,160	102,541	104,313	104,698	107,507	113,131	113,856	115,840	118,731	119,673	2.5	2.2	1.6
Angola	..	..	..	4,386	5,030	5,180	5,809	6,510	7,475	7,466	..	..	..	7.1
Benin	1,428	1,557	1,663	1,629	1,661	1,767	1,736	1,668	1,688	1,729	1,747	6.1	3.6	0.5
Botswana	717	770	762	944	1,126	1,219	1,318	1,454	1,588	1,801	..	12.2	12.1	11.3
Burkina Faso	1,830	1,912	2,104	2,120	2,083	2,286	2,515	2,559	2,748	2,743	2,789	3.8	4.0	2.8
Burundi	801	909	881	942	943	1,052	1,092	1,137	1,178	1,255	1,287	3.9	4.5	4.4
Cameroon	8,668	9,788	10,047	10,826	11,458	12,334	13,325	12,455	11,492	11,104	10,970	11.5	6.8	-4.9
Cape Verde	154	167	172	189	196	213	219	234	242	255	265	10.2	6.4	4.8
Central African Republic	987	965	1,037	968	1,059	1,100	1,110	1,073	1,091	1,115	1,155	1.2	2.2	1.2
Chad	573	579	610	706	720	877	841	813	956	964	993	-5.4	8.7	5.2
Comoros	..	..	..	178	186	191	195	199	200	200	204	..	..	1.0
Congo, People's Republic of the	1,496	1,705	2,150	2,316	2,477	2,448	2,281	2,298	2,310	2,318	2,315	4.3	11.0	0.4
Cote d'Ivoire	9,324	9,725	9,879	9,760	9,667	10,028	10,395	10,374	10,183	10,049	9,436	4.7	1.0	-2.2
Djibouti	..	..	..	..	405	404	376	373	377	374	377	..	..	0.1
Equatorial Guinea	..	..	..	..	..	123	123	128	139	140	139	..	..	3.4
Ethiopia	4,678	4,775	4,851	5,098	4,989	4,650	4,959	5,409	5,616	5,747	5,602	2.8	0.4	3.1
Gabon	3,319	3,186	3,273	3,302	3,515	3,737	4,164	3,396	3,400	3,535	3,729	-5.2	2.6	-1.8
Gambia, The	140	154	173	164	169	170	175	185	200	210	219	2.8	3.6	5.9
Ghana	4,654	4,518	4,225	4,037	4,390	4,612	4,848	5,070	5,385	5,713	5,946	2.0	-0.5	5.4
Guinea	1,799	1,812	1,844	1,867	1,817	1,908	2,044	2,106	2,230	2,325	2,435	..	0.9	4.6
Guinea-Bissau	119	141	148	143	151	157	156	165	176	185	191	-0.8	4.5	5.3
Kenya	6,127	6,376	6,494	6,589	6,701	6,990	7,488	7,929	8,404	8,787	9,159	6.6	2.4	5.2
Lesotho	306	309	320	302	325	335	332	357	400	417	449	11.1	1.6	7.9
Liberia	1,265	1,250	1,225	1,206	1,180	1,171	1,151	1,139	..	..	..	2.8	-1.6	..
Madagascar	2,737	2,469	2,422	2,444	2,485	2,515	2,561	2,590	2,690	2,822	2,953	1.8	-1.1	3.8
Malawi	1,100	1,042	1,068	1,108	1,170	1,223	1,217	1,237	1,272	1,341	1,391	6.1	2.6	3.5
Mali	1,476	1,545	1,648	1,574	1,595	1,588	1,872	1,899	1,945	2,124	2,131	4.9	1.2	3.8
Mauritania	845	877	859	901	836	860	908	936	971	1,004	1,007	2.3	0.0	2.8
Mauritius	1,195	1,259	1,332	1,336	1,399	1,502	1,657	1,831	1,950	2,018	2,147	4.5	4.3	6.4
Mozambique	1,737	1,746	1,686	1,471	1,494	1,374	1,400	1,473	1,555	1,604	1,653	..	-5.0	4.3
Namibia	1,616	1,647	1,569	1,520	1,490	1,575	1,668	1,671	1,754	1,710	..	..	-1.3	1.2
Niger	2,479	2,508	2,477	2,432	2,020	2,083	2,217	2,162	2,271	2,190	2,258	7.6	-4.3	0.5
Nigeria	28,253	26,633	26,580	24,932	23,120	25,136	25,637	24,460	25,636	27,130	28,571	3.3	-3.0	3.3
Rwanda	1,784	1,941	1,973	2,097	1,999	2,058	2,166	2,158	2,159	2,011	1,958	8.2	2.5	-2.7
Sao Tome & Principe	52	37	47	43	40	43	44	43	43	44	45	9.9	-2.2	1.1
Senegal	3,646	3,627	4,165	4,270	4,070	4,223	4,418	4,599	4,836	4,763	4,977	0.8	3.2	2.8
Seychelles	226	210	207	212	219	240	246	256	272	287	302	8.9	1.3	5.4
Sierra Leone	575	625	625	606	619	599	587	619	619	615	630	2.5	0.4	1.4
Somalia	820	885	917	832	860	930	964	1,023	1,010	1,037	1,022	5.0	1.3	1.3
Sudan	8,589	8,769	9,880	10,084	9,579	8,977	9,851	9,962	9,773	10,496	9,883	-4.6	1.5	0.6
Swaziland	444	474	479	476	494	506	550	557	608	636	665	2.4	2.2	5.3
Tanzania	2,977	2,948	2,940	2,926	3,059	3,107	3,274	3,409	3,587	3,741	3,910	2.0	0.9	4.6
Togo	1,234	1,192	1,148	1,088	1,152	1,189	1,229	1,247	1,310	1,359	*1,385*	4.7	-1.0	3.3
Uganda	3,538	3,805	4,251	4,658	4,262	4,183	4,120	4,354	4,618	4,912	5,223	-3.0	3.7	6.1
Zaire	6,791	7,031	7,001	7,106	7,279	7,441	7,761	7,806	8,057	7,896	7,749	-1.3	1.7	0.1
Zambia	1,979	2,100	2,044	2,000	1,979	2,013	2,018	2,078	2,192	2,195	2,216	-0.3	-0.3	2.4
Zimbabwe	4,344	4,888	5,017	5,097	4,971	5,305	5,449	5,372	5,293	6,002	6,182	-0.1	3.1	3.7
NORTH AFRICA	135,911	130,774	137,005	141,956	144,793	149,014	150,129	151,709	153,650	158,811	162,411	7.8	2.3	2.1
Algeria	48,853	50,322	53,561	56,446	58,772	61,889	63,110	64,476	62,829	66,373	68,046	6.6	5.0	1.8
Egypt, Arab Republic of	24,099	25,054	27,731	29,867	31,686	33,778	34,672	35,545	36,939	37,819	38,004	10.5	7.3	2.5
Libya	40,168	32,616	31,540	31,193	28,724	26,183	23,905	23,140	23,302	23,452	..	9.0	-7.0	0.7
Morocco	15,290	14,867	16,297	16,206	16,888	17,938	19,352	18,944	20,848	21,095	22,022	5.9	3.4	3.7
Tunisia	7,501	7,915	7,876	8,245	8,724	9,226	9,090	9,604	9,732	10,072	10,722	6.1	4.0	3.8
ALL AFRICA	259,668	256,567	266,127	271,202	272,611	281,657	288,897	290,025	295,126	304,673	310,654	..	1.8	2.0
South Africa	73,240	80,016	79,297	77,392	81,372	80,682	80,889	82,554	85,614	87,408	..	2.6	1.5	2.9

Notes: Where only 1990 figures are missing, estimates are made for calculating the group average to maintain the same group composition over time. However, the estimated values are not shown separately in the table.

2-2. Value added in agriculture

	Millions of U.S. dollars, constant 1987 prices and exchange rates											Average annual percentage growth		
	1980	1981	1982	1983	1984	1985	1986	1987	1988	1989	1990	75-80	80-85	86-MR
SUB-SAHARAN AFRICA	39,717	38,993	41,644	40,508	39,815	40,509	43,665	43,924	45,462	47,463	46,556	1.9	0.4	1.5
excluding Nigeria	32,046	32,585	35,039	33,898	33,644	33,458	35,963	36,815	37,962	39,663	38,826	2.6	0.5	1.6
Angola	940	916	955	917	911	914	915	926	907	881	..	..	-0.6	-1.3
Benin	477	443	451	456	463	525	552	520	587	620	620	5.6	1.8	4.2
Botswana	96	86	83	69	59	54	61	59	69	69	..	-1.1	-11.4	5.2
Burkina Faso	618	668	687	689	681	730	810	775	883	857	827	-0.6	2.6	1.4
Burundi	435	496	459	479	462	522	544	572	581	568	598	1.3	2.1	1.8
Cameroon	2,414	2,732	2,836	2,621	2,853	2,534	2,904	3,063	2,967	2,908	2,966	5.9	0.8	-0.1
Cape Verde	30	29	23	23	23	29	31	35	37	38	..	..	-2.3	6.2
Central African Republic	363	356	362	347	380	394	425	415	438	443	443	1.1	1.6	1.5
Chad	306	272	286	320	274	378	311	300	392	345	376	-1.4	3.5	5.4
Comoros	..	..	..	58	60	63	65	71	73	75	..	..	..	4.7
Congo, People's Republic of the	218	228	239	250	246	248	250	274	293	309	320	2.6	2.6	6.3
Cote d' Ivoire	2,878	2,938	2,898	2,578	2,650	2,900	3,248	3,147	3,539	3,688	3,688	4.1	-1.1	4.2
Djibouti	..	..	..	..	10	10	9	9	9	9	..	..	..	-1.0
Equatorial Guinea	..	..	..	..	..	63	66	70	70	70	72	..	..	2.0
Ethiopia	2,089	2,140	2,112	2,212	1,993	1,669	1,823	2,086	2,070	2,189	2,164	1.2	-3.6	4.0
Gabon	..	..	..	..	..	..	..	..	..	..	..	..	..	..
Gambia, The	31	44	53	42	45	47	52	54	54	57	52	-3.4	5.5	0.8
Ghana	2,627	2,559	2,420	2,251	2,469	2,485	2,567	2,568	2,660	2,773	2,706	4.2	-1.3	1.8
Guinea	763	772	780	770	712	821	611	619	648	654	674	..	0.3	2.6
Guinea-Bissau	46	59	63	61	63	68	71	78	81	87	89	-7.0	6.1	5.9
Kenya	1,704	1,804	1,937	1,973	1,905	1,981	2,079	2,166	2,268	2,358	2,440	4.3	2.7	4.1
Lesotho	64	68	54	72	58	56	53	56	71	71	71	1.2	-2.3	8.4
Liberia	..	..	..	..	..	..	..	..	..	..	..	..	..	..
Madagascar	722	689	717	736	759	768	792	810	830	873	886	-0.4	1.8	3.0
Malawi	347	319	339	354	375	376	378	382	389	399	399	4.6	2.7	1.5
Mali	885	870	937	821	755	710	938	922	915	1,087	1,086	4.7	-4.6	4.7
Mauritania	259	283	287	331	270	276	302	310	308	313	268	2.9	0.9	-2.3
Mauritius	147	179	214	186	188	209	231	224	212	196	213	-3.5	5.2	-3.0
Mozambique	868	868	868	729	795	802	807	852	913	962	974	..	-2.4	5.1
Namibia	210	216	196	153	135	147	147	188	190	198	..	..	-9.3	9.4
Niger	701	695	678	755	679	780	841	729	..	..	..	4.7	1.6	..
Nigeria	7,671	6,408	6,605	6,610	6,170	7,051	7,702	7,109	7,500	7,800	..	-1.0	-1.5	0.9
Rwanda	838	786	899	942	858	810	834	820	801	709	747	9.1	0.4	-3.6
Sao Tome & Principe	18	16	17	17	16	17	17	16	16	17	17	..	-1.3	0.7
Senegal	802	756	943	989	816	881	970	997	1,092	1,000	1,070	-3.9	2.1	2.0
Seychelles	12	16	12	15	13	13	14	13	13	14	..	..	0.0	-1.2
Sierra Leone	181	183	189	187	188	208	202	216	232	221	225	11.5	2.2	2.5
Somalia	453	518	533	468	528	578	571	618	641	652	..	7.8	3.3	4.4
Sudan	4,580	4,376	6,192	5,643	5,383	4,725	5,510	5,679	5,337	6,251	4,982	-0.1	2.0	-1.1
Swaziland	..	..	..	..	..	..	..	..	..	..	..	..	..	..
Tanzania	1,433	1,447	1,467	1,509	1,569	1,663	1,759	1,836	1,918	2,006	2,064	-0.2	2.9	4.2
Togo	316	317	289	291	378	393	413	419	446	479	473	3.0	4.8	4.1
Uganda	2,026	2,164	2,288	2,466	2,208	2,260	2,275	2,398	2,536	2,678	2,753	-3.8	2.0	5.1
Zaire	1,876	1,914	1,975	2,017	2,070	2,127	2,177	2,221	2,287	2,350	..	1.1	2.6	2.6
Zambia	190	206	182	197	208	215	234	229	273	269	254	-0.2	2.1	3.3
Zimbabwe	547	624	580	489	601	745	698	572	718	730	752	-1.2	3.7	4.0
NORTH AFRICA	14,116	13,553	13,933	13,778	14,432	16,479	17,764	17,642	18,034	19,107	18,924	2.0	2.8	2.1
Algeria	4,740	4,748	4,368	4,273	4,575	5,779	6,089	6,495	6,164	6,935	6,588	4.4	2.5	2.3
Egypt, Arab Republic of	5,673	5,773	6,006	6,179	6,309	6,511	6,648	6,787	6,957	7,096	7,202	2.4	2.8	2.1
Libya	..	..	..	..	..	..	..	..	..	..	..	..	..	..
Morocco	2,598	1,855	2,503	2,244	2,327	2,756	3,768	2,880	3,784	3,884	3,622	4.9	2.5	2.2
Tunisia	1,105	1,177	1,056	1,082	1,221	1,433	1,259	1,480	1,128	1,192	1,513	0.3	4.2	1.5
ALL AFRICA	53,833	52,546	55,577	54,287	54,246	56,988	61,429	61,566	63,496	66,570	65,480	1.5	0.8	1.7
South Africa	4,138	4,507	4,113	3,187	3,522	4,224	4,505	4,713	4,762	5,255	..	2.3	-2.5	4.8

2-3. Value added in industry

	Millions of U.S. dollars, constant 1987 prices and exchange rates											*Average annual percentage growth*		
	1980	1981	1982	1983	1984	1985	1986	1987	1988	1989	1990	75–80	80–85	86–MR
SUB-SAHARAN AFRICA	37,091	36,368	36,418	36,038	36,398	37,507	38,635	38,612	39,499	39,585	40,457	6.2	0.1	1.2
excluding Nigeria	22,506	23,261	23,592	25,111	26,156	26,277	27,716	28,098	28,190	27,285	27,616	5.6	3.5	-0.4
Angola	1,450	1,337	1,260	1,499	1,840	1,928	2,297	2,779	3,403	3,445	..	..	7.6	15.2
Benin	118	134	184	189	207	213	185	193	205	209	218	1.4	13.1	4.1
Botswana	281	333	310	461	614	632	657	688	719	832	..	17.2	19.7	7.8
Burkina Faso	438	432	466	470	478	505	559	606	624	609	635	-1.0	3.0	2.6
Burundi	117	129	141	145	147	161	163	175	176	178	188	11.3	5.9	3.0
Cameroon	2,243	2,931	3,410	4,118	4,295	3,987	4,392	3,568	3,281	3,928	3,714	22.0	12.8	-2.4
Cape Verde	25	28	28	33	32	37	38	40	42	45	..	..	7.6	6.1
Central African Republic	132	121	121	132	135	140	134	140	144	165	173	3.8	2.1	6.9
Chad	68	91	101	123	144	147	161	151	165	192	131	-12.7	16.8	-1.6
Comoros	..	..	..	30	33	31	31	28	25	23	..	..	..	-9.8
Congo, People's Republic of the	539	519	730	857	931	886	809	822	847	925	933	5.7	13.4	4.1
Cote d'Ivoire	2,246	2,469	2,100	2,165	2,225	2,140	2,019	2,169	2,023	1,930	1,741	12.4	-1.5	-4.0
Djibouti	..	..	..	..	57	56	57	56	57	58	..	..	..	0.6
Equatorial Guinea	..	..	..	..	..	9	8	9	11	11	11	..	..	10.6
Ethiopia	651	673	694	730	769	774	803	839	850	864	835	3.4	3.8	1.1
Gabon	..	..	..	..	..	..	..	..	..	..	..	..	..	..
Gambia, The	16	13	11	14	13	13	15	16	16	19	19	8.5	-2.2	6.0
Ghana	877	737	613	539	588	691	744	828	889	925	964	-4.8	-5.5	6.5
Guinea	408	396	401	423	412	395	666	695	742	791	818	..	0.1	5.6
Guinea-Bissau	25	24	26	25	33	35	31	26	28	29	30	5.6	8.0	0.9
Kenya	1,010	1,050	1,068	1,073	1,096	1,160	1,206	1,270	1,338	1,415	1,488	7.1	2.4	5.4
Lesotho	80	69	90	49	68	81	76	86	101	131	157	29.7	-1.9	20.5
Liberia	..	..	..	..	..	..	..	..	..	..	..	..	..	..
Madagascar	363	281	241	244	274	282	293	307	312	315	335	2.8	-3.7	3.1
Malawi	179	174	174	180	179	192	189	192	206	222	245	4.1	1.4	6.9
Mali	119	153	160	170	203	216	237	225	222	234	260	-1.0	11.8	2.3
Mauritania	140	140	134	127	169	176	182	181	189	211	200	1.4	4.8	3.5
Mauritius	281	292	304	305	333	379	442	497	542	577	625	5.5	5.6	8.8
Mozambique	319	321	287	260	224	188	205	207	216	228	220	..	-10.4	2.4
Namibia	639	588	546	532	515	501	524	516	523	500	..	..	-4.6	-1.2
Niger	604	631	608	543	509	496	501	523	..	..	..	17.8	-4.9	..
Nigeria	14,585	13,107	12,826	10,927	10,243	11,230	10,919	10,514	11,309	12,300	..	7.0	-6.1	4.4
Rwanda	409	420	410	479	465	452	472	476	477	472	444	..	2.8	-1.3
Sao Tome & Principe	7	7	7	7	6	7	7	7	7	7	7	..	-1.3	0.1
Senegal	685	617	709	726	712	727	762	822	876	880	902	3.7	2.2	4.2
Seychelles	32	29	26	22	32	38	39	38	40	43	..	..	3.0	3.1
Sierra Leone	136	125	114	99	111	92	100	100	93	106	119	-4.4	-6.8	4.1
Somalia	87	73	84	69	72	73	95	99	90	94	..	-3.7	-3.1	-1.1
Sudan	1,815	1,977	2,193	2,475	2,330	2,346	2,489	2,501	2,475	2,585	2,432	2.2	5.6	-0.1
Swaziland	..	..	..	..	..	..	..	..	..	..	..	..	..	..
Tanzania	405	374	371	312	332	319	327	341	354	376	405	1.8	-4.8	5.4
Togo	300	254	261	244	221	237	242	253	279	288	269	6.7	-4.7	3.5
Uganda	166	161	185	206	199	180	164	199	246	284	305	-14.4	3.3	17.3
Zaire	1,753	1,762	1,702	1,770	1,991	1,997	2,094	2,113	2,072	1,961	..	-4.7	3.1	-2.1
Zambia	2,124	2,057	2,000	2,036	2,027	2,115	2,256	2,239	2,188	..	..	1.0	-0.1	-1.5
Zimbabwe	1,624	1,735	1,724	1,682	1,634	1,734	1,807	1,868	1,932	2,061	2,155	-1.0	0.4	4.6
NORTH AFRICA	30,435	33,050	34,749	38,119	40,840	43,172	43,321	41,195	41,648	40,960	41,757	9.6	7.3	-0.8
Algeria	15,991	18,063	19,441	22,065	23,879	25,155	25,112	22,666	22,180	21,349	21,747	7.8	9.7	-3.4
Egypt, Arab Republic of	6,969	7,224	7,390	7,900	8,633	9,314	9,471	9,685	10,050	10,222	9,982	15.1	6.0	1.6
Libya	..	..	..	..	..	..	..	..	..	..	..	..	..	..
Morocco	5,239	5,374	5,526	5,600	5,678	6,006	6,062	6,162	6,665	6,487	6,967	4.4	2.5	3.4
Tunisia	2,236	2,389	2,392	2,553	2,650	2,697	2,675	2,682	2,752	2,902	3,061	7.5	3.8	3.5
ALL AFRICA	67,525	69,418	71,167	74,157	77,238	80,678	81,956	79,807	81,147	80,545	82,214	7.2	3.6	0.2
South Africa	32,047	35,238	34,653	33,304	34,569	33,672	33,351	33,400	34,963	35,253	..	1.9	0.4	2.1

2–4. Value added in services

	Millions of U.S. dollars, constant 1987 prices and exchange rates											Average annual percentage growth		
	1980	1981	1982	1983	1984	1985	1986	1987	1988	1989	1990	75–80	80–85	86–MR
SUB-SAHARAN AFRICA	46,774	48,970	49,534	50,608	50,769	53,540	54,549	55,459	56,151	55,983	57,286	5.0	2.1	0.6
excluding Nigeria	40,522	42,313	42,851	43,840	44,476	47,232	48,143	49,077	49,913	49,570	50,886	5.5	2.2	0.7
Angola	2,928	3,014	2,663	2,249	2,544	2,620	2,815	2,900	2,993	3,097	..	..	-3.5	3.2
Benin	566	678	700	659	663	697	718	720	725	710	730	3.3	2.7	0.2
Botswana	365	384	394	434	476	556	600	708	800	900	..	13.9	8.4	14.3
Burkina Faso	690	733	851	881	857	939	1,014	1,028	1,064	1,089	1,114	11.3	6.0	2.5
Burundi	188	210	223	231	245	274	282	288	296	308	340	6.5	7.1	4.5
Cameroon	3,703	3,747	3,421	3,727	4,003	5,497	5,658	5,413	4,923	4,404	4,283	8.0	6.7	-7.3
Cape Verde	88	100	109	118	125	130	134	142	146	153	..	..	7.9	4.4
Central African Republic	423	434	475	401	448	466	440	420	428	430	431	0.1	1.2	-0.2
Chad	200	212	223	263	302	352	369	362	398	427	426	-7.6	12.3	4.6
Comoros	..	..	..	95	100	102	104	103	103	104	..	..	..	0.0
Congo, People's Republic of the	650	934	1,094	1,096	1,153	1,186	1,122	1,116	1,106	1,085	1,091	4.5	11.0	-0.8
Cote d'Ivoire	2,206	2,375	2,637	2,784	2,357	3,010	3,072	2,488	2,188	2,079	2,008	1.7	4.6	-9.8
Djibouti	..	..	..	..	264	266	251	248	252	250	..	..	..	0.1
Equatorial Guinea	..	..	..	..	..	35	34	35	41	40	41	..	..	5.0
Ethiopia	1,469	1,525	1,586	1,685	1,701	1,728	1,811	1,906	2,090	2,101	2,113	3.0	3.5	4.1
Gabon	..	..	..	..	..	..	..	..	..	..	..	..	..	..
Gambia, The	68	68	76	78	79	76	80	84	86	91	98	5.6	3.0	5.0
Ghana	1,226	1,267	1,221	1,249	1,332	1,432	1,525	1,668	1,798	1,904	2,067	1.6	2.7	7.7
Guinea	629	644	663	674	693	693	741	760	802	880	934	..	2.1	6.3
Guinea-Bissau	49	59	60	56	54	55	54	61	67	69	71	9.6	0.7	6.6
Kenya	2,609	2,807	2,864	2,997	3,083	3,250	3,459	3,640	3,842	4,046	4,242	7.5	4.2	5.3
Lesotho	117	127	127	133	146	144	155	163	172	168	168	10.1	4.4	1.9
Liberia	..	..	..	..	..	..	..	..	..	..	..	..	..	..
Madagascar	1,273	1,159	1,133	1,130	1,155	1,119	1,128	1,122	1,174	1,222	1,275	2.3	-1.9	3.4
Malawi	407	392	397	408	430	459	471	489	502	520	552	4.7	2.6	3.9
Mali	485	458	487	514	565	590	616	669	659	779	805	7.6	4.9	7.1
Mauritania	366	361	334	348	307	315	330	347	360	368	404	4.2	-3.3	4.7
Mauritius	601	621	635	660	685	707	741	808	867	920	963	5.8	3.3	6.7
Mozambique	364	370	358	333	338	248	241	266	280	294	313	..	-6.2	6.4
Namibia	636	695	744	751	772	780	802	825	843	872	..	..	3.9	2.8
Niger	1,139	1,158	1,181	1,048	768	745	807	840	..	..	..	6.2	-9.5	..
Nigeria	6,252	6,657	6,683	6,768	6,293	6,308	6,406	6,382	6,239	6,413	..	2.1	-0.3	-0.2
Rwanda	385	501	600	613	614	723	780	782	799	771	731	1.9	11.4	-1.4
Sao Tome & Principe	34	30	32	31	29	32	32	30	31	31	32	..	-1.3	0.4
Senegal	2,159	2,230	2,503	2,531	2,541	2,623	2,691	2,782	2,865	2,871	2,992	1.7	4.0	2.5
Seychelles	167	156	137	133	138	148	148	163	161	167	..	..	-2.9	3.7
Sierra Leone	180	204	229	250	237	218	208	211	211	233	244	-1.6	4.3	4.3
Somalia	259	224	244	242	232	243	249	269	249	259	..	2.0	-0.6	0.3
Sudan	7,675	7,921	7,920	8,465	8,394	8,108	7,671	8,172	8,664	9,074	9,396	6.5	1.5	5.2
Swaziland	..	..	..	..	..	..	..	..	..	..	..	..	..	..
Tanzania	883	894	907	893	910	926	940	966	1,002	1,046	1,082	4.2	0.8	3.7
Togo	618	622	600	553	553	559	575	575	585	594	612	4.8	-2.7	1.6
Uganda	705	700	726	764	736	765	777	823	883	945	983	-4.2	1.8	6.3
Zaire	2,727	2,863	2,827	2,876	2,975	2,850	3,030	3,194	3,152	3,102	..	-0.1	1.0	0.6
Zambia	1,160	1,119	1,111	1,127	1,104	1,138	1,161	1,152	1,165	..	..	2.5	-0.3	..
Zimbabwe	1,895	2,119	2,204	2,178	2,191	2,271	2,242	2,321	2,335	2,441	2,486	1.0	2.9	2.6
NORTH AFRICA	41,113	38,699	43,144	44,029	44,580	46,656	48,951	52,753	55,029	59,156	59,726	7.1	3.1	5.3
Algeria	21,847	18,552	20,271	19,456	18,623	19,078	20,358	23,122	23,789	26,707	26,422	5.0	-2.0	6.9
Egypt, Arab Republic of	9,705	10,216	12,434	13,663	14,491	15,550	16,086	16,545	17,339	18,106	18,544	12.3	10.5	3.8
Libya	..	..	..	..	..	..	..	..	..	..	..	..	..	..
Morocco	6,430	6,594	7,021	7,361	7,737	8,118	8,534	8,866	9,336	9,677	9,897	5.2	5.0	3.9
Tunisia	3,131	3,337	3,418	3,549	3,729	3,911	3,973	4,219	4,565	4,667	4,863	5.8	4.3	5.2
ALL AFRICA	87,886	87,670	92,678	94,637	95,349	100,196	103,499	108,212	111,181	115,139	117,012	5.4	2.4	2.9
South Africa	31,728	34,474	34,942	35,725	37,838	37,764	37,985	39,185	40,442	41,371	..	4.2	3.4	2.9

2–5. Gross domestic product

	Millions of U.S. dollars, current prices and exchange rates											Average annual percentage growth		
	1980	1981	1982	1983	1984	1985	1986	1987	1988	1989	1990	75–80	80–85	86–MR
SUB-SAHARAN AFRICA	212,432	202,392	197,714	189,133	187,264	185,259	157,051	138,316	150,954	156,160	163,219	14.5	-2.7	2.0
excluding Nigeria	109,120	107,163	104,583	99,363	94,239	95,028	110,438	113,856	121,214	126,566	129,631	13.1	-3.2	4.4
Angola	..	..	5,375	5,169	5,985	6,074	5,595	6,510	6,926	7,724	..	..	..	7.9
Benin	1,147	1,054	1,035	980	955	1,113	1,453	1,668	1,765	1,681	2,020	15.1	-1.4	6.9
Botswana	893	1,015	861	965	1,138	1,032	1,169	1,454	2,013	2,503	..	18.2	3.4	11.5
Burkina Faso	1,711	1,575	1,556	1,420	1,284	1,431	2,019	2,559	2,874	2,567	3,165	18.0	-4.5	9.4
Burundi	920	969	1,013	1,107	1,006	1,171	1,234	1,137	1,094	1,062	1,090	16.7	4.1	-3.1
Cameroon	7,499	8,416	7,764	7,851	7,991	8,148	10,776	12,455	12,667	11,083	12,393	20.4	0.8	1.6
Cape Verde	142	140	141	139	132	138	191	234	263	283	359	2.1	-1.0	15.7
Central African Republic	797	695	748	659	638	704	990	1,073	1,118	1,105	1,378	17.0	-2.8	7.1
Chad	727	617	587	586	647	730	752	813	1,053	1,015	1,273	5.7	0.5	13.6
Comoros	..	..	115	112	108	115	163	199	207	200	246	..	..	8.7
Congo, People's Republic of the	1,706	1,994	2,161	2,097	2,194	2,161	1,849	2,298	2,220	2,269	2,649	11.0	4.2	7.3
Cote d'Ivoire	10,514	8,433	7,567	6,775	6,567	6,984	9,369	10,374	10,310	9,308	..	25.0	-8.0	5.2
Djibouti	..	..	..	..	327	338	363	373	395	404	453	..	..	5.4
Equatorial Guinea	..	..	..	..	..	81	106	128	141	132	157	..	..	8.5
Ethiopia	4,106	4,301	4,429	4,846	4,831	4,778	5,233	5,409	5,685	6,034	6,047	9.7	3.5	4.1
Gabon	4,281	3,863	3,618	3,377	3,515	3,664	3,468	3,396	3,234	3,439	4,376	4.6	-3.2	4.9
Gambia, The	233	212	213	204	164	172	148	185	212	223	253	21.4	-6.4	13.5
Ghana	4,445	4,222	4,036	4,057	4,419	4,504	5,723	5,070	5,230	5,258	5,644	10.5	0.6	0.1
Guinea	1,764	1,756	1,749	1,912	1,981	1,982	2,013	2,106	2,430	2,751	2,998	..	3.0	11.2
Guinea-Bissau	105	155	166	164	139	158	126	165	155	169	195	2.6	4.9	9.4
Kenya	7,265	6,855	6,437	5,984	6,192	6,131	7,241	7,929	8,419	8,284	9,155	18.8	-3.4	5.3
Lesotho	368	374	342	351	308	244	271	357	427	455	515	21.1	-7.1	16.5
Liberia	1,117	1,095	1,122	1,067	1,094	1,095	1,085	1,139	..	..	..	10.4	-0.4	..
Madagascar	4,042	3,595	3,526	3,511	2,940	2,893	3,296	2,590	2,501	2,539	3,161	10.9	-6.3	-1.0
Malawi	1,238	1,238	1,181	1,223	1,208	1,131	1,181	1,237	1,387	1,581	1,743	15.5	-1.4	10.8
Mali	1,629	1,365	1,228	1,079	1,061	1,058	1,526	1,899	2,055	2,078	2,463	17.0	-8.3	11.0
Mauritania	709	748	750	788	727	715	843	936	976	1,005	1,058	6.6	0.0	5.4
Mauritius	1,132	1,142	1,078	1,090	1,041	1,076	1,463	1,831	2,069	2,075	2,519	17.0	-1.5	12.9
Mozambique	2,414	2,283	2,459	2,275	2,538	3,395	4,128	1,473	1,258	1,282	1,310	..	5.7	-21.6
Namibia	2,005	1,833	1,659	1,689	1,469	1,251	1,394	1,671	1,895	1,899	..	..	-8.2	9.5
Niger	2,538	2,171	1,964	1,777	1,461	1,440	1,858	2,162	2,331	2,043	2,335	21.0	-11.1	4.1
Nigeria	103,312	95,230	93,130	89,770	93,025	90,232	46,613	24,460	29,740	29,594	33,588	16.4	-2.2	-4.5
Rwanda	1,163	1,321	1,411	1,507	1,588	1,715	1,944	2,158	2,328	2,170	2,181	15.8	7.6	2.4
Sao Tome & Principe	43	28	35	35	33	35	64	43	43	41	42	2.4	-1.6	-8.5
Senegal	3,016	2,465	2,568	2,465	2,325	2,564	3,738	4,599	4,980	4,664	5,715	9.0	-2.9	9.0
Seychelles	147	154	148	147	151	169	212	256	283	292	320	28.5	1.8	10.0
Sierra Leone	1,101	1,190	1,335	1,486	1,088	1,523	1,433	619	1,144	941	956	10.5	4.3	-3.8
Somalia	604	699	774	734	788	878	934	1,023	1,046	1,132	949	-7.0	6.4	1.4
Sudan	7,944	8,908	7,395	7,378	9,082	6,666	9,228	9,962	8,954	16,348	12,381	16.0	-2.3	11.4
Swaziland	542	576	505	521	461	339	421	557	612	637	..	12.5	-8.2	14.9
Tanzania	5,138	5,927	6,272	6,328	5,813	6,904	4,883	3,409	3,137	2,865	2,619	15.4	4.2	-13.2
Togo	1,136	962	822	766	718	753	1,046	1,247	1,364	1,338	1,620	10.8	-8.2	9.9
Uganda	1,724	1,596	1,747	2,194	2,628	3,507	3,893	4,354	4,899	4,713	4,122	-2.8	16.3	2.0
Zaire	14,758	13,643	14,335	11,262	7,191	7,150	8,304	7,806	9,706	9,607	9,557	13.1	-15.2	5.0
Zambia	3,884	4,008	3,871	3,321	2,720	2,253	1,664	2,078	3,618	4,703	4,246	7.1	-10.9	30.9
Zimbabwe	5,355	6,423	6,846	6,225	5,091	4,349	4,976	5,372	5,892	5,878	6,009	3.5	-5.1	4.8
NORTH AFRICA	128,362	123,044	123,643	127,811	129,953	141,199	145,769	151,709	136,011	135,560	143,941	16.7	1.9	-1.4
Algeria	42,347	44,365	45,197	48,812	52,947	57,997	63,069	64,476	51,899	47,825	52,845	21.1	6.4	-6.3
Egypt, Arab Republic of	22,913	23,405	25,592	28,137	30,643	34,690	35,880	35,545	30,978	33,399	33,333	10.8	8.9	-2.1
Libya	35,539	31,565	29,297	28,821	25,579	27,362	21,013	23,140	21,097	21,878	..	17.4	-5.4	4.9
Morocco	18,821	15,280	15,424	13,942	12,751	12,870	16,995	18,944	21,985	22,386	24,969	16.2	-7.0	9.8
Tunisia	8,742	8,429	8,133	8,099	8,033	8,280	8,811	9,604	10,052	10,072	12,098	13.8	-1.2	7.1
ALL AFRICA	340,793	325,436	321,357	316,944	317,217	326,459	302,820	290,025	286,965	291,720	307,160	15.3	-0.9	0.3
South Africa	79,598	83,140	76,260	84,049	76,201	57,471	63,773	82,554	88,226	90,366	..	11.0	-5.0	13.8

2-6. Total consumption

	Percentage of GDP											Annual average		
	1980	1981	1982	1983	1984	1985	1986	1987	1988	1989	1990	75–79	80–85	86–MR
SUB-SAHARAN AFRICA	77.5	83.7	89.1	91.4	90.9	87.9	89.0	88.1	88.5	87.7	82.7	77.0	86.7	87.2
excluding Nigeria	84.3	85.2	87.6	90.8	89.6	86.7	87.5	89.2	89.4	89.8	86.4	78.1	87.4	88.4
Angola	..	..	..	..	..	..	..	..	..	..	..	..	..	..
Benin	106.3	114.9	102.6	99.9	106.4	98.9	97.5	96.6	98.3	99.1	97.7	99.1	104.8	97.8
Botswana	70.3	77.6	92.2	83.2	76.2	71.6	61.4	66.0	64.2	62.9	..	81.4	78.5	63.6
Burkina Faso	103.1	104.1	101.0	100.2	100.6	96.8	97.1	95.9	92.7	94.8	95.4	96.1	101.0	95.2
Burundi	100.9	96.2	102.7	93.4	94.2	96.2	98.8	93.1	98.4	95.6	98.9	95.3	97.3	97.0
Cameroon	84.3	77.7	76.9	71.2	67.3	64.1	68.5	80.4	87.1	79.7	81.4	83.6	73.6	79.4
Cape Verde	108.0	103.9	103.4	104.3	110.9	111.4	112.0	95.5	98.7	96.0	..	123.5	107.0	102.1
Central African Republic	109.6	101.9	106.8	101.2	100.3	100.3	101.7	101.2	100.6	99.8	101.7	100.5	103.3	101.0
Chad	116.5	110.3	109.8	108.6	103.4	119.3	122.1	117.7	113.4	113.5	115.4	100.2	111.3	116.4
Comoros	..	..	..	97.2	110.8	108.8	103.5	109.2	110.7	104.9	106.2	..	52.8	106.9
Congo, People's Republic of the	58.6	54.2	53.5	55.4	53.6	68.9	84.4	77.2	81.2	71.4	69.5	88.5	57.4	76.7
Cote d'Ivoire	77.8	81.2	79.7	81.1	77.6	74.2	81.4	83.4	82.8	88.5	86.1	72.3	78.6	84.4
Djibouti	..	..	..	..	103.3	104.0	103.3	100.8	104.5	104.6	..	..	34.6	103.3
Equatorial Guinea	..	..	..	..	..	99.0	97.1	101.4	107.2	103.4	106.3	..	16.5	103.1
Ethiopia	95.2	96.4	98.0	97.3	97.6	97.2	97.8	96.5	93.7	94.9	97.0	94.6	97.0	96.0
Gabon	38.8	41.0	43.1	46.8	45.8	49.0	72.1	71.5	75.5	67.4	60.5	40.1	44.1	69.4
Gambia, The	99.3	95.8	90.2	95.7	95.1	93.6	94.8	93.1	92.9	91.7	91.0	96.8	94.9	92.7
Ghana	95.1	96.0	96.3	96.7	93.4	92.4	92.3	91.8	89.3	94.0	89.2	91.4	95.0	91.3
Guinea	78.4	83.4	83.2	83.9	86.2	87.0	81.3	81.5	84.6	80.6	79.9	..	83.7	81.6
Guinea-Bissau	106.0	98.8	105.2	103.6	108.3	111.0	101.2	96.4	105.9	114.5	111.2	106.4	105.5	105.8
Kenya	81.8	80.3	81.9	79.6	80.6	75.4	78.2	80.8	80.1	80.5	82.5	80.4	80.0	80.4
Lesotho	159.6	168.3	173.5	199.0	194.0	178.4	175.7	175.8	156.9	169.3	177.6	168.4	178.8	171.1
Liberia	72.7	81.2	87.5	90.0	85.6	85.7	81.6	..	..	..	..	70.1	83.8	..
Madagascar	101.4	99.8	101.0	98.6	96.3	97.4	95.6	95.3	93.4	90.9	91.8	96.7	99.1	93.4
Malawi	89.2	88.2	84.9	84.8	85.2	87.1	89.6	86.9	90.8	95.5	90.2	82.4	86.6	90.7
Mali	101.9	100.3	99.5	104.8	103.4	114.2	101.2	93.8	92.6	88.2	94.7	99.2	104.0	94.1
Mauritania	93.1	87.4	97.0	112.1	101.9	91.2	84.6	86.3	93.9	92.1	97.2	97.2	97.1	90.8
Mauritius	89.5	85.2	84.6	82.9	81.3	78.4	71.4	72.6	74.5	76.9	78.6	78.1	83.7	74.8
Mozambique	99.5	100.0	103.3	110.8	106.2	103.1	101.1	112.0	116.5	116.6	111.8	..	103.8	111.6
Namibia	62.4	88.4	93.6	96.9	95.9	83.9	83.4	96.2	86.8	84.6	..	..	86.8	87.8
Niger	77.4	91.3	92.2	92.5	101.6	97.6	94.4	95.5	93.3	97.6	..	90.0	92.1	95.2
Nigeria	70.5	82.0	90.7	92.0	92.3	89.2	92.6	83.1	85.2	79.0	..	75.6	86.1	85.0
Rwanda	95.8	98.6	94.8	95.6	91.2	91.8	91.7	93.7	93.6	93.7	96.2	91.2	94.7	93.8
Sao Tome & Principe	114.9	129.8	124.0	112.8	112.1	118.1	108.6	114.5	102.3	140.0	129.5	99.2	118.6	119.0
Senegal	100.4	107.5	101.0	100.4	97.8	101.4	94.4	93.9	92.5	94.5	91.3	91.8	101.4	93.3
Seychelles	72.9	82.5	91.2	101.0	91.8	92.8	94.6	92.7	92.4	95.7	87.9	54.4	88.7	92.6
Sierra Leone	99.1	97.6	96.8	96.7	89.1	92.0	90.4	88.9	84.8	95.0	94.9	94.7	95.2	90.8
Somalia	112.9	116.0	112.8	126.6	122.3	111.5	116.9	109.5	•107.4	126.0	..	104.6	117.0	115.0
Sudan	56.8	62.3	82.4	124.5	126.8	103.8	99.6	97.1	102.5	98.6	108.9	..	92.8	101.3
Swaziland	92.6	98.6	98.0	101.1	104.6	95.8	79.5	85.7	89.6	..	..	75.2	98.5	84.9
Tanzania	90.2	87.9	86.4	91.6	92.8	92.6	80.5	99.9	105.4	105.9	..	84.9	90.2	97.9
Togo	75.2	76.5	82.3	79.1	80.9	80.0	87.7	88.4	89.4	86.1	88.9	74.3	79.0	88.1
Uganda	95.4	85.0	104.3	96.1	93.8	92.2	91.6	93.9	99.2	100.2	100.7	..	94.5	97.1
Zaire	88.9	89.2	90.6	89.1	87.7	83.6	85.6	88.7	87.9	88.4	..	94.6	88.2	87.6
Zambia	80.7	93.2	92.0	84.8	83.5	84.6	77.4	82.0	81.3	96.5	83.0	76.9	86.5	84.1
Zimbabwe	84.2	84.2	84.8	87.2	80.5	77.7	76.3	76.8	75.4	78.6	82.6	80.7	83.1	77.9
NORTH AFRICA	51.8	53.9	55.7	55.4	59.1	59.4	66.6	66.3	66.5	66.9	64.2	55.9	55.9	66.1
Algeria	56.9	59.3	60.8	60.3	62.6	63.6	70.6	68.1	70.0	69.0	61.8	62.2	60.6	67.9
Egypt, Arab Republic of	84.8	85.9	84.8	82.2	86.0	85.4	86.2	93.4	91.8	93.1	90.1	84.4	84.9	90.9
Libya	42.0	52.0	66.1	70.1	..	..	..	..	..	..	..	53.7	..	..
Morocco	86.3	88.5	86.2	84.8	85.3	83.9	83.5	83.3	79.4	81.5	80.4	88.0	85.8	81.6
Tunisia	76.0	76.1	78.8	79.0	79.7	79.6	83.8	80.4	80.2	81.4	80.0	77.6	78.2	81.2
ALL AFRICA	67.7	72.3	76.2	76.8	77.9	75.7	78.3	76.9	77.9	77.7	73.7	69.4	74.4	76.9
South Africa	63.5	67.3	70.7	72.0	72.5	71.3	72.8	75.5	74.7	75.8	..	69.9	69.6	74.7

2-7. General government consumption

	Percentage of GDP											Annual average		
	1980	1981	1982	1983	1984	1985	1986	1987	1988	1989	1990	75-79	80-85	86-MR
SUB-SAHARAN AFRICA	12.1	12.7	13.2	13.8	14.0	12.5	14.4	15.3	14.9	14.4	33.9	12.5	13.1	18.6
excluding Nigeria	15.3	15.5	14.9	14.6	14.9	14.8	15.6	15.8	15.9	15.8	18.3	14.8	15.0	16.3
Angola	..	..	..	..	..	..	..	..	..	..	..	..	..	..
Benin	10.6	11.2	10.5	11.0	10.2	15.3	15.3	15.9	13.7	10.9	10.7	10.4	11.5	13.3
Botswana	19.8	25.7	30.6	28.8	27.9	26.7	23.8	23.8	22.7	19.6	..	21.8	26.6	22.5
Burkina Faso	9.6	9.6	14.4	15.0	13.6	12.1	12.9	13.4	12.7	13.1	12.9	11.2	12.4	13.0
Burundi	13.1	16.0	15.0	13.3	13.0	12.7	15.5	15.9	15.5	14.1	15.0	11.6	13.9	15.2
Cameroon	8.7	8.7	8.7	8.9	9.4	9.0	8.7	10.9	11.3	11.8	11.7	10.1	8.9	10.9
Cape Verde	14.7	15.1	19.1	20.7	22.9	23.8	27.4	23.4	24.2	19.6	..	21.3	19.4	23.7
Central African Republic	15.1	15.0	15.9	16.9	14.2	13.8	15.0	13.5	13.3	13.2	13.6	14.6	15.2	13.7
Chad	..	..	7.8	8.6	14.2	16.6	19.8	22.7	17.9	21.3	22.9	19.7	7.9	20.9
Comoros	..	..	..	28.4	28.3	29.7	27.6	26.5	29.3	29.0	30.0	..	14.4	28.5
Congo, People's Republic of the	17.6	13.4	13.5	15.5	14.8	16.5	25.0	20.6	21.0	18.7	18.6	19.7	15.2	20.8
Cote d'Ivoire	17.8	17.4	17.2	16.8	15.3	13.9	15.2	16.4	17.2	17.5	18.0	16.3	16.4	16.9
Djibouti	..	..	..	..	36.9	39.1	39.4	35.6	34.1	33.6	..	..	12.7	35.7
Equatorial Guinea	..	..	..	..	..	23.5	28.9	28.0	36.6	34.6	34.2	..	3.9	32.5
Ethiopia	15.2	15.7	16.2	17.3	18.4	19.5	18.9	19.3	23.6	25.8	26.4	14.7	17.0	22.8
Gabon	13.2	14.2	15.7	17.3	18.5	18.6	25.3	23.7	23.4	19.3	19.0	13.3	16.3	22.1
Gambia, The	20.1	23.1	19.9	20.6	18.2	16.4	22.8	20.0	16.9	16.7	16.4	15.4	19.7	18.5
Ghana	11.2	8.8	6.5	5.9	7.3	9.4	11.1	10.0	10.0	10.3	7.5	11.9	8.2	9.8
Guinea	20.8	17.4	19.4	18.9	14.4	14.5	9.5	10.7	10.6	10.4	11.2	..	17.6	10.5
Guinea-Bissau	29.0	28.5	29.4	25.5	24.7	24.2	13.7	11.7	16.9	14.1	12.6	21.9	26.9	13.8
Kenya	19.8	18.6	18.4	18.4	17.4	17.5	18.3	18.6	18.4	18.7	18.4	18.3	18.3	18.4
Lesotho	35.8	33.4	31.9	31.6	29.6	33.2	33.9	30.9	28.8	26.0	26.0	19.0	32.6	29.1
Liberia	16.3	19.3	21.7	19.1	17.1	21.0	17.1	..	..	..	..	13.0	19.1	..
Madagascar	12.1	11.6	10.6	9.6	9.6	9.8	8.8	9.1	8.1	8.9	8.6	11.4	10.5	8.7
Malawi	19.3	17.9	17.5	16.4	15.7	17.7	19.7	19.1	16.3	16.3	15.5	15.5	17.4	17.4
Mali	10.4	9.9	9.8	10.9	10.8	11.8	11.0	11.0	11.3	10.4	11.0	9.5	10.6	10.9
Mauritania	25.3	21.7	17.9	18.4	17.2	14.8	13.6	13.2	14.0	13.2	9.7	30.4	19.2	12.7
Mauritius	14.1	13.9	13.9	13.4	12.8	11.5	10.5	11.5	12.6	12.3	12.1	12.7	13.3	11.8
Mozambique	23.3	25.7	23.6	28.6	26.0	22.4	25.4	16.1	17.5	20.2	20.3	..	24.9	19.9
Namibia	16.5	25.1	27.3	29.6	30.8	28.3	29.5	33.6	30.3	28.4	..	..	26.3	30.5
Niger	10.3	10.9	11.7	11.4	10.2	10.8	11.5	11.7	10.4	12.1	..	12.2	10.9	11.4
Nigeria	8.9	9.7	11.4	13.0	13.2	10.1	11.8	13.3	11.2	8.9	..	9.9	11.1	11.3
Rwanda	12.5	20.0	12.2	11.8	10.2	11.3	11.9	13.0	12.9	14.4	18.4	15.9	13.1	14.1
Sao Tome & Principe	23.6	38.8	33.9	35.4	37.8	37.4	29.4	32.4	27.4	28.6	30.4	7.4	34.5	28.6
Senegal	22.0	20.4	18.2	18.0	18.5	16.8	15.4	15.6	14.7	15.2	14.3	16.9	19.0	15.0
Seychelles	28.7	31.7	34.9	32.8	30.7	34.6	38.8	29.3	27.3	28.6	25.5	19.5	32.2	29.9
Sierra Leone	8.4	7.0	8.6	8.9	6.9	7.2	6.7	6.1	10.2	9.6	9.9	9.9	7.8	8.5
Somalia	15.6	22.1	13.3	19.8	17.0	18.5	23.6	24.5	20.6	25.3	..	22.0	17.7	23.5
Sudan	16.0	15.9	10.8	9.2	9.7	9.6	13.6	12.9	14.0	14.6	14.2	12.4	11.9	13.8
Swaziland	24.6	26.7	25.8	23.4	27.5	22.1	22.9	21.2	21.7	..	..	19.4	25.0	21.9
Tanzania	13.0	12.4	13.8	13.4	15.6	15.4	14.8	11.5	10.0	10.4	..	16.5	13.9	11.7
Togo	22.4	19.1	19.1	17.2	16.7	16.6	20.0	21.0	17.9	17.6	18.6	21.2	18.5	19.0
Uganda	..	..	..	3.1	9.7	9.0	8.6	7.7	7.4	6.9	6.8	..	3.6	7.5
Zaire	8.4	10.0	9.5	7.5	6.6	7.7	8.0	9.9	12.7	8.9	..	9.9	8.3	9.9
Zambia	25.5	28.3	27.7	24.1	25.1	23.9	26.9	22.2	15.3	12.6	15.5	25.6	25.8	18.5
Zimbabwe	19.7	17.2	19.8	18.4	21.3	22.2	21.7	27.6	23.4	24.1	24.3	16.6	19.8	24.2
NORTH AFRICA	15.2	16.1	16.3	16.0	16.1	16.3	17.1	16.7	16.5	16.6	15.2	17.2	16.0	16.4
Algeria	13.8	13.8	14.8	14.8	15.0	15.7	17.8	18.5	18.7	19.5	18.2	13.3	14.6	18.6
Egypt, Arab Republic of	15.7	19.0	17.8	17.2	18.0	17.2	16.5	14.0	13.5	12.7	10.0	21.4	17.5	13.3
Libya	21.8	27.2	34.6	36.5	..	..	..	..	..	..	..	26.1	..	..
Morocco	18.3	19.1	18.3	16.8	15.6	15.8	15.4	15.7	15.4	15.9	15.9	20.3	17.3	15.6
Tunisia	14.5	14.8	16.5	16.9	16.5	16.5	17.3	16.3	16.0	17.0	16.2	15.5	15.9	16.6
ALL AFRICA	63.1	66.4	69.0	70.8	67.2	61.2	67.9	71.2	71.2	70.7	58.7	66.5	66.3	67.9
South Africa	13.6	14.1	15.6	15.7	17.0	17.5	18.3	18.9	18.2	19.6	..	14.4	15.6	18.7

2–8. Gross domestic investment

				Percentage of GDP							Annual average		
	1980	1981	1982	1983	1984	1985	1986	1987	1988	1989	1990	75–79	80–85	86–MR
SUB-SAHARAN AFRICA	20.2	20.5	17.2	13.7	10.4	11.6	14.6	15.6	15.6	15.6	14.2	21.5	15.6	15.1
excluding Nigeria	19.9	19.6	19.0	15.9	15.1	15.7	16.7	16.5	16.5	16.4	15.7	19.3	17.6	16.4
Angola	..	..	..	..	..	..	..	..	..	..	..	..	..	..
Benin	18.6	19.2	34.1	11.6	7.4	8.9	13.5	12.9	12.9	8.9	12.0	21.8	16.6	12.0
Botswana	41.0	43.6	44.2	29.4	24.4	30.1	17.9	6.3	10.3	23.9	..	39.8	35.4	14.6
Burkina Faso	18.2	17.0	21.6	20.6	17.0	25.9	22.9	20.0	22.2	22.8	19.9	24.1	20.0	21.6
Burundi	13.9	17.0	14.5	22.8	18.4	13.9	11.6	22.7	15.0	16.7	19.3	11.3	16.7	17.1
Cameroon	18.9	24.7	23.4	24.4	20.8	24.9	30.8	24.1	15.7	18.5	16.5	20.7	22.8	21.1
Cape Verde	41.9	45.3	52.9	48.8	44.0	45.1	45.8	44.3	41.7	42.3	..	32.6	46.3	43.5
Central African Republic	7.0	8.7	6.7	11.8	12.3	14.5	12.2	13.7	11.5	11.2	11.1	11.7	10.2	11.9
Chad	..	..	..	3.1	5.4	8.2	9.1	12.3	7.8	9.0	10.3	16.2	2.8	9.7
Comoros	..	..	..	29.0	45.8	29.6	23.6	23.3	16.0	13.9	14.7	..	17.4	18.3
Congo, People's Republic of the	35.8	48.2	59.7	38.4	30.4	30.3	29.5	19.7	18.6	16.0	15.9	30.0	40.5	19.9
Cote d'Ivoire	28.2	25.9	23.2	20.6	10.9	12.6	11.1	12.2	14.4	8.5	7.7	26.1	20.2	10.8
Djibouti	..	..	..	..	28.5	23.8	16.1	18.6	15.5	18.5	..	..	8.7	17.2
Equatorial Guinea	..	..	..	..	..	9.3	12.7	24.2	21.0	21.3	24.3	..	1.5	20.7
Ethiopia	10.0	10.4	11.8	11.2	12.3	14.0	12.7	14.6	15.3	13.3	11.3	9.0	11.6	13.5
Gabon	28.1	36.3	35.0	35.3	33.5	37.3	45.0	28.2	31.9	25.3	22.4	52.4	34.3	30.5
Gambia, The	26.2	24.5	20.6	17.3	19.2	15.8	20.4	18.5	18.0	22.0	20.7	19.4	20.6	19.9
Ghana	5.6	4.6	3.4	3.7	6.9	9.6	9.4	10.4	10.9	13.5	15.1	8.9	5.6	11.9
Guinea	15.8	13.4	14.1	14.1	10.1	9.4	15.5	17.7	19.5	18.4	17.4	..	12.8	17.7
Guinea-Bissau	29.6	25.7	28.3	22.7	30.0	32.0	24.3	33.3	34.2	35.6	22.4	19.0	28.0	30.0
Kenya	29.2	27.7	21.8	20.8	20.7	26.0	21.8	24.3	25.0	24.6	23.7	22.8	24.4	23.9
Lesotho	42.4	42.9	49.7	33.6	41.6	50.0	45.4	44.9	46.2	54.9	52.6	28.1	43.4	48.8
Liberia	27.3	16.3	14.3	11.8	10.2	8.7	9.7	..	..	..	..	31.6	14.8	..
Madagascar	15.0	11.5	8.5	8.4	8.6	8.5	9.0	10.1	13.3	13.5	16.9	10.0	10.1	12.6
Malawi	24.7	17.6	21.4	22.8	12.9	18.6	12.3	15.4	18.7	20.3	19.1	30.7	19.7	17.1
Mali	17.0	17.5	17.6	14.6	15.2	19.5	22.9	23.1	26.2	27.5	21.4	16.1	16.9	24.2
Mauritania	36.2	41.9	47.1	17.8	25.1	24.3	23.0	20.5	17.7	14.7	14.5	34.5	32.1	18.0
Mauritius	20.7	25.3	18.2	17.5	22.0	23.5	21.9	25.3	30.6	30.8	30.3	30.0	21.2	27.8
Mozambique	18.9	20.3	19.3	10.0	10.6	6.9	9.7	24.0	33.4	35.5	37.1	..	14.3	28.0
Namibia	33.2	30.8	23.1	17.8	17.2	14.0	12.7	15.9	20.2	16.6	..	..	22.7	16.4
Niger	36.6	20.3	18.2	12.8	3.2	12.7	10.1	9.2	11.0	9.5	..	19.4	17.3	10.0
Nigeria	20.5	21.4	15.4	11.4	6.0	7.5	9.7	11.4	12.3	12.5	..	24.1	13.7	11.5
Rwanda	16.1	13.3	17.8	13.5	15.8	17.3	15.9	15.6	15.7	15.6	12.5	14.3	15.6	15.0
Sao Tome & Principe	34.2	47.0	49.9	29.5	47.8	37.0	14.5	17.2	28.1	27.6	19.9	25.2	40.9	21.5
Senegal	15.3	11.9	11.3	11.9	11.7	9.8	11.0	11.7	12.5	10.8	12.7	16.7	12.0	11.7
Seychelles	38.3	32.6	32.3	21.2	21.7	22.7	22.8	18.6	20.0	19.8	21.2	31.0	28.1	20.5
Sierra Leone	16.2	19.1	13.4	14.3	12.7	10.0	11.2	10.4	11.6	11.4	11.5	13.0	14.3	11.2
Somalia	42.4	27.6	29.3	22.4	24.2	29.8	25.2	33.3	23.9	30.3	..	25.1	29.3	28.2
Sudan	15.1	14.3	22.8	16.0	13.8	4.5	12.8	10.3	10.0	9.1	9.3	17.1	14.4	10.3
Swaziland	40.7	31.0	32.2	35.0	31.6	29.6	22.2	15.3	16.6	..	..	31.6	33.4	18.0
Tanzania	23.0	20.6	21.0	13.6	15.3	15.7	19.5	22.5	19.8	24.7	..	24.3	18.2	21.6
Togo	30.1	30.2	26.3	22.1	21.2	28.8	24.0	20.2	20.2	21.4	22.5	37.7	26.4	21.7
Uganda	..	..	..	9.1	8.8	9.9	12.5	12.9	10.1	9.9	12.3	..	4.6	11.5
Zaire	10.0	10.5	8.3	9.3	10.5	12.5	13.2	14.2	14.4	14.5	..	15.7	10.2	14.1
Zambia	23.3	19.3	16.8	13.8	14.7	14.9	23.8	13.9	11.4	9.9	14.3	25.4	17.1	14.7
Zimbabwe	18.8	23.1	21.2	15.9	19.0	21.1	19.4	19.1	19.7	20.7	21.4	17.6	19.8	20.1
NORTH AFRICA	32.3	32.8	33.4	32.5	31.4	29.8	28.5	24.7	26.0	26.8	28.1	36.3	32.0	26.8
Algeria	39.1	37.0	37.3	37.6	35.1	33.2	33.5	30.0	30.4	31.1	33.0	45.9	36.5	31.6
Egypt, Arab Republic of	27.5	29.5	30.1	28.7	27.5	26.7	23.7	18.0	24.2	23.6	23.1	31.1	28.3	22.5
Libya	22.1	30.6	27.9	25.2	..	..	..	..	..	..	..	26.2	..	..
Morocco	24.2	26.1	28.2	24.0	25.3	25.0	22.8	21.1	21.1	24.0	25.7	27.5	25.5	22.9
Tunisia	29.4	32.3	31.7	29.6	32.0	26.6	23.5	20.6	19.4	22.7	26.7	29.9	30.2	22.6
ALL AFRICA	24.0	24.5	22.6	20.3	18.1	18.6	20.8	20.0	20.3	20.7	20.6	26.0	21.3	20.5
South Africa	30.4	32.9	25.0	25.6	24.8	20.1	19.3	19.3	21.5	20.8	..	28.2	26.5	20.2

2-9. Gross public investment

	Percentage of GDP											Annual average		
	1980	1981	1982	1983	1984	1985	1986	1987	1988	1989	1990	75–79	80–85	86–MR
SUB-SAHARAN AFRICA	..	..	..	..	..	..	..	..	..	..	..	..	..	..
excluding Nigeria	..	..	..	..	..	..	..	..	..	..	..	..	..	..
Angola	..	..	..	..	..	..	..	..	..	..	..	..	..	..
Benin	..	..	..	..	..	6.0	8.7	8.7	8.6	7.8	7.5	..	..	8.3
Botswana	13.3	15.9	..	..	..	..	..	..	..	..	..	14.4	..	..
Burkina Faso	..	..	10.5	11.7	12.2	10.8	15.5	18.7	13.8	9.9	9.3	..	..	13.4
Burundi	12.8	11.9	13.8	16.8	14.9	11.9	11.4	16.4	13.4	13.7	15.1	..	13.7	14.0
Cameroon	10.1	15.6	15.5	16.1	..	..	..	..	..	..	..	..	..	..
Cape Verde	..	..	..	..	..	..	..	..	..	..	..	..	..	..
Central African Republic	..	..	..	..	..	..	..	..	..	..	..	..	..	..
Chad	..	..	..	2.9	5.2	7.8	8.7	11.8	7.5	8.5	9.8	..	..	9.3
Comoros	..	..	..	17.7	26.6	20.0	14.3	..	..	..	..	..	..	..
Congo, People's Republic of the	..	..	..	..	..	..	..	..	..	..	..	..	..	..
Cote d'Ivoire	9.0	8.8	6.8	6.3	4.6	3.7	3.6	4.5	4.1	2.2	2.2	11.2	6.5	3.3
Djibouti	..	..	..	..	..	..	..	..	..	..	..	..	..	..
Equatorial Guinea	..	..	..	..	..	10.1	9.1	16.8	16.5	15.9	17.2	..	..	15.1
Ethiopia	..	..	..	..	..	11.8	10.7	12.6	13.4	12.0	10.1	..	..	11.8
Gabon	8.9	11.3	12.3	16.1	8.2	10.6	12.6	3.2	2.5	2.6	4.2	24.1	11.2	5.0
Gambia, The	17.0	14.5	12.6	11.7	16.2	10.6	14.9	14.1	10.7	9.7	9.5	..	13.8	11.8
Ghana	..	..	..	..	..	..	..	..	..	..	..	..	..	..
Guinea	..	..	..	..	..	..	5.1	6.0	7.2	6.8	7.1	..	..	6.4
Guinea-Bissau	..	..	..	..	..	..	..	..	..	..	..	..	..	..
Kenya	10.4	10.4	8.6	6.9	7.5	10.7	8.1	7.1	8.3	8.1	9.5	..	9.1	8.2
Lesotho	..	..	..	..	..	13.8	13.9	14.2	13.1	13.8	..	12.0	..	13.7
Liberia	..	..	..	..	..	..	..	..	..	..	..	..	..	..
Madagascar	..	..	..	..	..	..	..	..	..	..	..	..	..	..
Malawi	17.5	10.2	8.4	8.3	9.8	8.3	10.0	5.0	8.2	8.6	7.9	16.3	10.4	7.9
Mali	..	..	..	..	..	..	..	..	..	..	..	..	..	..
Mauritania	..	..	..	..	..	..	..	..	10.4	8.1	..	..	..	..
Mauritius	8.4	8.5	6.4	6.4	5.7	6.0	7.0	7.3	12.2	7.1	11.2	..	6.9	9.0
Mozambique	..	..	..	..	..	..	..	..	..	..	..	..	..	..
Namibia	..	..	..	..	..	..	..	..	..	..	..	..	..	..
Niger	..	..	..	..	..	..	..	..	..	..	..	..	..	..
Nigeria	..	14.3	9.6	7.2	3.6	4.4	6.4	7.8	7.2	..	..	..	..	7.1
Rwanda	..	..	..	..	..	..	..	..	..	..	..	..	..	..
Sao Tome & Principe	..	..	..	..	..	..	..	..	..	..	..	..	..	..
Senegal	5.9	4.2	3.9	4.0	4.0	3.9	4.0	4.1	3.9	4.0	3.8	..	4.3	4.0
Seychelles	..	..	..	14.3	18.3	7.3	7.9	12.8	9.6	10.8	11.0	..	..	10.4
Sierra Leone	11.4	6.9	5.0	3.8	1.3	..	..	..	..	..	..	5.1	4.7	..
Somalia	..	..	..	..	..	..	..	..	..	..	..	..	..	..
Sudan	7.0	6.8	5.2	4.7	4.0	3.1	..	..	..	..	..	..	5.2	..
Swaziland	..	..	..	..	..	..	..	..	..	..	..	..	..	..
Tanzania	11.6	5.1	4.1	2.3	2.0	1.8	1.8	2.2	2.3	..	..	..	4.5	2.1
Togo	21.9	17.9	15.7	9.6	13.0	14.9	14.5	9.3	9.9	..	..	..	15.5	11.2
Uganda	..	..	..	..	5.6	4.9	6.6	6.0	5.3	4.9	5.2	..	..	5.6
Zaire	5.1	5.0	2.4	2.9	3.9	3.4	4.0	4.9	6.7	..	..	..	3.8	5.2
Zambia	..	..	..	..	..	..	..	..	..	..	..	..	..	..
Zimbabwe	4.7	5.3	9.9	11.7	9.8	9.5	7.3	7.6	6.7	5.7	..	..	8.5	6.8
NORTH AFRICA	..	..	..	..	..	..	..	..	..	..	..	..	..	..
Algeria	..	..	..	..	..	..	..	..	..	..	..	..	..	..
Egypt, Arab Republic of	..	..	..	..	..	..	..	..	..	..	..	..	..	..
Libya	19.4	..	..	..	..	..	..	..	..	..	..	21.5	..	..
Morocco	..	..	..	..	..	..	..	..	..	..	..	..	..	..
Tunisia	15.0	16.2	18.6	17.6	17.1	14.5	13.5	11.0	9.6	10.0	11.7	17.7	16.5	11.2
ALL AFRICA	..	..	..	..	..	..	..	..	..	..	..	..	..	..
South Africa	13.0	12.3	12.0	11.1	9.9	10.2	8.6	7.4	6.7	7.1	..	14.4	11.4	7.4

2-10. Gross private investment

	Percentage of GDP											Annual average		
	1980	1981	1982	1983	1984	1985	1986	1987	1988	1989	1990	75–79	80–85	86–MR
SUB-SAHARAN AFRICA	..	..	..	..	..	..	..	..	..	..	..	..	..	..
excluding Nigeria	..	..	..	..	..	..	..	..	..	..	..			
Angola	..	..	..	..	..							..	..	..
Benin	..	..	..	..	..	2.8	4.1	4.7	3.9	3.7	4.3	..	..	4.1
Botswana	21.8	22.9	..	..	..	..	..	..	..	..	..	14.1	..	..
Burkina Faso	..	..	9.5	8.3	5.0	10.2	7.6	8.2	8.6	9.0	8.0	..	..	8.3
Burundi	1.1	1.6	1.4	2.5	2.7	2.4	2.6	4.5	1.7	3.2	3.3	..	2.0	3.0
Cameroon	7.9	6.6	6.6	7.4	..	..	..	..	..	..	..	..	..	..
Cape Verde	..	..	..	..	..	..	..	..	..	..	..	..	..	..
Central African Republic	..	..	..	..	..	..	2.5	1.9	1.8	2.3	1.7	..	..	2.0
Chad	..	..	..	0.1	0.3	0.4	0.4	0.5	0.4	0.4	0.5	..	..	0.4
Comoros	..	..	..	9.0	6.9	6.0	6.6	..	..	..	..	..	..	..
Congo, People's Republic of the	..	..	..	..	..	..	..	..	..	..	..	..	..	..
Cote d'Ivoire	17.1	15.5	14.9	11.9	7.7	7.7	8.3	6.7	6.9	6.3	6.3	14.1	12.5	6.9
Djibouti	..	..	..	..	..				..	..	..	..	..	..
Equatorial Guinea	..	..	..	..	..	-0.8	3.5	7.3	4.5	5.4	7.1	..	..	5.6
Ethiopia	..	..	..	..	..	2.2	2.0	2.0	1.9	1.3	1.2	..	..	1.7
Gabon	18.4	21.8	20.0	20.3	22.9	25.7	32.1	25.7	30.7	23.5	18.2	23.6	21.5	26.0
Gambia, The	9.3	10.1	8.0	5.6	3.0	5.2	5.4	4.4	7.3	12.4	11.2	..	6.9	8.1
Ghana	..	..	..	..	..	..	..	..	..	..	..	..	..	..
Guinea	..	..	..	..	..	..	8.2	10.2	10.6	9.6	10.3	..	..	9.8
Guinea-Bissau	..	..	..	..	..	..	..	..	..	..	..	..	..	..
Kenya	12.6	13.0	10.4	11.1	10.5	7.2	11.5	12.5	11.8	11.2	10.7	..	10.8	11.5
Lesotho	..	..	..	..	..	36.4	30.7	30.9	32.9	40.9	..	..	..	33.8
Liberia	..	..	..	..	..	..	..	..	..	..	..	..	..	..
Madagascar	..	..	..	..	..	..	..	..	..	..	..	..	..	..
Malawi	4.7	4.9	6.1	5.4	3.3	5.1	2.0	8.5	7.2	7.3	8.3	9.1	4.9	6.7
Mali	..	..	..	..	..	..	..	..	11.2	12.7	13.1	..	..	..
Mauritania	..	..	..	..	..	..	..	..	5.9	5.4	..	..	..	..
Mauritius	14.9	13.5	11.5	11.6	12.3	12.6	12.8	14.3	16.6	19.6	20.2	18.4	12.7	16.7
Mozambique	..	..	..	..	..	..	..	..	..	..	..	..	..	..
Namibia	..	..	..	..	..	..	..	..	..	..	..	..	..	..
Niger	..	..	..	..	..	..	..	..	..	..	..	..	..	..
Nigeria	..	6.8	5.5	4.0	2.4	2.3	3.1	4.8	4.5	..	..	..	3.5	4.1
Rwanda	..	..	..	..	..	..	..	..	..	..	..	..	..	..
Sao Tome & Principe	..	..	..	..	..	..	..	..	..	..	..	..	..	..
Senegal	9.8	8.4	8.2	9.0	8.3	7.6	8.0	8.2	8.6	8.8	8.9	..	8.5	8.5
Seychelles	..	..	..	7.8	2.9	15.4	14.4	4.7	8.2	7.0	8.4	..	..	8.5
Sierra Leone	3.5	11.4	7.8	8.8	10.8	..	..	..	..	..	..	6.9	..	..
Somalia	..	..	..	..	..	..	..	..	..	..	..	..	..	..
Sudan	4.5	3.3	12.9	11.9	11.6	8.4	..	..	..	..	..	7.6	8.8	..
Swaziland	27.3	19.5	20.6	29.8	28.0	22.3	17.3	..	..	..	..	..	24.6	..
Tanzania	8.9	12.5	14.5	8.7	11.4	12.2	16.2	18.7	16.2	..	..	10.1	11.4	17.0
Togo	8.0	9.2	8.6	9.8	9.3	9.6	8.8	8.6	8.6	..	..	..	9.1	8.7
Uganda	..	..	..	..	3.2	4.9	6.0	6.9	4.8	5.0	7.0	..	..	5.9
Zaire	3.7	4.6	6.9	7.2	6.7	7.7	8.8	9.0	7.9	..	..	..	6.1	8.6
Zambia	..	..	..	..	..	..	..	..	..	..	..	..	..	..
Zimbabwe	10.6	13.4	10.1	8.0	8.7	6.6	8.6	8.0	6.8	8.7	..	..	9.6	8.0
NORTH AFRICA	..	..	..	..	..	..	..	..	..	..	..	..	..	..
Algeria	22.7	21.0	18.2	15.9	16.2	16.3	20.2	17.5	16.6	18.0	22.4	31.7	18.4	18.9
Egypt, Arab Republic of	..	..	..	..	..	..	..	..	..	..	..	..	..	..
Libya	1.8	..	..	..	..	..	..	..	..	..	..	4.0	..	..
Morocco	..	..	..	..	..	..	..	..	..	..	..	..	..	..
Tunisia	13.3	14.8	15.4	14.2	13.6	12.3	10.5	9.3	9.7	10.7	11.5	11.7	13.9	10.3
ALL AFRICA	..	..	..	..	..	..	..	..	..	..	..	..	..	..
South Africa	13.4	15.3	15.8	15.5	14.4	12.9	11.5	11.7	13.2	13.4	..	13.6	14.6	12.5

2-11. Gross domestic saving

	Percentage of GDP											Annual average		
	1980	1981	1982	1983	1984	1985	1986	1987	1988	1989	1990	75-79	80-85	86-MR
SUB-SAHARAN AFRICA	21.7	14.8	10.7	9.8	10.9	12.4	11.4	13.0	12.3	13.1	16.6	18.9	13.4	13.3
excluding Nigeria	13.6	11.8	12.1	11.6	14.2	14.1	13.2	12.2	11.6	11.1	12.5	14.2	12.9	12.1
Angola	..	..	..	..	..	..	..	..	..	..	..	..	..	..
Benin	-6.3	-14.9	-2.6	0.1	-6.4	1.1	2.5	3.4	1.7	0.9	2.3	0.9	-4.8	2.2
Botswana	28.5	22.4	7.8	16.8	23.8	28.4	38.6	34.0	35.8	37.1	..	18.9	21.3	36.4
Burkina Faso	-3.1	-4.1	-1.0	-0.2	-0.6	3.2	2.9	4.1	7.3	5.2	4.6	3.9	-1.0	4.8
Burundi	-0.9	3.8	-2.7	6.6	5.8	3.8	1.1	6.9	1.6	4.4	1.1	4.9	2.7	3.0
Cameroon	15.7	22.3	23.1	28.8	32.7	35.9	31.5	19.6	12.9	20.3	18.6	16.4	26.4	20.6
Cape Verde	-8.0	-3.9	-3.4	-4.3	-10.9	-11.4	-12.0	4.5	1.3	4.0	..	-23.5	-7.0	-0.6
Central African Republic	-9.6	-1.9	-6.8	-1.2	-0.3	-0.3	-1.7	-1.2	-0.6	0.2	-1.7	-0.5	-3.3	-1.0
Chad	-16.9	-10.7	-9.8	-8.6	-3.4	-19.3	-22.1	-17.7	-13.4	-13.5	-15.4	-1.7	-11.5	-16.4
Comoros	..	..	..	2.8	-10.8	-9.1	-3.5	-9.2	-10.7	-4.9	-6.2	..	..	-6.9
Congo, People's Republic of the	35.7	30.1	46.5	44.6	46.4	31.1	15.6	22.8	18.8	28.6	30.5	11.5	39.1	23.3
Cote d'Ivoire	22.2	18.8	20.3	18.9	22.4	25.8	18.6	16.6	17.2	11.5	13.9	27.7	21.4	15.6
Djibouti	..	..	..	..	-3.3	-4.0	-3.3	-0.8	-4.5	-4.6	..	..	..	-3.3
Equatorial Guinea	..	..	..	..	..	1.0	2.9	-1.4	-7.2	-3.3	-6.3	..	..	-3.1
Ethiopia	4.9	3.6	2.0	2.7	1.9	2.8	2.2	3.5	4.4	5.4	3.0	5.4	3.0	3.7
Gabon	61.2	59.0	56.9	53.2	54.2	51.0	27.9	28.5	24.5	32.6	39.5	59.9	55.9	30.6
Gambia, The	0.7	4.2	9.8	4.3	4.9	6.4	5.2	6.9	7.1	8.3	9.0	3.2	5.1	7.3
Ghana	4.9	4.0	3.7	3.3	6.6	7.6	7.7	8.2	10.7	6.0	10.8	8.6	5.0	8.7
Guinea	21.6	16.6	16.7	16.1	13.8	13.0	18.7	18.5	15.4	19.4	20.1	..	16.3	18.4
Guinea-Bissau	-6.0	1.2	-5.2	-3.6	-8.3	-11.0	-1.3	3.6	-5.9	-14.4	-11.2	-6.4	-5.5	-5.8
Kenya	18.1	19.6	18.1	20.4	19.4	24.9	21.9	19.2	19.8	18.8	18.4	19.6	20.1	19.6
Lesotho	-59.7	-68.3	-73.5	-99.0	-94.1	-78.4	-75.7	-75.8	-56.9	-69.3	-77.6	-68.4	-78.8	-71.1
Liberia	27.3	18.8	12.5	10.0	14.4	14.3	18.4	..	..	..	..	29.9	16.2	..
Madagascar	-1.4	0.2	-1.0	1.4	3.7	2.6	4.4	4.7	6.6	9.1	8.2	3.3	0.9	6.6
Malawi	10.8	11.8	15.1	15.2	14.8	12.9	10.1	13.1	9.2	4.5	9.8	17.6	13.4	9.3
Mali	-1.9	-0.3	0.5	-4.8	-3.4	-14.2	-1.2	6.2	7.4	11.8	5.3	0.8	-4.0	5.9
Mauritania	6.9	12.6	3.0	-12.1	-1.9	8.8	15.4	13.7	6.1	7.9	2.8	2.8	2.9	9.2
Mauritius	10.5	14.8	15.4	17.1	18.7	21.6	28.6	27.4	25.5	23.1	21.4	21.9	16.3	25.2
Mozambique	0.5	0.0	-3.3	-10.8	-6.2	-3.1	-1.1	-12.1	-16.4	-16.6	-11.8	0.0	-3.8	-11.6
Namibia	37.6	11.6	6.4	3.1	4.1	16.1	16.6	3.8	13.2	15.4	..	..	13.2	12.2
Niger	22.6	8.7	7.8	7.5	-1.6	2.4	5.6	4.5	6.7	2.4	..	10.0	7.9	4.8
Nigeria	29.5	18.0	9.3	8.0	7.7	10.8	7.4	16.9	14.8	21.0	..	24.4	13.9	15.0
Rwanda	4.2	1.4	5.2	4.4	8.8	8.2	8.3	6.3	6.4	6.3	3.8	8.8	5.3	6.2
Sao Tome & Principe	-14.9	-29.8	-24.0	-12.8	-12.1	-18.1	-8.6	-14.5	-2.3	-40.0	-34.9	0.8	-18.6	-20.1
Senegal	-0.4	-7.5	-1.0	-0.4	2.2	-1.4	5.6	6.1	7.5	5.5	8.7	8.2	-1.4	6.7
Seychelles	27.1	17.0	8.8	-1.0	8.2	7.2	5.4	7.3	7.6	4.3	12.1	25.6	11.2	7.4
Sierra Leone	-0.8	4.4	1.9	7.5	11.1	8.0	9.6	11.1	9.0	4.9	5.1	4.1	5.4	7.9
Somalia	-12.9	-16.0	-12.8	-26.6	-22.3	16.8	2.8	8.8	6.5	-6.9	..	-4.6	-12.3	2.8
Sudan	3.4	1.0	8.3	1.5	6.2	-3.8	5.3	6.9	1.4	2.1	1.9	8.6	2.8	3.5
Swaziland	7.4	1.4	2.0	-1.1	-4.6	-3.2	11.5	15.7	14.8	..	..	24.8	0.3	14.0
Tanzania	9.8	12.1	13.6	8.4	7.2	7.4	5.5	0.1	-5.4	-5.9	..	15.1	9.8	-1.4
Togo	24.8	23.5	17.7	20.9	19.1	20.0	12.3	11.6	10.6	13.9	11.1	25.7	21.0	11.9
Uganda	..	..	..	3.9	6.2	7.8	8.4	6.1	0.8	-0.2	-0.7	..	..	2.9
Zaire	10.2	8.0	7.1	8.6	12.6	14.4	13.9	12.2	12.2	11.9	..	5.0	10.1	12.5
Zambia	19.3	6.8	8.0	15.2	16.5	15.4	22.6	18.0	18.7	3.5	17.0	23.1	13.5	15.9
Zimbabwe	15.8	15.8	15.3	12.8	19.5	22.3	23.7	23.2	24.6	21.4	19.4	19.3	16.9	22.5
NORTH AFRICA	28.4	27.5	27.0	28.5	26.4	26.3	22.2	21.8	21.5	20.5	24.7	24.7	27.3	22.1
Algeria	43.1	40.7	39.2	39.7	37.4	36.4	29.4	31.9	30.0	31.0	38.2	37.8	39.4	32.1
Egypt, Arab Republic of	15.2	14.1	15.2	17.8	14.0	14.5	13.8	6.6	8.2	6.9	9.9	15.6	15.1	9.1
Libya	56.9	46.3	46.3	38.0	..	..	..	..	..	..	..	46.1	..	..
Morocco	13.7	11.5	13.8	15.2	14.7	16.1	16.5	16.7	20.6	18.5	19.6	12.0	14.2	18.4
Tunisia	24.0	23.9	21.2	21.0	20.3	20.4	16.2	19.6	19.8	18.6	20.0	22.4	21.8	18.8
ALL AFRICA	23.8	18.9	16.1	16.4	16.6	17.8	16.3	17.3	16.4	16.4	20.9	20.7	18.2	17.5
South Africa	38.9	31.5	25.0	29.6	27.0	29.7	29.3	27.1	26.6	26.3	..	32.3	30.3	27.3

2–12. Gross national saving

	Percentage of GDP											Annual average		
	1980	1981	1982	1983	1984	1985	1986	1987	1988	1989	1990	75–79	80–85	86–MR
SUB-SAHARAN AFRICA	17.1	11.3	7.5	6.7	7.6	8.7	7.7	8.0	7.0	7.6	8.3	15.4	9.8	7.7
excluding Nigeria	8.9	7.7	7.6	7.2	9.2	9.1	8.7	7.4	6.6	6.1	8.1	10.0	8.3	7.4
Angola	..	..	..	..	..	..	..	..	..	..	..	..	..	..
Benin	2.8	-3.9	6.4	1.1	-4.2	3.4	5.2	6.1	5.1	2.3	3.7	6.5	0.9	4.5
Botswana	20.7	19.8	6.4	11.7	13.0	14.3	26.0	22.0	19.6	24.8	..	10.1	14.3	23.1
Burkina Faso	3.2	2.9	4.1	5.3	4.5	10.2	10.2	8.5	10.9	8.4	7.9	9.6	5.0	9.2
Burundi	-1.2	4.0	-3.3	6.0	4.8	3.0	0.0	5.0	0.4	3.6	0.7	3.2	2.2	1.9
Cameroon	6.8	13.4	16.6	22.5	26.1	29.2	25.8	14.8	8.3	16.6	13.1	8.7	19.1	15.7
Cape Verde	20.5	19.2	17.4	17.6	2.5	2.3	1.7	18.0	16.1	19.0	..	-10.7	13.2	13.7
Central African Republic	-11.4	-3.2	-9.6	-4.9	-3.5	-3.5	-4.9	-5.3	7.6	4.8	2.4	-2.6	-6.0	0.9
Chad	-18.1	-10.9	-10.1	-9.6	-5.1	-19.1	-24.0	-20.2	-16.3	-16.7	-18.0	-3.9	-12.1	-19.0
Comoros	..	..	..	0.5	-13.8	-10.4	-5.0	-9.3	-9.9	-4.2	-5.1	..	..	-6.7
Congo, People's Republic of the	22.3	21.0	36.4	34.4	35.2	18.7	15.2	9.3	2.4	14.6	16.2	2.4	28.0	11.6
Cote d'Ivoire	10.0	6.8	8.4	6.7	10.8	12.0	6.7	3.1	4.0	-3.3	..	12.7	9.1	2.6
Djibouti	..	..	..	..	-2.9	-4.2	-3.0	0.3	-2.4	-2.4	..	..	..	-1.9
Equatorial Guinea	..	..	..	..	..	-1.5	2.7	-7.2	-14.2	-9.4	-3.9	..	..	-6.4
Ethiopia	5.5	4.0	2.8	4.2	3.7	5.2	5.7	5.8	7.2	7.3	5.2	5.8	4.2	6.2
Gabon	47.6	48.1	46.0	42.1	45.2	41.4	15.9	17.0	11.1	19.8	26.1	49.1	45.1	18.0
Gambia, The	-2.5	0.4	4.9	-2.5	-2.1	-5.2	-8.0	0.3	1.7	-0.1	5.5	1.4	-1.2	-0.1
Ghana	4.5	3.7	3.5	2.4	5.5	6.5	6.5	9.6	11.5	7.9	12.2	8.1	4.3	9.5
Guinea	14.0	8.1	6.5	8.0	6.7	5.9	10.5	10.2	7.4	10.4	11.5	..	8.2	10.0
Guinea-Bissau	-6.6	0.2	-13.6	-8.6	-11.7	-14.4	-2.8	-0.7	-7.2	-15.0	-15.8	-9.6	-9.1	-8.3
Kenya	15.4	17.9	15.4	18.2	17.0	22.6	19.2	16.3	16.6	15.8	16.5	15.3	17.7	16.9
Lesotho	12.5	9.9	27.6	9.9	14.2	16.8	19.2	9.0	16.6	-1.3	19.0	11.5	15.1	12.5
Liberia	22.5	14.2	2.0	-2.8	-0.3	5.9	9.4	..	..	..	..	26.0	6.9	..
Madagascar	-3.1	-2.8	-4.2	-2.1	-1.3	-1.0	0.3	-0.8	1.2	3.3	5.2	1.7	-2.4	1.8
Malawi	3.8	6.1	10.1	10.7	11.2	9.2	6.1	9.5	6.3	7.6	12.0	16.1	8.5	8.3
Mali	-0.4	-0.3	0.5	-5.1	-3.3	-11.6	0.2	6.7	8.4	12.9	6.5	2.4	-3.4	6.9
Mauritania	-2.3	6.8	-7.1	-20.9	-10.6	-1.1	5.2	-0.1	-3.6	-0.8	-5.5	-8.5	-5.9	-0.9
Mauritius	10.6	13.3	12.4	14.8	16.2	19.4	26.9	27.4	26.8	25.4	24.3	22.2	14.4	26.1
Mozambique	-1.9	-3.1	-8.0	-16.4	-10.1	-7.3	-5.8	-27.8	-25.2	-28.8	-22.2	..	..	-22.0
Niger	18.8	5.0	0.9	0.6	-7.2	-4.4	0.1	-1.4	2.2	-2.4	..	4.9	2.3	-0.4
Nigeria	25.5	15.1	7.3	6.1	5.8	8.2	5.1	11.1	8.3	13.9	..	21.9	11.4	9.6
Rwanda	4.0	1.8	5.5	4.3	8.6	8.1	8.2	6.2	6.3	6.1	3.4	8.6	5.4	6.0
Sao Tome & Principe	-7.5	-21.1	-23.7	-8.3	5.5	-23.6	-14.8	-20.2	-7.8	-43.6	-44.5	2.2	-13.1	-26.2
Senegal	-4.4	-12.3	-5.6	-4.8	-3.2	-6.8	0.8	1.5	3.0	1.6	5.7	5.7	-6.2	2.5
Seychelles	22.5	13.8	3.9	-6.2	2.8	3.2	-1.1	0.7	-0.3	-2.0	15.9	20.2	6.7	2.7
Sierra Leone	-3.0	2.7	-0.4	5.6	9.6	4.5	7.5	10.0	4.1	-0.7	-3.6	2.2	3.2	3.5
Somalia	-11.0	-15.1	-13.9	-26.6	-22.6	12.1	-3.1	2.8	1.1	-14.3	..	-2.8	-12.8	-3.4
Sudan	5.0	1.8	9.3	3.0	5.2	-2.1	5.1	6.3	-0.4	-0.4	-0.4	10.1	3.7	2.1
Swaziland	5.6	2.7	4.9	3.7	3.4	7.0	14.7	16.2	18.2	..	..	20.4	4.5	16.4
Tanzania	10.0	12.2	13.6	8.4	8.1	10.2	8.5	1.8	-4.1	-6.7	..	15.4	10.4	-0.1
Togo	21.4	19.0	12.4	14.9	13.4	15.8	9.2	8.0	7.7	11.6	13.8	24.0	16.1	10.1
Uganda	-0.8	-15.5	-15.2	-10.4	5.5	6.2	7.1	7.4	1.8	0.6	0.1	..	..	3.4
Zaire	7.3	6.1	5.4	6.5	6.1	6.5	8.4	7.5	8.4	8.5	..	1.9	6.3	8.2
Zambia	7.1	0.1	0.4	6.2	5.1	3.7	2.8	1.6	6.9	-5.8	4.2	11.9	3.8	1.9
Zimbabwe	12.2	11.3	9.7	7.0	15.7	17.3	18.0	19.0	21.7	18.6	15.4	15.7	12.2	18.5
Namibia	27.8	5.3	-1.0	-1.0	-1.2	5.3	6.5	-2.0	3.9	0.0	..	..	5.9	2.1
NORTH AFRICA	29.2	27.2	26.2	28.5	26.5	24.8	20.7	20.1	19.2	18.4	23.3	25.9	27.1	20.4
Algeria	40.8	38.6	36.9	37.6	35.1	34.6	28.3	30.3	26.9	28.2	34.8	36.8	37.3	29.7
Egypt, Arab Republic of	20.6	16.0	15.4	20.3	17.0	12.5	8.7	1.4	3.7	3.4	6.7	18.8	17.0	4.8
Libya	53.6	41.7	39.1	28.3	..	..	..	..	..	..	..	39.9	..	..
Morocco	15.9	13.3	14.9	17.0	16.7	17.6	20.6	21.0	21.8	19.4	23.6	15.5	15.9	21.3
Tunisia	24.5	24.3	22.0	21.9	20.9	19.3	15.5	19.6	20.2	18.7	21.3	22.1	22.2	19.1
ALL AFRICA	20.8	16.3	13.4	14.1	14.2	14.7	13.3	13.6	12.2	12.2	15.0	18.5	15.6	13.3
South Africa	34.6	26.9	20.7	25.3	22.7	24.7	24.1	22.8	22.9	22.4	..	27.7	25.8	23.0

2–13. Resource balance

	Percentage of GDP											Annual average		
	1980	*1981*	*1982*	*1983*	*1984*	*1985*	*1986*	*1987*	*1988*	*1989*	*1990*	*75–79*	*80–85*	*86–MR*
SUB-SAHARAN AFRICA	1.0	-6.2	-7.0	-4.4	-0.2	0.1	-4.0	-3.3	-4.0	-3.0	-3.3	-3.6	-2.8	-3.5
excluding Nigeria	-6.9	-8.8	-7.8	-5.3	-2.1	-2.9	-4.7	-5.1	-5.7	-5.9	-4.9	-6.9	-5.6	-5.3
Angola	..	..	..	..	..	..	..	..	..	..	..	..	..	..
Benin	-24.8	-34.1	-36.8	-11.5	-13.8	-7.9	-10.9	-9.5	-11.2	-8.1	-9.8	-20.8	-21.5	-9.9
Botswana	-12.5	-21.2	-36.4	-12.5	-0.6	-1.7	20.7	27.7	25.5	13.1	..	-20.9	-14.1	21.8
Burkina Faso	-21.3	-21.1	-22.5	-20.8	-17.7	-22.7	-20.0	-15.8	-14.9	-17.6	-15.4	-20.2	-21.0	-16.7
Burundi	-14.8	-13.2	-17.2	-16.3	-12.5	-10.0	-10.5	-15.8	-13.4	-12.4	-18.2	-6.5	-14.0	-14.0
Cameroon	-3.1	-2.3	-0.3	4.4	11.9	11.0	0.7	-4.5	-2.8	1.8	2.1	-4.4	3.6	-0.5
Cape Verde	-49.9	-49.2	-56.3	-53.2	-54.9	-56.5	-57.8	-39.8	-40.4	-38.3	..	-56.1	-53.3	-44.1
Central African Republic	-16.6	-10.6	-13.5	-13.1	-12.6	-14.7	-13.9	-14.9	-12.1	-10.9	-12.9	-12.1	-13.5	-12.9
Chad	-16.9	-10.7	-9.8	-11.6	-8.8	-27.5	-31.2	-30.0	-21.2	-22.4	-25.7	-17.9	-14.2	-26.1
Comoros	..	..	..	-26.2	-56.6	-38.7	-27.1	-32.5	-26.6	-18.7	-20.9	..	..	-25.2
Congo, People's Republic of the	-0.1	-18.1	-13.2	6.2	16.0	0.8	-13.8	3.1	0.2	12.6	14.6	-18.5	-1.4	3.3
Cote d'Ivoire	-6.1	-7.1	-2.9	-1.7	11.5	13.2	7.5	4.4	2.8	3.0	6.1	1.6	1.2	4.8
Djibouti	..	..	..	..	-31.8	-27.8	-19.5	-19.4	-20.1	-23.0	..	..	..	-20.5
Equatorial Guinea	..	..	..	..	..	-8.3	-9.8	-25.5	-28.2	-24.7	-30.6	..	..	-23.8
Ethiopia	-5.2	-6.8	-9.8	-8.5	-10.4	-11.2	-10.5	-11.1	-11.0	-7.9	-8.3	-3.6	-8.6	-9.7
Gabon	33.1	22.7	21.9	17.9	20.7	13.7	-17.1	0.3	-7.4	7.4	17.1	7.5	21.7	0.1
Gambia, The	-25.5	-20.4	-10.9	-13.0	-14.3	-9.4	-15.2	-11.6	-10.9	-13.7	-11.8	-16.2	-15.6	-12.6
Ghana	-0.7	-0.6	0.4	-0.4	-0.3	-1.9	-1.7	-2.3	-0.3	-7.5	..	-0.3	-0.6	-2.9
Guinea	5.8	3.2	2.6	2.0	3.6	3.6	3.2	0.8	-4.1	1.0	2.6	..	3.5	0.7
Guinea-Bissau	-35.6	-24.5	-33.4	-26.2	-38.3	-43.1	-25.5	-29.7	-40.2	-50.0	-33.6	-25.4	-33.5	-35.8
Kenya	-11.1	-8.1	-3.7	-0.4	-1.4	-1.1	0.2	-5.1	-5.2	-5.7	-5.3	-3.2	-4.3	-4.2
Lesotho	-102.1	-111.2	-123.2	-132.5	-135.6	-128.4	-121.1	-120.8	-103.1	-124.2	-130.2	-96.5	-122.2	-119.9
Liberia	0.0	2.5	-1.8	-1.8	4.1	5.7	8.8	..	..	..	..	-1.7	1.4	..
Madagascar	-16.4	-11.3	-9.4	-7.0	-4.9	-6.0	-4.7	-5.4	-6.7	-4.5	-8.7	-6.7	-9.2	-6.0
Malawi	-14.0	-5.8	-6.3	-7.6	2.0	-5.7	-2.1	-2.3	-9.5	..	..	-13.1	-6.2	-4.7
Mali	-18.8	-17.8	-17.1	-19.4	-18.6	-33.8	-24.1	-16.8	-18.8	-15.7	-16.1	-15.3	-20.9	-18.3
Mauritania	-29.3	-29.3	-44.1	-29.9	-26.9	-15.5	-7.5	-6.8	-11.6	-6.7	-11.7	-31.7	-29.2	-8.9
Mauritius	-10.3	-10.5	-2.8	-0.4	-3.3	-1.9	6.7	2.1	-5.1	-7.7	-8.9	-8.1	-4.9	-2.6
Mozambique	-18.4	-20.3	-22.6	-20.8	-16.8	-10.0	-10.8	-36.1	-49.8	-52.1	-49.0	..	-18.1	-39.6
Namibia	4.4	-19.2	-16.8	-14.7	-13.1	2.2	3.8	-12.1	-7.0	-1.2	..	..	-9.5	-4.1
Niger	-14.1	-11.6	-10.4	-5.3	-4.7	-10.4	-4.5	-4.7	-4.2	-7.1	..	-9.4	-9.4	-5.1
Nigeria	9.1	-3.5	-6.1	-3.4	1.7	3.3	-2.3	5.5	2.4	8.4	..	0.3	0.2	3.5
Rwanda	-11.9	-11.9	-12.6	-9.2	-9.0	-9.1	-7.6	-9.3	-9.2	-9.3	-8.7	-5.5	-10.3	-8.8
Sao Tome & Principe	-49.1	-76.8	-73.8	-42.3	-59.9	-55.1	-23.1	-31.7	-30.4	-67.6	-54.8	-24.4	-59.5	-41.5
Senegal	-15.7	-19.3	-12.3	-12.3	-9.5	-11.2	-5.4	-5.6	-5.0	-5.3	-4.0	-8.5	-13.4	-5.1
Seychelles	-11.2	-15.6	-23.5	-22.2	-13.5	-15.5	..	..	..	..	..	-5.5	-16.9	..
Sierra Leone	-17.0	-14.7	-11.5	-6.8	-1.6	-2.0	-1.6	0.7	-2.6	-6.4	-6.4	-8.9	-8.9	-3.3
Somalia	-55.3	-43.6	-42.1	-49.1	-46.5	-13.0	-22.4	-24.5	-17.4	-37.2	..	-29.7	-41.6	-25.4
Sudan	-11.6	-13.3	-14.6	-14.4	-7.6	-8.4	-7.6	-3.4	-8.6	-7.0	-7.3	-8.5	-11.6	-6.8
Swaziland	-33.2	-29.7	-30.3	-36.1	-36.2	-32.8	-10.8	0.4	-1.7	..	..	-6.8	-33.1	-4.1
Tanzania	-13.2	-8.5	-7.4	-5.2	-8.1	-8.3	-14.1	-22.4	-25.2	-30.5	..	-9.2	-8.4	-23.1
Togo	-5.3	-6.7	-8.5	-1.3	-2.1	-8.8	-11.7	-8.6	-9.5	-7.4	-11.4	-11.9	-5.5	-9.7
Uganda	..	..	..	-5.2	-2.6	-2.1	-4.1	-6.8	-9.3	-10.1	-13.0	..	..	-8.6
Zaire	0.2	-2.5	-1.2	-0.7	2.1	1.9	0.7	-2.0	-2.2	-2.7	..	-10.7	..	-1.6
Zambia	-4.0	-12.5	-8.8	1.4	1.8	0.5	-1.2	4.1	7.3	-6.5	2.6	-2.3	-3.6	1.3
Zimbabwe	-3.0	-7.3	-5.9	-3.1	0.5	1.2	4.3	4.1	4.9	0.7	-2.0	1.7	-2.9	2.4
NORTH AFRICA	-3.9	-5.4	-6.4	-4.0	-5.0	-3.5	-6.3	-2.9	-4.5	-6.4	-3.4	-11.6	-4.7	-4.7
Algeria	4.0	3.7	1.9	2.2	2.3	3.2	-4.1	1.9	-0.4	-0.2	5.2	-8.2	2.9	0.5
Egypt, Arab Republic of	-12.4	-15.4	-14.9	-10.9	-13.5	-12.1	-9.9	-11.4	-16.0	-16.8	-13.2	-15.5	-13.2	-13.4
Libya	34.8	15.7	18.4	12.8	..	..	..	..	..	..	..	19.9	..	..
Morocco	-10.5	-14.6	-14.5	-8.8	-10.6	-9.0	-6.3	-4.4	-0.5	-5.5	-6.1	-15.5	-11.3	-4.6
Tunisia	-5.4	-8.5	-10.5	-8.6	-11.7	-6.1	-7.3	-1.0	0.4	-4.1	-6.7	-7.5	-8.5	-3.7
ALL AFRICA	-0.5	-6.0	-6.8	-4.3	-1.9	-1.3	-5.0	-3.1	-4.2	-4.5	-3.3	-6.0	-3.5	-4.0
South Africa	8.5	-1.4	..	4.0	2.1	9.6	10.0	7.9	5.1	5.5	..	..	3.8	7.1

2–14. Exports of goods and nonfactor services

	Millions of U.S. dollars, current prices and exchange rates											Average annual percentage growth		
	1980	1981	1982	1983	1984	1985	1986	1987	1988	1989	1990	75–80	80–85	86–MR
SUB-SAHARAN AFRICA	54,972	43,479	36,007	33,605	36,875	36,713	30,563	34,608	35,960	39,091	38,522	8.5	-2.8	1.3
excluding Nigeria	27,979	25,085	23,344	22,882	24,588	23,694	25,153	26,651	28,307	28,928	30,727	5.4	3.0	0.8
Angola	..	..	..	..	..	..	..	..	..	..	..	..	..	..
Benin	323	299	320	241	235	363	375	455	476	306	378	12.6	-0.3	-9.9
Botswana	450	511	380	568	675	603	832	1,172	1,585	1,592	..	13.0	19.0	-0.4
Burkina Faso	183	174	152	133	168	163	189	265	284	255	354	13.9	-5.1	5.4
Burundi	81	88	103	97	112	121	149	110	136	106	86	0.6	11.0	3.5
Cameroon	1,807	2,193	2,019	2,247	2,649	2,798	2,548	2,090	2,095	2,175	2,360	14.4	15.0	-5.7
Cape Verde	24	30	32	34	30	31	34	52	44	41	64	7.6	10.6	-0.8
Central African Republic	208	178	166	159	150	178	186	197	196	213	224	-1.3	-3.2	-0.9
Chad	175	132	55	136	165	123	143	180	223	224	281	-0.2	7.0	10.1
Comoros	..	..	..	22	10	20	27	21	26	36	35	..	..	..
Congo, People's Republic of the	1,024	1,157	1,194	1,215	1,352	1,227	737	959	899	1,154	1,394	9.4	8.9	5.6
Cote d'Ivoire	3,578	2,966	2,756	2,474	3,007	3,201	3,678	3,672	3,298	3,219	3,739	3.4	1.3	2.1
Djibouti	..	..	..	..	161	151	164	178	190	188	..	..	..	0.7
Equatorial Guinea	..	..	15	18	29	24	35	45	51	41	42	..	..	1.2
Ethiopia	569	554	512	552	612	549	662	616	629	717	569	..	..	..
Gabon	2,770	2,447	2,229	2,080	2,167	1,997	1,158	1,351	1,216	1,885	2,589	-1.1	0.5	..
Gambia, The	109	88	99	110	80	89	103	117	142	150	178	1.6	-4.9	10.8
Ghana	376	201	135	225	329	436	917	1,074	1,076	1,081	..	-9.0	-10.3	10.7
Guinea	497	490	521	557	532	504	624	639	636	762	886	..	2.6	6.9
Guinea-Bissau	9	17	13	10	19	16	10	24	26	26	44	2.6	-6.5	20.7
Kenya	2,030	1,762	1,607	1,497	1,624	1,552	1,870	1,701	1,876	1,942	2,219	1.0	0.6	0.9
Lesotho	74	66	51	46	41	32	35	61	82	98	101	25.1	-8.3	17.4
Liberia	614	588	539	487	471	467	464	..	..	..	..	1.6	-8.4	11.8
Madagascar	539	414	396	371	387	332	389	405	398	450	474	4.4	2.8	-0.1
Malawi	307	318	265	254	343	274	271	301	322	..	..	12.1	3.8	5.1
Mali	263	201	188	206	233	220	257	320	314	337	430	5.9	7.8	0.9
Mauritania	265	342	305	366	336	409	468	470	490	499	495	7.6	4.3	11.6
Mauritius	579	511	509	509	506	576	885	1,214	1,382	1,400	1,673	..	-20.4	9.2
Mozambique	399	395	336	222	157	143	146	175	189	200	229	..	-4.2	-5.6
Namibia	1,475	1,121	978	879	776	728	888	897	958	1,041	..	1.8	-8.0	0.7
Niger	619	540	416	400	302	251	366	402	427	362	404	11.7	-12.3	5.2
Nigeria	26,993	18,394	12,663	10,723	12,287	13,019	5,410	7,957	7,653	10,163	..	13.5	2.5	-1.1
Rwanda	168	130	163	175	201	185	245	213	211	189	197	7.0	-1.6	0.2
Sao Tome & Principe	20	9	11	10	14	9	13	10	15	11	13	1.4	5.2	2.7
Senegal	853	796	884	816	887	765	998	1,150	1,253	1,241	1,506	..	..	..
Seychelles	100	88	78	61	74	81	..	..	..	..	..	-10.8	-10.6	-3.4
Sierra Leone	268	253	192	197	150	150	157	69	129	125	156	27.8	-20.2	-9.4
Somalia	200	174	201	173	115	55	65	68	50	84	91	1.1	-3.0	-3.5
Sudan	810	748	762	765	962	668	498	640	661	751	660	..	..	..
Swaziland	418	446	385	360	301	217	313	437	443	546	..	-5.8	-8.5	..
Tanzania	676	724	490	459	413	427	446	466	502	520	..	11.5	-4.4	3.0
Togo	580	445	412	348	368	369	466	531	596	604	669	..	..	..
Uganda	242	214	409	340	377	287	384	269	292	202	199	3.6	17.7	-0.7
Zaire	2,276	1,676	1,646	1,786	2,034	1,980	2,000	1,947	2,329	2,360	1,867	-2.6	-3.1	-3.1
Zambia	1,608	1,148	1,071	1,093	954	873	739	894	1,242	1,071	1,010	..	2.4	-3.7
Zimbabwe	1,623	1,618	1,503	1,328	1,358	1,302	1,535	1,679	1,824	1,753	1,877	..	3.6	6.6
NORTH AFRICA	28,324	29,715	26,875	26,679	26,191	26,443	20,216	23,351	25,489	26,762	32,005	1.5	5.7	5.3
Algeria	14,541	15,335	13,985	13,645	13,583	13,650	8,234	9,450	8,422	10,001	13,396	7.3	1.8	6.0
Egypt, Arab Republic of	6,992	7,811	6,919	7,170	6,849	6,908	5,645	6,289	7,350	7,234	7,012	..	..	..
Libya	23,523	16,872	15,447	13,440	..	..	..	..	..	..	..	5.2	4.5	6.8
Morocco	3,273	3,082	2,969	2,994	3,038	3,185	3,616	4,234	5,474	5,038	6,306	10.6	0.2	11.3
Tunisia	3,518	3,487	3,002	2,870	2,721	2,700	2,722	3,377	4,243	4,489	5,290	..	-0.6	3.5
ALL AFRICA	83,296	73,194	62,882	60,284	63,065	63,156	50,778	57,959	61,449	65,853	70,527	..	-0.6	3.5
South Africa	28,529	23,455	20,107	20,791	19,156	18,125	20,349	23,588	25,084	25,331	..	8.8	1	4.3

2–15. Imports of goods and nonfactor services

	Millions of U.S. dollars, current prices and exchange rates											Average annual percentage growth		
	1980	1981	1982	1983	1984	1985	1986	1987	1988	1989	1990	75–80	80–85	86–MR
SUB-SAHARAN AFRICA	52,864	55,815	49,691	41,862	37,195	36,445	36,731	38,985	41,580	43,433	43501	8.0	0.8	-11.2
excluding Nigeria	35,224	34,114	31,346	28,054	26,478	26,385	30,244	32,362	34,654	35,769	36577	7.7	11.3	-11.3
Angola	..	..	..	..	..	..	..	..	..	..	..		..	-3.8
Benin	608	658	700	354	367	445	522	604	658	429	563	11.0		..
Botswana	561	727	693	689	682	620	590	769	1,072	1,264	924	9.5	4.2	-9.3
Burkina Faso	546	506	503	429	397	488	595	660	695	710	842	5.8	1.1	17.7
Burundi	217	216	277	273	236	236	275	289	282	241	286	8.3	20.0	0.9
Cameroon	2,041	2,388	2,039	1,904	1,696	1,902	2,474	2,646	2,444	1,980	2130	10.3	-28.3	-2.9
Cape Verde	95	99	111	108	103	109	144	145	150	149	153	17.7	67.7	-10.1
Central African Republic	341	252	267	245	230	281	323	352	329	331	392	7.4	-16.4	-2.3
Chad	298	199	113	205	222	324	378	424	446	452	564	-4.0	10.6	-2.9
Comoros	..	..	..	51	71	64	71	86	81	73	87			2.6
Congo, People's Republic of the	1,026	1,517	1,480	1,086	1,001	1,210	992	887	894	848	974	-2.4	-27.8	..
Cote d'Ivoire	4,215	3,565	2,976	2,587	2,252	2,278	2,978	3,214	3,007	2,942	3129	13.0	-17.8	-6.7
Djibouti	..	..	..	..	265	245	235	251	269	281	..		..	-3.6
Equatorial Guinea	..	..	51	28	52	31	45	75	88	72	89		..	-2.8
Ethiopia	782	846	946	962	1,116	1,082	1,212	1,217	1,252	1,191	1072	..	..	6.9
Gabon	1,354	1,572	1,435	1,476	1,439	1,494	1,750	1,341	1,456	1,624	1811	-5.3	..	..
Gambia, The	168	131	122	136	103	105	126	138	165	180	209	11.7	28.1	..
Ghana	407	225	120	243	340	523	1,012	1,189	1,090	1,478	1192	-3.8	-30.2	4.7
Guinea	394	434	475	519	460	432	561	622	734	735	807	..	6.2	16.9
Guinea-Bissau	46	55	68	53	72	83	42	73	88	110	110	-2.4	..	4.8
Kenya	2,837	2,318	1,848	1,524	1,709	1,617	1,857	2,108	2,315	2,423	2679	6.4	-40.2	6.6
Lesotho	450	482	473	511	459	345	363	491	522	658	809	7.2	19.9	5.1
Liberia	614	561	559	506	426	405	369	..	..	..	..	..	..	1.8
Madagascar	1,202	820	729	616	531	503	541	544	561	560	743	8.2	..	..
Malawi	480	390	340	346	319	338	297	328	449	..	..	1.0	-0.6	4.3
Mali	570	443	398	416	430	578	625	640	679	653	825	11.3	1.1	11.3
Mauritania	473	561	635	602	532	520	531	533	603	567	618	-4.2	10.5	3.0
Mauritius	695	630	539	512	541	596	788	1,176	1,487	1,562	1893	2.5	-3.5	1.9
Mozambique	844	859	891	694	583	481	594	702	814	875	934	..	24.4	7.7
Namibia	1,387	1,473	1,255	1,127	963	701	834	1,099	1,090	1,065	1022	..	-14.5	5.3
Niger	976	792	620	495	372	400	449	504	526	508	584	8.5	5.6	-0.5
Nigeria	17,640	21,701	18,345	13,809	10,717	10,060	6,487	6,622	6,926	7,664	6925	8.5	-43.8	-5.5
Rwanda	307	287	341	313	312	341	392	413	425	392	383	11.9	75.6	-8.0
Sao Tome & Principe	41	30	37	25	34	29	27	27	29	42	41	16.4	39.6	-6.0
Senegal	1,327	1,276	1,201	1,120	1,108	1,055	1,202	1,408	1,504	1,486	1739	7.4	-38.3	6.0
Seychelles	117	112	112	94	95	108	..	..	..	..	..	..	..	0.3
Sierra Leone	455	427	345	298	168	176	181	66	159	187	214	6.6	..	..
Somalia	534	478	527	533	481	169	273	316	231	491	35	35.7	-20.3	7.3
Sudan	1,597	1,799	1,902	1,861	1,622	1,527	1,543	1,194	1,456	1,560	1286	3.8	55.1	9.8
Swaziland	598	617	538	548	468	337	363	435	453	543	449	..	..	-8.2
Tanzania	1,353	1,227	955	786	886	1,000	1,132	1,239	1,335	1,381	1272	1.6	..	..
Togo	640	510	482	358	383	435	589	639	726	704	854	17.4	8.1	..
Uganda	324	297	533	441	439	332	522	518	673	523	590	..	..	10.2
Zaire	2,245	1,984	1,810	1,862	1,872	1,845	1,946	2,099	2,527	2,596	2327	1.9	..	..
Zambia	1,764	1,649	1,412	1,046	904	861	760	808	976	1,351	928	-9.2	3.6	-1.6
Zimbabwe	1,783	2,089	1,910	1,522	1,330	1,249	1,321	1,458	1,535	1,713	1999	..	-15.4	-1.9
NORTH AFRICA	31,913	34,623	32,905	30,629	31,398	30,468	28,043	27,116	30,737	34,103	36274	..	-34.7	7.3
Algeria	12,857	13,689	13,116	12,589	12,375	11,804	10,804	8,224	8,644	10,080	10639	4.2	..	..
Egypt, Arab Republic of	9,822	11,423	10,732	10,250	10,974	11,115	9,183	10,357	12,311	12,829	11656	6.0	-41.6	0.6
Libya	11,167	11,913	10,056	9,752	..	..	..	..	..	..	..	..	..	..
Morocco	5,247	5,310	5,199	4,223	4,390	4,341	4,692	5,063	5,576	6,288	7850	1.5	-24.2	14.7
Tunisia	3,987	4,201	3,858	3,567	3,659	3,207	3,364	3,473	4,206	4,906	6130	11.3	-23.6	4.5
ALL AFRICA	84,777	90,438	82,596	72,492	68,592	66,912	64,774	66,101	72,317	77,535	79775	..	-3.8	-10.5
South Africa	21,775	24,644	20,089	17,449	17,577	12,698	13,946	17,100	20,560	20,353	..	2.5	-52.1	-8.7

Notes:
  Period growth rates are calculated based on imports at constant 1987 prices and exchange rates.

2–16. GDP growth

	Percentage annual change											Average annual		
	1980	1981	1982	1983	1984	1985	1986	1987	1988	1989	1990	75–80	80–85	86–MR
SUB-SAHARAN AFRICA	1.8	1.6	2.6	0.1	-1.1	3.8	4.6	-0.3	2.3	3.1	1.6	2.7	1.1	1.9
excluding Nigeria	1.4	3.8	3.4	1.7	0.4	2.7	5.2	0.6	1.7	2.5	0.8	2.5	2.2	1.6
Angola	..	..	..	..	14.7	3.0	12.1	12.1	14.8	-0.1	..	..	..	7.1
Benin	20.9	9.0	6.8	-2.0	2.0	6.4	-1.7	-3.9	1.2	2.4	1.1	6.1	3.6	0.5
Botswana	15.4	7.4	-1.1	23.9	19.2	8.3	8.2	10.3	9.2	13.4	..	12.2	12.1	11.3
Burkina Faso	-0.1	4.5	10.0	0.8	-1.8	9.8	10.0	1.8	7.4	-0.2	1.7	3.8	4.0	2.8
Burundi	0.6	13.5	-3.1	7.0	0.0	11.6	3.8	4.1	3.6	6.5	2.5	3.9	4.5	4.4
Cameroon	15.6	12.9	2.6	7.8	5.8	7.6	8.0	-6.5	-7.7	-3.4	-1.2	11.5	6.8	-4.9
Cape Verde	37.7	8.5	2.8	9.5	3.8	8.7	2.9	7.0	3.2	5.5	4.0	10.2	6.4	4.8
Central African Republic	-1.9	-2.2	7.5	-6.7	9.4	3.9	1.0	-3.4	1.6	2.3	3.6	1.2	2.2	1.2
Chad	-6.0	1.0	5.4	15.7	2.0	21.8	-4.1	-3.4	17.6	0.9	3.0	-5.4	8.7	5.2
Comoros	..	..	..	..	4.3	2.8	2.1	2.0	0.7	0.2	2.0	..	..	1.0
Congo, People's Republic of the	18.2	13.9	26.1	7.7	7.0	-1.2	-6.8	0.7	0.5	0.3	-0.1	4.3	11.0	0.4
Cote d'Ivoire	-0.9	4.3	1.6	-1.2	-1.0	3.7	3.7	-0.2	-1.8	-1.3	-6.1	4.7	1.0	-2.2
Djibouti	..	..	..	..	..	-0.4	-6.9	-0.6	0.9	-0.8	0.7	..	..	0.1
Equatorial Guinea	..	..	..	..	..	..	0.1	4.2	8.5	0.4	-0.2	..	..	3.4
Ethiopia	4.4	2.1	1.6	5.1	-2.1	-6.8	6.7	9.1	3.8	2.3	-2.5	2.8	0.4	3.1
Gabon	2.5	-4.0	2.7	0.9	6.5	6.3	11.4	-18.4	0.1	4.0	5.5	-5.2	2.6	-1.8
Gambia, The	-9.8	10.2	12.8	-5.3	3.0	0.6	2.8	6.0	8.0	4.7	4.5	2.8	3.6	5.9
Ghana	0.6	-2.9	-6.5	-4.5	8.8	5.1	5.1	4.6	6.2	6.1	4.1	2.0	-0.5	5.4
Guinea	..	0.7	1.8	1.2	-2.7	5.1	7.1	3.0	5.9	4.3	4.7	..	0.9	4.6
Guinea-Bissau	-18.8	18.8	4.5	-3.2	5.5	4.3	-1.0	6.0	6.8	5.0	3.1	-0.8	4.5	5.3
Kenya	4.8	4.1	1.9	1.5	1.7	4.3	7.1	5.9	6.0	4.6	4.2	6.6	2.4	5.2
Lesotho	-3.0	1.1	3.7	-5.7	7.6	3.2	-0.9	7.3	12.3	4.1	7.8	11.1	1.6	7.9
Liberia	-4.5	-1.2	-2.0	-1.6	-2.1	-0.8	-1.7	-1.0	..	..	..	2.8	-1.6	..
Madagascar	1.9	-9.8	-1.9	0.9	1.7	1.2	1.8	1.1	3.8	4.9	4.6	1.8	-1.1	3.8
Malawi	5.2	-5.3	2.5	3.7	5.7	4.5	-0.5	1.6	2.9	5.4	3.7	6.1	2.6	3.5
Mali	-1.3	4.6	6.7	-4.5	1.3	-0.4	17.9	1.4	2.4	9.2	0.3	4.9	1.2	3.8
Mauritania	4.0	3.8	-2.1	4.9	-7.3	2.8	5.6	3.1	3.7	3.4	0.3	2.3	0.0	2.8
Mauritius	-11.1	5.3	5.8	0.3	4.7	7.4	10.3	10.5	6.5	3.5	6.4	4.5	4.3	6.4
Mozambique	..	0.5	-3.4	-12.8	1.5	-8.0	1.9	5.2	5.6	3.1	3.0	..	-5.0	4.3
Namibia	..	2.0	-4.7	-3.1	-2.0	5.7	5.9	0.2	5.0	-2.5	..	..	-1.3	1.2
Niger	4.8	1.2	-1.2	-1.8	-16.9	3.1	6.4	-2.4	5.0	-3.5	3.1	7.6	-4.3	0.5
Nigeria	3.4	-5.7	-0.2	-6.2	-7.3	8.7	2.0	-4.6	4.8	5.8	5.3	3.3	-3.0	3.3
Rwanda	10.2	8.8	1.7	6.3	-4.7	3.0	5.2	-0.4	0.1	-6.9	-2.7	8.2	2.5	-2.7
Sao Tome & Principe	13.6	-27.7	26.8	-8.9	-7.7	8.5	0.9	-2.3	1.9	1.6	2.5	9.9	-2.2	1.1
Senegal	-2.7	-0.5	14.8	2.5	-4.7	3.8	4.6	4.1	5.1	-1.5	4.5	0.8	3.2	2.8
Seychelles	1.1	-7.0	-1.5	2.2	3.6	9.5	2.4	4.1	6.2	5.6	5.3	8.9	1.3	5.4
Sierra Leone	15.2	8.7	0.0	-3.1	2.3	-3.4	-1.9	5.4	0.0	-0.7	2.6	2.5	0.4	1.4
Somalia	-4.2	8.0	3.6	-9.2	3.4	8.1	3.7	6.1	-1.3	2.7	-1.5	5.0	1.3	1.3
Sudan	-40.8	2.1	12.7	2.1	-5.0	-6.3	9.7	1.1	-1.9	7.4	-5.8	-4.6	1.5	0.6
Swaziland	-4.7	6.7	1.2	-0.8	3.8	2.4	8.8	1.2	9.2	4.7	4.6	2.4	2.2	5.3
Tanzania	2.7	-1.0	-0.3	-0.5	4.6	1.5	5.4	4.1	5.2	4.3	4.5	2.0	0.9	4.6
Togo	14.7	-3.4	-3.7	-5.2	5.9	3.2	3.4	1.5	5.0	3.7	1.9	4.7	-1.0	3.3
Uganda	12.3	7.5	11.7	9.6	-8.5	-1.9	-1.5	5.7	6.1	6.4	6.3	-3.0	3.7	6.1
Zaire	6.7	3.5	-0.4	1.5	2.4	2.2	4.3	0.6	3.2	-2.0	-1.9	-1.3	1.7	0.1
Zambia	3.2	6.1	-2.7	-2.1	-1.1	1.7	0.2	3.0	5.5	0.1	0.9	-0.3	-0.3	2.4
Zimbabwe	10.5	12.5	2.6	1.6	-2.5	6.7	2.7	-1.4	-1.5	13.4	3.0	-0.1	3.1	3.7
NORTH AFRICA	3.8	-3.8	4.8	3.6	2.0	2.9	0.7	1.1	1.3	3.4	2.3	7.8	2.3	2.1
Algeria	0.9	3.0	6.4	5.4	4.1	5.3	2.0	2.2	-2.6	5.6	2.5	6.6	5.0	1.8
Egypt, Arab Republic of	10.8	4.0	10.7	7.7	6.1	6.6	2.6	2.5	3.9	2.4	0.5	10.5	7.3	2.5
Libya	0.6	-18.8	-3.3	-1.1	-7.9	-8.8	-8.7	-3.2	0.7	0.6	..	9.0	-7.0	0.7
Morocco	10.1	-2.8	9.6	-0.6	4.2	6.2	7.9	-2.1	10.1	1.2	4.4	5.9	3.4	3.7
Tunisia	7.3	5.5	-0.5	4.7	5.8	5.8	-1.5	5.7	1.3	3.5	6.4	6.1	4.0	3.8
ALL AFRICA	..	-1.2	3.7	1.9	0.5	3.3	2.6	0.4	1.8	3.2	2.0	..	1.8	2.0
South Africa	5.2	9.3	-0.9	-2.4	5.1	-0.8	0.3	2.1	3.7	2.1	..	2.6	1.5	2.9

2–17. GNP per capita

	U.S. dollars, Atlas method											Annual average		
	1980	1981	1982	1983	1984	1985	1986	1987	1988	1989	1990	75–79	80–85	86–MR
SUB-SAHARAN AFRICA	582	613	609	546	497	491	438	354	339	333	335	404	557	360
excluding Nigeria	420	438	425	387	350	329	339	349	360	364	360	307	392	355
Angola	..	..	..	..	..	638	648	683	616	609	..	..	106	639
Benin	315	341	331	281	259	259	274	298	346	347	362	203	298	325
Botswana	786	1,042	1,017	1,075	1,085	964	962	1,034	1,199	1,606	2,049	459	995	1,370
Burkina Faso	241	251	252	217	188	189	213	244	302	313	328	164	223	280
Burundi	202	248	246	244	233	249	245	244	234	218	211	135	237	230
Cameroon	755	902	903	867	823	811	888	915	980	994	941	433	844	944
Cape Verde	527	541	514	488	453	457	483	572	698	781	894	334	497	685
Central African Republic	316	328	336	281	278	269	285	315	373	381	393	227	301	349
Chad	158	159	150	144	134	153	145	142	179	187	189	155	150	169
Comoros	347	387	356	327	314	302	319	378	443	454	482	204	339	415
Congo, People's Republic of the	850	1,102	1,320	1,237	1,151	1,043	945	958	933	973	1,007	544	1,117	963
Cote d'Ivoire	1,177	1,149	994	789	692	654	717	765	832	788	729	711	909	766
Djibouti	..	..	..	..	..	..	937	982	..	..	..	..	..	960
Equatorial Guinea	..	..	..	..	..	..	..	268	304	305	325	..	..	..
Ethiopia	116	118	117	120	116	108	115	123	123	122	118	95	116	120
Gabon	3,886	4,280	4,344	3,813	3,574	3,550	3,636	2,886	2,774	3,006	3,234	3,345	3,908	3,107
Gambia, The	348	363	360	287	247	212	174	193	215	236	260	261	303	216
Ghana	406	410	377	345	365	368	390	393	401	383	392	319	379	392
Guinea	303	307	299	293	299	315	310	316	401	442	482	..	303	429
Guinea-Bissau	134	172	191	197	188	182	159	166	168	183	179	170	177	171
Kenya	419	433	399	351	324	310	325	341	365	368	368	284	373	353
Lesotho	413	479	549	512	481	394	340	344	407	438	470	295	471	400
Liberia	578	590	550	494	465	473	454	448	..	..	..	498	525	451
Madagascar	428	411	402	380	339	307	291	263	244	220	233	309	378	250
Malawi	180	184	188	185	180	170	155	150	157	173	195	143	181	166
Mali	237	241	221	173	157	146	177	200	225	260	271	162	196	227
Mauritania	438	482	454	469	422	411	428	419	469	504	501	351	446	464
Mauritius	1,179	1,259	1,219	1,118	1,083	1,100	1,228	1,500	1,831	2,030	2,263	946	1,160	1,770
Mozambique	..	..	189	160	176	182	218	152	112	81	77	..	118	128
Namibia	..	..	1,212	1,131	1,036	925	840	832	961	1,029	..	..	717	916
Niger	436	436	378	314	239	227	243	255	298	292	308	272	338	279
Nigeria	1,029	1,094	1,114	980	898	931	707	370	280	249	266	667	1,008	374
Rwanda	237	263	261	269	259	271	296	309	328	320	311	153	260	313
Sao Tome & Principe	505	336	389	352	351	314	370	428	454	423	393	380	374	413
Senegal	507	489	506	441	380	379	431	522	648	656	708	398	450	593
Seychelles	2,116	2,435	2,511	2,545	2,545	2,383	2,541	2,938	3,527	4,069	4,541	1,089	2,422	3,523
Sierra Leone	322	372	380	382	365	343	329	244	235	211	237	226	361	251
Somalia	141	159	166	148	146	160	154	173	165	..	..	160	153	164
Sudan	397	405	415	393	358	368	464	577	506	499	374	344	389	484
Swaziland	823	1,011	1,014	935	870	810	712	675	806	796	816	616	911	761
Tanzania	284	300	320	318	301	309	275	218	163	129	..	202	305	196
Togo	414	397	341	280	261	249	265	304	370	392	405	305	324	347
Uganda	168	146	144	147	161	187	226	261	276	..	..	233	159	255
Zaire	611	559	512	442	352	268	248	242	248	244	228	471	457	242
Zambia	598	717	657	558	457	370	256	241	293	396	418	520	560	321
Zimbabwe	707	858	897	849	729	619	560	538	575	654	644	560	776	594
NORTH AFRICA	1,274	1,344	1,407	1,359	1,321	1,332	1,321	1,348	1,312	1,276	1,230	857	1,340	1,298
Algeria	1,944	2,237	2,426	2,424	2,468	2,591	2,646	2,687	2,467	2,277	2,058	1,226	2,349	2,427
Egypt, Arab Republic of	502	549	603	616	638	662	674	694	664	639	603	385	595	655
Libya	9,754	9,288	9,258	8,575	7,305	6,753	5,796	5,737	5,334	5,315	..	6,773	8,489	5,546
Morocco	927	873	861	725	657	620	658	677	833	884	948	616	777	800
Tunisia	1,279	1,379	1,308	1,238	1,207	1,170	1,112	1,183	1,232	1,271	1,419	872	1,264	1,243
ALL AFRICA	733	772	782	722	675	672	627	566	545	532	522	503	726	558
South Africa	2,235	2,802	2,768	2,635	2,607	2,214	1,960	2,015	2,324	..	..	1,533	2,544	2,100

2-18. Total consumption per capita

	Current U.S. dollars											Annual average		
	1980	1981	1982	1983	1984	1985	1986	1987	1988	1989	1990	75–79	80–85	86–MR
SUB-SAHARAN AFRICA	465	464	468	438	416	397	332	284	288	276	279	320	441	292
excluding Nigeria	342	329	320	296	266	266	305	314	307	298	292	245	303	303
Angola	..	..	..	..	..	..	..	..	..	..	..	..	..	..
Benin	352	339	289	258	259	256	312	350	358	330	391	213	292	348
Botswana	698	847	819	802	842	691	646	841	1,096	1,291	..	410	783	969
Burkina Faso	253	230	215	190	170	176	244	288	299	280	336	165	206	289
Burundi	226	221	241	228	204	235	245	211	208	198	199	137	226	212
Cameroon	726	728	645	585	546	514	703	924	986	764	759	406	624	827
Cape Verde	530	500	485	466	458	480	647	658	742	755	878	393	486	736
Central African Republic	377	297	326	266	248	266	370	379	386	364	436	246	297	387
Chad	189	149	138	133	137	173	179	182	221	208	224	161	153	203
Comoros	..	..	..	293	313	320	410	516	521	455	558	..	..	492
Congo, People's Republic of the	614	639	661	642	629	768	780	856	839	785	875	516	659	827
Cote d'Ivoire	999	804	682	598	534	508	727	806	751	683	697	620	688	733
Djibouti	..	..	..	..	995	1,004	1,013	990	1,060	1,029	..	..	..	1,023
Equatorial Guinea	..	..	..	..	..	241	267	311	347	312	382	..	..	324
Ethiopia	104	107	109	115	112	107	114	113	111	116	115	88	109	114
Gabon	2,078	1,907	1,770	1,718	1,676	1,794	2,451	2,313	2,261	2,160	2,435	1,512	1,824	2,324
Gambia, The	368	307	282	279	216	215	182	216	240	238	272	271	278	229
Ghana	393	367	342	334	339	330	404	344	332	342	376	296	351	360
Guinea	252	276	271	268	261	275	320	326	380	399	419	..	267	369
Guinea-Bissau	138	186	207	199	172	197	141	173	174	202	221	175	183	182
Kenya	357	318	293	255	256	229	269	295	301	287	296	244	285	290
Lesotho	435	453	415	479	398	283	300	385	398	444	546	275	411	415
Liberia	432	458	491	464	440	426	390	..	..	..	..	358	452	78
Madagascar	471	401	387	367	292	279	303	231	209	200	245	311	366	237
Malawi	181	173	154	154	148	137	143	134	152	184	197	121	158	162
Mali	252	203	177	161	152	164	204	229	225	215	275	170	185	230
Mauritania	426	411	449	536	438	377	403	444	493	482	519	368	440	468
Mauritius	1,045	993	922	895	838	827	1,014	1,278	1,469	1,524	1,825	757	920	1,422
Mozambique	199	184	199	193	201	254	295	112	98	99	102	..	205	141
Namibia	955	1,209	1,121	1,143	934	679	741	992	985	934	..	..	1,007	913
Niger	357	347	306	268	234	214	259	295	301	268	..	255	288	281
Nigeria	859	895	937	886	891	807	419	191	230	206	..	557	879	261
Rwanda	216	244	242	252	245	258	283	312	326	296	289	151	243	301
Sao Tome & Principe	550	362	439	397	365	376	634	577	417	537	554	330	415	544
Senegal	547	468	445	413	368	409	539	637	659	608	717	386	442	632
Seychelles	1,790	2,117	2,245	2,470	2,316	2,239	2,809	3,277	3,735	3,992	4,148	..	2,196	3,592
Sierra Leone	336	348	380	413	271	331	346	128	247	227	206	228	347	231
Somalia	146	169	177	183	184	181	195	194	189	226	17	150	173	164
Sudan	341	397	355	360	384	487	581	654	383	463	332	325	387	483
Swaziland	896	979	826	850	753	532	534	663	719	..	..	497	806	639
Tanzania	256	279	281	291	263	302	180	153	150	125	..	184	279	152
Togo	331	277	247	214	198	198	291	338	361	328	396	230	244	343
Uganda	96	82	146	137	156	135	206	219	250	190	175	..	125	208
Zaire	488	414	445	343	234	198	221	210	233	225	..	490	354	222
Zambia	555	640	589	449	349	282	184	234	392	536	319	456	627	475
Zimbabwe	643	745	771	694	505	402	437	460	480	485	511	513	789	904
NORTH AFRICA	779	757	765	765	808	859	967	976	869	850	856			
Algeria	1,291	1,367	1,384	1,435	1,567	1,689	1,978	1,898	1,579	1,391	1,295	821	1,455	1,629
Egypt, Arab Republic of	475	480	504	524	581	637	649	681	570	610	610	320	534	624
Libya	4,912	5,165	5,820	5,800	..	..	..	..	..	..	..	3,718	3,616	0
Morocco	838	680	653	565	506	490	625	668	733	750	808	565	622	717
Tunisia	1,042	980	952	928	904	908	996	1,018	1,042	1,036	1,225	709	952	1,063
ALL AFRICA	526	521	525	501	491	485	453	415	398	383	386	357	508	407
South Africa	1,788	1,938	1,821	2,004	1,748	1,276	1,434	1,876	1,934	1,958	..	1,115	1,763	1,801

Technical Notes

Data are from the World Bank's data base (BESD). Estimates are based on data obtained from national sources, usually collected directly by World bank staff, who review the quality of national accounts data and, in some instances, adjust and update national series.

Most of the definitions are taken from the UN's System of National accounts, series F No. 2, revision 3, following from the World Bank's Statistical Manual Note.

Table 2-1. Gross domestic product (GDP)

GDP's shown at purchaser values (formerly estimated as GDP at market prices). GDP at market prices is the sum of GDP at factor cost plus indirect taxes minus subsidies. The new SNA methodology reports GDP at producer prices, which is the sum of GDP by industrial origin at producer prices (formerly estimated as GDP at factor cost) plus import duties. GDP is presented in constant 1987 prices. Constant price series in national currency based on years other than the 1987 base have been partially rebased to 1987. Rebasing of any series is accomplished by rescaling, which moves the year in which current and constant price versions of the same time series have the same value without altering the trend of either.

The components of GDP by industrial origin are presented in the form of value added. Value added is the measure of the output of an industry without double counting and thus equals value of gross output at producers value less the value of intermediate inputs used in the course of production which were produced by other industries.

Table 2-2. Value added in agriculture

This covers the value added in forestry, hunting, and fishing, as well as in agriculture.

Table 2-3. Value added in industry

Like Table 2-2, this comprises value added in mining, manufacturing, construction, electricity, water, and gas.

Table 2-4. Value added in services

This table consists of all other branches of economic activity, including government. Other items, such as imputed bank service charges (which are difficult to assess in the same fashion for all countries) and any corrections for statistical discrepancies, are not included in GDP by industrial origin (in other presentations, they may be included with services). GDP by industrial origins (value added) shown in these tables are calculated from annual data in constant price series to reflect changes both in prices and real growth in the sector relative to those for the economy as a whole. Producers' prices are valuation is usually used for production by industrial origin so that the distribution of the services of the production can be analyzed without the variations that indirect taxes cause in relative market prices. At the sector level, the difference between estimates at producer prices and purchaser values also includes distribution costs; at the national level, these distribution costs are included as a separate component of services.

While the SNA envisages estimates of GDP by industrial origin to be at producer prices, many countries still report it at factor cost. When countries report GDP on one basis but not the other (for example, at producer prices [or factor cost] but not at purchaser values [or market prices], the estimate provided can be converted to the other basis for total GDP by adding or subtracting import duties (or net indirect taxes). If national accounts at producer prices are not reported, components of GDP by industrial origin are shown at purchaser values; this substitution has been made for Botswana, Cameroon, Chad, the People's Republic of Congo, Gabon, Guinea, Madagascar, Mali, Morocco, Niger, Rwanda, Senegal, Togo, Zaire, and Zambia.

The sum of the components of GDP by industrial origin will not normally equal total GDP for several reasons. First, components of GDP y expenditure are individually rescaled and summed to provide a partially rebased series for total GDP. Second, total GDP is shown at purchaser value, while value added components are conventionally reported at producer prices. As explained above, the former excludes net indirect taxes, while the latter includes indirect taxes. Third, certain items, such as imputed bank charges, are added in total GDP.

Table 2-5. Gross domestic product (in current prices)

Is at purchaser values as in Table 2-1, but it is expressed in current prices converted to U.S. dollars at annual exchange rates. Shares of components are calculated as the percentage ratio of sector GDP by expenditure to total GDP. The percentage shares of components of GDP by expenditure are calculated from annual data in current prices. Because components of GDP by expenditure are individually rescaled, often times a rescaling deviation occurs between the new constant price GDP by industrial origin and the sum of the rescaled components of GDP by expenditure.

Table 2-6. Total consumption

Is the sum of general government consumption and private consumption. Private consumption, not separately shown here, is the market value of all goods and services purchased or received as income in kind by households and nonprofit institutions. It excludes purchases of dwellings, but includes imputed rent for owner-occupied dwellings. In practice, it includes any statistical discrepancy in the use of resources.

Table 2-7. General government consumption

Includes all current expenditure for purchases of goods and services by all levels of government, including capital expenditure on national defense and security. Other capital expenditure by government is included in investment.

Table 2-8. Gross domestic investment

Consists of gross domestic fixed capital formation plus net changes in the level of inventories. Gross domestic investment comprises outlays by the private (Table 2-9) and the public sectors (Table 2-10). Examples include improvements of land, dwellings, machinery, and other equipments. Notably, for some countries the sum of gross private investment and gross public investment does not add up to gross domestic investment. This is so because of statistical discrepancies.

Table 2-11. Gross domestic saving (GDS)

Is calculated by deducting total consumption from gross domestic product.

Table 2-12. Gross national saving (GNS)

Is gross domestic savings plus the sum of net factor income from abroad and net private transfers from abroad. However, the estimate here includes public, as well as private, net transfers from abroad.

Table 2-13. Resource balance

Indicates the difference between exports (f.o.b.) and imports (c.i.f.) of goods and nonfactor services (or the difference between gross domestic savings and gross domestic investment). For the preceding six components of GDP, figures are shown as percentages of GDP, calculated from current price series at purchase values converted to

US dollars at annual, single year exchang rates. (The same result is obtained if values in national currency are used.)

Tables 2-14 and 2-15. Exports and imports of goods and nonfactor services

These are the values of all goods and nonfactor services (GNFS) provided to or by the rest of the world. · They include merchandise, freight, insurance, travel, and other nonfactor services. The value of factor services, such as investment income, interest, and labor income, is not included. These series are generally estimated on the basis of foreign trade statistics from customs declarations. They may not be fully comparable with the series from the balance of payments, which are based on changes in ownership between residents of a country and the rest of the world, as explained below.

Table 2-16. GDP growth

Table 2-16 provides average annual growth rates calculated from GDP data at constant 1987 purchaser values (as shown in Table 2-1).

Table 2-17. GNP per capita

Figures are calculated using the *World Bank Atlas* method, as described in the technical notes for Table 1-1.; these are similar in concept to GNP per capita in current prices, except that the use of three-year averages of exchange rates smooths sharp fluctuations from year to year. Growth rates for GNP per capita in countries are, however, calculated from annual GNP per capita data in constant 1987 prices in national currencies, which avoids the problem of changing exchange rates. Growth rates for country groups are based on totals in U.S. dollars converted at 1987 exchange rates in every year.

Table 2-18. Total consumption per capita

This is the estimate of total consumption at constant 1987 prices divided by the corresponding midyear population.

3

Prices and Exchange Rates

Information on prices and exchange rates are important in monitoring national economic performance. Three sets of price deflators and six exchange rate indicators are provided in this chapter. The GDP deflator for national currency series shows changes in domestic prices only. The U.S. dollar series GDP deflator includes the effects of both domestic price changes, as reflected in the national currency series GDP implicit deflator, and changes in the exchange rate between national currencies and U.S. dollars. The consumer price index measures the change in prices of a selected bundle of consumer goods, which differs among countries.

The U.S. dollar exchange rate (units of national currency per U.S. dollar) is reported because of extensive use of U.S. dollars to denominate international transactions; U.S. dollars are also widely used for statistical comparisons across countries. The SDR exchange rate index (based on SDRs per unit of national currency) is a broader measure of the changes in the international value of domestic

currencies because it is based on five major currencies. For Sub-Saharan Africa, it may be more representative of movements in non-dual exchange rates than that expressed in U.S. dollars alone because a large share of the region's foreign trade and debt is not denominated in U.S. dollars. A decrease in the index shows that the currency has depreciated, which indicates that foreign goods have become relatively more expensive than domestic goods. We have included information on the parallel market exchange rate and the ratio of the parallel to the official exchange rates to provide a measure of the premium on the official rate. It is tempting to view the divergence between the official and parallel rates as a measure of the disequilibrium in the official exchange rate. However, this is not necessarily true. Conversion factors are sometimes used in lieu of official exchange rates when the latter are considered especially unrepresentative of rates effectively applied to international transactions.

3-1. GDP deflator (Local currency series)

	Index 1987=100											Average		
	1980	1981	1982	1983	1984	1985	1986	1987	1988	1989	1990	75–79	80–85	86–MR
SUB-SAHARAN AFRICA	52.7	56.2	63.3	72.6	77.1	83.6	93.0	100.0	108.9	121.5	134.2	10.6	10.5	9.8
excluding Nigeria	53.2	56.4	65.4	72.7	79.0	85.3	93.1	100.0	108.8	120.4	132.6	10.5	10.5	9.5
Angola	..	..	..	118.2	119.3	117.6	96.3	100.0	92.7	103.5	..	..	..	1.4
Benin	79.4	85.3	99.1	103.8	105.8	100.7	97.0	100.0	99.7	103.3	105.2	10.6	5.5	2.0
Botswana	54.3	56.4	57.2	61.0	63.6	74.8	93.1	100.0	117.5	152.2	..	10.1	6.0	17.8
Burkina Faso	66.0	75.0	81.1	85.0	90.5	94.8	94.8	100.0	102.9	104.3	107.4	11.9	7.2	3.0
Burundi	83.3	78.3	82.7	88.0	103.0	108.4	103.8	100.0	104.2	117.1	123.1	14.7	6.5	5.1
Cameroon	56.8	63.5	71.9	80.7	89.6	97.7	98.1	100.0	100.9	98.8	96.9	9.1	11.7	-0.4
Cape Verde	51.1	56.0	65.8	72.7	79.1	81.9	96.4	100.0	108.2	119.4	136.4	6.2	10.5	9.1
Central African Republic	58.4	67.0	81.1	88.7	90.1	98.5	105.4	100.0	100.9	103.1	105.5	13.6	10.8	0.3
Chad	89.2	96.4	105.3	105.3	130.6	124.4	103.0	100.0	109.2	111.7	107.0	8.9	7.6	1.9
Comoros	..	..	..	79.4	84.2	90.0	96.1	100.0	102.6	105.8	110.1	..	..	3.3
Congo, People's Rep of the	79.7	105.2	109.3	114.2	128.0	131.2	92.9	100.0	93.8	106.9	107.3	9.1	9.3	3.6
Cote d'Ivoire	78.9	78.1	83.4	87.6	98.5	102.4	102.8	100.0	100.0	97.1	91.4	17.4	6.0	-2.6
Djibouti	..	..	..	..	80.8	83.8	96.6	100.0	105.0	108.0	..	..	..	3.9
Equatorial Guinea	..	..	..	..	..	117.0	104.9	100.0	101.7	104.9	105.9	..	..	0.7
Ethiopia	87.8	90.1	91.3	95.0	96.8	102.8	105.5	100.0	101.2	105.0	110.3	7.2	3.0	1.4
Gabon	90.7	109.6	120.9	129.7	145.4	146.6	96.0	100.0	94.3	90.4	102.2	10.4	9.9	0.3
Gambia, The	43.5	44.5	45.1	54.0	58.9	74.8	91.4	100.0	*110.4*	*126.5*	135.9	11.9	11.3	10.8
Ghana	6.3	10.9	13.9	31.0	41.9	50.6	71.7	100.0	133.5	171.5	241.1	53.5	54.7	34.5
Guinea	..	..	..	..	..	..	78.7	100.0	122.3	148.3	184.2	..	..	23.3
Guinea-Bissau	7.9	8.4	9.8	12.0	19.8	28.7	53.9	100.0	174.1	296.0	399.6	4.4	30.2	66.4
Kenya	53.2	58.8	65.4	73.1	80.5	87.1	94.8	100.0	108.6	118.5	131.4	10.8	10.6	8.6
Lesotho	46.0	52.2	57.0	63.7	68.7	79.8	91.6	100.0	119.0	133.8	151.2	8.5	11.1	13.8
Liberia	88.3	87.6	91.6	88.5	92.7	93.6	94.3	100.0	..	..	..	6.0	1.2	..
Madagascar	29.5	37.4	48.2	58.5	64.5	71.2	81.3	100.0	121.2	134.3	151.4	8.8	19.5	16.6
Malawi	43.3	50.4	55.2	61.4	69.1	75.3	85.5	100.0	127.1	155.1	171.4	6.5	11.5	20.1
Mali	77.6	79.9	81.5	87.0	96.7	99.6	93.9	100.0	104.7	99.4	102.1	9.6	5.5	1.6
Mauritania	52.1	55.7	61.2	64.9	75.1	86.7	93.4	100.0	102.4	112.6	116.0	6.2	10.5	5.7
Mauritius	56.1	62.5	67.8	73.6	79.0	85.3	91.8	100.0	110.7	122.6	132.6	8.8	8.6	9.8
Mozambique	15.7	16.1	19.1	21.6	24.8	37.1	41.7	100.0	147.3	205.3	279.1	..	17.8	57.2
Namibia	47.5	48.0	56.2	60.7	69.7	85.5	93.8	100.0	120.6	143.0	..	..	12.5	15.6
Niger	72.0	78.3	86.7	92.6	105.1	103.4	96.6	100.0	101.7	99.0	101.2	11.4	8.2	0.8
Nigeria	40.9	45.0	46.4	54.6	62.8	64.8	65.9	100.0	121.4	181.5	212.7	12.4	10.4	34.2
Rwanda	76.0	79.3	83.3	85.1	99.8	105.9	98.7	100.0	103.4	107.7	110.7	7.7	7.0	3.1
Sao Tome and Principe	41.3	40.7	43.6	49.1	51.7	51.8	81.3	100.0	137.8	184.6	230.8	1.7	5.8	31.0
Senegal	57.7	62.1	67.9	74.0	83.5	91.1	98.0	100.0	102.1	103.5	106.5	7.1	9.8	2.0
Seychelles	77.1	85.0	86.6	90.1	90.0	92.1	97.4	100.0	105.5	108.1	108.3	17.5	3.2	2.9
Sierra Leone	6.3	6.5	8.1	9.7	13.8	25.1	40.0	100.0	143.6	210.1	398.4	16.3	30.7	70.5
Somalia	12.8	15.0	19.1	25.4	43.6	56.5	75.3	100.0	170.1	335.6	1059.6	12.0	36.7	91.5
Sudan	15.4	18.9	23.8	31.7	41.1	57.0	78.1	100.0	133.4	233.6	362.2	16.0	29.9	48.0
Swaziland	*49.1*	54.6	58.9	63.0	69.3	73.4	92.8	100.0	108.8	124.1	140.9	11.3	8.3	11.1
Tanzania	21.7	25.5	30.4	36.9	44.5	59.6	75.0	100.0	140.4	165.9	184.3	14.9	21.9	25.9
Togo	64.7	73.0	78.3	89.2	90.6	94.6	98.1	100.0	103.2	104.3	108.5	6.1	7.9	2.5
Uganda	0.8	1.5	2.1	3.0	5.2	13.2	30.9	100.0	262.8	499.7	679.8	48.7	66.3	118.0
Zaire	5.5	7.3	10.6	18.8	35.6	44.8	57.5	100.0	191.4	394.1	650.3	49.9	57.1	86.3
Zambia	16.3	17.5	18.5	22.0	26.2	36.9	67.6	100.0	143.8	290.1	527.2	13.6	17.0	67.8
Zimbabwe	46.4	53.2	60.7	72.6	75.2	80.0	89.5	100.0	108.9	121.5	138.3	10.6	11.9	11.2
NORTH AFRICA	58.5	64.2	73.5	80.4	86.2	90.3	93.9	100.0	105.2	115.4	122.6	8.7	7.9	7.2
Algeria	67.5	77.2	78.7	84.1	89.7	93.8	94.4	100.0	104.0	118.2	151.8	11.5	6.4	11.8
Egypt, Arab Republic of	53.8	54.3	58.9	63.6	70.7	77.1	86.9	100.0	116.0	134.4	161.2	11.9	7.9	16.6
Libyan Arab Republic	88.8	97.1	93.2	92.7	89.4	104.9	93.9	100.0	87.8	94.6	..	6.2	1.7	-1.1
Morocco	58.5	64.2	68.8	73.8	80.3	87.1	96.5	100.0	105.2	109.5	115.5	8.7	8.1	4.6
Tunisia	56.9	63.4	73.5	80.4	86.2	90.3	93.1	100.0	107.6	115.4	122.6	7.5	10.0	7.2
ALL AFRICA	54.3	58.8	65.8	73.1	79.1	86.7	93.1	100.0	108.7	119.0	134.2	10.5	9.9	9.5
South Africa	40.0	44.8	50.9	58.9	65.7	76.4	88.2	100.0	115.7	133.0	151.6	11.8	13.8	14.7

Notes: *Group data are medians of individual country values for each year. Group data include countries for which only 1990 data are missing.*

3-2. GDP deflator (U.S. dollar series)

	Index 1987=100											Average		
	1980	1981	1982	1983	1984	1985	1986	1987	1988	1989	1990	75–79	80–85	86–MR
SUB-SAHARAN AFRICA	105.3	91.5	93.4	89.7	91.6	83.4	89.1	100.0	103.0	98.2	110.9	9.0	-5.5	4.6
excluding Nigeria	103.4	89.9	91.3	89.4	91.5	83.2	88.9	100.0	102.8	97.9	111.3	9.0	-5.5	4.6
Angola	..	..	121.8	118.2	119.3	117.6	96.3	100.0	92.7	103.5	..	..	..	1.4
Benin	92.2	77.0	70.8	68.5	65.3	67.3	84.2	100.0	100.6	95.6	115.7	11.4	-5.8	6.1
Botswana	124.7	132.0	113.3	102.3	100.7	84.4	88.5	100.0	127.0	139.1	..	6.1	-7.9	17.3
Burkina Faso	92.6	81.8	73.7	67.0	62.2	63.4	82.3	100.0	103.9	98.2	118.5	13.6	-7.7	7.4
Burundi	114.4	107.4	113.5	117.0	106.5	111.0	112.3	100.0	91.7	91.2	88.9	11.2	-0.4	-5.5
Cameroon	86.5	86.0	77.3	72.5	69.7	66.1	80.9	100.0	110.2	99.8	102.8	9.0	-5.7	4.9
Cape Verde	92.0	83.2	81.6	73.4	67.4	64.7	87.1	100.0	108.8	110.9	141.1	-3.2	-6.9	11.3
Central African Republic	82.5	73.1	73.2	70.0	62.0	65.9	91.5	100.0	101.9	97.1	116.4	14.7	-4.6	4.6
Chad	126.8	106.6	96.3	83.1	89.9	83.2	89.4	100.0	110.2	105.2	118.1	9.7	-7.6	6.3
Comoros	..	..	67.0	63.1	58.4	60.6	83.9	100.0	103.2	99.2	120.9	..	..	7.5
Congo, People's Rep of the	112.7	112.0	98.2	90.0	88.0	87.8	80.6	100.0	94.6	100.8	118.5	9.8	-5.7	8.1
Cote d'Ivoire	107.2	83.1	74.4	68.4	67.6	68.5	88.9	100.0	101.3	92.3	102.2	17.3	-8.1	2.0
Djibouti	..	..	..	..	80.8	83.8	96.6	100.0	105.0	108.0	..	..	..	3.9
Equatorial Guinea	..	..	..	..	..	78.9	91.2	100.0	103.6	99.7	117.8	..	..	5.2
Ethiopia	87.7	89.9	91.2	94.9	96.8	102.9	105.6	100.0	101.3	105.0	110.4	7.3	3.1	1.4
Gabon	129.0	121.2	110.5	102.3	100.0	98.0	83.3	100.0	95.1	85.2	112.8	11.2	-5.6	4.6
Gambia, The	168.7	140.5	125.3	125.8	98.0	103.4	84.0	100.0	*109.2*	*107.3*	124.1	16.1	-9.6	8.9
Ghana	94.5	93.0	95.5	100.6	100.7	97.8	118.3	100.0	96.9	93.2	108.0	8.4	1.3	-2.5
Guinea	..	..	..	..	..	..	100.9	100.0	110.7	107.7	119.8	..	..	4.3
Guinea-Bissau	87.7	108.9	111.8	114.4	91.8	100.3	80.8	100.0	87.6	91.4	102.1	-0.3	0.5	3.8
Kenya	117.2	106.5	98.6	90.4	92.0	87.3	96.2	100.0	100.7	94.8	94.3	11.2	-5.5	-0.9
Lesotho	120.0	120.9	106.7	116.1	96.3	74.0	81.5	100.0	107.0	104.3	119.4	5.7	-8.3	8.4
Liberia	86.8	86.9	91.3	88.5	92.7	93.6	94.3	100.0	..	..	..	6.5	1.6	..
Madagascar	149.6	147.4	147.2	145.3	119.6	115.0	128.5	100.0	92.1	89.5	108.3	9.6	-5.4	-4.4
Malawi	117.9	124.5	115.8	115.7	108.5	97.1	101.6	100.0	109.5	124.3	138.9	8.7	-3.9	8.8
Mali	108.6	87.5	73.7	68.3	66.5	66.8	81.2	100.0	105.7	93.4	112.4	10.5	-9.1	6.0
Mauritania	85.7	87.1	89.3	89.4	86.6	82.7	92.6	100.0	100.6	99.5	105.5	4.6	-0.5	2.6
Mauritius	93.4	89.6	80.0	80.6	73.4	71.1	88.0	100.0	105.8	103.0	114.5	8.7	-5.4	5.7
Mozambique	139.7	131.5	146.4	155.5	170.9	249.9	298.5	100.0	81.6	80.1	87.7	..	11.3	-23.4
Namibia	123.7	111.0	105.0	110.6	96.4	77.5	82.2	100.0	107.1	111.9	..	..	-7.5	10.5
Niger	103.4	87.5	79.8	74.0	72.5	67.7	81.7	100.0	102.7	93.3	111.7	12.8	-7.6	5.7
Nigeria	309.7	304.4	286.4	309.3	341.8	304.0	152.5	100.0	107.4	98.7	106.6	13.7	1.0	-7.0
Rwanda	66.8	68.9	72.8	73.4	80.3	83.6	89.8	100.0	107.6	106.8	106.7	7.5	4.7	4.2
Sao Tome and Principe	64.4	57.4	57.7	62.9	63.5	62.9	114.2	100.0	86.5	80.3	87.3	-6.2	0.8	-7.3
Senegal	82.7	68.8	62.2	58.4	57.4	60.9	85.1	100.0	103.0	97.5	117.6	8.2	-5.9	6.4
Seychelles	67.5	75.6	74.0	74.7	71.3	72.2	88.2	100.0	109.8	107.2	113.6	17.0	0.5	5.9
Sierra Leone	216.1	219.6	242.6	273.9	197.9	244.3	272.5	100.0	199.4	162.0	147.4	9.0	1.2	-7.2
Somalia	72.8	79.8	84.9	88.2	91.5	93.7	96.3	100.0	103.3	108.7	94.1	-13.0	5.0	0.4
Sudan	46.1	52.8	46.5	44.1	53.4	67.2	86.9	100.0	56.3	65.2	52.2	10.4	5.5	-13.5
Swaziland	*128.3*	127.7	110.8	115.2	98.1	68.2	83.2	100.0	97.9	96.6	110.9	8.5	-10.6	5.5
Tanzania	166.7	194.4	206.4	209.8	184.6	217.7	147.1	100.0	91.0	74.4	60.7	11.7	3.5	-18.7
Togo	91.7	80.3	71.1	70.1	62.3	63.3	85.1	100.0	104.2	98.4	119.9	6.7	-7.3	6.9
Uganda	42.6	39.1	52.4	50.2	66.0	61.0	98.4	100.0	105.6	77.0	69.9	..	10.0	-9.0
Zaire	221.3	188.3	206.0	163.8	110.8	101.0	108.5	100.0	115.0	116.1	101.7	15.9	-15.1	0.2
Zambia	198.0	192.5	191.3	167.5	137.9	112.1	82.3	100.0	164.5	198.8	145.3	7.8	-10.7	20.0
Zimbabwe	120.3	128.2	133.2	119.2	99.4	82.5	89.4	100.0	100.3	95.5	93.8	5.9	-7.6	0.5
NORTH AFRICA	94.0	96.7	92.8	92.2	88.9	90.3	97.1	100.0	90.4	93.1	92.1	7.6	1.0	0.8
Algeria	84.8	86.2	82.5	84.6	86.9	90.3	97.1	100.0	84.8	75.3	81.7	12.6	1.0	-6.1
Egypt, Arab Republic of	94.0	92.5	92.0	94.2	96.7	102.7	103.5	100.0	83.9	88.3	92.1	1.1	1.7	-3.5
Libyan Arab Republic	88.4	96.7	92.8	92.2	88.9	104.4	87.8	100.0	90.4	93.1	..	6.2	1.7	0.8
Morocco	124.6	104.0	95.8	87.1	76.3	72.5	88.4	100.0	106.9	107.5	117.0	10.2	-10.1	6.5
Tunisia	116.1	106.1	102.9	97.9	91.8	89.6	97.1	100.0	103.8	100.6	115.6	7.6	-5.0	3.6
ALL AFRICA	103.4	93.0	92.8	90.0	91.5	84.4	89.4	100.0	102.8	97.9	110.9	9.0	-5.5	4.0
South Africa	109.3	104.4	96.1	108.5	91.3	70.0	78.8	100.0	103.1	103.4	..	8.8	-6.9	8.8

Notes: Group data are medians of individual country values for each year. Group data include countries for which only 1990 data are missing.

3-3. Consumer price index

	Index 1987=100											Average Percentage change		
	1980	1981	1982	1983	1984	1985	1986	1987	1988	1989	1990	75-79	80-85	86-MR
SUB-SAHARAN AFRICA	49.1	57.5	65.9	73.4	80.9	86.1	93.4	100.0	108.9	120.9	134.7	12.9	12.9	9.2
excluding Nigeria	49.3	58.1	66.2	75.4	80.3	85.2	93.9	100.0	108.6	120.9	133.8	12.8	12.3	9.0
Angola	..	..	..	..	..	..	..	..	..	..	..	..	..	..
Benin	..	..	..	..	..	..	..	..	..	..	..	..	..	..
Botswana	49.3	57.5	63.9	70.5	76.6	82.8	91.1	100.0	108.4	120.9	134.7	11.3	10.7	10.2
Burkina Faso	72.2	77.7	87.0	94.3	98.9	105.7	102.9	100.0	104.4	103.9	103.1	12.0	8.0	0.5
Burundi	60.3	67.5	71.4	77.3	88.5	91.7	93.4	100.0	104.5	116.7	124.9	17.3	8.9	7.6
Cameroon	53.1	58.8	66.6	77.7	86.5	87.6	94.4	100.0	108.6	108.6	..	11.4	11.5	5.2
Cape Verde	..	..	..	74.1	82.4	86.9	96.3	100.0	..	..	..	..	..	3.8
Central African Republic	..	71.5	81.0	92.9	95.2	105.2	107.5	100.0	96.0	96.7	96.7	..	9.8	-2.4
Chad	..	..	..	96.7	116.3	122.3	106.4	100.0	115.5	109.8	110.5	..	..	1.7
Comoros	..	..	..	..	..	..	..	..	..	..	..	..	..	..
Congo, People's Republic	56.1	65.6	74.1	79.8	90.0	95.5	97.8	100.0	103.7	108.0	..	10.4	11.1	3.4
Cote d'Ivoire	70.6	76.9	82.5	87.4	91.1	92.8	99.6	100.0	107.0	..	..	17.7	5.7	3.7
Djibouti	75.1	79.4	77.4	78.1	79.6	81.3	96.1	100.0	..	..	..	..	1.2	4.1
Equatorial Guinea	..	..	..	..	..	139.6	114.8	100.0	102.3	108.4	109.6	..	..	-0.1
Ethiopia	78.9	83.7	88.6	88.0	95.4	113.6	102.5	100.0	107.1	115.5	121.4	18.1	6.5	4.9
Gabon	59.7	64.9	75.7	83.6	88.5	95.0	101.0	100.0	90.2	96.5	104.8	12.9	10.0	0.4
Gambia, The	27.5	29.2	32.4	35.8	43.7	51.7	81.0	100.0	*111.7*	*120.9*	135.7	10.9	13.6	13.0
Ghana	6.3	13.7	16.7	37.3	52.1	57.4	71.5	100.0	131.4	164.5	225.8	77.2	57.3	32.3
Guinea	..	..	..	..	..	..	..	..	..	..	..	..	..	..
Guinea-Bissau	..	..	..	..	..	..	..	..	..	..	..	..	..	..
Kenya	48.9	54.7	65.9	73.4	80.9	91.5	95.1	100.0	108.3	118.9	132.9	13.4	13.4	8.8
Lesotho	40.7	45.8	51.3	60.3	66.9	75.8	89.5	100.0	111.5	127.9	142.7	14.2	13.4	12.5
Liberia	78.0	83.9	88.9	91.4	92.5	91.6	95.2	100.0	109.6	..	..	7.5	3.3	7.3
Madagascar	30.5	39.8	52.4	62.5	68.7	76.0	87.0	100.0	126.9	138.3	154.6	6.6	20.0	15.9
Malawi	37.9	42.4	46.5	52.8	63.4	70.0	79.9	100.0	133.9	150.6	168.3	..	13.4	20.9
Mali	..	..	..	..	..	..	..	..	..	..	..	..	..	..
Mauritania	..	..	..	..	..	..	92.5	100.0	101.3	114.4	122.0	..	..	7.1
Mauritius	63.4	72.6	80.9	85.4	91.7	97.9	99.5	100.0	109.2	123.0	139.6	10.8	8.7	9.2
Mozambique	..	..	..	..	..	..	..	..	..	..	..	..	..	..
Namibia	..	..	..	..	..	..	..	..	..	..	..	..	..	..
Niger	77.1	94.8	105.8	103.2	111.8	110.7	107.2	100.0	98.6	95.8	95.1	15.9	6.7	-2.8
Nigeria	36.5	44.1	47.5	58.5	81.6	86.1	90.7	100.0	138.3	208.0	223.6	17.8	19.9	28.9
Rwanda	70.9	75.5	85.0	90.6	95.5	97.1	96.1	100.0	103.0	104.0	108.4	12.6	6.9	2.8
Sao Tome and Principe	..	..	..	..	..	..	..	..	..	..	..	..	..	..
Senegal	56.1	59.4	69.7	77.8	86.9	98.2	104.3	100.0	98.2	98.6	98.9	6.5	12.3	-1.2
Seychelles	79.7	88.1	87.4	92.7	96.5	97.2	97.5	100.0	101.8	103.4	107.5	13.5	3.9	2.3
Sierra Leone	2.5	3.1	4.0	6.7	11.1	19.6	35.5	100.0	131.3	213.7	450.9	13.3	51.7	79.4
Somalia	9.0	13.0	16.0	21.8	41.7	57.5	78.0	100.0	181.9	..	..	13.7	45.3	52.7
Sudan	16.7	20.8	26.2	34.2	45.8	66.6	82.9	100.0	164.7	269.2	..	17.1	31.4	49.6
Swaziland	39.5	45.0	48.4	58.9	66.5	79.7	88.9	100.0	111.8	..	..	12.2	14.9	12.2
Tanzania	15.6	19.5	25.2	32.0	43.3	58.1	77.0	100.0	131.2	167.9	208.9	11.0	30.1	28.6
Togo	69.7	83.4	92.7	101.3	97.8	96.0	99.9	100.0	99.9	99.0	100.0	10.4	6.4	-0.1
Uganda	0.9	1.8	2.7	3.3	4.7	11.0	29.6	100.0	283.6	539.6	..	..	57.5	165.2
Zaire	5.8	7.9	10.8	19.0	28.9	35.8	52.5	100.0	182.7	372.9	676.1	70.6	47.3	90.1
Zambia	18.2	20.6	23.4	28.0	33.6	46.1	69.9	100.0	155.6	305.5	..	16.5	19.7	62.7
Zimbabwe	38.7	43.8	48.5	59.7	71.7	77.8	88.9	100.0	107.4	121.3	142.3	10.5	15.9	12.0
NORTH AFRICA	54.7	61.1	67.3	71.6	78.3	85.5	93.2	100.0	106.1	115.0	128.5	10.6	9.7	8.1
Algeria	53.5	61.3	65.4	69.3	75.0	82.8	93.1	100.0	105.9	115.8	135.0	12.8	8.5	9.3
Egypt, Arab Republic of	35.0	38.6	44.3	51.4	60.2	67.4	83.5	100.0	117.7	142.7	166.6	11.2	14.6	19.0
Libya	..	..	..	..	..	..	..	..	..	..	..	9.8	..	..
Morocco	56.0	63.0	69.6	73.9	83.1	89.6	97.4	100.0	102.4	105.6	112.9	10.0	9.7	3.6
Tunisia	55.8	60.8	69.1	75.3	81.7	88.2	93.3	100.0	106.4	114.2	122.0	6.2	9.8	6.9
ALL AFRICA	51.2	58.8	65.9	73.4	80.9	86.1	93.3	100.0	108.5	119.9	134.7	12.6	11.9	9.2
South Africa	37.7	43.5	49.9	56.0	62.4	72.6	86.1	100.0	112.8	129.4	148.0	11.3	13.6	14.3

Notes: Group data are medians of individual country values for each year. Group data include countries for which only 1990 data are missing.

3–4. Official exchange rate

	National currency per U.S. dollar											Average		
	1980	1981	1982	1983	1984	1985	1986	1987	1988	1989	1990	75–79	80–85	86–MR
SUB-SAHARAN AFRICA **excluding Nigeria**														
Angola	29.9	29.9	29.9	29.9	29.9	29.9	29.9	29.9	29.9	29.9	29.9	28.9	29.9	29.9
Benin	211.3	271.7	328.6	381.1	437.0	449.3	346.3	300.5	297.8	319.0	272.3	227.5	346.5	307.2
Botswana	0.8	0.8	1.0	1.1	1.3	1.9	1.9	1.7	1.8	2.0	1.9	0.8	1.2	1.9
Burkina Faso	211.3	271.7	328.6	381.1	437.0	449.3	346.3	300.5	297.8	319.0	272.3	227.5	346.5	307.2
Burundi	90.0	90.0	90.0	92.9	119.7	120.7	114.2	123.6	140.4	158.7	171.3	87.0	100.6	141.6
Cameroon	211.3	271.7	328.6	381.1	437.0	449.3	346.3	300.5	297.8	319.0	272.3	227.5	346.5	307.2
Cape Verde	40.2	48.7	58.3	71.7	84.9	91.6	80.1	72.5	72.1	78.0	70.0	32.6	65.9	74.5
Central African Republic	211.3	271.7	328.6	381.1	437.0	449.3	346.3	300.5	297.8	319.0	272.3	227.5	346.5	307.2
Chad	211.3	271.7	328.6	381.1	437.0	449.3	346.3	300.5	297.8	319.0	272.3	227.5	346.5	307.2
Comoros	211.3	271.7	328.6	381.1	437.0	449.3	346.3	300.5	297.8	319.0	272.3	227.5	346.5	307.2
Congo, People's Republic of	211.3	271.7	328.6	381.1	437.0	449.3	346.3	300.5	297.8	319.0	272.3	227.5	346.5	307.2
Cote d'Ivoire	211.3	271.7	328.6	381.1	437.0	449.3	346.3	300.5	297.8	319.0	272.3	227.5	346.5	307.2
Djibouti	177.7	177.7	177.7	177.7	177.7	177.7	177.7	177.7	177.7	177.7	177.7	177.7	177.7	177.7
Equatorial Guinea	110.6	184.6	219.7	286.9	321.5	449.3	346.3	300.5	297.8	319.0	272.3	69.1	262.1	307.2
Ethiopia	2.1	2.1	2.1	2.1	2.1	2.1	2.1	2.1	2.1	2.1	2.1	2.1	2.1	2.1
Gabon	211.3	271.7	328.6	381.1	437.0	449.3	346.3	300.5	297.8	319.0	272.3	227.5	346.5	307.2
Gambia, The	1.7	2.0	2.3	2.6	3.6	3.9	6.9	7.1	6.7	7.6	7.9	2.1	2.7	7.2
Ghana	2.8	2.8	2.8	8.8	36.0	54.4	89.2	153.7	202.3	270.0	326.3	1.6	17.9	208.3
Guinea	19.0	20.9	22.4	23.1	24.1	24.3	333.5	428.4	474.4	591.6	660.2	20.4	22.3	497.6
Guinea-Bissau	33.8	37.3	39.9	42.1	105.3	159.6	204.0	559.3	1,111.1	1,811.4	2,185.5	31.7	69.7	1,174.2
Kenya	7.4	9.0	10.9	13.3	14.4	16.4	16.2	16.5	17.7	20.6	22.9	7.8	11.9	18.8
Lesotho	0.8	0.9	1.1	1.1	1.5	2.2	2.3	2.0	2.3	2.6	2.6	0.8	1.3	2.4
Liberia	1.0	1.0	1.0	1.0	1.0	1.0	1.0	1.0	1.0	1.0	1.0	1.0	1.0	1.0
Madagascar	211.3	271.7	349.7	430.4	576.6	662.5	676.3	1,069.2	1,407.1	1,603.4	1,494.2	227.5	417.1	1,250.1
Malawi	0.8	0.9	1.1	1.2	1.4	1.7	1.9	2.2	2.6	2.8	2.7	0.9	1.2	2.4
Mali	211.3	271.7	328.6	381.1	437.0	449.3	346.3	300.5	297.8	319.0	272.3	227.5	346.5	307.2
Mauritania	45.9	48.3	51.8	54.8	63.8	77.1	74.4	73.9	75.3	83.1	80.6	45.2	56.9	77.4
Mauritius	7.7	8.9	10.9	11.7	13.8	15.4	13.5	12.9	13.4	15.2	14.9	6.4	11.4	14.0
Mozambique	32.4	35.3	37.8	40.2	42.4	43.2	40.4	290.7	524.6	744.9	929.1	30.9	38.6	506.0
Namibia	..	..	..	..	..	..	..	..	..	..	..	..	..	..
Niger	211.3	271.7	328.6	381.1	437.0	449.3	346.3	300.5	297.8	319.0	272.3	227.5	346.5	307.2
Nigeria	0.5	0.6	0.7	0.7	0.8	0.9	1.8	4.0	4.5	7.4	8.0	0.6	0.7	5.1
Rwanda	92.8	92.8	92.8	94.3	100.2	101.3	87.6	79.7	76.4	80.0	82.6	92.8	95.7	81.3
Sao Tome & Principe	34.8	38.4	41.0	42.3	44.2	44.6	38.6	54.2	86.3	124.7	143.3	32.9	40.9	89.4
Senegal	211.3	271.7	328.6	381.1	437.0	449.3	346.3	300.5	297.8	319.0	272.3	227.5	346.5	307.2
Seychelles	6.4	6.3	6.6	6.8	7.1	7.1	6.2	5.6	5.4	5.6	5.3	6.9	6.7	5.6
Sierra Leone	1.0	1.2	1.2	1.9	2.5	5.1	16.1	34.0	32.5	59.8	151.4	1.1	2.2	58.8
Somalia	6.3	6.3	10.8	15.8	20.0	39.5	72.0	105.2	170.5	490.7	..	6.3	16.4	209.6
Sudan	0.5	0.6	1.0	1.3	1.3	2.3	2.5	3.0	4.5	4.5	4.5	0.4	1.2	3.8
Swaziland	0.8	0.9	1.1	1.1	1.5	2.2	2.3	2.0	2.3	2.6	2.6	0.8	1.3	2.4
Tanzania	8.2	8.3	9.3	11.1	15.3	17.5	32.7	64.3	99.3	143.4	195.1	8.0	11.6	106.9
Togo	211.3	271.7	328.6	381.1	437.0	449.3	346.3	300.5	297.8	319.0	272.3	227.5	346.5	307.2
Uganda	0.1	0.5	0.9	1.5	3.6	6.7	14.0	42.8	106.1	223.1	428.9	0.1	2.2	163.0
Zaire	2.8	4.4	5.7	12.9	36.1	49.9	59.6	112.4	187.1	381.4	718.6	0.9	18.6	291.8
Zambia	0.8	0.9	0.9	1.3	1.8	3.1	7.8	9.5	8.3	13.8	30.3	0.7	1.5	13.9
Zimbabwe	0.6	0.7	0.8	1.0	1.3	1.6	1.7	1.7	1.8	2.1	2.5	0.6	1.0	1.9
NORTH AFRICA														
Algeria	3.8	4.3	4.6	4.8	5.0	5.0	4.7	4.8	5.9	7.6	9.0	4.0	4.6	6.4
Egypt, Arab Republic of	0.7	0.7	0.7	0.7	0.7	0.7	0.7	0.7	0.7	0.9	1.6	0.5	0.7	0.9
Libya	0.3	0.3	0.3	0.3	0.3	0.3	0.3	0.3	0.3	0.3	0.3	0.3	0.3	0.3
Morocco	3.9	5.2	6.0	7.1	8.8	10.1	9.1	8.4	8.2	8.5	8.2	4.2	6.9	8.5
Tunisia	0.4	0.5	0.6	0.7	0.8	0.8	0.8	0.8	0.9	0.9	0.9	0.4	0.6	0.9
ALL AFRICA														
South Africa	0.8	0.9	1.1	1.1	1.5	2.2	2.3	2.0	2.3	2.6	2.6	0.8	1.3	2.4

3–5. SDR exchange rate index

	SDRs per unit of national currency, index 1987=100											Average		
	1980	1981	1982	1983	1984	1985	1986	1987	1988	1989	1990	75–79	80–85	86–MR
SUB-SAHARAN AFRICA	..	..	..	..	..	..	..	..	..	..	..	..	..	..
excluding Nigeria	..	..	..	..	..	..	..	..	..	..	..	..	..	..
Angola	99	120	137	146	159	162	122	100	93	102	..	..	137	83
Benin	141	121	107	95	87	85	96	100	97	95	105	141	106	99
Botswana	215	221	192	185	165	113	99	100	89	84	86	219	182	92
Burkina Faso	141	121	107	95	87	85	96	100	97	95	105	141	106	99
Burundi	136	150	160	160	130	130	120	100	84	78	69	151	144	90
Cameroon	141	121	107	95	87	85	96	100	97	95	105	141	106	99
Cape Verde	179	163	146	122	108	101	100	100	97	94	99	242	136	98
Central African Republic	141	121	107	95	87	85	96	100	97	95	105	141	106	99
Chad	141	121	107	95	87	85	96	100	97	95	105	141	106	99
Comoros	141	121	107	95	87	85	96	100	97	95	105	141	106	99
Congo, People's Republic of th	141	121	107	95	87	85	96	100	97	95	105	141	106	99
Cote d'Ivoire	141	121	107	95	87	85	96	100	97	95	105	141	106	99
Djibouti	99	110	117	121	126	127	110	100	96	101	95	107	117	101
Equatorial Guinea	141	121	107	95	87	85	96	100	97	95	105	141	106	99
Ethiopia	99	110	117	121	126	127	110	100	96	101	95	107	117	101
Gabon	141	121	107	95	87	85	96	100	97	95	105	141	106	99
Gambia, The	408	390	362	324	249	262	112	100	101	94	86	368	333	99
Ghana	5,554	6,130	6,548	2,106	539	360	190	100	73	57	45	11,722	3,539	93
Guinea	2,227	2,460	2,627	2,714	2,830	2,857	156	100	84	74	59	..	2,619	94
Guinea-Bissau	1,631	1,802	1,925	1,944	845	569	333	100	47	31	23	..	1,453	107
Kenya	220	201	177	150	145	129	..	100	89	81	68	224	170	..
Lesotho	260	256	220	221	179	118	99	100	87	78	75	260	209	88
Liberia	99	110	117	121	126	127	110	100	96	101	95	107	117	101
Madagascar	503	432	358	300	234	206	174	100	73	67	68	501	339	97
Malawi	271	271	245	227	197	164	131	100	83	81	77	271	229	94
Mali	141	121	107	95	87	85	96	100	97	95	105	141	106	99
Mauritania	160	168	167	163	146	122	109	100	94	90	87	174	154	96
Mauritius	167	156	139	133	118	106	105	100	92	85	83	216	136	93
Mozambique	885	989	1,056	1,058	1,090	1,093	874	100	51	40	28	..	1,029	219
Namibia	..	..	..	..	..	..	..	..	..	..	..	..	..	..
Niger	141	121	107	95	87	85	96	100	97	95	105	141	106	99
Nigeria	730	713	698	671	661	572	252	100	85	55	48	684	674	108
Rwanda	85	94	100	102	100	100	100	100	100	100	91	91	97	98
Sao Tome & Principe	154	170	181	187	195	197	171	100	58	44	0	..	181	75
Senegal	141	121	107	95	87	85	96	100	97	95	105	141	106	99
Seychelles	87	97	100	100	100	100	100	100	100	100	100	87	97	100
Sierra Leone	2,915	2,915	2,915	2,221	1,549	829	404	100	95	53	20	3,139	2,224	135
Somalia	1,660	1,832	1,146	806	663	339	161	100	59	22	..	1,780	1,074	..
Sudan	559	576	351	262	273	157	124	100	60	63	60	819	363	81
Swaziland	260	256	220	221	179	118	99	100	87	78	75	260	209	88
Tanzania	779	851	811	698	530	468	217	100	62	45	31	858	689	91
Togo	141	121	107	95	87	85	96	100	97	95	105	141	106	99
Uganda	57,391	9,387	5,336	3,368	1,503	812	337	100	39	19	10	58,176	12,966	101
Zaire	3,988	2,817	2,289	1,055	393	287	208	100	58	30	15	14,956	1,805	82
Zambia	1,122	1,122	1,122	860	625	417	134	100	104	70	29	1,277	878	87
Zimbabwe	257	264	257	199	168	131	110	100	89	79	65	280	213	89
NORTH AFRICA	..	..	..	..	..	..	..	..	..	..	..	..	..	..
Algeria	126	123	124	123	123	123	114	100	79	64	52	129	123	82
Egypt, Arab Republic of	99	110	117	121	126	127	110	100	96	87	47	175	117	88
Libya	100	110	117	121	127	128	104	100	100	100	100	107	117	101
Morocco	211	177	163	142	120	106	101	100	98	99	97	212	153	99
Tunisia	203	184	164	148	135	126	115	100	93	88	90	212	160	97
ALL AFRICA	..	..	..	..	..	..	..	..	..	..	..	..	..	..
South Africa	260	256	220	221	179	118	99	100	87	78	75	260	209	88

Notes: New Ugandan shilling = 100 old Ugandan shilling was introduced in May, 1987.

3-6. Conversion factor

	Units of national currency per dollar										Average		
	1980	1981	1982	1983	1984	1985	1986	1987	1988	1989	75-79	80-85	86-MR
SUB-SAHARAN AFRICA	..	..	..	..	..	..	..	..	..	..	..	..	..
excluding Nigeria	..	..	..	..	..	..	..	..	..	..	..	..	..
Angola	29.9	29.9	29.9	29.9	29.9	29.9	29.9	29.9	29.9	29.9	28.9	29.9	29.9
Benin	211.3	271.7	328.6	381.1	437.0	449.3	346.3	300.5	297.8	319.0	227.5	346.5	315.9
Botswana	0.8	0.8	0.9	1.1	1.1	1.6	1.9	1.8	1.7	2.0	0.8	1.1	1.9
Burkina Faso	211.3	271.7	328.6	381.1	437.0	449.3	346.3	300.5	297.8	319.0	227.5	346.5	315.9
Burundi	90.0	90.0	90.0	93.0	119.7	120.7	114.2	123.6	140.4	158.7	87.0	100.6	134.2
Cameroon	209.2	235.3	296.7	354.7	409.5	471.1	386.6	318.7	291.7	315.4	230.1	329.4	328.1
Cape Verde	40.2	48.7	58.3	71.7	84.9	91.6	80.1	72.5	72.1	78.0	32.6	65.9	75.7
Central African Republic	211.3	271.7	328.6	381.1	437.0	449.3	346.3	300.5	297.8	319.0	227.5	346.5	315.9
Chad	211.3	271.7	328.6	381.1	437.0	449.3	346.3	300.5	297.8	319.0	227.5	346.5	315.9
Comoros	211.3	271.7	328.6	381.1	437.0	449.3	346.3	300.5	297.8	319.0	227.5	346.5	315.9
Congo, People's Republic of the	211.3	271.7	328.6	381.1	437.0	449.3	346.3	300.5	297.8	319.0	227.5	346.5	315.9
Cote d'Ivoire	211.3	271.7	328.6	381.1	437.0	449.3	346.3	300.5	297.8	319.0	227.5	346.5	315.9
Djibouti	177.7	177.7	177.7	177.7	177.7	177.7	177.7	177.7	177.7	177.7	69.1	262.1	315.9
Equatorial Guinea	110.6	184.6	219.7	286.9	321.5	449.3	346.3	300.5	297.9	319.0	69.1	262.1	315.9
Ethiopia	2.1	2.1	2.1	2.1	2.1	2.1	2.1	2.1	2.1	2.1	2.1	2.1	2.1
Gabon	211.3	271.7	328.6	381.1	437.0	449.3	346.3	300.5	297.8	319.0	227.5	346.5	315.9
Gambia, The	1.8	2.2	2.5	2.9	4.1	5.0	7.3	6.7	7.0	8.1	2.1	3.1	7.3
Ghana	9.6	17.2	21.4	45.4	61.3	76.2	89.3	147.0	202.3	270.0	4.1	38.5	177.2
Guinea	19.0	20.9	22.4	23.1	24.1	24.3	333.5	428.4	474.4	591.6	20.3	22.3	457.0
Guinea-Bissau	49.9	42.9	48.7	58.7	120.6	160.0	373.3	559.3	1,111.1	1,811.4	43.8	80.1	963.8
Kenya	7.4	9.0	10.9	13.3	14.4	16.4	16.2	16.5	17.7	20.6	7.8	11.9	17.7
Lesotho	0.8	0.9	1.1	1.1	1.5	2.2	2.3	2.0	2.3	2.6	0.8	1.3	2.3
Liberia	1.0	1.0	1.0	1.0	1.0	1.0	1.0	1.0	1.0	1.0	1.0	1.0	1.0
Madagascar	211.3	271.7	349.7	430.4	576.6	662.5	676.3	1,069.2	1,407.1	1,603.4	227.5	417.1	1,189.0
Malawi	0.8	0.9	1.1	1.2	1.4	1.7	1.9	2.2	2.6	2.8	0.9	1.2	2.3
Mali	211.3	271.7	328.6	381.1	437.0	449.3	346.3	300.5	297.8	319.0	227.5	346.5	315.9
Mauritania	45.9	48.3	51.8	54.8	63.8	77.1	74.4	73.9	75.3	83.1	45.2	56.9	76.6
Mauritius	7.7	8.9	10.9	11.7	13.8	15.4	13.5	12.9	13.4	15.3	6.4	11.4	13.8
Mozambique	32.4	35.3	37.8	40.2	42.4	43.2	40.4	290.7	524.6	744.9	30.9	38.6	400.2
Namibia	0.8	0.9	1.1	1.1	1.5	2.2	2.3	2.0	2.3	2.6	0.8	1.3	2.3
Niger	211.3	271.7	328.6	381.1	437.0	449.3	346.3	300.5	297.8	319.0	227.5	346.5	315.9
Nigeria	0.5	0.6	0.7	0.7	0.8	0.9	1.8	4.0	4.5	7.4	0.6	0.7	4.4
Rwanda	92.8	92.8	92.8	94.3	100.2	101.3	87.6	79.7	76.4	80.0	92.8	95.7	80.9
Sao Tome & Principe	34.8	38.4	41.0	42.3	44.2	44.6	38.6	54.2	86.3	124.7	32.9	40.9	76.0
Senegal	211.3	271.7	328.6	381.1	437.0	449.3	346.3	300.5	297.8	319.0	227.5	346.5	315.9
Seychelles	6.4	6.3	6.6	6.8	7.1	7.1	6.2	5.6	5.4	5.6	6.9	6.7	5.7
Sierra Leone	1.0	1.1	1.2	1.3	2.5	3.6	5.2	35.6	25.5	46.3	1.0	1.8	28.1
Somalia	28.8	31.5	37.6	47.8	79.1	100.0	130.0	166.0	273.0	512.0	11.2	54.1	270.3
Sudan	0.6	0.6	0.9	1.3	1.4	1.5	1.6	1.8	4.2	6.3	0.4	1.0	3.5
Swaziland	0.8	0.9	1.1	1.1	1.4	2.2	2.3	2.0	2.3	2.6	0.8	1.2	2.3
Tanzania	8.2	8.3	9.3	11.1	15.3	17.5	32.7	64.3	99.3	143.4	7.8	11.6	84.9
Togo	211.3	271.7	328.6	381.1	437.0	449.3	346.3	300.5	297.8	319.0	227.5	346.5	315.9
Uganda	1.0	2.0	2.0	3.0	4.0	11.0	16.0	51.0	127.0	331.0	0.0	3.8	131.3
Zaire	2.8	4.4	5.7	12.9	36.1	49.9	59.6	112.4	187.1	381.4	0.9	18.6	185.1
Zambia	0.8	0.9	0.9	1.3	1.8	3.1	7.8	9.5	8.3	13.8	0.7	1.5	9.8
Zimbabwe	0.6	0.7	0.8	1.0	1.3	1.6	1.7	1.7	1.8	2.1	0.6	1.0	1.8
NORTH AFRICA	..	..	..	..	..	..	..	..	..	..	..	..	..
Algeria	3.8	4.3	4.6	4.8	5.0	5.0	4.7	4.9	5.9	7.6	4.0	4.6	5.8
Egypt, Arab Republic of	0.7	0.7	0.8	0.9	0.9	1.0	1.1	1.3	1.8	1.9	0.6	0.8	1.5
Libya	0.3	0.3	0.3	0.3	0.3	0.3	0.3	0.3	0.3	0.3	0.3	0.3	0.3
Morocco	3.9	5.2	6.0	7.1	8.8	10.1	9.1	8.4	8.2	8.5	4.2	6.9	8.5
Tunisia	0.4	0.5	0.6	0.7	0.8	0.8	0.8	0.8	0.9	0.9	0.4	0.6	0.9
ALL AFRICA	..	..	..	..	..	..	..	..	..	..	..	..	..
South Africa	0.8	0.9	1.1	1.1	1.5	2.2	2.3	2.0	2.3	2.6	0.8	1.3	2.3

Note: The conversion factor is a measure derived by the World Bank, based on the official exchange rate, adjusted for certain countries to more accurately reflect the rate at which international transactions are carried out. (See technical notes).

3–7. Parallel market exchange rate

	National currency per U.S. dollar											Average		
	1980	1981	1982	1983	1984	1985	1986	1987	1988	1989	1990	75–79	80–85	86–MR
SUB-SAHARAN AFRICA	..	..	..	..	..	..	..	..	..	..	..	..	..	..
excluding Nigeria														
Angola	..	..	..	450.0	1,350.0	1,650.0	1,850.0	2,000.0	1,850.0	..	..	..	..	1,900.0
Benin	209.5	274.7	332.8	400.3	455.6	444.6	343.0	305.0	302.1	324.8	281.8	228.2	352.9	311.3
Botswana	0.8	1.0	1.1	1.3	2.2	2.6	2.6	2.2	2.1	2.3	1.9	1.0	1.5	2.2
Burkina Faso	209.5	274.7	332.8	400.3	455.6	444.6	343.0	305.0	302.1	324.8	281.8	228.2	352.9	311.3
Burundi	106.0	106.0	120.0	130.0	176.0	140.0	147.7	137.3	169.6	214.0	186.1	108.9	129.7	170.9
Cameroon	209.5	274.7	332.8	400.3	455.6	444.6	343.0	305.0	302.1	324.8	281.8	228.2	352.9	311.3
Cape Verde	..	..	..	..	..	..	..	..	..	..	..	..	..	..
Central African Republic	209.5	274.7	332.8	400.3	455.6	444.6	343.0	305.0	302.1	324.8	281.8	228.2	352.9	311.3
Chad	209.5	274.7	332.8	400.3	455.6	444.6	343.0	305.0	302.1	324.8	281.8	228.2	352.9	311.3
Comoros	..	..	..	..	..	..	..	..	..	..	..	..	..	..
Congo, People's Republic of the	209.5	274.7	332.8	400.3	455.6	444.6	343.0	305.0	302.1	324.8	281.8	228.2	352.9	311.3
Cote d'Ivoire	209.5	274.7	332.8	400.3	455.6	444.6	343.0	305.0	302.1	324.8	281.8	228.2	352.9	311.3
Djibouti	..	..	..	..	..	193.8	188.3	225.7	213.5	217.9	191.8	..	..	207.4
Equatorial Guinea	..	..	..	..	..	444.6	343.0	305.0	302.1	324.8	281.8	..	..	311.3
Ethiopia	2.8	3.1	3.3	3.5	4.0	4.8	3.8	4.6	6.6	5.9	6.0	4.0	3.6	5.4
Gabon	209.5	274.7	332.8	400.3	455.6	444.6	343.0	305.0	302.1	324.8	..	..	352.9	318.7
Gambia, The	1.7	2.2	2.3	2.9	4.8	3.7	8.3	7.7	8.6	7.4	8.3	1.9	2.9	8.1
Ghana	15.9	26.3	61.7	76.6	96.7	131.3	185.0	213.3	252.2	328.8	360.8	7.2	68.0	268.0
Guinea	41.7	73.1	98.3	128.1	283.4	310.7	396.3	443.3	538.9	580.1	693.3	48.0	155.9	530.4
Guinea-Bissau	..	..	..	..	..	..	..	..	1,800.0	..	..	..	..	..
Kenya	8.2	10.9	14.3	16.2	16.5	17.3	15.9	17.5	21.8	22.4	23.3	8.7	13.9	20.2
Lesotho	..	..	..	1.3	1.5	2.4	2.5	2.4	2.4	2.7	2.7	..	..	2.5
Liberia	..	..	..	..	..	..	..	..	1.5	..	..	..	..	..
Madagascar	265.0	384.0	700.0	884.0	880.0	691.7	815.0	850.0	1,671.7	1,639.1	1,589.2	267.5	634.1	1,313.0
Malawi	1.6	2.0	1.8	1.8	2.2	2.5	2.1	2.5	3.1	3.6	3.3	1.4	2.0	2.9
Mali	209.5	274.7	332.8	400.3	455.6	444.6	343.0	305.0	302.1	324.8	281.8	228.2	352.9	311.3
Mauritania	65.0	54.0	60.0	147.0	155.0	167.0	175.0	170.0	200.0	..	..	85.8	108.0	181.7
Mauritius	..	..	..	..	..	14.4	14.3	13.7	14.1	16.0	15.7	..	..	14.7
Mozambique	80.0	75.0	100.0	160.0	1,450.0	1,750.0	1,950.0	2,225.0	..	1,250.0	..	195.3	602.5	1,808.3
Namibia	..	..	..	..	..	..	..	..	..	..	..	..	..	..
Niger	209.5	274.7	332.8	400.3	455.6	444.6	343.0	305.0	302.1	324.8	281.8	228.2	352.9	311.3
Nigeria	0.9	0.9	1.1	1.8	3.2	3.8	4.1	6.7	6.7	10.7	9.3	1.0	2.0	7.5
Rwanda	115.0	112.0	136.0	147.0	176.0	138.3	109.0	101.0	98.7	109.8	104.2	131.0	137.4	104.5
Sao Tome & Principe	..	..	..	..	..	..	..	..	..	..	..	..	..	..
Senegal	209.5	274.7	332.8	400.3	455.6	444.6	343.0	305.0	302.1	324.8	281.8	228.2	352.9	311.3
Seychelles	..	..	..	..	..	..	..	..	..	..	5.9	..	..	..
Sierra Leone	1.4	1.7	1.9	3.4	4.3	7.7	12.5	100.0	131.6	180.9	470.6	1.1	3.4	179.1
Somalia	9.9	10.5	11.7	22.1	30.0	105.0	147.0	150.0	319.2	398.8	1,982.1	9.3	31.5	599.4
Sudan	1.0	0.9	1.4	1.8	2.5	3.3	6.4	5.2	11.2	15.9	43.6	0.6	1.8	16.5
Swaziland	..	..	..	..	..	2.4	2.5	2.4	2.4	3.0	2.7	..	..	2.6
Tanzania	21.0	27.6	32.6	39.6	57.1	66.5	161.0	175.0	211.0	263.5	292.4	17.8	40.7	220.6
Togo	209.5	274.7	332.8	400.3	455.6	444.6	343.0	305.0	302.1	324.8	281.8	228.2	352.9	311.3
Uganda	75.7	208.3	265.8	317.5	429.3	1,006.3	4,583.3	11,750.0	470.8	597.5	685.8	64.9	383.8	3,617.5
Zaire	6.4	10.4	13.5	28.0	36.2	50.9	65.7	91.0	235.8	469.4	738.1	2.8	24.2	320.0
Zambia	1.3	1.4	1.4	1.6	2.3	4.8	9.8	15.0	30.3	107.8	121.2	1.8	2.1	56.8
Zimbabwe	1.1	1.2	1.2	2.4	2.8	2.4	2.2	2.6	3.1	3.5	3.3	1.7	1.8	3.0
NORTH AFRICA	..	..	..	..	..	..	..	..	..	..	..	..	..	..
Algeria	10.9	13.6	16.1	17.3	21.6	24.6	21.0	23.6	29.7	37.1	29.8	8.0	17.3	28.2
Egypt, Arab Republic of	0.8	0.9	1.0	1.1	1.2	1.5	1.8	2.0	2.2	2.6	2.6	0.7	1.1	2.3
Libya	0.5	0.5	0.5	0.5	0.6	0.8	1.1	1.3	1.0	0.9	1.0	0.4	0.6	1.0
Morocco	4.1	5.4	6.4	7.6	9.2	10.1	9.2	8.6	8.5	9.2	9.3	4.5	7.1	9.0
Tunisia	0.4	0.5	0.6	0.7	0.9	0.9	0.8	0.8	0.9	1.0	0.9	0.4	0.7	0.9
ALL AFRICA	..	..	..	..	..	..	..	..	..	..	..	..	..	..
South Africa	0.9	1.0	1.2	1.3	1.5	2.4	2.5	2.4	2.4	2.7	2.7	..	1.4	2.5

Notes: Rates are annual averages of month–end estimates, based on a sample of transactions.
New Ugandan shilling = 100 old Ugandan shilling was introduced in 1987

3–8. Ratio of parallel market to official exchange rates

	Ratio of parallel market to official exchange rates.											*Average*		
	1980	1981	1982	1983	1984	1985	1986	1987	1988	1989	1990	75–79	80–85	86–MR
SUB-SAHARAN AFRICA	..	..	..	..	..	..	..	..	..	..	..	..	..	..
excluding Nigeria														
Angola	..	..	..	15.04	45.12	55.15	61.84	66.85	61.84	..	..	..	..	63.51
Benin	0.99	1.01	1.01	1.05	1.04	0.99	0.99	1.01	1.01	1.02	1.03	1.00	1.02	1.01
Botswana	1.03	1.15	1.07	1.15	1.71	1.35	1.36	1.29	1.14	1.12	1.03	1.17	1.28	1.19
Burkina Faso	0.99	1.01	1.01	1.05	1.04	0.99	0.99	1.01	1.01	1.02	1.03	1.00	1.02	1.01
Burundi	1.18	1.18	1.33	1.40	1.47	1.16	1.29	1.11	1.21	1.35	1.09	1.25	1.29	1.21
Cameroon	0.99	1.01	1.01	1.05	1.04	0.99	0.99	1.01	1.01	1.02	1.03	1.00	1.02	1.01
Cape Verde	..	..	..	..	..	..	..	..	..	..	..	..	..	..
Central African Republic	0.99	1.01	1.01	1.05	1.04	0.99	0.99	1.01	1.01	1.02	1.03	1.00	1.02	1.01
Chad	0.99	1.01	1.01	1.05	1.04	0.99	0.99	1.01	1.01	1.02	1.03	1.00	1.02	1.01
Comoros	..	..	..	..	..	..	..	..	..	..	..	..	..	..
Congo, People's Republic of the	0.99	1.01	1.01	1.05	1.04	0.99	0.99	1.01	1.01	1.02	1.03	1.00	1.02	1.01
Cote d'Ivoire	0.99	1.01	1.01	1.05	1.04	0.99	0.99	1.01	1.01	1.02	1.03	1.00	1.02	1.01
Djibouti	..	..	..	..	..	1.09	1.06	1.27	1.20	1.23	1.08	..	..	1.17
Equatorial Guinea	..	..	..	..	..	0.99	0.99	1.01	1.01	1.02	1.03	..	..	1.01
Ethiopia	1.36	1.49	1.60	1.70	1.94	2.34	1.85	2.21	3.20	2.86	2.92	1.94	1.74	2.61
Gabon	0.99	1.01	1.01	1.05	1.04	0.99	0.99	1.01	1.01	1.02	..	..	1.02	1.04
Gambia, The	0.98	1.09	0.99	1.08	1.33	0.95	1.20	1.09	1.29	0.98	1.06	0.92	1.08	1.12
Ghana	5.77	9.55	22.42	8.67	2.69	2.41	2.07	1.39	1.25	1.22	1.11	4.53	3.80	1.29
Guinea	2.20	3.49	4.40	5.55	11.76	12.77	1.19	1.03	1.14	0.98	1.05	2.35	6.99	1.07
Guinea-Bissau	..	..	..	..	..	..	..	..	1.62	..	..	..	..	..
Kenya	1.10	1.20	1.31	1.22	1.15	1.06	0.98	1.06	1.23	1.09	1.02	1.11	1.17	1.07
Lesotho	..	..	..	1.12	1.03	1.07	1.11	1.16	1.04	1.03	1.04	..	..	1.07
Liberia	..	..	..	..	..	..	..	..	1.50	..	..	..	..	..
Madagascar	1.25	1.41	2.00	2.05	1.53	1.04	1.21	0.79	1.19	1.02	1.06	1.18	1.52	1.05
Malawi	1.94	2.29	1.71	1.56	1.53	1.47	1.11	1.12	1.22	1.29	1.20	1.65	1.69	1.20
Mali	0.99	1.01	1.01	1.05	1.04	0.99	0.99	1.01	1.01	1.02	1.03	1.00	1.02	1.01
Mauritania	1.42	1.12	1.16	2.68	2.43	2.17	2.35	2.30	2.66	..	..	1.90	1.90	2.35
Mauritius	..	..	..	..	..	0.93	1.06	1.06	1.05	1.05	1.06	..	..	1.05
Mozambique	2.47	2.12	2.65	3.98	34.16	40.53	48.23	7.65	..	1.68	..	6.32	15.63	3.57
Namibia	..	..	..	..	..	..	..	..	..	..	..	..	..	..
Niger	0.99	1.01	1.01	1.05	1.04	0.99	0.99	1.01	1.01	1.02	1.03	1.00	1.02	1.01
Nigeria	1.65	1.50	1.69	2.49	4.20	4.22	2.33	1.66	1.47	1.46	1.16	1.58	2.79	1.46
Rwanda	1.24	1.21	1.46	1.56	1.76	1.37	1.24	1.27	1.29	1.37	1.26	1.41	1.44	1.29
Sao Tome & Principe	..	..	..	..	..	..	..	..	..	..	..	..	..	..
Senegal	0.99	1.01	1.01	1.05	1.04	0.99	0.99	1.01	1.01	1.02	1.03	1.00	1.02	1.01
Seychelles	..	..	..	..	..	..	..	..	..	..	..	..	..	..
Sierra Leone	1.36	1.49	1.50	1.83	1.73	1.51	0.78	2.94	4.05	3.02	3.11	1.03	1.58	3.05
Somalia	1.57	1.66	1.08	1.40	1.50	2.66	2.04	1.43	1.87	0.81	..	1.47	1.92	2.86
Sudan	1.93	1.68	1.49	1.40	1.89	1.42	2.55	1.72	2.49	3.54	9.70	1.73	1.57	4.33
Swaziland	..	..	..	..	..	1.07	1.11	1.17	1.07	1.13	1.04	..	..	1.10
Tanzania	2.56	3.33	3.51	3.56	3.73	3.81	4.92	2.72	2.13	1.84	1.50	2.23	3.51	2.06
Togo	0.99	1.01	1.01	1.05	1.04	0.99	0.99	1.01	1.01	1.02	1.03	1.00	1.02	1.01
Uganda	1020.18	416.23	282.66	206.35	119.36	149.74	327.38	274.27	4.44	2.68	1.60	828.49	172.23	22.20
Zaire	2.30	2.38	2.34	2.17	1.00	1.02	1.10	0.81	1.26	1.23	1.03	2.94	1.30	1.10
Zambia	1.69	1.62	1.46	1.31	1.26	1.53	1.25	1.58	3.67	7.81	4.00	2.37	1.46	4.08
Zimbabwe	1.66	1.73	1.58	2.37	2.25	1.48	1.33	1.58	1.74	1.67	1.36	2.63	1.85	1.53
NORTH AFRICA	..	..	..	..	..	..	..	..	..	..	..	..	..	..
Algeria	2.84	3.15	3.50	3.61	4.34	4.89	4.46	4.87	5.02	4.87	3.33	1.99	3.78	4.41
Egypt, Arab Republic of	1.09	1.25	1.49	1.59	1.75	2.12	2.57	2.90	3.20	3.04	1.69	1.61	1.55	2.50
Libya	1.67	1.75	1.76	1.84	2.00	2.76	3.37	4.27	3.57	2.91	3.51	1.50	1.96	3.52
Morocco	1.05	1.03	1.07	1.06	1.05	1.00	1.01	1.03	1.04	1.09	1.13	1.07	1.04	1.06
Tunisia	1.10	1.01	1.08	1.09	1.14	1.05	1.04	1.01	1.07	1.03	1.04	1.05	1.08	1.04
ALL AFRICA	..	..	..	..	..	..	..	..	..	..	..	..	..	..
South Africa	1.10	1.09	1.11	1.12	1.03	1.07	1.11	1.16	1.04	1.04	1.04	..	1.08	1.07

3–9. Real effective exchange rate index

	Index 1987=100											Average		
	1980	1981	1982	1983	1984	1985	1986	1987	1988	1989	1990	75-79	80-85	86-MR
SUB-SAHARAN AFRICA excluding Nigeria	..	..	..	..	..	..	..	..	..	..	..	..	..	..
Angola	..	..	..	..	..	..	..	..	..	..	..	..	..	..
Benin	..	..	..	..	..	..	..	..	..	..	..	..	..	..
Botswana	114.7	120.1	114.4	110.6	114.6	102.5	100.9	100.0	97.8	98.3	103.3	..	112.8	99.6
Burkina Faso	127.4	115.5	112.9	109.0	104.2	106.3	104.4	100.0	100.5	96.1	95.2	..	112.4	101.6
Burundi	100.2	120.6	132.7	143.4	133.0	135.5	116.6	100.0	88.1	90.5	77.7	..	127.6	94.6
Cameroon	81.4	74.7	73.1	75.9	77.2	80.7	89.3	100.0	96.4	89.2	92.5	..	77.2	93.5
Cape Verde	87.2	91.6	96.9	101.2	101.2	100.6	97.8	100.0	100.7	99.4	100.3	..	96.4	99.5
Central African Republic	100.7	97.5	96.4	94.0	91.7	94.0	100.0	100.0	97.2	92.4	95.0	..	95.7	96.9
Chad	..	..	..	..	..	..	..	..	..	..	..	..	..	..
Comoros	..	..	..	..	..	..	..	..	..	..	..	..	..	..
Congo, People's Republic	98.2	98.5	97.6	94.2	97.4	98.4	100.0	100.0	100.1	100.0	101.6	..	97.4	100.0
Cote d'Ivoire	102.7	88.1	80.3	77.4	74.4	74.9	90.0	100.0	100.8	95.7	96.9	..	83.0	96.7
Djibouti	..	..	..	..	..	..	..	..	..	..	..	..	..	..
Equatorial Guinea	..	..	..	..	..	..	..	..	..	..	..	..	..	..
Ethiopia	97.1	106.2	115.3	117.8	133.3	158.9	117.4	100.0	99.4	106.7	97.8	..	121.7	105.9
Gabon	107.0	95.2	96.1	94.5	90.6	93.4	101.7	100.0	85.6	87.2	93.8	..	96.1	93.7
Gambia, The	133.7	127.9	128.6	129.5	120.6	131.9	94.8	100.0	*107.7*	*103.8*	97.2	..	128.7	100.7
Ghana	427.5	951.9	1190.9	803.4	310.7	225.7	129.7	100.0	95.1	89.9	89.6	..	651.4	108.5
Guinea	..	..	..	..	..	..	..	..	..	..	..	..	..	..
Guinea-Bissau	..	..	..	..	..	..	..	..	..	..	..	..	..	..
Kenya	126.7	122.6	127.1	120.6	129.4	127.6	110.6	100.0	92.1	88.2	78.5	..	125.9	101.0
Lesotho	108.9	106.6	104.6	109.3	108.3	104.9	103.3	100.0	98.8	98.9	98.9	..	107.1	100.0
Liberia	99.5	106.0	114.3	119.9	124.3	123.9	107.8	100.0	100.1	107.5	120.2	..	115.0	102.9
Madagascar	168.9	178.9	188.8	190.5	163.8	155.6	146.8	100.0	86.6	82.8	87.5	..	174.8	111.3
Malawi	123.2	123.4	118.4	120.6	119.7	119.9	107.6	100.0	105.4	111.9	112.7	..	120.9	107.5
Mali	127.8	124.7	114.3	114.2	117.0	121.1	119.0	100.0	101.8	100.0	95.3	..	119.9	107.0
Mauritania	105.2	122.1	132.5	131.1	124.4	116.4	·105.8	100.0	91.4	90.6	87.1	..	122.4	99.3
Mauritius	122.4	127.0	120.9	121.5	117.5	114.0	110.0	100.0	97.3	97.9	99.8	..	120.5	102.4
Mozambique	..	..	..	..	..	..	..	..	..	..	..	..	..	..
Namibia	..	..	..	..	..	..	..	..	..	..	..	..	..	..
Niger	139.3	145.8	143.6	125.1	123.7	116.8	110.1	100.0	94.3	87.5	84.8	..	132.4	101.5
Nigeria	343.8	381.4	391.3	462.8	639.2	573.3	313.4	100.0	102.1	87.3	82.0	..	465.3	137.0
Rwanda	74.7	83.4	97.8	105.9	109.1	109.7	100.1	100.0	100.5	99.0	90.4	..	96.9	100.4
Sao Tome & Principe	..	..	..	..	..	..	..	..	..	..	..	..	..	..
Senegal	94.2	83.9	86.4	86.9	88.9	97.1	105.5	100.0	94.0	89.8	91.5	..	89.6	99.8
Seychelles	83.7	97.6	97.2	102.0	107.3	108.1	102.6	100.0	98.5	96.1	92.4	..	99.3	100.4
Sierra Leone	92.0	106.2	131.6	160.2	198.9	165.2	129.4	100.0	118.0	102.9	74.7	..	142.4	105.0
Somalia	194.3	230.0	184.9	204.2	326.0	179.8	118.5	100.0	124.0			..	219.9	114.2
Sudan	119.0	125.7	103.2	100.8	127.5	118.8	112.7	100.0	112.3	172.8	251.6	..	115.8	149.9
Swaziland	111.6	117.9	109.2	111.6	109.0	102.2	97.2	100.0	96.9	94.8	94.5	..	112.0	98.5
Tanzania	142.6	185.1	219.1	245.1	252.3	293.5	203.3	100.0	77.8	68.4	52.4	..	223.0	100.4
Togo	115.4	114.2	109.5	109.1	97.6	93.4	100.7	100.0	93.8	87.5	90.0	..	106.5	94.4
Uganda	441.5	316.8	108.8	85.7	58.3	76.1	80.1	100.0	91.9	78.2	47.8	..	181.2	79.6
Zaire	280.2	260.4	273.4	320.4	127.9	115.8	115.6	100.0	102.7	101.8	84.0	..	229.7	100.8
Zambia	233.8	239.1	266.5	247.3	213.2	197.1	94.9	100.0	154.0	205.1	171.5	..	232.8	145.1
Zimbabwe	123.7	127.7	143.7	127.8	128.2	114.0	104.9	100.0	92.5	87.9	76.7	..	64.1	88.8
NORTH AFRICA	..	..	..	..	..	..	..	..	..	..	..	..	..	..
Algeria	85.1	94.2	98.7	105.9	113.5	122.4	112.9	100.0	82.5	70.8	59.5	..	103.3	85.2
Egypt, Arab Republic of	62.5	67.9	74.6	84.3	98.2	102.6	98.5	100.0	107.4	125.0	97.9	..	81.7	105.7
Libya	..	..	..	..	..	..	..	..	..	..	..	..	..	..
Morocco	145.7	133.4	131.4	122.8	116.0	108.3	103.5	100.0	97.7	98.1	93.5	..	126.3	98.6
Tunisia	140.4	139.1	138.2	136.7	136.6	135.8	116.1	100.0	98.0	96.1	92.3	..	137.8	133.8
ALL AFRICA	..	..	..	..	..	..	..	..	..	..	..	..	..	..
South Africa	130.6	137.4	130.2	143.4	126.6	96.1	88.6	100.0	94.5	94.8	97.7	..	127.4	95.1

Technical Notes

Table 3-1. GDP deflator (national currency series)

The implicit GDP deflator is the most broadly based domestic price index, showing annual price movements for all goods and services produced in an economy. It is calculated by dividing, for each year of the period, the value of GDP at current purchaser values by the value of GDP at constant (1987) purchaser values, both in national currency. It is an appropriate deflator for GDP series in national currencies, but not for series in U.S. dollars.

Table 3-2. GDP deflator (U.S. dollar series)

Shown here is simply the ratio of GDP in current prices in U.S. dollars (converted at annual exchange rates) to GDP in constant 1987 prices (converted to U.S. dollars at a fixed (1987) exchange rate). Because it combines the effects of changes in domestic prices as well as exchange rates, it is not comparable with the implicit GDP deflator in national currencies reported in Table 3-1. Deflators are useful for converting GDP in current prices to GDP in constant prices (when both are expressed in the same currency). This is achieved by dividing the current price data by the index (divided by 100). To convert from constant to current price series, the index (divided by 100) is the multiplier. Data on consumer prices and exchange rates are drawn from IMF, *International Finance Statistics*. (IFS).

Table 3-3. Consumer price index

These are taken from Line 64 of the *IFS*. They are generally compiled using the Laspeyres formula: goods in the consumption basket selected according to consumption patterns in the base year, derived from household expenditure surveys, are weighted by their relative prices in the base year. The data often relate only to selected representative income groups in capital cities or major urban areas. Thus, the consumer price indexes shown for some countries may not represent recent price movements very accurately because the weights assigned to prices may be outdated since the underlying consumption basket may not be representative of overall, national consumption patterns.

Table 3-4. Official exchange rate

The official exchange rate is expressed as the annual average of the official market exchange rate in national currency per U.S. dollar (line rf of the *IFS*). The Uganda shilling was devalued in May 1987, and a new currency unit was introduced. 1 new shilling = 100 old shillings and US$1.00 = 60.00 new shillings. This introduces some degree of discontinuity in the series for Uganda which would also affect Tables 3-5 to 3-9.

Table 3-5. SDR exchange rate index

This index is based on the average annual exchange rate for SDRs per unit of national currency. Summary statistics for country groups for the SDR index are unweighted arithmetic means of the indexes, not of the exchange rates. Time series summary statistics are averages of the index numbers for the period shown, not growth rates.

Table 3-6. Conversion factor

Are the annual exchange rates used by the World Bank to convert national currency series into U.S. dollars series. For most countries, in most years, the conversion factor is identical to the average annual official exchange rate. However, where the official exchange rate is judged to diverge by an exceptionally large margin from the rate effectively applied to international transactions, a more appropriate conversion factor is estimated. An alternative conversion factor is used when there are egregious differences between the official and effective transaction rates (for example, Ghana, Guinea-Bissau, Somalia, and Uganda in 1985); officially recognized, multiple exchange rates with analytically significant spreads between them (for example, Egypt in 1985-87); and exchange rates that need to be adjusted to a fiscal year base (for example, Cameroon, The Gambia, Sierra Leone, and Sudan). The objective in estimating alternative conversion factors is to approximate as closely as possible exchange rates actually used. For example, where multiple exchange rates are maintained, a transaction-weighted rate is given. These conversion factors are uniformly used throughout the first two chapters.

National statistical compilers sometimes use an official exchange rate to assign a national currency value to international transactions originally denominated in foreign currencies. In these cases, the official rate must be used to convert the same items back to dollars, regardless of whether it was the rate actually applied to the international transactions, even if an alternative conversion factor is used for other components of GDP. This affects trade data for Ghana, Guinea-Bissau, and Somalia.

Table 3-7. Parallel market exchange rate

Data reported here are from "Pick's currency yearbooks" and "Currency Allerts." They are averages of month- end rates for the period covered, based on a sample of transactions. Since

rates vary among parallel market dealers, the rates are averages across dealers, usually in the capital city or financial center of the country in question. These rates include the rates at the Bureaux de Change that have been established in some countries with auction markets as semi-official foreign exchange windows for small transactions.

Table 3-8. Ratio of parallel to official market exchange rates

This provides a measure of the premium on the official exchange rate. The premium is usually high in the presence of an overvalued exchange rate. To narrow or eliminate the premium, it is important to pay particular attention to fiscal and monetary policy because direct devaluation merely to bring the official rate to the parallel rate does not always accomplish this where fiscal and monetary imbalances persist.

Table 3-9. Real effective exchange rate index

This gives a measure of price competitiveness of the country's exports relative to trading partners. A decline (increase) in the index indicates real depreciation (appreciation) of the exchange rate. Only countries that have granted permission to the reporting agency to publish the data are included for the period after 1988. The data have been rebased to 1987. That year, however, coincided with the early period of massive devaluations in the process of adjustment by several Sub-Saharan African countries. As a result, the very substantial devaluations that continued to take place after 1987 may not be very pronounced in the data. Relative movements in the inflation rates between a country and the trading partner(s) may diminish the real impact of a devaluation, particularly if inflationary tendencies are stronger domestically than abroad.

4

Money and Banking

Monetary variables directly affect prices and exchange rates and indirectly affect real economic performance. Money plays a vital role in any modern economy. Data in this chapter are concerned with the creation of the types of assets that transactors in the economy wish to hold from the types of liabilities that debtors are willing to incur. However, emphasis here is on the creation of the means of payment, that is, on the more liquid end of the liquidity spectrum for assets.

Money and the institutions that deal in money provide cover against credit risks, limit transactions costs, help with the mobilization of savings, allocate credit, and facilitate investment and hence growth of the economy. Data on money and banking assist in assessing the prevailing financial conditions of a country and in arriving at a proper evaluation of the financial policy options open to a country for achieving its macroeconomic objectives. The government usually intervenes in finance to control the supply of money and credit. The primary objective of such intervention is to maintain price stability. However, the government may also interverne to finance a budget deficit that in turn may threaten price stability. The government also ensures that financial institutions are properly supervised to ensure continued confidence in the financial system and avoid destabilizing runs on the banking system. Time series are provided for nine indicators in this section.

4–1. Domestic credit

	Level	Percentage annual change											Average		
	1980	1980	1981	1982	1983	1984	1985	1986	1987	1988	1989	1990	75–79	80–85	86–MR
SUB-SAHARAN AFRICA		18.7	23.6	19.6	14.4	10.3	13.6	14.1	6.1	7.2	12.2	11.4	26.8	17.1	9.7
excluding Nigeria		18.3	23.4	19.3	13.6	10.0	13.9	13.4	5.8	7.1	12.3	10.3	26.8	16.4	8.6
Angola	..	..	..	..	..	..	..	..	..	..	..	..	..	..	..
Benin	69,824	48.8	-2.0	69.1	14.4	-1.0	15.2	-30.0	0.3	6.0	-39.4	16.3	13.1	18.5	-11.8
Botswana	6	-27.2	1158.5	-44.6	-117.9	1593.7	222.8	138.0	53.7	29.3	27.4	25.9	-25.9	-81.9	-32.5
Burkina Faso	56,507	3.7	14.4	13.4	-5.8	-1.8	6.7	1.9	-8.3	6.9	29.2	-6.0	36.0	3.9	8.1
Burundi	13,106	19.6	39.7	8.7	20.1	6.7	11.7	-2.8	4.9	19.1	-0.5	..	48.7	15.6	8.6
Cameroon	363,804	27.8	17.1	32.2	24.4	4.5	14.2	19.3	-5.8	-7.1	21.7	-1.6	26.1	18.7	2.2
Cape Verde	1,125	39.3	72.6	13.1	26.1	15.0	21.7	22.0	13.9	8.9	19.4	17.0	..	25.3	13.4
Central African Republic	36,342	33.4	17.0	6.5	7.2	-2.7	9.6	3.4	-10.3	-0.7	12.3	-2.4	7.4	6.3	-1.0
Chad	48,884	-1.3	-10.4	-4.5	3.7	24.8	23.1	22.5	-4.6	-8.3	-13.5	-25.4	17.2	6.6	-10.9
Comoros	..	..	..	..	22.6	37.2	-30.7	2.8	8.9	25.3	23.3	18.4	..	..	19.9
Congo, People's Republic	78,653	17.9	25.7	53.2	12.9	28.8	6.0	2.4	-8.4	3.2	2.2	-4.2	13.7	25.5	-1.0
Cote d'Ivoire	835,066	23.2	23.1	6.8	19.5	0.5	-2.3	4.3	1.5	5.8	-7.4	-7.2	26.2	9.2	-1.8
Djibouti	..	..	..	..	..	..	12.8	13.6	-7.2	2.8	3.0	-2.5	..	..	-0.3
Equatorial Guinea	..	..	..	..	..	..	..	13.5	-13.0	-2.3	9.5	-5.6	..	..	-1.9
Ethiopia	2,785	17.6	10.5	15.8	15.5	9.6	8.5	9.8	11.2	10.8	13.3	19.3	30.3	12.5	13.3
Gabon	173,174	12.1	-2.4	-9.8	37.3	12.4	33.3	17.3	4.4	-4.4	3.1	-14.4	27.1	13.0	-2.6
Gambia, The	196	23.3	20.4	23.7	26.7	17.1	26.5	-29.0	-47.0	17.5	-10.5	-60.6	34.9	22.8	-25.8
Ghana	9,494	28.2	63.1	21.6	72.2	50.2	59.7	53.1	72.4	-4.8	24.3	4.0	49.9	51.3	18.2
Guinea	..	..	..	..	..	..	..	..	10.8	..	..	..	..	..	10.8
Guinea-Bissau	..	..	..	..	28.2	24.4	33.5	30.5	131.9	71.3	..	..	..	..	99.3
Kenya	16,230	13.1	24.9	28.6	-0.4	10.3	12.4	27.5	19.8	6.9	4.1	21.8	23.7	13.6	11.4
Lesotho	58	..	78.1	24.7	5.8	4.7	30.8	28.7	24.4	39.6	19.9	-12.8	..	21.7	18.6
Liberia	284	18.7	14.1	19.1	17.3	3.9	14.9	8.3	15.9	24.7	15.4	..	30.3	13.7	19.2
Madagascar	340,636	49.5	23.6	18.2	22.1	19.7	11.6	14.2	23.3	2.8	-2.6	..	26.9	19.3	6.8
Malawi	333	12.0	29.0	17.7	17.1	2.3	13.0	21.9	1.4	-15.8	15.9	1.3	22.8	14.7	-0.2
Mali	137,926	5.2	8.0	14.7	12.9	-15.8	13.6	8.6	-5.7	-21.4	0.2	-16.0	11.3	5.4	-11.2
Mauritania	11,711	13.4	17.0	20.0	10.0	8.9	2.6	6.0	10.0	6.1	28.8	19.9	20.7	11.8	16.1
Mauritius	4,435	13.9	33.1	16.9	16.7	15.1	8.8	8.6	6.1	17.2	12.2	15.9	36.2	17.4	13.2
Mozambique	..	..	..	..	..	..	..	..	..	..	..	..	..	..	..
Namibia	..	..	..	..	..	..	..	..	..	..	..	..	..	..	..
Niger	82,308	55.6	20.2	28.0	3.2	-8.1	-4.4	0.6	-10.2	-16.3	-3.0	-14.0	36.5	6.7	-10.8
Nigeria	10,689	23.4	47.3	36.0	28.9	10.3	4.9	14.1	10.4	26.0	-9.5	34.3	63.9	24.6	12.6
Rwanda	3,481	11.8	54.4	53.5	46.0	13.0	22.7	5.6	22.8	23.5	18.6	15.2	-6.4	36.9	20.2
Sao Tome & Principe	..	..	..	..	14.2	-58.1	39.5	230.7	15.4	-0.4	..	..	..	..	7.2
Senegal	293,567	17.2	25.7	19.6	8.2	2.7	8.4	0.9	0.6	6.9	-7.7	-8.0	23.5	11.8	-1.9
Seychelles	190	12.2	23.2	14.1	8.2	8.7	19.4	12.6	5.5	25.4	22.9	11.4	28.9	13.3	17.6
Sierra Leone	413	34.6	33.5	33.9	24.5	27.5	49.2	69.1	50.3	54.1	59.4	37.4	31.9	31.9	51.4
Somalia	3,880	31.2	17.2	10.5	4.7	82.8	19.8	20.7	148.1	48.1	93.7	..	35.5	24.7	87.4
Sudan	1,955	34.4	28.8	25.1	-1.7	15.3	47.4	35.4	42.1	17.4	21.3	..	26.8	18.6	25.5
Swaziland	37	-0.5	131.6	34.6	18.2	11.3	11.1	16.7	-6.2	-3.2	-30.3	40.3	34.8	31.1	-6.1
Tanzania	18,673	24.3	21.7	21.0	15.1	21.7	33.5	10.2	54.5	38.2	..	..	27.6	21.4	46.1
Togo	69,726	11.9	10.5	4.8	-6.8	-12.6	-5.8	61.0	-2.3	7.2	-24.7	14.0	25.8	-3.2	-4.2
Uganda	211	63.8	104.2	35.3	37.9	43.4	149.7	84.3	..	..	..	..	25.0	59.5	..
Zaire	3,723	22.0	43.1	87.0	43.7	139.1	52.6	64.6	113.0	109.6	-2.7	362.9	41.2	72.9	95.7
Zambia	1,863	17.3	21.3	28.7	9.3	11.7	18.8	38.1	20.8	160.7	-18.3	..	23.3	17.1	46.1
Zimbabwe	1,148	32.0	24.3	32.5	12.4	-2.4	11.9	6.7	25.0	16.4	24.4	27.6	..	14.6	22.7
NORTH AFRICA		17.7	27.1	23.1	19.7	17.4	14.4	10.7	8.8	10.9	24.1	12.5	24.6	21.3	11.2
Algeria	101,540	17.2	12.0	31.0	24.6	20.5	12.3	10.7	9.3	11.7	8.1	12.5	25.2	21.4	10.3
Egypt, Arab Republic of	14,065	42.1	27.1	23.1	18.6	20.9	19.4	18.8	17.3	20.2	25.0	26.3	29.3	21.5	22.2
Libya	1,215	-41.3	141.8	-7.9	5.2	17.4	2.5	-8.5	6.0	10.9	82.9	..	24.6	17.4	27.1
Morocco	31,215	17.7	18.3	18.4	19.7	8.5	14.4	11.0	7.1	8.8	10.3	2.3	20.4	15.8	7.6
Tunisia	1,573	19.1	29.7	25.6	21.1	15.8	16.2	8.3	8.8	4.3	24.1	6.2	15.4	21.3	11.2
ALL AFRICA		17.9	23.9	19.3	16.9	10.8	13.9	10.8	7.9	8.8	10.3		26.2	17.4	10.8
South Africa	19,433	23.2	33.4	8.6	15.0	26.4	21.2	4.5	15.7	33.1	32.8	19.1	9.1	19.4	26.5

Notes: Levels for 1980 are expressed in millions of units of national currency. Group data are medians of individual country values in each year or period.

4–2. Credit to the private sector

	Level	Percentage annual change										Average		
	1980	1980	1981	1982	1983	1984	1985	1986	1987	1988	1989	1990	75–79	80–85	86–MR
SUB-SAHARAN AFRICA		14.1	19.9	11.4	10.2	6.5	14.4	11.1	7.6	14.7	16.7	13.0	20.7	12.1	13.0
excluding Nigeria		13.8	17.5	10.8	10.3	6.5	14.7	11.0	8.8	13.2	17.1	14	20.1	11.5	13.4
Angola	..	..	..	..	..	..	..	..	..	..	..	..	..	..	..
Benin	85,000	33.8	2.4	44.7	5.6	-12.1	24.4	-32.8	-3.8	12.9	-31.1	-2.4	18.3	10.9	-8.4
Botswana	93	10.2	45.9	-0.9	14.9	32.0	-11.0	19.6	20.4	22.9	35.5	52.1	11.3	14.4	31.5
Burkina Faso	59,026	5.5	5.1	14.4	3.9	-2.8	23.3	6.4	6.3	8.4	20.0	-1.3	27.5	7.4	9.3
Burundi	6,414	14.3	44.4	-9.5	-2.5	-29.1	4.6	29.3	2.0	34.0	31.3	..	54.7	-4.7	23.9
Cameroon	416,613	28.7	34.3	21.3	19.2	-0.3	9.0	12.3	2.9	0.9	-13.3	0.8	31.8	15.4	-3.2
Cape Verde	506	-14.3	42.3	11.4	52.4	17.6	46.8	21.6	23.9	-30.1	29.4	19.7	17.3	31.7	5.0
Central African Republic	23,468	50.2	4.1	24.2	1.6	-0.7	14.4	-8.7	-7.9	4.2	-1.6	-3.5	6.7	8.0	-1.6
Chad	37,479	-1.8	-16.6	-4.1	8.2	41.5	41.4	15.5	-1.1	-1.7	-59.5	-4.8	16.7	12.1	-25.0
Comoros	..	..	..	..	26.9	41.2	-46.0	16.7	18.8	44.3	-7.6	43.4	..	..	21.3
Congo, People's Republic	55,996	22.8	68.2	39.2	15.9	18.8	11.5	0.8	-7.9	-6.2	-36.0	6.5	9.6	27.5	-14.5
Cote d'Ivoire	866,500	11.9	9.0	6.0	7.7	-2.1	-2.0	2.1	7.6	-0.1	-6.0	-5.8	28.7	3.8	-1.6
Djibouti	..	..	..	..	..	..	13.2	7.5	-0.2	1.9	3.9	-5.1	..	..	0.6
Equatorial Guinea	..	..	..	..	..	..	..	28.1	-10.1	-4.6	8.6	1.1	..	..	-0.9
Ethiopia	289	-29.8	27.8	4.7	-0.3	-6.6	3.5	0.4	37.6	-25.3	1.0	4.9	2.1	3.5	-1.1
Gabon	142,586	15.6	19.9	8.2	23.9	9.9	20.4	10.9	-12.8	-12.9	-18.3	0.9	15.8	15.8	-12.0
Gambia	99	18.6	6.3	-1.0	33.3	14.9	34.0	-9.3	-3.7	13.2	12.3	15.7	38.3	16.6	9.8
Ghana	940	18.1	42.8	16.1	82.2	110.6	78.4	74.0	26.8	40.2	151.0	14.3	29.2	63.6	57.1
Guinea	..	..	..	..	..	..	..	..	119.3	..	..	..	..	..	..
Guinea-Bissau	..	..	..	..	14.8	83.6	122.3	192.2	696.7	89.9	..	..	..	..	289.0
Kenya	11,759	20.3	10.8	10.2	7.1	10.2	15.0	16.4	6.5	16.2	16.7	11.9	26.0	10.2	13.5
Lesotho	21	-10.1	73.2	26.4	10.2	32.1	30.5	1.5	24.6	28.9	17.6	19.9	29.0	29.5	22.8
Liberia	89	-39.2	3.2	-17.9	-4.6	6.4	2.2	-4.1	21.1	-17.1	65.0	..	18.5	-3.5	17.2
Madagascar	163,693	25.8	10.3	19.9	25.9	24.3	16.6	15.0	17.1	3.6	10.4	..	15.1	20.5	9.4
Malawi	184	7.7	4.2	14.1	16.3	-10.2	-7.0	11.1	-13.2	27.9	46.0	35.5	31.0	4.1	24.6
Mali	81,992	7.8	6.6	8.7	7.0	-22.8	21.7	18.1	-6.8	-24.0	13.0	-0.2	9.1	1.5	-5.8
Mauritania	10,081	13.4	11.7	13.3	8.7	8.1	11.1	4.9	10.1	8.5	11.8	27.5	12.4	10.4	13.4
Mauritius	1,881	9.3	20.1	8.9	13.7	21.8	35.5	17.9	29.2	27.1	21.4	20.9	21.4	18.2	24.5
Mozambique	..	..	..	..	..	..	..	..	..	..	..	..	..	..	..
Namibia	..	..	..	..	..	..	..	..	..	..	..	..	..	..	..
Niger	88,814	18.5	13.6	8.3	2.7	-12.9	-9.7	9.2	-4.1	..	..	-22.9	29.4	-0.3	..
Nigeria	6,744	31.6	32.2	18.5	4.8	6.8	8.5	30.2	7.3	16.4	14.2	9.1	32.1	12.4	12.4
Rwanda	6,207	46.1	24.5	3.9	4.0	23.0	30.6	0.2	1.1	21.5	7.8	-16.9	31.0	14.5	4.7
Sao Tome & Principe	..	..	..	..	18.5	20.4	16.0	48.0	45.3	17.8	..	..	..	..	30.8
Senegal	261,519	16.8	19.9	8.1	5.1	-0.7	5.6	0.2	2.9	7.9	-3.3	-5.6	21.6	6.5	0.7
Seychelles	160	3.0	-3.0	-7.5	-4.4	-12.4	-13.1	-13.2	-2.4	8.6	32.0	8.0	29.4	-8.0	12.6
Sierra Leone	91	28.0	9.2	14.6	16.3	-15.9	21.5	215.9	44.4	94.5	124.6	18.6	16.0	7.3	73.3
Somalia	426	-5.2	34.9	182.6	41.2	62.5	8.0	1.7	354.5	59.2	202.9	..	-1.2	63.4	163.6
Sudan	526	14.1	32.9	34.0	35.7	18.7	21.1	26.8	51.1	19.8	22.7	..	24.9	28.8	28.4
Swaziland	98	14.9	34.7	6.1	4.3	6.5	2.0	3.9	25.1	28.4	28.5	38.6	20.1	8.8	29.7
Tanzania	1,137	10.5	7.1	40.2	10.4	-26.5	73.6	22.1	99.2	37.1	..	..	16.5	12.8	65.3
Togo	64,140	12.4	-3.6	8.2	-4.1	-0.2	2.4	33.0	7.4	6.2	-6.3	3.2	23.9	0.5	1.9
Uganda	49	85.2	118.9	20.3	66.0	3.7	174.1	103.1	182.9	210.9	172.7	66.6	14.3	54.8	158.9
Zaire	1,105	32.4	15.1	42.3	56.7	58.9	24.3	92.3	126.3	61.6	74.4	76.8	31.5	42.4	80.1
Zambia	509	4.8	52.0	19.0	14.3	16.0	10.8	44.3	31.1	77.1	58.4	90.4	4.9	20.0	63.6
Zimbabwe	610	9.1	39.5	8.9	38.6	-22.4	3.8	8.1	37.7	21.3	16.0	50.8	..	10.3	28.2
NORTH AFRICA		10.5	61.6	26.9	22.9	15.9	13.6	4.4	11.6	6.2	13.5	11.3	14.2	20.5	9.2
Algeria	68,530	14.2	29.2	27.4	17.9	17.3	11.9	1.3	2.1	6.3	9.1	17.1	19.5	20.5	8.3
Egypt, Arab Republic of	2,174	-9.3	95.1	30.8	23.9	20.5	22.5	27.0	15.5	16.5	17.9	19.7	27.7	32.8	17.3
Libya	1,145	6.8	91.4	-27.7	40.4	-1.1	-5.5	-0.3	18.9	-4.3	6.4	5.5	13.2	10.0	5.2
Morocco	12,449	13.3	16.1	18.1	16.2	14.7	15.6	..	..	..	..	..	14.2	16.2	..
Tunisia	1,354	22.3	31.8	26.4	21.8	14.4	15.2	7.5	7.8	6.2	26.9	5.4	13.5	21.5	12.2
ALL AFRICA		14.1	24.5	13.3	14.3	8.1	14.4	10.9	7.8	12.9	16.7	..	19.5	12.6	12.5
South Africa	16,115	29.1	34.9	21.2	18.4	29.3	17.0	5.8	16.0	35.4	34.5	16.2	10.3	23.5	27.1

Notes: Data exclude credit to other financial institutions. Levels for 1980 are expressed in millions of units of national currency. Group data are medians of individual country values for each year or period.

4–3. Credit to the government

	Level	Percentage annual change											Average		
	1980	1980	1981	1982	1983	1984	1985	1986	1987	1988	1989	1990	75–79	80–85	86–MR
SUB-SAHARAN AFRICA		22.8	36.0	23.3	18.4	11.8	8.3	26.1	14.0	17.0	-5.2	8.3	15.6	17.5	7.9
excluding Nigeria		23.7	31.9	22.9	17.9	11.7	10.3	26.4	15.6	12.1	-5.3	6.9	15.2	17.1	6.7
Angola	..	..	..	..	..	..	..	..	..	..	..	..	..	..	..
Benin	-15,176	-8.6	22.4	-45.2	-94.3	-2540.1	-61.0	44.0	50.5	-48.0	-182.0	-253.0	-7.4	-9.3	-33.7
Botswana	-92	17.2	-26.8	57.3	74.7	99.3	74.4	97.6	43.1	29.3	29.9	28.8	-23.7	-18.8	-48.6
Burkina Faso	-3,380	45.6	-145.8	-63.4	-1326.1	-10.0	194.6	26.7	49.5	11.0	2.4	5.9	-6.7	-11.5	-41.9
Burundi	4,630	24.5	57.9	22.6	35.1	16.5	12.3	-11.0	6.7	0.4	-31.3	22.8	26.7	-11.0	-5.6
Cameroon	-52,809	34.9	153.3	-13.5	-6.4	-31.4	-42.6	-125.4	-798.8	100.7	-87.0	73.3	-6.2	-7.8	-40.5
Cape Verde	26	-63.2	1542.5	-27.1	53.9	-24.7	-31.4	145.1	18.1	0.7	34.5	28.2	-27.0	37.7	19.0
Central African Republic	12,874	10.8	40.4	-17.5	18.5	-6.2	0.8	29.0	-14.0	-8.6	0.3	-29.1	8.6	3.5	-11.7
Chad	11,405	0.3	9.9	-5.6	-7.6	-24.7	-79.3	290.6	-44.5	-141.3	-332.3	-171.9	20.0	-26.6	-30.2
Comoros	..	..	..	..	12.0	26.2	16.9	-17.1	-11.0	-26.0	185.8	-24.1		..	15.7
Congo, People's Republic	22,657	7.3	-79.3	333.3	-6.1	107.9	-18.7	12.1	-11.2	57.9	44.9	-17.6	24.4	26.1	20.4
Cote d'Ivoire	-54,654	-52.0	-212.5	25.2	173.8	11.8	-5.9	10.3	-27.5	49.0	-13.1	-11.4	-4.8	-7.7	-1.1
Djibouti	..	..	..	..	..	..	13.6	-35.8	82.1	-1.0	1.2	-15.2	..	..	-40.2
Equatorial Guinea	..	..	..	..	..	..	..	-5.7	-18.2	2.1	-0.8	-24.1	..	..	-8.8
Ethiopia	1,146	15.1	-1.5	26.7	53.8	15.7	8.1	9.4	2.3	12.1	21.5	33.2	38.9	23.0	16.7
Gabon	30,588	-1.8	-106.7	1488.4	-38.6	-16.4	-160.6	208.6	188.6	23.1	22.6	-39.1	-5.3	-8.4	26.6
Gambia, The	25	-42.8	38.6	31.9	92.3	33.1	41.6	-106.2	637.7	-1.7	-23.5	250.9	-21.8	48.1	-64.7
Ghana	6,518	33.0	63.4	3.8	153.7	33.5	28.3	59.4	104.9	-5.5	-25.9	8.5	55.2	52.2	5.4
Guinea	..	..	..	..	..	..	..	..	-7.0	..	..	..	..	..	..
Guinea-Bissau	..	..	..	..	31.9	21.6	17.5	24.2	19.0	11.1			..	..	..
Kenya	3,959	8.6	71.1	58.0	-18.6	9.9	8.3	50.1	28.0	-7.7	-10.7	44.0	21.9	17.5	6.7
Lesotho	27		103.9	27.3	-0.9	-13.1	41.2	60.5	28.5	38.9	22.8	-32.3	..	18.7	14.1
Liberia	151	63.2	27.8	34.8	26.1	2.9	22.1	10.0	20.0	31.4	12.0		79.3	21.9	15.2
Madagascar	176,943	81.0	36.0	16.8	19.1	15.9	7.3	13.4	29.2	2.2	-14.2	..	64.7	18.3	2.8
Malawi	92	31.5	91.0	25.8	23.4	7.8	22.9	34.1	5.0	-32.7	-5.2	-41.4	15.6	27.8	-20.7
Mali	55,935	1.6	10.1	23.3	20.3	-8.1	6.1	-1.6	-4.4	-18.1	-14.8	-40.4	14.7	10.3	-19.8
Mauritania	1,630	13.0	49.4	51.2	14.5	11.8	-24.5	11.4	9.8	-4.4	113.8	0.1	-9.8	18.8	26.3
Mauritius	2,554	17.6	42.6	21.8	18.4	11.6	-6.8	0.7	-16.7	2.0	-5.4	3.6	58.3	16.7	-3.9
Mozambique	..	..	..	..	..	..	..	..	..	..	..	..	..	..	..
Namibia	..	..	..	..	..	..	..	..	..	..	..	..	..	..	..
Niger	-7,492	-67.3	-60.2	-647.7	9.3	23.2	20.5	-27.9	-40.6	8.9	96.2	7.9	-5.7	-10.3	14.9
Nigeria	3,539	6.8	78.0	64.0	49.7	15.2	2.7	2.9	12.4	29.9	-33.0	69.1	-10.1	39.8	9.1
Rwanda	-3,034	109.4	-8.5	-78.2	-456.2	-6.6	-4.7	50.9	140.3	24.3	32.5	60.8	-7.7	-11.7	52.2
Sao Tome & Principe	..	..	..	..	-71.6	-317.7	83.0	18.2	9.1	-24.8			..	..	..
Senegal	28,673	52.8	80.1	90.3	18.4	12.7	14.9	1.9	-4.9	4.0	-16.3	-15.3	60.8	38.0	-8.1
Seychelles	19	52.0	138.9	18.3	62.2	21.7	131.0	26.1	7.8	28.0	21.6	12.9	-23.1	57.1	18.8
Sierra Leone	318	37.4	40.8	38.6	26.1	34.7	51.4	57.0	52.6	46.3	46.0	43.7	39.2	36.4	46.9
Somalia	1,902	54.5	18.3	-6.6	-14.0	142.5	23.9	12.1	134.6	41.1	-30.1	..	-12.2	22.4	22.8
Sudan	1,141	65.9	22.7	13.6	-2.4	12.6	40.0	37.5	46.4	4.8	16.0	..	37.3	13.6	12.8
Swaziland	-61	26.6	-23.4	-45.6	-58.4	-55.1	-285.2	246.0	-174.7	281.3	148.4	37.6	-17.5	-20.4	-72.6
Tanzania	11,326	36.6	25.7	26.1	17.4	19.1	30.6	3.5	3.2	44.5	..		35.5	22.8	..
Togo	4,530	14.5	216.4	-11.0	-21.8	-92.5	-760.7	-320.1	-84.9	72.6	-701.7	-54.1	45.5	-11.0	..
Uganda	151	59.3	108.9	16.4	25.4	70.0	121.5	33.9	..	..	..	..	26.8	54.2	..
Zaire	2,612	18.5	54.0	99.5	41.8	159.4	57.1	61.1	112.0	116.3	-12.2	424.9	48.4	80.7	96.2
Zambia	1,354	22.8	9.8	33.8	7.0	9.7	23.0	35.2	15.6	208.3	-43.4	38.3	38.5	15.9	..
Zimbabwe	367	121.0	-22.9	90.7	-9.4	-12.0	-14.7	-2.2	93.9	21.9	42.7	17.0	..	3.3	39.1
NORTH AFRICA		13.9	16.5	33.6	15.5	27.3	15.7	13.2	15.0	19.5	9.7	6.3	31.2	20.4	13.3
Algeria	33,010	24.0	-23.8	43.8	45.7	28.6	13.1	31.9	21.9	19.5	6.8	6.3	43.6	24.1	13.3
Egypt, Arab Republic of	8,248	13.9	3.4	33.6	9.2	18.4	15.7	14.3	20.4	24.4	30.0	25.4	31.2	16.5	25.4
Libya	70	-93.0	960.1	50.1	-44.6	83.9	18.1	-21.2	-19.2	54.5	218.8	..	46.6	55.5	42.1
Morocco	18,766	20.9	19.8	10.4	26.1	5.1	14.0	12.4	6.0	8.5	9.7	-4.3	25.8	14.8	5.6
Tunisia	219	2.3	16.5	20.1	15.5	27.3	22.9	13.2	15.0	-6.2	5.6	13.0	29.8	20.4	5.1
ALL AFRICA		19.7	26.8	24.2	17.9	12.2	13.6	13.8	15.0	19.5	4.0	8.1	23.1	17.9	9.1
South Africa	3,319	1.0	26.2	-57.1	-34.4	-49.5	306.6	-21.9	9.0	-30.7	-64.3	620.8	4.8	-20.1	-0.7

Notes: Data exclude credit to other financial institutions. Levels for 1980 are expressed in millions of units of national currency. Group data are medians of individual country values for each year or period.

4–4. Net foreign assets

		1980	1981	1982	1983	1984	1985	1986	1987	1988	1989	1990	75–79	80–85	86–MR
		Millions of units of national currency											*Average*		
SUB-SAHARAN AFRICA excluding Nigeria															
Angola		..	..	..	..	..	..	..	..	..	..	..	..	..	..
Benin		-2825	13,490	-4994	-21940	-46566	-38666	-32819	-54643	-54395	-20869	6,027	3,364	-16917	-31340
Botswana		254	218	313	452	725	1,660	2,207	3,161	4,390	5,234	6,344	121	604	4,267
Burkina Faso		3,400	4,820	1,767	14,307	31,679	30,977	51,142	68,248	80,032	66,418	65,929	6,925	14,492	66,354
Burundi		5,132	2,513	-621	64	29	1,458	5,072	4,562	5,156	11,045	9,906	5,098	1,429	7,148
Cameroon	*	-33	2	-74	15	68	105	-71	-203	-116	-194	-185	-6315	14	-154
Cape Verde		1,784	1,815	2,482	3,086	3,546	4,041	4,244	5,196	5,870	5,370	5,012	1,331	2,792	5,138
Central African Republic		6,153	8,373	4,500	6,800	12,872	12,016	13,942	17,654	18,727	19,572	19,747	-1102	8,452	17,928
Chad		-3028	-3982	-1456	6,462	21,669	14,157	3,145	7,317	12,181	22,038	31,853	-2246	5,637	15,307
Comoros		..	..	4,224	4,794	1,621	5,306	4,997	6,622	6,849	8,345	6,914	..	2,658	6,745
Congo, People's Republic		2,874	10,673	-13340	-36540	-69078	-60497	-76964	-42327	-43906	-39793	-4190	-9865	-27651	-41436
Cote d'Ivoire	*	-209	-367	-394	-598	-477	-329	-331	-378	-485	-486	-495	8,625	-396	-435
Djibouti		..	..	..	..	21,273	25,605	28,693	32,463	35,535	35,825	41,607	..	7,813	34,824
Equatorial Guinea		..	..	..	..	..	-3426	-2143	-3940	-5330	-3184	-5820	..	-571	-4083
Ethiopia		65	278	115	18	-73	178	394	136	4	-26	-122	532	97	77
Gabon		-34	27,021	75,904	65,153	85,790	42,189	-2832	-55560	-56948	-46776	20,590	-4698	49,337	-28305
Gambia, The		-49	-104	-192	-244	-316	-357	-475	-339	*-221*	*-205*	-13	23	-210	-251
Ghana	*	0	0	0	-6	-18	-33	-56	-131	-153	-181	-152	169	-9	-134
Guinea		..	..	..	..	..	7,900	25,100	..	..	..	..	..	0	16,500
Guinea-Bissau		..	..	-1462	-4170	-6859	-6583	-2807	-23185	-20198	..	..	..	-3179	-15397
Kenya		1,830	128	-2167	-1027	-374	-1976	-411	-2159	-3651	-1295	-1683	2,164	-598	-1840
Lesotho		64	50	73	110	170	209	200	184	201	195	371	..	113	230
Liberia		-134	-180	-224	-247	-253	-294	-331	-412	-412	-416	..	13	-222	-393
Madagascar	*	-110	-157	-198	-428	-605	-701	-922	-1718	-1957	-1993	..	-110	-366	-1647
Malawi		-81	-120	-169	-219	-145	-242	-378	-258	14	-13	89	-16	-163	-109
Mali		-59005	-64799	-77157	-85975	-29196	-41929	-51241	-43334	-26668	13,851	27,069	-49123	-59677	-16065
Mauritania		-1144	-814	-5862	-6472	-9167	-9314	-11032	-9845	-11068	-10565	-15010	-1325	-5462	-11504
Mauritius		-101	-1280	-1334	-2068	-2057	-1513	280	3,244	5,864	8,282	11,875	371	-1392	5,909
Mozambique		..	..	..	..	..	..	..	..	..	..	..	..	..	..
Namibia		..	..	..	..	..	..	..	..	..	..	..	..	..	..
Niger		8,725	18,642	-24004	-19760	-2470	5,238	11,913	18,612	32,819	27,770	32,256	18,365	-2272	24,674
Nigeria		5,607	2,556	1,057	808	1,423	1,816	4,463	6,865	7,974	20,043	41,247	2,935	2,211	16,118
Rwanda		15,047	14,026	9,830	8,145	9,793	9,173	12,921	11,674	8,918	6,068	2,764	6,738	11,002	8,469
Sao Tome & Principe		..	..	-125	-97	-422	-351	-597	-891	-1202	..	..	..	-166	-897
Senegal	*	-87	-133	-173	-199	-225	-259	-208	-207	-246	-187	-155	-26612	-179	-201
Seychelles		164	110	82	68	72	68	62	78	57	50	83	70	94	66
Sierra Leone		-125	-252	-274	-647	-697	-1586	-8284		-12228	-18739	-58861	-6	-597	-21674
Somalia	*	0	0	-1	-2	-4	-5	-18	-20	-56	-214	..	615	-2	-77
Sudan		-349	-451	-1421	-2498	-2417	-3570	-4068	-4933	-1512	-644	..	-224	-1784	-2789
Swaziland		*109*	83	80	99	129	185	187	250	429	585	648	84	114	420
Tanzania	*	0	0	0	1	-6	-15	-45	-81	-154	..	..	301	-4	-94
Togo		4,613	32,104	47,310	51,965	67,995	79,183	60,687	65,183	43,663	69,568	74,021	8,447	47,195	62,624
Uganda		-6	-171	-248	-612	-1347	-3819	-2985	..	..	..	..	1	-1034	..
Zaire	*	0	-1	-5	-39	-35	-52	-73	-105	-225	-266	-811	-57	-22	-296
Zambia		-828	-1156	-1447	-1969	-2674	-6609	-14567	-10930	-20572	-13098	-88613	-330	-2447	-29556
Zimbabwe		173	5	-40	-384	-129	-39	-18	80	259	219	14	31	-69	111
NORTH AFRICA															
Algeria		16,506	18,825	13,966	11,351	9,321	14,890	9,324	9,146	9,278	6,520	6,525	9,758	14,143	8,158
Egypt, Arab Republic of		-1234	-1211	-461	668	150	641	1,386	2,476	2,220	-1476	-1229	-1364	-241	676
Libya		4,504	2,983	2,313	1,748	1,240	2,010	2,007	1,709	1,228	1,167	..	1,478	2,466	1,528
Morocco		239	-946	-3385	-6123	-7798	-8789	-5376	-3054	-523	453	14,836	1,675	-4467	1,267
Tunisia		191	237	255	391	290	201	49	192	550	679	596	131	261	413
ALL AFRICA															
South Africa		5,615	2,333	1,873	1,175	-391	-2672	218	3,639	1,188	269	894	912	1,322	1,242

Notes: Levels are expressed in millions of units of national currency (billions of units of national currency for those marked with an "").*

4–5. Growth of money supply

	Level	Percentage annual change											Average		
	1980	1980	1981	1982	1983	1984	1985	1986	1987	1988	1989	1990	75–79	80–86	86–MR
SUB-SAHARAN AFRICA		19.4	20.8	12.9	10.7	11.7	10.3	12.9	5.8	11.0	16.4	13.8	20.9	13.1	10.8
excluding Nigeria		19.2	21.9	13.2	10.4	12.0	10.4	16.1	5.0	10.6	16.1	11.9	18.9	13.4	10.7
Angola	..	..	..	..	..	..	..	..	..	..	..	..	..	..	..
Benin	45,407	34.6	33.1	38.1	-1.7	9.1	-2.7	-9.4	-21.6	16.3	17.3	23.9	6.7	13.4	9.1
Botswana	91	10.4	26.7	11.0	7.8	9.7	25.0	29.4	28.2	30.2	24.6	15.7	..	13.9	25.1
Burkina Faso	41,669	19.9	17.2	11.3	11.0	10.2	4.6	22.8	6.7	10.6	4.4	-1.6	11.5	10.8	5.4
Burundi	9,651	6.5	26.8	-11.5	26.1	6.5	25.1	8.1	-1.0	2.6	2.9	1.6	30.9	11.8	1.8
Cameroon	207,324	13.1	24.3	15.2	26.5	9.0	4.0	5.0	-13.6	-0.3	15.5	-6.5	24.9	16.1	-0.1
Cape Verde	2,302	26.3	10.9	26.4	22.6	6.2	15.3	16.1	1.6	5.7	6.2	8.0	..	16.7	5.5
Central African Republic	34,612	32.5	22.3	-4.2	10.4	7.7	6.8	1.3	2.6	-1.5	7.4	-3.7	18.5	7.3	1.5
Chad	26,478	-16.1	19.6	4.7	22.9	59.8	4.9	1.2	2.1	-8.4	2.7	-0.3	19.3	22.5	-1.4
Comoros	..	..	..	..	40.2	-14.2	14.8	0.8	8.0	13.7	15.5	6.2	..	..	11.5
Congo, People's Republic	54,344	37.2	38.2	29.9	-7.3	12.0	10.4	-12.8	5.0	-7.3	1.4	25.0	8.6	13.5	3.7
Cote d'Ivoire	438,730	1.1	5.8	-0.9	6.0	17.7	7.9	2.6	-5.9	-3.4	-11.5	3.0	25.0	7.2	-5.2
Djibouti	..	..	..	..	..	..	..	3.0	13.4	8.8	6.8	-7.0	8.6	..	..	3.2
Equatorial Guinea	..	..	..	..	..	..	..	..	23.3	-9.2	-37.5	..	..	..	..
Ethiopia	1,568	-0.2	9.7	10.0	13.2	7.8	17.0	21.1	2.1	11.4	16.1	22.0	14.9	11.2	12.9
Gabon	93,959	10.0	21.9	9.7	13.6	17.7	5.2	-13.7	-12.6	9.9	16.7	5.8	6.1	13.5	6.1
Gambia, The	61	6.1	25.6	13.2	15.0	-0.7	62.8	2.7	18.8	7.9	21.9	13.8	10.8	17.9	15.3
Ghana	6,085	30.0	54.7	19.0	49.2	60.6	42.7	44.0	52.6	45.0	52.7	10.8	51.1	43.9	41.0
Guinea	..	..	..	..	..	..	..	..	..	..	..	..	..	..	..
Guinea-Bissau	..	..	..	..	..	..	..	..	..	93.3	84.5			..	..
Kenya	8,434	-8.1	11.6	13.0	7.9	14.1	-1.3	35.6	8.0	1.3	..	27.2	22.4	9.6	10.9
Lesotho	49	..	20.8	31.7	9.7	22.0	28.8	16.2	1.4	40.2	11.5	7.8	..	21.6	16.4
Liberia	..	..	..	..	..	..	..	..	..	..	..	..	..	..	..
Madagascar	151,296	21.8	28.1	7.3	-7.4	24.5	-0.6	21.4	28.4	22.4	31.5	26.9	16.3	8.5	27.2
Malawi	97	7.3	18.1	13.9	-2.3	20.7	8.2	32.3	35.0	46.3	-2.0	3.5	6.9	10.7	19.1
Mali	59,517	4.8	1.2	13.4	18.9	31.8	6.2	3.3	-7.0	4.7	-3.5	-10.8	15.7	15.8	-3.4
Mauritania	5,677	11.7	34.8	-6.8	13.4	19.2	26.3	-6.4	17.6	4.7	7.3	13.1	13.0	14.2	9.7
Mauritius	1,720	20.6	-10.9	13.5	3.6	13.7	-0.6	19.3	35.8	15.6	18.1	23.7	10.5	5.1	21.8
Mozambique	..	..	..	..	..	..	..	..	..	..	..	..	..	..	..
Namibia	..	..	..	..	..	..	..	..	..	..	..	..	..	..	..
Niger	64,594	12.8	15.7	-5.1	-6.2	17.8	2.8	2.9	-11.9	..	..	-11.7	31.2	3.5	..
Nigeria	9,227	50.1	5.6	3.1	12.3	8.2	8.4	-4.3	17.7	43.9	20.4	33.8	22.1	7.7	29.1
Rwanda	12,026	6.9	-2.1	-2.7	7.5	8.3	10.2	17.9	2.6	3.0	-12.4	4.9	22.2	4.2	-1.6
Sao Tome & Principe	..	..	..	..	..	..	6.1	11.5	9.1	-6.0			..	..	..
Senegal	137,939	13.8	18.3	15.8	0.1	1.3	1.0	17.3	-5.5	0.2	7.4	-11.5	13.2	6.4	-1.4
Seychelles	159	38.4	-0.5	-9.2	-8.4	2.6	15.3	-0.2	0.1	21.0	16.9	-1.3	23.3	-1.9	10.7
Sierra Leone	153	19.6	-0.4	66.7	41.9	35.3	85.0	105.8	56.0	60.5	87.1	64.3	20.9	43.8	67.9
Somalia	2,783	19.2	32.0	9.8	6.9	23.6	83.2	24.3	147.4	51.2	207.7	116.9	30.1	23.8	122.0
Sudan	1,097	31.2	39.5	36.6	11.7	18.3	49.9	41.1	32.8	44.4	68.5	47.5	32.0	27.6	49.4
Swaziland	50	22.0	2.4	13.7	4.6	11.5	13.4	49.7	8.9	13.9	18.3	17.1	14.7	9.1	14.8
Tanzania	13,346	27.9	15.4	19.0	12.2	0.2	23.6	40.6	31.6	36.1	..	..	22.5	12.8	..
Togo	55,336	5.1	44.5	12.6	-7.8	9.2	-8.8	8.4	1.5	-29.3	-1.9	19.3	24.2	6.8	-6.9
Uganda	140	31.5	102.8	5.2	46.2	126.6	128.7	168.7	..	..	..	..	32.7	67.4	..
Zaire	2,710	72.6	55.0	76.6	69.9	38.3	29.0	59.7	90.8	119.2	75.4	175.8	39.8	55.2	108.8
Zambia	519	0.5	8.6	22.3	15.3	9.4	41.6	87.1	40.0	63.7	..	..	9.2	17.9	..
Zimbabwe	633	36.6	7.3	21.8	-9.1	15.2	16.1	9.7	11.0	30.9	18.9	26.9	9.2	8.8	22.3
NORTH AFRICA		21.0	16.0	24.9	14.5	7.6	16.4	2.5	9.3	12.8	9.2	7.9	22.7	16.5	6.9
Algeria	84,434	16.9	16.0	28.0	21.9	18.1	12.1	1.2	9.3	12.7	-0.9	7.9	22.7	20.1	6.9
Egypt, Arab Republic of	6,775	55.6	12.9	24.9	14.5	13.8	18.1	8.7	14.2	12.8	9.2	16.6	24.1	16.9	12.7
Libya	2,899	29.0	21.2	-8.0	-10.8	-6.0	28.8	-12.9	13.1	-12.4	16.9	3.1	25.8	0.1	3.9
Morocco	25,312	8.4	14.6	3.6	13.7	7.6	16.4	16.8	8.9	13.8	10.3	18.3	16.4	10.4	12.6
Tunisia	951	21.0	22.5	24.9	16.8	6.8	13.5	2.5	0.7	17.3	1.2	6.1	13.8	16.5	6.7
ALL AFRICA		19.6	19.6	13.2	11.7	11.5	13.4	8.7	8.9	12.7	15.5	11.9	20.1	13.4	10.7
South Africa	8,398	35.5	34.2	16.4	26.4	41.2	-8.9	8.8	38.0	24.7	8.5	15.0	9.2	22.4	20.1

Notes: Levels for 1980 are expressed in millions of units of national currency. Group data are medians of individual country values in each year or period.

4–6. Discount rate

						Percent							Average	
	1980	1981	1982	1983	1984	1985	1986	1987	1988	1989	1990	75–79	80–85	86–MR
SUB-SAHARAN AFRICA	8.5	10.3	11.5	10.5	10.5	10.5	8.8	8.8	9.5	11.0	11.5	6.7	10.6	9.7
excluding Nigeria	8.5	9.8	10.8	10.5	10.5	10.5	8.8	8.8	9.5	11.0	11.5	6.9	10.7	9.7
Angola	..	..	..	..	..	..	..	..	..	..	..	..	..	..
Benin	10.5	10.5	12.5	10.5	10.5	10.5	8.5	8.5	9.5	11.0	11.0	8.0	10.8	9.7
Botswana	5.8	8.5	12.0	10.5	9.0	9.0	9.0	8.5	6.5	6.5	8.5	7.1	9.1	7.8
Burkina Faso	10.5	10.5	12.5	10.5	10.5	10.5	8.5	8.5	9.5	11.0	11.0	8.0	10.8	9.7
Burundi	7.0	7.0	7.0	7.0	7.0	7.0	5.0	7.0	7.0	..	..	5.8	7.0	6.3
Cameroon	8.5	8.5	8.5	8.5	8.5	9.0	8.0	8.0	9.5	9.5	..	6.7	8.6	8.8
Cape Verde	..	..	..	..	..	..	..	..	..	..	..	..	..	..
Central African Republic	8.5	8.5	8.5	8.5	8.5	9.0	8.0	8.0	9.5	9.5	..	6.7	8.6	8.8
Chad	8.5	8.5	8.5	9.0	9.0	9.0	8.0	8.0	9.5	9.5	..	6.7	8.8	8.8
Comoros	..	..	..	10.0	10.0	10.0	10.0	8.5	8.5	..	..	..	..	9.0
Congo, People's Republic of the	8.5	8.5	8.5	8.5	8.5	9.0	8.0	8.0	9.5	9.5	..	6.7	8.6	8.8
Cote d'Ivoire	10.5	10.5	12.5	10.5	10.5	10.5	8.5	8.5	9.5	11.0	11.0	8.0	10.8	9.7
Djibouti	..	..	..	..	..	..	..	..	..	..	..	..	..	..
Equatorial Guinea	..	..	..	..	..	9.0	8.0	8.0	9.5	9.5	..	..	..	8.8
Ethiopia	..	..	..	..	..	6.0	6.0	3.0	3.0	3.0	3.0	..	..	3.6
Gabon	8.5	8.5	8.5	8.5	8.5	9.0	8.0	8.0	9.5	9.5	..	6.7	8.6	8.8
Gambia, The	8.0	9.5	9.5	9.5	9.5	15.0	20.0	21.0	19.0	15.0	16.5	6.0	10.2	18.3
Ghana	13.5	19.5	10.5	14.5	18.0	18.5	20.5	23.5	26.0	26.0	33.0	10.2	15.8	25.8
Guinea	..	..	..	..	..	..	..	..	..	..	..	..	..	..
Guinea-Bissau	..	..	..	..	..	..	..	..	..	..	..	..	..	..
Kenya	8.0	12.5	15.0	15.0	12.5	12.5	12.5	12.5	16.0	16.5	19.4	7.1	12.6	15.4
Lesotho	8.0	12.0	12.0	12.0	15.0	12.0	9.5	9.0	15.5	17.0	15.8	..	11.8	13.4
Liberia	..	..	..	..	..	..	..	..	..	..	..	..	..	..
Madagascar	5.5	8.0	12.5	13.0	13.0	11.5	11.5	11.5	11.5	..	..	5.5	10.6	11.5
Malawi	10.0	10.0	10.0	10.0	10.0	11.0	11.0	14.0	11.0	11.0	14.0	7.0	10.2	12.2
Mali	10.5	10.5	12.5	10.5	10.5	10.5	8.5	8.5	9.5	11.0	11.0	8.0	10.8	9.7
Mauritania	6.0	6.0	6.0	6.0	6.0	6.5	6.5	6.5	6.5	..	..	5.0	6.1	6.5
Mauritius	10.5	12.0	12.0	11.0	11.0	11.0	11.0	10.0	10.0	12.0	12.0	7.7	11.3	11.0
Mozambique	..	..	..	..	..	..	..	..	..	..	..	..	..	..
Namibia	..	..	..	..	..	..	..	..	..	..	..	..	..	..
Niger	10.5	10.5	12.5	10.5	10.5	10.5	8.5	8.5	8.5	11.0	11.0	8.0	10.8	9.5
Nigeria	6.0	6.0	8.0	8.0	10.0	10.0	10.0	10.0	..	..	..	4.2	8.0	10.0
Rwanda	9.0	9.0	9.0	9.0	9.0	9.0	9.0	9.0	9.0	9.0	14.0	5.8	9.0	10.0
Sao Tome & Principe	..	..	..	..	..	..	..	..	..	..	..	..	..	..
Senegal	10.5	10.5	12.5	10.5	10.5	10.5	8.5	8.5	9.5	11.0	11.0	8.0	10.8	9.7
Seychelles	..	6.0	6.0	6.0	6.0	6.0	6.0	6.0	6.0	6.0	9.5	..	5.0	6.7
Sierra Leone	12.0	12.0	12.0	14.0	14.0	14.0	16.0	16.0	16.0	16.0	55.0	7.6	13.0	23.8
Somalia	4.0	6.0	8.0	8.0	8.0	12.0	12.0	12.0	45.0	45.0 ..		3.6	7.7	28.5
Sudan	..	..	..	..	..	..	..	..	..	..	..	..	..	..
Swaziland	7.0	10.5	16.0	13.5	19.0	12.5	9.5	9.0	11.0	12.0	12.0	8.5	13.1	10.7
Tanzania	4.8	4.0	4.0	4.0	4.0	4.3	6.5	11.3	12.7	15.2	..	4.8	4.2	11.4
Togo	10.5	10.5	12.5	10.5	10.5	10.5	8.5	8.5	9.5	11.0	11.0	8.0	10.8	9.7
Uganda	8.0	10.0	11.0	15.5	24.0	24.0	36.0	31.0	45.0	55.0	50.0	..	15.4	43.4
Zaire	12.0	12.0	15.0	20.0	20.0	26.0	26.0	26.0	26.0	50.0	..	..	17.5	32.0
Zambia	6.5	7.5	7.5	10.0	14.5	25.0	30.0	15.0	15.0	..	..	5.7	11.8	20.0
Zimbabwe	4.5	9.0	9.0	9.0	9.0	9.0	9.0	9.0	9.0	9.0	10.3	4.5	8.3	9.3
NORTH AFRICA	5.8	6.0	7.0	7.0	7.0	8.5	8.5	8.5	8.5			5.0	6.9	8.5
Algeria	2.8	2.8	2.8	2.8	2.8	2.8	5.0	5.0	5.0	..	..	2.8	2.8	5.0
Egypt, Arab Republic of	11.0	12.0	13.0	13.0	13.0	13.0	13.0	13.0	13.0	14.0	14.0	7.0	12.5	13.4
Libya	5.0	5.0	5.0	5.0	5.0	5.0	5.0	5.0	5.0	..	..	5.0	5.0	5.0
Morocco	6.0	6.0	7.0	7.0	7.0	8.5	8.5	8.5	8.5	..	..	4.5	6.9	8.5
Tunisia	5.8	7.0	7.0	7.0	7.0	9.3	9.3	9.3	9.3	..	..	5.5	7.2	9.3
ALL AFRICA	8.5	9.0	10.0	10.0	10.0	10.5	8.5	8.5	9.5	11.0	12.0	6.7	10.6	9.7
South Africa	6.5	14.5	14.4	17.8	20.8	13.0	9.5	9.5	14.5	18.0	18.0	7.3	14.5	13.9

Notes: Group data are medians of individual country values in each year or period.

4–7. Real discount rate

	Percent											Average		
	1980	1981	1982	1983	1984	1985	1986	1987	1988	1989	1990	75–79	80–85	86–MR
SUB-SAHARAN AFRICA excluding Nigeria														
Angola	..	..	..	..	..	..	..	..	..	..	..	..	..	..
Benin	..	..	..	..	..	..	..	..	..	..	..	..	..	..
Botswana	-6.9	-6.8	0.8	0.0	0.4	0.8	-0.9	-1.2	-1.7	-4.5	-2.6	-3.8	-2.0	-2.2
Burkina Faso	-1.5	2.7	0.4	2.0	5.4	3.4	11.4	11.7	4.9	11.5	11.6	-2.9	2.1	10.2
Burundi	4.4	-4.5	1.2	-1.3	-6.4	3.3	3.1	-0.1	2.3	..	..	-9.6	-0.6	..
Cameroon	-1.0	-2.0	-4.2	-7.0	-2.6	7.6	0.2	1.9	0.8	9.5	..	-4.2	-1.5	3.1
Cape Verde	..	..	..	..	..	..	..	..	..	..	..	..	..	..
Central African Republic	..	..	-4.2	-5.3	5.8	-1.3	5.6	16.1	14.0	8.8	..	..	..	8.9
Chad	..	..	..	..	-9.4	3.7	24.2	14.9	-5.2	15.1	-0.6	..	..	9.7
Comoros	..	..	..	..	..	..	..	..	..	..	..	..	..	..
Congo, People's Republic of the	1.1	-7.2	-3.8	0.6	-3.7	2.7	5.4	5.6	5.6	5.1	..	-4.1	-1.7	5.4
Cote d'Ivoire	-3.6	1.5	4.8	4.4	6.0	8.5	1.1	8.0	2.3	..	..	-6.8	3.6	3.8
Djibouti	..	..	..	..	..	..	..	..	..	..	..	..	..	..
Equatorial Guinea	..	..	..	..	..	..	31.4	24.0	7.0	3.4	-1.1	..	..	12.9
Ethiopia	..	..	..	..	..	-11.0	17.5	5.6	-3.8	-4.5	..	..	..	3.7
Gabon	-3.4	-0.2	-7.0	-1.7	2.5	1.5	1.5	9.1	21.4	2.4	..	-7.8	-1.4	8.6
Gambia, The	1.1	3.4	-1.2	-1.0	-10.3	-2.8	-23.4	-2.0	6.5	6.2	..	-6.7	-1.8	-3.2
Ghana	-24.4	-44.8	-9.6	-48.6	-15.5	7.4	-3.3	-11.7	-4.1	0.6	..	-31.7	-22.6	-4.6
Guinea	..	..	..	..	..	..	..	..	..	..	..	..	..	..
Guinea-Bissau	..	..	..	..	..	..	..	..	..	..	..	..	..	..
Kenya	-5.1	0.6	-4.5	3.1	2.1	-0.5	8.2	7.0	7.1	6.1	6.9	-6.0	-0.7	7.1
Lesotho	-6.6	-0.4	-0.1	-4.7	3.6	-1.2	-7.2	-2.5	3.6	2.0	3.7	..	-1.6	-0.1
Liberia	..	..	..	..	..	..	..	..	..	..	..	..	..	..
Madagascar	-10.8	-17.3	-14.6	-5.3	2.9	0.9	-2.6	-3.0	-12.1	..	..	-1.6	-7.4	-5.9
Malawi	..	-1.6	0.2	-3.1	-8.4	0.4	-2.7	-8.9	-17.1	-1.3	..	..	-2.1	-6.0
Mali	..	..	..	..	..	..	..	..	..	..	..	..	..	..
Mauritania	..	..	..	..	..	..	..	-1.5	5.1	-11.5	..	..	..	-2.6
Mauritius	-22.2	-2.2	0.6	5.1	3.4	4.0	9.2	9.4	0.8	-0.6	-1.3	-3.8	-1.9	3.5
Mozambique	..	..	..	..	..	..	..	..	..	..	..	..	..	..
Namibia	..	..	..	..	..	..	..	..	..	..	..	..	..	..
Niger	0.2	-10.1	0.8	13.3	2.0	11.5	12.1	16.3	10.0	14.2	11.9	-5.4	2.9	12.9
Nigeria	-3.6	-12.3	0.3	-12.3	-21.2	4.2	4.5	-9.3	..	..	..	-13.6	-7.5	-2.4
Rwanda	1.6	2.4	-3.2	2.3	3.4	7.1	10.2	4.7	5.9	7.9	9.4	-8.4	2.3	7.6
Sao Tome & Principe	..	..	..	..	..	..	..	..	..	..	..	..	..	..
Senegal	1.6	4.3	-4.2	-1.0	-1.1	-2.2	2.2	13.2	11.5	10.5	..	-2.2	-0.4	9.4
Seychelles	..	-4.1	6.9	-0.1	1.9	5.2	5.7	3.4	4.1	4.4	5.3	..	1.6	..
Sierra Leone	-0.8	-9.2	-11.7	-32.4	-31.6	-35.4	-35.9	-58.8	-11.7	-28.7	-26.5	-6.7	-20.2	-32.3
Somalia	-34.5	-26.6	-12.6	-20.6	-43.5	-18.7	-17.5	-12.6	-20.3	..	..	-10.2	-26.1	..
Sudan	..	..	..	..	..	..	..	..	..	..	..	..	..	..
Swaziland	*-11.3*	-3.0	7.9	-6.7	5.3	-6.1	-1.8	-3.1	-0.7	..	..	-2.7	-2.3	-1.9
Tanzania	-19.6	-17.2	-19.3	-18.1	-23.2	-22.2	-19.6	-14.3	-14.1	-10.0	..	-7.8	-19.9	-14.5
Togo	-1.6	-7.7	1.2	1.0	14.5	12.5	4.2	8.4	9.7	11.9	9.9	-3.1	3.3	8.8
Uganda	..	-47.3	-25.6	-6.9	-13.1	-46.7	-49.4	-61.3	-48.9	-18.5	..	..	-23.3	-44.5
Zaire	-23.6	-17.3	-15.9	-32.0	-21.2	1.8	-14.1	-33.8	-31.1	-26.5	..	-34.5	-18.0	-26.4
Zambia	-4.6	-4.9	-5.4	-8.0	-4.6	-8.9	-14.4	-19.6	-26.1	..	..	-7.9	-6.1	-20.0
Zimbabwe	-0.9	-3.7	-1.5	-11.5	-9.3	0.5	-4.7	-3.1	1.5	-3.4	-6.1	-5.7	-4.4	-3.2
NORTH AFRICA														
Algeria	-6.2	-10.3	-3.7	-3.0	-5.0	-7.0	-6.6	-2.3	-0.9	..	..	-8.0	-5.9	-3.2
Egypt, Arab Republic of	-8.0	1.5	-1.6	-2.7	-3.4	0.8	-8.8	-5.6	-4.0	-6.0	-2.4	-3.4	-2.2	-5.3
Libya	..	..	..	..	..	..	..	..	..	..	..	-2.5	..	..
Morocco	-3.1	-5.8	-3.2	0.7	-4.8	0.7	-0.2	5.6	6.0	..	..	-4.5	-2.6	3.8
Tunisia	-3.9	-1.8	-5.9	-1.8	-1.3	1.1	3.3	1.9	2.7	..	..	-1.4	-2.3	2.6
ALL AFRICA														
South Africa	-6.4	-0.6	-0.3	4.9	8.3	-2.8	-7.7	-5.7	1.5	2.9	3.2	-4.0	0.5	-1.2

Note: Real discount rate in each year is the nominal discount rate deflated by the annual change in the CPI.

4–8. Commercial bank lending rate

	Percent											Average		
	1980	1981	1982	1983	1984	1985	1986	1987	1988	1989	1990	75–79	80–85	86–MR
SUB-SAHARAN AFRICA	10.7	12.0	12.3	13.2	13.1	13.4	13.0	12.0	12.7	12.5	12.9	—	12.2	12.8
excluding Nigeria	10.8	12.0	12.0	13.0	13.0	13.0	13.0	12.0	12.7	12.5	12.5	9.3	12.3	12.8
Angola	..	..	..	..	..	..	..	..	..	..	..	..	..	..
Benin	9.4	10.0	11.5	10.5	10.0	10.0	8.8	8.0	7.1	8.8	..	7.5	10.2	8.2
Botswana	8.5	9.6	24.2	13.4	12.0	11.5	11.0	10.0	7.8	7.7	7.9	..	13.2	8.9
Burkina Faso	9.4	10.0	11.5	10.5	10.0	10.0	8.8	8.0	7.3	8.8	..	7.5	10.2	8.2
Burundi	12.0	12.0	12.0	12.0	12.0	12.0	12.0	12.0	12.0	..	..	12.0	12.0	12.0
Cameroon	13.0	13.0	13.0	14.5	14.5	14.5	13.5	13.0	13.5	14.0	..	..	13.8	13.5
Cape Verde	6.5	6.5	6.5	6.5	6.5	10.0	10.0	10.0	10.0	10.0	10.0	6.5	7.1	10.0
Central African Republic	10.5	12.0	12.0	12.5	12.5	12.5	12.0	11.4	12.3	12.5	..	9.0	12.0	12.1
Chad	11.0	11.0	11.0	11.5	11.5	11.5	11.0	10.5	10.8	11.5	..	9.5	11.3	11.0
Comoros	..	..	..	15.0	15.0	15.0	15.0	13.0	13.0	..	..	..	..	13.7
Congo, People's Republic of the	11.0	11.0	11.0	12.0	12.0	12.0	11.5	11.1	11.8	12.5	..	11.0	11.5	11.7
Cote d'Ivoire	9.4	10.0	11.5	10.5	10.0	10.0	8.8	8.0	7.1	8.8	..	7.5	10.2	8.2
Djibouti	..	..	..	..	..	..	..	..	..	..	..	..	..	..
Equatorial Guinea	..	..	..	..	..	15.0	14.5	13.0	15.5	15.5	..	..	..	14.6
Ethiopia	..	..	..	..	..	8.5	7.3	6.0	6.0	6.0	6.0	..	..	6.3
Gabon	12.5	12.5	12.5	13.0	13.0	12.7	11.5	11.1	11.8	12.5	..	9.5	12.7	11.7
Gambia, The	15.0	18.0	18.0	18.0	18.0	14.5	28.0	27.9	29.5	26.8	26.5	15.0	16.9	27.7
Ghana	19.0	19.0	19.0	19.0	21.2	21.2	20.0	25.5	25.6	..	..	19.0	19.7	23.7
Guinea	..	..	..	..	..	..	..	..	..	..	..	..	..	..
Guinea-Bissau	..	..	..	..	..	..	..	21.0	21.0	26.3	..	..	..	21.0
Kenya	10.6	12.4	14.5	15.8	14.4	14.0	14.0	14.0	15.0	17.3	18.8	10.0	13.6	15.8
Lesotho	11.0	15.0	17.0	15.4	17.6	19.7	13.4	11.1	13.7	18.8	20.4	..	16.0	15.5
Liberia	18.4	21.5	18.2	20.7	20.6	19.3	14.4	13.6	13.4	13.8	..	..	19.8	13.8
Madagascar	9.5	11.3	15.6	19.0	19.5	15.2	14.5	..	..	..	..	9.5	15.2	..
Malawi	16.7	18.5	18.5	18.3	16.5	18.4	19.0	19.5	22.3	23.0	21.0	..	17.8	21.0
Mali	9.4	10.0	11.5	10.5	10.0	10.0	8.8	8.0	6.6	8.8	..	7.5	10.2	8.1
Mauritania		12.0	12.0	12.0	12.0	12.0	12.0	12.0	12.0	..	..	..	10.0	12.0
Mauritius	..	12.2	13.4	15.1	13.3	13.8	14.3	14.1	15.0	16.1	18.0	..	11.3	15.5
Mozambique	..	..	..	..	..	..	..	..	..	..	..	..	..	..
Namibia	..	..	..	..	..	..	..	..	..	..	..	..	..	..
Niger	9.4	10.0	11.5	10.5	10.0	10.0	8.8	8.0	8.0	8.8	..	7.5	10.2	8.4
Nigeria	8.4	8.9	9.5	10.0	10.2	9.4	..	14.0	..	..	..	6.7	9.4	..
Rwanda	13.5	13.5	13.5	13.5	13.5	13.9	14.0	13.0	12.0	12.0	13.2	12.8	13.6	12.8
Sao Tome & Principe	..	..	..	..	..	..	..	..	..	..	..	..	..	..
Senegal	9.4	10.0	11.5	10.5	10.0	10.0	8.8	8.0	7.0	8.8	..	7.5	10.2	8.2
Seychelles	..	11.5	11.5	14.0	13.2	13.0	13.0	13.0	13.0	13.0	..	..	10.5	13.0
Sierra Leone	11.0	15.0	15.0	17.3	18.0	17.0	17.2	28.5	28.0	29.7	52.5	10.1	15.6	31.2
Somalia	7.5	10.0	11.5	12.0	12.0	19.0	20.6	22.0	33.7	..	..	7.1	12.0	25.4
Sudan	..	..	..	..	..	..	..	..	..	..	..	..	..	..
Swaziland	9.5	13.5	18.0	18.0	22.0	17.0	12.5	11.9	15.0	14.5	14.5	10.3	16.3	13.7
Tanzania	11.5	12.0	12.0	13.0	13.0	12.3	18.5	27.5	29.6	31.0	..	9.0	12.3	26.7
Togo	9.4	10.0	11.5	10.5	10.0	10.0	8.8	8.0	7.1	8.8	..	7.5	10.2	8.2
Uganda	10.8	12.5	14.5	16.2	21.9	24.0	33.3	34.7	35.0	40.0	38.7	..	16.7	36.3
Zaire	..	..	..	..	..	..	..	..	..	..	..	..	..	..
Zambia	9.5	9.5	9.5	13.0	14.5	18.6	27.4	21.2	18.4	..	..	8.3	12.4	22.3
Zimbabwe	17.5	19.4	23.0	23.1	23.0	17.2	13.0	13.0	13.0	13.0	11.7	17.5	20.5	12.7
NORTH AFRICA	7.2	7.6	7.8	7.8	7.8	8.7	9.0	10.1	9.5	18.3	19.0	7.2	7.8	9.5
Algeria	..	..	..	..	..	..	..	..	..	..	..	..	..	..
Egypt, Arab Republic of	13.3	15.0	15.0	15.0	15.0	15.0	15.0	16.3	17.0	18.3	19.0	9.8	14.7	17.1
Libya	7.0	7.0	7.0	7.0	7.0	7.0	7.0	7.0	7.0	..	..	7.0	7.0	7.0
Morocco	7.0	7.0	7.0	7.0	7.0	7.8	8.8	9.0	9.0	..	..	7.0	7.1	8.9
Tunisia	7.3	8.1	8.5	8.5	8.5	9.6	9.2	11.1	9.9	..	..	7.3	8.4	10.1
ALL AFRICA	10.6	11.8	12.0	13.0	12.8	12.6	12.5	12.0	12.2	12.8	13.2	9.0	12.0	12.4
South Africa	9.5	14.0	19.3	16.7	22.3	21.5	14.3	12.5	15.3	19.8	21.0	11.7	17.2	16.6

Notes: Group data are medians of individual country values in each year or period.

4–9. Commercial bank deposit rate

	Percent											Average		
	1980	*1981*	*1982*	*1983*	*1984*	*1985*	*1986*	*1987*	*1988*	*1989*	*1990*	*75–79*	*80–85*	*86–MR*
SUB-SAHARAN AFRICA	6.2	7.2	7.8	7.5	7.6	9.0	8.1	7.5	8.0	8.0	8.4	5.9	7.5	7.5
excluding Nigeria	6.2	7.3	7.8	7.5	7.5	8.7	8.1	7.4	8.0	8.0	8.4	6.0	7.5	7.4
Angola	..	..	..	..	..	..	..	..	..	..	..	..	..	..
Benin	6.2	6.3	7.8	7.5	7.3	7.3	6.1	5.3	5.3	6.4	7.0	6.0	7.1	6.0
Botswana	5.0	8.7	10.8	11.9	10.0	9.0	8.7	7.5	5.0	5.6	6.1	..	9.2	6.6
Burkina Faso	6.2	6.3	7.8	7.5	7.3	7.3	6.1	5.3	5.3	6.4	7.0	6.0	7.1	6.0
Burundi	2.5	4.5	5.0	4.5	4.5	4.5	6.0	5.3	4.0	..	..	2.5	4.3	5.1
Cameroon	7.5	7.5	7.5	7.5	7.5	7.5	7.4	7.1	7.2	7.5	..	..	7.5	7.3
Cape Verde	..	..	..	..	..	4.0	4.0	4.0	4.0	4.0	4.0	..	..	4.0
Central African Republic	5.5	7.5	7.5	7.5	7.5	7.5	7.4	7.2	7.4	7.5	..	..	7.2	7.4
Chad	5.5	5.5	5.5	5.5	5.5	5.5	5.5	5.3	4.3	4.3	..	..	5.5	4.9
Comoros	..	..	..	7.5	7.5	7.5	7.5	6.5	6.5	..	..	..	..	6.8
Congo, People's Republic of the	6.5	6.5	6.5	7.5	7.5	8.3	8.1	7.8	7.8	8.0	..	5.7	7.1	7.9
Cote d'Ivoire	6.2	6.3	7.8	7.5	7.3	7.3	6.1	5.3	5.3	6.4	7.0	6.0	7.1	6.0
Djibouti	..	..	..	..	..	..	..	..	..	..	..	..	..	..
Equatorial Guinea	..	..	..	..	..	7.5	8.5	6.0	6.5	6.5	..	..	..	6.9
Ethiopia	..	..	..	..	..	6.0	6.4	6.7	6.7	6.7	2.4	..	..	5.8
Gabon	7.5	7.5	7.5	7.5	7.5	7.7	8.0	7.9	8.2	8.8	..	7.0	7.5	8.2
Gambia, The	5.0	8.5	8.5	8.5	9.0	9.8	16.1	15.8	*15.0*	*12.9*	10.8	5.0	8.2	14.1
Ghana	11.5	11.5	11.5	11.5	15.0	15.8	17.0	17.6	16.5	..	..	11.5	12.8	17.0
Guinea	..	..	..	..	..	..	..	..	..	..	..	..	..	..
Guinea-Bissau	..	..	..	..	17.0	17.0	17.0	24.3	28.0	37.9	..	..	..	26.8
Kenya	5.8	8.8	12.2	13.3	11.8	11.3	11.3	10.3	10.3	12.0	13.7	5.1	10.5	11.5
Lesotho	..	9.6	11.8	9.4	..	10.4	10.0	7.0	9.6	12.8	13.0	..	..	10.5
Liberia	10.3	11.5	10.2	10.3	9.8	9.3	7.3	5.9	5.4	6.8	..	..	10.2	6.4
Madagascar	5.6	7.4	8.7	11.2	12.8	12.3	11.5	11.5	11.5	..	..	5.5	9.7	6.9
Malawi	7.9	9.8	9.8	9.9	11.8	12.5	12.8	14.3	13.5	12.8	12.1	..	10.3	13.1
Mali	6.2	6.3	7.8	7.5	7.3	7.3	6.1	5.3	5.3	6.4	7.0	6.0	7.1	6.0
Mauritania	..	5.5	5.5	5.5	5.5	7.2	6.6	6.0	6.0	..	..	..	4.9	6.2
Mauritius	..	9.3	11.1	12.1	10.3	9.5	9.5	9.4	10.0	11.1	12.6	..	10.5	10.5
Mozambique	..	..	..	..	..	..	..	..	..	..	..	..	..	..
Namibia	..	..	..	..	..	..	..	..	..	..	..	..	..	..
Niger	6.2	6.3	7.8	7.5	7.3	7.3	6.1	5.3	5.3	6.4	7.0	6.0	7.1	6.0
Nigeria	5.3	5.7	7.6	7.4	8.3	9.1	9.2	13.1	..	..	..	3.4	7.2	11.2
Rwanda	6.3	6.3	6.3	6.3	6.3	6.3	6.3	6.3	6.3	6.3	6.9	..	6.3	6.4
Sao Tome & Principe	3.0	3.0	3.0	3.0	3.0	..	..	..	..	..	..	3.0	2.5	..
Senegal	6.2	6.3	7.8	7.5	7.3	7.3	6.1	5.3	5.3	6.4	7.0	6.0	7.1	6.0
Seychelles	..	9.0	9.0	9.1	9.5	9.6	10.0	10.0	10.0	10.0	..	..	9.2	10.0
Sierra Leone	9.2	10.0	10.0	11.0	12.0	11.3	14.2	12.7	16.3	20.0	40.5	..	10.6	20.7
Somalia	4.5	5.5	7.5	8.5	8.5	14.0	15.3	16.3	20.6	25.0	..	4.0	8.1	19.3
Sudan	6.0	8.6	10.5	13.5	13.5	..	..	..	..	..	..	..	8.7	..
Swaziland	*4.5*	9.0	12.0	12.5	16.5	10.2	5.8	4.8	9.2	8.9	8.9	7.0	10.8	7.5
Tanzania	4.0	4.0	4.0	4.0	4.0	4.5	8.5	15.8	17.5	17.0	..	4.0	4.1	14.7
Togo	6.2	6.3	7.8	7.5	7.3	7.3	6.1	5.3	5.3	6.4	7.0	6.0	7.1	6.0
Uganda	6.8	7.2	9.0	10.7	16.0	19.0	30.0	27.5	26.0	36.2	35.0	..	11.5	30.9
Zaire	..	..	..	..	..	..	..	..	..	..	..	..	..	..
Zambia	7.0	6.2	6.0	7.0	7.7	15.3	17.7	13.2	11.4	..	..	5.7	8.2	14.1
Zimbabwe	3.5	7.5	14.5	12.8	10.3	10.0	10.3	9.6	9.7	8.9	8.8	3.6	9.8	9.5
NORTH AFRICA	5.0	5.8	6.0	6.0	6.0	6.8	7.7	7.9	8.0	..	..	4.3	5.9	7.8
Algeria	..	..	..	..	..	..	..	..	..	..	..	..	..	..
Egypt, Arab Republic of	8.3	10.0	11.0	11.0	11.0	11.0	11.0	11.0	11.0	11.7	12.0	5.2	10.4	11.3
Libya	5.1	5.5	5.5	5.5	5.5	5.5	5.5	5.5	5.5	..	..	4.0	5.4	5.5
Morocco	4.9	6.0	6.4	6.5	6.5	8.0	8.5	8.5	8.5	..	..	4.5	6.4	8.5
Tunisia	2.5	4.0	4.5	4.5	4.5	5.4	6.8	7.2	7.4	..	..	2.5	4.2	7.1
ALL AFRICA	6.2	6.9	7.8	7.5	7.5	8.2	8.1	7.4	8.0	8.4	8.8	5.7	7.5	7.4
South Africa	5.5	8.2	13.0	13.7	18.3	17.0	11.0	8.7	13.5	18.1	18.9	7.2	12.6	14.0

Note: Group data are medians of individual country values in each year or period.

Technical Notes

The data for domestic credit, central money supply, and bank discount rates are from the *IFS*.

Table 4-1. Domestic credit

Domestic credit includes all domestic assets of the banking system; it is the sum of the claims on the central government (net), on state and local governments, on nonfinancial public enterprises, on the private sector, and on other financial institutions (line 32 of the *IFS*). Domestic credit is made up of credit to the private sector and credit to the government.

Table 4-2. Credit to the private sector

Credit to the private sector is taken from line 32d of the *IFS*. Excessive credit to the government can easily crowd out credit to the private sector.

Table 4-3. Credit to the government

This is taken from line 32an of the *IFS*. Negative numbers for net claims on the central government indicate that government is a net depositor to the banking system. The government's financial position with the monetary system is always presented on a net basis because its recourse to the monetary system cannot always be analyzed meaningfully in terms of liquidity preferences or by considering debtor and creditor positions separately.

Movements in net claims on the central government (that is, claims or credits less government deposits) indicate the impact of government operations on the liquidity of the rest of the economy.

Table 4-4. Net foreign assets (*IFS* line 31n)

As with credit to the government, the financial position of the foreign sector with the monetary system is also presented on a net basis for the same reason noted above. Movements in the net foreign assets (that is, foreign assets less foreign liabilities) indicate the direct monetary impact of a country's transactions with the rest of the world.

Table 4-5. Growth of money supply

This is the annual percentage change in money (M1), defined as the sum of currency outside of banks and demand deposits other than those of the central government (line 34 of the *IFS*). This is a liability of the monetary system. The liability side of the monetary survey is completed by addition of quasi-money (*IFS* line 35) which includes time, savings and foreign currency deposits and other net balancing items (line 37r). Apart from net foreign assets, money supply and its components have been presented not in level form, but as growth rates. This is because the important consideration from the point of view of macroeconomic stability is not the stock of money per se, but the rate of growth of money stock.

Table 4-6. Discount rate

The discount rate reported here is the nominal interest rate at which the monetary authorities lend to (or discount eligible paper from) deposit money banks (line 60 of the *IFS*).

Table 4-7. Real discount rate

This is computed from Table 4-6 using the formula:

$$\{[1+(i/100)]/[1+(\pi/100)]-1\}*100$$

where i is nominal interest rate and π is inflation rate based on the CPI.

Table 4-8. Commercial bank lending rate (*IFS* line 60p)

Bank lending rate is the rate charged borrowers by commercial banks for short and medium term use of funds.

Table 4-9. Commercial bank deposit rate (*IFS* line 60*l*)

Deposit rate is the rate paid depositors on time, saving, and demand deposits by deposit money banks and similiar financial institutions.

Group data in this section are for the most part medians of the individual country values in each year, or simple arithmetic averages.

5

___

External Sector

The external sector provides data on economic and financial relations between African countries and the rest of the world, with detailed accounting of commodity trade, one of the principal components of the current account within the balance of payments framework. Commodity trade and price data can also provide a partial basis for analyzing Africa's constraints and performance in the international marketplace, including its terms of trade. Commodity exports are a major source of foreign exchange. Other sources of foreign exchange include receipts from factor and nonfactor services, borrowing from abroad, incoming foreign investent, and foreign transfers and grants.

The balance of payments is a system of accounts, covering a given period, that is intended to record systematically: flows of real resources, including the services of the original factors of production, between the domestic economy of a country and the rest of the world; changes in the country's foreign assets and liabilities that arise from economic transactions; and transfer payments, which are the counterpart of real resources or financial claims provided to, or received from, the rest of the world that carry no provision for repayment.

The tables provide gross entries for goods and services and net entries for unrequited transfers (official and private) and other financial flows; a table for current account balance as traditionally defined — with transfers above the line — is also shown. The information is presented for broad aggregates; fuller detail can be found in the IMF's *Balance of Payments Statistics* publications.

Unit values for exports (f.o.b.) and imports (c.i.f.) measure changes in the aggregate price level of a country's merchandise exports and imports over time. Unit values reflect average price changes for broad groups of commodities, rather than for any single commodity. The terms of trade indicate relative movements in export and import unit values (here, they are based on merchandise trade only). If the prices of exports rise while the prices of imports rise more slowly, stay constant, or decline, the same quantity of exports "buys" a bigger quantity of imports. The effect of such price changes is equivalent to an increase in the real value of output — or increased productivity in value terms — of the export sector. Were import prices to rise more quickly than export prices, the reverse would be true. Export figures for specific commodities show physical quantities rather than value in either current or constant prices. Most of the key nonagricultural primary commodities are exported from a few countries with substantial mineral resources.   Variations in export prices and earnings for the five major oil-exporting countries in Sub-Saharan Africa — which in the 1980s have accounted for about half of Sub-Saharan export earnings — have dominated trends in this region as a whole.

5–1. Merchandise exports, f.o.b.

	Millions of U.S. dollars (current prices and exchange rates)											Average annual percentage growth		
	1980	1981	1982	1983	1984	1985	1986	1987	1988	1989	1990	75–80	80–85	86–MR
SUB-SAHARAN AFRICA	48,743	38,662	31,272	29,298	32,672	33,530	27,026	29,573	29,689	31,933	..	..	-6.7	5.2
excluding Nigeria	22,815	20,547	19,109	18,954	20,813	20,416	21,011	22,029	22,792	24,063	..	..	-1.5	4.5
Angola	..	..	1,714	1,959	2,205	2,301	1,346	2,322	2,492	..	..	..	..	36.1
Benin	222	184	144	176	170	301	304	364	377	218	264	13.8	4.3	-7.7
Botswana	545	401	461	640	678	728	852	1,587	1,469	1,820	1,753	32.1	10.0	17.1
Burkina Faso	161	159	126	113	141	136	149	230	249	216	304	16.8	-3.7	14.6
Burundi	66	75	88	81	88	114	129	98	124	93	73	15.5	9.2	-11.4
Cameroon	1,418	1,763	1,617	1,830	2,080	2,337	2,293	1,827	1,645	1,807	1,909	25.4	9.3	-3.7
Cape Verde	9	6	4	3	7	6	5	12	5	11	13	..	-5.2	19.7
Central African Republic	147	118	124	123	114	131	129	127	134	148	151	21.3	-1.9	4.7
Chad	71	83	58	78	110	62	99	109	146	155	193	1.6	1.3	18.5
Comoros	11	16	20	19	7	16	20	12	21	18	17	..	-2.4	0.9
Congo, People's Republic of the	911	1,073	1,109	1,066	1,268	1,145	673	877	843	1,155	1,350	30.9	4.7	18.2
Cote d'Ivoire	3,013	2,435	2,347	2,066	2,625	2,761	3,187	2,950	2,774	2,808	3,120	18.3	-1.0	-0.9
Djibouti	..	..	..	..	27	30	32	40	42	41	..	..	..	8.0
Equatorial Guinea	15	16	15	18	21	24	35	38	45	33	37	..	10.6	-0.2
Ethiopia	459	411	376	392	449	359	446	384	374	436	337	13.6	-2.6	-4.3
Gabon	2,084	2,200	2,160	2,000	2,018	1,951	1,074	1,286	1,196	1,626	2,471	12.7	-1.9	20.9
Gambia, The	48	45	59	55	91	63	65	75	83	100	111	-1.3	10.0	14.6
Ghana	1,104	711	607	439	566	632	773	827	881	807	891	7.5	-10.3	2.6
Guinea	500	493	444	501	511	514	603	628	603	721	841	..	1.0	8.4
Guinea-Bissau	..	..	12	9	17	12	10	15	16	14	19	..	..	13.8
Kenya	1,261	1,081	936	927	1,034	943	1,170	909	1,017	926	1,010	12.9	-4.5	-2.7
Lesotho	58	45	37	31	28	22	25	47	64	66	59	34.6	-16.6	22.8
Liberia	600	529	477	421	447	430	408	375	..	..	..	7.9	-6.4	..
Madagascar	436	332	327	310	337	291	323	327	284	313	304	8.3	-5.6	-1.6
Malawi	281	273	240	246	312	245	248	278	297	283	344	13.2	-0.7	6.9
Mali	205	154	146	167	192	176	206	256	251	269	345	19.6	0.1	11.4
Mauritania	196	270	240	315	294	372	419	402	438	448	432	-0.3	11.2	1.7
Mauritius	434	327	366	368	374	433	675	891	998	993	1,186	8.7	1.2	13.1
Mozambique	281	281	229	132	96	77	79	97	103	104	127	..	-25.4	10.6
Namibia	..	..	..	..	..	..	..	..	..	..	..	..	..	..
Niger	576	485	381	335	303	259	332	412	369	311	312	35.5	-14.6	-3.9
Nigeria	25,929	18,115	12,163	10,344	11,859	13,115	6,015	7,545	6,897	7,870	13,585	22.2	-12.9	18.2
Rwanda	134	113	108	124	143	126	184	121	118	105	103	18.1	1.5	-12.3
Sao Tome & Principe	17	7	9	9	12	7	10	7	10	5	4	25.3	-7.7	-18.0
Senegal	422	561	502	606	598	515	657	673	763	778	847	-4.5	4.0	6.7
Seychelles	6	5	4	5	5	5	4	8	17	14	15	6.4	-1.5	34.5
Sierra Leone	213	152	110	107	133	132	126	139	104	112	142	13.5	-7.8	0.2
Somalia	133	175	171	98	55	91	95	94	58	61	58	9.8	-15.7	-13.1
Sudan	594	538	432	581	722	595	497	482	486	550	443	4.7	3.5	-1.0
Swaziland	368	388	324	304	231	177	278	424	466	486	557	11.7	-14.0	16.5
Tanzania	583	613	413	383	399	328	336	347	386	415	434	7.2	-11.4	7.2
Togo	476	378	345	274	291	282	362	403	325	331	396	26.3	-9.9	-0.2
Uganda	319	229	347	368	381	381	382	341	293	249	194	4.6	7.3	-15.4
Zaire	2,269	1,678	1,601	1,686	1,919	1,853	1,844	1,731	2,178	2,201	2,138	22.6	-1.6	5.5
Zambia	1,457	996	942	923	893	797	692	852	1,189	1,340	1,254	11.6	-9.2	17.8
Zimbabwe	1,445	1,451	1,312	1,154	1,174	1,120	1,323	1,452	1,665	1,590	1,633	8.4	-5.7	5.3
NORTH AFRICA	22,078	22,847	21,376	20,391	20,688	20,807	15,815	16,175	16,901	18,691	..	20.4	-1.8	5.6
Algeria	13,652	14,117	13,509	12,742	12,792	13,034	8,065	9,029	7,620	9,534	12,964	23.5	-1.7	10.6
Egypt, Arab Republic of	3,854	3,999	3,847	3,740	3,958	3,928	3,577	2,264	3,274	2,914	3,390	17.1	0.1	1.5
Libya	21,919	14,731	13,701	12,348	11,028	10,353	5,814	5,828	5,644	7,283	11,362	25.3	-12.6	16.9
Morocco	2,414	2,283	2,043	2,058	2,161	2,145	2,410	2,781	3,608	3,312	4,210	11.3	-2.1	13.8
Tunisia	2,158	2,448	1,977	1,850	1,776	1,700	1,763	2,101	2,399	2,931	3,515	22.8	-6.1	18.7
ALL AFRICA	70,822	61,509	52,648	49,689	53,360	54,338	42,841	45,749	46,590	50,624	..	19.0	-5.0	5.3
South Africa	25,698	20,632	17,328	18,241	16,948	16,244	18,330	21,088	22,432	22,399	23,383	25.9	-7.8	5.6

5-2. Merchandise imports, f.o.b.

	Millions of U.S. dollars (current prices and exchange rates)											Average annual percentage growth		
	1980	1981	1982	1983	1984	1985	1986	1987	1988	1989	1990	75–80	80–85	86–MR
SUB-SAHARAN AFRICA	40,287	43,908	37,624	31,213	28,217	26,493	24,747	27,013	28,974	28,944	..	..	-9.8	6.2
excluding Nigeria	25,534	24,961	22,730	19,780	19,350	18,994	21,045	22,916	24,703	25,252	..	..	-6.6	6.4
Angola	..	..	1,274	1,135	1,559	1,402	1,086	1,303	1,372	..	..	..	..	12.4
Benin	499	522	576	251	266	327	403	464	508	317	428	17.1	-13.2	-2.6
Botswana	603	687	580	615	583	494	608	804	987	1,185	1,606	29.2	-4.0	26.2
Burkina Faso	368	348	360	309	270	353	437	475	487	502	593	16.6	-3.2	6.9
Burundi	168	161	214	184	184	150	165	159	166	151	189	25.6	-0.9	2.2
Cameroon	1,452	1,611	1,285	1,166	1,195	1,088	1,477	1,734	1,484	1,275	1,372	24.6	-6.7	-4.5
Cape Verde	80	86	97	105	82	87	86	93	102	110	122	..	1.0	9.1
Central African Republic	185	145	150	138	140	168	201	198	178	186	212	18.1	-1.9	0.4
Chad	55	81	82	99	128	166	212	226	228	240	263	-15.1	22.4	5.0
Comoros	22	25	25	29	33	28	29	44	44	36	43	..	6.2	6.1
Congo, People's Republic of the	545	804	664	650	618	630	512	420	523	503	425	15.2	-0.3	-1.9
Cote d'Ivoire	2,614	2,068	1,790	1,635	1,487	1,410	1,640	1,864	1,696	1,720	1,701	22.0	-11.2	-0.1
Djibouti	..	..	..	..	239	219	207	222	239	249	..	..	..	6.5
Equatorial Guinea	58	49	50	27	36	25	27	48	57	44	63	..	-15.1	17.4
Ethiopia	692	744	848	856	1,026	975	1,087	1,081	1,099	1,034	890	22.5	8.0	-4.3
Gabon	686	841	723	725	733	855	979	732	791	752	760	4.4	2.0	-4.7
Gambia, The	138	129	94	90	99	75	85	95	106	125	141	22.1	-10.5	13.8
Ghana	908	954	589	500	533	669	713	952	993	1,002	1,199	6.0	-9.4	11.5
Guinea	339	426	378	366	407	396	462	491	592	577	664	..	1.8	9.3
Guinea-Bissau	..	..	62	58	60	60	51	45	59	69	68	..	..	10.5
Kenya	2,345	1,834	1,468	1,198	1,348	1,270	1,455	1,623	1,802	1,963	2,009	23.9	-11.3	8.7
Lesotho	424	449	447	483	433	324	342	452	559	593	621	21.6	-3.9	15.8
Liberia	478	424	390	375	325	264	259	312	..	..	..	9.7	-10.3	..
Madagascar	764	511	452	378	360	336	331	315	319	314	461	22.9	-14.1	6.8
Malawi	308	244	214	216	162	177	154	178	253	302	325	10.8	-10.8	22.5
Mali	308	269	233	241	258	328	339	335	359	339	432	23.3	0.6	5.1
Mauritania	321	386	427	378	302	334	401	359	349	349	402	6.5	-1.9	-0.2
Mauritius	516	478	397	386	416	459	617	908	1,166	1,204	1,466	13.9	-2.9	22.3
Mozambique	720	721	752	573	486	381	488	592	694	761	796	..	-12.4	13.1
Namibia	..	..	..	..	..	..	..	..	..	..	..	..	..	..
Niger	677	592	515	332	270	346	310	410	392	369	433	37.2	-16.1	5.8
Nigeria	14,753	18,946	14,894	11,433	8,867	7,499	3,702	4,097	4,271	3,692	4,932	20.5	-15.6	4.8
Rwanda	196	207	215	198	198	219	259	267	279	254	228	19.0	1.0	-3.0
Sao Tome & Principe	15	22	27	18	24	20	23	14	14	13	13	15.6	3.0	-11.1
Senegal	875	1,020	815	917	819	796	883	943	1,010	1,004	1,059	7.0	-2.9	4.4
Seychelles	84	79	83	74	74	84	89	96	135	140	158	23.6	-0.8	16.4
Sierra Leone	386	282	260	133	150	141	111	115	138	174	177	22.2	-19.5	14.4
Somalia	402	371	471	362	466	331	334	350	234	352	211	25.5	-1.6	-8.7
Sudan	1,339	1,540	1,544	1,350	1,206	981	897	707	1,040	1,040	880	9.8	-6.7	3.5
Swaziland	537	502	438	464	371	272	296	369	441	515	632	31.7	-11.5	20.3
Tanzania	1,089	1,061	952	708	760	869	913	1,000	1,033	1,070	1,290	13.7	-6.7	7.9
Togo	524	414	408	292	263	304	419	444	353	344	502	25.2	-11.9	1.1
Uganda	318	278	338	343	386	392	447	530	597	616	567	6.6	6.0	6.5
Zaire	1,519	1,421	1,297	1,213	1,176	1,247	1,283	1,376	1,645	1,683	1,539	3.5	-4.5	5.8
Zambia	1,114	1,065	1,004	711	612	571	518	585	687	774	977	3.1	-14.2	16.8
Zimbabwe	1,339	1,534	1,472	1,070	989	919	1,012	1,071	1,164	1,319	1,518	9.5	-9.6	10.7
NORTH AFRICA	33,686	39,827	36,235	33,587	34,397	31,161	28,013	26,637	30,124	34,221	38,465	15.0	-2.6	9.3
Algeria	9,596	10,088	9,889	9,516	9,235	8,811	7,879	6,616	6,675	8,372	8,777	13.8	-2.1	4.6
Egypt, Arab Republic of	6,814	7,918	8,418	8,869	10,201	10,516	9,525	7,952	9,841	10,201	10,632	11.1	8.9	4.8
Libya	10,368	14,563	10,976	8,978	8,464	5,754	4,434	5,391	5,753	6,517	7,582	20.5	-12.7	13.5
Morocco	3,770	3,840	3,815	3,301	3,569	3,513	3,477	3,850	4,360	4,991	6,282	10.5	-2.0	15.5
Tunisia	3,139	3,418	3,137	2,923	2,929	2,567	2,698	2,829	3,496	4,139	5,193	20.1	-4.3	18.4
ALL AFRICA	73,973	83,735	73,859	64,801	62,613	57,653	52,759	53,650	59,098	63,165	70,764	16.3	-6.2	7.8
South Africa	18,268	20,622	16,683	14,202	14,774	10,402	11,130	13,925	17,210	16,810	17,045	13.8	-10.7	11.0

5–3. Exports of total services

	Millions of U.S. dollars (current prices and exchange rates)											Average annual percentage growth		
	1980	1981	1982	1983	1984	1985	1986	1987	1988	1989	1990	75–80	80–85	86–MR
SUB-SAHARAN AFRICA	7,038	6,799	5,431	5,029	4,937	4,862	5,308	6,136	6,626	..	..	..	-7.9	11.7
excluding Nigeria	5,217	5,178	4,697	4,519	4,446	4,466	5,010	5,866	6,222	..	..	..	-3.6	11.4
Angola	..	..	..	..	..	..	..	..	..	..	..	..	..	..
Benin	77	77	59	55	66	77	99	112	119	..	..	17.9	-1.6	9.4
Botswana	203	203	185	196	200	161	217	297	330	355	497	16.6	-3.2	20.2
Burkina Faso	65	50	57	44	34	37	52	49	49	53	65	25.1	-11.3	5.4
Burundi	17	19	23	24	22	15	14	15	15	24	25	33.7	-0.5	18.1
Cameroon	410	455	416	430	508	531	615	424	473	..	..	25.3	4.9	-12.3
Cape Verde	14	20	29	35	25	27	36	45	44	56	..	..	12.9	14.1
Central African Republic	58	60	47	39	38	53	59	71	..	..	..	14.2	-5.6	..
Chad	0	4	4	29	38	38	48	73	81	44	..	-57.2	146.5	-1.9
Comoros	3	2	4	4	4	5	8	16	19	22	22	..	13.9	25.4
Congo, People's Republic of the	119	101	97	93	87	84	111	128	100	90	..	14.2	-6.1	-8.4
Cote d'Ivoire	627	480	497	472	408	438	539	614	628	529	564	21.7	-6.4	-0.6
Djibouti	..	..	..	..	..	..	..	..	..	..	..	..	..	..
Equatorial Guinea	..	..	..	..	..	..	6	6	6	..	..	..	..	..
Ethiopia	129	154	166	184	182	212	138	319	289	286	..	1.3	9.3	23.3
Gabon	349	333	190	218	186	168	142	131	228	308	164	24.2	-14.0	12.2
Gambia, The	18	20	25	27	28	24	29	50	64	68	71	12.0	7.6	23.6
Ghana	110	121	107	39	46	44	45	79	78	82	93	0.2	-21.7	16.0
Guinea	..	..	..	..	..	..	..	..	..	..	..	..	..	..
Guinea-Bissau	..	..	6	7	8	7	..	..	..	..	..	..	..	..
Kenya	800	717	694	598	629	663	732	830	874	1,008	1,223	16.1	-4.1	13.0
Lesotho	305	336	388	423	368	260	289	392	417	413	484	16.4	-1.2	11.5
Liberia	13	12	35	40	40	38	59	58	..	..	..	10.4	30.1	..
Madagascar	82	66	55	48	58	63	80	105	132	146	..	7.9	-5.0	22.3
Malawi	34	45	35	37	38	38	28	44	38	..	..	-7.5	0.2	16.6
Mali	58	46	44	42	41	59	71	87	88	78	95	25.3	-1.0	4.8
Mauritania	73	69	66	39	36	31	26	37	39	39	..	28.5	-17.5	13.7
Mauritius	145	182	145	140	133	148	217	332	404	454	567	15.9	-2.5	25.0
Mozambique	171	179	171	166	118	107	113	..	..	..	..	..	-9.8	..
Namibia	..	..	..	..	..	..	..	..	..	..	..	..	..	..
Niger	68	58	59	52	45	57	40	61	50	58	..	15.1	-4.9	9.3
Nigeria	1,820	1,621	734	511	491	396	298	270	404	704	1,265	18.0	-28.2	46.9
Rwanda	49	63	49	37	40	44	53	56	57	52	47	49.7	-6.0	-3.2
Sao Tome & Principe	6	4	3	2	2	2	4	2	2	5	4	68.4	-16.5	11.4
Senegal	409	442	402	367	318	341	420	490	505	477	..	18.7	-5.5	4.3
Seychelles	97	93	81	79	97	114	125	148	168	190	230	30.8	2.7	15.8
Sierra Leone	63	52	38	35	41	28	27	44	52	..	..	25.0	-12.7	39.8
Somalia	71	80	85	79	52	37	54	..	..	..	..	20.3	-12.4	..
Sudan	231	225	250	250	230	220	225	192	172	280	41	21.3	-0.5	-26.2
Swaziland	82	110	87	108	115	95	102	148	179	199	258	14.7	3.1	24.0
Tanzania	179	196	117	108	107	108	110	102	121	123	140	7.4	-11.8	7.0
Togo	95	113	105	87	94	111	131	133	162	159	197	22.5	0.1	10.5
Uganda	11	45	35	17	41	27	25	..	..	..	..	0.8	9.6	..
Zaire	135	151	84	116	141	153	189	262	185	165	171	-10.1	2.2	-6.4
Zambia	168	173	137	102	80	71	48	49	61	87	..	16.0	-18.0	21.9
Zimbabwe	274	228	262	215	195	333	205	198	208	..	..	15.0	0.9	0.6
NORTH AFRICA	6,938	7,380	6,995	6,784	7,097	6,932	7,636	8,328	10,112	11,118	14,473	21.3	-0.4	17.0
Algeria	848	955	856	866	778	722	721	675	542	607	571	20.3	-4.0	-5.6
Egypt, Arab Republic of	2,590	2,651	3,077	3,104	3,724	3,657	4,137	4,130	4,982	6,617	9,221	23.8	8.2	23.1
Libya	1,446	1,790	1,031	837	720	526	629	845	889	566	784	27.2	-20.4	0.4
Morocco	856	801	902	873	855	1,015	1,165	1,411	1,798	1,700	2,111	13.2	2.9	14.7
Tunisia	1,198	1,183	1,129	1,103	1,020	1,011	984	1,267	1,901	1,629	1,785	20.0	-3.7	15.5
ALL AFRICA	13,976	14,180	12,426	11,813	12,034	11,793	12,944	14,464	16,738	17,672	20,696	18.4	-3.9	12.1
South Africa	3,560	3,530	3,236	3,200	3,049	2,606	2,726	3,110	3,244	3,544	4,195	14.5	-5.6	10.4

5-4. Imports of total services

| | Millions of U.S. dollars (current prices and exchange rates) | | | | | | | | | | | Average annual percentage growth | | |
	1980	1981	1982	1983	1984	1985	1986	1987	1988	1989	1990	75-80	80-85	86-MR
SUB-SAHARAN AFRICA	19,944	19,029	16,897	15,240	14,799	15,520	15,953	18,812	19,303	..	..	..	-5.9	10.0
excluding Nigeria	12,653	12,633	12,038	11,859	11,757	12,330	13,820	15,050	16,090	..	..	..	-1.0	7.9
Angola	..	..	..	..	..	..	..	..	..	..	..	..	..	..
Benin	116	153	163	144	149	153	196	229	239	..	..	13.9	3.5	10.3
Botswana	351	261	233	350	399	353	401	590	792	712	782	27.4	5.0	16.5
Burkina Faso	228	204	193	163	139	146	181	213	235	237	273	21.8	-9.7	9.7
Burundi	47	63	78	106	96	109	126	163	141	119	123	20.9	18.0	-3.5
Cameroon	774	1,065	1,083	1,145	1,185	1,104	1,220	1,471	1,416	..	..	22.0	6.3	7.8
Cape Verde	8	20	19	20	17	15	23	26	21	26	..	..	8.6	1.0
Central African Republic	144	97	119	117	99	122	157	176	..	..	..	18.4	-2.2	..
Chad	28	26	23	81	96	161	178	211	233	221	..	-20.3	48.8	7.7
Comoros	12	26	26	24	39	38	45	45	46	43	50	21.8	1.3
Congo, People's Republic of the	650	842	855	907	525	763	891	818	873	797	..	15.0	-1.6	-2.7
Cote d'Ivoire	2,147	1,780	1,709	1,539	1,355	1,469	2,028	2,309	2,373	2,369	2,653	26.3	-7.7	5.8
Djibouti	..	..	..	..	..	..	..	..	..	..	..	..	..	..
Equatorial Guinea	..	..	..	..	..	..	..	47	57	50	..	..	..	..
Ethiopia	204	212	229	263	272	162	172	366	403	379	167	6.1	-0.7	27.9
Gabon	1,240	1,223	1,259	1,331	1,290	1,331	1,147	1,143	1,090	1,352	1,491	13.1	1.6	7.2
Gambia, The	44	44	48	48	26	19	22	64	63	66	65	28.9	-15.0	24.2
Ghana	355	381	316	224	280	284	344	376	400	408	429	4.5	-6.6	5.4
Guinea	..	..	..	..	..	..	..	..	..	..	..	..	..	..
Guinea-Bissau	..	..	21	18	26	31	31	33	37	49	35	..	..	..
Kenya	750	741	600	555	618	641	693	825	895	941	1,077	11.6	-3.9	10.7
Lesotho	58	64	62	63	56	45	57	76	84	91	104	19.3	-4.8	15.1
Liberia	97	80	166	264	222	211	264	263		..	..	16.1	23.7	..
Madagascar	357	316	301	293	306	300	366	410	443	475	..	18.4	-2.8	9.0
Malawi	330	278	226	244	273	267	254	244	230	..	..	37.2	-2.9	-4.8
Mali	229	201	187	194	192	282	332	355	372	353	434	16.2	2.8	5.5
Mauritania	172	199	222	249	225	298	330	306	307	252	..	5.9	9.7	-7.8
Mauritius	202	203	191	171	175	187	231	319	393	423	497	18.8	-2.7	19.9
Mozambique	130	173	201	210	179	217	259	..	..	..	..	..	8.1	..
Namibia	..	..	..	..	..	..	..	..	..	..	..	..	..	..
Niger	339	282	302	206	192	188	102	245	219	203	..	29.9	-12.0	21.5
Nigeria	7,291	6,395	4,859	3,381	3,042	3,190	2,132	3,762	3,212	3,918	4,877	11.7	-17.5	18.5
Rwanda	139	138	140	129	128	131	171	171	165	142	151	29.2	-1.7	-4.2
Sao Tome & Principe	7	8	11	9	11	10	14	9	9	9	9	23.5	8.8	-8.5
Senegal	462	611	532	516	508	501	658	720	761	720	..	13.6	-0.5	3.3
Seychelles	48	47	49	47	54	67	85	102	102	114	130	39.0	6.2	10.1
Sierra Leone	108	97	108	63	80	75	167	105	55	..	..	17.0	-8.0	-42.6
Somalia	139	149	139	124	137	123	130	180	165	206	..	14.2	-2.7	..
Sudan	343	489	568	597	748	773	859	323	341	496	178	11.0	16.6	-23.8
Swaziland	122	151	149	122	119	95	120	172	195	283	277	17.2	-6.1	24.2
Tanzania	323	284	221	191	264	309	328	420	471	479	481	16.5	-1.6	9.4
Togo	227	204	195	177	169	193	242	258	271	266	314	26.9	-4.2	5.7
Uganda	132	114	187	125	135	131	100	236	260	261	243	9.3	0.2	..
Zaire	1,364	1,256	1,129	1,114	1,292	1,193	1,286	1,412	1,558	1,569	1,549	6.4	-1.7	4.9
Zambia	872	761	612	575	478	667	553	553	893	915	..	11.3	-7.7	22.0
Zimbabwe	561	748	728	686	528	629	541	578	645	..	..	9.6	-1.5	9.1
NORTH AFRICA	14,770	16,168	16,473	15,896	16,894	16,073	14,720	12,046	13,288	15,007	16,849	23.6	1.5	5.0
Algeria	4,956	5,203	4,989	4,415	4,442	4,309	3,900	3,464	3,917	3,390	3,671	27.3	-3.6	-1.4
Egypt, Arab Republic of	3,147	3,537	4,792	5,229	6,675	6,799	6,252	3,725	3,859	6,035	7,312	30.4	18.2	8.3
Libya	3,650	4,275	3,642	3,748	3,420	2,314	1,638	1,801	2,071	1,871	1,880	20.2	-8.0	3.2
Morocco	2,037	2,174	2,009	1,508	1,374	1,612	1,864	1,937	2,185	2,431	2,572	18.3	-7.8	9.1
Tunisia	980	978	1,041	996	983	1,039	1,067	1,119	1,256	1,280	1,415	17.3	0.7	7.3
ALL AFRICA	34,714	35,197	33,370	31,136	31,693	31,593	30,673	30,858	32,590	33,383	32,960	18.1	-2.4	2.2
South Africa	7,720	8,371	7,317	7,425	6,910	5,899	6,861	7,549	7,424	7,755	8,397	15.8	-5.3	4.4

5–5. Private transfers

	Millions of U.S. dollars (current prices and exchange rates)											Average		
	1980	1981	1982	1983	1984	1985	1986	1987	1988	1989	1990	75–79	80–85	86–MR
SUB-SAHARAN AFRICA	-1238	-622	-460	-260	5	372	378	291	662	561	793	-641	-367	537
excluding Nigeria	-828	-181	-72	115	306	626	486	310	695	579	807	-431	-6	575
Angola	..	..	27	24	28	21	141	52	33	..	..	0	..	..
Benin	107	127	100	24	38	62	80	81	82	66	70	41	76	76
Botswana	-1	-2	0	0	-7	-3	-3	7	-17	-31	-41	3	-2	-17
Burkina Faso	112	120	89	89	71	102	160	123	113	97	114	49	97	122
Burundi	4	5	2	3	3	10	8	7	10	9	10	3	5	9
Cameroon	3	11	-16	-3	-7	-33	-66	-133	-144	-83	-84	-17	-8	-102
Cape Verde	40	36	32	35	22	22	29	34	40	43	43	14	31	38
Central African Republic	-17	-14	-17	-15	-11	-12	-19	-24	-28	-25	-29	-11	-14	-25
Chad	-4	-1	-1	-3	-2	7	-5	-10	-17	-20	-13	-9	-1	-13
Comoros	0	0	-2	-2	-3	-1	-2	1	.3	3	3	0	-1	2
Congo, People's Republic of the	-64	-32	-47	-41	-45	-37	-41	-57	-57	-42	-42	-29	-45	-48
Cote d'Ivoire	-716	-495	-391	-320	-291	-279	-427	-501	-514	-470	-540	-371	-415	-490
Djibouti	0	0	0	0	-11	-12	-12	-12	-1	-1	-3	0	-4	-6
Equatorial Guinea	..	..	0	0	0	2	4	-3	-4	-2	8	0	..	1
Ethiopia	20	25	45	85	107	145	210	163	217	187	205	18	71	196
Gabon	-157	-93	-84	-95	-92	-109	-169	-148	-155	-135	-147	-78	-105	-151
Gambia, The	4	4	3	3	5	6	11	13	13	7	14	0	4	12
Ghana	-3	-4	-1	-2	21	33	72	202	172	202	202	1	7	170
Guinea	-3	0	0	0	0	0	-15	-38	-27	-48	-44	-1	0	-34
Guinea-Bissau	0	0	-14	-11	-5	-3	-2	-2	2	1	-2	0	-6	-1
Kenya	27	99	83	63	60	81	58	72	89	102	168	0	69	98
Lesotho	2	2	3	3	3	2	2	0	4	4	5	2	2	3
Liberia	-29	-30	-45	-39	-44	-28	-25	-21	0	..	..	-26	-36	..
Madagascar	-20	-16	-17	-9	-1	24	21	34	38	47	68	-19	-6	42
Malawi	13	12	12	8	12	11	13	14	15	99	98	3	11	48
Mali	40	32	25	23	21	47	46	37	45	51	63	22	31	49
Mauritania	-28	-18	-28	-27	-20	-21	-23	-21	-22	-25	-18	-25	-24	-22
Mauritius	10	12	14	16	19	22	30	41	72	68	82	5	16	59
Mozambique	-25	-29	-24	-20	-26	-25	-23	-25	53	58	64	0	-25	25
Namibia	0	0	0	0	0	0	0	0	0	..	..	0	0	..
Niger	-57	-52	-53	-49	-43	-59	-43	-50	-35	-40	-42	-29	-52	-42
Nigeria	-410	-442	-388	-374	-300	-254	-108	-19	-33	-19	-14	-211	-361	-39
Rwanda	-3	-3	5	6	2	4	7	7	11	8	6	0	2	8
Sao Tome & Principe	1	1	0	1	3	0	-1	0	0	0	0	0	1	0
Senegal	-20	-10	-5	-2	0	8	11	30	32	25	34	2	-5	26
Seychelles	-1	-3	-3	-3	-2	-1	-5	-2	-5	-5	-3	-1	-2	-4
Sierra Leone	8	9	5	3	8	2	2	0	0	3	5	4	6	2
Somalia	57	54	14	19	163	19	5	-13	6	-3	-4	24	54	-2
Sudan	209	305	350	415	395	430	350	250	445	293	188	157	351	305
Swaziland	-2	1	0	-2	0	3	2	4	2	0	-4	-1	0	1
Tanzania	22	23	25	19	63	236	251	230	232	182	428	19	65	265
Togo	1	-1	-2	-3	-2	8	10	7	8	12	14	-1	0	10
Uganda	-2	0	19	66	33	70	99	110	119	98	79	-8	31	101
Zaire	-79	-4	-9	3	-91	-55	-62	-70	-67	-109	-81	-35	-39	-78
Zambia	-183	-156	-56	-49	-45	-33	-42	-20	-25	-30	-45	-114	-87	-32
Zimbabwe	-121	-124	-128	-114	-38	-45	-27	-32	-13	-19	-15	-50	-95	-21
NORTH AFRICA	3285	2283	2084	2618	4053	4255	5017	5146	5145	5459	6260	1807	3096	5406
Algeria	277	304	347	237	186	367	765	522	385	535	332	325	286	508
Egypt, Arab Republic of	2791	2230	2133	3191	3957	3522	2995	3033	3406	3556	3769	1321	2971	3352
Libya	-1089	-1570	-1597	-2045	-1240	-859	-490	-470	-496	-472	-446	-641	-1400	-475
Morocco	1004	988	840	888	847	965	1394	1579	1303	1356	2012	624	922	1529
Tunisia	301	331	361	346	304	259	354	481	547	485	593	177	317	492
ALL AFRICA	2048	1660	1624	2358	4059	4627	5395	5437	5807	6019	7053	1165	2729	5942
South Africa	94	90	117	140	125	84	76	97	90	129	107	30	108	100

5–6. Official transfers

	Millions of U.S. dollars (current prices and exchange rates)											Average		
	1980	*1981*	*1982*	*1983*	*1984*	*1985*	*1986*	*1987*	*1988*	*1989*	*1990*	*75–79*	*80–85*	*86–MR*
SUB-SAHARAN AFRICA	2,772	2,918	2,719	3,142	3,185	3,429	4,156	4,790	5,267	6,130	6,109	1,724	3,027	5,290
excluding Nigeria	2,940	3,034	2,760	3,162	3,211	3,431	4,161	4,795	5,246	5,984	6,011	1,738	3,090	5,239
Angola	..	..	0	0	0	0	0	0	0	0	..	..	..	..
Benin	63	82	65	55	38	29	35	59	73	108	59	66	55	66
Botswana	65	51	23	47	43	42	54	167	185	251	316	20	45	194
Burkina Faso	211	181	189	166	159	164	238	236	261	461	272	125	178	294
Burundi	32	37	15	27	41	78	103	106	87	132	148	21	38	115
Cameroon	83	63	57	75	57	0	0	0	0	0	0	36	56	0
Cape Verde	29	21	36	39	39	37	42	47	39	36	12	..	33	35
Central African Republic	97	74	72	78	65	69	102	125	169	130	163	55	76	138
Chad	28	44	62	114	88	134	190	239	278	231	219	84	78	231
Comoros	11	24	19	20	31	32	32	39	41	41	41	..	23	39
Congo, People's Republic of the	63	44	29	37	42	40	60	68	64	93	74	40	43	72
Cote d'Ivoire	10	15	30	27	28	26	71	143	61	74	107	33	23	91
Djibouti	..	..	..	..	46	52	48	54	47	49	64	..	..	52
Equatorial Guinea	..	..	5	6	7	8	20	29	50	40	47	..	..	37
Ethiopia	60	60	68	93	162	298	293	212	188	209	188	43	123	218
Gabon	33	28	24	6	25	14	22	24	11	9	(12)	37	22	11
Gambia, The	38	55	33	20	10	8	7	36	42	34	45	10	27	33
Ghana	83	87	84	74	141	110	123	123	196	220	214	52	96	175
Guinea	17	..	0	0	0	0	42	83	84	98	117	..	..	85
Guinea-Bissau	..	..	45	43	29	31	51	52	50	64	67	..	..	57
Kenya	120	119	52	119	119	113	151	143	257	281	207	63	107	208
Lesotho	173	134	103	129	96	72	79	112	134	211	246	37	118	156
Liberia	36	68	93	114	104	92	96	45	..	..	..	31	85	..
Madagascar	67	82	88	75	78	74	132	120	158	155	171	72	77	147
Malawi	50	47	37	30	25	25	30	30	81	55	102	29	36	60
Mali	110	98	89	101	130	197	186	216	257	218	270	82	121	229
Mauritania	118	117	94	86	107	134	115	99	105	120	0	133	109	88
Mauritius	11	5	20	9	9	14	20	25	22	7	9	6	11	17
Mozambique	56	57	79	90	168	139	219	304	377	388	448	..	98	347
Namibia	..	..	..	..	..	..	..	..	..	..	..	..	..	..
Niger	154	161	150	136	146	212	148	142	144	132	182	106	160	150
Nigeria	(168)	(117)	(41)	(20)	(26)	(2)	(5)	(5)	21	145	99	(14)	(62)	51
Rwanda	107	106	105	112	99	112	117	119	139	129	138	80	107	128
Sao Tome & Principe	(0)	0	1	6	6	5	6	2	1	2	2	2	3	2
Senegal	140	177	182	158	139	162	187	213	205	265	320	102	160	238
Seychelles	15	13	10	14	15	14	16	24	29	32	29	7	13	26
Sierra Leone	45	34	46	33	25	17	5	7	8	15	41	14	33	15
Somalia	143	127	163	148	194	204	305	343	244	357	265	66	163	303
Sudan	84	122	174	462	309	288	412	280	369	299	341	20	240	340
Swaziland	79	71	60	67	65	49	41	47	83	105	110	23	65	77
Tanzania	107	108	94	85	96	130	223	477	389	470	539	104	103	420
Togo	86	69	69	68	75	69	101	97	72	94	109	52	73	94
Uganda	38	150	107	104	68	48	35	66	129	159	179	12	86	114
Zaire	267	248	160	173	174	199	184	220	226	276	217	69	203	224
Zambia	7	33	28	39	10	6	22	8	59	109	147	17	20	69
Zimbabwe	58	91	45	41	88	65	58	80	66	79	92	..	65	75
NORTH AFRICA	195	81	639	686	736	1,222	1,378	1,142	1,087	1,225	1,611	479	593	1,288
Algeria	24	5	(18)	1	(5)	11	(1)	(5)	5	6	1	14	3	1
Egypt, Arab Republic of	2	1	527	601	686	1,097	1,209	974	698	756	1,110	487	486	949
Libya	(46)	(76)	(78)	(58)	(81)	(45)	(36)	(56)	(37)	(16)	(35)	(102)	(64)	(36)
Morocco	114	104	165	101	93	111	160	191	303	265	320	31	114	248
Tunisia	101	47	44	41	42	48	45	37	118	215	215	48	54	126
ALL AFRICA	2,967	2,998	3,358	3,828	3,921	4,651	5,533	5,931	6,354	7,355	7,720	2,203	3,620	6,579
South Africa	145	229	135	56	(25)	(10)	11	116	86	72	10	85	88	59

5–7. Current account

	Millions of U.S. dollars (current prices and exchange rates)											Average		
	1980	1981	1982	1983	1984	1985	1986	1987	1988	1989	1990	75–79	80–85	86–MR
SUB-SAHARAN AFRICA	(3,441)	(15,701)	(16,382)	(10,107)	(2,877)	(838)	(5,364)	(6,700)	(7,555)	(4,964)	(1,574)	..	(8,224)	(5,231)
excluding Nigeria	(8,390)	(9,032)	(8,723)	(5,369)	(3,515)	(3,408)	(3,461)	(4,602)	(5,400)	(5,595)	(6,524)	..	(6,406)	(5,117)
Angola	..	..	(425)	26	(18)	204	(303)	449	(469)	..	..	..	..	..
Benin	(134)	(197)	(328)	(48)	(86)	(13)	(59)	(38)	(52)	12	(94)	(63)	(134)	(46)
Botswana	(143)	(295)	(145)	(82)	(70)	81	111	663	188	498	137	(47)	(109)	320
Burkina Faso	(49)	(42)	(92)	(60)	(3)	(60)	(21)	(51)	(49)	88	(111)	(57)	(51)	(29)
Burundi	(96)	(89)	(164)	(156)	(126)	(42)	(38)	(96)	(71)	(12)	(56)	(20)	(112)	(55)
Cameroon	(395)	(448)	(352)	(55)	201	328	(610)	(1,225)	(913)	(204)	(278)	(130)	(120)	(646)
Cape Verde	4	(22)	(15)	(13)	6	(9)	2	19	4	10	(8)	..	(10)	6
Central African Republic	(43)	(4)	(43)	(29)	(33)	(49)	(87)	(75)	(15)	(75)	(97)	(18)	(34)	(70)
Chad	12	23	19	38	9	(87)	(59)	(26)	26	(51)	(79)	(28)	2	(38)
Comoros	(9)	(8)	(11)	(11)	(33)	(14)	(16)	(21)	(7)	5	(9)	..	(14)	(9)
Congo, People's Republic of the	(167)	(461)	(332)	(401)	210	(161)	(601)	(223)	(445)	(63)	(123)	(190)	(218)	(291)
Cote d'Ivoire	(1,827)	(1,411)	(1,016)	(929)	(73)	68	(298)	(967)	(1,120)	(1,148)	(1,104)	(605)	(865)	(927)
Djibouti	..	..	..	..	(57)	(42)	(21)	(15)	(24)	(23)	(25)	..	..	(22)
Equatorial Guinea	(43)	(33)	(30)	(9)	(8)	(1)	5	(24)	(17)	(17)	(19)	..	(21)	(14)
Ethiopia	(126)	(214)	(331)	(246)	(254)	(123)	(75)	(264)	(276)	(169)	(180)	(66)	(216)	(193)
Gabon	384	403	309	72	113	(162)	(1,057)	(581)	(602)	(192)	224	109	186	(442)
Gambia, The	(74)	(50)	(22)	(33)	8	7	4	18	34	17	36	(18)	(27)	22
Ghana	29	(421)	(109)	(174)	(39)	(134)	(43)	(97)	(66)	(99)	(229)	(12)	(141)	(107)
Guinea	(9)	(81)	(89)	85	58	69	(56)	(74)	(210)	(126)	(103)	..	5	(114)
Guinea-Bissau	..	..	(35)	(29)	(36)	(45)	(23)	(13)	(29)	(39)	(19)	..	..	(25)
Kenya	(886)	(558)	(302)	(45)	(123)	(110)	(37)	(494)	(460)	(587)	(477)	(295)	(338)	(411)
Lesotho	56	4	22	41	6	(12)	(3)	24	(25)	10	69	(7)	20	15
Liberia	46	75	3	(103)	(1)	57	15	(118)	..	..	..	26	13	..
Madagascar	(557)	(363)	(299)	(247)	(193)	(184)	(141)	(140)	(149)	(128)	(153)	(121)	(307)	(142)
Malawi	(260)	(146)	(117)	(138)	(48)	(124)	(89)	(55)	(53)	(116)	(47)	(125)	(139)	(72)
Mali	(124)	(140)	(115)	(103)	(66)	(132)	(161)	(96)	(90)	(75)	(94)	(61)	(113)	(103)
Mauritania	(133)	(147)	(277)	(213)	(111)	(116)	(194)	(147)	(96)	(19)	(199)	(89)	(166)	(131)
Mauritius	(119)	(156)	(43)	(23)	(55)	(29)	95	63	(63)	(104)	(119)	(72)	(71)	(26)
Mozambique	(367)	(407)	(497)	(415)	(308)	(301)	(359)	(389)	(281)	(376)	(335)	..	(383)	(348)
Namibia	..	..	..	..	..	..	..	..	..	..	..	..	..	..
Niger	(276)	(181)	(233)	(62)	1	(64)	25	(90)	(83)	(111)	(65)	(88)	(136)	(65)
Nigeria	5,127	(6,164)	(7,285)	(4,354)	115	2,566	366	(69)	(194)	1,090	5,126	(683)	(1,666)	1,264
Rwanda	(48)	(67)	(87)	(49)	(42)	(64)	(69)	(134)	(119)	(102)	(85)	6	(59)	(102)
Sao Tome & Principe	1	(18)	(25)	(9)	(11)	(16)	(19)	(13)	(11)	(11)	(12)	4	(13)	(13)
Senegal	(386)	(462)	(266)	(304)	(272)	(272)	(267)	(256)	(266)	(179)	(130)	(149)	(327)	(220)
Seychelles	(16)	(19)	(41)	(26)	(13)	(19)	(33)	(21)	(28)	(23)	(17)	(6)	(22)	(25)
Sierra Leone	(165)	(132)	(170)	(18)	(23)	4	141	(30)	(3)	(102)	(95)	(93)	(84)	(18)
Somalia	(136)	(83)	(177)	(142)	(139)	(103)	(126)	(114)	(101)	(153)	(81)	(74)	(130)	(115)
Sudan	(564)	(839)	(1,117)	(423)	(462)	(354)	(430)	(432)	(630)	(924)	(876)	(411)	(627)	(658)
Swaziland	(132)	(83)	(114)	(109)	(80)	(42)	7	80	95	(7)	12	(20)	(93)	37
Tanzania	(521)	(407)	(523)	(305)	(359)	(375)	(321)	(265)	(376)	(359)	(293)	(230)	(415)	(323)
Togo	(95)	(44)	(87)	(43)	26	(27)	(56)	(62)	(57)	(14)	(100)	(123)	(45)	(58)
Uganda	(83)	32	(16)	10	(10)	3	(37)	(153)	(214)	(251)	(255)	(9)	(11)	(182)
Zaire	(292)	(604)	(591)	(349)	(324)	(289)	(414)	(644)	(581)	(611)	(643)	(487)	(408)	(579)
Zambia	(537)	(734)	(565)	(271)	(153)	(398)	(350)	(248)	(295)	(183)	(343)	(265)	(443)	(284)
Zimbabwe	(244)	(636)	(709)	(460)	(100)	76	7	48	117	(104)	(271)	(63)	(371)	(41)
NORTH AFRICA	6,248	(8,235)	(6,091)	(4,116)	(4,957)	(666)	(5,362)	(1,668)	(3,722)	(5,053)	1,498	(2,958)	(2,970)	(2,861)
Algeria	249	90	(183)	(85)	74	1,015	(2,230)	141	(2,040)	(1,081)	1,420	(2,006)	193	(758)
Egypt, Arab Republic of	(436)	(2,135)	(1,806)	(921)	(1,819)	(2,112)	(2,148)	(880)	(539)	(1,994)	(1,425)	(1,217)	(1,538)	(1,397)
Libya	8,214	(3,964)	(1,560)	(1,643)	(1,457)	1,906	(156)	(1,045)	(1,823)	(1,028)	2,203	1,981	250	(370)
Morocco	(1,419)	(1,839)	(1,875)	(889)	(986)	(889)	(211)	176	467	790	(200)	(1,328)	(1,316)	(112)
Tunisia	(361)	(387)	(667)	(578)	(770)	(587)	(618)	(60)	213	160	(500)	(387)	(558)	(225)
ALL AFRICA	2,807	(23,936)	(22,473)	(14,224)	(7,834)	(1,504)	(10,726)	(8,368)	(11,276)	(10,017)	75	(7,584)	(11,194)	(8,092)
South Africa	3,508	(4,512)	(3,184)	10	(1,588)	2,622	3,152	2,936	1,218	1,579	2,253	233	(524)	2,228

5-8. Net foreign direct investment

| | Millions of U.S. dollars (current prices and exchange rates) | | | | | | | | | | | Average | | |
	1980	1981	1982	1983	1984	1985	1986	1987	1988	1989	1990	75-79	80-85	86-MR
SUB-SAHARAN AFRICA excluding Nigeria	..	..	..	..	..	..	..	..	..	..	..	..	..	..
Angola	..	..	347	361	331	278	234	119	131	..	..	..	..	97
Benin	4	2	(1)	(1)	(1)	1	1	1	1	1	2	2	1	1
Botswana	109	88	21	23	62	52	70	114	40	98	148	31	59	94
Burkina Faso	0	2	2	2	2	(1)	3	6	2	2	2	2	1	3
Burundi	1	1	2	0	1	1	2	1	1	1	1	..	1	1
Cameroon	105	31	28	58	92	21	0	31	34	32	33	26	56	26
Cape Verde	..	..	..	..	..	..	..	3	0	(1)	2	..	..	..
Central African Republic	5	6	9	4	5	2	7	9	(13)	(12)	..	6	5	(2)
Chad	(0)	(0)	(0)	(0)	9	53	28	0	(13)	6	19	20	10	8
Comoros	..	..	..	..	..	..	..	8	4	3	0	..	..	..
Congo, People's Republic of the	40	31	35	56	35	13	22	43	9	(1)	(1)	8	35	15
Cote d'Ivoire	95	33	47	38	22	29	71	88	56	78	(48)	57	44	49
Djibouti	..	..	..	..	..	..	..	..	..	0	0	..	..	..
Equatorial Guinea	..	..	..	..	..	0	0	0	0	0	10	..	..	2
Ethiopia	..	..	..	..	..	..	..	..	..	0	0	..	..	..
Gabon	24	47	127	106	5	11	104	82	121	(39)	(77)	56	53	38
Gambia, The	..	2	..	..	1	2	6	1	1	15	9	..	..	7
Ghana	16	16	16	2	2	6	4	5	5	15	15	16	10	9
Guinea	34	..	0	0	0	0	5	5	7	10	11	..	..	8
Guinea-Bissau	..	..	..	..	..	..	..	..	..	0	1	..	..	..
Kenya	78	8	3	9	4	13	28	41	(2)	69	23	44	19	32
Lesotho	4	5	3	5	2	5	2	6	21	13	17	..	4	12
Liberia	..	..	35	49	36	(16)	(17)	39				..	..	..
Madagascar	..	..	..	..	..	..	..	..	6	22		(1)	..	..
Malawi	9	1	..	3	..	1	..	0	..	..	..	6	..	..
Mali	2	4	2	3	10	3	(8)	(6)	1	15	(6)	(4)	4	(1)
Mauritania	27	12	15	1	9	7	3	1	1	3	7	(10)	12	3
Mauritius	1	1	2	2	5	8	7	17	24	35	41	2	3	25
Mozambique	0	0	0	0	0	0	0	6	5	3	9	..	0	5
Namibia	..	..	..	..	..	..	..	..	..	..	..	..	..	..
Niger	44	(7)	25	0	(1)	(10)	..	..	..	..	..	21	9	..
Nigeria	(740)	546	433	344	200	478	167	603	377	1,882	588	343	210	723
Rwanda	16	18	21	11	15	15	18	18	21	16	8	6	16	16
Sao Tome & Principe	..	..	..	..	..	..	..	..	(0)	0	0	..	..	..
Senegal	13	20	10	(36)	27	(19)	(13)	3	0	(10)	(8)	15	2	(6)
Seychelles	6	3	5	6	6	1	8	14	18	15	19	5	4	15
Sierra Leone	(19)	8	5	2	6	(31)	(140)	39	(23)	5	3	13	(5)	(23)
Somalia	..	..	(1)	(8)	(15)	(1)	..	..	..	..	..	..	..	..
Sudan	0	0	0	0	0	0	0	0	0	0	0	..	0	0
Swaziland	17	32	(16)	(6)	..	10	28	39	39	62	40	24	..	42
Tanzania	..	..	..	..	..	..	..	..	..	0	5	..	..	..
Togo	42	10	16	2	(10)	17	7	7	..	..	8	34	13	..
Uganda	..	..	0	1	0	0	0	0	0	0	0	1	..	0
Zaire	6	6	6	5	6	6	5	10	11	12	13	66	6	10
Zambia	62	(38)	39	26	17	52	28	75	93	..	..	32	26	39
Zimbabwe	2	4	(1)	(2)	(2)	3	7	(31)	(40)	(10)	16	..	0	(11)
NORTH AFRICA	45	325	827	854	1,403	1,528	1,171	795	1,167	459	408	217	830	800
Algeria	315	(1)	(65)	(14)	(14)	(2)	11	(11)	8	4	(4)	117	36	1
Egypt, Arab Republic of	541	747	885	966	1,275	1,289	1,275	869	973	124	136	582	951	675
Libya	(1,136)	(769)	(411)	(327)	(17)	119	(177)	(213)	42	90	54	(595)	(423)	(41)
Morocco	89	59	80	46	47	20	1	60	85	167	165	36	57	95
Tunisia	235	291	339	183	112	102	62	91	59	74	57	77	210	68
ALL AFRICA	..	..	..	..	..	..	..	..	..	..	..	..	..	..
South Africa	(765)	(579)	295	(87)	251	(497)	(116)	(163)	98	7	(5)	(197)	(230)	(36)

5–9. Net long–term borrowing

	Millions of U.S. dollars (current prices and exchange rates)											Average		
	1980	1981	1982	1983	1984	1985	1986	1987	1988	1989	1990	75–79	80–85	86–MR
SUB-SAHARAN AFRICA	8,345	9,557	10,087	7,772	5,345	3,665	4,996	6,280	5,553	5,564	5,165	4,633	7,462	5,511
excluding Nigeria	6,835	7,051	7,204	5,954	5,546	4,775	4,897	5,371	5,148	4,544	5,659	4,100	6,227	5,124
Angola	43	58	71	179	227	1,236	667	719	378	212	1,702	3	302	736
Benin	66	100	220	92	16	11	40	53	43	151	88	51	84	75
Botswana	21	26	55	25	60	41	17	64	14	29	(37)	16	38	17
Burkina Faso	59	61	65	82	41	39	71	92	70	80	60	38	58	75
Burundi	41	26	52	99	68	56	88	112	93	93	66	20	57	91
Cameroon	493	318	164	341	207	(164)	77	83	372	542	333	285	226	281
Cape Verde	3	21	22	17	15	20	9	5	7	7	6	4	16	7
Central African Republic	33	44	18	23	25	42	70	88	79	47	114	17	31	80
Chad	(0)	11	4	14	4	2	26	47	56	84	85	27	6	60
Comoros	13	11	16	18	23	22	23	13	8	5	8	7	17	11
Congo, People's Republic of the	453	229	503	278	209	203	132	151	330	(41)	(7)	104	313	113
Cote d'Ivoire	1,158	1,187	1,632	672	951	684	380	544	519	441	947	571	1,047	566
Djibouti	8	(1)	7	13	39	30	19	21	12	4	7	2	16	13
Equatorial Guinea	36	24	30	11	(7)	7	15	16	24	14	5	1	17	15
Ethiopia	93	361	104	182	173	246	241	288	289	109	108	77	193	207
Gabon	(109)	(161)	(94)	(67)	55	133	361	208	299	93	(111)	182	(40)	170
Gambia, The	55	50	37	6	11	10	25	32	8	25	0	13	28	18
Ghana	143	65	51	345	255	239	297	216	195	218	206	76	183	227
Guinea	53	73	40	58	(3)	60	154	58	184	204	99	47	47	140
Guinea-Bissau	66	19	16	15	31	57	20	41	32	38	33	14	34	33
Kenya	487	248	407	368	95	140	232	223	363	245	387	285	291	290
Lesotho	12	18	42	19	11	29	14	39	40	44	42	8	22	36
Liberia	91	125	114	118	105	48	30	27	7	(2)	(1)	68	100	12
Madagascar	413	289	274	200	137	117	144	245	142	165	83	93	238	156
Malawi	156	112	41	66	90	27	53	38	73	84	89	89	82	67
Mali	100	104	141	161	125	90	151	91	101	130	96	48	120	114
Mauritania	133	128	208	159	84	49	164	111	47	41	47	75	127	82
Mauritius	124	119	65	(8)	35	4	(10)	41	81	10	48	47	56	34
Mozambique	0	0	0	82	1,145	348	366	338	159	173	165	0	262	240
Namibia	..	..	..	..	..	..	..	..	..	..	..	..	..	..
Niger	233	323	21	110	57	67	131	144	100	104	104	78	135	117
Nigeria	1,510	2,506	2,883	1,819	(202)	(1,110)	98	909	405	1,020	(494)	534	1,234	388
Rwanda	31	24	29	36	44	69	64	90	73	48	52	24	39	65
Sao Tome & Principe	9	7	8	7	14	7	10	7	11	17	15	3	9	12
Senegal	230	282	314	355	176	134	311	285	113	249	61	118	248	204
Seychelles	12	7	14	11	10	15	26	12	6	0	4	2	11	9
Sierra Leone	59	59	70	36	21	24	6	7	20	3	30	32	45	13
Somalia	125	431	213	207	139	137	88	67	62	53	37	75	209	61
Sudan	790	745	926	589	252	80	59	160	324	191	170	470	564	181
Swaziland	22	11	19	27	18	12	7	(15)	(12)	(5)	(20)	25	18	(9)
Tanzania	0	0	0	0	0	0	0	0	0	0	0	0	0	0
Togo	104	26	34	71	27	8	13	0	87	36	59	139	45	39
Uganda	122	183	169	148	54	73	62	340	100	234	296	81	125	206
Zaire	333	400	231	218	162	85	130	275	173	194	23	453	238	159
Zambia	429	538	194	197	276	248	201	74	151	80	38	264	314	109
Zimbabwe	93	349	657	377	72	(6)	(85)	(76)	(82)	97	123	70	257	(4)
NORTH AFRICA	4,486	3,503	4,629	3,181	3,886	3,197	3,101	20,646	3,860	1,617	111	5,758	3,814	5,867
Algeria	916	246	(338)	206	567	484	960	735	1,432	407	(589)	2,498	347	589
Egypt, Arab Republic of	1,870	1,514	2,738	1,909	1,783	1,761	1,248	19,169	1,540	607	266	1,801	1,929	4,566
Libya	..	..	..	..	..	..	..	..	..	..	..	..	..	..
Morocco	1,378	1,417	1,922	565	1,096	636	444	682	635	463	440	1,059	1,169	533
Tunisia	322	326	307	501	440	316	449	60	254	140	(6)	400	369	180
ALL AFRICA	12,831	13,059	14,716	10,954	9,231	6,862	8,097	26,926	9,413	7,181	5,276	10,391	11,275	11,379
South Africa	..	..	..	..	..	..	..	..	..	..	..	..	..	..

5-10. Other capital flows

	Millions of U.S. dollars (current prices and exchange rates)											Average		
	1980	1981	1982	1983	1984	1985	1986	1987	1988	1989	1990	75-79	80-85	86-MR
SUB-SAHARAN AFRICA	(16,524)	(21,138)	(25,592)	(19,245)	(9,861)	(6,223)	(10,900)	(13,797)	(14,707)	(15,023)	(11,459)	..	(16,430)	(13,177)
excluding Nigeria	(14,989)	(15,468)	(15,117)	(11,423)	(8,980)	(7,410)	(7,662)	(9,817)	(9,922)	(10,923)	(11,720)	..	(12,231)	(10,009)
Angola	(43)	(58)	(839)	(514)	(625)	(1,331)	(1,163)	(406)	(1,027)	(206)	(1,702)	..	(568)	(901)
Benin	(194)	(384)	(397)	(137)	(108)	(9)	(101)	(13)	(93)	(242)	(289)	(113)	(205)	(147)
Botswana	(364)	(335)	(276)	(254)	(316)	(267)	(283)	(75)	(249)	(205)	(281)	(143)	(302)	(219)
Burkina Faso	(123)	(120)	(159)	(180)	(80)	(101)	(158)	(182)	(154)	71	(173)	(93)	(127)	(119)
Burundi	(146)	(81)	(186)	(253)	(186)	(108)	(157)	(198)	(181)	(149)	(119)	(57)	(160)	(161)
Cameroon	(1,133)	(686)	(489)	(659)	121	438	(479)	(782)	(1,358)	(675)	(719)	(435)	(401)	(803)
Cape Verde	7	(50)	(50)	(43)	(13)	(47)	14	(21)	(5)	25	(18)	1	(33)	(1)
Central African Republic	(108)	(80)	(47)	(59)	(67)	(73)	(165)	(183)	(74)	(132)	(204)	(49)	(72)	(152)
Chad	21	12	13	7	(24)	(123)	(94)	(96)	(2)	(183)	(187)	(76)	(16)	(113)
Comoros	(18)	(23)	(31)	(31)	(50)	(42)	(42)	(50)	(22)	(8)	(12)	(7)	(33)	(27)
Congo, People's Republic of the	(716)	(776)	(787)	(702)	(25)	(373)	(753)	(409)	(784)	(10)	(226)	(307)	(563)	(436)
Cote d'Ivoire	(2,981)	(2,629)	(2,677)	(1,658)	(1,031)	(633)	(747)	(1,601)	(1,681)	(1,649)	(1,979)	(1,219)	(1,935)	(1,531)
Djibouti	(8)	1	(7)	(13)	(85)	(78)	(43)	(45)	(45)	(29)	(31)	(2)	(32)	(39)
Equatorial Guinea	(84)	(56)	(60)	(18)	(2)	(10)	(8)	(36)	(46)	(25)	(32)	(1)	(38)	(29)
Ethiopia	(188)	(589)	(518)	(338)	(357)	(381)	(486)	(511)	(469)	(273)	(262)	(142)	(395)	(400)
Gabon	373	399	132	130	14	(256)	(1,422)	(755)	(1,078)	(213)	191	(116)	132	(655)
Gambia, The	(127)	(122)	(51)	(27)	(5)	(2)	(23)	(34)	8	(20)	11	(32)	(56)	(11)
Ghana	(34)	(455)	(170)	(531)	(442)	(554)	(319)	(343)	(377)	(485)	(502)	(147)	(364)	(405)
Guinea	(133)	(150)	(122)	28	61	12	(243)	(160)	(372)	(367)	(216)	(75)	(51)	(272)
Guinea-Bissau	(66)	(18)	(35)	(31)	(64)	(118)	(46)	(56)	(72)	(70)	(58)	(14)	(55)	(60)
Kenya	(1,335)	(653)	(701)	(613)	(265)	(253)	(309)	(600)	(842)	(1,037)	(924)	(715)	(637)	(742)
Lesotho	(4)	(19)	(31)	(9)	(14)	(49)	(29)	(19)	(82)	(44)	(10)	(16)	(21)	(37)
Liberia	(35)	(46)	(144)	(283)	(122)	27	5	(183)	(6)	(5)	1	(80)	(101)	(38)
Madagascar	(1,094)	(657)	(579)	(433)	(369)	(270)	(338)	(429)	(327)	(329)	(361)	(201)	(567)	(357)
Malawi	(444)	(261)	(138)	(193)	(181)	(136)	(114)	(123)	(232)	(165)	(185)	(213)	(225)	(164)
Mali	(230)	(238)	(259)	(268)	(232)	(218)	(252)	(167)	(249)	(289)	(238)	(107)	(241)	(239)
Mauritania	(319)	(316)	(480)	(348)	(182)	(140)	(345)	(266)	(128)	(85)	(235)	(159)	(297)	(212)
Mauritius	(308)	(226)	(108)	(1)	(105)	(43)	(2)	(179)	(311)	(258)	(396)	(108)	(132)	(229)
Mozambique	(335)	(340)	(356)	(482)	(1,477)	(628)	(749)	(733)	(443)	(552)	(522)	..	(603)	(600)
Namibia	..	..	..	..	..	..	..	..	..	..	..	..	..	..
Niger	(568)	(501)	(216)	(202)	(101)	(138)	(131)	(248)	(200)	(191)	(185)	(203)	(288)	(191)
Nigeria	(16)	(4,550)	(8,490)	(6,076)	367	2,709	579	(1,628)	539	(2,997)	2,717	(1,579)	(2,798)	(374)
Rwanda	(131)	(109)	(99)	(77)	(109)	(146)	(176)	(225)	(182)	(114)	(143)	(54)	(112)	(168)
Sao Tome & Principe	4	(18)	(31)	(14)	(20)	(23)	(27)	(16)	(17)	(24)	(26)	(4)	(17)	(22)
Senegal	(633)	(763)	(594)	(625)	(464)	(382)	(560)	(534)	(405)	(478)	(202)	(287)	(577)	(436)
Seychelles	(41)	(23)	(60)	(40)	(28)	(35)	(66)	(51)	(47)	(42)	(44)	(14)	(38)	(50)
Sierra Leone	(195)	(180)	(230)	(68)	(38)	13	271	(76)	(6)	(106)	(127)	(140)	(116)	(9)
Somalia	(261)	(550)	(456)	(311)	(242)	(273)	(175)	(162)	(234)	(218)	(165)	(158)	(349)	(191)
Sudan	(1,346)	(1,549)	(1,760)	(1,272)	(718)	(320)	(501)	(372)	(674)	(943)	(942)	(862)	(1,161)	(687)
Swaziland	(210)	(78)	(108)	(152)	(90)	(58)	(32)	41	59	(113)	(19)	(89)	(116)	(13)
Tanzania	(455)	(410)	(522)	(346)	(391)	(369)	(344)	(196)	(378)	(339)	(347)	(218)	(415)	(321)
Togo	(262)	(173)	(175)	(156)	(47)	(82)	(53)	(23)	(58)	(91)	(206)	(297)	(149)	(86)
Uganda	(215)	(189)	(219)	(167)	(93)	(42)	(21)	(475)	(306)	(453)	(563)	(89)	(154)	(363)
Zaire	(721)	(878)	(762)	(601)	(433)	(391)	(488)	(990)	(645)	(876)	(609)	(1,033)	(631)	(722)
Zambia	(1,056)	(1,188)	(803)	(490)	(388)	(818)	(447)	(323)	(590)	(328)	(454)	(540)	(790)	(428)
Zimbabwe	(251)	(1,025)	(1,512)	(737)	(102)	(104)	123	136	215	(107)	(464)	(171)	(622)	(19)
NORTH AFRICA	(6,679)	(8,063)	(8,661)	(6,784)	(8,149)	(8,881)	(8,788)	(22,904)	(7,471)	(7,142)	(286)	(10,283)	(7,869)	(9,318)
Algeria	(2,324)	(274)	1,289	144	(146)	(487)	(1,703)	(230)	(2,720)	(1,391)	1,875	(4,725)	(300)	(834)
Egypt, Arab Republic of	(3,506)	(4,473)	(5,441)	(4,676)	(4,983)	(5,509)	(5,026)	(21,751)	(3,328)	(2,558)	(2,036)	(4,273)	(4,765)	(6,940)
Libya	2,943	951	864	470	282	(575)	(190)	168	(475)	(1,410)	991	2,069	822	(183)
Morocco	(2,841)	(3,195)	(3,901)	(1,425)	(2,079)	(1,530)	(647)	(697)	(386)	(1,344)	(800)	(2,462)	(2,495)	(775)
Tunisia	(952)	(1,071)	(1,472)	(1,297)	(1,222)	(780)	(1,221)	(393)	(562)	(439)	(316)	(893)	(1,132)	(586)
ALL AFRICA	(23,203)	(29,201)	(34,252)	(26,029)	(18,010)	(15,104)	(19,688)	(36,700)	(22,179)	(22,165)	(11,745)	(20,651)	(24,300)	(22,496)
South Africa	3,482	(2,887)	(2,581)	(897)	(1,313)	3,645	3,428	1,677	1,887	1,045	1,902	559	(92)	1,988

Note: Includes all capital account flows, except changes in reserves, that are not included in the foreign investment (Table 5-8) or long-term borrowing (Table 5-9) tables.

5–11. Use of reserves

	Millions of U.S. dollars (current prices and exchange rates)											Average		
	1980	1981	1982	1983	1984	1985	1986	1987	1988	1989	1990	75–79	80–85	86–MR
SUB-SAHARAN AFRICA	(4,780)	4,935	2,563	(195)	(609)	(859)	440	304	(90)	(2,113)	(3,743)	(263)	176	(1,041)
excluding Nigeria	(407)	269	453	(637)	(126)	(370)	(38)	351	(527)	(928)	(1,428)	(242)	(136)	(514)
Angola	..	..	4	..	(49)	(21)	41	(17)	(49)	6	..	..	..	(5)
Benin	10	(84)	150	1	(7)	15	(1)	80	4	(102)	(105)	4	14	(25)
Botswana	(90)	74	(55)	(124)	(124)	(254)	(307)	(562)	(382)	(576)	(307)	..	(96)	(427)
Burkina Faso	(15)	(14)	0	(36)	(34)	(4)	(63)	(33)	(33)	65	(1)	3	(17)	(13)
Burundi	(8)	35	31	3	8	(9)	(30)	12	(16)	(43)	5	(17)	10	(14)
Cameroon	(139)	111	54	(206)	219	(32)	208	557	(38)	103	(75)	6	1	151
Cape Verde	6	(8)	(13)	(13)	8	(18)	20	(33)	(3)	22	(2)	..	(6)	1
Central African Republic	(27)	(25)	21	(3)	(4)	20	(2)	(11)	6	(21)	7	(8)	(3)	(4)
Chad	8	(0)	(2)	(17)	(20)	20	19	(24)	16	(42)	(4)	(0)	(2)	(7)
Comoros	4	(4)	(4)	(2)	6	(6)	(3)	(9)	(4)	(5)	5	..	(1)	(3)
Congo, People's Republic of the	(56)	(55)	82	33	9	4	1	8	1	11	(111)	(6)	3	(18)
Cote d'Ivoire	98	1	19	(19)	15	11	1	(2)	15	19	24	14	21	11
Djibouti	..	..	..	..	10	(6)	(3)	(10)	(8)	(2)	..	..	2	(6)
Equatorial Guinea	(5)	1	(0)	1	(0)	(2)	2	5	(6)	6	2	0	(1)	2
Ethiopia	31	(14)	(83)	91	70	(12)	(170)	40	96	5	27	7	14	(0)
Gabon	(96)	(118)	(144)	97	(39)	51	100	116	(56)	33	(221)	12	(42)	(6)
Gambia, The	2	(21)	8	12	(2)	3	4	(18)	(17)	3	(15)	2	0	(9)
Ghana	96	47	7	(10)	(146)	(175)	25	(25)	(110)	(153)	(53)	(44)	(30)	(63)
Guinea	(37)	4	7	2	1	2	(28)	(22)	29	(27)	(4)	..	(4)	(10)
Guinea–Bissau	(0)	1	16	13	3	(16)	(3)	(2)	(11)	6	(5)	..	3	(3)
Kenya	117	162	11	(191)	(43)	10	(12)	158	(21)	(135)	(36)	(91)	11	(10)
Lesotho	(45)	(1)	(8)	(26)	(8)	(4)	(10)	2	4	4	(21)	(1)	(15)	(4)
Liberia	10	3	0	(13)	20	2	3	0	0	(7)	0	(5)	4	(1)
Madagascar	(124)	(5)	(6)	13	(38)	30	(53)	(45)	(36)	(30)	(103)	11	(22)	(53)
Malawi	(19)	(3)	20	13	(43)	16	28	(30)	(106)	35	(49)	7	(3)	(24)
Mali	(3)	9	(1)	(1)	(32)	7	52	13	(57)	(69)	(55)	(2)	(3)	(23)
Mauritania	(25)	(28)	20	25	22	32	17	(7)	16	(22)	17	(4)	8	4
Mauritius	(64)	49	1	16	(10)	(2)	(100)	(184)	(143)	(108)	(189)	14	(2)	(145)
Mozambique	32	67	141	15	(23)	21	(24)	(1)	1	0	(12)	..	42	(7)
Namibia	..	..	..	..	..	..	..	..	..	..	..	..	..	..
Niger	(15)	(3)	63	(30)	(46)	(17)	(25)	(14)	(17)	24	(16)	(15)	(8)	(10)
Nigeria	(4,373)	4,666	2,110	441	(483)	(489)	478	(47)	437	(1,185)	(2,315)	(20)	312	(526)
Rwanda	(36)	(0)	37	18	(8)	1	(25)	16	31	52	2	(30)	2	15
Sao Tome & Principe	12	7	2	2	5	(1)	1	4	4	5	1	(5)	5	3
Senegal	(4)	1	(4)	(2)	12	5	5	10	(27)	(61)	(19)	(5)	1	(18)
Seychelles	(8)	5	0	2	2	0	1	(4)	4	(4)	(4)	(1)	0	(1)
Sierra Leone	11	18	14	(12)	12	(33)	39	20	(72)	(12)	(48)	(5)	(14)	(15)
Somalia	(1)	(35)	(66)	30	21	(33)	39	20	(72)	(12)	(48)	(5)	(14)	(15)
Sudan	8	35	283	(260)	(4)	114	(13)	220	280	172	103	19	29	152
Swaziland	(39)	48	9	(22)	8	7	(4)	(15)	(10)	(49)	(10)	(20)	2	(17)
Tanzania	66	(3)	2	(41)	(32)	6	(23)	69	(2)	20	(49)	12	(1)	3
Togo	(21)	(92)	(38)	(41)	(57)	(30)	23	46	86	(41)	(39)	(1)	(46)	15
Uganda	(10)	(38)	(35)	(28)	(29)	28	78	18	9	32	(12)	2	(18)	25
Zaire	(89)	132	66	(30)	59	(11)	61	(61)	119	(58)	70	(27)	21	26
Zambia	(27)	45	(5)	4	58	(120)	132	75	(51)	(64)	(73)	21	(8)	4
Zimbabwe	87	(36)	(147)	99	68	(32)	39	(19)	(24)	84	(54)	(39)	6	5
NORTH AFRICA	(8,396)	4,000	2,886	1,367	2,098	(3,489)	847	204	1,278	(13)	(1,266)	(1,351)	(256)	210
Algeria	(1,341)	(120)	1,070	421	333	(1,020)	1,498	352	759	101	(138)	(104)	(110)	514
Egypt, Arab Republic of	(658)	(78)	(13)	(880)	(107)	(347)	(356)	(834)	(277)	168	(209)	(673)	(347)	(301)
Libya	(6,407)	4,145	2,013	1,786	1,721	(2,362)	(212)	1,000	1,390	(292)	(1,159)	(507)	149	145
Morocco	45	120	(24)	76	50	15	8	(132)	(133)	75	6	(39)	47	(35)
Tunisia	(35)	(67)	(159)	35	100	225	(92)	(182)	(461)	(65)	234	(28)	5	(113)
ALL AFRICA	(13,176)	8,936	5,450	1,172	1,489	(4,348)	1,286	508	1,188	(2,126)	(5,009)	(1,614)	(80)	(831)
South Africa	(791)	1,046	897	(995)	525	526	160	(1,422)	766	(527)	(355)	129	202	(276)

Note: Excludes IMF credit transactions, which appear in Table 5-9: Long-term borrowing.

5-12. Import coverage ratio of imports

	Reserves in months of imports of goods and services											Average		
	1980	1981	1982	1983	1984	1985	1986	1987	1988	1989	1990	75-79	80-85	86-MR
SUB-SAHARAN AFRICA	3	1	1	1	1	2	2	2	2	2	..	..	1	2
excluding Nigeria	1	1	1	1	1	2	2	2	2	2	..	..	1	2
Angola	..	..	..	..	..	..	..	..	..	..	..	..	..	..
Benin	0	1	0	0	0	0	0	0	0	0	1	1	0	0
Botswana	4	3	4	5	6	11	14	18	15	18	17	4	6	16
Burkina Faso	1	2	1	2	3	3	5	6	5	4	4	2	2	5
Burundi	5	3	1	1	1	1	3	2	3	4	4	7	2	3
Cameroon	1	0	0	1	0	1	0	0	1	0	..	1	1	0
Cape Verde	6	4	4	4	5	7	6	8	8	7	6	8	5	7
Central African Republic	2	3	2	2	3	2	2	3	4	3	..	1	2	3
Chad	1	1	1	2	2	1	0	1	2	3	..	1	1	2
Comoros	2	2	3	2	1	2	3	4	3	5	4	..	2	4
Congo, People's Republic of the	1	1	0	0	0	0	0	0	0	0	..	0	0	0
Cote d'Ivoire	0	0	0	0	0	0	0	0	0	0	0	1	0	0
Djibouti	..	..	..	..	2	2	3	3	3	2	..	..	2	3
Equatorial Guinea	..	..	..	0	0	1	1	0	1	0	..	..	1	0
Ethiopia	1	4	2	2	0	2	2	1	1	0	0	5	2	1
Gabon	1	1	2	1	1	1	1	0	0	0	..	1	1	0
Gambia, The	0	0	1	0	0	0	2	2	1	1	..	3	0	2
Ghana	2	1	2	2	4	6	6	2	2	3	2	2	3	3
Guinea	..	..	..	..	..	..	..	..	..	..	..	..	..	..
Guinea-Bissau	..	..	..	..	..	..	4	2	2	..	..	..	..	3
Kenya	2	1	1	3	2	2	2	1	1	1	1	3	2	1
Lesotho	1	1	1	1	1	1	2	2	1	1	1	..	1	1
Liberia	0	0	0	0	0	0	0	0	..	..	..	1	0	0
Madagascar	0	0	0	1	1	1	2	3	4	4	..	1	1	3
Malawi	1	1	1	0	2	1	1	1	4	2	3	2	1	2
Mali	0	0	0	0	1	0	0	0	1	2	3	0	0	1
Mauritania	3	3	3	2	2	1	1	1	1	2	1	2	2	1
Mauritius	2	1	1	0	0	1	2	3	3	4	5	2	1	3
Mozambique	..	..	..	..	..	..	..	..	..	..	..	..	..	..
Namibia	..	..	..	..	..	..	..	..	..	..	..	..	..	..
Niger	1	1	0	1	2	3	6	5	5	4	5	3	2	5
Nigeria	6	2	1	1	1	2	2	2	1	3	5	4	2	3
Rwanda	7	6	4	4	4	4	5	4	3	2	1	4	5	3
Sao Tome & Principe	..	..	..	..	..	..	..	..	..	..	..	..	..	..
Senegal	0	0	0	0	0	0	0	0	0	0	0	0	0	0
Seychelles	2	1	1	1	1	1	1	1	0	1	1	2	1	1
Sierra Leone	1	1	0	1	0	1	1	0	0	0	0	1	1	0
Somalia	0	1	0	0	0	0	0	0	0	0	..	4	0	0
Sudan	0	0	0	0	0	0	0	0	0	0	0	0	0	0
Swaziland	3	2	2	2	2	3	3	3	3	3	3	4	2	3
Tanzania	0	0	0	0	0	0	1	0	1	0	1	2	0	1
Togo	1	3	3	4	6	7	6	6	4	6	5	2	4	5
Uganda	0	1	2	2	2	1	1	1	1	0	1	1	1	1
Zaire	1	1	0	1	1	1	1	1	1	1	1	1	1	1
Zambia	0	0	0	1	1	2	1	1	1	1	1	1	1	1
Zimbabwe	1	1	1	1	0	1	1	1	1	1	1	1	1	1
NORTH AFRICA	5	3	3	2	2	3	3	3	2	2	..	3	3	3
Algeria	3	3	2	2	1	3	2	2	1	1	1	2	2	1
Egypt, Arab Republic of	1	1	1	1	1	1	1	1	1	1	2	1	1	1
Libya	11	6	6	5	4	9	12	10	7	6	7	6	7	8
Morocco	1	0	0	0	0	0	0	1	1	1	3	1	0	1
Tunisia	2	1	2	2	1	1	1	2	2	2	1	2	1	2
ALL AFRICA	4	2	2	2	1	2	2	2	2	2	..	3	2	2
South Africa	0	0	0	0	0	0	0	0	0	0	0	0	0	0

Note: Based on total reserves, excluding gold, at year-end and on imports of all goods and services at current prices and exchange rates.

5-13. Export unit values

	Index 1987=100											Average annual percentage growth		
	1980	1981	1982	1983	1984	1985	1986	1987	1988	1989	1990	75-80	80-85	86-MR
SUB-SAHARAN AFRICA	128	154	135	122	119	112	89	100	103	104	..	..	-4.3	5.2
excluding Nigeria	128	114	110	104	101	95	100	100	109	107	..	..	-5.3	3.0
Angola	..	..	..	..	..	..	..	..	..	..	..	..	..	..
Benin	71	60	54	51	48	77	87	100	115	99	121	7.8	-0.9	6.8
Botswana	114	107	89	81	78	72	82	100	134	160	..	11.8	-9.2	25.8
Burkina Faso	75	63	64	72	80	78	83	100	114	101	117	5.8	3.0	7.2
Burundi	136	92	100	105	106	102	144	100	112	90	72	17.0	-2.7	-13.9
Cameroon	87	86	77	73	70	66	81	100	110	100	103	7.4	-5.6	4.9
Cape Verde	89	89	89	78	73	66	80	100	106	94	145	16.1	-6.1	12.1
Central African Republic	76	63	73	68	64	73	87	100	102	97	116	19.8	-0.6	5.7
Chad	126	106	81	83	90	83	89	100	110	105	118	8.2	-7.0	6.3
Comoros	..	..	..	115	72	88	113	100	..	..	..	..	..	..
Congo, People's Republic of the	149	154	145	126	128	124	77	100	83	99	122	16.7	-4.5	9.5
Cote d'Ivoire	123	95	87	85	94	100	102	100	91	80	80	15.2	-3.0	-6.7
Djibouti	..	..	..	..	80	83	96	100	105	108	..	..	..	4.1
Equatorial Guinea	..	..	..	..	..	104	88	100	104	103	95	..	..	1.9
Ethiopia	..	..	..	..	..	..	..	..	..	..	..	..	..	..
Gabon	181	185	171	148	147	137	83	100	96	..	..	18.5	-6.2	7.5
Gambia, The	116	76	79	92	103	105	129	100	131	121	137	16.5	1.6	3.2
Ghana	44	26	15	46	62	77	107	100	95	92	..	4.4	20.5	-5.0
Guinea	..	..	..	..	..	..	92	100	105	94	106	..	..	2.2
Guinea-Bissau	29	80	67	55	77	87	49	100	100	96	93	9.1	15.9	13.3
Kenya	138	125	110	105	113	101	111	100	106	116	125	13.3	-5.2	3.9
Lesotho	119	125	95	120	98	75	78	100	108	123	116	6.4	-7.8	10.4
Liberia	..	..	..	..	..	..	..	..	..	..	..	..	..	..
Madagascar	103	107	111	118	117	104	124	100	103	91	96	8.5	1.1	-6.0
Malawi	106	134	124	115	117	89	91	100	105	..	..	4.9	-3.9	7.3
Mali	98	79	74	73	78	71	79	100	94	91	111	11.6	-4.6	6.0
Mauritania	91	95	93	86	84	93	101	100	105	103	104	0.1	-0.9	0.9
Mauritius	87	83	74	73	70	71	86	100	102	94	104	2.2	-4.2	3.3
Mozambique	90	100	79	83	93	87	97	100	103	101	104	..	-1.0	1.5
Namibia	135	110	100	100	90	80	87	100	113	122	..	..	-8.8	11.9
Niger	96	85	85	77	64	59	91	100	103	88	98	26.6	-9.2	0.3
Nigeria	130	199	171	154	153	143	61	100	87	99	..	9.8	-1.3	14.4
Rwanda	114	87	108	108	126	112	129	100	125	121	94	12.1	2.8	-4.3
Sao Tome & Principe	141	102	80	94	102	95	97	100	133	98	104	15.8	-5.0	1.1
Senegal	101	95	79	72	76	78	88	100	104	99	122	2.8	-5.8	6.6
Seychelles	..	..	..	..	..	..	..	..	..	..	..	..	..	..
Sierra Leone	189	199	183	210	159	191	219	100	177	219	236	25.1	-1.4	9.7
Somalia	121	142	169	142	122	139	93	100	101	151	..	-6.7	0.3	15.8
Sudan	109	118	145	123	142	120	91	100	118	135	134	3.9	2.5	11.4
Swaziland	..	..	..	..	..	..	..	..	..	..	..	..	..	..
Tanzania	112	99	96	96	99	92	107	100	108	..	..	8.8	-2.7	0.7
Togo	107	94	87	83	88	85	96	100	107	106	123	5.3	-4.0	5.8
Uganda	..	..	..	..	..	..	..	..	..	..	..	..	..	..
Zaire	221	188	206	164	111	101	109	100	115	120	105	17.6	-15.1	1.2
Zambia	144	118	95	107	101	94	78	100	148	129	120	14.2	-6.9	11.9
Zimbabwe	150	139	126	111	121	100	93	100	124	123	126	..	-7.1	8.6
NORTH AFRICA	162	171	151	141	131	127	93	100	100	104	113	15.9	-5.8	4.2
Algeria	210	220	182	168	158	154	92	100	86	96	121	19.9	-7.2	5.2
Egypt, Arab Republic of	128	145	144	135	121	117	96	100	106	104	93	14.8	-3.0	-0.1
Libya	..	..	..	..	..	..	..	..	..	..	..	..	..	..
Morocco	106	100	92	85	84	85	94	100	109	116	120	6.3	-4.7	6.5
Tunisia	130	124	115	109	100	96	92	100	102	104	119	11.3	-6.0	5.6
ALL AFRICA	141	161	142	131	125	119	91	100	102	104	..	13.6	-4.8	4.2
South Africa	124	108	93	101	86	74	84	100	101	93	..	14.2	-8.7	3.1

5–14. Import unit values

					Index 1987=100							Average annual percentage growth		
	1980	1981	1982	1983	1984	1985	1986	1987	1988	1989	1990	75–80	80–85	86–MR
SUB-SAHARAN AFRICA	102	99	98	94	86	85	89	100	107	111	..	..	-4.4	5.4
excluding Nigeria	126	119	117	110	96	93	97	100	107	115	..	..	-5.4	3.4
Angola	..	..	..	..	..	..	..	..	..	..	..	..	..	..
Benin	64	63	57	55	52	64	84	100	105	102	123	7.8	-0.9	6.8
Botswana	106	124	116	114	115	85	88	100	120	115	..	11.8	-9.2	25.8
Burkina Faso	95	82	84	82	81	77	84	100	103	103	116	5.8	3.0	7.2
Burundi	104	107	113	102	91	95	102	100	99	100	112	17.0	-2.7	-13.9
Cameroon	87	86	77	73	70	66	81	100	110	100	103	7.4	-5.6	4.9
Cape Verde	103	107	101	91	84	85	96	100	107	113	109	16.1	-6.1	12.1
Central African Republic	78	68	76	72	65	76	84	100	102	97	116	19.8	-0.6	5.7
Chad	126	108	69	83	90	83	89	100	110	105	118	8.2	-7.0	6.3
Comoros	..	..	..	75	69	70	87	100			..	..	..	..
Congo, People's Republic of the	113	113	76	71	68	81	85	100	100	96	118	16.7	-4.5	9.5
Cote d'Ivoire	105	93	87	84	81	84	83	100	99	97	108	15.2	-3.0	-6.7
Djibouti	..	..	..	..	80	83	96	100	110	112	..	..	..	4.1
Equatorial Guinea	..	..	..	..	..	95	77	100	103	106	102	..	..	1.9
Ethiopia	..	..	..	..	..	..	..	..	..	..	..	..	..	..
Gabon	77	67	64	61	68	69	91	100	122	..	..	18.5	-6.2	7.5
Gambia, The	64	60	62	95	79	84	92	100	110	114	130	16.5	1.6	3.2
Ghana	37	24	21	46	62	77	107	100	95	92	..	4.4	20.5	-5.0
Guinea	..	..	..	..	..	..	92	100	105	105	111	..	..	2.2
Guinea-Bissau	79	101	90	73	85	96	49	100	107	107	111	9.1	15.9	13.3
Kenya	105	109	104	105	100	102	100	100	101	109	115	13.3	-5.2	3.9
Lesotho	98	98	91	100	87	68	78	100	99	129	162	6.4	-7.8	10.4
Liberia	..	..	..	..	..	..	..	..	..	..	..	..	..	..
Madagascar	112	117	109	108	99	93	104	100	105	104	115	8.5	1.1	-6.0
Malawi	90	94	86	86	85	74	88	100	113	..	..	4.9	-3.9	7.3
Mali	116	94	86	80	75	75	94	100	103	101	107	11.6	-4.6	6.0
Mauritania	118	113	108	105	98	95	99	100	111	100	109	0.1	-0.9	0.9
Mauritius	98	100	95	88	85	88	91	100	106	108	122	2.2	-4.2	3.3
Mozambique	110	110	102	100	97	92	89	100	109	109	115	..	-1.0	1.5
Namibia	104	104	97	104	85	66	78	100	102	101	..	..	-7.7	8.1
Niger	152	120	92	77	68	64	89	100	115	123	140	26.6	-9.2	0.3
Nigeria	78	80	79	77	76	77	69	100	107	107	..	9.8	-1.3	14.4
Rwanda	104	99	96	94	83	83	90	100	107	106	114	12.1	2.8	-4.3
Sao Tome & Principe	91	89	82	77	72	73	81	100	93	96	114	15.8	-5.0	1.1
Senegal	111	98	93	87	80	81	86	100	106	104	124	2.8	-5.8	6.6
Seychelles	..	..	..	..	..	..	..	..	..	..	..	..	..	..
Sierra Leone	191	211	212	251	188	216	300	100	245	253	265	25.1	-1.4	9.7
Somalia	128	129	127	124	121	122	80	100	114	167	..	-6.7	0.3	15.8
Sudan	177	169	172	152	125	156	155	100	158	166	176	3.9	2.5	11.4
Swaziland	..	..	..	..	..	..	..	..	..	..	..	..	..	..
Tanzania	101	105	99	95	94	92	93	100	104	..	..	8.8	-2.7	0.7
Togo	115	98	89	85	82	82	88	100	103	99	108	5.3	-4.0	5.8
Uganda	..	..	..	..	..	.:.	..	..	..	..	..	..	..	..
Zaire	221	188	206	164	111	101	109	100	115	139	133	17.6	-15.1	1.2
Zambia	166	185	203	178	158	124	97	100	121	200	119	14.2	-6.9	11.9
Zimbabwe	99	91	83	73	80	69	83	100	75	77	88	..	-7.1	8.6
NORTH AFRICA	113	109	108	99	95	92	95	100	110	118	122	15.9	-5.8	4.2
Algeria	136	124	121	109	105	101	110	100	113	123	131	19.9	-7.2	5.2
Egypt, Arab Republic of	76	84	91	86	81	79	75	100	114	123	110	14.8	-3.0	-0.1
Libya	..	..	..	..	..	..	..	..	..	..	..	..	..	..
Morocco	117	116	110	101	101	100	100	100	103	111	122	6.3	-4.7	6.5
Tunisia	112	104	95	90	87	88	94	100	105	106	122	11.3	-6.0	5.6
ALL AFRICA	82	81	80	75	82	81	82	90	97	103	..	14.0	-4.8	7.9
South Africa	105	105	101	106	89	75	85	100	98	97	..	14.2	-8.7	3.1

5–15. Terms of trade

					Index 1987=100							Average annual percentage growth		
	1980	1981	1982	1983	1984	1985	1986	1987	1988	1989	1990	75–80	80–85	86–MR
SUB-SAHARAN AFRICA	135	168	150	139	144	136	101	100	98	96	..	..	-1.5	-1.4
excluding Nigeria	106	99	98	98	107	105	105	100	104	97	..	..	0.5	-1.9
Angola	..	..	..	..	..	..	..	..	..	..	..	-0.7	0.9	-1.3
Benin	111	95	94	93	92	120	104	100	109	97	99	0.3	-5.7	13.9
Botswana	108	86	77	71	68	84	94	100	112	139	..	-5.6	6.4	0.1
Burkina Faso	79	77	77	88	98	102	99	100	111	99	101	0.4	0.2	-15.5
Burundi	131	86	89	103	117	108	142	100	113	90	64	-4.7	0.0	0.0
Cameroon	100	100	100	100	100	100	100	100	100	100	100	13.0	-1.2	7.8
Cape Verde	86	83	88	85	87	78	83	100	99	83	133	9.6	0.4	-0.7
Central African Republic	97	93	96	95	99	96	104	100	100	100	100	-4.3	-0.3	0.0
Chad	100	98	118	100	100	100	100	100	100	100	100	..	..	..
Comoros	..	..	..	154	104	126	130	100	..	..	..	0.9	4.9	3.0
Congo, People's Republic of the	131	136	191	178	189	153	90	100	83	103	103	4.1	1.4	-11.1
Cote d'Ivoire	117	102	100	101	116	119	122	100	92	82	74	..	..	-1.5
Djibouti	..	..	..	..	100	100	100	100	96	97	..	..	..	-4.3
Equatorial Guinea	..	..	..	..	..	109	115	100	101	97	93	..	..	..
Ethiopia	..	..	..	..	..	..	..	..	..	..	..	10.7	-4.7	-7.4
Gabon	237	275	268	241	217	199	92	100	79	..	..	0.6	-5.7	-5.0
Gambia, The	183	126	127	98	130	125	141	100	120	106	106	4.0	-2.3	0.0
Ghana	119	109	73	100	100	100	100	100	100	100	..	..	..	-2.1
Guinea	..	..	..	..	..	..	100	100	100	90	95	..	..	..
Guinea-Bissau	37	79	74	75	90	91	100	100	93	89	84	-5.0	15.1	-4.4
Kenya	130	114	106	100	113	100	111	100	105	106	108	-0.5	-4.0	0.1
Lesotho	122	128	105	120	113	111	100	100	109	95	72	-7.2	-2.2	-7.0
Liberia	..	..	..	..	..	..	..	..	..	..	..	..	..	..
Madagascar	92	92	102	110	118	112	120	100	99	88	83	-6.5	5.3	-8.2
Malawi	118	142	144	133	138	120	104	100	93	..	..	-6.9	-0.2	-5.7
Mali	85	85	86	92	104	95	85	100	92	91	104	0.4	3.7	3.1
Mauritania	77	84	86	82	86	98	102	100	95	102	96	-10.0	3.5	-0.9
Mauritius	89	83	78	83	82	81	95	100	96	88	85	-8.5	-1.2	-3.4
Mozambique	82	91	77	83	96	94	109	100	95	93	90	..	2.7	-4.5
Namibia	129	106	104	96	106	121	112	100	112	121	..	..	-1.2	3.6
Niger	63	71	92	101	95	93	101	100	90	72	70	9.2	8.6	-10.2
Nigeria	168	250	216	200	202	186	88	100	81	93	..	4.4	-0.6	-0.3
Rwanda	110	88	112	115	151	135	143	100	117	114	83	0.4	8.0	-9.1
Sao Tome & Principe	155	115	98	122	141	131	121	100	143	103	91	3.9	-0.1	-5.2
Senegal	91	97	85	83	95	97	102	100	98	95	98	0.1	0.5	-1.3
Seychelles	..	..	..	..	..	..	..	..	..	..	..	..	..	..
Sierra Leone	99	95	86	84	85	88	73	100	72	87	89	14.6	-2.6	2.5
Somalia	94	110	133	115	101	114	116	100	89	90	..	1.5	1.5	-8.5
Sudan	62	70	85	81	114	77	59	100	75	81	76	1.6	7.5	3.2
Swaziland	..	..	..	..	..	..	..	..	..	..	..	-1.7	-0.3	-4.7
Tanzania	110	94	97	100	106	100	114	100	104	..	..	3.2	2.5	1.6
Togo	93	96	98	98	106	104	109	100	103	107	114	..	..	..
Uganda	..	..	..	..	..	..	..	..	..	87	79	11.7	0.0	-5.9
Zaire	100	100	100	100	100	100	100	100	100	65	101	-1.5	-1.2	0.1
Zambia	86	64	47	60	64	76	81	100	122	160	144	..	-0.7	10.2
Zimbabwe	152	152	152	152	152	144	113	100	165	160	144	4.7	-1.7	-2.9
NORTH AFRICA	144	157	140	142	138	138	101	100	91	88	92	..	-1.5	-0.4
Algeria	155	177	151	153	150	153	83	100	77	78	92	8.3	-2.9	-9.3
Egypt, Arab Republic of	168	172	158	156	151	148	128	100	93	84	85	3.3	..	..
Libya	..	..	..	..	..	..	..	..	105	104	98	-2.8	-1.1	1.3
Morocco	91	86	83	84	84	85	94	100	97	98	98	2.0	-1.0	-0.3
Tunisia	116	119	121	121	116	110	98	100	95	93	..	4.3	-1.5	-3.0
ALL AFRICA	139	164	145	140	141	137	101	100	95	96	..	2.7	-3.1	-0.9
South Africa	118	103	92	96	97	98	99	100	103	96	..			

5-16. Value of merchandise exports

	Millions of U.S. dollars										Average annual percentage growth		
	1980	1981	1982	1983	1984	1985	1986	1987	1988	1989	75-80	80-85	86-MR
SUB-SAHARAN AFRICA	49,308	39,691	33,297	29,990	32,690	33,099	25,940	29,409	28,876	30,789	17.3	-7.4	5.1
excluding Nigeria	17,939	15,335	13,810	13,508	14,534	13,942	15,897	17,202	17,601	17,467	11.9	-4.0	5.1
Angola	1,902	1,874	1,645	1,840	2,053	2,261	1,316	2,190	1,400	1,350	14.3	3.6	-3.6
Benin	63	34	24	67	167	123	100	70	60	50	15.5	29.9	-20.0
Botswana	503	400	457	636	674	744	865	1,587	1,418	1,360	30.3	11.6	13.3
Burkina Faso	90	75	56	57	79	70	83	155	142	75	13.4	-3.0	-3.8
Burundi	65	71	88	80	98	111	169	90	133	78	16.0	10.7	-17.5
Cameroon	1,384	1,122	1,000	939	882	722	781	829	924	900	26.1	-10.9	5.5
Cape Verde	4	3	4	3	3	6	4	8	3	5	9.1	5.1	-3.1
Central African Republic	115	79	109	75	86	92	131	130	130	134	15.9	-3.5	0.7
Chad	71	83	58	104	131	88	99	111	141	137	9.2	9.0	12.9
Comoros	20	16	20	19	7	16	20	12	21	18	16.6	-9.9	2.5
Congo, People's Republic of the	911	1,073	977	1,066	1,183	1,087	776	517	751	912	35.7	3.7	9.0
Cote d'Ivoire	3,142	2,535	2,235	2,067	2,698	2,939	3,354	3,110	3,100	2,970	19.6	-0.6	-3.6
Djibouti	19	9	13	11	13	14	20	20	20	20	-19.3	-1.7	0.0
Equatorial Guinea	14	16	17	18	20	23	39	39	49	41	0.8	9.6	3.9
Ethiopia	425	389	404	402	417	338	464	371	446	420	11.5	-2.7	-1.1
Gabon	2,173	2,200	2,160	1,975	2,018	1,974	1,271	1,288	1,200	1,160	16.0	-2.3	-3.4
Gambia, The	31	27	44	48	47	43	35	40	46	40	-2.5	10.2	5.6
Ghana	1,148	1,063	873	503	540	623	862	909	1,014	1,020	7.2	-14.9	6.3
Guinea	390	490	410	400	518	493	450	520	490	430	19.7	3.8	-1.9
Guinea-Bissau	11	14	12	9	17	12	15	15	15	13	16.5	2.1	-4.2
Kenya	1,389	1,188	977	983	1,083	958	1,200	961	1,071	1,110	13.9	-5.9	-1.2
Lesotho	58	50	37	31	29	23	26	40	40	40	37.7	-16.8	13.8
Liberia	589	529	477	428	452	436	408	382	430	370	7.8	-5.8	-1.7
Madagascar	402	316	310	296	333	274	304	332	274	312	8.3	-5.0	-1.1
Malawi	285	270	246	229	309	253	245	278	284	267	13.4	-0.7	2.8
Mali	205	154	146	165	205	176	206	256	249	271	26.4	0.6	8.3
Mauritania	194	261	232	305	297	374	349	428	354	238	-0.8	11.9	-12.5
Mauritius	431	324	367	361	373	435	675	901	979	987	8.8	1.3	13.0
Mozambique	281	281	229	132	96	77	79	97	103	101	10.5	-25.4	8.3
Namibia	..	..	..	..	680	727	879	890	940	920	..	..	1.9
Niger	566	455	332	299	274	209	243	310	290	250	46.4	-17.2	0.2
Nigeria	24,999	18,087	13,705	10,662	12,020	13,113	5,899	7,383	7,000	9,000	21.9	-12.6	12.9
Rwanda	112	110	103	80	145	131	189	114	108	88	18.1	4.0	-20.9
Sao Tome & Principe	20	14	9	6	7	6	10	7	10	5	26.4	-21.6	-15.8
Senegal	477	500	548	543	534	554	620	606	550	600	0.1	2.7	-1.9
Seychelles	21	17	15	20	26	28	18	22	31	31	38.8	9.0	21.8
Sierra Leone	204	153	89	92	148	106	145	132	115	138	15.4	-9.1	-2.8
Somalia	133	152	199	111	56	91	89	104	85	82	9.0	-14.5	-4.4
Sudan	543	658	499	624	629	367	333	504	509	672	2.2	-5.2	23.6
Swaziland	369	391	325	304	237	176	267	406	453	450	11.5	-14.0	18.2
Tanzania	508	613	455	366	403	354	345	310	276	260	4.5	-9.0	-9.2
Togo	335	211	177	162	191	190	204	244	242	210	23.9	-8.8	0.8
Uganda	345	242	350	385	385	387	436	319	274	273	4.0	6.1	-14.4
Zaire	1,639	662	569	1,134	1,004	950	1,092	970	1,108	1,254	12.8	-2.2	5.6
Zambia	1,299	1,074	1,022	825	655	543	403	873	1,178	1,347	9.5	-15.9	48.0
Zimbabwe	1,423	1,406	1,273	1,128	1,148	1,109	1,301	1,419	1,360	1,300	9.3	-5.5	-0.4
NORTH AFRICA	45,221	35,747	32,530	30,542	30,143	28,093	22,192	23,987	22,982	24,166	21.9	-8.1	2.2
Algeria	15,618	13,320	11,414	11,177	11,886	10,149	7,831	8,186	8,164	8,600	25.2	-6.9	2.8
Egypt, Arab Republic of	3,046	3,233	3,120	3,215	3,140	1,838	2,214	2,037	2,120	2,565	13.6	-7.1	4.9
Libya	21,919	14,371	13,951	12,216	11,148	12,314	7,747	8,766	6,700	6,760	23.0	-10.2	-6.6
Morocco	2,403	2,320	2,059	2,062	2,172	2,165	2,640	2,827	3,603	3,308	10.4	-2.0	9.6
Tunisia	2,235	2,503	1,986	1,872	1,797	1,627	1,760	2,171	2,395	2,933	23.7	-7.3	17.7
ALL AFRICA	94,529	75,438	65,827	60,532	62,833	61,192	48,132	53,396	51,858	54,955	19.3	-7.7	3.8
South Africa	12,548	11,076	9,635	9,672	9,334	9,326	10,861	12,718	13,263	15,316	24.0	-5.5	11.3

Note: Values cover the international movement of goods across customs borders. Figures may, therefore, differ from those referring to the Balance of Payments (Table 5-1).

5–17. Value of merchandise imports

	Millions of U.S. dollars										Average annual percentage growth		
	1980	*1981*	*1982*	*1983*	*1984*	*1985*	*1986*	*1987*	*1988*	*1989*	*75–80*	*80–85*	*86–MR*
SUB-SAHARAN AFRICA	43,462	48,024	39,073	30,680	26,787	27,322	27,054	28,619	29,735	30,145	15.6	-11.6	3.7
excluding Nigeria	24,275	22,820	20,516	18,178	17,609	17,749	19,348	21,241	22,740	23,291	14.4	-6.8	6.4
Angola	1,341	1,678	876	682	721	665	530	451	450	460	29.7	-16.5	-4.2
Benin	331	544	464	294	288	298	314	340	340	335	12.0	-7.9	2.0
Botswana	691	799	688	736	707	583	713	936	1,031	1,050	28.4	-3.2	13.4
Burkina Faso	358	338	346	288	253	333	405	434	489	410	20.7	-4.0	1.6
Burundi	168	161	214	183	186	186	205	212	206	188	25.0	2.3	-2.8
Cameroon	1,602	1,428	1,211	1,217	1,106	1,151	1,705	1,749	1,271	1,320	23.6	-6.7	-10.3
Cape Verde	68	71	70	79	83	83	107	100	106	123	10.7	4.6	4.9
Central African Republic	81	95	127	85	87	113	252	204	201	150	4.2	2.9	-14.5
Chad	74	108	109	157	182	240	288	366	419	435	-10.2	25.0	14.7
Comoros	33	34	33	34	43	36	37	52	60	60	12.6	3.4	17.3
Congo, People's Republic of the	545	804	744	688	595	576	576	529	544	524	25.4	-2.0	-2.5
Cote d'Ivoire	3,015	2,384	2,090	1,808	1,511	1,742	2,054	2,241	2,340	2,380	22.7	-11.4	5.0
Djibouti	125	120	226	221	228	201	188	201	205	210	-3.4	13.0	3.6
Equatorial Guinea	26	31	42	25	25	25	41	50	30	31	18.3	-3.8	-12.6
Ethiopia	722	739	787	876	943	989	1,101	1,101	1,075	1,100	19.2	7.1	-0.3
Gabon	674	841	723	853	888	976	866	732	930	950	3.1	6.4	5.3
Gambia, The	163	122	97	115	98	93	100	127	137	161	22.8	-9.0	16.2
Ghana	1,129	1,106	705	542	608	865	783	894	907	940	4.7	-9.2	5.8
Guinea	270	320	310	300	360	420	430	470	470	465	14.8	7.5	2.4
Guinea–Bissau	55	50	50	55	48	60	60	70	70	70	11.4	1.2	4.7
Kenya	2,588	2,069	1,613	1,358	1,551	1,437	1,613	1,756	1,993	2,100	21.2	-10.7	9.6
Lesotho	464	516	524	564	504	363	400	420	430	440	22.7	-3.4	3.1
Liberia	534	477	428	412	363	284	259	308	220	217	9.4	-10.8	-8.3
Madagascar	600	540	425	387	366	402	353	302	364	340	15.8	-8.9	0.7
Malawi	440	350	311	311	269	287	258	298	409	505	15.9	-8.0	26.3
Mali	440	385	332	353	368	470	496	479	513	500	24.8	0.7	0.9
Mauritania	286	265	273	227	213	234	221	235	240	222	10.1	-5.1	0.3
Mauritius	619	554	464	435	472	529	684	1,013	1,286	1,326	14.0	-3.7	24.9
Mozambique	800	801	836	636	540	424	543	625	715	680	18.0	-12.4	8.4
Namibia	..	..	..	..	520	578	680	888	861	830	..	..	5.8
Niger	594	510	466	324	285	345	330	370	375	370	45.7	-12.9	3.6
Nigeria	15,025	20,453	15,003	9,062	5,868	6,205	4,029	3,917	3,800	3,600	16.6	-21.9	-3.6
Rwanda	243	256	276	267	295	294	352	357	370	333	22.0	3.9	-1.3
Sao Tome & Principe	19	17	15	10	12	10	17	14	14	18	17.3	-12.5	1.7
Senegal	1,052	861	992	1,039	1,010	812	961	1,023	1,180	1,150	12.3	-2.2	7.1
Seychelles	99	93	98	88	88	99	105	114	153	164	25.1	-0.8	17.7
Sierra Leone	414	312	240	166	166	154	152	137	152	189	19.9	-18.6	7.9
Somalia	348	512	330	180	104	112	284	132	130	133	16.9	-27.1	-20.5
Sudan	1,576	1,578	1,285	1,354	1,147	757	961	929	1,060	1,210	7.7	-12.2	8.6
Swaziland	538	506	440	551	447	323	352	435	516	500	26.1	-7.4	13.0
Tanzania	1,226	1,212	1,131	804	918	974	838	976	823	840	13.0	-6.4	-1.6
Togo	550	433	391	284	271	288	312	424	487	482	30.4	-13.2	15.5
Uganda	293	345	377	377	344	298	307	555	544	652	7.9	0.2	25.1
Zaire	842	672	480	498	659	997	884	756	771	849	-2.1	2.4	-1.0
Zambia	1,111	1,062	1,001	703	608	692	603	739	839	873	3.6	-11.8	13.2
Zimbabwe	1,290	1,472	1,430	1,052	959	897	985	1,046	1,070	1,090	10.7	-9.3	3.3
NORTH AFRICA	29,893	36,663	34,702	34,839	34,401	28,958	29,076	26,625	30,423	30,784	12.2	-1.0	3.1
Algeria	10,544	11,295	10,731	10,397	10,289	9,841	9,234	7,029	7,396	8,380	13.4	-1.9	-2.4
Egypt, Arab Republic of	4,860	8,839	9,078	10,274	10,766	5,495	8,680	7,596	8,657	7,434	4.1	3.9	-3.3
Libya	6,777	8,382	7,175	7,467	6,221	7,176	4,192	4,723	5,910	5,100	15.2	-1.6	8.5
Morocco	4,185	4,356	4,316	3,599	3,907	3,849	4,069	4,230	4,772	5,492	10.2	-2.6	10.7
Tunisia	3,527	3,791	3,402	3,102	3,218	2,597	2,901	3,047	3,688	4,378	20.7	-5.9	15.3
ALL AFRICA	73,355	84,687	73,775	65,519	61,188	56,280	56,130	55,244	60,158	60,929	14.1	-6.7	3.4
South Africa	18,553	21,077	16,971	14,528	14,956	10,319	11,980	14,100	17,362	17,034	19.9	-11.1	13.5

Note: *Values cover the international movement of goods across customs borders. Figures may, therefore, differ from those referring to the Balance of Payments (Table 5-2).*

5–18. Forest products exports

	Thousands of cubic meters										Average annual percentage growth		
	1980	1981	1982	1983	1984	1985	1986	1987	1988	1989	75–80	80–85	86–MR
SUB-SAHARAN AFRICA	7,240	5,829	5,952	5,804	6,426	5,653	5,060	5,263	5,632	5,454	1.7	-2.7	3.0
excluding Nigeria	4,760	3,726	3,760	3,794	3,813	3,191	3,110	2,801	3,056	2,919	0.4	-5.3	-1.0
Angola	0	0	0	0	0	0	0	0	0	0	..	..	..
Benin	0	0	0	0	0	0	0	0	0	0	..	..	..
Botswana	0	0	0	0	0	0	0	0	0	0	..	..	..
Burkina Faso	0	0	0	0	0	0	0	0	0	0	..	..	..
Burundi	0	0	0	0	0	0	0	0	0	0	..	..	..
Cameroon	934	592	585	496	623	911	499	521	652	539	11.0	-0.4	4.6
Cape Verde	0	0	0	0	0	0	0	0	0	0	..	..	..
Central African Republic	177	164	133	132	125	101	95	74	53	53	5.1	-9.8	-18.6
Chad	0	0	0	0	0	0	0	0	0	0	..	..	..
Comoros	0	0	0	0	0	0	0	0	0	0	..	..	..
Congo, People's Republic of the	385	308	293	273	337	345	355	643	941	1,014	13.0	-1.0	42.3
Cote d'Ivoire	3,394	2,558	2,643	2,709	2,697	1,959	1,579	1,175	1,108	1,108	2.8	-7.1	-10.6
Djibouti	0	0	0	0	0	0	0	0	0	0	..	..	..
Equatorial Guinea	16	54	97	78	83	83	133	133	133	133	-16.0	30.0	0.1
Ethiopia	0	0	0	0	0	0	0	0	0	0	..	..	..
Gabon	1,150	1,177	1,212	1,189	1,592	1,146	1,035	1,282	965	965	0.0	2.5	-4.8
Gambia, The	0	0	0	0	0	0	0	0	0	0	..	..	..
Ghana	183	114	98	114	138	225	296	514	531	371	-20.9	5.1	7.4
Guinea	0	10	14	14	14	8	8	8	8	8	..	..	0.0
Guinea-Bissau	6	2	2	2	2	2	2	2	2	2	0.0	-17.3	0.0
Kenya	14	26	13	14	36	3	3	2	2	2	-20.5	-18.8	-15.7
Lesotho	0	0	0	0	0	0	0	0	0	0	..	..	..
Liberia	524	284	252	236	192	266	378	255	701	729	10.3	-12.4	34.7
Madagascar	0	1	1	1	1	0	1	2	2	2	-18.4	4.1	14.5
Malawi	0	2	2	2	2	0	0	0	0	0	..	..	..
Mali	0	0	0	0	0	0	0	0	0	0	..	..	..
Mauritania	0	0	0	0	0	0	0	0	0	0	..	..	..
Mauritius	0	0	0	0	0	0	0	0	0	0	..	..	..
Mozambique	31	22	13	4	4	3	4	5	10	2	-22.2	-39.2	-20.1
Namibia	0	0	0	0	0	0	0	0	0	0	..	..	..
Niger	0	0	0	0	0	0	0	0	0	0	..	..	..
Nigeria	11	27	102	52	61	60	60	17	17	17	-33.3	34.1	-31.4
Rwanda	0	0	0	0	0	0	0	0	0	0	..	..	..
Sao Tome & Principe	0	0	0	0	0	0	0	0	0	0	..	..	..
Senegal	0	0	0	0	0	0	0	0	0	0	..	..	..
Seychelles	0	0	0	0	0	0	0	0	0	0	..	..	..
Sierra Leone	0	0	0	1	0	1	3	3	3	3	..	..	0.0
Somalia	0	0	0	0	0	0	0	0	0	0	..	..	..
Sudan	0	0	0	0	0	0	0	0	0	0	..	..	..
Swaziland	265	364	355	355	355	355	355	355	355	355	1.2	4.0	0.0
Tanzania	9	3	2	2	2	9	9	6	6	6	-4.1	-2.2	-12.9
Togo	0	0	0	0	0	0	0	0	0	0	..	..	..
Uganda	0	0	0	0	0	0	0	0	0	0	..	..	..
Zaire	116	112	99	118	150	162	226	226	141	143	7.8	8.0	-16.7
Zambia	0	0	0	0	0	0	0	0	0	0	..	..	..
Zimbabwe	24	23	51	31	28	24	30	54	13	13	..	0.2	-32.8
NORTH AFRICA	5	5	4	6	8	10	4	4	3	3	16.8	16.8	-11.2
Algeria	0	0	0	0	0	0	0	0	0	0	..	..	..
Egypt, Arab Republic of	0	0	0	0	0	0	0	0	0	0	..	..	..
Libya	0	0	0	0	0	0	0	0	0	0	..	..	..
Morocco	5	5	4	6	8	10	4	4	3	3	16.8	16.8	-11.2
Tunisia	0	0	0	0	0	0	0	0	0	0	..	..	..
ALL AFRICA	7,245	5,834	5,956	5,809	6,434	5,663	5,064	5,267	5,635	5,456	1.7	-2.7	3.0
South Africa	362	166	201	165	164	146	157	950	1,001	1,001	31.6	-12.7	75.2

5-19. Petroleum exports

	Thousands of metric tons									Average annual percentage growth		
	1980	1981	1982	1983	1984	1985	1986	1987	1988	75-80	80-85	86-MR
SUB-SAHARAN AFRICA	115,835	78,840	67,712	66,910	76,597	85,764	85,768	83,535	90,472	2.7	-4.5	2.7
excluding Nigeria	1,061	1,040	1,177	1,150	1,492	1,532	1,450	1,381	1,358	..	8.6	-3.2
Angola	6,204	5,930	5,365	6,885	7,300	8,850	9,650	12,750	15,750	1.1	7.9	27.8
Benin	0	0	0	0	0	0	0	0	0	..	..	..
Botswana	0	0	0	0	0	0	0	0	0	..	..	..
Burkina Faso	0	0	0	0	0	0	0	0	0	..	..	..
Burundi	0	0	0	0	0	0	0	0	0	.	..	..
Cameroon	2,676	4,115	4,621	4,995	6,662	8,402	8,163	7,939	8,104	..	..	..
Cape Verde	0	0	0	0	0	0	0	0	0	..	..	..
Central African Republic	0	0	0	0	0	0	0	0	0	..	..	..
Chad	0	0	0	0	0	0	0	0	0	..	..	..
Comoros	0	0	0	0	0	0	0	0	0	.	..	..
Congo, People's Republic of the	3,000	4,205	4,515	5,295	6,140	6,000	6,952	6,895	7,038	9.7	14.6	0.6
Cote d'Ivoire	120	200	97	350	400	400	366	243	200	..	30.7	-26.1
Djibouti	0	0	0	0	0	0	0	0	0	..	..	..
Equatorial Guinea	0	0	0	0	0	0	0	0	0	..	..	..
Ethiopia	0	0	0	0	0	0	0	0	0	..	..	..
Gabon	7,560	6,245	6,515	6,820	6,960	7,742	7,352	7,057	7,895	-7.0	1.4	3.6
Gambia, The	0	0	0	0	0	0	0	0	0	..	..	..
Ghana	88	50	0	0	0	0	0	0	0	..	..	..
Guinea	0	0	0	0	0	0	0	0	0	..	..	..
Guinea-Bissau	0	0	0	0	0	0	0	0	0	..	..	..
Kenya	0	0	0	0	0	0	0	0	0	..	..	..
Lesotho	0	0	0	0	0	0	0	0	0	..	..	..
Liberia	0	0	0	0	0	0	0	0	0	..	..	..
Madagascar	0	0	0	0	0	0	0	0	0	..	..	..
Malawi	0	0	0	0	0	0	0	0	0	..	..	..
Mali	0	0	0	0	0	0	0	0	0	..	..	..
Mauritania	0	0	0	0	0	0	0	0	0	..	..	..
Mauritius	0	0	0	0	0	0	0	0	0	..	..	..
Mozambique	0	0	0	0	0	0	0	0	0	..	..	..
Namibia	0	0	0	0	0	0	0	0	0	..	..	..
Niger	0	0	0	0	0	0	0	0	0	..	..	..
Nigeria	98,010	61,420	50,140	46,760	54,705	61,640	60,364	55,452	58,431	3.4	-7.5	-1.6
Rwanda	0	0	0	0	0	0	0	0	0	..	..	..
Sao Tome & Principe	0	0	0	0	0	0	0	0	0	..	..	..
Senegal	0	0	0	0	0	0	0	0	0	..	..	..
Seychelles	0	0	0	0	0	0	0	0	0	..	..	..
Sierra Leone	0	0	0	0	0	0	0	0	0	..	..	..
Somalia	0	0	0	0	0	0	0	0	0	..	..	..
Sudan	0	0	0	0	0	0	0	0	0	..	..	..
Swaziland	0	0	0	0	0	0	0	0	0	..	..	..
Tanzania	0	0	0	0	0	0	0	0	0	..	..	..
Togo	0	0	0	0	0	0	0	0	0	..	..	..
Uganda	0	0	0	0	0	0	0	0	0	..	..	..
Zaire	853	790	1,080	800	1,092	1,132	1,084	1,138	1,158	..	6.1	3.4
Zambia	0	0	0	0	0	0	0	0	0	..	..	..
Zimbabwe	0	0	0	0	0	0	0	0	0	..	..	..
NORTH AFRICA	126,441	96,015	83,731	87,621	90,943	88,076	87,532	85,014	83,118	2.3	-5.4	-2.6
Algeria	35,775	30,714	24,228	27,288	25,793	24,023	20,916	22,789	23,464	-0.9	-6.6	5.9
Egypt, Arab Republic of	8,007	7,185	7,055	9,235	14,530	15,100	13,350	16,000	12,750	39.9	17.2	-2.3
Libya	78,050	53,125	48,700	46,870	46,480	44,730	48,958	41,960	42,620	2.6	-8.8	-6.7
Morocco	0	0	0	0	0	0	0	0	0	..	..	..
Tunisia	4,609	4,991	3,748	4,228	4,140	4,223	4,308	4,265	4,284	3.0	-2.5	-0.3
ALL AFRICA	242,276	174,855	151,443	154,531	167,540	173,840	173,300	168,549	173,590	2.5	-4.9	0.1
South Africa	0	0	0	0	0	0	0	0	0	..	..	..

5-20. Copper exports

			Thousands of metric tons							Average annual percentage growth		
	1980	*1981*	*1982*	*1983*	*1984*	*1985*	*1988*	*1987*	*1988*	*75–80*	*80–85*	*86–MR*
SUB-SAHARAN AFRICA	1,124	1,056	1,160	1,102	1,070	1,051	1,044	1,024	932	..	..	..
excluding Nigeria	1,122	1,055	1,160	1,102	1,070	1,051	1,044	1,024	932	..	..	..
Angola	0	0	0	0	0	0	0	0	0	..	..	..
Benin	0	0	0	0	0	0	0	0	0	..	..	..
Botswana	20	17	19	20	21	19	17	19	25	21.3	1.5	19.9
Burkina Faso	0	0	0	0	0	0	0	0	0	..	..	..
Burundi	0	0	0	0	0	0	0	0	0	..	..	..
Cameroon	0	0	0	0	0	0	0	0	0	..	..	..
Cape Verde	0	0	0	0	0	0	0	0	0	..	..	..
Central African Republic	0	0	0	0	0	0	0	0	0	..	..	..
Chad	0	0	0	0	0	0	0	0	0	..	..	..
Comoros	0	0	0	0	0	0	0	0	0	..	..	..
Congo, People's Republic of the	1	0	0	0	0	0	0	0	0	-9.4	..	..
Cote d'Ivoire	0	0	0	0	0	0	0	0	0	..	..	..
Djibouti	0	0	0	0	0	0	0	0	0	..	..	..
Equatorial Guinea	0	0	0	0	0	0	0	0	0	..	..	..
Ethiopia	0	0	0	0	0	0	0	0	0	..	..	..
Gabon	1	1	0	0	0	0	0	0	0	..	..	..
Gambia, The	0	0	0	0	0	0	0	0	0	..	..	..
Ghana	0	0	0	0	0	0	0	0	0	..	..	..
Guinea	0	0	0	0	0	0	0	0	0	..	..	..
Guinea-Bissau	0	0	0	0	0	0	0	0	0	..	..	..
Kenya	0	0	0	0	0	0	0	0	0	..	..	..
Lesotho	0	0	0	0	0	0	0	0	0	..	..	..
Liberia	0	0	0	0	0	0	0	0	0	..	..	..
Madagascar	0	0	0	0	0	0	0	0	0	..	..	..
Malawi	0	0	0	0	0	0	0	0	0	..	..	..
Mali	0	0	0	0	0	0	0	0	0	..	..	..
Mauritania	1	0	0	0	0	0	0	0	0	..	..	..
Mauritius	0	0	0	0	0	0	0	0	0	..	..	..
Mozambique	0	0	0	0	0	0	0	0	0	..	..	..
Namibia	41	39	44	47	46	49	43	37	38	1.9	4.3	-6.2
Niger	0	0	0	0	0	0	0	0	0	..	..	..
Nigeria	0	0	0	0	0	0	0	0	0	..	..	..
Rwanda	0	0	0	0	0	0	0	0	0	..	..	..
Sao Tome & Principe	0	0	0	0	0	0	0	0	0	..	..	..
Senegal	0	0	0	0	0	0	0	0	0	..	..	..
Seychelles	0	0	0	0	0	0	0	0	0	..	..	..
Sierra Leone	0	0	0	0	0	0	0	0	0	..	..	..
Somalia	0	0	0	0	0	0	0	0	0	..	..	..
Sudan	0	0	0	0	0	0	0	0	0	..	..	..
Swaziland	0	0	0	0	0	0	0	0	0	..	..	..
Tanzania	0	0	0	0	0	0	0	0	0	..	..	..
Togo	0	0	0	0	0	0	0	0	0	..	..	..
Uganda	0	0	0	0	0	0	0	0	0	..	..	..
Zaire	461	463	515	486	498	499	528	483	461	-2.4	1.6	-6.6
Zambia	617	556	603	571	530	505	466	499	424	-1.8	-3.4	-4.7
Zimbabwe	23	18	23	25	20	28	32	22	22	..	4.3	-16.2
NORTH AFRICA	6	7	21	22	23	28	18	17	13	15.0	36.9	-14.5
Algeria	0	0	0	0	0	0	0	0	0	0.0	..	0.0
Egypt, Arab Republic of	0	0	0	0	0	4	0	0	0	..	..	..
Libya	0	0	0	0	0	0	0	0	0	..	..	..
Morocco	6	7	21	22	22	24	18	17	13	15.7	34.6	-14.7
Tunisia	0	0	0	0	0	0	0	0	0	..	..	..
ALL AFRICA	1,130	1,063	1,181	1,124	1,093	1,079	1,062	1,041	945	..	..	..
South Africa	121	115	120	142	112	117	119	117	104	-0.8	-0.2	-6.5

5-21. Iron exports

	Thousands of metric tons									Average annual percentage growth		
	1980	1981	1982	1983	1984	1985	1986	1987	1988	75-80	80-85	86-MR
SUB-SAHARAN AFRICA	17,482	19,674	15,994	15,637	17,718	16,892	15,504	14,903	14,805	-3.8	-1.4	-2.3
excluding Nigeria	17,482	19,611	15,994	15,574	17,718	16,892	15,504	14,903	14,805	-3.8	-1.4	-2.3
Angola	0	63	0	63	0	0	0	0	0	..	..	..
Benin	0	0	0	0	0	0	0	0	0	..	..	..
Botswana	0	0	0	0	0	0	0	0	0	..	..	..
Burkina Faso	0	0	0	0	0	0	0	0	0	..	..	..
Burundi	0	0	0	0	0	0	0	0	· 0	..	..	..
Cameroon	0	0	0	0	0	0	0	0	0	..	..	..
Cape Verde	0	0	0	0	0	0	0	0	0	..	..	..
Central African Republic	0	0	0	0	0	0	0	0	0	..	..	..
Chad	0	0	0	0	0	0	0	0	0	..	..	..
Comoros	0	0	0	0	0	0	0	0	0	..	..	..
Congo, People's Republic of the	0	0	0	0	0	0	0	0	0	..	..	..
Cote d'Ivoire	0	0	0	0	0	0	0	0	0	..	..	..
Djibouti	0	0	0	0	0	0	0	0	0	..	..	..
Equatorial Guinea	0	0	0	0	0	0	0	0	0	..	..	..
Ethiopia	0	0	0	0	0	0	0	0	0	..	..	..
Gabon	0	0	0	0	0	0	0	0	0	..	..	..
Gambia, The	0	0	0	0	0	0	0	0	0	..	..	..
Ghana	0	0	0	0	0	0	0	0	0	..	..	..
Guinea	0	0	0	0	0	0	0	0	0	..	..	..
Guinea-Bissau	0	0	0	0	0	0	0	0	0	..	..	..
Kenya	0	0	0	0	0	0	0	0	0	..	..	..
Lesotho	0	0	0	0	0	0	0	0	0	..	..	..
Liberia	11,695	13,865	10,924	10,522	11,303	10,787	9,700	9,052	8,783	-0.6	-3.0	-4.8
Madagascar	0	0	0	0	0	0	0	0	0	..	..	..
Malawi	0	0	0	0	0	0	0	0	0	..	..	..
Mali	0	0	0	0	0	0	0	0	0	..	..	..
Mauritania	5,673	5,746	5,070	4,812	6,175	6,045	5,804	5,851	6,022	-4.7	1.4	1.9
Mauritius	0	0	0	0	0	0	0	0	0	..	..	..
Mozambique	0	0	0	0	0	0	0	0	0	..	..	..
Namibia	0	0	0	0	0	0	0	0	0	..	..	..
Niger	0	0	0	0	0	0	0	0	0	..	..	..
Nigeria	0	0	0	0	0	0	0	0	0	..	..	..
Rwanda	0	0	0	0	0	0	0	0	0	..	..	..
Sao Tome & Principe	0	0	0	0	0	0	0	0	0	..	..	..
Senegal	0	0	0	0	0	0	0	0	0	..	..	..
Seychelles	0	0	0	0	0	0	0	0	0	..	..	..
Sierra Leone	0	0	0	240	240	60	0	0	0	..	..	..
Somalia	0	0	0	0	0	0	0	0	0	..	..	..
Sudan	0	0	0	0	0	0	0	0	0	..	..	..
Swaziland	114	0	0	0	0	0	0	0	0	-39.1	..	..
Tanzania	0	0	0	0	0	0	0	0	0	..	..	..
Togo	0	0	0	0	0	0	0	0	0	..	..	..
Uganda	0	0	0	0	0	0	0	0	0	..	..	..
Zaire	0	0	0	0	0	0	0	0	0	..	..	..
Zambia	0	0	0	0	0	0	0	0	0	..	..	..
Zimbabwe	0	0	0	0	0	0	0	0	0	..	..	..
NORTH AFRICA	784	742	710	699	487	4	23	6	0	-4.6	-54.6	..
Algeria	699	739	710	699	487	4	23	6	0	1.7	-53.9	..
Egypt, Arab Republic of	0	0	0	0	0	0	0	0	0	..	..	..
Libya	0	0	0	0	0	0	0	0	0	..	..	..
Morocco	85	3	0	0	0	0	0	0	0	-24.8	..	..
Tunisia	0	0	0	0	0	0	0	0	0	..	..	..
ALL AFRICA	18,266	20,416	16,704	16,336	18,205	16,896	15,527	14,909	14,805	-3.8	-2.1	-2.4
South Africa	10,733	9,316	7,605	4,914	7,497	6,426	5,607	5,544	6,225	46.4	-9.9	5.4

5–22. Manganese exports

	Thousands of metric tons									Average annual percentage growth		
	1980	1981	1982	1983	1984	1985	1986	1987	1988	75–80	80–85	86–MR
SUB-SAHARAN AFRICA	2,389	1,715	1,526	2,156	2,409	2,482	2,760	2,529	2,529	13.0	4.5	–4.3
excluding Nigeria	252	172	113	128	237	252	277	239	239	2.9	3.1	–7.1
Angola	0	0	0	0	0	0	0	0	0	..	..	..
Benin	0	0	0	0	0	0	0	0	0	..	..	..
Botswana	0	0	0	0	0	0	0	0	0	..	..	..
Burkina Faso	0	0	0	0	0	0	0	0	0	..	..	..
Burundi	0	0	0	0	0	0	0	0	0	..	..	..
Cameroon	0	0	0	0	0	0	0	0	0	..	..	..
Cape Verde	0	0	0	0	0	0	0	0	0	..	..	..
Central African Republic	0	0	0	0	0	0	0	0	0	..	..	..
Chad	0	0	0	0	0	0	0	0	0	..	..	..
Comoros	0	0	0	0	0	0	0	0	0	..	..	..
Congo, People's Republic of the	0	0	0	0	0	0	0	0	0	..	..	..
Cote d'Ivoire	0	0	0	0	0	0	0	0	0	..	..	..
Djibouti	0	0	0	0	0	0	0	0	0	..	..	..
Equatorial Guinea	0	0	0	0	0	0	0	0	0	..	..	..
Ethiopia	0	0	0	0	0	0	0	0	0	..	..	..
Gabon	2,137	1,543	1,413	2,028	2,172	2,230	2,483	2,290	2,290	14.6	4.7	–4.0
Gambia, The	0	0	0	0	0	0	0	0	0	..	..	..
Ghana	236	142	97	127	237	252	277	239	239	7.8	6.3	–7.1
Guinea	0	0	0	0	0	0	0	0	0	..	..	..
Guinea-Bissau	0	0	0	0	0	0	0	0	0	..	..	..
Kenya	0	0	0	0	0	0	0	0	0	..	..	..
Lesotho	0	0	0	0	0	0	0	0	0	..	..	..
Liberia	0	0	0	0	0	0	0	0	0	..	..	..
Madagascar	0	0	0	0	0	0	0	0	0	..	..	..
Malawi	0	0	0	0	0	0	0	0	0	..	..	..
Mali	0	0	0	0	0	0	0	0	0	..	..	..
Mauritania	0	0	0	0	0	0	0	0	0	..	..	..
Mauritius	0	0	0	0	0	0	0	0	0	..	..	..
Mozambique	0	0	0	0	0	0	0	0	0	..	..	..
Namibia	0	0	0	0	0	0	0	0	0	..	..	..
Niger	0	0	0	0	0	0	0	0	0	..	..	..
Nigeria	0	0	0	0	0	0	0	0	0	..	..	..
Rwanda	0	0	0	0	0	0	0	0	0	..	..	..
Sao Tome & Principe	0	0	0	0	0	0	0	0	0	..	..	..
Senegal	0	0	0	0	0	0	0	0	0	..	..	..
Seychelles	0	0	0	0	0	0	0	0	0	..	..	..
Sierra Leone	0	0	0	0	0	0	0	0	0	..	..	..
Somalia	0	0	0	0	0	0	0	0	0	..	..	..
Sudan	0	0	0	0	0	0	0	0	0	..	..	..
Swaziland	0	0	0	0	0	0	0	0	0	..	..	..
Tanzania	0	0	0	0	0	0	0	0	0	..	..	..
Togo	0	0	0	0	0	0	0	0	0	..	..	..
Uganda	0	0	0	0	0	0	0	0	0	..	..	..
Zaire	16	30	16	1	0	0	0	0	0	–20.7	..	..
Zambia	0	0	0	0	0	0	0	0	0	..	..	..
Zimbabwe	0	0	0	0	0	0	0	0	0	..	..	..
NORTH AFRICA	112	100	82	58	70	47	51	44	47	13.0	–15.2	–3.3
Algeria	0	0	0	0	0	0	0	0	0	..	..	..
Egypt, Arab Republic of	0	0	0	0	0	0	0	0	0	..	..	..
Libya	0	0	0	0	0	0	0	0	0	..	..	..
Morocco	112	100	82	58	70	47	51	44	47	13.0	–15.2	–3.3
Tunisia	0	0	0	0	0	0	0	0	0	..	..	..
ALL AFRICA	2,501	1,815	1,608	2,214	2,478	2,529	2,811	2,573	2,577	13.0	3.8	–4.3
South Africa	3,326	3,155	2,869	1,996	3,038	2,890	2,416	1,562	1,562	15.0	–3.3	–19.6

5-23. Phosphates exports

	Thousands of metric tons									Average annual percentage growth		
	1980	1981	1982	1983	1984	1985	1986	1987	1988	75–80	80–85	86–MR
SUB-SAHARAN AFRICA	4,274	3,371	3,258	3,279	4,121	3,698	3,619	3,962	4,715	9.2	-0.3	14.1
excluding Nigeria	4,274	3,371	3,258	3,279	4,121	3,698	3,619	3,962	4,715	9.2	-0.3	14.1
Angola	0	0	0	0	0	0	0	0	0	..	..	..
Benin	0	0	0	0	0	0	0	0	0	..	..	..
Botswana	0	0	0	0	0	0	0	0	0	..	..	..
Burkina Faso	0	0	0	0	0	0	0	0	0	..	..	..
Burundi	0	0	0	0	0	0	0	0	0	..	..	..
Cameroon	0	0	0	0	0	0	0	0	0	..	..	..
Cape Verde	0	0	0	0	0	0	0	0	0	..	..	..
Central African Republic	0	0	0	0	0	0	0	0	0	..	..	..
Chad	0	0	0	0	0	0	0	0	0	..	..	..
Comoros	0	0	0	0	0	0	0	0	0	..	..	..
Congo, People's Republic of the	0	0	0	0	0	0	0	0	0	..	..	..
Cote d'Ivoire	0	0	0	0	0	0	0	0	0	..	..	..
Djibouti	0	0	0	0	0	0	0	0	0	..	..	..
Equatorial Guinea	0	0	0	0	0	0	0	0	0	..	..	..
Ethiopia	0	0	0	0	0	0	0	0	0	..	..	..
Gabon	0	0	0	0	0	0	0	0	0	..	..	..
Gambia, The	0	0	0	0	0	0	0	0	0	..	..	..
Ghana	0	0	0	0	0	0	0	0	0	..	..	..
Guinea	0	0	0	0	0	0	0	0	0	..	..	..
Guinea-Bissau	0	0	0	0	0	0	0	0	0	..	..	..
Kenya	0	0	0	0	0	0	0	0	0	..	..	..
Lesotho	0	0	0	0	0	0	0	0	0	..	..	..
Liberia	0	0	0	0	0	0	0	0	0	..	..	..
Madagascar	0	0	0	0	0	0	0	0	0	..	..	..
Malawi	0	0	0	0	0	0	0	0	0	..	..	..
Mali	0	0	0	0	0	0	0	0	0	..	..	..
Mauritania	0	0	0	0	0	0	0	0	0	..	..	..
Mauritius	0	0	0	0	0	0	0	0	0	..	..	..
Mozambique	0	0	0	0	0	0	0	0	0	..	..	..
Namibia	0	0	0	0	0	0	0	0	0	..	..	..
Niger	0	0	0	0	0	0	0	0	0	..	..	..
Nigeria	0	0	0	0	0	0	0	0	0	..	..	..
Rwanda	0	0	0	0	0	0	0	0	0	..	..	..
Sao Tome & Principe	0	0	0	0	0	0	0	0	0	..	..	..
Senegal	1,378	1,155	1,203	1,271	1,360	1,253	1,353	1,453	1,847	-1.5	0.2	16.8
Seychelles	0	0	0	0	0	0	0	0	0	..	..	..
Sierra Leone	0	0	0	0	0	0	0	0	0	..	..	..
Somalia	0	0	0	0	0	0	0	0	0	..	..	..
Sudan	0	0	0	0	0	0	0	0	0	..	..	..
Swaziland	0	0	0	0	0	0	0	0	0	..	..	..
Tanzania	0	0	0	0	0	0	0	0	0	..	..	..
Togo	2,896	2,215	2,055	2,008	2,761	2,445	2,266	2,509	2,868	18.3	-0.6	12.5
Uganda	0	0	0	0	0	0	0	0	0	..	..	..
Zaire	0	0	0	0	0	0	0	0	0	..	..	..
Zambia	0	0	0	0	0	0	0	0	0	..	..	..
Zimbabwe	0	0	0	0	0	0	0	0	0	..	..	..
NORTH AFRICA	18,932	17,702	16,110	16,784	16,975	16,888	15,890	15,284	16,560	4.9	-1.9	2.1
Algeria	768	791	704	583	568	821	818	800	877	19.9	-2.4	3.5
Egypt, Arab Republic of	258	229	291	340	267	149	183	180	268	6.2	-5.9	20.8
Libya	0	0	0	0	0	0	0	0	0	..	..	..
Morocco	16,457	15,636	13,976	14,653	14,976	14,790	13,696	13,061	14,260	5.5	-1.7	2.0
Tunisia	1,449	1,046	1,139	1,208	1,165	1,128	1,193	1,245	1,156	-4.5	-2.5	-1.6
ALL AFRICA	23,206	21,072	19,368	20,063	21,096	20,586	19,510	19,246	21,275	5.6	-1.6	4.4
South Africa	4	105	200	303	528	500	949	1,061	1,268	-33.8	135.3	15.6

5-24. Cocoa exports

				Thousands of metric tons						Average annual percentage growth		
	1980	1981	1982	1983	1984	1985	1986	1987	1988	1989	75–80	80–85	86–MR
SUB-SAHARAN AFRICA	869	1,091	934	889	1,012	968	1,106	1,077	1,072	1,131	-3.5	0.8	0.6
excluding Nigeria	607	769	696	566	752	753	822	834	723	893	-2.5	2.3	1.1
Angola	0	0	0	0	0	0	0	0	0	0	..	..	..
Benin	5	0	0	3	10	16	13	6	1	0	38.3	..	-80.5
Botswana	0	0	0	0	0	0	0	0	0	0	..	..	..
Burkina Faso	0	0	0	0	0	0	0	0	0	0	..	..	..
Burundi	0	0	0	0	0	0	0	0	0	0	..	..	..
Cameroon	105	102	79	91	105	96	106	129	135	109	1.8	-0.7	1.2
Cape Verde	0	0	0	0	0	0	0	0	0	0	..	..	..
Central African Republic	0	0	0	0	0	0	0	0	0	0	-32.7	..	..
Chad	0	0	0	0	0	0	0	0	0	0	..	..	..
Comoros	0	0	0	0	0	0	0	0	0	0	-11.6	..	..
Congo, People's Republic of the	2	2	2	1	2	2	1	1	1	1	-1.0	-5.1	-4.4
Cote d'Ivoire	332	500	387	345	518	503	550	561	451	559	7.2	6.1	-1.7
Djibouti	0	0	0	0	0	0	0	0	0	0	..	..	..
Equatorial Guinea	7	10	8	10	8	9	7	8	8	6	-3.2	3.8	-5.0
Ethiopia	0	0	0	0	0	0	0	0	0	0	..	..	..
Gabon	4	4	3	3	2	2	2	2	2	2	-2.3	-18.9	0.5
Gambia, The	0	0	0	0	0	0	0	0	0	0	..	..	..
Ghana	218	207	260	166	162	188	211	219	223	294	-11.4	-5.3	10.5
Guinea	4	4	4	4	4	4	3	3	3	3	4.2	-50.0	2.0
Guinea-Bissau	0	0	0	0	0	0	0	0	0	0	..	..	..
Kenya	0	0	0	0	0	0	0	0	0	0	-4.2	-24.7	-7.9
Lesotho	0	0	0	0	0	0	0	0	0	0	..	..	..
Liberia	4	7	5	6	6	5	4	3	4	3	7.2	4.1	-4.8
Madagascar	2	2	1	2	2	2	2	3	4	3	2.6	5.3	8.7
Malawi	0	0	0	0	0	0	0	0	0	0	..	..	..
Mali	0	0	0	0	0	0	0	0	0	0	..	..	..
Mauritania	0	0	0	0	0	0	0	0	0	0	..	..	..
Mauritius	0	0	0	0	0	0	0	0	0	0	..	..	..
Mozambique	0	0	0	0	0	0	0	0	0	0	..	..	..
Namibia	0	0	0	0	0	0	0	0	0	0	..	..	..
Niger	0	0	0	0	0	0	0	0	0	0	..	..	..
Nigeria	151	214	155	228	151	116	175	112	212	126	-9.7	-5.4	-3.4
Rwanda	0	0	0	0	0	0	0	0	0	0	..	..	..
Sao Tome & Principe	7	7	6	4	4	3	3	3	4	4	8.1	-16.1	18.2
Senegal	0	0	0	0	0	0	0	0	0	0	-3.5	..	..
Seychelles	0	0	0	0	0	0	0	0	0	0	..	..	..
Sierra Leone	8	9	9	8	10	10	9	9	9	8	9.2	3.6	-2.4
Somalia	0	0	0	0	0	0	0	0	0	0	..	..	..
Sudan	0	0	0	0	0	0	0	0	0	0	..	..	..
Swaziland	0	0	0	0	0	0	0	0	0	0	..	..	..
Tanzania	1	1	1	2	1	1	1	1	1	2	15.9	3.9	7.0
Togo	15	18	10	9	21	7	13	12	11	7	-2.4	-9.5	-19.1
Uganda	0	0	0	0	0	0	0	0	0	0	21.1	6.6	15.7
Zaire	4	4	4	4	4	5	5	5	4	4	-2.6	1.2	-6.9
Zambia	0	0	0	0	0	0	0	0	0	0	..	13.8	78.8
Zimbabwe	0	0	0	0	0	0	0	0	0	0	..	..	50.0
NORTH AFRICA	0	0	0	0	0	0	0	1	0	1	..	..	50.0
Algeria	0	0	0	0	0	0	0	0	0	0	..	..	47.0
Egypt, Arab Republic of	0	0	0	0	0	0	0	0	0	0	..	..	..
Libya	0	0	0	0	0	0	0	0	0	0	..	..	..
Morocco	0	0	0	0	0	0	0	1	0	1	..	..	57.0
Tunisia	0	0	0	0	0	0	0	0	0	0	..	..	..
ALL AFRICA	869	1,091	934	889	1,012	969	1,106	1,078	1,073	1,131	-3.5	0.8	0.6
South Africa	0	0	1	0	1	1	1	1	2	1	-19.5	9.4	15.3

5-25. Coffee exports

	Thousands of metric tons										Average annual percentage growth		
	1980	1981	1982	1983	1984	1985	1986	1987	1988	1989	75–80	80–85	86–MR
SUB-SAHARAN AFRICA	895	965	1,053	939	914	973	1,076	910	959	974	-3.9	0.4	-2.4
excluding Nigeria	751	823	926	813	784	851	931	799	850	882	-2.5	1.0	-1.0
Angola	47	45	46	27	23	19	19	11	11	8	-19.3	-18.6	-23.6
Benin	0	1	2	1	2	0	0	0	3	3	-29.1	8.1	158.8
Botswana	0	0	0	0	0	0	0	0	..	..	..	..	..
Burkina Faso	0	0	0	0	0	0	0	0	0	0	..	..	..
Burundi	19	27	30	25	29	34	37	27	37	29	-2.1	9.1	-3.9
Cameroon	92	93	77	94	103	101	124	98	95	79	-0.1	3.0	-12.9
Cape Verde	0	0	0	0	0	0	0	0	0	0	..	..	..
Central African Republic	11	11	20	13	12	17	10	8	15	20	-1.9	5.9	29.9
Chad	0	0	0	0	0	0	0	0	0	0	..	..	..
Comoros	0	0	0	0	0	0	0	0	0	0	-21.2	..	..
Congo, People's Republic of the	2	2	2	1	3	1	1	0	0	1	14.1	-8.1	10.5
Cote d'Ivoire	207	231	273	223	188	241	230	165	235	180	-4.8	-0.2	-3.8
Djibouti	0	0	0	0	0	0	0	0	0	0	..	..	..
Equatorial Guinea	0	0	1	1	1	1	1	1	1	1	-38.4	38.2	-20.7
Ethiopia	76	86	84	93	87	68	74	74	84	102	7.3	-1.2	11.6
Gabon	1	1	1	1	1	1	2	1	2	2	33.4	5.3	8.8
Gambia, The	0	0	0	0	0	0	0	0	0	0	..	..	..
Ghana	0	1	1	1	0	0	1	1	1	1	-49.1	13.5	6.5
Guinea	3	3	3	5	0	1	4	5	6	10	0.4	-34.7	33.3
Guinea-Bissau	0	0	0	0	0	0	0	0	0	0	..	..	..
Kenya	80	86	101	90	97	105	127	100	88	104	2.7	4.6	-6.9
Lesotho	0	0	0	0	0	0	0	0	0	0	..	..	..
Liberia	13	8	10	7	5	11	8	5	4	5	23.6	-7.1	-17.8
Madagascar	69	57	54	50	51	42	47	47	43	48	-0.5	-8.1	-0.6
Malawi	0	1	1	1	2	3	4	5	4	4	18.7	42.3	-3.9
Mali	0	0	0	0	0	0	0	0	0	0	..	..	..
Mauritania	0	0	0	0	0	0	0	0	0	0	..	..	..
Mauritius	0	0	0	0	0	0	0	0	0	0	..	..	..
Mozambique	0	0	0	0	0	0	0	0	0	0	..	..	..
Namibia	0	0	0	0	0	0	0	0	0	0	..	..	..
Niger	0	0	0	0	0	0	0	0	0	0	..	..	..
Nigeria	2	2	2	3	0	0	0	1	1	3	-4.2	-49.3	62.7
Rwanda	22	29	27	29	32	34	41	46	40	28	-1.9	7.2	-11.8
Sao Tome & Principe	0	0	0	0	0	0	0	0	0	0	-5.0	-1.5	0.0
Senegal	1	0	0	0	0	0	0	0	0	0	143.7	..	..
Seychelles	0	0	0	0	0	0	0	0	0	0	..	..	..
Sierra Leone	10	9	9	6	2	10	7	6	8	5	13.0	-13.3	-6.0
Somalia	0	0	0	0	0	0	0	0	0	0	..	..	..
Sudan	0	0	0	0	0	0	0	0	0	0	..	..	..
Swaziland	0	0	0	0	0	0	0	0	0	0	..	..	..
Tanzania	43	61	52	48	53	44	49	44	50	49	-4.1	-1.3	1.1
Togo	9	10	10	6	3	10	8	14	11	13	2.2	-10.9	11.8
Uganda	110	128	175	144	133	152	141	151	144	176	-9.1	4.5	6.5
Zaire	74	68	68	63	77	66	130	89	68	98	1.1	-0.7	-10.5
Zambia	0	0	0	0	0	0	0	0	0	0	..	..	-42.4
Zimbabwe	3	6	7	7	10	12	11	12	9	7	-0.4	27.8	-12.8
NORTH AFRICA	0	0	0	0	0	0	0	0	0	2	..	..	..
Algeria	0	0	0	0	0	0	0	0	0	0	..	..	..
Egypt, Arab Republic of	0	0	0	0	0	0	0	0	0	2	..	..	..
Libya	0	0	0	0	0	0	0	0	0	0	..	..	..
Morocco	0	0	0	0	0	0	0	0	0	0	..	..	..
Tunisia	0	0	0	0	0	0	0	0	0	0	..	..	..
ALL AFRICA	895	965	1,053	939	914	973	1,076	910	960	976	-3.9	0.4	-2.4
South Africa	0	1	1	0	0	0	0	0	2	1	45.4	-17.1	54.2

5–26. Cotton exports

	Thousands of metric tons										Average annual percentage growth		
	1980	1981	1982	1983	1984	1985	1986	1987	1988	1989	75–80	80–85	86–MR
SUB-SAHARAN AFRICA	465	400	407	519	582	492	685	694	686	771	0.9	4.8	3.5
excluding Nigeria	440	375	380	495	553	472	667	671	663	713	0.5	5.2	1.9
Angola	0	0	1	1	1	1	1	1	1	2	..	..	23.1
Benin	8	8	5	11	22	22	38	42	40	42	-8.5	29.1	2.6
Botswana	0	1	1	0	0	0	0	0	0	0	76.6	..	..
Burkina Faso	28	22	19	23	29	25	45	65	55	53	15.7	1.2	3.6
Burundi	1	1	2	2	0	0	0	3	1	0	10.2	-20.6	-15.1
Cameroon	26	25	25	23	28	19	18	21	22	55	17.0	-3.6	41.7
Cape Verde	0	0	0	0	0	0	0	0	0	0	..	..	..
Central African Republic	14	14	6	12	11	15	15	10	7	8	-7.0	0.2	-18.1
Chad	35	32	22	35	57	33	36	33	43	48	-4.8	5.7	11.9
Comoros	0	0	0	0	0	0	0	0	0	0	..	..	..
Congo, People's Republic of the	0	0	0	0	0	0	0	0	0	0	..	..	..
Cote d'Ivoire	39	39	37	49	45	54	80	68	96	112	25.1	6.9	14.5
Djibouti	0	0	0	0	0	0	0	0	0	0	..	..	..
Equatorial Guinea	0	0	0	0	0	0	0	0	0	0	..	..	..
Ethiopia	6	5	7	3	2	0	0	0	0	0	5.0	..	..
Gabon	0	0	0	0	0	0	0	0	0	0	..	..	..
Gambia, The	0	0	0	0	0	1	1	0	0	1	..	..	8.6
Ghana	0	0	0	0	0	0	0	0	0	0	..	..	..
Guinea	0	0	0	0	0	0	0	0	0	0	..	..	..
Guinea-Bissau	0	1	0	0	1	0	0	0	1	1	..	..	42.3
Kenya	4	3	0	1	0	2	0	0	0	0	3.2	..	..
Lesotho	0	0	0	0	0	0	0	0	0	0	..	..	..
Liberia	0	0	0	0	0	0	0	0	0	0	..	..	..
Madagascar	1	4	4	2	3	0	8	6	1	1	..	-12.2	-54.6
Malawi	3	0	0	0	2	7	2	1	0	1	-2.4	..	..
Mali	53	45	57	44	49	50	69	78	71	102	16.9	-0.6	11.6
Mauritania	0	0	0	0	0	0	0	0	0	0	..	..	..
Mauritius	0	0	0	0	0	0	0	0	0	0	..	..	..
Mozambique	6	15	14	13	6	5	1	4	3	5	-13.4	-10.3	67.3
Namibia	0	0	0	0	0	0	0	0	0	0	..	..	..
Niger	0	0	0	0	0	0	0	2	1	3	14.2	..	64.5
Nigeria	0	0	0	0	0	0	0	0	0	1	..	..	..
Rwanda	0	0	0	0	0	0	0	0	0	0	..	..	..
Sao Tome & Principe	0	0	0	0	0	0	0	0	0	0	..	..	..
Senegal	6	4	11	14	9	10	13	5	12	13	-0.1	16.2	8.0
Seychelles	0	0	0	0	0	0	0	0	0	0	..	..	..
Sierra Leone	0	0	0	0	0	0	0	0	0	0	..	..	..
Somalia	0	0	0	0	0	0	0	0	0	0	..	..	..
Sudan	132	65	91	170	211	115	203	204	177	140	-2.4	10.4	-11.8
Swaziland	4	7	2	3	2	5	2	5	5	5	5.3	-8.3	22.3
Tanzania	31	44	39	40	27	26	32	44	53	55	-7.8	-6.5	20.0
Togo	5	9	12	12	10	20	35	30	29	34	14.9	22.4	-1.3
Uganda	2	1	2	7	7	7	4	4	2	2	-38.3	40.9	-27.8
Zaire	2	0	0	0	0	0	0	0	0	0	..	..	..
Zambia	5	2	2	4	1	8	2	3	2	8	..	7.6	34.4
Zimbabwe	54	54	50	51	58	67	81	65	65	80	9.3	4.1	-0.2
NORTH AFRICA	167	182	200	209	174	144	146	131	86	64	-2.9	-2.4	-25.0
Algeria	0	0	0	0	0	0	0	0	0	0	..	..	..
Egypt, Arab Republic of	164	178	200	209	174	144	146	130	80	58	-2.9	-1.9	-27.6
Libya	0	0	0	0	0	0	0	0	0	0	..	..	..
Morocco	3	5	0	0	0	0	0	2	6	6	0.0	..	..
Tunisia	0	0	0	0	0	0	0	0	0	0	..	..	..
ALL AFRICA	632	583	607	728	757	636	831	825	772	835	-0.2	2.9	-0.5
South Africa	0	0	0	0	0	0	0	0	0	0	-3.8	-31.6	..

5–27. Groundnut exports

	Thousands of metric tons										Average annual percentage growth		
	1980	1981	1982	1983	1984	1985	1986	1987	1988	1989	75–80	80–85	86–MR
SUB-SAHARAN AFRICA	554	320	623	646	415	196	318	370	651	528	-14.9	-11.8	23.2
excluding Nigeria	552	318	618	645	415	195	318	369	650	528	-14.7	-11.7	23.2
Angola	1	1	1	0	0	0	0	0	0	0	-15.6	35.4	..
Benin	2	0	3	3	1	5	0	5	2	2	3.0	-49.9	291.0
Botswana	1	0	0	0	0	0	0	0	0	0	..	..	..
Burkina Faso	1	0	1	1	0	0	4	6	4	1	-50.2	..	-38.7
Burundi	0	0	0	0	0	0	0	0	0	0	..	..	..
Cameroon	1	0	1	0	0	1	0	0	0	0	-58.3	-0.1	-15.0
Cape Verde	0	0	0	0	0	0	0	0	0	0	..	..	..
Central African Republic	0	0	0	0	0	0	0	0	0	0	..	..	..
Chad	0	0	0	0	2	0	0	0	3	0	..	..	..
Comoros	0	0	0	0	0	0	0	0	0	0	..	..	..
Congo, People's Republic of the	0	0	1	0	0	0	0	0	0	0	..	..	..
Cote d'Ivoire	0	0	0	0	0	1	0	0	1	0	15.2	..	..
Djibouti	0	0	0	0	0	0	0	0	0	0	..	..	..
Equatorial Guinea	0	0	0	0	0	0	0	0	0	0	..	..	..
Ethiopia	1	3	2	1	15	8	0	0	0	0	-31.7	49.6	..
Gabon	0	0	0	0	0	0	0	0	0	0	..	..	..
Gambia, The	67	26	43	69	52	32	25	17	38	21	-11.6	-3.3	2.3
Ghana	2	0	0	0	0	0	0	0	0	0	..	..	..
Guinea	0	0	0	0	0	0	0	0	0	0	..	..	..
Guinea-Bissau	8	4	10	8	8	4	2	5	2	3	-4.4	-2.5	-6.6
Kenya	0	0	0	0	0	0	0	0	0	0	7.6	-36.8	-13.4
Lesotho	0	0	0	0	0	0	0	0	0	0	..	..	..
Liberia	0	0	0	0	0	0	0	0	0	0	..	..	..
Madagascar	4	0	0	0	0	0	0	0	0	0	-12.3	-56.2	..
Malawi	28	13	9	6	1	9	20	19	36	1	-7.1	-30.1	-52.7
Mali	15	17	9	15	10	11	17	19	17	15	-16.8	-7.5	-3.6
Mauritania	0	0	0	0	0	0	0	0	0	0	..	..	..
Mauritius	0	0	0	0	0	0	0	0	0	0	..	..	..
Mozambique	10	9	9	6	1	1	4	4	2	3	-3.2	-38.8	-11.2
Namibia	0	0	0	0	0	0	0	0	0	0	..	..	..
Niger	1	2	0	0	0	0	0	1	1	1	-34.8	-69.4	32.5
Nigeria	1	0	3	0	0	0	0	0	1	0	..	..	..
Rwanda	0	0	0	0	0	0	0	0	0	0	..	..	..
Sao Tome & Principe	0	0	0	0	0	0	0	0	0	0	..	..	..
Senegal	175	56	350	431	188	94	200	213	376	340	-21.1	2.2	24.2
Seychelles	0	0	0	0	0	0	0	0	0	0	..	..	..
Sierra Leone	0	0	0	0	0	0	0	0	0	0	..	..	..
Somalia	0	0	0	0	0	0	0	0	0	0	..	..	..
Sudan	232	183	180	101	135	23	31	73	164	136	-7.1	-31.1	69.2
Swaziland	0	0	0	0	0	0	0	0	0	0	..	..	..
Tanzania	1	0	0	0	0	0	0	0	0	0	..	..	-80.5
Togo	0	0	0	1	0	6	13	4	0	0	..	..	..
Uganda	0	0	0	0	0	0	0	0	0	0	..	..	..
Zaire	0	0	0	0	0	0	0	0	0	0	..	..	..
Zambia	0	0	0	0	0	0	0	0	0	0	-27.9	..	-17.6
Zimbabwe	3	5	4	2	1	0	2	4	4	4	-11.5	-56.6	30.2
NORTH AFRICA	11	10	4	4	3	2	3	1	0	2	1.3	-29.7	-6.6
Algeria	0	0	0	0	0	0	0	0	0	0	..	..	..
Egypt, Arab Republic of	11	10	4	4	3	2	3	1	0	2	1.4	-29.7	-6.5
Libya	0	0	0	0	0	0	0	0	0	0	..	..	..
Morocco	0	0	0	0	0	0	0	0	0	0	..	..	..
Tunisia	0	0	0	0	0	0	0	0	0	0	..	..	..
ALL AFRICA	565	330	627	650	418	198	321	370	651	530	-14.8	-12.1	23.0
South Africa	45	94	52	23	13	31	35	19	26	55	-6.3	-21.8	18.7

5-28. Oil palm products exports

	Thousands of metric tons										Average annual percentage growth		
	1980	1981	1982	1983	1984	1985	1986	1987	1988	1989	75–80	80–85	86–MR
SUB-SAHARAN AFRICA	280	192	181	158	173	142	221	265	213	198	-15.9	-10.4	-5.5
excluding Nigeria	163	136	110	93	109	93	124	138	87	96	-11.9	-9.9	-11.4
Angola	0	0	0	0	0	0	0	0	0	0	..	..	..
Benin	13	3	0	3	4	4	2	12	9	9	-4.5	-7.8	50.0
Botswana	0	0	0	0	0	0	0	0	0	0	..	..	..
Burkina Faso	0	0	0	0	0	0	0	0	0	0	..	..	..
Burundi	0	0	0	0	0	0	0	0	0	0	..	..	..
Cameroon	21	7	15	11	20	13	20	32	21	23	-3.1	1.2	-0.2
Cape Verde	0	0	0	0	0	0	0	0	0	0	..	..	..
Central African Republic	0	0	0	0	0	0	0	0	0	0	..	..	..
Chad	0	0	0	0	0	0	0	0	0	0	..	..	..
Comoros	0	0	0	0	0	0	0	0	0	0	..	..	..
Congo, People's Republic of the	0	0	0	0	0	0	0	0	0	0	-18.9	..	..
Cote d'Ivoire	99	88	68	57	67	56	105	110	61	73	-12.0	-10.5	-15.6
Djibouti	0	0	0	0	0	0	0	0	0	0	..	..	..
Equatorial Guinea	0	0	0	0	0	0	0	0	0	0	..	..	..
Ethiopia	0	0	0	0	0	0	0	0	0	0	..	..	..
Gabon	0	0	0	0	2	4	4	2	1	8	..	..	15.8
Gambia, The	1	2	0	0	0	0	0	0	0	0	4.2	..	..
Ghana	0	0	0	0	0	3	0	0	0	0	..	..	..
Guinea	15	4	12	7	6	0	3	4	2	1	12.0	-48.6	-24.0
Guinea-Bissau	6	9	7	5	7	2	8	5	6	5	11.6	-16.5	-9.2
Kenya	0	0	0	0	0	0	0	0	0	0	..	..	..
Lesotho	0	0	0	0	0	0	0	0	0	0	..	..	..
Liberia	6	4	5	6	5	4	2	5	6	8	37.1	-3.5	46.1
Madagascar	0	0	0	0	0	0	0	0	0	0	..	..	..
Malawi	0	0	0	0	0	0	0	0	0	0	..	..	..
Mali	0	0	0	0	0	0	0	0	0	0	..	..	..
Mauritania	0	0	0	0	0	0	0	0	0	0	..	..	..
Mauritius	0	0	0	0	0	0	0	0	0	0	..	..	..
Mozambique	0	0	0	0	0	0	0	0	0	0	..	..	..
Namibia	0	0	0	0	0	0	0	0	0	0	..	..	..
Niger	0	0	0	0	0	0	0	0	0	0	..	..	..
Nigeria	96	49	57	54	42	32	74	92	103	70	-21.5	-15.6	-0.3
Rwanda	0	0	0	0	0	0	0	0	0	0	..	..	..
Sao Tome & Principe	0	1	1	0	0	0	0	0	0	0	-9.6	..	..
Senegal	0	0	0	0	0	1	0	0	0	0	..	..	..
Seychelles	0	0	0	0	0	0	0	0	0	0	..	..	..
Sierra Leone	1	3	7	8	13	8	2	0	2	1	-39.7	55.3	..
Somalia	0	0	0	0	0	0	0	0	0	0	..	..	..
Sudan	0	0	0	0	0	0	0	0	0	0	..	..	..
Swaziland	0	0	0	0	0	0	0	0	0	0	..	..	..
Tanzania	1	0	0	0	0	0	0	0	0	0	..	..	..
Togo	10	15	6	2	0	0	1	1	0	0	-1.1	-71.1	-67.1
Uganda	0	0	0	0	0	0	0	0	0	0	..	..	..
Zaire	10	6	4	5	6	14	2	1	2	0	..	5.8	-53.1
Zambia	0	0	0	0	0	0	0	0	0	0	..	..	..
Zimbabwe	0	0	0	0	0	0	0	0	0	0	..	..	..
NORTH AFRICA	0	0	0	0	0	0	0	0	0	0	..	..	..
Algeria	0	0	0	0	0	0	0	0	0	0	..	..	..
Egypt, Arab Republic of	0	0	0	0	0	0	0	0	0	0	..	..	..
Libya	0	0	0	0	0	0	0	0	0	0	..	..	..
Morocco	0	0	0	0	0	0	0	0	0	0	..	..	..
Tunisia	0	0	0	0	0	0	0	0	0	0	..	..	..
ALL AFRICA	280	192	181	158	173	142	221	265	213	198	-15.9	-10.4	-5.5
South Africa	0	0	0	0	0	0	0	0	0	0	..	..	..

5-29. Sisal exports

| | Thousands of metric tons | | | | | | | | | | Average annual percentage growth | | |
	1980	1981	1982	1983	1984	1985	1986	1987	1988	1989	75-80	80-85	86-MR
SUB-SAHARAN AFRICA	109	114	118	81	82	64	52	53	58	56	-9.6	-10.9	2.8
excluding Nigeria	106	111	112	79	81	64	52	53	58	56	-7.9	-10.3	2.9
Angola	3	2	6	2	1	0	0	0	0	0	-26.7	-43.2	..
Benin	0	0	0	0	0	0	0	0	0	0	..	..	..
Botswana	0	0	0	0	0	0	0	0	0	0	..	..	..
Burkina Faso	0	0	0	0	0	0	0	0	0	0	..	..	..
Burundi	0	0	0	0	0	0	0	0	0	0	..	..	..
Cameroon	0	0	0	0	0	0	0	0	0	0	..	..	..
Cape Verde	0	0	0	0	0	0	0	0	0	0	..	..	..
Central African Republic	0	0	0	0	0	0	0	0	0	0	..	..	..
Chad	0	0	0	0	0	0	0	0	0	0	..	..	..
Comoros	0	0	0	0	0	0	0	0	0	0	..	..	..
Congo, People's Republic of the	0	0	0	0	0	0	0	0	0	0	..	..	..
Cote d'Ivoire	0	0	0	0	0	0	0	0	0	0	..	..	..
Djibouti	0	0	0	0	0	0	0	0	0	0	..	..	..
Equatorial Guinea	0	0	0	0	0	0	0	0	0	0	..	..	..
Ethiopia	0	0	0	0	0	0	0	0	0	0	..	..	..
Gabon	0	0	0	0	0	0	0	0	0	0	..	..	..
Gambia, The	0	0	0	0	0	0	0	0	0	0	..	..	..
Ghana	0	0	0	0	0	0	0	0	0	0	..	..	..
Guinea	0	0	0	0	0	0	0	0	0	0	..	..	..
Guinea-Bissau	0	0	0	0	0	0	0	0	0	0	..	..	..
Kenya	40	36	40	39	39	40	32	28	31	33	-2.1	0.4	2.1
Lesotho	0	0	0	0	0	0	0	0	0	0	..	..	..
Liberia	0	0	0	0	0	0	0	0	0	0	..	..	..
Madagascar	10	13	15	11	13	8	9	7	9	7	-11.7	-4.0	-6.9
Malawi	0	0	0	0	0	0	0	0	0	0	..	..	..
Mali	0	0	0	0	0	0	0	0	0	0	..	..	..
Mauritania	0	0	0	0	0	0	0	0	0	0	..	..	..
Mauritius	0	0	0	0	0	0	0	0	0	0	..	..	..
Mozambique	7	6	6	3	2	0	0	0	1	1	-5.1	-46.4	243.7
Namibia	0	0	0	0	0	0	0	0	0	0	..	..	..
Niger	0	0	0	0	0	0	0	0	0	0	..	..	..
Nigeria	0	0	0	0	0	0	0	0	0	0	..	..	..
Rwanda	0	0	0	0	0	0	0	0	0	0	..	..	..
Sao Tome & Principe	0	0	0	0	0	0	0	0	0	0	..	..	..
Senegal	0	0	0	0	0	0	0	0	0	0	..	..	..
Seychelles	0	0	0	0	0	0	0	0	0	0	..	..	..
Sierra Leone	0	0	0	0	0	0	0	0	0	0	..	..	..
Somalia	0	0	0	0	0	0	0	0	0	0	..	..	..
Sudan	0	0	0	0	0	0	0	0	0	0	..	..	..
Swaziland	0	0	0	0	0	0	0	0	0	0	..	..	..
Tanzania	48	55	51	27	27	15	12	18	18	16	-10.9	-21.6	9.7
Togo	0	0	0	0	0	0	0	0	0	0	..	..	..
Uganda	0	0	0	0	0	0	0	0	0	0	..	..	..
Zaire	0	0	0	0	0	0	0	0	0	0	..	..	..
Zambia	0	0	0	0	0	0	0	0	0	0	..	..	..
Zimbabwe	0	0	0	0	0	0	0	0	0	0	..	..	..
NORTH AFRICA	0	0	0	0	0	0	0	0	0	0	..	..	..
Algeria	0	0	0	0	0	0	0	0	0	0	..	..	..
Egypt, Arab Republic of	0	0	0	0	0	0	0	0	0	0	..	..	..
Libya	0	0	0	0	0	0	0	0	0	0	..	..	..
Morocco	0	0	0	0	0	0	0	0	0	0	..	..	..
Tunisia	0	0	0	0	0	0	0	0	0	0	..	..	..
ALL AFRICA	109	114	118	81	82	64	52	53	58	56	-9.6	-10.9	2.8
South Africa	0	1	0	0	0	1	1	1	1	0	-2.4	13.6	-15.0

5–30. Tea exports

	1980	1981	1982	1983	1984	1985	1986	1987	1988	1989	75–80	80–85	86–MR
	Thousands of metric tons										Average annual percentage growth		
SUB-SAHARAN AFRICA	180	168	190	200	195	226	224	231	241	257	7.0	4.8	4.6
excluding Nigeria	179	167	189	199	193	225	224	231	241	256	7.0	4.8	4.6
Angola	0	0	0	0	0	0	0	0	0	0	..	..	..
Benin	0	0	0	0	0	0	0	0	0	0	..	..	..
Botswana	0	0	0	0	0	0	0	0	0	0	18.7	24.2	-10.2
Burkina Faso	0	0	0	0	0	0	0	0	0	0	..	..	..
Burundi	1	2	2	2	3	4	3	4	4	4	8.7	21.3	1.1
Cameroon	1	1	1	1	2	1	0	0	0	0	18.1	1.0	41.9
Cape Verde	0	0	0	0	0	0	0	0	0	0	..	..	..
Central African Republic	0	0	0	0	0	0	0	0	0	0	..	..	..
Chad	0	0	0	0	0	0	0	0	0	0	..	..	..
Comoros	0	0	0	0	0	0	0	0	0	0	..	..	..
Congo, People's Republic of the	0	0	0	0	0	0	0	0	0	0	..	..	..
Cote d'Ivoire	0	0	0	0	0	0	0	0	0	0	..	..	..
Djibouti	0	0	0	0	0	0	0	0	0	0	..	..	..
Equatorial Guinea	0	0	0	0	0	0	0	0	0	0	..	..	..
Ethiopia	0	0	0	0	0	0	0	0	0	0	..	..	..
Gabon	0	0	0	0	0	0	0	0	0	0	..	..	..
Gambia, The	0	0	0	0	0	0	0	0	0	0	..	..	..
Ghana	0	0	0	0	0	0	0	0	0	0	..	..	..
Guinea	0	0	0	0	0	0	0	0	0	0	..	..	..
Guinea-Bissau	0	0	0	0	0	0	0	0	0	0	..	..	..
Kenya	84	84	91	107	103	139	133	150	155	163	11.6	9.8	6.6
Lesotho	0	0	0	0	0	0	0	0	0	0	..	..	..
Liberia	0	0	0	0	0	0	0	0	0	0	..	..	..
Madagascar	0	0	0	0	0	0	0	0	0	0	..	..	-39.0
Malawi	31	31	36	36	37	37	40	33	37	42	3.7	4.1	2.4
Mali	0	0	0	0	0	0	0	0	0	0	..	..	..
Mauritania	0	0	0	0	0	0	0	0	0	0	..	..	..
Mauritius	4	4	4	5	7	7	6	7	5	5	9.2	15.8	-10.3
Mozambique	30	16	25	13	8	2	2	1	1	1	22.0	-38.3	-17.6
Namibia	0	0	0	0	0	0	0	0	0	0	..	..	..
Niger	0	0	0	0	0	0	0	0	0	0	..	..	..
Nigeria	0	0	0	0	0	0	0	0	0	0	..	..	..
Rwanda	7	6	7	7	8	11	10	9	12	13	8.3	8.7	10.1
Sao Tome & Principe	0	0	0	0	0	0	0	0	0	0	..	..	..
Senegal	0	0	0	0	0	0	0	0	0	0	..	..	..
Seychelles	0	0	0	0	0	0	0	0	0	0	..	..	..
Sierra Leone	0	0	0	0	0	0	0	0	0	0	..	..	..
Somalia	0	0	0	0	0	0	0	0	0	0	..	..	..
Sudan	0	0	0	0	0	0	0	0	0	0	..	..	..
Swaziland	0	0	0	0	0	0	0	0	0	0	..	..	..
Tanzania	13	14	12	17	11	11	11	12	10	10	6.3	-3.6	-5.5
Togo	0	0	0	0	0	0	0	0	0	0	..	..	..
Uganda	1	1	1	1	3	1	3	2	3	3	-50.0	29.0	7.7
Zaire	1	2	3	2	3	2	3	2	1	3	-20.4	10.8	-7.9
Zambia	0	0	0	0	0	0	0	0	0	0	..	..	..
Zimbabwe	6	6	7	8	10	10	12	10	12	13	10.6	11.8	4.5
NORTH AFRICA	0	0	0	0	0	0	0	0	0	0	..	..	..
Algeria	0	0	0	0	0	0	0	0	0	0	..	..	..
Egypt, Arab Republic of	0	0	0	0	0	0	0	0	0	0	..	..	..
Libya	0	0	0	0	0	0	0	0	0	0	..	..	..
Morocco	0	0	0	0	0	0	0	0	0	0	..	..	..
Tunisia	0	0	0	0	0	0	0	0	0	0	..	..	..
ALL AFRICA	180	168	190	200	195	226	224	231	241	257	7.0	4.8	4.6
South Africa	2	2	2	1	1	1	1	1	1	1	120.8	-23.4	14.8

5–31. Sugar exports

	Thousands of metric tons										Average annual percentage growth		
	1980	1981	1982	1983	1984	1985	1986	1987	1988	1989	75–80	80–85	86–MR
SUB-SAHARAN AFRICA	1,373	1,303	1,435	1,437	1,369	1,393	1,601	1,593	1,477	1,374	6.5	0.6	-5.2
excluding Nigeria	1,362	1,280	1,422	1,414	1,333	1,367	1,564	1,575	1,458	1,361	6.7	0.4	-4.8
Angola	0	0	0	0	0	0	0	0	0	0	..	..	..
Benin	0	0	0	0	0	0	0	0	0	0	..	..	..
Botswana	0	0	0	0	0	0	0	0	0	0	..	..	..
Burkina Faso	2	0	0	0	0	0	0	0	0	0	211.8	..	..
Burundi	0	0	0	0	0	0	0	0	0	0	..	..	..
Cameroon	9	12	7	14	4	0	21	0	1	0	65.6	-45.6	-79.7
Cape Verde	0	0	0	0	0	0	0	0	0	0	..	..	..
Central African Republic	0	0	0	0	0	0	0	0	0	0	..	..	..
Chad	0	0	0	0	0	0	0	0	0	0	..	..	..
Comoros	0	0	0	0	0	0	0	0	0	0	..	..	..
Congo, People's Republic of the	0	11	5	7	32	26	16	18	18	13	-64.9	157.1	-6.4
Cote d'Ivoire	11	58	73	70	43	21	21	28	7	18	149.4	7.7	-16.4
Djibouti	0	0	0	0	0	0	0	0	0	0	..	..	..
Equatorial Guinea	0	0	0	0	0	0	0	0	0	0	..	..	..
Ethiopia	11	7	11	16	22	24	24	25	25	0	..	25.8	2.7
Gabon	2	0	1	2	0	0	0	0	0	0	..	..	..
Gambia, The	0	0	0	0	0	0	0	0	0	0	..	..	..
Ghana	0	0	0	0	0	0	0	0	0	0	..	..	..
Guinea	0	0	0	0	0	0	0	0	0	0	..	..	..
Guinea-Bissau	0	0	0	0	0	0	0	0	0	0	..	..	..
Kenya	56	77	12	4	0	0	0	0	0	0	181.1	-82.7	-16.0
Lesotho	0	0	0	0	0	0	0	0	0	0	..	..	..
Liberia	0	0	0	0	0	0	0	0	0	0	..	..	..
Madagascar	26	12	11	35	31	12	0	52	19	37	-10.0	0.0	..
Malawi	92	123	78	91	79	100	100	94	99	61	20.2	-2.2	-13.3
Mali	0	0	0	0	0	0	0	0	0	0	..	..	..
Mauritania	0	0	0	0	0	0	0	0	0	0	..	..	..
Mauritius	618	433	597	607	531	540	626	657	653	637	4.2	-0.1	0.4
Mozambique	64	63	29	25	16	17	20	10	37	15	6.3	-26.6	4.9
Namibia	0	0	0	0	0	0	0	0	0	0	..	..	..
Niger	0	0	0	0	1	0	0	0	0	0	..	..	..
Nigeria	0	0	0	0	0	0	0	0	0	0	..	..	..
Rwanda	0	0	0	0	0	0	0	0	0	0	..	..	..
Sao Tome & Principe	0	0	0	0	0	0	0	0	0	0	..	..	..
Senegal	0	0	0	0	0	0	0	0	0	0	..	..	..
Seychelles	0	0	0	0	0	0	0	0	0	0	..	..	..
Sierra Leone	0	0	0	0	0	0	0	0	0	0	..	..	..
Somalia	0	0	0	0	0	0	0	0	0	0	..	..	..
Sudan	0	0	0	0	0	0	0	0	0	0	..	..	..
Swaziland	300	327	379	352	370	380	498	435	404	407	10.6	4.3	-6.6
Tanzania	13	3	10	9	11	12	11	10	11	11	-9.2	10.3	2.4
Togo	0	0	0	0	0	0	0	0	0	0	..	..	..
Uganda	0	0	0	0	0	0	0	0	0	0	..	..	..
Zaire	0	0	0	0	0	0	0	0	0	0	..	..	..
Zambia	0	2	0	0	6	9	37	24	4	4	..	..	-55.6
Zimbabwe	169	175	223	205	223	252	229	241	198	171	4.8	7.8	-10.2
NORTH AFRICA	23	37	22	20	0	5	5	1	3	14	-16.6	-46.3	53.8
Algeria	0	0	0	0	0	0	0	0	0	0	..	..	..
Egypt, Arab Republic of	10	24	22	20	0	0	1	0	0	14	-22.3	..	..
Libya	0	0	0	0	0	0	0	0	0	0	..	..	..
Morocco	0	0	0	0	0	0	0	0	1	0	..	..	..
Tunisia	13	13	0	0	0	4	4	1	2	0	-9.4	..	-81.4
ALL AFRICA	1,395	1,340	1,457	1,457	1,369	1,398	1,606	1,595	1,480	1,388	5.5	0.2	-5.0
South Africa	786	737	878	588	693	1,025	874	1,105	909	867	-3.0	2.1	-2.2

5-32. Tobacco exports

	Thousands of metric tons										Average annual percentage growth		
	1980	1981	1982	1983	1984	1985	1986	1987	1988	1989	75-80	80-85	86-MR
SUB-SAHARAN AFRICA	170	187	147	144	172	175	171	173	178	172	5.7	-0.5	0.5
excluding Nigeria	167	184	144	141	168	171	170	172	178	171	6.1	-0.4	0.5
Angola	2	2	2	2	2	2	0	0	0	0	-3.1	5.9	..
Benin	0	0	0	0	0	0	0	0	0	0	-69.1	..	..
Botswana	0	0	0	0	0	0	0	0	0	0	..	1.2	..
Burkina Faso	0	0	0	0	0	0	0	0	0	0	..	..	..
Burundi	0	0	0	0	0	0	0	0	0	0	..	..	..
Cameroon	2	1	1	1	1	1	1	1	1	1	-3.2	-5.6	-7.9
Cape Verde	0	0	0	0	0	0	0	0	0	0	..	..	..
Central African Republic	1	1	1	1	0	0	0	1	0	0	2.2	-22.8	-21.0
Chad	0	0	0	0	0	0	0	0	0	0	..	..	..
Comoros	0	0	0	0	0	0	0	0	0	0	..	..	..
Congo, People's Republic of the	0	0	0	0	0	0	0	0	0	0	-33.8	-24.6	..
Cote d'Ivoire	0	0	0	0	0	0	0	0	0	0	..	..	..
Djibouti	0	0	0	0	0	0	0	0	0	0	..	..	..
Equatorial Guinea	0	0	0	0	0	0	0	0	0	0	..	..	..
Ethiopia	0	0	0	0	0	0	0	0	0	0	..	..	..
Gabon	0	0	0	0	0	0	0	0	0	0	..	..	..
Gambia, The	0	0	0	0	0	0	0	0	0	0	..	..	..
Ghana	0	0	0	0	0	0	0	0	0	0	-47.3	..	..
Guinea	0	0	0	0	0	0	0	0	0	0	..	..	..
Guinea-Bissau	0	0	0	0	0	0	0	0	0	0	..	..	..
Kenya	0	0	0	0	0	0	0	0	1	1	-2.0	..	16.2
Lesotho	0	0	0	0	0	0	0	0	0	0	..	..	..
Liberia	0	0	0	0	0	0	0	0	0	0	..	52.8	..
Madagascar	0	0	0	1	1	1	1	1	1	1	-38.5	53.2	-5.9
Malawi	61	40	44	47	69	60	59	62	60	56	13.7	4.8	-1.8
Mali	0	0	0	0	0	0	0	0	0	0	..	..	..
Mauritania	0	0	0	0	0	0	0	0	0	0	..	..	..
Mauritius	0	0	0	0	0	0	0	0	0	0	..	..	..
Mozambique	0	0	0	0	0	0	0	0	0	0	..	..	..
Namibia	0	0	0	0	0	0	0	0	0	0	..	..	..
Niger	0	1	1	0	1	0	0	0	0	0	..	..	..
Nigeria	0	0	0	0	0	0	0	0	0	0	..	..	..
Rwanda	0	0	0	0	0	0	0	0	0	0	..	..	..
Sao Tome & Principe	0	0	0	0	0	0	0	0	0	0	..	..	..
Senegal	0	0	0	0	0	0	0	0	0	0	..	..	..
Seychelles	0	0	0	0	0	0	0	0	0	0	..	..	..
Sierra Leone	0	0	0	0	0	0	0	0	0	0	..	..	-31.9
Somalia	0	0	0	0	0	0	0	0	0	0	..	..	..
Sudan	0	0	0	0	0	0	0	0	0	0	..	..	..
Swaziland	0	0	0	0	0	0	0	0	0	0	1.7	-14.4	-32.7
Tanzania	8	11	10	5	5	8	8	7	9	6	-7.2	-9.2	-5.4
Togo	0	0	0	0	0	0	0	0	0	0	..	..	..
Uganda	0	0	0	1	1	1	1	1	0	0	-26.1	..	..
Zaire	0	0	0	0	0	0	0	0	0	0	..	..	..
Zambia	3	2	1	2	2	2	1	2	3	2	-19.4	-4.9	34.5
Zimbabwe	93	129	86	84	90	98	99	99	104	105	6.1	-2.3	2.3
NORTH AFRICA	2	2	1	0	1	1	2	1	1	1	32.6	-16.5	-26.5
Algeria	0	0	0	0	0	0	0	0	0	0	..	..	..
Egypt, Arab Republic of	0	0	0	0	0	0	0	0	0	0	..	..	..
Libya	0	0	0	0	0	0	0	0	0	0	..	..	..
Morocco	0	0	0	0	0	0	0	0	0	0	..	..	..
Tunisia	2	2	1	0	1	1	2	1	1	1	65.0	-20.6	-33.0
ALL AFRICA	172	189	147	144	173	175	173	174	179	173	5.8	-0.5	0.2
South Africa	7	6	6	7	5	8	8	4	3	9	0.5	0.5	-2.4

5-33. Meat exports

| | Thousands of metric tons | | | | | | | | | | Average annual percentage growth | | |
	1980	1981	1982	1983	1984	1985	1986	1987	1988	1989	75-80	80-85	86-MR
SUB-SAHARAN AFRICA	44	38	41	45	53	46	36	29	23	20	-12.5	4.1	-18.0
excluding Nigeria	43	38	41	45	53	46	36	29	23	20	-12.3	4.1	-18.0
Angola	0	0	0	0	0	0	0	0	0	0	..	..	..
Benin	0	0	0	0	0	0	0	0	0	0	..	..	..
Botswana	17	25	31	30	24	24	27	16	14	16	-9.8	4.8	-15.9
Burkina Faso	0	1	0	0	0	0	0	0	0	0	-6.1	-9.7	..
Burundi	0	0	0	0	0	0	0	0	0	0	..	..	..
Cameroon	0	0	0	0	0	0	0	0	0	0	-43.5	..	..
Cape Verde	0	0	0	0	0	0	0	0	0	0	..	..	..
Central African Republic	2	2	1	0	0	0	0	0	0	0	-19.5	..	..
Chad	0	0	0	0	0	0	0	0	0	0	..	..	..
Comoros	0	0	0	0	0	0	0	0	0	0	..	..	..
Congo, People's Republic of the	0	0	0	0	0	0	0	0	0	0	..	..	..
Cote d'Ivoire	0	0	0	0	0	0	0	0	0	0	-12.3	13.4	..
Djibouti	0	0	0	0	0	0	0	0	0	0	..	..	..
Equatorial Guinea	0	0	0	0	0	0	0	0	0	0	..	..	..
Ethiopia	1	2	1	3	3	1	0	0	0	0	-15.6	-8.9	..
Gabon	0	0	0	0	0	0	0	0	0	0	..	..	..
Gambia, The	0	0	0	0	0	0	0	0	0	0	..	..	..
Ghana	0	0	0	0	0	0	0	0	0	0	..	..	..
Guinea	0	0	0	0	0	0	0	0	0	0	..	..	..
Guinea-Bissau	0	0	0	0	0	0	0	0	0	0	..	..	..
Kenya	0	1	1	1	0	0	0	0	0	0	-42.8	-12.7	-19.8
Lesotho	0	0	0	0	0	0	0	0	0	0	..	..	..
Liberia	0	0	0	0	0	0	0	0	0	0	..	..	..
Madagascar	7	2	1	0	3	1	0	0	0	0	23.8	-20.0	21.0
Malawi	0	0	0	0	0	0	0	0	0	0	..	..	..
Mali	0	0	0	0	0	0	0	0	0	0	..	..	..
Mauritania	0	0	0	0	0	0	0	0	0	0	..	..	..
Mauritius	0	0	0	0	0	0	0	0	0	0	..	24.1	-53.5
Mozambique	0	0	0	0	0	0	0	0	0	0	..	..	..
Namibia	0	0	0	0	0	0	0	23	23	31	..	..	..
Niger	0	0	0	0	1	0	0	0	0	0	..	..	..
Nigeria	0	0	0	0	0	0	0	0	0	0	..	..	..
Rwanda	0	0	0	0	0	0	0	0	0	0	..	..	..
Sao Tome & Principe	0	0	0	0	0	0	0	0	0	0	..	..	..
Senegal	0	0	0	0	0	0	0	0	0	0	-13.0	..	..
Seychelles	0	0	0	0	0	0	0	0	0	0	..	..	..
Sierra Leone	0	0	0	0	0	0	0	0	0	0	..	..	..
Somalia	0	0	0	0	0	0	0	0	0	0	..	..	..
Sudan	0	0	0	0	2	2	0	0	0	0	-20.5	..	..
Swaziland	3	1	2	2	1	2	3	1	0	0	14.0	-4.9	..
Tanzania	0	0	0	0	0	0	0	0	0	0	-41.5	..	..
Togo	0	0	0	0	0	0	0	0	0	0	..	..	..
Uganda	0	0	0	0	0	0	0	0	0	0	..	..	..
Zaire	0	0	0	0	0	0	0	0	0	0	..	..	..
Zambia	0	0	0	0	0	0	0	0	0	0	..	..	-9.4
Zimbabwe	13	3	3	9	18	16	5	11	9	4	-16.6	25.4	-9.8
NORTH AFRICA	3	6	3	3	1	0	0	0	0	2	12.5	-46.0	119.1
Algeria	0	0	0	0	0	0	0	0	0	0	-56.9	..	..
Egypt, Arab Republic of	0	0	0	0	0	0	0	0	0	2	25.2	-0.9	140.4
Libya	0	0	0	0	0	0	0	0	0	0	..	..	..
Morocco	3	6	3	3	0	0	0	0	0	0	14.0	-66.2	-0.9
Tunisia	0	0	0	0	0	0	0	0	0	0	-10.2	18.7	66.6
ALL AFRICA	47	44	44	48	53	47	36	29	23	22	-11.7	1.8	-16.1
South Africa	37	18	14	12	6	5	4	4	4	3	9.7	-32.2	-5.8

5-34. Primary commodities exports

| | Millions of U.S. dollars | | | | | | | | | | Average annual percentage growth | | |
	1980	1981	1982	1983	1984	1985	1986	1987	1988	1989	75-80	80-85	86-MR
SUB-SAHARAN AFRICA	16,454	13,990	12,963	12,468	13,399	12,918	14,547	14,003	14,784	14,663	10.3	-3.9	0.8
excluding Nigeria	14,389	12,383	11,588	10,993	11,988	11,562	12,975	12,641	13,117	13,217	10.4	-3.5	0.9
Angola	191	125	122	84	91	77	62	27	36	21	-8.0	-15.4	-25.4
Benin	57	24	21	31	80	74	71	76	81	78	19.8	16.4	3.8
Botswana	183	215	183	169	149	154	190	174	377	346	13.6	-5.6	29.3
Burkina Faso	80	63	48	53	73	50	51	87	82	84	10.9	-5.1	15.3
Burundi	65	72	86	80	96	104	160	78	130	73	13.2	9.4	-16.9
Cameroon	867	577	519	555	598	615	742	668	738	657	17.9	-4.3	-2.6
Cape Verde	4	4	4	4	3	3	4	6	3	6	32.9	-7.6	8.6
Central African Republic	98	89	79	75	66	81	74	52	56	63	17.2	-5.3	-3.9
Chad	115	125	121	162	184	134	66	79	100	97	13.7	6.5	15.1
Comoros	7	15	18	15	6	14	21	9	18	13	9.7	1.1	-5.9
Congo, People's Republic of the	75	53	43	36	57	56	63	90	114	122	17.1	-4.0	24.5
Cote d'Ivoire	2,633	2,095	1,744	1,611	2,179	2,409	2,708	2,370	2,138	1,998	19.8	-1.2	-9.7
Djibouti	4	3	3	4	4	5	5	6	7	7	69.4	8.2	15.9
Equatorial Guinea	14	20	22	23	25	27	34	31	25	21	1.8	11.3	-15.0
Ethiopia	392	344	370	362	380	306	446	298	344	380	13.6	-2.7	-3.4
Gabon	411	361	299	319	282	269	308	314	333	340	23.0	-7.7	3.6
Gambia, The	33	21	18	27	30	19	14	9	22	11	-7.2	-3.3	4.0
Ghana	1,105	708	691	455	552	623	808	1,001	890	894	10.5	-10.9	1.8
Guinea	515	516	475	525	536	540	492	539	532	572	19.1	1.3	4.5
Guinea-Bissau	9	14	8	7	13	12	9	9	10	12	17.2	2.8	9.7
Kenya	729	665	618	649	765	711	937	709	769	804	15.4	1.0	-3.7
Lesotho	15	13	14	20	21	17	13	10	11	11	11.2	6.8	-5.6
Liberia	592	528	468	425	445	441	414	373	481	515	8.1	-5.8	9.6
Madagascar	367	286	287	270	306	246	293	335	230	229	9.0	-5.2	-10.6
Malawi	254	241	221	232	300	237	232	259	277	245	13.4	1.1	2.3
Mali	195	204	199	176	228	159	185	202	195	248	19.9	-2.2	8.8
Mauritania	207	247	214	239	280	317	356	348	371	382	-0.2	7.8	2.8
Mauritius	308	207	248	250	221	217	294	368	374	362	4.6	-4.3	6.6
Mozambique	211	205	169	106	82	78	87	121	107	106	7.4	-20.9	4.7
Namibia	288	240	228	221	197	212	220	277	295	318	12.9	-6.0	12.4
Niger	577	450	359	339	308	317	339	377	321	315	48.0	-11.3	-3.7
Nigeria	521	492	392	482	384	339	397	264	446	307	3.8	-7.4	-2.5
Rwanda	78	83	96	84	86	91	172	115	107	89	10.2	2.3	-18.5
Sao Tome & Principe	19	13	12	11	10	7	6	6	6	5	24.7	-14.7	-3.8
Senegal	314	249	392	404	383	323	431	455	523	582	-4.2	4.3	11.0
Seychelles	5	4	3	4	3	3	2	7	14	11	18.2	-7.2	72.6
Sierra Leone	75	52	53	59	61	86	81	76	67	63	13.5	3.8	-8.2
Somalia	125	153	243	95	55	103	97	102	83	86	10.5	-13.3	-5.6
Sudan	556	479	497	507	598	359	331	512	505	461	4.2	-4.2	10.3
Swaziland	291	276	216	227	227	192	239	266	262	267	11.0	-7.2	3.2
Tanzania	438	495	368	297	327	284	363	264	274	305	5.3	-9.9	-4.8
Togo	212	172	134	120	182	172	190	188	210	183	15.3	-2.8	-0.1
Uganda	347	245	354	365	416	435	412	319	275	275	4.1	8.2	-12.7
Zaire	988	817	795	805	814	782	959	820	971	1,025	0.4	-3.3	3.8
Zambia	1,442	1,099	1,016	1,040	842	782	685	822	1,100	1,217	11.6	-10.4	22.3
Zimbabwe	735	876	722	665	655	653	706	767	773	779	3.1	-4.3	3.1
NORTH AFRICA	2,933	2,947	2,456	2,326	2,438	1,922	2,294	2,367	2,876	2,989	2.5	-7.5	10.4
Algeria	193	199	148	105	110	98	88	71	102	107	-5.6	-14.6	10.2
Egypt, Arab Republic of	753	876	795	829	892	400	636	609	668	809	-1.8	-8.4	8.5
Libya	0	0	1	2	0	0	1	2	3	2	-34.0	2.5	9.0
Morocco	1,730	1,559	1,267	1,189	1,200	1,202	1,294	1,356	1,738	1,697	7.1	-7.3	11.2
Tunisia	256	313	246	201	236	222	275	329	365	375	-0.6	-4.9	10.9
ALL AFRICA	19,387	16,937	15,419	14,794	15,837	14,840	16,841	16,370	17,660	17,652	8.9	-4.4	2.2
South Africa	4,779	4,213	3,587	3,103	2,866	2,782	3,029	3,352	4,002	4,598	13.4	-10.8	15.4

Note: Discrepancies may occur between aggregated total merchandise trade (Tables 5-16 and 5-17), as reported originally from the trading countries, and total commodity trade (Tables 5-34 to 5-42), as estimated by the FAO.

5–35. Primary commodities imports

	Millions of U.S. dollars										Average annual percentage growth		
	1980	1981	1982	1983	1984	1985	1986	1987	1988	1989	75–80	80–85	86–MR
SUB-SAHARAN AFRICA	8,201	8,974	7,862	7,108	6,787	6,779	6,315	6,348	6,690	6,930	18.5	-5.3	3.4
excluding Nigeria	4,672	4,730	4,277	4,015	4,105	4,342	4,401	4,447	4,917	5,024	13.0	-2.4	5.1
Angola	386	448	359	306	373	376	263	345	410	505	38.4	-2.4	23.8
Benin	87	109	134	102	94	56	65	76	85	77	14.8	-8.1	6.2
Botswana	96	115	113	140	132	106	120	159	161	159	23.9	3.3	9.0
Burkina Faso	81	91	95	81	94	96	97	99	118	117	22.2	2.1	7.7
Burundi	34	36	45	32	34	38	30	25	30	21	23.4	0.0	-8.2
Cameroon	189	188	176	206	178	197	320	317	298	314	17.6	0.5	-1.2
Cape Verde	31	27	27	29	25	25	37	34	30	35	12.3	-3.2	-2.9
Central African Republic	28	36	28	32	19	26	34	31	31	34	3.8	-5.6	0.1
Chad	7	12	20	17	39	37	16	17	21	20	-18.3	40.4	9.2
Comoros	12	17	14	13	16	10	15	12	18	21	17.0	-3.3	15.0
Congo, People's Republic of the	92	79	101	103	124	123	128	114	128	123	25.0	8.5	0.0
Cote d'Ivoire	619	622	531	487	452	436	534	624	599	684	23.5	-7.7	7.2
Djibouti	78	82	73	85	81	78	87	93	100	97	32.5	0.4	3.9
Equatorial Guinea	10	13	12	6	5	7	7	7	12	11	37.3	-14.3	24.7
Ethiopia	114	104	105	149	132	319	315	198	370	277	26.4	19.5	2.4
Gabon	126	142	147	135	142	150	158	155	158	140	16.1	2.3	-3.4
Gambia, The	42	48	47	39	48	52	55	55	72	61	23.6	2.6	5.8
Ghana	272	245	210	146	125	127	150	191	229	241	7.8	-16.2	17.5
Guinea	76	61	40	50	65	66	79	83	93	102	24.6	-1.0	9.4
Guinea-Bissau	13	23	12	12	10	12	12	23	26	30	2.5	-7.8	33.0
Kenya	250	164	164	159	223	173	189	176	175	198	20.0	-2.7	1.4
Lesotho	116	117	120	149	133	125	127	113	126	124	21.2	2.9	0.5
Liberia	115	119	109	121	115	94	86	79	88	109	18.2	-2.9	8.5
Madagascar	87	124	139	101	66	69	69	64	45	58	15.8	-9.2	-8.3
Malawi	42	43	31	32	27	28	22	30	28	38	7.4	-9.4	16.5
Mali	79	66	80	64	103	106	129	80	99	111	1.5	7.8	-2.4
Mauritania	92	102	130	145	119	126	108	123	135	147	6.9	6.5	10.7
Mauritius	188	176	150	127	131	129	123	155	179	204	15.3	-8.1	18.3
Mozambique	168	157	128	172	177	180	142	202	209	185	-0.3	2.9	8.6
Namibia	23	25	25	24	24	24	25	27	29	29	11.3	0.4	4.6
Niger	102	135	109	91	101	150	126	121	133	121	31.5	2.6	-0.3
Nigeria	2,736	3,387	2,803	2,343	1,866	1,591	1,045	970	778	824	28.8	-12.5	-8.9
Rwanda	42	39	45	40	50	65	57	41	41	43	2.9	8.4	-8.0
Sao Tome & Principe	7	6	5	5	5	6	5	7	7	9	13.1	-2.5	19.5
Senegal	292	337	272	286	337	266	289	284	347	394	9.9	-1.2	12.0
Seychelles	22	20	22	18	19	19	22	26	33	30	16.9	-3.6	12.7
Sierra Leone	98	86	89	60	48	68	92	83	89	103	21.4	-10.8	4.1
Somalia	152	207	185	123	140	116	160	148	114	115	14.1	-8.0	-11.9
Sudan	410	356	281	269	244	399	294	261	295	270	14.6	-3.7	-1.3
Swaziland	40	61	62	59	64	52	39	50	50	50	12.2	4.2	8.2
Tanzania	189	133	141	100	114	106	101	97	106	82	1.1	-10.0	-5.2
Togo	95	118	117	89	83	82	83	93	134	131	28.1	-5.7	19.2
Uganda	48	43	34	24	24	21	29	44	31	38	14.9	-16.3	4.8
Zaire	185	304	210	231	235	304	310	310	293	330	-4.9	5.3	1.3
Zambia	158	90	76	64	71	97	87	73	95	74	13.5	-9.1	-2.1
Zimbabwe	101	89	70	66	108	71	61	62	75	71	12.0	-3.5	6.5
NORTH AFRICA	8,675	10,950	9,537	9,810	10,520	7,688	8,838	8,011	9,235	10,350	12.1	-2.0	6.4
Algeria	2,574	2,841	2,631	2,709	2,505	2,911	2,511	2,365	2,532	3,507	13.4	0.8	11.3
Egypt, Arab Republic of	2,756	4,246	3,761	3,946	4,656	1,800	3,173	2,655	3,084	3,135	10.0	-5.0	1.1
Libya	1,453	1,684	1,381	1,434	1,417	1,250	1,337	1,258	1,349	1,465	16.5	-3.5	3.5
Morocco	1,170	1,356	1,087	992	1,181	1,107	1,094	1,083	1,310	1,222	7.3	-2.2	5.4
Tunisia	722	823	677	729	761	620	723	650	960	1,021	17.7	-2.6	15.3
ALL AFRICA	16,875	19,924	17,399	16,919	17,307	14,467	15,152	14,359	15,925	17,280	14.9	-3.4	5.1
South Africa	1,323	1,495	1,200	1,551	1,923	1,143	1,160	1,367	1,441	1,486	8.8	0.8	8.3

Note: *Discrepancies may occur between aggregated total merchandise trade (Tables 5-16 and 5-17), as reported originally from the trading countries, and total commodity trade (Tables 5-34 to 5-42), as estimated by the FAO.*

5–36. Food exports

	Millions of U.S. dollars										Average annual percentage growth		
	1980	1981	1982	1983	1984	1985	1986	1987	1988	1989	75–80	80–85	86–MR
SUB-SAHARAN AFRICA	8,858	7,738	7,424	6,831	7,868	7,741	9,358	8,204	7,936	7,506	9.9	-2.0	-6.7
excluding Nigeria	7,597	6,778	6,630	5,930	6,990	6,906	8,325	7,448	7,049	6,905	10.2	-1.4	-6.0
Angola	170	103	100	78	87	74	59	24	33	17	-2.5	-13.2	-29.4
Benin	43	13	16	18	47	43	41	26	22	20	23.0	11.8	-21.2
Botswana	41	89	90	83	58	64	82	75	57	61	-1.8	2.7	-11.0
Burkina Faso	37	30	23	21	25	20	16	15	11	12	4.5	-9.8	-10.5
Burundi	60	70	83	74	91	100	156	70	125	67	13.5	9.7	-17.8
Cameroon	638	414	341	377	431	439	591	484	447	331	17.7	-4.6	-16.6
Cape Verde	3	3	4	3	2	2	4	5	3	6	28.8	-5.6	9.3
Central African Republic	37	26	40	31	28	40	33	21	29	30	12.2	1.1	0.5
Chad	76	85	95	101	85	86	21	33	29	31	19.6	2.1	11.4
Comoros	7	15	18	14	6	14	21	9	18	13	9.7	0.9	-5.9
Congo, People's Republic of the	15	15	14	11	24	20	16	13	12	11	8.4	8.1	-10.9
Cote d'Ivoire	1,955	1,647	1,377	1,218	1,803	2,087	2,353	2,015	1,724	1,570	19.8	1.4	-12.8
Djibouti	3	2	3	3	4	4	3	4	4	4	..	11.0	10.9
Equatorial Guinea	12	15	12	14	17	20	16	13	13	9	2.1	9.2	-16.8
Ethiopia	315	277	299	297	309	246	381	232	278	314	11.4	-2.6	-3.9
Gabon	14	17	11	11	11	12	17	14	13	20	54.7	-6.3	4.6
Gambia, The	33	21	17	27	29	18	13	8	22	10	-7.2	-4.3	2.9
Ghana	789	496	471	293	406	429	532	565	509	523	8.9	-11.1	-1.5
Guinea	33	28	29	33	21	18	25	25	27	33	13.3	-10.4	9.2
Guinea-Bissau	9	12	7	6	12	11	8	8	9	10	18.0	2.8	6.6
Kenya	591	543	528	570	688	626	846	612	661	689	16.8	3.1	-5.2
Lesotho	6	6	7	9	7	5	3	1	1	1	3.6	-1.9	-31.3
Liberia	51	38	37	36	39	44	28	20	19	18	29.9	-1.9	-12.9
Madagascar	335	250	256	249	284	224	264	300	206	207	10.2	-4.7	-10.5
Malawi	247	238	220	231	294	220	229	256	272	240	13.5	0.3	2.0
Mali	113	137	132	138	130	82	111	90	94	108	18.1	-4.9	-0.2
Mauritania	46	77	68	104	131	161	209	208	226	192	6.9	26.6	-1.7
Mauritius	307	206	247	249	217	216	292	365	370	357	4.6	-4.5	6.4
Mozambique	165	151	130	78	69	65	81	108	91	90	8.9	-19.4	1.6
Namibia	55	59	57	35	33	43	55	107	105	128	8.5	-9.3	28.4
Niger	82	84	76	46	80	63	65	48	49	53	16.8	-5.5	-5.4
Nigeria	424	411	328	424	325	290	351	222	381	222	3.1	-6.5	-8.0
Rwanda	58	67	69	61	63	69	160	104	100	78	8.3	1.6	-19.7
Sao Tome & Principe	19	13	12	11	10	7	6	6	6	5	24.7	-14.7	-3.8
Senegal	205	160	296	301	277	227	338	394	450	506	-5.7	6.4	14.4
Seychelles	5	4	3	4	3	3	2	6	14	11	19.5	-6.6	74.6
Sierra Leone	59	39	41	32	37	60	57	50	39	32	20.4	-1.0	-18.1
Somalia	115	150	241	93	53	99	91	96	75	82	10.7	-12.9	-5.3
Sudan	257	298	312	210	222	151	106	239	203	190	2.6	-10.6	17.2
Swaziland	204	179	142	153	132	94	147	171	167	172	13.9	-12.5	4.6
Tanzania	320	351	267	205	251	224	293	192	183	210	7.1	-8.4	-9.9
Togo	69	54	41	34	59	53	65	67	59	54	17.4	-3.5	-6.8
Uganda	340	242	350	353	403	424	407	314	272	273	7.0	7.8	-12.6
Zaire	195	137	135	143	224	196	349	185	133	155	-0.1	4.5	-24.1
Zambia	5	6	3	4	6	11	23	13	10	11	-15.6	11.7	-23.5
Zimbabwe	354	524	436	383	371	388	454	484	479	464	0.4	-2.0	0.6
NORTH AFRICA	1,182	1,192	988	959	957	885	1,124	1,305	1,437	1,439	3.9	-5.9	8.7
Algeria	120	124	72	38	49	56	26	30	30	35	-7.3	-18.7	8.5
Egypt, Arab Republic of	207	237	233	246	237	103	151	232	192	236	-6.9	-9.4	12.2
Libya	..	..	1	2	..	..	..	0	1	0	..	..	..
Morocco	696	600	510	542	494	559	726	771	924	884	12.8	-4.5	8.0
Tunisia	160	231	174	135	177	168	221	272	291	284	3.4	-2.3	8.6
ALL AFRICA	10,040	8,930	8,412	7,790	8,824	8,626	10,482	9,509	9,373	8,945	9.1	-2.5	-4.8
South Africa	2,188	2,012	1,606	1,093	823	839	1,059	1,211	1,212	1,795	8.4	-20.1	17.2

Note: Discrepancies may occur between aggregated total merchandise trade (Tables 5-16 and 5-17), as reported originally from the trading countries, and total commodity trade (Tables 5-34 to 5-42), as estimated by the FAO.

5-37. Food imports

	Millions of U.S. dollars										Average annual percentage growth		
	1980	1981	1982	1983	1984	1985	1986	1987	1988	1989	75–80	80–85	86–MR
SUB-SAHARAN AFRICA	7,290	8,000	7,030	6,392	5,951	5,900	5,513	5,454	5,755	6,008	19.8	-5.7	3.2
excluding Nigeria	4,085	4,136	3,780	3,589	3,701	3,853	3,836	3,843	4,273	4,388	13.6	-1.9	5.2
Angola	373	438	353	299	365	368	255	337	400	498	43.8	-2.2	24.3
Benin	84	106	130	100	94	55	64	75	83	76	14.8	-7.6	6.2
Botswana	95	113	111	138	130	104	117	155	157	155	24.2	3.2	8.9
Burkina Faso	73	83	86	73	87	87	85	84	104	103	22.8	2.6	8.2
Burundi	29	31	39	27	28	33	24	19	24	15	23.0	0.1	-11.1
Cameroon	146	129	134	155	124	146	265	260	240	250	18.4	0.1	-2.5
Cape Verde	29	25	26	28	24	24	36	33	29	34	12.6	-3.0	-3.0
Central African Republic	24	30	25	30	16	22	29	26	26	29	2.5	-5.6	-0.2
Chad	6	10	19	16	37	36	16	17	20	20	-19.6	45.0	9.4
Comoros	12	17	14	13	15	9	15	12	17	21	21.2	-4.7	15.1
Congo, People's Republic of the	82	67	91	91	115	113	117	104	117	112	23.4	9.7	-0.3
Cote d'Ivoire	557	571	488	451	418	396	479	570	559	643	23.8	-7.5	9.0
Djibouti	64	64	52	52	52	58	65	69	76	73	26.5	-3.1	4.4
Equatorial Guinea	10	13	12	6	5	7	7	7	12	11	37.3	-14.3	24.7
Ethiopia	98	89	86	130	110	291	297	181	349	250	30.3	20.5	1.4
Gabon	117	130	134	124	129	136	136	136	139	121	16.8	1.8	-3.2
Gambia, The	39	44	45	37	46	50	53	53	69	59	22.8	3.7	5.9
Ghana	161	131	115	108	106	93	89	122	144	143	7.7	-9.3	17.2
Guinea	74	58	37	46	61	62	75	79	90	100	25.6	-1.6	10.3
Guinea-Bissau	13	23	12	12	10	12	12	22	26	30	2.4	-7.8	33.2
Kenya	203	130	138	130	188	142	155	132	125	151	21.0	-2.1	-1.3
Lesotho	115	116	118	142	128	120	122	107	121	119	21.1	1.9	0.6
Liberia	105	109	101	109	109	90	83	76	85	107	18.1	-1.9	9.0
Madagascar	70	111	128	88	55	61	64	58	37	52	14.7	-8.6	-10.3
Malawi	33	37	23	25	20	22	17	24	21	31	5.9	-10.0	18.4
Mali	75	63	77	61	99	102	125	75	95	107	2.1	7.9	-2.3
Mauritania	90	100	128	144	118	123	104	119	132	144	6.9	6.4	11.2
Mauritius	162	153	130	110	112	106	98	125	145	165	14.0	-8.8	18.4
Mozambique	121	104	98	141	157	161	120	191	196	174	8.9	9.1	12.1
Namibia	23	25	25	24	24	24	25	27	29	29	11.3	0.4	4.6
Niger	82	122	93	79	83	130	88	76	96	84	26.5	2.9	0.9
Nigeria	2,487	3,100	2,537	2,134	1,517	1,284	903	774	586	639	31.6	-14.8	-12.3
Rwanda	40	37	43	37	48	62	53	38	37	40	2.9	8.6	-8.3
Sao Tome & Principe	7	6	5	5	5	6	5	7	7	9	13.1	-2.9	20.5
Senegal	281	326	259	272	317	241	254	252	314	361	11.9	-2.3	13.6
Seychelles	21	19	21	17	18	18	21	25	32	29	17.1	-3.5	13.2
Sierra Leone	96	84	87	58	46	66	91	82	87	102	21.9	-11.0	4.1
Somalia	136	172	160	98	114	90	135	120	87	88	13.4	-10.3	-14.9
Sudan	394	317	259	252	226	374	263	236	261	237	15.8	-3.7	-2.1
Swaziland	38	60	61	57	63	51	38	49	49	49	11.5	4.7	8.4
Tanzania	162	118	126	86	99	87	84	70	84	63	-1.2	-10.9	-6.8
Togo	91	112	113	86	80	77	80	90	129	126	29.2	-5.8	19.2
Uganda	45	39	31	21	20	18	24	37	23	30	17.4	-18.1	1.9
Zaire	154	280	187	215	216	276	278	270	248	284	-7.0	6.7	-0.2
Zambia	142	77	69	56	62	47	40	31	35	39	15.7	-16.7	0.5
Zimbabwe	58	40	29	36	81	43	32	30	42	37	6.7	2.2	7.8
NORTH AFRICA	7,199	9,081	7,768	7,898	8,506	5,908	6,863	6,021	6,784	8,033	12.0	-3.3	6.1
Algeria	2,202	2,341	2,210	2,192	1,971	2,413	2,025	1,910	2,038	2,995	13.3	-0.2	13.2
Egypt, Arab Republic of	2,348	3,645	3,221	3,326	3,975	1,335	2,606	2,076	2,296	2,368	10.5	-7.0	-1.8
Libya	1,315	1,517	1,217	1,233	1,244	1,087	1,175	1,096	1,186	1,301	18.2	-4.3	3.9
Morocco	852	1,037	726	656	822	687	639	580	634	712	4.6	-5.2	4.2
Tunisia	482	541	394	492	495	386	419	359	630	658	16.2	-3.3	21.1
ALL AFRICA	14,490	17,080	14,798	14,290	14,457	11,807	12,376	11,474	12,539	14,042	15.5	-4.4	4.8
South Africa	585	785	645	990	1,261	698	686	838	897	939	7.1	8.1	10.6

Note: Discrepancies may occur between aggregated total merchandise trade (Tables 5-16 and 5-17), as reported originally from the trading countries, and total commodity trade (Tables 5-34 to 5-42), as estimated by the FAO.

5-38. Minerals, ores and metals exports

| | Millions of U.S. dollars | | | | | | | | | | Average annual percentage growth | | |
	1980	1981	1982	1983	1984	1985	1986	1987	1988	1989	75-80	80-85	86-MR
SUB-SAHARAN AFRICA	5,088	4,317	3,896	3,849	3,497	3,482	3,400	3,763	4,444	4,675	10.1	-7.0	11.9
excluding Nigeria	4,723	4,002	3,607	3,542	3,233	3,235	3,145	3,496	4,105	4,339	10.1	-7.0	11.9
Angola	2	4	2	2	1	1	1	1	1	1	-42.1	-21.4	0.0
Benin	2	1	1	0	0	0	0	0	0	0	92.4	-37.3	-24.2
Botswana	137	119	85	79	82	85	104	96	316	282	24.7	-9.6	52.1
Burkina Faso	0	0	0	0	0	0	0	0	0	0	..	0.0	32.0
Burundi	0	0	0	0	0	0	0	0	0	0	4.2	6.1	0.0
Cameroon	25	31	65	79	75	59	65	71	125	121	-0.3	22.9	27.8
Cape Verde	0	1	0	1	0	0	0	0	0	0	38.9	-16.4	-24.2
Central African Republic	0	3	3	3	1	1	2	0	1	2	..	11.6	8.1
Chad	0	0	1	1	2	3	2	3	3	3	0.0	63.0	6.7
Comoros	..	..	..	..	0	..	..	..	..	..	..	..	..
Congo, People's Republic of the	2	1	1	1	1	1	1	1	1	1	-14.3	-8.8	0.0
Cote d'Ivoire	8	7	5	4	4	5	7	4	5	5	8.1	-10.1	-5.6
Djibouti	0	0	0	0	0	0	0	0	0	0	-50.0	-13.5	17.6
Equatorial Guinea	..	..	..	..	..	..	..	..	..	..	..	..	..
Ethiopia	0	1	0	..	1	1		1	1	1	..	..	..
Gabon	264	228	190	202	161	165	177	187	205	205	23.3	-9.1	5.4
Gambia, The													
Ghana	280	195	210	150	131	171	240	352	290	302	30.7	-10.9	5.1
Guinea	478	483	441	491	513	521	466	514	504	538	19.9	2.1	4.2
Guinea-Bissau	..	..	..	..	..	..	..	..	..	..	..	..	..
Kenya	33	46	23	20	15	23	24	24	24	24	21.6	-13.4	-0.3
Lesotho	..	..	..	..	..	..	..	..	..	..	..	..	..
Liberia	344	349	337	285	291	285	253	228	236	290	1.1	-4.6	4.5
Madagascar	14	16	14	10	9	15	17	18	15	15	-3.5	-4.8	-6.2
Malawi	0	0	0	0	0	0	0	0	0	0	..	0.0	0.0
Mali	0	0	0	2	0	0	0	0	0	0	10.4	5.4	0.0
Mauritania	160	170	145	135	148	155	147	139	145	190	-2.2	-1.8	8.5
Mauritius	..	0	..	..	3	0	1	1	1	1	..	..	36.4
Mozambique	25	19	15	8	3	6	4	5	8	8	26.1	-32.2	26.1
Namibia	163	111	101	116	94	98	95	100	120	120	18.1	-7.9	9.2
Niger	491	363	278	291	224	254	274	326	270	259	58.6	-12.6	-3.5
Nigeria	71	50	31	25	26	20	12	8	9	9	9.6	-21.8	-9.5
Rwanda	12	11	21	19	16	14	3	2	1	1	9.8	5.6	-32.1
Sao Tome & Principe	..	..	..	..	..	..	..	..	..	..	..	..	..
Senegal	95	79	78	77	85	77	71	50	51	51	-1.3	-2.4	-9.0
Seychelles	0	0	0	0	0	0	0	0	0	0	8.1	-9.4	0.0
Sierra Leone	14	12	11	26	24	25	23	26	27	31	-3.0	19.2	9.2
Somalia	0	..	..	..	..	..	..	..	..	..	..	..	..
Sudan	3	2	1	1	1	0	4	1	2	2	0.2	-28.2	-10.1
Swaziland	18	14	14	14	9	8	8	8	8	8	-10.9	-14.0	0.0
Tanzania	29	27	15	11	12	22	19	16	15	15	50.0	-11.3	-6.8
Togo	135	105	78	68	105	93	89	87	109	90	13.7	-5.6	2.7
Uganda	3	1	0	0	2	1	0	0	0	0	-27.3	-6.6	0.0
Zaire	740	636	625	623	550	550	570	595	790	830	0.4	-5.3	15.2
Zambia	1,428	1,091	1,010	1,031	834	765	660	805	1,086	1,194	11.7	-10.6	23.1
Zimbabwe	275	249	198	190	172	155	157	198	198	199	2.8	-10.8	7.4
NORTH AFRICA	1,203	1,185	975	829	906	757	751	754	1,100	1,105	3.5	-9.0	16.6
Algeria	73	75	76	67	61	41	61	40	72	72	-0.2	-9.9	11.3
Egypt, Arab Republic of	75	134	121	102	135	75	128	165	277	271	59.7	-0.6	31.9
Libya	0	0	0	0	0	0	0	0	0	0	..	2.0	0.0
Morocco	974	908	720	608	662	601	517	502	688	686	3.8	-9.6	12.3
Tunisia	81	67	58	52	48	41	45	46	63	76	-9.0	-12.1	21.3
ALL AFRICA	6,291	5,502	4,871	4,679	4,402	4,238	4,151	4,517	5,545	5,780	8.6	-7.4	12.7
South Africa	2,006	1,689	1,508	1,504	1,492	1,470	1,537	1,668	2,218	2,218	20.4	-5.4	14.9

Note: *Discrepancies may occur between aggregated total merchandise trade (Tables 5-16 and 5-17), as reported originally from the trading countries, and total commodity trade (Tables 5-34 to 5-42), as estimated by the FAO.*

5–39. Minerals, ores and metals imports

	Millions of U.S. dollars										Average annual percentage growth		
	1980	1981	1982	1983	1984	1985	1986	1987	1988	1989	75-80	80-85	86-MR
SUB-SAHARAN AFRICA	683	660	557	434	570	585	549	627	658	651	11.2	-4.1	5.8
excluding Nigeria	409	374	314	235	220	281	367	392	421	409	9.3	-10.2	4.1
Angola	11	9	5	6	6	7	6	6	6	6	-8.2	-9.0	0.0
Benin	2	3	4	2	0	0	1	1	1	1	18.4	-35.3	13.9
Botswana	..	..	..	..	..	..	..	..	..	..	..	..	..
Burkina Faso	4	4	4	4	5	6	10	12	10	10	9.8	6.5	-1.7
Burundi	4	3	4	4	5	5	5	6	5	5	26.0	5.7	-0.7
Cameroon	39	56	37	47	52	49	49	53	55	60	15.6	3.3	6.7
Cape Verde	..	..	..	..	..	..	..	..	..	..	..	..	..
Central African Republic	4	3	3	3	3	4	4	5	5	5	15.7	0.1	1.6
Chad	1	1	1	1	1	1	1	1	1	1	-14.0	-0.5	0.0
Comoros	0	0	0	0	0	0	0	0	0	0	-32.7	0.0	0.0
Congo, People's Republic of the	8	9	8	10	7	7	8	8	8	8	49.8	-3.5	0.0
Cote d'Ivoire	55	44	38	31	30	28	50	47	36	36	23.1	-12.7	-11.9
Djibouti	1	1	1	1	2	1	1	1	1	1	-0.1	13.3	0.0
Equatorial Guinea	..	..	..	..	..	..	..	..	..	..	..	..	..
Ethiopia	4	5	5	4	9	5	5	5	9	9	-6.0	6.0	30.8
Gabon	7	8	10	8	10	11	18	16	16	16	5.9	9.0	-4.8
Gambia, The	1	1	1	0	1	1	1	1	1	1	44.8	-7.9	6.4
Ghana	102	105	89	29	10	28	50	59	68	80	11.6	-34.0	16.8
Guinea	..	..	..	..	..	..	..	..	..	..	..	..	..
Guinea-Bissau	0	0	0	0	0	0	0	0	0	0	..	0.0	0.0
Kenya	33	24	18	20	21	20	25	33	35	35	28.3	-8.2	11.9
Lesotho	..	..	..	..	..	..	..	..	..	..	..	..	..
Liberia	6	6	3	7	5	3	3	3	2	2	11.5	-8.5	-8.5
Madagascar	8	4	3	3	2	3	3	2	3	3	20.0	-16.1	7.7
Malawi	6	5	5	4	4	5	5	6	6	6	14.8	-5.2	9.5
Mali	3	2	2	2	3	4	3	4	3	3	3.5	5.1	-5.9
Mauritania	2	2	2	2	1	1	2	1	1	1	7.8	-6.9	-18.3
Mauritius	7	5	7	5	5	5	6	9	11	11	17.7	-6.9	22.9
Mozambique	47	52	30	32	19	19	22	10	11	11	-18.7	-19.2	-17.7
Namibia	..	..	..	..	..	..	..	..	..	..	..	..	..
Niger	19	12	13	10	16	19	36	43	35	35	65.6	2.0	-3.0
Nigeria	210	203	182	128	275	231	100	152	152	152	15.2	3.0	13.2
Rwanda	2	2	2	2	2	2	2	3	3	3	7.9	-2.6	4.0
Sao Tome & Principe	0	0	0	0	0	0	0	0	0	0	10.4	9.7	0.0
Senegal	4	4	5	6	12	17	27	24	24	24	-9.6	35.1	-3.1
Seychelles	1	1	1	1	0	1	1	1	1	1	33.7	-10.3	2.9
Sierra Leone	2	1	1	1	1	1	1	1	1	1	8.8	-8.0	5.6
Somalia	1	0	1	1	1	1	1	1	1	1	-21.1	4.4	4.0
Sudan	8	12	7	7	6	4	6	2	10	10	11.0	-16.1	33.3
Swaziland	..	..	..	..	..	..	..	..	..	..	..	..	..
Tanzania	23	10	13	11	13	14	9	17	15	15	14.9	-5.5	14.1
Togo	2	4	3	2	2	4	3	2	4	5	9.9	2.8	22.2
Uganda	3	3	4	4	4	3	5	7	8	8	-3.6	2.5	19.4
Zaire	21	19	17	16	18	19	22	32	36	36	13.8	-2.3	17.2
Zambia	9	8	3	2	3	45	42	37	55	30	2.5	14.5	-5.9
Zimbabwe	26	28	26	19	16	16	17	19	20	20	17.6	-11.7	6.2
NORTH AFRICA	668	758	725	801	858	854	975	996	1,181	1,032	17.5	5.0	3.5
Algeria	181	193	125	150	164	202	204	204	188	188	15.4	0.7	-3.2
Egypt, Arab Republic of	110	150	136	177	192	129	144	170	241	238	6.2	5.2	20.4
Libya	71	66	86	126	120	120	115	115	115	115	10.8	14.6	0.0
Morocco	151	168	195	200	217	277	302	319	420	246	28.5	11.6	-3.4
Tunisia	155	181	184	149	166	127	210	188	217	246	29.9	-4.2	6.3
ALL AFRICA	1,351	1,418	1,282	1,235	1,428	1,439	1,524	1,624	1,839	1,683	13.9	0.9	4.3
South Africa	419	389	327	277	367	269	276	324	343	343	9.6	-7.1	7.3

Note: Discrepancies may occur between aggregated total merchandise trade (Tables 5-16 and 5-17), as reported originally from the trading countries, and total commodity trade (Tables 5-34 to 5-42), as estimated by the FAO.

5–40. Agricultural raw materials exports

	Millions of U.S. dollars										Average annual percentage growth		
	1980	1981	1982	1983	1984	1985	1986	1987	1988	1989	75–80	80–85	86–MR
SUB-SAHARAN AFRICA	2,504	1,932	1,639	1,784	2,028	1,689	1,784	2,028	2,396	2,475	12.1	–4.8	12.2
excluding Nigeria	2,064	1,600	1,347	1,517	1,758	1,414	1,500	1,691	1,955	1,964	11.5	–4.2	10.0
Angola	19	18	20	3	3	3	2	2	3	4	–13.2	–38.5	20.3
Benin	12	10	5	13	33	31	30	50	59	59	6.4	31.6	24.9
Botswana	6	8	8	7	8	6	5	3	4	4	27.6	–0.4	–3.4
Burkina Faso	43	34	25	32	47	30	35	71	70	71	23.4	–1.6	23.7
Burundi	4	3	3	5	4	3	4	8	5	5	11.0	4.0	9.1
Cameroon	205	132	113	99	92	117	87	113	167	206	23.7	–10.8	34.6
Cape Verde	0	0	0	0	0	0	0	0	0	0	..	..	..
Central African Republic	61	60	35	41	37	40	40	30	27	31	21.2	–9.2	–7.9
Chad	39	40	25	59	97	45	43	44	68	63	6.4	13.0	17.7
Comoros	..	..	..	..	..	..	..	..	..	..	..	..	..
Congo, People's Republic of the	59	37	28	25	32	35	47	76	101	110	24.4	–8.7	33.1
Cote d'Ivoire	670	441	363	389	372	317	348	351	410	424	19.7	–11.3	7.7
Djibouti	1	0	0	1	1	1	1	2	2	2	..	12.2	26.6
Equatorial Guinea	2	6	10	8	8	7	18	18	12	12	–9.5	20.3	–13.7
Ethiopia	77	66	70	66	71	59	65	66	65	65	27.1	–3.3	–0.3
Gabon	133	116	98	106	111	92	115	112	115	115	20.9	–5.3	0.3
Gambia, The	0	0	0	0	1	1	1	1	1	1	..	46.8	14.5
Ghana	36	16	10	12	15	24	37	84	91	68	–13.6	–6.0	21.5
Guinea	4	5	5	1	1	1	1	1	1	1	0.0	–30.0	0.0
Guinea-Bissau	0	2	1	0	2	1	1	1	2	2	0.0	9.1	29.6
Kenya	106	77	67	60	61	61	67	73	84	91	8.7	–9.6	11.0
Lesotho	9	7	7	11	14	12	11	10	10	10	17.5	12.5	–0.8
Liberia	198	141	95	104	115	112	132	125	227	207	25.6	–9.1	21.5
Madagascar	17	19	18	11	13	7	13	18	10	8	1.6	–16.3	–18.1
Malawi	7	3	1	1	6	17	3	3	5	5	7.8	22.0	22.7
Mali	81	67	67	36	98	77	74	112	101	140	23.8	0.8	19.6
Mauritania	1	1	1	1	1	1	1	1	1	1	14.5	4.8	0.0
Mauritius	1	1	1	1	1	1	1	2	3	3	7.1	16.1	33.5
Mozambique	21	35	24	20	11	7	2	9	8	8	–5.5	–23.7	45.4
Namibia	70	70	70	70	70	70	70	70	70	70	7.5	0.0	0.0
Niger	3	3	5	1	4	1	1	3	2	4	68.7	–23.9	60.7
Nigeria	26	30	33	33	33	29	34	35	56	76	0.1	2.6	33.8
Rwanda	8	4	7	5	7	9	9	9	7	10	53.5	3.5	–1.1
Sao Tome & Principe	..	..	..	..	..	..	..	..	..	..	..	..	..
Senegal	13	10	18	26	21	20	22	11	22	25	8.9	13.6	10.4
Seychelles	0	0	0	0	0	..	..	..	..	..	..	..	..
Sierra Leone	2	1	1	1	0	0	1	1	1	1	–3.9	–35.8	22.3
Somalia	10	3	2	2	2	4	6	7	7	4	8.5	–14.3	–12.0
Sudan	296	178	185	296	375	208	220	272	300	268	4.8	2.7	7.1
Swaziland	70	83	60	60	86	89	84	87	87	87	16.2	3.9	1.0
Tanzania	89	117	86	81	64	38	51	56	75	79	–2.6	–16.0	17.5
Togo	8	13	15	18	17	27	36	34	42	39	30.5	22.1	4.3
Uganda	4	2	3	12	11	10	5	5	3	3	–32.4	34.3	–20.1
Zaire	52	44	35	40	40	36	41	40	49	40	3.7	–5.5	1.4
Zambia	9	2	2	6	2	7	2	4	4	12	52.4	–2.0	75.1
Zimbabwe	106	103	88	92	112	109	95	85	97	116	18.7	1.4	7.4
NORTH AFRICA	548	570	492	535	575	280	418	307	336	443	–1.4	–8.9	2.7
Algeria	1	1	0	0	0	2	1	1	1	1	–23.8	1.7	13.8
Egypt, Arab Republic of	471	504	441	482	520	222	357	212	199	301	–2.8	–9.7	–5.6
Libya	..	0	..	..	..	..	1	2	2	1	..	..	–1.7
Morocco	60	51	36	39	44	42	51	83	125	127	13.0	–5.9	36.8
Tunisia	16	15	15	15	11	13	10	11	11	14	8.1	–4.8	12.2
ALL AFRICA	3,052	2,502	2,132	2,319	2,603	1,969	2,202	2,335	2,732	2,918	8.8	–5.5	10.5
South Africa	586	513	473	507	551	473	433	473	572	585	13.7	–2.2	11.5

Note: Discrepancies may occur between aggregated total merchandise trade (Table 5-16 and 5-17), as reported originally from the trading countries, and total commodity trade (Table 5-34 to 5-42), as estimated by the FAO.

5–41. Agricultural raw materials imports

	Millions of U.S. dollars										Average annual percentage growth		
	1980	1981	1982	1983	1984	1985	1986	1987	1988	1989	75–80	80–85	86–MR
SUB-SAHARAN AFRICA	227	311	273	281	265	290	250	262	272	267	9.0	2.2	2.4
excluding Nigeria	177	217	180	189	182	205	194	207	218	223	10.7	0.7	4.9
Angola	2	1	1	2	2	2	2	2	4	2	-1.2	0.4	2.6
Benin	1	0	0	0	0	0	0	0	0	0	..	..	0.0
Botswana	2	2	2	3	3	2	2	4	4	4	11.4	10.5	16.6
Burkina Faso	4	4	5	4	2	2	2	3	4	4	32.4	-15.6	26.9
Burundi	2	2	2	1	1	0	0	1	0	1	23.4	-22.7	20.4
Cameroon	4	4	4	3	2	2	6	5	3	3	12.3	-16.8	-18.0
Cape Verde	1	1	1	1	1	1	1	1	1	1	6.8	-6.8	-1.0
Central African Republic	0	3	0	0	0	0	0	0	0	0	..	-26.1	37.4
Chad	1	1	1	1	1	1	..	..	..	..	-0.5	-3.4	..
Comoros	..	..	..	1	1	1	0	..	..	..	..	..	..
Congo, People's Republic of the	2	2	2	3	2	3	3	1	3	3	62.7	2.4	14.9
Cote d'Ivoire	7	7	5	6	4	13	5	7	4	5	12.3	3.4	-7.8
Djibouti	13	17	20	32	26	19	21	23	23	23	..	11.6	2.8
Equatorial Guinea	..	..	..	..	..	..	..	..	..	..	..	..	..
Ethiopia	12	11	14	14	14	24	13	13	12	18	34.8	12.5	9.1
Gabon	2	3	2	3	2	3	4	4	3	3	31.9	3.7	-5.0
Gambia, The	3	3	2	2	2	1	2	2	2	2	31.6	-15.6	0.0
Ghana	9	10	6	9	9	6	11	10	18	18	-13.1	-5.0	24.1
Guinea	2	3	3	4	4	4	4	4	3	3	8.9	12.9	-12.2
Guinea-Bissau	..	..	..	..	..	0	0	0	..	..	..	..	..
Kenya	13	11	8	9	14	11	10	11	15	13	1.9	0.5	10.3
Lesotho	1	1	2	7	6	5	5	5	5	5	30.3	68.3	0.0
Liberia	4	4	5	5	1	1	0	0	0	0	48.2	-33.3	-4.0
Madagascar	9	10	9	10	8	5	2	3	5	3	23.6	-9.1	15.9
Malawi	4	1	4	3	3	1	1	0	1	1	11.4	-9.7	2.3
Mali	1	1	1	1	1	1	1	1	1	1	-23.8	8.6	6.0
Mauritania	..	..	0	0	..	2	3	3	3	3	..	..	1.5
Mauritius	19	19	14	12	15	18	18	21	23	28	31.5	-3.2	15.4
Mozambique	..	2	1	..	..	..	..	2	2	..	..	..	..
Namibia	..	..	..	..	..	..	..	..	..	..	..	..	..
Niger	1	1	3	2	2	2	2	2	2	2	15.0	13.6	0.0
Nigeria	40	83	83	81	75	76	42	44	40	33	2.7	8.7	-7.8
Rwanda	..	..	..	0	1	0	1	1	1	1	..	..	-20.7
Sao Tome & Principe	0	0	0	0	0	0	0	0	0	0	..	..	..
Senegal	7	7	8	7	8	8	8	8	9	9	-14.8	2.7	3.2
Seychelles	0	0	0	0	0	0	0	0	0	0	..	..	0.0
Sierra Leone	0	0	0	1	1	1	0	0	0	0	4.5	15.3	0.0
Somalia	14	34	25	25	25	25	25	28	26	26	26.6	5.7	0.8
Sudan	7	28	15	10	12	21	25	23	25	24	-8.5	7.6	-1.0
Swaziland	2	2	2	2	1	1	1	1	1	1	..	-11.3	-7.3
Tanzania	4	5	2	3	3	5	7	10	7	4	15.1	-1.3	-17.1
Togo	1	1	1	1	0	0	0	0	0	0	13.9	-25.2	12.2
Uganda	0	0	0	0	0	0	0	0	..	..	-18.6	..	..
Zaire	10	6	7	1	1	9	10	9	9	10	16.8	-18.9	-0.4
Zambia	8	5	5	5	6	5	5	5	5	5	3.2	-3.9	1.8
Zimbabwe	17	20	14	11	11	11	12	13	13	14	18.2	-11.0	3.7
NORTH AFRICA	808	1,111	1,043	1,112	1,156	927	999	996	1,271	1,284	9.7	2.5	10.5
Algeria	192	307	296	368	371	296	282	251	307	324	12.8	8.8	6.4
Egypt, Arab Republic of	298	451	404	444	490	337	424	410	547	529	8.1	2.8	10.0
Libya	67	100	78	76	52	43	47	47	49	49	1.8	-11.4	1.3
Morocco	166	151	166	137	142	143	153	184	256	265	12.4	-3.2	21.8
Tunisia	84	101	99	88	101	108	94	104	113	118	13.1	3.2	8.2
ALL AFRICA	1,035	1,421	1,316	1,392	1,420	1,217	1,249	1,258	1,542	1,552	9.5	2.5	8.9
South Africa	319	321	228	284	295	177	198	205	201	204	11.4	-8.2	0.7

Note: Discrepancies may occur between aggregated total merchandise trade (Tables 5-16 and 5-17), as reported originally from the trading countries, and total commodity trade (Tables 5-34 to 5-42), as estimated by the FAO.

5-42. Fuel exports

| | Millions of U.S. dollars | | | | | | | | | | Average annual percentage growth | | |
	1980	1981	1982	1983	1984	1985	1986	1987	1988	1989	75-80	80-85	86-MR
SUB-SAHARAN AFRICA	29,823	23,692	18,828	15,635	17,637	18,732	9,199	11,538	11,543	14,151	22.1	-9.2	13.8
excluding Nigeria	1,060	1,210	1,068	906	898	952	926	753	915	985	22.4	-4.5	3.9
Angola	1,483	1,539	1,307	1,615	1,839	2,028	1,195	2,050	2,153	2,420	14.1	6.8	24.2
Benin	2	0	2	9	16	9	3	4	12	10	88.2	98.0	57.6
Botswana	..	..	..	..	..	..	..	..	..	..	..	..	..
Burkina Faso	0	0	0	0	..	..	..	..	..	..	..	..	..
Burundi	0	0	1	0	0	0	0	0	..	..	11.7	3.5	..
Cameroon	405	550	483	447	384	427	170	145	116	117	282.1	-2.5	-12.7
Cape Verde	0	0	0	..	0	..	..	..	..	..	..	..	..
Central African Republic	..	0	..	..	1	18	..	..	..	..	..	..	..
Chad	0	..	..	13	19	..	..	..	..	..	..	..	..
Comoros	0	0	0	..	..	..	..	2	..	..	..	..	..
Congo, People's Republic of the	856	913	867	960	1,085	1,014	692	653	634	730	44.1	4.3	1.3
Cote d'Ivoire	70	191	298	237	262	259	409	245	360	400	5.9	23.0	3.2
Djibouti	13	6	20	9	8	7	8	8	8	8	20.5	-7.7	2.5
Equatorial Guinea	..	..	..	..	..	..	..	..	..	..	..	..	..
Ethiopia	32	30	31	33	31	33	11	21	13	13	37.9	1.2	0.0
Gabon	1,745	1,786	1,802	1,652	1,684	1,629	723	896	779	1,200	16.2	-1.7	14.8
Gambia, The	..	..	..	0	..	..	..	..	..	..	..	..	..
Ghana	4	104	69	86	28	32	23	26	29	29	-27.4	22.2	8.6
Guinea	..	0	..	..	..	..	..	..	..	..	..	..	..
Guinea-Bissau	..	0	0	0	..	..	..	..	..	..	..	..	..
Kenya	439	367	257	194	183	156	133	124	154	154	25.1	-19.4	6.7
Lesotho	..	..	..	..	..	..	..	..	..	..	..	..	..
Liberia	7	0	7	1	0	0	1	1	1	1	..	-81.1	0.0
Madagascar	23	26	25	21	8	11	7	7	6	6	-4.2	-18.7	-5.8
Malawi	1	0	0	0	0	0	0	0	0	0	37.1	-5.6	0.0
Mali	0	0	0	0	0	0	..	..	..	..	..	..	..
Mauritania	2	17	0	3	3	3	1	2	2	2	4.6	0.2	31.6
Mauritius	0	..	0	0	..	..	..	..	..	..	..	..	..
Mozambique	14	13	15	7	2	9	8	8	1	1	-11.2	-23.2	-51.8
Namibia	..	..	..	..	..	..	..	..	..	..	..	..	..
Niger	7	4	2	8	3	2	8	8	2	2	..	-13.2	-42.1
Nigeria	24,274	17,694	13,300	10,055	11,747	12,682	5,493	7,041	6,945	8,700	22.3	-12.7	14.6
Rwanda	0	0	0	0	..	..	..	..	9	..	..	..	..
Sao Tome & Principe	..	..	..	0	..	..	..	..	..	..	..	..	..
Senegal	90	210	106	78	75	169	122	114	118	120	22.0	-0.6	-0.1
Seychelles	15	12	11	15	20	23	13	15	14	16	34.7	11.3	4.9
Sierra Leone	0	2	..	4	1	1	0	0	0	0	..	..	-10.9
Somalia	6	0	2	0	0	0	0	0	0	0	..	-47.4	0.0
Sudan	6	22	30	9	3	1	..	4	..	..	-13.3	-32.5	..
Swaziland	..	..	..	..	..	..	..	..	..	..	..	..	..
Tanzania	25	1	8	20	16	6	3	2	2	2	0.7	7.2	-6.0
Togo	87	3	1	2	0	0	1	1	0	..	..	-62.2	..
Uganda	3	11	2	2	..	..	..	..	..	..	..	..	..
Zaire	202	206	190	165	231	221	164	146	172	200	74.6	1.9	8.0
Zambia	5	4	7	2	0	0	0	0	1	1	33.1	-48.7	44.8
Zimbabwe	18	16	17	16	13	10	11	19	19	19	9.6	-10.3	17.6
NORTH AFRICA	40,538	32,087	28,198	24,992	25,311	22,684	16,598	17,609	16,867	18,350	26.1	-10.1	2.6
Algeria	15,382	13,030	11,244	10,975	11,595	9,901	7,641	7,978	7,743	8,170	29.4	-7.1	1.7
Egypt, Arab Republic of	1,957	2,087	2,069	2,005	1,808	1,253	1,135	728	704	807	56.6	-7.4	-10.0
Libya	21,910	15,513	13,886	11,079	11,027	10,759	7,333	8,317	7,960	8,700	22.9	-12.8	4.8
Morocco	117	105	88	82	86	84	62	77	75	87	52.3	-6.3	10.2
Tunisia	1,172	1,352	911	852	796	686	427	508	386	587	28.2	-11.6	7.0
ALL AFRICA	70,361	55,779	47,025	40,627	42,949	41,415	25,797	29,147	28,410	32,502	24.4	-9.7	6.9
South Africa	966	1,270	1,155	1,167	1,229	1,364	1,609	1,772	1,622	1,850	68.5	4.8	3.4

Note: Discrepancies may occur between aggregated total merchandise trade (Tables 5-16 and 5-17), as reported originally from the trading countries, and total commodity trade (Tables 5-34 to 5-42), as estimated by the FAO.

5-43. Direction of trade matrix, imports, 1981

Exporters		Importers															
		DZA	ANG	BEN	BWA	HVO	BDI	CMR	CPV	CAF	TCD	COM	CGO	CIV	DJI	EGY	GNQ
Algeria	DZA	**	0.12	2.77	..	..	..	..	..	..	..	..	..	1.48	..	..	..
Angola	ANG	0.39	**	..	..	..	..	..	0.37	..	..	..	..	..	..	..	..
Benin	BEN	0.00	..	**	..	0.10	..	0.00	..	..	..	..	0.03	0.00	..	..	..
Botswana	BWA	..	..	..	**	..	..	..	..	..	..	..	..	..	..	..	..
Burkina Faso	HVO	..	..	0.03	..	**	..	..	..	..	..	..	0.00	1.03	..	..	**
Burundi	BDI	..	..	..	..	..	**	0.01	..	..	1.39	..	..	..	0.00	..	..
Cameroon	CMR	..	0.01	0.05	..	0.03	..	**	..	13.48	39.52	..	2.26	0.31	..	0.02	0.33
Cape Verde	CPV	..	0.02	..	..	..	..	..	**	0.12	..	..	..	..	..	..	..
Central African Republic	CAF	..	..	..	..	..	..	..	..	**	0.55	..	..	0.01	..	..	..
Chad	TCD	..	..	..	..	..	..	1.04	..	2.86	**	..	..	..	..	..	..
Comoros	COM	..	..	..	..	..	..	..	..	..	..	**	..	..	..	..	..
Congo, People's Republic of the	CGO	0.01	0.05	0.00	..	..	..	..	..	..	0.59	..	**	0.00	..	..	..
Cote d'Ivoire	CIV	0.33	..	2.06	..	33.45	..	0.66	..	1.04	..	..	0.61	**	..	..	..
Djibouti	DJI	..	..	..	..	..	..	..	..	..	..	..	..	..	**	..	..
Egypt, Arab Republic of	EGY	0.00	..	0.00	..	..	..	..	..	..	..	..	0.01	0.00	0.01	**	..
Equatorial Guinea	GNQ	..	..	..	..	..	..	0.02	..	..	..	..	..	..	..	..	**
Ethiopia	ETH	..	..	..	..	..	..	..	..	..	..	..	..	..	8.24	0.09	..
Gabon	GAB	0.01	0.41	..	..	..	..	..	..	..	..	..	..	0.01	..	..	..
Gambia, The	GMB	..	..	..	..	..	..	..	..	..	..	..	..	..	..	..	..
Ghana	GHA	0.00	0.00	..	..	..	..	0.00	..	..	..	..	..	0.00	..	0.03	..
Guinea	GIN	..	..	..	..	..	..	2.02	..	..	..	..	..	..	..	0.00	..
Guinea-Bissau	GNB	..	0.00	..	..	..	..	..	..	..	..	..	..	..	..	..	..
Kenya	KEN	..	0.01	0.00	0.47	0.01	18.32	0.03	0.01	0.03	0.04	9.73	0.01	0.02	9.69	0.06	0.27
Lesotho	LSO	..	..	..	..	..	..	..	..	..	..	..	..	..	..	..	..
Liberia	LBR	..	..	..	..	..	..	0.00	..	0.01	..	..	0.00	0.02	..	0.00	..
Libya	LBY	0.00	..	..	..	..	..	..	..	..	2.59	..	..	..	..	0.00	..
Madagascar	MDG	0.09	..	..	..	..	..	..	..	..	..	1.00	..	..	..	..	..
Malawi	MWI	..	..	..	..	..	..	0.01	..	..	..	..	..	..	..	..	..
Mali	MLI	0.00	..	..	..	0.19	..	..	..	..	..	..	..	1.44	..	..	..
Mauritania	MRT	..	..	..	..	..	..	..	..	..	..	..	0.09	..	..	..	..
Mauritius	MUS	..	..	..	0.04	..	0.00	0.00	..	..	..	2.56	0.02	0.00	0.01	0.00	..
Morocco	MAR	..	..	..	..	0.00	..	0.31	..	..	..	..	0.59	0.43	..	0.05	..
Mozambique	MOZ	0.01	..	..	..	..	..	..	..	..	..	..	..	..	..	0.00	..
Namibia	NAM	..	..	..	..	..	..	..	..	..	..	..	..	..	..	..	..
Niger	NER	0.00	..	0.04	..	0.27	0.00	0.02	..	..	0.01	..	0.01	0.02	..	..	..
Nigeria	NGA	0.00	..	0.89	..	..	..	0.03	0.10	..	..	..	..	3.82	..	0.00	..
Rwanda	RWA	..	..	..	..	..	0.20	..	..	..	..	..	..	..	..	..	..
Sao Tome & Principe	STP	..	..	..	..	..	..	..	..	..	..	..	..	..	..	..	..
Senegal	SEN	0.01	..	0.66	..	1.05	0.00	0.17	0.45	0.86	0.18	..	0.37	1.76	..	0.00	0.00
Seychelles	SYC	..	..	..	..	..	..	..	..	..	..	..	..	..	..	..	..
Sierra Leone	SLE	..	..	..	..	..	..	..	..	..	..	..	..	..	..	..	..
Somalia	SOM	..	..	..	..	..	..	..	..	..	..	..	..	..	0.51	0.00	..
South Africa	ZAF	..	..	..	..	..	..	..	..	..	..	..	..	..	..	..	..
Sudan	SDN	0.04	0.08	..	..	..	..	..	..	..	..	..	..	..	..	0.27	..
Swaziland	SWZ	..	..	..	..	..	..	..	..	..	..	..	..	..	..	..	..
Tanzania	TZA	0.26	..	..	..	..	7.83	..	..	..	..	..	..	..	..	0.02	..
Togo	TGO	..	..	0.32	..	0.95	..	0.00	..	..	..	..	0.02	0.42	..	..	..
Tunisia	TUN	0.48	..	..	..	..	..	..	..	..	..	..	..	0.10	..	0.13	..
Uganda	UGA	..	..	..	..	..	..	..	..	..	..	..	..	..	..	0.01	..
Zaire	ZAR	..	..	..	..	..	0.77	0.02	..	1.77	..	..	0.97	..	..	..	..
Zambia	ZMB	..	0.03	..	3.90	..	1.91	0.00	..	..	..	..	..	..	..	0.03	..
Zimbabwe	ZWE	0.00	0.22	..	68.55	..	0.66	0.06	..	0.06	..	0.56	0.03	0.01	..	0.07	..
Total Sub-Saharan Africa	SSA	1.16	0.84	4.04	72.96	36.05	29.69	4.09	0.93	20.23	42.29	13.85	4.41	8.89	18.44	0.60	0.60
European Community	EEC	67.68	50.12	44.14	11.33	50.81	35.65	62.48	54.35	66.37	52.33	73.52	71.14	49.91	47.29	43.70	92.49
North America	NNA	10.29	18.61	2.95	10.64	7.75	2.50	13.39	..	0.71	1.40	0.20	3.62	6.62	3.01	19.67	1.60
Rest of World	ROW	20.87	30.44	48.87	5.08	5.39	32.16	20.04	44.72	12.69	3.99	12.42	20.84	34.59	31.26	36.03	5.31
World	TOT	100	100	100	100	100	100	100	100	100	100	100	100	100	100	100	100

Note: ** means "not applicable."

(Table continues on the following page)

5-43. (continued)

Percentage of total imports

	ETH	GAB	GMB	GHA	GIN	GNB	KEN	LSO	LBR	LBY	MDG	MWI	MLI	MRT	MUS	MAR	MOZ	NAM	NER	NGA
DZA	..	..	2.77	1.77	0.09	..	0.28	..	0.02	0.02	..	..	0.37	0.00	0.44	..	4.81	..	0.02	0.00
ANG	..	..	..	0.00	..	..	..	..	..	..	..	..	..	..	..	..	..	..	..	0.01
BEN	..	..	..	0.04	..	..	..	..	..	..	..	..	0.00	..	..	..	..	..	0.65	0.01
BWA	..	..	..	..	..	..	..	..	..	..	..	..	..	..	..	..	..	..	..	..
HVO	..	..	..	0.03	..	..	..	..	..	..	..	..	0.37	..	..	..	..	..	0.46	..
BDI	..	..	..	..	..	..	0.03	..	..	..	..	..	..	..	..	..	..	..	..	..
CMR	..	2.44	..	0.00	0.39	..	..	..	..	..	0.06	0.00	0.24	..	..	0.00	0.00	..	..	0.03
CPV	..	..	..	..	..	..	..	..	..	..	..	..	..	..	..	..	..	..	..	..
CAF	..	..	..	..	..	..	..	..	..	..	..	..	..	0.00	..	..	..	..	..	0.00
TCD	..	..	..	..	..	..	..	..	..	..	..	..	..	..	..	..	..	..	..	..
COM	..	..	..	..	..	..	..	..	..	..	0.03	..	..	..	0.00	..	..	..	0.02	0.03
CGO	..	..	..	..	..	..	..	..	..	..	..	..	..	..	..	0.01	..	..	..	..
CIV	..	1.01	..	0.97	..	..	..	..	0.38	..	..	..	28.83	0.88	..	0.45	..	..	8.24	0.15
DJI	0.36	..	..	..	..	..	0.00	..	..	0.00	..	..	..	..	..	..	..	..	..	..
EGY	0.02	..	..	..	..	..	0.01	..	..	0.00	..	..	..	0.41	0.02	0.03	..	..	..	0.01
GNQ	..	..	..	..	..	..	..	..	..	..	..	..	..	..	..	..	..	..	..	..
ETH	**	..	..	..	..	..	0.05	..	..	..	..	..	..	..	..	..	..	..	..	..
GAB	..	**	..	..	0.76	..	..	..	..	..	..	..	..	..	..	0.13	..	..	..	0.14
GMB	..	..	**	0.78	0.90	0.26	..	..	0.00	..	..	..	0.00	..	..	..	..	..	..	0.01
GHA	..	..	0.14	**	0.00	..	0.00	..	0.01	0.00	..	..	0.00	..	..	..	0.00	..	..	0.00
GIN	..	..	..	..	**	0.09	..	..	0.01	..	..	..	..	..	0.00	0.02	..	..	0.00	..
GNB	..	..	0.06	..	0.02	**	..	..	..	..	..	..	..	..	..	..	..	..	..	..
KEN	0.50	0.00	0.00	0.00	0.01	..	**	0.42	0.00	0.00	0.27	0.63	0.06	0.00	3.13	0.01	3.43	..	0.01	0.03
LSO	..	..	..	..	..	..	..	**	..	..	..	..	..	..	..	..	..	..	..	..
LBR	..	..	0.02	0.21	0.55	..	..	..	**	0.02	..	0.01	0.01	0.00	..	..	..	..	..	0.03
LBY	..	..	..	..	..	..	..	..	..	**	..	..	..	..	..	0.00	..	..	..	..
MDG	..	..	..	..	..	..	..	..	..	..	**	..	..	..	0.23	0.02	..	..	..	..
MWI	0.01	0.06	..	..	..	..	0.06	..	0.09	..	..	**	..	..	0.16	..	0.25	..	..	..
MLI	..	..	..	0.03	..	..	..	..	0.02	..	..	..	**	..	..	..	..	..	..	0.09
MRT	..	..	..	..	..	..	..	..	..	..	..	..	..	**	..	..	..	..	..	..
MUS	..	0.00	0.00	..	0.00	..	0.02	..	..	0.00	0.12	0.01	..	..	**	0.00	..	..	0.00	0.00
MAR	..	0.40	0.27	..	0.49	..	..	..	0.00	0.31	0.00	..	0.02	0.24	0.17	**	..	..	..	0.06
MOZ	..	..	..	0.00	..	0.45	0.27	..	..	..	..	1.33	..	..	..	..	**	..	..	..
NAM	..	..	..	..	..	..	..	..	..	..	..	..	..	..	..	..	..	**	..	..
NER	..	0.00	..	0.01	0.00	..	..	..	..	0.47	..	..	0.40	..	..	..	..	..	**	0.47
NGA	..	..	..	25.97	..	..	..	..	0.01	..	..	0.00	..	..	..	..	..	..	0.03	**
RWA	..	..	..	..	..	..	0.05	..	..	0.00	..	..	..	..	..	..	..	..	..	..
STP	..	..	..	..	..	..	..	..	..	..	..	..	..	..	..	..	..	..	..	0.00
SEN	0.00	0.25	6.81	0.02	3.54	15.47	0.00	..	0.02	..	..	0.05	12.45	11.63	0.00	0.04	..	..	0.85	0.01
SYC	..	..	..	..	..	..	0.01	..	..	..	..	..	..	..	0.05	..	..	..	..	..
SLE	..	..	..	..	..	..	..	..	..	..	..	..	..	..	..	..	..	..	..	..
SOM	..	..	0.00	..	..	..	0.02	..	..	..	..	..	..	..	..	..	..	..	..	..
ZAF	..	..	..	..	..	..	..	..	..	..	..	..	..	..	..	..	..	..	..	..
SDN	0.03	..	..	..	..	..	..	..	..	..	..	..	..	..	..	0.00	..	..	..	..
SWZ	..	..	..	..	..	..	..	..	..	..	..	..	..	..	..	..	..	..	..	..
TZA	0.06	..	..	0.00	..	..	0.02	..	..	..	0.00	0.07	..	..	0.03	..	0.40	..	..	0.00
TGO	..	0.01	..	0.86	..	..	..	..	0.06	..	..	..	0.12	..	..	..	..	..	0.41	0.03
TUN	..	..	..	..	..	..	..	..	..	0.75	..	..	..	..	..	0.10	..	..	..	..
UGA	..	..	..	0.00	..	..	0.08	..	..	0.05	..	..	..	..	..	..	..	..	..	..
ZAR	..	0.19	..	..	..	..	0.01	..	..	..	..	..	..	..	..	..	..	..	..	..
ZMB	..	..	..	..	..	..	0.17	..	..	..	..	3.71	..	..	..	..	0.01	0.17	..	..
ZWE	0.00	0.08	..	0.07	..	..	0.19	7.04	..	0.04	0.01	12.44	0.17	..	0.94	0.01	2.43	14.44	..	0.01
SSA	0.96	4.04	7.04	29.00	6.17	16.27	0.97	7.46	0.59	0.58	0.48	18.26	42.64	12.51	4.54	0.68	6.52	14.61	10.77	0.94
EEC	36.11	65.60	49.70	33.53	53.35	59.33	36.91	38.72	30.21	63.48	49.96	46.99	47.45	60.23	27.42	51.11	37.49	12.04	73.99	54.71
NNA	13.62	16.63	3.50	14.43	15.82	..	9.01	36.17	7.83	6.25	7.20	3.45	1.55	7.24	5.22	11.45	7.56	54.08	3.22	9.56
ROW	49.32	13.73	39.76	23.04	24.66	24.39	53.11	17.65	61.37	29.69	42.35	31.29	8.35	20.02	62.81	36.76	48.43	19.27	12.02	34.79
TOT	100	100	100	100	100	100	100	100	100	100	100	100	100	100	100	100	100	100	100	100

Note: ** means "not applicable."

(Table continues on the following page)

5–43. (continued)

Percentage of total imports

	RWA	STP	SEN	SYC	SLE	SOM	ZAF	SDN	SWZ	TZA	TGO	TUN	UGA	ZAR	ZMB	ZWE	SSA	EEC	NNA	ROW	TOT
DZA	..	..	3.33	..	..	..	..	..	..	..	..	0.20	..	..	..	..	0.36	1.03	1.32	0.23	0.71
ANG	0.00	..	..	..	..	..	..	..	..	..	..	..	..	0.01	0.00	..	0.00	0.04	0.25	0.03	0.07
BEN	..	..	0.02	..	..	..	..	..	..	..	0.20	..	..	..	..	..	0.02	0.00	0.00	0.00	0.00
BWA	..	..	..	..	..	..	..	..	..	..	..	..	..	..	..	..	..	..	..	..	..
HVO	..	..	0.01	..	..	..	..	..	..	..	..	0.16	..	..	..	..	0.06	0.00	0.00	0.00	0.00
BDI	0.47	..	..	..	..	..	..	..	..	0.00	..	..	..	0.22	..	..	0.01	0.00	0.01	0.00	0.00
CMR	0.01	..	0.15	..	0.00	..	..	0.01	..	0.00	0.06	0.03	..	0.00	..	..	0.20	0.08	0.13	0.01	0.06
CPV	..	..	..	..	..	..	..	..	..	..	..	..	..	0.01	..	..	0.00	0.00	..	..	0.00
CAF	..	..	..	..	..	..	0.00	0.01	..	..	..	..	..	0.01	..	..	0.00	0.01	0.00	0.00	0.00
TCD	..	..	..	..	..	..	..	..	..	..	..	..	..	..	..	..	0.04	0.01	..	0.00	0.00
COM	..	..	0.00	..	..	..	..	..	..	..	..	..	..	..	..	..	0.01	0.00	0.00	0.00	0.00
CGO	..	0.36	0.00	..	..	..	0.01	..	0.66	..	..	0.03	..	0.14	..	0.15	0.01	0.07	0.04	0.03	0.05
CIV	..	..	3.28	..	..	..	..	..	..	..	2.50	0.06	..	..	..	..	0.82	0.23	0.09	0.05	0.14
DJI	..	..	0.00	..	..	3.28	..	..	..	..	..	..	..	..	..	..	0.04	0.00	..	0.00	0.00
EGY	0.02	..	..	..	0.04	0.01	..	0.72	..	0.01	..	0.08	0.00	0.00	0.00	..	0.04	0.22	0.04	0.20	0.17
GNQ	..	..	..	..	..	..	..	..	..	..	..	..	..	..	..	..	0.00	0.00	0.00	0.00	0.00
ETH	..	..	..	..	..	..	..	0.09	..	..	..	..	..	..	..	..	0.05	0.02	0.02	0.02	0.02
GAB	..	..	1.56	..	..	..	..	..	..	0.13	0.03	..	..	0.76	..	..	0.13	0.13	0.10	0.06	0.09
GMB	..	..	0.04	..	0.03	..	..	..	..	..	..	..	..	..	..	..	0.03	0.00	0.00	0.00	0.00
GHA	..	..	..	..	0.00	0.00	..	..	..	..	0.00	2.17	..	..	..	..	0.02	0.07	0.06	0.05	0.06
GIN	..	..	0.00	..	0.09	..	..	..	..	..	..	..	..	..	..	..	0.08	0.03	0.04	0.01	0.02
GNB	..	..	0.12	..	..	..	..	..	..	..	..	..	..	..	..	..	0.00	0.00	..	0.00	0.00
KEN	26.41	..	0.00	4.63	0.01	1.06	0.00	1.55	1.22	1.39	0.00	0.02	38.95	1.09	0.60	0.17	0.80	0.06	0.02	0.05	0.06
LSO	..	..	..	..	..	..	..	..	..	..	..	..	..	..	..	..	..	..	..	..	..
LBR	..	..	0.00	..	0.33	..	..	..	..	..	0.00	0.04	..	0.01	0.00	..	0.03	0.05	0.04	0.00	0.03
LBY	..	..	..	..	..	..	..	0.01	..	..	..	0.08	..	..	..	..	0.00	1.25	1.30	0.36	0.83
MDG	..	..	..	..	..	..	..	..	..	..	..	..	..	..	..	..	0.00	0.02	0.01	0.02	0.02
MWI	..	..	..	..	0.39	..	0.09	..	..	0.00	..	..	..	0.08	0.55	4.89	0.08	0.02	0.02	0.01	0.01
MLI	..	..	..	..	..	..	..	..	..	..	..	..	..	..	..	..	0.08	0.01	0.00	0.00	0.01
MRT	..	..	0.03	..	..	..	..	..	..	..	..	..	..	0.14	..	..	0.01	0.03	..	0.01	0.01
MUS	0.00	..	0.00	1.32	..	..	0.04	..	..	0.01	..	..	..	..	0.01	0.00	0.01	0.04	0.01	0.00	0.02
MAR	..	..	0.48	..	..	..	..	0.00	..	..	0.13	0.55	..	0.17	..	..	0.10	0.19	0.02	0.11	0.12
MOZ	..	..	..	..	..	..	..	..	..	0.41	..	..	..	..	0.00	5.87	0.09	0.01	0.02	0.01	0.02
NAM	..	..	..	..	..	..	..	..	..	..	..	..	..	..	..	..	..	..	..	..	..
NER	..	..	0.00	..	0.00	..	..	..	..	..	..	0.02	..	0.00	..	..	0.19	0.03	0.00	0.02	0.02
NGA	..	..	3.11	..	16.21	..	..	..	..	..	..	0.24	..	..	..	..	1.13	1.01	1.89	0.69	1.03
RWA	**	..	..	0.77	..	..	..	..	..	0.03	..	..	0.09	0.07	..	..	0.01	0.01	0.01	0.00	0.01
STP	..	**	..	..	..	..	..	..	..	..	..	..	..	..	..	..	0.00	0.00	..	0.00	0.00
SEN	..	..	**	0.01	0.17	..	..	..	..	..	1.53	0.01	0.00	0.08	0.01	..	0.43	0.03	0.00	0.02	0.03
SYC	..	..	..	**	..	..	..	..	..	..	..	..	..	..	..	..	0.00	0.00	0.00	0.00	0.00
SLE	..	..	..	..	**	..	..	..	..	..	..	..	..	..	..	..	..	0.01	0.01	0.01	0.01
SOM	..	..	..	0.00	..	**	..	0.00	..	0.00	..	..	0.00	..	0.01	..	0.00	0.00	0.00	0.02	0.01
ZAF	..	..	..	..	..	..	**	..	..	..	..	..	..	..	..	..	..	0.58	0.59	1.80	1.11
SDN	..	..	..	..	..	..	..	**	..	..	..	0.09	..	..	..	..	0.00	0.03	0.02	0.05	0.03
SWZ	..	..	..	..	..	..	..	..	**	..	..	..	..	..	..	..	..	..	..	..	0.03
TZA	1.45	..	..	0.84	..	0.14	..	0.23	0.80	**	..	..	3.29	0.39	0.24	0.05	0.10	0.04	0.01	0.03	0.03
TGO	..	..	0.00	..	..	..	..	..	..	..	**	..	..	0.00	..	..	0.08	0.02	0.00	0.01	0.01
TUN	..	..	..	..	..	..	..	..	..	..	..	**	..	..	..	..	0.01	0.22	0.13	0.04	0.12
UGA	0.34	..	..	..	0.00	..	..	0.23	..	0.01	..	..	**	..	..	0.00	0.02	0.02	0.03	0.00	0.01
ZAR	..	..	..	..	..	..	0.00	..	..	..	..	..	..	**	0.08	..	0.03	0.09	0.00	0.01	0.04
ZMB	..	..	..	..	..	..	0.04	..	0.08	0.61	..	..	..	..	**	..	0.05	0.06	0.02	0.02	0.03
ZWE	..	..	0.00	0.23	0.00	0.00	1.83	0.08	4.89	..	..	0.01	0.01	2.50	6.61	**	0.44	0.05	0.03	0.08	0.07
SSA	28.69	0.36	8.32	7.80	17.24	4.48	2.01	2.21	7.65	2.46	7.07	0.27	42.36	5.54	8.10	11.13	5.10	2.34	2.88	1.31	2.04
EEC	33.34	97.69	61.17	36.10	47.94	48.73	51.05	36.40	37.37	40.97	62.23	69.59	40.82	48.95	35.95	49.91	49.68	51.07	15.39	27.44	34.09
NNA	3.45	..	5.72	6.96	10.15	14.83	20.28	12.19	17.08	6.16	5.52	8.78	2.38	15.99	9.05	8.31	9.57	10.34	34.49	16.56	17.44
ROW	34.52	1.95	24.78	49.13	24.67	31.96	26.67	49.19	37.90	50.41	25.18	21.36	14.44	29.53	46.90	30.64	35.65	36.24	47.24	54.69	46.43
TOT	100	100	100	100	100	100	100	100	100	100	100	100	100	100	100	100	100	100	100	100	100

Note: ** means "not applicable."

5-44. Direction of trade matrix, imports, 1985

Exporters		DZA	ANG	BEN	BWA	HVO	BDI	CMR	CPV	CAF	TCD	COM	CGO	CIV	DJI	EGY	GNQ
		**	**	**	**	**	**	**	**	**	**	**	**	**	**	**	**
Algeria	DZA	**	..	..	..		..	..	..	..	..	..	..	..	..	..	..
Angola	ANG	..	**	..	..		..	0.08	..		..	..	0.02				
Benin	BEN	..	..	**	..	0.01	..	0.01	..	0.02	..	..	0.05	0.03	..	..	..
Botswana	BWA	..	..	..	**	..	..		..		..	..					
Burkina Faso	HVO	..	..	0.06	..	**	..	..	..	..	..	..	..	0.11	..	0.02	..
Burundi	BDI	..	..	..	..	..	**	0.02	..	..	..	..	..	..	..	..	..
Cameroon	CMR	0.03	0.01	0.15	..	0.01	..	**	..	6.79	15.32	..	2.84	1.17	..	0.00	13.68
Cape Verde	CPV	0.02	0.12	..	..	..	..	..	**	..	..	..	..	..	..	..	..
Central African Republic	CAF	..	..	..	..	..	..	..	..	**	0.19	..	..	0.00	..	..	..
Chad	TCD	..	..	..	..	..	..	0.14	..	0.01	**	..	0.06	..	..	..	..
Comoros	COM	..	..	..	..	..	..	..	..	..	..	**	..	..	..	..	..
Congo, People's Republic of the	CGO	0.01	0.92	..	..	..	..	..	..	..	1.00	..	**	0.03	..	0.00	..
Cote d'Ivoire	CIV	0.10	..	3.62	..	33.33	..	1.16	..	..	..	..	..	**	..	..	..
Djibouti	DJI	..	..	..	..	..	0.52	..	..	..	..	..	..	..	**	0.00	..
Egypt, Arab Republic of	EGY	0.03	..	..	..	..	0.00	0.00	..	..	..	..	..	0.00	0.01	**	..
Equatorial Guinea	GNQ	..	..	..	..	..	..	0.01	..	..	..	..	..	..	..	..	**
Ethiopia	ETH	..	..	..	..	..	..	..	..	..	..	..	..	..	4.34	0.01	..
Gabon	GAB	0.06	..	0.02	..	..	..	0.41	..	..	..	..	..	1.96	..	0.01	..
Gambia, The	GMB	..	..	..	..	..	..	..	..	..	..	..	..	..	..	..	..
Ghana	GHA	..	..	0.04	..	0.00	..	..	..	..	..	..	0.00	0.03	..	0.01	..
Guinea	GIN	..	..	..	..	..	..	2.12	..	..	..	..	..	0.00	..	..	..
Guinea-Bissau	GNB	..	0.00	..	..	..	..	..	..	..	..	..	..	..	..	..	..
Kenya	KEN	..	..	..	..	..	12.36	..	..	..	..	6.31	..	..	0.86	0.19	..
Lesotho	LSO																
Liberia	LBR	..	..	0.01	..	..	..	0.02	..	..	..	..	..	..	..	0.00	..
Libya	LBY	0.00	..	..	..	..	..	..	..	..	0.69	..	..	..	..	0.00	..
Madagascar	MDG	..	..	..	..	..	..	..	..	..	..	0.45	..	..	..	..	..
Malawi	MWI	..	..	..	1.01	..	..	..	..	..	..	..	..	..	..	..	..
Mali	MLI	0.07	..	..	..	0.47	..	..	..	..	..	..	0.01	0.22	..	..	..
Mauritania	MRT	0.17	..	0.02	..	..	..	0.04	..	..	..	..	0.03	0.78	..	0.00	..
Mauritius	MUS	0.00	..	..	..	..	0.00	0.00	..	0.00	..	2.70	0.00	0.00	..	0.00	..
Morocco	MAR	..	..	0.25	..	..	..	0.64	..	..	..	..	1.10	0.51	..	0.02	..
Mozambique	MOZ	..	..	..	..	..	..	..	..	..	..	..	0.04	..	..	0.00	..
Namibia	NAM	..	..	..	..	..	..	..	..	..	..	..	..	..	..	..	..
Niger	NER	0.08	..	0.17	..	0.40	..	0.00	..	..	..	..	..	0.25	..	..	..
Nigeria	NGA	..	0.00	0.42	0.00	0.00	..	0.20	..	4.18	..	0.17	0.00	13.40	..	0.00	..
Rwanda	RWA	..	..	..	..	..	0.35	0.00	..	..	..	..	..	..	..	..	..
Sao Tome & Principe	STP	..	..	..	..	..	..	..	..	..	..	..	..	..	..	..	..
Senegal	SEN	0.00	0.00	1.15	..	0.98	0.01	0.75	0.22	0.21	0.17	..	0.86	2.08	0.00	0.00	0.01
Seychelles	SYC	..	..	..	..	..	..	..	..	..	..	..	..	..	..	..	..
Sierra Leone	SLE	..	..	0.00	..	..	..	..	..	..	0.00	..	..	0.01	..	..	..
Somalia	SOM	..	..	..	..	..	..	0.01	..	..	..	..	..	..	0.04	0.03	..
South Africa	ZAF	..	..	..	..	..	..	..	..	..	..	..	..	..	..	..	..
Sudan	SDN	..	..	..	..	..	..	..	..	0.01	..	..	..	..	..	0.29	..
Swaziland	SWZ	..	..	..	..	..	..	..	..	..	..	..	..	..	..	..	..
Tanzania	TZA	0.01	..	..	0.04	..	1.40	..	..	..	..	..	..	0.02	..	0.01	..
Togo	TGO	..	..	0.29	..	0.86	..	0.01	..	0.10	0.11	..	0.04	0.05	..	..	..
Tunisia	TUN	0.69	0.00	0.04	..	..	..	0.04	..	..	..	..	0.06	0.09	..	0.04	..
Uganda	UGA	..	..	..	..	..	..	..	..	..	..	..	0.00	..	..	0.01	..
Zaire	ZAR	..	..	..	..	..	1.74	..	..	1.58	..	..	2.96	..	..	..	..
Zambia	ZMB	..	0.06	0.05	1.96	..	0.97	0.06	..	..	..	..	..	..	..	0.03	..
Zimbabwe	ZWE	0.03	0.52	0.00	35.81	..	0.77	0.02	0.03	0.24	0.30	0.10	0.06	0.02	..	0.00	..
Total Sub-Saharan Africa	SSA	0.57	1.64	5.99	38.82	36.06	18.13	5.05	0.25	13.12	17.09	9.72	6.96	20.17	5.24	0.63	13.69
European Community	EEC	66.50	53.20	44.86	28.15	47.78	49.28	71.19	83.08	74.11	59.44	60.92	76.05	56.92	49.07	41.67	75.03
North America	NNA	8.32	10.79	17.02	15.68	10.61	4.10	6.65	..	1.17	19.05	4.00	3.61	5.94	1.63	20.52	1.72
Rest of World	ROW	24.61	34.37	32.13	17.35	5.56	28.49	17.11	16.67	11.61	4.42	25.35	13.38	16.97	44.06	37.19	9.56
World	TOT	100	100	100	100	100	100	100	100	100	100	100	100	100	100	100	100

Note: ** means "not applicable."

(Table continues on the following page)

5-44. (continued)

Percentage of total imports

	ETH	GAB	GMB	GHA	GIN	GNB	KEN	LSO	LBR	LBY	MDG	MWI	MLI	MRT	MUS	MAR	MOZ	NAM	NER	NGA
DZA	..	..	..	..	..	..	..	..	..	..	..	..	..	..	..	..	..	..	..	..
ANG	..	..	..	..	..	..	..	..	..	..	..	..	..	..	..	..	..	..	..	0.00
BEN	..	..	..	0.00	..	..	..	..	0.00	..	..	..	0.06	..	..	..	..	..	1.27	0.00
BWA	..	..	..	..	..	..	..	..	..	..	..	..	..	..	..	..	..	..	..	..
HVO	..	..	..	..	..	..	..	..	..	..	..	..	0.14	..	0.00	..	..	..	0.40	0.01
BDI	..	..	..	..	..	..	0.14	..	..	..	..	..	..	..	..	..	..	..	..	..
CMR	..	3.54	..	0.00	0.32	..	0.03	..	..	..	..	..	0.00	..	..	0.04	..	..	0.01	0.34
CPV	..	..	..	..	..	..	..	..	..	..	..	..	..	..	..	..	..	..	..	..
CAF	..	..	..	..	..	..	..	..	..	..	..	..	..	..	..	..	..	..	..	0.01
TCD	..	..	..	..	..	..	..	..	..	..	..	..	..	..	..	..	..	..	..	0.02
COM	..	..	..	..	..	..	..	..	0.00	..	0.00	..	..	..	0.10	..	..	..	..	0.00
CGO	..	..	..	..	..	..	..	..	..	..	..	..	0.00	0.00	0.00	0.44	..	..	..	0.00
CIV	..	1.50	..	3.28	..	..	..	..	0.59	..	..	..	20.94	..	..	0.36	..	..	9.17	0.26
DJI	0.14	..	..	..	..	..	..	..	..	0.00	..	..	..	..	0.03	..	..	..	..	..
EGY	..	..	..	0.00	..	..	0.01	..	..	0.00	..	0.02	..	0.00	0.01	0.03	0.02	..	..	0.00
GNQ	..	..	..	..	..	..	..	..	0.00	..	..	..	0.07	..	..	..	..	..	..	0.01
ETH	**	..	..	..	..	..	0.03	..	..	..	..	..	..	..	..	..	..	..	..	0.00
GAB	..	**	..	..	0.01	..	..	..	..	..	..	..	0.01	0.04	0.00	1.17	..	..	..	0.01
GMB	..	..	**	0.07	0.97	0.23	..	..	0.00	..	..	..	0.11	0.01	..	..	..	..	..	0.00
GHA	..	..	0.01	**	..	..	..	..	0.00	..	..	..	..	..	..	..	..	..	0.01	0.00
GIN	..	..	..	..	**	0.10	..	..	0.02	..	..	..	0.46	..	..	..	..	..	..	..
GNB	..	..	0.03	..	0.01	**	..	..	..	..	..	..	..	..	..	..	..	..	..	0.02
KEN	0.32	..	..	..	..	..	**	..	..	..	..	..	..	..	1.10	..	1.37	..	..	0.00
LSO	..	..	..	..	..	..	..	**	..	..	..	..	..	..	..	..	..	..	..	..
LBR	..	..	0.01	0.03	0.15	..	..	..	**	0.00	..	..	0.00	0.02	..	0.00	..	..	..	0.14
LBY	..	..	0.00	..	..	..	..	..	..	**	..	..	..	..	..	0.00	..	..	..	..
MDG	..	..	..	..	..	0.00	..	..	..	..	**	..	..	..	0.29	..	..	..	..	..
MWI	..	..	..	..	..	..	0.00	..	..	..	..	**	..	..	..	..	0.91	..	..	..
MLI	..	0.03	..	..	0.02	..	..	..	0.02	..	..	..	**	0.02	..	0.14	..	..	0.08	0.01
MRT	..	..	..	0.05	..	..	..	..	0.04	..	..	..	..	**	..	..	..	..	..	..
MUS	0.00	..	..	0.01	0.00	..	0.02	..	..	.	0.14	0.06	0.00	..	**	..	..	..	..	0.00
MAR	..	0.60	..	..	1.63	..	..	..	..	0.73	..	..	0.00	0.10	0.09	**	..	..	..	0.00
MOZ	..	0.01	..	..	..	0.24	0.01	..	0.00	..	..	0.24	..	..	..	..	**	..	..	..
NAM	..	..	..	..	..	..	..	..	..	..	..	..	..	..	..	..	..	**	..	..
NER	..	..	..	0.06	..	..	..	..	..	..	0.00	..	0.18	..	..	..	..	..	**	0.44
NGA	..	0.01	..	25.61	0.00	0.10	0.00	0.00	0.01	..	..	..	0.00	..	..	..	..	..	0.95	**
RWA	..	..	..	..	..	..	0.21	..	..	0.00	..	..	..	..	..	..	..	..	..	..
STP	..	..	..	..	..	..	..	..	0.00	..	..	..	..	..	..	..	..	..	..	..
SEN	..	0.20	4.91	0.01	1.08	3.47	0.00	..	0.01	..	0.00	..	9.67	6.59	..	0.01	..	..	0.98	0.14
SYC	..	..	..	..	..	..	..	..	..	..	..	..	..	..	0.02	..	..	..	..	..
SLE	..	..	0.13	0.00	0.01	..	..	..	0.11	..	..	..	..	..	..	..	..	..	..	0.00
SOM	..	..	..	0.00	..	..	0.01	..	..	0.01	..	..	..	..	..	..	..	..	..	..
ZAF	..	..	..	..	..	..	..	..	..	..	..	..	..	..	..	..	..	..	..	..
SDN	0.01	..	..	..	..	..	..	..	..	..	..	0.00	0.00	..	..	..	..	..	..	0.00
SWZ	..	..	..	..	..	..	..	..	..	..	..	..	..	..	..	..	..	..	..	..
TZA	0.02	..	..	..	..	..	0.07	0.01	..	..	0.01	0.37	..	..	0.06	..	0.56	..	..	0.00
TGO	..	0.02	..	0.09	0.04	..	..	..	0.00	0.00	..	..	0.25	0.00	..	0.12	..	..	1.05	0.03
TUN	..	0.06	..	0.01	0.38	0.97	0.02	..	0.11	0.32	0.00	..	0.01	..	..	0.15	0.02	..	0.05	0.00
UGA	0.00	..	..	..	..	..	0.08	..	..	0.11	..	..	0.08	..	..	..	..	..	..	..
ZAR	..	0.14	..	..	..	..	0.03	..	..	..	..	..	..	..	..	..	..	..	..	..
ZMB	0.01	..	..	..	..	..	0.20	5.64	..	..	..	2.65	..	..	..	..	0.02	0.02	..	..
ZWE	0.32	0.11	..	0.10	0.00	..	0.23	1.13	..	0.00	0.06	11.10	..	..	0.40	0.03	3.32	2.81	..	0.01
SSA	0.83	5.54	5.09	29.32	2.60	4.14	1.07	6.78	0.80	0.12	0.21	14.42	31.99	6.68	2.01	2.30	6.18	2.83	13.93	1.45
EEC	40.04	71.73	55.35	39.67	54.88	72.22	35.55	41.20	24.39	56.89	47.20	53.90	50.41	70.15	36.41	58.32	39.58	19.08	67.61	52.34
NNA	22.22	11.16	11.13	9.59	18.64	..	7.74	25.99	5.97	7.74	10.38	4.38	7.48	9.44	2.77	11.63	15.99	71.09	5.13	11.29
ROW	36.92	11.56	28.43	21.42	23.88	23.64	55.64	26.03	68.84	35.24	42.20	27.30	10.12	13.72	58.80	27.75	38.25	7.00	13.32	34.92
TOT	100	100	100	100	100	100	100	100	100	100	100	100	100	100	100	100	100	100	100	100

Note: ** means "not applicable."

(Table continues on the following page)

5-44. (continued)

Percentage of total imports

	RWA	STP	SEN	SYC	SLE	SOM	ZAF	SDN	SWZ	TZA	TGO	TUN	UGA	ZAR	ZMB	ZWE	SSA	EEC	NNA	ROW	TOT
DZA	..	..	..	..	..	..	..	..	..	..	..	4.82	..	..	..	..	..	1.49	0.37	0.25	0.71
ANG	..	..	..	..	..	..	..	..	..	..	..	..	..	..	0.00	..	0.00	0.12	0.24	0.06	0.12
BEN	0.01	..	0.01	..	..	..	..	0.00	..	..	0.23	0.00	..	..	..	..	0.02	0.02	0.00	0.00	0.01
BWA	..	..	..	..	..	..	..	..	..	..	..	..	..	..	..	..	..	..	..	..	0.01
HVO	..	..	0.00	..	..	..	..	..	..	..	0.17	0.01	..	..	..	..	0.02	0.01	0.00	0.00	0.00
BDI	2.11	..	..	..	..	..	..	0.04	..	0.12	..	..	0.20	0.21	0.00	0.05	0.04	0.01	0.00	0.01	0.01
CMR	..	..	0.02	..	..	..	..	..	..	..	1.44	0.03	..	0.01	..	..	0.43	0.14	0.02	0.01	0.07
CPV	..	..	..	..	..	..	..	..	..	..	..	..	..	..	..	..	0.01	0.00	..	0.00	0.00
CAF	0.00	..	..	..	..	..	..	0.08	..	..	..	..	..	0.14	..	..	0.01	0.01	0.00	0.00	0.01
TCD	..	..	..	..	..	..	..	0.00	..	..	0.00	..	..	..	..	..	0.01	0.01	0.00	0.00	0.00
COM	..	..	..	..	..	..	..	..	..	..	..	0.01	..	..	..	..	0.00	0.00	0.00	0.00	0.00
CGO	..	..	0.00	..	..	..	0.00	..	1.30	0.03	0.00	0.08	..	0.36	..	..	0.06	0.06	0.16	0.01	0.06
CIV	..	..	5.87	..	..	..	..	..	..	..	5.55	..	..	..	..	..	1.27	0.28	0.09	0.06	0.16
DJI	..	..	..	3.74	..	1.12	..	..	..	..	..	0.01	..	..	..	..	0.03	0.00	0.00	0.00	0.00
EGY	..	..	0.00	..	..	0.00	0.00	..	..	..	..	0.10	0.02	..	..	..	0.00	0.13	0.00	0.14	0.10
GNQ	..	..	..	..	..	..	..	..	..	..	..	..	..	..	..	..	0.00	0.00	..	0.00	0.00
ETH	..	..	..	..	..	..	..	0.42	..	0.01	..	..	0.09	..	..	..	0.07	0.03	0.01	0.02	0.02
GAB	..	0.16	1.59	..	..	..	..	..	..	..	0.04	0.00	..	..	..	0.00	0.17	0.15	0.12	0.07	0.11
GMB	..	..	0.01	..	0.00	0.00	..	..	..	..	..	..	..	0.00	..	0.00	0.02	0.00	0.00	0.00	0.00
GHA	..	..	..	..	0.04	..	..	..	..	..	6.01	..	..	0.00	..	..	0.09	0.04	0.01	0.02	0.03
GIN	..	..	0.00	..	0.04	..	..	..	..	..	0.05	..	..	..	..	..	0.12	0.04	0.03	0.00	0.03
GNB	..	0.00	0.00	..	..	..	..	..	..	..	..	..	..	..	..	..	0.01	0.00	..	0.00	0.00
KEN	19.37	..	..	..	..	1.13	0.02	1.78	..	1.29	..	..	32.20	0.87	0.23	..	0.73	0.07	0.01	0.04	0.05
LSO	..	..	..	..	..	..	..	..	..	..	..	..	..	..	..	..	..	..	..	..	..
LBR	..	..	0.00	..	0.61	..	..	..	..	..	0.10	..	..	..	..	..	0.04	0.05	0.02	0.00	0.02
LBY	..	..	..	..	..	..	..	0.01	..	..	..	0.07	..	..	..	..	0.00	0.91	0.74	0.29	0.60
MDG	..	..	..	..	..	..	..	..	..	..	..	..	..	..	..	..	0.00	0.02	0.01	0.01	0.02
MWI	..	..	..	..	..	..	0.20	..	..	0.04	..	..	..	..	3.43	1.35	0.09	0.02	0.01	0.01	0.01
MLI	..	..	0.14	..	..	..	..	..	..	..	..	0.05	..	..	..	..	0.02	0.01	0.00	0.01	0.01
MRT	..	..	0.09	..	..	..	..	..	..	..	..	..	..	..	..	..	0.05	0.02	0.00	0.03	0.02
MUS	..	..	0.00	1.33	..	0.00	0.02	..	..	0.08	..	0.00	..	0.02	0.00	0.00	0.01	0.05	0.02	0.00	0.02
MAR	..	..	1.01	..	..	..	..	0.00	..	..	0.48	0.78	..	0.23	..	..	0.17	0.20	0.02	0.11	0.12
MOZ	..	..	0.02	..	..	..	..	..	..	0.07	..	0.00	..	..	..	0.03	0.01	0.00	0.00	0.01	0.01
NAM	..	..	..	..	..	..	..	..	..	..	..	..	..	..	..	..	..	..	..	..	..
NER	..	..	0.01	..	..	..	..	..	..	..	0.10	..	..	..	..	..	0.13	0.02	0.00	0.00	0.01
NGA	..	..	1.86	..	20.75	..	..	0.01	..	..	0.03	..	..	0.01	0.00	..	1.56	1.33	0.62	0.22	0.72
RWA	**	..	..	..	..	..	..	..	..	0.01	..	..	0.05	0.02	..	..	0.01	0.02	0.00	0.00	0.01
STP	..	**	..	..	..	..	..	..	..	..	..	..	..	..	..	..	0.00	0.00	..	0.00	0.00
SEN	0.00	..	**	..	1.04	..	0.00	..	0.03	..	0.92	0.12	..	0.12	..	..	0.51	0.03	0.00	0.02	0.03
SYC	..	..	..	**	..	..	..	..	..	..	..	..	..	..	..	..	0.00	0.00	0.00	0.00	0.00
SLE	..	..	0.01	..	**	..	..	0.00	..	..	..	..	..	0.00	..	..	0.01	0.01	0.00	0.01	0.01
SOM	..	..	..	..	..	**	..	..	0.49	..	..	..	..	..	..	..	0.00	0.00	0.00	0.01	0.01
ZAF	..	..	..	..	..	..	**	..	..	..	..	..	..	..	..	..	..	0.55	0.36	1.56	0.91
SDN	..	..	..	..	..	..	..	**	..	0.00	0.00	0.04	..	..	..	..	0.00	0.02	0.00	0.04	0.02
SWZ	..	..	..	..	..	..	..	..	**	..	..	..	..	..	..	..	..	..	..	..	..
TZA	0.75	..	..	..	..	0.14	..	0.13	0.13	**	..	..	0.70	0.04	0.18	0.04	0.05	0.03	0.00	0.01	0.02
TGO	0.00	..	0.00	..	..	..	..	..	..	..	**	0.13	..	0.00	..	..	0.04	0.02	0.00	0.01	0.01
TUN	..	..	0.04	..	0.02	..	..	0.00	..	..	0.02	**	..	..	..	..	0.03	0.19	0.05	0.05	0.10
UGA	0.15	..	..	..	..	..	..	0.00	..	0.26	..	0.01	**	..	0.00	0.00	0.01	0.03	0.03	0.01	0.02
ZAR	..	..	..	..	..	..	0.00	..	..	..	..	..	..	**	0.04	..	0.08	0.12	0.01	0.02	0.05
ZMB	0.11	..	..	..	..	..	0.06	..	0.07	0.52	..	..	0.04	0.24	**	2.86	0.12	0.03	0.00	0.03	0.03
ZWE	0.55	..	0.01	0.26	0.03	0.01	1.31	0.14	2.62	0.52	..	0.01	0.20	1.28	8.15	**	0.51	0.06	0.02	0.05	0.05
SSA	23.06	0.16	9.64	5.33	22.51	2.41	1.62	2.61	4.64	2.96	14.65	0.49	33.48	3.32	12.04	4.34	6.36	2.90	1.45	0.80	1.77
EEC	49.29	92.05	60.35	63.38	46.99	45.37	54.60	36.31	39.80	36.30	52.64	68.11	42.49	57.23	44.20	54.25	49.48	55.54	18.13	28.30	35.87
NNA	3.30	..	9.81	1.98	8.12	17.67	16.73	17.75	4.60	6.35	4.49	12.24	1.93	11.06	13.90	12.69	10.22	9.13	34.59	16.63	18.00
ROW	24.35	7.79	20.19	29.31	22.38	34.55	27.05	43.32	50.96	54.39	28.22	19.16	22.10	28.39	29.86	28.72	33.94	32.43	45.84	54.27	44.36
TOT	100	100	100	100	100	100	100	100	100	100	100	100	100	100	100	100	100	100	100	100	100

Note: ** means "not applicable."

5-45. Direction of trade matrix, imports, 1990

Importers — *Percentage of total imports*

Exporters		DZA	ANG	BEN	BWA	HVO	BDI	CMR	CPV	CAF	TCD	COM	CGO	CIV	DJI	EGY	GNQ
Algeria	DZA	**	..	..	..	..	..	0.00	..	..	..	..	0.01	..	..	0.03	..
Angola	ANG	..	**	..	..	..	..	0.00	0.92	..	..	..	0.06	..	..	..	..
Benin	BEN	..	..	**	..	0.01	..	0.01	..	0.04	..	..	..	0.05	..	0.00	..
Botswana	BWA	..	..	..	**	..	..	..	..	..	..	..	..	..	..	..	..
Burkina Faso	HVO	..	..	0.11	..	**	..	0.00	..	..	..	..	0.00	0.19	..	..	..
Burundi	BDI	..	..	..	..	..	**	..	..	..	..	..	..	..	..	..	..
Cameroon	CMR	0.01	0.39	0.85	..	0.01	..	**	..	24.60	8.88	..	1.15	1.69	..	..	61.66
Cape Verde	CPV	0.04	0.15	..	..	..	..	..	**	0.01	..	..	..	..	..	..	..
Central African Republic	CAF	..	..	..	..	..	..	0.01	..	**	0.26	..	..	0.00	..	0.00	..
Chad	TCD	..	..	..	..	..	..	0.13	..	0.01	**	..	..	..	..	..	..
Comoros	COM	..	..	..	..	..	..	..	..	..	..	**	..	..	..	0.00	..
Congo, People's Republic of the	CGO	0.04	0.25	0.02	..	..	..	..	..	..	..	..	**	0.12	..	..	..
Cote d'Ivoire	CIV	0.05	..	6.26	..	32.97	..	0.60	1.74	..	..	..	0.07	**	..	0.02	..
Djibouti	DJI	..	..	..	..	..	0.27	0.02	..	..	..	..	0.00	..	**	..	..
Egypt, Arab Republic of	EGY	0.06	..	0.02	..	..	0.01	0.00	..	..	0.14	..	..	0.06	0.09	**	..
Equatorial Guinea	GNQ	..	..	..	..	..	..	0.00	..	..	..	..	..	..	..	..	**
Ethiopia	ETH	..	..	..	..	..	..	..	..	:.	..	..	..	..	4.85	0.01	..
Gabon	GAB	0.08	..	0.02	..	..	..	0.39	..	..	..	..	..	2.68	..	..	..
Gambia, The	GMB	0.00	..	..	..	..	..	..	..	..	..	..	..	..	..	..	..
Ghana	GHA	..	0.01	0.26	..	0.04	..	..	..	..	..	..	0.03	0.07	..	0.01	..
Guinea	GIN	..	..	..	..	..	..	3.66	..	0.00	..	..	0.00	..	..	..	..
Guinea-Bissau	GNB	..	0.00	..	..	..	..	..	..	..	..	..	..	..	..	0.00	..
Kenya	KEN	..	..	..	..	9.25	..	..	..	..	..	2.93	..	..	0.84	0.22	..
Lesotho	LSO	..	..	..	..	..	..	..	..	..	..	..	..	..	..	..	..
Liberia	LBR	..	..	0.01	..	..	..	0.01	..	..	0.00	..	0.23	..	..	0.01	..
Libya	LBY	..	0.00	..	..	0.00	..	..	..	0.00	0.73	..	..	..	..	0.01	..
Madagascar	MDG	0.00	..	0.00	..	..	0.02	0.00	..	..	..	2.71	..	0.00	0.01	0.00	0.00
Malawi	MWI	..	..	..	1.22	..	..	..	..	..	..	..	..	..	..	..	..
Mali	MLI	0.29	..	..	..	1.07	..	0.00	..	..	..	..	0.00	0.67	..	..	..
Mauritania	MRT	0.00	0.00	0.04	..	0.00	0.00	0.41	0.03	0.02	0.07	..	0.02	1.92	..	0.00	..
Mauritius	MUS	0.00	0.00	..	0.13	0.00	0.01	0.00	..	..	..	1.94	0.00	0.00	0.01	0.00	..
Morocco	MAR	0.38	0.48	0.31	..	0.13	..	0.48	..	0.47	0.13	0.60	0.59	0.62	0.02	0.01	0.30
Mozambique	MOZ	..	0.01	..	..	..	..	0.00	..	..	..	..	0.02	..	..	0.00	..
Namibia	NAM	..	..	..	..	..	..	..	..	..	..	..	..	..	..	..	..
Niger	NER	..	..	0.34	..	0.46	..	..	..	..	..	..	0.01	0.17	..	0.00	..
Nigeria	NGA	0.00	0.08	0.40	..	0.00	..	1.28	..	..	0.29	0.18	..	8.44	..	0.00	..
Rwanda	RWA	..	..	..	0.00	0.00	0.04	0.00	..	..	0.00	..	0.00	..	0.01	0.00	..
Sao Tome & Principe	STP	..	..	..	..	..	..	..	..	..	..	..	..	..	..	..	..
Senegal	SEN	0.00	0.00	1.16	..	0.80	..	1.10	0.04	0.14	0.60	..	0.58	1.38	..	0.00	0.01
Seychelles	SYC	..	0.00	..	..	..	..	..	..	..	..	..	..	..	..	0.00	..
Sierra Leone	SLE	..	..	0.00	..	..	..	..	..	..	..	..	0.00	0.04	..	..	..
Somalia	SOM	..	..	..	..	..	..	..	..	..	..	..	0.00	..	0.35	0.00	..
South Africa	ZAF	..	..	..	..	..	..	..	..	..	..	..	0.00	0.00	..	..	..
Sudan	SDN	..	..	..	..	..	..	..	..	0.03	..	..	..	..	..	..	..
Swaziland	SWZ	..	..	..	..	..	..	..	..	..	..	..	..	..	..	..	..
Tanzania	TZA	0.00	..	..	0.01	..	1.40	..	..	..	..	..	..	0.02	..	0.01	..
Togo	TGO	..	..	0.51	..	0.87	..	0.00	..	0.12	0.20	..	0.09	0.04	..	..	..
Tunisia	TUN	0.88	..	0.15	..	0.11	..	0.75	..	..	..	..	0.09	0.44	0.18	0.03	..
Uganda	UGA	..	..	..	..	..	..	..	..	..	..	..	..	..	..	0.00	..
Zaire	ZAR	..	..	..	..	..	1.54	..	..	1.26	..	..	2.82	..	..	..	..
Zambia	ZMB	..	0.17	0.16	2.11	..	2.08	0.16	..	..	..	..	0.36	..	..	..	..
Zimbabwe	ZWE	0.03	0.24	0.00	29.63	..	2.36	0.32	..	0.04	..	0.00	..	0.01	0.01	0.18	..
Total Sub-Saharan Africa	SSA	0.56	1.30	10.15	33.11	36.23	16.98	8.14	2.72	26.29	10.30	7.77	5.44	17.51	6.07	0.46	61.67
European Community	EEC	66.01	67.74	50.56	32.65	51.43	56.59	70.90	79.13	63.80	73.20	73.00	65.12	60.34	41.79	44.42	34.86
North America	NNA	12.80	10.08	6.32	6.99	3.52	0.59	5.57	5.28	1.04	6.15	0.01	13.81	5.06	2.47	20.11	0.07
Rest of World	ROW	20.63	20.89	32.97	27.25	8.82	25.84	15.39	12.87	8.86	10.34	19.23	15.63	17.10	49.66	35.02	3.40
World	TOT	100	100	100	100	100	100	100	100	100	100	100	100	100	100	100	100

Note: ** means "not applicable."

(Table continues on the following page)

5–45. (continued)

Percentage of total imports

	ETH	GAB	GMB	GHA	GIN	GNB	KEN	LSO	LBR	LBY	MDG	MWI	MLI	MRT	MUS	MAR	MOZ	NAM	NER	NGA
DZA	..	..	..	..	..	..	..	..	..	..	0.00	..	..	4.55	..	0.44	..	..	..	..
ANG	..	..	..	0.00	..	..	..	..	..	..	..	..	..	..	..	..	..	..	..	0.00
BEN	..	..	..	0.00	..	..	..	..	0.00	..	..	..	0.00	0.00	..	0.06	..	..	2.26	0.06
BWA	..	..	..	..	..	..	..	..	..	..	..	..	..	..	..	..	..	..	..	..
HVO	..	..	..	0.44	..	..	..	..	..	..	..	..	0.19	..	0.02	0.01	..	..	0.71	0.06
BDI	..	..	..	..	..	..	..	..	..	..	..	..	..	..	0.00	0.00	..	..	..	..
CMR	..	5.78	..	0.02	0.38	..	..	..	0.14	0.02	..	..	0.00	0.00	0.00	0.03	0.39	..	0.07	0.32
CPV	..	..	..	..	..	0.04	..	..	0.00	..	..	..	..	..	..	..	..	..	..	..
CAF	..	..	..	..	..	0.00	..	..	0.00	..	..	..	..	..	0.03	0.01	..	..	..	..
TCD	..	..	..	..	..	..	..	..	0.00	..	..	..	..	..	..	0.04	..	..	..	0.05
COM	..	..	..	..	..	..	..	..	0.00	..	0.00	..	..	..	0.00	..	..	..	..	..
CGO	0.02	..	..	0.03	0.01	..	..	..	..	..	..	..	0.00	0.02	0.00	0.08	..	..	..	0.00
CIV	..	2.14	..	1.86	..	..	..	..	0.57	..	0.28	..	27.17	0.16	1.78	0.25	..	..	14.28	0.25
DJI	0.16	..	..	..	..	..	..	..	..	0.00	..	..	..	..	..	..	..	..	..	..
EGY	0.23	..	0.00	..	0.01	..	0.00	..	0.00	0.11	..	0.00	..	0.01	0.07	0.07	0.00	..	0.05	0.01
GNQ	..	..	..	..	..	..	..	..	0.00	..	..	..	..	..	..	..	..	..	..	..
ETH	**	..	..	..	..	..	0.13	..	..	..	..	..	0.00	..	0.00	0.00	..	..	..	0.00
GAB	..	**	..	..	0.00	..	..	..	..	..	..	..	0.06	..	..	0.25	..	..	..	0.00
GMB	0.00	..	**	0.03	1.43	0.23	..	..	0.00	..	..	..	..	..	0.00	..	..	..	..	0.00
GHA	0.00	..	0.05	**	0.00	..	..	..	0.00	0.00	..	..	0.02	..	0.00	0.03	..	..	0.00	0.02
GIN	..	..	..	..	**	0.10	..	..	0.01	..	..	..	2.46	0.00	0.00	0.00	..	..	..	..
GNB	..	..	0.03	..	0.01	**	..	..	..	..	..	..	..	..	..	..	..	..	..	0.00
KEN	0.32	..	..	..	..	..	**	..	..	..	..	..	..	..	1.14	..	0.73	..	..	..
LSO	..	..	..	..	..	..	..	**	..	..	..	..	..	..	..	..	..	..	..	..
LBR	..	..	0.01	0.02	0.14	0.00	..	..	**	0.00	..	..	0.00	0.00	..	0.01	..	..	..	0.12
LBY	0.19	0.00	0.00	0.01	0.00	..	..	..	0.00	**	..	..	..	0.00	..	0.14	0.00	..	..	0.00
MDG	0.00	0.00	..	..	0.01	..	0.03	0.03	..	..	**	..	0.01	0.13	0.55	0.01	0.75	0.00	0.00	..
MWI	..	..	..	..	..	..	0.00	..	..	..	..	**	..	..	0.01	..	1.87	..	..	..
MLI	..	0.00	..	..	..	..	..	..	0.05	..	..	..	**	0.01	..	0.23	..	..	0.06	0.00
MRT	..	0.00	0.00	0.03	0.01	..	..	..	0.13	0.00	..	..	0.01	**	..	..	..	..	..	..
MUS	0.00	0.00	..	0.00	0.00	..	0.05	..	..	..	1.73	0.05	0.00	0.00	**	0.00	0.00	..	..	0.00
MAR	..	1.05	0.04	0.10	1.18	..	0.00	..	0.01	1.92	0.05	..	0.84	0.97	0.11	**	0.02	..	0.24	0.25
.MOZ	..	0.00	..	0.00	..	0.14	0.01	..	0.00	..	0.15	0.45	..	..	0.00	0.01	**	..	..	0.00
NAM	..	..	..	..	..	..	..	..	..	..	..	..	..	..	..	..	..	**	..	..
NER	..	..	..	0.00	..	..	..	..	..	0.00	..	..	0.41	0.01	..	..	..	..	**	0.26
NGA	0.00	0.00	0.01	9.99	0.01	0.00	..	12.89	0.05	..	..	..	..	0.00	0.00	0.04	0.00	..	2.02	**
RWA	0.00	0.00	..	0.00	..	..	3.47	..	0.00	0.00	0.00	..	0.00	0.00	0.00	0.00	..	..	..	..
STP	..	..	..	..	..	..	..	..	0.00	..	..	..	..	..	0.00	..	..	..	..	..
SEN	0.00	0.25	3.15	0.01	1.72	5.22	..	..	0.03	0.00	0.00	..	5.63	0.54	0.00	0.01	..	..	0.22	0.04
SYC	..	..	..	..	..	..	..	..	..	..	..	..	..	..	0.01	..	..	..	..	..
SLE	..	..	0.09	..	0.01	..	..	..	0.04	..	..	..	..	..	..	..	..	..	..	0.00
SOM	..	..	..	0.00	0.06	..	..	..	0.00	..	..	..	..	..	0.00	..	..	..	0.00	..
ZAF	..	..	..	..	..	..	..	..	..	..	..	..	..	..	5.35	..	..	..	..	..
SDN	0.02	..	..	0.00	..	..	..	..	..	..	..	..	0.00	..	0.01	0.00	..	..	..	..
SWZ	..	..	..	..	..	..	..	..	..	..	..	..	..	..	..	..	..	..	..	..
TZA	0.01	..	0.00	..	..	..	0.25	0.00	..	..	0.00	0.17	0.00	..	0.03	0.05	0.24	..	..	0.00
TGO	..	0.03	..	3.73	0.06	..	..	..	0.00	0.00	..	..	0.34	0.00	..	0.06	..	..	1.75	0.03
TUN	..	0.02	..	0.65	0.09	0.84	..	..	0.00	3.12	..	..	..	0.52	..	0.35	..	..	0.04	0.01
UGA	0.00	..	..	0.00	..	..	0.08	..	..	0.12	..	..	0.00	..	0.00	0.01	..	..	..	..
ZAR	..	0.18	..	..	0.00	..	0.03	..	..	..	..	..	..	..	0.01	..	..	..	..	..
ZMB	0.03	..	..	..	..	..	0.15	7.70	..	..	..	3.22	..	..	..	..	0.04	0.01	..	0.01
ZWE	0.22	..	..	0.17	..	..	..	3.28	0.00	0.05	..	10.13	..	..	0.18	0.06	6.92	0.27	0.11	0.01
SSA	0.78	8.38	3.34	16.33	3.86	5.74	4.18	23.90	1.03	0.19	2.17	14.01	36.32	0.89	3.80	1.25	10.93	0.28	21.48	1.25
EEC	44.53	71.00	57.25	48.29	66.07	66.38	42.41	35.33	29.92	63.93	60.66	57.70	46.44	70.29	38.94	66.36	40.09	73.71	62.90	54.86
NNA	15.27	7.10	0.13	11.62	10.47	1.25	6.81	4.99	1.37	0.77	2.46	6.36	2.39	3.89	1.01	10.24	9.33	22.22	5.20	10.26
ROW	39.42	13.52	39.28	23.76	19.59	26.62	46.60	35.79	67.69	35.11	34.71	21.93	14.85	24.93	56.25	22.15	39.65	3.79	10.41	33.62
TOT	100	100	100	100	100	100	100	100	100	100	100	100	100	100	100	100	100	100	100	100

Note: ** means "not applicable."

(Table continues on the following page)

5-45. (continued)

Percentage of total imports

	RWA	STP	SEN	SYC	SLE	SOM	ZAF	SDN	SWZ	TZA	TGO	TUN	UGA	ZAR	ZMB	ZWE	SSA	EEC	NNA	ROW	TOT
DZA	0.03	..	0.01	..	..	..	..	..	..	0.00	..	1.66	..	..	0.00	0.00	0.05	0.58	0.40	0.14	0.37
ANG	..	..	1.87	0.00	..	..	..	..	..	..	..	..	..	..	0.00	..	0.07	0.10	0.30	0.03	0.11
BEN	0.00	..	0.01	..	0.00	..	..	0.00	..	..	0.20	0.00	..	..	..	..	0.03	0.00	0.00	0.00	0.00
BWA	..	..	..	..	..	..	..	..	..	..	..	..	..	..	..	..	..	..	..	..	..
HVO	0.02	..	0.00	..	..	..	..	..	..	..	0.15	0.15	..	..	..	..	0.05	0.01	0.00	0.00	0.00
BDI	1.05	..	..	..	..	..	..	..	..	..	..	..	..	..	..	..	0.01	0.00	0.00	0.00	0.00
CMR	0.02	..	1.98	..	..	..	..	..	..	..	0.34	0.06	..	..	0.00	..	0.73	0.11	0.02	0.02	0.07
CPV	0.00	..	0.00	..	..	..	..	..	..	..	..	0.02	..	..	..	..	0.01	0.00	0.00	0.00	0.00
CAF	0.03	..	0.00	..	..	..	..	0.05	..	..	..	0.01	..	..	..	..	0.00	0.01	0.00	0.00	0.00
TCD	..	..	..	..	..	..	..	0.01	..	..	0.00	..	..	..	..	..	0.01	0.00	0.00	0.00	0.00
COM	..	..	0.00	..	..	..	..	..	..	..	..	..	..	..	..	..	0.00	0.00	0.00	0.00	0.00
CGO	..	..	0.02	..	..	..	0.00	..	..	..	0.06	0.01	..	0.09	..	0.01	0.03	0.05	0.06	0.00	0.03
CIV	0.01	..	5.65	..	0.23	..	..	..	..	0.00	5.92	0.23	..	..	..	0.01	1.60	0.14	0.03	0.07	0.11
DJI	0.30	..	..	..	..	6.42	..	..	..	..	..	..	..	..	..	..	0.07	0.00	0.00	0.00	0.00
EGY	..	..	0.00	..	0.00	0.01	0.00	..	..	0.00	..	0.38	0.06	0.00	..	0.17	0.02	0.13	0.04	0.12	0.11
GNQ	..	..	..	..	..	..	..	..	..	..	..	..	..	..	..	..	0.00	0.00	0.00	0.00	0.00
ETH	0.00	..	..	..	..	..	0.00	0.76	..	0.01	..	0.00	0.07	..	..	..	0.07	0.01	0.01	0.01	0.01
GAB	0.00	0.04	1.70	..	..	..	..	..	..	..	0.02	0.03	..	..	..	0.00	0.20	0.08	0.11	0.03	0.07
GMB	..	..	0.00	..	0.00	..	..	..	..	..	..	..	..	0.00	..	..	0.02	0.01	0.00	0.01	0.01
GHA	0.00	..	0.09	..	..	..	..	0.00	..	0.00	6.44	0.00	..	..	..	0.00	0.14	0.06	0.03	0.03	0.04
GIN	..	..	0.01	..	0.03	..	..	..	..	..	0.05	0.00	..	..	..	0.02	0.17	0.02	0.02	0.01	0.02
GNB	..	0.00	0.00	..	..	..	..	..	..	..	..	0.00	..	..	..	..	0.00	0.00	0.00	0.00	0.00
KEN	17.60	..	..	..	..	1.19	0.01	2.79	..	1.23	..	0.01	20.29	0.58	0.16	..	0.62	0.04	0.01	0.02	0.03
LSO	..	..	..	..	..	..	..	..	..	..	..	..	..	..	..	..	..	..	..	..	..
LBR	..	..	0.01	..	0.26	..	..	..	..	..	0.08	0.00	..	..	..	..	0.03	0.06	0.01	0.07	0.06
LBY	0.00	..	0.00	..	..	..	..	0.01	..	0.00	..	0.53	..	..	..	..	0.01	0.66	0.00	0.12	0.31
MDG	..	..	0.00	0.12	..	0.30	..	0.00	0.00	0.15	0.00	0.00	..	0.00	..	..	0.05	0.02	0.02	0.01	0.01
MWI	..	..	..	..	..	..	0.22	..	..	0.07	..	..	..	..	1.26	0.84	0.10	0.01	0.01	0.01	0.01
MLI	0.00	..	0.05	..	..	..	..	..	..	..	0.10	0.08	..	..	..	..	0.06	0.01	0.00	0.01	0.01
MRT	..	..	0.04	..	0.01	..	..	..	..	..	0.21	0.01	..	0.00	..	..	0.13	0.02	0.00	0.01	0.01
MUS	0.00	..	..	2.45	..	0.00	0.05	0.00	0.35	0.02	0.01	0.00	0.01	0.01	0.04	0.35	0.05	0.07	0.02	0.01	0.04
MAR	..	..	0.58	..	0.14	..	..	0.04	..	0.16	0.35	1.08	..	2.35	..	..	0.34	0.22	0.03	0.09	0.13
MOZ	0.06	..	..	..	..	0.10	0.04	..	..	0.20	0.00	0.00	..	..	..	0.02	0.01	0.00	0.00	0.02	0.01
NAM	..	..	..	..	..	..	..	..	..	..	..	..	..	..	..	..	..	..	..	..	..
NER	..	..	0.07	..	..	..	..	..	..	..	0.12	..	..	..	0.00	..	0.07	0.01	0.01	0.00	0.01
NGA	..	..	3.59	..	22.91	..	..	..	..	0.05	0.03	..	..	..	..	0.00	1.13	0.36	0.96	0.08	0.38
RWA	**	..	0.00	..	..	0.00	..	..	0.03	0.00	0.00	0.00	0.04	0.10	0.00	..	0.23	0.00	0.00	0.00	0.00
STP	..	**	..	..	..	..	..	..	..	..	..	..	..	..	..	..	0.00	0.00	..	0.00	0.02
SEN	0.01	..	**	..	0.26	0.00	..	..	0.01	..	0.29	0.14	0.00	..	0.00	0.00	0.30	0.03	0.00	0.01	0.02
SYC	..	..	..	**	..	..	..	..	..	0.00	..	..	..	..	..	..	0.00	0.01	0.00	0.00	0.01
SLE	..	..	0.02	..	**	..	..	0.00	..	..	..	..	..	0.00	..	..	0.01	0.01	0.00	0.00	0.01
SOM	0.02	..	..	..	..	**	..	0.00	..	0.01	..	0.00	0.03	..	..	..	0.00	0.00	..	0.01	0.00
ZAF	..	0.00	..	..	..	..	**	..	..	..	..	0.00	..	..	..	..	0.18	0.45	0.30	1.26	0.73
SDN	0.00	..	..	..	..	0.03	..	**	..	0.01	0.00	0.06	..	..	..	..	0.00	0.01	0.00	0.03	0.02
SWZ	..	..	..	..	..	..	..	..	**	..	..	..	..	..	..	..	..	..	..	..	..
TZA	0.71	..	..	..	..	0.12	..	0.17	0.04	**	..	0.06	0.36	0.24	0.10	0.01	0.06	0.02	0.00	0.01	0.01
TGO	0.00	..	0.00	..	..	..	..	..	..	0.00	**	0.02	..	..	0.00	..	0.18	0.01	0.01	0.01	0.01
TUN	0.00	..	0.11	..	0.02	..	..	0.10	..	0.01	0.26	**	..	..	0.20	0.00	0.10	0.20	0.01	0.06	0.10
UGA	0.09	..	..	..	..	0.00	..	0.01	..	0.15	..	0.00	**	..	0.00	..	0.01	0.01	0.00	0.00	0.01
ZAR	..	..	..	..	..	..	0.00	..	..	..	..	0.01	..	**	0.03	..	0.07	0.07	0.03	0.01	0.04
ZMB	0.00	..	..	0.00	..	..	..	..	0.08	0.86	..	0.61	0.07	0.33	**	4.41	0.24	0.03	0.00	0.06	0.04
ZWE	0.75	..	0.00	0.12	0.03	1.10	..	0.08	4.94	0.25	0.47	0.03	0.20	0.76	10.75	**	0.81	0.04	0.02	0.03	0.04
SSA	20.68	0.04	15.12	2.69	23.74	9.27	0.33	3.87	5.47	3.01	14.49	1.57	21.06	2.11	12.35	5.68	7.39	1.44	1.70	0.63	1.24
EEC	54.08	57.64	64.03	49.39	47.38	53.29	59.68	40.79	41.05	49.22	48.16	73.39	43.95	50.07	48.53	47.68	50.91	61.11	17.31	31.53	40.98
NNA	0.91	30.35	5.02	1.74	11.90	4.27	15.47	4.88	13.93	6.05	4.87	4.78	6.57	8.49	12.25	19.76	7.22	8.19	35.18	16.31	16.61
ROW	24.32	11.97	15.83	46.18	16.98	33.18	24.52	50.46	39.55	41.71	32.48	20.25	28.42	39.33	26.87	26.87	34.48	29.25	45.80	51.53	41.17
TOT	100	100	100	100	100	100	100	100	100	100	100	100	100	100	100	100	100	100	100	100	100

Note: ** means "not applicable."

5-46. Direction of trade matrix, exports, 1981

Importers   *Percentage of total exports*

Exporters		DZA	ANG	BEN	BWA	HVO	BDI	CMR	CPV	CAF	TCD	COM	CGO	CIV	DJI	EGY	GNQ
Algeria	DZA	**	0.01	0.15	..	..	..	..	..	..	..	..	..	0.25	..	..	..
Angola	ANG	2.92	**	..	..	..	..	..	0.03	..	..	..	..	..	..	..	..
Benin	BEN	0.74	..	**	..	0.88	..	0.22	..	..	..	..	0.68	0.29	..	..	..
Botswana	BWA	..	..	..	**	..	..	..	..	..	..	..	..	..	..	..	..
Burkina Faso	HVO	..	..	0.33	..	**	..	..	..	..	..	..	..	0.01	31.27	..	..
Burundi	BDI	..	..	..	..	..	**	0.17	..	..	0.98	..	..	..	0.00	..	..
Cameroon	CMR	..	0.01	0.03	..	0.01	..	**	..	1.02	1.78	..	1.39	0.62	..	0.25	0.01
Cape Verde	CPV	..	10.34	..	..	..	..	..	**	3.45	..	..	..	..	..	..	..
Central African Republic	CAF	..	..	..	..	..	..	..	..	**	0.32	..	..	0.34	..	..	..
Chad	TCD	..	..	..	..	..	..	22.86	..	3.40	**	..	..	..	..	..	..
Comoros	COM	..	..	..	..	..	..	..	..	..	..	**	..	..	..	..	..
Congo, People's Republic of the	CGO	0.08	0.09	0.00	..	..	..	..	..	..	..	0.03	**	0.01	..	..	..
Cote d'Ivoire	CIV	1.32	..	0.58	..	3.78	..	0.40	..	0.03	..	..	0.16	**	..	..	..
Djibouti	DJI	..	..	..	..	..	..	..	..	..	..	..	..	..	**	..	..
Egypt, Arab Republic of	EGY	0.01	..	0.00	..	..	..	..	..	..	..	..	0.00	0.00	0.00	**	..
Equatorial Guinea	GNQ	..	..	..	..	..	..	0.89	..	..	..	..	..	..	..	..	**
Ethiopia	ETH	..	..	..	..	..	..	..	..	..	..	..	..	..	5.03	2.56	..
Gabon	GAB	0.03	0.35	..	..	..	..	..	..	..	..	..	..	0.02	..	..	..
Gambia, The	GMB	..	..	..	..	..	..	..	..	..	..	..	..	..	..	..	..
Ghana	GHA	0.00	0.00	..	..	..	..	0.00	..	..	..	..	..	0.00	..	0.31	..
Guinea	GIN	..	..	..	..	..	..	7.59	..	..	..	..	..	..	..	0.03	..
Guinea-Bissau	GNB	..	0.01	..	..	..	..	..	..	..	..	..	..	..	..	..	..
Kenya	KEN	..	0.01	0.00	0.02	0.00	2.43	0.05	0.00	0.00	0.00	0.41	0.01	0.04	1.97	0.61	0.01
Lesotho	LSO	..	..	..	..	..	..	..	..	..	..	..	..	..	..	..	..
Liberia	LBR	..	..	..	..	..	..	0.01	..	0.00	..	..	0.00	0.09	..	0.02	..
Libya	LBY	0.00	..	..	..	..	..	..	..	..	0.01	..	..	..	..	0.00	..
Madagascar	MDG	3.00	..	..	..	..	..	..	..	..	..	..	0.16	..	..	..	..
Malawi	MWI	..	..	..	..	..	..	0.07	..	..	..	..	..	..	..	..	..
Mali	MLI	0.20	..	..	..	0.51	..	..	..	..	..	..	..	30.18	..	..	..
Mauritania	MRT	..	..	..	..	..	..	..	..	..	..	..	0.23	..	..	..	..
Mauritius	MUS	..	..	..	0.01	..	0.00	0.00	..	..	..	0.39	0.04	0.00	0.00	0.01	..
Morocco	MAR	..	..	..	..	0.00	..	0.22	..	..	..	..	0.18	0.43	..	0.25	..
Mozambique	MOZ	0.26	..	..	..	..	..	..	..	..	..	..	..	..	..	0.03	..
Namibia	NAM	..	..	..	..	..	..	..	..	..	..	..	..	..	..	..	..
Niger	NER	0.00	..	0.06	..	0.17	0.00	0.05	..	..	0.00	..	0.01	0.09	..	..	..
Nigeria	NGA	0.00	..	0.03	..	..	..	0.00	0.00	..	..	..	..	0.44	..	0.00	..
Rwanda	RWA	..	..	..	..	..	0.28	..	..	..	..	..	..	..	..	..	..
Sao Tome & Principe	STP	..	..	..	..	..	..	..	..	..	..	..	..	..	..	..	..
Senegal	SEN	0.11	..	0.93	..	0.60	0.00	0.53	0.09	0.15	0.02	..	0.51	7.87	..	0.00	0.00
Seychelles	SYC	..	..	..	..	..	..	..	..	..	..	..	..	..	..	..	..
Sierra Leone	SLE	..	..	..	..	..	..	..	..	..	..	..	..	..	..	..	..
Somalia	SOM	..	..	..	..	..	..	..	..	..	..	..	..	..	0.80	0.02	..
South Africa	ZAF	..	..	..	..	..	..	..	..	..	..	..	..	..	..	..	..
Sudan	SDN	0.60	0.19	..	..	..	..	..	..	..	..	..	..	..	..	4.83	..
Swaziland	SWZ	..	..	..	..	..	..	..	..	..	..	..	..	..	..	..	..
Tanzania	TZA	4.76	..	..	..	..	2.19	..	..	..	..	..	..	..	..	0.38	..
Togo	TGO	..	..	1.08	..	1.31	..	0.02	..	..	..	..	0.07	4.49	..	..	..
Tunisia	TUN	2.14	..	..	..	..	..	..	..	..	..	..	..	0.10	..	0.69	..
Uganda	UGA	..	..	..	..	..	..	..	..	..	..	..	..	..	..	0.28	..
Zaire	ZAR	..	..	..	..	..	0.18	0.04	..	0.22	..	..	0.98	..	..	..	..
Zambia	ZMB	..	0.06	..	0.37	..	0.46	0.00	..	..	..	..	..	..	..	0.61	..
Zimbabwe	ZWE	0.02	0.25	..	3.20	..	0.08	0.07	..	0.00	..	0.02	0.02	0.02	..	0.60	..
Total Sub-Saharan Africa	SSA	0.31	0.03	0.08	0.12	0.27	0.12	0.17	0.00	0.04	0.06	0.02	0.08	0.52	0.12	0.18	0.00
European Community	EEC	1.07	0.11	0.05	0.00	0.02	0.01	0.15	0.01	0.01	0.00	0.01	0.08	0.18	0.02	0.79	0.01
North America	NNA	0.32	0.08	0.01	0.00	0.01	0.00	0.06	..	0.00	0.00	0.00	0.01	0.05	0.00	0.69	0.00
Rest of World	ROW	0.24	0.05	0.04	0.00	0.00	0.01	0.04	0.01	0.00	0.00	0.00	0.02	0.09	0.01	0.48	0.00
World	TOT	0.54	0.08	0.04	0.00	0.02	0.01	0.08	0.01	0.00	0.00	0.00	0.04	0.12	0.01	0.62	0.00

Note: ** means "not applicable."

(Table continues on the following page)

5-46. (continued)

Percentage of total exports

	ETH	GAB	GMB	GHA	GIN	GNB	KEN	LSO	LBR	LBY	MDG	MWI	MLI	MRT	MUS	MAR	MOZ	NAM	NER	NGA
DZA	..	..	0.02	0.16	0.00	..	0.04	..	0.00	0.02	..	..	0.01	0.00	0.01	..	0.25	..	0.00	0.00
ANG	..	..	..	0.00	..	..	..	..	..	..	..	..	..	..	..	..	..	..	..	0.07
BEN	..	..	..	1.46	..	..	..	..	..	..	..	..	0.04	..	..	..	..	..	8.02	6.31
BWA	..	..	..	..	..	..	..	..	..	..	..	..	..	..	..	..	..	..	..	..
HVO	..	..	..	0.54	..	..	..	..	..	..	..	..	1.56	..	..	..	..	..	2.43	..
BDI	..	..	..	..	..	..	0.83	..	..	..	..	..	..	..	..	..	..	..	..	..
CMR	..	1.72	..	0.00	0.12	..	..	..	..	..	0.02	0.00	0.07	..	..	0.02	0.00	..	..	0.46
CPV	..	..	..	..	..	..	..	..	..	..	..	..	..	..	..	..	..	..	..	..
CAF	..	..	..	..	..	..	..	..	..	..	..	..	..	0.01	..	..	..	..	..	0.21
TCD	..	..	..	..	..	..	..	..	..	..	..	..	..	..	..	..	..	..	..	..
COM	..	..	..	..	..	..	..	..	..	..	0.43	..	..	..	0.03	..	..	..	0.36	17.66
CGO	..	..	..	..	..	..	..	..	..	..	..	..	..	..	..	0.06	..	..	..	..
CIV	..	0.31	..	0.45	..	..	..	..	0.29	..	..	..	3.51	0.14	..	0.79	..	..	1.25	0.98
DJI	10.42	..	..	..	..	..	0.07	..	..	0.38	..	..	..	..	..	..	..	..	..	..
EGY	0.00	..	..	..	..	..	0.01	..	..	0.00	..	..	..	0.05	0.00	0.05	..	..	..	0.04
GNQ	..	..	..	..	..	..	..	..	..	..	..	..	..	..	..	..	..	..	..	..
ETH	**	..	..	..	..	..	0.24	..	..	..	..	..	..	..	..	..	..	..	..	..
GAB	..	**	..	..	0.15	..	..	..	..	..	..	..	..	..	..	0.33	..	..	..	1.34
GMB	..	..	**	27.79	9.17	0.42	..	..	0.02	..	..	..	0.00	..	..	..	..	..	..	3.00
GHA	..	..	0.01	**	0.00	..	0.00	..	0.01	0.00	..	..	0.00	..	..	..	0.00	..	..	0.01
GIN	..	..	..	..	**	0.01	..	..	0.06	..	..	..	..	..	0.00	0.18	..	..	0.00	..
GNB	..	..	0.34	..	0.39	**	..	..	..	..	..	..	..	..	..	..	..	..	..	..
KEN	0.30	0.00	0.00	0.00	0.00	..	**	0.01	0.00	0.04	0.09	0.09	0.02	0.00	0.98	0.03	1.98	..	0.00	0.40
LSO	..	..	..	..	..	..	..	**	..	..	..	..	..	..	..	..	..	..	..	..
LBR	..	..	0.00	0.46	0.35	..	..	..	**	0.51	..	0.00	0.01	0.00	..	..	..	..	..	0.84
LBY	..	..	..	..	..	..	..	..	..	**	..	..	..	..	..	0.00	..	..	..	..
MDG	..	..	..	..	..	..	..	..	..	..	**	..	..	..	0.27	0.26	..	..	..	..
MWI	0.03	0.17	..	..	..	..	0.43	..	0.61	..	..	**	..	..	0.21	..	0.61	..	..	..
MLI	..	..	..	0.31	..	..	..	..	0.36	..	..	..	**	..	..	..	..	..	0.32	..
MRT	..	..	..	..	..	..	..	..	..	..	..	..	..	**	..	..	..	..	..	..
MUS	..	0.00	0.00	..	0.00	..	0.13	..	..	0.00	0.15	0.01	..	..	**	0.00	..	..	0.00	0.00
MAR	..	0.14	0.01	..	0.07	..	..	..	0.00	1.98	0.00	..	0.00	0.04	0.03	**	..	..	..	0.47
MOZ	..	..	..	0.00	..	0.08	1.62	..	..	..	..	0.73	..	..	..	..	**	..	..	..
NAM	..	..	..	..	..	..	..	..	..	..	..	..	..	..	..	..	..	**	..	..
NER	..	0.00	..	0.02	0.00	..	..	..	..	14.57	..	..	0.26	..	..	..	..	..	**	16.84
NGA	..	..	..	1.60	..	..	..	..	0.00	..	..	0.00	..	..	..	..	..	..	0.00	**
RWA	..	..	..	..	..	..	0.79	..	..	0.09	..	..	..	..	..	..	..	..	..	..
STP	..	..	..	..	..	..	..	..	..	..	..	..	..	..	..	..	..	..	..	0.00
SEN	0.00	0.39	1.29	0.04	2.40	1.68	0.00	..	0.06	..	..	0.02	7.69	9.38	0.00	0.32	..	..	0.66	0.29
SYC	..	..	..	..	..	..	0.57	..	..	..	..	..	..	..	1.15	..	..	..	..	..
SLE	..	..	..	..	..	..	..	..	..	..	..	..	..	..	..	..	..	..	..	..
SOM	..	..	0.00	..	..	..	0.29	..	..	..	..	..	..	..	..	..	..	..	..	..
ZAF	..	..	..	..	..	..	..	..	..	..	..	..	..	..	..	..	..	..	..	..
SDN	0.03	..	..	..	..	..	..	..	..	..	..	..	..	..	..	0.02	..	..	..	..
SWZ	..	..	..	..	..	..	..	..	..	..	..	..	..	..	..	..	..	..	..	..
TZA	0.07	..	..	0.00	..	..	0.06	..	..	0.00	0.02	..	..	..	0.02	..	0.48	..	..	0.03
TGO	..	0.03	..	4.93	..	..	..	..	0.59	..	..	..	0.19	..	..	..	..	..	0.77	2.42
TUN	..	..	..	..	..	..	..	..	..	4.85	..	..	..	..	..	0.21	..	..	..	..
UGA	..	..	..	0.00	..	..	0.61	..	..	2.64	..	..	..	..	..	..	..	..	..	..
ZAR	..	0.22	..	..	..	..	0.01	..	..	..	..	..	..	..	..	..	..	..	..	..
ZMB	..	..	..	..	..	..	0.50	..	..	..	..	0.99	..	..	..	..	0.01	0.01	..	..
ZWE	0.00	0.05	..	0.07	..	..	0.27	0.13	..	0.46	0.00	1.65	0.04	..	0.26	0.02	1.26	0.26	..	0.14
SSA	0.02	0.08	0.02	0.90	0.05	0.02	0.05	0.00	0.03	0.22	0.01	0.08	0.35	0.13	0.04	0.08	0.12	0.01	0.11	0.41
EEC	0.04	0.08	0.01	0.06	0.03	0.01	0.11	0.00	0.09	1.45	0.03	0.01	0.02	0.04	0.02	0.36	0.04	0.00	0.04	1.44
NNA	0.03	0.04	0.00	0.05	0.02	..	0.05	0.00	0.05	0.28	0.01	0.00	0.00	0.01	0.01	0.16	0.02	0.00	0.00	0.49
ROW	0.04	0.01	0.00	0.03	0.01	0.00	0.12	0.00	0.14	0.50	0.02	0.01	0.00	0.01	0.03	0.19	0.04	0.00	0.01	0.67
TOT	0.04	0.04	0.01	0.06	0.02	0.00	0.10	0.00	0.11	0.78	0.02	0.01	0.02	0.02	0.02	0.24	0.04	0.00	0.02	0.90

Note: ** means "not applicable."

(Table continues on the following p g page)

5–46. (continued)

Percentage of total exports

	RWA	STP	SEN	SYC	SLE	SOM	ZAF	SDN	SWZ	TZA	TGO	TUN	UGA	ZAR	ZMB	ZWE	SSA	EEC	NNA	ROW	TOT
DZA	..	..	0.24	..	..	..	..	..	..	..	..	0.05	..	..	..	..	1.14	51.02	33.22	14.62	100
ANG	0.00	..	..	..	..	..	..	..	..	..	..	..	..	0.01	0.00	..	0.11	19.91	62.93	17.05	100
BEN	..	..	0.48	..	..	..	..	..	..	..	..	2.94	..	..	..	..	21.31	47.50	0.53	30.66	100
BWA	..	..	..	..	..	..	..	..	..	..	..	..	..	..	..	..	..	..	..	..	..
HVO	..	..	0.11	..	..	..	..	..	..	..	..	0.96	..	..	..	..	37.21	32.74	0.05	30.00	100
BDI	1.23	..	..	..	..	..	..	..	..	0.02	..	..	..	3.49	..	..	6.72	23.07	43.95	26.26	100
CMR	0.00	..	0.12	..	0.00	..	..	0.02	..	0.00	0.03	0.08	..	0.00	..	..	7.45	48.08	38.19	6.28	100
CPV	..	..	..	..	..	..	..	..	..	..	..	..	..	3.45	..	..	17.24	82.76	..	..	100
CAF	..	..	..	..	..	..	0.30	0.31	..	..	..	..	..	0.19	..	..	1.37	67.02	8.91	22.70	100
TCD	..	..	..	..	..	..	..	..	..	..	..	..	..	..	..	..	26.26	58.05	..	15.69	100
COM	..	..	0.02	..	..	..	..	..	..	..	..	..	..	..	..	..	18.50	65.20	13.92	2.38	100
CGO	..	0.01	0.00	..	..	..	0.15	..	0.03	..	..	0.09	..	0.17	..	0.08	0.42	54.47	13.80	31.31	100
CIV	..	..	1.22	..	..	..	..	..	..	..	0.45	0.08	..	..	..	..	13.56	59.08	11.69	15.66	100
DJI	..	..	0.00	..	..	55.62	..	..	..	..	..	..	..	..	..	..	66.12	7.27	..	26.60	100
EGY	0.00	..	..	..	0.00	0.00	..	0.39	..	0.00	..	0.08	0.00	0.00	0.00	..	0.51	44.24	4.56	50.69	100
GNQ	..	..	..	..	..	..	..	..	..	..	..	..	..	..	..	..	0.89	97.72	0.69	0.70	100
ETH	..	..	..	..	..	..	..	0.42	..	..	..	..	..	..	..	..	5.69	31.30	20.64	42.37	100
GAB	..	..	0.86	..	..	..	..	..	..	..	0.04	0.06	..	0.51	..	..	3.26	49.30	19.30	28.14	100
GMB	..	..	1.06	..	0.26	..	..	..	..	..	..	..	..	..	..	..	41.72	40.87	0.55	16.86	100
GHA	..	..	0.00	..	0.00	..	0.00	..	..	0.00	0.93	..	..	..	..	..	0.98	41.23	18.73	39.06	100
GIN	..	..	0.01	..	0.06	..	..	..	..	..	..	..	..	..	..	..	7.73	48.25	32.84	11.18	100
GNB	..	..	7.13	..	..	..	..	..	..	..	..	..	..	..	..	..	7.88	61.98	..	30.13	100
KEN	4.16	..	0.00	0.21	0.00	0.37	0.01	2.33	0.04	1.19	0.00	0.05	9.88	1.05	0.41	0.07	28.55	34.17	4.43	32.86	100
LSO	..	..	..	..	..	..	..	..	..	..	..	..	..	..	..	..	..	..	..	..	..
LBR	..	..	0.00	..	0.17	..	..	..	..	0.00	0.04	..	..	0.02	0.00	..	2.02	66.47	26.03	5.49	100
LBY	..	..	..	..	..	..	0.00	..	..	..	..	0.02	..	..	..	..	0.01	52.73	28.05	19.22	100
MDG	..	..	..	..	..	..	..	..	..	..	..	..	..	..	..	..	0.43	33.31	14.53	51.73	100
MWI	..	..	..	..	0.38	..	4.90	..	..	0.01	..	..	..	0.34	1.57	8.12	12.56	37.80	28.54	21.10	100
MLI	..	..	..	..	..	..	..	..	..	..	..	..	..	..	..	..	31.68	44.68	0.00	23.63	100
MRT	..	..	0.11	..	..	..	..	..	..	..	..	..	..	0.62	..	..	0.95	71.64	..	27.41	100
MUS	0.00	..	0.00	0.22	..	1.70	..	..	..	0.02	..	..	..	..	0.03	0.00	1.00	85.88	5.21	7.91	100
MAR	..	..	0.20	..	..	..	0.00	..	..	..	0.03	0.78	..	0.09	..	..	1.91	54.36	3.58	40.16	100
MOZ	..	..	..	..	..	..	..	..	..	1.31	..	..	..	..	0.01	8.56	12.31	25.27	25.59	36.83	100
NAM	..	..	..	..	..	..	..	..	..	..	..	..	..	..	..	..	..	..	..	..	..
NER	..	..	0.01	..	0.00	..	..	..	..	..	0.02	..	..	0.00	..	..	17.55	45.69	0.02	36.74	100
NGA	..	..	0.15	..	0.23	..	..	..	..	..	0.01	..	..	..	..	..	2.47	34.51	33.08	29.95	100
RWA	**	..	..	0.38	..	..	..	..	..	0.23	..	..	0.25	0.77	..	..	2.70	45.76	36.10	15.44	100
STP	..	**	..	..	..	..	..	..	..	..	..	..	..	..	..	..	0.00	92.22	..	7.78	100
SEN	..	..	**	0.00	0.09	..	..	..	..	..	1.38	0.08	0.00	0.18	0.01	..	36.26	37.95	0.15	25.64	100
SYC	..	..	..	**	..	..	..	..	..	..	..	..	..	..	..	..	1.72	2.30	1.15	94.83	100
SLE	..	..	..	..	**	..	..	..	..	..	..	..	..	..	..	..	..	51.62	11.26	37.13	100
SOM	..	..	..	0.00	..	**	..	0.00	..	0.01	..	..	0.01	..	0.03	..	1.13	15.15	0.16	83.57	100
ZAF	..	..	..	..	..	..	**	..	..	..	..	..	..	..	..	..	..	18.37	9.57	72.07	100
SDN	..	..	..	..	..	..	..	**	..	..	..	0.44	..	..	..	..	0.22	28.74	8.09	62.95	100
SWZ	..	..	..	..	..	..	..	..	**	..	..	..	..	..	..	..	..	..	..	..	..
TZA	0.48	..	..	0.08	..	0.10	..	0.75	0.06	**	..	..	1.77	0.79	0.34	0.04	7.30	45.38	4.10	43.21	100
TGO	..	..	0.02	..	..	..	..	..	..	..	**	..	..	0.00	..	..	15.91	61.58	0.16	22.35	100
TUN	..	..	..	..	..	..	..	..	.	..	..	**	..	..	..	..	0.10	64.35	19.26	16.30	100
UGA	0.24	..	..	..	0.00	..	..	1.54	..	0.03	..	..	**	..	..	0.00	2.43	45.88	37.31	14.38	100
ZAR	..	..	..	..	..	..	0.01	..	..	..	..	..	..	**	0.09	..	1.74	84.52	1.61	12.14	100
ZMB	..	..	..	..	..	..	0.97	..	0.01	0.94	..	..	..	..	**	..	3.34	63.48	11.31	21.88	100
ZWE	..	..	0.00	0.01	0.00	0.00	21.63	0.11	0.16	..	..	0.02	0.00	2.16	3.99	**	14.24	27.42	7.87	50.48	100
SSA	0.14	0.00	0.21	0.01	0.12	0.05	0.81	0.10	0.01	0.06	0.08	0.02	0.33	0.16	0.17	0.13	5.64	40.35	25.35	28.66	100
EEC	0.01	0.00	0.09	0.00	0.02	0.03	1.24	0.10	0.00	0.06	0.04	0.35	0.02	0.09	0.04	0.04	3.29	52.72	8.11	35.88	100
NNA	0.00	..	0.02	0.00	0.01	0.02	0.96	0.07	0.00	0.02	0.01	0.09	0.00	0.06	0.02	0.01	1.24	20.88	35.54	42.35	100
ROW	0.01	0.00	0.03	0.00	0.01	0.02	0.47	0.10	0.00	0.06	0.01	0.08	0.00	0.04	0.04	0.02	1.73	27.47	18.28	52.51	100
TOT	0.01	0.00	0.05	0.00	0.01	0.02	0.83	0.09	0.00	0.05	0.02	0.17	0.02	0.06	0.04	0.02	2.26	35.19	17.97	44.58	100

Note: ** means "not applicable."

5–47. Direction of trade matrix, exports, 1985

Exporters		DZA	ANG	BEN	BWA	HVO	BDI	CMR	CPV	CAF	TCD	COM	CGO	CIV	DJI	EGY	GNQ
		Importers							*Percentage of total exports*								
Algeria	DZA	**	..	..	..	..	..	..	..	..	..	..	..	..	..	..	..
Angola	ANG	..	**	..	..	..	..	0.05	..	..	..	..	0.00	..	..	..	..
Benin	BEN	..	..	**	..	0.02	..	0.07	..	0.01	..	..	0.19	0.26	..	..	..
Botswana	BWA	..	..	..	**	..	..	..	..	..	..	..	..	..	..	..	..
Burkina Faso	HVO	..	..	0.37	..	**	..	..	..	..	..	..	..	2.55	..	3.71	..
Burundi	BDI	..	..	..	..	..	**	0.28	..	..	..	..	..	..	..	..	..
Cameroon	CMR	0.21	0.01	0.05	..	0.00	..	**	..	0.58	1.69	..	1.26	1.38	..	0.04	0.27
Cape Verde	CPV	38.78	32.65	..	..	..	..	..	**	..	..	..	..	..	..	..	..
Central African Republic	CAF	..	..	..	..	..	..	..	..	**	0.27	..	..	0.00	..	..	..
Chad	TCD	..	..	..	..	..	..	4.30	..	0.01	**	..	0.71	..	..	..	..
Comoros	COM	..	..	..	..	..	..	..	..	..	..	**	..	..	..	..	..
Congo, People's Republic of the	CGO	0.04	1.09	..	..	..	..	..	..	..	0.12	..	**	0.03	..	0.03	..
Cote d'Ivoire	CIV	0.27	..	0.49	..	2.89	..	0.56	..	..	..	..	..	**	..	..	..
Djibouti	DJI	..	..	..	..	..	3.31	..	..	..	..	..	..	..	**	0.23	..
Egypt, Arab Republic of	EGY	0.12	..	..	..	..	0.00	0.00	..	..	..	..	..	0.00	0.00	**	..
Equatorial Guinea	GNQ	..	..	..	..	..	..	0.28	..	..	..	..	..	..	..	..	**
Ethiopia	ETH	..	..	..	..	..	..	..	..	..	..	..	..	..	3.61	0.42	..
Gabon	GAB	0.23	..	0.00	..	..	..	0.29	..	..	..	..	..	1.38	..	0.05	..
Gambia, The	GMB	..	..	..	..	..	..	..	..	..	..	..	..	..	..	..	..
Ghana	GHA	..	..	0.04	..	0.00	..	..	..	..	..	..	0.00	0.10	..	0.25	..
Guinea	GIN	..	..	..	..	..	..	6.32	..	..	..	..	..	0.01	..	..	..
Guinea–Bissau	GNB	..	0.01	..	..	..	..	..	..	..	..	..	..	..	..	..	..
Kenya	KEN	..	..	..	..	..	1.92	..	..	..	..	0.25	..	..	0.25	2.43	..
Lesotho	LSO	..	..	..	..	..	..	..	..	..	..	..	..	..	..	..	..
Liberia	LBR	..	..	0.01	..	..	..	0.05	..	..	..	..	..	..	..	0.01	..
Libya	LBY	0.00	..	..	..	..	..	..	..	..	0.01	..	..	..	..	0.00	..
Madagascar	MDG	..	..	..	..	..	..	..	..	..	..	0.06	..	..	..	..	..
Malawi	MWI	..	..	..	0.46	..	..	..	..	..	..	..	..	..	..	..	..
Mali	MLI	4.49	..	..	..	0.97	..	..	..	..	..	..	0.03	2.46	..	..	..
Mauritania	MRT	3.78	..	0.03	..	..	..	0.15	..	..	..	..	0.04	2.96	..	0.00	..
Mauritius	MUS	0.00	..	..	..	..	0.00	0.01	..	0.00	..	0.23	0.00	0.00	..	0.06	..
Morocco	MAR	..	..	0.05	..	..	..	0.42	..	..	..	..	0.27	0.33	..	0.10	..
Mozambique	MOZ	..	..	..	..	..	..	..	..	..	..	..	0.15	..	..	0.01	..
Namibia	NAM	..	..	..	..	..	..	..	..	..	..	..	..	..	..	..	..
Niger	NER	3.36	..	0.33	..	0.49	..	0.02	..	..	..	..	..	1.70	..	..	..
Nigeria	NGA	..	0.00	0.01	0.00	0.00	..	0.02	..	0.03	..	0.00	0.00	1.44	..	0.00	..
Rwanda	RWA	..	..	..	..	..	0.40	0.03	..	..	..	..	..	..	..	..	..
Sao Tome & Principe	STP	..	..	..	..	..	..	..	..	..	..	..	..	..	..	..	..
Senegal	SEN	0.03	0.01	0.85	..	0.47	0.00	1.98	0.04	0.04	0.04	..	0.85	5.48	0.00	0.02	0.00
Seychelles	SYC	..	..	..	..	..	..	..	..	..	..	..	..	..	..	..	..
Sierra Leone	SLE	..	..	0.00	..	..	..	..	..	..	0.00	..	..	0.14	..	..	..
Somalia	SOM	..	..	..	..	..	..	0.16	..	..	..	..	..	..	0.09	3.37	..
South Africa	ZAF	..	..	..	..	..	..	..	..	..	..	..	..	..	..	..	..
Sudan	SDN	..	..	..	..	..	..	..	..	0.00	..	..	..	..	..	8.92	..
Swaziland	SWZ	..	..	..	..	..	..	..	..	..	..	..	..	..	..	..	..
Tanzania	TZA	0.21	..	..	0.01	..	0.73	..	..	..	..	..	..	0.11	..	0.48	..
Togo	TGO	..	..	0.57	..	1.09	..	0.06	..	0.05	0.07	..	0.10	0.37	..	..	..
Tunisia	TUN	3.31	0.00	0.01	..	..	..	0.03	..	..	..	..	0.02	0.07	..	0.29	..
Uganda	UGA	..	..	..	..	..	..	..	..	..	..	..	0.00	..	..	0.45	..
Zaire	ZAR	..	..	..	..	..	0.27	..	..	0.17	..	..	1.66	..	..	..	..
Zambia	ZMB	..	0.18	0.04	0.43	..	0.31	0.18	..	..	..	..	..	..	..	0.69	..
Zimbabwe	ZWE	0.24	0.70	0.00	3.85	..	0.12	0.03	0.00	0.03	0.04	0.00	0.03	0.02	..	0.01	..
Total Sub-Saharan Africa	SSA	0.15	0.07	0.07	0.12	0.29	0.08	0.22	0.00	0.04	0.07	0.01	0.12	0.89	0.05	0.24	0.01
European Community	EEC	0.85	0.11	0.03	0.00	0.02	0.01	0.15	0.01	0.01	0.01	0.00	0.06	0.12	0.02	0.77	0.00
North America	NNA	0.21	0.04	0.02	0.00	0.01	0.00	0.03	..	0.00	0.01	0.00	0.01	0.03	0.00	0.75	0.00
Rest of World	ROW	0.25	0.06	0.02	0.00	0.00	0.01	0.03	0.00	0.00	0.00	0.00	0.01	0.03	0.02	0.56	0.00
World	TOT	0.46	0.07	0.02	0.01	0.01	0.01	0.08	0.01	0.01	0.01	0.00	0.03	0.08	0.02	0.66	0.00

Note: ** *means "not applicable."*

(Table continues on the following page)

5–47. (continued)

Percentage of total exports

	ETH	GAB	GMB	GHA	GIN	GNB	KEN	LSO	LBR	LBY	MDG	MWI	MLI	MRT	MUS	MAR	MOZ	NAM	NER	NGA
DZA	..	..	..	..	..	..	..	..	..	..	..	..	..	..	..	..	..	..	..	..
ANG	..	..	..	..	..	..	..	..	..	..	..	..	..	..	..	..	..	..	..	0.00
BEN	..	..	..	0.00	..	..	..	..	0.00	..	..	..	0.15	..	..	..	..	..	2.13	0.12
BWA	..	..	..	..	..	..	..	..	..	..	..	..	..	..	..	..	..	..	..	..
HVO	..	..	..	..	..	..	..	..	..	..	..	..	0.95	..	0.01	..	..	..	1.73	1.16
BDI	..	..	..	..	..	..	1.78	..	..	..	..	..	..	..	..	..	..	..	..	..
CMR	..	2.44	..	0.00	0.09	..	0.03	..	..	..	..	..	0.00	..	..	0.13	..	..	0.00	1.83
CPV	..	..	..	..	..	..	..	..	..	..	..	..	..	..	..	..	..	..	..	..
CAF	..	..	..	..	..	..	..	..	..	..	..	..	..	..	..	..	..	..	..	0.36
TCD	..	..	..	..	..	..	..	..	..	..	..	..	..	..	..	..	..	..	..	2.91
COM	..	..	..	..	..	..	..	..	0.22	..	0.05	..	..	..	2.79	..	..	..	..	1.19
CGO	..	..	..	..	..	..	..	..	..	..	..	..	0.00	0.00	0.00	1.42	..	..	..	0.00
CIV	..	0.42	..	0.84	..	..	..	..	0.41	..	..	..	2.88	..	..	0.44	..	..	0.80	0.59
DJI	6.86	..	..	..	..	..	..	..	..	0.30	..	..	..	..	0.61	..	..	..	..	..
EGY	..	..	..	0.00	..	..	0.01	..	..	0.01	..	0.00	..	0.00	0.00	0.05	0.00	..	..	0.00
GNQ	..	..	..	..	..	..	..	..	0.01	..	..	..	1.00	..	..	..	..	..	..	1.26
ETH	**	..	..	..	..	..	0.14	..	..	..	..	..	..	..	..	..	..	..	..	0.00
GAB	..	**	..	..	0.00	..	..	..	..	..	..	..	0.00	0.01	0.00	2.05	..	..	..	0.02
GMB	..	..	**	2.04	12.31	0.43	..	..	0.07	..	..	..	1.67	0.08	..	..	..	..	..	0.03
GHA	..	..	0.00	**	..	..	..	..	0.01	..	..	..	..	..	..	..	..	..	0.00	0.03
GIN	..	..	..	..	**	0.01	..	..	0.07	..	..	..	0.40	..	..	..	..	..	..	..
GNB	..	..	0.31	..	0.21	**	..	..	..	..	..	..	..	..	..	..	..	..	..	17.15
KEN	0.37	..	..	..	..	..	**	..	..	..	..	..	..	..	..	0.47	0.55	..	..	0.01
LSO	..	..	..	..	..	..	..	**	..	..	..	..	..	..	..	..	..	..	..	..
LBR	..	..	0.00	0.05	0.12	..	..	..	**	0.00	..	..	0.00	0.01	..	0.00	..	..	..	2.02
LBY	..	..	0.00	..	..	..	..	..	..	**	..	..	..	..	..	0.00	..	..	..	..
MDG	..	..	..	..	..	..	0.00	..	..	..	**	..	..	..	..	0.43	..	..	..	..
MWI	..	..	..	..	..	..	0.03	..	..	..	..	**	..	..	..	..	1.52	..	..	..
MLI	..	0.20	..	..	0.06	..	..	..	0.25	..	..	..	**	0.06	..	3.88	..	..	0.17	0.35
MRT	..	..	..	0.11	..	..	..	..	0.23	..	..	..	..	**	..	..	..	..	..	..
MUS	0.00	..	..	0.01	0.00	..	0.07	..	..	..	0.12	0.02	0.00	..	**	..	..	..	..	0.01
MAR	..	0.23	..	..	0.26	..	..	..	..	1.66	..	..	0.00	0.01	0.02	**	..	..	..	0.01
MOZ	..	0.05	..	..	..	0.10	0.14	..	0.00	..	..	0.21	..	..	..	..	**	..	..	..
NAM	..	..	..	..	..	..	..	..	..	..	..	..	..	..	..	..	..	**	..	..
NER	..	..	..	0.21	..	..	..	..	..	0.02	..	..	0.35	..	..	..	..	..	**	13.69
NGA	..	0.00	..	1.46	0.00	0.00	0.00	0.00	0.00	..	..	..	0.00	..	..	..	..	..	0.02	**
RWA	..	..	..	..	..	..	2.28	..	..	0.00	..	..	..	..	..	..	..	..	..	..
STP	..	..	..	..	..	..	..	..	0.00	..	..	..	..	..	..	..	..	..	..	..
SEN	..	0.30	0.93	0.02	0.69	0.33	0.01	..	0.04	..	0.00	..	7.28	3.77	..	0.05	..	..	0.47	1.73
SYC	..	..	..	..	..	..	..	..	..	..	..	..	..	..	0.36	..	..	..	..	..
SLE	..	..	0.09	0.01	0.02	..	..	..	1.48	..	..	..	..	..	..	..	..	..	..	0.04
SOM	..	..	..	0.00	..	..	0.10	..	..	0.39	..	..	..	..	..	..	..	..	..	..
ZAF	..	..	..	..	..	..	..	..	..	..	..	..	..	..	..	..	..	..	..	..
SDN	0.02	..	..	..	..	..	..	..	..	..	..	0.00	0.00	..	..	..	..	..	..	0.02
SWZ	..	..	..	..	..	..	..	..	..	..	..	..	..	..	..	..	..	..	..	..
TZA	0.07	..	..	..	..	..	0.35	0.00	..	..	0.01	0.15	..	..	0.08	..	0.75	..	..	0.04
TGO	..	0.08	..	0.32	0.07	..	..	..	0.03	0.00	..	..	0.51	0.00	..	2.03	..	..	1.33	0.91
TUN	..	0.03	..	0.00	0.08	0.03	0.01	..	0.12	0.90	0.00	..	0.00	..	..	0.30	0.01	..	0.01	0.00
UGA	0.01	..	..	..	..	..	0.30	..	..	1.41	..	..	0.08	..	..	..	..	..	..	..
ZAR	..	0.12	..	..	..	..	0.05	..	..	..	..	..	..	..	..	..	..	..	..	..
ZMB	0.03	..	..	..	..	..	0.59	0.31	..	..	..	0.63	..	..	..	..	0.02	0.00	..	..
ZWE	0.38	0.09	..	0.08	0.00	..	0.34	0.03	..	0.01	0.02	1.30	..	..	0.17	0.10	1.33	0.08	..	0.06
SSA	0.03	0.14	0.02	0.68	0.03	0.01	0.05	0.01	0.05	0.02	0.00	0.05	0.40	0.06	0.03	0.25	0.07	0.00	0.11	0.29
EEC	0.07	0.09	0.01	0.05	0.03	0.01	0.08	0.00	0.08	0.43	0.03	0.01	0.03	0.03	0.02	0.32	0.02	0.00	0.03	0.52
NNA	0.08	0.03	0.00	0.02	0.02	..	0.03	0.00	0.04	0.12	0.01	0.00	0.01	0.01	0.00	0.13	0.02	0.01	0.00	0.23
ROW	0.05	0.01	0.00	0.02	0.01	0.00	0.10	0.00	0.18	0.22	0.02	0.00	0.01	0.01	0.03	0.12	0.02	0.00	0.00	0.28
TOT	0.06	0.05	0.01	0.04	0.02	0.00	0.08	0.00	0.11	0.27	0.02	0.01	0.02	0.02	0.02	0.19	0.02	0.00	0.01	0.36

Note: ** means "not applicable."

(Table continues on the following page)

5-47. (continued)

Percentage of total exports

	RWA	STP	SEN	SYC	SLE	SOM	ZAF	SDN	SWZ	TZA	TGO	TUN	UGA	ZAR	ZMB	ZWE	SSA	EEC	NNA	ROW	TOT
DZA	..	..	..	..	..	..	..	..	..	..	..	0.96	..	..	..	..	..	73.98	11.98	14.04	100
ANG	..	..	..	..	..	..	..	..	..	..	..	..	..	..	0.00	..	0.05	34.14	45.74	20.07	100
BEN	0.01	..	0.03	..	..	..	..	0.00	..	..	0.64	0.00	..	..	..	..	3.63	92.73	0.12	3.53	100
BWA	..	..	..	..	..	..	..	..	..	..	..	..	..	..	..	..	..	..	..	..	..
HVO	..	..	0.00	..	..	..	..	..	..	..	1.26	0.57	..	..	..	..	8.03	57.51	1.23	33.23	100
BDI	3.21	..	..	..	..	..	..	0.55	..	0.97	..	..	0.47	2.05	0.00	0.21	9.52	41.64	5.94	42.89	100
CMR	..	..	0.01	..	..	..	..	..	..	..	0.52	0.07	..	0.01	..	..	10.19	75.12	8.37	6.32	100
CPV	..	..	..	..	..	..	..	..	..	..	..	..	..	..	..	..	32.65	26.53	..	40.82	100
CAF	0.00	..	..	..	..	..	..	1.24	..	..	..	..	..	1.68	..	..	3.56	90.85	0.01	5.58	100
TCD	..	..	..	..	..	..	..	0.13	..	..	0.03	..	..	..	..	..	8.10	88.16	0.80	2.94	100
COM	..	..	..	..	..	..	..	..	..	..	..	1.45	..	..	..	..	4.25	54.28	39.29	2.18	100
CGO	..	..	0.00	..	..	..	0.01	..	0.03	0.02	0.00	0.19	..	0.36	..	..	1.67	34.54	60.04	3.75	100
CIV	..	..	1.57	..	..	..	..	..	..	..	..	0.81	..	..	..	..	12.26	60.76	12.05	14.93	100
DJI	..	..	..	9.67	..	15.51	..	..	..	..	..	0.85	..	..	..	..	35.96	7.62	0.77	55.65	100
EGY	..	..	0.00	..	..	0.00	0.00	..	..	..	..	0.14	0.00	..	..	..	0.03	43.90	0.96	55.11	100
GNQ	..	..	..	..	..	..	..	..	..	..	..	..	..	..	..	..	2.54	96.09	..	1.37	100
ETH	..	..	..	..	..	..	1.81	..	..	0.04	..	..	0.07	..	..	..	5.67	48.88	10.53	34.92	100
GAB	..	0.00	0.62	..	..	..	..	..	..	..	0.01	0.01	..	..	..	0.00	2.33	48.78	25.04	23.85	100
GMB	..	..	0.15	..	0.01	0.00	..	..	..	..	..	..	..	0.00	..	0.00	16.78	43.13	0.67	39.42	100
GHA	..	..	..	..	0.02	..	..	..	..	..	5.67	..	..	0.00	..	..	5.87	51.33	11.18	31.62	100
GIN	..	..	0.01	..	0.02	..	..	..	..	..	0.05	..	..	..	..	..	6.87	57.42	28.29	7.42	100
GNB	..	0.00	0.04	..	..	..	..	..	..	..	..	..	..	..	..	..	17.72	61.37	..	20.91	100
KEN	3.43	..	..	..	..	0.38	0.16	2.70	..	1.25	..	..	8.70	0.99	0.11	..	21.39	45.19	5.76	27.66	100
LSO	..	..	..	..	..	..	..	..	..	..	..	..	..	..	..	..	..	..	..	..	..
LBR	..	..	0.01	..	0.23	..	..	..	..	..	0.10	..	..	..	..	..	2.60	70.23	21.82	5.35	100
LBY	..	..	..	..	..	..	..	0.00	..	..	..	0.02	..	..	..	..	0.01	52.73	28.05	19.22	100
MDG	..	..	..	..	..	..	..	..	..	..	..	..	..	..	..	..	0.49	56.76	13.97	28.78	100
MWI	..	..	..	..	..	..	6.85	..	..	0.15	..	..	..	..	6.90	2.55	11.60	59.84	11.18	17.38	100
MLI	..	..	0.90	..	..	..	..	..	..	..	..	0.99	..	..	..	..	5.45	58.14	0.10	36.31	100
MRT	..	..	0.18	..	..	..	..	..	..	..	..	..	..	..	..	..	3.69	41.99	0.00	54.32	100
MUS	..	..	0.00	0.19	..	0.00	0.33	..	..	0.17	..	0.00	..	0.04	0.00	0.00	0.87	77.77	16.22	5.14	100
MAR	..	..	0.36	..	..	..	..	0.00	..	..	0.10	0.92	..	0.12	..	..	2.17	58.78	3.06	35.99	100
MOZ	..	..	0.14	..	..	..	..	..	..	0.54	..	0.02	..	..	..	0.11	1.45	23.52	12.76	62.27	100
NAM	..	..	..	..	..	..	..	..	..	..	..	..	..	..	..	..	..	..	..	..	..
NER	..	..	0.05	..	..	..	..	..	..	..	0.20	..	..	..	..	..	17.04	72.90	0.13	9.93	100
NGA	..	..	0.11	..	0.26	..	..	0.00	..	..	0.00	..	..	0.00	0.00	..	3.37	64.54	19.58	12.52	100
RWA	**	..	..	..	..	..	..	..	..	0.08	..	..	0.10	0.13	..	..	3.02	92.07	2.87	2.05	100
STP	..	**	..	..	..	..	..	..	..	..	..	..	..	..	..	..	0.00	62.93	..	37.07	100
SEN	0.00	..	**	..	0.32	..	0.01	..	0.00	..	0.74	0.58	..	0.24	..	..	26.62	40.82	0.32	32.24	100
SYC	..	..	..	**	..	..	..	..	..	..	..	..	..	..	..	..	0.36	3.61	2.53	93.50	100
SLE	..	..	0.05	..	**	..	..	0.00	..	..	..	..	..	0.00	..	..	1.84	53.71	12.38	32.07	100
SOM	..	..	..	..	..	**	..	..	0.10	..	..	..	..	..	..	..	0.45	10.36	0.06	89.13	100
ZAF	..	..	..	..	..	..	**	..	..	..	..	..	..	..	..	..	..	21.33	8.97	69.70	100
SDN	..	..	..	..	..	..	..	**	..	0.01	0.00	0.25	..	..	..	..	0.05	24.93	1.70	73.32	100
SWZ	..	..	..	..	..	..	..	..	**	..	..	..	..	..	..	..	..	..	..	..	..
TZA	0.45	..	..	..	..	0.16	..	0.68	0.01	**	..	..	0.64	0.14	0.30	0.05	4.74	57.65	2.89	34.73	100
TGO	0.00	..	0.00	..	..	..	..	..	..	..	**	1.62	..	0.01	..	..	5.58	52.72	7.33	34.37	100
TUN	..	..	0.02	..	0.00	..	..	0.00	..	..	0.00	**	..	..	..	..	0.45	68.23	10.96	20.36	100
UGA	0.07	..	..	..	..	..	0.01	..	..	0.65	..	0.05	**	..	0.00	0.00	1.11	53.67	28.66	16.56	100
ZAR	..	..	..	..	..	..	0.03	..	..	..	..	..	..	**	0.02	..	2.29	82.60	3.43	11.68	100
ZMB	0.04	..	..	..	..	..	1.07	..	0.00	1.03	..	..	0.02	0.57	**	2.60	6.97	36.65	2.97	53.41	100
ZWE	0.10	..	0.01	0.02	0.00	0.00	10.81	0.21	0.06	0.51	..	0.02	0.05	1.46	3.90	**	15.03	40.88	8.47	35.62	100
SSA	0.12	0.00	0.24	0.01	0.11	0.02	0.40	0.12	0.00	0.09	0.20	0.04	0.27	0.11	0.17	0.06	5.59	57.46	18.68	18.27	100
EEC	0.01	0.00	0.07	0.01	0.01	0.02	0.66	0.08	0.00	0.05	0.03	0.27	0.02	0.10	0.03	0.04	2.15	54.36	11.55	31.93	100
NNA	0.00	..	0.02	0.00	0.00	0.02	0.40	0.08	0.00	0.02	0.01	0.10	0.00	0.04	0.02	0.02	0.89	17.81	43.92	37.38	100
ROW	0.01	0.00	0.02	0.00	0.00	0.01	0.27	0.08	0.00	0.06	0.02	0.06	0.01	0.04	0.02	0.02	1.19	25.67	23.62	49.52	100
TOT	0.01	0.00	0.04	0.00	0.01	0.02	0.43	0.08	0.00	0.05	0.02	0.14	0.01	0.06	0.03	0.02	1.56	35.11	22.86	40.47	100

Note: ** means "not applicable."

5-48. Direction of trade matrix, exports, 1990

		Importers								Percentage of total exports							
Exporters		DZA	ANG	BEN	BWA	HVO	BDI	CMR	CPV	CAF	TCD	COM	CGO	CIV	DJI	EGY	GNQ
Algeria	DZA	**	..	..	..	..	..	0.00	..	..	..	..	0.00	..	..	0.03	..
Angola	ANG	..	**	..	..	..	..	0.00	0.03	..	..	..	0.01	..	..	..	..
Benin	BEN	..	..	**	..	0.06	..	0.11	..	0.07	..	..	..	0.92	..	0.00	..
Botswana	BWA	..	..	..	**	..	..	..	..	..	..	..	..	..	..	..	..
Burkina Faso	HVO	..	..	0.28	..	**	..	0.01	..	..	..	..	0.01	2.09	..	..	..
Burundi	BDI	..	..	..	..	..	**	..	..	..	..	..	..	..	..	..	..
Cameroon	CMR	0.04	0.28	0.15	..	0.00	..	**	..	1.79	0.53	..	0.34	1.34	..	..	3.12
Cape Verde	CPV	30.93	19.86	..	..	..	..	..	**	0.19	..	..	..	..	..	..	..
Central African Republic	CAF	..	..	..	..	..	..	0.10	..	**	0.32	..	..	0.00	..	0.01	..
Chad	TCD	..	..	..	..	..	..	1.92	..	0.03	**	..	..	..	..	..	..
Comoros	COM	..	..	..	..	..	..	..	..	..	..	**	..	..	..	0.13	..
Congo, People's Republic of the	CGO	0.38	0.37	0.01	..	..	..	..	..	..	..	..	**	0.20	..	..	..
Cote d'Ivoire	CIV	0.13	..	0.72	..	4.23	..	0.22	0.06	..	..	..	0.01	**	..	0.06	..
Djibouti	DJI	..	..	..	..	..	1.20	0.59	..	..	..	..	0.03	..	**	..	..
Egypt, Arab Republic of	EGY	0.15	..	0.00	..	..	0.00	0.00	..	..	0.01	..	..	0.03	0.01	**	0.00
Equatorial Guinea	GNQ	..	..	..	..	..	..	0.21	..	..	..	..	..	..	..	..	**
Ethiopia	ETH	..	..	..	..	..	..	..	..	..	..	..	..	..	4.06	0.31	..
Gabon	GAB	0.32	..	0.00	..	..	..	0.22	..	..	..	..	..	2.02	..	..	..
Gambia, The	GMB	0.00	..	..	..	..	..	..	..	..	..	..	..	..	..	..	..
Ghana	GHA	..	0.01	0.08	..	0.01	..	..	..	..	..	..	0.01	0.09	..	0.07	..
Guinea	GIN	..	..	..	..	..	..	8.09	..	0.00	..	..	0.00	..	..	..	..
Guinea-Bissau	GNB	..	0.02	..	..	..	..	..	..	..	..	..	..	..	..	0.41	..
Kenya	KEN	..	..	..	..	..	1.78	..	..	..	..	0.23	..	..	0.24	2.26	..
Lesotho	LSO	..	..	..	..	..	..	..	..	..	..	..	..	..	..	..	..
Liberia	LBR	..	..	0.00	..	..	..	0.01	..	..	0.00	..	0.08	..	..	0.04	..
Libya	LBY	..	0.00	..	..	0.00	..	..	..	0.00	0.01	..	..	..	..	0.01	..
Madagascar	MDG	0.00	..	0.00	..	..	0.01	0.00	..	..	..	0.57	..	0.00	0.00	0.00	0.00
Malawi	MWI	..	..	..	1.17	..	..	..	..	..	..	..	..	..	..	..	..
Mali	MLI	10.18	..	..	..	1.79	..	0.01	..	..	..	..	0.00	4.34	..	..	..
Mauritania	MRT	0.00	0.00	0.03	..	0.00	0.00	1.10	0.01	0.01	0.02	..	0.02	6.92	..	0.01	..
Mauritius	MUS	0.00	0.00	..	0.03	0.00	0.00	0.00	..	..	..	0.14	0.00	0.00	0.00	0.00	..
Morocco	MAR	0.81	0.17	0.03	..	0.01	..	0.14	..	0.02	0.00	0.01	0.09	0.25	0.00	0.02	0.01
Mozambique	MOZ	..	0.03	..	..	..	..	0.01	..	..	..	..	0.04	..	..	0.09	..
Namibia	NAM	..	..	..	..	..	..	..	..	..	..	..	..	..	..	..	..
Niger	NER	..	..	0.51	..	0.77	..	..	..	..	..	..	0.01	1.14	..	0.08	..
Nigeria	NGA	0.00	0.01	0.01	..	0.00	..	0.13	..	..	0.00	0.00	..	1.17	..	0.00	..
Rwanda	RWA	..	..	..	0.01	0.00	0.06	0.00	..	..	0.00	..	0.00	..	0.01	0.00	..
Sao Tome & Principe	STP	..	..	..	..	..	..	..	..	..	..	..	..	..	..	..	..
Senegal	SEN	0.03	0.01	0.69	..	0.53	..	2.13	0.01	0.03	0.12	..	0.56	3.58	..	0.07	0.00
Seychelles	SYC	..	0.00	..	..	..	..	..	..	..	..	..	..	..	..	0.04	..
Sierra Leone	SLE	..	..	0.00	..	..	..	..	..	..	0.00	..	..	0.37	..	..	..
Somalia	SOM	..	..	..	..	..	..	..	..	..	0.00	..	..	..	0.78	0.04	..
South Africa	ZAF	..	..	..	..	..	..	..	..	..	0.00	..	..	0.00	..	..	..
Sudan	SDN	..	..	..	..	..	..	..	..	0.01	..	..	..	..	..	..	..
Swaziland	SWZ	..	..	..	..	..	..	..	..	..	..	..	..	..	..	..	..
Tanzania	TZA	0.10	..	..	0.01	..	0.70	..	..	..	..	..	..	0.07	..	0.23	..
Togo	TGO	..	..	0.69	..	1.32	..	0.02	..	0.07	0.09	..	0.21	0.26	..	..	..
Tunisia	TUN	2.35	..	0.02	..	0.01	..	0.28	..	..	..	..	0.02	0.22	0.02	0.10	..
Uganda	UGA	..	..	..	..	..	..	..	..	..	..	..	..	..	..	0.19	..
Zaire	ZAR	..	..	..	..	..	0.26	..	..	0.16	..	..	1.49	..	..	..	..
Zambia	ZMB	..	0.19	0.05	0.47	..	0.33	0.16	..	..	..	..	0.17	..	..	..	..
Zimbabwe	ZWE	0.21	0.27	0.00	6.34	..	0.35	0.30	..	0.00	..	0.00	..	0.02	0.00	1.43	..
Total Sub-Saharan Africa	SSA	0.12	0.05	0.10	0.24	0.39	0.09	0.26	0.01	0.10	0.03	0.02	0.09	0.74	0.04	0.13	0.17
European Community	EEC	0.45	0.08	0.01	0.01	0.02	0.01	0.07	0.01	0.01	0.01	0.00	0.03	0.08	0.01	0.37	0.00
North America	NNA	0.22	0.03	0.00	0.00	0.00	0.00	0.01	0.00	0.00	0.00	0.00	0.02	0.02	0.00	0.42	0.00
Rest of World	ROW	0.14	0.02	0.01	0.01	0.00	0.00	0.01	0.00	0.00	0.00	0.00	0.01	0.02	0.01	0.29	0.00
TOTAL IMPORTS	TOT	0.28	0.05	0.01	0.01	0.01	0.01	0.04	0.00	0.00	0.00	0.00	0.02	0.05	0.01	0.34	0.00

Note: ** means "not applicable."

(Table continues on the following page)

5-48. (continued)

Percentage of total exports

	ETH	GAB	GMB	GHA	GIN	GNB	KEN	LSO	LBR	LBY	MDG	MWI	MLI	MRT	MUS	MAR	MOZ	NAM	NER	NGA
DZA	..	..	..	..	..	..	..	..	..	..	0.00	..	..	0.14	..	0.24	..	..	..	..
ANG	..	..	..	0.00	..	..	..	..	..	..	..	..	..	..	..	..	..	..	..	0.00
BEN	..	..	..	0.02	..	..	..	..	0.01	..	..	..	0.02	0.00	..	4.24	..	..	6.99	3.83
BWA	..	..	..	..	..	..	..	..	..	..	..	..	..	..	..	..	..	..	..	..
HVO	..	..	..	3.71	..	..	..	..	..	..	..	..	0.67	..	0.12	0.59	..	..	1.29	2.31
BDI	..	..	..	..	..	..	..	..	..	..	..	..	..	..	0.00	0.00	..	..	..	..
CMR	..	1.97	..	0.01	0.08	..	..	..	0.26	0.04	..	..	0.00	0.00	0.00	0.08	0.13	..	0.01	0.82
CPV	..	..	..	..	..	0.35	..	..	0.09	..	..	..	..	..	..	..	..	..	..	..
CAF	..	..	..	..	..	0.00	..	..	0.00	..	..	..	..	..	0.34	0.90	..	..	..	..
TCD	..	..	..	..	..	..	..	..	0.00	..	..	..	..	..	..	2.81	..	..	..	2.84
COM	..	..	..	..	..	..	..	..	0.23	..	0.08	..	..	..	0.14	..	..	..	..	..
CGO	0.02	..	..	0.03	0.01	..	..	..	..	..	..	..	0.00	0.01	0.00	0.50	..	..	..	0.01
CIV	..	0.46	..	0.70	..	..	..	..	0.66	..	0.04	..	4.21	0.02	0.64	0.48	..	..	1.17	0.41
DJI	3.80	..	..	..	..	..	..	..	..	0.17	..	..	..	..	..	..	..	..	..	0.01
EGY	0.08	..	0.00	..	0.00	..	0.00	..	0.00	0.15	..	0.00	..	0.00	0.02	0.12	0.00	..	0.00	0.01
GNQ	..	..	..	..	..	..	..	..	0.01	..	..	..	..	..	..	..	..	..	..	..
ETH	**	..	..	..	..	..	0.84	..	..	..	..	..	0.00	..	0.00	0.00	..	..	..	0.00
GAB	..	**	..	..	0.00	..	..	..	..	..	..	..	0.01	..	..	0.71	..	..	..	0.01
GMB	0.00	..	**	0.23	3.97	0.14	..	..	0.02	..	..	..	0.01	..	0.00	0.12	..	..	0.00	0.09
GHA	0.00	..	0.01	**	0.00	..	..	..	0.01	0.01	..	..	0.01	..	0.00	0.12	..	..	..	0.09
GIN	..	..	..	..	**	0.02	..	..	0.08	..	..	..	2.26	0.00	0.00	0.03	..	..	..	1.36
GNB	..	0.71	..	..	0.47	**	..	..	..	..	..	..	..	..	1.32	..	..	0.51	..	0.01
KEN	0.34	..	..	..	..	..	**	..	..	..	..	..	..	..	..	..	..	..	..	..
LSO	..	..	..	..	..	..	..	**	..	..	..	..	..	..	..	..	..	..	..	..
LBR	..	..	0.00	0.01	0.04	0.00	..	..	**	0.00	..	..	0.00	0.00	0.00	0.05	..	..	..	0.37
LBY	0.02	0.00	0.00	0.00	0.00	..	..	..	0.00	**	..	..	..	0.00	..	0.09	0.00	..	..	0.00
MDG	0.00	0.00	..	..	0.01	..	0.18	0.00	..	..	**	..	0.02	0.12	1.73	0.16	1.42	0.00	0.00	..
MWI	..	..	..	..	..	..	0.02	..	..	..	..	**	..	..	0.04	..	4.58	..	..	..
MLI	..	0.00	..	..	..	..	..	..	0.72	..	..	..	**	0.02	..	5.71	..	..	0.06	0.10
MRT	..	0.00	0.00	0.09	0.01	..	..	..	1.10	0.00	..	..	0.02	**	..	0.04	..	..	..	..
MUS	0.00	0.00	..	0.00	0.00	..	0.10	..	..	..	0.75	0.01	0.00	0.00	**	0.00	0.00	..	..	0.00
MAR	..	0.18	0.00	0.03	0.13	..	0.00	..	0.01	2.30	0.01	..	0.11	0.09	0.03	**	0.00	..	0.02	0.32
MOZ	..	0.01	..	0.00	..	0.04	0.04	..	0.00	..	0.21	0.30	..	..	0.01	0.15	**	..	..	0.00
NAM	..	..	..	..	..	..	..	..	..	..	..	..	..	..	..	..	..	**	..	..
NER	..	..	..	0.00	..	..	..	..	..	0.01	..	..	0.84	0.02	..	..	..	..	**	5.62
NGA	0.00	0.00	0.00	1.05	0.00	0.00	..	0.06	0.02	..	..	..	..	0.00	0.00	0.02	0.00	..	0.05	**
RWA	0.00	0.00	..	0.01	..	..	56.38	..	0.00	0.01	0.00	..	0.00	0.00	0.00	0.00	..	..	..	..
STP	..	..	..	..	..	..	..	..	0.00	..	..	..	..	..	0.00	..	..	..	..	..
SEN	0.00	0.28	0.80	0.01	1.19	0.77	..	..	0.17	0.00	0.00	..	4.54	0.31	0.00	0.06	..	..	0.10	0.31
SYC	..	..	..	..	..	..	..	..	..	..	..	..	..	..	0.09	..	..	..	..	..
SLE	..	..	0.08	..	0.02	..	..	..	0.85	..	..	..	..	..	..	..	..	..	0.00	0.01
SOM	..	..	..	0.00	0.22	..	..	..	0.02	..	..	..	..	..	0.00	0.28	..	..	..	..
ZAF	..	..	..	..	..	..	..	..	..	..	..	..	..	..	..	..	..	..	..	..
SDN	0.04	..	..	0.00	..	..	..	..	..	..	..	..	0.00	..	0.03	0.00	..	..	..	..
SWZ	..	..	..	..	..	..	..	..	..	..	..	..	..	..	..	..	..	..	..	..
TZA	0.02	..	0.00	..	..	..	1.39	0.00	..	..	0.00	0.10	0.00	..	0.10	0.85	..	0.43	..	0.03
TGO	..	0.07	..	16.50	0.09	..	..	..	0.06	0.00	..	..	0.62	0.00	..	1.25	..	..	1.68	0.55
TUN	..	0.00	..	0.25	0.01	0.02	..	..	0.00	4.63	..	..	..	0.06	..	0.68	..	..	0.00	0.01
UGA	0.01	..	..	0.00	..	..	1.02	..	..	3.56	..	..	0.00	..	0.00	0.33	..	..	..	..
ZAR	..	0.11	..	..	0.00	..	0.05	..	..	..	..	..	..	..	0.01	..	..	..	..	0.01
ZMB	0.02	..	..	..	..	..	0.26	0.35	..	..	..	0.59	..	..	0.00	..	3.76	0.04	0.02	0.02
ZWE	0.19	..	..	0.16	..	..	..	0.14	0.00	0.17	..	1.79	..	..	0.16	0.27	..	..	..	..
SSA	0.02	0.15	0.01	0.52	0.04	0.01	0.24	0.03	0.10	0.02	0.03	0.08	0.48	0.01	0.12	0.20	0.20	0.00	0.15	0.17
EEC	0.04	0.04	0.01	0.05	0.02	0.00	0.07	0.00	0.09	0.24	0.02	0.01	0.02	0.02	0.04	0.32	0.02	0.01	0.01	0.23
NNA	0.03	0.01	0.00	0.03	0.01	0.00	0.03	0.00	0.01	0.01	0.00	0.00	0.00	0.00	0.00	0.12	0.01	0.01	0.00	0.10
ROW	0.03	0.01	0.00	0.02	0.01	0.00	0.08	0.00	0.20	0.13	0.01	0.00	0.01	0.01	0.05	0.11	0.02	0.00	0.00	0.14
TOT	0.03	0.02	0.01	0.04	0.01	0.00	0.07	0.00	0.12	0.16	0.02	0.01	0.02	0.01	0.04	0.20	0.02	0.01	0.01	0.17

Note: ** means "not applicable"

(Table continues on the following page)

5-48. (continued)

Percentage of total exports

	RWA	STP	SEN	SYC	SLE	SOM	ZAF	SDN	SWZ	TZA	TGO	TUN	UGA	ZAR	ZMB	ZWE	SSA	EEC	NNA	ROW	TOT
DZA	0.00	..	0.00	..	..	..	..	..	..	0.00	..	0.69	..	..	0.00	0.00	0.15	63.25	21.43	15.17	100
ANG	..	..	0.63	0.00	..	..	..	..	..	..	..	..	..	..	0.00	..	0.67	35.46	52.97	10.90	100
BEN	0.00	..	0.16	..	0.00	..	..	0.00	..	..	1.53	0.03	..	..	..	..	13.72	41.42	22.72	22.14	100
BWA	..	..	..	..	..	..	..	..	..	..	..	..	..	..	..	..	..	..	..	..	..
HVO	0.03	..	0.00	..	..	..	..	..	..	..	0.69	4.99	..	..	..	..	11.22	51.99	0.77	36.02	100
BDI	2.57	..	..	..	..	..	..	..	..	..	..	..	..	..	..	..	2.57	82.31	4.13	10.99	100
CMR	0.00	..	1.11	..	..	..	..	..	..	..	0.11	0.14	..	..	0.00	..	12.04	68.65	7.10	12.21	100
CPV	0.02	..	0.05	..	..	..	..	..	..	..	..	10.58	..	..	..	..	20.56	30.08	2.95	46.41	100
CAF	0.06	..	0.00	..	..	..	..	0.48	..	..	..	0.51	..	..	..	..	1.30	84.99	1.91	11.80	100
TCD	..	..	..	..	..	..	..	0.12	..	..	0.02	..	..	..	..	..	4.93	67.52	2.05	25.50	100
COM	..	..	0.00	..	..	..	..	..	..	..	..	..	..	..	..	..	0.45	75.23	19.35	4.97	100
CGO	..	..	0.02	..	..	..	0.00	..	..	..	0.04	0.03	..	0.15	..	0.01	0.87	57.76	37.12	4.25	100
CIV	0.00	..	2.01	..	0.02	..	..	..	..	0.00	1.19	0.33	..	..	..	0.00	16.76	52.85	6.33	24.06	100
DJI	1.22	..	..	..	..	43.71	..	..	..	..	..	..	..	..	..	..	50.55	8.84	0.00	40.60	100
EGY	..	..	0.00	..	0.00	0.00	0.00	..	..	0.00	..	0.55	0.01	0.00	..	0.04	0.22	50.56	6.84	42.39	100
GNQ	0.01	..	..	..	..	..	..	..	..	..	..	..	..	..	..	..	0.24	93.45	0.22	6.10	100
ETH	0.00	..	..	..	..	..	0.00	2.04	..	0.04	..	0.01	0.08	..	..	..	7.06	45.56	9.14	38.24	100
GAB	0.00	0.00	0.91	..	..	..	..	..	..	..	0.01	0.06	..	..	..	0.00	3.18	48.47	31.52	16.82	100
GMB	..	..	0.01	..	0.00	..	..	..	..	..	..	0.00	..	0.00	..	..	4.37	53.39	0.10	42.13	100
GHA	0.00	..	0.09	..	..	..	..	0.00	..	0.00	3.32	0.02	..	..	..	0.00	3.72	57.31	12.28	26.69	100
GIN	..	..	0.02	..	0.01	..	..	..	..	..	0.05	0.00	..	..	..	0.03	10.57	54.63	23.58	11.22	100
GNB	..	0.00	0.61	..	..	..	..	..	..	..	..	0.51	..	..	..	..	3.17	81.22	1.26	14.36	100
KEN	3.18	..	..	..	..	0.36	0.14	2.51	..	1.16	..	0.04	8.07	0.92	0.10	..	20.73	45.42	5.74	28.10	100
LSO	..	..	..	..	..	..	..	..	..	..	..	..	..	..	..	..	..	..	..	..	..
LBR	..	..	0.01	..	0.03	..	..	..	..	..	0.03	0.01	..	..	..	..	0.59	44.17	3.43	51.82	100
LBY	..	..	0.00	..	..	..	..	0.00	..	0.00	..	0.26	..	..	..	..	0.03	85.52	0.00	14.44	100
MDG	..	..	0.00	0.04	..	0.25	..	0.00	0.00	0.38	0.00	0.02	..	0.01	..	..	4.76	51.02	26.64	17.58	100
MWI	..	..	..	..	..	..	8.51	..	..	0.24	..	..	..	..	2.90	2.35	11.30	47.60	11.07	30.04	100
MLI	0.00	..	0.24	..	..	..	..	..	..	..	0.27	1.48	..	..	..	..	7.54	33.47	5.94	53.05	100
MRT	..	..	0.11	..	0.01	..	..	..	..	..	0.30	0.08	..	0.01	..	..	9.77	50.87	4.46	34.90	100
MUS	0.00	..	..	0.28	..	0.00	0.54	0.00	0.02	0.01	0.00	0.02	0.00	0.01	0.03	0.26	1.66	78.79	13.18	6.37	100
MAR	..	..	0.17	..	0.01	..	..	0.01	..	0.04	0.06	1.29	..	0.94	..	..	2.90	67.52	3.91	25.67	100
MOZ	0.03	..	..	..	..	0.09	1.19	..	..	0.54	0.00	0.00	..	..	..	0.06	1.41	17.65	8.31	72.63	100
NAM	..	..	..	..	..	..	..	..	..	..	..	..	..	..	..	..	..	..	..	..	..
NER	..	..	0.34	..	..	..	..	..	..	..	0.31	..	..	..	0.00	..	9.57	71.69	16.62	2.12	100
NGA	..	..	0.35	..	0.43	..	..	..	..	0.00	0.00	..	..	..	..	0.00	3.30	39.12	49.85	7.73	100
RWA	**	..	0.00	..	..	0.00	..	..	0.01	0.02	0.00	0.00	0.12	1.15	0.02	..	57.81	26.95	8.26	6.99	100
STP	..	**	..	..	..	..	..	..	..	..	..	..	..	..	..	..	0.00	98.66	..	1.34	100
SEN	0.00	..	**	..	0.09	0.00	..	..	0.00	..	0.30	1.10	0.00	..	0.00	0.00	16.53	60.22	1.48	21.76	100
SYC	..	..	..	**	..	..	..	..	..	0.00	..	..	..	..	..	..	0.09	52.70	0.59	46.61	100
SLE	..	..	0.10	..	**	..	..	0.00	..	..	..	..	..	0.00	..	..	1.43	53.93	15.61	29.03	100
SOM	0.03	..	..	..	..	**	..	0.00	..	0.05	..	0.03	0.08	..	..	..	1.18	39.08	..	59.73	100
ZAF	..	0.00	..	..	..	..	**	..	..	..	..	0.00	..	..	..	..	0.28	24.91	8.04	66.78	100
SDN	0.00	..	..	..	..	0.02	..	**	..	0.01	0.00	0.59	..	..	..	..	0.11	36.05	2.66	61.17	100
SWZ	..	..	..	..	..	..	..	..	**	..	..	..	..	..	..	..	..	..	..	..	..
TZA	0.33	..	..	..	..	0.10	..	0.40	0.01	**	..	0.78	0.37	0.98	0.17	0.03	5.22	49.91	3.53	41.34	100
TGO	0.00	..	0.01	..	..	..	..	..	..	0.00	**	0.43	..	..	0.00	..	22.21	32.30	11.51	33.98	100
TUN	0.00	..	0.04	..	0.00	..	..	0.03	..	0.00	0.05	**	..	..	0.04	0.00	1.09	77.17	1.04	20.71	100
UGA	0.10	..	..	..	..	0.00	..	0.05	..	0.88	..	0.02	**	..	0.00	..	2.07	73.64	10.46	13.83	100
ZAR	..	..	..	..	..	..	0.03	..	..	..	..	0.03	..	**	0.02	..	2.10	76.23	13.24	8.43	100
ZMB	0.00	..	..	0.00	..	..	..	..	0.00	0.66	..	2.34	0.02	0.43	**	2.86	6.60	30.85	1.92	60.62	100
ZWE	0.10	..	0.00	0.01	0.00	0.26	..	0.06	0.22	0.18	0.23	0.13	0.06	0.93	5.51	**	21.13	39.87	9.95	29.05	100
SSA	0.10	0.00	0.45	0.01	0.14	0.07	0.10	0.09	0.01	0.08	0.25	0.19	0.22	0.09	0.22	0.12	6.53	47.12	26.80	19.55	100
EEC	0.01	0.00	0.06	0.00	0.01	0.01	0.52	0.03	0.00	0.04	0.02	0.28	0.01	0.06	0.03	0.03	1.37	60.58	8.27	29.79	100
NNA	0.00	0.00	0.01	0.00	0.01	0.01	0.33	0.01	0.00	0.01	0.01	0.04	0.01	0.03	0.02	0.03	0.48	20.03	41.46	38.03	100
ROW	0.00	0.00	0.01	0.00	0.00	0.01	0.21	0.04	0.00	0.03	0.02	0.08	0.01	0.05	0.01	0.02	0.92	28.86	21.77	48.45	100
TOT	0.01	0.00	0.04	0.00	0.01	0.01	0.36	0.03	0.00	0.03	0.02	0.15	0.01	0.05	0.02	0.03	1.10	40.62	19.57	38.71	100

Note: ** means "not applicable"

5-49. Direction of trade matrix, current U.S. dollars, 1981

Importers   *Millions of current U.S. dollars*

Exporters		DZA	ANG	BEN	BWA	HVO	BDI	CMR	CPV	CAF	TCD	COM	CGO	CIV	DJI	EGY	GNQ
Algeria	DZA	**	2	20	..	..	..	..	..	..	..	..	..	33	..	..	..
Angola	ANG	40	**	..	..	..	..	..	0	..	..	..	..	..	..	..	..
Benin	BEN	0	..	**	..	0	..	0	..	..	..	..	0	0	..	..	..
Botswana	BWA	..	..	..	**	..	..	..	..	..	..	..	..	..	..	..	..
Burkina Faso	HVO	..	..	0	..	**	..	..	..	..	..	..	0	23	..	..	..
Burundi	BDI	..	..	..	..	..	**	0	..	..	1	..	..	..	0	..	..
Cameroon	CMR	..	0	0	..	0	..	**	..	11	20	..	16	7	..	3	0
Cape Verde	CPV	..	0	..	..	..	..	..	**	0	..	..	..	..	..	..	..
Central African Republic	CAF	..	..	..	..	..	..	..	..	**	0	..	..	0	..	..	..
Chad	TCD	..	..	..	..	..	..	16	..	2	**	..	..	..	..	..	..
Comoros	COM	..	..	..	..	..	..	..	..	..	..	**	..	..	..	..	..
Congo, People's Republic of the	CGO	1	1	0	..	..	..	..	..	..	0	..	**	0	..	..	..
Cote d'Ivoire	CIV	34	..	15	..	96	..	10	..	1	..	..	4	**	..	..	..
Djibouti	DJI	..	..	..	..	..	..	..	..	..	..	..	..	..	**	..	..
Egypt, Arab Republic of	EGY	0	..	0	..	..	..	..	..	..	..	..	0	0	0	**	..
Equatorial Guinea	GNQ	..	..	..	..	..	..	0	..	..	..	..	..	..	..	..	**
Ethiopia	ETH	..	..	..	..	..	..	..	..	..	..	..	..	..	20	10	..
Gabon	GAB	1	6	..	..	..	..	..	..	..	..	..	..	0	..	..	..
Gambia, The	GMB	..	..	..	..	..	..	..	..	..	..	..	..	..	..	..	..
Ghana	GHA	0	0	..	..	..	..	0	..	..	..	..	..	0	..	3	..
Guinea	GIN	..	..	..	..	..	..	31	..	..	..	..	..	..	..	0	..
Guinea-Bissau	GNB	..	0	..	..	..	..	..	..	..	..	..	..	..	..	..	..
Kenya	KEN	..	0	0	0	0	29	1	0	0	0	5	0	0	23	7	0
Lesotho	LSO	..	..	..	..	..	..	..	..	..	..	..	..	..	..	..	..
Liberia	LBR	..	..	..	..	..	..	0	..	0	..	..	0	0	..	0	..
Libya	LBY	0	..	..	..	..	..	..	..	..	1	..	..	..	..	0	..
Madagascar	MDG	10	..	..	..	..	..	..	..	..	..	0	..	..	..	..	..
Malawi	MWI	..	..	..	..	..	..	0	..	..	..	..	..	..	..	..	..
Mali	MLI	0	..	..	..	1	..	..	..	..	..	..	..	32	..	..	..
Mauritania	MRT	..	..	..	..	..	..	..	..	..	..	..	1	..	..	..	..
Mauritius	MUS	..	..	..	0	..	0	0	..	..	..	1	0	0	0	0	..
Morocco	MAR	..	..	..	..	0	..	5	..	..	..	..	4	10	..	6	..
Mozambique	MOZ	1	..	..	..	..	..	..	..	..	..	..	..	..	..	0	..
Namibia	NAM	..	..	..	..	..	..	..	..	..	..	..	..	..	..	..	..
Niger	NER	0	..	0	..	1	0	0	..	..	0	..	0	0	..	..	..
Nigeria	NGA	0	..	6	..	..	..	0	0	..	..	..	..	85	..	0	..
Rwanda	RWA	..	..	..	..	..	0	..	..	..	..	..	..	..	..	..	..
Sao Tome & Principe	STP	..	..	..	..	..	..	..	..	..	..	..	..	..	..	..	..
Senegal	SEN	1	..	5	..	3	0	3	0	1	0	..	3	39	..	0	0
Seychelles	SYC	..	..	..	..	..	..	..	..	..	..	..	..	..	..	..	..
Sierra Leone	SLE	..	..	..	..	..	..	..	..	..	..	..	..	..	..	..	..
Somalia	SOM	..	..	..	..	..	..	..	..	..	..	..	..	..	1	0	..
South Africa	ZAF	..	..	..	..	..	..	..	..	..	..	..	..	..	..	..	..
Sudan	SDN	4	1	..	..	..	..	..	..	..	..	..	..	..	..	31	..
Swaziland	SWZ	..	..	..	..	..	..	..	..	..	..	..	..	..	..	..	..
Tanzania	TZA	27	..	..	..	..	12	..	..	..	..	..	..	..	..	2	..
Togo	TGO	..	..	2	..	3	..	0	..	..	..	..	0	9	..	..	..
Tunisia	TUN	48	..	..	..	..	..	..	..	..	..	..	..	2	..	15	..
Uganda	UGA	..	..	..	..	..	..	..	..	..	..	..	..	..	..	1	..
Zaire	ZAR	..	..	..	..	..	1	0	..	2	..	..	7	..	..	..	..
Zambia	ZMB	..	0	..	2	..	3	0	..	..	..	..	..	..	..	4	..
Zimbabwe	ZWE	0	3	..	42	..	1	1	..	0	..	0	0	0	..	8	..
Total Sub-Saharan Africa	SSA	117	12	29	45	103	46	64	1	17	21	7	30	199	44	69	0
European Community	EEC	6,795	727	314	7	145	56	974	54	56	26	36	490	1,115	113	5,021	41
North America	NNA	1,033	270	21	7	22	4	209	0	1	1	0	25	148	7	2,260	1
Rest of World	ROW	2,095	442	348	3	15	50	312	44	11	2	6	143	773	75	4,141	2
WORLD	TOT	10,040	1,451	711	61	286	156	1,559	98	85	50	49	688	2,234	239	11,492	44

Note: ** means "not applicable."

(Table continues on the following page)

5–49. (continued)

Millions of current U.S. dollars

	ETH	GAB	GMB	GHA	GIN	GNB	KEN	LSO	LBR	LBY	MDG	MWI	MLI	MRT	MUS	MAR	MOZ	NAM	NER	NGA
DZA	..	..	3	21	0	..	5	..	0	3	..	..	1	0	2	..	33	..	0	0
ANG	..	..	..	0	..	..	..	..	..	..	..	..	..	..	..	..	..	..	..	1
BEN	..	..	..	0	..	..	..	..	..	..	..	..	0	..	..	..	..	..	3	2
BWA	..	..	..	..	..	..	..	..	..	..	..	..	..	..	..	..	..	..	..	..
HVO	..	..	..	0	..	..	..	..	..	..	..	..	1	..	..	..	..	..	2	..
BDI	..	..	..	..	..	..	1	..	..	..	..	..	..	..	..	..	..	..	..	..
CMR	..	19	..	0	1	..	..	..	..	..	0	0	1	..	..	0	0	..	..	5
CPV	..	..	..	..	..	..	..	..	..	..	..	..	..	..	..	..	..	..	..	..
CAF	..	..	..	..	..	..	..	..	..	..	..	..	..	0	..	..	..	..	..	0
TCD	..	..	..	..	..	..	..	..	..	..	..	..	..	..	..	..	..	..	..	..
COM	..	..	..	..	..	..	..	..	..	..	0	..	..	..	0	..	..	..	0	5
CGO	..	..	..	..	..	..	..	..	..	..	..	..	..	..	..	1	..	..	..	..
CIV	..	8	..	12	..	..	..	..	7	..	..	..	89	4	..	20	..	..	32	25
DJI	3	..	..	..	..	..	0	..	..	0	..	..	..	..	..	..	..	..	..	..
EGY	0	..	..	..	..	..	0	..	..	0	..	..	..	..	2	0	1	..	..	1
GNQ	..	..	..	..	..	..	..	..	..	..	..	..	..	..	..	..	..	..	..	..
ETH	**	..	..	..	..	..	1	..	..	..	..	..	..	..	..	..	..	..	..	..
GAB	..	**	..	..	3	..	..	..	..	..	..	..	..	..	..	6	..	..	..	23
GMB	..	..	**	9	3	0	..	..	..	..	..	..	0	..	..	..	..	..	..	1
GHA	..	..	0	**	0	..	0	..	0	0	..	..	0	..	..	..	0	..	..	0
GIN	..	..	..	..	**	0	..	..	0	..	..	..	..	..	0	1	..	..	0	..
GNB	..	..	0	..	0	**	..	..	..	..	..	..	..	..	..	..	..	..	..	..
KEN	3	0	0	0	0	..	**	0	0	1	1	1	0	0	11	0	23	..	0	5
LSO	..	..	..	..	..	..	..	**	..	..	..	..	..	..	..	..	..	..	..	..
LBR	..	..	0	2	2	..	..	..	**	3	..	0	0	0	..	..	..	..	..	4
LBY	..	..	..	..	..	..	..	..	..	**	..	..	..	..	..	0	..	..	..	..
MDG	..	..	..	..	..	..	..	..	..	..	**	..	..	..	1	1	..	..	..	..
MWI	0	0	..	..	..	..	1	..	2	..	..	**	..	..	1	..	2	..	..	..
MLI	..	..	..	0	..	..	..	..	0	..	..	..	**	..	..	..	..	..	0	..
MRT	..	..	..	..	..	..	..	..	..	..	..	..	..	**	..	..	..	..	..	..
MUS	..	0	0	..	0	..	0	..	..	0	0	0	..	..	**	0	..	..	0	0
MAR	..	3	0	..	2	..	..	..	0	45	0	..	0	1	1	**	..	..	..	10
MOZ	..	..	..	0	..	0	5	..	..	..	..	2	..	..	..	..	**	..	..	..
NAM	..	..	..	..	..	..	..	..	..	..	..	..	..	..	..	..	..	**	..	..
NER	..	0	..	0	0	..	..	..	..	68	..	..	1	..	..	..	..	..	**	78
NGA	..	..	..	308	..	..	..	..	0	..	..	0	..	..	..	..	..	..	0	**
RWA	..	..	..	..	..	..	1	..	..	0	..	..	..	..	..	..	..	..	..	..
STP	..	..	..	..	..	..	..	..	..	..	..	..	..	..	..	..	..	..	..	0
SEN	0	2	6	0	12	8	0	..	0	..	..	0	38	47	0	2	..	..	3	1
SYC	..	..	..	..	..	..	0	..	..	..	..	..	..	..	0	..	..	..	..	..
SLE	..	..	..	..	..	..	..	..	..	..	..	..	..	..	..	..	..	..	..	..
SOM	..	..	0	..	..	..	0	..	..	..	..	..	..	..	..	..	..	..	..	..
ZAF	..	..	..	..	..	..	..	..	..	..	..	..	..	..	..	..	..	..	..	..
SDN	0	..	..	..	..	..	..	..	..	..	..	..	..	..	..	0	..	..	..	..
SWZ	..	..	..	..	..	..	..	..	..	..	..	..	..	..	..	..	..	..	..	..
TZA	0	..	..	0	..	..	0	..	..	..	0	0	..	..	0	..	3	..	..	0
TGO	..	0	..	10	..	..	..	..	1	..	..	..	0	..	..	..	..	..	2	5
TUN	..	..	..	..	..	..	..	..	..	109	..	..	..	..	..	5	..	..	..	..
UGA	..	..	..	0	..	..	2	..	..	7	..	..	..	..	..	..	..	..	..	..
ZAR	..	2	..	..	..	..	0	..	..	..	..	..	..	..	..	..	..	..	..	..
ZMB	..	..	..	..	..	..	3	..	..	..	..	6	..	..	..	..	0	0	..	..
ZWE	0	1	..	1	..	..	4	2	..	6	0	22	1	..	3	0	16	3	..	2
SSA	7	32	7	344	21	9	19	2	12	84	2	32	132	50	17	30	44	3	42	158
EEC	254	516	47	398	181	32	707	9	598	9,212	208	82	147	243	101	2,281	254	3	285	9,198
NNA	96	131	3	171	54	0	173	9	155	907	30	6	5	29	19	511	51	13	12	1,607
ROW	347	108	37	274	84	13	1,017	4	1,216	4,308	176	54	26	81	231	1,641	329	5	46	5,849
TOT	703	787	94	1,188	339	54	1,915	24	1,981	14,512	415	174	309	404	368	4,463	679	24	386	16,812

Note: ** means "not applicable."

(Table continues on the following page)

5-49. (continued)

Millions of current U.S. dollars

	RWA	STP	SEN	SYC	SLE	SOM	ZAF	SDN	SWZ	TZA	TGO	TUN	UGA	ZAR	ZMB	ZWE	SSA	EEC	NNA	ROW	TOT
DZA	..	..	31	..	..	..	..	..	..	..	..	6	..	..	..	..	151	6,784	4,418	1,944	13,296
ANG	0	..	..	..	..	..	..	..	..	..	..	..	..	0	0	..	1	270	853	231	1,355
BEN	..	..	0	..	..	..	..	..	..	..	1	..	..	..	..	..	7	15	0	10	31
BWA	..	..	..	..	..	..	..	..	..	..	..	..	..	..	..	..	0	..	0	0	..
HVO	..	..	0	..	..	..	..	..	..	..	1	..	..	..	..	..	27	24	0	22	73
BDI	1	..	..	..	..	..	..	..	..	0	..	..	..	2	..	..	5	16	31	19	71
CMR	0	..	1	..	0	..	..	0	..	0	0	1	..	0	..	..	83	536	425	70	1,114
CPV	..	..	..	..	..	..	..	..	..	..	..	..	..	0	..	..	1	2	0	0	3
CAF	..	..	..	..	..	..	0	0	..	..	..	..	..	0	..	..	1	57	8	19	85
TCD	..	..	..	..	..	..	..	..	..	..	..	..	..	..	..	..	19	41	0	11	71
COM	..	..	0	..	..	..	..	..	..	..	..	..	..	..	..	..	5	17	4	1	27
CGO	..	0	0	..	..	..	1	..	0	..	..	1	..	2	..	1	4	488	124	281	896
CIV	..	..	31	..	..	..	..	..	..	..	11	2	..	..	..	..	344	1,499	297	397	2,537
DJI	..	..	0	..	..	13	..	..	..	..	..	..	..	..	..	..	16	2	0	6	24
EGY	0	..	..	..	0	0	..	13	..	0	..	3	0	0	0	..	16	1,430	148	1,639	3,233
GNQ	..	..	..	..	..	..	..	..	..	..	..	..	..	..	..	..	0	26	0	0	26
ETH	..	..	..	..	..	..	..	2	..	..	..	..	..	..	..	..	22	123	81	166	392
GAB	..	..	15	..	..	..	..	..	..	..	1	1	..	9	..	..	55	838	328	478	1,700
GMB	..	..	0	..	0	..	..	..	..	..	..	..	..	..	..	..	14	14	0	6	33
GHA	..	..	0	..	0	..	0	..	..	0	10	..	..	..	..	..	10	431	196	409	1,046
GIN	..	..	0	..	0	..	..	..	..	..	..	..	..	..	..	..	32	200	136	46	415
GNB	..	..	1	..	..	..	..	..	..	..	..	..	..	..	..	..	1	10	0	5	16
KEN	49	..	0	2	0	4	0	27	1	14	0	1	116	12	5	1	336	402	52	387	1,177
LSO	..	..	..	..	..	..	..	..	..	..	..	..	..	..	..	..	0	..	0	0	0
LBR	..	..	0	..	1	..	..	..	..	0	0	..	..	0	0	..	11	352	138	29	529
LBY	..	..	..	..	..	..	..	0	..	..	..	3	..	..	..	..	2	8,213	4,368	2,993	15,575
MDG	..	..	..	..	..	..	..	..	..	..	..	..	..	..	..	..	1	106	46	164	317
MWI	..	..	..	..	1	..	14	..	..	0	..	..	..	1	4	23	35	105	79	59	277
MLI	..	..	..	..	..	..	..	..	..	..	..	..	..	..	..	..	34	47	0	25	106
MRT	..	..	0	..	..	..	..	..	..	..	..	..	..	2	..	..	2	187	0	72	261
MUS	0	..	0	1	..	..	6	..	..	0	..	..	..	..	0	0	3	278	17	26	324
MAR	..	..	5	..	..	..	..	0	..	..	1	18	..	2	..	..	43	1,224	81	904	2,251
MOZ	..	..	..	..	..	..	..	..	..	4	..	..	..	..	0	27	39	80	81	116	316
NAM	..	..	..	..	..	..	..	..	..	..	..	..	..	..	..	..	0	..	0	0	..
NER	..	..	0	..	0	..	..	..	..	..	0	..	..	0	..	..	81	212	0	171	464
NGA	..	..	29	..	44	..	..	..	..	..	1	..	..	..	..	..	475	6,632	6,357	5,756	19,220
RWA	**	..	..	0	..	..	..	..	..	0	..	..	0	1	..	..	3	50	39	17	109
STP	..	**	..	..	..	..	..	..	..	..	..	..	..	..	..	..	0	13	0	1	14
SEN	..	..	**	0	0	..	..	..	..	..	7	0	0	1	0	..	181	190	1	128	500
SYC	..	..	..	**	..	..	..	..	..	..	..	..	..	..	..	..	0	0	0	17	17
SLE	..	..	..	..	**	..	..	..	..	..	..	..	..	..	..	..	0	78	17	56	150
SOM	..	..	..	0	..	**	..	0	..	0	..	..	..	0	..	..	2	23	0	127	152
ZAF	..	..	..	..	..	..	**	..	..	..	..	..	..	..	..	..	0	3,822	1,990	14,994	20,806
SDN	..	..	..	..	..	..	..	**	..	..	..	3	..	..	..	..	1	182	51	399	634
SWZ	..	..	..	..	..	..	..	..	**	..	..	..	..	..	..	..	0	..	0	0	..
TZA	3	..	..	0	..	1	..	4	0	**	..	..	10	4	2	0	41	253	23	241	557
TGO	..	..	0	..	..	..	..	..	..	..	**	..	..	0	..	..	33	128	0	46	208
TUN	..	..	..	..	..	..	..	..	..	..	..	**	..	..	..	..	2	1,449	434	367	2,252
UGA	1	..	..	..	0	..	..	4	..	0	..	..	**	..	..	0	6	122	99	38	265
ZAR	..	..	..	..	..	..	0	..	..	..	..	..	..	**	1	..	12	579	11	83	685
ZMB	..	..	..	..	..	..	6	..	0	6	..	..	..	..	**	..	22	413	74	142	651
ZWE	..	..	0	0	0	0	283	1	2	..	..	0	0	28	52	**	186	358	103	660	1,307
SSA	53	0	78	4	46	18	310	39	3	25	32	9	126	62	64	51	2,153	15,399	9,671	10,936	38,159
EEC	62	19	576	19	129	199	7,872	646	16	411	281	2,253	122	552	284	230	20,961	335,794	51,654	228,540	636,950
NNA	6	0	54	4	27	60	3,127	216	7	62	25	284	7	180	71	38	4,037	68,013	115,793	137,964	325,808
ROW	64	0	233	26	66	130	4,112	873	16	506	114	691	43	333	370	141	15,039	238,317	158,603	455,514	867,473
TOT	186	19	942	53	269	407	15,421	1,774	43	1,004	451	3,237	299	1,127	789	461	42,190	657,523	335,722	832,955	1,868,390

Note: ** means "not applicable."

5-50. Direction of trade matrix, current U.S. dollars, 1985

		Importers															*Millions of current U.S. dollars*
Exporters		DZA	ANG	BEN	BWA	HVO	BDI	CMR	CPV	CAF	TCD	COM	CGO	CIV	DJI	EGY	GNQ
Algeria	DZA	**	..	..	..	..	..	..	..	..	..	..	..	..	..	..	..
Angola	ANG	..	**	..	..	..	..	1	..	..	..	..	0	..	..	..	..
Benin	BEN	..	..	**	..	0	..	0	..	0	..	..	0	0	..	..	..
Botswana	BWA	..	..	..	**	..	..	..	..	..	..	..	..	..	..	..	..
Burkina Faso	HVO	..	..	0	..	**	..	..	..	..	..	..	..	2	..	2	..
Burundi	BDI	..	..	..	..	..	**	0	..	..	..	..	..	..	..	..	..
Cameroon	CMR	3	0	1	..	0	..	**	..	7	20	..	15	17	..	0	3
Cape Verde	CPV	2	2	..	..	..	..	..	**	..	..	..	..	..	..	..	..
Central African Republic	CAF	..	..	..	..	..	..	..	..	**	0	..	..	0	..	..	..
Chad	TCD	..	..	..	..	..	..	2	..	0	**	..	0	..	..	..	..
Comoros	COM	..	..	..	..	..	..	..	..	..	..	**	..	..	..	..	..
Congo, People's Republic of the	CGO	0	12	..	..	..	..	..	..	..	1	..	**	0	..	0	..
Cote d'Ivoire	CIV	8	..	14	..	85	..	16	..	..	..	..	..	**	..	..	..
Djibouti	DJI	..	..	..	..	..	1	..	..	..	..	..	..	..	**	0	..
Egypt, Arab Republic of	EGY	2	..	..	..	..	0	0	..	..	..	..	..	0	0	**	..
Equatorial Guinea	GNQ	..	..	..	..	..	..	0	..	..	..	..	..	..	..	..	**
Ethiopia	ETH	..	..	..	..	..	..	..	..	..	..	..	..	..	12	1	..
Gabon	GAB	5	..	0	..	..	..	6	..	..	..	..	..	28	..	1	..
Gambia, The	GMB	..	..	..	..	..	..	..	..	..	..	..	..	..	..	..	..
Ghana	GHA	..	..	0	..	0	..	..	..	..	..	..	0	0	..	1	..
Guinea	GIN	..	..	..	..	..	..	30	..	..	..	..	0	..	..	..	..
Guinea-Bissau	GNB	..	0	..	..	..	..	..	..	..	..	..	..	..	..	..	..
Kenya	KEN	..	..	..	..	..	18	..	..	..	..	2	..	..	2	23	..
Lesotho	LSO	..	..	..	..	..	..	..	..	..	..	..	..	..	..	..	..
Liberia	LBR	..	..	0	..	..	..	0	..	..	..	..	..	..	..	0	..
Libya	LBY	0	..	..	..	..	..	..	..	..	..	1	..	..	..	0	..
Madagascar	MDG	..	..	..	..	..	..	..	..	..	..	0	..	..	..	..	..
Malawi	MWI	..	..	..	1	..	..	..	..	..	..	..	..	..	..	..	..
Mali	MLI	6	..	..	..	1	..	..	..	..	..	..	0	3	..	..	..
Mauritania	MRT	14	..	0	..	..	..	1	..	..	..	..	0	11	..	0	..
Mauritius	MUS	0	..	..	..	..	0	0	..	0	..	1	0	0	..	0	..
Morocco	MAR	..	..	1	..	..	..	9	..	..	..	..	6	7	..	2	..
Mozambique	MOZ	..	..	..	..	..	..	..	..	..	..	..	0	..	..	0	..
Namibia	NAM	..	..	..	..	..	..	..	..	..	..	..	..	..	..	..	..
Niger	NER	7	..	1	..	1	..	0	..	..	..	..	..	4	..	..	..
Nigeria	NGA	..	0	2	0	0	..	3	..	4	..	0	0	189	..	0	..
Rwanda	RWA	..	..	..	..	..	1	0	..	..	..	..	..	..	..	..	..
Sao Tome & Principe	STP	..	..	..	..	..	..	..	..	..	..	..	..	..	..	..	..
Senegal	SEN	0	0	5	..	3	0	11	0	0	0	..	5	29	0	0	0
Seychelles	SYC	..	..	..	..	..	..	..	..	..	..	..	..	..	..	..	..
Sierra Leone	SLE	..	..	0	..	..	..	..	..	..	0	..	..	0	..	..	..
Somalia	SOM	..	..	..	..	..	..	0	..	..	..	..	..	..	0	4	..
South Africa	ZAF	..	..	..	..	..	..	..	..	..	..	..	..	..	..	..	..
Sudan	SDN	..	..	..	..	..	..	..	..	0	..	..	..	..	..	35	..
Swaziland	SWZ	..	..	..	..	..	..	..	..	..	..	..	..	..	..	..	..
Tanzania	TZA	1	..	..	0	..	2	..	..	..	..	..	..	0	..	1	..
Togo	TGO	..	..	1	..	2	..	0	..	0	0	..	0	1	..	..	..
Tunisia	TUN	57	0	0	..	..	..	1	..	..	..	..	0	1	..	5	..
Uganda	UGA	..	..	..	..	..	..	..	..	..	..	..	0	..	..	2	..
Zaire	ZAR	..	..	..	..	..	3	..	..	2	..	..	16	..	..	..	..
Zambia	ZMB	..	1	0	2	..	1	1	..	..	..	..	..	..	..	3	..
Zimbabwe	ZWE	2	7	0	37	..	1	0	0	0	0	0	0	0	..	0	..
Total Sub-Saharan Africa	SSA	47	21	24	40	92	27	71	0	13	23	4	37	285	15	76	3
European Community	EEC	5,519	689	178	29	122	73	1,004	83	76	79	23	405	803	138	4,997	17
North America	NNA	690	140	68	16	27	6	94	0	1	25	2	19	84	5	2,461	0
Rest of World	ROW	2,043	445	128	18	14	42	241	17	12	6	10	71	240	124	4,459	2
WORLD	TOT	8,299	1,296	397	103	255	149	1,410	100	103	132	37	532	1,411	281	11,992	23

Note: ** means "not applicable."

(Table continues on the following page)

5-50. (continued)

Millions of current U.S. dollars

	ETH	GAB	GMB	GHA	GIN	GNB	KEN	LSO	LBR	LBY	MDG	MWI	MLI	MRT	MUS	MAR	MOZ	NAM	NER	NGA
DZA	..	..	..	..	..	..	..	..	..	..	..	..	..	..	..	..	..	..	..	..
ANG	..	..	..	..	..	..	..	..	..	..	..	..	..	..	..	..	..	..	..	0
BEN	..	..	..	0	..	..	..	..	0	..	..	..	0	..	..	..	..	..	3	0
BWA	..	..	..	..	..	..	..	..	..	..	..	..	..	..	..	..	..	..	..	..
HVO	..	..	..	..	..	..	..	..	..	..	..	..	1	..	0	..	..	..	1	1
BDI	..	..	..	..	..	..	2	..	..	..	..	..	..	..	..	..	..	..	..	..
CMR	..	29	..	0	1	..	0	..	..	..	..	..	0	..	..	2	..	..	0	22
CPV	..	..	..	..	..	..	..	..	..	..	..	..	..	..	..	..	..	..	..	..
CAF	..	..	..	..	..	..	..	..	..	..	..	..	..	..	..	..	..	..	..	0
TCD	..	..	..	..	..	..	..	..	..	..	..	..	..	..	..	..	..	..	..	1
COM	..	..	..	..	..	..	..	..	0	..	0	..	..	..	0	..	..	..	..	0
CGO	..	..	..	..	..	..	..	..	..	..	..	..	0	0	0	15	..	..	..	0
CIV	..	12	..	25	..	..	..	..	12	..	..	..	85	..	..	13	..	..	23	17
DJI	2	..	..	..	..	..	..	..	..	0	..	..	..	..	0	..	..	..	..	..
EGY	..	..	..	0	..	..	0	..	..	0	..	0	..	0	0	1	0	..	..	0
GNQ	..	..	..	..	..	..	..	..	0	..	..	..	0	..	..	..	..	..	..	0
ETH	**	..	..	..	..	..	0	..	..	..	..	..	..	..	..	..	..	..	..	0
GAB	..	**	..	..	0	..	..	..	..	..	..	..	0	0	0	41	..	..	..	0
GMB	..	..	**	1	3	0	..	..	0	..	..	..	0	0	..	..	..	..	..	0
GHA	..	..	0	**	..	..	..	..	0	..	..	..	..	..	..	..	..	..	0	0
GIN	..	..	..	..	**	0	..	..	0	..	..	..	2	..	..	..	..	..	..	..
GNB	..	..	0	..	0	**	..	..	..	..	..	..	..	..	..	..	..	..	..	1
KEN	4	..	..	..	..	..	**	..	..	..	..	..	..	..	5	..	5	..	..	0
LSO	..	..	..	..	..	..	..	**	..	..	..	..	..	..	..	..	..	..	..	..
LBR	..	..	0	0	1	..	..	..	**	0	..	..	0	0	..	0	..	..	..	9
LBY	..	..	0	..	..	..	..	..	..	**	..	..	..	..	..	0	..	..	..	..
MDG	..	..	..	..	..	..	0	..	..	..	**	..	..	..	1	..	..	..	..	..
MWI	..	..	..	..	..	..	0	..	..	..	..	**	..	..	..	..	3	..	..	..
MLI	..	0	..	..	0	..	..	..	0	..	..	..	**	0	..	5	..	..	0	0
MRT	..	..	..	0	..	..	..	..	1	..	..	..	..	**	..	..	..	..	..	..
MUS	0	..	..	0	0	..	0	..	..	..	1	0	0	..	**	..	..	..	..	0
MAR	..	5	..	6	..	..	..	..	..	36	..	..	0	0	0	**	..	..	..	0
MOZ	..	0	..	..	..	0	0	..	0	..	..	0	..	..	..	..	**	..	..	..
NAM	..	..	..	..	..	..	..	..	..	..	..	..	..	..	..	..	..	**	..	..
NER	..	..	..	0	..	..	..	..	..	0	..	..	1	..	..	..	..	..	**	29
NGA	..	0	..	192	0	0	0	0	0	..	..	..	0	..	..	..	..	..	2	**
RWA	..	..	..	..	..	..	3	..	..	0	..	..	..	..	..	..	..	..	..	..
STP	..	..	..	..	..	..	..	..	0	..	..	..	..	..	..	..	..	..	..	..
SEN	..	2	5	0	4	2	0	..	0	..	0	..	39	20	..	0	..	..	3	9
SYC	..	..	..	..	..	..	..	..	..	..	..	..	..	..	0	..	..	..	..	..
SLE	..	..	0	0	0	..	..	..	2	..	..	..	..	..	..	..	..	..	..	0
SOM	..	..	..	0	..	..	0	..	..	0	..	..	..	..	..	..	..	..	..	..
ZAF	..	..	..	..	..	..	..	..	..	..	..	..	..	..	..	..	..	..	..	..
SDN	0	..	..	..	..	..	..	..	..	..	..	0	0	..	..	..	..	..	..	0
SWZ	..	..	..	..	..	..	..	..	..	..	..	..	..	..	..	..	..	..	..	..
TZA	0	..	..	..	..	..	1	0	..	..	0	0	..	..	0	..	2	..	..	0
TGO	..	0	..	1	0	..	..	..	0	0	..	..	1	0	..	4	..	..	3	2
TUN	..	0	..	0	1	0	0	..	2	16	0	..	0	..	..	5	0	..	0	0
UGA	0	..	..	..	..	..	1	..	..	5	..	..	0	..	..	..	..	..	..	..
ZAR	..	1	..	..	..	..	0	..	..	..	..	..	..	..	..	..	..	..	..	..
ZMB	0	..	..	..	..	..	3	1	..	..	..	3	..	..	..	..	0	0	..	..
ZWE	4	1	..	1	0	..	3	0	..	0	0	12	..	..	2	1	13	1	..	1
SSA	9	46	5	220	9	2	15	2	16	6	1	16	129	21	8	81	24	1	36	94
EEC	446	592	56	297	190	37	505	11	499	2,797	170	60	203	215	150	2,049	151	5	173	3,406
NNA	248	92	11	72	64	0	110	7	122	381	37	5	30	29	11	409	61	19	13	735
ROW	411	95	29	160	82	12	790	7	1,409	1,733	152	31	41	42	242	975	146	2	34	2,272
TOT	1,114	826	102	749	345	51	1,420	26	2,047	4,917	359	112	404	307	411	3,514	382	27	255	6,507

Note: ** means "not applicable."

(Table continues on the following page)

5-50. (continued)

Millions of current U.S. dollars

	RWA	STP	SEN	SYC	SLE	SOM	ZAF	SDN	SWZ	TZA	TGO	TUN	UGA	ZAR	ZMB	ZWE	SSA	EEC	NNA	ROW	TOT
DZA	..	..	..	..	..	..	..	..	..	..	..	124	..	..	..	..	0	9,500	1,539	1,803	12,841
ANG	..	..	..	..	..	..	..	..	..	..	..	..	..	..	0	..	1	743	996	437	2,177
BEN	0	..	0	..	..	..	..	0	..	..	1	0	..	..	..	..	6	141	0	5	153
BWA	..	..	..	..	..	..	..	..	..	..	..	..	..	..	..	..	0	..	0	0	..
HVO	..	..	0	..	..	..	..	..	..	..	1	0	..	..	..	..	5	34	1	20	59
BDI	4	..	..	..	..	..	..	1	..	1	..	..	1	2	0	0	11	47	7	48	112
CMR	..	..	0	..	..	..	..	..	..	..	6	1	..	0	..	..	122	899	100	76	1,197
CPV	..	..	..	..	..	..	..	..	..	..	..	..	..	..	..	..	2	1	0	2	5
CAF	0	..	..	..	..	..	..	1	..	..	..	..	..	2	..	..	3	84	0	5	92
TCD	..	..	..	..	..	..	..	0	..	..	0	..	..	..	..	..	4	40	0	1	46
COM	..	..	..	..	..	..	..	..	..	..	..	0	..	..	..	..	1	8	6	0	15
CGO	..	..	0	..	..	..	0	..	0	0	0	2	..	4	..	..	18	376	653	41	1,087
CIV	..	..	46	..	..	..	..	..	..	24	..	..	..	..	..	..	360	1,783	354	438	2,934
DJI	..	..	..	2	..	4	..	..	..	..	..	0	..	..	..	..	8	2	0	13	24
EGY	..	..	0	..	..	0	0	..	..	..	..	3	0	..	..	..	0	807	18	1,013	1,838
GNQ	..	..	..	..	..	..	..	..	..	..	..	..	..	..	..	..	1	26	0	0	27
ETH	..	..	..	..	..	..	..	6	..	0	..	..	0	..	..	..	19	165	36	118	338
GAB	..	0	12	..	..	..	..	..	..	..	0	0	..	..	..	0	47	976	501	477	2,000
GMB	..	..	0	..	0	0	..	..	..	..	..	..	..	..	0	0	5	12	0	11	27
GHA	..	..	..	..	0	..	..	..	..	..	26	..	..	0	..	..	27	234	51	144	455
GIN	..	..	0	..	0	..	..	..	..	..	0	..	..	..	..	..	33	272	134	35	474
GNB	..	0	0	..	..	..	..	..	..	..	..	..	..	..	..	..	2	5	0	2	9
KEN	33	..	..	..	..	4	1	26	..	12	..	..	83	10	1	..	205	433	55	265	958
LSO	..	..	..	..	..	..	..	..	..	..	..	..	..	..	..	..	0	..	0	0	..
LBR	..	..	0	..	1	..	..	..	..	..	0	..	..	..	..	..	11	306	95	23	436
LBY	..	..	..	..	..	..	0	..	..	..	..	2	..	..	..	..	1	5,763	3,065	2,100	10,929
MDG	..	..	..	..	..	..	..	..	..	..	..	..	..	..	..	..	1	156	38	79	274
MWI	..	..	..	..	..	..	16	..	..	0	..	..	..	..	16	6	26	136	25	40	227
MLI	..	..	1	..	..	..	..	..	..	..	..	1	..	..	..	..	7	72	0	45	124
MRT	..	..	1	..	..	..	..	..	..	..	..	..	..	..	..	..	14	157	0	203	373
MUS	..	..	0	1	..	0	1	..	..	1	..	0	..	0	0	0	4	336	70	22	433
MAR	..	..	8	..	..	..	0	..	..	..	2	20	..	3	..	..	47	1,277	66	782	2,173
MOZ	..	..	0	..	..	..	..	..	..	1	..	0	..	..	..	0	2	30	16	80	129
NAM	..	..	..	..	..	..	..	..	..	..	..	..	..	..	..	..	0	..	0	0	..
NER	..	..	0	..	..	..	..	..	..	..	0	..	..	..	..	..	36	152	0	21	209
NGA	..	..	15	..	34	..	..	0	..	..	0	..	..	0	0	..	442	8,463	2,568	1,641	13,114
RWA	**	..	..	..	..	..	..	..	..	0	..	..	0	0	..	..	4	120	4	3	130
STP	..	**	..	..	..	..	..	..	..	..	..	..	..	..	..	..	0	5	0	3	7
SEN	0	..	**	..	2	..	0	..	0	..	4	3	..	1	..	..	143	219	2	173	536
SYC	..	..	..	**	..	..	..	..	..	..	..	..	..	..	..	..	0	1	1	26	28
SLE	..	..	0	..	**	..	..	0	..	..	..	..	..	0	..	..	3	80	18	48	148
SOM	..	..	..	..	..	**	..	..	0	..	..	..	..	..	..	..	0	11	0	97	109
ZAF	..	..	..	..	..	..	**	..	..	..	..	..	..	..	..	..	0	3,500	1,472	11,434	16,405
SDN	..	..	..	..	..	..	..	**	..	0	0	1	..	..	..	..	0	98	7	289	394
SWZ	..	..	..	..	..	..	..	..	**	..	..	..	..	..	..	..	0	..	0	0	..
TZA	1	..	..	..	..	0	..	2	0	**	..	..	2	0	1	0	13	164	8	99	284
TGO	0	..	0	..	..	..	..	..	..	..	**	3	..	0	..	..	11	106	15	69	201
TUN	..	..	0	..	0	..	..	0	..	..	0	**	..	..	..	..	8	1,181	190	352	1,731
UGA	0	..	..	..	..	..	..	0	..	2	..	0	**	..	0	0	4	205	109	63	382
ZAR	..	..	..	..	..	..	0	..	..	..	..	..	..	**	0	..	22	785	33	111	950
ZMB	0	..	..	..	..	..	5	..	0	5	..	0	0	3	**	12	33	173	14	251	471
ZWE	1	..	0	0	0	0	103	2	1	5	..	0	1	14	37	**	144	391	81	341	956
SSA	39	0	76	3	37	8	127	38	1	28	63	13	87	36	55	19	1,796	18,444	5,997	5,864	32,102
EEC	84	9	472	39	77	147	4,298	527	9	338	226	1,747	110	624	202	232	13,981	353,169	75,041	207,448	649,639
NNA	6	0	77	1	13	57	1,317	258	1	59	19	314	5	121	64	54	2,888	58,072	143,191	121,881	326,031
ROW	41	1	158	18	37	112	2,129	629	11	507	121	491	57	309	137	123	9,588	206,206	189,756	397,828	803,378
TOT	169	10	783	61	164	325	7,871	1,451	22	932	429	2,565	259	1,090	458	428	28,253	635,891	413,986	733,020	1,811,150

Note: ** means "not applicable."

5–51. Direction of trade matrix, current U.S. dollars, 1990

Importers   *Millions of current U.S. dollars*

Exporters		DZA	ANG	BEN	BWA	HVO	BDI	CMR	CPV	CAF	TCD	COM	CGO	CIV	DJI	EGY	GNQ
Algeria	DZA	**	..	..	..	..	..	0	..	..	..	..	0	..	..	4	..
Angola	ANG	..	**	..	..	..	..	0	1	..	..	..	0	..	..	..	..
Benin	BEN	..	..	**	..	0	..	0	..	0	..	..	..	1	..	0	..
Botswana	BWA	..	..	..	**	..	..	..	..	..	..	..	..	..	..	..	..
Burkina Faso	HVO	..	..	0	..	**	..	0	..	..	..	..	0	3	..	..	..
Burundi	BDI	..	..	..	..	..	**	..	..	..	..	..	..	..	..	..	..
Cameroon	CMR	1	6	3	..	0	..	**	..	40	12	..	8	30	..	..	69
Cape Verde	CPV	4	2	..	..	..	..	..	**	0	..	..	..	..	..	..	..
Central African Republic	CAF	..	..	..	..	..	..	0	..	**	0	..	..	0	..	0	..
Chad	TCD	..	..	..	..	..	..	2	..	0	**	..	..	..	..	..	..
Comoros	COM	..	..	..	..	..	..	..	..	..	..	**	..	..	..	0	..
Congo, People's Republic of the	CGO	4	4	0	..	..	..	..	..	..	..	..	**	2	..	..	..
Cote d'Ivoire	CIV	4	..	25	..	148	..	8	2	..	..	..	0	**	..	2	..
Djibouti	DJI	..	..	..	..	..	1	0	..	..	..	..	0	..	**	..	..
Egypt, Arab Republic of	EGY	5	..	..	..	..	0	0	..	..	0	..	..	1	0	**	0
Equatorial Guinea	GNQ	..	..	..	..	..	..	0	..	..	..	..	..	..	..	..	**
Ethiopia	ETH	..	..	..	..	..	..	..	..	..	..	..	..	..	15	1	..
Gabon	GAB	7	..	0	..	..	..	5	..	..	..	..	..	47	..	..	..
Gambia, The	GMB	0	..	..	..	..	..	..	..	..	..	..	..	..	..	..	..
Ghana	GHA	..	0	1	..	0	..	..	..	..	..	..	0	1	..	1	..
Guinea	GIN	..	..	..	..	..	..	48	..	0	..	..	0	..	..	..	..
Guinea-Bissau	GNB	..	0	..	..	..	..	..	..	..	..	..	..	..	..	0	..
Kenya	KEN	..	..	..	..	..	20	..	..	..	..	3	..	..	3	25	..
Lesotho	LSO	..	..	..	..	..	..	..	..	..	..	..	..	..	..	..	..
Liberia	LBR	..	..	0	..	..	..	0	..	..	0	..	2	..	..	1	..
Libya	LBY	..	0	..	..	0	..	..	..	0	1	..	..	..	..	1	...
Madagascar	MDG	0	..	0	..	..	0	0	..	..	..	2	..	0	0	0	0
Malawi	MWI	..	..	..	4	..	..	..	..	..	..	..	..	..	..	..	..
Mali	MLI	27	..	..	..	5	..	0	..	..	..	..	0	12	..	..	..
Mauritania	MRT	0	0	0	..	0	0	5	0	0	0	..	0	34	..	0	..
Mauritius	MUS	0	0	..	0	0	0	0	..	..	..	2	0	0	0	0	..
Morocco	MAR	35	8	1	..	1	..	6	..	1	0	1	4	11	0	1	0
Mozambique	MOZ	..	0	..	..	..	..	0	..	..	..	..	0	..	..	0	..
Namibia	NAM	..	..	..	..	..	..	..	..	..	..	..	..	..	..	..	..
Niger	NER	..	..	1	..	2	..	..	..	..	..	..	0	3	..	0	..
Nigeria	NGA	0	1	2	..	0	..	17	..	..	0	0	..	148	..	0	..
Rwanda	RWA	..	..	..	0	0	0	0	..	..	0	..	0	..	0	0	..
Sao Tome & Principe	STP	..	..	..	..	..	..	..	..	..	..	..	..	..	..	..	..
Senegal	SEN	0	0	5	..	4	..	14	0	0	1	..	4	24	..	0	0
Seychelles	SYC	..	0	..	..	..	..	..	..	..	..	..	..	..	..	0	..
Sierra Leone	SLE	..	..	0	..	..	..	..	..	..	0	..	..	1	..	..	..
Somalia	SOM	..	..	..	..	..	..	..	..	..	0	..	..	..	1	0	..
South Africa	ZAF	..	..	..	..	..	..	..	..	..	0	..	..	0	..	..	..
Sudan	SDN	..	..	..	..	..	..	..	..	0	..	..	..	..	..	..	..
Swaziland	SWZ	..	..	..	..	..	..	..	..	..	..	..	..	..	..	..	..
Tanzania	TZA	0	..	..	0	..	3	..	..	..	..	..	..	0	..	1	..
Togo	TGO	..	..	2	..	4	..	0	..	0	0	..	1	1	..	..	..
Tunisia	TUN	82	..	1	..	0	..	10	..	..	..	..	1	8	1	4	..
Uganda	UGA	..	..	..	..	..	..	..	..	..	..	..	..	..	..	0	..
Zaire	ZAR	..	..	..	..	..	3	..	..	2	..	..	18	..	..	..	..
Zambia	ZMB	..	3	1	6	..	4	2	..	..	..	..	2	..	..	..	..
Zimbabwe	ZWE	3	4	0	89	..	5	4	..	0	..	0	..	0	0	20	..
Total Sub-Saharan Africa	SSA	52	21	41	100	163	36	106	3	42	14	7	36	307	19	53	69
European Community	EEC	6,174	1,072	203	99	232	120	927	96	103	97	63	427	1,058	128	5,110	39
North America	NNA	1,198	159	25	21	16	1	73	6	2	8	0	90	89	8	2,313	0
Rest of World	ROW	1,929	331	132	82	40	55	201	16	14	14	16	102	300	152	4,029	4
WORLD	TOT	9,353	1,582	402	302	450	211	1,307	121	162	133	86	655	1,753	306	11,504	112

Note: ** *means "not applicable."*

(Table continues on the following page)

5-51. (continued)

Millions of current U.S. dollars

	ETH	GAB	GMB	GHA	GIN	GNB	KEN	LSO	LBR	LBY	MDG	MWI	MLI	MRT	MUS	MAR	MOZ	NAM	NER	NGA
DZA	..	..	..	..	..	..	..	..	..	..	0	..	..	18	..	30	..	..	..	..
ANG	..	..	..	0	..	..	..	..	..	..	..	..	..	..	..	..	..	..	..	0
BEN	..	..	..	0	..	..	..	..	0	..	..	..	0	0	..	4	..	..	6	4
BWA	..	..	..	..	..	..	..	..	..	..	..	..	..	..	..	..	..	..	..	..
HVO	..	..	..	6	..	..	..	..	..	..	..	..	1	..	0	1	..	..	2	4
BDI	..	..	..	..	..	..	..	..	..	..	..	..	..	0	0	..	..	..	..	..
CMR	..	44	..	0	2	..	..	..	6	1	..	..	0	0	0	2	3	..	0	18
CPV	..	..	..	..	..	0	..	..	0	..	..	..	..	..	..	..	..	..	..	..
CAF	..	..	..	..	..	0	..	..	0	..	..	..	..	..	0	1	..	..	..	..
TCD	..	..	..	..	..	..	..	..	0	..	..	..	..	..	..	3	..	..	..	3
COM	..	..	..	..	..	..	..	..	0	..	0	..	..	..	0	..	..	..	..	..
CGO	0	..	..	0	0	..	..	..	..	..	..	..	0	0	0	5	..	..	..	0
CIV	..	16	..	24	..	..	..	..	23	..	1	..	148	1	22	17	..	..	41	14
DJI	2	..	..	..	..	..	..	..	..	0	..	..	..	..	..	..	..	..	..	..
EGY	3	..	0	..	0	..	0	..	0	5	..	0	..	0	1	4	0	..	0	0
GNQ	..	..	..	..	..	..	..	..	..	..	..	..	..	..	..	..	..	..	..	..
ETH	**	..	..	..	..	..	3	..	..	..	..	..	0	..	0	0	..	..	..	0
GAB	..	**	..	..	0	..	..	..	..	..	..	..	0	..	..	17	..	..	..	0
GMB	0	..	**	0	7	0	..	..	0	..	..	..	..	..	0	..	..	..	..	0
GHA	0	..	0	**	0	..	..	..	0	0	..	..	0	..	0	2	..	..	0	1
GIN	..	..	..	..	**	0	..	..	0	..	..	..	13	0	0	0	..	..	..	..
GNB	..	..	0	..	0	**	..	..	..	..	..	..	..	..	..	..	..	..	..	0
KEN	4	..	..	..	..	..	**	..	..	..	..	..	..	..	14	..	6	..	..	0
LSO	..	..	..	..	..	..	..	**	..	..	..	..	..	..	..	..	..	..	..	..
LBR	..	..	0	0	1	0	..	..	**	0	..	..	0	0	0	1	..	..	..	7
LBY	2	0	0	0	0	..	..	..	0	**	..	..	..	0	..	9	0	..	..	0
MDG	0	0	..	..	0	..	1	0	..	..	**	..	0	0	7	1	6	0	0	..
MWI	..	..	..	..	..	..	0	..	..	..	..	**	..	..	0	..	14	..	..	..
MLI	..	0	..	..	..	..	..	..	2	..	..	..	**	0	..	15	..	..	0	0
MRT	..	0	0	0	0	..	..	..	5	0	..	..	0	**	..	0	..	..	..	..
MUS	0	0	..	0	0	..	1	..	..	..	9	0	0	0	**	0	0	..	..	0
MAR	..	8	0	1	6	..	0	..	1	100	0	..	5	4	1	**	0	..	1	14
MOZ	..	0	..	0	..	0	0	..	0	..	1	1	..	..	0	1	**	..	..	0
NAM	..	..	..	..	..	..	..	..	..	..	..	..	..	..	..	..	..	**	..	..
NER	..	..	..	0	..	..	..	..	..	0	..	..	2	0	..	..	..	..	**	15
NGA	0	0	0	132	0	0	..	8	2	..	..	..	..	0	0	3	0	..	6	**
RWA	0	0	..	0	..	..	83	..	0	0	0	..	0	0	0	0	..	..	..	..
STP	..	..	..	..	..	..	..	..	0	..	..	..	..	0	..	..	..	..	..	..
SEN	0	2	5	0	8	5	..	..	1	0	0	..	31	2	0	0	..	..	1	2
SYC	..	..	..	..	..	..	..	..	..	..	..	..	..	0	..	..	..	..	..	..
SLE	..	..	0	..	0	..	..	..	2	..	..	..	..	..	..	..	..	..	..	0
SOM	..	..	..	0	0	..	..	..	0	..	..	..	..	..	0	..	..	..	0	..
ZAF	..	..	..	..	..	..	..	..	..	..	..	..	..	..	68	..	..	..	..	..
SDN	0	..	..	0	..	..	..	..	..	..	..	..	0	0	..	0	..	..	..	..
SWZ	..	..	..	..	..	..	..	..	..	..	..	..	..	..	..	..	..	..	..	..
TZA	0	..	0	..	..	..	6	0	..	..	0	0	0	..	0	4	2	..	..	0
TGO	..	0	..	49	0	..	..	..	0	0	..	..	2	0	..	4	..	..	5	2
TUN	..	0	..	9	0	1	..	..	0	162	..	..	..	2	..	24	..	..	0	0
UGA	0	..	..	0	..	..	2	..	0	6	..	..	0	..	0	1	..	..	..	..
ZAR	..	1	..	..	0	..	1	..	..	..	..	..	..	..	0	..	..	..	..	..
ZMB	0	..	..	..	..	..	4	5	..	..	..	8	..	..	0	..	0	0	..	0
ZWE	3	..	..	2	..	..	..	2	0	2	..	25	..	..	2	4	53	1	0	0
SSA	9	64	6	215	18	6	100	15	42	10	11	35	198	3	48	83	84	1	62	70
EEC	518	538	99	637	308	67	1,015	21	1,219	3,320	316	144	253	273	492	4,436	307	155	180	3,085
NNA	178	54	0	153	49	1	163	3	56	40	13	16	13	15	13	685	72	47	15	577
ROW	458	102	68	314	91	27	1,115	22	2,757	1,823	181	55	81	97	710	1,480	304	8	30	1,891
TOT	1,163	758	172	1,319	467	100	2,393	61	4,074	5,194	521	249	545	388	1,263	6,685	767	210	287	5,624

Note: ** means "not applicable."

(Table continues on the following page)

5-51. (continued)

Millions of current U.S. dollars

	RWA	STP	SEN	SYC	SLE	SOM	ZAF	SDN	SW	TZA	TGO	TUN	UGA	ZAR	ZMB	ZWE	SSA	EEC	NNA	ROW	TOT
DZA	0	..	0	..	..	..	..	..	..	0	..	85	..	..	0	0	18	7,798	2,643	1,870	12,329
ANG	..	..	23	0	..	..	..	..	..	..	..	..	..	..	0	..	25	1,311	1,958	403	3,696
BEN	0	..	0	..	0	..	..	0	..	..	1	0	..	..	..	..	13	38	21	20	93
BWA	..	..	..	..	..	..	..	..	..	..	..	..	..	..	..	..	0	..	0	0	..
HVO	0	..	0	..	..	..	..	..	..	..	1	8	..	..	..	..	18	82	1	57	157
BDI	2	..	..	..	..	..	..	..	..	..	..	..	..	..	..	..	2	67	3	9	81
CMR	0	..	25	..	..	..	..	..	..	..	2	3	..	..	0	..	268	1,526	158	271	2,223
CPV	0	..	0	..	..	..	..	..	..	..	..	1	..	..	..	..	2	4	0	6	12
CAF	0	..	0	..	..	..	..	1	..	..	..	1	..	..	..	..	1	92	2	13	108
TCD	..	..	..	..	..	..	..	0	..	..	0	..	..	..	..	..	4	62	2	23	91
COM	..	..	0	..	..	..	..	..	..	..	..	..	..	..	..	..	0	17	4	1	23
CGO	..	..	0	..	..	..	0	..	..	..	0	0	..	..	2	0	9	627	403	46	1,085
CIV	0	..	70	..	1	..	..	..	..	0	42	12	..	..	..	0	589	1,856	222	845	3,512
DJI	1	..	..	..	..	21	..	..	..	..	..	..	..	..	..	..	24	4	0	20	48
EGY	..	..	0	..	0	0	0	..	..	0	..	19	0	0	..	2	8	1,799	243	1,509	3,559
GNQ	0	..	..	..	..	..	..	..	..	..	..	..	..	..	..	..	0	28	0	2	29
ETH	0	..	..	..	..	..	0	7	..	0	..	0	0	..	..	..	26	167	33	140	366
GAB	0	0	21	..	..	..	..	..	..	..	0	1	..	..	..	0	74	1,130	735	392	2,330
GMB	..	..	0	..	0	..	..	..	..	..	..	0	..	0	..	..	7	90	0	71	168
GHA	0	..	1	..	..	..	..	0	..	0	45	0	..	..	..	0	51	783	168	365	1,366
GIN	..	..	0	..	0	..	..	..	..	..	..	0	0	..	..	0	63	324	140	66	592
GNB	..	0	0	..	..	..	..	..	..	..	..	..	0	..	..	..	0	6	0	1	8
KEN	35	..	..	..	..	4	2	27	..	13	..	0	88	10	1	..	227	498	63	308	1,096
LSO	..	..	..	..	..	..	..	..	..	..	..	..	..	..	..	..	0	..	0	0	..
LBR	..	..	0	..	1	..	..	..	..	..	1	0	..	..	..	..	11	815	63	956	1,846
LBY	0	..	0	..	..	..	..	0	..	0	..	27	..	..	..	..	3	8,934	0	1,509	10,446
MDG	..	..	0	0	..	1	..	0	0	2	0	0	..	0	..	..	19	207	108	71	405
MWI	..	..	..	..	..	..	27	..	..	1	..	..	..	..	9	7	36	150	35	94	314
MLI	0	..	1	..	..	..	..	..	..	..	1	4	..	..	..	..	20	90	16	143	270
MRT	..	..	1	..	0	..	..	..	..	..	1	0	..	0	..	..	48	248	22	170	487
MUS	0	..	..	3	..	0	6	0	0	0	0	0	0	0	0	3	20	947	158	77	1,202
MAR	..	..	7	..	0	..	..	0	..	2	2	56	..	41	..	..	125	2,924	169	1,111	4,330
MOZ	0	..	..	..	..	0	4	..	..	2	0	0	..	..	..	0	5	66	31	270	372
NAM	..	..	..	..	..	..	..	..	..	..	..	..	..	..	..	..	0	..	0	0	..
NER	..	..	1	..	..	..	..	..	..	..	1	..	..	..	..	0	25	190	44	6	265
NGA	..	..	45	..	54	..	..	..	..	..	1	0	..	..	..	0	416	4,928	6,281	974	12,599
RWA	**	..	0	..	..	0	..	..	0	0	0	0	..	0	2	0	85	40	12	10	147
STP	..	**	..	..	..	..	..	..	..	..	..	..	..	..	..	..	0	22	0	0	22
SEN	0	..	**	..	1	0	..	..	0	..	2	7	0	..	0	0	112	407	10	147	676
SYC	..	..	..	**	..	..	..	..	..	0	..	..	..	..	..	..	0	53	1	47	101
SLE	..	..	0	..	**	..	..	0	..	..	..	..	..	0	..	..	3	97	28	52	180
SOM	0	..	..	..	..	**	..	0	..	0	..	0	0	..	..	..	2	54	0	83	139
ZAF	..	0	..	..	..	..	**	..	..	..	..	0	..	..	..	..	68	6,053	1,954	16,231	24,306
SDN	0	..	..	..	..	0	..	**	..	0	0	3	..	..	..	..	1	194	14	330	539
SWZ	..	..	..	..	..	..	..	..	**	..	..	..	..	..	..	..	0	..	0	0	..
TZA	1	..	..	..	..	0	..	2	0	**	..	3	2	4	1	0	22	211	15	175	423
TGO	0	..	0	..	..	..	..	..	..	0	**	1	..	..	0	..	66	96	34	101	298
TUN	0	..	1	..	0	..	..	1	..	0	2	**	..	..	1	0	38	2,702	36	725	3,502
UGA	0	..	..	..	..	0	..	0	..	2	..	0	**	..	0	..	4	132	19	25	179
ZAR	..	..	..	..	..	..	0	..	..	..	..	0	..	**	0	..	26	945	164	104	1,240
ZMB	0	..	..	0	..	..	..	..	0	9	..	32	0	6	**	39	89	417	26	820	1,353
ZWE	1	..	0	0	0	4	..	1	3	3	3	2	1	13	78	**	298	563	141	410	1,412
SSA	41	0	188	4	56	31	40	38	3	31	102	81	92	37	89	50	2,712	19,582	11,136	8,126	41,555
EEC	107	26	798	68	113	175	7,105	402	25	510	339	3,771	192	869	351	419	18,684	828,655	113,101	407,451	1,367,890
NNA	2	14	63	2	28	14	1,842	48	9	63	34	246	29	147	89	174	2,651	111,045	229,858	210,812	554,366
ROW	48	5	197	63	40	109	2,919	498	24	432	229	1,041	124	682	195	236	12,653	396,648	299,203	665,884	1,374,389
TOT	198	45	1,246	137	238	329	11,906	986	62	1,036	705	5,139	436	1,735	724	879	36,699	1,355,930	653,298	1,292,273	3,338,200

Note: ** means "not applicable."

131

Technical Notes

Balance of payments

The primary source of statistics for the balance of payments tables is the data compiled by the IMF for its *Balance of Payments Yearbooks,* with data on reserves and gold from the IMF's *International Financial Statistics.* Supplementary data, usually the most recent estimates, are obtained from national sources or estimated by World Bank staff. The general methodology underlying the presentation is described in the IMF's *Balance of Payments Manual* (fourth edition). For net long-term borrowing, data are reported to the World Bank's Debtor Reporting System (DRS). Any difference between long-term capital data in the IMF statistics for the balance of payments and in the DRS is shown as "other capital flows" in Tables 5-10. Values are in current U.S. dollars.

It is not yet possible to reconcile related measures from the data series for balance of payments, foreign trade, and national accounts. This reflects differences in definitions used, tinting, recording, and valuation of transactions, as well as the nature of basic data sources.

Balances can be computed for various definitions, including the trade balance (usually the difference between merchandise imports and exports); the resource gap (the difference between imports and exports of goods and nonfactor services); total to be financed (the resource gap less net factor income from abroad, net official private transfers, and, sometimes, official grants other than those for capital formation); and the current account balance (the total to be financed less official capital grants). The current account balance after net official transfers is shown here. However, because net official transfers may be used to finance balance of payments deficits in lieu of long-term loans, it may be analytically useful to consider other definitions of the balance as well, for example, the total to be financed, which puts net official transfers "below the line."

Tables 5-1, 5-2. Merchandise exports and imports

These tables are both valued f.o.b. (free on board) and comprise all transactions involving a change of ownership of goods, including nonmonetary gold, between residents of a country and those in the rest of the world. These transactions include those in which ownership changes even though goods do not cross customs borders. The few types of goods not covered by the merchandise account include travelers' purchases abroad (which are included in travel, a nonfactor service) and purchases by diplomatic and military personnel (which are included in nonfactor services).

Tables 5-3, 5-4. Exports and imports of total services

Service exports and imports imnclude total nonfactor and factor services, based on transactions involving ownership changes as explained above for goods. Nonfactor services comprise shipment, passenger and other transport services, travel, and current account transactions not separately reported (for example not classified as merchandise, nonfactor services, or transfers). These include transactions with nonresidents by government agencies and their personnel abroad, and also transactions by private residents with foreign governments and government personnel stationed in the reporting country. Factor services comprise services of labor and capital, thus covering income from direct investment abroad, interest, dividends, and property and labor income. Net interest is recorded on an accrual basis; that is, interest obligations are included whether payments are made or not. Because the data on trade in this chapter are derived according to methodologies different from those in Chapter 1, the two series cannot be compared directly. For example, the value of nonfactor services cannot be derived simply by subtracting merchandise trade (Tables 5-1 and 5-2) from exports and import of goods and nonfactor services (Tables 2-13 and 2-14). Current transfers comprise net transfer payments — between private persons, unofficial organizations, and governments of the reporting country and the rest of the world — that carry no provisions for repayment. They are classified as either private or official.

Table 5-5. Net private transfers

These inflows less outflows of unrequited transfers from private sources (in the recipient and donor country). They include workers' remittances if migrants are employed or expect to be employed for more than a year in their new economy, where they are considered residents; if migrants' stays are shorter, their remittances are included in services as labor income. Included also are transfers by migrants, gifts, dowries, and inheritances, alimony, and other support remittances.

Table 5-6. Net official transfers

This is the official counterpart of Table 5-5 and represents inflows of unrequited transfers from official sources less outflows of unrequited transfers from official sources in the reporting country to the rest of the world. They include transfers on both current and capital accounts, such as government grants of real resources and financial items such as subsidies to current budgets, grants of technical assistance, and government contributions to international organizations for administrative expenses.

Table 5-7. Current account balance

As presented here, is the difference between exports of goods and all services plus inflows of unrequited transfers (official and private) and imports of goods and all services plus outflows of unrequited transfers to the rest of the world.

Table 5-8. Net foreign direct investment

This is is the net amount invested or reinvested by nonresidents to acquire a lasting interest in enterprises in which they exercise significant managerial control. Investment includes equity capital, reinvested earnings, and other capital. The net figures subtract the value of direct investment abroad by residents of the reporting country.

Table 5-9. Net long-term borrowing

Net Long-term borrowings is calculated as disbursements less the repayment of principal (amortization) of public, publicly guaranteed, and private nonguaranteed borrowings that have an original or extended maturity of more than a year and that are repayable in foreign currencies, goods, or services. These data are as reported in the accord with the data on external debt, discussed in Chapter 3.

Table 5-10. Other capital flows

Other capital flows comprise the net balance of inflows and outflows of capital not elsewhere included. It covers, for example, changes in the stock of short-term debt, arrears and other liabilities (all adjusted for valuation changes resulting from exchange rate changes and other factors), and errors and omissions, as well as the differences between long-term capital flows as reported to the DRS (Table 2-9) and the similar item reported in the IMF's *Balance of Payments Yearbook*.

Table 5-11. Use of reserves

This reflects the variation from year to year of the net balance of international reserve assets and is valued throughout at year-end London prices (for example, US$37.37 an ounce in 1970 and US$484.10 in 1987). Positive numbers represent a decrease or use of reserves; negative numbers represent an increase in reserves.

Table 5-12. Import coverage ratio of imports

This gives the number of months, at current levels, that can adequately be covered by available foreign exchange reserves.

Prices

Tables 5-13, 5-14. Export and import unit values

The indexes for total export and import unit values are World Bank estimates figured from international prices for primary commodities and unit values for manufactures. These indexes are calculated by dividing the values of merchandise exports and imports (expressed in current U.S. dollars) by the volume of merchandise exports (f.o.b.) and imports (c.i.f.) (expressed in constant 1980 U.S. dollars) in the corresponding years (trade values are given in Tables 5-16 and 5-17, discussed below). Because of the way these trade unit value indexes are calculated, they reflect the composition of imports and exports in each year (that is, they are Paasche indexes, which having changing weights). These indexes thus reflect changes in the composition of trade and may not give a reliable trend in unit values when trade composition changes dramatically, as it has for countries where, for example, oil exports have grown from a minimal or nonexistent share of exports to the dominant share. By contrast, this index reflects more accurately shifts in a country's actual composition of trade than would an index using weights based on trade shares in a single year.

Alternative indexes trade unit values indexes could be calculated. For example, an index could be based on individual price series for major commodities weighted by relative trade shares in the base year (this would be a Laspeyres index); the comprehensiveness of such an index would depend on the level of detail available for individual traded goods. Fixed weights would eliminate the effects of large changes in trade composition over time but may reflect less accurately the actual composition of trade in any year other than the base year. It thus poses the problem of choosing the appropriate base year in such cases. Indexes could also be calculated from trade data in current and constant prices from the national accounts, which include nonfactor services; their reliability would depend on the implicit price indexes for nonfactor services, which are generally considered difficult to establish.

Table 5-15. Terms of trade

Shown here are the "net barter" terms of trade. They measure the relative movement of export unit values (or prices) against that of imports. The series is calculated as the ratio of a country's export unit value index to its import unit value index, times 100. It shows changes over a base year (here, 1987) in the level of export unit values as a percentage of import unit values. A similar terms of trade index could be calculated from fixed weight price indexes, as discussed above.

There are other definitions of terms of trade. One of the most common is the income terms of trade, which is also referred to as the capacity to import. It is usually calculated by deflating the value of exports of goods and nonfactor services (in current prices) by a price index (or unit value index) for imports.

Commodity trade

Statistics on merchandise trade are primarily from the UN trade data system. This accords with the *Yearbook of International Trade Statistics*, which is based on countries' customs returns. For the most recent years, statistics are often from secondary sources, such as the IMF, the World Bank, and UN Conference on Trade and Development (UNCTAD). Secondary sources are based on aggregated reports from national authorities that become available before detailed figures submitted to the United Nations are released. In some cases, these estimates contain adjustments to include significant components of a country's foreign trade not regularly reported in customs data.

The tables on selected commodity exports give data for sixteen major African primary exports. Figures are shown in cubic meters for data on forest products exports and metric tons for all other commodity tables. The data for forest products exports (Table 5-18) were taken from the Food and Agriculture Organization (FAO) *Yearbook of Forest Products*. The data for the tables on petroleum, metals, and minerals (Tables 5-18 through 5-22) are from a database compiled and maintained by the World Bank. Sources of the data include UNCTAD, the UN Trade Analysis and Reporting System (TARS), *World Metal Statistics*, and *Metallstatistik*, an annual publication of the Metallgesellschaft AG. All volumes shown refer to metal content weight. Since trade figures for these commodities are not always reported, some of the data represent best estimates and should be treated with caution.

The tables for agricultural commodity exports (Tables 5-23 through 5-32) have been drawn entirely from FAO computer files used for its *Trade Yearbook*. Most of the FAO data come from information provided by governments and other national and international organizations. Occasionally, unofficial data sources are used to supplement data from official sources. Where reliable sources are not available, estimates have been made based on the trade returns of trading partners. All tables on agricultural exports are given in volume terms (metric tons).

Tables 5-16, 5-17. Value of total merchandise exports (f.o.b.) value of total merchandise imports (c.i.f.)

Merchandise trade covers international movements of goods across customs borders. Imports are valued c.i.f. (cost, insurance, and freight) and exports f.o.b. (free on board). Figures for these two tables represent the sum of the United Nations Standard International Trade Classificaton, Revision 2 (SITC, Rev.2), sections 0 to 9. Data are from a database compiled by UNCTAD and used for its *Commodity Yearbook*.

Table 5-18. Forest products exports

Exports of forest production is given as an aggregate that includes all wood removed from forests and wood from trees outside the forest, whether in its natural form or partially processed (such as bark removed, split, and squared) (SITC 245, 246, and 247). It includes both coniferous (broadleaved or hardwoods) and nonconiferous (softwoods) woods. It further accounts for exports of sawnwood and sleepers (SITC 248). Finally, wood-based panels are included, an aggregate comprising veneer sheets, plywood, particle board, and fiberwood (compressed or noncompressed) (SITC 634 and 641).

Table 5-19. Petroleum exports

This table contains the volumes of crude petroleum exported. Cote d'Ivoire, a country classified as a middle-income oil importer, exports petroleum, due to a lack of refining capability, and imports refined oil.

Table 5-20. Copper exports

The table presents the unweighted sum of the metal content weights of copper ore and concentrate and of unrefined copper (blister), plus refined copper, metal, and alloys, unwrought. This is a different specification than the one adopted for the 1989 edition of this book; the reason for this change being the importance of refined copper exports for some African countries (for instance, Zaire and Zambia).

Table 5-21. Iron exports

These are exports of the metal content weight of iron ore.

Table 5-22. Manganese exports

This consists of the metal content weights of manganese ore and manganese concentrate.

Table 5-23. Phosphates exports

Volume of phosphates exports is expressed as the weight of mineral content in phosphate rock.

Table 5-24. Cocoa exports

Are given as an aggregate of the subcommodities cocoa beans, cocoa powder and cake, cocoa paste, cocoa butter, and chocolate products not elsewhere specified.

Table 5-25. Coffee exports

Only green and roasted beens are reported here.

Table 5-26. Cotton exports

This refers to cotton lint only.

Table 5-27. Groundnut exports

Groundnut exports include the weight of groundnuts in shelled equivalent, using a conversion factor of 70 percent to convert groundnuts in the shell to the shelled equivalent, and groundnu oil and groundnut cake, which have been added without conversion.

Table 5-28. Oil palm products exports

Oil palm products exports consist of the simple aggregate of palm oil and palm kernels.

Table 5-29. Sisal exports

Only sisal fiber exports are included.

Table 5-30. Tea exports

These are export of processed tea.

Table 5-31. Sugar exports

Figures on this table are shown in terms of raw sugar equivalent. The conversion factor to express refined sugar as the equivalent of raw sugar is 1.087 for all countries.

Table 5-32. Tobacco exports

Only tobacco leaves are covered.

Table 5-33. Meat exports

Meat exports are defined by the SITC category 011; that is, fresh, chilled, or frozen meat. Two new sets of tables are included in this chapter that were not in the *1989 African Economic and Financial Data*: disaggregated trade for some selected group of commodities, and direction of trade (on the international and intra-regional level) matrixes for Africa. Tables 5-34 to 5-39 are based on UNCTAD secretariat compilations that try to adjust the figures in order to overcome some discrepancies between aggregated total merchandise trade and total commodity trade, as reported originally from the trading countries. Adjustments are done using the best available estimates from all sources, including data available from the United Nations Statistical Office, the IMF, FAO and the UNCTAD secretariat.

Tables 5-34, 5-35. Primary commodities exports and imports

These represent total nonfuel primary commodities: the sum of agricultural primary commodities andmineral commodities defined as SITC sections 0, 1, 2 (less groups 233, 244, 266, 267), and 4; division 68; and item 522.56.

Table 5-36, 5-37. Food exports and imports

Data reported on these tables are the sum of SITC sections 0, 1, and 4 and division 22. Data refer to the sum of food, beverages, tobacco, oilseeds and oleaginous fruits, animal and vegetable oils, and fats

Table 5-38, 5-39. Minerals, ores and metals exports and imports

These are the sum of SITC divisions 27, 28, and 68 and item 522.56.

Table 5-40, 5-41. Agricultural raw materials exports and imports

Synthetics are excluded in these tables which represent the sum of SITC section 2 (less divisions 22, 27, and 28 and groups 233, 244, 266, and 267).

Three different kinds of "direction of trade" matrices are provided. On all of them, importers are listed in the top row, and exporters are listed in the left side column. The list of countries includes 52 African countries, the sum of the values for the sub-Saharan countries, the sum of European Community countries, North America

Table 5-42. Fuel exports

Figures are defined as SITC section 3.(sum of Canada, Mexico, and the United States), total exports and total imports, and "rest of the world," which was calculated as a residual. All of these tables were compiled using exports f.o.b. values taken from the IMF Direction of Trade computer files. Each of the matrixes (percentage of imports, percentage of exports, and current value) has a three page tables for 1981, 1985, and 1990 — so that changes in patterns of trade during the past decade can be better analyzed. The tables do not

begin with 1980 since data for that year were incomplete.

Tables 5-43, 5-44 and 5-45. Direction of trade, percent of imports

These tables show, for each importing country, the percentage of the value of its total imports that originates from each of the exporting countries for 1981, 1985 and 1990, respectively. They are calculated from Tables 5-49 to 5-51.

Tables 5-46, 5-47 and 5-48. Direction of trade, percentage of exports

As with the foregoing, these tables show for each exporter, the percentage of the value of total exports, f.o.b., that goes to each of its trade partners for 1981, 1985 and 1990, respectively. These are also calculated from Tables 5-49 to 5-51 below.

Table 5-49, 5-50 and 5-51. Direction of trade, millions of current U.S. dollars

These are the value of trade in goods and services to or from the countries indicated. They form the basis for the calculations in the previous six tables.

6

External Debt and Related Flows

The tables in this chapter provide a consistent presentation of the structure and terms of external debt and debt servicing. No data are presented on debt owed to domestic lenders. The aggregates and ratios provide various measures of a country's external debt situation.

These include the size of debt and its servicing requirements, the amount of debt relative to GDP, the ratio of debt-servicing payments to exports, and the interest rate and terms of the stock of debt (including grace period, maturity, and grant element).

Unlike presentations of debt data in other publications, these tables include IMF purchases, repurchases and net purchases as long- or short-term lending, repayments, or net lending. In a parallel manner, charges for IMF purchases are counted as interest on debt. IMF concessional and nonconcessional transactions are also included as appropriate in the lending data in these tables. While IMF purchases and repurchases are not strictly lending (they are swaps of currency) they do add to or subtract from the resources available for consumption or investment of a nation and do impose a liability against future income streams. For this reason, IMF transactions are included here.

6-1. Gross disbursements: official concessional long-term loans

	Millions of U.S. dollars (current prices and exchange rates)											Average		
	1980	1981	1982	1983	1984	1985	1986	1987	1988	1989	1990	75-79	80-85	86-MR
SUB-SAHARAN AFRICA	2,954	3,077	3,066	2,880	3,354	2,909	4,221	4,687	4,680	4,949	..	1,812	3,025	4,616
excluding Nigeria	2,905	3,074	3,066	2,813	3,354	2,893	4,221	4,687	4,656	4,858	..	1,790	2,999	4,588
Angola	..	..	..	..	..	..	..	..	..	..	..	..	..	..
Benin	44	21	37	50	28	32	64	61	51	136	..	26	35	78
Botswana	9	5	9	14	15	13	3	18	21	38	..	12	11	20
Burkina Faso	49	58	34	48	43	51	82	100	76	87	..	33	47	86
Burundi	44	29	51	80	56	58	99	131	105	96	..	16	53	108
Cameroon	132	125	90	72	64	60	74	54	75	169	..	115	91	93
Cape Verde	3	6	8	7	14	19	10	7	11	8	..	3	10	9
Central African Republic	28	29	16	24	33	43	56	96	91	66	..	8	29	77
Chad	5	4	0	12	6	9	30	46	59	91	..	18	6	57
Comoros	13	11	13	16	22	21	21	13	8	5	..	7	16	12
Congo, People's Republic of the	49	102	117	44	48	66	55	95	56	35	..	60	71	60
Cote d'Ivoire	94	43	110	69	43	39	53	157	43	23	..	50	66	69
Djibouti	2	1	4	14	39	30	23	30	22	13	..	2	15	22
Equatorial Guinea	10	4	14	2	1	8	18	23	25	19	..	1	7	21
Ethiopia	71	236	89	207	114	232	236	297	324	262	..	71	158	280
Gabon	16	5	7	10	24	25	29	53	· 39	18	..	10	15	35
Gambia, The	30	25	13	10	12	12	37	42	20	37	..	11	17	34
Ghana	142	81	64	64	88	123	215	305	397	525	..	54	94	361
Guinea	64	104	62	53	52	78	168	159	233	267	..	50	69	207
Guinea-Bissau	48	16	11	16	19	29	20	40	24	39	..	8	23	31
Kenya	182	152	209	121	169	107	212	213	264	408	..	90	157	274
Lesotho	9	12	20	18	20	26	17	25	33	46	..	7	18	30
Liberia	49	49	39	50	68	33	33	29	3	1	..	23	48	17
Madagascar	187	113	150	121	84	119	153	253	191	180	..	48	129	194
Malawi	62	43	41	47	91	46	118	93	106	123	..	42	55	110
Mali	84	105	114	124	102	105	174	133	142	178	..	41	106	157
Mauritania	102	112	123	100	80	77	178	157	111	105	..	62	99	138
Mauritius	18	30	23	21	16	20	20	48	45	35	..	10	21	37
Mozambique	0	0	0	3	816	304	364	266	154	126	..	..	187	228
Namibia	..	..	..	..	..	..	..	..	..	..	..	..	..	..
Niger	68	70	48	52	43	63	111	145	155	106	..	26	57	129
Nigeria	49	3	0	67	0	16	0	0	24	91	..	22	23	29
Rwanda	33	25	26	37	41	78	76	100	85	68	..	24	40	82
Sao Tome & Principe	8	4	6	6	5	8	7	9	12	18	..	2	6	12
Senegal	129	190	117	148	131	108	341	326	291	346	..	42	137	326
Seychelles	6	5	5	3	8	8	14	10	5	6	..	2	6	9
Sierra Leone	44	15	61	20	21	35	27	6	20	7	..	17	33	15
Somalia	88	224	121	95	122	100	104	87	64	75	..	88	125	83
Sudan	295	374	454	425	281	98	208	198	293	219	..	269	321	230
Swaziland	17	7	4	6	9	6	13	12	14	18	..	12	8	14
Tanzania	148	224	206	188	82	101	158	128	219	155	..	190	158	165
Togo	43	17	44	57	38	50	87	44	114	83	..	35	42	82
Uganda	31	37	152	54	64	103	83	156	220	188	..	17	74	162
Zaire	176	156	142	142	126	114	187	354	213	297	..	130	143	263
Zambia	272	160	124	96	133	169	164	99	130	66	..	58	159	115
Zimbabwe	1	45	88	67	83	67	79	67	92	70	..	0	59	78
NORTH AFRICA	2,250	2,334	1,785	1,107	1,311	1,222	1,084	1,470	1,338	1,097	..	2,216	1,667	1,078
Algeria	74	65	5	4	20	7	37	242	119	96	..	92	29	124
Egypt, Arab Republic of	1,228	1,085	963	685	906	697	490	698	795	576	..	1,675	927	640
Libya	..	..	..	..	..	..	..	..	..	..	..	..	..	..
Morocco	744	961	614	261	230	380	368	317	203	176	..	304	532	266
Tunisia	204	223	203	157	155	138	189	213	221	249	..	145	180	218
ALL AFRICA	5,204	5,411	4,851	3,987	4,665	4,131	5,305	6,157	6,018	6,046	..	4,028	4,689	5,694
South Africa	..	..	..	..	..	..	..	..	..	..	..	..	..	..

6-2. Gross disbursements: official nonconcessional long-term loans

| | *Millions of US dollars, current prices and exchange rates* | | | | | | | | | | | *Average* | | |
	1980	1981	1982	1983	1984	1985	1986	1987	1988	1989	1990	75–79	80–85	88–MR
SUB-SAHARAN AFRICA	2,433	3,581	3,204	4,134	2,919	2,231	2,510	2,450	2,299	1,923	..	1,347	3,084	2,296
excluding Nigeria	2,360	3,395	2,917	3,432	2,542	1,854	1,823	1,974	1,921	1,266	..	1,293	2,750	1,746
Angola	..	..	..	..	..	..	..	..	..	..	..	..	..	..
Benin	24	7	11	6	1	5	7	6	5	12	..	4	9	8
Botswana	15	19	17	20	44	52	25	75	29	26	..	5	28	39
Burkina Faso	18	22	20	22	6	5	14	13	14	9	..	5	16	13
Burundi	1	1	2	11	11	10	6	11	5	2	..	4	6	6
Cameroon	128	140	67	89	108	100	172	199	251	219	..	58	105	210
Cape Verde	0	14	14	10	1	1	0	0	0	0	..	0	7	0
Central African Republic	11	21	4	7	8	15	29	6	3	1	..	7	11	10
Chad	0	8	1	0	5	8	1	2	1	1	..	5	4	1
Comoros	0	0	2	2	2	2	4	0	0	0	..	0	1	1
Congo, People's Republic of the	35	16	21	116	28	72	60	61	108	16	..	33	48	61
Cote d'Ivoire	174	473	442	524	361	180	230	416	367	233	..	120	359	312
Djibouti	3	0	1	1	0	0	0	0	0	0	..	1	1	0
Equatorial Guinea	23	20	5	5	0	6	0	0	1	0	..	1	10	0
Ethiopia	7	93	33	4	7	29	75	11	7	22	..	16	29	29
Gabon	19	40	20	24	43	45	72	81	173	85	..	58	32	103
Gambia, The	4	18	20	2	4	2	9	7	0	1	..	4	8	4
Ghana	55	33	18	340	233	139	84	155	139	58	..	46	136	109
Guinea	8	4	16	15	15	9	37	12	6	12	..	18	11	17
Guinea-Bissau	0	4	4	1	10	12	2	1	1	2	..	2	5	2
Kenya	164	169	288	306	357	234	96	87	183	79	..	132	253	111
Lesotho	1	0	21	1	7	13	5	9	9	4	..	0	7	7
Liberia	49	85	94	82	69	31	11	3	12	0	..	28	68	7
Madagascar	103	122	108	54	65	65	88	70	29	11	..	12	86	50
Malawi	80	81	38	52	51	42	26	16	22	5	..	24	57	17
Mali	15	4	29	23	33	15	13	3	13	12	..	4	20	10
Mauritania	41	51	87	50	18	31	36	29	21	1	..	20	46	22
Mauritius	64	113	40	45	61	70	39	37	61	16	..	22	66	38
Mozambique	0	0	0	79	132	15	11	23	10	40	..	..	38	21
Namibia	..	..	..	..	..	..	..	..	..	..	..	..	..	..
Niger	33	89	19	68	35	29	21	30	6	23	..	14	46	20
Nigeria	73	186	287	702	377	377	687	476	378	657	..	54	334	550
Rwanda	0	0	1	1	0	0	0	0	0	0	..	0	0	0
Sao Tome & Principe	2	4	4	3	5	0	3	1	0	0	..	0	3	1
Senegal	124	133	214	174	90	105	67	138	30	20	..	40	140	64
Seychelles	6	2	4	6	2	5	4	3	2	3	..	0	4	3
Sierra Leone	22	46	8	24	20	0	9	0	0	0	..	11	20	2
Somalia	20	77	60	115	24	42	23	7	0	0	..	4	56	8
Sudan	481	262	482	249	47	3	2	3	89	17	..	140	254	28
Swaziland	12	14	26	33	14	9	15	9	4	4	..	5	18	8
Tanzania	102	71	53	191	95	54	76	25	9	2	..	62	94	28
Togo	29	26	7	36	33	18	16	5	22	6	..	15	25	12
Uganda	106	193	114	126	34	22	30	98	54	4	..	39	99	47
Zaire	171	319	136	156	187	206	154	179	113	136	..	137	196	146
Zambia	133	513	128	222	221	98	201	46	49	16	..	198	219	78
Zimbabwe	77	88	238	137	55	55	50	97	73	168	..	0	108	97
NORTH AFRICA	1,784	1,712	2,903	2,422	3,120	2,848	2,725	2,684	3,063	4,792	..	190	2,465	3,316
Algeria	492	415	544	770	817	592	585	759	1,503	2,905	..	283	605	1,438
Egypt, Arab Republic of	817	680	1,419	1,022	1,252	1,296	1,025	838	500	592	..	204	1,081	739
Libya	..	..	..	..	..	..	..	..	..	..	..	..	..	..
Morocco	356	458	770	423	719	691	667	763	733	855	..	182	570	755
Tunisia	119	159	170	207	332	269	448	324	327	440	..	89	209	385
ALL AFRICA	4,217	5,293	6,107	6,556	6,039	5,079	5,235	5,134	5,362	6,715	..	1,537	5,549	5,612
South Africa	..	..	..	..	..	..	..	..	..	..	..	..	..	..

6-3. Gross disbursements: private long-term loans

	Millions of U.S. dollars (current prices and exchange rates)											Average		
	1980	1981	1982	1983	1984	1985	1986	1987	1988	1989	1990	75-79	80-85	86-MR
SUB-SAHARAN AFRICA	6,275	6,503	7,539	5,174	4,330	3,890	3,615	3,280	3,375	3,014	..	3,254	5,618	3,321
excluding Nigeria	4,644	3,551	4,102	2,961	2,684	2,625	2,955	2,398	2,752	2,237	..	2,625	3,428	2,585
Angola	..	..	..	..	..	..	..	..	..	..	..	..	..	..
Benin	4	79	181	47	9	2	1	2	1	11	..	23	54	4
Botswana	3	3	33	4	17	4	7	6	3	0	..	1	10	4
Burkina Faso	6	3	24	19	5	2	1	0	0	4	..	4	10	1
Burundi	0	0	3	16	12	1	0	0	6	0	..	4	5	1
Cameroon	364	188	206	348	236	147	263	236	431	345	..	167	248	319
Cape Verde	0	0	0	0	1	1	1	0	0	0	..	0	0	0
Central African Republic	6	0	2	4	0	1	1	1	1	0	..	5	2	1
Chad	0	6	3	2	0	0	0	3	1	0	..	7	2	1
Comoros	0	0	1	0	0	0	0	0	0	0	..	0	0	0
Congo, People's Republic of the	412	224	489	335	378	315	263	304	444	83	..	59	359	273
Cote d'Ivoire	1,445	1,282	1,681	689	1,068	1,129	1,002	918	914	912	..	625	1,216	936
Djibouti	5	0	5	1	2	1	0	0	0	0	..	0	2	0
Equatorial Guinea	5	4	14	2	0	1	1	1	0	0	..	1	4	0
Ethiopia	33	58	17	35	131	87	75	129	135	13	..	5	60	88
Gabon	135	16	68	69	183	231	383	97	115	30	..	249	117	156
Gambia, The	22	8	15	2	0	0	0	0	0	0	..	1	8	0
Ghana	0	1	16	50	20	50	105	25	42	36	..	12	23	52
Guinea	57	29	19	32	13	21	3	3	38	0	..	12	29	11
Guinea-Bissau	21	1	2	0	4	18	0	6	0	0	..	24	8	1
Kenya	365	183	172	215	58	212	337	230	256	107	..	243	201	233
Lesotho	5	8	6	14	1	4	2	14	15	8	..	2	6	10
Liberia	11	3	0	8	0	0	0	0	0	0	..	41	4	0
Madagascar	155	96	45	43	6	16	8	12	17	2	..	46	60	10
Malawi	48	35	6	2	8	4	1	1	9	11	..	37	17	5
Mali	10	3	5	24	5	1	3	1	0	0	..	2	8	1
Mauritania	16	9	19	29	17	6	10	1	2	0	..	33	16	3
Mauritius	61	10	41	3	45	7	12	37	120	48	..	24	28	54
Mozambique	0	0	0	0	198	76	101	86	18	41	..	..	46	61
Namibia	..	..	..	..	..	..	..	..	..	..	..	..	..	..
Niger	190	249	112	73	27	30	67	50	28	49	..	52	113	48
Nigeria	1,631	2,952	3,437	2,212	1,646	1,265	660	882	622	777	..	629	2,191	735
Rwanda	0	2	4	3	9	2	0	4	0	0	..	2	3	1
Sao Tome & Principe	0	0	0	0	6	0	0	0	0	0	..	0	1	0
Senegal	141	47	29	74	17	20	68	34	13	8	..	80	55	31
Seychelles	0	0	6	2	4	7	15	5	7	5	..	0	3	8
Sierra Leone	42	45	15	1	3	0	0	0	0	0	..	27	18	0
Somalia	27	173	42	4	2	7	0	0	0	0	..	0	42	0
Sudan	145	183	122	0	0	0	0	0	0	0	..	110	75	0
Swaziland	0	0	1	1	5	15	1	0	0	0	..	6	4	0
Tanzania	218	82	125	52	49	18	4	0	0	0	..	70	91	1
Togo	50	1	0	0	0	0	0	0	0	0	..	117	9	0
Uganda	46	13	30	30	9	41	6	51	4	0	..	21	28	15
Zaire	249	109	43	19	0	0	6	8	2	58	..	262	70	18
Zambia	294	158	139	55	61	51	67	8	36	57	..	176	126	42
Zimbabwe	55	242	361	656	75	99	144	126	99	411	..	75	248	195
NORTH AFRICA	5,332	5,170	5,997	5,892	5,853	5,870	5,556	4,895	6,117	4,493	..	4,633	5,686	5,265
Algeria	2,832	2,317	2,068	2,748	3,339	3,389	3,923	3,574	4,290	3,055	..	2,789	2,782	3,710
Egypt, Arab Republic of	1,278	1,877	2,326	2,034	1,663	1,742	914	669	1,216	978	..	737	1,820	944
Libya	..	..	..	..	..	..	..	..	..	..	..	..	..	..
Morocco	935	671	1,339	560	458	356	354	390	257	209	..	808	720	302
Tunisia	288	305	265	549	394	384	365	262	356	251	..	299	364	308
ALL AFRICA	11,607	11,673	13,536	11,066	10,183	9,760	9,171	8,175	9,492	7,507	..	7,887	11,304	8,586
South Africa	..	..	..	..	..	..	..	..	..	..	..	..	..	..

6-4. Amortization: official concessional long-term loans

	Millions of U.S. dollars (current prices and exchange rates)											Average		
	1980	1981	1982	1983	1984	1985	1986	1987	1988	1989	1990	75-79	80-85	86-MR
SUB-SAHARAN AFRICA	245	241	248	325	388	472	742	680	701	664	..	204	320	697
excluding Nigeria	224	219	218	297	366	437	726	675	686	650	..	188	294	684
IDA-eligible countries	167	151	161	228	287	363	636	579	590	578	..	147	226	596
Angola	..	..	..	..	..	..	..	..	..	..	..	..	..	..
Benin	1	1	2	3	3	4	12	11	9	5	..	2	2	9
Botswana	0	0	0	2	2	3	4	4	6	5	..	0	1	5
Burkina Faso	4	0	2	1	6	4	9	10	18	13	..	2	3	13
Burundi	1	1	1	2	7	9	11	14	12	12	..	1	4	12
Cameroon	14	21	15	17	19	23	36	37	29	13	..	9	18	29
Cape Verde	0	0	0	0	1	1	1	1	1	1	..	0	0	1
Central African Republic	0	0	0	5	6	3	5	6	5	4	..	0	2	5
Chad	3	1	0	0	1	5	4	3	2	3	..	1	2	3
Comoros	0	0	0	0	1	0	1	0	0	0	..	0	0	0
Congo, People's Republic of the	11	17	17	17	22	14	5	4	5	4	..	4	16	5
Cote d'Ivoire	18	17	16	18	16	14	21	24	17	10	..	15	17	18
Djibouti	2	1	1	1	1	1	2	7	8	8	..	1	1	6
Equatorial Guinea	0	0	0	0	0	0	2	2	2	1	..	0	0	2
Ethiopia	9	12	13	13	20	29	47	48	67	52	..	9	16	54
Gabon	5	5	4	7	11	5	5	4	5	6	..	5	6	5
Gambia, The	0	0	1	1	4	1	4	7	6	6	..	0	1	6
Ghana	17	19	24	29	34	39	47	49	47	40	..	22	27	46
Guinea	43	41	34	24	55	36	32	77	46	40	..	31	39	49
Guinea-Bissau	0	0	0	0	0	2	2	1	1	3	..	0	0	2
Kenya	8	9	10	19	22	34	39	42	42	29	..	7	17	38
Lesotho	0	0	0	1	2	3	4	4	4	5	..	0	1	4
Liberia	1	0	1	2	4	1	2	2	4	1	..	8	2	2
Madagascar	6	2	2	4	7	7	17	23	28	22	..	6	5	23
Malawi	2	2	2	3	4	6	10	8	8	9	..	2	3	9
Mali	4	4	4	6	8	21	18	15	31	23	..	4	8	22
Mauritania	3	4	6	7	10	26	28	40	41	28	..	2	9	34
Mauritius	2	2	3	5	6	8	10	13	15	16	..	2	4	14
Mozambique	0	0	0	0	0	26	60	1	2	5	..	..	4	17
Namibia	..	..	..	..	..	..	..	..	..	..	..			
Niger	16	6	4	4	6	9	11	13	13	8	..	3	8	11
Nigeria	21	22	30	28	22	35	16	5	15	14	..	16	26	13
Rwanda	0	1	1	2	3	6	7	10	9	14	..	0	2	10
Sao Tome & Principe	0	0	0	0	0	0	0	2	1	1	..	0	0	1
Senegal	8	4	2	5	11	16	28	45	44	45	..	5	8	41
Seychelles	0	0	0	0	0	1	1	0	1	2	..	0	0	1
Sierra Leone	0	1	0	1	4	2	9	2	0	0	..	1	1	3
Somalia	2	1	2	4	3	2	5	6	1	3	..	2	2	4
Sudan	18	21	28	28	16	12	124	39	50	43	..	19	21	64
Swaziland	2	2	2	3	3	4	5	6	7	6	..	1	3	6
Tanzania	4	8	6	7	12	11	22	20	24	19	..	6	8	21
Togo	2	1	0	3	4	6	10	12	12	11	..	2	3	11
Uganda	3	1	9	22	15	7	12	11	11	79	..	5	10	28
Zaire	3	2	3	29	14	25	39	39	34	25	..	2	13	34
Zambia	7	8	3	2	3	9	12	9	7	20	..	4	5	12
Zimbabwe	5	4	0	0	0	2	3	4	11	10	..	5	2	7
NORTH AFRICA	350	372	400	367	398	489	469	440	484	548	..	270	396	485
Algeria	73	67	68	103	130	114	84	93	78	89	..	55	93	86
Egypt, Arab Republic of	171	201	232	176	188	257	200	157	201	258	..	146	204	204
Libya	..	..	..	..	..	..	..	..	..	..	..	..	..	..
Morocco	64	60	55	34	19	57	93	73	77	59	..	38	48	76
Tunisia	42	44	45	54	61	61	92	117	128	142	..	31	51	120
ALL AFRICA	595	613	648	692	786	961	1,211	1,120	1,185	1,212	..	474	716	1,182
Namibia	..	..	..	..	..	..	..	..	..	..	..	..	..	..
South Africa	..	..	..	..	..	..	..	..	..	..	..	..	..	..

6-5. Amortization: official nonconcessional long-term loans

	Millions of U.S. dollars (current prices and exchange rates)											Average		
	1980	1981	1982	1983	1984	1985	1986	1987	1988	1989	1990	75-79	80-85	86-MR
SUB-SAHARAN AFRICA	780	807	761	871	1,122	1,738	1,876	1,955	2,236	2,210	..	204	1,013	2,069
excluding Nigeria	755	780	722	811	1,055	1,248	1,775	1,824	1,946	1,976	..	188	895	1,880
Angola	..	..	..	..	..	..	..	..	..	..	..	..	..	..
Benin	1	3	3	4	2	4	5	4	5	4	..	0	3	5
Botswana	6	2	3	4	4	8	12	28	27	27	..	2	5	24
Burkina Faso	4	5	2	1	2	2	5	4	5	4	..	1	3	5
Burundi	1	1	0	5	5	1	3	3	5	4	..°	2	2	4
Cameroon	32	23	34	37	38	48	67	82	70	54	..	12	35	68
Cape Verde	0	0	1	1	2	1	2	2	2	2	..	0	1	2
Central African Republic	6	5	2	5	10	12	10	8	10	14	..	2	7	11
Chad	3	6	0	0	3	4	2	1	2	5	..	2	3	3
Comoros	0	0	0	0	0	0	0	0	0	0	..	0	0	0
Congo, People's Republic of the	17	15	21	18	14	16	7	10	18	24	..	9	17	15
Cote d'Ivoire	37	49	52	46	77	157	207	228	320	275	..	26	70	258
Djibouti	1	1	0	0	0	0	0	0	0	0	..	0	0	0
Equatorial Guinea	1	4	2	0	6	8	3	6	1	4	..	0	4	4
Ethiopia	1	3	8	25	32	39	45	36	33	41	..	1	18	39
Gabon	14	14	16	29	32	27	16	9	15	23	..	8	22	16
Gambia, The	0	0	3	6	2	3	17	8	6	5	..	2	2	9
Ghana	41	22	18	47	25	16	42	203	295	196	..	11	28	184
Guinea	21	15	13	9	21	8	19	33	28	23	..	7	15	26
Guinea-Bissau	0	0	0	1	3	1	1	2	2	2	..	0	1	2
Kenya	41	45	60	92	130	163	210	244	209	244	..	34	89	227
Lesotho	0	0	0	9	7	2	3	3	8	4	..	0	3	5
Liberia	5	7	12	18	28	15	12	3	7	3	..	5	14	6
Madagascar	3	16	16	17	28	53	57	40	60	73	..	4	22	58
Malawi	5	13	21	16	29	24	49	53	48	43	..	4	18	48
Mali	3	3	1	2	4	6	18	23	21	21	..	3	3	21
Mauritania	10	11	7	9	16	35	25	30	46	31	..	9	15	33
Mauritius	3	17	12	24	41	59	57	51	62	61	..	2	26	58
Mozambique	0	0	0	0	0	2	2	5	4	4	..	..	0	4
Namibia	..	..	..	..	..	..	..	..	..	..	..	..	..	..
Niger	2	17	23	2	5	10	19	31	40	28	..	0	10	30
Nigeria	25	27	39	60	67	490	101	131	290	234	..	17	118	189
Rwanda	0	0	0	0	0	0	0	0	0	0	..	1	0	0
Sao Tome & Principe	1	1	1	2	2	1	1	1	0	1	..	0	1	1
Senegal	20	18	22	20	28	59	98	122	123	87	..	8	28	108
Seychelles	0	0	0	1	1	2	2	2	1	3	..	0	1	2
Sierra Leone	19	13	7	3	13	6	26	2	5	1	..	5	10	9
Somalia	9	11	8	4	3	9	34	21	1	16	..	1	7	18
Sudan	106	49	98	55	59	9	22	2	8	3	..	33	63	9
Swaziland	3	3	5	5	7	8	14	17	17	13	..	1	5	15
Tanzania	46	43	23	40	40	30	44	33	22	28	..	16	37	32
Togo	8	10	10	16	28	43	58	30	39	34	..	6	19	40
Uganda	13	48	28	30	47	76	94	72	87	84	..	9	40	84
Zaire	185	172	56	34	113	165	164	205	153	370	..	35	121	223
Zambia	87	115	129	155	118	53	189	34	29	28	..	0	110	70
Zimbabwe	0	0	5	19	30	63	114	133	112	89	..	0	20	112
NORTH AFRICA	519	562	474	577	910	1,476	2,157	2,137	2,113	2,429	..	170	753	2,209
Algeria	171	185	219	324	528	580	698	808	891	1,086	..	30	335	871
Egypt, Arab Republic of	148	164	97	68	81	252	523	407	480	515	..	87	135	481
Libya	..	..	..	..	..	..	..	..	..	..	..	..	..	..
Morocco	139	124	109	113	204	510	751	693	534	624	..	34	200	651
Tunisia	61	89	49	72	97	134	185	229	208	204	..	19	84	207
ALL AFRICA	1,299	1,369	1,235	1,448	2,032	3,214	4,033	4,092	4,349	4,639	..	374	1,766	4,278
South Africa	..	..	..	..	..	..	..	..	..	..	..	..	..	..

6-6. Amortization: private long-term loans

	Millions of U.S. dollars (current prices and exchange rates)											Average		
	1980	1981	1982	1983	1984	1985	1986	1987	1988	1989	1990	75–79	80–85	86–MR
SUB-SAHARAN AFRICA	1,974	2,363	2,404	2,922	3,788	4,278	3,288	2,404	2,273	1,867	..	1,928	2,955	2,458
excluding Nigeria	1,777	1,777	1,633	1,848	1,652	2,036	2,160	2,096	1,934	1,630	..	1,784	1,787	1,955
Angola	..	..	..	..	..	..	..	..	..	..	..	..	..	..
Benin	3	3	4	4	17	19	19	3	0	0	..	1	8	6
Botswana	0	0	0	6	11	16	1	3	4	4	..	1	5	3
Burkina Faso	2	2	3	5	5	11	8	4	2	1	..	1	5	4
Burundi	3	2	2	2	1	4	6	8	7	6	..	2	2	7
Cameroon	85	91	150	115	143	399	330	287	286	131	..	34	164	258
Cape Verde	0	0	0	0	0	0	0	0	0	0	..	0	0	0
Central African Republic	1	2	1	2	1	1	1	2	1	2	..	1	1	1
Chad	0	0	1	0	3	6	0	0	0	1	..	1	2	0
Comoros	0	0	0	0	0	0	0	0	0	0	..	0	0	0
Congo, People's Republic of the	12	79	84	180	207	221	233	294	258	151	..	19	130	234
Cote d'Ivoire	500	545	533	546	429	492	675	696	465	556	..	185	508	598
Djibouti	0	0	1	2	2	1	2	2	2	1	..	0	1	2
Equatorial Guinea	0	1	1	1	1	0	0	0	0	0	..	0	1	0
Ethiopia	7	11	15	24	27	34	53	64	77	104	..	4	20	74
Gabon	260	203	169	134	152	136	103	11	7	33	..	115	176	38
Gambia, The	0	0	8	0	0	0	0	2	1	1	..	0	1	1
Ghana	42	4	3	7	17	19	35	53	75	90	..	9	15	63
Guinea	11	7	10	10	7	4	2	6	19	13	..	6	8	10
Guinea-Bissau	3	3	2	1	1	1	0	1	0	0	..	0	1	0
Kenya	171	204	211	204	225	223	207	147	148	100	..	125	206	150
Lesotho	3	3	4	5	8	10	3	2	4	6	..	0	5	4
Liberia	12	4	7	1	0	0	0	0	0	0	..	14	4	0
Madagascar	24	25	20	1	1	22	25	24	27	18	..	3	16	23
Malawi	28	31	22	16	27	36	34	12	9	3	..	9	27	14
Mali	2	2	1	2	3	3	3	7	2	1	..	0	2	3
Mauritania	13	30	8	4	5	4	7	6	1	7	..	30	10	5
Mauritius	14	16	24	49	40	26	17	17	68	13	..	6	28	29
Mozambique	0	0	0	0	0	4	5	9	8	7	..	..	1	7
Namibia	..	..	..	..	..	..	..	..	..	..	..	..	..	..
Niger	40	61	131	76	37	37	39	38	35	38	..	11	64	38
Nigeria	197	586	771	1,074	2,136	2,242	1,128	308	339	237	..	144	1,168	503
Rwanda	2	2	1	3	3	5	5	4	3	3	..	0	3	3
Sao Tome & Principe	0	0	0	0	0	0	0	0	0	0	..	0	0	0
Senegal	137	66	22	16	23	25	38	57	64	59	..	38	48	55
Seychelles	0	0	0	1	1	2	3	3	7	8	..	0	1	5
Sierra Leone	29	33	7	4	5	4	1	2	0	1	..	17	14	1
Somalia	0	31	1	0	0	0	0	0	0	0	..	1	5	0
Sudan	7	3	7	2	1	0	5	0	0	0	..	28	3	1
Swaziland	3	5	5	5	0	5	4	12	2	2	..	1	4	5
Tanzania	38	47	27	22	11	8	2	0	0	0	..	26	25	1
Togo	9	8	7	4	12	14	23	8	0	2	..	23	9	8
Uganda	17	18	10	22	35	25	13	4	6	0	..	5	21	6
Zaire	90	37	26	34	40	34	38	11	4	17	..	39	43	17
Zambia	175	170	65	18	11	9	27	39	59	60	..	134	75	46
Zimbabwe	34	31	42	324	142	177	198	257	284	193	..	1	125	233
NORTH AFRICA	3,736	4,098	4,768	5,055	4,508	4,332	4,046	3,793	4,424	5,302	..	1,384	4,416	4,391
Algeria	2,237	2,300	2,668	2,889	2,950	2,810	2,803	2,939	3,512	4,039	..	669	2,642	3,323
Egypt, Arab Republic of	838	1,045	1,167	1,278	1,195	1,131	780	257	441	713	..	483	1,109	548
Libya	..	..	..	..	..	..	..	..	..	..	..	..	..	..
Morocco	475	525	696	601	81	111	189	213	156	194	..	162	415	188
Tunisia	186	228	237	286	282	280	275	384	315	357	..	70	250	333
ALL AFRICA	5,710	6,460	7,172	7,976	8,296	8,609	7,334	6,197	6,697	7,169	..	3,312	7,371	6,849
South Africa	..	..	..	..	..	..	..	..	..	..	..	..	..	..

6–7. Amortization: long–term loans

	Millions of U.S. dollars (current prices and exchange rates)											Average		
	1980	1981	1982	1983	1984	1985	1986	1987	1988	1989	1990	75–79	80–85	86–MR
SUB-SAHARAN AFRICA	2,997	3,410	3,416	4,123	5,298	6,490	5,905	5,038	5,208	4,738	..	1,556	4,289	5,222
excluding Nigeria	2,755	2,775	2,575	2,961	3,073	3,722	4,660	4,594	4,564	4,253	..	1,379	2,977	4,518
Angola	..	..	..	..	..	..	..	..	..	..	..	..	..	..
Benin	6	7	9	11	22	27	36	19	13	9	..	3	14	19
Botswana	6	2	4	12	17	27	17	36	38	36	..	3	11	32
Burkina Faso	11	8	8	8	13	17	22	18	25	18	..	4	11	21
Burundi	4	4	3	9	14	14	19	25	23	22	..	4	8	22
Cameroon	131	135	199	168	200	470	433	406	384	197	..	55	217	355
Cape Verde	0	0	1	1	2	2	2	4	4	3	..	0	1	3
Central African Republic	7	6	3	12	16	17	16	15	15	19	..	3	10	16
Chad	5	7	1	0	7	15	5	4	5	8	..	4	6	5
Comoros	0	0	0	0	1	0	1	0	0	0	..	0	0	0
Congo, People's Republic of the	41	112	122	215	243	251	244	308	281	179	..	32	164	253
Cote d'Ivoire	555	611	601	610	522	664	903	948	801	841	..	226	594	873
Djibouti	2	2	2	3	3	2	4	9	10	9	..	1	2	8
Equatorial Guinea	2	5	3	2	7	8	5	8	3	5	..	1	4	5
Ethiopia	17	25	35	63	79	102	145	148	177	197	..	14	54	167
Gabon	279	222	189	170	195	168	123	23	28	63	..	129	204	59
Gambia, The	0	1	11	8	6	4	21	17	12	12	..	2	5	16
Ghana	100	45	45	83	75	74	123	305	417	328	..	42	70	293
Guinea	76	64	57	43	82	48	53	116	93	75	..	45	62	84
Guinea-Bissau	3	3	2	2	4	3	3	4	3	5	..	1	3	4
Kenya	220	258	281	315	376	420	456	433	400	372	..	166	312	415
Lesotho	3	3	5	15	17	14	10	9	17	15	..	1	10	13
Liberia	18	12	20	21	31	15	14	5	11	4	..	26	20	8
Madagascar	33	42	38	23	37	82	98	86	115	112	..	14	42	103
Malawi	35	47	44	35	60	65	93	72	65	55	..	16	48	71
Mali	9	9	7	10	15	30	39	45	54	45	..	7	13	46
Mauritania	26	44	20	20	31	65	60	76	87	66	..	42	34	72
Mauritius	19	35	39	77	86	93	84	82	145	89	..	10	58	100
Mozambique	0	0	0	0	0	31	67	16	14	17	..	..	5	28
Namibia	..	..	..	..	..	..	..	..	..	..	..	..	..	..
Niger	58	84	158	83	48	56	69	81	89	74	..	14	81	78
Nigeria	243	635	841	1,162	2,225	2,768	1,245	445	644	485	..	177	1,312	705
Rwanda	3	2	3	5	6	11	13	14	12	17	..	2	5	14
Sao Tome & Principe	1	1	2	2	2	2	1	2	1	2	..	0	2	2
Senegal	165	88	45	41	62	100	164	225	231	191	..	51	84	203
Seychelles	0	0	0	2	3	5	6	6	9	13	..	0	2	8
Sierra Leone	48	47	14	8	22	11	36	5	6	3	..	23	25	12
Somalia	11	43	10	8	7	11	40	27	2	18	..	3	15	22
Sudan	131	74	132	84	76	21	151	42	58	46	..	80	86	74
Swaziland	8	10	12	13	10	17	23	35	25	21	..	3	12	26
Tanzania	88	97	57	69	64	49	69	53	47	47	..	47	71	54
Togo	19	18	17	23	45	63	91	50	51	48	..	31	31	60
Uganda	33	67	46	73	97	108	119	88	104	163	..	20	71	118
Zaire	277	210	85	98	167	225	241	254	191	413	..	76	177	275
Zambia	269	293	196	175	132	71	228	82	94	108	..	173	189	128
Zimbabwe	40	35	47	343	172	242	316	395	407	292	..	5	146	352
NORTH AFRICA	4,605	5,034	5,641	5,998	5,817	6,297	6,676	6,375	7,028	8,293	..	1,823	5,565	7,093
Algeria	2,482	2,552	2,955	3,317	3,608	3,504	3,585	3,840	4,481	5,221	..	754	3,069	4,282
Egypt, Arab Republic of	1,157	1,410	1,495	1,522	1,464	1,640	1,508	826	1,127	1,486	..	715	1,448	1,237
Libya	..	..	..	..	..	..	..	..	..	..	..	..	..	..
Morocco	678	710	861	747	304	678	1,033	979	770	879	..	234	663	915
Tunisia	290	361	331	412	441	476	551	730	651	707	..	120	385	660
ALL AFRICA	7,603	8,443	9,057	10,121	11,115	12,787	12,581	11,413	12,236	13,031	..	3,379	9,854	12,315
South Africa	..	..	..	..	..	..	..	..	..	..	..	..	..	..

6–8. Interest payments: official concessional long–term loans

	Millions of U.S. dollars (current prices and exchange rates)											Average		
	1980	1981	1982	1983	1984	1985	1986	1987	1988	1989	1990	75–79	80–85	86–MR
SUB-SAHARAN AFRICA	258	208	210	209	224	254	350	368	412	412	..	143	227	386
excluding Nigeria	240	191	195	193	212	241	338	363	403	401	..	127	212	376
Angola	..	..	..	..	..	..	..	..	..	..	..	..	..	..
Benin	1	2	2	3	2	4	5	5	5	4	..	1	2	5
Botswana	1	1	1	1	2	2	2	3	2	3	..	0	1	3
Burkina Faso	2	2	2	3	2	4	5	7	7	8	..	1	3	7
Burundi	1	1	2	2	4	4	6	8	10	9	..	0	2	8
Cameroon	15	14	17	18	18	19	24	24	14	10	..	8	17	18
Cape Verde	0	0	0	0	0	0	1	1	1	1	..	0	0	1
Central African Republic	0	1	1	1	1	2	3	5	5	4	..	0	1	4
Chad	0	0	0	0	0	2	1	3	3	1	..	0	0	2
Comoros	0	0	1	1	1	1	1	1	0	1	..	0	1	1
Congo, People's Republic of the	12	9	8	9	8	9	1	3	10	6	..	3	9	5
Cote d'Ivoire	14	14	15	12	12	11	17	10	5	7	..	11	13	10
Djibouti	1	0	0	0	1	1	2	3	3	2	..	1	1	3
Equatorial Guinea	0	0	0	0	0	0	0	0	1	0	..	0	0	0
Ethiopia	9	9	9	10	13	13	18	24	38	29	..	8	11	27
Gabon	3	3	3	2	3	3	2	2	2	4	..	3	3	3
Gambia, The	0	1	1	1	1	1	1	2	3	3	..	0	1	2
Ghana	14	15	17	19	12	14	16	20	24	23	..	14	15	21
Guinea	12	12	12	10	10	10	6	14	13	15	..	8	11	12
Guinea-Bissau	0	0	0	0	0	1	1	2	2	2	..	0	0	2
Kenya	11	13	15	17	19	22	28	28	31	25	..	7	16	28
Lesotho	0	0	1	1	1	1	2	2	2	2	..	0	1	2
Liberia	2	1	1	1	1	1	2	2	3	1	..	2	1	2
Madagascar	5	4	3	4	6	6	9	15	18	17	..	4	5	15
Malawi	4	5	4	4	5	6	9	8	7	9	..	3	5	8
Mali	2	2	4	5	6	10	10	12	14	12	..	2	5	12
Mauritania	7	8	14	11	9	13	13	12	11	12	..	3	10	12
Mauritius	2	2	3	3	4	4	5	7	9	8	..	1	3	7
Mozambique	0	0	0	0	0	11	26	7	8	9	..	..	2	13
Namibia	..	..	..	..	..	..	..	..	..	..	..	..	..	..
Niger	2	3	4	4	4	4	6	11	11	6	..	2	4	9
Nigeria	18	17	15	16	12	13	12	5	9	11	..	16	15	9
Rwanda	1	2	2	2	3	3	4	7	8	7	..	1	2	7
Sao Tome & Principe	0	0	0	0	0	1	0	0	1	0	..	0	0	0
Senegal	8	6	4	6	8	4	19	23	31	76	..	3	6	37
Seychelles	0	0	0	0	0	0	1	1	2	2	..	0	0	2
Sierra Leone	1	1	0	1	1	1	3	0	0	0	..	1	1	1
Somalia	2	3	4	5	3	3	3	3	3	4	..	1	3	3
Sudan	32	24	10	8	8	10	43	16	18	10	..	18	15	22
Swaziland	1	2	1	1	1	1	1	3	2	2	..	0	1	2
Tanzania	8	8	10	10	11	7	9	12	11	11	..	5	9	11
Togo	1	1	1	2	4	4	5	6	11	7	..	1	2	7
Uganda	2	0	2	3	13	6	6	7	8	16	..	2	4	9
Zaire	47	7	11	5	8	7	7	21	20	9	..	7	14	14
Zambia	16	14	8	4	2	7	4	13	14	9	..	5	9	10
Zimbabwe	1	1	2	4	5	8	11	10	12	15	..	1	4	12
NORTH AFRICA	317	307	309	290	266	258	263	217	296	376	..	266	291	288
Algeria	33	34	40	35	34	19	19	17	27	27	..	23	33	23
Egypt, Arab Republic of	179	188	162	171	179	173	163	104	151	218	..	172	175	159
Libya	..	..	..	..	..	..	..	..	..	..	..	..	..	..
Morocco	73	51	72	45	11	24	30	36	49	61	..	48	46	44
Tunisia	32	34	35	39	42	42	51	60	69	70	..	23	37	63
ALL AFRICA	575	515	519	499	490	512	613	585	708	788	..	409	518	674
South Africa	..	..	..	..	..	..	..	..	..	..	..	..	..	..

6–9. Interest payments: official nonconcessional long–term loans

	Millions of U.S. dollars (current prices and exchange rates)											Average		
	1980	1981	1982	1983	1984	1985	1986	1987	1988	1989	1990	75–79	80–85	86–MR
SUB-SAHARAN AFRICA	539	595	763	897	1,177	1,318	1,522	1,602	1,947	1,580	..	193	882	1,663
excluding Nigeria	492	548	705	795	1,035	1,157	1,359	1,267	1,258	1,163	..	166	789	1,262
Angola	..	..	..	..	..	..	..	..	..	..	..	..	..	..
Benin	1	1	2	3	2	3	3	3	2	2	..	0	2	3
Botswana	5	5	6	7	9	15	22	28	28	26	..	3	8	26
Burkina Faso	2	3	2	3	1	4	6	7	6	8	..	0	3	7
Burundi	1	1	1	1	2	2	4	4	5	4	..	0	1	4
Cameroon	29	35	37	41	46	47	66	78	72	62	..	9	39	70
Cape Verde	0	0	1	2	3	2	1	3	2	1	..	0	1	2
Central African Republic	1	1	3	7	6	6	7	5	3	5	..	0	4	5
Chad	1	1	1	1	1	0	1	1	1	1	..	0	1	1
Comoros	0	0	0	0	0	1	0	0	0	0	..	0	0	0
Congo, People's Republic of the	14	13	14	10	9	17	33	25	24	32	..	5	13	29
Cote d'Ivoire	63	70	95	121	157	189	258	198	221	198	..	21	116	219
Djibouti	0	0	0	0	0	0	0	0	0	0	..	0	0	0
Equatorial Guinea	0	1	1	1	1	1	2	3	2	0	..	0	1	2
Ethiopia	7	7	14	16	13	11	13	13	11	12	..	3	11	12
Gabon	17	14	13	12	13	13	13	23	56	91	..	8	14	46
Gambia, The	1	1	2	3	2	2	6	3	3	3	..	0	2	4
Ghana	14	12	12	19	33	50	67	68	70	67	..	3	23	68
Guinea	10	7	7	8	9	7	8	28	14	16	..	7	8	17
Guinea-Bissau	0	0	0	0	0	0	0	2	1	1	..	0	0	1
Kenya	59	63	76	88	108	123	144	149	135	121	..	26	86	137
Lesotho	0	0	2	3	1	2	2	3	3	3	..	0	1	3
Liberia	7	10	17	23	26	20	13	4	5	0	..	4	17	6
Madagascar	4	14	23	14	15	38	46	78	52	84	..	1	18	65
Malawi	7	18	16	20	22	23	30	25	25	22	..	3	18	26
Mali	1	1	2	3	4	7	8	7	6	5	..	0	3	7
Mauritania	4	9	9	13	14	14	17	19	23	15	..	3	11	19
Mauritius	9	15	22	22	25	27	30	30	32	28	..	2	20	30
Mozambique	0	0	0	0	0	4	4	5	12	20	..	..	1	10
Namibia	..	..	..	..	..	..	..	..	..	..	..	..	..	..
Niger	5	8	13	9	8	17	23	38	37	12	..	1	10	28
Nigeria	47	47	58	102	142	161	163	335	689	417	..	27	93	401
Rwanda	0	0	0	0	0	0	0	0	0	0	..	0	0	0
Sao Tome & Principe	0	0	0	0	0	0	0	0	0	2	..	0	0	1
Senegal	17	20	29	40	47	45	82	92	80	66	..	5	33	80
Seychelles	0	0	0	1	1	1	2	2	2	2	..	0	1	2
Sierra Leone	4	4	6	6	9	3	12	2	2	0	..	2	5	4
Somalia	0	1	4	7	10	6	19	6	0	10	..	0	5	9
Sudan	25	39	56	45	41	57	24	19	3	15	..	9	44	15
Swaziland	6	5	6	6	8	7	9	11	11	9	..	1	6	10
Tanzania	26	23	23	22	21	16	24	29	25	23	..	9	22	25
Togo	11	10	11	20	26	32	36	24	57	25	..	2	18	36
Uganda	4	6	21	33	44	42	32	26	22	26	..	0	25	27
Zaire	73	56	52	52	160	197	114	120	116	60	..	16	98	103
Zambia	64	67	91	89	95	57	121	35	28	34	..	23	77	55
Zimbabwe	0	7	15	24	43	49	57	51	61	52	..	0	23	55
NORTH AFRICA	333	556	601	808	932	1,090	1,502	1,101	1,657	1,893	..	130	720	1,538
Algeria	128	147	160	190	227	256	298	296	359	388	..	32	185	335
Egypt, Arab Republic of	87	274	265	409	358	418	627	315	612	668	..	40	302	556
Libya	..	..	..	..	..	..	..	..	..	..	..	..	..	..
Morocco	75	87	129	151	274	326	460	343	516	668	..	37	174	497
Tunisia	43	48	47	58	73	90	117	147	170	169	..	21	60	151
ALL AFRICA	872	1,151	1,364	1,705	2,109	2,408	3,024	2,703	3,604	3,473	..	323	1,602	3,201
South Africa	..	..	..	..	..	..	..	..	..	..	..	..	..	..

6–10. Interest payments: private long–term loans

	Millions of U.S. dollars (current prices and exchange rates)											Average		
	1980	1981	1982	1983	1984	1985	1986	1987	1988	1989	1990	75–79	80–85	86–MR
SUB-SAHARAN AFRICA	1,482	1,742	1,999	1,982	2,208	2,260	1,459	1,089	1,535	1,577	..	454	1,946	1,415
excluding Nigeria	1,016	1,137	1,199	1,102	1,114	1,136	1,119	876	797	726	..	403	1,117	879
Angola	..	..	..	..	..	..	..	..	..	..	..	..	..	..
Benin	1	1	1	7	13	7	14	7	0	6	..	0	5	7
Botswana	1	1	3	4	5	4	3	3	3	3	..	0	3	3
Burkina Faso	3	1	3	2	3	2	1	1	0	0	..	0	2	1
Burundi	1	1	0	0	2	2	2	3	2	1	..	0	1	2
Cameroon	77	89	97	81	102	71	99	77	107	40	..	20	86	81
Cape Verde	0	0	0	0	0	0	0	0	0	0	..	0	0	0
Central African Republic	0	0	0	0	0	1	1	0	0	0	..	1	0	0
Chad	0	0	0	0	0	0	0	0	0	0	..	0	0	0
Comoros	0	0	0	0	0	0	0	0	0	0	..	0	0	0
Congo, People's Republic of the	12	72	72	78	81	107	58	57	50	57	..	9	70	56
Cote d'Ivoire	306	365	470	426	461	491	549	355	261	260	..	105	420	356
Djibouti	0	0	0	1	0	1	1	0	0	0	..	0	0	0
Equatorial Guinea	0	0	0	0	0	0	0	0	0	0	..	0	0	0
Ethiopia	3	4	7	8	14	17	20	20	32	34	..	1	9	27
Gabon	100	71	80	39	44	41	35	20	20	21	..	37	63	24
Gambia, The	0	0	1	1	0	0	1	2	0	0	..	0	0	1
Ghana	7	2	1	10	6	6	15	19	16	16	..	4	5	16
Guinea	2	3	3	3	2	2	0	0	5	3	..	2	3	2
Guinea-Bissau	1	1	1	0	0	1	0	0	0	0	..	0	1	0
Kenya	113	110	118	90	75	72	68	80	70	76	..	41	96	73
Lesotho	1	1	2	3	2	1	0	1	2	2	..	0	2	1
Liberia	16	11	5	0	0	0	0	0	0	0	..	5	5	0
Madagascar	19	19	26	20	22	21	17	21	19	23	..	3	21	20
Malawi	25	31	20	13	12	11	9	4	4	5	..	7	19	5
Mali	1	1	0	1	2	1	1	1	1	0	..	0	1	1
Mauritania	4	4	2	3	4	2	5	1	1	1	..	3	3	2
Mauritius	15	27	25	16	13	13	9	8	12	13	..	3	18	10
Mozambique	0	0	0	0	0	4	2	3	4	6	..	..	1	4
Namibia	..	..	..	..	..	..	..	..	..	..	..	..	..	..
Niger	58	56	55	39	28	24	24	28	32	21	..	12	43	26
Nigeria	466	605	800	880	1,095	1,125	340	213	738	851	..	51	828	536
Rwanda	0	0	0	0	0	1	1	1	1	0	..	0	0	1
Sao Tome & Principe	0	0	0	0	0	1	0	0	0	0	..	0	0	0
Senegal	46	30	15	9	20	21	17	25	24	22	..	19	24	22
Seychelles	0	0	0	1	1	1	1	2	3	3	..	0	0	2
Sierra Leone	5	8	2	2	1	1	0	0	0	0	..	4	3	0
Somalia	0	0	2	4	0	0	0	0	0	0	..	0	1	0
Sudan	5	54	0	30	0	41	2	0	0	0	..	12	22	0
Swaziland	2	3	2	1	1	1	2	2	1	1	..	0	1	1
Tanzania	15	16	14	8	3	2	1	0	0	0	..	7	9	0
Togo	8	10	13	7	11	8	7	4	6	5	..	5	9	6
Uganda	0	1	1	3	6	3	3	1	2	0	..	1	2	2
Zaire	99	76	38	70	71	64	55	30	12	5	..	52	70	26
Zambia	63	48	42	35	16	5	15	15	26	20	..	47	35	19
Zimbabwe	9	24	77	87	92	88	81	84	80	81	..	3	63	81
NORTH AFRICA	2,105	2,107	2,108	1,974	2,004	1,920	2,033	1,945	2,167	2,352	..	776	2,036	2,124
Algeria	1,275	1,180	1,227	1,050	1,115	1,134	1,246	1,262	1,425	1,459	..	501	1,163	1,348
Egypt, Arab Republic of	193	228	283	379	431	435	422	229	276	320	..	103	325	312
Libya	..	..	..	..	..	..	..	..	..	..	..	..	..	..
Morocco	483	559	463	436	324	234	228	311	314	404	..	131	416	314
Tunisia	154	141	135	110	134	118	138	143	152	170	..	41	132	150
ALL AFRICA	3,587	3,850	4,107	3,956	4,213	4,181	3,492	3,034	3,702	3,929	..	1,230	3,982	3,539
South Africa	..	..	..	..	..	..	..	..	..	..	..	..	..	..

6–11. Interest payments: long–term loans

	Millions of U.S. dollars (current prices and exchange rates)											Average		
	1980	1981	1982	1983	1984	1985	1986	1987	1988	1989	1990	75–79	80–85	86–MR
SUB-SAHARAN AFRICA	2,277	2,547	2,978	3,092	3,613	3,830	3,330	3,059	3,895	3,574	..	604	3,056	3,464
excluding Nigeria	1,746	1,878	2,105	2,095	2,365	2,531	2,815	2,506	2,460	2,294	..	511	2,120	2,519
Angola	..	..	..	..	..	..	..	..	..	..	..	..	..	..
Benin	3	3	6	13	17	14	22	15	8	12	..	2	9	14
Botswana	7	7	10	13	15	21	28	34	34	33	..	4	12	32
Burkina Faso	6	6	8	8	6	10	12	14	14	16	..	3	7	14
Burundi	3	2	3	4	8	9	12	15	17	15	..	1	5	15
Cameroon	121	138	151	139	166	136	189	179	193	111	..	38	142	168
Cape Verde	0	0	1	2	3	3	2	3	4	2	..	0	1	3
Central African Republic	1	2	4	8	8	9	11	11	9	9	..	1	5	10
Chad	1	1	1	1	1	2	2	4	4	2	..	1	1	3
Comoros	0	0	1	1	2	2	1	1	0	1	..	0	1	1
Congo, People's Republic of the	38	94	94	97	99	132	92	84	84	95	..	17	92	89
Cote d'Ivoire	383	449	580	559	629	691	823	563	487	465	..	138	549	585
Djibouti	1	1	1	1	1	2	3	3	4	2	..	1	1	3
Equatorial Guinea	0	1	1	1	1	1	2	4	2	1	..	0	1	2
Ethiopia	19	21	30	34	39	41	51	57	82	76	..	11	31	66
Gabon	120	88	96	53	61	57	51	45	79	116	..	49	79	73
Gambia, The	1	3	4	4	4	2	8	7	6	6	..	0	3	7
Ghana	34	29	31	48	51	70	97	107	111	106	..	22	44	105
Guinea	24	22	22	22	21	20	14	43	32	34	..	16	22	31
Guinea-Bissau	1	1	1	1	1	2	1	5	3	3	..	0	1	3
Kenya	182	185	209	195	202	217	240	258	236	222	..	74	198	239
Lesotho	1	2	5	6	4	4	4	6	7	7	..	0	4	6
Liberia	25	22	23	24	28	21	15	6	7	1	..	11	24	7
Madagascar	28	37	53	38	43	65	73	114	89	125	..	8	44	100
Malawi	36	54	41	38	39	40	47	37	36	36	..	13	41	39
Mali	4	4	7	9	12	18	19	19	20	18	..	2	9	19
Mauritania	15	21	26	27	27	30	34	33	36	28	..	9	24	33
Mauritius	26	45	49	42	43	44	44	45	52	49	..	6	41	48
Mozambique	0	0	0	0	0	20	31	15	24	35	..	..	3	26
Namibia	..	..	..	..	..	..	..	..	..	..	..	..	..	..
Niger	65	66	72	52	40	45	53	77	79	39	..	15	57	62
Nigeria	531	669	873	998	1,249	1,299	515	553	1,435	1,280	..	93	936	946
Rwanda	2	2	2	3	4	4	5	7	8	8	..	1	3	7
Sao Tome & Principe	0	0	0	1	1	1	1	1	1	3	..	0	1	1
Senegal	70	56	49	56	76	70	118	140	136	164	..	27	63	139
Seychelles	0	0	1	1	2	2	4	5	7	7	..	0	1	6
Sierra Leone	10	13	8	9	11	5	15	2	3	1	..	6	9	5
Somalia	2	4	10	16	13	8	22	9	3	14	..	1	9	12
Sudan	63	117	66	83	49	108	69	35	21	26	..	38	81	38
Swaziland	9	9	9	8	10	9	12	15	14	12	..	2	9	13
Tanzania	48	46	47	40	35	25	34	41	36	34	..	22	40	36
Togo	19	21	25	29	40	43	48	35	74	37	..	8	30	48
Uganda	6	8	25	38	63	51	41	34	32	42	..	3	32	37
Zaire	220	138	101	127	239	267	176	172	148	74	..	75	182	142
Zambia	142	129	141	128	114	68	141	64	67	63	..	76	120	84
Zimbabwe	10	32	95	115	141	144	149	145	153	147	..	3	89	149
NORTH AFRICA	2,754	2,971	3,019	3,070	3,203	3,270	3,800	3,265	4,120	4,621	..	1,171	3,048	3,951
Algeria	1,436	1,361	1,427	1,274	1,376	1,409	1,564	1,576	1,811	1,873	..	556	1,381	1,706
Egypt, Arab Republic of	459	690	710	958	968	1,026	1,213	650	1,039	1,206	..	314	802	1,027
Libya	..	..	..	..	..	..	..	..	..	..	..	..	..	..
Morocco	631	697	665	632	609	584	718	690	879	1,133	..	216	636	855
Tunisia	229	223	217	207	250	251	306	350	391	409	..	85	229	364
ALL AFRICA	5,031	5,518	5,996	6,163	6,815	7,099	7,129	6,324	8,015	8,195	..	1,775	6,104	7,416
South Africa	..	..	..	..	..	..	..	..	..	..	..	..	..	..

6-12. Total external debt service payments: long-term loans

	Millions of U.S. dollars (current prices and exchange rates)											Average		
	1980	1981	1982	1983	1984	1985	1986	1987	1988	1989	1990	75-79	80-85	86-MR
SUB-SAHARAN AFRICA	5,275	5,957	6,394	7,215	8,912	10,319	9,234	8,098	9,103	8,312	..	2,340	7,345	8,687
excluding Nigeria	4,501	4,653	4,680	5,055	5,438	6,253	7,475	7,100	7,024	6,547	..	2,070	5,097	7,036
Angola	..	..	..	..	..	..	..	..	..	..	..	..	..	..
Benin	9	10	15	24	39	41	58	33	21	21	..	5	23	33
Botswana	13	9	14	25	32	47	45	69	72	69	..	7	23	64
Burkina Faso	17	14	15	15	19	27	34	32	38	34	..	6	18	35
Burundi	7	6	7	13	22	23	31	40	40	37	..	3	13	37
Cameroon	252	273	350	308	366	606	622	584	577	309	..	89	359	523
Cape Verde	0	0	2	3	5	5	4	7	7	5	..	0	3	6
Central African Republic	8	8	7	20	24	25	27	26	24	28	..	6	15	26
Chad	6	8	2	1	8	17	8	7	9	10	..	5	7	9
Comoros	0	1	1	2	3	2	2	1	0	1	..	0	1	1
Congo, People's Republic of the	78	206	216	312	342	384	336	392	366	274	..	49	256	342
Cote d'Ivoire	939	1,060	1,182	1,169	1,151	1,354	1,726	1,510	1,289	1,306	..	350	1,142	1,458
Djibouti	3	3	3	4	4	4	7	13	13	12	..	2	4	11
Equatorial Guinea	2	5	4	3	9	9	6	11	5	6	..	0	5	7
Ethiopia	36	46	65	96	118	143	196	205	259	272	..	26	84	233
Gabon	399	310	285	223	256	225	174	68	107	179	..	177	283	132
Gambia, The	1	3	14	12	10	6	29	24	18	18	..	2	8	22
Ghana	134	74	75	131	126	144	220	412	528	434	..	66	114	398
Guinea	100	85	79	64	103	68	67	158	124	109	..	62	83	115
Guinea-Bissau	4	4	3	3	4	5	4	9	6	8	..	1	4	7
Kenya	402	443	490	510	577	637	696	691	635	594	..	218	510	654
Lesotho	5	4	9	21	21	19	14	15	24	22	..	1	13	19
Liberia	43	34	43	45	59	36	28	11	18	5	..	37	43	15
Madagascar	61	79	91	61	80	147	171	201	204	237	..	23	86	203
Malawi	71	100	85	73	99	105	140	109	101	90	..	29	89	110
Mali	13	13	14	19	27	48	58	65	75	63	..	9	22	65
Mauritania	41	64	46	46	58	95	94	109	123	94	..	51	58	105
Mauritius	44	80	89	119	129	137	128	127	197	139	..	15	99	148
Mozambique	0	0	0	0	0	51	98	30	38	51	..	..	9	54
Namibia	..	..	..	..	..	..	..	..	..	..	..	..	..	..
Niger	122	150	229	135	88	101	122	158	168	113	..	29	138	140
Nigeria	774	1,304	1,714	2,160	3,474	4,066	1,760	998	2,080	1,765	..	270	2,249	1,650
Rwanda	4	5	5	8	10	15	18	22	20	24	..	2	8	21
Sao Tome & Principe	1	1	2	3	3	3	1	3	2	4	..	0	2	3
Senegal	235	144	94	97	138	170	282	364	367	355	..	80	146	342
Seychelles	0	0	1	3	5	8	10	11	17	20	..	0	3	14
Sierra Leone	57	60	22	18	33	17	51	7	9	4	..	31	34	18
Somalia	13	47	20	24	19	20	62	37	5	32	..	4	24	34
Sudan	194	191	198	167	125	129	220	77	79	72	..	126	167	112
Swaziland	17	19	21	21	20	26	34	51	39	33	..	4	21	39
Tanzania	136	144	104	109	98	74	102	95	83	80	..	75	111	90
Togo	38	39	43	52	85	106	139	84	124	85	..	38	60	108
Uganda	39	75	71	112	160	159	159	122	136	205	..	26	102	155
Zaire	497	348	186	225	406	492	417	426	339	487	..	150	359	417
Zambia	412	422	337	303	246	139	368	146	161	171	..	257	310	212
Zimbabwe	50	67	142	458	313	386	465	540	560	439	..	9	236	501
NORTH AFRICA	7,360	8,005	8,659	9,068	9,020	9,566	10,476	9,640	11,147	12,914	..	2,990	8,613	11,044
Algeria	3,917	3,913	4,381	4,591	4,985	4,913	5,149	5,416	6,292	7,094	..	1,310	4,450	5,987
Egypt, Arab Republic of	1,616	2,101	2,205	2,480	2,432	2,666	2,721	1,475	2,166	2,692	..	1,025	2,250	2,263
Libya	..	..	..	..	..	..	..	..	..	..	..	..	..	..
Morocco	1,308	1,407	1,525	1,379	913	1,262	1,750	1,669	1,648	2,012	..	450	1,299	1,770
Tunisia	518	584	548	619	690	726	856	1,080	1,041	1,117	..	205	614	1,023
ALL AFRICA	12,634	13,962	15,053	16,283	17,931	19,886	19,710	17,738	20,250	21,226	..	5,330	15,958	19,731
South Africa	..	..	..	..	..	..	..	..	..	..	..	..	..	..

6–13. Interest payments: short–term loans

	Millions of U.S. dollars (current prices and exchange rates)											Average		
	1980	1981	1982	1983	1984	1985	1986	1987	1988	1989	1990	78–79	80–85	86–MR
SUB-SAHARAN AFRICA	1,025	1,327	1,050	903	1,179	870	728	470	585	506	..	520	1,059	572
excluding Nigeria	645	840	672	483	479	434	428	430	545	475	..	276	592	469
Angola	..	..	..	..	..	..	..	..	..	..	..	..	..	..
Benin	11	13	10	7	7	7	7	8	7	5	..	5	9	7
Botswana	2	1	1	0	1	0	0	0	0	0	..	0	1	0
Burkina Faso	5	6	5	3	3	3	3	4	5	5	..	6	4	4
Burundi	2	2	2	1	1	2	2	2	2	1	..	1	2	2
Cameroon	28	31	37	36	36	35	40	65	74	57	..	15	34	59
Cape Verde	0	0	0	0	0	0	0	1	0	0	..	1	0	0
Central African Republic	2	2	2	1	1	1	2	2	2	2	..	1	2	2
Chad	0	0	0	0	0	0	0	0	0	2	..	1	0	0
Comoros	0	0	0	0	0	0	0	1	1	3	..	0	0	1
Congo, People's Republic of the	31	30	20	17	18	35	46	52	46	46	..	12	25	47
Cote d'Ivoire	90	168	127	91	80	75	80	31	42	52	..	65	105	51
Djibouti	1	1	1	1	2	3	2	1	2	3	..	1	2	2
Equatorial Guinea	1	1	1	1	1	1	0	0	0	0	..	1	1	0
Ethiopia	9	10	8	6	7	6	6	6	8	8	..	6	8	7
Gabon	33	32	21	20	25	22	24	30	32	45	..	23	25	33
Gambia, The	3	4	3	2	4	3	2	2	2	1	..	1	3	1
Ghana	18	35	33	14	17	18	13	10	9	4	..	31	23	9
Guinea	9	10	8	6	6	6	5	6	4	4	..	4	7	5
Guinea-Bissau	1	1	1	2	4	3	2	1	0	4	..	1	2	2
Kenya	58	68	42	36	40	35	29	35	46	51	..	38	47	40
Lesotho	1	1	1	0	0	0	0	0	0	0	..	0	1	0
Liberia	11	13	9	5	5	4	4	4	4	0	..	7	8	3
Madagascar	29	28	12	11	12	7	6	4	1	4	..	5	16	3
Malawi	16	14	9	8	6	5	6	6	5	5	..	8	10	5
Mali	3	8	6	2	4	5	4	5	4	4	..	2	5	4
Mauritania	7	12	11	8	9	7	6	6	9	8	..	5	9	7
Mauritius	8	7	5	4	5	4	3	3	3	4	..	6	5	3
Mozambique	0	0	0	0	0	7	6	8	9	12	..	..	1	9
Namibia	..	..	..	..	..	..	..	..	..	..	..	..	..	..
Niger	19	23	16	9	7	7	8	7	7	9	..	18	13	8
Nigeria	379	487	378	420	700	436	300	40	40	31	..	244	467	103
Rwanda	3	4	3	2	3	3	2	2	3	5	..	2	3	3
Sao Tome & Principe	0	0	0	0	0	0	0	0	0	1	..	0	0	0
Senegal	24	39	29	19	24	20	17	21	23	24	..	14	26	21
Seychelles	37	6	1	1	1	2	2	3	1	4	..	28	8	3
Sierra Leone	6	9	8	6	5	4	4	6	5	1	..	2	6	4
Somalia	0	0	0	0	0	1	0	0	1	0	..	2	0	0
Sudan	70	112	98	59	47	20	27	20	100	25	..	44	68	43
Swaziland	2	2	1	3	2	1	1	1	1	2	..	2	2	1
Tanzania	26	32	24	19	21	25	20	20	22	7	..	22	25	17
Togo	14	17	12	8	7	6	6	6	6	6	..	8	11	6
Uganda	5	6	4	3	2	2	2	2	3	4	..	3	4	3
Zaire	45	53	37	21	24	23	22	28	34	26	..	33	34	27
Zambia	0	0	0	0	0	0	0	0	0	0	..	68	0	0
Zimbabwe	15	41	65	52	43	27	21	20	22	33	..	4	41	24
NORTH AFRICA	669	910	788	818	917	717	559	535	738	482	..	354	803	578
Algeria	116	404	184	136	141	128	36	65	272	126	..	195	185	125
Egypt, Arab Republic of	422	380	473	545	640	467	390	293	305	300	..	75	488	322
Libya	..	..	..	..	..	..	..	..	..	..	..	..	..	..
Morocco	105	110	115	118	120	102	112	159	143	34	..	58	112	112
Tunisia	26	16	15	19	16	20	21	18	18	22	..	26	19	20
ALL AFRICA	1,694	2,237	1,838	1,721	2,095	1,587	1,287	1,004	1,323	988	..	874	1,862	1,150
South Africa	..	..	..	..	..	..	..	..	..	..	..	..	..	..

6–14. Net flows: long– and short–term loans

	Millions of US dollars (current prices and exchange rates)											Average		
	1980	1981	1982	1983	1984	1985	1986	1987	1988	1989	1990	75–79	80–85	86–MR
SUB-SAHARAN AFRICA	8,664	9,754	10,393	8,064	5,299	4,059	6,432	8,421	6,410	5,392	..	2,889	7,705	6,664
excluding Nigeria	7,154	7,248	7,510	6,245	5,500	4,524	4,991	5,377	4,615	4,767	..	2,510	6,364	4,938
Angola	..	..	..	..	..	..	..	..	..	..	..	..	..	..
Benin	66	100	220	92	16	48	46	66	-21	134	..	34	90	56
Botswana	21	26	55	25	60	38	18	64	14	29	..	6	38	31
Burkina Faso	62	76	70	82	41	57	80	113	58	76	..	23	65	82
Burundi	41	26	52	97	66	74	77	131	68	81	..	13	59	89
Cameroon	493	318	164	341	207	-30	322	10	373	378	..	156	249	271
Cape Verde	3	20	22	16	14	20	13	7	2	3	..	3	16	6
Central African Republic	39	44	19	23	25	47	80	83	83	41	..	9	33	72
Chad	0	11	4	14	4	4	30	50	57	94	..	3	17	58
Comoros	13	11	16	18	23	23	25	18	1	6	..	3	17	12
Congo, People's Republic of the	455	231	505	280	211	685	135	272	-85	2	..	52	395	81
Cote d'Ivoire	1,158	1,187	1,632	672	951	779	444	1,022	635	934	..	448	1,063	759
Djibouti	8	-1	7	13	39	54	-23	44	10	25	..	-1	20	14
Equatorial Guinea	36	24	30	8	-7	-6	13	17	22	14	..	1	14	16
Ethiopia	93	361	104	182	173	256	247	300	327	64	..	48	195	234
Gabon	-109	-161	-94	-67	55	144	538	173	296	231	..	133	-39	310
Gambia, The	55	50	37	6	11	-4	25	29	8	22	..	7	26	21
Ghana	98	70	53	372	265	181	276	151	120	255	..	36	173	201
Guinea	53	73	40	58	-3	82	151	87	184	224	..	-6	50	162
Guinea-Bissau	66	19	16	15	29	44	-5	53	22	30	..	5	32	25
Kenya	490	246	387	327	208	234	91	317	242	289	..	187	315	235
Lesotho	12	18	42	19	11	29	14	39	43	39	..	7	22	34
Liberia	91	125	114	119	105	56	30	27	10	-3	..	46	102	16
Madagascar	413	288	265	195	118	121	145	238	121	82	..	58	233	146
Malawi	156	112	41	66	90	65	53	47	27	80	..	57	88	52
Mali	100	104	141	161	125	91	155	82	96	140	..	23	120	118
Mauritania	133	128	208	159	84	50	168	114	84	35	..	16	127	100
Mauritius	124	119	65	-8	35	15	-26	36	96	-6	..	38	58	25
Mozambique	0	0	0	82	1145	364	420	393	175	224	..	0	265	303
Namibia	..	..	..	..	..	..	..	..	..	..	..	..	..	..
Niger	233	323	21	110	57	104	154	97	128	87	..	24	141	116
Nigeria	1,510	2,506	2,883	1,819	-202	-465	1,442	3,043	1,795	625	..	379	1,342	1,726
Rwanda	31	24	29	36	44	59	64	102	75	54	..	14	37	73
Sao Tome & Principe	9	7	8	7	14	7	11	10	11	27	..	1	9	15
Senegal	230	282	314	355	176	84	374	321	63	155	..	77	240	228
Seychelles	12	7	14	11	10	20	41	8	6	0	..	0	12	14
Sierra Leone	59	59	70	37	22	48	67	53	9	17	..	23	49	36
Somalia	125	431	213	207	140	123	73	73	48	57	..	18	207	63
Sudan	790	745	926	589	252	-174	-133	113	346	213	..	160	521	135
Swaziland	22	11	19	27	18	20	9	-15	-16	15	..	12	20	-2
Tanzania	380	279	327	362	162	170	100	140	232	-139	..	114	280	83
Togo	104	26	34	71	27	17	25	-11	96	118	..	104	46	57
Uganda	150	176	250	136	9	54	14	214	182	40	..	17	129	112
Zaire	319	374	236	219	147	160	115	431	170	89	..	313	243	201
Zambia	429	538	194	197	283	367	596	-6	304	45	..	141	335	235
Zimbabwe	93	340	640	517	40	-56	-60	-132	-103	466	..	69	262	43
NORTH AFRICA	4,761	4,183	5,044	3,425	4,471	3,946	3,648	448	3,777	1,979	..	3,696	4,305	2,463
Algeria	916	246	-338	206	567	587	2,250	-1102	1,737	626	..	2,131	364	878
Egypt, Arab Republic of	2,166	2,231	3,213	2,219	2,361	2,288	748	1,059	1,316	774	..	608	2,413	974
Libya	..	..	..	..	..	..	..	..	..	..	..	..	..	..
Morocco	1,357	1,380	1,862	498	1,103	743	153	423	425	300	..	744	1,157	325
Tunisia	322	326	307	501	440	328	496	67	300	279	..	214	371	286
ALL AFRICA	13,425	13,937	15,437	11,488	9,770	8,004	10,080	8,868	10,187	7,371	..	6,585	12,010	9,126
South Africa	..	..	..	..	..	..	..	..	..	..	..	..	..	..

6–15. Net flows: long–term loans

	Millions of U.S. dollars (current prices and exchange rates)											Average		
	1980	1981	1982	1983	1984	1985	1986	1987	1988	1989	1990	75–79	80–85	86–MR
SUB–SAHARAN AFRICA	8,664	9,754	10,393	8,064	5,299	2,539	4,442	5,382	5,146	5,153	..	4,039	7,452	5,031
excluding Nigeria	7,154	7,248	7,510	6,245	5,500	3,648	4,340	4,468	4,766	4,113	..	3,648	6,218	4,422
Angola	..	..	..	..	..	..	..	..	..	..	..	..	..	..
Benin	66	100	220	92	16	11	36	51	43	151	..	29	84	70
Botswana	21	26	55	25	60	41	17	64	14	29	..	15	38	31
Burkina Faso	62	76	70	82	41	40	74	95	66	82	..	35	62	79
Burundi	41	26	52	97	66	55	85	117	93	77	..	19	56	93
Cameroon	493	318	164	341	207	-164	77	83	372	537	..	169	226	267
Cape Verde	3	20	22	16	14	19	8	4	8	5	..	4	16	6
Central African Republic	39	44	19	23	25	42	70	88	79	47	..	12	32	71
Chad	0	11	4	14	4	2	26	47	56	84	..	20	6	53
Comoros	13	11	16	18	23	22	24	13	8	5	..	7	17	12
Congo, People's Republic of the	455	231	505	280	211	202	133	153	327	-45	..	112	314	142
Cote d'Ivoire	1,158	1,187	1,632	672	951	684	382	544	522	328	..	491	1,047	444
Djibouti	8	-1	7	13	39	30	19	21	12	4	..	2	16	14
Equatorial Guinea	36	24	30	8	-7	7	15	16	24	14	..	1	16	17
Ethiopia	93	361	104	182	173	246	241	289	289	100	..	77	193	230
Gabon	-109	-161	-94	-67	55	133	361	208	299	71	..	182	-40	235
Gambia, The	55	50	37	6	11	10	25	32	8	26	..	13	28	23
Ghana	98	70	53	372	265	237	280	181	160	291	..	72	183	228
Guinea	53	73	40	58	-3	60	154	58	184	204	..	31	47	150
Guinea–Bissau	66	19	16	15	29	56	19	43	22	36	..	10	34	30
Kenya	490	246	387	327	208	133	189	98	303	222	..	199	299	203
Lesotho	12	18	42	19	11	29	14	39	41	43	..	7	22	34
Liberia	91	125	114	119	105	48	30	27	5	-3	..	65	100	15
Madagascar	413	288	265	195	118	118	151	248	121	81	..	66	233	150
Malawi	156	112	41	66	90	27	53	38	73	85	..	84	82	62
Mali	100	104	141	161	125	90	151	91	101	145	..	47	120	122
Mauritania	133	128	208	159	84	49	164	111	47	41	..	58	127	91
Mauritius	124	119	65	-8	35	3	-13	41	81	10	..	46	56	30
Mozambique	0	0	0	82	1145	364	410	359	167	190	..	0	265	282
Namibia	..	..	..	..	..	..	..	..	..	..	..	..	..	..
Niger	233	323	21	110	57	67	131	144	100	105	..	37	135	120
Nigeria	1,510	2,506	2,883	1,819	-202	-1109	102	914	380	1,040	..	391	1,235	609
Rwanda	31	24	29	36	44	69	64	90	73	51	..	23	39	69
Sao Tome & Principe	9	7	8	7	14	7	10	8	11	17	..	3	9	11
Senegal	230	282	314	355	176	133	313	274	104	183	..	93	248	218
Seychelles	12	7	14	11	10	15	26	12	6	0	..	2	11	11
Sierra Leone	59	59	70	37	22	24	1	1	14	4	..	24	45	5
Somalia	125	431	213	207	140	137	88	67	62	57	..	75	209	68
Sudan	790	745	926	589	252	80	59	160	324	190	..	394	564	183
Swaziland	22	11	19	27	18	12	7	-15	-7	1	..	25	18	-3
Tanzania	380	279	327	362	162	124	170	100	182	111	..	242	272	141
Togo	104	26	34	71	27	6	12	0	86	41	..	115	44	35
Uganda	150	176	250	136	9	58	1	217	174	29	..	40	130	105
Zaire	319	374	236	219	147	95	106	287	138	78	..	399	232	152
Zambia	429	538	194	197	283	248	203	71	121	30	..	235	315	106
Zimbabwe	93	340	640	517	40	-20	-42	-102	-143	357	..	66	268	17
NORTH AFRICA	4,761	4,183	5,044	3,425	4,471	3,650	2,692	2,674	3,493	1,661	..	4,188	4,256	2,630
Algeria	916	246	-338	206	567	484	960	735	1,432	407	..	1,269	347	883
Egypt, Arab Republic of	2,166	2,231	3,213	2,219	2,361	2,101	924	1,380	1,385	660	..	1,748	2,382	1,087
Libya	..	..	..	..	..	..	..	..	..	..	..	..	..	..
Morocco	1,357	1,380	1,862	498	1,103	750	356	491	425	361	..	890	1,158	408
Tunisia	322	326	307	501	440	316	451	68	252	233	..	281	369	251
ALL AFRICA	13,425	13,937	15,437	11,488	9,770	6,189	7,134	8,056	8,639	6,815	..	8,227	11,708	7,661
South Africa	..	..	..	..	..	..	..	..	..	..	..	..	..	..

6–16. Net transfers: long– and short–term loans

| | *Millions of U.S. dollars (current prices and exchange rates)* | | | | | | | | | | | *Average* | | |
	1980	1981	1982	1983	1984	1985	1986	1987	1988	1989	1990	75–79	80–85	86–MR
SUB-SAHARAN AFRICA	5,362	5,880	6,365	4,069	507	–641	2,375	4,892	1,930	1,313	..	3,936	3,590	2,627
excluding Nigeria	4,763	4,530	4,733	3,668	2,657	1,559	1,748	2,442	1,611	1,999	..	3,612	3,652	1,950
Angola	..	..	..	..	..	..	..	..	..	..	..	..	..	..
Benin	51	85	203	71	–8	27	17	43	–36	117	..	49	72	35
Botswana	13	18	45	12	44	18	–10	30	–20	–5	..	12	25	–1
Burkina Faso	51	64	58	71	32	44	65	95	40	55	..	36	53	63
Burundi	37	22	47	92	56	63	63	113	49	65	..	19	53	73
Cameroon	344	149	–24	165	5	–201	94	–233	106	210	..	226	73	44
Cape Verde	3	20	21	14	11	17	11	3	–2	0	..	4	14	3
Central African Republic	36	40	13	13	16	37	67	71	72	30	..	15	26	60
Chad	–1	10	3	13	3	2	28	46	53	90	..	26	5	54
Comoros	13	10	15	17	21	21	24	16	0	2	..	6	16	11
Congo, People's Republic of the	387	107	391	166	95	518	–3	136	–215	–139	..	105	277	–55
Cote d'Ivoire	685	569	925	22	242	13	–459	428	106	417	..	410	409	123
Djibouti	6	–3	5	10	36	49	–28	39	3	19	..	1	17	9
Equatorial Guinea	35	22	27	6	–9	–8	11	13	20	13	..	1	12	14
Ethiopia	66	331	65	142	127	209	190	236	237	–19	..	65	157	161
Gabon	–262	–281	–211	–139	–31	66	463	98	185	70	..	142	–143	204
Gambia, The	51	44	31	0	4	–9	15	21	0	16	..	13	20	13
Ghana	46	6	–10	309	197	93	166	34	0	146	..	50	107	86
Guinea	20	41	10	31	–30	56	132	39	149	187	..	31	21	127
Guinea-Bissau	65	17	14	12	24	39	–7	47	19	23	..	13	28	20
Kenya	250	–7	136	97	–34	–19	–178	25	–39	16	..	235	71	–44
Lesotho	10	15	37	13	7	24	9	33	35	32	..	8	18	27
Liberia	55	90	81	89	73	31	12	17	–2	–3	..	57	70	6
Madagascar	356	224	201	145	63	49	67	120	31	–46	..	85	173	43
Malawi	103	44	–9	21	45	20	1	4	–13	40	..	76	37	8
Mali	93	92	129	150	109	68	132	58	71	119	..	46	107	95
Mauritania	111	96	171	125	48	13	128	75	39	–2	..	65	94	60
Mauritius	90	67	11	–54	–13	–32	–72	–11	41	–59	..	42	11	–26
Mozambique	0	0	0	82	1,145	337	383	371	142	178	..	0	261	268
Namibia	..	..	..	..	..	..	..	..	..	..	..	..	..	..
Niger	149	234	–66	49	11	52	93	14	41	39	..	43	71	47
Nigeria	599	1,350	1,631	401	–2,150	–2,199.9	627	2,450	319	–686	..	324	–61	677
Rwanda	26	18	24	32	38	52	56	92	64	41	..	24	32	63
Sao Tome & Principe	9	6	8	6	13	6	10	9	10	24	..	3	8	13
Senegal	135	188	236	280	77	–5	239	160	–96	–33	..	88	152	68
Seychelles	–26	1	12	9	7	16	35	0	–3	–11	..	2	3	5
Sierra Leone	44	38	54	22	6	40	48	45	1	15	..	26	34	27
Somalia	122	427	203	190	127	114	50	63	45	43	..	74	197	50
Sudan	657	516	762	448	156	–302	–229	58	225	163	..	423	373	54
Swaziland	11	0	9	17	6	10	–4	–32	–31	1	..	23	9	–16
Tanzania	306	201	256	303	106	120	46	79	174	–179	..	253	215	30
Togo	70	–12	–4	34	–20	–32	–29	–51	16	76	..	129	6	3
Uganda	139	163	221	96	–57	2	–29	178	148	–7	..	53	94	72
Zaire	54	183	99	71	–116	–130	–83	231	–12	–11	..	377	27	31
Zambia	287	409	54	69	169	299	456	–70	236	–18	..	190	214	151
Zimbabwe	67	266	480	351	–144	–228	–230	–297	–278	286	..	66	132	–130
NORTH AFRICA	1,338	302	1,238	–464	352	–41	–711	–3,352	–1,081	–3,124	..	4,664	454	–2,067
Algeria	–636	–1,519	–1949	–1,205	–950	–950	651	–2,743	–346	–1,373	..	1,916	–1,201	–953
Egypt, Arab Republic of	1,285	1,161	2,030	717	753	795	–855	117	–29	–732	..	1,601	1,123	–375
Libya	..	..	..	..	..	..	..	..	..	..	..	..	..	..
Morocco	622	573	1,083	–252	374	57	–676	–426	–597	–867	..	838	409	–641
Tunisia	67	87	74	276	175	58	170	–301	–109	–153	..	309	123	–98
ALL AFRICA	6,700	6,182	7,603	3,605	858	–682	1,664	1,539	850	–1,811	..	8,600	4,044	560
South Africa	..	..	..	..	..	..	..	..	..	..	..	..	..	..

6–17. Net transfers: long–term loans

	Millions of U.S. dollars (current prices and exchange rates)											Average		
	1980	1981	1982	1983	1984	1985	1986	1987	1988	1989	1990	75–79	80–85	86–MR
SUB-SAHARAN AFRICA	6,387	7,207	7,415	4,972	1,685	-1,290	1,113	2,322	1,251	1,580	..	3,463	4,396	1,566
excluding Nigeria	5,408	5,370	5,405	4,151	3,136	1,117	1,526	1,962	2,306	1,819	..	3,145	4,098	1,903
Angola	..	..	..	..	..	..	..	..	..	..	..	..	..	..
Benin	63	97	214	78	-1	-3	14	36	36	138	..	28	75	56
Botswana	15	19	45	13	45	21	-11	30	-20	-4	..	11	26	-1
Burkina Faso	56	70	63	74	35	30	62	81	52	66	..	33	55	65
Burundi	38	24	49	93	57	46	73	101	76	62	..	19	51	78
Cameroon	372	180	13	201	41	-300	-112	-96	179	425	..	147	84	99
Cape Verde	3	20	21	14	11	17	6	0	4	3	..	4	14	4
Central African Republic	38	42	15	15	18	34	59	77	71	38	..	12	27	61
Chad	-1	10	3	13	3	0	24	43	52	82	..	20	5	50
Comoros	13	11	15	17	22	20	23	12	8	5	..	6	16	12
Congo, People's Republic of the	417	137	411	183	113	70	41	69	242	-140	..	102	222	53
Cote d'Ivoire	775	737	1,052	113	322	-7	-441	-19	35	-137	..	382	499	-141
Djibouti	7	-2	7	11	37	28	16	18	8	2	..	1	15	11
Equatorial Guinea	36	23	28	7	-8	6	13	13	22	13	..	1	15	15
Ethiopia	74	341	74	149	134	205	189	232	207	25	..	66	163	163
Gabon	-228	-249	-189	-120	-6	76	310	163	220	-45	..	140	-119	162
Gambia, The	54	47	34	2	7	8	17	25	1	20	..	12	25	16
Ghana	64	41	23	323	214	167	183	74	49	186	..	54	139	123
Guinea	29	51	18	37	-24	40	140	16	153	170	..	16	25	120
Guinea-Bissau	65	17	15	15	29	54	18	38	19	32	..	10	32	27
Kenya	308	61	178	132	7	-84	-51	-160	68	0	..	162	100	-36
Lesotho	10	16	38	13	7	24	9	33	33	36	..	6	18	28
Liberia	66	103	91	94	78	27	15	21	-3	-3	..	56	77	8
Madagascar	384	252	212	156	75	53	78	134	33	-44	..	60	189	50
Malawi	119	58	1	29	51	-13	6	1	37	49	..	72	41	23
Mali	96	100	135	152	113	72	132	72	81	127	..	45	111	103
Mauritania	119	108	182	132	57	19	130	78	11	13	..	51	103	58
Mauritius	98	74	15	-50	-8	-41	-56	-4	29	-39	..	41	15	-18
Mozambique	0	0	0	82	1,145	344	379	345	143	155	..	0	262	256
Namibia	..	..	..	..	..	..	..	..	..	..	..	..	..	..
Niger	168	257	-51	58	18	22	78	67	20	65	..	34	79	58
Nigeria	979	1,837	2,010	821	-1,450	-2,407	-413	360	-1,056	-240	..	318	298	-337
Rwanda	29	22	26	33	41	65	58	82	65	43	..	22	36	62
Sao Tome & Principe	9	7	8	6	13	6	9	7	10	14	..	3	8	10
Senegal	160	226	266	299	100	63	195	134	-32	19	..	73	186	79
Seychelles	11	7	13	10	9	12	22	7	-2	-6	..	2	10	5
Sierra Leone	50	47	62	27	11	19	-15	-2	11	3	..	20	36	-1
Somalia	122	428	203	191	128	129	66	58	59	43	..	74	200	56
Sudan	727	628	860	507	203	-28	-10	125	303	165	..	359	483	146
Swaziland	13	2	10	19	8	3	-4	-30	-21	-11	..	24	9	-17
Tanzania	332	233	280	322	127	99	136	59	146	77	..	227	232	104
Togo	84	5	9	42	-14	-37	-36	-34	12	4	..	109	15	-14
Uganda	144	169	225	98	-54	8	-40	183	142	-13	..	38	98	68
Zaire	100	236	136	92	-93	-172	-70	115	-10	4	..	335	50	10
Zambia	287	409	54	69	169	180	63	7	54	-33	..	205	194	23
Zimbabwe	82	307	546	402	-101	-164	-191	-247	-296	210	..	63	179	-131
NORTH AFRICA	2,007	1,212	2,026	354	1,268	380	-1108	-591	-627	-2,960	..	3,371	1,208	-1,321
Algeria	-520	-1,116	-1,765	-1,069	-809	-925	-604	-841	-379	-1,466	..	926	-1,034	-822
Egypt, Arab Republic of	1,707	1,541	2,503	1,262	1,393	1,075	-289	731	346	-546	..	1,501	1,580	60
Libya	..	..	..	..	..	..	..	..	..	..	..	..	..	..
Morocco	727	683	1,198	-134	494	166	-361	-199	-454	-772	..	721	522	-447
Tunisia	93	103	90	295	191	65	146	-282	-138	-176	..	222	139	-113
ALL AFRICA	8,394	8,419	9,441	5,326	2,954	-910	5	1,732	624	-1,380	..	6,834	5,604	245
South Africa	..	..	..	..	..	..	..	..	..	..	..	..	..	..

6-18. Official concessional long-term debt

	Millions of U.S. dollars (current prices and exchange rates)											Average		
	1980	1981	1982	1983	1984	1985	1986	1987	1988	1989	1990	75-79	80-85	86-MR
SUB-SAHARAN AFRICA	16,143	18,044	20,171	21,697	23,353	27,694	33,076	40,742	43,678	46,419	..	8,765	21,184	40,979
excluding Nigeria	15,599	17,556	19,734	21,237	22,943	27,244	32,524	40,123	43,077	45,853	..	8,436	20,719	40,394
Angola	..	..	..	..	..	..	..	..	..	..	..	..	..	..
Benin	182	191	217	254	260	304	379	472	488	660	..	116	235	500
Botswana	62	66	73	84	96	108	109	123	135	165	..	105	82	133
Burkina Faso	239	246	250	282	299	375	480	621	645	565	..	125	282	578
Burundi	127	148	190	258	282	350	460	644	704	782	..	40	226	648
Cameroon	833	863	891	886	849	952	1,067	1,108	1,069	1,220	..	444	879	1,116
Cape Verde	20	25	32	37	45	66	77	90	97	101	..	11	38	91
Central African Republic	75	100	110	121	141	198	277	413	486	558	..	36	124	434
Chad	113	107	91	98	96	106	140	201	246	296	..	78	102	221
Comoros	43	52	65	79	96	121	146	172	173	149	..	21	76	160
Congo, People's Republic of the	421	473	548	540	515	608	700	886	914	949	..	311	518	862
Cote d'Ivoire	511	475	529	522	529	653	841	1,097	998	1,033	..	329	537	992
Djibouti	16	12	14	24	54	87	111	148	154	132	..	15	35	136
Equatorial Guinea	37	37	48	50	43	49	64	92	112	136	..	25	44	101
Ethiopia	601	804	869	1,043	1,105	1,365	1,629	2,014	2,235	2,415	..	410	965	2,073
Gabon	125	106	99	91	92	133	180	259	269	538	..	96	108	312
Gambia, The	77	98	108	114	115	130	170	224	227	255	..	26	107	219
Ghana	858	868	879	873	873	977	1,240	1,662	1,937	2,164	..	607	888	1,751
Guinea	692	948	934	911	834	922	1,132	1,339	1,483	1,428	..	598	874	1,346
Guinea-Bissau	85	94	100	112	121	159	193	260	272	317	..	18	112	261
Kenya	787	874	1,038	1,084	1,162	1,369	1,691	2,061	2,172	2,274	..	457	1,052	2,050
Lesotho	49	59	77	93	108	137	154	190	211	251	..	25	87	202
Liberia	251	299	327	366	422	482	547	620	599	571	..	154	358	584
Madagascar	528	608	736	724	729	885	1,108	1,448	1,589	1,800	..	207	702	1,486
Malawi	296	320	348	383	449	525	680	859	936	1,032	..	227	387	877
Mali	647	709	782	858	1,043	1,247	1,514	1,833	1,856	1,993	..	406	881	1,799
Mauritania	539	628	730	808	848	928	1,102	1,357	1,385	1,447	..	280	747	1,323
Mauritius	85	104	115	122	122	150	172	236	249	266	..	47	116	231
Mozambique	0	0	0	3	792	1,400	1,739	2,225	2,409	2,532	..	..	366	2,226
Namibia	..	..	..	..	..	..	..	..	..	..	..	..	..	..
Niger	172	225	257	296	325	403	525	709	817	734	..	110	280	696
Nigeria	544	488	437	460	410	450	552	619	601	566	..	478	465	585
Rwanda	155	169	188	217	241	329	417	558	608	601	..	72	217	546
Sao Tome & Principe	20	22	27	32	34	43	51	62	72	88	..	5	30	68
Senegal	453	607	685	776	841	1,001	1,426	1,909	2,070	2,466	..	207	727	1,968
Seychelles	19	20	22	23	26	39	55	76	75	77	..	4	25	71
Sierra Leone	174	173	225	233	194	239	277	315	324	318	..	92	206	309
Somalia	563	764	842	806	852	1,076	1,206	1,420	1,445	1,481	..	398	817	1,388
Sudan	1,865	2,136	2,673	3,018	3,353	3,450	3,577	3,881	4,049	4,281	..	961	2,749	3,947
Swaziland	101	93	88	83	79	94	114	139	136	148	..	48	90	134
Tanzania	1,336	1,465	1,563	1,725	1,632	1,815	1,956	2,250	2,711	2,838	..	1,039	1,589	2,439
Togo	273	249	280	324	247	308	415	504	598	589	..	131	280	527
Uganda	252	212	348	378	423	551	660	936	1,127	1,245	..	205	361	992
Zaire	1,018	1,104	1,198	1,247	1,269	1,455	1,727	2,234	2,422	2,612	..	621	1,215	2,249
Zambia	881	948	1,001	1,067	1,060	1,295	1,527	1,829	1,889	1,615	..	467	1,042	1,715
Zimbabwe	18	55	137	192	247	360	489	647	684	731	..	42	168	638
NORTH AFRICA	15,588	16,935	17,898	18,458	18,589	20,471	22,239	25,212	25,588	26,064	..	10,314	17,990	24,776
Algeria	1,252	1,151	988	837	573	513	512	816	727	738	..	984	886	698
Egypt, Arab Republic of	9,146	9,797	10,368	10,694	11,136	12,135	13,076	14,839	15,267	15,429	..	6,652	10,546	14,653
Libya	..	..	..	..	..	..	..	..	..	..	..	..	..	..
Morocco	3,779	4,520	4,988	5,379	5,358	6,047	6,597	7,135	7,220	7,407	..	1,685	5,012	7,090
Tunisia	1,411	1,467	1,554	1,548	1,522	1,776	2,054	2,422	2,374	2,490	..	993	1,546	2,335
ALL AFRICA	31,731	34,979	38,069	40,155	41,942	48,165	55,315	65,954	69,266	72,483	..	19,079	39,174	65,755
South Africa	..	..	..	..	..	..	..	..	..	..	..	..	..	..

6-19. Official nonconcessional long-term debt

	Millions of U.S. dollars (current prices and exchange rates)											Average		
	1980	1981	1982	1983	1984	1985	1986	1987	1988	1989	1990	75-79	80-85	86-MR
SUB-SAHARAN AFRICA	10,929	13,317	15,086	19,263	20,413	24,753	36,458	45,629	43,749	47,366	..	5,197	41,772	80,978
excluding Nigeria	10,468	12,704	14,235	17,790	18,797	22,991	28,017	34,365	32,984	32,679	..	4,870	34,869	55,954
Angola	..	..	..	..	..	..	..	..	..	..	..	..	..	..
Benin	44	41	49	45	40	48	56	67	62	112	..	9	45	74
Botswana	59	74	86	100	120	191	236	336	317	304	..	42	105	298
Burkina Faso	39	48	56	65	60	77	99	128	123	85	..	14	58	109
Burundi	18	16	16	21	25	37	44	58	56	53	..	4	22	53
Cameroon	406	476	482	499	494	646	872	1,180	1,254	1,863	..	186	501	1,292
Cape Verde	0	13	26	33	28	27	28	29	25	23	..	1	21	26
Central African Republic	47	78	89	91	84	106	138	158	124	98	..	21	83	130
Chad	41	34	23	22	23	30	32	38	34	36	..	36	29	35
Comoros	0	0	2	4	5	8	13	15	14	13	..	2	3	14
Congo, People's Republic of the	182	186	175	257	233	345	692	1,108	1,141	1,126	..	119	230	1,017
Cote d'Ivoire	783	1,136	1,468	1,858	2,104	2,702	3,248	4,407	4,349	4,362	..	342	1,675	4,092
Djibouti	5	4	4	4	2	3	3	3	3	0	..	3	4	2
Equatorial Guinea	24	38	37	39	31	69	78	84	80	73	..	7	40	79
Ethiopia	97	182	201	172	142	147	190	188	153	131	..	47	157	166
Gabon	205	203	190	163	156	208	300	850	1,266	1,333	..	165	188	937
Gambia, The	13	29	45	38	37	41	52	63	54	49	..	6	34	55
Ghana	210	211	205	488	638	822	967	1,074	857	699	..	127	429	899
Guinea	179	156	157	154	148	188	424	469	431	507	..	153	164	458
Guinea-Bissau	7	10	14	11	54	67	71	87	87	90	..	6	27	84
Kenya	773	847	1,046	1,216	1,333	1,611	1,740	1,903	1,738	1,502	..	453	1,138	1,721
Lesotho	2	2	23	13	11	24	29	41	39	39	..	1	13	37
Liberia	197	285	354	411	420	487	544	629	617	631	..	81	359	605
Madagascar	138	415	614	757	901	1,095	1,366	1,693	1,546	1,410	..	44	653	1,504
Malawi	217	255	259	286	265	320	338	363	306	253	..	80	267	315
Mali	27	24	50	66	90	108	114	110	104	96	..	15	61	106
Mauritania	107	148	223	253	235	330	421	444	394	357	..	66	216	404
Mauritius	170	250	271	278	268	323	355	409	378	320	..	49	260	366
Mozambique	0	0	0	79	309	447	480	710	718	732	..	0	139	660
Namibia	..	..	..	..	..	..	..	..	..	..	..	..	..	..
Niger	99	152	129	195	235	338	423	520	465	374	..	32	191	446
Nigeria	461	613	851	1,473	1,616	1,762	8,441	11,264	10,765	14,687	..	327	1,129	11,289
Rwanda	1	1	1	2	2	2	2	2	1	1	..	1	2	2
Sao Tome & Principe	4	6	9	10	14	13	23	23	23	22	..	0	9	23
Senegal	335	456	660	807	787	1,045	1,166	1,425	1,258	1,175		118	682	1,256
Seychelles	6	8	11	16	16	19	23	27	27	26	..	0	13	26
Sierra Leone	92	122	117	130	149	166	198	234	212	210	..	63	129	214
Somalia	23	88	117	320	328	405	417	452	465	448	..	5	214	446
Sudan	1,859	1,784	2,175	2,656	2,508	2,797	3,040	3,439	3,429	3,471	..	717	2,297	3,345
Swaziland	65	68	85	107	94	106	124	140	116	103	..	16	88	121
Tanzania	382	395	413	551	570	672	1,461	1,683	1,587	1,561	..	258	497	1,573
Togo	243	314	294	365	393	468	494	565	485	381	..	56	346	481
Uganda	268	447	421	507	490	477	458	509	442	338	..	86	435	437
Zaire	1,950	2,126	2,067	2,673	2,711	3,361	4,093	5,022	4,717	4,772	..	832	2,481	4,651
Zambia	1,068	1,423	1,366	1,627	1,768	2,044	2,539	2,973	2,867	2,809	..	607	1,549	2,797
Zimbabwe	83	153	205	401	476	571	626	707	620	691	..	0	315	661
NORTH AFRICA	8,616	11,301	14,287	16,981	19,939	24,931	27,570	35,217	35,758	36,247		2,402	40,468	64,012
Algeria	2,260	2,412	2,670	2,912	2,960	3,360	3,788	4,419	4,895	7,059	..	644	2,762	5,040
Egypt, Arab Republic of	4,711	6,891	8,892	10,595	12,491	15,447	16,051	20,734	20,657	18,318	..	787	9,838	18,940
Libya	..	..	..	..	..	..	..	..	..	..	..	..	..	..
Morocco	1,095	1,390	2,003	2,628	3,515	4,862	5,986	7,884	8,051	8,532	..	637	2,582	7,613
Tunisia	550	608	722	846	973	1,262	1,745	2,180	2,155	2,338	..	334	827	2,105
ALL AFRICA	19,545	24,618	29,373	36,244	40,352	49,684	64,028	80,846	79,507	83,613	..	7,599	87,090	144,990
South Africa	..	..	..	..	..	..	..		..	..		..	..	..

6-20. Private long-term debt

| | *Millions of U.S. dollars (current prices and exchange rates)* | | | | | | | | | | | *Average* | | |
	1980	1981	1982	1983	1984	1985	1986	1987	1988	1989	1990	75-79	80-85	86-MR
SUB-SAHARAN AFRICA	19,423	22,045	25,889	27,500	26,682	30,343	30,896	38,844	39,205	37,198	..	10,040	25,314	36,536
excluding Nigeria	15,047	15,437	16,758	15,953	15,916	17,999	19,565	21,195	20,330	20,376	..	8,919	16,185	20,367
Angola	..	..	..	..	..	..	..	..	..	..	..	..	..	..
Benin	118	170	321	325	287	317	340	395	362	285	..	41	256	346
Botswana	8	10	41	38	40	32	39	49	45	40	..	2	28	43
Burkina Faso	20	17	34	44	39	37	35	37	32	36	..	6	32	35
Burundi	8	5	5	17	25	28	27	24	20	14	..	8	14	21
Cameroon	1,003	963	947	1,026	997	813	987	1,029	1,137	1,116	..	400	958	1,067
Cape Verde	0	0	0	0	1	2	3	3	3	3	..	0	1	3
Central African Republic	48	36	35	31	27	25	25	26	24	22	..	44	34	24
Chad	54	50	47	43	36	30	34	43	39	8	..	37	43	31
Comoros	0	0	1	1	0	0	0	0	0	0	..	0	0	0
Congo, People's Republic of the	647	699	1,034	1,038	1,107	1,401	1,387	1,456	1,505	1,471	..	221	988	1,455
Cote d'Ivoire	3,494	3,876	4,758	4,553	4,834	5,660	6,195	6,674	6,798	7,201	..	1,592	4,529	6,717
Djibouti	5	4	7	6	6	7	5	3	1	1	..	0	5	3
Equatorial Guinea	7	10	21	21	19	8	8	9	7	5	..	1	14	7
Ethiopia	49	93	101	109	210	280	314	410	460	359	..	17	140	386
Gabon	955	679	538	427	421	604	982	1,029	863	743	..	926	604	904
Gambia, The	24	30	35	35	33	38	19	17	26	25	..	1	32	22
Ghana	115	97	107	148	148	193	265	290	252	188	..	128	134	249
Guinea	167	163	156	159	153	196	87	92	133	93	..	129	166	101
Guinea-Bissau	36	30	28	24	15	38	43	50	36	25	..	8	28	38
Kenya	1,329	1,215	1,118	1,081	820	853	1,025	1,215	1,257	1,273	..	733	1,069	1,192
Lesotho	11	16	18	26	14	8	7	21	29	32	..	2	15	22
Liberia	156	149	143	172	165	174	182	196	194	188	..	72	160	190
Madagascar	347	498	468	439	380	365	380	406	345	300	..	67	416	358
Malawi	192	187	164	144	120	93	63	57	53	62	..	96	150	59
Mali	36	30	29	47	42	44	49	48	25	21	..	23	38	36
Mauritania	134	99	105	129	128	136	133	123	111	41	..	125	122	102
Mauritius	165	154	167	119	121	104	103	132	182	214	..	44	138	158
Mozambique	0	0	0	0	184	858	1,013	994	892	922	..	..	174	955
Namibia	..	..	..	..	..	..	..	..	..	..	..	..	..	..
Niger	432	531	447	392	334	369	377	392	355	362	..	106	417	372
Nigeria	4,376	6,608	9,131	11,547	10,766	12,344	11,331	17,649	18,875	16,821	..	1,121	9,129	16,169
Rwanda	8	6	8	7	12	12	9	11	7	5	..	6	9	8
Sao Tome & Principe	0	1	1	0	6	6	1	1	1	0	..	0	2	1
Senegal	461	367	311	299	300	290	357	365	271	217	..	243	338	302
Seychelles	0	0	6	7	9	16	30	36	33	30	..	0	6	32
Sierra Leone	110	111	106	95	75	84	88	100	90	88	..	85	97	91
Somalia	28	170	211	214	214	84	88	47	35	35	..	3	153	51
Sudan	854	1,394	1,399	1,105	1,238	1,338	1,571	2,049	1,804	1,888	..	535	1,221	1,828
Swaziland	24	18	12	7	11	23	23	12	10	8	..	13	16	13
Tanzania	547	525	582	572	566	597	382	414	281	247	..	216	565	331
Togo	415	292	254	161	104	86	67	64	54	52	..	252	219	59
Uganda	147	96	117	107	75	99	96	148	140	130	..	67	107	129
Zaire	1,567	1,357	1,261	961	855	807	822	808	774	815	..	1,712	1,134	805
Zambia	731	651	693	596	561	622	603	629	585	571	..	717	642	597
Zimbabwe	595	644	921	1,230	1,185	1,225	1,303	1,294	1,060	1,243	..	241	967	1,225
NORTH AFRICA	21,590	21,234	21,689	21,427	21,683	25,135	28,608	31,920	31,499	30,508	..	12,306	22,126	30,633
Algeria	13,539	12,527	11,319	10,579	10,652	12,640	15,344	18,197	17,832	16,884	..	8,070	11,876	17,064
Egypt, Arab Republic of	2,593	3,373	4,631	5,266	5,578	6,522	7,008	7,276	7,040	7,246	..	1,405	4,660	7,143
Libya	..	..	..	..	..	..	..	..	..	..	..	..	..	..
Morocco	4,029	3,936	4,379	4,049	4,022	4,312	4,383	4,533	4,754	4,621	..	2,115	4,121	4,573
Tunisia	1,429	1,399	1,360	1,534	1,431	1,660	1,872	1,913	1,873	1,756	..	716	1,469	1,854
ALL AFRICA	41,014	43,279	47,578	48,927	48,365	55,478	59,504	70,764	70,704	67,705	..	22,346	47,440	67,169
South Africa	..	..	..	..	..	..	..	..	..	..	..	..	..	..

6–21. Total external debt

	Millions of U.S. dollars (current prices and exchange rates)											Average		
	1980	1981	1982	1983	1984	1985	1986	1987	1988	1989	1990	75–79	80–85	86–MR
SUB-SAHARAN AFRICA	56,203	64,391	70,744	79,803	83,386	96,474	113,813	138,755	141,541	146,995	..	23,339	75,167	135,276
excluding Nigeria	47,269	52,255	57,790	61,263	64,849	76,923	89,770	107,562	109,594	114,163	..	20,035	60,058	105,272
Angola	..	..	..	..	..	..	..	..	..	..	..	..	..	..
Benin	417	486	665	706	674	812	944	1,141	1,060	1,177	..	201	627	1,081
Botswana	133	158	203	226	261	334	387	513	502	513	..	154	219	479
Burkina Faso	334	346	373	418	429	535	670	866	878	756	..	174	406	793
Burundi	166	179	228	306	344	446	555	763	794	867	..	57	278	745
Cameroon	2,513	2,548	2,717	2,739	2,722	2,940	3,710	4,039	4,224	4,743	..	1,132	2,697	4,179
Cape Verde	20	39	58	70	75	97	115	133	129	130	..	13	60	127
Central African Republic	195	233	253	258	265	348	468	626	671	716	..	108	259	620
Chad	218	201	168	169	158	186	237	320	357	368	..	158	183	321
Comoros	44	55	69	86	104	133	166	203	199	176	..	24	82	186
Congo, People's Republic of the	1,496	1,475	1,942	2,007	2,049	3,033	3,480	4,351	4,158	4,316	..	743	2,000	4,076
Cote d'Ivoire	5,848	6,651	7,862	7,819	8,106	9,747	11,088	13,555	13,977	15,412	..	2,676	7,672	13,508
Djibouti	32	30	32	46	86	144	125	183	185	180	..	21	62	168
Equatorial Guinea	76	92	117	122	116	132	159	196	211	228	..	36	109	199
Ethiopia	804	1,139	1,239	1,387	1,524	1,869	2,215	2,710	2,981	3,013	..	507	1,327	2,730
Gabon	1,513	1,135	1,000	914	920	1,207	1,941	2,544	2,801	3,176	..	1,322	1,115	2,616
Gambia, The	137	176	207	212	230	245	270	327	322	342	..	41	201	315
Ghana	1,314	1,462	1,397	1,598	1,898	2,174	2,652	3,134	3,113	3,078	..	1,020	1,641	2,994
Guinea	1,117	1,361	1,345	1,329	1,226	1,438	1,735	2,036	2,220	2,176	..	938	1,303	2,042
Guinea-Bissau	132	139	157	185	240	304	329	427	431	458	..	35	193	411
Kenya	3,530	3,405	3,540	3,787	3,689	4,309	4,834	5,787	5,731	5,690	..	1,870	3,710	5,511
Lesotho	71	83	121	135	136	173	194	256	285	324	..	28	120	265
Liberia	686	814	903	1,005	1,076	1,247	1,439	1,685	1,707	1,761	..	345	955	1,648
Madagascar	1,257	1,612	1,920	2,102	2,160	2,460	3,009	3,728	3,638	3,607	..	369	1,919	3,496
Malawi	821	812	857	885	876	1,018	1,161	1,373	1,345	1,394	..	454	878	1,318
Mali	733	835	880	992	1,244	1,468	1,756	2,067	2,039	2,157	..	457	1,025	2,005
Mauritania	845	973	1,151	1,296	1,339	1,502	1,773	2,044	2,072	2,010	..	502	1,184	1,975
Mauritius	467	546	585	568	550	629	668	811	857	832	..	174	558	792
Mozambique	0	0	0	82	1,365	2,863	3,525	4,261	4,418	4,737	..	..	718	4,235
Namibia	..	..	..	..	..	..	..	..	..	..	..	..	..	..
Niger	863	1,022	957	950	956	1,208	1,448	1,697	1,742	1,578	..	329	993	1,616
Nigeria	8,934	12,136	12,954	18,540	18,537	19,551	24,043	31,193	31,947	32,832	..	3,304	15,109	30,004
Rwanda	190	197	218	242	291	369	456	610	658	652	..	89	251	594
Sao Tome & Principe	24	34	38	44	54	62	77	93	104	131	..	6	43	101
Senegal	1,468	1,667	1,858	2,074	2,200	2,559	3,222	4,020	3,880	4,139	..	658	1,971	3,815
Seychelles	84	37	51	55	71	98	148	175	171	168	..	194	66	166
Sierra Leone	430	563	620	640	617	724	855	1,009	994	1,057	..	259	599	979
Somalia	660	1,056	1,222	1,410	1,498	1,639	1,800	2,009	2,071	2,137	..	418	1,248	2,004
Sudan	5,163	6,192	7,216	7,600	8,612	9,127	9,870	11,563	11,961	12,965	..	2,538	7,318	11,590
Swaziland	206	185	199	235	192	238	278	309	270	281	..	83	209	285
Tanzania	2,572	2,694	2,985	3,380	3,431	3,867	4,167	4,839	5,139	4,918	..	1,646	3,155	4,766
Togo	1,045	970	956	915	807	937	1,065	1,235	1,224	1,186	..	485	938	1,178
Uganda	733	794	938	1,020	1,031	1,171	1,286	1,659	1,799	1,809	..	375	948	1,638
Zaire	4,860	4,976	4,990	5,146	5,150	6,027	7,060	8,744	8,742	8,843	..	3,357	5,192	8,347
Zambia	3,266	3,633	3,708	3,799	3,824	4,639	5,725	6,607	6,863	6,874	..	2,182	3,812	6,517
Zimbabwe	786	1,250	1,845	2,304	2,253	2,465	2,708	2,914	2,671	3,088	..	305	1,817	2,845
NORTH AFRICA	52,966	56,213	62,696	65,129	68,931	79,881	89,617	101,114	101,568	102,616	..	26,896	64,303	98,729
Algeria	19,377	18,397	17,728	16,285	15,944	18,374	22,796	24,748	25,074	26,067	..	10,818	17,684	24,671
Egypt, Arab Republic of	20,384	23,576	28,795	31,598	34,864	40,218	42,997	49,121	49,485	48,799	..	9,094	29,906	47,601
Libya	..	..	..	..	..	..	..	..	..	..	..	..	..	..
Morocco	9,678	10,632	12,401	13,187	14,027	16,409	17,926	20,504	20,334	20,851	..	4,806	12,722	19,904
Tunisia	3,527	3,608	3,772	4,059	4,096	4,880	5,898	6,741	6,675	6,899	..	2,178	3,990	6,553
ALL AFRICA	109,169	120,604	133,440	144,932	152,317	176,355	203,430	239,869	243,109	249,611	..	40,934	******	234,005
South Africa	..	..	..	..	..	..	..	..	..	..	..	..	..	..

6-22. Structure of external debt

	Bilateral				Multilateral				Private				Total	
	Concessional		Nonconcessional		Concessional		Nonconcessional		Guaranteed		Other			
	1980	1989	1980	1989	1980	1989	1980	1989	1980	1989	1980	1989	1980	1989
SUB-SAHARAN AFRICA	10,641	25,046	5,849	31,054	5,501	21,374	5,077	16,315	9,666	18,672	19,460	34,329	56,194	146,990
excluding Nigeria	10,228	24,592	5,828	19,424	5,370	21,263	4,637	13,258	9,286	8,330	11,911	27,291	47,260	114,158
Angola	..	..	..	..	..	..	..	..	..	..	..	..	..	..
Benin	82	256	24	74	100	404	20	38	116	285	75	121	417	1,178
Botswana	28	69	9	53	34	96	50	252	8	40	4	4	133	514
Burkina Faso	89	101	30	18	150	464	9	67	8	34	47	72	333	756
Burundi	49	224	1	2	78	559	17	52	8	13	12	19	165	869
Cameroon	554	849	205	1,012	279	370	202	852	517	627	756	1,033	2,513	4,743
Cape Verde	3	34	0	10	17	67	0	13	0	3	0	3	20	130
Central African Republic	17	224	28	59	58	334	19	39	46	22	27	38	195	716
Chad	32	48	34	30	81	248	7	6	53	8	11	28	218	368
Comoros	21	55	0	0	21	94	0	13	0	0	1	13	43	175
Congo, People's Republic of	354	795	108	726	66	155	74	399	565	948	329	1,292	1,496	4,315
Cote d'Ivoire	351	827	355	2,046	160	206	428	2,315	1,556	600	2,997	9,416	5,847	15,410
Djibouti	14	53	5	0	2	79	0	0	5	1	6	47	32	180
Equatorial Guinea	30	79	13	62	8	57	11	11	7	5	7	15	76	229
Ethiopia	261	1,446	18	22	340	969	79	110	39	211	67	255	804	3,013
Gabon	103	508	173	1,012	22	30	32	321	456	584	728	721	1,514	3,176
Gambia, The	32	67	0	19	45	188	13	30	16	6	31	31	137	341
Ghana	624	549	60	72	234	1,615	150	627	115	172	131	45	1,314	3,080
Guinea	598	905	108	406	93	523	72	100	163	63	83	178	1,117	2,175
Guinea-Bissau	56	124	5	74	29	193	1	16	34	25	7	26	132	458
Kenya	428	977	228	213	359	1,297	544	1,290	657	599	1,313	1,315	3,529	5,691
Lesotho	4	23	2	9	45	229	0	29	9	32	10	2	70	324
Liberia	179	371	50	109	73	200	147	522	57	65	180	494	686	1,761
Madagascar	329	807	63	1,214	199	993	75	195	280	191	311	207	1,257	3,607
Malawi	102	211	112	59	194	821	105	194	47	22	261	88	821	1,395
Mali	453	1,231	8	41	194	762	19	55	35	13	24	54	733	2,156
Mauritania	404	1,002	54	194	135	445	52	163	120	38	79	167	844	2,009
Mauritius	39	196	36	44	45	70	134	277	29	136	183	109	466	832
Mozambique	0	2,200	0	658	0	332	0	74	0	654	0	819	0	4,737
Namibia	..	..	..	..	..	..	..	..	..	..	..	..	..	..
Niger	42	140	70	289	130	594	29	86	60	1	532	468	863	1,578
Nigeria	413	454	21	11,630	131	111	440	3,057	380	10,342	7,549	7,238	8,934	32,832
Rwanda	51	120	1	0	104	481	0	1	8	5	26	45	190	652
Sao Tome & Principe	9	31	4	21	11	57	0	1	0	0	0	20	24	130
Senegal	221	1,376	169	752	232	1,090	166	423	327	135	353	364	1,468	4,140
Seychelles	16	57	4	5	2	20	2	21	0	25	59	40	83	168
Sierra Leone	103	128	42	122	71	190	50	87	110	88	53	440	429	1,055
Somalia	400	798	9	306	163	683	14	142	28	35	47	173	661	2,137
Sudan	1,361	2,851	1,298	2,538	504	1,430	561	934	771	685	668	4,527	5,163	12,965
Swaziland	65	103	34	14	36	45	31	89	0	8	39	21	205	280
Tanzania	950	1,500	76	1,222	386	1,338	305	339	457	234	397	284	2,571	4,917
Togo	155	101	210	294	118	488	33	87	307	15	221	201	1,044	1,186
Uganda	153	299	183	98	100	946	85	240	141	127	72	98	734	1,808
Zaire	673	1,186	1,589	4,064	346	1,426	360	709	1,059	440	833	1,018	4,860	8,843
Zambia	778	1,080	327	1,226	103	535	741	1,583	480	385	838	2,065	3,267	6,874
Zimbabwe	15	591	83	235	3	140	0	456	592	750	93	915	786	3,087
NORTH AFRICA	13,116	22,462	6,333	25,561	2,473	3,602	2,283	10,688	13,658	17,823	15,102	23,031	52,965	103,167
Algeria	1,239	624	1,990	5,094	14	114	270	1,965	9,474	10,912	6,390	7,890	19,377	26,599
Egypt, Arab Republic of	7,012	12,686	3,986	15,736	2,134	2,743	725	2,583	1,867	4,839	4,660	10,213	20,384	48,800
Libya	..	..	..	..	..	..	..	..	..	..	..	..	..	..
Morocco	3,549	6,951	145	4,233	230	456	950	4,299	1,567	1,124	3,236	3,798	9,677	20,861
Tunisia	1,316	2,201	212	498	95	289	338	1,841	750	948	816	1,130	3,527	6,907
ALL AFRICA	23,757	47,508	12,182	56,615	7,974	24,976	7,360	27,003	23,324	36,495	34,562	57,560	109,159	250,157
South Africa	..	..	..	..	..	..	..	..	..	..	..	..	..	..

6–23. Structure of external debt service payments

| | Bilateral | | | | Multilateral | | | | Private | | | | Total | |
| | Concessional | | Nonconcessional | | Concessional | | Nonconcessional | | Guaranteed | | Other | | | |
	1980	1989	1980	1989	1980	1989	1980	1989	1980	1989	1980	1989	1980	1989
SUB-SAHARAN AFRICA	381	545	464	720	121	530	845	3,074	1,319	1,300	3,164	2,646	6,294	8,815
excluding Nigeria	357	533	449	487	106	517	789	2,656	1,282	816	2,159	2,011	5,142	7,020
Angola	..	..	..	..	..	..	..	..	..	..	..	..	..	..
Benin	1	2	1	0	1	7	1	6	2	5	14	5	20	25
Botswana	1	5	1	12	0	4	10	41	1	7	2	0	15	69
Burkina Faso	3	6	4	4	3	15	2	8	2	1	9	5	23	39
Burundi	1	8	0	0	0	13	1	8	4	6	2	2	8	37
Cameroon	22	7	21	8	7	15	39	107	58	32	133	196	280	365
Cape Verde	0	0	0	2	0	1	0	1	0	0	0	0	0	4
Central African Republic	0	2	0	2	0	6	6	18	1	2	2	2	9	32
Chad	1	0	0	0	2	4	3	5	0	1	0	2	6	12
Comoros	0	0	0	0	0	0	0	0	0	0	0	3	0	3
Congo, People's Republic of	22	6	13	3	1	4	18	54	20	109	35	144	109	320
Cote d'Ivoire	29	5	55	12	4	12	45	461	336	33	560	835	1,029	1,358
Djibouti	2	5	1	0	0	5	0	0	0	1	1	3	4	14
Equatorial Guinea	0	0	1	0	0	1	0	4	0	0	1	0	2	5
Ethiopia	11	58	1	16	7	23	7	37	5	79	13	67	44	280
Gabon	6	6	28	82	2	3	3	32	200	24	193	75	432	222
Gambia, The	0	3	0	0	0	6	1	8	0	1	3	1	4	19
Ghana	24	33	15	6	7	29	40	256	25	54	42	56	153	434
Guinea	55	43	7	6	0	12	23	33	13	10	10	10	108	114
Guinea-Bissau	0	2	0	0	0	4	0	3	3	0	1	3	4	12
Kenya	14	29	38	45	5	25	61	320	130	82	212	144	460	645
Lesotho	0	1	0	2	0	6	0	5	4	7	1	0	5	21
Liberia	3	2	0	0	1	0	12	3	9	0	29	0	54	5
Madagascar	8	15	2	82	3	24	5	75	29	19	43	25	90	240
Malawi	4	5	7	11	3	12	5	55	14	2	55	10	88	95
Mali	4	13	0	0	1	22	4	26	3	1	3	4	15	66
Mauritania	7	20	1	8	3	20	12	38	11	2	14	14	48	102
Mauritius	2	20	4	8	1	5	8	81	6	18	31	12	52	144
Mozambique	0	8	0	15	0	6	0	10	0	5	0	20	0	64
Namibia	..	..	..	..	..	..	..	..	..	..	..	..	..	..
Niger	3	5	5	11	16	9	2	29	7	2	110	67	143	123
Nigeria	24	12	15	233	15	13	56	418	37	484	1,005	635	1,152	1,795
Rwanda	0	8	0	0	1	13	0	1	3	3	3	5	7	30
Sao Tome & Principe	0	0	1	3	0	1	0	0	0	0	0	1	1	5
Senegal	13	77	19	35	3	45	18	118	94	36	113	69	260	380
Seychelles	0	3	0	1	0	1	0	4	0	10	37	5	37	24
Sierra Leone	0	0	2	0	1	0	20	2	34	1	6	1	63	4
Somalia	3	1	0	9	1	6	9	17	0	0	0	0	13	33
Sudan	37	18	30	2	13	36	102	16	8	0	74	25	264	97
Swaziland	2	4	6	5	1	3	3	17	0	3	6	2	18	34
Tanzania	7	0	11	0	5	30	60	51	28	0	50	7	161	88
Togo	2	5	17	17	1	13	2	42	5	3	26	10	53	90
Uganda	3	80	0	0	2	15	17	110	17	0	5	4	44	209
Zaire	48	4	136	15	2	31	122	416	91	22	143	26	542	514
Zambia	16	6	22	37	6	23	128	26	93	44	145	35	410	171
Zimbabwe	3	18	0	28	3	7	0	112	26	191	32	116	64	472
NORTH AFRICA	647	799	466	2,566	21	126	384	1,756	3,453	4,124	3,057	4,021	8,028	13,392
Algeria	104	110	230	1,154	2	6	69	320	2,193	3,243	1,435	2,407	4,033	7,240
Egypt, Arab Republic of	342	423	184	842	9	53	50	341	830	431	623	902	2,038	2,992
Libya	..	..	..	..	..	..	..	..	..	..	..	..	..	..
Morocco	131	70	24	465	5	50	189	827	266	179	797	441	1,412	2,032
Tunisia	70	196	28	105	5	17	76	268	164	271	202	271	545	1,128
ALL AFRICA	1,028	1,344	930	3,286	142	656	1,229	4,830	4,772	5,424	6,221	6,667	14,322	22,207
South Africa	..	..	..	..	..	..	..	..	..	..	..	..	..	..

Millions of U.S. dollars (current prices and exchange rates)

6–24. Terms of external financing, 1989

	Concessional terms				Nonconcessional terms				Structure of financing (percentage of total)		
	Interest (percent)	Grace period (years)	Maturity (years)	Grant element (percent)	Interest (percent)	Grace period (years)	Maturity (years)	Grant element (percent)	Grants	Concessional loans	Nonconcessional loans
SUB-SAHARAN AFRICA	1.6	9	34	69	8.1	4	15	10	47	34	19
excluding Nigeria	1.6	9	34	69	8.1	4	15	10	51	36	13
Angola	..	..	..	..	..	..	..	..	..	..	..
Benin	1.3	9	34	72	5.8	2	11	17	43	53	4
Botswana	0.6	9	27	69	7.3	5	22	17	59	14	27
Burkina Faso	2.0	8	32	63	9.0	5	15	5	46	54	1
Burundi	1.2	10	37	75	0.0	0	0	0	61	39	0
Cameroon	4.3	8	21	41	8.0	5	16	11	28	12	60
Cape Verde	0.8	10	40	81	0.0	0	0	0	82	18	0
Central African Republic	1.2	10	38	75	6.5	3	11	16	47	53	0
Chad	1.2	10	40	75	0.0	0	0	0	53	47	0
Comoros	0.8	7	30	73	0.0	0	0	0	83	17	0
Congo, People's Republic of the	3.9	7	21	42	10.2	2	5	-1	37	43	20
Cote d'Ivoire	5.0	6	20	34	7.9	6	19	12	36	14	50
Djibouti	1.3	9	33	71	0.0	0	0	0	52	48	0
Equatorial Guinea	4.1	6	13	32	0.0	0	0	0	87	13	0
Ethiopia	1.5	8	32	66	7.6	6	17	14	37	49	14
Gabon	5.5	6	17	28	8.0	4	15	11	30	26	44
Gambia, The	1.0	10	39	74	0.0	0	0	0	47	*53*	*0*
Ghana	1.4	10	37	73	7.7	6	20	15	37	49	14
Guinea	1.6	10	33	69	7.4	5	20	16	34	64	2
Guinea-Bissau	0.9	10	37	77	6.5	0	15	16	36	42	23
Kenya	0.9	10	38	78	8.0	2	12	9	43	43	14
Lesotho	2.0	10	33	66	8.5	1	8	4	79	17	4
Liberia	0.0	0	0	0	0.0	0	0	0	100	0	0
Madagascar	0.7	10	29	71	0.0	0	0	0	58	42	0
Malawi	0.8	10	39	80	0.0	0	0	0	66	34	0
Mali	1.0	9	33	73	0.0	0	0	0	58	42	0
Mauritania	2.5	7	27	57	0.0	0	0	0	43	57	0
Mauritius	4.9	9	19	36	7.0	3	12	14	30	55	15
Mozambique	1.0	10	40	78	0.0	0	0	0	69	31	0
Niger	2.0	10	31	63	10.1	6	16	-1	56	34	10
Nigeria	2.2	10	32	65	8.1	4	16	10	18	14	68
Rwanda	1.2	9	36	73	8.8	3	13	5	55	43	1
Sao Tome & Principe	0.5	11	35	80	0.0	0	0	0	65	35	0
Senegal	1.5	9	33	70	6.7	5	18	20	52	46	1
Seychelles	4.2	9	19	40	8.5	3	12	7	36	22	42
Sierra Leone	1.5	12	22	67	0.0	0	0	0	31	69	0
Somalia	0.8	10	40	81	0.0	0	0	0	72	28	0
Sudan	1.1	10	38	76	0.0	0	0	0	66	34	0
Swaziland	1.8	10	36	65	7.4	5	20	16	61	31	8
Tanzania	0.8	10	43	81	0.0	0	0	0	84	16	0
Togo	1.4	9	36	72	0.0	0	0	0	58	42	0
Uganda	2.4	7	24	54	0.0	0	0	0	42	58	0
Zaire	1.1	10	41	78	0.0	0	0	0	62	38	0
Zambia	0.0	0	0	0	9.1	2	7	2	82	0	18
Zimbabwe	3.0	9	26	53	8.8	2	9	4	34	14	51
NORTH AFRICA	2.9	7	24	50	8.3	3	13	8	15	10	75
Algeria	0.0	0	0	0	8.2	3	13	8	2	0	98
Egypt, Arab Republic of	2.5	9	28	58	8.9	2	7	4	46	21	34
Libya	..	..	..	..	..	..	..	..	..	..	..
Morocco	3.0	5	17	42	8.4	4	17	9	21	19	60
Tunisia	3.5	7	24	47	8.5	4	13	8	10	24	66
ALL AFRICA	1.8	9	32	66	8.3	3	13	8	34	24	42
Namibia	..	..	..	..	..	..	..	..	..	..	..
South Africa	..	..	..	..	..	..	..	..	..	..	..

Note: Data are averages for new commitments of public and publicly guaranteed long–term loans only, excluding IMF purchases, weighted by the U.S. dollar value of the loans.

6–25. External debt and debt service ratios, 1989

	Debt–GDP ratio		Total external debt per capita (U.S. dollars)	Percentage of debt disbursed	Debt–export ratio		Debt service–export ratio	
	Concessional	Nonconcessional			Concessional	Nonconcessional	Ex ante	Ex post
SUB-SAHARAN AFRICA	29	63	324	84	117	253	46	21
excluding Nigeria	35	53	332	83	146	218	39	21
Angola	..	..	..	..	..	..	..	..
Benin	39	31	264	73	199	156	27	6
Botswana	7	14	435	61	8	16	4	3
Burkina Faso	22	7	89	60	211	71	21	13
Burundi	74	8	168	71	667	71	37	31
Cameroon	11	32	424	75	56	163	29	14
Cape Verde	36	10	369	69	150	43	16	8
Central African Republic	50	14	249	83	261	74	16	13
Chad	29	7	68	47	149	36	5	5
Comoros	75	13	398	75	376	67	28	2
Congo, People's Republic of the	42	148	2,020	84	77	274	74	22
Cote d'Ivoire	11	154	1,370	93	33	457	78	41
Djibouti	33	12	456	54	65	24	7	6
Equatorial Guinea	103	70	573	80	350	236	33	15
Ethiopia	40	10	63	64	334	83	44	38
Gabon	16	77	2,948	92	28	139	24	9
Gambia, The	115	39	415	71	152	52	11	10
Ghana	41	17	220	71	243	103	27	49
Guinea	52	27	403	71	192	101	36	15
Guinea-Bissau	187	83	487	69	1,229	547	105	32
Kenya	27	41	251	79	118	177	34	31
Lesotho	55	16	193	52	53	15	6	5
Liberia			731	97				
Madagascar	71	71	330	83	392	393	88	52
Malawi	65	23	175	78	304	107	20	27
Mali	96	8	270	79	577	47	13	18
Mauritania	144	56	1,078	78	297	116	38	19
Mauritius	13	27	793	84	19	40	7	10
Mozambique	198	172	317	88	933	812	180	19
Namibia	..	..	..	..	..	..	..	..
Niger	36	41	219	81	199	229	49	31
Nigeria	2	109	298	90	7	383	72	21
Rwanda	28	2	98	61	372	31	15	15
Sao Tome & Principe	215	104	1,126	70	926	448	116	43
Senegal	53	36	592	82	196	133	30	28
Seychelles	26	31	2,512	73	38	45	9	10
Sierra Leone	34	78	269	82	263	610	31	3
Somalia	131	58	362	83	2,188	969	174	47
Sudan	26	53	544	90	568	1,153	114	10
Swaziland	23	21	383	79	22	20	5	5
Tanzania	99	73	213	81	527	386	86	15
Togo	44	45	351	84	120	122	13	17
Uganda	26	12	112	70	458	207	62	75
Zaire	27	65	265	90	109	261	53	20
Zambia	34	112	911	92	107	347	32	11
Zimbabwe	12	40	332	77	40	129	22	24
NORTH AFRICA	23	67	973	83	87	255	50	43
Algeria	2	53	1,097	78	7	250	70	70
Egypt, Arab Republic of	46	100	978	89	149	322	41	26
Libya	..	..	..	..	..	..	..	..
Morocco	33	60	870	85	148	268	51	40
Tunisia	25	44	884	66	55	97	25	24
ALL AFRICA	27	65	446	84	104	253	48	30
South Africa	..	..	..	..	..	..	..	..

Technical Notes

Data on debt and related flows are drawn largely from the World Bank's Debtor Reporting System (DRS), to which member countries submit detailed accounts on the annual status, transactions, and terms of debt and related flows. The DRS is concerned solely with developing economies and does not collect data on external debt for other groups of borrowers or from economies that are not members of the World Bank. World Bank and IMF staff estimates based on other sources of data supplement DRS data, especially for recent years, on debt not guaranteed by debtor governments and on short-term debt. Thus, the figures in this chapter are based mostly on data supplied by *debtor* countries. Other data series on debt, on which the World Bank may base some of its estimates, are maintained by the Organization for Economic Cooperation and Development (OECD) and the Bank for International Settlements (BIS) from data provided by *creditor* governments and agencies. No figures are given for Angola or Libya, which do not report debt information to the DRS. Mozambique has only recently begun reporting debt data to the DRS. Data are in U.S. dollars converted from other foreign currencies at official exchange rates for each corresponding year (annual average rates for disbursements, debt service payments, and other flows and year end rates for stocks of debt). For all tables, summary statistics for country groups are totals or weighted averages based on group totals.

The following definitions apply throughout the chapter. "Official" and "private" refer to the *source* of the foreign loans. Official loans are from multilateral organizations (including the IMF) and from foreign governments; these loans are either made directly to the government of the borrowing country or guaranteed by it or its agencies when made to a third party. Private loans are from the private sector, including foreign parent companies and their affiliates, suppliers, financial markets (such as commercial banks), and other sources. These private loans may or may not be guaranteed by creditor or debtor governments and agencies. "Public and publicly guaranteed" loans, as defined by the DRS, refer to loans from both official and private foreign sources that are made to, or guaranteed by, the debtor government or its agencies. All loans from foreign official sources are public or publicly guaranteed. Some loans from foreign private sources are made to, or guaranteed by, the debtor government or its agencies (these are labeled "private guaranteed" by the DRS). Some loans from foreign private sources are not public or publicly guaranteed (these are labeled "private non-guaranteed" by DRS).

However, guarantees for private foreign loans may also be provided by creditor governments or their agencies. When guaranteed by creditor governments, private loans may be eligible for rescheduling under the Paris Club; other private loans must be rescheduled under other auspices. Because of the recent importance of rescheduling for Africa, this chapter presents *estimates* of private foreign loans that are guaranteed by creditor governments in Tables 6-22 and 6-23, where they are labeled as "private guaranteed." The remaining private source loans are labeled as "private other." Other sources, including the OECD and the BIS, may publish other data on private loans guaranteed by creditor governments, which are based on reports made directly by creditor governments, and which may diverge — in some cases significantly — from the estimates shown here.

Concessional loans carry a grant element of 25 percent or more (based on a standard 10 percent discount rate), which is consistent with the DAC definition of ODA (see Chapter 12).

Nonconcessional loans carry a grant element of less than 25 percent. In this chapter, private loans are shown separately from other nonconcessional loans except in summary Tables 6-24 and 6-25. Long-term loans have an original or extended maturity greater than one year, while the maturity on short-term loans is one year or less. Data on short-term loans are included in Tables 6-13, 6-16, 6-21, 6-22, and 6-25 (for debt only).

Tables 6-1, 6-2 and 6-3. Gross disbursements of official concessional, official nonconcessional, and private long-term loans

Gross disbursements are from commitments of long-term external loans by official concessional, official nonconcessional, and private sources. Data are shown separately for official concessional loans, official nonconcessional loans, and private loans. Gross disbursements of official non-concessional loans include IMF purchases (total drawings on the General Resources Account plus drawings on enlarged access resources and all the special facilities of the IMF during the year speci-fied), except drawings in the reserve tranche. Dis-bursements under the IMF's Trust Fund and Structural Adjustment Facility (SAF) are classified as concessional.

Table 6-4, 6-5 and 6-6. Amortization: official nonconcessional and private long-term loans

Amortization is the actual repayment (including repurchases of drawings from the IMF as defined above) of principal made in foreign currencies, goods, or services on outstaning long-term official concessional, as described above.

Table 6-7. Amortization: long-term loans

This is the sum of Tables 6-4 to 6-6.

Tables 6-8, 6-9 and 6-10. Interest payments

These are actual payments made in foreign currencies, goods, and services to various lenders described above on interest obligations (including IMF charges on drawings as defined above) due on disbursed debt and on commitment charges due on undisbursed debt (where information is available), that is, on long-term **official concessional, official nonconcessional, and private loans.**

Table 6-11. Interest payments: long-term loans

These are all interest payments on all long-term loans outstanding, both concessional and non-concessional, and on private and official loans.

Table 6-12. Total external debt service payments: long-term loans

Total external debt service payments includes the sum of amortization on long-term loans and interest payments on long-term loans.

Table 6-13. Interest payments: short-term loans

These are estimated for the respective year based on the estimated year-end stock of short-term debt (which may include interest arrears on long-term debt) and the annual average six-month LIBOR on notes denominated in U.S. dollars as reported in the *IFS* (with no adjustment for spreads). Actual payments may be different because LIBOR only approximates actual interest rates on short-term loans, and because not all interest due on short-term loans is actually paid.

Table 6-14. Net flows: long- short-term loans

Represent all disbursements of long and short-term loans net of all repayments of principal on long- and short-term loans.

Table 6-15. Net flows: long-term loans

Are for long-term loans only.

Table 6-16. Net transfers: long- and short-term loans

Net transfers are Are net flows less interest payments.

Table 6-17. Net transfers: long-term loans

Are net transfers for long term loans only.

The tables on **total external debt** sum three tables plus an estimate of short-term debt, which includes interest in arrears on public and publicly guaranteed long term loans. The time series for debt outstanding and disbursed reflects changes in the valuation of year-end debt stocks (because of U.S. dollar exchange rate fluctuation) and debt cancellation, as well as net disbursements. Therefore, changes in debt stocks from year to year cannot be used as a measure of net borrowing or vice versa.

Tables 6-18, 6-19 and 6-20. Official concessional, offical non-concessional and private long-term debt

These three tables almost sum up to total external debt.

Table 6-21. Total external debt.

When tables 6-18 to 6-20 are supplemented with estimates of total short-term debt, they sum up to total external debt.

Table 6-22. Structure of external debt

Table 6-22 summarizes debt structure for two years, 1980 and 1989. The columns cover type of creditor and concessionality. For creditor types in this table, "private guaranteed debt" represents an estimate of loans from private foreign lenders that are guaranteed by a public entity of the creditor government (rather than guaranteed by an entity of the *debtor* government, which is the definition of "private guaranteed" used by the DRS, although such debt will usually also be guaranteed by the debtor government). Some of the service on this debt, as well as that on official debt from creditor governments, may be eligible for rescheduling under agreements reached within the framework of the Paris Club. (The column includes loans from, or guaranteed by, all official bilateral sources, irrespective of whether the creditor government formally participates in the Paris Club discussions, since debtor governments are expected to seek similar rescheduling terms from official bilateral creditors or guarantors.) "Private other" represents

long-term loans from private foreign lenders that are not guaranteed by a public entity of the creditor country, plus all short-term loans. Some of this debt may be eligible for rescheduling under the auspices of the London Club.

The separation of all foreign private loans to a borrowing country into creditor-guaranteed private and other private has been estimated on the basis of source and type of interest rates. All suppliers' credits and loans from financial institutions that carry a fixed interest rate are classified as "private guaranteed" on the basis of information on loans actually rescheduled by the Paris Club. All other foreign private loans, including debtor governments' obligations as compensation for nationalization and bonds, are classified as "private other." The amounts of debt and debt service in each private category are therefore approximate estimates that may be subject to errors; for example, the creditor guaranteed debt is based on the total value of each guaranteed loan, even though the guarantee may apply to only a portion of it. The estimates are provided to help evaluate overall debt strategies and should be supplemented by detailed data from other sources when used for detailed country analysis.

Table 6-23. Structure of external debt service payments

This is a summary table that compares debt service payments (on long-term loans only) in two years, 1980 and 1989. Debt service payments on short-term loans are excluded to be consistent with Table 6-12, total debt service payments. Debt service payments are actual repayments of principal (amortization) and actual payments of interest. The column headings have the same definitions given above for Table 6-22, structure of external debt, except that they exclude short-term loans and the estimates for "private guaranteed" and "private other" are based on the same methodology.

Table 6-24. Terms of external financing, 1989

Presented on this table are the average interest rates, grace periods, maturities, and grant elements shown separately for long-term loans, including official concessional, official nonconcessional, and private; short-term loans are excluded. Grant elements are calculated using a standard 10 percent discount rate. The indicators are weighted averages across all loans in each category. For the column on structure of financing (that is, total flows), grants are based on sources for Chapter 12 (Aid Flows) and are not comparable with net official transfers in Table 5-6.

Table 6-25. External debt and debt service ratios, 1989

This include the ratio of debt outstanding and disbursed to gross domestic product; per capita debt; the ratio of debt outstanding and disbursed to debt outstanding, including undisbursed; the ratio of debt outstanding and disbursed to exports of goods and all services, including receipts of worker remittances; and the ratio of total debt

service paid to exports of goods and all services, more commonly called the debt service ratio. Ratios are shown separately for official concessional debt and for all nonconcessional (including private) debt. The stock of external debt includes short- and long-term loans, whereas debt service payments are for long-term loans only. The mid-year series used to calculate per capita figures are based on slightly earlier estimates than those shown in Table 1-2. The data for exports of goods and all services, plus receipts of workers remittances, are taken from the files used for the *World Debt Tables* and may contain later estimates for some countries than the comparable balance of payments data in Chapter 5. For Burkina Faso, Ethiopia, Ghana, Guinea, Mozambique, and Sierra Leone, the export data cover only goods and nonfactor services.

Additional information, definitions, and methodology are available in the World Bank, *World Debt Tables,* and the IMF, *International Financial Statistics.*

7

![black bar]

Government Finance

The data in this chapter pertain exclusively to central government operations; state and local government operations are not covered. Public enterprises — commercial entities owned or controlled by government — are not included both because they sell goods and services and because coherent and comprehensive data are often unavailable. (Public enterprises are covered in Chapter 10.)

The focus of this chapter is on the principal financial transactions of government taxing, borrowing, spending, and lending — rather than on the production and consumption of goods and services, the use of labor, or other government activities. Spending covers both current and capital transactions. Definitions and concepts generally conform to those in the IMF's *A Manual on Government Finance Statistics (GFS),* which provides a framework that facilitates the analysis of government transactions.

The basic *GFS* framework consists of revenue, grants, expenditure, and lending minus repayments. Data are compiled on a cash or payments basis and represent payments made to, or received from, the rest of the economy or the world by each government during the fiscal period indicated.

The data cover major government finance indicators during 1980-90 — fiscal deficit or surplus, expenditure and lending minus repayments, revenue, grants, and domestic and foreign financing —

expressed as a percentage of GDP (in purchaser values). The chapter also includes information on the major components of revenue and expenditure by functional and economic categories, shown as percentages of total revenue, total expenditure, and total expenditure and lending minus repayments, respectively.

Measures of fiscal deficit or surplus are among the single most important indicators of government fiscal performance. The measure is usually calculated as the difference between total revenue (including grants) and total expenditure (including lending minus repayments). As such, it measures government net financing requirements. *GFS* methodology recommends grouping grants receipts with revenue because they can be spent without incurring an obligation for future payments but lists them separately because grants can sometimes be treated as financing items. Financing includes all government borrowing from others (at home and abroad) *minus* amortization (government repayment of its borrowing from others and changes in cash balances). Other measures of fiscal balance include the fiscal deficit or surplus without grants, which measures the government's ability to operate without foreign transfers, and the fiscal deficit or surplus excluding interest payments from expenditure, referred to as the primary deficit or surplus.

Revenue is divided between taxes — unrequited compulsory payments to government — and nontax revenue. It includes only nonrepayable receipts other than grants. Tax revenue is also classified according to the base upon which the tax is levied (for example, income and profits).

Expenditure is classified by function (such as health and education) and by economic categories (such as wages, purchases, and interest payments). Lending minus repayments — government lending less repayment of past government lending — is grouped with expenditure, except in certain cases (see technical notes).

The data have limitations, particularly for intercountry comparisons. Coverage (that is, whether based on consolidated accounts or only budgetary accounts) of central government varies among countries. Underlying government finance data are reported by fiscal year (which differs from country to country and may not be consistent with the GDP data on a calendar year basis used to calculate ratios in this chapter). Some 1989 and 1990 data are still considered provisional, and data gaps remain for many countries, so interpretation of broad trends should be appropriately guarded.

Data on state and local governments are excluded because they are not systematically compiled, although in some countries, such as Nigeria, state and local governments carry out a large proportion of total government operations.

7-1. Government deficit/surplus (including grants)

	Percentage of total revenue											Average		
	1980	1981	1982	1983	1984	1985	1986	1987	1988	1989	1990	75-79	80-85	86-MR
SUB-SAHARAN AFRICA	-6.1	-7.3	-7.7	-6.3	-5.0	-5.1	-5.8	-6.0	..	..	..	-5.4	-6.2	-5.2
excluding Nigeria	-6.2	-7.2	-7.7	-6.2	-5.0	-5.2	-5.9	-5.8	..	..	..	-5.3	-6.2	-5.2
Angola	..	..	..	..	..	..	..	..	..	..	..	..	..	..
Benin	-6.0	-0.4	-4.9	-5.4	-4.7	-2.1	-2.2	-5.7	-5.1	..	..	1.1	-3.9	-4.3
Botswana	-0.2	-2.3	-2.5	9.8	14.5	24.9	24.1	19.0	26.0	..	..	-1.3	7.4	23.0
Burkina Faso	0.2	-1.1	-1.2	0.1	-0.6	1.0	-0.1	0.3	..	..	..	-0.3	-0.3	0.1
Burundi	-3.9	-5.7	-7.5	-12.2	-8.7	-5.2	-4.3	-12.8	-7.9	..	..	-2.7	-7.2	-8.3
Cameroon	0.5	-3.0	-2.4	1.2	1.6	0.8	0.6	-3.4	-3.7	-3.2	..	-0.4	-0.2	-2.4
Cape Verde	..	..	..	..	..	..	..	..	..	..	..	..	..	..
Central African Republic	..	-3.9	0.8	-0.6	-0.3	-0.1	-0.1	..	..	..	..	..	-0.9	-0.1
Chad	..	..	..	-0.2	-1.2	-1.6	-3.3	-11.5	..	..	..	-1.8	-1.0	-7.4
Comoros	..	..	-10.8	-14.9	-18.3	-15.7	-8.6	-12.4	..	..	..	..	-14.9	-10.5
Congo, People's Republic of the	-5.2	-1.7	-13.3	-2.8	-2.4	-1.0	-12.4	-11.5	-20.5	..	..	-5.6	-4.4	-14.8
Cote d'Ivoire	-10.5	-11.7	-14.0	-10.3	-2.9	-3.4	..	..	-8.5	-6.1	-12.2	-8.7	-8.8	-9.0
Djibouti	..	..	..	..	4.7	1.5	-2.3	-8.9	-1.0	..	..	..	3.1	-4.1
Equatorial Guinea	..	..	..	..	..	..	..	..	..	..	..	..	..	..
Ethiopia	-4.5	-3.8	-5.4	-13.5	-6.2	-8.8	-7.5	-6.7	-7.4	-9.0	-15.7	-4.4	-7.0	-9.3
Gabon	6.1	0.8	3.0	-1.3	0.2	0.1	-8.1	-13.1	-8.7	-5.4	..	-10.2	1.5	-8.8
Gambia, The	-4.5	-10.9	-6.4	-9.5	-5.5	-6.8	-7.4	-6.1	-0.4	1.9	..	-6.4	-7.2	-3.0
Ghana	-4.2	-6.5	-5.6	-2.7	-1.8	-2.2	0.1	0.5	0.4	0.7	..	-8.8	-3.8	0.4
Guinea	-0.2	0.4	-0.3	-0.7	-0.3	-1.9	-5.4	-4.9	-6.7	-6.1	..	..	-0.5	-5.8
Guinea-Bissau	-22.6	-27.3	-25.8	-23.1	-27.6	-28.4	-16.0	-19.4	-18.4	-17.5	..	..	-25.8	-17.8
Kenya	-4.5	-6.5	-7.8	-4.8	-4.8	-6.2	-4.4	-6.4	-4.2	-4.9	..	-5.0	-5.8	-5.0
Lesotho	-14.1	-17.9	-7.4	-5.0	-2.8	-5.1	-16.4	-22.1	-18.6	-7.3	..	-6.6	-8.7	-16.1
Liberia	-7.9	-10.1	-10.4	-9.6	-5.6	-8.0	-8.4	-7.4	-5.5	-14.7	..	-4.7	-8.6	-9.0
Madagascar	-9.5	-12.1	-7.1	-5.4	-3.9	-3.8	-3.2	-3.5	-3.4	-3.1	..	..	-7.0	-3.3
Malawi	-15.9	-12.4	-7.6	-7.1	-5.2	-8.4	-9.9	-8.3	-5.6	-0.6	..	-8.0	-9.4	-6.1
Mali	-4.6	-3.9	-7.8	-8.4	-7.6	-9.8	-8.2	-5.4	-4.5	..	..	-1.4	-7.0	-6.0
Mauritania	-13.7	-3.4	-10.2	-15.0	-9.4	-4.5	-1.5	-1.5	2.0	..	..	-5.5	-9.4	-0.3
Mauritius	-10.3	-12.7	-11.8	-7.7	-4.5	-3.5	-1.8	0.2	0.3	-0.1	-0.9	-8.1	-8.4	-0.4
Mozambique	..	..	..	..	..	..	..	..	..	..	..	..	..	..
Namibia	..	..	-7.3	-7.8	-1.9	0.9	6.2	-4.3	0.2	3.2	..	..	-4.0	1.3
Niger	-4.7	-10.8	-7.0	-7.1	-6.7	-5.7	-4.0	-4.5	-3.2	..	..	-2.4	-7.0	-3.9
Nigeria	-3.1	-11.8	-7.4	-9.4	-4.1	-2.5	-3.4	-9.9	-7.6	-6.3	..	-4.0	-6.4	-6.8
Rwanda	-1.7	-3.9	-4.2	-4.6	-3.3	-3.9	-4.7	-7.9	..	..	..	-1.6	-3.6	-6.3
Sao Tome & Principe	..	..	..	..	..	..	..	..	..	..	..	..	..	..
Senegal	0.9	-3.4	-6.2	-5.9	-8.1	..	..	1.9	..	..	..	-1.0	-4.5	1.9
Seychelles	-10.0	-8.3	-15.2	-9.2	-13.0	-10.6	-14.8	-1.6	-3.7	-7.3	..	-0.5	-11.1	-6.8
Sierra Leone	-12.8	-9.3	-10.4	-14.5	-7.5	-7.8	-12.6	-17.7	..	..	..	-9.2	-10.4	-15.1
Somalia	-7.1	-4.6	-5.3	-3.6	-5.6	-8.2	-5.1	-8.0	-5.1	-3.0	..	-6.6	-5.7	-5.3
Sudan	-3.3	-6.6	-4.6	-3.7	-7.0	-13.9	-10.2	-9.3	..	..	..	-5.0	-6.5	-9.7
Swaziland	6.5	-9.8	-5.8	-3.4	-0.5	-3.7	-5.1	1.9	4.3	1.1	0.2	-2.0	-2.8	0.5
Tanzania	-8.4	-6.7	-11.5	-7.7	-5.9	-4.1	-4.2	-2.6	-1.9	..	..	-8.0	-7.4	-2.9
Togo	-2.0	-5.7	-1.8	-1.9	-2.5	-5.6	-4.6	-0.6	-0.8	-3.2	..	-20.5	-3.2	-2.3
Uganda	-3.1	-4.0	-3.9	-2.3	-2.3	-2.7	-2.5	-2.3	-3.2	-1.7	..	-3.4	-3.1	-2.4
Zaire	-0.8	-3.6	-4.2	-2.2	-3.0	-0.8	-5.0	-9.7	-3.5	..	..	-6.6	-2.4	-6.1
Zambia	-18.5	-12.9	-18.6	-7.8	-8.4	-15.2	-21.6	-12.9	-11.6	-4.2	..	-14.5	-13.6	-12.6
Zimbabwe	-10.9	-5.9	-10.5	-6.2	-10.1	-7.3	-7.7	-10.9	-9.4	-8.9	-7.6	-7.7	-8.5	-8.9
NORTH AFRICA	-7.3	-7.4	-11.4	-8.6	-7.5	-7.1	-8.1	-4.9	..	..	..	-11.0	-8.2	-6.5
Algeria	..	..	..	..	..	..	..	..	..	..	..	..	..	..
Egypt, Arab Republic of	-9.3	-6.3	-17.1	-9.8	-11.4	-10.4	-12.1	-5.8	-8.6	-6.4	..	-16.5	-10.7	-8.2
Libya	..	..	..	..	..	..	..	..	..	..	..	..	..	..
Morocco	-9.7	-13.4	-11.4	-7.7	-6.0	-7.3	-7.7	-4.4	..	..	..	-12.5	-9.3	-6.1
Tunisia	-2.8	-2.5	-5.8	-8.3	-4.9	-3.7	-4.6	-4.4	-3.8	-4.3	..	-3.9	-4.7	-4.3
ALL AFRICA	-6.2	-7.3	-8.0	-6.5	-5.1	-5.3	-6.0	-5.9	-4.8	..	..	-5.8	-6.4	-5.3
South Africa	-2.3	-3.8	-3.7	-5.1	-4.6	-3.7	-5.3	-6.8	-5.0	-1.9	..	..	-3.9	-4.8

7–2. Government deficit/surplus (excluding grants)

	Percentage of total revenue											Average		
	1980	1981	1982	1983	1984	1985	1986	1987	1988	1989	1990	75–79	80–85	86–MR
SUB-SAHARAN AFRICA	-9.2	-9.9	-10.5	-8.8	-7.8	-7.7	-8.2	-9.3	-8.5	..	..	..	-9.0	-8.7
excluding Nigeria	-9.3	-9.8	-10.6	-8.8	-8.0	-7.9	-8.4	-9.3	-8.5	..	..	..	-9.1	-8.8
Angola	..	..	..	..	..	..	..	..	..	..	..	0.9	-9.8	-7.3
Benin	-11.5	-8.2	-11.1	-11.0	-10.4	-6.4	-5.3	-7.4	-9.2	..	..	-1.3	2.9	19.9
Botswana	-5.5	-7.4	-8.5	5.2	11.4	22.4	21.1	15.3	23.3	..	..	-5.2	-0.5	0.0
Burkina Faso	0.1	-1.8	-1.3	-0.1	-0.7	0.9	-0.1	0.2	..	..	..	-2.7	-11.2	-12.2
Burundi	-7.7	-10.7	-11.5	-15.8	-12.7	-8.6	-8.0	-16.8	-11.8	..	..	-0.4	-0.6	-2.5
Cameroon	0.5	-3.0	-2.4	-0.9	1.5	0.8	0.5	-3.4	-3.7	-3.2	..	..	..	..
Cape Verde	..	..	..	..	..	..	..	..	..	..	..	..	-2.5	-1.3
Central African Republic	..	-6.4	-1.3	-2.0	-1.4	-1.2	-1.3	..	..	..	..	-1.8	..	..
Chad	..	..	..	-5.6	-6.5	-8.7	-20.2	-29.1	..	..	..	..	-23.8	-24.7
Comoros	-7.8	-8.0	-23.4	-31.1	-38.0	-34.2	-25.4	-23.9	..	..	..	-5.6	-4.8	-14.9
Congo, People's Republic of the	-5.9	-1.8	-13.4	-3.2	-3.3	-1.3	-12.4	-11.6	-20.8	..	..	-8.7	-9.0	-8.4
Cote d'Ivoire	-10.5	-11.9	-14.2	-10.6	-3.2	-3.6			-13.5	-16.2	-12.2	..	0.6	-8.7
Djibouti	..	..	..	..	2.2	-0.9	-6.0	-17.2	-3.0	..	..	..	..	..
Equatorial Guinea	..	..	..	..	..	..	..	..	..	..	..	..	..	..
Ethiopia	-6.5	-5.9	-8.2	-16.1	-8.8	-15.2	-11.6	-9.6	-9.7	-11.8	-19.4	-6.3	-10.1	-12.4
Gabon	5.7	0.4	3.0	-1.6	-0.1	-0.2	-8.7	-13.6	-9.2	-6.0	..	-10.2	1.2	-9.4
Gambia, The	-7.7	-15.4	-15.5	-12.3	-9.3	-10.5	-12.9	-19.0	-10.9	-5.6	..	-6.4	-11.8	-12.1
Ghana	-4.2	-6.5	-5.7	-2.7	-2.1	-2.7	-0.7	-0.3	-0.7	-0.8	..	-8.8	-4.0	-0.6
Guinea	-0.3	0.4	-0.4	-0.8	-0.3	-1.9	-7.3	-8.8	-9.9	-9.4	..	..	-0.5	-8.9
Guinea-Bissau	-57.4	-40.6	-45.9	-38.7	-46.5	-50.1	-32.4	-43.7	-39.5	-51.9	..	..	-46.5	-41.9
Kenya	-5.2	-7.1	-8.3	-5.4	-5.0	-6.4	-4.6	-7.6	-5.7	-4.9	..	-6.7	-6.2	-5.7
Lesotho	-21.6	-22.1	-8.9	-6.9	-7.9	-5.9	-20.8	-23.7	-22.3	-11.0	..	-8.2	-12.2	-19.4
Liberia	-10.0	-12.3	-14.1	-12.7	-8.9	-10.0	-10.7	-8.9	-6.8	-15.9	..	-4.7	-11.3	-10.6
Madagascar	-9.5	-12.1	-7.1	-5.9	-4.6	-4.2	-3.9	-4.2	-4.1	-3.9	..	..	-7.2	-4.0
Malawi	-20.3	-16.4	-10.8	-9.5	-7.6	-9.9	-12.3	-11.3	-7.7	-6.7	..	-9.3	-12.4	-9.5
Mali	-11.6	-11.6	-15.4	-18.2	-16.6	-18.2	-13.7	-12.0	-10.3	..	..	-13.6	-15.3	-12.0
Mauritania	-29.0	-17.3	-22.1	-23.6	-23.0	-14.9	-6.8	-8.5	-10.2	..	..	-5.5	-21.6	-8.5
Mauritius	-10.3	-12.8	-12.4	-7.8	-4.9	-4.5	-3.0	-0.6	-0.5	-0.5	-1.3	-14.1	-8.8	-1.2
Mozambique	..	..	..	..	..	..	..	..	..	..	..	..	..	..
Namibia	..	..	-20.1	-23.0	-19.5	-13.1	-9.5	-13.3	-7.2	0.3	..	..	..	..
Niger	-4.7	-10.8	-7.0	-8.8	-10.1	-9.3	-9.1	-9.8	-7.7	..	..	-2.4	-8.5	-8.9
Nigeria	-3.1	-11.8	-7.4	-9.4	-4.1	-2.5	-3.4	-9.9	-7.6	-6.3	..	-4.0	-6.4	-6.8
Rwanda	-1.7	-7.6	-7.8	-8.2	-6.3	-7.0	-7.7	-10.6	..	..	..	-1.6	-6.4	-9.2
Sao Tome & Principe	..	..	..	..	..	..	..	..	..	..	..	..	..	..
Senegal	0.8	-3.6	-7.4	-7.4	-10.6	-1.1	-1.5	0.8	..	..	..	-1.7	-4.8	-0.3
Seychelles	-12.0	-10.6	-17.0	-12.7	-15.6	-13.2	-17.2	-4.6	-5.3	-8.9	..	-0.9	-13.5	-9.0
Sierra Leone	-13.5	-10.6	-11.1	-15.2	-8.9	-8.7	-14.0	-22.0	..	..	..	-9.7	-11.3	-18.0
Somalia	-9.8	-6.6	-9.0	-6.8	-8.8	-15.8	-13.7	-25.1	-16.3	-29.1	..	-6.8	-9.5	-21.1
Sudan	-6.0	-7.6	-7.4	-5.9	-8.9	-15.4	-12.0	-11.6	..	..	..	-6.9	-8.5	-11.8
Swaziland	4.7	-10.8	-6.8	-4.4	-2.2	-5.1	-6.3	1.3	3.9	0.2	-1.1	-2.0	-4.1	-0.4
Tanzania	-11.4	-10.8	-14.3	-10.0	-7.3	-5.7	-5.2	-7.7	-7.7	..	..	-8.0	-9.9	-6.8
Togo	-2.0	-7.3	-3.6	-4.2	-5.9	-8.3	-8.9	-2.9	-2.8	-5.6	..	-20.6	-5.2	-5.0
Uganda	-3.2	-4.1	-4.7	-2.4	-2.7	-2.9	-3.2	-2.7	-4.0	-3.5	..	-4.5	-3.3	-3.3
Zaire	-2.9	-5.5	-5.4	-3.9	-5.6	-3.3	-6.6	-10.0	-6.4	..	..	-7.4	-4.4	-7.7
Zambia	-19.4	-13.6	-19.4	-9.1	-8.9	-15.4	-23.0	-13.3	-13.2	-6.3	..	-14.5	-14.3	-14.0
Zimbabwe	-10.9	-5.9	-10.8	-6.6	-11.3	-9.6	-9.0	-11.8	-10.5	-9.6	-8.6	-7.7	-9.2	-9.9
NORTH AFRICA	-7.5	-7.5	-11.5	-8.8	-7.5	-7.4	-8.5	-5.8	..	..	..	-11.2	-8.4	-7.1
Algeria	..	..	..	..	..	..	..	..	..	..	..	..	..	..
Egypt, Arab Republic of	-9.3	-6.4	-17.1	-10.2	-11.4	-11.0	-13.1	-8.2	-9.7	-8.0	..	-16.5	-10.9	-9.7
Libya	..	..	..	..	..	..	..	..	..	..	..	..	..	..
Morocco	-9.7	-13.4	-11.4	-7.7	-6.0	-7.3	-7.7	-4.4	..	..	..	-13.0	-9.3	-6.1
Tunisia	-3.4	-2.7	-5.9	-8.5	-5.1	-3.8	-4.6	-4.6	-4.1	-5.8	..	-3.9	-4.9	-4.8
ALL AFRICA	-9.0	-9.7	-10.6	-8.8	-7.8	-7.7	-8.2	-9.0	-8.4	..	..	..	-8.9	-8.6
South Africa	-2.3	-3.8	-3.7	-5.1	-4.6	-3.7	-5.3	-6.8	-5.0	-1.9	..	..	-3.9	-4.8

7–3. Government prime deficit/surplus (–/+)

	Percentage of total revenue											Average		
	1980	1981	1982	1983	1984	1985	1986	1987	1988	1989	1990	75–79	80–85	86–MR
SUB-SAHARAN AFRICA	-1.0	-1.7	-1.2	1.6	5.2	6.3	4.9	5.1	..	..	..	..	1.5	5.1
excluding Nigeria	-1.0	-1.5	-1.3	1.5	4.7	5.8	4.5	4.1	..	..	..	..	1.3	4.4
Angola	..	..	..	..	..	..	..	..	..	..	..	..	..	..
Benin	-4.7	1.4	-2.5	0.7	9.2	8.9	6.1	2.2	2.9	..	..	1.3	2.2	3.7
Botswana	1.5	-0.6	0.2	12.7	17.6	28.7	27.9	22.3	30.0	..	..	-0.3	10.0	26.7
Burkina Faso	0.5	1.6	1.5	2.2	5.0	10.9	7.6	8.7	..	..	..	0.2	3.6	8.2
Burundi	-0.1	-3.8	-5.8	-9.5	-3.7	1.3	2.3	-6.9	-0.1	..	..	-2.7	-3.6	-1.6
Cameroon	1.1	-1.9	-1.4	3.5	4.1	4.8	4.3	-3.4	-3.7	2.9	..	-0.2	1.7	0.0
Cape Verde	..	..	..	..	..	..	..	..	..	..	..	..	..	..
Central African Republic	..	-2.7	5.6	5.3	8.2	9.7	9.6	..	..	..	..	..	5.2	9.6
Chad	..	..	..	3.7	0.9	0.2	-1.7	-10.7	..	..	..	-1.8	1.6	-6.2
Comoros	-7.8	-8.0	-9.1	-12.9	-15.9	-13.2	-5.1	-11.8	..	..	..	..	-11.2	-8.5
Congo, People's Republic of the	-0.4	5.2	-7.7	4.5	7.4	11.9	6.4	9.0	5.4	..	..	-5.4	3.5	6.9
Cote d'Ivoire	-3.3	1.7	4.2	10.9	24.5	25.8	..	..	19.0	3.9	-12.2	-8.7	10.6	3.6
Djibouti	..	..	..	..	4.7	2.3	-1.5	-0.5	0.4	..	..	..	3.5	-0.5
Equatorial Guinea	..	..	..	..	..	..	..	..	..	..	..	..	..	..
Ethiopia	-1.5	-0.4	-2.2	-11.1	-1.3	-2.0	-2.3	-0.7	-5.1	-6.2	-12.1	-3.8	-3.1	-5.3
Gabon	10.1	5.4	8.0	4.0	5.7	5.5	-1.2	1.4	11.5	16.7	..	-10.2	6.5	7.1
Gambia, The	-3.1	-8.2	-2.2	-2.9	0.3	-3.6	-1.0	6.5	11.7	18.8	..	-6.2	-3.3	9.0
Ghana	11.0	6.3	14.7	-2.7	10.7	8.4	15.5	10.4	8.3	9.9	..	-7.6	8.1	11.1
Guinea	-0.2	4.5	2.5	2.8	3.8	0.7	4.9	4.4	5.5	3.1	..	..	2.3	4.5
Guinea-Bissau	-21.8	-26.1	-24.9	-22.5	-25.2	-24.8	-11.4	-10.9	2.8	16.9	..	..	-24.2	-0.6
Kenya	2.1	1.1	3.7	9.4	10.6	8.5	13.8	9.6	14.1	-4.9	..	-3.7	5.9	8.2
Lesotho	-11.6	-13.6	2.1	5.0	4.4	2.6	-14.9	-15.8	-11.2	3.6	..	-6.2	-1.9	-9.6
Liberia	0.9	-4.2	-0.6	2.4	14.3	14.2	5.3	7.8	-4.2	-2.2	..	-3.7	4.5	1.7
Madagascar	-7.6	-9.3	-6.6	0.4	4.4	4.7	6.4	7.5	-2.7	-2.3	..	..	-2.3	2.2
Malawi	-7.8	1.2	7.5	6.5	10.9	11.0	10.4	12.9	14.9	16.8	..	-6.4	4.9	13.7
Mali	-4.0	-3.1	-6.7	-7.2	-5.7	-6.4	-5.7	-0.1	-1.5	..	..	-1.4	-5.5	-2.4
Mauritania	-12.2	0.0	-7.4	-10.4	-4.8	2.9	10.0	5.6	14.2	..	..	-5.2	-5.3	9.9
Mauritius	1.6	1.0	5.6	10.4	15.4	17.0	18.1	17.5	13.6	13.3	10.4	-6.8	8.5	14.6
Mozambique	..	..	..	..	..	..	..	..	..	..	..	..	..	..
Namibia	..	..	-7.1	-7.7	-1.5	1.3	6.5	-4.0	0.4	3.2	..	..	-3.7	1.5
Niger	0.7	-6.2	-1.0	0.0	4.4	7.1	8.6	9.5	11.3	..	..	-1.7	0.8	9.8
Nigeria	0.5	-8.0	3.1	5.6	21.4	23.8	20.9	35.8	37.3	42.1	..	-3.6	7.7	34.0
Rwanda	0.3	-2.3	-1.9	-1.9	0.5	-0.2	-0.9	-3.6	..	..	..	-1.5	-0.9	-2.3
Sao Tome & Principe	..	..	..	..	..	..	..	..	..	..	..	..	..	..
Senegal	28.0	17.1	7.9	9.3	6.1	13.2	12.3	3.0	..	..	..	0.2	13.6	7.7
Seychelles	-8.0	-6.0	-12.7	-5.3	-7.8	-3.2	-9.9	14.3	12.3	6.0	-5.6	-0.4	-7.2	3.4
Sierra Leone	-5.8	-1.8	-2.4	-5.9	2.5	1.0	1.2	2.1	..	..	..	-8.5	-2.1	1.7
Somalia	-4.3	-2.7	-1.7	-0.5	2.6	0.9	8.3	1.1	8.7	9.4	..	-6.5	-0.9	6.9
Sudan	2.8	-0.7	1.2	3.2	6.8	10.6	14.3	8.2	..	..	..	-3.9	4.0	11.3
Swaziland	6.8	-8.2	-1.9	0.9	4.0	2.1	2.0	8.3	10.3	6.0	5.0	-1.7	0.6	6.3
Tanzania	-1.6	0.8	-4.5	1.2	3.7	5.6	4.5	10.7	14.0	..	..	-7.0	0.9	9.7
Togo	4.9	2.9	6.0	16.5	10.7	9.9	-4.6	-0.6	13.8	10.4	..	-19.8	8.5	4.8
Uganda	-3.1	-4.0	-1.2	8.5	12.0	8.5	9.9	3.1	2.0	6.0	..	-3.4	3.4	5.2
Zaire	6.7	7.5	7.2	18.7	31.6	37.9	31.3	-8.9	3.3	..	..	-5.7	18.3	8.6
Zambia	-11.0	-5.2	-11.9	5.4	-4.9	-4.3	-10.7	-12.3	-11.3	-2.2	..	-11.6	-5.3	-9.1
Zimbabwe	-4.2	2.6	-2.2	3.5	0.3	4.8	4.9	1.6	3.5	5.2	6.9	-6.1	0.8	4.4
NORTH AFRICA	-2.5	-1.1	-5.5	-1.0	1.4	2.9	2.7	6.6	..	..	..	..	-1.0	4.6
Algeria	..	..	..	..	..	..	..	..	..	..	..	..	..	..
Egypt, Arab Republic of	-6.3	-1.3	-13.2	-3.1	-4.2	-3.0	-4.5	3.4	1.1	-4.8	..	-14.7	-5.2	-1.2
Libya	..	..	..	..	..	..	..	..	..	..	..	..	..	..
Morocco	-2.6	-3.9	-2.5	3.3	7.3	8.5	9.6	11.9	..	..	..	-11.1	1.7	10.7
Tunisia	1.3	2.0	-0.8	-3.2	1.1	3.3	2.9	4.5	5.1	4.8	..	-2.9	0.6	4.3
ALL AFRICA	-1.1	-1.6	-1.5	1.4	4.9	6.1	4.8	5.2	-4.8	..	..	..	1.3	5.1
South Africa	4.7	4.3	5.2	4.8	6.7	8.1	6.8	5.7	7.8	12.8	..	..	5.6	8.3

Note: The prime deficit/surplus excludes the payment of interest on past debt from total spending.

7-4. Government expenditure and lending minus repayments

	Percentage of total revenue											Average		
	1980	1981	1982	1983	1984	1985	1986	1987	1988	1989	1990	75–79	80–85	86–MR
SUB-SAHARAN AFRICA	29.5	29.5	31.2	30.1	29.8	29.2	29.5	29.8	..	..	..	..	29.9	29.4
excluding Nigeria	29.7	29.6	31.5	30.3	30.2	29.6	29.8	29.9	..	..	..	..	30.2	29.5
Angola	..	..	..	..	..	..	..	..	..	..	..	..	..	..
Benin	24.6	25.7	28.6	30.0	29.0	22.3	21.5	19.5	20.5	..	..	20.1	26.7	20.5
Botswana	42.7	42.2	51.4	43.2	46.3	42.6	43.5	49.1	50.9	..	..	32.5	44.7	47.8
Burkina Faso	11.7	12.5	11.9	10.0	11.8	10.1	11.5	11.4	..	..	..	12.2	11.3	11.5
Burundi	21.7	24.1	28.5	30.6	25.7	21.5	23.9	32.3	28.2	..	..	18.4	25.3	28.1
Cameroon	14.2	18.8	19.3	22.9	22.7	22.3	21.6	24.3	22.3	20.4	..	13.8	20.1	22.1
Cape Verde	..	..	..	..	..	..	..	..	..	..	..	..	17.0	13.2
Central African Republic	20.0	21.4	15.9	16.9	14.2	13.8	13.2	..	..	..	..	14.1		
Chad	..	..	..	9.7	13.2	15.4	26.9	38.0	..	..	..	14.1	12.8	32.4
Comoros	25.0	30.0	36.1	46.7	52.6	46.8	41.5	35.4	..	..	..	..	39.5	38.4
Congo, People's Republic of the	49.6	38.4	48.1	42.3	38.3	39.0	43.8	32.3	33.3	38.7	30.6	34.0	42.6	35.8
Cote d'Ivoire	33.8	37.6	39.4	38.7	31.6	30.4	31.0	31.0	31.0	..	..	28.6	35.2	31.0
Djibouti	..	..	..	..	38.5	38.3	38.6	44.9	31.6	..	..	..	38.4	38.4
Equatorial Guinea	..	..	..	..	..	..	..	..	..	..	..	..	..	..
Ethiopia	25.3	26.0	28.7	37.7	30.2	33.7	34.3	34.8	38.4	41.5	45.6	19.1	30.3	38.9
Gabon	33.0	39.5	38.1	40.8	39.3	39.3	56.4	35.8	35.3	29.5	..	36.5	38.4	39.3
Gambia, The	31.1	32.0	32.0	29.9	31.4	30.5	27.7	43.3	40.8	28.8	..	23.9	31.1	35.1
Ghana	11.1	11.0	11.2	8.2	10.1	14.0	14.3	14.4	14.2	14.4	..	13.1	10.9	14.3
Guinea	32.5	27.4	49.6	33.5	27.0	42.4	23.0	20.2	21.8	20.0	..	..	35.4	21.2
Guinea-Bissau	72.8	54.5	57.4	49.3	58.5	61.7	40.5	56.8	52.8	65.8	..	..	59.0	54.0
Kenya	27.1	29.0	29.5	25.7	25.2	26.4	24.9	28.7	27.0	..	..	21.1	27.2	26.9
Lesotho	58.0	55.9	45.5	49.8	55.5	49.6	62.8	64.9	60.3	50.1	..	31.7	52.4	59.5
Liberia	28.1	32.2	35.2	34.3	29.3	28.9	27.3	24.8	25.5	34.3	..	23.2	31.3	28.0
Madagascar	25.1	24.3	19.4	17.1	18.0	17.0	16.0	18.5	..	..	..	..	20.1	17.3
Malawi	39.4	35.7	29.4	28.7	27.5	32.1	34.1	31.2	24.1	22.9	..	24.2	32.1	28.1
Mali	22.5	23.4	28.4	31.5	30.8	34.9	30.2	27.7	29.0	..	..	..	28.6	29.0
Mauritania	45.6	37.0	42.0	45.3	46.6	38.5	31.7	33.8	34.2	..	..	41.5	42.5	33.2
Mauritius	31.2	33.0	31.4	31.0	27.5	26.1	23.9	22.6	23.7	23.7	24.5	24.2	30.0	23.7
Mozambique	..	..	..	..	..	..	..	..	..	..	..	..	..	..
Namibia	..	..	44.5	50.3	49.1	45.3	44.1	49.1	41.6	39.3	..	..	47.3	43.5
Niger	19.1	23.6	18.4	19.0	19.2	20.2	20.8	20.7	19.0	..	..	12.5	19.9	20.2
Nigeria	21.6	25.5	20.6	21.0	14.4	13.6	18.7	27.6	25.3	23.4	..	18.8	19.4	23.8
Rwanda	14.5	19.7	19.5	19.1	17.5	19.2	21.5	23.2	..	..	..	11.3	18.3	22.3
Sao Tome & Principe	..	..	..	..	..	..	..	..	..	..	..	..	..	..
Senegal	23.3	26.1	27.6	26.8	29.5	2.2	20.6	20.3	..	..	..	14.7	22.6	20.4
Seychelles	50.0	51.5	59.2	52.0	55.7	57.4	60.2	53.0	56.7	67.3	54.7	27.1	54.3	58.4
Sierra Leone	29.9	27.7	22.4	23.5	17.3	14.7	19.1	28.4	..	..	..	23.2	22.6	23.8
Somalia	18.0	16.9	18.4	18.9	18.1	20.8	24.3	31.2	27.0	36.4	..	15.9	18.5	29.7
Sudan	20.0	25.9	19.3	19.1	21.3	25.0	20.5	20.4	..	..	..	17.1	21.8	20.4
Swaziland	30.5	36.0	36.7	35.4	34.0	36.3	31.9	27.9	26.7	31.1	33.0	28.8	35.0	30.1
Tanzania	28.7	27.7	31.6	26.2	23.5	21.5	20.3	21.4	21.0	..	..	24.9	26.5	20.9
Togo	32.3	32.8	32.0	31.4	35.2	36.3	37.8	31.3	29.3	29.0	..	..	33.3	31.9
Uganda	6.3	5.3	11.3	11.4	12.3	9.8	8.4	5.6	8.5	7.3	..	7.8	9.4	7.5
Zaire	12.1	13.5	12.9	11.8	15.9	15.3	16.7	20.0	17.5	..	..	11.6	13.6	18.1
Zambia	44.3	36.7	42.8	33.4	31.0	37.4	46.3	34.9	30.4	16.4	..	35.3	37.6	32.0
Zimbabwe	35.0	31.4	40.0	36.2	43.1	40.1	39.1	44.9	43.7	43.9	43.3	27.9	37.6	43.0
NORTH AFRICA	38.7	42.3	47.3	43.4	42.0	40.6	41.3	36.5	..	..	..	35.5	42.4	38.9
Algeria	..	..	..	..	..	..	..	..	..	..	..	..	..	..
Egypt, Arab Republic of	48.0	53.0	63.9	55.6	54.7	52.3	53.5	45.2	45.6	42.9	..	44.7	54.6	46.8
Libya	..	..	..	..	..	..	..	..	..	..	..	..	..	..
Morocco	33.3	39.2	37.7	32.5	29.8	30.6	28.9	27.9	..	..	..	32.3	33.8	28.4
Tunisia	34.7	34.6	40.3	42.1	41.5	38.9	41.3	36.3	35.8	36.4	..	29.5	38.7	37.5
ALL AFRICA	30.2	30.5	32.4	31.1	30.7	30.0	30.4	30.3	..	..	..	..	30.8	30.0
South Africa	25.6	25.9	27.1	28.4	28.8	30.3	31.3	32.9	32.3	31.3	..	20.6	27.7	32.0

7–5. Government interest payments

	Percentage of total revenue											Average		
	1980	1981	1982	1983	1984	1985	1986	1987	1988	1989	1990	75–79	80–85	86–MR
SUB-SAHARAN AFRICA	1.2	1.5	1.8	2.3	2.7	3.1	3.0	3.3	..	..	..	..	2.1	3.5
excluding Nigeria	1.2	1.5	1.8	2.3	2.6	3.0	2.9	3.0	..	..	..	..	2.1	3.3
Angola	..	..	..	..	..	..	..	..	..	..	..	..	..	..
Benin	0.3	0.4	0.7	1.8	4.0	2.4	1.8	1.5	1.6	..	..	0.1	1.6	1.6
Botswana	0.7	0.7	1.4	1.2	1.5	1.6	1.6	1.6	2.0	..	..	1.0	1.2	1.8
Burkina Faso	0.0	0.3	0.3	0.2	0.7	1.0	0.9	1.0	..	..	..	0.5	0.4	0.9
Burundi	..	0.4	0.5	0.8	1.3	1.4	1.6	1.9	2.2	..	..	..	0.9	1.9
Cameroon	0.1	0.2	0.2	0.5	0.6	0.9	0.8	1.1	1.1	1.2	..	0.2	0.4	1.0
Cape Verde	..	..	..	..	..	..	..	..	..	..	..	..	..	..
Central African Republic	..	0.3	0.8	1.0	1.2	1.4	1.3	..	..	..	..	..	0.9	1.3
Chad	..	..	..	0.4	0.3	0.3	0.4	0.3	..	..	..	..	0.3	0.4
Comoros	..	..	0.6	1.0	1.3	1.2	1.4	0.2	..	..	..	..	1.0	0.8
Congo, People's Republic of the	2.4	2.6	2.6	3.1	3.8	5.0	8.2	6.6	8.6	..	..	1.2	3.3	7.8
Cote d'Ivoire	2.4	4.0	7.2	8.2	8.6	8.9	..	..	8.5	9.9	11.4	..	6.5	9.9
Djibouti	..	..	0.0	0.0	0.0	0.3	0.3	..	0.4	..	..	..	0.1	0.4
Equatorial Guinea	..	..	..	..	..	..	..	..	..	..	..	..	..	..
Ethiopia	0.7	0.9	0.9	0.9	1.5	2.3	1.8	2.1	..	..	..	0.5	1.2	1.9
Gabon	1.3	1.8	1.9	2.2	2.2	2.1	3.9	5.2	7.1	6.5	..	..	1.9	5.7
Gambia, The	0.4	0.8	1.3	2.0	1.8	1.0	1.8	5.5	4.9	4.9	..	0.1	1.2	4.3
Ghana	1.7	1.4	2.3	1.4	1.3	1.5	2.2	1.4	1.1	1.3	..	1.2	1.6	1.5
Guinea	..	1.1	1.4	1.2	1.1	1.1	1.8	1.9	2.7	1.8	..	..	1.2	2.0
Guinea-Bissau	0.6	0.7	0.5	0.3	1.4	2.2	1.9	4.8	..	..	..	..	0.9	3.4
Kenya	1.8	2.2	3.4	3.7	3.9	3.9	4.5	4.6	5.0	..	..	1.2	3.1	4.7
Lesotho	1.5	2.4	4.3	5.0	4.0	3.8	1.0	4.1	4.5	5.5	..	0.3	3.5	3.8
Liberia	2.5	1.9	3.4	4.1	5.8	6.4	3.7	3.8	..	4.3	..	1.0	4.0	3.9
Madagascar	0.5	0.7	0.1	1.0	1.5	1.4	1.5	2.0	2.0	2.0	..	0.2	0.9	1.9
Malawi	3.2	4.9	4.4	3.9	4.4	6.2	6.9	6.6	4.9	4.0	..	1.5	4.5	5.6
Mali	0.1	0.2	0.3	0.4	0.6	1.2	0.8	1.5	0.9	..	..	..	0.5	1.0
Mauritania	1.0	1.2	1.2	2.1	2.1	2.8	3.6	..	..	..	..	0.7	1.8	3.6
Mauritius	3.7	4.5	5.5	5.6	5.5	5.4	4.7	3.9	3.2	3.2	2.8	1.3	5.0	3.5
Mozambique	..	..	..	..	..	..	..	..	..	..	..	..	..	..
Namibia	..	..	2.1	3.3	5.3	4.3	3.6	3.2	2.7	2.6	..	..	3.8	3.0
Niger	1.0	1.1	1.1	1.4	2.1	2.6	2.6	2.9	2.8	..	..	0.7	1.6	2.8
Nigeria	0.8	1.0	2.2	3.1	3.7	3.6	4.6	12.6	11.4	11.3	..	0.5	2.4	10.0
Rwanda	0.3	0.3	0.5	0.5	0.7	0.7	0.8	1.0	..	..	..	0.1	0.5	0.9
Sao Tome & Principe	..	..	..	..	..	..	..	..	..	..	..	..	..	..
Senegal	6.3	5.3	3.9	4.1	4.2	3.9	3.2	..	..	..	..	4.8	4.6	3.2
Seychelles	0.0	1.2	1.5	2.0	2.9	4.3	2.9	8.4	9.0	8.9	..	0.2	2.0	7.3
Sierra Leone	0.0	0.0	0.0	2.0	1.7	1.3	2.6	5.6	..	..	..	1.3	0.8	4.1
Somalia	0.0	0.0	0.0	0.0	1.5	1.9	3.3	2.8	3.7	4.5	..	0.1	0.6	3.6
Sudan	1.2	1.5	1.1	1.3	2.9	6.1	5.0	3.6	..	..	..	1.0	2.4	4.3
Swaziland	1.1	0.6	1.4	1.5	1.6	2.1	2.3	1.8	1.6	1.5	1.6	0.3	1.4	1.7
Tanzania	2.0	2.1	2.2	2.3	2.3	2.1	1.8	2.8	3.4	..	..	1.0	2.1	2.7
Togo	..	2.8	2.5	5.8	4.7	5.6	5.2	0.0	4.3	4.0	..	0.7	4.3	3.4
Uganda	0.0	0.0	0.3	1.2	1.8	1.1	1.0	0.3	0.4	0.6	..	..	0.7	0.6
Zaire	0.9	1.5	1.5	2.5	5.5	5.9	6.1	4.0	1.2	..	..	0.8	3.0	3.8
Zambia	3.3	2.8	2.9	4.4	1.1	4.1	4.3	0.2	0.1	..	..	2.9	3.1	1.5
Zimbabwe	2.4	2.7	3.3	3.5	4.5	4.9	4.9	5.6	5.7	6.2	6.3	1.7	3.5	5.7
NORTH AFRICA	2.2	2.6	2.6	3.2	3.5	3.8	4.1	4.0	..	..	..	1.4	3.0	4.0
Algeria	..	..	..	..	..	..	..	..	..	..	..	..	..	..
Egypt, Arab Republic of	2.8	2.7	2.5	3.7	4.0	3.8	4.1	4.2	4.5	..	..	1.9	3.3	4.2
Libya	..	..	..	..	..	..	..	..	..	..	..	..	..	..
Morocco	2.4	3.7	3.4	3.6	4.0	4.8	5.0	4.5	..	..	..	1.3	3.6	4.8
Tunisia	1.4	1.6	2.0	2.2	2.5	2.7	3.1	3.3	3.2	3.3	..	1.0	2.1	3.2
ALL AFRICA	1.3	1.6	1.9	2.4	2.7	3.1	3.0	3.4	..	..	..	..	2.2	3.5
South Africa	1.8	2.1	2.4	2.8	3.3	3.6	3.8	4.1	4.1	4.6	..	1.4	2.7	4.2

7–6. Government revenue (excluding grants)

	Percentage of total revenue											Average		
	1980	1981	1982	1983	1984	1985	1986	1987	1988	1989	1990	75–79	80–85	86–MR
SUB-SAHARAN AFRICA	19.4	18.8	19.2	19.5	20.2	20.3	20.2	19.6	..	..	..	..	19.6	20.1
excluding Nigeria	19.4	18.9	19.4	19.7	20.5	20.5	20.3	19.6	..	..	..	..	19.7	20.2
Angola	..	..	..	..	..	..	..	..	..	..	..	..	..	..
Benin	13.1	17.6	17.4	13.8	11.2	11.9	11.6	12.1	11.3	..	..	15.5	14.2	11.6
Botswana	37.2	34.8	42.9	48.4	57.7	65.0	64.6	64.4	74.2	..	..	26.4	47.7	67.7
Burkina Faso	11.7	10.7	10.6	9.9	11.1	11.0	11.3	11.7	..	..	..	11.3	10.8	11.5
Burundi	14.0	13.4	15.4	12.5	14.1	13.9	16.9	13.9	16.6	..	..	11.2	13.9	15.8
Cameroon	14.7	15.9	17.0	22.0	24.2	23.1	22.1	18.7	17.1	17.2	..	13.2	19.5	18.8
Cape Verde	..	..	..	..	..	..	..	..	..	..	..	..	..	..
Central African Republic	..	15.0	14.6	14.5	14.2	13.2	11.9	..	..	..	..	..	14.3	11.9
Chad	..	..	..	3.8	6.5	6.5	6.5	8.9	..	..	..	9.6	5.6	7.7
Comoros	10.0	12.0	13.3	16.1	14.9	12.6	16.0	11.4	..	..	..	..	13.1	13.7
Congo, People's Republic of the	43.7	35.8	35.3	33.7	33.7	34.2	35.5	19.7	..	..	..	22.7	36.1	27.6
Cote d'Ivoire	23.3	25.7	24.4	25.8	28.4	30.4	..	..	26.9	23.9	27.8	21.0	26.3	26.2
Djibouti	..	..	..	..	40.6	37.4	32.6	30.1	28.6	..	..	..	39.0	30.4
Equatorial Guinea	..	..	..	..	..	..	..	..	..	..	..	..	..	..
Ethiopia	18.8	20.1	20.3	21.5	22.8	22.9	25.2	25.4	28.8	29.9	26.2	13.7	21.1	27.1
Gabon	38.8	40.0	41.1	39.2	39.2	39.1	41.3	24.5	25.1	24.1	..	27.0	39.6	28.8
Gambia, The	23.4	16.6	16.5	17.2	18.3	17.0	18.9	25.5	22.7	24.5	23.0	16.1	18.2	22.9
Ghana	6.9	4.5	5.6	5.5	8.0	10.8	13.7	14.1	13.4	13.6	..	7.3	6.9	13.7
Guinea	1.6	2.0	2.9	1.7	1.7	1.4	9.6	8.4	6.3	6.6	..	1.4	1.9	7.7
Guinea-Bissau	15.4	14.0	11.5	10.6	11.9	11.6	8.1	13.2	13.2	13.9	..	..	12.5	12.1
Kenya	21.9	21.9	21.2	20.3	20.2	20.0	20.3	21.1	21.4	..	..	16.4	20.9	21.0
Lesotho	36.4	33.8	36.5	42.9	47.6	43.7	42.0	41.3	38.0	39.1	..	23.6	40.2	40.1
Liberia	18.1	19.9	21.1	21.5	20.4	18.9	16.7	15.9	18.7	18.4	..	17.1	20.0	17.4
Madagascar	15.6	14.6	11.8	11.7	13.6	12.7	11.9	14.5	12.8	11.1	..	18.7	13.4	12.6
Malawi	19.1	19.3	18.6	19.2	19.9	22.2	21.8	19.9	16.4	16.3	..	14.7	19.7	18.6
Mali	10.9	11.8	13.1	13.3	14.3	16.8	16.6	15.7	18.7	..	..	10.2	13.3	17.0
Mauritania	16.6	18.4	18.6	20.7	22.2	22.3	21.8	22.8	22.7	..	..	20.8	19.8	22.5
Mauritius	20.8	20.2	18.9	23.2	22.6	21.6	21.0	22.1	23.2	23.1	23.2	17.2	21.2	22.5
Mozambique	..	..	..	..	..	..	..	..	..	..	..	..	..	..
Namibia	..	..	24.4	27.3	29.6	32.2	34.6	35.7	34.4	39.6	..	..	28.4	36.1
Niger	14.4	12.7	11.4	10.2	11.0	10.6	11.5	11.6	9.8	..	..	10.2	11.7	11.0
Nigeria	18.5	13.7	13.2	11.5	10.3	11.2	15.3	17.7	14.3	16.5	..	15.2	13.1	15.9
Rwanda	12.8	12.2	11.7	10.9	11.3	12.2	13.8	12.5	..	..	..	9.7	11.8	13.2
Sao Tome & Principe	..	..	..	..	..	..	..	..	..	..	..	..	..	..
Senegal	24.1	22.5	20.2	19.5	18.9	17.7	16.9	18.3	..	..	..	17.0	20.5	17.6
Seychelles	38.0	40.9	42.2	39.3	40.2	44.2	43.0	48.4	51.5	58.4	..	19.4	40.8	50.3
Sierra Leone	16.4	17.1	11.3	8.3	8.4	6.0	5.2	6.4	8.0	8.5	..	14.6	11.2	7.0
Somalia	8.2	10.3	9.5	12.1	6.4	6.3	8.2	6.3	5.4	4.7	..	11.2	8.8	6.2
Sudan	14.1	15.4	11.9	13.3	12.5	9.7	8.7	9.2	..	..	..	12.8	12.8	8.9
Swaziland	28.9	26.2	32.7	31.0	31.8	31.3	25.5	29.2	30.5	31.2	31.9	26.4	30.3	29.7
Tanzania	17.3	16.9	17.7	16.8	16.2	15.1	13.3	14.3	15.2	..	..	15.5	16.6	14.3
Togo	30.3	25.5	28.4	27.2	29.3	31.7	28.9	26.5	23.9	22.8	..	28.0	28.7	25.6
Uganda	3.1	1.1	6.6	8.9	9.5	6.9	5.2	3.0	4.4	4.9	..	5.3	6.0	4.4
Zaire	9.2	7.9	7.5	7.9	10.3	12.0	10.1	10.0	11.0	..	..	6.1	9.1	10.4
Zambia	25.0	23.2	23.4	24.2	22.1	22.0	23.3	21.6	17.2	10.1	..	21.8	23.3	18.0
Zimbabwe	24.1	25.5	29.1	29.6	31.8	30.4	30.1	33.1	33.1	34.3	34.7	21.2	28.4	33.1
NORTH AFRICA	26.5	34.8	35.8	34.6	34.5	32.8	32.1	30.7	..	..	..	25.7	33.2	31.4
Algeria	..	..	..	..	..	..	..	..	..	..	..	..	..	..
Egypt, Arab Republic of	24.5	46.6	46.7	45.4	43.3	41.3	40.4	37.1	35.9	34.9	..	30.1	41.3	37.1
Libya	..	..	..	..	..	..	..	..	..	..	..	..	..	..
Morocco	23.6	25.8	26.3	24.7	23.8	23.3	21.3	23.4	..	..	..	21.5	24.6	22.3
Tunisia	31.3	31.9	34.3	33.6	36.5	33.7	34.5	31.6	31.6	30.6	..	25.5	33.6	32.1
ALL AFRICA	19.9	20.0	20.4	20.6	21.3	21.2	21.1	20.4	..	..	..	..	20.6	20.8
South Africa	23.3	22.0	23.3	23.3	24.2	26.6	26.0	26.1	27.3	29.3	..	17.3	23.8	27.2

7–7. Grants to government

	Percentage of total revenue											Average		
	1980	1981	1982	1983	1984	1985	1986	1987	1988	1989	1990	75–79	80–85	86–MR
SUB-SAHARAN AFRICA	3.3	2.7	3.2	2.9	3.3	3.2	3.1	3.7	..	..	..	..	3.2	3.8
excluding Nigeria	3.4	2.8	3.3	3.0	3.4	3.3	3.2	3.8	..	..	..	..	3.3	3.9
Angola	..	..	..	..	..	..	..	..	..	..	..	..	..	..
Benin	5.5	7.8	6.2	5.6	5.8	4.3	3.1	1.8	4.1	..	..	5.9	5.9	3.0
Botswana	5.3	5.0	6.0	4.6	3.1	2.5	3.0	3.7	2.7	..	..	5.0	4.4	3.1
Burkina Faso	0.2	0.7	0.1	0.2	0.1	0.1	0.0	0.0	..	..	..	0.3	0.2	0.0
Burundi	3.8	5.1	4.0	3.6	4.0	3.4	3.7	4.0	3.9	..	..	4.9	4.0	3.9
Cameroon	0.0	0.0	0.0	2.1	0.1	0.0	0.1	0.0	0.0	0.0	..	0.3	0.4	0.0
Cape Verde	..	..	..	..	..	..	..	..	..	..	..	..	..	..
Central African Republic	..	2.5	2.0	1.4	1.1	1.1	1.2	..	..	..	..	..	1.6	1.2
Chad	..	..	..	5.3	5.3	7.1	16.9	17.6	..	..	..	2.9	5.9	17.3
Comoros	..	..	12.6	16.2	19.8	18.5	16.9	11.5	..	..	..	..	16.7	14.2
Congo, People's Republic of the	0.7	0.1	0.2	0.4	0.9	0.3	0.0	0.1	0.3	..	..	0.0	0.4	0.2
Cote d'Ivoire	0.0	0.2	0.2	0.3	0.3	0.2	0.0	..	5.0	10.1	..	0.0	0.2	7.6
Djibouti	..	..	..	..	2.5	2.4	3.7	8.3	2.0	..	..	..	2.5	4.7
Equatorial Guinea	..	..	..	..	..	..	..	..	..	..	..	..	..	..
Ethiopia	2.0	2.1	2.9	2.6	2.5	6.4	4.1	2.9	2.3	2.8	3.7	1.4	3.1	3.1
Gabon	0.4	0.4	0.0	0.3	0.3	0.3	0.5	0.6	0.5	0.6	..	..	0.3	0.6
Gambia, The	3.2	4.5	9.1	2.8	3.9	3.8	5.5	12.9	10.5	7.6	..	2.4	4.6	9.1
Ghana	0.0	0.1	0.1	0.0	0.3	0.5	0.8	0.8	1.1	1.5	..	0.1	0.2	1.0
Guinea	0.1	0.1	0.1	0.1	0.0	0.0	1.9	3.9	3.2	3.3	..	0.0	0.1	3.1
Guinea-Bissau	34.8	13.2	20.1	15.6	18.9	21.7	16.3	24.3	21.2	34.4	..	..	20.7	24.1
Kenya	0.7	0.6	0.6	0.6	0.2	0.2	0.2	1.2	1.5	..	..	0.5	0.5	0.9
Lesotho	7.4	4.2	1.5	1.9	5.1	0.8	4.4	1.6	3.6	3.7	..	2.9	3.5	3.3
Liberia	2.1	2.2	3.7	3.1	3.3	2.1	2.3	1.6	1.3	1.1	..	1.7	2.7	1.6
Madagascar	..	..	..	0.5	0.7	0.4	0.7	0.7	0.7	0.8	..	..	0.5	0.7
Malawi	4.4	3.9	3.2	2.4	2.4	1.5	2.4	3.1	2.1	6.0	..	2.4	3.0	3.4
Mali	6.9	7.6	7.6	9.8	9.0	8.3	5.5	6.6	5.8	..	..	1.3	8.2	6.0
Mauritania	15.3	13.9	11.9	8.6	13.5	10.4	5.3	7.1	12.2	..	..	15.5	12.3	8.2
Mauritius	0.0	0.1	0.6	0.2	0.4	1.0	1.2	0.8	0.8	0.4	0.4	0.1	0.4	0.7
Mozambique	..	..	..	..	..	..	..	..	..	..	..	..	..	..
Namibia	..	..	12.8	15.2	17.6	14.0	15.7	9.1	7.4	2.8	..	..	14.9	8.7
Niger	0.0	0.0	0.0	1.7	3.4	3.6	5.1	5.3	4.6	..	..	0.2	1.4	5.0
Nigeria	0.0	0.0	0.0	0.0	0.0	0.0	0.0	0.0	0.0	0.0	0.0	..	0.0	0.0
Rwanda	0.0	3.7	3.6	3.6	3.0	3.1	3.0	2.7	..	..	..	0.2	3.4	2.8
Sao Tome & Principe	..	..	..	..	..	..	..	..	..	..	..	..	..	..
Senegal	0.1	0.2	1.2	1.4	2.4	1.1	1.5	1.1	..	..	..	0.0	1.1	1.3
Seychelles	2.0	2.3	1.8	3.4	2.5	2.6	2.4	3.0	1.6	1.6	..	7.5	2.4	2.1
Sierra Leone	0.6	1.3	0.6	0.8	1.4	0.8	1.4	4.3	..	..	..	1.4	0.9	2.8
Somalia	2.8	2.0	3.6	3.2	3.2	7.6	8.6	17.1	11.2	26.1	..	0.5	3.7	15.7
Sudan	2.7	1.0	2.8	2.2	1.9	1.5	1.8	2.3	..	..	..	0.2	2.0	2.1
Swaziland	1.8	1.0	1.0	1.0	1.6	1.4	1.2	0.6	0.4	1.0	1.3	0.8	1.3	0.9
Tanzania	3.0	4.1	2.8	2.3	1.4	1.6	1.1	5.1	5.7	..	..	2.0	2.5	4.0
Togo	0.0	1.6	1.8	2.2	3.4	2.8	4.3	2.2	2.0	2.4	..	0.1	2.0	2.7
Uganda	0.1	0.1	0.8	0.2	0.4	0.2	0.7	0.4	0.9	1.8	..	0.0	0.3	0.9
Zaire	2.1	1.9	1.2	1.7	2.6	2.5	1.6	0.3	2.9	..	..	1.1	2.0	1.6
Zambia	0.8	0.7	0.8	1.3	0.5	0.3	1.3	0.5	1.7	2.0	..	0.9	0.7	1.4
Zimbabwe	0.0	0.0	0.3	0.4	1.2	2.3	1.3	0.9	1.1	0.7	0.9	..	0.7	1.0
NORTH AFRICA	0.2	0.1	0.1	0.2	0.1	0.2	0.3	0.9	..	..	..	0.7	0.1	0.6
Algeria	..	..	..	..	..	..	..	..	..	..	..	..	..	..
Egypt, Arab Republic of	0.0	0.1	0.0	0.4	0.0	0.7	1.0	2.4	1.0	1.6	..	1.5	0.2	1.5
Libya	..	..	..	..	..	..	..	..	..	..	..	..	..	..
Morocco	0.0	0.0	0.0	0.0	0.0	0.0	0.0	0.0	0.0	0.0	..	0.0	0.0	0.0
Tunisia	0.6	0.1	0.2	0.1	0.1	0.0	0.1	0.2	0.4	1.5	..	0.6	0.2	0.5
ALL AFRICA	3.0	2.5	3.0	2.7	3.1	3.0	2.9	3.5	..	..	..	..	3.0	3.6
South Africa	0.0	0.0	0.0	0.0	0.0	0.0	0.0	0.0	..	..	..	0.0	0.0	0.0

7–8. Foreign financing

	Percentage of total revenue											Average		
	1980	1981	1982	1983	1984	1985	1986	1987	1988	1989	1990	75–79	80–85	86–MR
SUB-SAHARAN AFRICA	3.2	3.6	4.5	3.6	3.4	4.3	3.0	4.2	..	..	..	..	3.8	3.5
excluding Nigeria	3.3	3.6	4.6	3.7	3.5	4.4	3.1	4.1	..	..	..	..	3.9	3.5
Angola	..	..	..	..	..	..	..	..	..	..	..	..	..	..
Benin	3.3	1.9	2.3	2.9	2.7	2.6	2.9	4.7	..	..	..	0.7	2.6	2.6
Botswana	1.5	1.5	7.4	1.9	2.6	0.8	3.3	2.8	2.7	..	..	2.9	2.6	2.9
Burkina Faso	0.4	0.7	0.8	0.4	0.6	-0.4	-0.4	-2.0	..	..	..	..	0.4	0.3
Burundi	2.0	1.7	4.7	9.4	6.7	3.8	4.6	11.9	7.5	..	..	1.6	4.7	5.2
Cameroon	0.6	4.1	3.1	0.8	1.1	0.9	1.1	1.6	..	2.7	..	0.8	1.8	1.8
Cape Verde	..	..	..	..	..	..	..	..	..	..	..	..	..	..
Central African Republic	..	2.1	0.2	0.2	-0.1	-0.7	-0.9	..	..	..	..	..	0.3	0.1
Chad	..	..	..	0.4	0.6	2.0	2.7	8.7	..	..	..	1.0	1.0	1.4
Comoros	6.8	7.7	10.4	14.4	19.1	14.7	4.4	11.3	..	..	..	..	12.2	11.8
Congo, People's Republic of the	3.8	0.8	12.2	4.5	0.9	2.3	-17.0	1.3	..	..	..	0.0	4.1	-7.8
Cote d'Ivoire	6.3	7.3	11.2	3.9	0.5	2.6	..	..	5.6	6.6	-4.2	6.1	5.3	2.7
Djibouti	..	..	..	..	..	..	-0.3	7.3	..	..	..	..	..	-0.3
Equatorial Guinea	..	..	..	..	..	..	..	..	..	..	..	..	..	..
Ethiopia	1.8	1.5	5.2	4.2	2.1	3.4	4.4	3.5	3.6	4.6	3.7	1.5	3.0	3.5
Gabon	0.0	0.0	0.0	0.0	0.0	0.2	8.1	5.9	8.3	13.4	..	12.2	0.0	8.9
Gambia, The	1.2	7.8	6.8	5.2	3.2	4.4	0.7	19.3	-0.4	0.9	..	3.3	4.8	4.7
Ghana	0.7	0.5	0.4	0.5	0.7	1.0	-1.1	-0.1	0.2	0.3	..	0.1	0.6	0.3
Guinea	..	6.4	2.0	1.9	0.6	1.3	5.1	5.0	5.7	6.5	..	..	2.5	2.9
Guinea-Bissau	9.4	10.0	9.8	8.1	17.6	20.0	10.2	4.0	..	..	..	..	12.5	12.6
Kenya	2.4	3.0	2.9	2.3	7.9	10.6	9.5	12.5	6.9	..	..	1.6	4.8	6.0
Lesotho	3.7	2.7	2.6	6.6	1.3	-1.0	5.9	9.7	6.6	..	..	2.8	2.6	3.0
Liberia	2.7	5.6	3.7	3.7	1.8	4.8	6.3	3.7	..	..	..	3.9	3.7	4.3
Madagascar	5.0	5.9	4.1	3.1	2.2	2.5	2.3	3.6	3.8	3.6	..	..	3.8	3.3
Malawi	8.3	3.0	5.0	6.6	3.3	3.5	7.5	6.7	2.3	3.3	..	4.9	5.0	4.8
Mali	4.3	4.3	7.0	7.3	7.0	8.7	8.0	4.9	3.7	..	..	-0.2	6.4	7.1
Mauritania	15.3	10.6	13.9	11.6	7.3	18.9	-5.9	-2.3	-5.3	..	..	3.5	13.0	9.4
Mauritius	2.5	6.9	6.8	-1.4	-1.0	4.3	-0.6	0.6	2.2	-0.6	-0.1	1.9	3.0	0.3
Mozambique	..	..	..	..	..	..	..	..	..	..	..	..	..	..
Namibia	..	..	..	..	..	..	..	..	..	..	..	..	..	..
Niger	4.0	6.8	5.4	6.2	5.4	3.4	3.8	5.3	3.4	..	..	2.1	5.2	5.2
Nigeria	0.5	0.9	0.4	0.3	-0.2	0.3	0.0	7.6	0.9	3.5	..	0.9	0.3	3.0
Rwanda	2.6	0.9	1.6	1.8	2.3	3.5	3.5	4.8	..	..	..	2.4	2.1	2.3
Sao Tome & Principe	..	..	..	..	..	..	..	..	..	..	..	..	..	..
Senegal	-2.7	1.0	3.1	4.4	4.0	3.3	2.2	3.6	..	..	..	0.0	2.2	3.0
Seychelles	5.0	4.7	12.8	5.4	6.5	2.5	10.4	-0.9	0.5	1.9	..	0.2	6.1	3.0
Sierra Leone	3.8	1.2	2.1	2.3	0.0	1.1	0.6	1.4	..	..	..	3.4	1.7	1.2
Somalia	3.1	3.1	5.9	4.5	1.5	5.8	5.3	2.6	3.0	5.7	..	5.2	4.0	4.3
Sudan	2.8	2.4	1.8	2.9	5.3	9.6	6.7	4.1	..	..	..	1.6	4.1	4.8
Swaziland	0.0	1.3	3.1	0.2	-0.8	0.4	2.9	1.4	..	-0.7	-0.6	3.4	0.7	0.7
Tanzania	2.0	1.2	2.1	1.4	0.3	0.7	0.3	1.0	..	..	..	2.1	1.3	1.0
Togo	1.6	3.0	1.0	1.9	2.0	0.8	3.2	3.3	2.4	5.2	..	19.0	1.7	2.0
Uganda	0.0	0.0	0.0	0.2	-0.1	0.6	0.9	0.1	1.7	2.1	..	0.3	0.1	0.3
Zaire	0.3	1.2	0.3	-0.6	2.9	1.2	4.3	8.1	..	..	..	1.1	0.9	1.6
Zambia	8.8	7.1	3.1	2.9	2.6	8.5	2.4	-1.2	0.6	..	..	2.1	5.5	4.4
Zimbabwe	2.3	3.3	2.5	0.7	5.0	7.0	3.1	2.1	1.6	1.0	1.4	1.9	3.5	1.9
NORTH AFRICA	3.3	4.6	4.5	3.3	2.7	2.6	1.2	0.7	..	..	..	4.6	3.5	1.0
Algeria	..	..	..	..	..	..	..	..	..	..	..	..	..	..
Egypt, Arab Republic of	2.3	2.1	2.6	1.4	0.9	1.5	0.6	0.7	-0.6	-0.7	..	5.0	1.8	0.0
Libya	..	..	..	..	..	..	..	..	..	..	..	..	..	..
Morocco	5.3	9.0	7.0	3.3	4.7	3.5	-0.1	0.6	..	..	..	6.5	5.5	0.2
Tunisia	2.3	2.6	4.1	5.2	2.4	2.9	3.3	0.7	2.0	1.2	..	2.4	3.2	1.8
ALL AFRICA	3.2	3.6	4.5	3.6	3.3	4.2	2.9	3.9	..	..	..	..	3.7	3.3
South Africa	-0.2	0.4	0.1	0.1	0.2	-0.3	0.0	0.0	-0.2	-0.1	..	0.1	0.0	-0.1

Note: *Negative values indicate that amortizations exceed new borrowings.*

7-9. Taxes on income and profits

	Percentage of total revenue											Average		
	1980	1981	1982	1983	1984	1985	1986	1987	1988	1989	1990	75-79	80-85	86-MR
SUB-SAHARAN AFRICA	25.2	26.9	25.7	27.0	26.5	25.7	25.1	23.9	..	..	..	..	26.2	25.8
excluding Nigeria	23.3	24.8	24.1	25.5	25.3	25.0	24.5	23.4	..	..	..	..	24.6	25.0
Angola	..	..	..	..	..	..	..	..	..	..	..	..	..	..
Benin	10.6	12.7	14.1	22.0	22.9	20.5	23.3	..	..	..	..	16.5	17.1	23.3
Botswana	33.1	36.6	28.4	27.1	33.5	29.7	38.1	43.2	51.9	..	..	28.2	31.4	44.4
Burkina Faso	17.8	18.0	15.9	17.6	17.4	12.7	15.0	16.2	..	..	..	14.8	16.6	15.6
Burundi	19.2	22.5	23.4	24.7	20.7	18.8	17.2	18.2	19.7	..	..	18.1	21.5	18.4
Cameroon	21.7	28.2	38.9	58.9	47.8	57.2	38.4	30.8	42.1	45.2	..	15.1	42.1	39.1
Cape Verde	..	28.7	37.3	..	..	..	21.4	21.1	..	..	..	..	33.0	21.3
Central African Republic	..	17.7	16.2	16.7	16.2	18.7	19.1	..	..	..	..	..	17.1	19.1
Chad	..	..	..	8.1	8.2	15.2	19.8	14.6	..	..	..	17.4	10.5	17.2
Comoros	3.0	3.4	3.8	4.1	7.7	11.7	12.8	11.3	..	..	..	..	5.6	12.0
Congo, People's Republic of the	39.4	25.7	15.1	13.2	14.2	12.5	19.0	28.6	..	..	..	27.2	20.0	23.8
Cote d'Ivoire	12.3	13.2	13.2	13.9	11.4	8.9	..	..	..	..	..	..	12.2	..
Djibouti	15.2	14.1	12.6	11.2	12.7	15.6	16.2	..	16.4	..	..	15.7	13.6	16.3
Equatorial Guinea	..	..	..	..	..	..	..	..	..	..	..	..	..	..
Ethiopia	20.8	24.5	27.6	25.6	26.7	28.5	26.4	30.2	..	..	..	19.9	25.6	28.3
Gabon	36.5	51.0	48.8	48.2	45.3	44.9	51.8	21.4	..	..	..	41.4	45.8	36.6
Gambia, The	15.4	22.7	16.8	12.8	13.9	16.0	15.3	12.7	11.8	9.4	12.1	12.8	16.3	12.2
Ghana	20.5	24.8	28.7	17.0	18.7	20.0	19.4	21.5	28.7	23.8	..	19.7	21.6	23.3
Guinea	14.5	9.2	28.1	19.4	23.5	21.2	1.7	2.1	..	..	..	20.7	19.3	1.9
Guinea-Bissau	14.5	14.7	13.3	8.0	12.9	14.5	15.6	7.2	5.5	..	..	..	13.0	9.4
Kenya	29.1	29.1	26.8	28.6	27.9	29.8	29.7	28.0	28.4	..	..	33.4	28.6	28.7
Lesotho	13.9	12.2	12.6	10.0	9.1	11.1	10.7	11.8	10.9	..	..	11.2	11.5	11.1
Liberia	32.9	32.4	35.3	38.7	37.5	38.1	39.7	34.1	33.9	34.0	..	37.9	35.8	35.4
Madagascar	14.1	16.1	14.0	13.7	14.8	12.4	13.9	11.1	11.4	..	..	10.6	14.2	12.2
Malawi	33.7	28.9	34.3	33.9	34.5	34.6	35.5	33.7	..	..	..	38.3	33.3	34.6
Mali	17.8	18.7	15.4	15.6	10.9	9.2	9.8	8.1	10.8	..	..	21.1	14.6	9.5
Mauritania	23.0	23.7	26.0	27.7	25.4	24.0	29.8	..	..	..	..	19.8	25.0	29.8
Mauritius	15.3	17.6	17.1	13.3	13.1	11.1	8.6	10.0	10.9	12.3	15.0	28.1	14.6	11.3
Mozambique	..	..	..	..	..	..	..	..	..	..	..	..	..	..
Namibia	..	..	12.7	20.9	26.5	34.1	35.8	34.2	30.5	40.8	..	..	23.6	35.3
Niger	23.8	20.6	18.8	20.8	19.2	22.1	21.5	19.8	26.1	..	..	27.4	20.9	22.5
Nigeria	87.6	97.0	79.5	75.3	67.2	50.5	44.2	39.9	73.8	..	..	70.2	76.2	52.6
Rwanda	17.8	25.3	19.7	21.2	18.0	16.9	15.5	18.6	..	..	..	16.3	19.8	17.0
Sao Tome & Principe	..	..	..	..	..	..	..	..	..	..	..	..	..	..
Senegal	18.4	23.6	20.3	19.0	19.9	21.5	20.1	..	..	..	..	21.1	20.5	20.1
Seychelles	28.0	27.0	25.5	24.3	22.6	21.6	19.9	19.7	12.8	15.1	..	24.2	24.8	16.9
Sierra Leone	22.4	23.9	23.7	27.4	24.9	26.8	26.8	20.1	..	26.3	..	24.7	24.9	24.4
Somalia	6.7	6.4	4.8	6.3	7.6	5.7	8.9	7.2	9.2	..	..	7.0	6.3	8.4
Sudan	14.2	15.0	15.7	16.0	19.4	20.2	17.5	14.9	..	..	..	11.5	16.1	17.5
Swaziland	24.0	32.1	23.5	23.8	24.5	25.5	27.7	37.9	34.1	94.2	95.2	30.2	25.6	57.8
Tanzania	33.1	32.1	32.1	32.1	28.5	25.6	31.0	23.4	23.0	..	..	26.3	30.6	25.8
Togo	34.4	30.6	33.7	34.0	36.9	33.1	30.5	32.7	32.1	37.7	..	34.1	33.8	33.2
Uganda	11.5	16.6	9.2	4.7	6.9	6.0	5.5	6.0	6.8	..	..	8.7	9.1	6.1
Zaire	30.4	35.7	33.4	88.3	88.8	85.6	84.8	86.2	77.6	..	..	33.5	60.3	82.9
Zambia	38.1	35.2	32.6	34.8	29.5	28.2	26.7	22.8	34.6	..	..	36.9	33.1	28.0
Zimbabwe	46.1	47.7	46.7	41.9	42.1	42.4	42.8	45.9	47.3	45.1	44.8	49.5	44.5	45.2
NORTH AFRICA	19.9	17.3	15.6	16.3	14.7	15.7	16.7	15.4	..	..	..	15.4	16.6	16.1
Algeria	..	..	..	..	..	..	..	..	..	..	..	..	..	..
Egypt, Arab Republic of	26.1	18.3	16.5	17.7	13.2	14.5	15.7	14.1	14.2	..	..	10.2	17.7	14.6
Libya	..	..	..	..	..	..	..	..	..	..	..	..	..	..
Morocco	19.0	18.3	15.5	17.5	18.6	18.5	18.9	18.9	..	..	..	21.3	17.9	18.9
Tunisia	14.6	15.3	14.7	13.6	12.2	14.3	15.5	13.3	11.9	12.9	..	14.6	14.1	13.4
ALL AFRICA	24.8	26.1	24.9	26.1	25.5	24.9	24.4	23.2	..	..	..		25.4	25.4
South Africa	55.7	53.2	52.2	52.8	52.1	53.2	51.9	50.5	48.0	48.1	..	55.4	53.2	49.6

Note: Total revenue does not include grants.

7–10. Taxes on international trade and transactions

	Percentage of total revenue										Average		
	1980	1981	1982	1983	1984	1985	1986	1987	1988	1989	1990	75–79	80–85	86–MR
SUB-SAHARAN AFRICA	36.7	34.2	33.9	34.2	33.6	34.3	33.4	31.9	..	..	..	..	34.5	31.5
excluding Nigeria	37.4	34.5	34.4	34.8	34.2	35.0	34.0	32.7	..	..	..	..	35.0	32.0
Angola	..	..	..	..	..	..	..	..	..	..	..	..	..	..
Benin	73.3	64.5	68.2	59.1	57.0	46.5	46.0	..	..	..	..	51.3	61.4	46.0
Botswana	38.8	38.1	33.8	31.0	20.8	13.9	13.4	13.8	11.6	..	..	34.4	29.4	12.9
Burkina Faso	43.6	44.0	42.4	38.2	30.0	34.8	38.9	22.5	..	..	..	49.4	38.8	30.7
Burundi	39.3	24.1	28.8	23.2	35.7	37.0	39.6	30.7	30.6	..	..	44.3	31.3	33.7
Cameroon	38.4	34.1	25.9	19.0	18.1	15.2	16.1	16.0	13.5	11.0	..	42.0	25.1	14.1
Cape Verde	..	52.1	48.3	..	..	..	38.4	38.2	..	..	..	..	..	..
Central African Republic	..	43.6	36.9	31.2	35.4	42.9	39.9	..	..	..	..	..	38.0	39.9
Chad	..	..	..	42.0	47.6	44.5	38.4	41.4	..	..	..	50.1	44.7	39.9
Comoros	..	78.3	76.5	65.8	67.3	66.4	61.2	54.0	..	..	..	..	70.8	57.6
Congo, People's Republic of the	10.5	25.7	14.2	17.0	12.8	12.5	16.7	26.1	..	..	..	24.1	15.4	21.4
Cote d'Ivoire	40.7	41.8	39.9	34.7	26.7	30.5	..	..	..	..	..	..	35.7	..
Djibouti	4.1	3.7	5.9	5.1	5.2	5.3	5.3	..	6.0	..	..	..	4.9	5.6
Equatorial Guinea	..	..	..	..	..	..	..	..	..	..	..	..	..	..
Ethiopia	35.6	28.3	24.5	23.0	24.6	19.8	19.5	19.0	..	..	..	38.1	26.0	19.2
Gabon	18.0	16.6	16.2	16.2	15.1	16.5	19.4	25.8	..	..	..	22.5	16.4	22.6
Gambia, The	65.2	63.0	68.5	70.4	73.2	66.2	71.5	75.2	71.7	49.0	52.9	63.5	67.8	64.1
Ghana	44.2	28.0	19.0	49.0	37.9	42.6	40.8	42.5	35.2	39.6	..	45.8	36.8	39.5
Guinea	58.6	60.3	27.9	34.5	50.7	57.7	8.4	11.0	15.4	14.2	..	47.5	48.3	12.2
Guinea-Bissau	36.2	38.4	45.0	45.0	19.8	40.9	17.8	39.7	37.1	..	..	..	37.6	31.5
Kenya	18.5	22.0	25.4	21.3	21.5	19.0	21.0	20.3	18.2	..	..	20.3	21.3	19.9
Lesotho	65.7	57.3	57.5	68.5	70.2	67.8	55.6	52.6	52.4	..	..	50.8	64.5	53.6
Liberia	33.6	36.3	31.2	27.3	29.5	28.3	28.6	26.9	34.6	30.6	..	32.6	31.1	30.2
Madagascar	23.4	18.8	20.0	31.8	28.6	39.2	36.5	39.0	44.7	..	..	19.9	27.0	40.0
Malawi	21.9	23.5	22.6	21.1	19.6	21.5	16.7	16.0	..	..	..	17.0	21.7	16.3
Mali	17.8	20.8	18.6	21.2	18.8	21.7	30.7	27.5	10.5	..	..	27.4	19.8	22.9
Mauritania	34.0	42.1	49.1	44.0	33.8	40.5	39.2	..	..	..	..	26.7	40.6	39.2
Mauritius	51.6	47.9	48.6	47.9	49.9	48.6	53.3	50.5	50.8	53.2	47.2	41.9	49.1	51.0
Mozambique	..	..	..	..	..	..	..	..	..	..	..	..	..	..
Namibia	..	..	4.9	4.5	3.4	4.4	4.6	3.4	4.3	..	..	..	4.3	4.1
Niger	36.4	38.3	43.3	38.6	36.8	35.4	38.7	33.6	32.4	..	..	32.3	38.1	34.9
Nigeria	13.2	21.6	20.1	14.9	13.9	11.7	16.4	6.6	17.0	..	..	16.6	15.9	13.3
Rwanda	42.4	34.3	36.5	35.6	42.0	41.3	47.7	39.0	..	..	..	55.3	38.7	43.3
Sao Tome & Principe	..	..	..	..	..	..	..	..	..	..	..	..	..	..
Senegal	34.2	32.1	33.5	34.7	41.9	38.7	33.7	..	..	..	..	44.5	35.8	33.7
Seychelles	28.0	29.0	31.5	33.0	31.0	33.3	36.4	43.5	52.1	14.2	..	37.0	31.0	36.6
Sierra Leone	49.6	44.4	48.7	36.6	35.8	38.6	40.0	55.3	29.8	44.6	..	46.3	42.3	42.5
Somalia	53.8	53.3	50.7	34.2	43.2	42.3	47.5	50.5	..	..	..	41.3	46.3	49.0
Sudan	41.9	42.5	49.7	53.4	49.0	53.6	56.6	37.6	..	..	..	45.2	47.3	49.2
Swaziland	67.4	57.2	66.6	67.2	61.9	58.8	49.6	41.8	42.8	13.9	12.2	58.4	63.2	32.1
Tanzania	17.6	10.8	7.0	6.6	6.9	8.4	7.0	13.6	11.8	..	..	20.5	9.6	10.8
Togo	32.0	34.8	33.3	28.2	25.1	29.1	32.3	32.5	35.7	34.6	..	33.2	30.4	33.8
Uganda	44.3	23.9	49.5	66.9	66.2	69.6	75.3	49.8	33.9	..	..	52.4	53.4	53.0
Zaire	38.4	30.8	25.7	24.4	24.2	19.2	15.1	14.6	9.6	..	..	40.2	27.1	13.1
Zambia	8.3	7.7	8.8	10.2	16.3	22.4	33.7	32.0	15.8	..	..	7.1	12.3	27.2
Zimbabwe	4.4	9.1	11.1	15.0	14.8	15.5	16.4	15.0	15.0	17.0	17.5	4.1	11.6	16.2
NORTH AFRICA	21.6	21.9	22.2	21.8	20.9	19.7	17.5	16.3	..	..	..	..	21.3	16.9
Algeria	..	..	..	..	..	..	..	..	..	..	..	..	..	..
Egypt, Arab Republic of	19.6	19.6	19.2	15.8	16.5	15.2	13.3	11.5	12.5	..	..	26.0	17.6	12.4
Libya	..	..	..	..	..	..	..	..	..	..	..	..	..	..
Morocco	20.5	20.6	20.3	18.2	17.7	15.9	14.2	12.6	..	..	..	18.2	18.8	13.4
Tunisia	24.6	25.5	27.3	31.4	28.4	28.2	25.1	24.7	26.8	27.9	..	24.9	27.6	26.1
ALL AFRICA	35.4	33.2	33.0	33.2	32.6	33.2	32.1	30.6	..	..	..	..	33.4	30.3
South Africa	3.3	4.5	4.9	3.3	2.5	2.9	3.7	3.7	5.9	4.9	..	5.8	3.5	4.6

Note: Total revenue does not include grants.

7–11. Import duties

	Percentage of total revenue											Average		
	1980	1981	1982	1983	1984	1985	1986	1987	1988	1989	1990	75–79	80–85	86–MR
SUB-SAHARAN AFRICA	26.1	27.1	27.5	26.6	24.6	25.2	26.1	25.0	..	..	..	..	26.2	25.4
excluding Nigeria	26.5	27.3	27.8	27.0	25.0	25.6	26.4	25.6	..	..	..	..	26.5	25.8
Angola	..	..	..	..	..	..	..	..	..	..	..	..	..	..
Benin	67.1	60.7	65.0	56.0	52.3	42.7	42.2	..	..	..	..	46.5	57.3	42.2
Botswana	38.7	37.9	33.6	30.9	20.7	13.8	13.3	13.7	11.6	..	..	33.9	29.3	12.9
Burkina Faso	38.0	38.8	38.0	34.0	26.3	30.0	34.5	20.1	..	..	..	43.2	34.2	27.3
Burundi	27.7	22.5	22.8	21.5	18.9	17.0	17.9	22.5	20.3	..	..	24.1	21.7	20.2
Cameroon	28.3	24.6	21.6	16.2	15.8	12.7	14.1	2.2	2.6	3.0	..	33.5	19.9	5.5
Cape Verde	..	22.3	20.4	..	..	..	16.0	15.4	..	..	..	..	21.4	15.7
Central African Republic	..	33.1	27.1	18.9	25.1	31.2	33.7	..	..	..	..	..	27.1	33.7
Chad	..	..	..	38.6	31.0	27.7	37.7	39.7	..	..	..	42.3	32.4	38.7
Comoros	..	55.7	41.8	44.7	55.4	47.1	46.3	45.0	..	..	..	..	48.9	45.6
Congo, People's Republic of the	10.5	19.5	14.2	17.0	12.8	12.5	16.7	26.1	27.4	..	..	23.7	14.4	23.4
Cote d'Ivoire	30.8	31.8	30.8	27.1	19.1	21.9	..	..	25.9	30.3	25.1	..	26.9	27.1
Djibouti	3.9	3.6	5.3	4.9	5.1	5.2	5.1	..	..	..	..	..	4.7	5.1
Equatorial Guinea	..	..	..	..	..	..	..	..	..	..	..	..	..	..
Ethiopia	14.7	15.5	14.3	13.6	13.3	12.2	9.8	13.6	..	..	..	21.6	13.9	11.7
Gabon	15.8	15.3	14.9	15.0	14.0	14.9	18.4	23.8	..	..	..	20.0	15.0	21.1
Gambia, The	54.0	62.0	63.7	70.4	64.5	62.1	68.5	73.6	60.9	47.2	52.9	54.1	62.8	60.6
Ghana	12.2	14.6	11.9	17.6	14.5	17.7	20.4	16.9	18.0	..	..	15.7	14.8	18.4
Guinea	..	..	6.5	9.0	18.3	24.9	8.0	..	..	..	..	21.1	14.7	8.0
Guinea-Bissau	18.1	19.3	25.1	17.3	11.2	19.3	15.1	11.8	15.6	12.4	..	..	18.4	13.8
Kenya	17.3	21.5	24.7	20.5	20.4	16.4	17.7	17.9	17.1	..	..	19.8	20.1	17.6
Lesotho	..	..	56.5	65.5	70.1	67.7	55.5	52.5	52.4	..	..	50.2	64.9	53.5
Liberia	32.6	35.5	30.6	26.7	29.3	27.9	28.4	26.8	34.3	24.8	..	31.7	30.4	28.6
Madagascar	21.3	16.1	16.5	24.4	22.0	27.7	25.3	25.7	34.9	..	..	16.9	21.3	28.6
Malawi	21.9	23.5	22.6	21.1	19.6	17.2	15.8	15.9	..	..	..	17.0	21.0	15.9
Mali	13.8	16.9	16.7	18.9	11.8	10.8	24.5	23.0	5.1	..	..	19.5	14.8	17.6
Mauritania	30.0	33.9	41.6	31.7	23.6	25.5	23.1	..	..	..	..	25.6	31.0	23.1
Mauritius	35.4	34.4	31.0	33.4	35.8	37.9	41.7	39.5	40.9	44.6	41.9	29.4	34.7	41.7
Mozambique	..	..	..	..	..	..	..	..	..	..	..	..	..	..
Namibia	0.0	0.0	0.0	0.0	0.0	0.0	0.0	0.0	0.0	0.0	0.0	..	0.0	0.0
Niger	31.5	33.1	38.1	31.8	31.1	30.0	33.5	..	..	..	..	27.3	32.6	33.5
Nigeria	13.1	21.6	20.1	14.9	13.9	11.5	16.2	6.5	17.0	..	..	16.6	15.9	13.2
Rwanda	23.3	24.3	27.2	25.7	27.8	27.2	26.6	28.4	..	..	..	28.5	25.9	27.5
Sao Tome & Principe	..	..	..	..	..	..	..	..	..	..	..	..	..	..
Senegal	32.4	31.0	32.7	34.1	41.4	38.5	33.6	..	..	..	..	40.6	35.0	33.6
Seychelles	28.0	28.6	31.2	32.9	31.0	33.3	36.4	43.5	52.1	14.2	..	36.5	30.8	36.6
Sierra Leone	36.6	37.6	38.1	33.1	31.0	36.4	38.6	52.8	28.8	43.5	..	33.8	35.5	40.9
Somalia	52.5	51.1	46.2	51.7	45.6	46.4	43.8	42.4	39.1	38.6	..	40.9	48.9	41.0
Sudan	40.1	43.0	45.7	42.2	37.3	50.1	54.9	35.3	..	..	..	35.2	41.7	46.8
Swaziland	58.4	47.8	65.8	67.2	61.9	58.8	49.1	40.8	38.4	38.8	55.2	42.4	60.0	44.5
Tanzania	11.3	7.9	6.7	6.1	6.6	8.4	7.0	13.0	11.8	..	..	12.1	7.8	10.6
Togo	23.1	28.4	27.5	23.3	18.7	23.5	26.2	26.7	27.5	26.2	..	23.4	24.1	26.7
Uganda	9.5	18.8	21.0	12.1	10.3	8.8	6.2	11.5	7.2	..	..	10.3	13.4	8.3
Zaire	20.4	25.4	21.8	28.8	31.2	37.3	33.3	42.5	36.6	..	..	20.7	27.5	37.5
Zambia	8.3	7.6	8.6	4.9	7.6	13.0	16.7	17.9	14.8	..	..	6.9	8.3	16.5
Zimbabwe	4.4	9.1	11.1	15.0	14.8	15.1	16.0	14.6	14.5	16.4	17.0	4.1	11.6	15.7
NORTH AFRICA	20.2	20.5	21.1	21.2	20.3	19.1	16.7	15.8	..	..	..	19.9	20.4	16.3
Algeria	..	..	..	..	..	..	..	..	..	..	..	..	..	..
Egypt, Arab Republic of	17.8	17.8	17.6	15.7	16.5	15.2	12.4	11.5	12.1	..	..	19.9	16.7	12.0
Libya	..	..	..	..	..	..	..	..	..	..	..	..	..	..
Morocco	18.9	19.4	19.3	17.2	16.6	14.8	13.4	12.0	..	..	..	16.8	17.7	12.7
Tunisia	23.8	24.5	26.6	30.8	27.8	27.2	24.3	23.9	26.0	27.1	..	23.1	26.8	25.3
ALL AFRICA	25.6	26.5	27.0	26.2	24.3	24.7	25.4	24.1	..	..	..	..	25.7	24.7
South Africa	..	..	..	..	..	..	..	..	..	..	..	..	..	..

Note: Total revenue does not include grants.

7-12. Export duties

	Percentage of total revenue											Average		
	1980	1981	1982	1983	1984	1985	1986	1987	1988	1989	1990	75–79	80–85	86–MR
SUB-SAHARAN AFRICA	7.6	3.6	4.1	5.2	6.5	7.3	7.4	6.7	..	..	..	..	5.8	7.0
excluding Nigeria	7.9	3.7	4.3	5.3	6.7	7.6	7.6	7.0	..	..	..	..	6.0	7.2
Angola	..	..	..	..	..	..	..	..	..	..	..	..	..	..
Benin	2.4	1.1	0.7	0.9	..	..	..	..	..	..	..	2.2	1.3	..
Botswana	0.2	0.2	0.2	0.1	0.1	0.1	0.0	0.0	0.0	..	..	0.5	0.1	0.0
Burkina Faso	2.9	2.2	1.5	1.6	1.5	2.0	1.4	1.2	..	..	..	3.4	2.0	1.3
Burundi	12.6	1.5	5.8	1.1	16.6	19.9	21.6	3.1	10.4	..	..	23.8	9.6	11.7
Cameroon	9.8	9.5	4.3	2.7	2.1	2.3	1.9	1.5	6.2	7.6	..	8.3	5.1	4.3
Cape Verde	..	0.2	..	..	..	..	..	..	..	..	..	..	..	..
Central African Republic	..	10.4	9.8	12.3	10.4	11.8	6.1	..	..	..	..	..	10.9	6.1
Chad	..	..	..	3.5	16.6	16.8	0.7	1.7	..	..	..	..	12.3	1.2
Comoros	..	20.8	34.4	17.6	10.4	17.4	13.6	8.5	..	..	..	..	20.1	11.1
Congo, People's Republic of the	0.2	0.2	0.1	0.1	0.1	0.1	0.1	0.1	0.3	0.0	0.0	0.4	0.1	0.1
Cote d'Ivoire	9.9	10.0	9.1	7.7	7.6	8.7	..	..	..	..	1.1	..	8.8	1.1
Djibouti	0.0	0.0	0.1	0.1	0.1	0.1	0.1	..	..	..	..	0.0	0.1	0.1
Equatorial Guinea	..	..	..	..	..	..	..	..	..	..	..	..	..	..
Ethiopia	20.9	12.8	10.2	9.4	11.3	7.6	9.6	5.4	..	..	..	16.5	12.0	7.5
Gabon	2.2	1.3	1.2	1.1	1.1	1.6	1.0	1.9	..	..	..	2.0	1.4	1.5
Gambia, The	10.9	0.6	4.3	0.4	8.7	4.1	3.1	1.6	2.3	1.8	0.0	9.4	4.8	1.8
Ghana	31.4	6.2	..	27.5	22.9	24.7	20.4	25.6	17.2	..	..	30.1	22.5	21.1
Guinea	..	..	19.2	22.8	0.0	0.1	0.3	..	..	..	..	24.8	10.5	0.3
Guinea-Bissau	2.1	3.1	4.0	5.8	4.4	1.5	2.6	27.9	21.5	..	..	..	3.5	17.4
Kenya	1.2	0.5	0.7	0.8	1.1	2.7	3.3	2.5	1.0	..	..	0.5	1.2	2.3
Lesotho	..	..	1.0	3.1	0.1	0.1	0.1	0.1	..	..	..	0.6	1.1	0.1
Liberia	0.7	0.5	0.5	0.4	0.1	0.3	0.1	0.1	0.3	..	..	0.5	0.4	0.1
Madagascar	2.1	2.7	3.5	7.3	6.7	11.5	11.1	13.3	9.8	..	..	3.1	5.6	11.4
Malawi	..	..	..	..	..	..	0.9	0.0	..	..	..	..	..	0.5
Mali	3.5	3.7	1.9	2.0	6.5	10.5	5.7	3.9	5.8	..	..	7.7	4.7	5.1
Mauritania	4.0	8.3	7.5	11.9	10.3	15.0	16.1	..	..	..	..	0.7	9.5	16.1
Mauritius	15.9	13.0	17.0	14.1	13.6	10.3	11.1	10.6	9.5	8.2	4.8	12.5	14.0	8.8
Mozambique	..	..	..	..	..	..	..	..	..	..	..	..	..	..
Namibia	..	..	4.9	4.5	3.4	4.4	4.6	..	..	..	..	..	4.3	4.6
Niger	4.1	5.2	5.3	6.7	5.8	5.4	5.2	..	..	..	..	4.2	5.4	5.2
Nigeria	0.0	0.0	0.0	0.0	0.0	0.1	0.2	0.1	0.0	0.0	0.0	0.0	0.0	0.1
Rwanda	19.1	8.4	9.3	9.9	14.2	14.1	21.2	10.6	..	..	..	26.9	12.5	15.9
Sao Tòme & Principe	..	..	..	..	..	..	..	..	..	..	..	..	..	..
Senegal	1.8	1.0	0.8	0.6	0.3	0.2	0.1	..	..	..	..	3.8	0.8	0.1
Seychelles	0.0	0.4	0.3	0.0	0.0	0.0	0.0	0.0	0.0	0.0	0.0	0.5	0.1	0.0
Sierra Leone	12.7	6.6	7.7	3.5	4.4	2.2	1.4	1.8	0.3	0.4	..	12.3	6.2	1.0
Somalia	1.3	2.2	4.5	2.9	0.9	1.6	0.8	0.7	0.2	0.2	..	..	2.2	0.5
Sudan	1.7	2.9	4.0	1.7	1.6	1.3	1.7	2.2	..	..	..	3.6	2.4	1.7
Swaziland	9.0	9.4	0.8	0.1	0.0	0.0	0.5	1.0	4.3	35.9	52.8	16.0	3.2	18.9
Tanzania	6.4	2.6	0.2	0.1	0.1	0.0	0.0	0.0	0.0	0.0	0.0	8.4	1.6	0.0
Togo	4.6	1.1	0.6	0.6	0.7	0.9	0.9	0.9	0.0	0.0	0.0	4.8	1.4	0.4
Uganda	33.6	4.0	27.4	30.5	45.7	59.3	67.3	37.4	26.6	..	..	42.0	33.4	43.8
Zaire	17.9	5.3	3.8	18.4	14.9	26.6	21.0	28.2	24.7	..	..	19.4	14.5	24.6
Zambia	0.0	0.0	0.0	5.3	8.7	8.3	13.7	14.1	1.0	..	..	0.0	3.7	9.6
Zimbabwe	0.0	0.0	0.0	0.0	0.0	0.0	0.0	0.0	0.0	0.0	0.0	0.0	0.0	0.0
NORTH AFRICA	1.3	1.4	1.1	0.5	0.6	0.5	0.6	0.3	..	..	..	1.6	0.9	0.5
Algeria	..	..	..	..	..	..	..	..	..	..	..	..	..	..
Egypt, Arab Republic of	1.8	1.8	1.6	0.1	0.0	0.0	0.9	0.0	0.4	..	..	1.7	0.9	0.4
Libya	..	..	..	..	..	..	..	..	..	..	..	..	..	..
Morocco	1.2	1.3	1.0	0.9	1.1	1.1	0.7	0.5	..	..	..	1.2	1.1	0.6
Tunisia	0.9	1.0	0.7	0.6	0.6	0.5	0.3	0.4	0.3	0.3	..	1.8	0.7	0.3
ALL AFRICA	7.0	3.4	3.8	4.7	5.9	6.7	6.8	6.1	..	..	..	..	5.4	6.4
South Africa	..	..	..	..	..	..	..	..	..	..	..	..	..	..

Note: Total revenue does not include grants.

181

7-13. Nontax revenue

	Percentage of total revenue											Average		
	1980	1981	1982	1983	1984	1985	1986	1987	1988	1989	1990	75–79	80–85	86–MR
SUB-SAHARAN AFRICA	13.5	13.4	14.4	14.4	16.2	18.7	17.5	18.5	..	..	..	..	15.1	17.1
excluding Nigeria	12.7	12.7	13.2	13.2	15.4	17.6	16.5	17.0	..	..	..	..	14.2	15.8
Angola	..	..	..	..	..	..	..	..	..	..	..	..	..	..
Benin	3.0	4.4	3.0	3.9	3.0	4.4	7.5	..	..	..	..	6.2	3.6	7.5
Botswana	26.6	22.8	35.4	39.5	44.0	55.0	47.1	41.4	44.2	..	..	35.1	37.2	44.2
Burkina Faso	10.5	12.5	11.3	8.4	10.1	24.8	18.1	20.7	..	..	..	8.3	12.9	19.4
Burundi	5.6	10.9	10.4	7.8	5.9	7.5	11.0	13.0	12.9	..	..	4.8	8.0	12.3
Cameroon	7.9	11.2	10.3	3.4	15.4	8.0	25.4	1.6	3.2	..	..	5.3	9.4	10.1
Cape Verde	..	..	..	..	..	..	..	..	..	..	..	..	..	..
Central African Republic	..	9.8	19.6	20.0	16.2	9.8	7.3	..	..	..	..	..	15.1	7.3
Chad	..	..	..	25.0	20.9	20.6	17.0	13.6	..	..	..	11.0	22.2	15.3
Comoros	..	13.4	14.1	23.7	18.3	12.2	15.0	22.3	..	..	..	..	16.3	18.6
Congo, People's Republic of the	19.0	27.3	63.5	67.6	70.2	72.1	56.8	41.2	..	..	..	23.3	53.3	49.0
Cote d'Ivoire	7.2	6.0	7.2	14.6	33.6	31.3	..	..	24.4	19.9	27.1	..	16.6	23.8
Djibouti	13.2	12.8	11.9	8.7	9.0	11.4	6.9	12.7	8.2	..	..	11.6	11.2	9.3
Equatorial Guinea	..	..	..	..	..	..	..	..	..	..	..	..	..	..
Ethiopia	15.4	20.8	22.1	26.8	23.2	25.1	30.6	25.8	30.6	36.5	24.2	16.9	22.2	29.5
Gabon	30.9	25.1	27.0	26.1	33.2	31.7	19.2	27.3	..	..	..	25.8	29.0	23.2
Gambia, The	14.5	8.2	9.4	9.9	6.0	6.4	5.1	5.8	2.8	9.5	7.2	19.8	9.1	6.1
Ghana	6.9	8.2	12.9	16.9	17.5	14.0	11.2	10.6	7.8	..	..	9.7	12.7	9.9
Guinea	29.2	27.5	35.8	39.9	15.6	10.2	5.4	10.8	19.4	12.6	..	26.1	26.4	12.0
Guinea-Bissau	26.9	22.1	13.0	15.2	37.4	33.5	41.5	35.6	0.1	0.1	..	..	24.7	19.3
Kenya	12.6	10.0	9.3	12.7	9.9	12.1	10.6	9.9	8.7	..	..	12.4	11.1	9.7
Lesotho	8.1	15.9	13.1	9.6	12.1	10.5	11.2	12.9	12.1	..	..	29.6	11.6	12.1
Liberia	7.6	3.8	1.9	3.0	3.7	2.9	4.3	4.4	4.2	14.9	..	4.4	3.8	7.0
Madagascar	2.1	4.8	3.2	3.0	3.4	2.0	2.1	1.9	1.9	..	..	12.0	3.1	2.0
Malawi	12.9	16.3	10.4	13.1	12.7	14.8	18.2	16.8	..	..	..	16.7	13.4	17.5
Mali	7.7	7.5	8.2	11.0	13.0	14.7	13.1	9.1	..	..	..	7.7	10.3	11.1
Mauritania	16.0	19.9	13.0	11.9	17.0	11.7	13.1	..	..	..	..	20.4	14.9	13.1
Mauritius	11.6	12.5	12.0	13.1	8.9	12.0	10.4	12.8	10.5	6.9	7.9	9.4	11.7	9.7
Mozambique	..	..	..	..	..	..	..	..	..	..	..	..	..	..
Namibia	..	..	65.9	58.9	51.2	45.3	42.2	40.9	42.9	33.4	..	..	55.3	39.8
Niger	15.3	14.7	10.8	9.1	12.7	12.7	13.2	21.0	16.7	..	..	14.5	12.5	17.0
Nigeria	40.4	36.0	50.2	51.6	38.9	53.1	47.4	62.9	54.5	..	..	16.1	45.0	54.9
Rwanda	14.0	16.9	14.4	11.5	10.0	11.4	8.8	7.1	..	..	..	6.5	13.0	8.0
Sao Tome & Principe	..	..	..	..	..	..	..	..	..	..	..	..	..	..
Senegal	6.3	7.0	7.9	7.8	6.2	6.8	4.7	..	..	..	..	6.8	7.0	4.7
Seychelles	15.0	16.3	15.3	13.9	16.1	18.7	16.6	20.0	21.8	19.9	..	24.3	15.9	19.6
Sierra Leone	10.1	9.8	1.8	8.1	5.5	5.4	7.0	2.9	20.2	3.1	..	10.6	6.8	8.3
Somalia	16.1	11.0	12.2	11.9	34.3	74.4	63.9	78.2	49.2	..	..	17.9	26.6	63.8
Sudan	16.0	20.8	19.7	14.2	15.2	13.2	9.7	34.7	..	..	..	14.6	17.2	19.2
Swaziland	6.3	7.9	7.8	7.1	10.0	8.4	8.4	8.2	10.0	0.3	0.2	7.9	7.9	5.4
Tanzania	7.9	4.1	9.1	4.8	5.0	5.6	5.5	5.9	10.4	..	..	14.0	6.1	7.3
Togo	11.1	11.4	9.4	16.4	19.9	22.4	22.2	9.5	18.2	40.8	..	11.2	15.1	22.7
Uganda	3.1	6.0	2.4	1.7	2.0	1.7	1.9	13.4	8.0	..	..	6.3	2.8	7.8
Zaire	11.9	12.5	9.6	2.1	1.5	0.6	4.2	0.9	0.4	..	..	2.6	6.4	1.8
Zambia	7.3	6.9	7.6	5.4	6.6	7.3	4.7	6.6	8.6	4.2	..	11.5	6.9	6.0
Zimbabwe	20.2	11.4	9.8	10.3	10.1	9.9	9.4	10.2	11.7	10.9	..	16.9	12.0	10.5
NORTH AFRICA	27.9	25.3	25.0	23.5	25.8	25.3	23.2	23.1	..	..	..	20.2	25.5	23.1
Algeria	..	..	..	..	..	..	..	..	..	..	..	..	..	..
Egypt, Arab Republic of	49.5	35.7	32.8	34.9	38.2	34.7	35.2	33.9	36.3	..	..	27.0	37.6	35.2
Libya	..	..	..	..	..	..	..	..	..	..	..	..	..	..
Morocco	12.3	16.4	18.6	14.9	12.9	14.6	8.2	10.1	..	..	..	16.2	15.0	9.1
Tunisia	21.9	23.8	23.7	20.8	26.2	26.5	26.1	25.4	26.6	22.8	..	17.4	23.8	25.2
ALL AFRICA	14.8	14.4	15.3	15.2	17.0	19.3	18.0	18.9	..	..	..	..	16.0	17.6
South Africa	12.7	11.9	10.6	10.3	8.4	8.3	9.1	8.4	7.9	7.5	..	12.2	10.4	8.2

Note: Total revenue does not include grants.

7–14. Government expenditure: wages and salaries

	Percentage of total expenditure and lending minus repayments											Average		
	1980	1981	1982	1983	1984	1985	1986	1987	1988	1989	1990	75–79	80–85	86–MR
SUB-SAHARAN AFRICA	26.8	27.0	26.2	27.0	27.2	26.9	24.8	25.0	..	..	..	..	26.9	25.2
excluding Nigeria	27.4	27.7	26.8	27.6	27.7	27.3	25.3	25.5	..	..	..	..	27.4	25.8
Angola	..	..	..	..	..	..	..	..	..	..	..	..	..	..
Benin	..	..	..	32.2	30.0	33.4	40.6	46.5	39.1	..	..	30.7	31.9	42.0
Botswana	24.9	26.7	24.9	26.3	24.3	23.5	20.8	20.2	19.3	..	..	24.0	25.1	20.1
Burkina Faso	49.0	46.6	49.4	59.7	50.3	57.6	46.4	51.6	..	..	..	..	52.1	49.0
Burundi	..	25.4	22.8	19.1	20.9	23.3	23.2	19.1	22.2	..	..	..	22.3	21.5
Cameroon	31.6	26.4	24.5	22.3	24.2	23.9	27.3	22.8	..	33.7	..	34.0	25.5	27.9
Cape Verde	..	..	..	..	..	..	..	..	..	..	..	..	..	..
Central African Republic	..	53.5	60.6	56.4	58.9	56.1	55.5	..	..	..	..	..	57.1	55.5
Chad	..	..	..	30.4	16.9	16.3	13.5	11.0	..	..	..	..	21.2	12.3
Comoros	..	..	19.1	16.7	15.2	19.6	27.0	21.4	..	..	..	..	17.6	24.2
Congo, People's Republic of the	20.6	20.0	15.9	17.1	18.2	20.1	28.6	37.5	37.4	..	..	..	18.6	34.5
Cote d'Ivoire	25.0	24.0	24.2	25.8	34.4	26.3	..	..	37.4	..	..	..	26.6	37.4
Djibouti	29.0	35.6	43.3	45.6	53.2	54.6	51.5	43.7	60.6	..	..	38.0	43.5	51.9
Equatorial Guinea	..	..	..	..	..	..	..	..	..	..	..	..	..	..
Ethiopia	33.4	32.7	33.3	25.1	36.5	33.4	31.5	33.0	25.8	26.2	27.3	37.6	32.4	28.8
Gabon	21.1	18.1	16.1	15.6	15.5	16.6	17.0	28.8	31.4	31.3	..	10.8	17.2	27.1
Gambia, The	23.9	25.2	26.2	26.9	27.3	20.6	19.0	12.2	11.3	19.4	..	23.3	25.0	15.5
Ghana	26.4	28.5	25.8	25.7	24.7	28.6	35.7	33.6	33.0	30.8	..	26.0	26.6	33.3
Guinea	39.9	39.5	21.8	30.0	37.3	29.5	15.6	11.7	18.1	18.7	..	..	33.0	16.0
Guinea-Bissau	23.6	29.2	25.7	26.8	20.5	19.3	21.5	10.2	9.4	8.8	..	..	24.2	12.5
Kenya	25.3	27.2	27.6	31.1	31.7	29.7	33.7	31.5	32.0	..	..	29.2	28.8	32.4
Lesotho	33.1	32.9	33.9	31.1	30.5	39.5	29.0	24.9	29.1	29.6	..	32.4	33.5	28.1
Liberia	30.1	39.2	39.8	37.1	39.4	36.6	36.2	37.1	39.0	30.6	..	27.9	37.0	35.7
Madagascar	27.8	28.6	33.8	34.1	32.4	33.5	32.7	27.5	..	..	..	..	31.7	30.1
Malawi	12.9	13.9	19.8	19.3	18.2	17.6	17.8	20.7	17.8	15.7	..	14.3	17.0	18.0
Mali	31.4	29.3	24.2	23.6	25.8	24.3	26.8	26.9	25.0	..	..	54.3	26.4	26.3
Mauritania	31.8	32.4	29.0	27.0	24.8	27.1	30.2	..	..	..	..	30.8	28.7	30.2
Mauritius	28.1	26.2	29.5	31.9	32.8	30.9	30.5	31.0	33.9	34.3	38.2	29.8	29.9	33.6
Mozambique	..	..	..	..	..	..	..	..	..	..	..	..	..	..
Namibia	..	..	19.0	19.0	21.7	19.0	23.8	22.3	24.2	24.0	..	..	19.7	23.6
Niger	16.4	13.6	17.1	17.2	18.8	19.1	19.3	21.0	23.0	..	..	19.0	17.0	21.1
Nigeria	7.5	7.2	7.9	7.6	10.5	11.1	7.9	5.4	6.1	..	..	11.7	8.6	6.5
Rwanda	29.6	30.4	29.1	28.6	29.4	26.2	25.9	24.9	..	..	..	33.0	28.9	25.4
Sao Tome & Principe	..	..	..	..	..	..	..	..	..	..	..	..	..	..
Senegal	44.4	43.3	34.3	34.2	32.0	41.9	4.4	..	..	..	..	..	38.4	4.4
Seychelles	29.0	28.1	27.3	29.5	27.0	23.5	22.6	27.2	24.9	20.8	..	35.8	27.4	23.9
Sierra Leone	24.6	26.6	30.0	30.4	37.1	29.5	15.8	10.0	..	..	..	27.9	29.7	12.9
Somalia	..	..	..	..	19.1	11.9	7.3	4.2	4.1	2.6	..	..	15.5	4.6
Sudan	11.5	10.1	8.5	..	..	..	..	..	..	..	..	11.0	..	..
Swaziland	35.8	29.6	33.2	36.8	36.9	32.4	35.1	37.6	39.1	35.6	31.9	29.2	34.1	35.9
Tanzania	18.6	21.1	20.4	22.9	22.3	25.6	24.8	19.2	18.2	..	..	25.4	21.8	20.7
Togo	25.8	27.6	31.4	28.7	24.8	22.2	20.7	28.0	29.8	28.8	..	16.2	26.7	26.8
Uganda	10.0	12.0	15.1	10.4	10.9	19.1	11.7	6.7	8.4	10.4	..	..	12.9	9.3
Zaire	42.0	31.9	27.3	19.1	12.3	12.2	14.1	20.2	18.8	..	..	36.8	24.1	17.7
Zambia	22.4	32.9	29.6	31.4	30.7	25.6	22.3	25.8	22.2	..	..	25.8	28.8	23.4
Zimbabwe	30.7	30.0	25.7	26.1	24.4	24.2	25.3	26.4	32.8	32.0	33.5	31.6	26.9	30.0
NORTH AFRICA	22.9	23.7	23.6	26.1	26.2	25.6	25.0	26.9	..	..	..	23.5	24.7	25.9
Algeria	..	..	..	..	..	..	..	..	..	..	..	..	..	..
Egypt, Arab Republic of	9.3	16.0	15.2	16.6	17.0	18.5	17.0	18.2	18.6	..	..	16.4	15.4	18.0
Libya	..	..	..	..	..	..	..	..	..	..	..	..	..	..
Morocco	32.9	30.9	30.7	36.6	37.0	32.9	32.6	36.0	..	..	..	27.8	33.5	34.3
Tunisia	26.5	24.3	25.1	25.0	24.4	25.3	25.2	26.4	27.0	27.3	..	26.1	25.1	26.5
ALL AFRICA	26.5	26.8	26.0	27.0	27.1	26.8	24.9	25.1	..	..	..	..	26.7	25.3
South Africa	..	..	..	..	..	..	..	..	..	..	..	..	..	..

7–15. Government expenditure: trends in real wages and salaries

	Index 1980=100											Average		
	1980	1981	1982	1983	1984	1985	1986	1987	1988	1989	1990	75–79	80–85	86–MR
SUB-SAHARAN AFRICA excluding Nigeria	..	..	..	..	..	..	..	..	..	..	..	..	..	..
Angola	..	..	..	..	..	..	..	..	..	..	..	..	..	..
Benin	100	112	125	141	129	118	138	138	123	..	..	83	121	80
Botswana	100	115	130	142	169	163	159	195	214	..	..	66	136	189
Burkina Faso	100	106	117	119	117	126	138	163	..	..	..	..	114	150
Burundi*	..	100	103	99	91	95	109	126	133	..	..	..	97	122
Cameroon	100	125	122	141	161	166	205	199	197	196	..	87	136	199
Cape Verde	..	..	..	..	..	..	..	..	..	..	..	..	..	..
Central African Republic	..	100	90	83	80	77	73	..	..	..	..	..	86	73
Chad*	..	..	..	100	72	90	140	173	..	..	..	..	87	157
Comoros*	..	..	100	116	124	147	184	127	..	..	..	..	122	155
Congo, People's Republic of the	100	85	107	110	113	125	185	181	187	..	..	..	107	184
Cote d'Ivoire	100	112	120	124	129	104	..	..	150	..	..	..	115	150
Djibouti	100	89	141	146	145	147	131	128	126	..	..	..	128	128
Equatorial Guinea	..	..	..	..	..	..	..	..	..	..	..	..	..	..
Ethiopia	100	103	117	122	139	131	135	157	140	158	165	83	119	151
Gabon	100	98	86	87	92	106	150	139	143	132	..	74	95	141
Gambia, The	100	119	140	127	139	103	91	96	88	118	..	77	121	98
Ghana	100	104	90	63	80	134	181	177	182	198	..	166	95	185
Guinea	100	90	102	101	103	137	430	395	689	758	..	..	105	568
Guinea-Bissau	100	110	106	92	88	92	67	47	44	54	..	..	98	53
Kenya	100	120	125	124	127	131	149	167	167	..	..	86	121	161
Lesotho	100	97	84	80	92	110	103	98	119	105	..	50	94	106
Liberia	100	147	161	143	128	117	107	99	..	..	..	79	133	103
Madagascar	100	90	83	75	76	75	70	69	..	..	..	..	83	70
Malawi	100	94	112	111	106	125	133	144	115	103	..	71	108	124
Mali	100	102	109	112	122	130	146	137	139	..	..	101	112	141
Mauritania	100	93	92	97	88	82	79	..	..	..	..	89	92	79
Mauritius	100	104	118	126	120	115	115	125	159	159	169	97	114	145
Mozambique	..	..	..	..	..	..	..	..	..	..	..	..	..	..
Namibia*	..	..	100	109	119	102	134	137	133	120	..	..	108	131
Niger	100	103	100	102	96	108	120	124	131	..	..	75	102	125
Nigeria	100	107	95	87	76	82	82	79	86	..	..	135	91	82
Rwanda	100	152	146	149	135	137	158	165	..	..	..	76	136	162
Sao Tome & Principe	..	..	..	..	..	..	..	..	..	..	..	..	..	..
Senegal	100	108	104	103	102	104	11	..	..	..	..	..	104	11
Seychelles	100	100	110	106	108	106	110	120	120	118	..	67	105	117
Sierra Leone	100	103	109	109	100	65	44	44	..	..	..	94	98	44
Somalia	..	..	..	..	100	78	57	45	38	33	..	..	89	43
Sudan	100	92	82	..	..	..	..	..	..	..	..	97	91	..
Swaziland	100	107	120	128	127	123	127	120	131	145	142	84	117	133
Tanzania	100	109	120	110	101	107	102	87	85	..	..	127	108	92
Togo	100	107	115	97	101	96	96	110	115	113	..	87	103	109
Uganda	100	125	138	97	73	148	81	35	65	75	..	..	113	64
Zaire	100	92	77	46	44	44	38	67	59	..	..	92	67	55
Zambia	100	129	131	107	96	98	92	76	62	..	..	103	110	76
Zimbabwe	100	98	110	103	112	111	116	137	176	179	176	84	106	157
NORTH AFRICA	..	..	..	..	..	..	..	..	..	..	..	..	..	..
Algeria	..	..	..	..	..	..	..	..	..	..	..	..	..	..
Egypt, Arab Republic of	100	198	249	256	274	303	293	282	275	..	..	160	230	283
Libya	..	..	..	..	..	..	..	..	..	..	..	..	..	..
Morocco	100	108	112	115	111	108	110	114	..	..	..	79	109	112
Tunisia	100	96	115	126	128	131	137	133	136	142	..	80	116	137
ALL AFRICA	..	..	..	..	..	..	..	..	..	..	..	..	..	..
South Africa	..	..	..	..	..	..	..	..	..	..	..	..	..	..

Note: Countries marked with an asterisk (*) are indexed using a year other than 1980, due to unavailable 1980 information.

7-16. Government expenditure: other goods and services

	Percentage of total expenditure and lending minus repayments											Average		
	1980	1981	1982	1983	1984	1985	1986	1987	1988	1989	1990	75–79	80–85	86–MR
SUB-SAHARAN AFRICA	19.4	19.0	20.2	17.7	17.7	17.6	19.8	18.9	..	..	..	..	20.2	17.7
excluding Nigeria	19.7	19.4	20.4	17.5	18.0	18.0	20.2	19.4	..	..	..	..	20.4	17.5
Angola	..	..	..	..	..	..	..	..	..	..	..	..	..	..
Benin												9.1	..	..
Botswana	15.7	16.0	15.5	16.7	16.1	16.7	21.9	29.1	24.1	..	..	14.0	16.1	25.0
Burkina Faso	14.0	12.0	13.5	15.2	8.0	8.1	9.1	9.2	..	..	..	..	11.8	9.1
Burundi	..	13.8	18.4	16.9	15.9	16.0	16.1	9.2	13.4	..	..	..	16.2	12.9
Cameroon	23.1	29.6	20.7	22.0	20.7	17.4	21.2	12.1	..	10.1	..	24.3	22.2	14.5
Cape Verde	..	..	..	..	..	..	..	..	..	..	..	..	15.4	17.7
Central African Republic	..	13.2	17.1	17.5	13.6	15.8	17.7	..	..	..	..	..	10.4	5.6
Chad	..	..	..	15.3	6.5	9.4	5.4	5.9	..	..	..	..	20.4	41.8
Comoros	..	..	42.9	15.7	10.2	12.8	42.1	41.6	..	..	..	..	10.1	11.6
Congo, People's Republic of the	6.9	12.8	10.8	9.1	10.0	10.7	13.1	10.0	11.6	..	..	..	9.9	..
Cote d'Ivoire	10.2	12.1	9.5	7.8	11.9	7.8	..	..	..	..	..	24.8	25.6	25.2
Djibouti	18.0	27.6	26.4	26.5	26.3	28.6	26.1	21.8	27.6	..	..	37.2	41.2	36.5
Equatorial Guinea	..	..	..	..	..	..	..	..	..	..	..			
Ethiopia	46.0	44.1	41.4	34.7	35.3	45.6	40.2	32.9	..	..	..	7.0	18.8	20.6
Gabon	16.7	18.1	20.1	20.9	19.9	17.2	15.4	23.1	22.3	21.7	..	30.5	21.5	18.3
Gambia, The	19.2	21.4	27.9	22.0	19.5	19.2	25.3	11.3	..	..	..	21.0	24.8	18.4
Ghana	20.9	20.0	23.7	..	32.2	27.1	17.1	17.4	21.6	17.5	..	..	14.2	20.9
Guinea	..	18.0	23.2	5.4	13.4	10.9	24.8	26.3	14.8	17.8	..	..	12.0	10.4
Guinea-Bissau	10.7	12.1	14.1	14.2	11.0	9.9	13.0	7.9	..	..	..	21.0	23.6	19.7
Kenya	27.2	23.0	23.4	25.0	23.1	19.6	20.3	19.4	19.4	..	..	19.6	19.0	28.7
Lesotho	14.5	15.6	16.0	22.3	21.9	23.7	28.8	27.5	36.3	22.1	..	17.0	13.9	13.7
Liberia	13.6	10.9	18.6	17.3	10.6	12.1	12.5	19.8	..	9.0	..	..	10.1	9.5
Madagascar	..	9.1	9.7	10.2	9.3	12.2	10.0	9.0	..	..	..	28.8	27.3	28.0
Malawi	19.5	33.9	28.2	31.9	26.7	23.7	26.1	30.0	..	..	..	13.5	10.7	12.6
Mali	12.4	13.5	9.6	8.8	9.9	10.2	11.4	13.7	12.8	..	..	32.5	13.3	12.8
Mauritania	18.1	15.0	12.3	11.9	10.8	11.4	12.8	..	..	..	..	8.8	7.9	9.3
Mauritius	8.3	8.5	6.8	6.9	8.2	8.5	8.2	8.4	8.8	10.5	10.5	..	..	..
Mozambique	..	..	..	..	..	..	..	..	..	..	..	..	17.3	24.0
Namibia	..	..	16.3	16.6	15.6	20.7	23.2	23.7	25.8	23.3	..	18.2	13.4	14.5
Niger	12.7	9.7	16.2	10.8	13.8	17.4	14.5	14.5	14.5	..	..	17.0	11.4	8.8
Nigeria	11.3	7.1	13.4	22.3	9.0	5.4	7.9	3.3	15.2	..	..	24.6	18.2	15.2
Rwanda	27.2	14.9	18.7	17.6	16.1	14.4	16.2	14.2	..	..	..	..	..	..
Sao Tome & Principe	..	..	..	..	..	..	..	..	..	..	..	..	17.0	15.1
Senegal	27.1	20.4	14.1	15.2	11.8	13.2	15.1	..	..	..	..	22.5	25.1	24.9
Seychelles	20.0	21.4	24.9	32.1	25.5	26.6	26.4	28.7	22.9	21.7	..	16.5	14.9	15.5
Sierra Leone	11.0	12.0	13.0	13.0	24.9	15.5	18.6	12.4	..	..	..	..	33.7	33.6
Somalia	..	..	..	..	..	33.7	34.3	32.8	33.6	..	..	33.3	..	..
Sudan	33.4	22.5	23.1	..	..	..	..	..	..	..	..	16.4	19.8	17.1
Swaziland	19.5	26.7	18.0	17.4	19.9	17.5	18.6	18.3	21.0	16.4	11.3	29.7	32.8	34.2
Tanzania	33.2	33.7	35.0	30.8	32.7	31.6	39.3	34.7	28.5	..	..	11.2	19.7	24.5
Togo	19.9	23.2	18.9	11.3	23.1	21.5	21.4	20.4	27.8	28.6	..	..	..	..
Uganda	..	..	..	..	..	..	..	..	..	..	..	27.9	21.1	25.8
Zaire	23.2	23.4	29.8	22.0	12.3	16.2	13.2	12.6	51.7	..	..	24.9	19.6	13.0
Zambia	23.2	33.2	24.1	7.0	17.5	12.4	9.8	16.8	12.4	..	..	21.6	18.0	16.8
Zimbabwe	24.6	18.8	15.9	17.1	16.7	15.2	15.7	17.2	16.4	17.1	17.8	11.8	13.8	14.3
NORTH AFRICA	13.4	12.8	12.7	14.7	14.4	14.9	14.0	14.6	..	..	..			
Algeria	..	..	..	..	..	..	..	..	..	..	..	13.3	18.2	20.7
Egypt, Arab Republic of	14.7	17.0	15.9	18.4	21.6	21.9	20.5	22.8	18.7	..	..	..	..	..
Libya	..	..	..	..	..	..	..	..	..	..	..	12.4	13.4	14.4
Morocco	13.7	12.3	11.5	13.3	12.9	16.4	14.4	14.5	..	..	..	9.7	9.9	6.3
Tunisia	11.8	9.2	10.7	12.3	8.8	6.4	6.9	6.5	6.1	6.0	..	..	18.4	19.1
ALL AFRICA	18.9	18.5	19.6	17.4	17.4	17.4	19.3	18.5	..	..	..	..	..	..
South Africa	..	..	..	..	..	..	..	..	..	..	..	..	..	..

7–17. Government expenditure: interest payments

	Percentage of total expenditure and lending minus repayments											Average		
	1980	1981	1982	1983	1984	1985	1986	1987	1988	1989	1990	75–79	80–85	86–MR
SUB-SAHARAN AFRICA	5.1	5.7	6.5	7.9	10.2	11.4	10.8	11.1	..	..	..	..	7.4	11.1
excluding Nigeria	5.2	5.7	6.4	7.7	9.7	11.0	10.4	10.0	..	..	..	..	7.3	10.4
Angola	..	..	..	..	..	..	..	..	..	..	..	..	..	..
Benin	1.3	1.8	2.5	6.0	13.9	11.0	8.3	7.9	8.0	..	..	0.7	6.1	8.1
Botswana	1.7	1.7	2.7	2.9	3.2	3.7	3.8	3.3	4.0	..	..	3.0	2.6	3.7
Burkina Faso	0.3	2.7	2.7	2.1	5.6	9.9	7.8	8.5	..	..	..	4.2	3.9	8.1
Burundi	..	1.8	1.7	2.7	5.0	6.5	6.6	5.9	7.7	..	..	..	3.6	6.8
Cameroon	0.6	1.0	1.0	2.3	2.5	4.0	3.7	..	..	6.0	..	1.5	1.9	4.9
Cape Verde	..	..	..	..	..	..	..	..	..	..	..	..	..	..
Central African Republic	..	1.2	4.9	5.9	8.6	9.9	9.7	..	..	..	..	..	6.1	9.7
Chad	..	..	..	3.9	2.1	1.8	1.6	0.8	..	..	..	..	2.6	1.2
Comoros	..	..	1.7	2.1	2.4	2.5	3.4	0.6	..	..	..	..	2.2	2.0
Congo, People's Republic of the	4.8	6.9	5.5	7.3	9.9	12.9	18.8	20.5	25.8	..	..	..	7.9	21.7
Cote d'Ivoire	7.2	13.5	18.2	21.2	27.3	29.2	..	..	27.5	..	..	..	19.4	27.5
Djibouti	0.0	0.0	0.0	0.0	0.0	0.7	0.8	..	1.4	..	..	0.3	0.1	1.1
Equatorial Guinea	..	..	..	..	..	..	..	..	..	..	..	..	..	..
Ethiopia	3.0	3.4	3.2	2.4	4.9	6.8	5.2	6.0	..	..	..	2.8	3.9	5.6
Gabon	4.0	4.6	5.1	5.3	5.5	5.4	7.0	14.4	20.2	22.1	..	..	5.0	15.9
Gambia, The	1.3	2.6	4.2	6.6	5.7	3.2	6.4	12.6	12.1	16.9	..	0.5	3.9	12.0
Ghana	15.2	12.8	20.3	0.0	12.5	10.6	15.5	9.9	8.0	9.2	..	9.4	11.9	10.6
Guinea	..	4.1	2.8	3.5	4.1	2.5	10.4	9.3	12.2	9.2	..	..	3.4	10.3
Guinea-Bissau	0.8	1.2	0.8	0.6	2.4	3.6	4.7	8.5	..	..	..	..	1.6	6.6
Kenya	6.6	7.6	11.4	14.3	15.4	14.7	18.2	16.0	18.3	..	..	5.9	11.7	17.5
Lesotho	2.5	4.4	9.5	10.1	7.2	7.7	1.5	6.3	7.4	10.9	..	1.0	6.9	6.6
Liberia	8.8	5.9	9.8	12.1	19.9	22.1	13.7	15.2	..	12.5	..	4.2	13.1	13.8
Madagascar	1.9	2.8	0.5	5.8	8.3	8.4	9.6	11.0	..	..	..	..	4.6	10.3
Malawi	8.2	13.6	15.1	13.6	16.1	19.3	20.3	21.2	20.5	17.4	..	6.3	14.3	19.8
Mali	0.6	0.8	1.1	1.2	1.8	3.4	2.5	5.3	3.0	..	..	0.7	1.5	3.6
Mauritania	1.5	3.4	2.9	4.6	4.6	7.3	11.5	..	..	..	..	2.1	4.0	11.5
Mauritius	12.0	13.7	17.5	18.1	19.9	20.5	19.8	17.3	13.4	13.4	11.2	5.2	16.9	15.0
Mozambique	..	..	..	..	..	..	..	..	..	..	..	..	..	..
Namibia	..	..	0.1	0.2	0.4	0.4	0.3	0.2	0.3	..	..	..	0.3	0.3
Niger	5.5	4.7	6.0	7.2	11.1	12.8	12.5	14.0	14.5	..	..	5.6	7.9	13.7
Nigeria	3.6	3.8	10.5	15.0	25.4	26.2	24.3	45.7	44.8	48.4	..	3.2	14.1	40.8
Rwanda	2.1	1.6	2.3	2.6	3.8	3.7	3.8	4.3	..	..	..	1.2	2.7	4.0
Sao Tome & Principe	..	..	..	..	..	..	..	..	..	..	..	..	..	..
Senegal	27.1	20.4	14.1	15.2	14.2	17.5	15.4	..	..	..	..	..	18.1	15.4
Seychelles	2.0	2.3	2.5	3.9	5.2	7.4	4.8	15.9	16.0	13.3	..	0.7	3.9	12.5
Sierra Leone	7.0	7.5	8.0	8.6	10.0	8.9	13.8	19.9	..	..	..	6.0	8.3	16.8
Somalia	..	..	..	..	8.2	9.1	13.4	9.1	13.7	12.4	..	0.5	8.7	12.2
Sudan	6.0	5.8	5.8	6.9	13.9	24.5	24.5	17.5	..	..	..	6.1	10.5	21.0
Swaziland	0.3	1.6	3.9	4.2	4.6	5.8	7.1	6.4	6.0	4.9	4.8	1.2	3.4	5.8
Tanzania	6.8	7.4	6.9	8.9	9.6	9.7	8.7	13.3	15.9	..	..	4.2	8.2	12.6
Togo	6.8	8.5	7.7	18.5	13.2	15.5	0.0	0.0	14.6	13.6	..	1.7	11.7	7.1
Uganda	..	..	2.7	10.7	14.3	11.2	12.3	5.4	5.2	7.7	..	..	9.7	7.6
Zaire	7.5	11.1	11.4	21.0	34.6	38.7	36.3	0.8	6.8	..	..	7.4	20.7	14.6
Zambia	7.6	7.7	6.7	13.2	3.5	10.9	10.9	0.6	0.3	..	..	8.4	8.3	4.0
Zimbabwe	6.8	8.5	8.3	9.7	10.4	12.1	12.6	12.5	12.9	14.1	14.6	6.0	9.3	13.4
NORTH AFRICA	4.7	6.3	5.9	7.6	8.8	10.0	10.8	11.5	..	..	..	..	7.2	11.1
Algeria	..	..	..	..	..	..	..	..	..	..	..	..	..	..
Egypt, Arab Republic of	2.9	5.1	3.9	6.7	7.2	7.3	7.6	9.2	9.8	..	..	4.3	5.5	8.9
Libya	..	..	..	..	..	..	..	..	..	..	..	..	..	..
Morocco	7.1	9.4	9.0	11.0	13.3	15.7	17.2	16.3	..	..	..	4.2	10.9	16.8
Tunisia	4.1	4.5	4.9	5.1	6.0	7.0	7.5	9.0	8.9	9.1	..	3.3	5.3	8.6
ALL AFRICA	5.1	5.7	6.5	7.9	10.1	11.3	10.8	11.1	..	..	..	..	7.8	11.2
South Africa	7.0	8.2	8.9	9.9	11.4	11.8	12.2	12.5	12.8	14.7	..	6.5	9.5	13.0

7–18. Government expenditure: subsidies and current transfers

| | Percentage of total expenditure and lending minus repayments | | | | | | | | | | | Average | | |
	1980	1981	1982	1983	1984	1985	1986	1987	1988	1989	1990	75–79	80–85	86–MR
SUB-SAHARAN AFRICA	..	10.5	11.7	11.3	11.7	11.3	12.3	10.9	..	..	..	..	11.4	11.2
excluding Nigeria	..	10.7	12.0	11.7	11.5	11.3	12.3	11.0	..	..	..	..	11.5	11.2
Angola	..	..	..	..	..	..	..	..	..	..	..	14.2	..	..
Benin	..	..	..	..	..	..	..	..	..	..	..	14.2	..	..
Botswana	16.8	19.2	23.2	23.9	25.5	26.4	27.7	21.4	22.9	..	..	13.9	22.5	24.0
Burkina Faso	13.9	12.6	14.0	17.0	16.0	11.3	13.9	15.8	..	..	..	11.2	14.1	14.8
Burundi	..	6.7	4.3	4.0	4.0	7.1	6.2	5.4	6.3	..	..	..	5.2	6.0
Cameroon	11.2	9.5	5.6	7.3	10.3	13.1	5.6	5.0	..	12.7	..	9.1	9.5	7.8
Cape Verde	..	..	..	..	..	..	..	..	..	..	..	..	..	..
Central African Republic	..	14.6	10.0	9.9	11.6	9.4	9.3	..	..	..	..	..	11.1	9.3
Chad	..	..	..	4.7	2.8	3.9	1.6	1.6	..	..	..	..	3.8	1.6
Comoros	..	..	5.0	4.3	3.6	3.2	4.3	7.4	..	..	..	..	4.0	5.9
Congo, People's Republic of the	9.3	9.6	7.6	13.1	10.2	10.4	11.4	11.2	10.9	..	..	..	10.0	11.1
Cote d'Ivoire	12.2	10.2	9.5	9.4	8.8	10.2	..	..	..	..	..	..	10.0	..
Djibouti	..	5.5	5.4	2.5	8.3	5.2	8.2	..	6.3	..	..	7.9	5.4	7.3
Equatorial Guinea	..	..	..	..	..	..	..	..	..	..	..	5.5	6.2	6.7
Ethiopia	4.0	4.8	5.0	10.9	5.8	6.7	6.8	6.6	..	..	..	5.5	6.2	6.7
Gabon	5.0	5.8	6.0	6.4	7.2	6.9	4.0	5.8	4.9	4.9	..	7.0	6.2	4.9
Gambia, The	4.2	8.3	12.5	5.8	8.4	6.4	5.5	3.0	..	..	..	6.4	7.6	4.2
Ghana	25.2	18.0	18.9	21.8	15.5	10.0	10.0	9.0	7.8	..	..	14.4	18.2	8.9
Guinea	..	14.3	33.0	42.6	29.3	50.6	8.1	..	..	..	..	..	34.0	8.1
Guinea-Bissau	5.0	6.7	5.8	6.8	3.3	3.0	4.8	2.1	..	..	..	..	5.1	3.4
Kenya	12.1	13.4	16.2	12.4	15.4	17.6	13.4	13.0	14.6	..	..	14.1	14.5	13.7
Lesotho	15.0	14.0	13.1	9.5	6.9	7.4	7.0	5.5	4.8	5.1	..	8.3	11.0	5.6
Liberia	4.8	4.1	6.5	6.9	6.5	6.3	6.8	8.0	..	6.0	..	6.9	5.9	6.9
Madagascar	..	5.0	5.3	6.4	6.7	6.1	8.2	7.3	..	..	..	..	5.9	7.7
Malawi	5.0	5.3	6.8	6.4	7.2	7.0	7.2	6.4	..	..	..	7.4	6.3	6.8
Mali	10.2	9.5	8.4	7.3	3.9	8.0	8.9	3.9	2.1	..	..	19.0	7.9	5.0
Mauritania	2.8	6.2	6.1	7.3	7.0	7.2	7.5	..	..	..	..	13.3	6.1	7.5
Mauritius	24.4	25.0	24.9	23.8	24.2	23.5	22.9	20.9	22.4	20.1	21.7	29.2	24.3	21.6
Mozambique	..	..	..	..	..	..	..	..	..	..	..	..	..	..
Namibia	..	..	33.3	40.9	33.5	30.9	29.9	28.1	28.9	37.0	..	..	34.7	30.9
Niger	13.2	7.0	7.4	7.9	8.9	9.8	6.8	6.9	7.4	..	..	16.0	9.0	7.0
Nigeria	9.8	3.1	0.8	1.1	17.3	9.9	14.4	6.9	..	..	..	7.0	7.0	10.7
Rwanda	5.2	8.5	6.6	10.4	7.6	7.0	7.7	13.5	..	..	..	5.2	7.6	10.6
Sao Tome & Principe	..	..	..	..	..	..	..	..	..	..	..	..	..	..
Senegal	6.2	3.2	7.5	6.4	12.9	12.8	10.3	..	..	..	..	..	8.2	10.3
Seychelles	7.0	8.8	10.7	12.4	20.7	14.4	15.7	12.1	14.3	16.4	..	7.0	12.3	14.6
Sierra Leone	..	4.8	5.2	5.3	6.2	4.3	26.1	11.2	..	..	..	6.6	5.0	18.6
Somalia	..	..	..	..	..	24.6	20.8	23.8	19.9	..	..	6.9	24.6	21.5
Sudan	27.8	23.6	28.4	..	..	..	..	..	..	..	..	20.4	..	..
Swaziland	5.4	2.6	6.6	8.1	7.4	7.4	10.7	12.3	12.3	12.3	11.6	5.0	6.3	11.9
Tanzania	3.9	4.0	16.2	15.7	15.0	12.3	10.4	9.8	13.4	..	..	9.2	11.2	11.2
Togo	..	11.8	11.9	14.6	15.7	10.8	21.3	14.1	3.1	3.0	..	8.0	12.6	10.4
Uganda	..	..	..	..	..	..	..	..	..	..	..	..	..	..
Zaire	7.7	5.2	8.7	5.5	2.1	1.3	1.7	1.2	2.8	..	..	8.4	5.1	1.9
Zambia	21.1	14.9	18.6	15.6	14.9	13.8	17.9	23.2	26.8	..	..	14.1	16.5	22.6
Zimbabwe	32.3	31.4	32.7	30.5	34.3	34.1	34.4	31.0	20.8	18.0	16.0	29.3	32.5	24.0
NORTH AFRICA	18.1	25.1	25.1	22.4	25.8	23.1	22.8	21.3	..	..	..	24.4	23.3	22.1
Algeria	..	..	..	..	..	..	..	..	..	..	..	..	..	..
Egypt, Arab Republic of	17.9	30.9	35.5	30.0	34.3	26.6	28.1	23.1	27.9	..	..	35.4	29.2	26.3
Libya	..	..	..	..	..	..	..	..	..	..	..	..	..	..
Morocco	14.6	14.4	14.2	14.1	15.0	15.1	12.0	11.6	..	..	..	12.7	14.6	11.8
Tunisia	21.7	30.0	25.5	23.2	28.1	27.7	28.3	29.2	31.7	35.0	..	25.0	26.0	31.1
ALL AFRICA	..	11.8	12.9	12.4	13.0	12.4	13.3	11.9	..	..	..	..	12.5	12.3
South Africa	26.8	28.2	29.3	29.7	29.5	29.9	25.1	25.2	24.4	22.8	..	28.9	28.9	24.4

7–19. Government expenditure: capital

	Percentage of total expenditure and lending minus repayments											Average		
	1980	1981	1982	1983	1984	1985	1986	1987	1988	1989	1990	75–79	80–85	86–MR
SUB-SAHARAN AFRICA	28.9	29.9	28.0	27.7	27.1	27.4	26.8	29.2	..	..	..	..	28.2	27.3
excluding Nigeria	28.1	29.1	27.3	27.6	26.9	27.0	26.5	29.1	..	..	..	..	27.7	27.2
Angola	..	..	..	..	..	..	..	..	..	..	..	..	..	..
Benin	51.5	57.0	46.8	39.8	34.8	24.5	25.4	24.1	..	..	..	29.8	42.4	24.8
Botswana	27.5	26.5	25.2	18.8	18.2	20.6	18.7	19.0	29.8	..	..	32.2	22.8	22.5
Burkina Faso	19.8	16.7	12.6	8.6	5.8	9.6	7.4	14.5	..	..	..	13.3	12.2	11.0
Burundi	..	45.3	48.9	58.0	56.5	51.1	48.8	54.1	44.8	..	..	..	51.9	49.2
Cameroon	32.8	41.3	42.4	31.7	34.8	40.6	36.3	36.0	36.0	36.8	..	31.0	37.3	36.3
Cape Verde	..	..	..	..	..	..	..	..	..	..	..	..	..	..
Central African Republic	..	6.0	6.9	9.0	6.8	7.3	7.1	..	..	..	..	..	7.2	7.1
Chad	..	..	..	41.2	37.0	50.6	65.6	71.7	..	..	..	21.1	42.9	68.6
Comoros	27.0	30.0	32.5	38.5	43.3	37.6	23.2	28.7	..	..	..	..	34.8	25.9
Congo, People's Republic of the	27.5	48.3	58.1	51.0	45.4	42.9	22.7	13.6	14.3	..	..	23.2	45.5	16.9
Cote d'Ivoire	25.8	41.5	35.8	32.1	20.8	18.9	..	..	15.0	..	..	..	29.2	15.0
Djibouti	26.0	23.0	21.7	20.8	11.3	10.5	10.6	30.8	4.1	..	..	22.8	18.9	15.2
Equatorial Guinea	..	..	..	..	..	..	..	..	..	..	..	..	..	..
Ethiopia	14.1	15.3	16.9	16.5	20.4	18.9	22.4	21.8	33.2	33.6	31.7	15.0	17.0	28.5
Gabon	44.9	48.0	50.1	51.9	48.6	52.2	44.8	26.6	22.4	17.6	..	..	49.3	27.8
Gambia, The	49.8	39.9	23.5	37.1	33.3	41.6	25.9	42.3	28.6	30.5	..	34.1	37.5	31.8
Ghana	10.3	17.4	9.6	8.9	12.3	15.2	13.4	20.0	19.9	18.7	..	23.0	12.3	18.0
Guinea	23.3	24.2	19.3	18.5	15.9	6.5	41.1	43.9	45.8	46.4	..	..	17.9	44.3
Guinea-Bissau	60.0	50.7	53.6	51.6	64.4	60.4	57.1	63.1	67.8	58.0	..	..	56.8	61.5
Kenya	21.6	21.6	14.5	14.5	11.9	15.8	12.0	17.8	14.3	..	..	20.3	16.6	14.7
Lesotho	37.5	36.3	27.5	26.8	33.6	19.0	29.0	35.7	34.3	32.2	..	37.4	30.1	32.8
Liberia	32.3	31.6	19.1	19.0	16.7	14.8	23.1	13.2	13.8	10.5	..	37.2	22.3	15.1
Madagascar	40.0	38.5	31.1	34.0	36.3	35.2	34.3	37.5	..	..	..	..	35.9	35.9
Malawi	42.1	32.7	28.2	29.6	32.6	29.8	27.7	20.5	24.2	26.8	..	37.8	32.5	24.8
Mali	45.3	46.9	56.7	59.3	58.5	54.3	50.3	50.1	57.0	..	..	12.4	53.5	52.5
Mauritania	12.4	27.6	32.8	37.4	40.3	29.4	25.2	24.6	23.6	..	..	10.5	30.0	24.5
Mauritius	14.7	14.3	12.1	8.9	8.8	13.9	12.8	18.3	18.1	17.5	17.7	19.5	12.1	16.9
Mozambique	..	..	..	..	..	..	..	..	..	..	..	..	..	..
Namibia	..	..	26.0	16.4	17.1	18.6	15.2	19.1	15.2	9.2	..	..	19.5	14.7
Niger	46.9	50.4	31.9	54.4	43.9	39.3	46.7	45.0	40.5	..	..	36.3	44.5	44.1
Nigeria	57.2	58.0	52.9	28.3	36.9	38.8	37.5	32.9	26.6	22.9	..	37.6	45.4	30.0
Rwanda	34.4	20.8	42.3	40.6	42.8	47.0	43.5	42.5	..	..	..	32.2	38.0	43.0
Sao Tome & Principe	..	..	..	..	..	..	..	..	..	..	..	..	..	..
Senegal	18.0	13.8	16.7	16.1	20.3	13.7	12.7	19.4	..	..	..	..	16.4	16.1
Seychelles	28.0	30.9	27.2	14.4	17.4	20.6	24.8	11.6	11.8	16.0	..	27.4	23.1	16.1
Sierra Leone	20.0	20.3	22.0	22.6	21.9	22.6	14.8	25.0	..	..	..	18.8	21.6	19.9
Somalia	5.2	7.7	6.5	31.6	27.7	43.8	43.7	52.9	48.5	..	..	16.5	20.4	48.4
Sudan	22.6	22.4	23.0	22.6	18.5	12.3	7.8	19.4	..	..	..	33.0	20.2	13.6
Swaziland	30.0	29.4	29.5	26.3	24.3	32.3	24.1	20.8	17.7	19.0	26.4	32.5	28.6	21.6
Tanzania	40.5	35.8	25.5	23.8	20.5	20.8	16.8	23.2	23.3	..	..	32.4	27.8	21.1
Togo	35.0	27.1	28.8	26.1	22.3	27.3	36.7	30.8	25.5	25.9	..	36.0	27.8	29.7
Uganda	12.4	16.5	16.7	13.6	11.6	15.3	26.7	46.1	44.2	34.7	..	19.3	14.4	37.9
Zaire	19.6	28.3	22.5	27.8	29.5	34.7	34.0	33.3	20.0	..	..	19.7	27.1	29.1
Zambia	9.1	10.6	12.2	12.2	12.0	24.1	24.6	38.3	22.9	45.5	..	13.8	13.4	32.8
Zimbabwe	5.1	4.9	8.0	7.6	6.6	7.3	6.8	7.2	8.8	9.6	9.3	7.2	6.6	8.3
NORTH AFRICA	22.6	26.9	26.3	21.1	20.2	20.0	20.6	20.9	..	..	..	29.7	22.8	20.8
Algeria	..	..	..	..	..	..	..	..	..	..	..	..	..	..
Egypt, Arab Republic of	9.9	17.0	16.9	11.6	11.8	11.8	12.2	15.1	14.4	13.7	..	17.4	13.2	13.8
Libya	..	..	..	..	..	..	..	..	..	..	..	..	..	..
Morocco	31.0	32.8	34.0	24.5	21.7	19.1	23.7	21.7	..	..	..	41.3	27.2	22.7
Tunisia	27.1	30.8	27.9	27.1	27.1	28.9	25.9	26.0	24.1	20.8	..	30.4	28.2	24.2
ALL AFRICA	28.4	29.7	27.9	27.2	26.6	26.8	26.3	28.6	..	..	..	..	27.8	26.7
South Africa	11.6	11.9	12.4	15.0	10.2	10.5	9.7	7.2	7.0	7.1	..	12.6	11.9	7.8

7–20. Government expenditure: defense

	Percentage of total expenditure and lending minus repayments											Average		
	1980	1981	1982	1983	1984	1985	1986	1987	1988	1989	1990	75–79	80–85	86–MR
SUB-SAHARAN AFRICA	11.9	11.4	9.6	9.5	10.0	8.5	9.6	7.9	..	..	..	..	10.1	9.0
excluding Nigeria	12.2	11.7	9.7	9.6	9.9	8.4	10.0	8.5	..	..	..	..	10.2	9.5
Angola	..	..	..	..	..	..	..	..	..	..	..	..	..	..
Benin	..	..	..	..	..	..	..	..	..	..	..	6.2	..	..
Botswana	8.5	7.8	5.8	6.2	6.0	5.8	7.4	..	..	..	..	5.9	6.7	7.4
Burkina Faso	17.7	17.3	17.8	20.7	17.7	18.7	22.1	17.3	..	..	..	20.4	18.3	19.7
Burundi	..	..	..	..	..	..	..	..	..	..	..	12.0	..	..
Cameroon	9.1	5.0	5.3	8.2	7.9	8.3	6.7	..	..	6.6	..	8.7	7.3	6.7
Cape Verde	..	..	..	..	..	..	..	..	..	..	..	..	..	..
Central African Republic	..	10.0	..	..	..	..	..	..	..	..	..	..	10.0	..
Chad	..	..	..	..	..	..	..	..	..	..	..	22.9	..	..
Comoros	..	..	..	..	3.1	..	..	4.3	..	..	..	..	3.1	4.3
Congo, People's Republic of the	..	..	..	..	..	..	..	..	..	..	..	12.5	..	..
Cote d'Ivoire	3.5	3.9	4.0	3.6	3.9	..	..	..	..	..	..	..	3.8	..
Djibouti	..	..	..	..	..	..	..	..	..	..	..	27.9	..	..
Equatorial Guinea	..	..	..	..	..	..	..	..	..	..	..	..	..	..
Ethiopia	..	..	..	..	..	..	..	..	..	..	..	..	..	..
Gabon	..	..	..	..	..	..	..	..	..	..	..	..	..	..
Gambia, The	..	..	..	..	..	..	..	..	..	..	..	..	..	..
Ghana	3.7	6.1	6.0	..	5.8	7.2	6.3	6.2	3.1	..	..	5.5	5.8	5.2
Guinea	..	..	..	..	..	..	..	..	..	..	..	..	..	..
Guinea-Bissau	..	..	..	16.1	6.9	4.7	6.6	4.1	..	4.0	..	..	9.2	4.9
Kenya	15.3	10.0	12.4	13.5	12.4	8.4	8.7	8.9	12.1	..	..	10.9	12.0	9.9
Lesotho	..	..	..	7.6	7.6	9.4	8.3	..	..	..	..	..	8.2	8.3
Liberia	5.2	10.3	12.7	7.5	7.0	8.8	7.1	8.3	..	..	..	3.7	8.6	7.7
Madagascar	..	..	..	..	..	..	..	..	..	..	..	8.8	7.5	6.1
Malawi	11.3	8.4	7.5	6.2	5.7	5.8	6.6	5.6	..	..	..	8.8	7.5	6.1
Mali	10.5	9.9	8.4	7.9	7.8	8.1	8.1	8.4	7.9	..	..	18.2	8.8	8.1
Mauritania	..	..	..	13.5	..	..	..	..	..	..	..	31.2	13.5	..
Mauritius	0.7	2.0	0.8	0.8	0.9	0.8	0.8	0.8	0.8	1.0	1.5	0.6	1.0	1.0
Mozambique	..	..	..	..	..	..	..	..	..	..	..	..	..	..
Namibia	..	..	..	..	..	..	..	..	..	..	..	..	..	..
Niger	3.6	2.6	3.2	3.3	3.8	3.8	3.6	3.9	..	..	..	4.4	3.4	3.8
Nigeria	8.5	8.8	8.6	8.7	11.3	9.4	5.4	2.7	3.9	..	..	16.4	9.2	4.0
Rwanda	12.9	10.6	10.5	10.5	9.4	8.6	8.8	..	..	..	..	13.5	10.4	8.8
Sao Tome & Principe	..	..	..	..	..	..	..	..	..	..	..	..	..	..
Senegal	16.7	11.6	9.8	9.6	8.6	10.8	10.6	..	..	..	..	..	11.2	10.6
Seychelles	..	..	..	..	..	..	..	..	..	..	..	..	..	..
Sierra Leone	3.4	4.7	5.2	4.0	4.2	4.8	2.6	1.9	..	..	..	3.5	4.4	2.3
Somalia	19.2	22.7	16.8	20.0	16.3	10.0	8.9	6.0	10.5	..	..	20.5	17.5	8.5
Sudan	12.9	11.7	8.4	8.9	12.0	12.0	10.0	10.7	..	..	..	11.7	..	..
Swaziland	7.7	5.5	5.7	6.0	5.6	5.2	5.4	5.0	5.3	5.5	4.7	5.3	5.9	5.2
Tanzania	9.2	11.9	12.5	13.9	13.1	14.1	..	..	..	..	..	15.4	12.4	..
Togo	7.4	7.1	7.0	6.8	6.2	6.9	7.6	11.1	11.2	11.1	..	9.3	6.9	10.3
Uganda	24.4	30.3	16.2	14.3	16.6	15.6	26.3	13.9	15.9	..	..	19.2	19.6	18.7
Zaire	8.5	3.9	7.9	0.0	12.3	7.4	12.2	..	14.0	..	..	10.8	6.7	13.1
Zambia	..	..	..	..	..	..	..	..	..	..	..	..	..	..
Zimbabwe	24.9	19.2	15.6	16.7	15.0	14.1	15.6	16.1	15.0	15.0	..	18.4	17.6	15.4
NORTH AFRICA	9.3	11.6	11.1	13.0	15.7	16.1	15.1	17.2	..	..	..	9.7	13.2	14.5
Algeria	..	..	..	..	..	..	..	..	12.9	..	..	7.6	12.8	15.1
Egypt, Arab Republic of	9.3	11.6	11.1	13.0	15.7	16.1	15.1	17.2	12.9	..	..	7.6	12.8	15.1
Libya	..	..	..	..	..	..	..	..	..	..	..	..	..	..
Morocco	17.8	16.3	16.6	14.5	14.8	16.3	14.4	15.2	..	..	..	15.5	16.1	14.8
Tunisia	11.1	7.8	10.0	11.3	7.5	6.7	5.7	5.6	..	..	..	6.1	9.1	5.6
ALL AFRICA	11.7	11.4	9.7	9.8	10.5	9.1	10.0	8.8	..	..	..	..	10.3	9.5
South Africa	..	..	13.4	12.6	12.1	11.5	12.5	12.6	..	..	..	..	12.4	12.5

7–21. Government expenditure: trends in real defense spending

	Index 1980=100											Average		
	1980	1981	1982	1983	1984	1985	1986	1987	1988	1989	1990	75–79	80–85	86–MR
SUB-SAHARAN AFRICA	..	..	..	..	..	..	..	..	..	..	..	..	..	..
excluding Nigeria	..	..	..	..	..	..	..	..	..	..	..	..	..	..
Angola	..	..	..	..	..	..	..	..	..	..	..	..	..	..
Benin	..	..	..	..	..	..	..	..	..	..	..	..	..	..
Botswana	100	99	88	98	122	119	167	..	..	..	..	56	104	167
Burkina Faso	100	109	117	115	114	113	182	152	..	..	..	101	111	167
Burundi	..	..	..	..	..	..	..	..	..	..	..	..	..	..
Cameroon	100	83	93	182	184	203	177	..	..	134	..	81	141	156
Cape Verde	..	..	..	..	..	..	..	..	..	..	..	..	..	..
Central African Republic	..	..	..	..	..	..	..	..	..	..	..	..	..	..
Chad	..	..	..	..	..	..	..	..	..	..	..	..	..	..
Comoros*	..	..	..	..	100	..	..	101	..	..	..	..	100	101
Congo, People's Republic of the	..	..	..	..	..	..	..	..	..	..	..	..	..	..
Cote d'Ivoire	100	128	138	122	103	..	..	..	..	..	..	..	118	..
Djibouti	..	..	..	..	..	..	..	..	..	..	..	..	..	..
Equatorial Guinea	..	..	..	..	..	..	..	..	..	..	..	..	..	..
Ethiopia	..	..	..	..	..	..	..	..	..	..	..	..	..	..
Gabon	..	..	..	..	..	..	..	..	..	..	..	..	..	..
Gambia, The	..	..	..	..	..	..	..	..	..	..	..	..	..	..
Ghana	100	160	151	..	137	241	228	236	122	..	..	257	158	195
Guinea	..	..	..	..	..	..	..	..	..	..	..	..	..	..
Guinea-Bissau*	..	..	..	100	54	41	37	34	..	44	..	..	65	39
Kenya	100	73	93	89	82	61	64	78	105	..	..	57	83	82
Lesotho*	..	..	..	100	118	133	151	..	..	..	..	..	117	151
Liberia	100	227	299	168	134	162	122	129	..	..	..	61	182	126
Madagascar	..	..	..	..	..	..	..	..	..	..	..	..	..	..
Malawi	100	65	49	41	38	47	56	44	..	..	..	53	57	50
Mali	100	103	114	112	110	130	133	128	131	..	..	101	112	131
Mauritania*	..	..	..	100	..	..	..	..	..	..	..	180	100	..
Mauritius	100	312	127	129	136	123	118	124	152	191	..	71	155	146
Mozambique	..	..	..	..	..	..	..	..	..	..	..	..	..	..
Namibia	..	..	..	..	..	..	..	..	..	..	..	..	..	..
Niger	100	90	85	90	89	99	103	104	..	..	..	81	92	103
Nigeria	100	115	91	87	73	62	50	35	48	..	..	173	88	44
Rwanda	100	121	121	125	99	103	123	..	..	..	..	72	111	123
Sao Tome & Principe	..	..	..	..	..	..	..	..	..	..	..	..	..	..
Senegal	100	77	79	78	73	71	68	..	..	..	..	..	80	68
Seychelles	..	..	..	..	..	..	..	..	..	..	..	..	..	..
Sierra Leone	100	105	111	117	93	87	59	70	..	..	..	103	102	65
Somalia	100	119	100	111	90	69	74	68	102	..	..	109	98	82
Sudan	100	119	72	77	109	121	89	87	..	..	..	94	100	88
Swaziland	100	92	96	96	89	91	90	75	82	104	..	79	94	88
Tanzania	100	123	149	135	120	119	..	..	..	..	..	167	124	..
Togo	100	101	94	85	92	109	129	159	157	160	..	184	97	151
Uganda	100	133	152	138	116	124	189	76	127	..	..	172	127	131
Zaire	100	55	110	..	215	132	161	..	218	..	..	134	123	189
Zambia	..	..	..	..	..	..	..	..	..	..	..	..	..	..
Zimbabwe	100	78	83	81	85	80	88	103	99	103	..	60	84	99
NORTH AFRICA	..	..	..	..	..	..	..	..	..	..	..	..	..	..
Algeria	..	..	..	..	..	..	..	..	..	..	..	..	..	..
Egypt, Arab Republic of	100	143	181	199	251	262	258	264	189	..	..	73	189	237
Libya	..	..	..	..	..	..	..	..	..	..	..	..	..	..
Morocco	100	105	112	84	82	99	90	89	..	..	..	82	97	89
Tunisia	100	74	110	135	94	83	74	67	..	..	..	48	99	70
ALL AFRICA	..	..	..	..	..	..	..	..	..	..	..	..	..	..
South Africa*	..	..	100	97	100	98	111	120	..	..	..	..	99	115

Note: Countries marked with an asterisk (*) are indexed using a year other than 1980, due to unavailable information on 1980.

7-22. Government expenditure: education

	Percentage of total expenditure and lending minus repayments											Average		
	1980	1981	1982	1983	1984	1985	1986	1987	1988	1989	1990	75–79	80–85	86–MR
SUB-SAHARAN AFRICA	13.9	13.7	14.4	14.7	13.3	12.9	12.6	12.3	..	..	..	..	13.9	12.5
excluding Nigeria	14.3	14.0	14.7	15.0	13.6	13.1	13.0	12.8	..	..	..	..	14.2	12.9
Angola	..	..	..	..	..	..	..	..	..	..	..	..	..	..
Benin	..	..	..	..	..	..	..	..	..	..	..	17.9	..	..
Botswana	19.2	19.0	16.1	17.2	15.2	16.1	17.2	14.0	16.6	..	..	18.3	17.1	15.9
Burkina Faso	16.1	14.8	16.3	19.6	16.3	18.4	17.1	13.6	..	..	..	15.6	16.9	15.3
Burundi	..	..	..	..	..	..	..	..	..	..	..	18.2	..	..
Cameroon	12.3	7.4	10.1	11.4	10.9	13.7	11.6	12.7	16.3	11.9	..	14.8	11.0	13.1
Cape Verde	..	..	..	..	..	..	..	..	..	..	..	..	..	..
Central African Republic	..	18.1	..	..	..	..	..	..	..	..	..	..	18.1	..
Chad	..	..	..	..	..	..	..	..	..	..	..	14.0	..	..
Comoros	..	..	..	..	19.4	..	..	25.1	..	..	..	..	19.4	25.1
Congo, People's Republic of the	..	..	..	..	..	..	..	..	..	..	..	17.5	..	..
Cote d'Ivoire	14.8	18.8	18.6	18.5	20.5	..	..	..	..	..	..	..	18.2	..
Djibouti	..	..	..	..	..	..	..	..	..	..	..	6.7	..	..
Equatorial Guinea	..	..	..	..	..	..	..	..	..	..	..	..	..	..
Ethiopia	9.3	9.9	10.3	8.0	10.8	10.9	10.2	10.6	..	..	..	11.5	9.9	10.4
Gabon	..	..	..	..	..	..	..	..	..	..	..	..	..	..
Gambia, The	12.7	14.2	16.4	16.9	12.3	8.9	8.1	4.6	5.0	6.8	..	9.2	13.6	6.1
Ghana	21.6	16.5	18.3	19.5	19.6	17.2	23.1	22.8	24.7	..	..	17.7	18.8	23.5
Guinea	..	..	..	..	..	..	..	..	..	..	..	..	..	..
Guinea-Bissau	..	..	..	11.9	10.8	9.5	7.4	4.8	..	2.5	..	..	10.7	4.9
Kenya	18.3	19.2	18.6	20.1	19.1	19.1	22.1	20.8	21.9	..	..	19.1	19.1	21.6
Lesotho	11.0	13.0	15.3	17.4	12.4	15.1	11.3	14.1	16.2	14.4	..	20.5	14.0	14.0
Liberia	10.7	14.6	14.4	14.3	13.6	15.1	13.1	15.2	..	..	..	12.7	13.8	14.1
Madagascar	14.7	12.8	14.8	17.1	15.7	15.7	16.1	13.5	..	..	..	..	15.1	14.8
Malawi	7.9	11.0	14.0	13.5	12.4	10.8	10.7	9.9	..	..	..	9.9	11.6	10.3
Mali	14.9	13.0	10.5	10.0	9.6	9.0	9.3	9.7	8.9	..	..	22.4	11.2	9.3
Mauritania	..	..	..	..	..	..	..	..	..	..	..	10.0	..	..
Mauritius	15.4	13.9	13.4	14.3	14.4	13.9	13.1	11.9	12.3	13.6	14.6	13.7	14.2	13.1
Mozambique	..	..	..	..	..	..	..	..	..	..	..	..	..	..
Namibia	..	..	..	..	..	..	..	..	..	..	..	..	..	..
Niger	17.3	8.4	12.1	13.7	13.5	12.2	11.7	12.0	..	..	..	16.1	12.8	11.9
Nigeria	5.2	7.8	7.9	7.4	8.0	8.0	4.8	2.7	2.0	..	..	9.8	7.4	3.2
Rwanda	18.6	19.3	17.5	16.6	17.5	15.1	15.8	..	..	..	..	17.8	17.4	15.8
Sao Tome & Principe	..	..	..	..	..	..	..	..	..	..	..	..	..	..
Senegal	22.8	22.0	17.1	17.4	14.7	17.0	16.9	..	..	..	..	13.2	18.5	16.9
Seychelles	..	..	..	..	..	..	..	..	..	..	..	13.2	..	..
Sierra Leone	10.2	14.3	15.8	13.9	15.7	12.9	9.0	4.1	..	..	..	12.4	13.8	6.6
Somalia	6.1	7.0	5.2	5.5	3.6	2.6	1.7	0.8	0.6	..	..	11.4	5.0	1.0
Sudan	9.6	8.0	5.3	..	..	..	..	..	..	..	..	5.9	..	..
Swaziland	22.4	19.0	16.4	19.3	20.7	19.4	21.1	23.5	23.0	21.2	19.6	16.1	19.5	21.7
Tanzania	13.4	12.8	12.5	13.8	12.0	7.4	..	..	..	..	..	13.4	12.0	..
Togo	15.4	16.6	22.9	19.7	14.8	11.7	13.1	19.9	12.1	11.7	..	8.1	16.8	14.2
Uganda	14.5	12.3	12.2	10.9	11.6	12.7	15.0	10.4	12.5	..	..	15.4	..	..
Zaire	18.9	20.2	16.3	..	1.9	2.5	1.5	5.9	6.1	..	..	15.9	12.0	4.5
Zambia	9.5	11.8	13.8	14.0	15.1	11.4	7.9	10.9	9.1	..	..	13.6	12.6	9.3
Zimbabwe	15.4	18.7	19.8	19.6	18.8	19.4	21.1	19.8	20.1	21.3	..	12.5	18.6	20.6
NORTH AFRICA	12.3	12.8	12.5	13.6	13.9	13.3	13.5	13.9	..	..	..	14.1	13.0	13.7
Algeria	..	..	..	..	..	..	..	..	..	..	..	..	..	..
Egypt, Arab Republic of	4.3	7.4	8.0	8.9	9.0	9.7	9.3	10.6	10.6	..	..	8.3	7.9	10.2
Libya	..	..	..	..	..	..	..	..	..	..	..	..	..	..
Morocco	17.2	16.6	16.3	18.5	19.1	16.5	16.9	17.0	..	..	..	14.8	17.4	17.0
Tunisia	15.5	14.4	13.1	13.4	13.5	13.7	14.2	14.2	..	..	..	19.4	13.9	14.2
ALL AFRICA	13.7	13.6	14.2	14.6	13.4	12.9	12.7	12.5	..	..	..	..	13.8	12.6
South Africa	..	..	16.7	16.7	16.8	17.6	..	17.6	..	..	..	..	16.9	17.6

7–23. Government spending: real per capita education spending

	Constant 1987 U.S. dollars											Average		
	1980	1981	1982	1983	1984	1985	1986	1987	1988	1989	1990	75–79	80–85	86–MR
SUB-SAHARAN AFRICA	..	..	..	..	..	..	..	..	..	..	..	..	..	..
excluding Nigeria	..	..	..	..	..	..	..	..	..	..	..	..	..	..
Angola	..	..	..	..	..	..	..	..	..	..	..	..	..	..
Benin	..	..	..	..	..	..	..	..	..	..	..	12.3	..	..
Botswana	60.1	64.9	64.4	67.3	70.9	68.6	78.8	76.4	95.3	..	..	33.7	66.0	83.5
Burkina Faso	5.0	4.9	5.5	5.5	5.2	5.3	6.0	4.6	..	..	..	5.0	5.2	5.3
Burundi	..	..	..	..	..	..	..	..	..	..	..	6.2	..	..
Cameroon	15.9	13.9	19.8	27.6	27.0	34.5	30.1	34.1	36.1	22.5	..	14.3	23.1	30.7
Cape Verde	..	..	..	..	..	..	..	..	..	..	..	..	..	..
Central African Republic	..	15.5	..	..	..	..	..	..	..	..	..	..	..	..
Chad	..	..	..	..	..	..	..	..	..	..	..	3.6	..	..
Comoros	..	..	..	..	49.5	..	..	41.2	..	..	..	..	49.5	41.2
Congo, People's Republic of the	..	..	..	..	..	..	..	..	..	..	..	49.2	..	..
Cote d'Ivoire	53.9	75.9	76.7	70.6	60.9	..	..	..	..	..	..	..	67.6	..
Djibouti	..	..	..	..	..	..	..	..	..	..	..	..	..	..
Equatorial Guinea	..	..	..	..	..	..	..	..	..	..	..	..	..	..
Ethiopia	2.9	3.2	3.6	3.7	3.9	3.9	3.9	4.3	..	..	..	2.6	3.5	4.1
Gabon	..	..	..	..	..	..	..	..	..	..	..	..	..	..
Gambia, The	8.3	10.1	12.8	10.9	8.1	5.3	4.1	4.0	4.4	4.3	..	4.9	9.3	4.2
Ghana	10.3	7.4	7.6	5.5	7.1	8.6	11.9	12.0	13.1	..	..	10.2	7.7	12.3
Guinea	..	..	..	..	..	..	..	..	..	..	..	..	..	..
Guinea-Bissau	..	..	..	9.7	11.0	10.3	5.1	4.8	..	3.1	..	..	10.3	4.3
Kenya	17.7	19.9	19.2	17.7	16.1	16.9	19.0	21.0	21.1	..	..	13.1	17.9	20.4
Lesotho	26.4	30.7	32.9	39.0	31.5	32.2	29.2	36.9	41.0	29.2	..	23.8	32.1	34.1
Liberia	19.8	29.8	29.1	26.0	19.8	21.9	16.9	17.1	..	..	..	20.6	24.4	17.0
Madagascar	11.3	8.3	7.3	7.2	6.8	6.3	6.1	5.6	..	..	..	..	7.9	5.8
Malawi	4.9	5.8	6.0	5.8	5.2	5.3	5.4	4.5	..	..	..	3.9	5.5	5.0
Mali	7.4	6.8	7.0	6.9	6.4	6.7	6.8	6.5	6.0	..	..	..	6.9	6.4
Mauritania	..	..	..	..	..	..	..	..	..	..	..	17.7	..	..
Mauritius	59.6	57.8	54.4	57.5	52.8	52.0	49.0	46.2	52.8	60.8	70.0	44.3	55.7	55.8
Mozambique	..	..	..	..	..	..	..	..	..	..	..	..	..	..
Namibia	..	..	..	..	..	..	..	..	..	..	..	..	..	..
Niger	14.6	8.5	8.8	9.8	7.9	7.5	7.7	7.4	..	..	..	8.0	9.5	7.6
Nigeria	3.4	5.6	4.5	3.9	2.5	2.5	2.1	1.6	1.1	..	..	5.8	3.7	1.6
Rwanda	9.3	14.0	12.2	11.5	10.4	9.7	11.7	..	..	..	..	5.9	11.2	11.7
Sao Tome & Principe	..	..	..	..	..	..	..	..	..	..	..	..	..	..
Senegal	34.2	34.9	32.0	31.6	26.8	2.3	22.2	..	..	..	..	..	27.0	22.2
Seychelles	..	..	..	..	..	..	..	..	..	..	..	56.5	..	..
Sierra Leone	4.7	6.6	5.7	5.0	4.2	2.7	2.4	1.7	..	..	..	4.4	4.8	2.0
Somalia	1.9	2.1	1.8	1.7	1.0	0.9	0.7	0.4	0.3	..	..	2.5	1.6	0.4
Sudan	14.7	15.4	8.3	..	..	..	..	..	..	..	..	8.4	..	..
Swaziland	53.6	58.5	49.5	54.9	59.4	59.1	55.8	51.7	53.0	57.1	..	36.9	55.8	54.4
Tanzania	6.3	5.6	6.0	5.3	4.2	2.3	..	..	..	..	..	5.6	4.9	..
Togo	23.0	23.3	29.1	22.4	19.3	15.7	18.6	22.9	13.2	12.7	..	16.5	22.1	16.9
Uganda	2.1	1.4	3.1	3.0	3.5	3.0	2.9	1.4	2.5	..	..	3.8	..	..
Zaire	5.5	6.6	4.9	0.0	0.7	0.8	0.6	2.7	2.4	..	..	4.8	3.1	1.9
Zambia	13.6	15.2	18.9	13.8	12.9	11.4	8.6	9.2	7.3	..	..	17.1	14.3	8.4
Zimbabwe	32.8	38.4	50.5	44.1	47.9	46.9	49.2	51.3	48.7	57.1	..	20.8	43.4	51.6
NORTH AFRICA	..	..	..	..	..	..	..	..	..	..	..	..	..	..
Algeria	..	..	..	..	..	..	..	..	..	..	..	..	..	..
Egypt, Arab Republic of	11.2	21.4	30.6	30.9	31.8	33.1	32.2	31.6	32.8	..	..	16.8	26.5	32.2
Libya	..	..	..	..	..	..	..	..	..	..	..	..	..	..
Morocco	42.3	44.7	45.5	43.0	41.4	38.5	39.7	36.5	..	..	..	31.9	42.6	38.1
Tunisia	61.3	57.8	59.2	65.0	66.7	64.6	68.2	61.9	..	..	..	58.1	62.4	65.0
ALL AFRICA	..	..	..	..	..	..	..	..	..	..	..	..	..	..
South Africa	..	..	1197.6	1498.5	1845.5	2441.9	..	..	..	..	..	..	1745.9	..

7-24. Government expenditure: health

	Percentage of total expenditure and lending minus repayments											Average		
	1980	1981	1982	1983	1984	1985	1986	1987	1988	1989	1990	75–79	80–85	86–MR
SUB-SAHARAN AFRICA	4.7	4.8	5.0	5.2	5.0	4.9	4.7	4.8	..	..	..	..	4.9	4.7
excluding Nigeria	4.8	5.0	5.1	5.3	5.1	5.0	4.8	5.0	..	..	..	..	4.9	4.7
Angola	..	..	..	..	..	..	..	..	..	..	..	..	..	..
Benin	..	..	..	..	..	..	..	..	..	..	..	5.7	..	..
Botswana	4.7	5.4	4.5	5.0	4.2	4.5	5.5	4.1	5.5	..	..	5.5	4.7	5.0
Burkina Faso	6.1	5.5	6.8	6.8	5.4	6.0	5.0	5.1	..	..	..	5.5	6.1	5.1
Burundi	..	..	..	..	..	..	..	..	..	..	..	5.9	..	..
Cameroon	5.1	2.7	3.6	3.2	4.2	4.9	3.3	3.4	3.5	3.3	..	4.6	3.9	3.4
Cape Verde	..	..	..	..	..	..	..	..	..	..	..	..	..	..
Central African Republic	..	5.2	..	..	..	..	..	..	..	..	..	..	5.2	..
Chad	..	..	..	..	..	..	..	..	..	..	..	4.0	..	..
Comoros	..	..	..	..	5.6	..	..	7.2	..	..	..	..	5.6	7.2
Congo, People's Republic of the	..	..	..	..	..	..	..	..	..	..	..	5.3	..	..
Cote d'Ivoire	3.6	3.2	3.1	3.0	4.0	..	..	..	..	..	..	..	3.4	..
Djibouti	..	..	..	..	..	..	..	..	..	..	..	5.8	..	..
Equatorial Guinea	..	..	..	..	..	..	..	..	..	..	..	..	..	..
Ethiopia	3.5	3.7	3.4	2.7	3.4	3.4	3.3	3.6	..	..	..	4.3	3.3	3.4
Gabon	..	..	..	..	..	..	..	..	..	..	..	..	..	..
Gambia, The	7.6	7.0	7.5	8.0	7.0	5.8	..	..	..	..	..	7.4	7.2	..
Ghana	6.8	6.2	5.7	7.2	8.3	9.4	8.0	7.9	8.6	..	..	7.0	7.3	8.2
Guinea	..	..	..	..	..	..	..	..	..	..	..	..	..	..
Guinea-Bissau	..	..	..	7.9	9.6	4.8	6.8	5.0	..	1.4	..	..	7.5	4.4
Kenya	7.3	7.3	6.9	6.8	6.5	6.2	6.3	5.9	5.8	..	..	7.0	6.8	6.0
Lesotho	3.6	4.8	6.2	7.2	5.4	6.7	5.8	..	..	..	..	5.3	5.6	5.8
Liberia	4.7	7.0	6.7	6.7	5.8	5.1	5.3	6.6	..	..	..	7.2	6.0	5.9
Madagascar	4.8	2.9	3.8	4.7	4.7	5.1	5.0	5.1	..	..	..	..	4.3	5.1
Malawi	4.9	5.1	5.1	6.8	8.0	6.7	7.0	5.8	..	..	..	5.3	6.1	6.4
Mali	3.0	4.6	2.8	2.5	1.8	1.7	2.4	2.6	2.0	..	..	5.9	2.7	2.4
Mauritania	..	..	..	..	..	..	..	..	..	..	..	2.9	..	..
Mauritius	6.5	6.1	6.4	7.2	7.8	7.5	7.4	7.3	7.3	8.6	8.4	7.5	6.9	7.8
Mozambique	..	..	..	..	..	..	..	..	..	..	..	..	..	..
Namibia	..	..	..	..	..	..	..	..	..	..	..	..	..	..
Niger	3.9	2.4	2.7	3.4	4.1	3.4	3.6	4.1	..	..	..	4.5	3.3	3.9
Nigeria	1.8	2.0	2.6	2.3	1.4	2.0	2.2	0.8	1.7	..	..	1.9	2.0	1.6
Rwanda	4.5	3.2	3.3	3.2	3.2	3.2	3.4	..	..	..	..	5.4	3.4	3.4
Sao Tome & Principe	..	..	..	..	..	..	..	..	..	..	..	..	..	..
Senegal	4.7	4.5	3.9	4.7	4.0	3.2	3.3	..	..	..	..	..	4.1	3.3
Seychelles	..	..	..	..	..	..	..	..	..	..	..	10.0	..	..
Sierra Leone	4.8	6.9	6.9	5.8	7.2	4.9	3.8	1.7	..	..	..	4.5	6.1	2.8
Somalia	2.4	2.6	1.9	1.9	1.3	1.0	0.7	0.4	0.3	..	..	4.9	1.9	0.5
Sudan	1.4	1.4	1.2	..	..	..	..	..	..	..	..	1.6	..	..
Swaziland	6.5	4.9	6.5	6.8	6.3	7.2	8.0	8.9	8.2	8.0	7.8	5.2	6.4	8.2
Tanzania	6.0	5.8	5.4	5.3	5.6	5.1	..	..	..	..	..	6.8	5.5	..
Togo	5.6	5.2	6.1	5.7	5.4	3.6	3.8	5.2	4.0	4.2	..	3.9	5.3	4.3
Uganda	4.9	5.7	4.2	3.8	2.5	3.5	2.4	4.1	2.9	..	..	6.2	..	..
Zaire	2.5	2.6	3.2	..	2.9	3.6	3.4	4.7	4.3	..	..	3.1	3.0	4.1
Zambia	5.1	6.0	7.7	6.4	6.8	5.4	4.3	6.4	7.8	..	..	6.0	6.2	6.2
Zimbabwe	5.4	6.7	5.8	5.6	5.7	6.0	6.3	6.4	6.9	6.9	..	5.8	5.9	6.7
NORTH AFRICA	3.7	4.1	3.7	3.7	3.8	3.6	3.4	3.7	..	..	..	4.1	3.8	3.5
Algeria	..	..	..	..	..	..	..	..	..	..	..	..	..	..
Egypt, Arab Republic of	1.1	1.9	2.1	2.4	2.2	2.2	2.0	2.2	2.2	..	..	2.6	2.0	2.1
Libya	..	..	..	..	..	..	..	..	..	..	..	..	..	..
Morocco	3.4	3.0	2.9	2.9	3.1	2.8	2.9	3.0	..	..	..	3.3	3.0	3.0
Tunisia	6.5	7.2	6.2	5.8	6.2	5.8	5.4	5.8	..	..	..	6.4	6.3	5.6
ALL AFRICA	4.6	4.7	4.8	5.0	4.8	4.7	4.5	4.6	..	..	..	..	5.1	4.6
South Africa	..	..	9.2	9.7	9.4	9.0	9.6	9.4	..	..	..	..	9.3	9.5

7-25. Government expenditure: real per capita health spending

	Constant 1987 U.S. dollars											Average		
	1980	1981	1982	1983	1984	1985	1986	1987	1988	1989	1990	75–79	80–85	86–MR
SUB-SAHARAN AFRICA	..	..	..	..	..	..	..	..	..	..	..	..	..	..
excluding Nigeria	..	..	..	..	..	..	..	..	..	..	..	..	..	..
Angola	..	..	..	..	..	..	..	..	..	..	..	..	..	..
Benin	..	..	..	..	..	..	..	..	..	..	..	3.9	..	..
Botswana	14.6	18.2	18.0	19.5	19.4	19.3	25.2	22.2	31.2	..	..	10.0	18.2	26.2
Burkina Faso	1.9	1.8	2.3	1.9	1.7	1.7	1.8	1.7	..	..	..	1.7	1.9	1.7
Burundi	..	..	..	..	..	..	..	..	..	..	..	2.0	..	..
Cameroon	6.6	5.1	7.1	7.8	10.5	12.3	8.6	9.2	7.8	6.3	..	4.4	8.2	8.0
Cape Verde	..	..	..	..	..	..	..	..	..	..	..	..	..	..
Central African Republic	..	4.5	..	..	..	..	..	..	..	..	..	..	..	..
Chad	..	..	..	..	..	..	..	..	..	..	..	1.0	..	..
Comoros	..	..	..	..	14.2	..	..	11.9	..	..	..	..	14.2	11.9
Congo, People's Republic of the	..	..	..	..	..	..	..	..	..	..	..	14.6	..	..
Cote d'Ivoire	13.0	12.9	12.8	11.5	11.8	..	..	..	..	..	..	..	12.4	..
Djibouti	..	..	..	..	..	..	..	..	..	..	..	..	..	..
Equatorial Guinea	..	..	..	..	..	..	..	..	..	..	..	..	..	..
Ethiopia	1.1	1.2	1.2	1.3	1.2	1.2	1.2	1.4	..	..	..	1.0	1.2	1.3
Gabon	..	..	..	..	..	..	..	..	..	..	..	..	..	..
Gambia, The	5.0	5.0	5.9	5.2	4.6	3.4	4.1	4.0	4.4	4.3	..	4.0	4.8	4.2
Ghana	3.3	2.8	2.3	2.0	3.0	4.7	4.1	4.1	4.5	..	..	4.0	3.0	4.3
Guinea	..	..	..	..	..	..	..	..	..	..	..	..	..	..
Guinea-Bissau	..	..	..	6.5	9.7	5.2	4.7	5.0	..	1.7	..	..	7.2	3.8
Kenya	7.1	7.6	7.1	6.0	5.5	5.5	5.4	5.9	5.6	..	..	4.9	6.4	5.7
Lesotho	8.6	11.4	13.2	16.1	13.7	14.3	15.0	36.9	41.0	29.2	..	6.3	12.9	30.5
Liberia	8.6	14.2	13.7	12.3	8.4	7.4	6.8	7.5	..	..	..	11.6	10.8	7.1
Madagascar	3.7	1.9	1.8	2.0	2.0	2.1	1.9	2.1	..	..	..	..	2.2	2.0
Malawi	3.0	2.7	2.2	2.9	3.4	3.3	3.6	2.7	..	..	..	2.1	2.9	3.1
Mali	1.5	2.4	1.9	1.7	1.2	1.2	1.8	1.7	1.4	..	..	..	1.7	1.6
Mauritania	..	..	..	..	..	..	..	..	..	..	..	5.1	..	..
Mauritius	25.3	25.5	26.3	28.9	28.7	28.0	27.5	28.3	31.5	38.3	40.6	23.8	27.1	33.2
Mozambique	..	..	..	..	..	..	..	..	..	..	..	..	..	..
Namibia	..	..	..	..	..	..	..	..	..	..	..	..	..	..
Niger	3.3	2.5	2.0	2.5	2.4	2.1	2.4	2.5	..	..	..	2.2	2.5	2.5
Nigeria	1.1	1.5	1.5	1.2	0.4	0.6	1.0	0.4	0.9	..	..	1.1	1.1	0.8
Rwanda	2.3	2.3	2.3	2.2	1.9	2.1	2.5	..	..	..	..	1.8	2.2	2.5
Sao Tome & Principe	..	..	..	..	..	..	..	..	..	..	..	..	..	..
Senegal	7.0	7.1	7.3	8.5	7.2	0.4	4.4	..	..	..	..	..	6.3	4.4
Seychelles	..	..	..	..	..	..	..	..	..	..	..	71.6	..	..
Sierra Leone	2.2	3.2	2.5	2.1	1.9	1.0	1.0	0.7	..	..	..	1.6	2.2	0.9
Somalia	0.8	0.8	0.6	0.6	0.4	0.3	0.3	0.2	0.1	..	..	1.1	0.6	0.2
Sudan	2.1	2.7	1.8	..	..	..	..	..	..	..	..	2.3	..	..
Swaziland	15.6	14.9	19.7	19.5	17.9	21.9	21.1	19.6	19.0	21.6	..	11.9	18.2	20.3
Tanzania	2.8	2.5	2.6	2.0	2.0	1.6	..	..	..	..	..	2.8	2.2	..
Togo	8.4	7.4	7.7	6.5	7.1	4.9	5.3	6.0	4.4	4.6	..	7.9	7.0	5.1
Uganda	0.7	0.6	1.1	1.1	0.8	0.8	0.5	0.5	0.6	..	..	1.5	..	..
Zaire	0.7	0.9	1.0	0.0	1.0	1.2	1.3	2.2	1.7	..	..	1.0	0.8	1.7
Zambia	7.2	7.7	10.4	6.3	5.8	5.4	4.7	5.4	6.3	..	..	7.5	7.2	5.5
Zimbabwe	11.4	13.6	14.8	12.6	14.5	14.5	14.8	16.6	16.7	18.6	..	9.6	13.6	16.7
NORTH AFRICA	..	..	..	..	..	..	..	..	..	..	..	..	..	..
Algeria	..	..	..	..	..	..	..	..	..	..	..	..	..	..
Egypt, Arab Republic of	2.9	5.6	8.0	8.2	7.9	7.6	6.9	6.5	6.8	..	..	5.3	6.7	6.7
Libya	..	..	..	..	..	..	..	..	..	..	..	..	..	..
Morocco	8.3	8.2	8.0	6.8	6.7	6.4	6.7	6.5	..	..	..	7.0	7.4	6.6
Tunisia	25.9	28.9	28.1	28.1	30.5	27.3	26.1	25.1	..	..	..	19.1	28.1	25.6
ALL AFRICA	..	..	..	..	..	..	..	..	..	..	..	..	..	..
South Africa	..	..	663.1	867.5	1039.3	1254.5	..	..	..	..	..	..	956.1	..

7–26. Government expenditure: economic services

	Percentage of total expenditure and lending minus repayments											Average		
	1980	1981	1982	1983	1984	1985	1986	1987	1988	1989	1990	75–79	80–85	86–MR
SUB-SAHARAN AFRICA	22.8	20.3	20.3	21.1	19.8	20.2	22.2	22.3	..	..	..	..	21.2	21.3
excluding Nigeria	21.1	18.7	18.6	19.7	19.3	19.8	21.2	21.6	..	..	..	..	20.0	20.8
Angola	..	..	..	..	..	..	..	..	..	..	..	..	..	..
Benin	..	..	..	..	..	..	..	..	..	..	..	17.6	..	..
Botswana	23.3	24.2	29.7	24.2	26.1	27.0	26.6	19.1	17.1	..	..	28.5	25.8	20.9
Burkina Faso	20.1	19.2	17.0	14.6	11.5	6.5	6.4	6.8	..	..	..	23.3	14.8	6.6
Burundi	..	..	..	..	..	..	..	..	..	..	..	33.5	..	..
Cameroon	23.8	10.0	9.1	25.5	31.9	32.2	33.6	34.6	14.8	47.8	..	25.2	22.1	32.7
Cape Verde	..	..	..	..	..	..	..	..	..	..	..	..	..	..
Central African Republic	..	20.1	..	..	..	..	..	..	..	..	..	..	20.1	..
Chad	..	..	..	..	..	..	..	..	..	..	..	29.8	..	..
Comoros	..	..	..	..	55.1	..	..	43.5	..	..	..	..	55.1	43.5
Congo, People's Republic of the	..	..	..	..	..	..	..	..	..	..	..	..	..	..
Cote d'Ivoire	12.2	10.6	10.1	10.0	31.4	..	..	..	..	..	..	..	14.8	..
Djibouti	..	..	..	..	..	..	..	..	..	..	..	14.5		
Equatorial Guinea	..	..	..	..	..	..	..	..	..	..	..	..	..	..
Ethiopia	22.1	22.8	23.0	20.4	23.7	24.7	30.3	30.2	..	..	..	21.7	22.8	30.2
Gabon	..	..	..	..	..	..	..	..	..	..	..	..	..	..
Gambia, The	46.3	41.4	23.6	36.6	38.5	40.0	..	..	..	..	..	35.8	37.7	..
Ghana	20.3	22.0	18.9	22.7	18.4	22.7	15.1	15.0	18.4	..	..	20.4	20.8	16.2
Guinea	..	..	..	..	..	..	..	..	..	..	..	..	..	..
Guinea-Bissau	..	..	..	16.0	46.3	50.5	37.7	37.2	..	..	..	..	37.6	37.5
Kenya	25.1	28.1	25.2	24.0	21.5	25.5	21.3	20.4	17.7	..	..	26.7	24.9	19.8
Lesotho	..	..	36.0	29.4	34.5	23.6	22.0	..	..	..	..	28.7	30.8	22.0
Liberia	33.7	28.4	23.9	26.5	24.9	29.2	31.8	25.8	..	..	..	31.0	27.7	28.8
Madagascar	5.8	4.7	5.2	29.7	33.6	28.6	29.6	32.7	..	..	..	..	17.9	31.2
Malawi	38.4	38.0	32.9	35.5	35.4	29.8	33.4	26.7	..	..	..	38.0	35.0	30.0
Mali	10.6	4.6	8.1	7.0	6.8	8.9	17.0	18.4	5.2	..	..	12.4	7.7	13.6
Mauritania	..	..	..	21.6	..	..	..	..	..	..	..	12.0	..	..
Mauritius	10.2	11.6	8.9	9.9	11.7	13.5	12.5	22.3	23.0	14.8	15.8	15.7	11.0	17.7
Mozambique	..	..	..	..	..	..	..	..	..	..	..	..	..	..
Namibia	..	..	..	..	..	..	..	..	..	..	..	..	..	..
Niger	31.2	4.6	5.9	8.3	6.9	8.5	6.2	4.9	..	..	..	34.1	10.9	5.5
Nigeria	55.0	51.8	52.8	48.8	29.8	28.9	41.4	34.6	17.4	..	..	26.4	44.5	31.1
Rwanda	40.9	17.3	19.9	17.7	17.2	13.7	13.4	..	..	..	..	37.1	21.1	13.4
Sao Tome & Principe	..	..	..	..	..	..	..	..	..	..	..	..	..	..
Senegal	14.2	11.7	14.7	19.0	21.2	..	..	..	..	..	..	..	16.2	..
Seychelles	..	..	..	..	..	..	..	..	..	..	..	27.3	..	..
Sierra Leone	16.1	25.6	32.7	30.3	18.9	9.8	17.6	26.7	..	..	..	23.6	22.2	22.2
Somalia	11.2	11.9	10.1	12.3	8.3	5.4	6.9	4.4	..	..	..	21.5	9.9	5.6
Sudan	19.4	21.7	20.7	..	..	..	..	..	..	..	..	39.6	..	..
Swaziland	27.3	22.7	27.6	32.2	27.6	31.5	27.2	24.5	21.3	20.3	18.2	28.4	28.1	22.3
Tanzania	43.0	38.8	29.8	28.3	26.7	24.5	..	..	..	..	..	37.7	31.9	..
Togo	34.6	25.0	22.2	18.3	19.8	23.5	31.8	31.1	39.5	3.8	..	26.8	23.9	26.6
Uganda	10.8	14.0	11.8	8.0	8.5	10.6	14.8	29.1	24.0	..	..	15.9	..	..
Zaire	13.2	16.1	16.8	10.8	12.1	16.9	16.3	27.2	25.9	..	..	16.6	14.3	23.1
Zambia	27.2	21.9	21.8	14.3	15.2	16.2	21.9	10.4	26.1	..	..	21.3	19.4	19.4
Zimbabwe	18.0	18.8	21.9	19.0	24.0	24.8	24.2	22.6	21.2	20.3	..	22.7	21.1	22.1
NORTH AFRICA	18.8	22.0	22.2	20.5	21.4	22.4	20.6	18.5	..	..	..	22.6	21.2	19.5
Algeria	..	..	..	..	..	..	..	..	..	..	..	..	..	..
Egypt, Arab Republic of	3.5	6.0	5.8	7.1	7.3	7.3	8.0	8.1	8.7	..	..	17.8	6.2	8.3
Libya	..	..	..	..	..	..	..	..	..	..	..	..	..	..
Morocco	27.6	28.1	30.7	28.7	25.7	25.7	26.2	21.4	..	..	..	23.9	27.7	23.8
Tunisia	25.2	31.9	30.2	25.6	31.1	34.2	27.4	26.0	..	..	..	26.2	29.7	26.7
ALL AFRICA	22.3	20.5	20.5	21.0	20.0	20.5	22.0	21.8	..	..	..	..	21.2	21.1
South Africa	..	..	..	..	..	..	..	..	..	..	..	..	..	..

7-27. Government expenditure: agriculture

	Percentage of total expenditure and lending minus repayments											Average		
	1980	1981	1982	1983	1984	1985	1986	1987	1988	1989	1990	75-79	80-85	86-MR
SUB-SAHARAN AFRICA	7.1	6.2	6.7	6.1	6.6	6.4	8.0	7.4	..	..	..	..	6.7	7.5
excluding Nigeria	7.3	6.4	6.8	6.2	6.6	6.5	7.8	7.4	..	..	..	..	6.8	7.5
Angola	..	..	..	..	..	..	..	..	..	..	..	..	..	..
Benin	..	..	..	..	..	..	..	..	..	..	..	7.9	..	..
Botswana	8.4	7.8	7.9	7.0	8.1	8.9	10.5	9.6	9.7	..	..	8.5	8.0	9.9
Burkina Faso	5.7	4.9	4.7	5.0	4.2	4.8	4.3	4.9	..	..	..	4.0	4.9	4.6
Burundi	..	..	..	..	..	..	..	..	..	..	..	12.5	..	..
Cameroon	2.2	1.3	1.2	7.1	6.4	7.6	7.0	7.2	4.1	3.2	..	5.5	4.3	5.4
Cape Verde	..	..	..	..	..	..	..	..	..	..	..	..	..	..
Central African Republic	..	10.8	..	..	..	..	..	..	..	..	..	..	..	..
Chad	..	..	..	..	..	..	..	..	..	..	..	24.3	..	..
Comoros	..	..	..	..	9.3	..	..	..	..	..	..	..	9.3	..
Congo, People's Republic of the	..	..	..	..	..	..	..	..	..	..	..	3.0	..	..
Cote d'Ivoire	3.1	..	..	..	..	..	..	..	..	..	..	..	3.1	..
Djibouti	..	..	..	..	..	..	..	..	..	..	..	1.1	..	..
Equatorial Guinea	..	..	..	..	..	..	..	..	..	..	..	..	..	..
Ethiopia	6.4	5.6	6.5	6.2	7.4	9.3	13.1	10.8	..	..	..	8.4	6.9	12.0
Gabon	..	..	..	..	..	..	..	..	..	..	..	..	..	..
Gambia, The	17.7	13.4	10.4	15.5	14.7	9.8	..	..	..	..	..	14.4	13.6	..
Ghana	12.0	11.8	10.5	9.3	4.8	5.9	4.4	4.3	3.3	..	..	8.7	9.1	4.0
Guinea	..	..	..	..	..	..	..	..	..	..	..	..	..	..
Guinea-Bissau	..	..	..	..	..	..	19.8	18.7	..	..	..	..	..	19.3
Kenya	7.7	10.4	8.4	9.9	7.4	10.1	9.5	11.2	7.1	..	..	8.1	9.0	9.2
Lesotho	..	..	10.4	8.3	6.4	7.8	7.5	..	..	..	..	12.5	8.2	7.5
Liberia	4.5	4.6	6.9	5.3	5.2	5.6	7.1	8.4	..	..	..	6.7	5.4	7.7
Madagascar	2.3	1.9	2.3	6.8	15.3	11.9	11.5	11.3	..	..	..	..	6.8	11.4
Malawi	8.9	13.5	14.8	16.2	12.0	8.2	13.1	11.3	..	..	..	12.4	12.3	12.2
Mali	8.0	4.0	5.4	4.2	0.0	4.8	8.3	4.7	1.9	..	..	8.5	4.4	5.0
Mauritania	..	..	..	..	..	..	..	..	..	..	..	6.5	..	..
Mauritius	6.0	5.8	5.9	6.4	6.6	7.1	5.5	8.2	8.0	7.8	7.2	7.6	6.3	7.3
Mozambique	..	..	..	..	..	..	..	..	..	..	..	..	..	..
Namibia	..	..	..	..	..	..	..	..	..	..	..	..	..	..
Niger	6.5	1.9	2.5	2.8	2.7	2.2	2.0	1.8	..	..	..	7.3	3.1	1.9
Nigeria	3.3	3.0	4.4	4.1	7.2	4.6	12.5	7.9	3.0	..	..	1.6	4.4	7.8
Rwanda	12.4	4.5	5.0	4.7	4.4	3.6	4.2	..	..	..	..	8.6	5.8	4.2
Sao Tome & Principe	..	..	..	..	..	..	..	..	..	..	..	..	..	..
Senegal	4.3	5.0	7.9	7.4	7.3	..	..	..	..	..	..	..	6.4	..
Seychelles	..	..	..	..	..	..	..	..	..	..	..	6.6	..	..
Sierra Leone	..	..	..	9.5	5.8	2.1	7.0	6.4	..	..	..	5.9	5.8	6.7
Somalia	2.5	2.9	2.8	4.4	2.7	1.3	1.9	1.0	..	..	..	10.4	2.7	1.4
Sudan	9.2	..	7.5	..	..	..	..	..	..	..	..	12.2	..	..
Swaziland	11.8	9.6	11.2	9.0	7.4	6.0	6.0	6.4	6.9	7.2	7.2	9.1	9.2	6.8
Tanzania	10.9	10.7	7.0	6.7	7.6	6.3	..	..	..	..	..	11.6	8.2	..
Togo	..	5.0	7.5	6.0	9.1	8.1	15.0	14.5	19.3	1.9	..	5.3	7.2	12.7
Uganda	6.8	10.1	5.7	3.8	3.1	4.3	4.7	..	..	..	..	10.3	..	..
Zaire	1.1	1.9	3.0	0.0	3.2	4.6	2.8	4.1	3.9	..	..	1.0	2.3	3.6
Zambia	19.2	12.5	15.0	11.0	12.8	10.0	15.1	5.2	20.4	..	..	9.0	13.4	13.6
Zimbabwe	7.0	7.9	9.4	5.5	10.1	10.2	11.1	9.4	10.1	10.1	..	8.4	8.3	10.1
NORTH AFRICA	7.3	9.0	8.1	7.5	8.8	5.5	5.7	5.3	..	..	..	5.9	7.7	5.5
Algeria	..	..	..	..	..	..	..	..	..	..	..	..	..	..
Egypt, Arab Republic of	2.3	3.9	3.2	3.9	3.7	3.6	3.5	3.7	3.9	..	..	4.1	3.5	3.7
Libya	..	..	..	..	..	..	..	..	..	..	..	..	..	..
Morocco	6.4	7.0	5.6	5.4	5.6	5.0	6.2	5.5	..	..	..	3.9	5.8	5.8
Tunisia	13.2	16.0	15.4	13.2	17.0	7.9	7.4	6.7	..	..	..	9.6	13.8	7.1
ALL AFRICA	7.2	6.6	6.9	6.3	6.9	6.3	7.7	7.2	..	..	..	..	6.7	7.2
South Africa	..	..	0.8	7.2	6.6	7.0	4.3	4.3	..	..	..	..	5.4	4.3

Technical Notes

Definitions have been taken, where possible, from IMF, *A Manual on Government Finance Statistics* (1986). Data are presented for 46 countries, 3 of which are in North Africa. Of the 43 countries of Sub-Saharan Africa, 41 have been included in the *GFS*, and, except for Namibia, South Africa, and Cape Verde, *GFS* data are reported here whenever possible. *GFS* data are usually supplemented with data from IMF, World Bank, or staff reports, or from other national government sources. Although Namibia and South Africa are included in the *GFS*, central bank data were used instead. These data were very similar to the *GFS* data, but coverage was greater, internal consistency was higher, and this source was more up-to-date. Data on Cape Verde are from IMF staff reports. Other countries are not included here due to lack of reliable, consistent data that could meet international standards.

The data cover budgetary central government or consolidated central government only, not state and local government. Data cover only central government budgetary transactions in Ghana, Guinea Bissau, Kenya, Malawi, Mauritius, Nigeria, Sierra Leone, Somalia, Sudan, Swaziland, Tanzania, Uganda, and Zimbabwe. Data for all other countries cover consolidated central government transactions.

Data are presented on an actual cash basis; where total expenditures taken from sources other than the *GFS Yearbook* (especially in later years) were originally reported on a commitment basis, they have been adjusted (taking account of expenditure arrears as well as other adjustments) to approximate cash expenditures.

Data are largely from the 1987 *GFS Yearbook*. The statistics are compiled by IMF correspondents in each government, central bank, or statistical office. For more recent years and in cases in which data were missing, series were updated based on information from various sources, including World Bank and IMF documents. Data from various sources have been harmonized to produce a consistent and comparable time series.

No attempt was made to reconcile *GFS* data with the System of National Accounts (SNA). The fundamental difference between the two systems is that *GFS* focuses on government financial transactions, whereas the SNA considers government transactions as part of total demand and value added. (For further discussion, see World Bank 1988b, box 2.1, p. 45.) Indicators calculated as ratios to GDP use GDP at purchaser values or market prices (see technical notes to Chapter 1). Because GDP at purchaser values includes import duties (and GDP at market prices includes indirect taxes), ratios for revenues tend to understate tax burdens, especially where such taxes are an important source of government revenue.

The economic classification of expenditures (for example, on wages) is presented as a percentage of total expenditure and lending minus repayments, because lending minus repayments is itself a separate economic classification. The functional classification of expenditures (for example, in agriculture) is presented as a percentage of total expenditures only because lending minus repayments is listed separately from expenditures in the various functional categories.

Social sector spending by central governments are included and can be quite useful in monitoring the social impacts of government policies. The data on central government education spending differ in most instances from Unesco education spending data in that Unesco attempts to include all public education spending. Hence, Unesco education spending statistics should in all cases exceed the expenditure data presented here. This, however, is not the case. In about 25 percent of the instances in Africa Unesco data were equal to or less than central government education spending reported here. This indicates inconsistent reporting in the Unesco data set. Sometimes Unesco data cover only central government, and sometimes that spending may not include all education spending claimed by the central government.

Fiscal year data are compared with the calendar year GDP data that correspond either to the second half of the fiscal year or to the calendar year in which most of the fiscal year falls. Fiscal years do not correspond to calendar years in Botswana, Cameroon, Egypt, Ethiopia, The Gambia, Ghana (before 1982), Kenya, Lesotho, Liberia, Malawi, Mauritius, Niger, Nigeria, Senegal, Sierra Leone, Sudan, Swaziland, Tanzania, Uganda, and Zimbabwe (after 1985).

Average annual growth rates are calculated from government expenditures at constant prices using the least-squares method. Expenditures are deflated by the implicit GDP deflator for data in national currency (see Table 3-1).

Summary statistics for country groups are simple averages, that is, each country receives equal weighting. Sub-Saharan groups include only those countries for which data are available for every year for which a group average is provided. For instance, the Central African Republic is omitted from the regional averages in Table 7-1 because data for it are not available for 1980 and 1987. North African group averages are shown for any year in which Egypt, Morocco, and Tunisia have data, and no average is shown for years in which data are missing for any of these countries. For instance, in a number of tables, Moroccan data are unavailable for 1987; nonetheless, Morocco was included in the North African averages for 1980-86, and no average was calculated for 1987.

Table 7-1. Government deficit/surplus (including grants)

Surplus/deficit is calculated as receipts from revenue plus grants less expenditures and lending minus repayments. It represents the net financing requirement of the central government.

Table 7-2. Government deficit/surplus (excluding grants)

This is calculated as above except that grants are excluded from receipts. It is a measure of the ability of a government to fund its activities from its own resources. Because some budgetary grants may be tied to certain expenditures that would not otherwise be incurred, excluding grants may overstate the deficit or understate the surplus if no account is taken of the expenditures dependent on these grants.

Table 7-3. Government prime deficit/surplus

The prime deficit or surplus is the government deficit or surplus (including grants) minus interest expenditures on both domestic and foreign debt. In countries with large government interest payments, this ratio may provide a more reliable indicator for monitoring fiscal stabilization efforts.

Table 7-4. Government expenditure and lending minus repayments

This represents total government outlays for current or capital purposes. Expenditure includes all nonrepayable payments by government. Lending minus repayments comprises government transactions in debt and equity claims upon others, acquired for purposes of public policy rather than for managing government liquidity or earning a return. It consists of gross lending and acquisition of financial equity minus repayments of past government lending and government sales of equities. (This definition differs from the concept of lending minus repayments adopted in the SNA, which is gross government lending minus repayments of past government lending minus net government borrowing.) In determining a government's deficit or surplus, lending minus repayments is grouped with expenditures rather than with financing.

Table 7-5. Government interest payments

Include interest on all borrowings, both domestic and foreign, but exclude commission charges paid for assistance in placing debt (which would be classified as expenditures for payment of other goods and services).

Table 7-6. Government revenue (excluding grants)

Refers to current revenues (tax and nontax) and capital revenues, such as proceeds from the sale of real assets, including land. They do not include grant receipts from other governments or international organizations.

Table 7-7. Grants to government

These are unrequited, nonrepayable, noncompulsory government receipts from other governments or international institutions. Grants of goods and services in kind are not included here.

Table 7-8. Foreign financing

This includes all government financing transactions — not including grants with nonresident individuals, enterprises, governments, international organizations, and other entities. It may be affected by trading in outstanding government securities between residents and nonresidents. The data also reflect changes, resulting from transactions but not revaluations, in government holdings of foreign exchange, deposits in nonresident financial institutions, and securities issued by nonresident entities held by government for liquidity purposes (reserves).

Table 7-9. Taxes on income and profits

Are levied on the actual or presumptive net income (after personal deductions and exemptions) of individuals and profits (after costs) of enterprises. Also included are taxes levied on capital gains that are realized on land sales, securities, and other assets.

Table 7-10. Taxes on international trade and transactions

Include import duties, export duties, profits of export or import monopolies remitted to government,

and monopoly profits of monetary authorities made in foreign exchange transactions, as well as taxes levied on the sale of foreign exchange.

Table 7-11. Import duties

Include all levies collected on imported goods (other than consumption or commodity taxes that are also levied on domestic goods), whether imposed to generate revenue or to protect domestic markets. Duties include those imposed under the customs tariff schedule and charges such as consular fees and tonnage charges.

Table 7-12. Export duties

Include all levies based on the export of goods. Rebates on exported goods comprising repayments of previously paid general consumption taxes, excises, or import duties are not netted out of this category but are deducted from the gross receipts of the respective taxes as appropriate.

Table 7-13. Nontax revenue

Is all nonrepayable government receipts, other than compulsory unrequited receipts (taxes) and revenue from capital sales or government grants, plus all fines and penalties other than for noncompliance with taxes. For some mineral-exporting countries in Africa this category is quite large, since royalties on the extraction of minerals, such as petroleum in Nigeria and Egypt and bauxite in Guinea, make up significant portions of total government revenues.

Table 7-14. Government expenditure: wages and salaries

Are payments in cash, but not in kind, to employees in return for services, before withholding taxes and employee contributions to social security and pension funds are deducted. Included are basic wages and salaries; pay for overtime, weekends, and nights; cost of living allowances; local allowances and expatriation allowances; and similar compensation. Reimbursement to employees for expenses incurred as part of their employment are excluded.

Table 7-15. Government expenditure: trends in real wages and salaries

Includes expenditure on wages and salaries, as discussed above, deflated by national price deflators. For most countries the trend is shown in index numbers beginning with 100 in 1980. For Burundi, Central African Republic, Chad, Namibia, and Somalia, the beginning year of indexation is after 1980 due to missing data.

Table 7-16. Government expenditure: other goods and services

Includes expenditures for all goods and services (except fixed capital assets and wages and salaries) bought on the market, goods and services to be used to produce fixed capital assets, strategic or emergency stocks, stocks held by market regulatory organizations, and land and intangible assets. This category encompasses purchases of materials, office supplies, fuel and lighting, travel services, and payment of rent, as well as payments in kind to certain civil servants.

Table 7-17. Government expenditure: interest payments

Are payments for the use of all borrowed money, excluding commission charges paid for assistance in the placing of debt, which would be classified as expenditures for payment of other goods and services.

Table 7-18. Government expenditure: subsidies and current transfers

Are all unrequited, nonrepayable government payments for current purposes. Transfers for capital purposes (that is, to permit the recipient to acquire capital assets) are excluded as also are transfers in kind.

Table 7-19. Government expenditure: capital

Represents payments for acquiring land, buildings, and other nonfinancial assets to be used for more than one year in the process of production, including transfers for capital assets.

For the tables showing, government expenditure by function data are expressed as a percentage of total expenditure. The indicator shows the relative priority accorded the use of government resources to specific purposes, such as health, education, and defense. Expenditures are classified by their purpose; for instance, spending on education includes any expenditure for the general purpose of education, whether funded through the ministry of education or through some other government institution. Conventional government accounts are not usually suitable for functional monitoring, since they reflect the structure rather than purposes of government expenditure. Because some state and local governments provide more services, such as education and health, than others, comparisons of functional expenditures across countries on the basis of data for the central government alone may be misleading. Because these data reflect only actual financial transactions, current expenditures do not include the consumption of fixed capital assets; the SNA, in contrast, includes such depreciation in government consumption.

Table 7-20. Government expenditure: defense

Consists of expenditures made by the central government for military and civil defense and administration, foreign military aid, defense-related applied research and experimental development, and all other defense affairs not classified elsewhere.

Table 7-21. Government expenditure: trends in real defense spending

Deflates defense spending by national price deflators and presents the data in indexes, with 1980 indexed as 100. For Comoros, Guinea-Bissau, Lesotho, and Mauritania, data limitations force the series to be indexed to a different year.

Table 7-22. Government expenditure: education

Includes all capital and current expenditures made by the central government for preprimary through tertiary education and for educational services not definable by level or classified elsewhere.

Table 7-23. Government expenditure: real per capita education spending

Presents per capita education spending by central government in 1987 U.S. dollars. Data are calculated using the conversion factors in Table 3-6.

Table 7-24. Government expenditure: health

Consists of all expenditures made by the central government for hospitals, clinics, and public health affairs and services; for medical, dental, and paramedical practitioners; for medications, prostheses, medical equipment, and appliances; for applied research and experimental development; and for health affairs and services not classified elsewhere.

Table 7-25. Government expenditure: real per capita health spending

Presents government health spending on per capita basis in 1987 U.S. dollars. Data are calculated using the conversion factors in Table 3-6.

Table 7-26. Government expenditure: economic services

Consists of all expenditures associated with the regulation, and more efficient operation, of business. Objectives include promoting economic development, redressing regional imbalances, and creating employment opportunities. These expenditures finance services rendered to industries by general government bodies, such as research, trade promotion, surveys, inspections, agricultural land management, and extension services.

Table 7-27. Government expenditure: agriculture

Includes all capital and current expenditure on forestry, fishing, and hunting affairs and services and related expenditures not classified elsewhere. Typical expenditures cover land management, farm price administration and subsidies, agricultural extension, pest control, administration of commercial and sport fishing, and agricultural research.

8

Agriculture

Agriculture is Africa's most important sector. It accounts for roughly 35 percent of GDP, 40 percent of exports, and 75 percent of employment. African agriculture has two major components: food production and export commodities. Food production, including meat, is the livelihood for most Africans. Export crops provide many African countries with their main source of foreign exchange and thus the capacity to import, invest, and develop. The information in this chapter provides a basis for assessing recent trends in producer prices, aggregate agricultural production and trade, cereal imports, and food aid in Africa.

The data on producer prices are one measure of the incentives offered to producers for specific commodities in each of 35 countries. Official producer prices (announced or controlled by the government) are distinguished from farmgate prices (actually received by farmers, in either open or parallel markets). Because some agricultural production is sold outside of the official market and because official prices are not always effectively enforced, official and farmgate prices may differ.

The data on producer price shares are another measure of price incentives that compare the price received by farmers with the export or import price. For example, a producer price share of 0.8 indicates that farmers receive 80 percent of the value that the crop has on the international market. The other 20 percent goes to pay transport, marketing, processing, and other costs, as well as taxes levied by government agencies.

The data in this chapter are estimates based on a variety of sources whose quality and reliability vary from country to country and year to year. Furthermore, production and export data are probably underestimated for two reasons. It is difficult to estimate production levels of staple food crops, especially roots and tubers, when much of the output is consumed directly by farmers, rather than marketed. Moreover, parallel market activity, including trade, may not be fully accounted for. Because this is one of the first systematic compendiums of comparative data on agricultural prices for Africa, data cover a longer period — 1975-1990 — than for most of the other series in this volume.

8-1. Nominal producer prices

		Local currency per kilogram										
	Category	1980	1981	1982	1983	1984	1985	1986	1987	1988	1989	1990
ALGERIA												
Official producer price												
Wheat (hard)	F1	1.25	1.25	1.40	1.40	1.60	2.00	2.20	2.70	2.70	4.00	..
Citrus (oranges)	F2	1.05	1.20	1.25	..	..	..	..	..	..	..	..
Dates	F3	4.50	4.50	5.50	..	..	..	..	..	..	..	..
Barley	NT1	0.80	0.80	0.80	0.80	1.00	1.40	1.35	1.74	1.80	1.85	1.70
Potatoes	NT2	1.30	1.30	1.60	..	..	..	..	..	..	..	..
Farmgate price												
Wheat (hard)	F1	1.25	1.25	1.40	1.40	1.60	2.00	2.20	2.70	2.70	4.00	..
Citrus (oranges)	F2	..	..	..	1.30	1.35	1.40	1.60	1.70	1.80	1.90	2.00
Dates (high quality)	F3	..	..	..	6.50	7.00	10.00	11.30	11.50	11.70	11.90	13.80
Barley	NT1	0.80	0.80	0.80	0.80	1.00	1.40	1.35	1.74	1.80	1.85	1.70
Potatoes	NT2	..	..	..	1.90	1.90	2.50	2.60	2.80	3.00	3.20	3.40
ANGOLA												
Official producer price												
Coffee	X1	20.43	23.45	58.60	58.60	58.60	58.60	58.60	58.60	69.00	69.00	69.00
Maize	F1	4.50	4.50	4.50	4.50	4.50	4.50	4.50	4.50	5.00	5.00	5.00
Millet	F2	4.00	4.00	10.00	10.00	10.00	10.00	10.00	10.00	11.00	11.00	11.00
Wheat	F3	4.50	4.50	10.00	17.50	17.50	17.50	17.50	17.50	18.00	18.00	18.00
Cassava	NT1	2.10	2.41	2.50	5.00	5.00	5.00	5.00	5.00	6.00	6.00	6.00
Sweet potatoes	NT2	2.50	2.50	6.00	6.00	6.00	6.00	6.00	6.00	7.00	7.00	7.00
Farmgate price												
Coffee	X1	..	..	..	..	..	..	..	..	..	..	..
Maize	F1	..	..	..	..	..	..	..	..	..	..	..
Millet	F2	..	..	..	..	..	..	..	..	..	..	..
Wheat	F3	..	..	..	..	..	..	..	..	..	..	..
Cassava	NT1	..	..	..	..	..	..	..	..	..	..	..
Sweet potatoes	NT2	..	..	..	..	..	..	..	..	..	..	..
BENIN												
Official producer price												
Cotton (seed cotton)	X1	65.00	80.00	85.00	100.00	100.00	110.00	110.00	100.00	95.00	95.00	95.00
Palm kernels	X2	35.00	37.50	42.00	45.00	60.00	60.00	20.00	20.00	30.00	30.00	30.00
Maize	F1	40.00	43.00	..	..	..	..	..	..	..	..	..
Sorghum	F2	46.00	50.50	..	..	..	..	..	..	..	..	..
Cassava	NT1	30.00	35.00	..	..	..	..	..	..	..	..	..
Yams	NT2	32.00	34.00	..	..	..	..	..	..	..	..	..
Farmgate price												
Cotton (seed cotton)	X1	65.00	80.00	85.00	100.00	100.00	110.00	110.00	100.00	95.00	95.00	95.00
Palm kernels	X2	35.00	37.50	42.00	45.00	60.00	60.00	20.00	20.00	30.00	30.00	30.00
Maize	F1	40.00	43.00	70.00	80.00	94.00	83.00	73.00	75.00	80.00	85.00	90.00
Sorghum	F2	46.00	50.50	80.00	90.00	112.00	81.00	87.00	90.00	95.00	100.00	105.00
Cassava	NT1	30.00	35.00	45.00	50.00	66.00	56.00	37.00	35.00	38.00	40.00	42.00
Yams	NT2	32.00	34.00	47.00	58.00	78.00	87.00	82.00	85.00	87.00	89.00	93.00
BOTSWANA												
Official producer price												
Groundnuts (in shell)	X1	0.22	0.24	0.29	0.36	0.40	0.42	0.45	0.46	0.50	0.53	0.56
Sorghum	F1	0.12	0.13	0.18	0.20	0.26	0.27	0.30	0.35	0.38	0.41	0.44
Maize	F2	0.12	0.13	0.16	0.19	0.23	0.24	0.26	0.32	0.34	0.37	0.40
Farmgate price												
Groundnuts (in shell)	X1	..	..	..	..	..	..	..	..	..	..	..
Sorghum	F1	0.12	0.13	0.18	0.20	0.26	0.27	0.30	0.35	0.38	0.41	0.44
Maize	F2	0.12	0.13	0.16	0.19	0.23	0.24	0.26	0.32	0.34	0.37	0.40
BURKINA FASO												
Official producer price												
Cotton (seed cotton)	X1	55.00	62.00	62.00	70.00	90.00	100.00	100.00	95.00	95.00	95.00	95.00
Groundnuts (shelled)	X2	81.93	130.80	138.70	138.70	138.75	150.00	90.00	90.00	95.00	95.00	95.00
Sesame seed	X3	70.00	83.70	89.00	96.00	96.00	113.00	75.00	50.00	60.00	80.00	80.00
Sorghum	F1	45.00	50.00	60.00	64.00	80.00	90.00	40.00	40.00	50.00	45.00	45.00
Millet	F2	45.00	50.00	60.00	66.00	80.00	80.00	40.00	50.00	50.00	45.00	45.00
Maize	F3	45.00	50.00	55.00	60.00	85.00	80.00	40.00	50.00	50.00	45.00	45.00
Farmgate price												
Cotton (seed cotton)	X1	55.00	62.00	62.00	70.00	90.00	100.00	100.00	95.00	95.00	95.00	95.00
Groundnuts (shelled)	X2	81.93	130.80	138.70	138.70	138.75	150.00	90.00	90.00	95.00	95.00	95.00
Sesame seed	X3	70.00	83.70	89.00	96.00	96.00	113.00	75.00	50.00	60.00	80.00	80.00
Sorghum	F1	..	55.00	50.00	70.00	70.00	..	..	60.00	..	..	..
Millet	F2	..	..	..	..	..	..	..	..	..	..	..
Maize	F3	..	50.00	45.00	..	..	..	..	55.00	..	..	..

(Table continues on the following page

8-1. (continued)

	Category	Local currency per kilogram										
		1980	1981	1982	1983	1984	1985	1986	1987	1988	1989	1990
BURUNDI												
Official producer price												
Coffee (Arabica, dry cherry)	X1	118.00	118.00	118.00	118.00	128.00	125.00	160.00	160.00	162.00	177.00	..
Tea (green leaves)	X2	10.00	10.00	10.00	10.00	13.00	15.00	18.00	18.00	..	..	..
Cotton (grain)	X3	29.00	29.00	35.00	35.00	35.00	35.00	35.00	40.00	40.00	..	..
Maize	F1	..	..	..	..	..	..	..	..	..	..	..
Sorghum	F2	..	..	..	..	..	..	..	..	..	..	..
Rice	F3	..	..	..	..	..	..	..	..	..	..	..
Millet	F4	..	..	..	..	..	..	..	..	..	..	..
Bananas	NT1	..	..	..	..	..	..	..	..	..	..	..
Cassava	NT2	..	..	..	..	..	..	..	..	..	..	..
Farmgate price												
Coffee (Arabica, dry cherry)	X1	118.00	118.00	118.00	118.00	128.00	125.00	160.00	160.00	162.00	177.00	..
Tea (green leaves)	X2	10.00	10.00	10.00	10.00	13.00	15.00	18.00	18.00	..	..	..
Cotton (grain)	X3	29.00	29.00	35.00	35.00	35.00	35.00	35.00	40.00	40.00	..	..
Maize	F1	25.00	25.00	25.70	28.90	32.50	37.00	37.60	39.40	42.30	45.10	47.70
Sorghum	F2	20.00	20.00	20.30	19.80	22.00	25.10	26.20	27.00	28.10	29.30	30.60
Rice	F3	25.00	25.00	25.00	25.00	28.00	31.50	32.10	33.60	35.10	36.70	38.30
Millet	F4	20.00	20.00	20.30	19.80	22.00	25.10	26.40	27.30	28.40	29.60	31.00
Bananas	NT1	6.00	6.00	6.40	6.90	7.00	7.40	7.60	7.80	8.10	8.40	8.70
Cassava	NT2	10.90	8.70	7.20	7.90	8.50	8.70	9.30	9.70	10.00	10.20	10.40
CAMEROON												
Official producer price												
Coffee (Arabica)	X1	320.00	330.00	350.00	370.00	430.00	450.00	475.00	475.00	475.00	480.00	480.00
Cocoa (grade 1, superior)	X2	300.00	310.00	330.00	370.00	410.00	420.00	420.00	420.00	420.00	430.00	430.00
Cotton (seed cotton, nonselected)	X3	70.00	80.00	95.00	105.00	117.00	130.00	130.00	130.00	130.00	130.00	140.00
Maize	F1	..	..	..	..	..	..	..	..	..	..	..
Sorghum	F2	..	..	..	..	..	..	..	..	..	..	..
Millet	F3	..	..	..	..	..	..	..	..	..	..	..
Rice (paddy)	F4	42.50	55.00	62.00	62.00	78.00	78.00	78.00	78.00	78.00	..	..
Cassava	NT1	..	..	..	..	..	..	..	..	..	..	..
Plantains	NT2	..	..	..	..	..	..	..	..	..	..	..
Farmgate price												
Coffee (Arabica)	X1	320.00	330.00	350.00	370.00	430.00	450.00	475.00	475.00	475.00	480.00	480.00
Cocoa (grade 1, superior)	X2	300.00	310.00	330.00	370.00	410.00	420.00	420.00	420.00	420.00	430.00	430.00
Cotton (seed cotton, nonselected)	X3	70.00	80.00	95.00	105.00	117.00	130.00	130.00	130.00	130.00	130.00	140.00
Maize	F1	60.00	65.00	70.00	72.00	73.00	75.00	79.00	83.00	86.10	88.90	91.80
Sorghum	F2	40.00	45.00	50.00	..	95.00	..	..	..	..	..	..
Millet	F3	40.00	45.00	50.00	51.00	51.50	52.00	53.00	56.00	58.10	59.90	61.60
Rice (paddy)	F4	105.00	124.00	130.00	132.00	135.00	138.00	146.00	154.00	159.60	165.10	170.60
Cassava	NT1	19.00	24.00	30.00	31.00	31.50	33.00	34.00	36.00	38.40	40.50	42.40
Plantains	NT2	25.00	35.00	45.00	50.00	55.00	62.00	69.00	75.00	81.50	88.10	94.70
CENTRAL AFRICAN REPUBLIC												
Official producer price												
Coffee (Robusta, cherries)	X1	120.00	120.00	130.00	135.00	135.00	135.00	135.00	135.00	190.00	190.00	195.80
Cotton (seed cotton)	X2	60.00	60.00	70.00	80.00	90.00	100.00	100.00	100.00	100.00	100.00	105.60
Sorghum	F1	35.00	35.00	40.00	40.00	60.00	..	..	..	..	..	..
Maize	F2	40.00	40.00	40.00	50.00	60.00	..	..	..	..	..	..
Groundnuts (unshelled)	F3	35.00	35.00	45.00	45.00	55.00	..	..	..	..	..	..
Cassava	NT1	30.00	30.00	35.00	35.00	40.00	..	..	..	..	..	..
Yams	NT2	25.00	25.00	25.00	25.00	25.00	..	..	..	..	..	..
Farmgate price												
Coffee (Robusta, cherries)	X1	120.00	120.00	130.00	135.00	135.00	135.00	135.00	135.00	190.00	190.00	195.80
Cotton (seed cotton)	X2	60.00	60.00	70.00	80.00	90.00	100.00	100.00	100.00	100.00	100.00	105.60
Sorghum	F1	..	..	..	..	..	115.89	103.45	128.34	107.66	107.66	107.70
Maize	F2	..	..	..	..	..	83.33	65.29	67.69	104.31	104.31	112.10
Groundnuts (unshelled)	F3	..	..	..	..	..	120.00	150.00	165.00	170.00	175.00	180.00
Cassava	NT1	..	..	..	..	..	81.98	76.22	89.50	57.45	57.45	57.50
Yams	NT2	..	..	..	..	..	97.36	107.09	91.00	124.45	124.45	124.50

(Table continues on the following page

8-1. (continued)

		Local currency per kilogram										
	Category	1980	1981	1982	1983	1984	1985	1986	1987	1988	1989	1990
CHAD												
Official producer price												
Cotton (seed cotton, avg. white/yellow)	X1	80.00	80.00	80.00	80.00	100.00	98.60	98.80	97.80	96.90	97.10	99.90
Sorghum	F1	..	..	..	..	..	..	..	..	..	..	..
Millet	F2	55.40	59.80	60.00	65.00	68.00	72.00	74.00	78.00	80.00	85.00	87.00
Groundnuts	F3	64.87	75.70	81.95	80.13	119.23	140.00	91.30	102.95	72.27	69.38	72.70
Farmgate price												
Cotton (seed cotton, avg. white/yellow)	X1	80.00	80.00	80.00	80.00	100.00	98.60	98.80	97.80	96.90	97.10	99.90
Sorghum	F1	..	..	..	..	..	200.00	90.00	..	..	..	..
Millet	F2	..	..	..	..	..	..	..	..	..	..	..
Groundnuts	F3	..	..	..	..	..	..	..	..	..	..	..
COMOROS												
Official producer price												
Vanilla (green)	X1	1,050.00	1,150.00	1,200.00	1,500.00	2,000.00	1,750.00	2,000.00	2,000.00	1,800.00	2,500.00	1,156.20
Cloves	X2	..	..	..	..	..	..	..	..	..	..	..
Ylang Ylang (flower)	X3	..	..	..	..	..	..	..	..	..	..	..
Copra	X4	..	..	..	..	..	..	..	..	..	..	..
Bananas	F1	..	..	..	..	..	..	..	..	..	..	..
Cassava	NT1	..	..	..	..	..	..	..	..	..	..	..
Farmgate price												
Vanilla (green)	X1	..	..	..	..	..	..	..	..	..	..	..
Cloves	X2	1,250.00	1,250.00	2,000.00	2,350.00	1,150.00	1,100.00	1,250.00	800.00	709.00	..	..
Ylang Ylang (flower)	X3	45.00	50.00	55.00	55.00	55.00	80.00	90.00	65.00	65.00	..	..
Copra	X4	40.00	40.00	40.00	65.00	65.00	72.50	77.50	45.00	50.00	..	..
Bananas	F1	50.00	72.10	72.60	73.10	73.40	73.60	73.80	74.00	76.90	79.10	80.50
Cassava	NT1	40.00	47.30	47.50	47.70	47.90	48.10	48.50	48.70	49.70	50.50	51.10
CONGO, PEOPLE'S REPUBLIC OF THE												
Official producer price												
Coffee (Robusta, shelled)	X1	172.00	180.00	201.00	201.00	210.00	210.00	430.00	430.00	430.00	430.00	..
Cocoa (superior quality)	X2	220.00	235.00	240.00	240.00	260.00	260.00	320.00	320.00	320.00	320.00	..
Maize	F1	43.00	47.00	59.00	65.00	68.00	73.00	73.00	85.00	85.00	85.00	89.80
Cassava	NT1	100.00	100.00	100.00	102.40	104.40	106.50	108.60	110.80	114.00	116.60	118.60
Plantains	NT2	67.50	75.00	82.50	82.50	82.50	82.50	82.50	82.50	84.90	86.50	87.70
Farmgate price												
Coffee (Robusta, shelled)	X1	172.00	180.00	201.00	201.00	210.00	210.00	430.00	430.00	430.00	430.00	..
Cocoa (superior quality)	X2	220.00	235.00	240.00	240.00	260.00	260.00	320.00	320.00	320.00	320.00	..
Maize	F1	43.00	47.00	59.00	65.00	68.00	73.00	73.00	85.00	85.00	85.00	89.80
Cassava	NT1	..	..	..	..	..	..	..	..	..	..	..
Plantains	NT2	..	..	..	..	..	..	..	..	..	..	..
CÔTE D'IVOIRE												
Official producer price												
Coffee (Robusta, green)	X1	310.56	301.64	303.99	306.09	358.25	354.30	399.50	400.00	400.00	430.00	451.20
Cocoa (beans)	X2	300.00	300.00	300.00	350.00	375.00	400.00	400.00	400.00	400.00	400.00	468.20
Palm oil (fresh fruit bunch)	X3	10.00	15.00	15.00	18.50	22.50	20.00	21.00	21.00	..	..	..
Rice (paddy)	F1	50.00	60.00	69.00	68.00	80.00	80.00	84.00	90.00	93.70	98.30	103.10
Maize	F2	30.00	30.00	40.00	40.00	40.00	40.00	50.00	..	..	..	..
Cassava	NT1	..	..	..	..	..	..	20.00	..	..	..	..
Yams	NT2	..	..	..	..	..	..	..	..	..	..	..
Farmgate price												
Coffee (Robusta, green)	X1	310.56	301.64	303.99	306.09	358.25	354.30	399.50	400.00	400.00	430.00	451.20
Cocoa (beans)	X2	300.00	300.00	300.00	350.00	375.00	400.00	400.00	400.00	400.00	400.00	468.20
Palm oil (fresh fruit bunch)	X3	10.00	15.00	15.00	18.50	22.50	20.00	21.00	21.00	..	..	..
Rice (paddy)	F1	..	..	..	..	..	..	..	..	..	..	..
Maize	F2	68.00	72.00	58.00	65.00	..	..	40.00	40.00	..	..	..
Cassava	NT1	49.00	48.00	32.00	40.00	43.00	36.00	46.00	46.00	46.30	46.80	47.20
Yams	NT2	59.00	60.00	72.00	87.00	93.00	75.00	99.90	110.00	116.40	122.50	128.60

(Table continues on the following page

8–1. (continued)

		Local currency per kilogram										
	Category	1980	1981	1982	1983	1984	1985	1986	1987	1988	1989	1990
EGYPT, ARAB REPUBLIC OF												
Official producer price												
Cotton	X1	0.30	0.37	0.40	0.44	0.48	0.52	0.57	0.62	0.66	0.70	0.74
Rice (96% humidity)	X2	0.08	0.09	0.10	0.11	0.11	0.13	0.17	0.20	0.20	0.28	0.28
Wheat (94% humidity)	F1	0.08	0.08	0.08	0.08	0.12	0.17	0.17	0.20	0.27	0.40	..
Sugarcane	F2	0.01	0.02	0.02	0.02	0.02	0.02	0.03	0.03	0.03	0.04	0.05
Broadbeans	NT1	0.10	0.23	0.24	0.24	0.26	0.28	0.35	0.48	0.48	0.48	0.48
Farmgate price												
Cotton	X1	0.30	0.37	0.40	0.44	0.48	0.52	0.57	0.62	0.66	0.70	0.74
Rice (96% humidity)	X2	0.08	0.10	0.13	0.13	0.13	0.21	0.25	0.21	0.26	..	0.32
Wheat (94% humidity)	F1	0.09	0.09	0.08	0.11	0.12	0.17	0.22	0.22	0.24	..	..
Sugarcane	F2	0.02	0.02	0.02	0.02	0.02	0.03	0.03	..	..	..	..
Broadbeans	NT1	0.20	0.23	0.24	0.25	0.28	0.32	0.46	0.55	0.55	..	..
EQUATORIAL GUINEA												
Official producer price												
Cocoa (first grade dried beans)	X1	190.00	270.00	310.00	440.00	550.00	500.00	450.00	400.00	300.00		..
Coffee (Robusta, cherry)	X2	225.00	225.00	225.00	225.00	225.00	300.00	250.00	150.00	125.00	..	..
Cassava	NT1	..	..	..	..	..	..	..	..	..	..	..
Plantains	NT2	..	..	..	..	..	..	..	..	..	..	..
Farmgate price												
Cocoa (first grade dried beans)	X1	190.00	270.00	310.00	440.00	550.00	500.00	450.00	400.00	300.00		..
Coffee (Robusta, cherry)	X2	..	..	..	..	..	..	..	..	..		..
Cassava	NT1	..	..	..	..	..	..	..	..	..		..
Plantains	NT2	..	..	..	..	..	..	..	..	..		..
ETHIOPIA												
Official producer price												
Coffee (Arabica, beans)	X1	2.22	2.78	2.14	2.27	2.43	3.34	2.27	2.56	2.39	2.42	2.54
Sesame seed	X2	1.10	1.15	1.45	1.41	1.60	2.09	1.45	1.45	1.64	1.50	1.60
Sorghum (mixed)	F1	0.21	0.21	0.23	0.23	0.23	0.23	0.23	0.25	0.25	0.29	0.51
Maize	F2	0.17	0.17	0.20	0.20	0.20	0.20	0.20	0.22	0.22	0.23	0.36
Barley (non-white mixed)	NT1	0.26	0.26	0.26	0.26	0.26	0.26	0.26	0.28	0.28	0.31	0.52
Teff (mixed types)	NT2	0.36	0.36	0.39	0.39	0.39	0.39	0.39	0.42	0.53	0.48	0.73
Farmgate price												
Coffee (Arabica, beans)	X1	2.22	2.78	2.14	2.27	2.43	3.34	2.27	2.56	2.39	2.42	2.54
Sesame seed	X2	1.10	1.15	1.45	1.41	1.60	2.09	1.45	1.45	1.64	1.50	1.60
Sorghum (mixed)	F1	..	0.53	..	..	..	..	..	..	..	..	..
Maize	F2	..	0.40	..	..	..	..	..	..	..	..	..
Barley (non-white mixed)	NT1	..	0.36	..	..	..	..	..	..	..	..	..
Teff (mixed types)	NT2	..	0.46	..	..	..	..	..	..	..	..	..
GABON												
Official producer price												
Cocoa (first quality)	X1	320.00	320.00	345.00	375.00	420.00	430.00	430.00	..			..
Coffee (merchant, processed)	X2	180.00	180.00	200.00	215.00	250.00	260.00	260.00	..	..		..
Maize	F1	54.50	63.60	68.20	68.20	71.44	72.20	74.10	74.10	77.10	79.70	81.80
Cassava	NT1	139.50	143.00	143.00	150.00	157.00	164.00	171.00	178.00	184.70	191.10	197.40
Taro (cocoyam)	NT2	153.00	218.00	241.00	248.00	274.20	301.60	331.70	364.90	389.20	415.20	441.90
Yams	NT3	124.50	125.00	126.00	127.50	129.00	130.30	131.60	132.90	134.90	136.40	137.80
Farmgate price												
Cocoa (first quality)	X1	..	..	..	..	..	..	..	..	..		..
Coffee (merchant, processed)	X2	..	..	..	..	..	..	..	..	..		..
Maize	F1	..	..	..	..	..	..	..	..	..		..
Cassava	NT1	..	..	..	..	..	..	..	..	..		..
Taro (cocoyam)	NT2	..	..	..	..	..	..	..	..	..		..
Yams	NT3	..	..	..	..	..	..	..	..	..		..

(Table continues on the following page

8-1. (continued)

	Category	1980	1981	1982	1983	1984	1985	1986	1987	1988	1989	1990
GAMBIA, THE												
Official producer price												
Groundnuts (unshelled)	X1	0.46	0.50	0.52	0.45	0.62	1.26	1.80	1.50	1.10	1.65	1.75
Cotton (seed cotton)	X2	0.53	0.53	0.56	0.61	0.70	1.28	1.35	1.10	1.80	2.20	..
Palm kernels	X3	0.32	0.32	0.32	0.32	0.32	0.32	0.32	0.45	0.45	0.50	0.50
Millet	F1	0.52	0.47	0.76	0.97	0.76	0.97	1.13	1.20	1.20	1.51	1.90
Rice (paddy)	F2	0.46	0.51	0.51	0.51	0.60	0.90	0.95	0.95	0.95	0.95	..
Maize	F3	0.49	0.49	0.39	0.39	0.39	0.80	..	..	..	..	..
Sorghum	F4	0.32	0.32	0.52	0.41	0.35	0.79	0.88	1.00	1.00	1.20	1.50
Farmgate price												
Groundnuts (unshelled)	X1	0.46	0.50	0.52	0.45	0.62	1.26	1.80	1.50	1.10	1.65	1.75
Cotton (seed cotton)	X2	0.53	0.53	0.56	0.61	0.70	1.28	1.35	1.10	1.80	2.20	..
Palm kernels	X3	..	..	..	..	..	..	..	..	..	..	..
Millet	F1	..	..	..	..	..	..	..	..	..	..	..
Sorghum	F2	..	..	..	..	..	..	..	..	..	..	..
Rice (paddy)	F3	..	..	..	..	..	..	..	..	..	..	..
Maize	F4	..	..	..	..	..	..	..	..	..	..	..
GHANA												
Official producer price												
Cocoa	X1	4.00	12.00	12.00	20.00	30.00	56.60	85.50	150.00	165.00	174.40	..
Maize	F1	..	..	..	..	..	..	..	..	..	..	..
Millet	F2	..	..	..	..	..	..	..	..	..	..	..
Groundnuts	F3	..	..	..	..	..	..	..	..	..	..	..
Cassava	NT1	..	..	..	..	..	..	..	..	..	..	..
Plantains	NT2	..	..	..	..	..	..	..	..	..	..	..
Farmgate price												
Cocoa	X1	4.00	12.00	12.00	20.00	30.00	56.60	85.50	150.00	165.00	174.40	..
Maize	F1	4.13	7.74	7.98	38.53	23.41	20.40	32.96	53.77	68.24	54.31	..
Millet	F2	5.34	9.47	13.51	48.92	47.90	31.94	43.42	63.24	102.60	114.81	..
Groundnuts	F3	8.44	18.16	28.98	72.38	70.01	72.71	62.62	128.43	147.53	199.16	..
Cassava	NT1	1.52	3.73	4.21	16.49	9.32	8.76	15.52	39.59	51.48	27.64	..
Plantains	NT2	1.93	2.98	4.93	17.62	19.56	17.27	21.41	41.32	43.70	61.50	..
GUINEA												
Official producer price												
Coffee (Robusta)	X1	49.00	49.00	43.00	45.00	55.00	70.00	400.00	400.00	450.00	450.00	500.00
Palm kernels	X2	6.00	6.00	7.00	7.00	10.00	13.00	60.00	60.00	67.50	67.50	75.00
Rice (paddy)	F1	9.00	9.00	9.00	12.00	12.00	15.00	85.70	85.70	96.40	96.40	107.10
Maize	F2	7.00	7.00	7.00	10.00	10.00	13.00	..	..	..	..	..
Groundnuts (unshelled)	F3	11.00	11.00	11.00	15.00	15.00	20.00	..	..	..	..	..
Cassava	NT1	5.00	5.00	5.00	7.00	7.00	7.00	..	..	..	..	..
Plantains	NT2	4.50	4.50	4.50	14.00	14.00	14.00	..	..	..	..	..
Farmgate price												
Coffee (Robusta)	X1	49.00	49.00	43.00	45.00	55.00	70.00	400.00	400.00	450.00	450.00	500.00
Palm kernels	X2	6.00	6.00	7.00	7.00	10.00	13.00	60.00	60.00	67.50	67.50	75.00
Rice (paddy)	F1	..	..	..	..	..	..	..	..	..	..	..
Maize	F2	..	..	..	..	..	..	74.30	74.30	83.60	83.60	92.80
Groundnuts (unshelled)	F3	..	..	..	..	..	..	114.30	114.30	128.60	128.60	142.80
Cassava	NT1	..	..	..	..	..	..	40.00	40.00	45.00	45.00	50.00
Plantains	NT2	..	..	..	..	..	..	80.00	80.00	90.00	90.00	100.00
GUINEA-BISSAU												
Official producer price												
Cashew nuts	X1	8.00	8.00	8.00	9.50	17.50	28.50	37.00	45.50	91.00	159.20	255.80
Groundnuts (unshelled, grade 1)	X2	7.50	7.50	7.50	9.20	15.50	25.00	32.50	40.00	80.00	140.00	225.00
Palm kernels	X3	4.52	5.50	5.50	6.00	11.50	19.00	24.70	30.40	60.80	106.40	171.00
Rice (paddy, grade 1)	F1	8.50	8.50	9.50	9.50	14.50	24.00	37.50	50.00	85.00	180.00	325.00
Sorghum	F2	9.00	9.00	8.50	8.50	13.50	21.00	32.80	43.70	74.30	157.40	284.30
Maize (grade 1)	F3	7.50	7.50	8.50	8.50	13.50	21.00	32.80	43.70	74.30	157.40	284.30
Farmgate price												
Cashew nuts	X1	8.00	8.00	8.00	9.50	17.50	28.50	37.00	230.00	..	..	..
Groundnuts (unshelled, grade 1)	X2	7.50	7.50	7.50	9.20	15.50	25.00	32.50	..	..	..	..
Palm kernels	X3	4.52	5.50	5.50	6.00	11.50	19.00	24.70	..	..	..	..
Rice (paddy, grade 1)	F1	8.50	8.50	9.50	9.50	14.50	24.00	37.50	50.00	85.00	180.00	325.00
Sorghum	F2	..	..	..	..	..	..	..	..	..	..	..
Maize (grade 1)	F3	..	..	..	..	..	..	..	..	..	..	..

(Table continues on the following page

8-1. (continued)

	Category	Local currency per kilogram										
		1980	1981	1982	1983	1984	1985	1986	1987	1988	1989	1990
KENYA												
Official producer price												
Coffee (Arabica, washed bean, grade 1-6)	X1	26.35	21.33	27.80	34.88	38.44	46.60	54.76	34.14	43.71	38.80	41.60
Tea	X2	15.91	17.74	19.41	21.84	51.84	33.66	33.82	25.00	26.77	26.80	27.00
Sugar (cane)	X3	0.13	0.15	0.17	0.23	0.23	0.27	0.30	0.30	0.36	0.39	0.41
Sisal	X4	4.23	4.12	5.03	6.25	6.74	7.07	7.43	7.05	7.45	7.50	7.60
Maize	F1	0.95	1.00	1.06	1.54	1.75	1.94	2.09	2.09	2.23	2.46	2.60
Wheat	F2	1.64	1.67	1.79	2.22	2.69	2.71	2.93	2.95	3.19	3.40	3.60
Farmgate price												
Coffee (Arabica, washed bean, grade 1-6)	X1	26.35	21.33	27.80	34.88	38.44	46.60	54.76	34.14	43.71	38.80	41.60
Tea	X2	15.91	17.74	19.41	21.84	51.84	33.66	33.82	25.00	26.77	26.80	27.00
Sugar (cane)	X3	0.13	0.15	0.17	0.23	0.23	0.27	0.30	0.30	0.36	0.39	0.41
Sisal	X4	4.23	4.12	5.03	6.25	6.74	7.07	7.43	7.05	7.45	7.50	7.60
Maize	F1	0.95	1.00	1.06	1.54	1.75	1.94	2.09	2.09	2.23	2.46	2.60
Wheat	F2	1.64	1.67	1.79	2.22	2.69	2.71	2.93	2.95	3.19	3.40	3.60
LESOTHO												
Official producer price												
Wheat	X1	0.18	0.30	0.24	0.25	0.33	0.36	0.39	0.45	0.48	0.55	0.60
Beans	X2	..	0.74	0.62	0.75	0.93	1.02	1.09	1.14	1.24	1.24	..
Peas	X3	..	0.45	0.44	0.56	0.68	0.68	0.68	..	..	..	..
Maize	X4	0.14	0.20	0.20	0.19	0.25	0.28	0.32	0.34	0.36	0.39	0.40
Sorghum	F1	0.15	0.33	0.21	0.20	0.21	0.24	0.25	0.29	0.30	0.31	0.33
Farmgate price												
Wheat	X1	..	0.30	0.24	0.25	..	..	..	..	..	..	..
Beans	X2	..	0.56	0.70	0.82	..	..	..	..	..	..	..
Peas	X3	..	0.48	0.44	0.56	..	..	..	..	..	..	..
Maize	X4	..	0.20	0.20	0.19	..	..	..	..	..	..	..
Sorghum	F1	..	0.33	0.21	0.20	..	..	..	..	..	..	..
LIBERIA												
Official producer price												
Rubber (nonspec. coagul.)	X1	..	..	..	..	..	..	..	..	..	..	..
Coffee (Robusta)	X2	1.98	1.76	1.21	1.21	1.32	1.10	1.43	1.54	1.60	2.00	2.00
Cocoa (fair average quality)	X3	1.81	1.59	1.10	1.21	0.99	0.99	1.05	1.10	..	..	..
Rice	F1	0.46	0.40	0.40	0.40	0.40	0.40	0.33	0.33	..	..	..
Cassava	NT1	..	..	..	..	..	..	..	..	..	..	..
Farmgate price												
Rubber (nonspec. coagul.)	X1	0.71	0.43	0.42	0.46	0.48	0.43	0.43	0.57	0.66	..	..
Coffee (Robusta)	X2	1.98	1.76	1.21	1.21	1.32	1.10	1.43	1.54	1.60	2.00	2.00
Cocoa (fair average quality)	X3	1.81	1.59	1.10	1.21	0.99	0.99	1.05	1.10	..	..	..
Rice	F1	0.46	0.40	0.40	0.40	0.40	0.40	0.33	0.33	..	..	..
Cassava	NT1	0.04	0.04	0.04	0.07	0.07	0.07	0.07	0.09	0.09	0.20	0.21
LIBYA												
Official producer price												
Wheat	F1	0.14	0.16	0.20	0.20	0.20	0.20	0.22	0.24	0.25	0.27	0.28
Olives	F2	0.07	0.07	0.08	0.08	0.08	0.08	0.08	0.09	0.10	0.11	0.12
Oranges	F3	0.14	0.17	0.18	0.18	0.18	0.18	0.19	0.20	0.23	0.26	0.30
Barley	NT1	0.11	0.13	0.15	0.15	0.15	0.15	0.16	0.18	0.19	0.20	0.21
Farmgate price												
Wheat	F1	..	..	..	..	..	..	..	..	..	..	..
Olives	F2	..	..	..	..	..	..	..	..	..	..	..
Oranges	F3	..	..	..	..	..	..	..	..	..	..	..
Barley	NT1	..	..	..	..	..	..	..	..	..	..	..
MADAGASCAR												
Official producer price												
Coffee (Robusta)	X1	215.00	250.00	260.00	280.00	330.00	395.00	600.00	800.00	950.00	950.00	950.00
Vanilla (green)	X2	600.00	700.00	700.00	1,000.00	1,000.00	1,000.00	1,100.00	1,200.00	1,700.00	2,000.00	2,000.00
Cloves	X3	395.00	430.00	435.00	435.00	435.00	435.00	525.00	600.00	600.00	600.00	600.00
Rice (paddy)	F1	43.00	47.00	60.00	65.00	75.00	83.00	100.00	120.00	180.00	250.00	283.00
Cassava	NT1	..	..	..	..	..	..	..	..	..	..	..
Sweet potatoes	NT2	..	..	..	..	..	..	..	..	..	..	..
Farmgate price												
Coffee (Robusta)	X1	..	..	..	..	..	..	..	..	..	..	..
Vanilla (green)	X2	600.00	700.00	700.00	1,000.00	1,000.00	1,000.00	1,100.00	1,200.00	1,700.00	2,000.00	2,000.00
Cloves	X3	395.00	430.00	435.00	435.00	435.00	435.00	525.00	..	..	..	..
Rice (paddy)	F1	43.00	47.00	60.00	81.00	90.00	103.00	215.00	..	..	..	..
Cassava	NT1	10.00	20.00	30.00	40.00	50.00	50.00	55.00	55.00	60.00	62.00	64.00
Sweet potatoes	NT2	30.00	35.00	40.00	45.00	50.00	60.00	60.00	60.00	64.50	69.10	73.60

(Table continues on the following page

8-1. (continued)

		Local currency per kilogram										
	Category	1980	1981	1982	1983	1984	1985	1986	1987	1988	1989	1990
MALAWI												
Official producer price												
Tobacco (flue-cured)	X1	..	..	..	..	..	..	..	..	..	..	..
Tobacco (Northen division dark-fired, G2)	X1	0.44	0.44	0.44	0.77	0.97	0.97	0.97	0.97	1.21	1.65	1.65
Tea (dry leaves)	X2	..	..	..	..	..	..	..	..	..	..	..
Groundnuts (shelled)	X3	0.33	0.37	0.55	0.60	0.70	0.75	0.75	0.75	0.85	0.95	..
Cotton (grade A)	X4	0.23	0.23	0.29	0.38	0.46	0.50	0.55	0.65	0.77	0.81	0.86
Maize	F1	0.07	0.07	0.11	0.11	0.12	0.12	0.12	0.17	0.24	0.26	0.27
Sorghum	F2	0.05	0.05	0.05	0.10	0.10	0.14	0.21	0.15	0.16	0.18	0.20
Rice (paddy, grade 1)	F3	0.10	0.10	0.10	0.12	0.17	0.19	0.22	0.27	0.30	0.35	0.37
Cassava	NT1	0.03	0.03	0.03	0.03	0.04	0.04	0.04	0.06	0.10	0.12	0.15
Farmgate price												
Tobacco (flue-cured)	X1	1.01	1.79	2.09	1.87	2.23	2.38	3.03	3.96	5.28	5.03	6.48
Tobacco (Northen division dark-fired, G2)	X1	0.44	0.44	0.44	0.77	0.97	0.97	0.97	0.97	1.21	1.65	1.65
Tea (dry leaves)	X2	0.84	0.90	1.19	1.60	2.98	1.81	1.50	1.64	2.12	2.68	2.23
Groundnuts (shelled)	X3	0.33	0.37	0.55	0.60	0.70	0.75	0.75	0.75	0.85	1.00	1.10
Cotton (seed cotton)	X4	0.23	0.23	0.29	0.38	0.46	0.50	0.55	0.65	0.77	0.81	0.86
Maize	F1	0.07	0.07	0.11	0.11	0.12	0.12	0.12	0.17	0.24	0.26	0.27
Sorghum	F2	0.05	0.05	0.05	0.10	0.10	0.14	0.21	0.15	0.16	0.18	0.20
Rice (paddy, grade 1)	F3	0.10	0.10	0.10	0.12	0.17	0.19	0.22	0.27	0.30	0.35	0.37
Cassava	NT1	0.03	0.03	0.03	0.03	0.04	0.04	0.04	0.06	0.10	0.12	0.15
MALI												
Official producer price												
Cotton (seed cotton)	X1	55.00	65.00	65.00	75.00	75.00	84.65	84.65	84.65	84.65	84.65	84.65
Groundnuts (unshelled)	X2	40.00	45.00	45.00	45.00	55.00	65.00	70.00	60.00	62.00	63.00	64.00
Millet	F1	35.00	42.50	45.00	50.00	50.00	55.00	55.00	55.00	58.00	60.00	61.00
Rice (paddy)	F2	37.50	50.00	55.00	60.00	65.00	70.00	70.00	70.00	73.00	75.00	80.00
Sorghum	F3	35.00	42.50	45.00	50.00	50.00	55.00	55.00	55.00	58.00	60.00	61.00
Maize	F4	35.00	45.00	47.50	50.00	50.00	55.00	55.00	55.00	58.00	60.00	61.00
Farmgate price												
Cotton (seed cotton)	X1	55.00	65.00	65.00	75.00	75.00	84.65	84.65	84.65	84.65	84.65	84.65
Groundnuts (unshelled)	X2	40.00	45.00	45.00	50.00	50.00	55.00	..	..	..	..	..
Millet	F1	35.00	42.50	45.00	50.00	50.00	55.00	55.00	..	..	..	..
Rice (paddy)	F2	37.50	50.00	55.00	60.00	65.00	70.00	70.00	70.00	..	..	..
Sorghum	F3	35.00	42.50	45.00	50.00	50.00	55.00	55.00		..	..	..
Maize	F4	35.00	45.00	47.50	50.00	50.00	55.00	55.00	..	..	..	..
MAURITANIA												
Official producer price												
Sorghum	F1	9.00	13.00	13.00	13.00	13.00	21.00	21.00	21.00	22.00	22.00	22.00
Millet	F2	8.50	13.00	13.00	13.00	13.00	21.00	21.00	21.00	22.00	22.00	21.00
Rice (paddy)	F3	10.00	12.50	12.50	12.50	12.50	14.00	18.50	18.50	19.00	19.00	21.00
Maize	F4	11.00	13.00	13.00	13.00	13.00	21.00	21.00	21.00	22.00	22.00	22.00
Farmgate price												
Sorghum	F1	9.00	13.00	13.00	13.00	13.00	21.00	21.00	21.00	22.00	22.00	22.00
Millet	F2	8.50	13.00	13.00	13.00	13.00	21.00	21.00	21.00	22.00	22.00	21.00
Rice (paddy)	F3	10.00	12.50	12.50	12.50	12.50	14.00	18.50	18.50	19.00	19.00	21.00
Maize	F4	11.00	13.00	13.00	13.00	13.00	21.00	21.00	21.00	22.00	22.00	22.00
MAURITIUS												
Official producer price												
Sugarcane	X1	0.20	0.20	0.25	0.26	0.27	0.29	0.30	0.32	0.33	0.35	0.36
Tea	X2	11.04	12.42	13.50	11.88	19.45	12.86	9.24	7.38	10.33	10.42	13.00
Maize (12% moisture)	F1	2.00	2.40	2.80	2.90	4.05	4.23	4.34	4.34	..	..	..
Rice (paddy, 14% moisture)	F2	1.50	..	..	8.05	7.32	7.32	7.32	7.32	7.32	..	..
Potatoes	NT1	3.00	2.60	2.60	2.60	2.60	2.00	2.00	2.50	2.50	2.75	2.80
Onions	NT2	4.15	4.35	5.02	5.33	5.03	4.72	4.17	4.78	5.83	5.74	5.80
Farmgate price												
Sugarcane	X1	..	..	..	..	..	..	..	..	..	..	..
Tea	X2											
Maize (12% moisture)	F1	..	..	..	..	..	..	..	..	..	..	..
Rice (paddy, 14% moisture)	F2	..	..	..	..	..	..	..	..	..	..	..
Potatoes	NT1	..	..	..	..	..	..	..	..	..	..	..
Onions	NT2	..	..	..	..	..	..	..	..	..	..	..

(Table continues on the following page

8–1. (continued)

	Category	1980	1981	1982	1983	1984	1985	1986	1987	1988	1989	1990
						Local currency per kilogram						
MOROCCO												
Official producer price												
Citrus (oranges)	X1	1.29	1.48	1.50	1.51	1.52	1.55	1.57	1.60	1.70	1.80	1.90
Bananas	X2	..	..	..	..	..	..	..	..	..	..	..
Cotton	X3	3.20	3.50	3.59	4.00	5.00	5.50	6.00	6.00	6.00	6.70	6.70
Wheat (hard)	F1	1.25	1.35	1.40	1.40	1.50	1.80	2.00	2.00	2.00	2.00	..
Sugarbeet (16.5% sugar)	F2	0.14	0.14	0.16	0.16	0.18	0.19	0.22	0.22	0.22	0.24	0.25
Barley	NT1	0.90	0.96	1.00	1.00	1.10	1.30	..	..	..	..	..
Farmgate price												
Citrus	X1	..	..	..	..	..	..	..	..	..	..	..
Bananas	X2	..	..	..	..	..	..	..	..	..	..	..
Cotton	X3	..	..	..	..	..	..	..	..	..	..	..
Wheat (hard)	F1	1.14	1.48	1.96	1.61	1.79	2.18	..	..	..	..	..
Sugarbeet (16.5% sugar)	F2	0.14	0.14	0.16	0.16	0.18	0.19	0.22	0.22	0.22	0.24	0.25
Barley	NT1	0.79	1.02	1.45	0.93	1.28	1.44	..	..	..	..	..
MOZAMBIQUE												
Official producer price												
Cashew nuts	X1	5.00	5.00	5.00	5.00	10.00	10.00	10.00	60.00	105.00	165.00	200.00
Cotton (seed, prime grade)	X2	11.00	11.00	11.00	12.50	12.50	16.00	16.00	65.00	175.00	246.00	270.00
Tea	X3	25.57	25.57	25.60	35.00	35.00	45.00	45.00	140.00	378.00	529.00	582.00
Maize	F1	4.00	4.00	6.00	6.00	6.00	13.00	13.00	40.00	65.00	110.00	126.00
Rice	F2	6.20	6.20	10.00	10.00	10.00	16.00	16.00	48.00	130.00	181.40	199.60
Cassava	NT1	2.00	3.00	4.50	4.50	4.50	..	..	..	..	..	..
Farmgate price												
Cashew nuts	X1	7.50	7.50	7.50	7.50	13.20	13.20	13.20	86.00	232.00	325.00	358.00
Cotton (seed, prime grade)	X2	11.00	11.00	11.00	12.50	12.50	16.00	16.00	65.00	175.00	..	..
Tea	X3	25.57	25.57	25.60	35.00	35.00	45.00	45.00	..	..	..	..
Maize	F1	4.00	4.00	6.00	6.00	6.00	13.00	13.00	40.00	65.00	110.00	126.00
Rice	F2	6.20	6.20	10.00	10.00	10.00	16.00	16.00	48.00	130.00	181.40	199.60
Cassava	NT1	2.00	3.00	4.50	4.50	4.50	6.00	6.00	15.00	40.00	56.00	62.00
NAMIBIA												
Official producer price												
Wheat	F1	0.21	0.24	0.25	0.28	0.30	0.32	0.35	0.37	0.39	0.42	0.45
Maize (white)	F2	0.12	0.13	0.15	0.17	0.19	0.22	0.24	0.26	0.28	0.30	0.32
Farmgate price												
Wheat	F1	..	..	..	..	..	..	..	..	..	..	..
Maize (white)	F2	..	..	..	..	..	..	..	..	..	..	..
NIGER												
Official producer price												
Cowpeas	X1	45.00	102.50	85.00	90.00	100.00	120.00	80.00	80.00	..	..	..
Cotton (unginned, top grade)	X2	62.00	80.00	120.00	120.00	120.00	130.00	130.00	110.00	100.00	100.00	100.00
Groundnuts (shelled)	X3	75.00	85.00	100.00	100.00	110.00	140.00	140.00	145.00	..	..	..
Millet	F1	40.00	70.00	80.00	80.00	100.00	80.00	..	..	..	..	..
Sorghum (red)	F2	40.00	50.00	70.00	70.00	100.00	80.00	..	..	..	..	..
Farmgate price												
Cowpeas	X1	..	..	..	..	..	..	..	..	..	..	..
Cotton (unginned, top grade)	X2	62.00	80.00	120.00	120.00	120.00	130.00	130.00	110.00	100.00	100.00	100.00
Groundnuts (shelled)	X3	..	..	..	..	..	..	..	..	..	..	..
Millet	F1	..	..	..	..	..	..	..	..	..	..	..
Sorghum (red)	F2	..	..	..	..	..	..	..	..	..	..	..

(Table continues on the following page

8-1. (continued)

	Category	Local currency per kilogram										
		1980	1981	1982	1983	1984	1985	1986	1987	1988	1989	1990
NIGERIA												
Official producer price												
Cocoa (bean)	X1	1.30	1.30	1.30	1.40	1.50	1.60	3.50	..	..	..	..
Palm kernels	X2	0.20	0.20	0.23	0.23	0.40	0.40	0.40	..	..	..	..
Cotton (seed cotton)	X3	0.40	0.47	0.51	0.56	0.70	0.85	1.00	..	..	..	..
Groundnuts (in shell)	X4	0.42	0.45	0.45	0.45	0.65	0.75	1.00	..	..	..	..
Sorghum	F1	0.21	0.22	0.22	0.22	0.36	0.50	0.58	..	..	..	..
Millet	F2	0.22	0.23	0.23	0.23	0.36	0.50	0.58	..	..	..	..
Maize	F3	0.20	0.21	0.21	0.21	0.35	0.45	0.52	..	..	..	..
Rice (paddy)	F4	0.33	0.40	0.40	0.40	0.50	0.70	1.00	..	..	..	..
Yams	NT1	0.40	0.57	0.58	0.58	0.68	0.90	1.05	..	..	..	..
Cassava (gari)	NT2	0.30	0.42	0.43	0.43	0.57	0.17	0.31	..	..	..	..
Farmgate price												
Cocoa (bean)	X1	1.30	1.30	1.30	1.40	1.50	1.60	3.50	7.50	11.00	24.00	25.00
Palm kernels	X2	0.20	0.20	0.23	0.23	0.40	0.40	0.40	0.85	1.00	1.20	1.50
Cotton (seed cotton)	X3	0.40	0.47	0.51	0.56	0.70	0.85	1.00	4.00	4.50	5.00	5.50
Groundnuts (in shell)	X4	0.42	0.45	0.45	0.45	0.65	0.75	1.00	2.08	2.25	2.30	2.50
Sorghum	F1	0.21	0.22	0.22	0.22	0.36	0.50	0.58	0.62	1.61	1.60	1.90
Millet	F2	0.22	0.23	0.23	0.23	0.36	0.50	0.58	0.60	1.62	1.60	1.90
Maize	F3	0.20	0.21	0.21	0.21	0.35	0.45	0.52	0.84	1.52	1.60	1.80
Rice (paddy)	F4	0.33	0.40	0.40	0.40	0.50	0.70	1.00	1.31	2.13	2.60	2.80
Yams	NT1	0.40	0.57	0.58	0.58	0.68	0.90	1.05	0.86	2.29	2.50	2.70
Cassava (gari)	NT2	0.30	0.42	0.43	0.43	0.57	0.17	0.31	0.48	0.55	0.70	0.80
RWANDA												
Official producer price												
Coffee (Arabica, merchant)	X1	164.40	164.40	164.40	164.40	164.40	164.40	168.90	168.90	168.90	168.90	135.00
Tea (green leaf, delivered)	X2	13.00	15.00	15.00	15.00	15.00	15.00	15.00	15.00	15.00	15.00	..
Beans (dry)	F1	..	..	..	..	..	..	..	..	..	..	..
Sorghum	F2	..	..	..	..	..	..	..	..	..	..	..
Maize	F3	..	..	..	..	..	..	..	..	..	..	..
Bananas	NT1	..	..	..	..	..	..	..	..	..	..	..
Sweet potatoes	NT2	..	..	..	..	..	..	..	..	..	..	..
Farmgate price												
Coffee (Arabica, merchant)	X1	164.40	164.40	164.40	164.40	164.40	164.40	168.90	168.90	168.90	168.90	135.00
Tea (green leaf, delivered)	X2	13.00	15.00	15.00	15.00	15.00	15.00	15.00	15.00	15.00	15.00	..
Beans (dry)	F1	27.60	15.80	21.05	23.28	33.74	35.77	22.28	28.55	..	..	..
Sorghum	F2	21.21	18.84	20.12	16.45	23.52	23.61	20.19	20.18	20.56	22.00	24.00
Maize	F3	14.96	10.37	6.78	10.46	17.01	21.75	15.63	15.38	13.32	16.00	18.00
Bananas	NT1	7.58	9.56	6.01	6.35	9.45	11.97	9.65	9.76	10.25	10.50	10.70
Sweet potatoes	NT2	7.05	4.81	4.32	6.45	7.63	9.93	6.13	6.23	5.26	5.50	6.00
SAO TOME & PRINCIPE												
Official producer price												
Cocoa	X1	..	..	..	..	..	..	..	..	..	..	..
Maize	F1	..	..	..	..	..	..	..	..	..	..	..
Cassava	NT1	..	..	..	..	..	..	..	..	..	..	..
Taro	NT2	..	..	..	..	..	..	..	..	..	..	..
Farmgate price												
Cocoa	X1	..	..	..	..	..	..	..	..	..	..	..
Maize	F1	..	..	..	..	..	..	..	..	..	..	..
Cassava	NT1	..	..	..	..	..	..	..	..	..	..	..
Taro	NT2	..	..	..	..	..	..	..	..	..	..	..
SENEGAL												
Official producer price												
Groundnuts (in shell)	X1	50.00	60.00	60.00	70.00	70.00	90.00	90.00	90.00	70.00	70.00	70.00
Cotton (seed cotton, first quality)	X2	60.00	68.00	70.00	70.00	70.00	100.00	100.00	100.00	100.00	100.00	100.00
Millet	F1	40.00	50.00	50.00	55.00	60.00	70.00	70.00	70.00	74.40	78.80	83.10
Rice (paddy)	F2	41.50	51.50	51.50	60.00	66.00	85.00	85.00	85.00	85.00	85.00	85.00
Maize	F3	37.00	47.00	47.00	50.00	60.00	70.00	70.00	70.00	77.00	79.70	84.60
Sorghum	F4	40.00	50.00	50.00	55.00	60.00	70.00	70.00	70.00	74.40	78.80	83.10
Farmgate price												
Groundnuts (in shell)	X1	50.00	60.00	60.00	70.00	70.00	90.00	90.00	90.00	70.00	70.00	70.00
Cotton (seed cotton, first quality)	X2	60.00	68.00	70.00	70.00	70.00	100.00	100.00	100.00'	100.00	100.00	100.00
Millet	F1	40.00	50.00	50.00	55.00	60.00	70.00	70.00	70.00	74.40	78.80	83.10
Rice (paddy)	F2	41.50	51.50	51.50	60.00	66.00	85.00	85.00	85.00	85.00	85.00	85.00
Maize	F3	37.00	47.00	47.00	50.00	60.00	70.00	70.00	70.00	77.00	79.70	84.60
Sorghum	F4	40.00	50.00	50.00	55.00	60.00	70.00	70.00	70.00	74.40	78.80	83.10

(Table continues on the following page

8–1. (continued)

	Category	Local currency per kilogram										
		1980	1981	1982	1983	1984	1985	1986	1987	1988	1989	1990
SIERRA LEONE												
Official producer price												
Cocoa	X1	1.81	1.43	1.43	2.98	4.85	6.61	29.76	29.76	29.76	44.09	99.21
Coffee (Robusta)	X2	1.76	1.32	1.43	3.80	5.29	8.82	52.91	52.91	52.91	70.55	88.19
Palm kernels	X3	0.18	0.16	0.22	0.44	0.66	0.88	1.32	2.65	2.65	8.82	22.05
Rice (paddy)	F1	0.43	0.52	0.62	0.93	1.10	1.30	2.78	7.40	22.20	29.04	37.04
Cassava	NT1	0.28	0.27	0.27	0.64	1.55	2.90	4.89	13.00	39.00	50.00	63.70
Farmgate price												
Cocoa	X1	1.81	1.43	1.43	2.98	4.85	6.61	29.76	29.76	29.76	44.09	99.21
Coffee (Robusta)	X2	1.76	1.32	1.43	3.80	5.29	8.82	52.91	52.91	52.91	70.55	88.19
Palm kernels	X3	0.18	0.16	0.22	0.44	0.66	0.88	1.32	2.65	2.65	8.82	22.05
Rice (paddy)	F1	..	..	..	..	..	..	..	..	..	..	..
Cassava	NT1	..	..	..	..	..	..	..	..	..	..	..
SOMALIA												
Official producer price												
Bananas	X1	0.66	1.70	2.00	2.39	3.46	9.68	13.22	13.22	31.68	..	..
Maize	F1	1.00	1.80	1.80	3.25	3.25	15.00	15.00	17.00	52.00	245.00	..
Sorghum	F2	1.00	1.50	1.50	2.65	2.72	13.00	13.00	15.00	35.00	155.00	..
Sesame	NT1	3.00	4.50	7.00	8.70	9.10	50.00	60.00	..	..	..	..
Farmgate price												
Bananas	X1	0.66	1.70	2.00	2.39	3.46	9.68	13.22	13.22	31.68	..	..
Maize	F1	1.00	1.80	..	..	..	15.00	15.00	17.00	52.00	245.00	..
Sorghum	F2	1.00	1.50	..	..	..	13.00	13.00	15.00	35.00	155.00	..
Sesame	NT1	..	..	..	..	..	..	..	..	..	..	..
SOUTH AFRICA												
Official producer price												
Maize	X1	0.12	0.13	0.16	0.17	0.22	0.22	0.27	0.31	0.28	0.26	0.28
Wheat	X2	0.21	0.23	0.29	0.27	0.29	0.31	0.36	0.39	0.34	0.38	0.38
Sugar cane	X3	0.03	0.02	0.03	0.03	0.03	0.03	0.04	0.03	0.04	0.05	0.05
Sorghum	F1	0.09	0.10	0.14	0.20	0.20	0.18	0.19	0.19	0.21	0.20	0.21
Barley	F2	0.18	0.21	0.25	0.25	0.27	0.24	0.30	0.32	0.32	0.35	0.36
Farmgate price												
Maize	X1	..	..	..	..	..	..	..	..	..	..	..
Wheat	X2	..	..	..	..	..	..	..	..	..	..	..
Sugar cane	X3	..	..	..	..	..	..	..	..	..	..	..
Sorghum	F1	..	..	..	..	..	..	..	..	..	..	..
Barley	F2	..	..	..	..	..	..	..	..	..	..	..
SUDAN												
Official producer price												
Cotton (seed cotton, long-staple, grade 1)	X1	0.47	0.71	0.73	0.89	1.08	1.64	1.91	2.78	5.05	5.85	..
Groundnuts (El-Obeid, in shell)	X2	0.12	0.14	0.20	0.28	0.41	0.48	1.22	1.22	..	..	..
Sesame (Gedaref, mixed)	X3	0.26	0.30	0.43	0.55	0.76	1.07	1.36	1.36	..	..	..
Gum arabic (El-Obeid)	X4	0.36	0.42	0.51	0.89	1.16	2.05	6.68	8.90	8.90	8.90	..
Sorghum	F1	0.22	0.25	0.28	0.30	..	..	0.35	0.38	..	..	..
Wheat	F2	0.12	0.16	0.23	0.28	..	0.70	0.77	0.85	2.40	3.00	..
Farmgate price												
Cotton (seed cotton, long-staple, grade 1)	X1	0.47	0.71	0.73	0.89	1.08	1.64	1.91	2.78	5.05	5.85	..
Groundnuts (El-Obeid, in shell)	X2	..	..	..	..	..	1.30	1.42	1.52	2.04	2.93	..
Sesame (El-Obeid, mixed)	X3	..	..	..	..	..	1.85	1.74	2.10	4.24	6.04	..
Gum arabic (El-Obeid)	X4	..	..	..	..	..	..	..	..	..	..	..
Sorghum	F1	..	..	..	..	..	0.51	0.29	0.76	0.96	1.11	..
Wheat	F2	0.12	0.16	0.23	0.28	..	0.70	0.77	0.85	2.40	3.00	..
SWAZILAND												
Official producer price												
Sugarcane (sucrose)	X1	..	..	..	..	..	..	..	..	..	..	..
Citrus	X2	..	..	..	..	..	..	..	..	..	..	..
Pineapple	X3	..	..	..	..	..	..	..	..	..	..	..
Cotton (seed cotton)	X4	0.45	0.47	0.52	0.63	0.83	0.83	0.83	..	..	..	..
Maize	F1	0.11	0.12	0.13	0.16	0.19	0.26	0.31	0.32	0.34	0.37	0.40
Farmgate price												
Sugarcane (sucrose)	X1	..	0.20	0.19	0.21	0.22	0.25	..	..	..	..	..
Citrus (average export)	X2	..	0.19	0.24	0.22	0.22	0.50	..	..	..	..	..
Pineapple	X3	..	0.05	0.05	0.07	0.07	0.07	..	..	..	..	..
Cotton (seed cotton)	X4	0.45	0.47	0.52	0.63	0.83	0.83	0.83	..	..	..	..
Maize	F1	0.11	0.12	0.13	0.16	0.19	0.26	0.31	0.32	0.34	0.37	0.40

(Table continues on the following page

8–1. (continued)

		Local currency per kilogram										
	Category	1980	1981	1982	1983	1984	1985	1986	1987	1988	1989	1990
TANZANIA												
Official producer price												
Coffee (Arabica) (parchment)	X1	12.36	13.90	15.17	22.87	29.68	45.80	50.75	66.00	90.00	120.00	125.00
Cotton (seed cotton, AR)	X2	3.20	3.70	4.70	6.00	8.40	13.00	16.90	19.45	22.35	28.00	41.00
Tea (green leaves)	X3	1.50	1.50	2.00	2.80	4.10	4.95	7.60	9.90	13.40	13.40	13.50
Maize	F1	1.00	1.50	1.75	2.20	4.00	5.25	6.30	8.20	9.00	11.00	13.00
Sorghum	F2	1.00	1.00	1.60	2.00	3.00	4.00	4.80	6.00	6.20	6.81	6.86
Rice (paddy)	F3	1.75	2.30	3.00	4.00	6.00	8.00	9.60	14.40	17.30	19.00	26.00
Millet	F4	1.50	1.50	1.50	2.00	3.00	4.00	4.80	6.00	6.60	7.25	7.30
Cassava (grade 1, Makopa)	NT1	0.65	0.70	0.90	1.20	2.00	3.00	3.60	4.50	4.95	5.45	5.50
Farmgate price												
Coffee (Arabica) (parchment)	X1	12.36	13.90	15.17	22.87	29.68	45.80	50.75	66.00	90.00	120.00	125.00
Cotton (seed cotton, AR)	X2	3.20	3.70	4.70	6.00	8.40	13.00	16.90	19.45	22.35	28.00	41.00
Tea (green leaves)	X3	1.50	1.50	2.00	2.80	4.10	4.95	7.60	9.90	13.40	13.40	13.50
Maize	F1	4.98	1.44	3.80	10.90	7.60	7.50	8.00	..	14.30	..	..
Sorghum	F2	4.68	..	..	..	..	4.00	4.80	6.00	..	..	..
Rice (paddy)	F3	4.23	..	4.06	9.12	10.80	19.00	20.50	..	22.55	..	..
Millet	F4	6.95	..	..	..	..	4.00	4.80	6.00	..	..	..
Cassava (grade 1, Makopa)	NT1	2.90	..	..	..	..	..	..	..	..	..	..
TOGO												
Official producer price												
Coffee (Robusta)	X1	200.00	215.00	235.00	290.00	315.00	365.00	400.00	400.00	350.00	175.00	..
Cocoa	X2	220.00	225.00	235.00	275.00	300.00	330.00	360.00	360.00	300.00	225.00	..
Cotton (seed cotton)	X3	60.00	65.00	65.00	75.00	90.00	105.00	105.00	95.00	95.00	95.00	..
Maize	F1	..	..	..	..	..	..	..	..	..	..	
Sorghum	F2	..	..	..	..	..	..	..	..	..	..	
Millet	F3	..	..	..	..	..	..	..	..	..	..	
Cassava	NT1	..	..	..	..	..	..	..	..	..	..	
Yams	NT2	..	..	..	..	..	..	..	..	..	..	
Farmgate price												
Coffee (Robusta)	X1	200.00	215.00	235.00	290.00	315.00	365.00	400.00	400.00	350.00	175.00	..
Cocoa	X2	220.00	225.00	235.00	275.00	300.00	330.00	360.00	360.00	300.00	225.00	..
Cotton (seed cotton)	X3	60.00	65.00	65.00	75.00	90.00	105.00	105.00	95.00	95.00	95.00	..
Maize	F1	68.36	95.52	99.86	104.20	75.00	47.00	73.00	72.00	79.00	60.00	60.00
Sorghum	F2	68.03	83.75	97.30	110.84	89.00	58.00	76.00	66.00	98.00	69.00	69.00
Millet	F3	66.65	69.52	73.20	76.87	89.00	67.90	59.00	61.00	62.60	62.70	62.80
Cassava	NT1	20.31	41.36	38.12	34.88	38.00	28.66	30.00	32.00	26.00	30.00	30.00
Yams	NT2	48.47	77.98	83.33	88.68	81.00	63.87	61.00	63.00	63.00	68.00	65.30
TUNISIA												
Official producer price												
Olives	X1	0.09	0.10	0.15	0.13	0.15	0.17	0.19	0.21	0.22	0.24	0.26
Citrus (oranges)	X2	0.13	0.12	0.17	0.19	0.14	0.16	0.19	0.19	0.20	0.21	0.21
Wheat	F1	0.09	0.10	0.11	0.13	0.14	0.15	0.16	0.17	0.18	0.19	0.20
Barley	NT1	0.06	0.07	0.08	0.10	0.10	0.11	0.11	0.12	0.13	0.14	0.15
Farmgate price												
Olives	X1	..	..	..	..	..	..	..	..	..	..	..
Citrus (oranges)	X2	..	..	..	..	..	..	..	..	..	..	..
Wheat	F1	..	..	..	..	..	..	..	..	..	..	..
Barley	NT1	..	..	..	..	..	..	..	..	..	..	..
UGANDA												
Official producer price												
Coffee (Robusta, Kiboko)	X1	0.20	0.50	0.80	1.30	2.70	4.70	8.50	24.00	60.00	60.00	120.00
Cotton (seed cotton, AR Safi)	X2	0.15	0.40	0.60	1.20	2.20	3.20	4.00	19.00	80.00	130.00	220.00
Tea (greenleaf)	X3	0.03	0.06	0.10	0.20	0.55	0.80	1.30	5.00	15.00	20.00	30.00
Millet	F1	0.16	0.22	0.27	0.32	1.42	1.73	7.38	17.62	43.69	56.47	75.00
Maize	F2	0.12	0.09	0.14	0.22	0.98	1.57	4.55	11.30	31.08	37.60	50.00
Sorghum	F3	0.13	0.20	0.26	0.30	1.38	1.64	5.45	18.30	45.37	58.65	77.89
Cassava	NT1	0.07	0.07	0.07	0.12	0.56	0.76	2.26	9.30	22.31	28.70	37.96
Plantains	NT2	0.07	0.07	0.06	0.19	0.72	0.85	3.90	7.54	21.00	30.00	35.00
Farmgate price												
Coffee (Robusta)	X1	0.20	0.50	0.80	1.30	2.70	4.70	8.50	24.00	60.00	60.00	120.00
Cotton (seed cotton)	X2	0.15	0.40	0.60	1.20	2.20	3.20	4.00	19.00	80.00	130.00	220.00
Tea (greenleaf)	X3	..	..	..	..	..	..	..	..	..	..	..
Millet	F1	0.16	0.22	0.27	0.32	1.42	1.73	7.38	17.62	43.69	56.47	75.00
Maize	F2	0.12	0.09	0.14	0.22	0.98	1.57	4.55	11.30	31.08	37.60	50.00
Sorghum	F3	0.13	0.20	0.26	0.30	1.38	1.64	5.45	18.30	45.37	58.65	77.89
Cassava	NT1	0.07	0.07	0.07	0.12	0.56	0.76	2.26	9.30	22.31	28.70	37.96
Plantains	NT2	0.07	0.07	0.06	0.19	0.72	0.85	3.90	7.54	21.00	30.00	35.00

(Table continues on the following page

8–1. (continued)

| | | \multicolumn{11}{c}{*Local currency per kilogram*} | | | | | | | | | |
	Category	1980	1981	1982	1983	1984	1985	1986	1987	1988	1989	1990
ZAIRE												
Official producer price												
Coffee (Arabica, green beans)	X1	4.00	5.00	..	..	..	..	..	..	..	..	..
Palm oil	X2	2.12	2.82	..	..	..	..	..	..	..	..	..
Rubber (natural)	X3	2.07	2.50	..	..	..	..	..	..	..	..	..
Cocoa (beans)	X4	2.00	3.00	..	..	..	..	..	..	..	..	..
Maize	F1	1.16	1.17	1.20	1.51	1.82	2.02	2.10	2.35	2.50	2.70	2.90
Rice (paddy)	F2	1.96	2.08	3.80	6.03	6.10	6.17	6.35	6.50	6.50	7.10	7.60
Cassava	NT1	1.29	1.48	1.94	3.21	3.50	3.70	4.20	4.50	4.50	4.50	4.90
Plantains	NT2	2.85	0.80	0.80	3.60	4.50	5.90	6.20	6.50	6.50	6.50	7.00
Farmgate price												
Coffee (Arabica, green beans)	X1	4.00	5.00	6.50	11.00	23.00	72.00	65.00	65.00	65.00	65.00	70.00
Palm oil	X2	2.12	2.82	4.53	7.92	8.75	9.80	10.20	10.70	10.70	10.70	11.70
Rubber (natural)	X3	2.07	2.50	5.20	33.00	35.00	38.40	43.00	46.40	46.40	46.40	46.40
Cocoa (beans)	X4	2.00	3.00	5.00	11.50	19.00	25.00	30.00	50.00	55.00	55.00	60.00
Maize	F1	1.16	1.17	..	3.20	4.00	5.00	6.60	15.00	..	..	..
Rice (paddy)	F2	1.96	2.08	5.00	..	10.00	10.00	11.50	16.00	..	..	..
Cassava	NT1	1.29	1.48	..	..	7.10	6.00	11.00	19.00	..	..	..
Plantains	NT2	2.85	0.80	..	..	..	..	..	..	..	..	..
ZAMBIA												
Official producer price												
Cotton (seed cotton)	X1	0.46	0.46	0.47	0.52	0.58	0.67	0.99	1.60	3.00	3.60	9.70
Tobacco (Virginia)	X2	1.57	1.65	2.40	2.70	2.80	3.45	5.12	5.22	14.00	14.40	60.00
Sunflower (seeds)	X3	0.33	0.35	0.42	0.43	0.43	0.56	0.84	1.40	1.80	3.25	6.01
Maize	F1	0.13	0.15	0.18	0.20	0.27	0.32	0.61	0.87	0.89	1.20	2.05
Wheat	F2	0.22	0.29	0.36	0.40	0.47	0.50	0.96	1.23	2.11	2.51	5.41
Cassava	NT1	0.14	0.12	0.15	0.15	0.20	0.30	0.60	0.70	1.00	1.40	3.20
Farmgate price												
Cotton (seed cotton)	X1	0.46	0.46	0.47	0.52	0.58	0.67	0.99	1.60	3.00	3.60	9.70
Tobacco (Virginia)	X2	1.57	1.65	2.40	2.70	2.80	3.45	5.12	5.22	14.00	14.40	60.00
Sunflower (seeds)	X3	0.33	0.35	0.42	0.43	0.43	0.56	0.84	1.40	1.80	3.25	6.01
Maize	F1	0.13	0.15	0.18	0.20	0.27	0.32	0.61	0.87	0.89	1.20	2.05
Wheat	F2	0.22	0.29	0.36	0.40	0.47	0.50	0.96	1.23	2.11	2.51	5.41
Cassava	NT1	..	..	..	..	..	..	..	..	..	..	..
ZIMBABWE												
Official producer price												
Tobacco	X1	0.80	1.84	1.67	1.89	2.07	2.68	3.13	2.18	3.94	4.00	4.30
Cotton (seed cotton)	X2	0.38	0.40	0.52	0.52	0.57	0.67	0.75	0.80	0.85	0.93	0.99
Sugarcane	X3	0.01	0.02	0.02	0.02	0.02	0.03	0.03	0.03	0.03	0.03	0.04
Maize	X4	0.09	0.12	0.12	0.12	0.14	0.18	0.18	0.18	0.20	0.22	0.22
Wheat	F1	0.16	0.17	0.19	0.22	0.25	0.29	0.30	0.32	0.37	0.40	0.43
Farmgate price												
Tobacco	X1	0.80	1.84	1.67	1.89	2.07	2.68	3.13	2.18	3.94	4.00	4.30
Cotton (seed cotton)	X2	0.38	0.40	0.52	0.52	0.57	0.67	0.75	0.80	0.85	0.93	0.99
Sugarcane	X3	0.01	0.02	0.02	0.02	0.02	0.03	0.03	0.03	0.03	0.03	0.04
Maize	X4	0.09	0.12	0.12	0.12	0.14	0.18	0.18	0.18	0.20	0.22	0.22
Wheat	F1	0.16	0.17	0.19	0.22	0.25	0.29	0.30	0.32	0.37	0.40	0.43

Notes: *The categories of crops are defined in the technical notes.*
Categories are mutually exclusive and ordering is intended to reflect relative importance of these crops as of 1986–88.
In many cases official markets operate simultaneously with parallel or open market activites. Where a large majority of markets production is believed to pass through the official channels, the official price is also reported as the farmgate price. In most cases, only very rough estimates of the share of marketed production passing through each channel is available.

(Table continues on the following page

8-2. Producer price shares

	Ratio of producer price to international reference price											Average		
	1980	1981	1982	1983	1984	1985	1986	1987	1988	1989	1990	75–79	80–85	86–MR
ANGOLA														
Official producer price														
Coffee	0.17	0.31	0.38	0.73	0.55	0.54	0.70	0.90	0.83	1.43	..	0.22	0.45	0.96
Farmgate price														
Coffee	..	..	..	..	..	..	..	..	..	..	..	..	..	..
BENIN														
Official producer prices														
Cotton (lint)	0.42	0.42	0.57	0.44	0.29	0.32	0.74	0.56	0.46	0.47	0.48	0.45	0.41	0.54
Palm oil	0.70	0.60	2.48	0.48	0.31	0.34	0.65	0.37	0.31	0.40	0.70	1.20	0.82	0.49
Farmgate prices														
Cotton (lint)	0.42	0.42	0.57	0.44	0.29	0.32	0.74	0.56	0.46	0.47	0.48	0.45	0.41	0.54
Palm oil	0.70	0.60	2.48	0.48	0.31	0.34	0.65	0.37	0.31	0.40	0.70	1.20	0.82	0.49
BOTSWANA														
Official producer prices														
Groundnuts (in shell)	..	..	0.78	0.46	0.56	1.26	..	0.48	..	..	..	..	0.61	..
Farmgate prices														
Groundnuts (in shell)	..	..	..	..	..	..	..	..	..	..	..	..	..	..
BURKINA FASO														
Official producer prices														
Cotton (lint)	0.46	0.37	0.34	0.29	0.23	0.34	0.69	0.55	0.52	0.47	..	0.42	0.34	0.56
Groundnuts (shelled)	0.50	0.60	0.83	0.93	1.38	..	1.49	0.76	0.84	0.74	..	0.46	0.85	0.96
Sesame seed	0.80	0.68	0.65	0.55	0.44	0.46	1.11	0.83	0.61	0.48	..	0.59	0.59	0.76
Farmgate prices														
Cotton (lint)	0.46	0.37	0.34	0.29	0.23	0.34	0.69	0.55	0.52	0.47	..	0.42	0.34	0.56
Groundnuts (shelled)	0.50	0.60	0.83	0.93	1.38	..	1.49	0.76	0.84	0.74	..	0.46	0.85	0.96
Sesame seed	0.80	0.68	0.65	0.55	0.44	0.46	1.11	0.83	0.61	0.48	..	0.59	0.59	0.76
BURUNDI														
Official producer prices														
Coffee (Arabica, green)	0.50	0.57	0.74	0.70	0.61	0.51	0.51	0.47	0.75	0.50	0.74	0.51	0.60	0.60
Tea (green leaves)	0.08	0.09	0.11	0.09	0.09	0.05	0.09	0.12	0.12	0.09	0.07	0.07	0.08	0.10
Cotton (lint)	0.60	0.58	0.81	0.61	0.41	0.44	0.61	0.59	0.45	0.49	..	0.66	0.57	0.54
Farmgate prices														
Coffee (Arabica, green)	0.50	0.57	0.74	0.70	0.61	0.51	0.51	0.47	0.75	0.50	0.74	0.51	0.60	0.60
Tea (green leaves)	0.08	0.09	0.11	0.09	0.09	0.05	0.09	0.12	0.12	0.09	0.07	0.07	0.08	0.10
Cotton (lint)	0.60	0.58	0.81	0.61	0.41	0.44	0.61	0.59	0.45	0.49	..	0.66	0.57	0.54
CAMEROON														
Official producer prices														
Coffee (Arabica)	0.41	0.57	0.48	0.44	0.42	0.39	0.47	0.75	0.82	0.86	1.60	0.39	0.45	0.90
Cocoa (grade 1, superior)	0.41	0.63	0.52	0.53	0.47	0.55	0.61	0.77	0.88	0.80	1.14	0.26	0.52	0.84
Cotton (lint)	0.39	0.31	0.30	0.24	0.42	0.55	0.42	0.43	0.39	0.42	0.36	0.42	0.37	0.40
Farmgate prices														
Coffee (Arabica)	0.41	0.57	0.48	0.44	0.42	0.39	0.47	0.75	0.82	0.86	1.60	0.39	0.45	0.90
Cocoa (grade 1, superior)	0.41	0.63	0.52	0.53	0.47	0.55	0.61	0.77	0.88	0.80	1.14	0.26	0.52	0.84
Cotton (lint)	0.39	0.31	0.30	0.24	0.42	0.55	0.42	0.43	0.39	0.42	0.36	0.42	0.37	0.40
CENTRAL AFRICAN REPUBLIC														
Official producer prices														
Coffee (Robusta, cherries)	0.20	0.25	0.20	0.16	0.15	0.14	0.14	0.24	0.25	0.37	0.72	0.29	0.18	0.34
Cotton (lint)	0.47	0.39	0.39	0.41	0.55	0.54	0.91	0.91	0.79	0.66	0.82	0.88	0.46	0.82
Farmgate prices														
Coffee (Robusta, cherries)	0.20	0.25	0.20	0.16	0.15	0.14	0.14	0.24	0.25	0.37	0.72	0.29	0.18	0.34
Cotton (lint)	0.47	0.39	0.39	0.41	0.55	0.54	0.91	0.91	0.79	0.66	0.82	0.88	0.46	0.82
CHAD														
Official producer prices														
Cotton (lint)	0.81	0.61	0.60	0.35	0.30	0.37	0.55	0.58	0.48	0.55	0.55	0.75	0.51	0.54
Farmgate prices														
Cotton (lint)	0.81	0.61	0.60	0.35	0.30	0.37	0.55	0.58	0.48	0.55	0.55	0.75	0.51	0.54
COMOROS														
Official producer prices														
Vanilla (dried)	0.28	0.35	0.32	0.29	0.30	0.35	0.38	0.46	0.46	0.37	..	0.43	0.32	0.42
Cloves	..	..	..	..	..	..	..	..	..	..	..	..	..	..
Ylang Ylang (essence)	..	..	..	..	..	..	..	..	..	..	..	..	..	..
Copra	..	..	..	..	..	..	..	..	..	..	..	..	..	..
Farmgate prices														
Vanilla (dried)	..	..	..	..	..	..	..	..	..	..	..	..	..	..
Cloves	0.49	0.72	0.49	0.71	1.40	0.94	1.01	1.59	1.14	1.36	..	0.62	0.79	1.28
Ylang Ylang (essence)	0.14	0.18	0.20	0.22	0.22	0.23	0.34	0.37	0.27	..	..	0.20	0.20	0.33
Copra	0.36	0.52	0.28	0.49	0.66	0.65	0.76	..	0.63	0.62	..	0.63	0.49	0.67

8-2. (continued)

	Ratio of producer price to international reference price											Average		
	1980	1981	1982	1983	1984	1985	1986	1987	1988	1989	1990	75–79	80–85	86–MR
CONGO, PEOPLE'S REPUBLIC OF THE														
Official producer prices														
Coffee (Robusta, shelled)	0.25	0.34	0.31	0.26	0.20	0.19	0.18	0.91	0.91	1.52	1.92	0.21	0.26	1.09
Cocoa (superior quality)	0.38	0.51	0.48	0.53	0.40	0.28	0.43	0.61	0.99	1.37	1.94	0.35	0.43	1.07
Farmgate prices														
Coffee (Robusta, shelled)	0.25	0.34	0.31	0.26	0.20	0.19	0.18	0.91	0.91	1.52	1.92	0.21	0.26	1.09
Cocoa (superior quality)	0.38	0.51	0.48	0.53	0.40	0.28	0.43	0.61	0.99	1.37	1.94	0.35	0.43	1.07
COTE D'IVOIRE														
Official producer prices														
Coffee (Robusta, green)	0.38	0.59	0.54	0.43	0.31	0.31	0.35	0.56	0.70	0.68	1.30	0.35	0.43	0.72
Cocoa (beans)	0.48	0.65	0.60	0.53	0.40	0.39	0.52	0.65	0.74	0.90	1.16	0.40	0.51	0.79
Palm oil	0.73	0.63	0.71	0.65	0.40	0.77	1.83	2.24	1.69	2.06	3.32	0.65	0.65	2.23
Farmgate prices														
Coffee (Robusta, green)	0.38	0.59	0.54	0.43	0.31	0.31	0.35	0.56	0.70	0.68	1.30	0.35	0.43	0.72
Cocoa (beans)	0.48	0.65	0.60	0.53	0.40	0.39	0.52	0.65	0.74	0.90	1.16	0.40	0.51	0.79
Palm oil	0.73	0.63	0.71	0.65	0.40	0.77	1.83	2.24	1.69	2.06	3.32	0.65	0.65	2.23
EGYPT, ARAB REPUBLIC OF														
Official producer prices														
Cotton (lint)	0.42	0.51	0.65	0.64	0.50	0.48	0.50	0.52	0.44	0.29	0.12	0.45	0.53	0.37
Rice (milled paddy)	0.21	0.22	0.41	0.49	0.59	0.69	0.85	1.03	0.95	0.73	0.46	0.37	0.44	0.80
Farmgate prices														
Cotton (lint)	0.42	0.51	0.65	0.64	0.50	0.48	0.50	0.52	0.44	0.29	0.12	0.45	0.53	0.37
Rice (milled paddy)	0.22	0.24	0.48	0.67	0.74	0.86	1.44	1.54	0.98	0.94	..	0.38	0.53	1.22
EQUATORIAL GUINEA														
Official producer prices														
Cocoa (first grade dried beans)	0.68	0.70	0.84	0.84	0.72	0.65	0.79	1.04	0.94	0.82	..	..	0.74	0.90
Coffee (Robusta, cherry)	0.12	1.12	1.04	0.97	0.47	0.34	0.35	0.45	0.27	0.26	..	..	0.67	0.33
Farmgate prices														
Cocoa (first grade dried beans)	0.68	0.70	0.84	0.84	0.72	0.65	0.79	1.04	0.94	0.82	..	..	0.74	0.90
Coffee (Robusta, cherry)	..	..	..	..	..	..	..	..	..	..	..	..	..	..
ETHIOPIA														
Official producer prices														
Coffee (Arabica, beans)	0.38	0.40	0.45	0.38	0.36	0.38	0.34	0.40	0.38	0.40	0.58	0.45	0.39	0.42
Sesame seed	0.55	0.62	0.77	0.76	1.02	0.95	1.41	0.96	0.98	0.94	0.71	0.51	0.78	1.00
Farmgate prices														
Coffee (Arabica, beans)	0.38	0.40	0.45	0.38	0.36	0.38	0.34	0.40	0.38	0.40	0.58	0.45	0.39	0.42
Sesame seed	0.55	0.62	0.77	0.76	1.02	0.95	1.41	0.96	0.98	0.94	0.71	0.51	0.78	1.00
GABON														
Official producer prices														
Cocoa (first quality)	0.55	0.61	0.55	0.51	0.34	0.39	0.56	0.69	..	..	..	0.57	0.49	0.63
Coffee (merchant, processed)	0.30	0.40	0.31	0.26	0.25	0.26	0.25	0.40	..	..	..	0.70	0.30	0.32
Farmgate prices														
Cocoa (first quality)	..	..	..	..	..	..	..	..	..	..	..	..	..	..
Coffee (merchant, processed)	..	..	..	..	..	..	..	..	..	..	..	..	..	..
GAMBIA, THE														
Official producer prices														
Groundnuts (unshelled)	0.86	0.51	0.83	0.72	0.35	0.46	0.41	0.97	0.77	0.69	..	0.54	0.62	0.71
Cotton (lint)	..	..	..	..	0.61	0.67	0.90	0.93	0.98	0.82	..	..	0.64	0.91
Palm kernels	0.49	0.64	0.19	..	0.19	0.28	..	..	..	..	..	0.48	0.36	..
Farmgate prices														
Groundnuts (unshelled)	0.86	0.51	0.83	0.72	0.35	0.46	0.41	0.97	0.77	0.69	..	0.54	0.62	0.71
Cotton (lint)	..	..	..	..	0.61	0.67	0.90	0.93	0.98	0.82	..	0.15	0.21	0.91
Palm kernels	..	..	..	..	..	..	..	..	..	..	..	..	..	..
GHANA														
Official producer prices														
Cocoa	0.43	0.70	2.73	0.86	0.24	0.26	0.27	0.23	0.35	0.40	..	0.30	0.87	0.25
Farmgate prices														
Cocoa	0.43	0.70	2.73	0.86	0.24	0.26	0.27	0.23	0.35	0.40	..	0.30	0.87	0.25
GUINEA														
Official producer prices														
Coffee (Robusta)	0.80	0.78	0.76	0.73	0.66	0.87	0.08	0.52	0.43	0.42	0.57	0.60	0.77	0.40
Palm kernels	1.06	0.75	0.76	0.82	0.65	1.11	0.34	0.99	0.63	0.57	0.57	1.08	0.86	0.62
Farmgate prices														
Coffee (Robusta)	0.80	0.78	0.76	0.73	0.66	0.87	0.08	0.52	0.43	0.42	0.57	0.60	0.77	0.40
Palm kernels	1.06	0.75	0.76	0.82	0.65	1.11	0.34	0.99	0.63	0.57	0.57	1.08	0.86	0.62

(Table continues on the following page)

8-2. (continued)

	Ratio of producer price to international reference price											Average		
	1980	1981	1982	1983	1984	1985	1986	1987	1988	1989	1990	75-79	80-85	86-MR
GUINEA-BISSAU														
Official producer prices														
Cashew nuts	0.48	0.31	0.27	0.32	0.18	0.14	0.16	0.08	0.05	0.07	0.10	1.00	0.28	0.09
Groundnuts (unshelled, grade 1)	0.76	0.47	0.67	0.61	0.25	0.30	0.66	0.33	0.23	0.21	0.27	0.63	0.51	0.34
Palm kernels	0.78	0.57	0.70	0.64	0.55	1.27	0.49	0.41	0.32	0.51	0.89	0.67	0.75	0.53
Farmgate prices														
Cashew nuts	0.48	0.31	0.27	0.32	0.18	0.14	0.16	0.08	0.25	..	..	1.00	0.28	0.16
Groundnuts (unshelled, grade 1)	0.76	0.47	0.67	0.61	0.25	0.30	0.66	0.33	..	..	..	0.63	0.51	0.50
Palm kernels	0.78	0.57	0.70	0.64	0.55	1.27	0.49	0.41	..	..	..	0.67	0.75	0.45
KENYA														
Official producer prices														
Coffee (Arabica, washed, g. 1-6)	1.06	1.02	0.74	0.79	0.82	0.87	0.75	1.38	0.62	1.04	..	0.82	0.88	0.95
Tea	0.90	0.99	0.95	0.81	0.55	1.76	1.19	1.40	0.97	0.80	..	1.03	0.99	1.09
Sugar (centrifugal, raw)	0.41	0.35	0.37	0.38	0.35	0.25	0.31	0.28	0.26	..	..	0.33	0.35	0.28
Sisal	0.86	0.86	0.76	0.81	0.96	0.93	1.02	1.03	0.92	0.75	..	1.02	0.87	0.93
Farmgate prices														
Coffee (Arabica, washed, g. 1-6)	1.06	1.02	0.74	0.79	0.82	0.87	0.75	1.38	0.62	1.04	..	0.82	0.88	0.95
Tea	0.90	0.99	0.95	0.81	0.55	1.76	1.19	1.40	0.97	0.80	..	1.03	0.99	1.09
Sugar (centrifugal, raw)	0.41	0.35	0.37	0.38	0.35	0.25	0.31	0.28	0.26	..	..	0.33	0.35	0.28
Sisal	0.86	0.86	0.76	0.81	0.96	0.93	1.02	1.03	0.92	0.75	..	1.02	0.87	0.93
LESOTHO														
Official producer prices														
Wheat (wheat equivalent)	..	..	1.46	1.77	1.34	1.03	1.09	1.57	1.35	1.03	..	..	1.40	1.26
Beans	..	..	1.82	1.43	1.25	1.39	1.49	1.78	1.68	1.58	1.59	..	1.48	1.62
Peas	1.32	1.39	1.68	1.67	1.50	..	..	..	..	..	..	0.98	1.51	..
Maize	..	..	..	0.89	0.65	..	..	..	..	..	..	..	..	..
Farmgate prices														
Wheat (wheat equivalent)	..	..	1.70	1.52	1.11	1.03	1.09	1.57	1.35	1.03	..	..	1.34	1.26
Beans	..	..	1.38	1.62	1.38	1.39	1.49	1.78	1.68	1.58	1.59	..	1.44	1.62
Peas	..	..	1.81	1.68	1.50	..	..	..	..	..	..	..	1.66	..
Maize	..	..	..	1.01	0.68	..	..	..	..	..	..	..	..	..
LIBERIA														
Official producer prices														
Rubber (nonspec. coagul.)	..	..	..	..	..	..	..	..	..	..	..	0.42	0.64	0.79
Coffee (Robusta)	0.77	0.85	0.78	0.49	0.43	0.54	0.58	0.68	0.90	1.01	..	0.42	0.64	0.79
Cocoa (fair average quality)	0.64	0.88	0.83	0.55	0.49	0.44	0.44	0.49	0.64	..	..	..	0.64	0.52
Farmgate prices														
Rubber (nonspec. coagul.)	0.44	0.56	0.43	0.34	0.43	0.52	0.48	0.45	0.53	0.61	..	0.39	0.45	0.52
Coffee (Robusta)	0.77	0.85	0.78	0.49	0.43	0.54	0.58	0.68	0.90	1.01	..	0.42	0.64	0.79
Cocoa (fair average quality)	0.64	0.88	0.83	0.55	0.49	0.44	0.44	0.49	0.64	..	..	..	0.64	0.52
MADAGASCAR														
Official producer prices														
Coffee (Robusta)	0.28	0.40	0.41	0.26	0.18	0.22	0.19	0.27	0.33	0.48	0.63	0.40	0.29	0.38
Vanilla (dried)	0.24	0.23	0.20	0.13	0.12	0.10	0.10	0.07	0.06	0.07	0.09	0.25	0.17	0.08
Cloves	0.25	0.17	0.16	0.12	0.13	0.21	0.24	0.17	0.15	0.19	0.17	0.31	0.18	0.18
Farmgate prices														
Coffee (Robusta)	0.28	0.40	0.41	0.26	0.18	0.22	0.19	0.27	0.33	..	..	0.40	0.29	0.26
Vanilla (dried)	0.05	0.05	0.04	0.03	0.03	0.02	0.02	0.01	0.01	0.01	0.02	0.05	0.04	0.02
Cloves	0.25	0.17	0.16	0.12	0.13	0.21	0.24	0.17	..	..	..	0.31	0.18	0.20
MALAWI														
Official producer prices														
Tobacco (flue-cured)	..	..	..	..	..	..	..	..	..	..	..	..	..	..
Tobacco (NDDF, G2)	0.28	0.19	0.11	0.14	0.20	0.45	0.36	0.24	0.19	..	0.27	..	0.23	0.26
Tea (dry leaves)	..	..	..	..	..	..	..	..	..	..	..	..	..	..
Groundnuts (shelled)	0.52	0.34	0.55	0.75	0.68	1.06	0.89	1.05	1.03	1.08	..	0.47	0.65	1.01
Cotton (lint)	0.36	..	..	2.37	0.56	0.50	1.12	1.08	..	0.39	0.42	0.40	0.95	0.75
Farmgate prices														
Tobacco (flue-cured)	0.81	0.34	0.52	0.58	0.55	0.54	0.52	0.47	0.51	0.66	0.49	..	0.56	0.53
Tobacco (NDDF, G2)	0.28	0.19	0.11	0.14	0.20	0.45	0.36	0.24	0.19	..	0.27	..	0.23	0.26
Tea (dry leaves)	0.84	0.85	0.74	0.76	0.53	1.20	1.06	0.82	0.76	0.80	0.86	0.47	0.82	0.86
Groundnuts (shelled)	0.52	0.34	0.55	0.75	0.68	1.06	0.89	1.05	1.03	1.08	..	0.47	0.65	1.01
Cotton (lint)	0.36	..	..	2.37	0.56	0.50	1.12	1.08	..	0.39	0.42	0.40	0.95	0.75

(Table continues on the following page)

8-2. (continued)

	Ratio of producer price to international reference price											Average		
	1980	1981	1982	1983	1984	1985	1986	1987	1988	1989	1990	75–79	80–85	86–MR
MALI														
Official producer prices														
Cotton (lint)	0.42	0.35	0.42	0.58	0.27	0.29	0.55	0.45	0.49	0.49	..	0.34	0.39	0.50
Groundnuts (unshelled)	..	0.34	0.74	0.77	0.43	0.46	0.67	1.39	0.80	0.76	..	0.45	0.55	0.91
Farmgate prices														
Cotton (lint)	0.42	0.35	0.42	0.58	0.27	0.29	0.55	0.45	0.49	0.49	..	0.34	0.39	0.50
Groundnuts (unshelled)	..	0.34	0.74	0.77	0.47	0.42	0.57	..	..	..	..	0.45	0.55	..
MAURITIUS														
Official producer prices														
Sugar (centrifugal, raw)	0.64	0.62	0.56	0.65	0.63	0.58	0.58	0.52	0.54	0.49	0.46	0.90	0.61	0.52
Tea	0.81	0.92	0.82	0.68	0.32	0.77	0.79	0.67	0.45	0.55	0.57	0.50	0.72	0.61
Farmgate prices														
Sugar (centrifugal, raw)	..	..	..	..	..	..	..	..	..	..	..	..	..	..
Tea	..	..	..	..	..	..	..	..	..	..	..	..	..	..
MOROCCO														
Official producer prices														
Citrus (oranges)	0.90	0.86	0.97	0.82	0.82	0.69	0.57	0.58	0.63	0.86	0.61	0.94	0.84	0.65
Cotton lint	0.73	0.64	..	..	..	..	..	0.42	0.37	0.32	0.54	0.71	..	0.41
Farmgate prices														
Citrus	..	..	..	..	..	..	..	..	..	..	..	..	..	..
Cotton lint	..	..	..	..	..	..	..	..	..	..	..	..	..	..
MOZAMBIQUE														
Official producer prices														
Cashew nuts	0.03	0.03	0.05	0.04	0.03	0.06	0.05	0.01	0.02	0.04	0.05	..	0.04	0.03
Cotton (seed, prime grade)	0.26	0.35	0.28	0.25	0.21	0.22	0.47	0.08	0.18	0.48	0.47	..	0.26	0.34
Tea	0.55	0.44	0.54	0.49	0.61	0.71	..	..	0.18	0.36	0.45	0.64	0.56	0.33
Farmgate prices														
Cashew nuts	0.04	0.05	0.08	0.07	0.05	0.08	0.06	0.01	0.03	0.09	0.10	..	0.06	0.06
Cotton (seed, prime grade)	0.26	0.35	0.28	0.25	0.21	0.22	0.47	0.08	0.18	0.48	..	..	0.26	0.30
Tea	0.55	0.44	0.54	0.49	0.61	0.71	..	..	..	..	..	0.64	0.56	..
NIGER														
Official producer prices														
Cowpeas	0.52	0.11	0.17	0.24	0.34	0.35	0.63	0.46	0.46	..	..	0.50	0.29	0.52
Cotton (lint)	0.38	0.44	..	..	0.41	0.52	1.11	1.03	1.16	1.21	..	0.35	0.45	1.13
Farmgate prices														
Cowpeas	..	..	..	..	..	..	..	..	..	..	..	..	..	..
Cotton (lint)	0.38	0.44	..	..	0.41	0.52	1.11	1.03	1.16	1.21	..	0.35	0.45	1.13
NIGERIA														
Official producer prices														
Cocoa (bean)	1.21	1.45	1.18	1.15	0.95	0.76	0.49	0.50	..	..	..	0.53	1.12	0.49
Palm kernels	1.26	1.50	1.57	1.04	1.05	2.09	2.34	1.22	..	..	..	1.08	1.42	1.78
Farmgate prices														
Cocoa (bean)	1.21	1.45	1.18	1.15	0.95	0.76	0.49	0.50	1.02	1.12	..	0.53	1.12	0.78
Palm kernels	1.26	1.50	1.57	1.04	1.05	2.09	2.34	1.22	1.38	1.09	1.35	1.08	1.42	1.47
RWANDA														
Official producer prices														
Coffee (Arabica, merchant)	0.90	0.90	0.78	0.92	0.91	0.91	0.54	0.90	0.90	0.89	..	0.58	0.89	0.81
Tea (green leaf, delivered)	0.08	0.09	0.15	0.21	0.20	0.21	0.11	0.14	0.17	0.13	..	0.07	0.16	0.14
Farmgate prices														
Coffee (Arabica, merchant)	0.90	0.90	0.78	0.92	0.91	0.91	0.54	0.90	0.90	0.89	..	0.58	0.89	0.81
Tea (green leaf, delivered)	0.08	0.09	0.15	0.21	0.20	0.21	0.11	0.14	0.17	0.13	..	0.07	0.16	0.14
SAO TOME & PRINCIPE														
Official producer prices														
Cocoa	0.69	1.35	1.25	0.93	0.76	..	..	..	..	..	..	0.36	0.99	..
Farmgate prices														
Cocoa	..	..	..	..	..	..	..	..	..	..	..	..	..	..
SENEGAL														
Official producer prices														
Groundnuts (shelled)	0.35	0.24	0.64	0.52	0.40	0.37	0.70	0.97	0.96	0.71	0.69	0.42	0.42	0.81
Cotton (cottonseed)	..	..	..	..	..	..	..	0.63	0.71	0.70	0.59	..	..	0.66
Farmgate prices														
Groundnuts (shelled)	0.35	0.24	0.64	0.52	0.40	0.37	0.70	0.97	0.96	0.71	0.69	0.42	0.42	0.81
Cotton (cottonseed)	..	..	..	..	..	..	..	0.63	0.71	0.70	0.59	..	..	0.66

(Table continues on the following page)

8-2. (continued)

	Ratio of producer price to international reference price											Average		
	1980	1981	1982	1983	1984	1985	1986	1987	1988	1989	1990	75–79	80–85	86–MR
SIERRA LEONE														
Official producer prices														
Cocoa	0.75	1.03	0.72	0.47	0.53	0.46	0.15	0.37	0.64	0.45	0.48	0.47	0.66	0.42
Coffee (Robusta)	0.64	0.83	0.63	0.42	0.66	0.38	0.21	0.51	0.92	0.58	0.81	0.36	0.60	0.61
Palm kernels	0.85	0.72	0.50	0.80	0.44	0.45	0.15	..	0.41	..	0.56	0.49	0.63	0.37
Farmgate prices														
Cocoa	0.75	1.03	0.72	0.47	0.53	0.46	0.15	0.37	0.64	0.45	0.48	0.47	0.66	0.42
Coffee (Robusta)	0.64	0.83	0.63	0.42	0.66	0.38	0.21	0.51	0.92	0.58	0.81	0.36	0.60	0.61
Palm kernels	0.85	0.72	0.50	0.80	0.44	0.45	0.15	..	0.41	..	0.56	0.49	0.63	0.37
SOMALIA														
Official producer prices														
Bananas	0.41	0.34	0.63	0.51	0.39	0.30	0.46	0.39	0.24	0.22	..	..	0.43	0.33
Farmgate prices														
Bananas	0.41	0.34	0.63	0.51	0.39	0.30	0.46	0.39	0.24	0.22	..	..	0.43	0.33
SOUTH AFRICA														
Official producer prices														
Maize	0.80	0.93	0.96	1.10	0.90	0.79	1.01	1.66	1.16	0.89	0.87	0.68	0.92	1.12
Wheat	1.27	1.33	1.25	1.55	1.15	0.97	1.24	1.97	1.41	0.85	1.14	0.93	1.25	1.32
Sugar (centrifugal, raw)	0.42	0.82	1.16	1.10	1.38	1.13	1.03	1.27	0.74	0.71	0.66	0.67	1.00	0.88
Farmgate prices														
Maize	..	..	..	..	..	..	..	..	..	..	..	..	..	..
Wheat	..	..	..	..	..	..	..	..	..	..	..	..	..	..
Sugar (centrifugal, raw)	..	..	..	..	..	..	..	..	..	..	..	..	..	..
SUDAN														
Official producer prices														
Cotton (lint)	0.92	0.88	0.88	0.70	0.75	0.48	0.96	0.80	0.38	0.29	..	1.03	0.77	0.61
Groundnuts (shelled)	0.50	0.31	0.54	0.36	0.33	0.33	0.30	1.19	1.40	..	..	0.55	0.40	0.96
Sesame (Gedaref, mixed)	0.45	0.71	0.47	0.37	0.46	0.37	0.53	0.57	0.50	..	..	0.46	0.47	0.53
Gum arabic (El-Obeid)	0.40	0.49	0.31	0.28	0.51	0.48	0.28	0.44	0.59	0.72	..	0.53	0.41	0.40
Farmgate prices														
Cotton (lint)	0.92	0.88	0.88	0.70	0.75	0.48	0.96	0.80	0.38	0.29	..	1.03	0.77	0.61
Groundnuts (shelled)	..	..	..	..	..	..	..	..	..	..	..	..	..	..
Sesame (El-Obeid, mixed)	..	..	..	..	..	..	..	..	..	..	..	..	..	..
Gum arabic (El-Obeid)	..	..	..	..	..	..	..	..	..	..	..	..	..	..
SWAZILAND														
Official producer prices														
Cotton (lint)	0.39	0.32	0.31	0.33	0.23	0.17	0.26	0.31	..	0.30	0.21	0.46	0.29	0.27
Farmgate prices														
Cotton (lint)	0.39	0.32	0.31	0.33	0.23	0.17	0.26	0.31	..	0.30	0.21	0.46	0.29	0.27
TANZANIA														
Official producer prices														
Coffee (Arabica) (parchment)	0.42	0.60	0.60	0.51	0.51	0.64	0.35	0.34	0.35	0.29	0.47	0.39	0.55	0.36
Cotton (lint)	0.97	0.89	1.13	1.11	0.92	2.16	1.01	0.66	0.40	0.24	0.15	0.79	1.20	0.49
Tea (green leaves)	0.11	0.13	0.11	0.14	0.08	0.17	0.10	0.11	0.06	0.06	0.04	0.11	0.12	0.07
Farmgate prices														
Coffee (Arabica) (parchment)	0.42	0.60	0.60	0.51	0.51	0.64	0.35	0.34	0.35	0.29	0.47	0.39	0.55	0.36
Cotton (lint)	0.97	0.89	1.13	1.11	0.92	2.16	1.01	0.66	0.40	0.24	0.15	0.79	1.20	0.49
Tea (green leaves)	0.11	0.13	0.11	0.14	0.08	0.17	0.10	0.11	0.06	0.06	0.04	0.11	0.12	0.07
TOGO														
Official producer prices														
Coffee (Robusta)	0.33	0.41	0.33	0.28	0.25	0.26	0.33	0.59	0.67	0.63	0.50	0.24	0.31	0.54
Cocoa	0.35	0.51	0.40	0.39	0.28	0.34	0.44	0.57	0.59	0.50	0.54	0.26	0.38	0.53
Cotton (lint)	0.43	0.37	0.34	0.27	0.22	0.29	0.50	0.70	0.46	0.57	0.56	0.50	0.32	0.56
Farmgate prices														
Coffee (Robusta)	0.33	0.41	0.33	0.28	0.25	0.26	0.33	0.59	0.67	0.63	0.50	0.24	0.31	0.54
Cocoa	0.35	0.51	0.40	0.39	0.28	0.34	0.44	0.57	0.59	0.50	0.54	0.26	0.38	0.53
Cotton (lint)	0.43	0.37	0.34	0.27	0.22	0.29	0.50	0.70	0.46	0.57	0.56	0.50	0.32	0.56
TUNISIA														
Official producer prices														
Olives	..	0.35	..	..	..	..	0.17	0.26	0.24	..	..	..	..	0.22
Citrus (oranges)	0.64	0.68	0.59	0.54	1.06	0.54	0.61	0.54	0.62	0.61	0.61	0.74	0.67	0.60
Farmgate prices														
Olives	..	..	..	..	..	..	..	..	..	..	..	..	..	..
Citrus (oranges)	..	..	..	..	..	..	..	..	..	..	..	..	..	..

(Table continues on the following page)

8–2. (continued)

	Ratio of producer price to international reference price											Average		
	1980	*1981*	*1982*	*1983*	*1984*	*1985*	*1986*	*1987*	*1988*	*1989*	*1990*	*75–79*	*80–85*	*86–MR*
UGANDA														
Official producer prices														
Coffee (Robusta, Kiboko)	0.31	0.21	0.27	0.22	0.13	0.17	0.12	0.10	0.12	0.18	0.19	0.13	0.22	0.14
Cotton (lint)	1.13	0.17	0.47	0.61	0.63	0.64	0.84	0.25	0.44	0.49	0.43	0.56	0.61	0.49
Tea (greenleaf)	0.57	0.09	0.10	0.07	0.04	0.10	0.05	0.03	0.05	0.08	0.08	0.10	0.16	0.06
Farmgate prices														
Coffee (Robusta)	0.31	0.21	0.27	0.22	0.13	0.17	0.12	0.10	0.12	0.18	0.19	0.13	0.22	0.14
Cotton (lint)	1.13	0.17	0.47	0.61	0.63	0.64	0.84	0.25	0.44	0.49	0.43	0.56	0.61	0.49
Tea (greenleaf)	0.57	0.09	0.10	0.07	0.04	0.10	0.05	0.03	0.05	0.08	0.08	0.10	0.16	0.06
ZAIRE														
Official producer prices														
Coffee (Arabica, green beans)	0.29	0.55	0.51	..	..	..	..	..	..	..	..	0.18	0.45	..
Palm oil	1.41	0.75		..	..	..	..	..	..	..	..	1.29	1.08	..
Rubber	0.51	0.35	0.41	..	..	..	..	..	..	..	..	0.41	0.42	..
Cocoa (bean)	0.34	0.39	0.51	..	..	..	..	..	..	..	..	0.17	0.41	..
Farmgate prices														
Coffee (Arabica, green beans)	0.29	0.55	0.51	0.27	0.12	0.18	0.48	0.31	0.20	0.12	0.10	0.18	0.32	0.24
Palm oil	1.41	0.75	..	0.46	0.76	0.71	0.86	0.33	0.19	0.03	0.06	1.29	0.82	0.29
Rubber	0.51	0.35	0.41	0.44	0.95	0.74	0.83	0.47	0.25	0.20	0.13	0.41	0.57	0.38
Cocoa (bean)	0.34	0.39	0.51	0.24	0.26	0.21	0.23	0.16	0.18	0.12	0.09	0.17	0.33	0.16
ZAMBIA														
Official producer prices														
Cotton (lint)	0.88	1.15	0.86	0.62	0.55	0.46	0.26	..	..	..	..	..	0.76	..
Tobacco (Virginia)	1.46	0.68	0.72	1.00	0.82	0.54	0.17	0.40	0.44	0.51	0.28	0.75	0.87	0.36
Sunflower (seeds)	..	..	..	..	..	0.10	0.05	..	..	..	..	..	..	..
Farmgate prices														
Cotton (lint)	0.88	1.15	0.86	0.62	0.55	0.46	0.26	..	..	..	..	..	0.76	..
Tobacco (Virginia)	1.46	0.68	0.72	1.00	0.82	0.54	0.17	0.40	0.44	0.51	0.28	0.75	0.87	0.36
Sunflower (seeds)	..	..	..	..	..	0.10	0.05	..	..	..	..	..	..	..
ZIMBABWE														
Official producer prices														
Tobacco	0.65	0.47	0.82	0.61	0.59	0.56	0.63	0.72	0.44	0.63	0.50	0.66	0.62	0.58
Cotton (lint)	1.07	1.12	1.30	0.92	0.88	1.04	1.29	0.95	0.84	0.83	0.64	0.98	1.05	0.91
Farmgate prices														
Tobacco	0.65	0.47	0.82	0.61	0.59	0.56	0.63	0.72	0.44	0.63	0.50	0.66	0.62	0.58
Cotton (lint)	1.07	1.12	1.30	0.92	0.88	1.04	1.29	0.95	0.84	0.83	0.64	0.98	1.05	0.91

Notes: *Wheat for Lesotho is shown in terms of wheat equivalent, which consists of the sum of wheat and flour, converted at the appropriate conversion factor. For Malawian tobacco, NDDF indicates Northen division, dark-fired.*

8-3. Agricultural production index

	Index (average 1986-88 = 100)											Average annual percentage growth		
	1980	1981	1982	1983	1984	1985	1986	1987	1988	1989	1990	75-80	80-85	86-MR
SUB-SAHARAN AFRICA	86	90	92	89	89	94	98	98	104	104	103	0.5	1.1	1.6
excluding Nigeria	86	90	92	89	89	94	98	98	104	105	103	0.5	1.0	1.6
Angola	105	99	99	99	99	98	100	100	99	97	97	-5.4	-1.0	-1.0
Benin	69	68	69	70	93	95	103	89	109	112	115	4.4	7.4	4.7
Botswana	94	119	124	114	109	104	99	85	116	117	116	-3.2	0.5	6.7
Burkina Faso	62	68	69	71	73	88	102	94	104	99	95	1.8	5.8	-0.9
Burundi	78	89	84	86	83	94	97	102	101	96	92	0.6	2.0	-1.6
Cameroon	86	88	88	81	91	92	102	93	105	98	101	0.3	1.1	0.3
Cape Verde	83	60	58	51	62	60	80	115	105	96	96	6.7	-4.6	1.8
Central African Republic	90	92	96	95	92	87	100	96	104	104	103	0.7	-0.3	1.5
Chad	96	92	96	105	84	97	95	99	105	102	109	1.3	-0.5	3.0
Comoros	92	80	86	92	87	92	98	100	102	104	106	1.2	0.9	2.0
Congo, People's Republic of the	84	88	90	92	94	97	97	100	103	101	105	1.7	2.8	1.7
Cote d' Ivoire	77	87	77	79	80	94	95	100	105	105	107	3.3	2.2	3.0
Djibouti	..	..	..	..	..	..	..	..	..	..	..	..	..	..
Equatorial Guinea	..	..	..	..	..	..	..	..	..	..	..	..	..	..
Ethiopia	98	98	106	97	89	94	103	98	99	103	106	3.3	-1.7	1.2
Gabon	90	88	90	91	92	92	97	99	104	105	107	5.0	0.9	2.5
Gambia, The	75	108	134	102	102	82	104	101	95	113	85	-11.4	-0.1	-3.0
Ghana	79	79	74	71	103	94	96	98	106	106	94	-3.4	4.8	0.4
Guinea	96	96	97	94	97	98	99	100	101	103	103	1.6	0.3	1.1
Guinea-Bissau	71	80	89	78	92	91	97	101	102	105	105	-0.6	4.5	2.0
Kenya	74	73	83	84	77	89	98	97	106	107	116	2.3	3.1	4.6
Lesotho	90	97	93	94	98	101	96	96	108	97	101	2.1	1.8	1.1
Liberia	86	87	89	88	94	96	98	99	103	92	76	2.4	2.3	-5.7
Madagascar	91	91	91	94	97	98	100	100	100	103	104	0.7	1.8	1.0
Malawi	88	91	97	95	99	99	98	97	104	110	111	3.8	2.5	3.8
Mali	82	89	93	93	85	89	98	94	109	113	110	2.9	0.7	4.3
Mauritania	96	98	95	90	91	96	97	100	103	105	102	5.1	-0.8	1.5
Mauritius	74	86	102	87	87	94	102	103	95	94	97	0.8	3.1	-1.8
Mozambique	104	105	103	96	92	94	100	99	101	104	105	0.4	-2.7	1.5
Namibia	89	92	89	81	82	87	90	106	104	108	111	-0.4	-1.8	4.5
Niger	119	115	114	113	81	87	98	86	116	108	111	9.1	-7.2	5.0
Nigeria	78	79	82	80	82	90	97	98	105	111	113	1.6	2.4	4.4
Rwanda	89	98	102	104	95	112	98	101	102	101	100	3.9	3.0	0.5
Sao Tome & Principe	110	115	110	112	95	100	99	93	108	108	100	-0.7	-3.0	1.7
Senegal	58	95	98	64	66	85	99	109	92	104	95	-11.8	1.2	-1.3
Seychelles	..	..	..	..	..	..	..	..	..	..	..	..	..	..
Sierra Leone	95	95	104	104	95	97	103	99	97	102	106	0.3	0.4	0.8
Somalia	82	84	87	83	85	94	98	99	103	105	105	1.9	1.9	2.0
Sudan	102	112	94	101	90	106	96	94	110	89	86	1.8	-1.1	-2.6
Swaziland	85	89	88	89	90	91	102	97	101	100	100	4.4	1.2	-0.1
Tanzania	84	88	88	92	94	95	99	100	101	110	102	3.2	2.6	1.6
Togo	86	87	84	79	84	96	97	101	102	114	114	2.2	1.0	4.5
Uganda	84	87	100	103	91	99	93	100	107	113	119	-4.9	2.7	6.3
Zaire	84	85	89	91	94	96	97	100	103	105	105	1.2	2.9	2.1
Zambia	74	74	70	76	80	87	93	91	117	115	94	-5.4	3.1	2.7
Zimbabwe	80	88	81	69	83	105	103	88	110	102	104	-1.2	3.0	1.8
NORTH AFRICA	86	81	83	90	88	100	98	104	99	107	106	0.8	3.0	2.0
Algeria	84	77	71	77	82	101	99	106	95	99	105	-1.3	3.6	0.5
Egypt, Arab Republic of	77	77	81	84	85	92	97	101	102	102	107	1.7	3.5	2.1
Libya	102	102	108	115	108	104	92	103	105	116	107	2.1	0.8	4.3
Morocco	69	59	76	71	74	85	101	90	108	110	103	3.6	4.6	2.2
Tunisia	100	89	77	101	93	116	99	118	82	107	109	-1.0	3.3	0.9
ALL AFRICA	86	89	91	89	89	95	98	99	103	105	103	0.5	1.3	1.6
South Africa	99	109	96	82	89	97	97	100	103	111	105	3.2	-2.5	2.8

8-4. Food production index

	Index (average 1986-88 = 100)											Average annual percentage growth		
	1980	1981	1982	1983	1984	1985	1986	1987	1988	1989	1990	75-80	80-85	86-MR
SUB-SAHARAN AFRICA	86	91	93	90	89	94	98	98	104	104	103	0.6	0.9	1.5
excluding Nigeria	86	91	93	90	89	94	98	98	104	104	102	0.6	0.9	1.5
Angola	97	96	97	98	98	98	100	101	100	98	98	-0.2	0.3	-0.5
Benin	75	73	73	73	94	96	101	91	108	113	114	4.7	5.7	4.6
Botswana	94	120	124	115	109	104	99	85	116	117	117	-3.2	0.5	6.8
Burkina Faso	66	72	72	74	75	90	101	94	105	100	93	1.4	5.1	-1.2
Burundi	81	86	86	85	83	94	97	102	101	96	92	0.1	1.8	-1.7
Cameroon	87	89	88	87	89	95	102	96	102	103	104	-0.8	1.3	1.1
Cape Verde	83	59	58	52	62	60	80	115	105	96	96	6.9	-4.4	1.9
Central African Republic	91	94	96	96	90	88	100	97	102	105	106	1.0	-0.7	1.7
Chad	100	96	97	101	84	98	98	98	104	99	105	3.5	-1.2	1.5
Comoros	93	81	86	93	87	92	98	100	102	104	106	1.4	0.8	2.0
Congo, People's Republic of the	83	86	89	90	94	95	97	100	103	101	105	1.4	2.8	1.7
Cote d' Ivoire	74	78	74	75	90	91	93	98	109	105	104	4.7	4.2	3.0
Djibouti	..	..	..	..	..	..	..	..	..	..	..	..	..	..
Equatorial Guinea	..	..	..	..	..	..	..	..	..	..	..	..	..	..
Ethiopia	97	96	105	98	89	95	103	97	99	103	105	3.5	-1.2	0.9
Gabon	90	89	90	91	92	92	97	99	104	104	106	4.9	0.7	2.4
Gambia, The	76	108	135	103	103	81	105	102	93	113	84	-11.6	-0.1	-3.5
Ghana	78	78	74	70	103	94	96	98	106	106	94	-3.3	5.0	0.4
Guinea	94	94	95	92	95	96	100	100	100	98	103	1.6	0.3	0.5
Guinea-Bissau	71	80	88	78	92	91	97	101	102	105	105	-0.9	4.5	2.0
Kenya	74	72	83	82	72	88	98	97	105	107	118	1.6	2.4	4.8
Lesotho	90	99	94	94	97	101	96	96	108	98	102	1.9	1.5	1.4
Liberia	82	87	90	91	92	94	96	100	104	98	78	2.2	2.4	-4.1
Madagascar	90	90	91	94	97	98	100	100	100	103	104	1.1	1.9	1.1
Malawi	91	96	100	96	98	97	99	97	104	107	105	2.8	0.9	2.1
Mali	83	94	98	96	87	90	98	92	109	111	107	1.9	0.5	3.6
Mauritania	96	98	95	90	91	96	97	100	103	105	102	5.1	-0.8	1.5
Mauritius	75	87	105	87	85	93	101	104	95	95	99	0.5	2.5	-1.4
Mozambique	103	104	102	96	95	96	100	99	101	105	106	0.1	-1.8	2.0
Namibia	87	90	87	80	81	87	90	106	104	109	111	-0.4	-1.2	4.6
Niger	120	116	115	113	81	88	98	86	116	109	112	9.3	-7.3	5.1
Nigeria	78	79	83	80	82	90	97	98	105	111	112	1.7	2.5	4.3
Rwanda	94	102	107	107	98	112	98	100	102	101	98	3.9	2.3	0.0
Sao Tome & Principe	110	115	110	112	95	100	99	93	108	108	100	-0.8	-3.0	1.7
Senegal	58	94	97	64	64	85	99	109	92	105	94	-11.8	1.0	-1.5
Seychelles	..	..	..	..	..	..	..	..	..	..	..	..	..	..
Sierra Leone	93	94	104	106	98	95	103	100	97	103	105	-0.4	0.9	0.7
Somalia	82	84	87	83	85	94	98	99	103	105	105	1.9	1.9	2.0
Sudan	104	116	93	98	85	104	96	93	112	89	87	2.7	-2.4	-2.3
Swaziland	82	87	87	87	89	90	102	97	101	100	100	3.9	1.5	-0.1
Tanzania	82	87	88	93	95	97	99	100	101	110	103	3.8	3.3	1.8
Togo	94	95	92	85	94	98	99	98	103	113	112	2.4	0.2	4.0
Uganda	84	90	99	102	90	97	92	100	108	113	117	-3.8	2.2	6.2
Zaire	83	84	88	90	93	95	97	100	103	105	106	1.5	2.9	2.2
Zambia	75	76	71	77	78	87	93	92	115	115	94	-5.7	2.7	2.4
Zimbabwe	79	103	90	68	76	111	107	81	112	101	106	-3.3	1.6	2.0
NORTH AFRICA	86	81	82	89	88	99	97	104	99	107	106	0.7	3.0	2.1
Algeria	87	79	70	76	82	102	100	106	94	98	105	-1.5	2.8	0.2
Egypt, Arab Republic of	71	73	78	82	83	90	95	101	104	103	109	0.9	4.8	2.9
Libya	103	105	109	117	109	104	92	103	105	117	107	2.4	0.8	4.5
Morocco	70	59	77	71	74	84	102	90	108	110	102	4.0	4.4	2.2
Tunisia	101	89	77	102	93	117	99	119	82	107	109	-1.1	3.3	0.8
ALL AFRICA	86	90	92	90	89	95	98	98	103	105	103	0.7	1.1	1.6
South Africa	98	109	96	80	88	96	97	100	103	112	105	3.3	-2.6	2.8

8–5. Nonfood production index

	Index (average 1986–88 = 100)											Average annual percentage growth		
	1980	1981	1982	1983	1984	1985	1986	1987	1988	1989	1990	75–80	80–85	86–MR
SUB-SAHARAN AFRICA	88	89	90	90	90	96	98	98	104	105	103	-2.7	1.3	1.8
excluding Nigeria	83	88	87	88	89	95	98	98	104	106	103	-0.4	2.1	1.8
Angola	229	138	127	107	113	101	112	93	95	78	78	-23.4	-12.9	-8.6
Benin	17	16	34	43	87	83	117	70	113	103	126	-4.9	46.4	5.3
Botswana	100	100	100	100	100	100	100	100	100	100	100	0.0	0.0	0.0
Burkina Faso	39	37	48	50	57	76	108	96	96	89	114	8.1	14.1	0.4
Burundi	57	115	62	96	79	94	93	107	100	92	98	6.7	5.3	-0.5
Cameroon	82	80	89	57	99	80	102	81	117	77	87	6.3	0.2	-3.5
Cape Verde	96	174	32	32	32	88	117	77	107	78	79	-5.6	-14.6	-7.3
Central African Republic	83	78	95	86	109	83	95	92	112	99	89	-1.3	2.6	-0.7
Chad	70	59	85	133	79	86	76	107	117	129	138	-13.2	7.1	14.7
Comoros	61	71	105	83	86	100	100	92	108	115	102	-5.5	8.3	2.8
Congo, People's Republic of the	179	171	143	198	140	200	109	90	101	102	102	8.3	0.8	-0.1
Cote d' Ivoire	89	123	89	98	44	107	103	108	90	109	118	-0.7	-5.9	2.8
Djibouti	..	..	..	..	..	..	..	..	..	..	..	..	..	..
Equatorial Guinea	..	..	..	..	..	..	..	..	..	..	..	..	..	..
Ethiopia	107	113	113	92	86	85	98	104	98	111	114	2.1	-5.9	3.7
Gabon	42	47	115	87	75	80	83	107	110	112	112	22.2	13.2	6.7
Gambia, The	65	124	112	36	93	107	75	39	187	187	187	..	1.3	40.6
Ghana	164	159	159	166	107	82	99	104	97	125	152	-11.1	-12.4	10.9
Guinea	157	157	159	162	164	165	88	88	125	261	103	0.9	1.1	15.3
Guinea-Bissau	69	89	103	60	100	100	100	100	100	100	100	58.6	4.7	0.0
Kenya	75	80	80	90	99	96	95	97	108	106	108	5.9	6.0	3.5
Lesotho	83	84	84	94	100	100	100	100	100	94	94	3.5	4.5	-1.9
Liberia	93	86	86	83	101	99	102	98	100	78	70	3.0	2.2	-9.4
Madagascar	92	97	94	93	98	98	105	96	98	107	99	-2.0	1.0	-0.2
Malawi	76	77	86	93	102	107	96	97	106	120	132	7.5	7.8	8.7
Mali	77	56	53	69	74	76	92	107	102	131	133	14.9	3.1	10.0
Mauritania	..	..	..	..	..	..	..	..	..	..	..	..	..	..
Mauritius	69	78	71	84	108	108	107	98	95	81	80	5.7	10.2	-7.4
Mozambique	117	127	111	94	58	62	104	104	92	87	90	3.5	-14.9	-4.5
Namibia	205	200	155	114	91	91	100	100	100	100	100	1.0	-17.5	0.0
Niger	51	44	46	73	62	73	99	100	100	76	52	-14.0	9.7	-14.4
Nigeria	84	74	60	53	61	60	86	102	112	118	137	-7.9	-6.6	11.3
Rwanda	57	69	58	84	69	104	93	103	104	102	115	3.2	10.2	4.1
Sao Tome & Principe	100	100	100	100	90	100	100	100	100	100	100	14.3	-0.9	0.0
Senegal	57	110	139	88	139	80	80	110	110	88	110	-9.5	5.8	4.1
Seychelles	..	..	..	..	..	..	..	..	..	..	..	..	..	..
Sierra Leone	131	121	114	75	39	133	103	85	112	80	117	11.9	-10.1	1.9
Somalia	76	58	91	76	76	76	76	114	109	59	59	6.4	2.0	-11.3
Sudan	80	71	101	127	136	128	98	108	94	97	76	-6.0	13.9	-5.9
Swaziland	109	101	101	101	100	100	100	100	100	100	100	9.2	-1.5	0.0
Tanzania	99	102	89	85	89	73	101	95	104	109	93	-1.7	-5.5	-0.3
Togo	49	47	49	47	37	84	86	116	98	121	119	-0.3	5.5	7.1
Uganda	86	64	107	105	101	108	95	104	101	115	127	-11.8	7.3	7.1
Zaire	90	91	102	98	102	101	99	100	101	107	101	-1.9	2.3	1.1
Zambia	60	53	43	59	104	84	93	67	141	123	99	3.7	12.1	7.7
Zimbabwe	81	60	65	70	95	93	94	100	106	104	100	3.6	6.4	1.6
NORTH AFRICA	84	82	87	89	89	100	99	101	100	101	106	2.2	3.3	1.4
Algeria	50	52	72	93	86	99	94	102	105	107	114	4.3	15.8	4.4
Egypt, Arab Republic of	144	135	122	108	108	119	113	99	88	82	83	6.7	-4.9	-7.8
Libya	96	75	96	91	88	97	98	101	102	103	105	-1.2	1.4	1.8
Morocco	50	58	55	63	79	91	94	101	105	106	111	-6.4	12.1	4.0
Tunisia	80	88	86	89	85	94	96	102	101	105	118	5.8	2.1	4.3
ALL AFRICA	88	89	89	90	90	97	98	98	104	104	103	-2.2	1.5	1.7
South Africa	112	105	106	108	106	107	99	97	103	104	107	2.8	-0.6	2.2

8-6. Food production per capita index

	Index (average 1986-88 = 100)											Average annual percentage growth		
	1980	1981	1982	1983	1984	1985	1986	1987	1988	1989	1990	75-80	80-85	86-MR
SUB-SAHARAN AFRICA	107	109	108	101	98	100	101	98	101	98	94	-2.3	-2.0	-1.5
excluding Nigeria	106	109	108	101	97	100	101	98	101	98	93	-2.3	-2.1	-1.5
Angola	116	111	110	108	106	103	102	101	97	93	91	-3.5	-2.1	-3.2
Benin	92	87	85	82	102	102	104	91	105	107	104	2.0	2.7	1.5
Botswana	122	150	150	133	123	112	103	85	112	109	105	-6.6	-3.1	2.9
Burkina Faso	78	84	82	82	81	95	104	94	102	95	85	-0.9	2.5	-3.8
Burundi	98	102	99	95	91	99	100	102	98	91	84	-2.2	-1.0	-4.6
Cameroon	107	108	103	99	98	102	106	96	99	96	95	-3.5	-1.7	-2.2
Cape Verde	98	68	66	57	67	63	82	115	102	92	89	6.0	-6.6	-0.8
Central African Republic	109	110	110	107	97	93	103	97	100	99	97	-1.4	-3.3	-1.0
Chad	118	111	109	111	91	103	100	98	101	94	98	1.4	-3.5	-1.0
Comoros	117	98	101	106	96	98	101	100	99	97	95	-2.7	-2.5	-1.5
Congo, People's Republic of the	102	104	104	102	103	101	100	100	100	95	96	-1.4	-0.2	-1.4
Cote d' Ivoire	97	98	90	87	101	98	97	98	105	97	93	0.8	0.2	-0.8
Djibouti	..	..	..	..	..	..	..	..	..	..	..	..	..	..
Equatorial Guinea	..	..	..	..	..	..	..	..	..	..	..	..	..	..
Ethiopia	114	110	118	108	96	100	106	97	97	97	97	1.0	-3.2	-1.8
Gabon	119	111	108	105	103	99	101	99	100	98	96	0.1	-3.2	-1.1
Gambia, The	93	129	156	116	112	86	108	102	91	106	77	-14.3	-3.1	-6.2
Ghana	100	97	88	81	114	100	99	98	103	100	86	-5.0	1.2	-2.7
Guinea	111	109	108	102	103	101	102	100	97	92	95	0.1	-2.0	-2.4
Guinea-Bissau	81	89	96	84	97	94	99	101	100	100	99	-5.5	2.6	0.0
Kenya	97	90	100	95	81	94	102	97	101	100	106	-2.2	-1.4	1.2
Lesotho	110	117	108	105	106	107	98	96	105	92	93	-0.5	-1.3	-1.4
Liberia	103	106	106	103	101	100	99	100	101	92	71	-0.9	-0.8	-7.1
Madagascar	112	108	106	106	107	104	103	100	97	96	95	-1.9	-1.1	-2.1
Malawi	116	118	120	110	109	104	102	97	100	99	94	-0.5	-2.5	-1.5
Mali	101	112	114	109	95	96	101	92	106	104	98	-0.2	-2.3	0.5
Mauritania	116	114	108	101	99	101	100	100	100	99	94	2.5	-3.4	-1.3
Mauritius	81	92	111	91	88	96	102	104	94	93	95	-1.1	1.4	-2.5
Mozambique	123	121	116	107	103	101	102	99	99	100	98	-2.7	-4.3	-0.7
Namibia	108	109	102	91	90	92	93	106	101	102	101	-3.1	-4.1	1.3
Niger	151	142	136	129	89	93	101	86	113	102	102	5.9	-10.4	1.9
Nigeria	97	96	97	91	91	97	100	98	101	104	102	-1.6	-0.8	0.9
Rwanda	118	124	127	122	108	120	102	100	98	94	88	0.6	-1.0	-3.3
Sao Tome & Principe	132	134	125	123	102	105	102	93	105	103	93	-3.7	-5.5	-0.7
Senegal	71	112	112	71	70	90	102	109	89	99	87	-14.3	-1.8	-4.2
Seychelles	..	..	..	..	..	..	..	..	..	..	..	..	..	..
Sierra Leone	109	108	117	117	106	100	106	100	94	98	98	-2.5	-1.4	-1.8
Somalia	105	103	103	95	94	100	101	99	100	99	95	-3.2	-1.6	-1.3
Sudan	129	139	108	111	93	110	98	93	109	84	80	-0.4	-5.4	-5.1
Swaziland	104	107	102	100	99	96	106	97	98	93	90	0.7	-1.8	-3.5
Tanzania	107	108	106	108	106	104	102	100	97	102	92	0.4	-0.5	-1.8
Togo	116	114	107	96	103	104	102	98	100	106	102	-0.4	-2.7	0.8
Uganda	108	112	119	118	100	105	96	100	104	105	105	-6.8	-1.3	2.4
Zaire	102	101	102	102	102	102	100	100	100	99	96	-1.4	-0.1	-1.0
Zambia	99	96	87	90	88	94	96	92	111	107	84	-8.8	-1.3	-1.3
Zimbabwe	98	123	105	77	83	118	111	81	108	95	96	-6.1	-1.4	-1.2
NORTH AFRICA	107	97	96	101	96	105	100	104	96	101	98	-2.3	-0.1	-0.7
Algeria	106	94	81	85	89	107	102	106	92	93	97	-4.6	-0.3	-2.5
Egypt, Arab Republic of	85	85	88	91	90	94	98	101	101	99	102	-1.4	2.1	0.5
Libya	138	134	134	137	123	113	95	103	102	109	96	-2.0	-3.5	0.8
Morocco	84	69	88	79	80	89	104	90	106	104	95	1.7	1.8	-0.4
Tunisia	121	104	87	112	100	123	102	119	80	102	101	-3.6	0.7	-1.6
ALL AFRICA	107	108	106	101	98	100	101	98	100	99	94	-2.3	-1.8	-1.4
South Africa	115	125	107	87	94	101	99	100	101	107	99	1.0	-4.7	0.6

8-7. Volume of food output, by major food crop

	Thousands of metric tons										Average annual percentage growth		
	1980	1981	1982	1983	1984	1985	1986	1987	1988	1989	75-80	80-85	6-MR
ALGERIA													
Wheat	1,511	1,218	977	790	887	1,478	1,229	1,175	614	1,103	-5.5	-3.6	-9.3
Citrus	422	355	319	255	285	244	253	277	312	..	-3.9	-9.8	11.0
Dates	201	195	206	182	183	199	189	224	196	200	6.7	-1.0	0.4
Barley	794	525	483	447	502	1,130	1,083	820	390	..	0.0	4.5	-40.0
Potatoes	591	528	415	491	821	815	812	905	899	..	0.5	9.3	5.2
ANGOLA													
Maize	360	250	250	275	260	250	280	300	270	204	-6.1	-4.5	-10.0
Millet	57	50	50	50	50	50	54	60	60	63	-9.4	-1.9	4.7
Cassava	1,850	1,900	1,950	1,950	1,950	1,950	1,970	1,970	1,980	1,920	1.3	1.0	-0.7
Sweet potatoes	180	180	180	180	180	180	180	180	180	170	2.5	0.0	-1.7
BENIN													
Palm oil	..	..	..	..	..	..	..	..	..	..	..	..	..
Maize	271	287	273	282	379	425	376	267	430	455	8.6	9.3	11.1
Sorghum	56	57	60	57	83	79	89	95	97	110	-0.5	8.2	6.8
Cassava	583	575	610	580	685	708	726	570	780	1,002	2.4	4.2	13.7
Yams	694	666	672	620	819	777	875	835	922	1,049	8.4	3.2	6.7
BOTSWANA													
Livestock (1000 heads)	3,853	3,883	3,922	3,939	3,914	3,976	4,075	4,157	4,205	4,267	0.8	0.5	1.5
Rabbits/chickens (1,000s)	913	1,126	1,246	1,061	814	1,120	1,279	1,383	1,400	1,400	6.4	-0.3	2.9
Sorghum	29	28	4	5	6	15	16	18	44	61	-23.1	-20.2	63.4
Maize	12	21	12	8	0	1	4	3	7	10	-35.7	-46.9	46.5
Millet	2	2	0	0	1	2	1	0	3	2	-18.3	-10.7	39.2
BURKINA FASO													
Groundnuts	54	78	71	82	83	123	152	146	161	131	-5.4	13.7	-3.5
Sorghum	547	659	609	611	594	798	1,011	848	1,009	991	-2.5	4.6	1.2
Millet	351	443	441	391	372	587	680	632	817	649	-0.5	5.7	1.2
Maize	105	119	111	71	77	142	155	131	227	257	8.8	-0.6	23.0
Rice	40	45	28	40	41	48	23	22	..	..	..	2.7	-6.8
BURUNDI													
Maize	140	146	144	148	139	157	164	174	206	138	-0.3	1.3	-3.4
Sorghum	52	53	52	53	49	59	61	63	113	72	-16.4	1.2	11.3
Rice	14	15	14	9	18	20	23	28	30	35	15.5	5.6	14.2
Millet	9	11	10	11	10	12	12	12	13	10	-20.3	3.6	-5.2
Bananas	1,100	1,239	1,220	1,160	1,197	1,384	1,434	1,484	1,574	1,608	3.4	2.9	4.1
Cassava	400	451	444	444	511	504	554	574	614	698	-2.3	4.5	7.9
CAMEROON													
Maize	414	431	503	500	409	337	360	410	420	430	-8.0	-3.3	5.7
Sorghum	331	262	285	324	250	333	260	225	230	240	3.9	0.1	-2.2
Millet	100	89	95	115	80	110	90	75	80	100	2.5	1.0	3.9
Rice	46	51	77	89	95	107	110	70	85	90	8.2	19.8	-4.0
Cassava	1,250	1,280	1,020	1,143	1,385	1,400	1,460	1,500	1,500	1,530	11.4	2.7	1.4
Plantains	1,020	1,030	1,000	950	970	980	980	1,000	1,100	1,150	5.0	-1.2	5.9
CENTRAL AFRICAN REPUBLIC													
Sorghum	36	43	45	40	32	40	60	39	45	50	2.2	-1.4	-3.9
Maize	41	46	48	40	42	46	94	66	70	70	-1.4	0.2	-8.0
Groundnuts	123	125	127	125	81	60	111	88	97	100	-1.4	-13.1	-2.1
Cassava	920	900	850	760	675	580	606	529	533	540	2.1	-9.0	-3.3
Yams	150	160	160	160	165	165	170	170	170	170	-3.6	1.6	0.0
CHAD													
Sorghum	250	143	156	221	164	273	354	293	330	289	-1.9	3.5	-4.8
Millet	200	114	124	110	90	253	270	225	367	257	-1.8	1.0	3.5
Groundnuts	99	86	73	78	77	77	105	96	79	80	3.8	-4.3	-9.5
COMOROS													
Bananas	33	..	..	34	37	38	39	..	..	..	..	..	..
Cassava	25	25	25	26	26	27	29	45	49	55	-18.2	1.6	22.2
CONGO, PEOPLE'S REPUBLIC OF THE													
Maize	9	11	6	7	7	9	7	9	9	9	-10.0	-4.7	7.4
Cassava	628	666	650	667	690	713	693	746	761	760	2.7	2.2	3.0
Plantains	56	58	51	55	56	54	59	64	65	66	8.8	-0.4	3.5
COTE D'IVOIRE													
Palm oil	189	153	169	168	167	161	211	227	190	167	2.1	-1.6	-8.5
Rice	420	390	450	360	514	540	560	580	597	650	-1.4	5.5	4.9
Maize	380	400	430	410	520	480	420	435	448	450	6.4	5.6	2.4
Cassava	1,010	1,080	1,105	1,060	1,250	1,250	1,250	1,294	1,333	1,300	2.3	4.3	1.5
Yams	2,040	2,130	2,280	2,170	2,470	2,500	2,300	2,381	2,452	2,370	-0.6	4.1	1.2

(Table continues on following page)

8-7. Volume of food output, by major food crop

| | \multicolumn{10}{c}{Thousands of metric tons} | \multicolumn{3}{c}{Average annual percentage growth} |
	1980	1981	1982	1983	1984	1985	1986	1987	1988	1989	75–80	80–85	6–MR
EGYPT, ARAB REPUBLIC OF													
Rice	2,382	2,236	2,441	2,442	2,236	2,311	2,445	2,406	2,132	2,680	0.6	-0.4	1.6
Wheat	1,736	1,938	2,017	1,996	1,815	1,872	1,928	2,721	2,839	3,183	-2.3	0.5	16.7
Sugarcane	8,618	8,805	8,740	8,424	8,633	9,429	9,684	10,162	10,832	10,795	1.6	1.0	4.0
Broadbeans	213	208	260	295	271	302	448	337	358	362	-2.4	7.9	-5.6
EQUATORIAL GUINEA													
Cassava	53	53	53	54	54	55	55	56	56	57	2.0	0.7	0.9
Plantains	..	..	..	..	..	..	..	..	..	..	..	..	..
ETHIOPIA													
Sorghum	1,411	1,203	1,356	1,202	507	905	1,092	950	964	964	15.7	-13.1	-3.5
Maize	948	1,200	1,603	1,533	1,088	1,037	1,788	1,560	1,600	1,600	-0.1	0.3	-3.0
Barley (nonwhite mixed)	1,075	936	1,168	814	842	914	1,041	1,024	1,098	1,100	9.9	-4.2	2.4
Teff (mixed)	..	..	..	..	..	..	..	..	..	..	..	..	..
GABON													
Oil palm	2	2	2	3	3	4	5	5	5	5	-2.3	15.5	0.0
Maize	10	10	10	10	10	10	10	10	12	12	6.3	0.5	7.6
Cassava	250	237	250	260	245	250	255	255	260	260	4.6	0.4	0.8
Yam	79	85	87	88	90	80	90	95	100	100	7.1	0.7	3.7
Plantain	175	157	150	148	145	142	140	138	135	132	7.3	-3.7	-2.0
GAMBIA, THE													
Groundnuts	60	109	151	114	105	76	110	120	98	133	-18.2	2.2	3.6
Palm oil	3	3	3	3	3	3	3	3	3	3	2.1	-4.1	0.0
Millet	25	35	42	26	39	55	51	50	48	56	-6.1	11.7	2.6
Rice	43	40	34	26	27	23	24	14	24	34	4.5	-12.0	16.7
Maize	6	13	17	9	13	27	17	15	16	16	14.1	20.7	-2.1
Sorghum	5	7	8	7	8	12	9	7	7	15	-6.3	16.6	17.5
GHANA													
Maize	382	378	346	172	696	584	559	598	751	749	3.4	9.7	11.7
Millet	..	..	..	..	..	..	..	..	..	..	..	..	..
Groundnuts	1,858	2,065	2,470	1,728	4,065	3,076	2,876	2,726	2,788	3,327	-0.5	12.7	4.7
Cassava	142	126	111	91	167	140	190	191	230	200	3.2	1.6	3.4
Plantains	734	829	745	342	1,943	1,629	1,087	1,078	1,135	1,036	-10.6	17.9	-0.9
GUINEA													
Palm kernels	40	40	40	40	40	40	40	40	40	40	1.9	0.0	0.0
Rice	480	485	490	396	403	437	510	515	521	525	-0.3	-3.5	1.0
Maize	90	90	90	90	100	100	100	90	80	108	5.6	2.4	1.2
Groundnuts	84	84	85	77	82	74	70	60	50	45	1.2	-2.3	-14.1
Cassava	480	485	490	494	496	470	450	420	400	358	-5.5	-0.1	-7.1
Plantains	350	350	350	350	350	350	350	350	350	350	4.6	0.0	0.0
GUINEA-BISSAU													
Groundnuts	30	30	35	22	30	27	29	30	35	30	-4.6	-2.8	2.6
Palm kernels	9	9	10	6	11	6	14	14	14	14	6.5	-4.6	0.0
Rice	42	80	103	85	105	115	125	142	146	162	-12.1	17.5	8.4
Sorghum	..	..	..	..	..	..	..	..	..	..	..	..	..
Maize	7	13	10	10	10	20	29	20	15	20	13.7	13.2	-13.4
KENYA													
Sugarcane	4,532	4,382	3,628	3,846	4,171	4,023	4,112	4,258	4,395	4,500	18.0	-1.9	3.1
Maize	1,620	1,768	2,502	2,300	1,422	2,430	2,898	2,416	2,761	2,925	-9.5	3.8	1.6
Wheat	216	214	248	253	145	201	216	207	243	258	4.8	-4.2	7.2
LESOTHO													
Wheat	28	17	14	15	17	18	11	19	21	19	-9.0	-5.8	19.4
Beans	4	5	2	1	3	4	..	..	..	..	-25.0	-5.1	..
Peas	3	5	3	4	..	..	..	..	..	..	-10.3	..	..
Maize	106	106	83	76	79	92	86	95	146	75	15.2	-4.5	0.0
Sorghum	59	48	26	31	34	55	33	31	55	28	17.7	-3.6	0.3
LIBERIA													
Rice	243	269	284	290	298	289	288	298	298	280	0.9	3.5	-0.8
Cassava	300	300	300	270	218	282	306	372	447	400	3.4	-3.8	10.4
LIBYA													
Wheat	141	123	188	210	184	149	160	190	193	195	9.8	4.7	6.3
Olives	..	..	..	..	..	..	..	..	..	..	..	..	..
MADAGASCAR													
Rice	2,109	2,011	1,970	2,147	2,131	2,178	2,230	2,296	2,149	2,380	0.8	1.2	1.3
Cassava	1,683	1,670	1,898	1,992	2,047	2,142	2,421	2,178	2,286	2,277	5.1	5.5	-1.4
Sweet potatoes	373	399	356	463	463	450	467	467	467	483	1.4	4.8	1.0

(Table continues on following page)

8-7. Volume of food output, by major food crop

	Thousands of metric tons										Average annual percentage growth		
	1980	1981	1982	1983	1984	1985	1986	1987	1988	1989	75-80	80-85	6-MR
MALAWI													
Groundnuts	177	180	170	170	170	180	180	190	192	193	1.2	-0.2	2.2
Maize	1,186	1,245	1,415	1,369	1,398	1,355	1,295	1,202	1,427	1,510	4.8	2.8	6.5
Sorghum	20	20	20	7	14	22	21	15	19	20	-34.5	-4.5	1.6
Cassava	292	295	296	144	259	209	218	169	135	155	2.4	-7.6	-11.8
MALI													
Groundnuts	135	128	94	75	54	85	107	101	83	115	-10.3	-13.6	0.2
Millet	407	546	608	594	507	871	806	694	965	862	-4.1	10.7	5.5
Rice	132	135	153	216	109	214	225	237	288	329	-9.4	6.3	14.3
Sorghum	301	404	449	504	370	471	465	513	711	716	-4.1	6.2	17.6
Maize	407	546	608	594	507	871	806	694	965	862	-4.1	10.7	5.5
MAURITANIA													
Sorghum	28	36	18	9	9	73	84	90	109	77	-8.9	-0.2	-0.7
Millet	3	4	2	1	1	8	9	7	7	8	-3.3	0.1	-3.5
Rice	11	15	20	22	20	25	33	51	51	46	24.4	15.9	10.5
Maize	5	4	4	3	3	1	3	1	7	3	12.0	-23.1	21.5
MAURITIUS													
Sugarcane	4,564	5,303	6,582	5,255	5,009	5,583	6,025	6,231	5,517	5,436	0.8	1.8	-4.2
Potatoes	..	..	..	..	..	..	..	..	..	..	..	..	..
Onions	..	..	..	..	..	..	..	..	..	..	..	..	..
MOROCCO													
Citrus	..	..	..	..		..		..	..	..	..	..	..
Wheat	1,811	892	2,183	1,970	1,989	2,358	3,809	2,427	4,019	3,927	1.4	10.9	6.1
Sugarbeet	2,193	2,115	2,314	2,589	2,526	..	..	..	..	..	5.2	..	..
Barley	2,210	1,039	2,334	1,228	1,405	..	..	..	..	..	2.8	..	..
MOZAMBIQUE													
Cashew nuts	71	71	61	36	20	25	30	35	40	45	-18.4	-23.8	14.5
Maize	380	370	350	330	330	340	350	271	322	330	5.0	-2.7	0.0
Rice	70	60	60	55	55	55	60	55	55	55	-2.2	-4.3	-2.6
Cassava	3,100	3,200	3,250	3,150	3,150	3,250	3,320	3,370	3,400	3,400	3.6	0.5	0.8
NAMIBIA													
Wheat	1	1	1	1	1	1	1	2	2	2	-50.0	10.4	15.0
Maize	50	48	48	48	50	52	55	62	65	65	-0.9	0.9	5.6
NIGER													
Cowpeas	266	275	272	269	195	115	297	209	357	360	6.7	-13.9	11.8
Groundnuts	126	102	88	74	30	55	60	41	45	80	18.8	-20.5	10.2
Sorghum	368	322	357	362	236	329	360	366	560	452	7.5	-4.1	11.7
Millet	1,364	1,314	1,293	1,325	779	1,450	1,383	997	1,766	1,293	15.0	-3.5	3.8
NIGERIA													
Groundnuts	471	419	396	591	546	532	696	612	540	700	1.7	5.3	-1.1
Palm oil	675	675	700	730	700	730	760	730	750	770	0.7	1.6	0.7
Sorghum	3,690	3,535	4,081	4,231	3,551	4,822	5,425	5,890	4,948	4,587	1.9	4.0	-6.6
Millet	2,450	2,452	2,339	3,339	2,115	3,683	4,001	4,397	3,816	3,500	-7.0	5.7	-5.3
Maize	653	653	626	1,027	1,196	1,826	1,735	1,357	1,821	1,600	-17.0	23.7	0.5
Rice	1,090	1,241	1,250	1,280	1,300	1,515	1,416	1,450	1,400	1,400	18.6	5.3	-0.7
Yams	17,000	17,500	18,500	16,625	18,500	19,250	19,750	16,000	16,000	16,000	2.6	2.0	-6.1
Cassava (gari)	11,000	11,000	11,700	9,950	11,800	13,500	14,700	14,000	15,000	16,500	0.3	3.1	4.2
RWANDA													
Sorghum	179	193	214	189	183	228	193	188	177	164	3.9	2.7	-5.4
Maize	85	85	92	110	102	99	90	91	88	89	4.8	4.4	-0.5
Plantains	2,063	2,321	2,378	2,363	2,056	2,107	2,100	2,130	2,140	2,150	3.5	-0.8	0.8
Sweet potatoes	871	958	1,027	923	812	980	893	895	1,032	810	6.0	0.0	-1.5
SENEGAL													
Groundnuts	523	872	1,004	512	682	587	841	963	723	844	-16.1	-2.4	-2.7
Millet	451	790	477	287	381	768	502	690	485	639	-0.4	-0.1	3.8
Rice	65	127	119	109	136	147	143	136	146	168	-7.1	12.8	5.8
Maize	57	95	76	61	98	147	108	114	123	131	0.9	14.2	7.0
Sorghum	102	196	108	65	90	182	132	111	110	127	-0.5	0.1	-1.3
SIERRA LEONE													
Palm oil	47	48	48	46	37	44	44	44	44	44	1.5	-3.3	0.0
Palm kernels	30	30	30	30	30	30	30	30	30	30	-9.8	0.0	0.0
Rice	513	500	583	609	504	428	525	466	420	430	-2.7	-2.4	-6.8
Cassava	95	97	100	105	100	110	112	116	116	116	2.5	2.5	1.1
SOMALIA													
Bananas	60	59	79	89	62	60	94	108	115	116	-10.1	0.7	7.2
Maize	110	142	150	236	270	280	336	286	353	302	0.8	22.3	-1.1
Sorghum	140	222	235	120	221	222	237	244	235	291	0.5	4.7	6.0
Sesame	38	53	57	36	40	57	45	45	46	47	0.8	1.8	1.8

(Table continues on following page)

8–7. Volume of food output, by major food crop

	1980	1981	1982	1983	1984	1985	1986	1987	1988	1989	75–80	80–85	6–MR
				Thousands of metric tons							Average annual percentage growth		
SOUTH AFRICA													
Maize	10,726	14,656	8,359	4,083	4,393	7,658	8,077	7,372	7,253	12,061	3.5	-15.8	12.6
Wheat	1,470	2,341	2,434	1,774	2,335	1,684	2,322	3,146	3,539	2,179	-3.6	1.0	-0.7
Sugarcane	14,062	19,532	19,340	13,423	22,356	18,803	18,287	21,066	19,864	18,500	-2.9	4.4	-0.2
Sorghum	701	542	276	194	472	602	446	506	483	466	12.6	-4.3	0.9
Barley	60	106	110	154	173	256	199	280	..	..	4.4	29.5	40.7
SUDAN													
Groundnuts	707	721	497	413	386	274	364	432	527	400	-3.3	-17.7	4.9
Sesame	221	242	163	206	133	132	216	233	195	..	-3.0	-11.2	-5.0
Sorghum	2,068	3,345	1,938	1,829	1,097	3,542	3,277	1,363	4,640	1,600	0.1	-2.0	-8.8
Wheat	233	218	163	141	169	79	199	157	181	258	-4.4	-16.5	9.6
SWAZILAND													
Sugarcane	2,782	3,250	3,479	3,562	3,586	3,386	4,084	4,000	4,000	3,800	7.2	3.8	-2.1
Citrus	40	48	52	47	43	..	..	..	..	..	-2.4	..	..
Maize	97	94	52	30	148	85	95	95	149	135	-2.0	0.5	16.3
TANZANIA													
Maize	1,726	1,839	1,654	1,651	1,939	2,093	2,210	2,359	2,339	3,159	4.5	3.3	11.2
Sorghum	510	425	580	475	455	615	650	663	420	503	19.8	2.7	-11.5
Rice	291	200	320	350	356	427	547	644	615	570	-0.4	11.3	0.8
Millet	340	280	390	320	305	410	380	291	280	300	17.3	2.9	-7.2
Cassava	4,828	6,168	6,343	7,118	6,603	6,840	6,227	6,000	6,200	6,300	-0.5	6.1	0.7
TOGO													
Maize	138	151	151	145	222	182	127	172	296	287	5.3	7.3	34.8
Sorghum	95	80	84	80	119	95	131	98	119	153	..	3.4	6.8
Millet	43	40	52	51	76	74	82	71	56	97	-21.4	14.0	3.0
Cassava	408	372	367	345	444	474	411	355	413	409	1.2	3.6	1.4
Yams	484	528	472	383	342	364	409	360	379	405	4.5	-8.0	0.2
TUNISIA													
Olive oil	115	70	55	150	95	105	114	95	54	110	-7.3	4.3	-6.5
Citrus	160	221	165	144	214	195	252	250	233	262	4.9	2.2	0.5
Wheat	869	963	916	618	711	1,380	474	1,360	220	420	-1.7	2.9	-19.6
Barley	..	..	..	..	..	..	..	..	..	..	..	..	..
UGANDA													
Millet	458	480	528	545	223	480	350	471	414	417	-7.1	-5.7	4.0
Maize	286	342	393	413	281	343	286	330	331	300	-12.3	1.1	1.5
Sorghum	299	320	400	407	164	310	280	286	289	260	-8.7	-5.0	-2.1
Cassava	2,072	3,000	3,127	3,239	1,881	2,700	1,871	2,819	2,502	2,500	-12.3	-0.1	7.8
Plantains	5,698	5,900	6,596	6,647	6,461	6,655	6,660	6,726	6,630	6,700	-8.7	3.1	0.0
ZAIRE													
Palm oil	168	165	155	145	153	160	155	165	178	178	-1.4	-1.5	5.0
Maize	594	639	666	673	704	726	728	730	730	790	4.0	3.8	2.5
Rice	234	245	251	271	286	297	299	300	300	315	2.3	5.1	1.6
Cassava	13,087	13,172	14,185	14,600	15,038	15,493	16,249	16,251	16,254	16,300	1.8	3.7	0.1
Plantains	1,434	1,450	1,460	1,470	1,480	1,490	1,500	1,510	1,550	1,530	0.5	0.7	0.9
ZAMBIA													
Sunflower seeds	28	19	27	35	43	42	31	17	16	18	13.8	14.4	-15.6
Maize	937	1,007	750	935	872	1,122	1,231	1,063	1,943	1,861	-11.6	2.0	20.2
Wheat	10	12	14	11	13	17	18	27	32	47	21.0	8.6	35.3
Cassava	180	190	200	210	210	210	220	230	240	260	1.6	3.3	5.6

(Table continues on following page)

8-7. Volume of food output, by major food crop

	Thousands of metric tons										Average annual percentage growth		
	1980	1981	1982	1983	1984	1985	1986	1987	1988	1989	75-80	80-85	6-MR
ZIMBABWE													
Sugarcane	2,528	3,551	3,587	3,438	3,459	3,650	4,135	3,339	3,199	3,622	0.6	5.0	-4.3
Maize	1,511	2,833	1,808	910	1,133	2,960	2,546	1,094	2,253	1,927	-6.1	-0.2	-1.1
Wheat	191	183	192	111	84	205	248	215	257	285	8.6	-7.0	6.1

Notes: Crops shown represent same major food crops, as the ones presented in Nominal Producer Prices Table (8-1), excluding beverages (coffee, tea, cocoa), cotton and tobacco.

The following commodities are in their least-processed form **unless otherwise indicated:**

    Cotton, seed cotton
    Groundnuts, unshelled
    Rice, paddy
    Sunflower, seeds
    Citrus, total for country
    Sesame, seeds
    Livestock = combined total head of cattle, sheep, goats, pigs, horses, asses and mules
    Chickens/rabbits = combined total

For South Africa, barley production is for white areas only.

8–8. Value of agriculture exports

	Millions of U.S. dollars (current prices and exchange rates)											Average annual percentage growth		
	1980	1981	1982	1983	1984	1985	1986	1987	1988	1989	1990	75–80	80–85	86–MR
SUB-SAHARAN AFRICA	9,900	8,515	8,022	7,635	8,833	8,280	9,811	8,840	8,655	8,688	8,437	9.6	-2.4	-3.1
excluding Nigeria	8,556	7,489	7,163	6,664	7,899	7,403	8,733	8,021	7,656	7,744	7,635	9.8	-1.8	-3.0
Angola	172	104	104	81	89	75	55	25	29	16	7	-2.4	-13.0	-36.5
Benin	55	22	20	30	79	73	69	74	77	75	89	12.9	17.6	5.4
Botswana	52	96	98	90	66	69	86	77	73	93	93	3.2	0.8	3.5
Burkina Faso	80	63	48	53	72	50	51	87	81	97	108	10.9	-5.1	17.5
Burundi	64	72	86	80	95	104	159	78	129	73	69	13.2	9.5	-15.9
Cameroon	699	470	390	427	473	469	625	527	510	661	524	17.7	-5.2	-1.2
Cape Verde	1	2	1	1	0	1	1	1	·1	2	2	43.5	-23.3	18.6
Central African Republic	61	51	55	53	46	61	50	36	40	59	30	13.2	-0.9	-5.0
Chad	115	125	120	161	180	132	64	77	97	95	88	14.2	6.1	9.0
Comoros	7	15	18	15	6	14	20	9	18	13	13	9.7	0.9	-5.9
Congo, People's Republic of the	13	12	10	7	17	15	12	10	10	8	11	6.6	4.1	-3.5
Cote d' Ivoire	2,009	1,696	1,412	1,280	1,866	2,144	2,420	2,067	1,737	1,619	1,748	19.9	1.5	-8.6
Djibouti	3	3	3	4	4	5	4	5	6	6	6	..	10.3	9.3
Equatorial Guinea	12	14	12	14	17	19	16	13	13	8	8	2.5	8.7	-16.4
Ethiopia	391	343	369	360	381	301	447	326	400	391	225	13.7	-2.9	-11.2
Gabon	14	10	7	7	7	8	10	6	8	7	3	48.9	-10.0	-19.3
Gambia, The	28	18	16	26	29	17	12	7	19	8	13	-9.1	-1.6	3.1
Ghana	744	436	422	269	382	403	504	538	481	425	387	7.2	-10.6	-7.4
Guinea	33	28	29	33	21	18	25	25	26	32	22	13.3	-10.4	0.2
Guinea-Bissau	6	8	7	6	12	8	7	13	11	13	13	7.8	8.1	11.5
Kenya	693	615	591	626	747	685	909	678	735	680	717	15.2	1.7	-4.6
Lesotho	16	14	12	21	21	15	12	16	18	21	23	12.2	4.2	16.2
Liberia	151	124	89	107	129	120	108	107	119	162	68	21.4	-2.5	-5.0
Madagascar	334	253	252	236	274	208	250	273	179	208	166	9.8	-6.1	-10.4
Malawi	251	239	220	231	297	229	232	258	275	249	380	13.5	0.7	10.0
Mali	192	201	197	174	228	157	182	226	203	228	287	20.7	-2.1	9.6
Mauritania	39	43	41	35	33	36	32	31	32	33	33	15.9	-3.9	1.5
Mauritius	302	200	242	248	211	207	283	356	356	346	365	4.5	-4.8	4.9
Mozambique	157	142	112	65	50	37	36	53	44	38	41	7.0	-26.7	-1.1
Namibia	125	129	127	105	103	113	125	177	175	197	187	7.9	-3.8	9.5
Niger	86	87	69	46	77	62	65	48	48	49	45	18.6	-6.6	-7.2
Nigeria	446	429	348	448	348	310	376	251	444	251	255	3.2	-6.1	-7.4
Rwanda	66	72	76	65	70	77	169	130	98	114	98	10.3	1.6	-11.4
Sao Tome & Principe	19	13	12	11	10	7	6	6	6	5	4	24.7	-14.8	-10.4
Senegal	115	64	167	190	157	103	105	118	132	209	214	-12.4	6.7	22.0
Seychelles	3	3	2	2	2	2	1	1	1	1	0	13.4	-14.9	-19.4
Sierra Leone	59	34	35	28	35	54	49	42	31	22	17	18.7	-1.7	-24.2
Somalia	125	150	240	92	50	99	94	99	75	73	73	11.2	-14.3	-7.8
Sudan	553	476	496	506	597	359	327	514	505	662	540	4.2	-4.1	13.4
Swaziland	211	194	147	157	136	100	150	189	175	180	208	14.0	-12.7	6.2
Tanzania	406	466	352	284	312	258	343	245	254	284	272	4.2	-10.0	-3.1
Togo	77	67	56	51	77	79	101	99	100	93	82	18.3	1.4	-4.8
Uganda	344	244	362	371	392	364	403	314	272	271	154	4.8	5.1	-18.8
Zaire	235	170	158	167	254	221	375	211	162	181	139	0.3	2.8	-19.3
Zambia	13	8	6	9	8	17	25	17	13	23	24	-2.6	4.9	2.7
Zimbabwe	453	620	517	471	480	494	543	565	619	611	778	2.4	-1.2	8.3
NORTH AFRICA	1,544	1,518	1,278	1,234	1,268	1,227	1,313	1,355	1,309	1,293	1,419	1.0	-4.8	1.1
Algeria	120	124	72	38	49	57	27	30	30	36	50	-7.2	-18.4	15.5
Egypt, Arab Republic of	677	741	673	726	756	662	669	673	514	532	481	-4.2	0.1	-8.6
Libya	..	0	..	..	..	..	1	2	2	1	1	..	..	-2.2
Morocco	606	436	375	364	311	367	456	458	572	520	637	12.4	-9.7	8.3
Tunisia	140	217	158	107	152	141	161	194	193	203	252	1.2	-4.0	9.8
ALL AFRICA	11,444	10,032	9,300	8,869	10,101	9,507	11,124	10,195	9,965	9,981	9,856	8.2	-2.7	-2.6
South Africa	2,517	2,288	1,830	1,334	1,128	1,070	1,233	1,366	1,430	1,923	1,671	9.9	-17.5	10.0

8–9. Volume of agricultural exports

| | Thousands of metric tons | | | | | | | | | Average annual percentage growth | | |
	1980	1981	1982	1983	1984	1985	1986	1987	1988	75–80	80–85	86–88
SUB-SAHARAN AFRICA	13,269	13,069	13,518	12,726	11,245	11,930	12,493	12,517	11,870	-0.8	-2.9	-2.5
excluding Nigeria	12,266	12,094	12,678	11,874	10,541	11,281	11,671	11,792	11,032	-0.4	-2.5	-2.8
Angola	71	67	70	46	40	36	34	26	26	-19.1	-14.2	-12.3
Benin	82	49	44	62	81	85	98	135	103	1.6	5.9	2.8
Botswana	26	37	45	44	39	51	60	36	31	-10.0	10.4	-28.0
Burkina Faso	374	321	202	206	256	237	192	201	196	-0.8	-8.1	0.9
Burundi	21	31	37	30	35	39	48	41	58	-14.4	10.0	10.2
Cameroon	361	336	295	320	358	341	385	351	397	-1.2	0.0	1.5
Cape Verde	10	12	13	11	8	8	8	9	6	-12.0	-6.7	-11.5
Central African Republic	33	34	33	30	28	37	31	24	32	-5.6	-0.3	1.8
Chad	459	426	422	432	335	327	289	237	265	3.2	-6.6	-4.2
Comoros	2	2	1	2	2	3	2	2	1	-1.6	8.5	-32.3
Congo, People's Republic of the	6	20	11	10	44	29	19	19	20	-24.8	34.2	1.6
Cote d' Ivoire	1,213	1,453	1,348	1,233	1,433	1,597	1,593	1,507	1,468	2.3	3.6	-4.0
Djibouti	25	24	33	68	54	79	59	69	85	..	28.8	19.9
Equatorial Guinea	7	10	8	11	11	10	8	9	9	-7.2	7.7	4.4
Ethiopia	244	246	280	320	305	361	344	392	425	-14.5	8.1	11.2
Gabon	11	10	9	11	7	10	11	8	9	13.5	-3.0	-11.5
Gambia, The	68	28	43	69	53	33	26	37	39	-11.6	-3.6	23.2
Ghana	224	212	265	173	166	196	224	236	264	-13.4	-5.1	8.6
Guinea	113	105	110	103	84	72	74	77	72	3.4	-8.2	-1.3
Guinea-Bissau	16	17	20	16	25	13	17	17	15	0.6	0.2	-3.8
Kenya	508	546	479	681	519	506	742	810	717	1.8	0.5	-1.7
Lesotho	37	37	35	45	36	24	13	2	2	-3.8	-5.6	-56.9
Liberia	105	102	97	96	114	115	114	110	109	0.9	2.3	-2.5
Madagascar	173	120	117	131	158	112	112	172	116	-5.5	-3.4	1.6
Malawi	301	260	213	336	333	333	334	267	260	11.3	5.0	-11.7
Mali	822	932	1,126	1,079	993	771	823	688	727	13.0	-0.5	-6.0
Mauritania	706	736	646	586	536	536	516	456	456	0.1	-6.7	-6.0
Mauritius	776	600	778	750	667	699	769	801	796	4.4	-0.7	1.7
Mozambique	235	220	177	101	74	75	59	58	81	-6.8	-23.9	17.0
Namibia	447	451	718	405	348	505	659	829	798	..	-2.1	10.0
Niger	538	476	338	304	510	417	336	242	248	5.5	-3.3	-14.0
Nigeria	554	541	455	465	253	233	374	321	387	-3.5	-17.2	1.8
Rwanda	33	38	37	37	41	47	54	57	53	-19.7	6.0	-0.3
Sao Tome & Principe	10	10	10	8	6	6	6	4	5	6.2	-12.5	-3.1
Senegal	237	122	427	492	224	130	240	242	427	-18.1	-3.0	33.2
Seychelles	4	4	3	4	2	3	4	3	1	-4.7	-7.9	-37.2
Sierra Leone	39	27	31	28	27	33	24	23	24	-7.3	-2.4	-0.4
Somalia	1,943	1,654	1,673	1,242	738	1,533	1,288	1,197	789	6.4	-10.6	-21.7
Sudan	1,255	1,212	1,480	1,080	1,008	907	735	1,213	1,134	6.6	-6.9	24.2
Swaziland	481	552	619	607	584	549	715	630	605	7.0	2.3	-8.0
Tanzania	317	364	307	202	227	211	228	329	262	-4.6	-10.4	7.0
Togo	57	74	62	60	56	71	101	98	84	0.9	0.6	-8.9
Uganda	113	130	201	185	184	162	150	153	156	-15.3	8.2	2.1
Zaire	185	177	164	151	154	169	207	161	158	-6.5	-2.7	-12.6
Zambia	9	6	7	9	17	30	98	58	46	-18.7	31.0	-31.6
Zimbabwe	489	709	779	914	471	773	991	1,061	791	-11.8	3.6	-10.7
NORTH AFRICA	2,922	2,716	2,504	2,348	2,281	2,392	1,999	2,287	2,555	-1.9	-4.4	13.1
Algeria	281	270	179	91	128	180	57	62	53	-16.4	-13.7	-3.5
Egypt, Arab Republic of	960	881	956	945	899	837	758	1,119	973	-1.8	-1.8	13.3
Libya	..	..	..	..	..	..	1	2	3	..	..	54.4
Morocco	1,518	1,342	1,221	1,080	1,020	1,095	1,013	882	1,318	4.8	-7.1	14.1
Tunisia	162	222	148	232	233	280	171	224	211	-7.5	10.0	10.9
ALL AFRICA	16,191	15,784	16,022	15,075	13,525	14,322	14,492	14,804	14,425	-1.0	-3.2	-0.2
South Africa	6,898	7,623	7,253	4,059	2,801	3,342	4,567	5,407	3,995	..	-18.6	-6.5

8–10. Volume of cereal imports

	Thousands of metric tons											Average annual percentage growth		
	1980	1981	1982	1983	1984	1985	1986	1987	1988	1989	1990	75–80	80–85	86–MR
SUB-SAHARAN AFRICA	8,264	8,354	8,633	8,003	9,173	11,001	8,441	7,744	8,336	7,362	7,697	17.8	4.8	-2.3
excluding Nigeria	5,840	5,658	5,943	5,911	6,985	8,455	6,577	6,446	7,061	6,146	6,373	14.4	7.3	-1.1
Angola	341	288	291	287	374	284	159	280	249	290	272	28.6	-0.4	11.8
Benin	61	89	104	114	91	67	73	77	136	105	126	24.3	1.7	15.0
Botswana	68	49	61	123	174	155	113	94	112	92	87	26.9	27.8	-5.3
Burkina Faso	77	48	89	82	148	205	123	94	130	120	145	28.7	26.3	6.0
Burundi	18	18	20	20	14	19	13	13	15	6	17	15.5	-1.6	-2.2
Cameroon	140	107	117	202	122	141	191	289	350	370	398	18.6	2.8	18.7
Cape Verde	65	56	57	71	66	67	81	61	49	67	71	12.2	2.6	-1.7
Central African Republic	12	19	15	15	13	22	40	35	40	27	37	-0.4	5.3	-3.7
Chad	16	30	57	31	85	101	36	59	61	40	36	13.2	40.2	-4.3
Comoros	14	33	28	23	33	19	35	19	34	33	25	8.3	4.4	-0.6
Congo, People's Republic of the	88	51	81	80	108	100	94	78	113	83	94	20.4	8.6	0.7
Cote d' Ivoire	469	573	541	597	536	554	580	760	496	613	502	41.2	2.1	-4.9
Djibouti	32	26	35	25	29	64	49	38	49	47	44	15.8	10.3	0.0
Equatorial Guinea	2	3	5	7	5	10	7	8	14	15	11	-1.8	32.4	18.7
Ethiopia	397	210	278	345	252	741	973	480	1,127	471	687	41.0	11.7	-6.9
Gabon	27	35	43	48	55	64	53	55	59	51	57	-15.4	18.2	0.7
Gambia, The	47	42	39	38	63	73	97	70	96	81	95	22.9	10.4	1.0
Ghana	247	163	171	230	193	137	145	223	257	244	337	23.3	-6.0	19.4
Guinea	171	130	94	112	162	140	151	172	178	283	210	22.2	-0.5	12.3
Guinea-Bissau	21	47	30	26	34	31	22	60	55	64	52	5.6	2.2	20.2
Kenya	387	149	275	161	556	279	179	257	86	150	188	35.2	5.2	-4.3
Lesotho	107	100	96	147	130	119	132	79	146	100	97	11.2	5.0	-3.7
Liberia	99	111	117	102	113	103	118	100	102	157	70	21.0	0.4	-5.6
Madagascar	110	279	391	265	162	195	212	178	86	103	183	18.0	2.4	-8.0
Malawi	36	74	26	20	21	29	16	61	103	101	115	-12.2	-13.6	56.5
Mali	87	97	177	172	254	319	193	80	114	92	61	3.5	30.6	-19.4
Mauritania	166	141	152	300	266	304	188	203	250	219	205	5.7	17.3	2.6
Mauritius	181	175	179	168	188	179	162	189	176	209	210	4.0	0.3	6.5
Mozambique	368	320	307	274	430	598	244	374	529	400	416	16.6	9.6	12.0
Namibia	..	..	..	..	..	..	..	..	..	..	..	..	..	..
Niger	90	141	149	128	90	300	68	48	159	100	86	30.0	13.8	12.7
Nigeria	1,828	2,216	2,159	1,475	1,529	1,957	1,369	595	504	423	502	31.4	-3.2	-20.9
Rwanda	16	15	14	24	25	33	27	11	10	10	21	-3.4	16.9	-5.7
Sao Tome & Principe	9	11	8	10	11	10	7	9	5	11	9	17.0	1.9	6.2
Senegal	452	485	494	544	661	540	502	431	431	516	534	12.6	5.6	3.1
Seychelles	9	7	9	6	9	7	9	10	13	14	12	4.0	-2.8	9.5
Sierra Leone	83	78	128	59	53	119	124	148	119	145	146	33.2	-0.4	3.2
Somalia	221	430	394	254	264	180	258	302	212	188	194	0.1	-8.0	-9.9
Sudan	236	295	437	452	518	1,561	658	748	727	589	586	16.1	37.6	-4.6
Swaziland	20	55	44	45	81	31	27	49	52	52	54	5.4	10.0	15.6
Tanzania	399	266	324	232	270	412	230	179	129	73	73	-6.4	-0.4	-27.4
Togo	41	61	56	81	87	57	61	71	136	112	111	66.5	9.2	18.0
Uganda	52	40	68	23	31	16	13	20	28	16	7	..	-20.0	-12.9
Zaire	350	552	323	323	291	320	408	476	415	323	336	-0.2	-6.6	-7.5
Zambia	498	250	206	210	240	201	165	135	119	123	100	25.0	-12.5	-10.4
Zimbabwe	156	28	11	75	371	153	54	47	93	52	83	5.6	31.2	9.9
NORTH AFRICA	12,987	14,274	14,871	15,896	17,586	18,192	17,725	18,063	19,123	21,053	19,071	10.4	7.0	3.0
Algeria	3,414	2,719	4,095	3,766	4,116	5,266	4,611	3,865	5,368	7,969	5,185	16.6	10.0	10.1
Egypt, Arab Republic of	6,028	7,199	6,800	8,114	8,616	8,903	8,407	9,348	8,560	8,514	8,580	7.7	7.9	-0.5
Libya	908	684	976	868	1,012	1,114	1,785	1,446	1,435	1,552	2,290	7.0	6.1	5.9
Morocco	1,821	2,724	1,975	2,015	2,770	2,177	1,610	2,236	1,643	1,363	1,578	7.3	2.8	-5.2
Tunisia	817	948	1,026	1,133	1,073	732	1,312	1,168	2,116	1,655	1,439	21.5	-0.2	5.5
ALL AFRICA	21,251	22,628	23,505	23,900	26,760	29,193	26,166	25,807	27,459	28,414	26,768	12.9	6.2	1.4
South Africa	159	480	302	1,517	3,260	763	731	530	369	376	876	9.0	54.3	0.2

8-11. Food aid

	Thousands of metric tons											Average annual percentage growth		
	1980	1981	1982	1983	1984	1985	1986	1987	1988	1989	1990	75–80	80–85	86–MR
SUB-SAHARAN AFRICA	1,576	2,307	2,329	2,502	2,636	4,797	3,841	3,253	3,703	2,678	2,587	13.4	18.8	-9.4
excluding Nigeria	1,557	2,271	2,244	2,426	2,565	4,700	3,774	3,176	3,591	2,591	2,467	13.3	18.6	-10.0
Angola	11	25	75	61	69	84	53	69	109	80	113	..	45.3	18.2
Benin	5	11	8	14	6	21	11	8	11	15	13	-9.7	17.8	10.2
Botswana	20	11	7	12	32	39	49	44	53	33	5	34.2	22.1	-38.4
Burkina Faso	37	51	81	45	57	128	116	22	42	49	44	17.3	18.8	-10.7
Burundi	8	12	9	7	11	17	6	2	4	6	2	19.8	9.9	-9.8
Cameroon	4	10	11	6	1	13	12	7	2	6	..	6.4	-2.0	-29.9
Cape Verde	34	31	54	35	63	50	51	59	54	54	55	36.6	10.6	0.5
Central African Republic	3	3	2	4	8	12	11	6	6	..	4	30.0	36.6	..
Chad	16	14	29	36	69	163	82	29	22	15	27	15.0	60.4	-24.8
Comoros	3	2	8	7	5	5	7	10	11	2	2	20.5	19.0	-32.6
Congo, People's Republic of the	4	2	0	9	1	0	2	1	1	2	7	15.4	-25.9	43.7
Cote d' Ivoire	2	..	1	..	..	..	1	..	1	19	26	-8.4	..	..
Djibouti	5	14	11	8	11	15	20	16	10	12	6	..	13.8	-23.0
Equatorial Guinea	0	2	8	12	8	7	5	1	2	3	1	..	78.1	-17.7
Ethiopia	111	228	190	356	172	869	799	570	824	578	538	17.1	33.3	-7.5
Gabon	..	..	..	..	0	..	..	..	..	..	..	..	..	..
Gambia, The	7	16	21	13	19	21	19	15	17	10	11	9.7	17.4	-13.7
Ghana	110	94	43	58	75	96	96	66	110	46	73	29.2	-3.0	-8.6
Guinea	24	34	39	25	43	52	55	92	26	42	25	-7.7	12.3	-21.1
Guinea-Bissau	18	26	30	35	19	31	18	10	13	8	14	13.4	6.0	-6.2
Kenya	86	173	127	165	122	340	139	107	119	112	62	71.3	18.9	-14.6
Lesotho	29	44	34	29	50	71	40	34	55	34	30	20.3	14.5	-5.6
Liberia	3	26	42	57	47	20	76	2	56	28	28	-3.7	37.6	7.8
Madagascar	14	27	87	141	74	98	65	151	81	76	31	28.4	46.7	-19.6
Malawi	5	17	2	3	4	5	5	10	105	223	175	100.5	-9.4	175.0
Mali	22	50	66	88	110	266	83	77	26	62	38	-11.8	54.2	-16.1
Mauritania	26	106	86	71	129	135	137	38	54	70	72	-5.6	27.8	-6.7
Mauritius	22	21	43	13	22	9	5	15	31	21	9	-9.8	-14.1	17.3
Mozambique	151	155	148	174	311	379	262	364	480	434	493	33.5	21.6	15.5
Namibia	..	..	..	..	..	..	..	..	..	1	4	..	..	..
Niger	9	11	71	12	13	221	107	17	23	83	35	-35.1	52.1	-6.4
Nigeria	..	..	1	..	..	0	0	..	..	..	..	..	..	..
Rwanda	14	15	13	13	25	35	25	16	8	2	7	-3.2	18.9	-36.5
Sao Tome & Principe	2	2	3	2	9	10	6	8	9	7	4	..	49.2	-6.4
Senegal	61	153	83	91	150	131	117	80	109	53	61	32.0	11.7	-15.8
Seychelles	2	1	1	0	2	1	2	1	0	0	0	63.3	-11.8	-34.3
Sierra Leone	36	12	29	29	16	21	49	43	58	38	37	21.6	-5.3	-6.4
Somalia	137	330	186	188	177	248	143	161	154	74	90	6.9	3.2	-15.6
Sudan	212	195	194	330	450	815	939	890	615	200	335	42.0	32.2	-29.9
Swaziland	1	1	1	4	10	1	0	3	8	15	7	..	33.3	118.3
Tanzania	89	236	308	171	141	125	66	55	76	76	22	-13.1	-1.2	-16.9
Togo	7	4	5	7	9	23	9	6	16	11	11	0.7	26.5	9.7
Uganda	17	57	49	14	10	31	7	15	29	17	35	..	-8.7	40.3
Zaire	69	77	97	110	53	138	101	56	177	55	107	109.9	7.2	1.0
Zambia	167	84	100	83	72	116	85	116	145	66	3	96.6	-6.8	-50.0
Zimbabwe	..	18	..	6	76	131	..	38	14	10	13	..	..	..
NORTH AFRICA	2,061	2,113	2,535	2,114	2,383	2,662	2,024	2,988	2,405	1,987	1,919	21.1	4.3	-5.0
Algeria	19	29	5	2	6	2	4	4	5	38	11	-18.8	-39.5	56.1
Egypt, Arab Republic of	1,758	1,865	1,957	1,816	1,783	1,951	1,799	1,977	1,646	1,427	1,210	22.3	0.9	-10.6
Libya	..	..	..	..	..	..	0	..	..	..	..	..	..	..
Morocco	119	120	477	142	448	518	142	611	340	237	219	20.4	33.3	-0.8
Tunisia	165	99	96	154	146	192	80	396	415	284	479	28.0	7.1	38.4
ALL AFRICA	3,637	4,420	4,865	4,616	5,019	7,460	5,865	6,241	6,108	4,665	4,505	17.3	11.9	-7.9
South Africa	..	..	..	..	..	..	..	..	..	..	..	..	..	..

8–12. Fertilizer consumption

	Thousands of metric tons										Average annual percentage growth		
	1980	*1981*	*1982*	*1983*	*1984*	*1985*	*1986*	*1987*	*1988*	*1989*	*75–80*	*80–85*	*86–MR*
SUB-SAHARAN AFRICA	948	1,040	959	1,008	1,000	1,187	1,074	1,100	1,165	1,279	4.6	3.1	6.0
excluding Nigeria	724	777	708	686	667	811	743	743	797	844	1.5	0.2	4.6
Angola	17	12	5	9	7	20	12	10	16	27	42.4	-0.4	32.6
Benin	1	3	3	5	7	11	11	9	7	3	-15.3	60.0	-32.1
Botswana	1	1	2	1	1	0	1	1	1	1	-12.0	-16.8	8.9
Burkina Faso	4	10	10	13	11	12	16	18	15	21	25.6	18.3	5.4
Burundi	1	1	1	3	2	2	3	3	3	5	11.8	18.7	13.3
Cameroon	32	35	42	46	43	57	52	50	39	29	23.9	10.7	-18.6
Cape Verde	0	..	..	..	0	0	0	0	..	..	1.8	..	..
Central African Republic	1	1	1	0	1	3	1	1	1	1	-23.0	8.6	0.9
Chad	1	5	5	6	7	7	4	5	5	5	..	39.5	3.7
Comoros	..	..	..	..	..	..	..	..	..	..	..	..	..
Congo, People's Republic of the	1	1	2	2	3	5	3	2	1	1	-34.2	58.7	-42.2
Cote d' Ivoire	53	49	34	38	42	42	29	33	41	41	7.3	-4.5	13.8
Djibouti	1	0	..	..	..	..	0	0	..	..			
Equatorial Guinea	0	..	..	..	..	..	..	..	..	..	0.0	..	..
Ethiopia	43	46	36	48	33	66	62	54	79	97	8.0	4.1	18.4
Gabon	0	2	0	2	3	3	2	2	1	1	-32.0	77.7	-22.8
Gambia, The	2	1	2	2	2	4	4	3	4	2	24.3	13.8	-12.6
Ghana	12	29	27	21	8	13	8	11	13	8	-11.7	-10.2	4.9
Guinea	0	1	1	..	0	0	1	1	1	1	-17.2	..	3.2
Guinea-Bissau	0	2	1	1	..	..	..	..	..	1			
Kenya	62	83	69	87	79	109	123	102	125	117	1.7	8.8	0.5
Lesotho	5	5	5	5	5	4	4	4	5	5	32.5	-3.3	6.3
Liberia	3	5	1	3	1	1	2	4	3	4	-7.8	-19.5	29.8
Madagascar	9	7	16	14	7	10	11	6	11	11	5.1	0.6	6.0
Malawi	33	34	32	43	45	34	37	48	51	55	12.1	3.5	12.7
Mali	14	9	11	10	50	20	15	16	13	11	31.6	21.4	-8.8
Mauritania	1	..	0	0	1	2	1	1	3	2	14.6	..	42.9
Mauritius	27	22	26	27	27	28	25	33	28	35	3.5	2.5	8.5
Mozambique	28	41	40	15	4	4	6	7	2	2	34.4	-40.2	-33.6
Namibia	..	..	..	..	..	..	..	..	..	..			
Niger	3	6	3	2	2	4	2	3	2	3	27.1	-4.6	7.7
Nigeria	174	213	202	264	277	292	262	293	312	378	21.2	11.0	12.3
Rwanda	0	0	1	1	2	1	1	2	1	2	-14.0	66.6	1.0
Sao Tome & Principe	..	..	..	..	..	..	..	..	..	..	..	..	..
Senegal	19	24	18	27	18	21	21	21	26	29	-15.0	-0.6	12.5
Seychelles	..	..	1	0	..	..	..	..	..	..	..	..	..
Sierra Leone	2	3	0	1	1	4	4	1	0	1	-1.2	5.5	-48.4
Somalia	1	1	1	2	4	4	2	4	2	3	-18.0	32.8	8.7
Sudan	81	75	79	38	44	93	46	50	47	49	-11.8	-4.6	1.5
Swaziland	20	17	14	17	9	9	12	7	8	8	16.5	-16.0	-11.5
Tanzania	36	29	24	23	35	39	45	48	41	49	2.3	2.8	0.7
Togo	3	2	3	3	7	10	11	11	12	12	4.7	33.2	3.5
Uganda	1	1	..	..	1	0	0	1	0	0	..	..	-21.8
Zaire	8	8	7	9	12	7	2	6	3	8	-8.5	2.1	31.7
Zambia	79	85	85	66	56	80	77	95	85	87	4.7	-3.9	2.6
Zimbabwe	173	173	151	155	146	170	158	140	166	170	2.1	-1.7	4.0
NORTH AFRICA	1,273	1,232	1,351	1,469	1,491	1,599	1,627	1,649	1,705	1,766	7.2	5.3	2.8
Algeria	236	166	126	160	204	283	272	241	170	215	10.7	5.2	-10.0
Egypt, Arab Republic of	664	708	827	899	851	864	867	897	1,034	1,045	6.1	5.7	7.3
Libya	53	74	88	91	101	60	72	89	88	79	7.8	4.6	2.4
Morocco	259	200	229	246	248	299	310	318	313	318	8.3	4.2	0.7
Tunisia	62	84	81	74	87	93	106	104	101	109	4.1	6.0	0.6
ALL AFRICA	2,221	2,272	2,310	2,477	2,491	2,786	2,701	2,750	2,870	3,045	6.1	4.3	4.1
South Africa	1,064	1,233	1,132	878	964	865	818	713	835	758	6.4	-5.6	-0.7

8–13. Fertilizer imports

	Thousands of metric tons										Average annual percentage growth		
	1980	1981	1982	1983	1984	1985	1986	1987	1988	1989	75–80	80–85	86–MR
SUB-SAHARAN AFRICA	789	854	854	879	901	1,116	875	947	968	1,025	5.7	5.7	5.1
excluding Nigeria	563	609	610	559	573	647	590	622	740	751	2.5	1.2	9.4
Angola	17	12	5	10	7	20	12	10	22	24	40.9	-0.1	32.4
Benin	1	3	3	5	7	12	13	8	7	3	-17.8	61.4	-34.1
Botswana	1	1	2	1	1	0	1	1	1	1	-12.0	-16.8	8.9
Burkina Faso	5	10	10	13	12	12	16	18	19	23	29.6	14.8	11.4
Burundi	1	1	1	3	2	2	3	3	3	5	11.8	19.7	13.3
Cameroon	32	27	42	46	43	67	45	50	39	29	26.6	15.8	-15.0
Cape Verde	0	..	..	..	0	0	0	0	..	..	1.8	..	..
Central African Republic	1	1	1	0	1	3	1	1	1	1	-23.0	8.6	0.9
Chad	1	5	5	6	7	7	4	5	5	5	..	39.5	3.7
Comoros	..	..	..	..	..	..	..	..	..	..	..	..	..
Congo, People's Republic of the	1	1	2	2	3	5	4	0	1	1	..	58.7	-37.9
Cote d' Ivoire	45	48	41	53	60	61	31	44	43	41	7.3	7.0	8.3
Djibouti	1	0	..	..	..	..	0	0	..	..	..	..	..
Equatorial Guinea	0	..	..	..	..	..	..	..	..	..	0.0	..	..
Ethiopia	50	6	36	60	36	79	62	54	79	97	17.3	26.5	18.4
Gabon	0	2	0	2	3	3	2	2	1	1	-32.7	77.7	-22.8
Gambia, The	2	1	2	2	2	6	3	3	4	2	24.3	19.6	-4.2
Ghana	12	47	9	21	9	12	8	11	13	23	-12.1	-10.7	40.9
Guinea	0	1	1	..	0	0	1	1	1	1	-18.7	..	3.2
Guinea-Bissau	0	2	1	1	..	..	..	..	..	1	..	..	..
Kenya	62	83	69	87	79	109	123	99	139	120	0.0	8.8	2.7
Lesotho	5	5	5	5	5	4	4	4	5	5	32.5	-3.3	6.3
Liberia	3	5	1	3	1	1	2	4	3	4	-7.8	-19.5	29.8
Madagascar	9	7	16	14	7	10	11	6	11	11	5.1	0.6	6.0
Malawi	33	34	32	43	58	29	37	48	51	55	13.0	3.6	12.7
Mali	14	9	11	10	50	20	15	16	13	11	31.6	21.4	-8.8
Mauritania	1	..	0	0	1	2	1	1	3	2	14.6	..	42.9
Mauritius	17	18	21	22	22	20	31	23	25	30	-0.8	4.1	0.2
Mozambique	20	39	37	14	12	3	6	7	2	2	56.1	-34.7	-32.2
Namibia	..	..	..	..	..	..	..	..	..	..	..	..	..
Niger	3	6	3	2	2	4	2	3	2	3	27.1	-4.6	7.7
Nigeria	177	204	195	260	272	375	221	263	165	220	17.4	15.1	-4.7
Rwanda	0	0	1	1	2	1	2	2	1	1	-14.0	66.6	-25.6
Sao Tome & Principe	..	..	..	..	..	..	..	..	..	..	..	..	..
Senegal	16	16	6	14	17	21	7	9	23	17	-9.9	6.8	44.1
Seychelles	..	..	1	0	..	..	..	..	..	..	..	..	..
Sierra Leone	2	3	0	1	1	4	4	1	0	1	2.9	6.4	-48.4
Somalia	2	0	1	2	2	1	2	4	2	3	..	2.4	8.7
Sudan	81	83	69	41	55	93	46	50	47	49	-12.7	-2.9	1.5
Swaziland	18	14	10	12	9	9	12	7	8	8	13.1	-13.0	-11.5
Tanzania	20	17	25	17	26	47	24	40	52	56	5.2	16.1	31.8
Togo	3	4	3	1	7	13	9	9	14	13	7.9	21.9	13.7
Uganda	1	1	..	..	1	0	0	1	0	0	..	..	-21.8
Zaire	8	8	7	9	12	7	2	6	3	8	-8.7	2.1	31.7
Zambia	69	64	94	50	32	10	66	94	85	94	3.5	-29.4	10.3
Zimbabwe	56	72	85	43	38	46	43	42	78	58	10.9	-9.6	16.0
NORTH AFRICA	588	576	382	394	413	565	521	499	449	448	3.6	-3.3	-5.4
Algeria	189	148	50	48	88	115	164	121	30	51	6.0	-10.9	-38.8
Egypt, Arab Republic of	182	207	76	107	118	221	91	115	150	168	-3.2	-1.1	23.5
Libya	53	74	78	85	69	61	72	95	80	74	7.2	1.5	-1.2
Morocco	133	105	137	115	128	159	183	159	166	147	9.3	3.9	-6.0
Tunisia	30	42	40	40	10	8	10	8	23	8	11.8	-26.5	3.0
ALL AFRICA	1,377	1,429	1,237	1,273	1,314	1,681	1,396	1,446	1,417	1,473	4.8	2.2	1.4
South Africa	229	331	313	184	186	192	161	186	130	174	2.0	-8.6	-1.2

8–14. Area under major crops

	Thousands of hectares										Average annual percentage growth		
	1980	1981	1982	1983	1984	1985	1986	1987	1988	1989	75–80	80–85	86–MR
SUB-SAHARAN AFRICA	141,431	141,999	142,383	142,877	144,216	144,863	145,617	145,938	146,693	146,822	0.7	0.5	0.3
excluding Nigeria	100,016	100,572	100,894	101,376	102,106	102,699	103,172	103,441	104,130	104,259	0.8	0.5	0.4
Angola	3,500	3,500	3,500	3,500	3,500	3,500	3,500	3,550	3,600	3,600	0.0	0.0	1.0
Benin	1,795	1,797	1,803	1,806	1,818	1,838	1,838	1,840	1,860	1,860	0.2	0.4	0.5
Botswana	1,360	1,360	1,360	1,360	1,360	1,360	1,360	1,360	1,380	1,380	0.3	0.0	0.6
Burkina Faso	2,785	2,835	2,885	2,935	2,985	3,035	3,085	3,140	3,564	3,564	1.9	1.7	5.8
Burundi	1,305	1,306	1,306	1,306	1,308	1,325	1,330	1,332	1,334	1,336	0.8	0.2	0.2
Cameroon	6,930	6,940	6,950	6,960	6,965	6,965	6,990	6,995	7,008	7,008	1.7	0.1	0.1
Cape Verde	40	40	40	40	40	40	40	40	39	39	0.0	0.0	-1.0
Central African Republic	1,945	1,945	1,960	1,970	1,982	1,983	2,004	2,005	2,006	2,006	0.6	0.5	0.0
Chad	3,150	3,150	3,150	3,150	3,150	3,155	3,205	3,205	3,205	3,205	0.9	0.0	0.0
Comoros	91	91	92	93	94	97	98	98	99	100	0.2	1.2	0.7
Congo, People's Republic of the	148	150	152	154	158	162	168	165	168	168	0.7	1.8	0.2
Cote d' Ivoire	3,095	3,130	3,170	3,219	3,486	3,580	3,620	3,640	3,660	3,660	1.2	3.1	0.4
Djibouti	..	..	..	..	..	..	..	..	..	..	..	..	..
Equatorial Guinea	230	230	230	230	230	230	230	230	230	230	0.0	0.0	0.0
Ethiopia	13,880	13,930	13,930	13,930	13,930	13,930	13,930	13,930	13,930	13,930	0.2	0.1	0.0
Gabon	452	452	452	452	452	452	452	452	452	452	4.0	0.0	0.0
Gambia, The	156	158	160	160	165	165	167	170	175	178	0.5	1.2	2.2
Ghana	2,800	2,760	2,730	2,670	2,690	2,690	2,690	2,690	2,690	2,720	-1.9	-0.9	0.3
Guinea	702	712	713	714	715	725	726	726	726	728	0.4	0.5	0.1
Guinea-Bissau	285	287	300	310	315	320	335	335	335	335	0.0	2.6	0.0
Kenya	2,270	2,310	2,310	2,310	2,335	2,370	2,370	2,420	2,425	2,428	0.2	0.7	0.7
Lesotho	292	298	288	283	297	300	300	320	320	320	-4.6	0.3	2.0
Liberia	371	371	371	371	371	371	371	371	373	373	0.3	0.0	0.2
Madagascar	3,000	3,000	3,000	3,011	3,020	3,040	3,065	3,067	3,078	3,092	1.9	0.3	0.3
Malawi	2,320	2,320	2,333	2,344	2,345	2,376	2,376	2,377	2,387	2,409	0.4	0.4	0.5
Mali	2,050	2,053	2,053	2,053	2,053	2,073	2,076	2,076	2,093	2,093	1.5	0.2	0.3
Mauritania	195	195	195	195	195	195	199	199	199	199	-0.3	0.0	0.0
Mauritius	107	107	107	107	107	107	107	107	106	106	0.1	0.0	-0.4
Mozambique	3,080	3,080	3,080	3,080	3,080	3,090	3,090	3,090	3,100	3,100	0.0	0.0	0.1
Namibia	657	657	657	662	662	662	662	662	662	662	0.1	0.2	0.0
Niger	3,552	3,560	3,550	3,540	3,535	3,530	3,540	3,592	3,600	3,605	9.1	-0.2	0.6
Nigeria	30,385	30,385	30,435	30,435	31,035	31,085	31,335	31,335	31,335	31,335	0.2	0.5	0.0
Rwanda	1,015	1,060	1,075	1,090	1,108	1,119	1,130	1,142	1,153	1,153	2.1	1.8	0.7
Sao Tome & Principe	36	36	36	36	36	37	37	37	37	37	0.0	0.4	0.0
Senegal	5,225	5,225	5,225	5,225	5,225	5,225	5,225	5,225	5,226	5,226	0.9	0.0	0.0
Seychelles	5	5	6	6	6	6	6	6	6	6	0.0	4.3	0.0
Sierra Leone	1,766	1,766	1,771	1,771	1,771	1,781	1,796	1,801	1,801	1,801	2.1	0.1	0.1
Somalia	1,000	1,005	1,010	1,015	1,020	1,025	1,030	1,035	1,039	1,039	0.5	0.5	0.3
Sudan	12,417	12,448	12,448	12,448	12,448	12,478	12,478	12,478	12,508	12,510	0.4	0.1	0.1
Swaziland	189	142	141	141	179	164	164	164	164	164	3.5	0.0	0.0
Tanzania	5,160	5,190	5,190	5,190	5,190	5,190	5,215	5,230	5,240	5,250	0.5	0.1	0.2
Togo	1,420	1,424	1,426	1,427	1,427	1,427	1,429	1,431	1,439	1,444	0.1	0.1	0.4
Uganda	5,680	5,760	5,840	6,300	6,500	6,600	6,705	6,705	6,705	6,705	0.9	3.5	0.0
Zaire	7,600	7,650	7,670	7,700	7,750	7,800	7,850	7,850	7,850	7,850	0.3	0.5	0.0
Zambia	5,108	5,158	5,158	5,158	5,158	5,188	5,188	5,208	5,238	5,268	0.4	0.2	0.5
Zimbabwe	2,539	2,678	2,782	2,682	2,682	2,734	2,767	2,769	2,810	2,810	0.1	1.0	0.6
NORTH AFRICA	24,738	24,917	25,031	24,844	25,170	25,239	25,428	25,827	25,939	26,281	-0.2	0.4	1.0
Algeria	7,509	7,510	7,509	7,231	7,510	7,511	7,533	7,624	7,611	7,605	-0.3	-0.1	0.3
Egypt, Arab Republic of	2,445	2,468	2,469	2,478	2,493	2,497	2,567	2,547	2,581	2,585	-3.1	0.4	0.3
Libya	2,080	2,085	2,092	2,105	2,115	2,127	2,137	2,145	2,145	2,150	0.3	0.5	0.2
Morocco	8,004	8,154	8,261	8,330	8,352	8,404	8,491	8,811	8,902	9,241	0.8	0.9	2.7
Tunisia	4,700	4,700	4,700	4,700	4,700	4,700	4,700	4,700	4,700	4,700	-0.6	0.0	0.0
ALL AFRICA	166,169	166,916	167,414	167,721	169,386	170,102	171,045	171,765	172,632	173,103	0.5	0.5	0.4
South Africa	13,254	13,214	13,169	13,169	13,169	13,169	13,169	13,169	13,174	13,174	-0.2	-0.1	0.0

8–15. Agricultural yields by major crop

		Thousands of hectograms per hectare											Average annual percentage growth		
	Category	1980	1981	1982	1983	1984	1985	1986	1987	1988	1989	1990	75–80	80–85	86–MR
ALGERIA															
Wheat	F1	7.3	6.7	6.0	5.6	5.7	8.9	8.1	7.8	6.0	7.8	..	-3.1	1.3	-3.7
Citrus	F2	1.0	0.9	0.8	0.6	0.7	0.6	0.6	0.6	0.7	..	..	-3.1	-10.0	12.0
Dates	F3	0.3	0.3	0.3	0.3	0.3	0.3	0.3	0.3	0.3	..	..	6.9	-0.6	-1.9
Barley	NT1	8.4	6.0	5.9	6.2	5.1	9.6	8.9	7.5	5.8	7.0	6.6	0.1	0.5	-6.6
Potatoes	NT2	77.7	63.7	56.3	63.9	72.5	83.6	84.0	84.2	92.1	85.8	88.2	-1.4	2.5	1.2
ANGOLA															
Coffee (green)	X1	2.2	1.4	1.0	0.7	0.8	0.7	0.8	0.5	0.5	0.5	..	-21.4	-19.7	-14.3
Maize	F1	6.0	4.2	4.2	4.6	4.3	4.2	3.5	3.5	3.0	2.9	..	-6.1	-4.5	-6.9
Millet	F2	7.1	6.3	6.3	6.3	6.7	6.7	6.0	6.0	6.0	5.7	..	-6.2	-0.4	-1.4
Wheat	F3	5.8	6.3	6.3	6.3	6.6	6.3	8.0	8.0	8.0	8.0	..	-12.9	0.9	0.0
Cassava	NT1	38.5	38.0	39.0	39.0	39.0	39.0	39.4	39.4	39.6	38.4	..	1.3	0.4	-0.7
Sweet potatoes	NT2	94.7	94.7	94.7	94.7	94.7	94.7	94.7	94.7	94.7	89.5	..	1.2	0.0	-1.7
BENIN															
Cotton	X1	6.6	7.8	11.5	11.2	15.6	10.7	12.8	9.6	10.9	12.0	..	-2.0	13.6	-0.8
Palm oil (fresh fruit bunch)	X2	..	..	..	..	..	..	..	..	..	..	..	..	..	..
Maize	F1	7.4	6.6	6.5	6.2	8.1	8.7	8.3	6.8	8.8	9.5	..	1.2	3.8	7.0
Sorghum	F2	6.3	6.1	6.4	5.4	7.5	7.9	8.0	8.1	7.3	7.9	..	-5.6	4.6	-1.5
Cassava	NT1	65.9	61.5	64.6	67.0	69.4	65.9	70.2	66.0	68.1	83.2	..	-3.4	1.2	5.6
Yams	NT2	97.2	83.9	84.1	73.9	101.7	102.9	107.7	102.4	105.5	117.6	..	0.5	2.1	3.0
BOTSWANA															
Sorghum	F1	2.2	2.3	1.0	1.5	1.2	1.8	1.6	1.6	1.8	4.1	..	-19.4	-7.7	33.4
Maize	F2	2.5	3.6	5.2	4.3	1.5	1.8	4.1	6.1	2.1	3.2	..	-28.7	-11.9	-16.2
Millet	F3	1.6	1.5	1.3	0.7	0.9	1.9	1.3	0.7	3.3	2.5	..	-20.9	-3.8	42.1
BURKINA FASO															
Cotton	X1	8.3	8.8	10.5	10.3	10.7	12.2	13.3	10.3	10.5	11.0	..	5.5	7.3	-5.3
Groundnuts	X2	5.1	6.1	4.6	6.0	5.8	7.4	6.6	6.3	6.6	7.4	..	1.3	5.9	3.9
Sorghum	F1	5.7	6.0	5.8	5.6	6.2	7.4	7.6	7.2	7.8	7.3	..	-0.5	3.8	-0.5
Millet	F2	4.9	4.8	4.9	4.2	5.1	6.0	5.8	5.4	6.4	5.1	..	3.9	3.3	-2.3
Maize	F3	9.0	8.3	8.2	5.6	6.4	9.9	9.4	7.4	8.2	11.6	..	7.4	-1.9	7.7
BURUNDI															
Coffee (green)	X1	6.3	8.0	6.0	11.6	8.3	10.2	8.4	9.6	9.3	8.1	..	4.2	9.6	-1.3
Tea	X2	4.0	6.0	5.2	4.6	7.2	8.5	7.5	9.0	7.4	7.7	..	-2.7	12.9	-1.1
Maize	F1	10.8	11.2	10.7	11.0	10.5	11.6	12.1	12.9	15.4	11.2	..	-1.3	0.6	-0.8
Sorghum	F2	10.0	10.0	10.0	10.0	10.0	10.0	10.0	10.0	14.6	12.4	..	-2.2	0.0	10.8
Rice	F3	32.9	30.0	40.0	25.7	30.0	44.2	33.8	32.2	25.0	35.0	..	9.7	3.0	-1.4
Millet	F4	10.0	10.0	10.0	10.0	10.0	10.0	10.0	10.0	10.0	8.0	..	4.0	0.0	-6.5
Bananas	NT1	49.9	74.8	55.5	52.7	54.4	55.4	55.2	55.0	55.2	56.0	..	-3.1	-1.4	0.5
Cassava	NT2	102.6	115.6	111.0	111.0	113.6	112.0	110.8	114.8	115.8	134.3	..	-0.9	1.1	6.0
CAMEROON															
Coffee (green)	X1	3.0	3.0	3.5	1.9	4.1	2.9	3.8	2.7	3.8	2.3	..	2.8	0.6	-10.3
Cocoa	X2	2.6	2.8	2.6	2.6	2.9	2.8	2.7	3.0	2.7	2.7	..	2.6	1.2	-0.8
Cotton	X3	12.9	12.6	13.3	12.1	12.1	12.9	11.8	11.2	10.2	9.4	..	16.6	-0.6	-7.4
Maize	F1	8.3	9.8	10.9	10.5	10.1	8.4	9.0	10.3	10.3	10.2	..	-7.3	0.3	4.0
Sorghum	F2	8.7	7.1	6.5	8.7	9.0	9.3	6.8	9.0	9.1	8.9	..	0.9	3.9	8.5
Millet	F3	7.6	6.9	6.2	8.7	8.4	9.2	7.5	7.5	7.3	9.1	..	-0.4	5.5	5.6
Rice	F4	..	..	..	..	..	..	..	..	..	..	..	..	..	..
Cassava	NT1	25.0	25.6	26.6	26.6	25.2	25.5	24.3	25.0	25.0	25.5	..	10.4	0.1	1.4
Plantains	NT2	52.3	52.8	52.1	50.0	49.7	49.7	49.5	50.5	55.0	54.8	..	2.8	-1.3	4.0
CENTRAL AFRICAN REPUBLIC															
Coffee (green)	X1	3.6	3.6	3.7	3.3	4.1	3.8	7.9	7.3	8.6	8.7	..	-1.0	1.6	4.4
Cotton	X2	3.4	4.4	5.5	4.9	4.7	6.2	4.0	4.6	3.8	3.7	..	6.5	9.4	-4.0
Sorghum	F1	6.5	7.0	7.0	6.7	5.7	10.0	12.0	8.3	11.3	11.1	..	1.1	4.2	0.8
Maize	F2	3.8	4.1	4.0	4.2	5.3	9.6	12.0	10.2	10.2	10.3	..	-2.4	16.9	-4.6
Groundnuts	F3	10.1	9.5	9.5	9.4	9.0	9.9	10.6	9.9	10.3	11.1	..	-2.4	-0.8	1.9
Cassava	NT1	30.7	31.3	35.4	36.2	37.5	38.0	37.2	32.1	32.0	33.8	..	0.8	4.8	-2.9
Yams	NT2	60.0	64.0	61.5	61.5	61.1	61.1	60.7	60.7	60.7	60.7	..	-0.1	-0.1	0.0
CHAD															
Cotton	X1	5.1	5.3	7.4	9.0	6.9	6.7	7.2	8.6	6.9	6.6	..	2.0	6.9	-4.8
Sorghum	F1	5.1	6.6	6.8	4.4	5.5	5.5	5.9	5.9	6.2	5.8	..	-0.8	-1.8	0.0
Millet	F2	4.7	6.1	6.2	3.5	2.3	5.6	5.6	5.0	8.0	6.4	..	-0.8	-7.0	8.9
Groundnuts	F3	5.7	5.0	7.3	6.7	6.7	6.1	7.8	8.7	6.9	7.0	..	0.7	3.3	-5.6
COMOROS															
Vanilla	X1	..	..	..	..	..	..	..	..	..	..	..	..	..	..
Cloves	X2	..	..	..	..	..	..	..	..	..	..	..	..	..	..
Ylang Ylang	X3	..	..	..	..	..	..	..	..	..	..	..	..	..	..
Bananas	F1	..	..	..	..	..	..	..	..	..	..	..	..	..	..
Cassava	NT1	25.0	25.0	25.0	26.0	26.0	27.0	29.0	26.5	28.8	25.0	..	-7.4	1.6	-3.5

237

(Table continues on the following page)

8–15. (continued)

	Category	Thousands of hectograms per hectare										Average annual percentage growth		
		1980	1981	1982	1983	1984	1985	1986	1987	1988	1989	1990	75–80	80–85	86–MR
CONGO, PEOPLE'S REPUBLIC OF THE															
Coffee (green)	X1	8.0	7.2	5.3	8.8	5.5	9.2	3.8	2.6	4.3	5.3	..	18.7	1.0	16.2
Cocoa (bean)	X2	5.6	5.3	5.9	3.8	4.7	4.4	3.3	2.7	3.4	4.2	..	-2.8	-5.4	10.3
Maize	F1	8.1	9.6	5.7	5.9	5.9	7.7	6.4	8.2	8.2	8.2	..	3.7	-4.5	7.4
Cassava	NT1	68.8	70.9	69.1	71.6	71.6	71.6	72.0	72.6	71.6	71.7	..	2.8	0.8	-0.2
Plantains	NT2	75.9	77.0	68.6	73.5	74.2	72.6	75.8	78.7	76.5	77.6	..	3.5	-0.7	0.4
COTE D'IVOIRE															
Coffee	X1	2.4	3.4	2.2	2.3	0.8	2.6	2.4	2.3	1.6	2.0	..	-6.5	-10.8	-8.4
Cocoa	X2	5.0	5.2	3.8	4.3	5.5	5.0	5.7	6.3	7.8	6.9	..	2.2	1.1	8.2
Palm oil	X3	..	..	..	..	..	..	..	..	..	..	..	..	..	..
Rice	F1	11.7	11.5	12.9	9.5	12.5	12.0	11.0	11.0	11.0	12.0	..	-1.4	0.3	2.7
Maize	F2	8.1	8.2	8.3	7.5	8.7	9.0	7.0	7.0	7.0	6.7	..	6.3	1.8	-1.2
Cassava	NT1	52.3	53.2	52.4	48.6	54.3	56.1	55.1	55.1	55.1	56.5	..	-0.9	1.0	0.8
Yams	NT2	90.7	98.2	99.1	90.4	96.9	100.8	95.0	95.2	95.0	94.8	..	-0.7	1.1	-0.1
EGYPT, ARAB REPUBLIC OF															
Cotton	X1	26.9	26.8	27.0	25.5	25.4	26.2	25.3	23.8	20.0	19.2	..	8.6	-1.0	-9.5
Rice	X2	58.3	55.7	56.7	57.7	54.1	59.5	57.7	58.3	54.1	64.9	..	2.0	0.1	2.8
Wheat	F1	31.2	33.0	35.0	36.0	36.7	37.6	38.0	47.2	47.6	49.4	..	-2.0	3.7	8.3
Sugar cane	F3	812.5	835.4	817.7	802.3	842.2	894.3	922.3	967.6	962.2	981.4	..	-0.7	1.4	1.8
Broadbeans	NT1	20.7	20.8	22.6	21.5	21.0	21.2	34.7	28.1	28.4	27.8	..	-1.1	0.3	-6.3
EQUATORIAL GUINEA															
Cocoa	X1	1.1	1.4	1.0	0.9	1.2	0.9	1.0	0.9	0.9	1.1	..	-3.7	-4.6	1.2
Coffee (green)	X2	3.4	3.8	3.8	3.7	3.8	3.8	3.8	3.8	3.8	3.8	..	0.8	1.4	0.0
Cassava	NT1	23.5	23.0	23.1	22.3	21.6	21.8	22.0	21.3	21.5	21.7	..	-0.4	-1.7	-0.3
Plantains	NT2	..	..	..	..	..	..	..	..	..	..	..	..	..	..
ETHIOPIA															
Coffee (green)	X1	4.2	4.5	4.5	4.2	4.5	4.5	4.5	4.5	4.5	5.0	..	3.7	1.0	3.2
Sorghum	F1	14.4	14.4	15.0	13.2	6.6	10.5	12.2	10.6	12.1	10.7	..	6.8	-10.9	-2.6
Maize	F2	12.9	18.4	19.6	18.7	11.5	12.0	17.2	17.0	17.5	17.8	..	-2.5	-5.1	1.2
Barley (non-white mixed)	NT1	12.9	11.5	12.9	10.2	10.2	9.9	10.9	12.7	12.2	12.2	..	6.3	-5.5	3.0
Teff (mixed)	NT2	..	..	..	..	..	..	..	..	..	..	..	..	..	..
GABON															
Coffee (green)	X2	2.4	2.3	5.3	4.2	3.6	3.7	3.9	3.9	4.1	4.2	..	1.6	9.9	2.9
Oil palm	X3	60.0	60.0	60.0	66.7	72.0	76.9	96.2	96.2	92.6	92.6	100.0	-0.4	5.6	0.4
Rubber	X4	..	..	..	..	..	..	..	..	..	..	..	..	..	..
Maize	F1	16.6	15.9	15.4	15.4	14.3	14.3	14.3	14.3	17.1	17.1	..	4.1	-3.0	7.6
Cassava	NT1	61.0	59.3	61.0	61.9	58.3	59.5	60.0	60.0	61.2	61.2	..	3.4	-0.4	0.8
Taro (cocoyam)	NT2	62.5	66.7	73.3	73.3	80.0	70.8	76.4	80.6	85.7	88.6	76.3	1.5	3.4	0.9
Yams	NT3	78.9	85.1	87.0	88.0	90.0	80.0	90.0	95.0	100.0	100.0	..	4.6	0.7	3.7
GAMBIA, THE															
Groundnuts	X1	8.7	13.5	15.9	11.7	11.5	13.0	13.7	12.6	10.4	15.1	..	-9.3	3.4	0.9
Cotton	X2	6.1	10.5	8.7	6.1	7.4	5.4	7.0	7.0	7.1	7.1	..	..	-5.5	0.6
Palm oil	X3	..	..	..	..	..	..	..	..	..	..	..	..	..	..
Millet	F1	9.3	12.3	11.0	10.4	11.8	11.0	11.3	11.2	11.0	9.5	..	1.3	1.9	-5.3
Rice	F2	19.7	14.2	12.4	17.6	25.7	19.2	16.0	9.9	13.2	14.3	..	7.3	5.9	-0.5
Maize	F3	10.7	16.4	18.1	12.3	13.6	15.9	15.5	11.9	12.3	13.8	..	11.8	3.0	-3.1
Sorghum	F4	8.0	10.8	9.5	10.0	11.4	9.2	10.0	7.4	8.8	10.4	..	1.0	2.6	2.9
GHANA															
Cocoa	X1	2.3	2.1	2.3	2.1	2.1	2.2	2.7	2.0	3.2	3.3	..	-3.6	-1.0	11.2
Maize	F1	8.7	10.2	9.3	4.3	9.6	10.1	11.8	10.9	13.9	13.2	..	-2.9	-0.5	5.9
Millet	F2	..	..	..	..	..	..	..	..	..	..	..	..	..	..
Groundnuts	F3	17.0	10.6	9.7	9.6	11.2	11.8	11.7	12.7	17.6	12.6	..	6.6	-4.7	5.7
Cassava	NT1	80.8	98.3	95.0	82.3	93.2	106.1	74.3	70.0	*78.8	80.2	..	3.7	3.1	3.5
Plantains	NT2	59.7	64.8	52.8	23.9	58.3	61.2	56.9	63.4	95.1	63.2	..	1.4	-2.8	7.4
GUINEA															
Coffee (green)	X1	3.2	3.2	3.1	2.9	2.8	2.7	2.7	2.6	2.5	2.5	..	-0.1	-3.7	-2.2
Palm kernels	X2	..	..	..	..	..	..	..	..	..	..	..	..	..	..
Rice	F1	9.0	9.0	9.0	7.2	7.3	7.8	9.0	9.0	9.0	9.0	..	0.0	-4.4	-0.1
Maize	F2	10.0	10.0	10.0	10.0	11.1	11.1	11.1	10.0	8.9	11.5	..	-3.3	2.4	-0.1
Groundnuts	F3	6.6	6.5	6.5	5.9	6.2	5.6	5.4	5.0	4.5	4.3	..	0.2	-3.1	-7.4
Cassava	NT1	70.0	70.0	70.1	69.9	69.5	65.2	64.3	60.0	57.1	50.0	..	0.0	-1.1	-7.7
Plantains	NT2	..	..	..	..	..	..	..	..	..	..	..	..	..	..
GUINEA-BISSAU															
Groundnuts	X1	3.5	3.5	4.1	2.6	3.5	5.5	5.5	5.7	6.6	5.7	..	-3.5	5.1	2.5
Palm kernels	X2	..	..	..	..	..	..	..	..	..	..	..	..	..	..
Rice	F1	7.0	8.9	7.2	7.1	7.5	11.9	11.9	11.8	11.8	13.7	..	-6.6	6.2	4.5
Sorghum	F2	6.4	6.7	6.5	6.6	6.4	5.7	5.9	6.2	5.8	5.8	..	-0.9	-2.0	-0.7
Millet	F3	6.0	7.0	6.5	6.5	6.4	6.7	7.3	9.0	8.3	8.3	..	2.3	0.7	3.2
Maize	F4	5.8	8.1	6.5	6.3	5.8	9.1	10.9	8.0	6.0	8.0	..	-1.2	3.6	-11.4

238

(Table continues on the following page)

8–15. (continued)

		Thousands of hectograms per hectare											Average annual percentage growth		
	Category	1980	1981	1982	1983	1984	1985	1986	1987	1988	1989	1990	75–80	80–85	86–MR
KENYA															
Coffee (green)	X1	8.9	8.5	6.7	6.4	7.9	6.2	7.3	6.7	8.0	6.7	..	3.9	-5.9	-0.6
Tea	X2	14.6	12.2	12.5	15.1	14.5	18.4	17.7	18.8	19.5	21.2	..	7.7	5.4	6.1
Sugar	X3	1,211.8	1,126.5	927.8	990.8	1,074.6	829.9	795.5	818.8	829.2	833.3	..	12.8	-5.5	1.5
Sisal	X4	9.9	10.3	12.5	12.8	13.5	11.8	12.2	11.8	10.6	11.9	..	0.9	5.1	-1.8
Maize	F1	12.0	15.8	20.7	17.7	14.4	17.2	20.3	17.2	19.0	18.8	..	-7.2	4.0	-1.3
Wheat	F2	21.6	21.5	20.8	21.1	13.8	17.0	15.6	13.1	16.1	16.8	..	5.6	-6.9	4.3
LESOTHO															
Wheat	X1	9.7	8.5	6.1	5.1	5.8	5.1	5.8	6.3	6.8	6.3	..	3.8	-12.3	3.5
Peas	X2	6.8	4.9	3.9	4.6	4.5	4.3	4.1	4.8	4.8	4.8	4.8	1.0	-6.7	3.1
Beans	X3	4.8	3.6	3.5	3.5	1.6	3.4	2.2	2.1	2.1	2.1	2.1	-2.3	-11.0	-0.8
Maize	X4	9.6	8.5	7.3	7.4	6.8	7.8	7.1	5.9	9.1	7.5	..	11.4	-4.6	6.3
Sorghum	F1	9.7	8.0	5.4	6.6	6.2	7.3	6.4	4.0	7.4	5.6	..	13.3	-5.6	2.1
LIBERIA															
Rubber	X1	7.6	7.7	6.7	8.1	9.4	9.7	10.1	10.7	10.8	11.8	10.0	-0.6	5.9	0.9
Coffee (green)	X2	4.6	3.4	4.7	3.8	5.8	4.5	4.8	5.0	2.5	2.5	..	7.5	3.9	-23.2
Cocoa	X3	2.3	2.7	1.8	2.3	2.5	1.9	1.5	1.4	1.7	1.6	..	-6.7	-2.7	3.6
Rice	F1	12.3	12.8	13.5	12.3	12.9	12.5	12.4	12.6	12.8	11.9	..	0.5	0.0	-1.0
Cassava	NT1	66.7	66.7	66.7	60.0	50.4	61.6	63.8	80.0	85.7	80.0	..	3.4	-3.7	7.7
LIBYA															
Wheat	F1	5.2	5.7	13.2	8.5	7.1	5.5	5.7	6.7	6.7	6.7	..	5.4	1.4	5.1
Olives	F2	..	..	..	..	..	..	..	..	..	..	..	..	..	..
MADAGASCAR															
Coffee (green)	X1	3.7	3.8	3.7	3.6	3.6	3.5	3.7	3.6	3.7	3.7	..	-1.7	-1.1	0.6
Vanilla	X2	0.4	0.6	0.6	0.7	0.9	0.7	0.3	0.7	0.8	0.8	..	-23.8	13.3	34.0
Cloves	X3	1.7	1.5	1.3	0.6	2.3	1.8	0.9	0.8	1.3	0.9	..	-5.7	2.3	3.5
Rice	F1	17.6	17.0	16.6	18.1	18.2	18.4	18.8	18.9	19.3	20.8	..	-1.4	1.5	3.3
Cassava	NT1	60.8	58.1	60.5	60.6	60.9	61.1	67.4	70.0	68.6	66.5	..	-1.9	0.5	-0.6
Sweet potatoes	NT2	48.6	46.5	41.2	48.0	47.6	49.6	49.9	50.6	51.9	53.0	..	-1.8	0.9	2.1
MALAWI															
Tobacco	X1	8.6	7.8	8.8	7.2	8.3	7.2	6.7	7.8	8.1	8.5	..	3.6	-2.5	7.6
Tea	X2	17.1	18.3	22.0	18.8	18.3	19.0	18.6	15.2	20.1	17.9	..	1.6	1.1	1.8
Groundnuts	X3	7.1	7.2	6.8	6.5	6.5	6.9	6.9	6.8	6.9	6.9	..	0.2	-1.3	-0.1
Cotton	X4	7.2	9.3	6.4	4.0	6.4	7.6	7.0	6.1	6.7	7.4	..	10.0	-3.6	2.6
Maize	F1	12.2	11.3	11.8	11.7	11.9	11.8	10.8	10.2	11.8	11.9	..	3.5	-0.1	4.3
Sorghum	F2	6.7	6.7	6.7	3.0	6.7	6.7	6.5	4.7	6.3	6.7	..	-6.2	-2.1	4.0
Cassava	NT1	64.9	65.6	65.8	24.2	31.7	26.1	29.9	26.1	21.8	21.3	..	0.0	-19.8	-11.4
MALI															
Cotton	X1	11.3	12.2	10.5	11.2	14.6	12.0	14.8	16.1	14.4	13.9	..	1.2	2.6	-3.1
Groundnuts	X2	8.3	7.5	6.5	6.3	6.5	9.5	11.5	8.0	9.2	11.5	..	-4.9	0.6	1.4
Millet	F1	6.2	7.8	7.5	7.3	5.6	10.4	9.4	8.9	9.7	8.8	..	0.6	4.6	-2.4
Rice	F2	9.7	11.7	8.4	11.5	6.6	11.6	11.8	14.5	13.4	15.4	..	-4.1	-1.5	7.4
Sorghum	F3	6.7	8.6	8.2	8.7	9.6	11.1	11.1	10.4	11.4	11.9	..	0.6	8.6	3.0
Maize	F4	11.1	8.8	18.8	11.4	11.4	12.8	16.5	15.1	18.8	18.2	..	12.9	2.9	5.2
MAURITANIA															
Sorghum	F1	3.2	3.0	1.5	1.0	1.0	4.9	6.0	7.8	6.6	5.2	..	-12.8	-4.1	-5.8
Rice	F2	32.0	43.0	50.0	53.7	43.9	50.0	47.1	46.4	42.5	46.0	..	-2.1	7.0	-1.6
Millet	F3	2.3	5.0	6.7	10.0	10.0	8.0	9.0	3.5	5.4	5.3	..	-7.4	28.2	-10.8
Maize	F4	6.5	5.2	5.7	5.0	5.0	3.3	7.5	5.0	6.4	6.0	..	11.6	-9.6	-4.2
MAURITIUS															
Sugarcane	X1	576.8	677.4	824.0	669.9	642.3	715.8	775.3	803.4	735.6	703.3	..	1.1	2.1	-3.7
Potatoes	NT1	165.6	207.2	230.6	202.3	252.2	270.4	211.9	195.5	190.2	211.5	206.9	1.7	8.7	0.3
Onions	NT2	..	..	..	..	..	..	..	..	..	..	..	..	..	..
MOROCCO															
Citrus	X1	..	..	13.0	10.0	10.7	12.5	17.1	10.6	17.3	14.9	..	..	..	..
Wheat	F1	10.6	5.4	13.0	10.0	10.7	12.5	17.1	10.6	17.3	14.9	..	2.9	7.7	0.8
Sugarbeet	F2	353.5	370.3	403.7	390.4	475.6	398.8	475.5	449.0	480.2	467.7	478.9	3.7	3.8	0.6
Barley	NT1	10.3	4.7	11.4	5.7	6.6	10.7	14.4	6.7	13.8	12.5	9.2	0.6	1.6	-2.6
MOZAMBIQUE															
Cashew nuts	X1	..	..	..	..	..	..	..	..	..	..	..	..	..	..
Cotton	X2	4.0	4.0	3.2	3.2	10.0	6.6	8.3	11.5	9.9	9.9	..	1.3	16.1	3.8
Tea	X3	10.3	11.7	11.1	7.9	8.5	7.8	7.1	6.0	5.0	5.0	..	1.3	-7.4	-11.8
Maize	F1	6.3	6.2	5.8	5.5	5.5	5.7	5.8	4.5	5.4	5.5	..	4.7	-2.7	0.0
Rice	F2	9.3	8.6	8.6	7.9	7.9	7.9	8.6	7.9	7.9	7.9	..	-3.6	-3.4	-2.6
Cassava	NT1	51.7	53.3	54.2	63.0	57.3	57.0	58.2	58.1	58.6	58.6	..	1.5	2.5	0.3
NAMIBIA															
Wheat	F1	10.0	10.0	10.0	10.0	12.0	12.0	12.0	10.0	10.0	10.0	..	0.0	4.3	-5.3
Maize	F2	5.0	4.8	5.3	4.8	5.0	5.2	5.0	5.2	5.4	5.4	..	-0.9	0.6	2.9

(Table continues on the following page)

8–15. (continued)

	Category	Thousands of hectograms per hectare										Average annual percentage growth		
		1980	1981	1982	1983	1984	1985	1986	1987	1988	1989	1990	75–80	80–85	86–MR
NIGER															
Cowpeas	X1	2.4	2.3	2.0	1.7	1.3	1.2	1.9	1.2	1.8	1.8	..	1.2	-14.5	3.4
Groundnuts	X3	6.7	4.9	4.6	4.6	2.1	4.6	6.0	2.6	3.5	7.3	..	28.7	-11.5	9.2
Millet	F1	4.4	4.3	4.2	4.2	2.6	4.6	4.3	3.3	5.0	3.8	..	4.3	-3.9	0.8
Sorghum	F2	4.8	3.3	3.1	3.3	2.1	2.9	3.2	2.7	3.8	2.9	..	6.3	-10.2	-0.2
NIGERIA															
Cocoa	X1	2.2	2.6	2.3	2.0	2.1	1.6	1.4	2.1	2.3	2.3	..	-4.5	-6.7	15.9
Palm oil	X2	..	..	..	..	..	..	..	..	..	..	..	..	..	..
Cotton	X3	1.9	1.9	1.4	1.5	1.0	1.2	1.8	3.2	3.1	3.5	..	-12.4	-11.0	21.9
Groundnuts	X4	8.4	6.4	8.0	9.1	8.7	7.7	8.2	6.8	7.0	8.8	..	19.3	1.7	2.1
Sorghum	F1	11.2	11.1	10.1	9.9	11.5	10.3	11.2	18.5	11.7	10.9	..	4.5	-1.0	-5.2
Millet	F2	8.7	7.9	6.8	8.4	9.1	9.9	10.3	11.9	9.9	10.3	..	4.5	3.8	-2.0
Maize	F3	14.0	14.9	11.3	9.7	11.4	11.7	10.1	11.9	11.7	10.7	..	-1.3	-5.2	1.5
Rice	F4	19.8	20.7	20.8	20.3	19.4	21.6	20.2	20.7	20.0	20.0	..	-1.3	0.6	-0.7
Yams	NT1	113.3	116.7	119.4	110.8	123.3	128.3	131.7	106.7	106.7	106.7	..	0.8	2.1	-6.1
Cassava (gari)	NT2	91.7	91.7	93.6	86.5	94.4	112.5	113.1	107.7	115.4	126.9	..	-2.2	3.0	4.2
RWANDA															
Coffee (green)	X1	6.9	8.2	6.8	9.0	7.8	7.8	7.5	8.0	8.7	9.3	..	3.3	2.2	7.9
Tea	X2	7.4	7.4	7.5	8.5	7.1	9.2	11.3	11.7	10.4	11.5	..	-9.6	3.1	-0.6
Sorghum	F1	12.4	10.5	12.1	10.8	9.9	12.4	12.9	12.1	11.8	10.9	..	1.7	-0.9	-5.1
Maize	F2	11.8	12.3	11.6	12.9	12.0	12.2	11.3	11.3	11.4	11.4	..	1.4	0.5	0.4
Plantains	NT1	91.9	95.6	95.5	95.6	81.1	95.8	95.5	95.1	94.7	94.3	..	1.3	-0.8	-0.4
Sweet potatoes	NT2	76.3	79.3	85.0	75.6	65.7	72.1	71.0	71.1	73.7	71.7	..	0.4	-2.7	0.7
SENEGAL															
Groundnuts	X1	4.9	8.6	8.7	4.9	7.8	9.7	10.4	11.4	8.0	10.8	..	-12.2	7.7	-2.5
Cotton	X2	6.9	12.8	11.2	9.1	10.9	7.2	9.2	12.5	11.7	12.0	..	-3.7	-1.4	7.6
Millet	F1	4.7	7.6	5.5	4.0	4.2	6.7	5.9	7.3	5.4	6.7	..	-2.6	-1.0	1.1
Rice	F2	9.6	16.7	17.7	20.9	20.6	18.8	20.0	18.3	18.6	21.2	..	-4.5	12.5	2.0
Maize	F3	7.3	12.2	9.8	8.6	11.9	14.5	11.4	11.5	11.2	14.1	..	-6.5	9.7	6.4
Sorghum	F4	7.7	13.6	9.0	8.7	9.0	9.6	9.6	8.7	8.4	9.7	..	-2.7	-0.6	-0.2
SIERRA LEONE															
Cocoa	X1	1.7	1.8	1.8	1.7	2.1	2.0	1.7	1.8	1.4	2.0	..	9.2	3.6	2.3
Coffee (green)	X2	5.1	4.6	4.3	2.7	2.0	3.9	5.0	5.1	3.3	3.0	..	13.7	-11.2	-17.8
Palm oil	X3	..	..	..	..	..	..	..	..	..	..	..	..	..	..
Palm kernels	X4	..	..	..	..	..	..	..	..	..	..	..	..	..	..
Rice	F1	12.5	12.5	14.6	16.5	15.8	12.6	15.4	13.0	14.0	13.0	..	-3.8	2.5	-4.3
Cassava	NT1	38.0	34.6	33.8	33.9	33.3	35.5	33.9	33.1	33.1	33.1	..	-5.0	-1.3	-0.7
SOMALIA															
Bananas	X1	232.3	203.4	281.1	317.5	207.3	222.2	184.1	177.0	180.0	178.5	..	1.0	-0.1	-0.8
Maize	F1	10.1	7.2	7.2	10.8	12.3	12.0	13.7	11.0	12.6	10.4	..	-1.4	8.5	-6.7
Sorghum	F2	3.1	4.3	4.4	3.6	4.1	5.0	6.1	4.7	4.1	5.3	..	-0.6	6.0	-5.7
Sesame	NT1	4.6	5.9	6.3	3.6	4.3	5.2	5.5	4.3	4.2	4.3	..	-9.1	-2.6	-7.5
SOUTH AFRICA															
Maize	X1	22.3	29.9	19.5	10.0	11.1	19.7	20.0	18.4	19.8	31.9	..	7.1	-11.5	16.0
Wheat	X2	9.1	13.1	12.3	9.8	12.2	8.6	12.1	16.3	17.8	11.9	..	-2.6	-2.0	0.5
Sugarcane	X3	661.4	758.3	726.3	578.5	908.8	699.0	677.3	794.9	749.6	685.2	..	-5.3	1.7	-0.2
Sorghum	F1	15.6	13.6	16.2	10.5	16.7	19.1	14.5	16.1	15.4	16.6	..	7.5	3.5	3.6
Barley	F2	8.8	15.4	17.2	19.5	19.9	25.3	21.9	28.0	15.8	29.5	28.9	4.8	19.3	6.3
SUDAN															
Cotton	X1	8.2	7.3	12.4	15.1	16.0	17.7	12.5	15.7	13.4	15.6	..	-4.5	20.0	5.3
Groundnuts	X2	7.9	7.2	6.4	5.4	5.2	6.9	6.7	6.3	8.6	7.3	..	-5.2	-5.2	5.6
Sesame	X3	2.6	2.9	1.9	2.3	1.7	1.3	2.3	2.4	2.4	2.7	..	0.4	-13.8	4.5
Gum arabic	X4	..	..	..	..	..	..	..	..	..	..	..	..	..	..
Sorghum	F1	7.1	8.6	5.3	5.0	3.3	6.6	6.6	4.0	7.9	4.5	..	-2.7	-9.1	-4.8
Wheat	F2	12.1	11.9	10.5	10.8	11.5	16.4	13.2	13.3	12.6	13.0	..	1.4	4.2	-1.0
SWAZILAND															
Sugarcane	X1	1,077.2	1,054.5	995.5	1,037.5	1,068.5	969.1	1,021.1	1,000.0	1,000.0	950.0	..	-1.1	-1.3	-2.1
Citrus	X2	..	..	..	..	..	..	..	..	..	..	..	..	..	..
Cotton	X3	14.5	13.9	13.3	13.3	13.3	13.3	13.3	13.3	13.3	13.3	..	6.4	-1.5	0.0
Maize	F1	13.6	16.8	8.9	6.8	17.9	13.1	14.6	14.6	19.9	16.9	..	-3.6	-0.8	7.7

(Table continues on the following page)

8–15. (continued)

	Category	Thousands of hectograms per hectare										Average annual percentage growth		
		1980	1981	1982	1983	1984	1985	1986	1987	1988	1989	1990	75–80	80–85	86–MR
TANZANIA															
Coffee (green)	X1	4.2	5.4	4.9	4.8	5.2	4.2	5.0	5.2	4.5	3.9	..	-1.8	-0.4	-8.3
Cotton	X2	4.0	3.4	3.6	3.1	3.2	2.3	5.1	4.0	6.1	7.4	..	-7.3	-8.3	16.5
Tea	X3	9.4	9.1	19.5	16.9	18.3	16.9	11.1	7.5	8.6	8.6	..	-1.0	15.0	-6.2
Maize	F1	12.3	13.6	13.4	13.4	13.7	13.3	11.6	13.7	12.6	16.2	..	1.0	1.1	9.7
Rice	F2	11.9	7.1	10.7	15.6	13.1	18.1	20.0	18.3	17.8	16.3	..	-3.5	13.1	-6.2
Sorghum	F3	6.9	6.1	18.0	10.0	9.9	13.8	8.1	8.7	8.2	9.8	..	9.3	13.2	5.0
Millet	F4	7.6	6.2	19.5	14.0	11.1	11.9	11.4	10.0	9.3	10.0	..	-1.9	11.0	-4.7
Cassava	NT1	107.3	137.1	107.6	106.0	95.7	103.9	87.5	85.7	88.6	90.0	..	7.8	-3.5	1.2
TOGO															
Coffee (green)	X1	3.8	3.2	3.1	2.0	0.9	3.3	3.3	4.2	4.9	3.7	..	-5.7	-13.1	4.6
Cocoa	X2	4.5	3.1	2.7	4.6	2.7	4.0	3.5	3.1	2.5	2.5	..	-1.2	-1.4	-11.4
Cotton	X3	7.7	8.1	9.0	10.4	8.1	12.6	9.2	12.9	9.9	9.7	..	15.0	7.7	-1.2
Maize	F1	9.2	9.9	8.6	6.7	9.3	9.1	6.5	7.7	11.1	10.7	..	-0.8	-1.5	20.9
Sorghum	F2	7.5	6.4	8.9	8.9	7.1	6.5	10.4	7.2	6.6	7.8	..	..	-1.2	-8.8
Millet	F3	2.6	4.2	10.4	9.3	13.0	11.3	7.0	5.5	4.8	7.7	..	-19.8	35.2	1.4
Cassava	NT1	103.3	86.3	33.8	35.3	55.8	76.6	73.4	78.8	67.7	74.3	..	-13.3	-7.6	-1.1
Yams	NT2	86.6	90.5	68.3	68.7	105.9	108.8	99.1	86.3	101.2	105.5	..	-2.1	4.7	3.5
TUNISIA															
Olive oil	X1	..	..	..	..	..	..	..	..	..	..	..	..	..	..
Citrus	X2	..	..	..	..	..	..	..	..	..	..	..	..	..	..
Wheat	F1	10.2	12.3	12.8	6.6	7.9	13.4	8.8	14.0	7.7	7.5	..	-0.4	-1.8	-10.0
Barley	F2	7.7	6.1	8.6	4.8	6.4	8.4	3.0	8.4	4.2	4.9	9.1	-3.8	-0.2	18.4
UGANDA															
Coffee (green)	X1	6.0	4.4	7.4	7.0	6.2	6.9	6.4	7.0	8.2	8.3	..	-8.3	4.9	10.2
Cotton	X2	0.4	1.4	1.1	3.4	5.9	4.6	3.1	2.3	1.8	2.2	..	-27.0	64.3	-12.1
Millet	F1	16.4	16.0	16.0	15.1	6.7	16.0	10.2	16.0	13.8	13.9	..	4.7	-7.7	8.0
Maize	F2	11.1	13.2	13.8	14.0	8.1	11.9	8.9	11.8	10.8	10.0	..	1.1	-3.1	2.7
Sorghum	F3	17.9	18.8	20.0	19.7	8.0	16.3	13.5	15.5	14.5	14.4	..	4.6	-8.4	1.5
Cassava	NT1	68.6	96.8	94.5	87.1	46.9	90.1	51.7	90.0	71.5	73.5	..	1.7	-2.5	8.6
Plantains	NT2	48.6	50.0	55.0	55.0	53.4	55.0	55.0	55.4	54.8	55.4	..	-10.3	2.4	0.1
ZAIRE															
Coffee (green)	X1	3.4	3.0	3.4	3.2	3.1	3.3	3.4	3.6	3.5	3.5	..	-4.3	-0.2	0.4
Palm oil	X2	..	..	..	..	..	..	..	..	..	..	..	..	..	..
Maize	F1	8.0	8.4	8.5	8.3	8.5	8.6	8.3	8.4	8.3	9.0	..	2.1	1.0	2.4
Rice	F2	8.0	8.2	8.1	8.5	8.8	8.9	8.7	8.7	8.7	9.1	..	0.6	2.3	1.3
Cassava	NT1	70.0	68.5	71.7	71.6	71.9	72.2	73.7	73.7	73.7	73.8	..	0.0	0.9	0.0
Plantains	NT2	47.8	48.3	48.7	49.0	49.3	49.7	50.0	50.3	51.7	51.0	..	-1.1	0.7	0.9
ZAMBIA															
Cotton	X1	5.0	4.7	5.4	6.2	8.4	7.3	6.4	7.5	7.5	5.9	..	-5.4	11.5	-2.5
Tobacco	X2	10.4	10.0	9.8	9.1	11.1	17.4	13.7	14.4	8.9	7.8	..	8.0	8.3	-19.6
Sunflower	X3	9.2	4.1	6.4	7.3	7.5	6.8	5.3	5.4	3.5	3.8	5.0	2.1	1.2	-4.6
Maize	F1	16.9	20.4	16.5	17.1	17.2	19.8	20.9	17.4	26.9	20.6	..	3.3	0.9	3.9
Wheat	F2	40.7	32.9	38.2	35.9	37.9	34.3	50.0	37.1	45.6	47.0	..	0.1	-1.4	0.2
Cassava	NT1	32.7	32.5	33.3	35.0	33.9	32.8	34.6	34.4	34.1	36.0	..	0.7	0.5	1.1
ZIMBABWE															
Tobacco	X1	19.5	18.1	19.4	20.7	24.4	20.3	19.8	20.0	20.5	22.5	..	7.1	3.4	4.2
Cotton	X2	18.5	14.5	12.8	12.2	19.2	19.8	18.7	11.5	11.3	11.0	..	0.8	3.3	-15.0
Sugar	X3	1,031.2	1,040.0	1,137.0	1,040.8	1,046.7	1,106.1	1,253.0	1,065.4	1,004.2	1,168.4	..	0.0	0.8	-2.7
Maize	F1	13.4	20.8	12.8	6.8	8.3	23.6	19.4	9.0	17.3	16.2	..	-6.0	-1.5	1.1
Wheat	F2	49.7	49.8	50.8	51.5	49.6	54.0	59.1	58.0	57.1	57.0	..	4.4	1.2	-1.2

Notes: The following commodities are in their least-processed form unless otherwise indicated:
Cotton, seed cotton
Groundnuts, unshelled
Coffee, green or roasted
Rice, paddy
Cloves, whole
Cocoa, beans
Tobacco, leaves
Sunflower, seeds
1 hectogram = 100 grams = 3.527 oz.

241

8-16. Incidence of drought

	1980	1981	1982	1983	1984	1985	1986	1987	1988	1989	1990
				D = significant shortage of rain							
SUB-SAHARAN AFRICA	..	..	..	..	..	..	..	..	..	..	..
excluding Nigeria	..	..	..	..	..	..	..	..	..	..	..
Angola	..	..	..	..	..	..	..	..	..	..	..
Benin	..	..	..	..	..	..	..	..	..	..	..
Botswana	..	..	D	D	D	D	D	D	..	..	..
Burkina Faso	..	..	..	D	D	..	..	..	..	..	..
Burundi	..	..	D	D	D	..	..	..	..	..	..
Cameroon	..	..	..	D	..	..	..	..	..	..	..
Cape Verde	..	D	D	D	D	D	..	..	..	..	..
Central African Republic	..	..	..	D	D	..	..	..	..	..	..
Chad	..	..	..	D	D	..	..	..	..	..	..
Comoros	..	..	..	..	..	..	..	..	..	..	..
Congo, People's Republic of the	..	..	..	..	..	..	..	..	..	..	..
Cote d' Ivoire	..	..	..	D	..	..	..	..	..	..	..
Djibouti	..	..	..	..	..	..	..	..	..	..	..
Equatorial Guinea	..	..	..	..	..	..	..	..	..	..	..
Ethiopia	D	D	..	..	D	D	..	D	D	..	..
Gabon	..	..	..	..	..	..	..	..	..	..	..
Gambia, The	..	..	..	..	..	..	..	..	..	..	..
Ghana	..	..	D	D	D	..	..	..	..	..	..
Guinea	..	..	..	..	..	..	..	..	..	..	..
Guinea-Bissau	..	..	..	..	..	..	..	..	..	..	..
Kenya	..	..	..	..	D	..	..	..	..	..	..
Lesotho	..	..	D	D	..	..	..	..	..	..	..
Liberia	..	..	..	..	..	..	..	..	..	..	..
Madagascar	..	..	..	..	..	..	..	..	..	..	..
Malawi	D	D	..	..	..	..	..	..	..	..	..
Mali	..	..	D	D	D	..	..	..	..	..	..
Mauritania	..	..	..	D	D	..	..	..	..	..	..
Mauritius	..	..	..	D	..	..	..	..	..	..	..
Mozambique	..	D	D	..	..	..	..	..	..	..	..
Namibia	..	..	..	..	..	..	..	..	..	..	..
Niger	..	..	..	D	D	..	..	D	..	..	D
Nigeria	..	..	..	..	..	..	..	..	..	..	..
Rwanda	..	..	..	..	D	..	..	..	..	..	..
Sao Tome & Principe	..	..	D	D	..	..	..	..	..	..	..
Senegal	D	..	..	D	D	..	..	..	..	..	..
Seychelles	..	..	..	..	..	..	..	..	..	..	..
Sierra Leone	..	..	..	..	..	..	..	..	..	..	..
Somalia	..	..	..	D	..	..	..	..	..	..	..
Sudan	..	..	..	..	D	..	..	D	..	D	D
Swaziland	..	..	D	..	..	..	..	D	..	..	..
Tanzania	..	..	..	..	D	D	..	..	..	..	..
Togo	..	..	..	D	..	..	..	..	..	..	..
Uganda	..	..	..	..	..	..	..	..	..	..	..
Zaire	..	..	..	..	..	..	..	..	..	..	..
Zambia	..	..	D	D	D	..	..	..	..	..	..
Zimbabwe	..	..	D	D	..	..	..	..	..	..	..
NORTH AFRICA	..	..	..	..	..	..	..	..	..	..	..
Algeria	..	..	..	..	..	..	..	..	D	D	..
Egypt, Arab Republic of	..	..	..	..	..	..	..	..	..	..	..
Libya	..	..	..	..	..	..	..	..	..	..	..
Morocco	..	..	..	..	..	..	..	..	..	..	..
Tunisia	..	..	..	..	..	..	D	..	D	D	..
ALL AFRICA	..	..	..	..	..	..	..	..	..	..	..
South Africa	..	..	..	..	..	..	..	..	..	..	..

Note: ".." indicates normal rainfall, insufficient information, or not applicable.

Technical Notes

Table 8-1. Nominal producer prices

Data on nominal producer prices are compiled from several sources including the World Bank, the Food and Agriculture Organization (FAO), IMF, the U.S. Department of Agricultural Producers, government publications, and direct contacts in African countries.

In general, the figures reflect the average annual price received by farmers in the most important producing regions. But given the wide regional and seasonal variation and the lack of precision in recording specifics about prices quoted, the data should be interpreted only as a rough indication of price levels for an entire country during an entire year.

Data series from different sources have sometimes been spliced when they seem reasonably consistent. Crop years for most countries span parts of two calendar years; planting takes place in the first calendar year, while harvest and marketing take place at the end of the first and beginning of the second year. For consistency, producer prices are listed corresponding to the calendar year during which planting decisions are made. For example, producer prices for the crop year 1987/88 are listed as 1987.

For each country, up to four export crops and five food crops are included, which represent the most important commodities for that country in terms of value of total production during the early 1980s. The food crops include up to three cereals of "traded" grains (those commonly imported or exported) and up to two "non-traded" staples, generally roots and tubers, which are not normally imported or exported by African countries. In the table, these categories of crops are designated by the following symbols: X1 through X4 for export crops; F1 through F3 for traded food crops; and

NT1 and NT2 for nontraded staple food crops. The categorization is consistent across countries, but the numbering of crops within categories in each country depends on which crops are most important.

Where commodities may be marketed in several different forms, the form is generally specified (for instance, shelled or unshelled groundnuts). When not specified, the form of the commodity is the most common (for instance, shelled and dried maize). Where commodities are graded, an average grade has been used unless otherwise specified.

Official producer prices are reported where governments announce them, whether or not they are effectively enforced. Farmgate, or market determined, prices are reported only if information is available. Where sources indicate a divergence between the officially announced price and the price generally received by farmers, the farmgate price given in the tables will be different from the official price.

Table 8-2. Producer price shares

Producer price shares for the major commodities that are exported or that substitute for imports (some food crops) are the ratio of the nominal producer price to the international reference price for the same commodity. The nominal producer price is, more often, the farmgate price, or, whenever it was not possible to collect the latter, the official producer price from Table 8-1. The international reference price is the export price of the commodity for each country, as reported by the World Bank, IMF, or government officials or as obtained by dividing the value of the commodity's exports by the volume of exports, both reported by the FAO. When data specific to the individual countries are not available, the international reference price represents the most commonly quoted price in international markets (for instance, the price of medium staple cotton in London). International prices are taken from the data compiled for the World Bank's *Commodity Trade and Price Trends*. When the two prices refer to different forms of the commodity (for example, groundnuts versus groundnut oil), the producer price is converted by a standard commodity-specific conversion factor to correspond to the form for which the international price is quoted. International prices are converted to national currencies at the official average annual exchange rate. No adjustments have been made for either international or domestic transport costs nor for domestic transport costs nor for domestic marketing and processing costs. Because costs of domestic transportation, marketing, and processing are high and vary widely among countries, different ratios for the same crop across countries may reflect differences in intermediate costs rather than government taxation. Ratios should be used cautiously for deriving measures of nominal or effective protection. (See Jaeger and Humphreys (1988) for a further discussion of this indicator and an analysis of the data.)

Because crops are generally marketed during the second half of a crop year, nominal producer prices are taken as a ratio to the international prices that prevailed during the calendar year corresponding to the second half of the crop year. (For instance, nominal producer prices for the crop year 1986/87 are taken as a ratio to the international prices for 1987.) In this way prices received by farmers for a particular crop year are compared with the international price that prevailed when production from that year was marketed.

Agricultural producion, food production, nonfood production, and food production per capita are indexes taken directly from databases used to prepare the *FAO Production Yearbook*. The index numbers reflect changes in production. They are calculated by multiplying annual production volumes for each commodity (in metric tons) by weights (derived from average prices based on national agricultural producer prices in 1979-81 converted to U.S. dollar equivalents by the ICP methodology) and summing the figures.

The total for each country represents the value of annual production in constant prices. The use of a single, uniform set of dollar prices to weight commodities across all countries — referred to as "international dollars" by the FAO — facilitates comparisons and makes it possible to aggregate across countries. It also helps minimize biases that may arise from converting each national price series into a uniform currency using official exchange rates.

The national index calculated from these totals is the value of annual production in constant prices divided by the base, a three-year average of the same indicator, multiplied by 100. In *African Economic and Financial Data* the series was based upon the 1979-81 period. In this volume, it has been rescaled to have the average of the 1986-88 three-year period be the base (that is, the average of the index of these three years equals 100). Production indexes based on nominal producer prices in national currency for the same base period may show slight differences from those shown here. (Some of the problems with using fixed weights to calculate indexes are discussed in more detail in the introduction to this book.)

The indexes shown in the tables are based on the following definitions of commodity groups, which conform to those established by the UN Statistical Office.

Table 8-3. Agricultural production index

These are derived from production figures for 197 primary commodities.

Table 8-4. Food production index

These indexes are based on 169 commodities that provide calories when consumed. Some of these (such as cottonseed, cocoa, and vanilla) are not, however, a significant part of African diets, but are produced primarily for export.

Table 8-5. Nonfood production index

Data in this table are derived from 29 products that are not considered nutritious, including coffee, rubber, cotton lint, and tobacco leaves.

Table 8-6. Food production per capita index

These are derived as the ratio of the food production index and estimated total mid-year population figures.

Table 8-7. Volume of food output, by major food crop

The table covers, with only a few differences, the same major food crops as presented in Table 8-1, excluding beverages (coffee, tea, cocoa), cotton, and tobacco. Included are also figures for livestock, which represent the combined total head of cattle, sheep, goats, pigs, horses, asses, and mules, and figures for the total head of rabbits.

Table 8-8. Value of agricultural exports

Value of agricultural exports is expressed in current U.S. dollars at f.o.b. prices.

Table 8-9. Volume of agricultural exports

This is a weighted sum across all commodities expressed in metric tons, with weights based on export unit values in 1979-81. Agricultural exports represent the sum of SITC section 0 (excluding division 03 and item 081.42), section 1 (divisions 21, 22, 26 (excluding groups 266, 267, and 269), and 29), subgroup 231.1, and section 4 (excluding subgroup 411.1). Growth rates for the value of agricultural exports are calculated from annual series in current U.S. dollars.

Table 8-10. Volume of cereal imports

These are volumes of total cereals (including SITC groups 041 and 046), aggregated as for agricultural exports. The trade data shown in these tables are from the FAO.

Table 8-11. Food aid

Data are deliveries of all cereals, converted to grain equivalent, as defined and reported by the FAO in *Food Aid in Figures*. Non-cereal food aid is not included. Data are compiled for "marketing years" July through June and shown in the tables under the calendar year corresponding to the second half of the split year (for instance, totals for 1988 refer to the 1987/88 marketing year).

Tables 8-12 and 8-13. Fertilizer consumption and imports

These are volumes and are based on FAO computer files used for its *Fertilizer Yearbook*. Figures are in metric tons and represent the aggregate of nitrogenous, phosphate, and potash fertilizers.

Table 8-14. Area under major crops

Reflects arable land and land under permanent crops, as defined by FAO.

Table 8-15. Agricultural yield, by major crop

This again, follows closely the selection of commodities of Table 8-1. Units are in thousands of hectograms (which are equivalent to hundreds of kilograms) per hectare. Most of the data come from the database for the *FAO Production Yearbook*, with additional information taken from World Bank agricultural sector reports, for some countries. The *FAO Production Yearbook* warns that "data on yields of permanent crops are not as reliable as those for temporary crops either because most of the area information may relate to planted area, as for grapes, or because of the scarcity and unreliability of the area figures reported by the countries, as, for example, for cocoa and coffee."

Table 8-16. Incidence of drought

This is the only indicator in this chapter based on subjective considerations. Data on rainfall levels from other sources are usually presented to suit different purposes, without considering seasonal and regional characteristics of the producing regions. A low rainfall level might not harm agricultural production, if it did not adversely affect the regions where the main crops are produced, whereas an average rainfall level might be associated with difficulties in the producing regions, due to delay, for example. Therefore, just presenting the annual rainfall levels would not necessarily enrich the agricultural data.

For each country, a binary classification was thus created. A **D** was assigned to a country if a significant shortage of rain unfavorably affected its agricultural production. For normal or average rainfall, the standard .. sign was given, as in the cases of insufficient information or not applicable. Specialists who work on the relevant countries were surveyed, as well as World Bank agricultural and environmental experts, in order to provide this information. Also the FAO, cross-checked the table.

9

Industry

This chapter provides data on the industrial sector of the economy, with emphasis on manufacturing activities. Information is provided on value added in manufacturing as a percentage of GDP, the distribution of manufacturing value added, and manufacturing earnings and output, as well as on capacity utilization in manufacturing industry. To facilitate comparability, data are provided in current U.S. dollars.

Capacity utilization in manufacturing data are based on surveys of manufacturing companies. Variations in coverage of such surveys reduces comparability across countries.

9-1. Value added in manufacturing compared with GDP

	Value added in manufacturing as percentage of GDP											Average		
	1980	1981	1982	1983	1984	1985	1986	1987	1988	1989	1990	75-79	80-85	86-90
SUB-SAHARAN AFRICA	..	..	..	..	..	..	..	..	..	..	..	..	..	..
excluding Nigeria	..	..	..	..	..	..	..	..	..	..	..	..	..	..
Angola	..	..	..	..	..	..	..	..	..	..	..	..	..	..
Benin	..	..	..	..	..	..	..	..	..	..	..	..	..	..
Botswana	7.3	8.6	10.8	8.0	7.0	5.3	6.2	6.1	5.9	5.5	..	11.9	11.1	10.4
Burkina Faso	..	..	..	..	..	..	..	..	..	..	..	..	..	..
Burundi	..	..	..	..	..	..	..	..	..	..	..	..	..	..
Cameroon	7.9	9.3	12.2	12.1	11.2	12.1	12.9	13.2	13.5	..	..	8.7	8.6	8.7
Cape Verde	6.4	5.0	5.9	6.4	5.9	7.1	6.6	7.5	8.3	8.7	..	..	1.3	2.3
Central African Republic	..	..	..	..	..	..	..	..	..	..	..	..	..	..
Chad	..	..	..	16.5	19.2	15.1	17.2	16.5	15.5	17.5	11.1	..	..	..
Comoros	..	..	..	3.2	3.3	3.4	3.5	3.6	3.7	3.5	..	..	..	..
Congo, People's Republic of	7.2	7.5	6.4	7.8	7.7	8.5	8.6	8.7	9.1	9.2	9.2	3.1	4.5	6.0
Cote d'Ivoire	..	..	..	..	..	..	..	..	..	..	..	..	..	..
Djibouti	..	..	..	..	..	..	..	..	..	..	..	..	..	..
Equatorial Guinea	..	..	..	..	..	..	..	..	..	..	..	..	..	..
Ethiopia	..	..	..	..	..	..	..	..	..	..	..	..	..	..
Gabon	..	..	..	..	..	..	..	..	..	..	..	..	..	..
Gambia, The	..	..	..	..	..	..	..	..	..	..	..	..	..	..
Ghana	11.0	9.2	7.8	7.3	7.5	8.9	9.4	9.9	9.8	9.6	9.6	13.9	13.1	12.0
Guinea	..	..	..	..	..	..	3.5	3.5	3.5	3.5	3.5	..	..	..
Guinea-Bissau	..	..	..	..	..	..	11.5	11.4	10.8	10.4	..	..	..	..
Kenya	..	..	..	..	..	..	..	..	..	..	..	..	..	..
Lesotho	..	..	..	..	..	..	..	..	..	..	..	..	..	..
Liberia	..	..	..	..	..	..	..	..	..	..	..	..	..	..
Madagascar	..	..	..	..	..	..	..	..	..	..	..	..	..	..
Malawi	..	..	..	..	..	..	..	..	..	..	..	..	..	..
Mali	..	..	..	5.7	7.2	7.2	6.8	6.3	6.2	5.8	6.0	..	..	..
Mauritania	..	..	..	..	..	..	..	..	..	..	..	..	..	..
Mauritius	..	..	..	..	..	..	..	..	..	..	..	..	..	..
Mozambique	..	..	..	..	..	..	..	..	..	..	..	..	..	..
Namibia	..	..	..	..	..	..	..	..	..	..	..	..	..	..
Niger	..	..	..	..	..	..	..	..	..	..	..	..	..	..
Nigeria	..	..	..	..	..	..	..	..	..	..	..	..	..	..
Rwanda	14.7	14.3	13.5	14.5	12.9	12.5	14.1	14.4	13.9	14.5	14.1	13.6	13.7	13.9
Sao Tome & Principe	..	..	..	..	..	..	..	..	..	..	..	..	..	..
Senegal	10.6	12.4	11.6	11.4	12.0	11.7	11.8	12.2	12.7	12.9	12.7	11.1	10.8	11.0
Seychelles	9.5	7.9	8.4	9.3	8.7	8.6	9.0	9.6	10.1	10.5	..	5.7	7.6	7.9
Sierra Leone	..	..	..	..	..	..	..	..	..	..	..	..	..	..
Somalia	..	..	..	..	..	..	..	..	..	..	..	..	..	..
Sudan	..	..	..	..	..	..	..	..	..	..	..	..	..	..
Swaziland	..	..	..	..	..	..	..	..	..	..	..	..	..	..
Tanzania	..	..	..	..	..	..	..	..	..	..	..	..	..	..
Togo	7.9	8.6	9.3	9.1	7.0	7.4	7.5	7.5	7.4	7.9	8.6	6.8	8.3	8.1
Uganda	..	..	..	..	..	..	..	..	..	..	..	..	..	..
Zaire	8.8	8.7	8.7	8.8	9.0	9.5	9.4	9.4	9.1	8.3	..	9.7	9.4	9.1
Zambia	24.4	25.8	25.6	24.1	24.5	26.4	26.6	28.0	31.4	31.5	30.8	23.9	24.0	24.4
Zimbabwe	..	..	..	..	..	..	..	..	..	..	..	..	..	..
NORTH AFRICA	..	..	..	..	..	..	..	..	..	..	..	..	..	..
Algeria	..	..	..	..	..	..	..	..	..	..	..	..	..	..
Egypt, Arab Republic of	..	..	..	..	..	..	..	..	..	..	..	..	..	..
Libya	..	..	..	..	..	..	..	..	..	..	..	..	..	..
Morocco	17.4	18.2	17.4	18.3	18.3	18.4	17.3	18.2	17.5	16.8	17.7	..	3.5	7.1
Tunisia	..	..	..	..	..	..	..	..	..	..	..	..	..	..
ALL AFRICA	..	..	..	..	..	..	..	..	..	..	..	..	..	..
South Africa	..	..	..	..	..	..	..	..	..	..	..	..	..	..

9-2. Structure of manufacturing value added

| | Distribution of manufacturing value added (percent) | | | | | | | | | | | |
| | Food, beverages & tobacco | | | Textile & clothing | | | Machinery & transport equipment | | | Chemicals | | |
	1970	1980	1988	1970	1980	1988	1970	1980	1988	1970	1987	1988
SUB-SAHARAN AFRICA	..	..	..	..	..	..	..	..	..	..	..	..
excluding Nigeria	..	..	..	..	..	..	..	..	..	..	..	..
Angola	..	..	..	..	..	..	..	..	..	..	6	..
Benin	..	59	..	..	14	..	..	0	..	..	6	..
Botswana	..	..	54	..	..	10	..	..	0	..	..	6
Burkina Faso	69	..	..	9	..	..	2	..	..	1	..	..
Burundi	53	..	..	25	..	..	0	..	..	6	..	..
Cameroon	47	56	..	16	9	..	5	4	..	4	4	..
Cape Verde	..	..	..	..	..	..	..	..	..	..	..	..
Central African Republic	..	..	..	..	..	..	..	..	..	..	..	..
Chad	..	..	..	..	..	..	..	..	..	..	..	..
Comoros	..	..	..	..	..	..	..	..	..	..	..	..
Congo, People's Republic of	65	..	..	4	..	..	1	..	..	8	..	..
Cote d'Ivoire	27	35	..	16	..	..	10	10	..	5	..	..
Djibouti	..	..	..	..	..	..	..	..	..	..	..	..
Equatorial Guinea	..	..	..	..	..	..	..	..	..	..	..	..
Ethiopia	46	49	48	31	29	19	0	0	2	2	3	4
Gabon	37	..	..	7	..	..	6	..	..	6	..	..
Gambia, The	..	35	..	..	2	..	..	0	..	..	3	..
Ghana	34	37	40	16	11	6	4	2	1	4	5	7
Guinea	..	..	..	..	..	..	..	..	..	..	..	..
Guinea-Bissau	..	..	..	..	..	..	..	..	..	..	..	..
Kenya	31	30	40	9	11	10	18	12	12	7	8	9
Lesotho	..	..	..	..	..	..	..	..	..	..	..	..
Liberia	..	27	..	..	..	..	..	..	..	..	..	..
Madagascar	36	27	..	28	44	..	6	5	..	7	5	..
Malawi	51	50	..	17	11	..	3	..	..	10	..	..
Mali	36	..	..	40	..	..	4	..	..	5	..	..
Mauritania	..	..	..	..	..	..	..	..	..	..	..	..
Mauritius	75	36	23	6	30	51	5	6	3	3	6	5
Mozambique	51	..	..	13	..	..	5	..	..	3	..	..
Namibia	..	..	..	..	..	..	..	..	..	..	..	..
Niger	..	..	..	..	..	..	..	..	..	..	..	..
Nigeria	36	..	..	26	..	..	1	..	..	6	..	..
Rwanda	86	58	65	0	..	3	3	..	0	2	..	5
Sao Tome & Principe	..	..	..	..	..	..	..	..	..	..	..	..
Senegal	51	48	48	19	19	15	2	4	6	6	8	7
Seychelles	..	..	..	..	..	..	..	..	0	..	..	4
Sierra Leone	..	..	65	..	..	1	..	..	0	..	..	4
Somalia	88	..	59	6	..	13	0	..	2	1	..	13
Sudan	39	..	..	34	..	..	3	..	..	5	..	..
Swaziland	..	..	..	..	..	..	..	..	..	..	..	..
Tanzania	36	..	..	28	..	..	5	..	..	..	..	..
Togo	..	..	..	..	..	..	..	..	..	4	..	..
Uganda	40	..	..	20	..	..	2	..	..	4	..	..
Zaire	38	44	..	16	20	..	7	..	..	10	10	..
Zambia	49	44	..	9	13	..	5	9	..	10	9	..
Zimbabwe	24	21	35	16	18	15	9	10	9	11	10	10
NORTH AFRICA	..	..	..	..	..	..	..	..	..	..	..	..
Algeria	32	27	20	20	18	17	9	10	13	4	3	3
Egypt, Arab Republic of	17	19	29	35	20	..	9	11	9	12	9	17
Libya	..	31	..	..	..	..	..	0	..	..	16	..
Morocco	..	32	..	..	12	..	..	9	..	13	9	..
Tunisia	29	18	20	18	19	20	4	7	4	13	15	9
ALL AFRICA	..	..	..	..	..	..	..	..	..	..	..	..
South Africa	15	15	14	13	11	8	17	16	2	10	11	11

Notes: Sector does not add up to 100 due to unclassified others that are left out. See the technical notes.

9-3. Manufacturing gross output per employee

	Current U.S. dollars									Average		
	1980	1981	1982	1983	1984	1985	1986	1987	1988	75–79	80–85	86–MR
SUB-SAHARAN AFRICA excluding Nigeria	..	..	..	..	..	..	..	..	..	..	..	..
Angola	..	..										
Benin	36,549	30,714	..	..	..	..	..	..	..	23,566	..	..
Botswana	..	..	..	..	..	..	..	..	..	..	..	..
Burkina Faso	..	..	..	..	..	..	..	..	..	..	..	..
Burundi	..	..	..	..	..	..	..	..	..	..	..	..
Cameroon	34,108	37,394	33,767	31,377	31,236	..	..	..	..	21,715	33,576	..
Cape Verde	..	..	..	..	..	..	..	..	..	..	..	..
Central African Republic	..	..	..	..	..	..	..	..	..	..	..	..
Chad	..	..	..	..	..	..	..	..	..	..	..	..
Comoros	..	..	..	..	..	..	..	..	..	..	..	..
Congo, People's Republic of	..	33,132	19,934	26,066	20,290	19,386	..	..	..	..	23,762	..
Cote d'Ivoire	59,619	51,560	50,879	..	..	..	..	..	..	38,547	54,019	..
Djibouti	..	..	..	..	..	..	..	..	..	..	..	..
Equatorial Guinea	..	..	..	..	..	..	..	..	..	..	..	..
Ethiopia	13,263	14,001	14,898	15,266	14,919	15,628	15,684	16,367	16,483	8,886	14,662	16,178
Gabon	..	..	..	..	..	..	..	..	..	..	..	..
Gambia, The	16,026	18,756	14,122	..	..	..	..	..	..	8,929	16,301	..
Ghana	..	..	..	..	..	..	..	..	..	..	..	..
Guinea	..	..	..	..	..	..	..	..	..	..	..	..
Guinea-Bissau	..	..	..	..	..	..	..	..	..	..	..	..
Kenya	..	..	..	..	..	..	..	..	..	..	..	..
Lesotho	..	..	17,479	22,088	14,474	9,753	..	..	..	..	15,949	..
Liberia	..	..	..	..	..	..	..	..	..	..	..	..
Madagascar	14,117	10,670	8,829	7,826	7,316	6,872	..	..	..	9,227	9,272	..
Malawi	..	..	..	..	..	..	..	..	..	..	..	..
Mali	..	..	..	..	..	..	..	..	..	..	..	..
Mauritania	..	..	..	..	..	..	..	..	..	..	..	..
Mauritius	..	..	..	..	..	..	..	..	..	..	..	..
Mozambique	..	..	..	..	..	..	..	..	..	..	..	..
Namibia	..	..	..	..	..	..	..	..	..	..	..	..
Niger	..	..	..	..	..	..	..	..	..	..	..	..
Nigeria	..	45,491	40,011	43,487	44,841	..	..	..	..	..	43,458	..
Rwanda	..	..	..	..	23,792	33,159	37,165	..	..	29,598	28,475	..
Sao Tome & Principe	..	..	..	..	..	..	..	..	..	..	..	..
Senegal	33,813	28,746	25,631	26,447	22,768	..	..	..	..	35,931	27,481	..
Seychelles	..	..	..	..	..	..	..	..	..	.	..	..
Sierra Leone	..	..	..	..	..	..	..	..	..	..	..	..
Somalia	..	..	..	..	..	..	3,051	..	..	5,158	..	..
Sudan	..	..	..	..	..	..	..	..	..	..	..	..
Swaziland	..	..	..	..	..	..	..	..	..	..	..	..
Tanzania	..	..	..	..	..	..	..	..	..	..	..	..
Togo	31,772	28,660	26,378	22,767	19,399	..	..	..	..	19,616	25,795	..
Uganda	..	..	..	..	..	..	..	..	..	..	..	..
Zaire	..	..	..	..	..	..	..	..	..	..	..	..
Zambia	28,293	27,434	28,012	..	..	..	..	..	..	21,273	27,913	..
Zimbabwe	..	..	..	..	..	..	..	..	..	..	..	..
NORTH AFRICA												
Algeria	29,243	..	..	..	..	..	..	..	..	21,827	29,243	..
Egypt, Arab Republic of	..											
Libya	69,698	..	..	..	..	..	..	..	..	40,607	69,698	..
Morocco	..	..	..	..	..	..	..	..	..	..	..	..
Tunisia	28,740	26,088	..	..	..	..	..	..	..	19,846	27,414	..
ALL AFRICA												
South Africa	..	..	..	..	..	..	..	..	..	..	..	..

9–4. Real annual earnings per employee in manufacturing

	Constant 1987 U.S. dollars									Average annual percentage growth		
	1980	1981	1982	1983	1984	1985	1986	1987	1988	75–80	80–85	86–88
SUB-SAHARAN AFRICA	..	..	..	..	..	..	..	..	..	..	..	..
excluding Nigeria	..	..	..	..	..	..	..	..	..	..	..	..
Angola	..	..	..	..	..	..	..	..	..	..	..	..
Benin	..	..	..	..	..	..	..	..	..	..	..	..
Botswana	7,258	7,113	5,485	4,256	3,965	2,665	2,137	..	..	-1.9	-18.2	..
Burkina Faso	5,569	4,312	3,469	2,905	..	..	..	..	..	15.5	..	..
Burundi	3,912	..	..	4,577	..	..	..	..	..	-12.0	..	..
Cameroon	9,211	8,183	6,450	5,150	4,463	..	..	..	..	3.5	..	..
Cape Verde	..	..	..	..	..	..	..	..	..	..	..	..
Central African Republic	..	4,469	3,216	2,838	..	1,931	3,329	..	..	..	..	..
Chad	..	..	..	..	..	..	..	..	..	..	..	..
Comoros	..	..	..	..	..	..	..	..	..	..	..	..
Congo, People's Republic of	..	5,655	5,044	4,568	4,197	3,232	..	..	..	..	..	..
Cote d'Ivoire	8,130	6,416	5,465	6,129	..	..	..	..	..	-0.2	..	..
Djibouti	..	..	..	..	..	..	..	..	..	..	..	..
Equatorial Guinea	..	..	..	..	..	..	..	..	..	..	..	..
Ethiopia	1,369	1,326	1,291	1,392	1,291	1,172	1,326	1,448	1,402	..	-2.2	2.8
Gabon	10,523	9,368	..	..	..	..	..	..	..	25.8	..	..
Gambia, The	5,572	4,619	3,106	..	..	..	..	..	..	..	..	..
Ghana	..	..	..	..	..	..	..	..	..	..	..	..
Guinea	..	..	..	..	..	..	..	..	..	..	..	..
Guinea-Bissau	..	..	..	..	..	..	..	..	..	..	..	..
Kenya	4,650	4,028	3,228	2,578	2,394	1,963	2,064	2,146	2,056	-5.5	-16.0	-0.2
Lesotho	..	..	3,235	2,892	1,759	1,180	..	..	..	..	..	..
Liberia	..	..	..	..	..	..	..	..	..	..	..	..
Madagascar	6,876	5,352	3,459	2,038	1,568	1,451	..	..	..	1.9	-29.0	..
Malawi	2,761	2,754	2,317	2,028	1,674	1,477	..	..	..	..	-12.7	..
Mali	..	..	..	..	..	..	..	..	..	..	..	..
Mauritania	..	..	..	..	..	..	..	..	..	..	..	..
Mauritius	..	..	..	..	..	..	..	..	..	..	..	..
Mozambique	..	..	..	..	..	..	..	..	..	..	..	..
Namibia	..	..	..	..	..	..	..	..	..	..	..	..
Niger	..	..	..	..	..	..	..	..	..	..	..	..
Nigeria	..	11,830	10,403	7,830	6,077	..	..	..	..	..	..	..
Rwanda	..	..	..	..	1,817	1,987	2,959	..	..	..	..	..
Sao Tome & Principe	..	..	..	..	..	..	..	..	..	..	..	..
Senegal	6,259	4,851	3,417	3,642	2,932	..	..	..	..	-4.1	..	..
Seychelles	4,091	4,644	4,922	5,055	4,752	5,332	6,157	..	..	..	4.1	..
Sierra Leone	..	..	..	..	..	..	..	..	..	..	..	..
Somalia	..	..	..	..	..	..	268	..	..	-23.5	..	..
Sudan	..	..	..	..	..	..	..	..	..	..	..	..
Swaziland	9,881	8,512	7,565	6,554	4,327	2,513	..	..	..	..	-22.7	..
Tanzania	7,544	6,192	4,624	3,405	2,242	1,792	..	..	..	..	-26.0	..
Togo	..	..	2,622	2,382	2,155	..	..	..	..	8.6	..	..
Uganda	..	..	..	..	..	..	..	..	..	..	..	..
Zaire	..	..	..	..	..	..	..	..	..	..	..	..
Zambia	17,820	16,814	15,137	..	..	..	..	..	..	-11.3	..	..
Zimbabwe	9,949	10,054	9,582	6,680	5,042	4,163	3,815	3,773	3,539	-5.4	-17.6	-3.7
NORTH AFRICA												
Algeria	12,186	..	..	..	..	..	..	..	..	1.5	..	..
Egypt, Arab Republic of	4,097	4,738	4,046	4,058	3,780	3,625	2,850	..	..	-7.1	-3.6	..
Libya	..	..	..	..	..	..	..	..	..	4.8	..	..
Morocco	7,959	5,803	4,859	4,176	2,919	2,705	2,627	2,978	..	..	-19.5	..
Tunisia	6,269	5,244	..	..	..	..	..	..	..	4.1	..	..
ALL AFRICA	..	..	..	..	..	..	..	..	..	..	..	..
South Africa	16,202	14,844	12,338	12,133	9,287	5,983	5,583	6,222	5,793	..	-16.7	1.9

Note: Earnings refer to wages and salaries only.

9–5. Employees earnings as percentage of value added in manufacturing

	Percent									Average		
	1980	1981	1982	1983	1984	1985	1986	1987	1988	75–79	80–85	86–88
SUB-SAHARAN AFRICA	..	..	..	..	..	..	..	..	..	..	..	..
excluding Nigeria	..	..	..	..	..	..	..	..	..	..	..	..
Angola	..	..	..	..	..	..	..	..	..	..	..	..
Benin	..	..	..	..	..	..	..	..	..	..	..	..
Botswana	53.4	42.6	37.4	40.3	41.1	40.3	36.1	..	..	37.4	42.5	36.1
Burkina Faso	..	..	..	..	..	..	..	..	..	..	..	..
Burundi	..	..	..	..	..	..	..	..	..	..	..	..
Cameroon	41.7	40.6	30.4	28.6	24.7	..	..	..	..	36.8	33.2	..
Cape Verde	..	..	..	..	..	..	..	..	..	..	..	..
Central African Republic	..	..	..	..	..	..	..	..	..	..	..	..
Chad	..	..	..	..	..	..	..	..	..	9.5	..	..
Comoros	..	..	..	..	..	..	..	..	..	..	..	..
Congo, People's Republic of	..	14.7	27.1	20.8	33.2	22.3	..	..	..	..	23.6	..
Cote d'Ivoire	..	..	..	..	..	..	..	..	..	..	..	..
Djibouti	..	..	..	..	..	..	..	..	..	..	..	..
Equatorial Guinea	..	..	..	..	..	..	..	..	..	..	..	..
Ethiopia	..	..	..	..	..	..	..	..	..	..	..	..
Gabon	47.8	51.6	56.1	..	..	..	..	..	..	57.7	51.8	..
Gambia, The	..	..	..	..	..	..	..	..	..	..	..	..
Ghana	14.0	14.6	23.0	13.8	7.3	8.4	12.1	..	..	15.9	13.5	12.1
Guinea	..	..	..	..	..	..	..	..	..	..	..	..
Guinea-Bissau	..	..	..	..	..	..	..	..	..	..	..	..
Kenya	..	..	..	..	..	..	..	..	..	..	..	..
Lesotho	..	..	..	..	..	..	..	..	..	..	..	..
Liberia	..	..	..	..	..	..	..	..	..	..	..	..
Madagascar	..	..	..	..	..	..	..	..	..	..	..	..
Malawi	..	..	..	..	..	..	..	..	..	..	..	..
Mali	62.9	55.7	..	..	..	..	..	..	..	49.6	59.3	..
Mauritania	..	..	..	..	..	..	..	..	..	..	..	..
Mauritius	..	..	..	..	..	..	..	..	..	..	..	..
Mozambique	..	..	..	..	..	..	..	..	..	..	..	..
Namibia	..	..	..	..	..	..	..	..	..	..	..	..
Niger	14.2	..	12.5	20.0	8.1	7.8	7.0	6.6	7.1	10.2	12.5	6.9
Nigeria	..	..	..	..	..	..	..	..	..	..	..	..
Rwanda	..	..	..	..	6.4	6.7	6.0	..	..	5.3	6.6	6.0
Sao Tome & Principe	..	..	..	..	..	..	..	..	..	..	..	..
Senegal	24.4	32.8	33.6	39.8	32.6	33.8	32.1	..	..	24.1	32.8	32.1
Seychelles	26.0	26.8	28.6	28.6	27.1	27.5	26.8	..	..	30.4	27.4	26.8
Sierra Leone	..	..	..	..	..	..	..	..	..	..	..	..
Somalia	..	..	..	..	..	..	..	..	..	..	..	..
Sudan	..	..	..	..	..	..	..	..	..	..	..	..
Swaziland	..	..	..	..	..	..	..	..	..	..	..	..
Tanzania	..	..	..	..	..	..	..	..	..	..	..	..
Togo	..	..	15.4	20.3	20.0	..	..	..	..	18.4	18.6	..
Uganda	..	..	..	..	..	..	..	..	..	..	..	..
Zaire	..	..	..	..	..	..	..	..	..	..	..	..
Zambia	26.7	25.0	24.4	..	..	..	..	..	..	31.3	25.4	..
Zimbabwe	..	..	..	..	..	..	..	..	..	..	..	..
NORTH AFRICA	..	..	..	..	..	..	..	..	..	..	..	..
Algeria	..	..	..	..	..	..	..	..	..	..	..	..
Egypt, Arab Republic of	..	..	..	..	..	..	..	..	..	..	..	..
Libya	..	..	..	..	..	..	..	..	..	..	..	..
Morocco	26.8	25.8	25.3	24.6	24.8	25.6	25.0	25.6	..	26.6	25.5	25.3
Tunisia	..	..	..	..	..	..	..	..	..	..	..	..
ALL AFRICA	..	..	..	..	..	..	..	..	..	..	..	..
South Africa	..	..	..	..	..	..	..	..	..	..	..	..

Note: Earnings refer to wages and salaries only.

9-6. Index of industrial production

	1987 = 100											Average annual percentage growth		
	1980	1981	1982	1983	1984	1985	1986	1987	1988	1989	1990	75-80	80-85	86-MR
SUB-SAHARAN AFRICA	..	..	..	..	..	..	..	..	..	..	..	..	..	..
excluding Nigeria	..	..	..	..	..	..	..	..	..	..	..	..	..	..
Angola	..	..	..	..	..	..	..	..	..	..	..	..	..	..
Benin	..	..	..	..	..	..	..	..	..	..	..	..	..	..
Botswana	..	..	..	..	..	..	..	..	..	..	..	..	..	..
Burkina Faso	..	..	..	..	..	..	..	..	..	..	..	..	..	..
Burundi	..	..	..	..	..	..	..	..	..	..	..	..	..	..
Cameroon	..	..	..	..	..	..	..	..	..	..	..	..	..	..
Cape Verde	..	..	..	..	..	..	..	..	..	..	..	..	..	..
Central African Republic	..	..	..	..	..	..	..	..	..	..	..	..	..	..
Chad	..	..	..	..	..	..	..	..	..	..	..	..	..	..
Comoros	..	..	..	..	..	..	..	..	..	..	..	..	..	..
Congo, People's Republic of	..	..	..	..	..	..	..	..	..	..	..	..	..	..
Cote d'Ivoire	100.2	101.2	97.3	82.8	89.7	92.5	100.0	100.0	97.2	95.3	..	15.2	-2.6	-2.8
Djibouti	..	..	..	..	..	..	..	..	..	..	..	..	..	..
Equatorial Guinea	..	..	..	..	..	..	..	..	..	..	..	..	..	..
Ethiopia	..	..	..	..	..	..	..	..	..	..	..	..	..	..
Gabon	..	..	..	..	..	..	..	..	..	..	..	..	..	..
Gambia, The	..	..	..	..	..	..	..	..	..	..	..	..	..	..
Ghana	..	..	..	..	..	..	..	..	..	..	..	..	..	..
Guinea	..	..	..	..	..	..	..	..	..	..	..	..	..	..
Guinea-Bissau	..	..	..	..	..	..	..	..	..	..	..	..	..	..
Kenya	74.1	77.8	78.5	82.0	85.4	89.4	94.6	100.0	106.0	112.2	118.2	12.0	3.7	4.1
Lesotho	..	..	..	..	..	..	..	..	..	..	..	..	..	..
Liberia	..	..	..	..	..	..	..	..	..	..	..	..	..	..
Madagascar	..	..	..	..	..	..	..	..	..	..	..	..	..	..
Malawi	86.6	95.5	89.8	103.0	101.9	102.2	103.8	100.0	106.1	114.9	130.7	5.4	3.4	2.7
Mali	65.6	65.7	71.9	80.3	101.5	98.4	107.2	100.0	98.2	99.4	116.2	..	10.3	-1.7
Mauritania	..	..	..	..	..	..	..	..	..	..	..	..	..	..
Mauritius	..	..	..	..	..	..	..	..	..	..	..	..	..	..
Mozambique	..	..	..	..	..	..	..	..	..	..	..	..	..	..
Namibia	..	..	..	..	..	..	..	..	..	..	..	..	..	..
Niger	..	..	..	..	..	..	..	..	..	..	..	..	..	..
Nigeria	97.4	94.6	100.5	84.8	75.2	85.9	85.5	100.0	110.2	120.8	128.0	10.7	-4.2	8.2
Rwanda	..	..	..	..	..	..	..	..	..	..	..	..	..	..
Sao Tome & Principe	..	..	..	..	..	..	..	..	..	..	..	..	..	..
Senegal	78.4	85.9	89.1	92.4	90.6	92.8	99.4	100.0	86.2	83.1	..	-1.3	3.0	-10.8
Seychelles	..	..	..	..	..	..	..	..	..	..	..	..	..	..
Sierra Leone	..	..	..	..	..	..	..	..	..	..	..	..	..	..
Somalia	..	..	..	..	..	..	..	..	..	..	..	..	..	..
Sudan	..	..	..	..	..	..	..	..	..	..	..	..	..	..
Swaziland	..	..	..	..	..	..	..	..	..	..	..	..	..	..
Tanzania	..	..	..	..	..	..	..	..	..	..	..	..	..	..
Togo	..	..	..	..	..	..	..	..	..	..	..	..	..	..
Uganda	..	..	..	..	..	..	..	..	..	..	..	..	..	..
Zaire	..	..	..	..	..	..	..	..	..	..	..	..	..	..
Zambia	99.0	93.3	97.7	94.8	89.1	100.0	86.0	..	..	..	..	-1.2	-0.3	..
Zimbabwe	..	..	..	..	..	..	..	..	..	..	..	..	..	..
NORTH AFRICA	..	..	..	..	..	..	..	..	..	..	..	..	..	..
Algeria	..	..	..	..	..	..	..	..	..	..	..	..	..	..
Egypt, Arab Republic of	..	..	..	..	..	..	..	..	..	..	..	..	..	..
Libya	..	..	..	..	..	..	..	..	..	..	..	..	..	..
Morocco	..	..	..	..	..	..	..	..	..	..	..	..	..	..
Tunisia	100.0	103.7	102.5	111.4	..	..	..	..	..	..	..	8.9	..	..
ALL AFRICA	..	..	..	..	..	..	..	..	..	..	..	..	..	..
South Africa	..	..	..	..	..	..	..	..	..	..	..	..	..	..

Notes: The base year is 1980 for Tunisia and 1985 for Zambia.

9–7. Capacity utilization in manufacturing

Percent

	1980	1981	1982	1983	1984	1985	1986	1987	1988	1989	1990
SUB-SAHARAN AFRICA	..	..	..	..	..	..	..	..	..	..	..
excluding Nigeria	..	..	..	..	..	..	..	..	..	..	..
Angola	..	..	..	..	..	..	..	..	..	..	..
Benin	..	..	..	..	..	..	..	..	..	..	..
Botswana	..	..	..	..	..	..	..	..	..	..	..
Burkina Faso	..	..	..	..	..	..	..	..	..	..	..
Burundi	35	37	43	45	42	47	51	..	..	..	..
Cameroon	..	..	..	..	..	..	..	..	..	..	..
Cape Verde	..	..	..	..	..	..	..	..	..	..	..
Central African Republic	..	..	..	..	..	..	..	..	..	..	..
Chad	..	..	..	..	..	..	..	..	..	..	..
Comoros	..	..	..	..	..	..	..	..	..	..	..
Congo, People's Republic of	..	..	..	..	..	..	..	..	..	..	..
Cote d'Ivoire	..	..	..	..	..	..	..	..	..	..	..
Djibouti	..	..	..	..	..	..	..	..	..	..	..
Equatorial Guinea	..	..	..	..	..	..	..	..	..	..	..
Ethiopia	..	..	..	..	..	..	..	..	..	..	..
Gabon	..	..	..	..	..	..	..	..	..	..	..
Gambia, The	..	..	..	..	..	..	..	..	..	..	..
Ghana	..	..	..	..	18	25	30	31	40	38	37
Guinea	..	..	..	..	..	..	..	..	..	..	..
Guinea-Bissau	..	..	..	..	..	..	..	..	..	..	..
Kenya	..	..	..	..	..	..	..	..	..	..	..
Lesotho	..	..	..	..	..	..	..	..	..	..	..
Liberia	..	..	..	..	..	..	..	..	..	..	..
Madagascar	..	..	..	..	..	..	..	..	..	..	..
Malawi	..	..	..	..	..	..	..	..	..	..	..
Mali	..	..	..	..	..	..	..	..	..	..	..
Mauritania	..	..	..	..	..	..	..	..	..	..	..
Mauritius	..	..	..	..	..	..	..	..	..	..	..
Mozambique	..	..	..	..	..	..	..	..	..	..	..
Namibia	..	..	..	..	..	..	..	..	..	..	..
Niger	48	46	32	41	39	44	46	57	56	54	..
Nigeria	..	..	..	..	..	38	38	38	40	42	37
Rwanda	37	46	32	41	39	44	..	..	..	..	..
Sao Tome & Principe	..	..	..	..	..	..	..	..	..	..	..
Senegal	..	..	..	..	..	..	..	..	..	..	..
Seychelles	..	..	..	..	..	..	..	..	..	..	..
Sierra Leone	..	..	..	..	..	..	..	..	..	..	..
Somalia	..	..	29	24	27	23	24	32	..	..	..
Sudan	..	..	..	..	..	..	..	..	..	..	..
Swaziland	..	..	..	..	..	..	..	..	..	..	..
Tanzania	55	50	47	43	44	45	31	30	..	..	..
Togo	..	..	..	..	..	..	..	..	..	..	..
Uganda	..	..	..	..	..	..	..	..	..	..	..
Zaire	..	..	..	..	..	..	..	..	..	..	..
Zambia	..	..	..	..	..	..	..	..	..	..	..
Zimbabwe	..	..	..	..	..	..	..	..	..	..	..
NORTH AFRICA	..	..	..	..	..	..	..	..	..	..	..
Algeria	..	..	..	..	..	..	..	..	..	..	..
Egypt, Arab Republic of	..	..	..	..	..	..	..	..	..	..	..
Libya	..	..	..	..	..	..	..	..	..	..	..
Morocco	..	..	..	..	..	..	..	..	..	..	..
Tunisia	..	..	..	..	..	..	..	..	..	..	..
ALL AFRICA	..	..	..	..	..	..	..	..	..	..	..
South Africa	..	..	..	..	..	..	..	..	..	..	..

Technical Notes

The United Nations Industrial Development Organization (UNIDO) is the primary source for the data in this chapter. For cross-country comparisons, UNIDO has standardized the coverage of establishments to those with five or more employees. Information on capacity utilization is drawn from various issues of the IMF's "Recent Economic Developments" and, in very limited cases, from country studies by World Bank staff.

Averages are arithmetic means for individual countries. When currency values are involved, the national currency is converted to current U.S. dollars to facilitate cross-country comparisons. Conversion factors are those in Table 3-6. These conversion factors approximate more closely the rate effectively applied to international transactions.

Table 9-1. Value added in manufacturing compared with GDP.

This is the current value of gross output in manufacturing less the current cost of materials, fuels, and other supplies consumed; contract and commission work done; repair and maintenance work done; and goods exported in the same condition as received.

Table 9-2. Structure of manufacturing value added

This shows the distribution of manufacturing value added among industries. The data are from UNIDO, and distribution calculations are from national currencies in current prices. The classification of manufacturing industries is in accordance with the UN International Standard Industrial Classification of All Economic Activities

(ISIC), Revision 2. "Food, beverages, and tobacco" comprise ISIC Division 31; "textiles and clothing," Division 32; "machinery and transport equipment," Major Groups 382-84; and "chemicals," Major Groups 351-52.

Table 9-3. Manufacturing gross output per employee

This is calculated by dividing the gross output in manufacturing for the year by the total number of employees in manufacturing firms. The term employee is defined as a person who works for a public or private employer and receives remuneration in wages, salary, commission, tips, piece rates, or pay in kind. In contrast to "persons engaged," the term employee excludes working proprietors, active business partners, and unpaid family workers.

Table 9-4. Real annual earnings per employee in manufacturing

This is derived by deflating nominal earnings per employee data from UNIDO by the consumer price index (CPI) of the country concerned. The base year used for the CPI calculation is 1987 in conformity with the currently adopted practice of the World Bank.

Table 9-5. Employee earnings as percentage of value added in manufacturing

This table is derived by dividing total nominal earnings of employees by nominal value added in manufacturing to show labor's share in income generated in the manufacturing sector.

Table 9-6. Index of industrial production

This relates the output of industrial sectors in one year to output in a base year. It shows the relative progress being made in industrial activities over the years. Industrial production indexes are calculated using the Laspeyres' formula (see "Index Numbers of Industrial Production," UN 1950). The formula, based on the weighted average of quantity relatives, is

$$I = \frac{\sum q_o p_o (\frac{q_n}{q_o})}{\sum q_o p_o}$$

or

$$I = \frac{\sum q_n p_o}{\sum q_o p_o}$$

where q_n is the quantity produced in the reporting period, q_o is the quantity produced in the base period, and p_o is the value added per unit in the base period. Apart from Tunisia and Zambia, the base year is 1987. For Tunisia the base year is 1980. For Zambia, the base year is 1985. No data are available for 1987 for these two countries.

Table 9-7. Capacity utilization in manufacturing.

This is the ratio of manufacturing output in a given year to the installed capacity of manufacturing equipment in the same period. Since units of measure differ, it has been necessary to first calculate the capacity utilization for individual products and then combine these as a weighted average for a given year. When installed capacity is given in daily, shift, or hourly bases, it is first converted to an annual measure by multiplying by the number of days, shifts, or hours worked per year. The resulting figure is then used as the donominator, while the output for the year is used as the numerator in the capacity utilization calculation.

10

Public Enterprises

Public enterprises (PEs) account for a significant share of output, investment, and employment in Sub-Saharan Africa. They usually dominate public utilities and mining, account on average for nearly half of the output in transportation and communications, and are important in other productive sectors.

Data presented here are mainly for nonfinancial PEs only and exclude financial PEs and public agencies. Most PEs listed are government majority-owned, most of which, in turn, are wholly owned.

This chapter provides data on the size and importance of the PE sector, PE financial results and financial flows between PEs and governments, and the extent of PE reform efforts. A measure of the place of PEs in the economy is the amount of resources they use — their share of total investment, credit, and employment — compared with their share of total goods and services produced (GDP). Another measure is PE financial flows, of which an important measure is PE net financial results, or aggregate sector profits less aggregate sector losses. PE financial results influence the level and composition of government expenditure, domestic credit, and external debt.

The data in this section have serious limitations. First, time-series data are incomplete; for many indicators, the data are available for one or two years only, and recent data are scarce.

Second, the quality of the data is sometimes inadequate; insufficient information on government lending to PEs, on cross-debts among public entities, and on PE arrears impairs the assessment of government and PE financial flows. Third, data consistency over time and comparability across countries for data series are compromised by varying definitions and accounting conventions. Trends shown for country groups may be distorted by changes in country coverage. National aggregates may be unduly biased by the inclusion or exclusion of some of large enterprises that dominate the sector but may not be representative of PE operations. The table notes provide details on data coverage for most indicators. Technical notes and sources offer more information for each of the indicators and on the nature of the data.

We have tried to minimize table notes and so have not included them here from the previous volume. However, we have tried to incorporate the major ones in the technical notes.

It should therefore be borne in mind that coverage may vary from year to year even within the same country. In some cases, only manufacturing PEs may be covered in some years, or agriculture PEs or a combination of all PEs. Despite these limitations, the data in this section are a step toward better monitoring of PE activities at the national and regional level.

257

10-1. Number of public enterprises

	1980	1981	1982	1983	1984	1985	1986	1987	1988	1989	1990	75-79	80-85	88-MR
SUB-SAHARAN AFRICA	..	..	..	..	..	..	..	..	..	..	..	..	..	..
excluding Nigeria	..	..	..	..	..	..	..	..	..	..	..	..	..	..
Angola	..	..	..	..	..	..	..	..	..	..	..	..	..	..
Benin	..	..	60	57	..	..	54	52	45	36	29	..	..	43
Botswana	9	..	..	..	..	..	47	48	48	48	48	..	..	48
Burkina Faso	..	..	..	..	..	..	35	48	49	49	49	..	..	46
Burundi	..	..	..	..	64	64	64	38	42	42	42	..	..	46
Cameroon	50	..	..	63	...	58	58	58	55	55	52	..	..	56
Cape Verde	..	..	..	..	..	..	..	..	..	..	..	..	..	..
Central African Republic	..	..	..	..	29	..	52	..	45	35	..	..	..	..
Chad	..	..	..	..	..	..	13	13	13	13	..	..	..	13
Comoros	..	..	..	..	..	..	10	10	12	12	12	..	..	11
Congo, People's Republic of the	..	94	94	94	94	94	123	122	82	82	82	..	..	98
Cote d'Ivoire	147	..	..	..	..	..	150	57	57	62	56	..	..	76
Djibouti	..	..	..	..	..	..	12	12	19	19	19	..	..	16
Equatorial Guinea	..	..	..	..	..	..	..	..	..	..	..	..	..	..
Ethiopia	..	..	..	..	108	..	60	59	60	57	58	..	..	59
Gabon	..	..	..	..	..	..	38	32	32	32	32	..	..	33
Gambia, The	..	..	..	..	..	20	19	16	16	16	13	..	..	16
Ghana	..	..	..	..	..	185	181	50	55	208	208	..	..	140
Guinea	174	..	..	..	..	101	183	85	188	27	48	..	..	106
Guinea-Bissau	..	..	..	..	..	36	23	23	22	22	22	..	..	22
Kenya	..	..	176	177	175	174	110	111	108	108	112	..	..	110
Lesotho	..	..	..	..	..	..	27	32	32	32	33	..	..	31
Liberia	22	..	..	..	..	21	21	16	16	16	16	..	..	17
Madagascar	136	..	..	..	..	167	184	68	104	104	104	..	..	113
Malawi	13	13	13	13	13	13	24	25	25	25	25	..	13	25
Mali	51	52	57	57	57	57	57	57	56	57	59	..	55	57
Mauritania	..	..	..	112	..	..	32	32	32	32	32	..	..	32
Mauritius	..	..	..	..	24	26	28	28	30	31	33	..	..	30
Mozambique	..	..	..	..	..	..	..	..	..	..	..	..	..	..
Namibia	..	..	..	..	..	..	..	..	..	..	..	..	..	..
Niger	47	..	..	..	..	44	23	23	23	23	23	..	..	23
Nigeria	..	107	..	110	..	..	83	83	99	94	94	..	..	91
Rwanda	..	40	40	40	40	..	29	29	29	29	29	..	..	29
Sao Tome & Principe	..	..	..	..	..	..	..	..	..	..	..	..	..	..
Senegal	..	..	83	85	85	85	85	87	47	87	87	..	..	79
Seychelles	..	..	..	..	..	..	39	34	35	35	35	..	..	36
Sierra Leone	..	..	..	..	23	26	26	22	22	25	25	..	..	24
Somalia	44	..	..	..	..	..	45	44	52	52	52	..	..	49
Sudan	..	..	..	..	138	..	200	40	38	38	38	..	..	71
Swaziland	..	..	..	..	..	..	13	14	14	14	14	..	..	14
Tanzania	..	398	433	448	460	420	166	188	197	197	197	..	..	189
Togo	..	..	80	80	80	..	65	47	47	42	43	..	..	49
Uganda	..	..	..	..	..	..	72	69	69	69	69	..	..	70
Zaire	..	138	..	..	..	..	129	40	40	40	40	..	..	58
Zambia	114	..	..	..	111	..	137	140	140	146	146	..	..	142
Zimbabwe	..	..	..	..	..	..	..	24	24	24	27	..	..	25
NORTH AFRICA	..	..	..	..	..	..	..	..	..	..	..	..	..	..
Algeria	..	..	..	..	..	..	..	..	..	..	..	..	..	..
Egypt, Arab Republic of	..	..	..	..	..	..	468	441	441	441	441	..	..	446
Libya	..	..	..	..	..	..	..	..	..	..	..	..	..	..
Morocco	..	..	..	..	..	..	73	73	73	73	77	..	..	74
Tunisia	..	..	..	..	..	..	104	106	105	107	107	..	..	106
ALL AFRICA	..	..	..	..	..	..	..	..	..	..	..	..	..	..
South Africa	..	..	..	..	..	..	29	26	26	26	26	..	..	27

10-2. Public enterprise contribution to gross domestic product

					Percent						
	1980	1981	1982	1983	1984	1985	1986	1987	1988	1989	1990
SUB-SAHARAN AFRICA	..	..	..	..	..	..	..	..	..	..	..
excluding Nigeria	..	..	..	..	..	..	..	..	..	..	..
Angola	..	..	..	..	..	..	..	..	..	..	..
Benin	..	..	..	..	..	..	..	..	..	..	..
Botswana	..	..	..	..	..	..	..	..	..	..	..
Burkina Faso	..	..	..	..	..	..	..	..	..	..	..
Burundi	..	..	..	..	..	..	5.0	..	..	..	..
Cameroon	..	..	..	..	..	..	..	..	..	..	..
Cape Verde	..	..	..	..	..	..	..	..	..	..	..
Central African Republic	..	..	3.5	4.4	4.3	4.9	3.7	3.9	4.0	..	..
Chad	..	..	..	..	..	..	..	..	..	..	..
Comoros	..	..	..	..	..	..	..	..	..	..	..
Congo, People's Republic of the	11.0	10.1	10.0	10.7	9.8	10.6	17.7	14.2	..	..	..
Cote d'Ivoire	..	..	..	..	..	..	..	..	..	..	..
Djibouti	..	..	..	..	..	..	..	..	..	..	..
Equatorial Guinea	..	..	..	..	..	..	..	..	..	..	..
Ethiopia	..	4.6	..	..	..	..	..	..	..	..	..
Gabon	..	..	..	..	..	..	..	..	..	..	..
Gambia, The	..	..	..	..	..	..	..	..	..	..	..
Ghana	..	..	..	..	4.6	5.5	10.6	11.9	..	..	..
Guinea	25.0	..	..	..	..	..	..	..	..	..	..
Guinea-Bissau	..	..	..	..	..	..	..	..	..	..	..
Kenya	..	..	..	..	8.0	12.0	11.7	11.7	10.9	11.4	11.7
Lesotho	..	..	..	..	..	..	..	..	..	..	..
Liberia	..	..	..	..	..	..	..	..	..	..	..
Madagascar	..	..	..	..	2.3	..	..	..	..	..	..
Malawi	9.5	7.1	..	6.8	..	..	..	..	..	..	..
Mali	12.1	..	..	..	..	..	..	..	..	..	..
Mauritania	..	..	..	25.0	..	..	..	..	..	..	..
Mauritius	..	..	..	..	7.2	..	..	..	..	..	..
Mozambique	..	..	..	..	..	..	..	..	..	..	..
Namibia	..	..	..	..	..	..	..	..	..	..	..
Niger	..	..	4.5	4.4	4.8	5.3	5.8	4.6	4.7	..	..
Nigeria	..	..	..	..	..	..	..	..	..	..	..
Rwanda	..	..	..	..	..	..	..	..	..	..	..
Sao Tome & Principe	..	..	..	..	..	..	..	..	..	..	..
Senegal	8.4	8.0	9.1	8.9	10.3	9.7	6.9	..	..	..	..
Seychelles	..	..	..	..	..	..	..	..	..	..	..
Sierra Leone	..	..	..	..	..	..	..	..	..	..	..
Somalia	2.9	1.3	1.5	..	..	..	..	..	..	..	..
Sudan	..	..	..	..	..	..	47.5	..	..	..	..
Swaziland	..	..	..	..	..	..	..	..	..	..	..
Tanzania	12.0	12.4	12.6	11.7	11.4	13.0	..	..	..	..	..
Togo	..	..	..	..	..	..	..	..	..	7.3	..
Uganda	..	..	..	..	..	..	..	..	..	..	..
Zaire	..	..	..	22.8	..	..	..	..	..	..	..
Zambia	..	35.0	26.8	30.9	31.5	35.0	..	..	..	..	..
Zimbabwe	..	..	..	..	..	..	..	..	..	..	..
NORTH AFRICA	..	..	..	..	..	..	..	..	..	..	..
Algeria	9.5	10.3	11.0	11.2	10.5	10.1	..	..	..	..	..
Egypt, Arab Republic of	20.1	19.6	17.9	17.5	..	..	..	..	..	..	..
Libya	..	..	..	..	..	..	..	..	..	..	..
Morocco	20.0	20.0	19.7	..	..	15.4	..	..	..	..	..
Tunisia	..	..	..	..	24.0	..	..	..	..	..	..
ALL AFRICA	..	..	..	..	..	..	..	..	..	..	..
South Africa	..	..	..	..	..	..	..	..	..	..	..

10–3. Public enterprise share of domestic investment

	1980	1981	1982	1983	1984	1985	1986	1987	1988	1989	1990
					Percent						
SUB-SAHARAN AFRICA	..	..	..	..	..	..	..	..	..	..	..
excluding Nigeria	..	..	..	..	..	..	..	..	..	..	..
Angola	..	..	..	..	..	..	..	..	..	..	..
Benin	..	..	..	..	..	..	..	..	..	..	..
Botswana	..	..	..	..	..	..	..	..	..	..	..
Burkina Faso	..	..	..	..	..	..	..	..	..	..	..
Burundi	42.8	25.1	41.3	26.4	35.4	43.9	41.5	..	..	..	..
Cameroon	..	..	..	..	..	..	..	..	..	..	..
Cape Verde	..	..	..	..	..	..	..	..	..	..	..
Central African Republic	..	..	..	..	..	..	17.0	..	..	..	..
Chad	..	..	..	..	..	..	..	..	..	..	..
Comoros	..	..	..	..	..	..	..	..	..	..	..
Congo, People's Republic of the	..	..	..	39.8	..	..	..	..	..	..	..
Cote d'Ivoire	7.7	6.4	23.2	22.9	26.1	18.8	20.4	..	..	..	..
Djibouti	..	..	..	..	..	..	..	..	..	..	..
Equatorial Guinea	..	..	..	..	..	..	..	..	..	..	..
Ethiopia	..	..	..	..	..	..	..	..	..	..	..
Gabon	..	..	..	..	..	..	..	..	..	..	..
Gambia, The	..	..	..	..	..	..	..	..	..	..	..
Ghana	27.6	26.2	28.7	17.4	..	..	..	..	..	..	..
Guinea	..	..	..	..	..	..	..	..	..	..	..
Guinea-Bissau	..	..	..	..	..	..	..	..	..	..	..
Kenya	19.4	20.3	22.7	20.8	19.8	12.9	20.0	14.9	13.9	16.3	21.4
Lesotho	..	..	..	..	..	..	..	..	..	..	..
Liberia	..	..	..	..	..	..	..	..	..	..	..
Madagascar	..	..	..	..	..	..	..	..	..	..	..
Malawi	27.7	17.9	7.5	3.7	..	..	..	..	..	..	..
Mali	8.1	..	..	..	..	..	..	..	..	..	..
Mauritania	..	..	..	..	..	..	..	..	..	..	..
Mauritius	..	..	..	..	7.2	..	..	..	..	..	..
Mozambique	..	..	..	..	..	..	..	..	..	..	..
Namibia	..	..	..	..	..	..	..	..	..	..	..
Niger	..	..	..	10.6	..	33.5	14.5	..	..	..	..
Nigeria	..	..	..	20.0	10.6	14.0	15.1	..	..	..	..
Rwanda	..	..	..	..	..	..	..	..	..	..	..
Sao Tome & Principe	..	..	..	..	..	..	..	..	..	..	..
Senegal	..	..	..	23.8	50.2	..	24.0	..	..	..	..
Seychelles	..	..	..	..	..	..	..	..	..	..	..
Sierra Leone	..	..	1.4	1.2	1.0	..	..	..	..	..	..
Somalia	..	..	..	..	..	..	..	..	..	..	..
Sudan	..	..	..	..	..	..	..	..	..	..	..
Swaziland	..	..	..	..	..	..	..	..	..	..	..
Tanzania	22.4	31.7	16.5	30.9	26.2	..	..	..	..	..	..
Togo	..	..	..	..	..	..	..	..	..	..	..
Uganda	..	..	..	..	..	..	..	..	..	..	..
Zaire	..	..	..	..	..	..	..	..	..	..	..
Zambia	54.8	49.6	50.0	58.8	57.2	..	..	..	..	..	..
Zimbabwe	..	..	..	..	..	..	..	..	..	..	..
NORTH AFRICA	..	..	..	..	..	..	..	..	..	..	..
Algeria	69.5	56.4	51.0	42.0	37.7	33.4	..	..	..	..	..
Egypt, Arab Republic of	..	..	..	..	..	..	..	..	..	..	..
Libya	..	..	..	..	..	..	..	..	..	..	..
Morocco	23.9	33.2	28.1	..	..	33.1	..	..	..	..	..
Tunisia	34.2	35.2	39.4	37.2	38.7	33.6	..	..	..	..	..
ALL AFRICA	..	..	..	..	..	..	..	..	..	..	..
South Africa	..	..	..	..	..	..	..	..	..	..	..

10–4. Public enterprise share of formal sector employment

	1980	1981	1982	1983	1984	1985	1986	1987	1988	1989	1990
SUB-SAHARAN AFRICA	..	..	..	..	..	..	..	..	..	..	..
excluding Nigeria	..	..	..	..	..	..	..	..	..	..	..
Angola	..	..	..	..	..	..	..	..	..	..	..
Benin	42.4	..	..	..	..	..	..	..	..	..	..
Botswana	..	..	..	..	..	..	..	..	..	..	..
Burkina Faso	..	..	..	..	..	..	..	..	..	..	..
Burundi	..	..	26.9	27.9	..	..	..	..	..	..	..
Cameroon	..	..	..	..	..	..	..	..	..	..	..
Cape Verde	..	..	..	..	..	..	..	..	..	..	..
Central African Republic	..	..	..	..	..	..	..	..	..	..	..
Chad	..	..	..	..	..	..	..	..	..	..	..
Comoros	..	..	..	..	..	..	..	..	..	..	..
Congo, People's Republic of the	..	..	..	..	..	21.8	18.9	..	..	..	..
Cote d'Ivoire	7.7	6.4	23.2	22.9	26.1	18.8	20.4	..	..	..	..
Djibouti	..	..	..	..	..	..	..	..	..	..	..
Equatorial Guinea	..	..	..	..	..	..	..	..	..	..	..
Ethiopia	..	..	..	..	..	..	..	..	..	..	..
Gabon	..	..	..	..	..	..	..	..	..	..	..
Gambia, The	..	..	..	..	..	..	..	..	..	..	..
Ghana	55.0	..	..	..	..	..	..	..	..	..	..
Guinea	68.8	67.9	67.3	..	..	..	..	..	..	..	..
Guinea-Bissau	..	..	..	..	..	..	..	..	..	..	..
Kenya	..	8.5	9.2	9.0	8.5	7.7	8.2	7.6	8.1	8.1	8.1
Lesotho	..	..	..	..	..	..	..	..	..	..	..
Liberia	..	..	..	..	..	..	..	..	..	..	..
Madagascar	..	..	..	5.1	2.1	1.8	..	..	..	..	..
Malawi	11.2	..	..	..	..	..	..	..	..	..	..
Mali	17.4	..	..	..	..	..	..	..	..	..	..
Mauritania	..	..	..	..	..	..	..	..	..	..	..
Mauritius	..	..	..	..	7.2	..	..	..	..	..	..
Mozambique	..	..	..	..	..	..	..	..	..	..	..
Namibia	..	..	..	..	..	..	..	..	..	..	..
Niger	..	..	..	..	..	..	..	..	..	..	..
Nigeria	..	..	..	..	..	..	..	..	..	..	..
Rwanda	..	..	..	..	..	..	..	..	..	..	..
Sao Tome & Principe	..	..	..	..	..	..	..	..	..	..	..
Senegal	..	..	..	..	..	..	..	..	..	..	..
Seychelles	..	..	..	..	..	..	..	..	..	..	..
Sierra Leone	..	..	17.1	..	..	..	..	..	..	..	..
Somalia	..	..	..	5.3	..	..	..	..	..	..	..
Sudan	..	..	..	..	..	..	..	..	..	..	..
Swaziland	..	..	..	..	..	..	..	..	..	..	..
Tanzania	..	..	..	..	..	..	..	..	..	..	..
Togo	..	..	..	24.0	..	..	..	..	..	..	..
Uganda	..	..	..	..	..	..	..	..	..	..	..
Zaire	..	..	..	..	..	..	10.0	..	..	..	..
Zambia	43.4	37.0	34.1	34.4	..	..	..	..	..	..	..
Zimbabwe	..	..	..	..	..	..	..	..	..	..	..
NORTH AFRICA	..	..	..	..	..	..	..	..	..	..	..
Algeria	..	..	..	..	..	..	..	..	..	..	..
Egypt, Arab Republic of	..	..	..	..	..	..	..	..	..	..	..
Libya	..	..	..	..	..	..	..	..	..	..	..
Morocco	..	..	..	..	..	..	..	..	..	..	..
Tunisia	..	..	..	..	..	..	..	..	..	..	..
ALL AFRICA	..	..	..	..	..	..	..	..	..	..	..
South Africa	..	..	..	..	..	..	..	..	..	..	..

10–5. Number of persons employed in the public enterprise sector

Thousands

	1980	1981	1982	1983	1984	1985	1986	1987	1988	1989	1990
SUB-SAHARAN AFRICA	..	..	..	..	..	..	..	..	..	..	..
excluding Nigeria	..	..	..	..	..	..	..	..	..	..	..
Angola	..	..	..	..	..	..	..	..	..	..	..
Benin	28.0	..	..	..	..	..	..	..	..	..	..
Botswana	..	..	..	..	..	..	..	..	..	..	..
Burkina Faso	..	..	..	..	..	..	..	..	..	..	..
Burundi	..	..	15.6	17.0	18.0	..	..	..	..	..	..
Cameroon	..	..	..	..	..	..	..	..	..	..	..
Cape Verde	..	..	..	..	..	..	..	..	..	..	..
Central African Republic	..	..	..	..	6.1	11.3	12.1	7.3	8.2	..	..
Chad	..	..	..	..	..	..	..	..	..	..	..
Comoros	..	..	..	..	..	..	..	..	..	..	..
Congo, People's Republic of the	30.1	31.8	35.0	37.1	40.1	28.8	29.6	29.3	..	..	..
Cote d'Ivoire	..	..	..	..	..	..	..	..	..	..	..
Djibouti	..	..	..	..	..	..	..	..	..	..	..
Equatorial Guinea	..	..	..	..	..	..	..	..	..	..	..
Ethiopia	80.6	83.3	86.2	..	..	..	..	..	..	..	..
Gabon	..	..	..	..	..	..	..	..	..	..	..
Gambia, The	..	..	..	..	..	10.7	8.0	..	..	..	..
Ghana	65.8	60.0	58.8	180.0	..	160.0	..	..	200.0	..	..
Guinea	108.4	111.8	116.3	..	..	..	..	..	..	..	..
Guinea-Bissau	4.9	..	..	..	3.1	..	2.5	..	..	..	..
Kenya	..	87.0	96.0	98.0	95.4	108.8	110.4	112.0	119.2	120.7	121.8
Lesotho	..	..	..	..	..	..	..	..	..	..	..
Liberia	..	..	..	..	..	..	..	..	..	..	..
Madagascar	..	..	..	5.0	21.5	20.0	77.0	..	..	..	..
Malawi	41.2	..	..	..	..	..	..	..	..	..	..
Mali	13.7	13.0	12.6	11.9	11.0	9.7	9.3	8.8	7.6	..	..
Mauritania	..	..	..	..	..	11.0	..	..	..	..	..
Mauritius	..	..	..	..	..	20.2	..	..	..	..	..
Mozambique	..	..	..	..	..	..	..	..	..	..	..
Namibia	..	..	..	..	..	..	..	..	..	..	..
Niger	..	..	..	10.9	10.6	11.4	11.2	11.2	10.8	..	..
Nigeria	..	400.0	360.0	448.0	460.0	..	..	..	300.0	..	..
Rwanda	..	..	..	..	..	..	..	..	..	..	..
Sao Tome & Principe	..	..	..	..	..	..	..	..	..	..	..
Senegal	30.6	..	..	..	..	..	30.8	30.2	..	..	..
Seychelles	..	..	..	..	..	..	..	..	..	..	..
Sierra Leone	..	..	12.2	..	..	..	..	..	..	..	..
Somalia	..	..	10.4	7.9	5.6	6.6	..	..	..	..	..
Sudan	..	..	..	..	117.6	..	..	..	..	..	..
Swaziland	..	..	..	..	..	..	..	..	..	..	..
Tanzania	..	..	..	..	..	..	..	..	..	..	..
Togo	..	..	12.8	12.7	11.9	..	..	..	..	..	..
Uganda	..	..	..	..	..	..	..	..	..	..	..
Zaire	..	..	..	..	..	..	150.0	..	..	..	..
Zambia	136.4	..	..	125.2	..	..	..	..	..	..	..
Zimbabwe	..	..	..	..	..	..	..	..	..	..	..
NORTH AFRICA	..	..	..	..	..	..	..	..	..	..	..
Algeria	..	..	..	..	..	..	..	..	..	..	..
Egypt, Arab Republic of	..	..	..	..	..	..	..	..	..	..	..
Libya	..	..	..	..	..	..	..	..	..	..	..
Morocco	..	..	..	..	..	..	..	..	..	..	..
Tunisia	..	..	..	..	..	..	..	..	..	..	..
ALL AFRICA	..	..	..	..	..	..	..	..	..	..	..
South Africa	..	..	..	..	..	..	..	..	..	..	..

10–6. Public enterprise share of domestic credit outstanding

	Percent											Average		
	1980	1981	1982	1983	1984	1985	1986	1987	1988	1989	1990	75–79	80–85	86–MR
SUB-SAHARAN AFRICA	..	..	..	..	..	..	..	..	..	..	..	..	..	..
excluding Nigeria	..	..	..	..	..	..	..	..	..	..	..	..	..	..
Angola	..	..	..	..	..	..	..	..	..	..	..	..	..	..
Benin	..	..	..	45.3	..	..	..	..	..	..	..	..	..	..
Botswana	27.3	6.5	18.2	-191.8	-14.1	-6.0	-3.4	-1.5	-1.3	-2.2	-1.7	10.1	-26.7	-2.0
Burkina Faso	..	..	..	..	..	..	..	..	..	..	..	..	..	..
Burundi	12.9	7.0	8.3	7.7	17.1	18.7	19.8	19.9	22.2	25.0	25.1	9.4	12.0	22.4
Cameroon	..	..	..	..	..	..	..	..	..	18.0	17.5	..	..	17.7
Cape Verde	52.2	39.7	47.7	37.2	42.3	38.3	32.1	26.4	46.5	42.0	38.5	19.9	42.9	37.1
Central African Republic	..	..	..	..	..	..	..	..	..	11.8	21.1	..	..	16.5
Chad	..	..	..	..	..	..	..	..	..	39.0	33.5	..	..	36.2
Comoros	..	..	..	..	..	..	..	..	..	..	..	..	..	..
Congo, People's Republic of the	..	..	..	..	..	..	..	..	..	13.9	12.3	..	..	13.1
Cote d'Ivoire	..	..	..	..	..	..	..	..	..	..	..	..	..	..
Djibouti	..	..	..	..	2.1	1.9	1.5	1.5	1.9	0.7	1.8	..	..	1.4
Equatorial Guinea	..	..	..	..	..	..	..	..	..	3.9	5.7	..	..	4.8
Ethiopia	..	..	..	..	..	..	..	..	..	..	..	..	..	..
Gabon	..	..	..	..	..	..	..	..	..	6.0	5.9	..	..	6.0
Gambia, The	..	..	..	..	..	..	..	..	..	..	..	..	..	..
Ghana	20.7	21.9	32.3	4.1	8.8	21.0	17.0	9.8	4.1	16.9	11.8	17.0	18.1	11.9
Guinea	..	..	..	..	..	..	..	..	..	..	..	..	..	..
Guinea-Bissau	..	..	..	..	..	..	13.9	15.5	23.4	..	..	..	..	..
Kenya	2.1	1.6	2.1	4.4	5.3	5.4	4.3	7.2	6.4	5.0	4.8	2.4	3.5	5.5
Lesotho	..	..	..	..	..	..	..	..	..	..	..	..	..	..
Liberia	15.2	11.5	12.1	11.1	11.3	8.7	9.1	5.7	5.9	4.7	..	..	11.7	6.3
Madagascar	..	..	..	14.7	14.6	14.1	..	..	..	..	..	..	..	..
Malawi	13.2	6.5	3.8	..	..	..	..	..	..	..	..	..	..	..
Mali	..	..	..	..	..	..	..	..	..	..	..	..	..	..
Mauritania	..	..	..	..	..	..	..	..	..	..	..	..	..	..
Mauritius	..	..	..	..	..	20.2	..	..	..	..	..	..	..	..
Mozambique	..	..	..	..	..	..	..	..	..	..	..	..	..	..
Namibia	..	..	..	..	..	..	..	..	..	..	..	..	..	..
Niger	27.3	26.3	23.9	23.7	19.0	18.0	28.5	..	..	..	..	..	23.0	28.5
Nigeria	..	..	..	..	..	..	..	..	..	..	..	..	..	..
Rwanda	6.0	4.7	5.0	7.1	5.2	4.1	..	..	..	..	..	..	5.4	..
Sao Tome & Principe	..	..	..	..	32.9	27.2	71.6	69.5	70.6	..	..	..	..	70.5
Senegal	39.5	42.4	39.1	34.3	26.1	25.3	..	..	..	..	..	..	34.5	..
Seychelles	..	..	..	..	..	..	..	..	..	..	..	..	..	..
Sierra Leone	..	..	..	..	..	..	..	..	..	..	..	..	..	..
Somalia	..	..	..	..	..	..	..	..	..	..	..	..	..	..
Sudan	21.3	22.5	28.8	13.2	13.6	19.7	20.4	20.3	18.1	15.1	..	22.2	19.9	18.5
Swaziland	..	..	..	..	..	..	..	..	..	..	..	..	..	..
Tanzania	..	..	22.0	16.9	22.8	..	..	..	..	..	..	..	..	..
Togo	..	..	..	..	25.4	18.1	24.5	31.6	..	..	..	..	..	28.1
Uganda	0.6	0.5	0.5	7.7	5.8	3.8	..	..	..	..	..	..	3.2	..
Zaire	0.1	0.6	1.3	0.7	0.6	0.3	0.4	0.2	0.5	1.1	1.6	1.9	0.6	0.8
Zambia	12.6	..	15.5	16.1	14.2	..	..	..	..	..	..	..	14.6	..
Zimbabwe	14.9	27.3	22.4	27.7	30.9	38.8	39.9	27.3	24.3	23.9	17.6	..	27.0	26.6
NORTH AFRICA	..	..	..	..	..	..	..	..	..	..	..	..	..	..
Algeria	..	..	..	..	..	..	..	..	..	..	..	..	..	..
Egypt, Arab Republic of	23.5	25.1	19.4	22.7	23.7	23.8	22.7	22.3	21.6	22.0	23.9	..	23.0	22.5
Libya	..	..	..	..	..	..	..	..	..	..	..	..	..	..
Morocco	..	..	..	..	..	..	..	..	..	..	..	..	..	..
Tunisia	..	..	..	..	..	..	..	..	..	..	..	..	..	..
ALL AFRICA	..	..	..	..	..	..	..	..	..	..	..	..	..	..
South Africa	..	..	..	..	..	..	..	..	..	..	..	..	..	..

10-7. Public enterprise share of external debt outstanding

| | Percent | | | | | | | | | | | Average | | |
	1980	1981	1982	1983	1984	1985	1986	1987	1988	1989	1990	75–79	80–85	86–MR
SUB-SAHARAN AFRICA	14.78	15.05	14.90	13.13	11.51	12.26	11.52	10.33	9.21	8.16	..	18.09	13.61	9.80
excluding Nigeria	16.66	15.74	14.92	13.76	11.86	12.39	11.81	10.83	9.62	8.58	..	18.80	14.22	10.21
Angola	..	..	..	..	..	..	..	..	..	..	..	..	..	..
Benin	33.31	36.00	32.17	30.32	28.47	28.01	28.27	28.81	27.89	26.06	..	20.2	31.4	27.8
Botswana	9.08	10.72	8.03	9.26	20.64	28.96	30.26	27.57	25.64	21.91	..	1.1	14.4	26.9
Burkina Faso	7.43	7.64	7.59	8.38	8.34	8.45	7.32	6.32	5.14	4.85	..	7.1	8.0	6.4
Burundi	1.03	0.95	1.05	3.20	2.59	2.19	1.89	0.88	0.69	0.52	..	3.9	1.8	1.2
Cameroon	39.65	38.53	32.12	28.57	23.89	24.08	21.67	21.53	17.68	10.96	..	37.9	31.1	19.2
Cape Verde	0.00	45.08	51.21	53.42	42.57	35.64	32.24	24.43	22.26	20.60	..	..	38.0	27.0
Central African Republic	24.15	12.55	18.68	16.92	11.63	12.44	13.12	13.42	11.54	11.60	..	38.5	16.1	12.4
Chad	33.94	27.66	16.55	14.12	14.70	15.43	20.82	23.84	20.85	7.36	..	24.9	20.4	17.7
Comoros	..	..	1.75	2.57	4.70	7.28	8.54	11.38	12.63	2.28	..	0.8	4.1	8.4
Congo, People's Republic of the	24.90	30.37	30.62	29.25	27.05	23.62	20.94	15.73	16.72	15.09	..	12.9	27.6	18.4
Cote d'Ivoire	24.10	19.83	16.06	15.71	13.30	11.45	9.94	8.00	5.76	4.97	..	29.6	16.7	8.0
Djibouti	..	..	..	..	..	..	..	..	..	..	..	..	..	..
Equatorial Guinea	8.33	12.23	7.27	5.56	5.33	3.56	3.47	3.42	3.04	0.79	..	..	7.0	2.9
Ethiopia	12.85	14.00	12.77	11.74	16.66	18.05	16.19	16.35	16.08	13.63	..	11.4	14.3	16.1
Gabon	14.22	14.49	12.26	9.64	7.10	7.17	7.01	6.77	5.46	4.77	..	12.5	10.8	6.2
Gambia, The	8.19	6.42	9.76	10.20	9.13	8.89	6.07	4.22	1.52	1.40	..	5.2	8.8	4.4
Ghana	14.43	14.82	16.52	14.81	10.75	10.27	9.24	8.82	8.22	7.15	..	9.6	13.6	8.7
Guinea	..	..	..	..	..	..	..	..	..	..	..	..	..	..
Guinea-Bissau	2.27	3.17	3.45	2.76	1.75	1.58	1.55	0.77	0.12	0.09	..	2.1	2.5	0.8
Kenya	17.31	17.80	16.73	14.99	13.04	12.65	15.22	14.68	13.58	15.38	..	18.9	15.4	14.3
Lesotho	0.57	0.36	0.17	0.22	0.96	4.16	3.86	3.60	2.73	2.50	..	1.8	1.1	3.4
Liberia	10.80	8.60	8.40	8.84	8.27	8.32	8.37	8.38	8.40	8.16	..	14.6	8.9	8.3
Madagascar	24.97	22.92	24.64	24.11	17.79	17.35	16.50	14.91	15.05	13.41	..	19.9	22.0	15.4
Malawi	16.51	16.19	13.92	10.66	7.45	5.92	4.78	4.72	4.22	4.48	..	11.4	11.8	4.8
Mali	3.68	2.51	2.22	2.06	1.37	1.28	1.16	0.87	0.50	0.51	..	5.2	2.2	0.9
Mauritania	7.77	10.00	15.50	19.41	19.28	20.81	20.73	20.32	19.11	17.11	..	14.4	15.5	19.6
Mauritius	3.79	3.06	2.84	2.23	3.26	3.67	3.88	6.06	16.99	18.61	..	3.9	3.1	9.8
Mozambique	..	..	..	..	..	12.20	13.64	10.53	8.74	9.48	..	..	12.2	10.9
Namibia	..	..	..	..	..	..	..	..	..	..	..	..	..	..
Niger	12.52	16.96	13.03	11.75	10.01	8.06	6.52	5.73	4.09	2.97	..	5.5	12.1	5.5
Nigeria	5.09	12.16	14.80	11.09	10.31	11.78	10.50	8.64	7.80	6.69	..	14.9	10.9	9.1
Rwanda	..	..	..	..	..	..	..	..	..	..	..	..	..	..
Sao Tome & Principe	..	..	..	..	..	..	..	..	..	..	..	..	..	..
Senegal	12.36	8.96	8.34	7.70	7.00	6.90	6.76	7.10	6.42	4.24	..	13.7	8.5	6.3
Seychelles	3.45	6.25	7.69	6.24	7.23	7.54	6.71	8.34	7.79	8.08	..	..	6.4	7.7
Sierra Leone	8.96	8.77	8.79	8.20	6.92	7.14	5.44	4.60	4.22	3.47	..	11.1	8.1	5.0
Somalia	3.03	1.99	1.11	0.77	0.71	0.74	0.76	0.78	0.78	0.78	..	3.6	1.4	0.8
Sudan	3.12	2.47	2.08	1.54	1.42	1.39	1.19	1.03	0.90	0.80	..	2.8	2.0	1.1
Swaziland	23.32	21.66	23.79	20.81	19.67	17.09	17.46	16.85	15.08	11.56	..	6.8	21.1	15.6
Tanzania	11.44	11.39	9.77	8.40	8.48	8.52	7.12	6.43	4.89	4.72	..	6.7	9.7	6.3
Togo	6.41	5.04	4.79	3.66	4.88	5.21	4.61	4.61	4.60	3.96	..	2.9	5.0	4.6
Uganda	4.37	3.49	2.54	2.47	2.82	3.93	4.49	4.35	3.95	4.17	..	3.2	3.3	4.2
Zaire	26.10	24.63	23.50	19.31	17.35	16.71	15.95	14.90	13.14	13.97	..	38.7	21.3	14.9
Zambia	17.10	17.89	19.52	18.65	17.81	18.33	15.60	15.25	13.57	12.91	..	31.0	18.2	15.1
Zimbabwe	2.58	13.00	24.29	25.32	23.20	22.39	19.17	17.07	14.06	10.23	..	11.6	18.5	16.6
NORTH AFRICA	39.97	37.02	33.20	31.78	27.65	25.63	24.24	22.65	20.41	20.07	..			
Algeria	66.87	65.47	62.30	64.36	56.19	46.26	36.40	36.20	28.96	27.55	..	62.9	60.2	35.1
Egypt, Arab Republic of	23.44	23.33	21.53	21.10	19.64	20.58	22.17	20.04	20.36	21.10	..	18.6	21.6	20.8
Libya	..	..	..	..	..	..	..	..	..	..	..	..	..	..
Morocco	24.23	20.25	19.03	17.50	15.11	14.51	13.36	11.90	9.64	8.76	..	25.2	18.4	11.6
Tunisia	30.93	30.83	32.12	30.61	27.69	27.03	25.41	24.71	21.45	18.66	..	24.5	29.9	23.5
ALL AFRICA	27.13	25.41	23.59	21.59	18.88	18.37	17.18	15.57	13.94	13.10				
South Africa											..	..	..	..

10–8. Public enterprise net financial results

Billions of local currencies, except otherwise indicated

	1980	1981	1982	1983	1984	1985	1986	1987	1988	1989	1990
SUB-SAHARAN AFRICA excluding Nigeria	..	..	..	..	..	..	..	..	..	..	..
Angola	..	..	..	..	..	..	..	..	..	..	..
Benin	..	..	..	-5.6	..	..	..	..	..	..	..
Botswana	..	..	..	..	..	..	..	..	..	..	..
Burkina Faso	..	..	..	..	..	..	..	..	..	..	..
Burundi	..	..	..	..	0.4	..	..	..	..	..	..
Cameroon	..	..	-48.6	-59.0	-39.9	..	..	..	..	..	..
Cape Verde	..	..	..	..	..	..	..	..	..	..	..
Central African Republic	..	..	-5.6	-2.3	-1.8	-6.4	-11.3	-15.3	-8.3	..	..
Chad	..	..	..	..	..	..	..	..	..	..	..
Comoros	..	..	..	..	..	..	..	..	..	..	..
Congo, People's Republic of the	..	-8.3	-24.6	-27.5	-28.0	-25.3	..	..	..	..	..
Cote d'Ivoire	..	..	-46.3	-106.9	-138.9	-156.7	..	..	..	..	..
Djibouti	..	..	..	..	..	..	..	..	..	..	..
Equatorial Guinea	..	..	..	..	..	..	..	..	..	..	..
Ethiopia	..	..	..	..	..	..	..	..	..	..	..
Gabon	..	..	..	..	..	..	..	..	..	..	..
Gambia, The *	..	-19.9	-39.1	-47.6	-33.7	-16.5	-26.3	..	..	..	..
Ghana	-0.1	-0.6	-2.9	-0.6	7.3	8.0	28.5	53.8	..	..	..
Guinea	2.4	..	0.1	..	-0.2	..	..	..	..	..	..
Guinea–Bissau	..	..	..	..	..	..	..	..	..	..	..
Kenya	..	..	..	..	0.2	..	..	..	..	..	..
Lesotho	..	..	..	..	..	..	..	..	..	..	..
Liberia	..	..	..	..	..	..	..	..	..	..	..
Madagascar	..	..	-1.3	..	..	..	..	..	..	..	..
Malawi *	-6.0	-7.0	..	-6.0	-1.0	-3.0	-23.0	..	..	..	..
Mali	..	-10.1	-3.7	-8.6	-7.8	-3.5	..	..	..	..	..
Mauritania	-97.0	80.0	-598.0	-246.0	..	..	..	..	..	..	..
Mauritius	..	..	..	-0.1	-0.2	-0.1	..	..	..	..	..
Mozambique	..	..	..	..	..	..	..	..	..	..	..
Namibia	..	..	..	..	..	..	..	..	..	..	..
Niger	..	-5.4	-13.2	-8.7	-5.7	2.0	0.1	-3.1	-1.2	..	..
Nigeria	..	..	..	0.4	1.4	..	0.6	..	..	..	..
Rwanda	..	..	0.3	0.4	..	..	..	..	..	..	..
Sao Tome & Principe	..	..	..	..	..	..	..	..	..	..	..
Senegal	..	-13.2	-1.4	-8.9	-10.8	-3.3	-11.1	..	..	..	..
Seychelles	..	..	..	..	..	..	..	..	..	..	..
Sierra Leone *	..	7.5	-15.6	-32.7	-7.9	51.4	..	..	..	..	..
Somalia	..	..	..	-0.1	-0.1	0.2	..	..	..	..	..
Sudan	..	..	..	..	..	..	..	..	..	..	..
Swaziland	..	..	..	..	..	..	..	..	..	..	..
Tanzania	..	..	..	..	..	..	..	..	..	..	..
Togo *	..	..	26.0	23.0	18.0	..	..	..	..	10.0	..
Uganda	..	..	..	..	..	..	..	..	..	..	..
Zaire	1.3	1.9	-1.4	0.6	6.5	11.8	6.3	..	..	..	..
Zambia	0.0	-0.1	-0.1	0.2	0.3	..	..	..	..	..	..
Zimbabwe	..	..	..	..	..	..	..	..	..	..	..
NORTH AFRICA	..	..	..	..	..	..	..	..	..	..	..
Algeria	..	..	..	..	..	..	..	..	..	..	..
Egypt, Arab Republic of	..	..	..	..	..	..	..	..	..	..	..
Libya	..	..	..	..	..	..	..	..	..	..	..
Morocco	..	..	..	..	..	..	..	..	..	..	..
Tunisia	..	..	..	..	..	..	..	..	..	..	..
ALL AFRICA	..	..	..	..	..	..	..	..	..	..	..
South Africa	..	..	..	..	..	..	..	..	..	..	..

Note: '*' = millions of local currency.

10–9. Public enterprise net financial results as ratio of GDP

Percent

	1980	1981	1982	1983	1984	1985	1986	1987	1988	1989	1990
SUB-SAHARAN AFRICA	..	..	..	..	..	..	..	..	..	..	..
excluding Nigeria	..	..	..	..	..	..	..	..	..	..	..
Angola	..	..	..	..	..	..	..	..	..	..	..
Benin	..	..	..	-1.5	..	..	..	..	..	..	..
Botswana	..	..	..	..	..	..	..	..	..	..	..
Burkina Faso	..	..	..	..	..	..	..	..	..	..	..
Burundi	..	..	..	..	0.4	..	..	..	..	..	..
Cameroon	..	..	-2.2	-2.2	-1.2	..	..	..	..	..	..
Cape Verde	..	..	..	..	..	..	..	..	..	..	..
Central African Republic	..	..	-2.6	-1.0	-0.7	-2.0	-3.3	-4.7	-2.5	..	..
Chad	..	..	..	..	..	..	..	..	..	..	..
Comoros	..	..	..	..	..	..	..	..	..	..	..
Congo, People's Republic of the	..	-1.5	-3.5	-3.4	-2.9	-2.6	..	..	..	..	..
Cote d'Ivoire	..	..	-1.9	-4.1	-4.8	-5.0	..	..	..	..	..
Djibouti	..	..	..	..	..	..	..	..	..	..	..
Equatorial Guinea	..	..	..	..	..	..	..	..	..	..	..
Ethiopia	..	..	..	..	..	..	..	..	..	..	..
Gabon	..	..	..	..	..	..	..	..	..	..	..
Gambia, The	..	-4.8	-8.7	-9.0	2.3	-2.6	-3.2	..	..	..	..
Ghana	-0.2	-0.9	-3.3	-0.3	2.7	2.3	5.6	7.2	..	..	..
Guinea	..	..	..	..	..	..	..	..	..	..	..
Guinea-Bissau	..	..	..	..	..	..	..	..	..	..	..
Kenya	..	..	..	..	0.3	..	..	..	..	..	..
Lesotho	..	..	..	..	..	..	..	..	..	..	..
Liberia	..	..	..	..	..	..	..	..	..	..	..
Madagascar	..	..	-0.1	..	..	..	..	..	..	..	..
Malawi	-0.6	-0.6	..	-0.4	-0.1	-0.2	-23.0	..	..	..	..
Mali	..	-2.7	-1.8	-0.9	-1.9	-1.6	-0.7	..	..	..	..
Mauritania	-0.3	0.2	-1.5	-0.6	..	..	..	..	..	..	..
Mauritius	..	..	..	-1.0	-1.2	-0.3	..	..	..	..	..
Mozambique	..	..	..	..	..	..	..	..	..	..	..
Namibia	..	..	..	..	..	..	..	..	..	..	..
Niger	..	-0.9	-2.1	-1.3	-0.9	0.3	0.0	-0.5	-0.2	..	..
Nigeria	..	..	..	0.7	2.3	..	1.0	..	..	..	..
Rwanda	..	..	0.2	0.3	1.0	1.0	1.0	1.0	..	..	..
Sao Tome & Principe	..	..	..	..	..	..	..	..	..	..	..
Senegal	..	-2.0	-0.2	-0.9	-1.1	-0.3	-0.9	..	..	..	..
Seychelles	..	..	..	..	..	..	..	..	..	..	..
Sierra Leone	..	0.6	-1.0	-1.7	-0.3	1.4	..	..	..	..	..
Somalia	..	..	..	-0.3	-0.1	0.2	..	..	..	..	..
Sudan	..	..	..	..	..	..	..	..	..	..	..
Swaziland	..	..	..	..	..	..	..	..	..	..	..
Tanzania	..	..	..	..	..	..	..	..	..	..	..
Togo	..	..	..	..	..	..	..	..	..	..	..
Uganda	..	..	..	..	..	..	..	..	..	..	..
Zaire	4.7	4.8	-2.8	0.6	3.6	4.9	1.7	..	..	..	..
Zambia	1.0	-3.5	-2.2	4.6	7.1	..	..	..	..	..	..
Zimbabwe	..	..	..	..	..	..	..	..	..	..	..
NORTH AFRICA	..	..	..	..	..	..	..	..	..	..	..
Algeria	..	..	..	..	..	..	..	..	..	..	..
Egypt, Arab Republic of	..	..	..	..	..	..	..	..	..	..	..
Libya	..	..	..	..	..	..	..	..	..	..	..
Morocco	..	..	..	..	..	..	..	..	..	..	..
Tunisia	..	..	..	..	..	..	..	..	..	..	..
ALL AFRICA	..	..	..	..	..	..	..	..	..	..	..
South Africa	..	..	..	..	..	..	..	..	..	..	..

10–10. Public enterprise net financial results as ratio of govt. expenditure

	Ratio								
	1980	1981	1982	1983	1984	1985	1986	1987	1988
SUB-SAHARAN AFRICA	..	..	..	..	..	..	..	..	..
excluding Nigeria	..	..	..	..	..	..	..	..	..
Angola	..	..	..	..	..	..	..	..	..
Benin	..	..	..	-5.0	..	..	..	..	..
Botswana	..	..	..	..	..	..	..	..	..
Burkina Faso	..	..	..	..	..	..	..	..	..
Burundi	..	..	..	..	1.3	..	..	..	..
Cameroon	..	..	-9.8	-9.6	-5.5	..	..	..	..
Cape Verde	..	..	..	..	..	..	..	..	..
Central African Republic	..	..	-14.0	-5.4	-4.6	..	..	..	..
Chad	..	..	..	..	..	..	..	..	..
Comoros	..	..	..	..	..	..	..	..	..
Congo, People's Republic of the	..	0.5	0.3	0.4	0.7	1.5	..	..	..
Cote d'Ivoire	..	..	-4.6	-10.3	-13.6	-16.1	..	..	..
Djibouti	..	..	..	..	..	..	..	..	..
Equatorial Guinea	..	..	..	..	..	..	..	..	..
Ethiopia	..	..	..	..	..	..	..	..	..
Gabon	..	..	..	..	..	..	..	..	..
Gambia, The	..	-11.6	-21.5	-24.4	-14.2	-6.1	-7.1	..	..
Ghana	-1.8	-7.9	-31.4	-3.6	..	..	..	..	..
Guinea	..	..	..	..	..	..	..	..	..
Guinea-Bissau	..	..	..	..	..	..	..	..	..
Kenya	..	..	..	..	1.0	..	..	..	..
Lesotho	..	..	..	..	..	..	..	..	..
Liberia	..	..	..	..	..	..	..	..	..
Madagascar	..	..	-0.5	..	..	..	..	..	..
Malawi	-1.7	-1.8	..	-1.4	-0.2	-0.5	-3.8	..	..
Mali	..	-23.7	-17.2	-12.0	-12.4	-11.1	..	..	..
Mauritania	-0.7	0.6	-3.7	-1.4	..	..	..	..	..
Mauritius	..	..	..	-3.3	-4.3	-1.2	..	..	..
Mozambique	..	..	..	..	..	..	..	..	..
Namibia	..	..	..	..	..	..	..	..	..
Niger	..	-3.9	-11.1	-8.0	-7.0	3.6	-2.3	..	..
Nigeria	..	..	..	3.1	13.2	..	4.9	..	..
Rwanda	..	..	1.7	2.2	6.0	6.0	6.0	6.0	..
Sao Tome & Principe	..	..	..	..	..	..	..	..	..
Senegal	..	..	-1.7	-1.7	-1.8	0.0	-3.0	..	..
Seychelles	..	..	..	..	..	..	..	..	..
Sierra Leone	..	1.8	-3.8	-8.0	-1.7	6.1	..	..	..
Somalia	..	..	..	-1.3	-0.7	1.5	..	..	..
Sudan	..	..	..	..	..	..	..	..	..
Swaziland	..	..	..	..	..	..	..	..	..
Tanzania	..	..	..	..	..	..	..	..	..
Togo	..	..	..	..	..	..	..	..	..
Uganda	..	..	..	..	..	..	..	..	..
Zaire	30.0	22.8	-13.1	3.7	17.1	21.5	8.9	..	..
Zambia	2.6	-9.5	-5.0	13.9	22.4	..	..	..	..
Zimbabwe	..	..	..	..	..	..	..	..	..
NORTH AFRICA	..	..	..	..	..	..	..	..	..
Algeria	..	..	..	..	..	..	..	..	..
Egypt, Arab Republic of	..	..	..	..	..	..	..	..	..
Libya	..	..	..	..	..	..	..	..	..
Morocco	..	..	..	..	..	..	..	..	..
Tunisia	..	..	..	..	..	..	..	..	..
ALL AFRICA	..	..	..	..	..	..	..	..	..
South Africa	..	..	..	..	..	..	..	..	..

10–11. Net financial flows between government and public enterprises

		Millions of local currency, except otherwise indicated							
	1980	1981	1982	1983	1984	1985	1986	1987	1988
SUB-SAHARAN AFRICA	..	..	..	..	..	..	..	..	..
excluding Nigeria	..	..	..	..	..	..	..	..	..
Angola	..	..	..	..	..	..	..	..	..
Benin *	..	..	-2.6	..	..	..	..	..	..
Botswana	..	..	..	..	..	..	..	..	..
Burkina Faso	..	..	..	..	..	..	..	..	..
Burundi	..	..	..	279.5	..	..	..	..	..
Cameroon	..	..	..	..	..	..	..	..	..
Cape Verde	..	..	..	..	..	..	..	..	..
Central African Republic	..	..	..	..	..	..	..	..	..
Chad	..	..	..	..	..	..	..	..	..
Comoros	..	..	..	..	..	..	..	..	..
Congo, People's Republic of the	..	..	..	..	..	..	..	..	..
Cote d'Ivoire	..	..	..	..	..	..	..	..	..
Djibouti	..	..	..	..	..	..	..	..	..
Equatorial Guinea	..	..	..	..	..	..	..	..	..
Ethiopia	..	..	..	..	..	..	..	..	..
Gabon	..	..	..	..	..	..	..	..	..
Gambia, The	..	..	..	..	..	..	..	..	..
Ghana	..	..	..	..	..	..	..	..	..
Guinea	..	..	..	..	..	..	..	..	..
Guinea-Bissau	..	..	..	..	..	..	..	..	..
Kenya	..	..	..	..	..	..	..	..	..
Lesotho	..	..	..	..	..	..	..	..	..
Liberia	..	..	..	..	..	..	..	..	..
Madagascar	..	..	..	..	..	..	..	..	..
Malawi	75.0	61.0	43.0	20.0	10.0	13.0	112.0	..	..
Mali	..	..	..	..	..	..	..	..	..
Mauritania	..	..	..	..	..	..	..	..	..
Mauritius	..	..	..	290.0	308.0	160.0	..	..	..
Mozambique	..	..	..	..	..	..	..	..	..
Namibia	..	..	..	..	..	..	..	..	..
Niger	..	..	..	..	..	..	..	..	..
Nigeria	..	..	..	..	..	..	..	..	..
Rwanda	..	..	..	..	..	..	..	..	..
Sao Tome & Principe	..	..	..	..	..	..	..	..	..
Senegal	..	..	..	..	..	..	..	..	..
Seychelles	..	..	..	..	..	..	..	..	..
Sierra Leone	..	..	..	21.0	..	..	..	..	..
Somalia	..	..	..	..	..	..	..	..	..
Sudan	..	..	..	..	..	..	..	..	..
Swaziland	..	..	..	..	..	..	..	..	..
Tanzania	..	447.0	654.0	635.0	465.0	677.0	793.0	..	..
Togo	..	..	..	..	..	..	..	..	..
Uganda	..	..	..	..	..	..	..	..	..
Zaire	..	..	..	..	..	..	..	..	..
Zambia	..	..	..	..	..	..	..	..	..
Zimbabwe	..	..	..	..	..	..	..	..	..
NORTH AFRICA	..	..	..	..	..	..	..	..	..
Algeria	..	..	..	..	..	..	..	..	..
Egypt, Arab Republic of	..	..	..	..	..	..	..	..	..
Libya	..	..	..	..	..	..	..	..	..
Morocco	..	..	..	..	..	..	..	..	..
Tunisia	..	..	..	..	..	..	..	..	..
ALL AFRICA	..	..	..	..	..	..	..	..	..
South Africa	..	..	..	..	..	..	..	..	..

Note: '*' = billions of local currency.

10–12. Public enterprise payments to government

	Billions of local currency											Average		
	1980	1981	1982	1983	1984	1985	1986	1987	1988	1989	1990	75–79	80–85	86–MR
SUB-SAHARAN AFRICA	..	..	..	..	..	..	..	..	..	..	..	..	..	..
excluding Nigeria	..	..	..	..	..	..	..	..	..	..	..	..	..	..
Angola	..	..	..	..	..	..	..	..	..	..	..	0.9	..	..
Benin	4.5	6.9	5.1	4.0	..	..	..	..	..	..	..	..	..	..
Botswana	..	..	..	..	..	..	..	..	..	..	..	2.1	2.7	2.5
Burkina Faso	1.5	3.4	1.4	3.7	2.9	3.2	3.0	2.1	..	..	..	0.2	0.7	..
Burundi	0.4	0.9	0.4	1.0	0.7	1.0	0.4	..	..	0.5	..	1.2	4.6	3.7
Cameroon	2.5	1.2	3.7	1.7	4.8	13.6	4.6	6.1	..	..	..	..	..	..
Cape Verde	..	..	..	..	..	..	..	..	..	..	..	..	1.0	..
Central African Republic	..	0.2	1.1	0.9	1.1	1.6	..	..	..	..	..	..	..	..
Chad	..	..	..	..	..	..	0.2	..	..	..	..	..	..	..
Comoros	..	..	..	..	..	..	..	..	..	..	..	..	..	..
Congo, People's Republic of the	0.2	0.0	0.1	4.6	..	..	..	..	..	..	..	..	..	..
Cote d'Ivoire	0.5	..	..	..	174.0	-4.7	..	..	..	..	..	..	..	..
Djibouti *	11.0	..	..	..	..	..	..	..	..	..	..	..	..	..
Equatorial Guinea	..	..	..	..	..	..	..	..	..	..	..	0.1	0.7	1.0
Ethiopia	0.3	0.6	0.7	1.0	0.9	0.8	1.1	1.0	..	..	..	..	..	..
Gabon	..	..	..	..	14.0	12.7	..	..	..	3.5	0.97	4.4	1.6	..
Gambia, The *	1.4	..	1.2	2.3	2.7	0.6	..	..	..	..	..	..	0.4	..
Ghana	0.2	0.2	0.2	1.0	0.3	0.5	0.5	..	..	..	..	1.3	2.5	..
Guinea	4.2	2.2	4.0	3.0	1.3	0.2	..	..	..	..	..	0.9	1.4	2.5
Guinea-Bissau	..	..	..	0.0	0.2	0.2	..	..	..	..	..	..	..	..
Kenya	1.0	1.2	1.2	1.8	1.6	..	1.9	2.1	2.4	3.7	..	..	..	9.8
Lesotho *	..	..	3.8	6.0	14.1	11.1	14.6	9.7	5.1	..	..	..	..	..
Liberia *	10.1	1.9	..	..	..	..	..	..	..	..	..	4.0	..	..
Madagascar	7.9	12.7	8.9	..	..	..	..	..	..	..	..	7.9	9.0	..
Malawi *	13.6	19.2	4.6	5.5	2.3	..	..	..	..	..	..	0.1	2.7	5.9
Mali	..	1.2	2.2	2.2	2.6	5.1	5.7	3.6	8.3	..	..	0.1	..	0.9
Mauritania	..	..	..	0.4	0.7	0.4	0.7	1.4	0.5	..	..	0.0	0.2	0.4
Mauritius	0.1	0.1	0.1	0.1	0.2	0.3	0.3	0.5	0.4	0.3	0.4	..	..	..
Mozambique	..	..	..	..	..	..	14.9	22	41.7	48.4	41.9	..	..	33.8
Namibia *	..	..	..	..	..	..	..	..	..	..	..	0.7	10.4	..
Niger	11.3	10.7	11.3	8.1	..	..	..	..	..	..	..	..	5.7	..
Nigeria	..	..	5.8	5.2	5.1	6.9	7.2	..	..	..	..	0.1	..	..
Rwanda	0.3	..	..	..	..	..	..	..	..	..	..	..	..	..
Sao Tome & Principe	..	..	..	..	..	..	..	..	..	..	..	0.3	0.5	..
Senegal	0.5	1.0	0.4	0.3	0.3	..	..	..	..	..	..	..	..	..
Seychelles	..	..	..	..	..	..	..	..	..	..	..	..	..	..
Sierra Leone *	..	..	..	3.0	..	..	..	..	..	..	..	..	0.8	..
Somalia	..	0.0	0.2	0.4	0.4	2.9	..	..	..	..	..	..	..	..
Sudan	..	..	..	..	..	..	..	..	..	..	..	3.9	8.9	19.9
Swaziland *	4.4	6.1	8.6	8.2	14.3	11.7	10.1	7.5	18.2	43.6	..	0.2	0.3	..
Tanzania	0.2	0.1	0.2	0.3	0.4	0.4	0.4	..	..	..	..	4.4	6.6	4.9
Togo	7.4	6.6	7.0	5.2	6.6	6.6	6.6	3.2	..	..	..	..	..	..
Uganda	..	..	..	..	..	..	..	..	..	..	..	1.0		
Zaire	..	..	2.1	1.1	2.9	5.2	..	..	..	..	..	18.2	89.1	102.1
Zambia *	72.1	31.3	48.5	139.4	180.8	62.4	52.5	167.1	86.6	..	..	0.1	0.2	..
Zimbabwe	0.1	0.1	0.2	0.2	0.2	0.2	..	..	..	..	..	..	..	..
NORTH AFRICA	..	..	..	..	..	..	..	..	..	..	..	..	..	..
Algeria	..	..	..	..	..	..	..	..	..	..	..	0.4	1.8	2.2
Egypt, Arab Republic of	1.6	1.7	1.6	2.0	2.1	1.9	2.2	1.9	2.2	2.5	..	..	..	..
Libya	..	..	..	..	..	..	..	..	..	..	..	0.9	1.8	0.8
Morocco	0.8	1.7	1.8	1.9	1.8	2.7	0.5	1.1	..	..	..	19.3	0.5	0.4
Tunisia	..	0.6	0.7	0.4	0.5	0.5	0.4	0.4	0.5	0.5	..	..	..	..
ALL AFRICA	..	..	..	..	..	..	..	..	..	..	..	..	..	..
South Africa	..	..	..	..	..	..	..	..	..	..	..	..	..	..

Note: '*' = millions of local currency.

10–13. Public enterprise payments as a share of government revenue

	1980	1981	1982	1983	1984	1985	1986	1987	1988	1989	1990
					Percent						
SUB-SAHARAN AFRICA	..	..	..	..	..	..	..	..	..	..	..
excluding Nigeria	..	..	..	..	..	..	..	..	..	..	..
Angola	..	..	..	..	..	..	..	..	..	..	..
Benin	9.3	9.0	6.0	5.2	..	..	..	..	..	..	..
Botswana	..	..	..	..	..	..	..	..	..	..	..
Burkina Faso	..	..	..	..	..	..	..	..	..	..	..
Burundi	..	..	..	5.8	3.2	4.0	..	..	..	..	..
Cameroon	..	0.3	0.7	..	0.7	..	..	..	..	..	..
Cape Verde	..	..	..	..	..	..	..	..	..	..	..
Central African Republic	..	..	2.8	2.3	2.6	..	..	..	..	..	..
Chad	..	..	..	..	..	..	..	..	..	..	..
Comoros	..	..	..	..	..	..	..	..	..	..	..
Congo, People's Republic of the	..	..	..	..	..	..	..	..	..	..	..
Cote d'Ivoire	..	..	..	..	..	..	..	..	..	..	..
Djibouti	..	..	..	..	..	..	..	..	..	..	..
Equatorial Guinea	..	..	..	..	..	..	..	..	..	..	..
Ethiopia	..	..	..	..	..	..	..	..	..	..	..
Gabon	..	..	..	..	..	..	..	..	..	..	..
Gambia, The	1.3	..	0.9	1.6	1.6	0.2	..	..	..	..	..
Ghana	5.8	6.3	3.5	9.5	1.3	1.4	0.6	..	..	..	..
Guinea	39.6	17.8	22.8	28.1	11.5	1.6	..	..	..	..	..
Guinea-Bissau	..	..	..	..	..	..	..	..	..	..	..
Kenya	..	..	..	..	..	..	..	..	..	..	..
Lesotho	..	..	..	..	..	..	..	..	..	..	..
Liberia	..	..	..	..	..	..	..	..	..	..	..
Madagascar	..	..	..	..	..	..	..	..	..	..	..
Malawi	..	..	..	..	..	..	..	..	..	..	..
Mali	..	3.0	5.5	4.7	5.1	..	..	..	..	..	..
Mauritania	..	..	..	..	..	..	..	..	..	..	..
Mauritius	..	..	..	4.6	6.7	8.0	..	..	..	..	..
Mozambique	..	..	..	..	..	..	..	..	..	..	..
Namibia	..	..	..	..	..	..	..	..	..	..	..
Niger	15.4	14.2	15.3	11.8	..	..	..	..	..	..	..
Nigeria	..	..	70.4	62.6	68.8	76.5	68.6	..	..	..	..
Rwanda	..	..	..	..	..	..	..	..	..	..	..
Sao Tome & Principe	..	..	..	..	..	..	..	..	..	..	..
Senegal	..	..	..	..	..	..	..	..	..	..	..
Seychelles	..	..	..	..	..	..	..	..	..	..	..
Sierra Leone	..	..	..	1.7	..	..	..	..	..	..	..
Somalia	..	1.4	5.9	8.2	5.9	20.7	..	..	..	..	..
Sudan	..	..	..	..	..	..	..	..	..	..	..
Swaziland	..	..	..	..	..	..	..	..	..	..	..
Tanzania	2.2	1.3	1.7	2.5	2.8	1.9	2.0	..	..	..	..
Togo	..	9.3	8.3	6.0	6.4	5.8	5.9	..	..	..	..
Uganda	..	..	..	..	..	..	..	..	..	..	..
Zaire	..	..	..	..	8.9	..	..	..	..	..	..
Zambia	9.1	3.8	5.6	13.0	15.5	..	..	..	..	..	..
Zimbabwe	..	..	..	..	..	..	..	..	..	..	..
NORTH AFRICA	..	..	..	..	..	..	..	..	..	..	..
Algeria	..	..	..	..	..	..	..	..	..	..	..
Egypt, Arab Republic of	..	..	..	..	..	..	..	..	..	..	..
Libya	..	..	..	..	..	..	..	..	..	..	..
Morocco	..	..	..	..	..	..	..	..	..	..	..
Tunisia	..	..	..	..	..	..	..	..	..	..	..
ALL AFRICA	..	..	..	..	..	..	..	..	..	..	..
South Africa	..	..	..	..	..	..	..	..	..	..	..

10-14. Government payments to public enterprises

	1980	1981	1982	1983	1984	1985	1986	1987	1988	1989	1990	75–79	80–85	:86–MR
SUB-SAHARAN AFRICA	..	..	..	..	..	..	..	..	..	..	..	..	..	..
excluding Nigeria	..	..	..	..	..	..	..	..	..	..	..	..	..	..
Angola	..	..	..	..	..	..	..	..	..	..	..	..	..	..
Benin	..	..	2.5	..	..	..	..	..	..	..	..	..	..	..
Botswana	..	..	..	..	..	..	..	..	..	..	..	..	..	..
Burkina Faso *	..	..	..	..	..	-8	72	..	..	..	..	..	..	..
Burundi	..	..	1.3	1.2	..	..	..	..	..	..	..	..	..	..
Cameroon	..	..	..	80.5	..	..	..	..	..	..	..	..	..	..
Cape Verde	..	..	..	..	..	..	..	..	..	..	..	..	..	..
Central African Republic	..	..	..	..	..	5.5	13.8	11.5	8.4	..	..	..	..	11.2
Chad	..	..	..	..	..	..	..	..	..	..	..	..	..	..
Comoros	..	..	..	..	..	..	..	..	..	..	..	..	..	..
Congo, People's Republic of the	..	4.6	12.5	6.9	6.9	6.7	..	..	..	..	..	..	7.5	..
Cote d'Ivoire	55.0	70.0	132.7	167.3	191.6	160.8	..	..	..	..	..	..	129.6	..
Djibouti	..	..	..	..	..	..	..	..	..	..	..	..	..	..
Equatorial Guinea	..	..	..	..	..	..	..	..	..	..	..	..	..	..
Ethiopia	..	..	0.0	0.7	0.1	0.1	0.1	0.0	..	..	..	..	..	0.1
Gabon	..	..	..	..	..	..	..	..	..	..	..	..	..	..
Gambia, The *	..	..	..	..	..	..	..	100.48	0.87	14.4	77.59	..	..	48.3
Ghana	0.1	0.2	0.1	0.1	0.7	1.9	3.7	0.6	..	..	..	..	0.5	2.2
Guinea	..	..	..	..	..	..	..	..	..	..	..	..	..	..
Guinea-Bissau	..	..	..	..	..	..	0.2	0.2	..	..	..	..	..	0.2
Kenya	..	0.5	1.0	0.5	0.5	0.7	72	..	..	..	..	..	0.6	..
Lesotho *	..	..	..	..	..	..	..	..	14.1	..	..	..	..	..
Liberia	..	..	..	..	..	..	..	..	..	..	..	..	..	..
Madagascar	..	..	..	..	..	..	..	..	..	..	..	..	..	..
Malawi *	75.0	61.0	43.0	20.0	10.0	13.0	112.0	..	..	..	..	..	37.0	..
Mali	..	..	..	..	..	..	0.1	0.1	..	..	..	..	..	0.1
Mauritania	..	..	..	1.0	..	..	..	..	..	..	..	..	..	..
Mauritius	..	..	0.4	0.5	0.4	0.1	0.3	0.4	0.1	0.0	..	..	..	0.2
Mozambique	..	..	..	..	..	..	..	..	..	..	..	..	..	..
Namibia	..	..	..	..	..	0.1	0.2	0.1	0.1	0.1	..	..	..	0.1
Niger	..	12.0	..	6.3	7.0	7.3	7.9	4.3	3.3	..	..	..	..	5.2
Nigeria	1.5	..	1.1	2.0	0.6	2.6	..	0.7	1.1	1.4	..	..	1.5	1.0
Rwanda	..	..	..	..	..	..	..	..	..	..	..	..	..	..
Sao Tome & Principe	..	..	..	..	..	..	..	..	..	..	..	..	..	..
Senegal *	..	24.6	22.6	22.6	22.4	22.1	21.6	22.1	..	..	..	..	22.9	21.9
Seychelles *	..	..	..	..	..	40.5	50.6	33.0	98.9	143.5	..	..	..	81.5
Sierra Leone *	..	..	..	24.0	35.0	..	..	..	..	..	..	..	..	..
Somalia	..	..	..	..	..	..	..	..	..	..	..	..	..	..
Sudan	..	..	..	..	..	..	..	..	..	..	..	..	..	..
Swaziland	..	..	..	..	..	..	..	..	..	..	..	..	..	..
Tanzania	..	0.6	0.9	1.0	0.9	1.1	1.2	..	..	..	..	..	0.9	..
Togo	..	..	..	..	..	..	..	16.8	..	..	..	..	..	..
Uganda	..	..	..	..	..	..	..	..	..	..	..	..	..	..
Zaire	..	..	..	..	..	..	..	..	..	..	..	..	..	..
Zambia *	279.1	28.8	114.6	20.2	26.7	..	568.8	4	..	..	..	..	93.9	286.4
Zimbabwe	..	..	..	..	..	..	..	..	..	..	..	..	..	..
NORTH AFRICA	..	..	..	..	..	..	..	..	..	..	..	..	..	..
Algeria	..	..	..	..	..	..	..	..	..	..	..	..	..	..
Egypt, Arab Republic of	..	..	..	..	..	..	..	2.6	4.7	2.1	..	..	..	3.1
Libya	..	..	..	..	..	..	..	..	..	..	..	..	..	..
Morocco	..	..	..	..	..	..	..	..	..	..	..	..	..	..
Tunisia	..	..	..	..	..	0.1	0.3	0.2	0.2	0.2	..	..	..	0.2
ALL AFRICA	..	..	..	..	..	..	..	..	..	..	..	..	..	..
South Africa	..	..	..	..	..	..	..	..	..	..	..	..	..	..

Notes: "*" = millions of local currency

10–15. Payments to public enterprise as a share of government expenditure

	Percent											Average		
	1980	1981	1982	1983	1984	1985	1986	1987	1988	1989	1990	75–79	80–85	86–MR
SUB-SAHARAN AFRICA	..	..	..	..	..	..	..	..	..	..	..	..	..	..
excluding Nigeria	..	..	..	..	..	..	..	..	..	..	..	..	..	..
Angola	..	..	..	..	..	..	..	..	..	..	..	..	..	..
Benin	7.3	9.4	4.9	3.6	..	..	..	..	..	..	..	..	..	..
Botswana	..	..	..	..	..	..	..	..	..	..	..	..	..	..
Burkina Faso	..	..	..	..	..	..	..	..	..	..	..	..	..	..
Burundi	..	..	5.4	4.2	..	..	..	..	..	..	..	..	..	..
Cameroon	..	..	..	13.1	..	..	..	..	..	..	..	..	..	..
Cape Verde	..	..	..	..	..	..	..	..	..	..	..	..	..	..
Central African Republic	..	..	..	..	..	12.6	30.6	..	..	..	..	..	..	..
Chad	..	..	..	..	..	..	..	..	..	..	..	..	..	..
Comoros	..	..	..	..	..	..	..	..	..	..	..	..	..	..
Congo, People's Republic of t	..	2.2	3.7	2.0	1.9	1.8	..	..	..	..	..	..	..	..
Cote d'Ivoire	6.2	7.8	13.2	16.2	18.7	16.5	..	..	..	..	..	..	13.1	..
Djibouti	..	..	..	..	..	..	..	..	..	..	..	..	..	..
Equatorial Guinea	..	..	..	..	..	..	..	..	..	..	..	..	..	..
Ethiopia	..	..	..	..	..	..	..	..	..	..	..	..	..	..
Gabon	..	..	..	..	..	..	..	..	..	..	..	..	..	..
Gambia, The	..	..	..	..	..	..	..	..	..	..	..	..	..	..
Ghana	3.1	2.6	1.4	0.6	2.5	3.9	5.0	0.6	..	..	..	..	2.4	..
Guinea	35.0	21.9	20.5	19.6	9.7	0.7	..	..	..	..	..	..	17.9	..
Guinea-Bissau	..	..	..	..	..	..	..	..	..	..	..	..	..	..
Kenya	..	2.4	4.9	2.3	2.2	2.5	2.7	..	..	..	..	..	..	..
Lesotho	..	..	..	..	..	..	..	..	..	..	..	..	..	..
Liberia	..	..	..	..	..	..	..	..	..	..	..	..	..	..
Madagascar	..	..	..	..	..	..	..	..	..	..	..	..	..	..
Malawi	20.9	15.5	10.7	4.5	2.0	2.2	18.4	..	..	..	..	..	9.3	..
Mali	..	..	..	..	..	..	..	..	..	..	..	..	..	..
Mauritania	..	..	..	5.5	..	..	..	..	..	..	..	..	..	..
Mauritius	..	..	..	10.6	13.0	10.1	..	..	..	..	..	..	..	..
Mozambique	..	..	..	..	..	..	..	..	..	..	..	..	..	..
Namibia	..	..	..	..	..	..	..	..	..	..	..	..	..	..
Niger	..	11.3	..	4.9	5.7	5.6	5.9	3.2	2.5	..	..	..	..	..
Nigeria	12.1	..	8.7	14.0	5.6	23.0	..	2.4	..	..	..	..	..	..
Rwanda	..	..	..	..	..	..	..	..	..	..	..	..	..	..
Sao Tome & Principe	..	..	..	..	..	..	..	..	..	..	..	..	..	..
Senegal	..	14.1	9.7	9.0	9.1	8.7	8.1	..	..	..	..	..	..	..
Seychelles	..	..	..	..	..	..	..	..	..	..	..	..	..	..
Sierra Leone	..	..	..	5.9	7.5	..	..	..	..	..	..	..	..	..
Somalia	..	..	..	..	..	..	..	..	..	..	..	..	..	..
Sudan	..	..	..	..	..	..	..	..	..	..	..	..	..	..
Swaziland	..	..	..	..	..	..	..	..	..	..	..	..	..	..
Tanzania	..	4.1	4.5	5.2	4.3	4.1	4.2	..	..	..	..	..	..	..
Togo	..	..	..	..	..	..	..	..	..	..	..	..	..	..
Uganda	..	..	..	..	..	..	..	..	..	..	..	..	..	..
Zaire	..	..	..	..	..	..	..	..	..	..	..	..	..	..
Zambia	..	..	..	..	..	..	..	..	..	..	..	..	..	..
Zimbabwe	..	..	..	..	..	..	..	..	..	..	..	..	..	..
NORTH AFRICA	..	..	..	..	..	..	..	..	..	..	..	..	..	..
Algeria	..	..	..	..	..	..	..	..	..	..	..	..	..	..
Egypt, Arab Republic of	..	..	..	..	..	..	..	..	..	..	..	..	..	..
Libya	..	..	..	..	..	..	..	..	..	..	..	..	..	..
Morocco	..	..	..	..	..	..	..	..	..	..	..	..	..	..
Tunisia	..	..	..	..	..	..	..	..	..	..	..	..	..	..
ALL AFRICA	..	..	..	..	..	..	..	..	..	..	..	..	..	..
South Africa	..	..	..	..	..	..	..	..	..	..	..	..	..	..

10–16. Subsidies to public enterprises

		Billions of local currency											Average		
		1980	1981	1982	1983	1984	1985	1986	1987	1988	1989	1990	75–79	80–85	86–MR
SUB-SAHARAN AFRICA		..	..	..	..	..	..	..	..	..	..	..	..	..	..
excluding Nigeria		..	..	..	..	..	..	..	..	..	..	..	..	..	..
Angola		..	..	..	..	..	..	..	..	..	..	..	..	..	..
Benin		..	..	0.2	..	..	..	..	..	..	..	..	..	..	..
Botswana	*	..	..	0.1	..	0.1	0.1	0.1	..	..	..	..	..	..	..
Burkina Faso		..	..	..	..	..	..	..	..	..	..	..	..	..	..
Burundi	*	..	..	120.0	24.0	141.0	..	..	..	..	..	..	..	..	..
Cameroon		..	..	..	25.0	..	..	..	..	..	..	..	..	..	..
Cape Verde		..	..	..	..	..	..	..	..	..	..	..	..	..	..
Central African Republic		..	..	1.8	0.5	4.1									
Chad		..	..	..	..	..	..	..	..	..	..	..	..	..	..
Comoros		..	..	..	..	..	..	..	..	..	..	..	..	..	..
Congo, People's Republic of the		..	4.6	11.6	6.8	6.2	6.8	..	..	..	..	..	..	7.2	..
Cote d'Ivoire		..	..	14.0	14.9	10.8	10.8	..	..	..	..	..	..	..	..
Djibouti		..	..	..	..	..	..	..	..	..	..	..	..	..	..
Equatorial Guinea		..	..	..	..	..	..	..	..	..	..	..	..	..	..
Ethiopia	*	..	..	25.4	284.9	44.5	36.4	62.5	57.3	..	..	..	..	..	59.9
Gabon		..	..	..	..	..	..	..	..	..	..	..	..	..	..
Gambia, The	*	..	5.0	1.2	..	0.4	16.3	..	..	..	..	..	..	..	..
Ghana		0.4	0.6	0.7	1.1	0.4	0.9	1.0	..	..	..	..	..	0.7	..
Guinea		..	..	..	..	..	..	..	..	..	..	..	..	..	..
Guinea-Bissau	*	..	9.0	48.0	83.0	34.0	64.0	42.0	152	567	..	..	..	47.6	253.7
Kenya	*	..	200.0	80.0	80.0	110.0	..	..	..	..	..	..	..	117.5	..
Lesotho	*	..	..	..	..	..	..	..	..	14.1	..	..	..	..	..
Liberia		..	..	..	..	..	..	..	..	..	..	..	..	..	..
Madagascar	*	750.0	159.0	136.0	20.0	..	..	..	..	..	..	..	..	..	..
Malawi	*	0.2	0.3	0.6	0.3	1.5	1.6	1.5	..	..	..	..	..	0.8	..
Mali	*	..	..	..	..	..	..	100	100	..	..	..	..	..	100.0
Mauritania		..	..	..	..	..	..	..	..	..	..	..	..	..	..
Mauritius		..	..	..	0.1	0.2	0.2	..	..	..	..	..	..	..	..
Mozambique		..	..	..	..	..	..	..	..	..	..	..	..	..	..
Namibia	*	..	..	..	..	..	..	66.7	61.4	44.2	43	45.8	..	..	52.2
Niger		2.6	2.4	2.4	1.3	1.7	2.1	2.9	..	..	..	..	..	2.1	..
Nigeria		..	..	..	..	..	..	..	..	..	..	..	..	..	..
Rwanda	*	42.0	284.0	526.0	218.0	56.0	..	..	..	..	..	..	..	225.2	..
Sao Tome & Principe		..	..	..	..	..	..	..	..	..	..	..	..	..	..
Senegal		..	4.8	7.2	2.7	7.4	4.5	7.6	..	..	..	..	..	5.3	..
Seychelles		..	..	..	..	..	..	..	..	..	..	..	..	..	..
Sierra Leone	*	..	6.0	6.0	..	..	..	..	..	..	..	..	..	..	..
Somalia		..	..	..	..	..	..	..	..	..	..	..	..	..	..
Sudan		..	..	..	..	..	..	..	..	..	..	..	..	..	..
Swaziland		..	..	..	..	..	..	..	..	..	..	..	..	..	..
Tanzania		0.2	0.3	0.6	..	..	..	..	..	..	..	..	..	..	..
Togo		..	..	..	..	..	0.4	..	3.7	..	..	..	..	..	..
Uganda		..	..	..	..	..	..	..	..	..	..	..	..	..	..
Zaire		..	..	..	..	..	..	0.3	..	..	..	..	..	..	..
Zambia	*	..	..	..	..	..	..	568.8	4	..	..	..	..	..	286.4
Zimbabwe		..	..	..	..	..	..	..	..	..	..	..	..	..	..
NORTH AFRICA		..	..	..	..	..	..	..	..	..	..	..	..	..	..
Algeria		..	..	..	..	..	..	..	..	..	..	..	..	..	..
Egypt, Arab Republic of		..	..	..	..	..	..	..	1.7	3.2	..	..	..	..	2.4
Libya		..	..	..	..	..	..	..	..	..	..	..	..	..	..
Morocco		..	..	..	..	..	..	..	..	..	..	..	..	..	..
Tunisia	*	..	..	..	..	..	6.8	6.4	6.6	51.3	64.8	..	..	..	32.3
ALL AFRICA		..	..	..	..	..	..	..	..	..	..	..	..	..	..
South Africa		..	..	..	..	..	..	..	..	..	..	..	..	..	..

Note: '*' = millions of local currency.

10–17. Subsidies to public enterprises as share of government expenditure

	Percent											Average		
	1980	1981	1982	1983	1984	1985	1986	1987	1988	1989	1990	75–79	80–85	86–MR
SUB-SAHARAN AFRICA	..	..	..	..	..	..	..	..	..	..	..	..	..	..
excluding Nigeria	..	..	..	..	..	..	..	..	..	..	..	..	..	..
Angola	..	..	..	..	..	..	..	..	..	..	..	..	..	..
Benin	..	..	0.2	..	..	..	..	..	..	..	..	..	..	..
Botswana *	..	..	..	..	..	..	..	..	..	..	..	..	..	..
Burkina Faso	..	..	..	..	..	..	..	..	..	..	..	..	..	..
Burundi *	..	..	0.5	0.1	0.5	..	..	..	..	..	..	..	..	..
Cameroon	..	..	..	7.3	..	..	..	..	..	..	..	..	..	..
Cape Verde	..	..	..	..	..	..	..	..	..	..	..	..	..	..
Central African Republic	..	..	4.6	1.3	10.3	..	..	..	..	..	..	..	..	..
Chad	..	..	..	..	..	..	..	..	..	..	..	..	..	..
Comoros	..	..	..	..	..	..	..	..	..	..	..	..	..	..
Congo, People's Republic of the	..	4.3	8.4	3.5	3.1	2.9	..	..	..	..	..	..	4.4	..
Cote d'Ivoire	..	..	3.0	3.2	1.4	1.3	..	..	..	..	..	..	2.2	..
Djibouti	..	..	..	..	..	..	..	..	..	..	..	..	..	..
Equatorial Guinea	..	..	..	..	..	..	..	..	..	..	..	..	..	..
Ethiopia *	..	..	1.0	7.5	1.5	1.1	1.7	1.5	..	..	..	..	2.8	1.6
Gabon	..	..	..	..	..	..	..	..	..	..	..	..	..	..
Gambia, The *	..	3.4	0.7	..	0.2	6.2	..	..	..	..	..	..	2.6	..
Ghana	8.9	9.8	8.5	8.4	1.9	2.2	1.6	..	..	..	..	..	6.6	..
Guinea	..	..	..	..	..	..	..	..	..	..	..	..	..	..
Guinea-Bissau *	..	0.5	2.2	3.6	0.9	1.1	0.2	0.3	0.6	..	..	..	1.7	0.4
Kenya *	..	1.6	0.5	0.5	0.6	..	..	..	..	..	..	..	0.8	..
Lesotho *	..	..	..	..	..	..	..	..	2.4	..	..	..	..	..
Liberia	..	..	..	..	..	..	..	..	..	..	..	..	..	..
Madagascar *	0.4	0.1	0.1	0.0	..	..	..	..	..	..	..	..	0.1	..
Malawi *	0.1	0.1	0.2	0.1	0.5	0.4	0.2	..	..	..	..	..	0.2	..
Mali *	..	..	..	..	..	..	0.1	0.1	..	..	..	..	..	0.1
Mauritania	..	..	..	..	..	..	..	..	..	..	..	..	..	..
Mauritius	..	..	..	4.5	6.2	5.9	..	..	..	..	..	..	..	..
Mozambique	..	..	..	..	..	..	..	..	..	..	..	..	..	..
Namibia *	..	..	..	..	..	..	4.7	3.7	2.5	2.2	..	..	..	3.3
Niger	5.1	4.7	4.3	2.3	2.6	2.9	2.2	..	..	..	..	..	3.7	..
Nigeria	..	..	..	..	..	..	..	..	..	..	..	..	..	..
Rwanda *	0.4	1.2	2.1	0.8	0.2	..	..	..	..	..	..	..	0.9	..
Sao Tome & Principe	..	..	..	..	..	..	..	..	..	..	..	..	..	..
Senegal	..	3.4	4.3	1.5	3.6	2.1	2.8	..	..	..	..	..	3.0	..
Seychelles	..	..	..	..	..	..	..	..	..	..	..	..	..	..
Sierra Leone *	..	2.1	2.2	..	..	..	..	..	..	..	..	..	..	..
Somalia	..	..	..	..	..	..	..	..	..	..	..	..	..	..
Sudan	..	..	..	..	..	..	..	..	..	..	..	..	..	..
Swaziland	..	..	..	..	..	..	..	..	..	..	..	..	..	..
Tanzania	2.8	3.7	4.2	..	..	..	..	..	..	..	..	..	..	..
Togo	..	..	..	..	..	0.3	..	3.1	..	..	..	..	..	..
Uganda	..	..	..	..	..	..	..	..	..	..	..	..	..	..
Zaire	..	..	..	..	..	..	0.4	..	..	..	..	..	..	..
Zambia *	..	..	..	..	..	..	9.5	0.1	..	..	..	..	..	4.8
Zimbabwe	..	..	..	..	..	..	..	..	..	..	..	..	..	..
NORTH AFRICA	..	..	..	..	..	..	..	..	..	..	..	..	..	..
Algeria	..	..	..	..	..	..	..	..	..	..	..	..	..	..
Egypt, Arab Republic of	..	..	..	..	..	..	..	8.1	12.9	..	..	..	..	10.5
Libya	..	..	..	..	..	..	..	..	..	..	..	..	..	..
Morocco	..	..	..	..	..	..	..	..	..	..	..	..	..	..
Tunisia *	..	..	..	..	..	0.3	0.2	0.2	1.7	1.8	..	..	..	1.0
ALL AFRICA	..	..	..	..	..	..	..	..	..	..	..	..	..	..
South Africa	..	..	..	..	..	..	..	..	..	..	..	..	..	..

10–18. Summary of key reforms implemented 1983–1990

	Privatization (sale of shares)		Liquidation (sale of assets)		Rehabilitation		Management contracts	Performance contracts	Number of PE studies for divestiture
	Completed	Under way	Completed	Under way	Completed	Under way			
SUB-SAHARAN AFRICA	..	..	..	..	..	..	..	..	..
excluding Nigeria	..	..	..	..	..	..	..	..	..
Angola	..	..	..	..	..	..	..	..	..
Benin	8	6	15	..	..	..	2	2	11
Botswana	..	..	..	..	..	..	..	..	..
Burkina Faso	..	..	..	..	..	..	..	..	..
Burundi	..	..	..	4	..	5	..	..	..
Cameroon	1	..	5	..	1	..	3	..	1
Cape Verde	..	..	..	..	..	..	..	..	..
Central African Republic	..	4	1	3	1	..	1	2	2
Chad	..	..	..	..	..	..	..	..	..
Comoros	..	..	..	..	..	..	..	..	..
Congo	..	..	..	..	7	..	..	..	..
Cote d' Ivoire	14	..	24	..	..	..	5	1	..
Djibouti	..	..	..	..	..	..	..	..	..
Equatorial Guinea	..	..	..	..	..	..	..	..	..
Ethiopia	..	..	..	..	..	..	..	..	..
Gabon	..	..	..	..	..	..	..	..	..
Gambia	1	3	1	..	1	..	1	3	3
Ghana	15	5	23	5	..	14	5	13	40
Guinea	19	11	70	15	..	..	..	..	..
Guinea-Bissau	..	..	..	..	1	..	..	..	..
Kenya	..	1	..	..	2	..	2	..	..
Lesotho	..	..	..	..	..	..	..	..	..
Liberia	..	..	..	..	..	..	..	..	7
Madagascar	34	37	12	..	..	..	..	..	35
Malawi	1	..	..	..	2	..	1	..	5
Mali	2	..	7	..	3	..	2	..	..
Mauritania	2	2	1	4	6	3	1	..	30
Mauritius	..	..	..	..	..	..	..	..	..
Mozambique	..	..	..	..	..	..	..	..	..
Namibia	..	..	..	..	..	..	..	..	..
Niger	12	6	4	..	7	..	3	..	22
Nigeria	2	6	..	4	..	..	..	..	..
Rwanda	1	..	..	..	..	..	..	..	..
Sao Tome & Principe	..	..	..	..	..	..	..	..	..
Senegal	4	18	18	5	4	..	2	9	..
Seychelles	..	..	..	..	..	..	..	..	..
Sierra Leone	1	..	..	5	6	6	4	..	10
Somalia	1	..	..	..	3	..	1	..	..
Sudan	3	1	..	..	10	..	1	..	..
Swaziland	..	..	..	..	..	..	..	..	..
Tanzania	1	2	..	..	..	..	2	..	..
Togo	6	..	12	7	..	..	7	..	7
Uganda	7	5	1	..	..	..	..	..	..
Zaire	1	..	3	..	2	..	8	..	..
Zambia	1	..	..	..	..	..	6	..	..
Zimbabwe	..	..	..	..	..	..	..	..	..
NORTH AFRICA	..	..	..	..	..	..	..	..	..
Algeria	..	..	..	..	..	..	..	..	..
Egypt	..	..	..	..	..	..	..	..	..
Libya	..	..	..	..	..	..	..	..	..
Morocco	..	..	..	..	..	..	..	..	..
Tunisia	..	..	..	..	..	..	..	..	..
ALL AFRICA	..	..	..	..	..	..	..	..	..
South Africa	..	..	..	..	..	..	..	..	..

10-19. Physical/financial restructuring and management reforms 1983-90

| | Restructuring | | | | Financial performance | | | Management, legal and institutional reforms | | | | |
	Physical investmen	Cross debts	Budget policy	Credit policy	Price-liberal-ization	Personne reduction	Accounting and auditing	PE class-ification	Government supervisory role	Autonomy to board of directors	Perform-ance contracts	Manage-ment contracts
SUB-SAHARAN AFRICA	..	..	..	..	..	..	..	..	..	..	..	..
excluding Nigeria	..	..	..	..	..	..	..	..	..	..	..	..
Angola	..	..	..	..	..	..	..	..	..	..	..	..
Benin	..	..	..	..	..	..	85	86	..	..	X	..
Botswana	..	..	..	..	..	..	..	..	..	..	..	..
Burkina Faso	..	..	..	..	..	..	..	..	..	..	..	..
Burundi	..	..	86	86	86	..	87	..	86	..	..	..
Cameroon	85	..	..	..	85	..	..	87	..	..	..	X
Cape Verde	..	..	..	..	..	..	..	..	..	..	..	..
Central African Republic	..	..	..	..	85	..	..	..	..	..	..	..
Chad	..	..	..	..	..	..	..	..	..	..	..	..
Comoros	..	..	..	..	..	..	..	..	..	..	..	..
Congo, People's Republic of	..	86	..	86	86	85	..	..	..	..	..	..
Cote d'Ivoire	86	..	..	86	..	..	..	..	87	..	..	X
Djibouti	..	..	..	..	..	..	..	..	..	..	..	..
Equatorial Guinea	..	..	..	..	..	..	..	..	..	..	..	..
Ethiopia	..	..	..	..	..	..	..	..	..	..	X	..
Gabon	..	..	..	..	..	..	..	..	..	..	..	..
Gambia, The	83	86	..	86	86	86	86	X	86	86	86,87	X
Ghana	87	85	..	..	84	87	87	..	87	87	..	82,83,84
Guinea	..	X	..	..	..	85	..	X	X	..	..	X
Guinea-Bissau	X	..	..	..	..	86	X	..	86	86	..	87
Kenya	X	..	..	85	..	..	..	..	86	..	..	X
Lesotho	..	..	..	..	..	..	..	..	..	..	..	..
Liberia	..	..	..	..	..	..	..	..	..	..	..	..
Madagascar	81,85	87	..	86	86	85,86	83,84	..	X	..	..	..
Malawi	X	..	..	..	85	83	..	..	..	..	..	X
Mali	86	..	X	X	85	83	X	..	..	X	..	X
Mauritania	X	84	..	..	85	..	..	..	..	..	..	X
Mauritius	..	..	..	..	..	..	..	..	..	..	..	..
Mozambique	..	..	..	..	..	..	..	..	..	..	..	..
Namibia	..	..	..	..	..	..	..	..	..	..	..	..
Niger	86	85	..	86	..	83,85	83	83	86	..	X	83
Nigeria	..	..	..	87	..	..	..	80	..	X	..	..
Rwanda	..	..	X	..	..	..	84	..	..	..	..	..
Sao Tome & Principe	..	..	..	..	..	..	85	..	..	..	..	..
Senegal	83,85	..	86	86	..	..	..	83,85,87	..	..	84,85,87	86
Seychelles	..	..	..	..	..	..	..	..	..	..	..	..
Sierra Leone	..	..	..	..	86	..	..	..	86	..	..	..
Somalia	86	..	..	..	..	..	..	86	85	..	..	..
Sudan	..	..	..	..	..	..	87	84	..	85	..	..
Swaziland	..	..	..	..	..	..	..	..	..	..	..	..
Tanzania	..	..	..	..	85	X	..	..	..	..	..	..
Togo	..	X	..	..	83	..	..	X	X	..	..	85
Uganda	..	..	..	..	..	..	..	..	..	..	..	..
Zaire	84	X	..	..	83	X	..	84	..	..	..	85
Zambia	..	..	..	..	..	..	..	..	X	X	..	..
Zimbabwe	..	..	..	..	..	..	..	..	..	..	..	..
NORTH AFRICA	..	..	..	..	..	..	..	..	..	..	..	..
Algeria	..	..	..	..	..	..	..	..	..	..	..	..
Egypt, Arab Republic of	..	..	..	..	..	..	..	..	..	..	..	..
Libya	..	..	..	..	..	..	..	..	..	..	..	..
Morocco	..	..	..	..	..	..	..	..	..	..	..	..
Tunisia	..	..	..	..	..	..	..	..	..	..	..	..
ALL AFRICA	..	..	..	..	..	..	..	..	..	..	..	..
South Africa	..	..	..	..	..	..	..	..	..	..	..	..

Technical Notes

In common usage, the term "public enterprise" is synonymous with the term" state-owned enterprise." They are generally majority-owned by government, and their borrowing is implicitly or explicitly guaranteed by government. Public enterprises (PEs) are singled out from other government activities because they are expected to earn most of their revenue from the sale of goods and services. PEs have a separate legal identity, and their accounts are conventionally separated from government finance accounts, in part because their productive activities use different accounting conventions.

Major mineral or commodity-exporting enterprises that weigh heavily on the size and performance of the sector are included in PE sectoral data for most countries; financial enterprises and regulatory, educational, health, and promotional agencies are excluded, except otherwise indicated in the table notes. This chapter contains data on more than 31 Sub-Saharan African countries, although for most indicators data are available for considerably fewer.

Data measuring the size and importance of the PE sector are drawn from nationally aggregated PE accounts and from World Bank and IMF staff reports. For some countries, the data cover only part of the PE sector; the resulting underestimation in the aggregate figures can usually be approximated from information in the table notes. Only a sample of PEs are covered in different tables for different countries.

Table 10-1. Number of PEs

For most countries, this measures the changes brought about by the creation or dissolution of PEs. In a few cases, improved monitoring or reclassification have resulted in revised figures, especially in recent years. Figures for the period from 1986 for most of the countries are from the *IMF's Government Finance Statistics Yearbooks* (various issues). Figures for 1986 for the Sudan, 1987 for Ghana, Guinea and Madagascar and 1988 for Ghana are from World Bank sources. Discrepancies result from coverage for different years/sources. In most cases the figures are for Central Government PEs, although sometimes figures for PEs operated by other tiers of government are included, figures for Botswana are for 1978. In a country like Zambia, the ZIMCO group represents 95 percent of PE turnover.

Table 10-2. PE contribution to GDP

This is the sum of PE value added as a share of total GDP (at purchaser values, as shown in Table 2-19). PE value added equals PE income (that is, sales plus royalties plus other trading income) less materials and services purchased outside the enterprise. (It can be estimated as wage payments plus the operating surplus.) Figures for Ethiopia are for manufacturing PEs only.

Table 10-3. PE share of domestic investment

Is the ratio of the addition to capital stock of public enterprises, excluding changes in inventories, to gross domestic investment, which does include changes in inventories (see Table 2-8 for discussion) but is used because it is the most common measure of total domestic investment. Data for Congo are for net investment.

Tables 10-4. PE share of formal sector employment

The PE share of formal sector employment is based on table 10-5 below.

Table 10-5. Number of persons employed in the PE sector

The number of people employed is defined as full-time employees, although seasonal and temporary workers also constitute part of the PE workforce. All employment data, including total formal sector employment, must be viewed as approximations, since survey techniques and accuracy may vary widely across countries, and these differences among countries will be reflected in the ratios. Formal sector implies wage employment, although definitions may vary.

Table 10-6. PE share of domestic credit outstanding

PEs borrow from government as well as from foreign and domestic financial markets. Data are available from World Bank and IMF country reports and, for some (non-CFA franc zone) countries, from line 32c of the *IFS* (which is generally the sum of central bank claims on PEs (line 12c) and deposit money bank claims on PEs (line 22c). Negative figures imply a large net government surplus to the Central Bank.

Table 10-7. PE share of external debt outstanding

The share of external debt attributable to PEs is defined as debt outstanding and disbursed that has been borrowed directly by PEs; it generally does not include debt that has been assumed or incurred by government on behalf of PEs. The figures may thus understate the actual share of PEs in external debt. These data are from the World Bank DRS. Totals are for longterm debt (see Tables 6-23, 6-24, and 6-25).

Table 10-8. PE net financial results

PE net financial results or aggregate sector profits less aggregate sector losses, as defined here exclude certain flows between PEs and government (subsidies, transfers, and taxes) but include interest payments and depreciation that are treated as costs of doing business. Taxes, subsidies, and transfers are excluded because they are not applied uniformly. For example, in some cases, some governments may collect taxes from some PEs and then provide subsidies, while in other cases, governments may forego taxes in lieu of paying subsidies to some PEs. Thus, financial results in most cases will equal the operating surplus or deficit plus interest payments and depreciation less subsidies, transfers, and taxes. Even though financial data for many countries are drawn from samples of enterprises, the results may be considered fairly indicative of general patterns and trends since the samples generally cover considerably more than half the PE sector. Exceptions are marked in the table notes. The data for these indicators are drawn largely from World Bank, IMF, and consultants' reports, as well as from aggregated PE accounts from country sources.

Tables 10-9 and 10-10. PE net financial results as ratio of GDP and of government expenditure

Although PE losses are partly financed from sources other than government, comparison with government expenditures is relevant because PEs are part of the public sector and the governments may eventually have to budget for PE losses. Data on government expenditure are based on Table 7-4.

Table 10-11. Net financial flows between government and PEs

This is the difference between total PE payments to government and total government payments to PEs (as defined below). Net financial flows exclude government loans to PEs, as well as interest and amortization payments to government. Implicit flows, such as the accumulation or retirement of arrears between PEs and government and government assumption of PE debt, are also excluded.

The poor data coverage for net financial flows can be overcome somewhat by estimating roughly comparable figures from the two component tables — PE payments to government and government payments to PEs — which have more data. (This is done by converting the respective flows to ratios to GDP (from Table 2-5), a common base, and comparing averages of country experiences.) Government assumption of PE debt are excluded.

Table 10-12. PE payments to government

Figures for PE payments to government (taxes, dividends, and net profits) may be underestimated because data on trading profits transferred to government are sometimes not available for major exporting PEs (for instance, the petroleum company in Cameroon).

Table 10-13. PE payments as a share of government revenue

PE payments to government are also shown as a share of government revenue (including grants) (from Table 7-6).

Table 10-14. Government payments to PEs

In the other direction government payments to PE consists of capital transfers (unrequited receipts to acquire capital or equity), debt servicing, and subsidies. Debt servicing takes two forms: government forgiveness of its own outstanding loans to PEs (through write-offs and equity conversions) and debt service payments on behalf of PEs to third parties, mainly domestic and external banks. Government assumption of PE debt is not available.

Table 10-15. Payments to PEs as a share of government expenditure

Payments to PEs are also shown as a share of government expenditure (current and capital from Table 7-4).

Table 10-16. Subsidies to PEs

These are operating subsidies. They may compensate PEs that provide social services on behalf of government, and they are sometimes used to cover operating losses. These subsidies may be difficult to distinguish from capital transfers owing to different accounting conventions and general lack of transparency in these flows.

Table 10-17. Subsidies to PEs as a share of government expenditure

Subsidies to PEs are also shown here, as a share of government expenditure (comparable with total government expenditure and lending minus repayments (see Table 7-4) less capital expenditure (see Table 7-23)) of which they are a component.

Table 10-18. Summary of key reforms implemented, 1983-90

This table provides a count of reform actions taken from 1983 to mid-1988, most since 1985. For some indicators, a second column shows the number of actions under-way but not fully implemented. More details on these reforms and the sources of data in the reforms tables are available in Candoy-Sekse (1988), Hemming and Mansoor (1988), and Swanson and Wolde-Semait (1989). Other sources are listed in the references at the end of the book.

Table 10-19. Physical and financial restructuring and management reforms, 1983-90

These reforms are designed to improve the performance and accountability of PEs through physical investment and financial restructuring as well as through management, legal, and institutional changes. Financial restructuring includes measures to decrease cross-debts among PEs, reduce or eliminate operating subsidies provided by government, and limit PE access to domestic bank lending for covering operating losses. Financial performance reforms aim to raise PE revenues or decrease expenditures; they include raising prices and reducing payrolls. The data also cover measures affecting the government's role in the sector (for example, policies to decrease government managerial intervention while promoting accountability of PEs through improved auditing, increased autonomy for PE boards of directors, and performance and management contracts). An X indicates that year of implementation is undetermined.

11

Labor Force and Employment

This chapter presents data on the level and structure of the labor force. The distribution of the labor force into various industrial activities is also given, as well as the participation rates of the population in economic activities. Information is also presented on minimum wage data.

The treatment of statistics on public sector employment is not homogenous among countries. The scope covered often varies. While some countries include education and health sectors, others leave them out. Staff of local, regional, and state or provincial governments are likewise treated differently. For these reasons data on public sector employment in this volume have been limited to number employed in the central government to permit greater comparability.

The stipulations on minimum wage take different forms among the countries where such practice exists. While some countries have a minimum wage per hour worked, others stipulate a minimum monthly wage for a worker. To permit some measure of comparability, we have computed and reported the annual earnings at minimum wage, irrespective of whether the minimum wage is per hour or per month. The annual earnings are further converted to U.S. dollars at the official exchange rate. These data should be used with caution since some countries have more than one minimum wage rate based on the industry and the

occupation within the industry, as well as the region of the country concerned.

The definition of labor force or economically active population is that used by the International Labour Organization (ILO), which follows the U.N. system of national accounts. The labor force is measured by dividing economically active persons into two categories: employed and unemployed. Caution in the use of the data is necessary for, as pointed out in the ILO's "World Labor Report 1," there are many persons who do not clearly come within one of these categories or the other. Many are visibly underemployed in that they work less than full time. Others work full time but earn less than a subsistence income. Some of the unemployed may even be voluntarily idle.

The comparability of the data is further hampered by the fact that practices vary among countries as regards the treatment of such groups as armed forces, inmates of institutions, persons living on reservations, persons seeking their first job, seasonal workers, and persons engaged in part-time economic activities. In some countries, all or part of these groups are included among the economically active, while in others they are treated as inactive. In addition, the extent to which family workers who assist in family enterprises are included among the enumerated economically active population, particularly females, varies considerably from country to country. Further, in some countries the statistics of the economically active relate only to employed and unemployed persons above a specified age, while in others there is no such age provision.

The reference period is also an important factor of difference, especially when it comes to the classification of the labor force according to industry. In some countries, such classification refers to the actual position of each individual on the day of the census or survey date, while in others the data recorded refer to the usual position of each person, generally without reference to any given period of time. The group summaries are all population weighted. When a country lacks data for a period, it is eliminated from the group before the group summary is calculated. This ensures that the same countries are used to represent a given group for all the periods shown. If data are missing for more than one-third of the countries in a group, group summaries are not computed for that indicator.

11-1. Number and gender structure of the labor force

	Total labor force						Percentage of total labor force that are females					
	Number in thousands			Average annual percentage growth			Percentage			Average annual percentage		
	1980	1985	1990	75–80	80–85	86–90	1980	1985	1990	75–79	80–85	86–90
SUB-SAHARAN AFRICA	155,591	174,991	197,901	2.7	2.4	2.5	39.3	38.5	37.6	39.6	38.9	38.0
excluding Nigeria	155,591	174,991	197,901	2.5	2.4	2.5	29.8	29.2	28.5	40.3	29.4	28.7
Angola	3,414	3,719	4,081	2.9	1.7	1.9	40.6	39.7	38.6	40.8	40.1	39.0
Benin	1,775	1,964	2,195	2.2	2.0	2.2	48.9	48.3	47.4	48.6	48.6	47.7
Botswana	321	381	446	2.9	3.5	3.1	37.8	36.3	34.9	39.5	37.1	35.4
Burkina Faso	3,421	3,765	4,167	1.9	1.9	2.0	47.8	47.0	46.2	48.0	47.4	46.5
Burundi	2,280	2,520	2,820	1.3	2.0	2.2	49.1	48.3	47.3	49.3	48.7	47.7
Cameroon	3,618	3,958	4,365	1.6	1.8	2.0	35.5	34.4	33.3	36.1	34.9	33.7
Cape Verde	102	121	141	1.0	3.5	3.0	27.7	28.8	29.1	26.5	28.3	29.0
Central African Republic	1,200	1,282	1,384	1.3	1.3	1.5	48.0	46.9	45.7	48.4	47.5	46.2
Chad	1,635	1,790	1,971	1.8	1.8	1.9	22.4	21.7	21.1	22.6	22.0	21.3
Comoros	181	204	231	3.1	2.4	2.5	42.4	41.4	40.4	42.5	41.9	40.8
Congo, People's Republic of	649	710	781	2.2	1.8	1.9	39.8	39.3	38.8	39.9	39.6	39.0
Cote d'Ivoire	3,547	4,053	4,599	2.4	2.7	2.5	34.9	34.7	34.2	35.9	34.8	34.4
Djibouti	..	..	..	..	..	..	..	..	..	..	..	..
Equatorial Guinea	159	169	182	1.2	1.3	1.4	41.3	40.6	39.9	41.5	41.0	40.2
Ethiopia	17,593	19,182	21,225	2.0	1.7	2.0	39.3	38.4	37.4	39.5	38.9	37.8
Gabon	502	518	536	0.9	0.6	0.7	39.4	38.3	37.3	39.6	38.9	37.7
Gambia, The	289	307	329	1.9	1.2	1.4	42.3	41.3	40.3	42.5	41.8	40.7
Ghana	4,353	4,963	5,686	2.7	2.7	2.7	41.4	40.6	39.7	41.7	41.0	40.0
Guinea	2,626	2,846	3,097	1.9	1.6	1.7	41.7	40.8	39.8	41.8	41.2	40.2
Guinea-Bissau	403	427	458	4.5	1.1	1.4	42.6	41.8	40.8	42.6	42.2	41.2
Kenya	7,072	8,389	10,011	3.7	3.5	3.5	41.9	40.9	39.9	42.0	41.4	40.3
Lesotho	662	730	808	2.1	2.0	2.0	45.7	44.6	43.4	46.4	45.2	43.8
Liberia	726	808	912	2.7	2.2	2.4	31.9	31.1	30.2	31.9	31.5	30.6
Madagascar	4,098	4,510	5,004	2.2	1.9	2.1	41.3	40.4	39.3	41.4	40.8	39.7
Malawi	2,703	3,074	3,495	2.6	2.6	2.6	43.9	42.6	41.2	44.3	43.2	41.7
Mali	2,296	2,598	2,959	1.9	2.5	2.6	17.4	16.8	16.2	17.4	17.1	16.4
Mauritania	516	590	679	1.8	2.7	2.8	20.0	21.1	22.2	20.5	20.6	21.8
Mauritius	331	390	440	3.4	3.3	2.4	22.9	24.8	26.5	22.2	23.9	25.8
Mozambique	6,904	7,671	8,437	4.5	2.1	1.9	49.8	48.7	47.4	49.9	49.2	47.9
Namibia	475	477	537	1.8	2.3	2.4	24.1	24.0	23.8	24.2	24.1	23.8
Niger	2,865	3,203	3,619	2.0	2.3	2.4	48.0	47.4	46.7	48.3	47.7	47.0
Nigeria	32,087	36,568	41,857	3.2	2.6	2.7	36.7	35.7	34.8	36.8	36.2	35.1
Rwanda	2,671	3,063	3,520	3.3	2.8	2.8	49.5	48.6	47.7	49.6	49.0	48.0
Sao Tome & Principe	..	..	..	..	..	..	..	..	..	..	..	..
Senegal	2,641	2,897	3,192	3.3	1.9	1.9	41.3	40.3	39.3	41.3	40.8	39.7
Seychelles	..	..	..	..	..	..	..	..	..	..	..	..
Sierra Leone	1,278	1,352	1,438	1.0	1.1	1.2	34.7	33.7	32.7	35.0	34.2	33.1
Somalia	1,808	1,999	2,143	3.6	2.0	1.4	40.6	39.7	38.7	40.8	40.1	39.0
Sudan	6,086	6,991	8,078	2.7	2.8	2.9	19.7	20.8	21.9	19.8	20.3	21.5
Swaziland	245	273	306	2.2	2.2	2.3	41.0	39.9	38.8	41.4	40.5	39.2
Tanzania	9,508	10,913	12,597	2.9	2.8	2.9	49.8	48.9	47.9	50.0	49.4	48.3
Togo	1,113	1,244	1,396	2.2	2.2	2.3	38.5	37.5	36.4	38.6	38.0	36.8
Uganda	6,163	7,054	8,129	2.9	2.7	2.8	42.8	41.9	41.1	42.9	42.4	41.4
Zaire	10,434	11,666	13,084	1.9	2.3	2.3	37.6	36.6	35.5	39.0	37.1	35.9
Zambia	1,912	2,242	2,644	2.8	3.2	3.3	27.3	28.2	29.0	27.4	27.8	28.7
Zimbabwe	2,979	3,410	3,921	3.0	2.7	2.8	36.7	35.7	34.6	37.0	36.2	35.0
NORTH AFRICA	23,699	27,475	31,887	3.1	3.0	3.0	11.8	12.8	13.7	10.9	12.4	13.4
Algeria	4,051	4,834	5,819	3.2	3.6	3.7	8.2	8.9	9.6	7.6	8.6	9.3
Egypt, Arab Republic of	11,298	12,837	14,574	2.4	2.6	2.5	8.6	9.3	10.1	8.1	9.0	9.8
Libya	755	904	1,076	3.7	3.7	3.5	7.3	8.1	9.1	6.9	7.7	8.7
Morocco	5,688	6,676	7,824	4.1	3.3	3.2	18.4	19.7	20.7	17.3	19.1	20.3
Tunisia	1,908	2,224	2,594	3.5	3.1	3.1	21.0	23.0	24.4	18.1	22.1	23.9
ALL AFRICA	179,290	202,466	229,788	2.7	2.5	2.5	35.7	35.0	34.3	35.8	35.4	34.6
South Africa	9,449	10,831	12,434	1.3	2.8	2.8	34.1	34.9	35.6	33.8	34.5	35.4

11-2. Age structure of the labor force

	Percentage distribution according to age groups											
	1980-85						1986-89					
	0-19	20-29	30-39	40-49	50-59	60+	0-19	20-29	30-39	40-49	50-59	60+
SUB-SAHARAN AFRICA	..	..	..	..	..	..	..	..	..	..	..	..
excluding Nigeria	..	..	..	..	..	..	..	..	..	..	..	..
Angola	..	..	..	..	..	..						
Benin							26.8	24.2	19.8	13.5	7.9	7.7
Botswana	18.3	31.7	17.7	12.7	9.0	10.5						
Burkina Faso	..	..	..	..		..	..	..	..	..	..	..
Burundi	..	..	..	..	..	..	24.8	30.1	19.3	11.3	7.8	6.7
Cameroon	..	..	..	..	..	..	..	..	..	..	..	..
Cape Verde	15.0	30.5	12.5	17.3	12.1	12.6						
Central African Republic	..	..	..	..	..	..	23.7	27.6	20.8	14.1	8.7	5.1
Chad	21.5	29.1	21.2	14.3	8.8	5.0						
Comoros	15.2	24.2	21.0	16.3	10.3	13.0	..	..	..	..	..	..
Congo, People's Republic of	7.7	26.2	23.2	18.0	13.2	11.8	..	..	..	..	..	..
Cote d'Ivoire	..	..	..	..	..	..	..	..	..	..	..	..
Djibouti	..	..	..	..	..	..	..	..	..	..	..	..
Equatorial Guinea	..	..	..	..	..	..	..	..	..	..	..	..
Ethiopia	25.7	23.8	20.6	14.5	8.6	6.8	..	..	..	..	..	..
Gabon	..	..	..	..	..	..	..	..	..	..	..	..
Gambia, The	19.6	28.7	20.3	13.3	8.0	10.1	..	..	..	..	..	..
Ghana	..	..	..	..	..	..	..	..	..	..	..	..
Guinea	20.3	23.7	20.9	15.8	10.6	8.6	..	..	..	..	..	..
Guinea-Bissau	..	..	..	..	..	..	..	..	..	..	..	..
Kenya	..	..	..	..	..	..	..	..	..	..	..	..
Lesotho	..	..	..	..	..	..	..	..	..	..	..	..
Liberia	12.5	25.8	23.7	16.6	10.3	10.9	..	..	..	..	..	..
Madagascar	..	..	..	..	..	..	..	..	..	..	..	..
Malawi	22.5	25.7	20.1	13.4	9.8	8.5	22.5	25.7	20.1	13.4	9.8	8.5
Mali	..	..	..	..	..	..	..	..	..	..	..	..
Mauritania	..	..	..	..	..	..	..	..	..	..	..	..
Mauritius	11.6	36.8	24.6	14.3	10.7	2.1	9.3	34.6	28.5	15.9	9.3	2.4
Mozambique	15.9	14.3	34.1	15.9	10.2	9.6	..	..	..	..	..	..
Namibia	..	..	..	..	..	..	..	..	..	..	..	..
Niger	..	..	..	..	..	..	..	..	..	..	..	..
Nigeria	9.6	23.7	27.6	20.4	11.1	7.5	7.9	21.9	26.1	22.8	13.5	7.9
Rwanda	..	..	..	..	..	..	..	..	..	..	..	..
Sao Tome & Principe	12.7	30.7	17.0	18.1	12.9	8.6						
Senegal	28.0	24.7	20.8	12.7	8.4	5.5	32.6	23.7	18.1	11.1	7.8	6.6
Seychelles	15.7	43.9	18.4	11.2	7.8	2.9	..	..	..	..	..	..
Sierra Leone	..	..	..	..	..	..	..	..	..	..	..	..
Somalia	..	..	..	..	..	..	..	..	..	..	..	..
Sudan	..	..	..	..	..	..	..	..	..	..	..	..
Swaziland	..	..	..	..	..	..	..	..	..	..	..	..
Tanzania	..	..	..	..	..	..	..	..	..	..	..	..
Togo	15.2	28.7	22.2	15.3	8.3	10.3	..	..	..	..	..	..
Uganda	..	..	..	..	..	..	..	..	..	..	..	..
Zaire	..	..	..	..	..	..	..	..	..	..	..	..
Zambia	18.1	27.7	18.9	14.9	10.0	10.4	..	..	..	..	..	..
Zimbabwe	15.3	31.8	20.3	15.1	9.7	7.7	14.5	27.5	12.5	18.8	18.3	8.4
NORTH AFRICA	18.2	28.1	18.9	15.3	10.9	7.7	..	..	..	..	..	..
Algeria	10.9	34.6	22.3	16.4	10.7	5.2	10.2	37.2	24.5	13.4	10.2	4.6
Egypt, Arab Republic of	19.9	24.2	18.0	16.7	12.0	9.2	..	..	..	..	..	..
Libya	..	..	..	..	..	..	..	..	..	..	..	..
Morocco	20.8	30.2	18.3	14.0	10.2	6.5	..	..	..	..	..	..
Tunisia	15.0	34.5	19.6	14.2	10.9	5.8	..	..	..	..	..	..
ALL AFRICA	..	..	..	..	..	..	..	..	..	..	..	..
South Africa	..	..	..	..	..	..	..	..	..	..	..	..

Note: Data do not include the armed forces and the unemployed.

11-3. Occupational distribution of labor force

Percentage of economically active population in indicated occupational groups (1970–85):

	Agricultural		Professional, technical		Administrative, managerial		Clerical, sales, services		Production, transport, laborers		Others	
	Female	Male	Female	Male	Female	Male	Female	Male	Female	Male	Female	Male
SUB-SAHARAN AFRICA	..	..	..	..	..	..	..	..	..	..	..	..
excluding Nigeria	..	..	..	..	..	..	..	..	..	..	..	..
Angola	..	..	..	..	..	..	..	..	..	..	..	..
Benin			..	..	..	..	..	..	..	..	..	..
Botswana	42.1	45.4	5.4	3.8	0.4	0.8	15.9	9.1	5.6	21.6	30.6	19.3
Burkina Faso	..	..	..	..	..	..	..	..	..	..	..	..
Burundi	..	..	..	..	..	..	..	..	..	..	..	..
Cameroon	88.6	64.6	0.9	3.3	0.0	0.2	3.9	9.0	2.5	16.6	4.1	6.3
Cape Verde	..	..	..	..	..	..	..	..	..	..	..	..
Central African Republic	..	..	..	..	..	..	..	..	..	..	..	..
Chad	..	..	..	..	..	..	..	..	..	..	..	..
Comoros	..	..	..	..	..	..	..	..	..	..	..	..
Congo, People's Republic of	..	..	..	..	..	..	..	..	..	..	..	..
Cote d'Ivoire	..	..	..	..	..	..	..	..	..	..	..	..
Djibouti	..	..	..	..	..	..	..	..	..	..	..	..
Equatorial Guinea	..	..	..	..	..	..	..	..	..	..	..	..
Ethiopia	..	..	..	..	..	..	..	..	..	..	..	..
Gabon	..	..	..	..	..	..	..	..	..	..	..	..
Gambia, The	..	..	..	..	..	..	..	..	..	..	..	..
Ghana	52.6	56.5	1.9	5.0	0.0	0.6	27.2	10.6	14.8	21.8	3.5	5.5
Guinea	..	..	..	..	..	..	..	..	..	..	..	..
Guinea-Bissau	..	..	..	..	..	..	..	..	..	..	..	..
Kenya	..	..	..	..	..	..	..	..	..	..	..	..
Lesotho	..	..	..	..	..	..	..	..	..	..	..	..
Liberia	..	..	..	..	..	..	..	..	..	..	..	..
Madagascar	..	..	..	..	..	..	..	..	..	..	..	..
Malawi	..	..	..	..	..	..	..	..	..	..	..	..
Mali	..	..	..	..	..	..	..	..	..	..	..	..
Mauritania	..	..	..	..	..	..	..	..	..	..	..	..
Mauritius	32.3	26.1	9.6	4.1	0.1	0.5	34.8	18.4	9.3	35.5	13.9	15.4
Mozambique	..	..	..	..	..	..	..	..	..	..	..	..
Namibia	..	..	..	..	..	..	..	..	..	..	..	..
Niger	..	..	..	..	..	..	..	..	..	..	..	..
Nigeria	..	..	..	..	..	..	..	..	..	..	..	..
Rwanda	..	..	..	..	..	..	..	..	..	..	..	..
Sao Tome & Principe	..	..	..	..	..	..	..	..	..	..	..	..
Senegal	..	..	..	..	..	..	..	..	..	..	..	..
Seychelles	22.7	26.2	11.8	4.1	1.4	3.3	40.7	11.6	10.9	46.4	12.5	8.4
Sierra Leone	..	..	..	..	..	..	..	..	..	..	..	..
Somalia	..	..	..	..	..	..	..	..	..	..	..	..
Sudan	..	..	..	..	..	..	..	..	..	..	..	..
Swaziland	..	..	..	..	..	..	..	..	..	..	..	..
Tanzania	..	..	..	..	..	..	..	..	..	..	..	..
Togo	..	..	..	..	..	..	..	..	..	..	..	..
Uganda	..	..	..	..	..	..	..	..	..	..	..	..
Zaire	..	..	..	..	..	..	..	..	..	..	..	..
Zambia	6.3	19.0	2.8	4.5	0.3	0.9	5.3	14.4	..	..	..	..
Zimbabwe	..	..	..	..	..	..	..	..	..	..	..	..
NORTH AFRICA	..	..	..	..	..	..	..	..	..	..	..	..
Algeria	21.2	51.0	16.6	2.8	1.1	0.1	37.5	15.9	14.3	17.7	9.3	12.5
Egypt, Arab Republic of	36.5	37.9	17.6	8.7	1.8	2.0	24.0	21.1	9.7	25.1	10.4	5.2
Libya	37.1	19.5	28.0	8.6	0.1	0.8	26.8	27.6	5.2	37.4	2.8	6.1
Morocco	37.8	53.9	3.9	4.0	4.6	2.7	..	12.3	19.6	19.1	..	8.0
Tunisia	31.1	30.9	1.6	2.4	9.3	8.7	10.1	11.6	42.0	37.1	5.9	9.3
ALL AFRICA	..	..	..	..	..	..	..	..	..	..	..	..
South Africa	25.6	30.0	5.8	3.3	0.1	1.4	46.4	17.9	6.8	42.9	15.3	4.5

11-4. Industrial structure of the labor force

	Percentage of females working in:									Percentage of males working in:								
	Agriculture			Industry			Services			Agriculture			Industry			Service		
	1980	1985	1987	1980	1985	1987	1980	1985	1987	1980	1985	1987	1980	1985	1987	1980	1985	1987
SUB-SAHARAN AFRICA	82	80	79	4	5	5	14	15	15	71	68	66	12	13	13	17	19	20
excluding Nigeria	86	84	82	4	4	4	10	12	12	72	69	66	11	12	12	17	19	20
Angola	89	88	87	2	2	2	9	10	11	63	61	61	15	15	15	22	24	24
Benin	75	70	69	3	4	4	22	26	27	66	62	60	10	11	12	24	27	28
Botswana	86	82	80	2	3	3	12	15	17	61	58	57	19	21	22	20	21	22
Burkina Faso	86	85	85	4	4	4	10	11	11	87	86	85	5	5	6	8	9	9
Burundi	98	98	98	1	1	1	1	1	1	88	87	86	4	4	5	9	9	9
Cameroon	78	76	74	3	4	4	19	21	21	65	60	58	11	14	15	23	26	27
Cape Verde	31	26	24	21	23	23	48	52	53	59	56	54	23	25	26	9	18	20
Central African Republic	74	72	71	4	4	4	22	24	25	69	64	61	9	9	9	22	27	30
Chad	86	85	85	1	1	1	13	13	14	82	78	75	6	7	8	12	15	17
Comoros	88	86	85	3	2	2	10	12	13	80	78	78	8	8	8	12	14	14
Congo, People's Republic of the	87	85	83	2	2	2	12	13	14	46	46	45	19	19	19	35	35	36
Cote d'Ivoire	75	72	71	5	6	6	20	22	23	60	54	52	10	11	12	30	34	36
Djibouti	88	87	86	20	2	2	10	11	12	72	71	70	11	11	11	17	18	19
Equatorial Guinea	88	83	81	2	4	4	10	14	15	52	46	44	17	20	20	31	34	36
Ethiopia	85	83	82	6	7	8	9	10	10	77	74	73	9	10	11	15	16	17
Gabon	86	85	84	3	3	3	12	12	13	67	64	62	16	17	18	16	19	20
Gambia, The	93	92	92	2	2	3	5	5	6	77	76	75	10	11	11	13	13	14
Ghana	49	49	48	19	17	17	32	34	34	56	55	54	20	21	21	24	24	25
Guinea	88	85	84	5	6	7	7	9	9	75	73	71	12	13	14	13	14	15
Guinea-Bissau	92	91	91	2	2	2	6	7	7	75	73	72	5	5	6	20	22	23
Kenya	86	84	83	3	3	3	11	13	13	77	76	75	10	10	11	13	14	14
Lesotho	90	87	85	2	2	3	9	11	12	23	80	79	6	6	6	11	14	15
Liberia	87	83	82	2	2	2	12	16	17	69	68	67	13	13	13	19	20	20
Madagascar	94	92	91	2	2	2	5	6	7	72	70	69	9	10	10	19	20	21
Malawi	94	92	92	2	3	3	4	5	5	75	70	68	12	13	14	14	17	18
Mali	78	77	24	2	2	2	11	13	14	87	85	24	2	2	2	11	13	14
Mauritania	87	85	84	3	4	5	10	11	12	65	62	61	11	11	12	25	26	27
Mauritius	31	27	26	13	14	14	56	59	60	27	25	24	28	27	27	46	48	49
Mozambique	97	97	97	1	1	1	2	2	2	72	70	69	14	15	15	14	15	15
Namibia	..	..	..	..	..	..	..	..	..	..	..	..	..	..	..	..	..	..
Niger	94	93	93	0	0	0	6	7	7	88	86	85	3	4	4	9	10	11
Nigeria	69	68	67	7	7	7	24	25	25	68	66	65	15	15	15	18	19	20
Rwanda	98	98	98	1	1	1	1	2	2	88	87	86	5	6	6	7	8	8
Sao Tome & Principe	77	74	72	4	4	5	19	22	23	39	35	34	21	24	26	41	40	40
Senegal	90	89	88	2	3	3	8	9	9	74	73	73	9	9	9	17	17	18
Seychelles	7	7	7	8	12	14	85	81	79	13	13	13	31	34	35	56	53	52
Sierra Leone	82	80	79	4	4	4	14	16	17	63	59	58	20	22	23	17	19	20
Somalia	90	87	86	2	2	2	9	11	12	66	63	63	13	14	1	21	23	23
Sudan	87	84	82	4	5	5	9	11	13	67	61	59	8	10	11	24	29	31
Swaziland	83	81	80	3	4	4	14	15	16	68	63	61	13	15	16	19	21	22
Tanzania	92	90	89	2	1	1	7	9	9	79	77	76	7	8	8	13	16	17
Togo	67	66	65	7	8	8	25	26	27	77	75	74	12	12	13	12	13	14
Uganda	89	86	85	2	3	3	9	12	12	84	82	81	6	7	7	10	12	12
Zaire	95	94	94	1	2	2	4	4	5	58	54	53	20	22	22	23	24	25
Zambia	84	83	82	3	3	3	13	14	15	69	66	65	13	13	14	19	20	21
Zimbabwe	82	81	80	4	4	4	15	15	16	68	65	64	15	15	15	18	20	21
NORTH AFRICA	24	20	19	22	25	26	54	55	56	42	39	38	24	25	26	34	35	36
Algeria	10	8	7	22	23	24	68	69	69	33	29	27	27	29	30	40	42	43
Egypt, Arab Republic of	20	17	16	16	19	19	64	65	65	45	46	45	22	22	22	33	33	33
Libya	40	32	31	13	15	16	47	54	54	16	13	12	30	32	32	53	55	56
Morocco	41	33	32	29	35	36	30	32	32	50	43	41	21	25	26	29	32	33
Tunisia	33	26	25	45	49	50	22	25	25	36	30	28	34	37	38	30	33	34
ALL AFRICA	71	69	67	8	9	9	21	23	23	65	63	61	14	15	15	21	22	23
South Africa	..	..	..	..	..	..	..	..	..	..	..	..	..	..	..	..	..	..

Note: Subgroup cells are population-weighted averages.

11–5. Labor force participation rate

	Percentage of population of all ages in the labor force											
	Total				Female				Male			
	1980	1985	1988	1990	1980	1985	1988	1990	1980	1985	1988	1990
SUB-SAHARAN AFRICA	43	42	41	40	34	32	31	30	53	52	51	51
excluding Nigeria	44	43	42	41	35	33	32	31	53	52	52	51
Angola	44	43	42	41	35	33	32	31	53	52	51	51
Benin	51	49	47	46	49	46	44	43	53	51	50	50
Botswana	35	34	34	34	25	24	23	23	46	45	45	45
Burkina Faso	56	54	53	53	53	51	49	48	59	58	58	57
Burundi	56	53	52	52	53	50	49	48	58	57	56	56
Cameroon	42	40	39	38	29	27	26	25	55	53	53	52
Cape Verde	35	37	38	38	18	20	21	21	54	57	58	58
Central African Republic	52	50	49	48	48	45	44	42	56	55	54	53
Chad	37	36	35	35	16	15	15	15	58	57	56	56
Comoros	47	46	45	45	40	38	37	36	55	54	54	54
Congo, People's Republic of the	42	41	40	39	33	32	31	30	52	50	49	49
Cote d'Ivoire	43	41	40	39	31	29	28	28	55	53	52	51
Djibouti	..	..	..	..	..	..	..	..	..	..	..	..
Equatorial Guinea	45	43	42	41	37	34	33	32	54	52	51	51
Ethiopia	46	44	43	42	36	34	32	32	56	55	54	53
Gabon	47	45	43	42	37	34	32	31	58	56	55	54
Gambia, The	50	48	47	46	41	39	38	*37*	58	57	56	56
Ghana	38	37	36	35	31	29	29	28	45	44	43	43
Guinea	49	47	46	45	40	38	36	35	57	56	55	55
Guinea-Bissau	50	48	47	46	41	39	38	37	59	58	57	57
Kenya	42	41	40	39	35	33	32	31	49	48	48	48
Lesotho	49	48	47	47	44	41	40	39	56	55	55	55
Liberia	39	37	36	35	25	23	22	21	53	51	50	50
Madagascar	47	45	44	43	39	36	35	34	56	54	53	53
Malawi	45	44	43	43	39	37	36	35	53	52	51	51
Mali	33	32	32	32	11	11	10	10	56	55	55	55
Mauritania	32	31	31	31	13	13	13	14	51	50	49	48
Mauritius	35	37	38	39	16	18	19	20	54	57	57	57
Mozambique	57	55	54	53	56	53	51	50	58	57	56	56
Namibia	32	31	30	30	15	15	14	14	48	47	47	46
Niger	54	52	52	51	51	49	48	47	57	56	55	55
Nigeria	40	38	38	37	29	27	26	25	51	50	49	49
Rwanda	52	51	50	49	51	48	47	46	53	53	52	52
Sao Tome & Principe	..	..	..	..	..	..	..	..	..	..	..	..
Senegal	47	45	44	43	38	36	35	34	55	54	54	53
Seychelles	..	..	..	..	..	..	..	..	..	..	..	..
Sierra Leone	39	38	37	36	26	25	24	23	52	51	50	50
Somalia	45	43	42	42	36	34	33	32	54	53	52	52
Sudan	33	32	32	32	13	14	14	14	52	51	51	51
Swaziland	44	42	41	40	36	33	32	31	53	51	50	50
Tanzania	50	49	47	47	49	47	45	44	51	50	50	49
Togo	44	42	41	41	33	31	30	29	54	53	53	52
Uganda	47	46	45	44	40	38	37	36	54	53	53	52
Zaire	40	39	38	38	30	28	27	26	51	50	50	49
Zambia	34	34	34	33	18	19	19	19	50	49	48	48
Zimbabwe	40	39	38	37	29	28	26	26	52	50	50	49
NORTH AFRICA	27	27	28	28	6	7	7	8	47	47	47	48
Algeria	22	22	23	23	4	4	4	4	40	41	41	41
Egypt, Arab Republic of	27	27	28	28	5	5	6	6	49	49	49	49
Libya	25	25	25	25	4	4	5	5	45	44	43	43
Morocco	29	30	31	32	11	12	13	13	48	49	50	50
Tunisia	30	31	32	33	13	15	16	16	47	48	49	49
ALL AFRICA	40	39	38	38	28	27	26	26	52	51	50	50
South Africa	33	33	34	34	22	23	24	24	44	44	44	44

11-6. Minimum wage

	Annual earnings at minimum wage in US Dollars at official exchange rate						
	1980	*1981*	*1982*	*1983*	*1984*	*1985*	*1986*
SUB-SAHARAN AFRICA	..	..	..	..	..	..	..
excluding Nigeria	..	..	..	..	..	..	..
Angola	..	..	..	..	..	..	..
Benin	509	396	327	443	386	376	..
Botswana	..	..	..	..	..	..	..
Burkina Faso	886	689	721	622	543	526	685
Burundi	288	288	504	488	379	376	..
Cameroon	710	603	601	599	622	605	785
Cape Verde	..	..	..	..	..	..	..
Central African Republic	738	574	475	409	357	347	..
Chad	473	367	304	262	228	222	288
Comoros	..	..	..	..	..	..	..
Congo, People's Republic of	1,226	953	788	680	645	628	814
Cote d'Ivoire	1,581	1,229	1,118	964	841	818	1,061
Djibouti	..	..	..	..	..	..	..
Equatorial Guinea	..	..	..	..	..	..	..
Ethiopia	..	290	290	290	290	290	290
Gabon	2,272	1,766	1,826	1,575	1,648	1,709	2,218
Gambia, The	..	..	824	714	526	513	..
Ghana	624	1,414	1,414	917	315	420	328
Guinea	696	630	590	572	543	508	..
Guinea-Bissau	..	..	..	..	..	..	..
Kenya	737	605	607	498	460	443	489
Lesotho	..	..	..	..	..	..	..
Liberia	648	648	648	648	648	648	648
Madagascar	653	599	549	446	367	336	367
Malawi	180	253	249	223	186	188	174
Mali	435	341	316	306	267	340	..
Mauritania	888	844	983	928	797	666	..
Mauritius	..	..	..	..	..	..	..
Mozambique	..	..	..	..	..	..	..
Namibia	..	..	..	..	..	..	..
Niger	100	834	690	595	519	505	655
Nigeria	1,547	2,443	2,229	2,075	1,963	1,682	1,114
Rwanda	349	349	349	343	323	320	..
Sao Tome & Principe	..	..	..	..	..	..	..
Senegal	1,317	1,075	962	954	832	851	1,104
Seychelles	..	..	..	..	..	..	..
Sierra Leone	514	..	..	..	..	..	..
Somalia	381	496	313	213	168	85	47
Sudan	672	634	357	258	331	262	336
Swaziland	..	..	..	..	..	..	..
Tanzania	703	869	776	646	636	556	297
Togo	743	578	526	453	395	385	499
Uganda	388	152	121	133	200	..	..
Zaire	..	346	196	84	61	..	..
Zambia	1,246	1,131	1,252	1,059	1,059	821	..
Zimbabwe	..	..	..	..	..	..	..
NORTH AFRICA	..	..	..	..	..	..	..
Algeria	..	..	..	..	..	..	..
Egypt, Arab Republic of	..	..	..	..	..	..	..
Libya	..	..	..	..	..	..	..
Morocco	..	..	..	..	..	..	..
Tunisia	..	..	..	..	..	..	..
ALL AFRICA	..	..	..	..	..	..	..
South Africa	..	..	..	..	..	..	..

11-7. Comparative minimum wage

	Ratio of minimum wage earnings to agriculture value added per worker						
	1980	1981	1982	1983	1984	1985	1986
SUB-SAHARAN AFRICA	..	..	..	..	..	..	..
excluding Nigeria	..	..	..	..	..	..	..
Angola	..	..	..	..	..	..	..
Benin	0.7	0.7	0.6	0.8	0.7	0.6	..
Botswana	..	..	..	..	..	..	..
Burkina Faso	4.7	3.9	4.6	4.4	4.2	3.5	..
Burundi	0.9	0.9	1.6	1.4	1.3	1.2	..
Cameroon	1.2	1.1	1.1	1.3	1.3	1.2	1.0
Cape Verde	..	..	..	..	..	..	..
Central African Republic	2.8	2.5	2.4	2.1	1.9	1.8	..
Chad	4.2	2.7	2.5	2.2	2.1	1.6	..
Comoros	..	..	..	..	..	..	..
Congo, People's Republic of the	1.1	1.1	1.0	0.9	0.8	0.8	..
Cote d'Ivoire	1.8	1.7	1.9	1.9	1.8	1.6	..
Djibouti	..	..	..	..	..	..	..
Equatorial Guinea	..	..	..	..	..	..	..
Ethiopia	1.6	1.6	1.6	1.5	1.6	1.7	..
Gabon	1.8	1.7	2.0	1.8	1.9	1.9	..
Gambia, The	..	2.5	2.2	1.7	2.1	2.0	..
Ghana	0.2	0.2	0.2	0.2	0.2	0.3	..
Guinea	1.8	1.7	1.7	1.6	1.3	1.3	..
Guinea-Bissau	..	..	..	..	..	..	..
Kenya	1.8	1.6	1.7	1.6	1.5	1.5	1.4
Lesotho	..	..	..	..	..	..	..
Liberia	0.8	1.0	1.1	1.0	0.9	0.9	0.9
Madagascar	2.1	2.0	1.9	1.5	1.5	..	..
Malawi	1.0	1.5	1.5	1.3	1.1	..	..
Mali	1.8	1.7	1.8	2.0	1.9	2.3	..
Mauritania	..	..	..	..	..	..	..
Mauritius	..	..	..	..	..	..	..
Mozambique	..	..	..	..	..	..	..
Namibia	..	..	..	..	..	..	..
Niger	..	..	..	..	..	..	..
Nigeria	1.4	2.4	1.9	1.7	1.5	1.3	..
Rwanda	1.7	1.6	..	..	..	..	..
Sao Tome & Principe	..	..	..	..	..	..	..
Senegal	4.4	4.7	3.4	3.6	4.3	3.9	3.0
Seychelles	..	..	..	..	..	..	..
Sierra Leone	1.3	..	..	..	..	..	..
Somalia	0.8	0.6	0.6	..	..	..	..
Sudan	1.2	1.0	0.7	0.6	0.7	0.8	0.6
Swaziland	..	..	..	..	..	..	..
Tanzania	2.2	2.3	1.8	1.5	1.6	1.2	..
Togo	1.7	1.5	1.7	1.4	1.4	1.4	..
Uganda	0.1	0.1	..	..	..	..	..
Zaire	..	..	1.0	0.7	0.5	0.4	..
Zambia	3.1	2.5	3.4	3.2	3.0	..	..
Zimbabwe	..	..	..	..	..	..	..
NORTH AFRICA	..	..	..	..	..	..	..
Algeria	..	..	..	..	..	..	..
Egypt, Arab Republic of	..	..	..	..	..	..	..
Libya	..	..	..	..	..	..	..
Morocco	..	..	..	..	..	..	..
Tunisia	..	..	..	..	..	..	..
ALL AFRICA	..	..	..	..	..	..	..
South Africa	..	..	..	..	..	..	..

11-8. Comparative average wage

	Average wages in manufacturing as a multiple of average agricultural income					
	1980	*1981*	*1982*	*1983*	*1984*	*1985*
SUB-SAHARAN AFRICA	..	..	..	..	..	..
excluding Nigeria	..	..	..	..	..	..
Angola	..	..	..	..	..	..
Benin	..	..	..	..	..	..
Botswana	..	..	..	..	..	..
Burkina Faso	..	..	..	..	..	..
Burundi	6.7	11.2	11.7	11.4	13.2	11.5
Cameroon	4.5	4.1	..	..	..	..
Cape Verde	..	..	..	..	..	..
Central African Republic	..	..	..	..	..	..
Chad	..	..	..	..	..	..
Comoros	..	..	..	..	..	..
Congo, People's Republic of the	..	..	..	..	..	..
Cote d'Ivoire	..	..	..	..	..	..
Djibouti	..	..	..	..	..	..
Equatorial Guinea	..	..	..	..	..	..
Ethiopia	..	..	..	..	..	..
Gabon	..	..	..	..	..	..
Gambia, The	..	..	..	2.5	2.8	4.5
Ghana	0.6	0.5	0.4	..	..	..
Guinea	..	..	..	..	..	..
Guinea-Bissau	..	..	..	..	..	..
Kenya	4.8	4.8	4.8	4.7	5.0	4.9
Lesotho	..	..	..	..	..	..
Liberia	..	..	..	..	..	..
Madagascar	..	..	..	..	..	..
Malawi	5.0	5.3	6.7	4.7	3.6	..
Mali	..	..	..	..	..	..
Mauritania	..	..	..	..	..	..
Mauritius	..	..	..	..	..	..
Mozambique	..	..	..	..	..	..
Namibia	..	..	..	..	..	..
Niger	..	..	..	..	..	..
Nigeria	1.9	..	..	..	..	..
Rwanda	..	..	..	..	..	..
Sao Tome & Principe	..	..	..	..	..	..
Senegal	..	..	..	..	..	..
Seychelles	..	..	..	..	..	..
Sierra Leone	2.2	2.0	..	..	..	..
Somalia	..	..	..	..	..	..
Sudan	..	..	..	..	..	..
Swaziland	..	..	..	..	..	..
Tanzania	3.9	3.7	..	..	..	..
Togo	..	..	..	..	..	..
Uganda	..	..	..	..	..	..
Zaire	..	..	..	..	..	..
Zambia	6.8	5.2	6.3	5.7	4.8	..
Zimbabwe	..	..	..	..	..	..
NORTH AFRICA	..	..	..	..	..	..
Algeria	..	..	..	..	..	..
Egypt, Arab Republic of	..	..	..	..	..	..
Libya	..	..	..	..	..	..
Morocco	..	..	..	..	..	..
Tunisia	..	..	..	..	..	..
ALL AFRICA	..	..	..	..	..	..
South Africa	..	..	..	..	..	..

11-9. Public sector employment

	Number of people employed by central government					
	1980	1981	1982	1983	1984	1985
SUB-SAHARAN AFRICA	..	..	..	..	..	..
excluding Nigeria		..	..		..	
Angola	..	..	..	..	..	..
Benin	26,240	..	..	..	..	..
Botswana	18,000	19,500	20,000	21,800	..	..
Burkina Faso	..	35,739	34,648	..	..	..
Burundi	41,947	..	..	..	..	..
Cameroon	33,400	36,900	40,200	43,900	47,800	..
Cape Verde	..	..	..	..	..	..
Central African Republic	..	..	..	..	..	..
Chad	..	..	..	..	..	..
Comoros	..	..	..	..	..	..
Congo, People's Republic of the	34,790	38,725	41,509	44,801	..	..
Cote d'Ivoire	..	..	..	..	..	..
Djibouti	..	..	..	..	..	..
Equatorial Guinea	..	..	..	..	..	..
Ethiopia	..	..	..	..	..	..
Gabon	21,866	22,861	24,249	25,680	..	..
Gambia, The	..	..	..	..	..	..
Ghana	..	..	..	..	..	..
Guinea	..	..	..	..	..	..
Guinea-Bissau	..	..	..	..	..	..
Kenya	214,800	214,500	216,700	226,400	221,100	..
Lesotho	..	..	..	..	11,475	..
Liberia	32,000	33,600	..	..	..	..
Madagascar	..	107,000	127,500	..	..	..
Malawi	39,824	43,345	45,333	50,368	..	..
Mali	44,786	45,758	47,725	49,116	50,924	51,731
Mauritania	..	..	..	..	..	..
Mauritius	..	..	..	..	..	..
Mozambique	..	..	..	..	..	..
Namibia	..	..	..	..	..	..
Niger	..	..	..	..	..	..
Nigeria	231,800	256,300	266,300	292,900	..	..
Rwanda	..	..	..	..	..	..
Sao Tome & Principe	..	..	..	..	..	..
Senegal	..	..	..	..	..	..
Seychelles	..	..	..	..	..	..
Sierra Leone	..	..	..	..	..	..
Somalia	53,866	54,024	43,802	..	..	..
Sudan	158,400	154,300	150,700	161,900	..	..
Swaziland	..	..	..	..	..	..
Tanzania	..	..	..	..	..	..
Togo	36,098	38,621	37,878	34,026	33,496	32,378
Uganda	..	..	..	..	..	..
Zaire	429,000	446,000	444,000	388,000	305,000	302,000
Zambia	..	..	..	..	..	..
Zimbabwe	..	..	..	..	..	..
NORTH AFRICA						
Algeria	..	..	..	..	..	..
Egypt, Arab Republic of	..	..	..	..	..	..
Libya	..	..	..	..	..	..
Morocco	..	..	..	..	..	..
Tunisia	..	..	..	..	..	..
ALL AFRICA	..	..	..	..	..	..
South Africa	..	..	..	..	..	..

Technical Notes

The sources for the tables in this chapter are various issues of the ILO's *Yearbook of Labor Statistics*, the ECA, the World Bank data files, and numerous reports and studies of individual countries.

Table 11-1. Number and gender structure of the labor force

This table provides the total number of persons in the labor force and the percentage that is female. "Labor force" refers to "economically active" persons, including the armed forces and the unemployed but excluding housewives and students. The "economically active" population comprises all persons of either gender who furnish the labor to produce economic goods and services, as defined by the UN system, of national accounts, during a specified period. The production of economic goods and services should include all production and processing of primary products, whether for the market, for barter, or for own consumption; the production of all other goods and services for the market; and, in the case of households that produce such goods and services for the markets, the corresponding production for own consumption.

Table 11-2. Age structure of the labor force

This table shows the distribution of the economically active population among various age groups. Taken from different issues of the ILO's *Yearbook of Labor Statistics*, the data are from the latest census or survey of the country concerned. These data include all persons who fulfill the requirements for inclusion among the "employed" or the "unemployed." The "unemployed" comprise all persons above a specified age who during the reference period were: without work, currently available for work, and seeking work for pay or profit. The definitions of "working age" are not uniform for all countries. However, the most common practice is to limit it to age group 14-64.

Table 11-3. Occupational distribution of the labor force

This table reflects the distribution of the total labor force into various occupations according to gender. The occupational statistics are based on the revised International Standard Classification of Occupations (ISCO) issued by ILO in 1968. The occupational groups shown include agricultural workers; professional and technical workers; administrative and managerial workers; clerical and related workers and sales and service workers; production and related workers, transport equipment operators and laborers; and "others". This last group refers to workers not classified by occupation and includes new workers seeking employment, workers reporting occupations unidentifiable or inadequately described, and workers not reporting any occupation.

Table 11-4. Industrial structure of the labor force

The industrial structure of the labor force can often give an indication of the relative level of development of the economy. This table shows the distribution of the labor force among the various sectors of economic activities according to gender. The "agriculture" sector includes farming, animal husbandry, hunting, forestry, and fishing. The "industry" sector includes mining and quarrying, manufacturing, construction and public works, electricity, water, and gas. All other branches of activity are included in "services".

Table 11-5. Labor force participation rate

This is the percentage of the population within each sex and age group that participates in economic activities (either employed or unemployed). Figures given are crude activity rates, that is, the ratios of the total economically active population to the total population of *all* ages. It should be recalled that the sex-age structure of the population, that is, the proportion of population in each sex-age group (particularly those under 15 years of age), will affect the participation rates shown. Further, the activity (participation) rate for females may be difficult to compare among countries, since in many countries relatively large numbers of women assist on farms or in other family enterprises without pay, and there are differences from one country to another in the criteria adopted for determining the extent to which such workers are to be counted among the "economically active."

Table 11-6. Minimum wage

Table 11-6 shows the annual earnings at the stipulated minimum wage rate converted to U.S. dollars at official exchange rates in the countries concerned. "Earnings" here are limited to wages and salaries of employees only. Thus it excludes remuneration for time not worked, such as for annual vacation, other paid leave or holidays, employers' contributions to social security and pension schemes and the benefits received by employees under these schemes, severance and termination pay, bonuses and gratuities, and housing and family allowances paid by the employer to the employee.

It should be borne in mind that wages do not reflect worker's disposable or net earnings since they may include gross wages before deductions such as taxes or social security contributions.

Table 11-7. Comparative minimum wage

This is earnings (as defined above) at minimum wage divided by value added per worker in agriculture then multiplied by 100. The former is given as a ratio of the latter.

Table 11-8. Comparative average wage

This table provides a direct comparison of wages in the agricultural and manufacturing sectors respectively. It divides average wages in agriculture by those in manufacturing. Each sector's average wage is calculated by the formula:

$$W_j = \frac{\sum W_{ij} L_{ij}}{\sum L_{ij}}$$

in which the sector wage W_j is a weighted average of the wage in sector j paid for each of the i types of labor, W_{ij}, where the weights are the sector employment shares of each type of labor. Measured sectorial differentials may, in some cases, reflect differences in the skill mix of employment between sectors, rather than differences in wages.

Table 11-9. Public sector employment

Table 11-9 refers to the number of persons engaged in the central administration (central government) alone. Persons employed in local, regional, or state governments are not included, neither are staff of public enterprises or corporations. Comparability of data presented here is limited to the extent that country reports include or exclude such persons as part-time workers, workers on contract appointments, and expatriate experts.

12

Aid Flows

Official development assistance (ODA) consists of concessional financial flows that aim to promote economic development and welfare. ODA disbursements from bilateral and multilateral sources have become increasingly important to Africa and have accounted for about half of the entire region's total net financial flows in 1987 and most of total net flows to Sub-Saharan Africa in 1986-87. For many countries, the foreign savings made available to them through ODA flows are equivalent to a sizable share of GDP and to the bulk of their domestic investment. Thus monitoring aid flows is of special importance because of their significance for the economic performance of the region.

The tables in this chapter show data on net ODA flows and their relative importance to key economic and demographic indicators in recipient countries, real growth in net ODA flows to Sub-Saharan Africa in the 1980s from major donors or donor groups, and the share of each donor's worldwide aid portfolio allocated to Sub-Saharan Africa. ODA disbursements are shown net of repayments of earlier concessional loans.

12-1. Net ODA from all donors

	Millions of U.S. dollars (current prices and exchange rates)										Average annual percentage growth		
	1980	1981	1982	1983	1984	1985	1986	1987	1988	1989	75–80	80–85	86–MR
SUB-SAHARAN AFRICA	7,390	7,314	7,496	7,305	7,595	8,622	10,587	11,918	13,469	13,800	20.5	2.5	9.6
excluding Nigeria	6,889	6,890	7,032	6,881	7,107	8,207	9,983	11,267	12,711	12,618	21.3	2.7	8.6
Angola	53	61	60	75	95	92	131	135	159	147	53.4	13.1	5.1
Benin	90	82	81	86	77	95	138	138	162	248	12.9	0.5	21.2
Botswana	106	97	101	104	102	96	102	156	151	160	19.6	-0.8	14.0
Burkina Faso	212	217	213	184	189	198	284	281	298	282	23.2	-2.6	0.4
Burundi	117	121	127	140	141	142	187	202	188	198	22.8	4.5	0.9
Cameroon	265	199	212	129	186	159	224	213	284	469	20.2	-8.9	28.4
Cape Verde	64	50	55	60	64	70	110	88	87	75	38.1	3.5	-11.0
Central African Republic	111	102	90	93	114	104	139	176	196	193	17.8	0.2	11.7
Chad	35	60	65	95	115	182	165	198	264	242	-5.6	35.1	15.5
Comoros	43	47	39	38	41	47	46	54	52	45	7.2	0.1	-1.5
Congo, People's Republic of the	92	81	93	108	98	71	110	152	89	89	10.9	-1.6	-11.3
Cote d'Ivoire	210	124	137	156	128	125	186	254	439	413	15.7	-6.6	34.1
Djibouti	73	65	59	66	102	82	115	106	93	76	11.9	6.0	-13.0
Equatorial Guinea	9	10	14	11	15	17	22	43	43	42	41.7	12.1	22.0
Ethiopia	212	245	200	339	364	715	636	634	970	742	10.2	24.9	9.3
Gabon	56	44	62	64	76	61	79	82	106	133	0.8	6.4	20.0
Gambia, The	54	68	48	42	53	50	101	100	82	93	48.2	-3.6	-4.4
Ghana	191	145	141	110	216	203	371	373	474	553	16.1	3.6	15.5
Guinea	89	106	90	68	123	119	175	213	262	348	41.3	4.7	25.5
Guinea-Bissau	59	65	65	64	55	58	71	107	99	102	26.5	-1.9	10.7
Kenya	397	449	485	400	411	438	455	572	808	972	27.1	0.1	30.0
Lesotho	94	104	93	108	101	94	88	107	108	128	26.9	0.1	12.1
Liberia	98	108	109	118	133	90	97	78	65	59	38.5	0.9	-15.4
Madagascar	230	234	242	183	153	188	316	321	304	323	24.7	-7.1	0.1
Malawi	143	137	121	117	158	113	198	280	366	399	21.1	-2.3	26.7
Mali	267	230	210	215	321	380	372	366	427	455	18.0	8.3	7.9
Mauritania	176	214	187	176	175	209	225	182	184	244	14.0	0.6	2.6
Mauritius	33	58	48	41	36	28	56	65	59	59	9.7	-6.6	0.4
Mozambique	169	144	208	211	259	300	422	651	893	768	45.1	14.2	23.6
Namibia	0	0	0	0	0	6	15	17	22	59	..	..	54.3
Niger	170	194	257	175	161	304	307	353	371	297	6.9	5.8	-0.5
Nigeria	36	41	37	48	33	32	59	69	120	346	-16.4	-2.3	79.2
Rwanda	155	153	151	150	165	181	211	245	252	235	14.9	2.8	3.6
Sao Tome & Principe	4	6	10	12	11	12	12	17	24	33	14.2	25.1	39.1
Senegal	263	398	285	323	368	295	567	641	568	651	20.6	1.3	3.0
Seychelles	22	17	18	16	15	22	28	24	21	20	31.1	-0.8	-12.0
Sierra Leone	91	60	82	66	61	66	87	68	102	101	42.2	-5.0	8.8
Somalia	433	374	462	343	350	353	511	580	433	421	24.1	-4.3	-8.4
Sudan	624	632	740	962	622	1,128	945	898	937	752	24.6	9.5	-6.2
Swaziland	50	37	28	33	30	26	35	45	38	30	31.7	-10.3	-5.9
Tanzania	679	703	684	594	558	487	681	882	982	920	21.3	-6.9	10.6
Togo	91	63	77	112	110	114	174	126	199	183	22.8	9.5	6.3
Uganda	114	136	133	137	163	182	198	279	363	406	23.0	8.7	27.4
Zaire	428	394	348	315	312	325	448	627	576	639	19.3	-6.0	10.3
Zambia	318	232	317	217	239	328	464	430	478	390	39.0	-0.4	-4.1
Zimbabwe	164	212	216	208	298	237	225	294	273	266	81.9	8.4	4.4
NORTH AFRICA	2,709	2,746	2,574	2,167	2,450	2,917	2,517	2,716	2,511	2,426	-1.8	-0.4	-1.9
Algeria	176	167	136	95	122	173	165	214	171	154	-2.3	-3.9	-4.3
Egypt, Arab Republic of	1,387	1,292	1,441	1,463	1,794	1,791	1,716	1,773	1,537	1,568	-9.0	6.7	-4.1
Libya	17	11	12	6	5	5	11	6	6	10	12.3	-22.2	-4.3
Morocco	897	1,037	774	398	352	785	403	447	481	454	28.4	-12.3	4.4
Tunisia	232	239	210	205	178	163	222	274	316	241	2.9	-7.4	3.9
ALL AFRICA	10,098	10,061	10,071	9,472	10,045	11,539	13,104	14,634	15,980	16,227	11.8	1.7	7.6
South Africa	..	..	..	..	..	..	..	..	..	..	..	..	..

12-2. Net ODA from DAC donors

	Millions of U.S. dollars (current prices and exchange rates)										Average annual percentage growth		
	1980	1981	1982	1983	1984	1985	1986	1987	1988	1989	75–80	80–85	86–MR
SUB-SAHARAN AFRICA	4,347	4,337	4,429	4,372	4,666	5,278	6,605	7,607	8,938	8,906	20.6	3.4	11.2
excluding Nigeria	4,018	4,068	4,100	4,076	4,302	4,978	6,136	7,076	8,320	8,008	21.8	3.6	10.1
Angola	36	39	40	46	60	60	94	98	106	88	54.7	11.9	-1.3
Benin	36	45	41	41	40	48	73	77	93	138	8.3	3.1	23.5
Botswana	84	76	83	75	65	59	82	124	125	120	18.9	-6.4	12.3
Burkina Faso	151	158	147	128	122	122	175	196	219	208	25.3	-5.5	6.4
Burundi	60	65	75	69	70	77	89	87	83	89	18.7	4.2	-0.5
Cameroon	172	134	155	109	155	126	176	180	240	300	22.3	-4.1	20.8
Cape Verde	39	36	43	45	39	41	76	63	59	49	73.1	1.5	-13.1
Central African Republic	75	73	69	65	68	61	85	109	107	99	19.2	-3.5	4.7
Chad	20	31	35	51	59	96	102	120	146	128	-2.4	33.2	9.1
Comoros	13	18	14	15	18	18	21	33	35	32	-5.7	4.6	14.1
Congo, People's Republic of the	55	43	60	55	67	47	101	131	77	79	7.2	1.3	-11.9
Cote d'Ivoire	152	91	102	141	114	138	138	221	226	260	17.7	-1.7	21.3
Djibouti	32	36	44	41	48	46	65	59	71	64	-4.5	7.9	1.5
Equatorial Guinea	1	4	5	4	8	7	10	22	24	20	..	34.0	21.9
Ethiopia	92	76	77	93	187	416	397	313	560	378	2.9	34.9	4.5
Gabon	49	36	58	57	68	52	59	70	99	121	4.2	6.4	28.5
Gambia, The	16	19	24	21	32	31	59	51	54	56	35.2	14.2	-0.7
Ghana	107	87	65	61	95	96	120	131	236	350	9.2	-1.0	46.2
Guinea	32	31	27	27	42	60	98	120	160	192	45.9	12.1	26.0
Guinea-Bissau	34	42	34	32	30	24	41	48	48	54	36.0	-7.4	8.7
Kenya	277	363	333	338	294	329	382	444	610	620	23.9	0.7	19.3
Lesotho	64	59	53	61	63	49	52	58	67	66	35.0	-2.9	8.4
Liberia	60	86	85	88	108	64	69	51	48	39	32.7	3.0	-16.6
Madagascar	91	94	159	117	98	99	176	181	214	176	25.0	0.8	1.5
Malawi	75	82	65	56	52	53	85	170	181	182	13.7	-9.0	26.5
Mali	131	133	96	97	224	251	204	222	260	301	20.1	14.8	14.1
Mauritania	54	67	62	72	69	100	105	98	111	160	32.0	10.2	14.9
Mauritius	25	48	31	25	24	22	48	50	45	50	16.3	-7.9	0.3
Mozambique	115	110	161	160	190	217	319	535	731	546	54.7	14.8	21.2
Namibia	0	0	0	0	0	3	6	16	17	36	..	..	69.6
Niger	105	123	123	107	102	206	184	215	242	200	8.1	8.0	3.8
Nigeria	17	17	17	29	15	16	39	51	97	310	-27.8	-0.8	98.6
Rwanda	97	103	99	95	96	102	124	138	137	131	13.9	0.1	1.8
Sao Tome & Principe	1	2	4	3	4	3	7	4	8	11	..	21.7	22.6
Senegal	182	214	189	212	246	196	316	359	368	536	18.8	2.6	17.5
Seychelles	18	14	15	14	14	12	21	19	18	15	27.7	-5.8	-9.8
Sierra Leone	57	34	56	36	22	30	51	44	52	72	44.7	-12.8	12.7
Somalia	139	140	141	152	193	163	354	398	311	267	42.2	5.4	-10.3
Sudan	272	295	357	438	309	646	467	441	498	434	38.1	14.3	-1.0
Swaziland	32	24	19	20	17	18	25	30	22	12	37.1	-9.9	-22.3
Tanzania	524	485	484	427	408	370	511	716	782	684	20.7	-6.6	10.1
Togo	52	37	50	49	53	53	92	86	128	108	26.1	3.3	9.3
Uganda	42	79	53	44	47	42	77	87	188	159	46.2	-4.8	34.0
Zaire	317	277	251	193	209	210	296	339	400	433	17.9	-8.6	14.0
Zambia	234	179	188	179	180	213	346	343	405	311	36.1	-1.4	-1.5
Zimbabwe	112	137	142	185	243	214	191	264	232	227	72.7	16.1	4.0
NORTH AFRICA	1,660	1,624	1,749	1,675	2,153	2,265	2,133	2,265	2,192	2,072	20.7	7.0	-1.2
Algeria	118	146	130	86	112	142	120	137	120	89	-0.8	-0.8	-9.6
Egypt, Arab Republic of	1,187	1,105	1,237	1,241	1,651	1,681	1,566	1,575	1,433	1,409	35.8	8.8	-4.0
Libya	10	2	2	2	2	3	8	2	2	7	36.2	-14.4	-8.1
Morocco	188	209	230	189	248	318	292	350	402	389	2.9	8.8	10.5
Tunisia	158	162	150	157	141	122	147	201	236	178	6.1	-4.7	7.6
ALL AFRICA	6,007	5,960	6,177	6,047	6,818	7,543	8,738	9,872	11,131	10,978	20.6	4.4	8.4
South Africa	..	..	..	..	..	..	..	..	..	..	..	..	..

12-3. Net ODA from non-DAC bilateral donors

	Millions of U.S. dollars (current prices and exchange rates)										Average annual percentage growth		
	1980	1981	1982	1983	1984	1985	1986	1987	1988	1989	75–80	80–85	86–MR
SUB-SAHARAN AFRICA	685	601	796	711	442	486	458	376	209	109	17.6	-7.6	-38.6
excluding Nigeria	647	585	791	689	420	484	441	370	212	108	17.6	-7.1	-38.0
Angola	1	0	1	0	1	0	1	2	3	3	..	..	48.7
Benin	2	1	0	2	0	3	3	1	1	0	..	..	..
Botswana	0	0	6	9	10	3	-1	0	1	-2	..	..	..
Burkina Faso	0	0	4	1	12	4	11	7	2	1	..	..	-55.5
Burundi	4	2	6	7	13	7	9	12	3	1	..	27.7	-52.6
Cameroon	23	0	-4	-6	8	3	3	0	-4	0	42.6	..	..
Cape Verde	2	0	1	0	1	2	2	1	1	0	..	..	-30.7
Central African Republic	2	0	1	0	0	0	3	8	2	-1	..	..	..
Chad	0	0	4	0	0	0	0	0	0	0	..	..	..
Comoros	17	13	10	6	5	4	2	0	0	0	..	-25.5	..
Congo, People's Republic of the	15	13	7	27	10	-1	-1	0	0	0	..	..	..
Cote d'Ivoire	0	0	0	0	0	0	0	0	0	0	..	..	..
Djibouti	33	14	2	12	34	12	29	24	3	1	..	-0.8	-69.1
Equatorial Guinea	0	0	0	0	0	0	0	0	0	0	..	..	..
Ethiopia	0	18	0	70	1	10	-1	-2	-1	0	..	..	..
Gabon	0	3	1	1	2	0	14	5	-2	-1	..	..	..
Gambia, The	7	21	4	1	1	1	-1	0	-2	-1	..	-46.8	..
Ghana	25	14	3	-5	-5	-6	3	-5	13	2	..	..	..
Guinea	0	25	29	-1	30	2	4	12	14	18	-35.5	..	54.5
Guinea-Bissau	1	0	5	6	2	3	4	5	6	2	-16.4	47.0	-11.3
Kenya	0	2	6	4	31	22	5	4	3	0	..	..	-69.9
Lesotho	0	3	4	6	6	6	3	4	3	3	..	..	-5.2
Liberia	9	2	1	0	0	0	0	0	0	0	..	..	..
Madagascar	48	55	3	-7	-8	-5	-2	-2	-2	-2	..	..	..
Malawi	0	0	0	0	0	0	0	0	0	0	..	..	..
Mali	33	7	40	32	9	27	40	8	5	2	13.3	-1.2	-60.6
Mauritania	86	97	76	46	50	60	63	12	-4	-5	7.4	-11.6	..
Mauritius	0	1	2	3	3	2	2	3	3	-1	..	..	..
Mozambique	20	1	6	1	3	6	7	3	3	3	..	-10.8	-19.2
Namibia	0	0	0	0	0	0	0	0	0	0	..	..	..
Niger	2	20	90	18	7	2	5	8	6	3	-34.4	-11.2	-22.8
Nigeria	0	0	0	0	0	0	0	0	0	0	..	..	..
Rwanda	1	1	0	2	6	6	6	6	3	6	-22.7	..	-7.5
Sao Tome & Principe	0	0	0	0	0	0	0	0	0	0	..	..	..
Senegal	2	54	16	48	59	38	33	30	24	12	..	56.9	-28.5
Seychelles	0	1	0	0	0	2	1	1	0	0	..	..	..
Sierra Leone	4	0	0	0	14	0	6	4	10	0	..	..	-54.8
Somalia	128	47	160	39	7	36	-9	1	4	1	20.3	-32.0	..
Sudan	160	115	166	358	118	215	193	210	106	26	14.6	6.8	-48.7
Swaziland	0	0	0	0	0	0	0	0	0	0	..	..	..
Tanzania	27	45	13	17	10	13	8	3	4	4	122.8	-20.6	-14.0
Togo	0	1	4	3	2	9	8	3	-2	-1	..	..	..
Uganda	1	0	1	4	-3	0	3	4	0	31	..	..	37.2
Zaire	5	15	6	0	0	0	0	0	0	0	..	..	..
Zambia	23	3	76	5	1	2	3	3	3	3	..	-37.0	0.4
Zimbabwe	5	8	44	0	1	-2	-2	2	-3	-1	..	..	..
NORTH AFRICA	739	788	494	104	57	393	190	214	35	8	-21.8	-30.2	-67.4
Algeria	41	2	-3	-4	0	9	28	52	27	22	..	..	-12.4
Egypt, Arab Republic of	4	-19	-18	-26	-25	-25	54	74	-17	-15	-65.0	..	..
Libya	0	0	0	0	0	0	0	0	0	0	..	..	..
Morocco	644	763	482	122	73	404	70	62	21	0	58.1	-26.4	-87.4
Tunisia	49	43	32	12	9	5	39	27	3	1	1.7	-38.6	-78.3
ALL AFRICA	1,424	1,389	1,290	815	499	879	648	590	244	118	-10.1	-15.6	-45.1
South Africa	..	..	..	..	..	..	..	..	..	..	..	..	..

12–4. Net ODA from multilateral donors

	Millions of U.S. dollars (current prices and exchange rates)										Average annual percentage growth		
	1980	1981	1982	1983	1984	1985	1986	1987	1988	1989	75–80	80–85	86–MR
SUB-SAHARAN AFRICA	2,357	2,377	2,272	2,223	2,487	2,858	3,524	3,935	4,321	4,785	21.1	3.1	10.6
excluding Nigeria	2,224	2,237	2,141	2,117	2,384	2,746	3,406	3,822	4,179	4,502	21.7	3.6	9.7
Angola	16	22	20	29	34	32	36	36	50	57	65.6	15.9	18.2
Benin	53	35	40	43	38	45	63	60	67	111	15.8	-1.4	19.8
Botswana	23	21	12	21	27	34	21	32	25	42	22.9	10.2	19.4
Burkina Faso	61	59	62	55	54	72	98	78	77	73	19.9	1.3	-8.6
Burundi	54	55	45	64	58	59	89	103	102	108	25.8	2.8	5.7
Cameroon	71	65	61	26	24	30	45	32	48	169	13.0	-20.8	54.6
Cape Verde	24	14	11	14	23	27	32	24	26	26	9.6	7.4	-5.4
Central African Republic	34	29	20	28	45	42	50	59	87	94	16.2	8.4	25.5
Chad	15	28	26	44	56	86	63	78	118	114	-5.5	37.9	24.7
Comoros	13	16	15	17	18	25	23	21	17	13	13.1	11.1	-18.0
Congo, People's Republic of the	22	26	27	27	20	25	10	20	12	10	7.6	0.0	-7.1
Cote d'Ivoire	58	32	35	15	14	14	49	33	213	153	8.4	-26.0	70.0
Djibouti	9	15	13	13	20	23	22	23	18	11	..	18.5	-21.0
Equatorial Guinea	8	6	9	7	7	10	11	21	20	22	54.9	4.5	22.0
Ethiopia	121	151	123	176	176	288	240	323	411	364	15.9	16.0	16.0
Gabon	7	4	4	6	6	10	6	7	9	13	31.4	9.8	28.2
Gambia, The	31	28	21	20	20	18	43	49	29	38	52.6	-9.9	-8.2
Ghana	59	44	73	54	125	113	247	247	225	201	23.4	19.0	-6.9
Guinea	57	51	35	42	51	57	73	82	89	139	75.0	0.7	22.3
Guinea-Bissau	24	24	27	26	22	31	27	54	45	46	27.6	3.1	15.9
Kenya	120	84	146	58	85	88	68	124	195	352	38.4	-6.7	71.4
Lesotho	31	42	36	41	32	39	32	45	39	59	15.7	1.6	18.3
Liberia	29	20	22	30	26	26	28	27	17	21	38.0	2.0	-13.0
Madagascar	91	85	80	73	64	93	142	142	92	150	12.5	-2.4	-2.7
Malawi	68	55	56	61	107	60	113	110	185	218	35.9	4.2	28.0
Mali	103	90	74	86	88	102	128	136	162	152	18.5	0.0	7.0
Mauritania	36	50	49	58	57	49	57	73	77	88	15.0	5.9	14.8
Mauritius	8	10	15	14	8	4	7	12	11	10	-3.1	-10.0	12.3
Mozambique	34	33	41	49	66	77	96	113	159	219	22.2	19.9	32.6
Namibia	0	0	0	0	0	3	9	1	5	23	..	..	58.0
Niger	64	51	44	50	52	96	118	130	124	95	8.5	6.7	-6.8
Nigeria	18	24	20	19	18	16	20	18	23	36	11.3	-3.9	21.4
Rwanda	58	50	52	53	63	73	81	101	112	97	21.4	5.5	6.8
Sao Tome & Principe	3	4	6	8	7	9	5	13	16	22	3.4	26.4	55.7
Senegal	79	129	80	62	64	60	218	252	177	103	25.4	-10.1	-23.1
Seychelles	3	2	3	2	2	9	6	5	2	5	71.1	11.0	-14.8
Sierra Leone	30	26	26	30	25	35	30	21	40	29	33.7	2.3	5.1
Somalia	166	188	160	152	150	154	167	181	118	154	18.5	-3.1	-6.5
Sudan	192	223	217	166	196	267	285	248	333	293	22.7	2.9	3.8
Swaziland	17	13	9	13	12	7	10	16	16	18	24.4	-11.5	19.9
Tanzania	128	173	187	150	140	104	162	163	196	232	20.1	-5.2	13.5
Togo	39	26	23	60	55	52	75	37	73	76	22.0	14.3	7.4
Uganda	70	57	79	89	118	140	117	188	175	215	33.6	17.9	19.2
Zaire	106	102	92	121	103	115	152	288	175	205	22.0	2.1	4.1
Zambia	62	50	52	33	58	113	115	83	71	76	44.0	8.9	-13.2
Zimbabwe	47	67	30	23	53	26	36	28	43	40	..	-10.9	8.1
NORTH AFRICA	311	335	332	388	240	258	194	236	283	346	7.9	-4.9	21.1
Algeria	17	19	9	13	10	22	18	25	24	42	-5.8	-1.3	29.0
Egypt, Arab Republic of	196	206	223	248	168	135	96	125	121	173	7.9	-6.5	19.0
Libya	7	9	10	3	3	2	3	4	4	3	5.3	-25.5	3.7
Morocco	66	65	63	87	31	63	41	36	57	64	52.2	-5.9	19.9
Tunisia	25	35	28	37	29	36	37	46	77	63	-9.8	4.2	23.9
ALL AFRICA	2,668	2,712	2,604	2,610	2,727	3,116	3,718	4,172	4,605	5,131	18.0	2.3	11.2
South Africa	..	..	..	..	..	..	..	..	..	..	..	..	..

12–5. Net ODA from all donors as a share of recipient GDP

	Percentage of GDP										Average		
	1980	*1981*	*1982*	*1983*	*1984*	*1985*	*1986*	*1987*	*1988*	*1989*	*75–80*	*80–85*	*86–MR*
SUB-SAHARAN AFRICA	**3.5**	**3.6**	**3.7**	**3.7**	**3.9**	**4.4**	**6.2**	**7.7**	**8.4**	**8.6**	**3.2**	**3.8**	**7.7**
excluding Nigeria	**7.3**	**7.5**	**7.6**	**7.9**	**8.7**	**9.7**	**9.8**	**10.7**	**12.1**	**11.9**	**5.9**	**8.1**	**11.1**
Angola	..	..	1.1	1.4	1.6	1.5	2.3	2.1	2.3	1.9	..	..	2.2
Benin	7.9	7.7	7.8	8.8	8.1	9.1	10.3	8.8	10.0	16.3	8.7	8.2	11.3
Botswana	11.9	9.5	11.8	10.7	9.0	9.3	8.7	10.7	7.5	6.4	15.1	10.4	8.3
Burkina Faso	12.4	13.8	13.7	12.9	14.6	13.8	14.0	11.2	10.8	10.9	11.3	13.5	11.7
Burundi	12.7	12.5	12.5	12.9	14.3	12.4	15.6	17.9	17.3	18.1	10.9	12.9	17.2
Cameroon	3.5	2.4	2.7	1.6	2.3	1.9	2.1	1.7	2.2	4.2	4.5	2.4	2.6
Cape Verde	45.3	36.1	39.0	43.1	48.3	50.5	57.4	37.4	32.9	26.4	29.0	43.7	38.5
Central African Republic	13.9	14.6	12.0	14.1	17.8	14.8	14.0	16.8	17.8	17.9	10.6	14.5	16.6
Chad	4.9	9.7	11.0	16.2	17.8	24.9	21.9	24.4	25.1	23.9	12.5	14.1	23.8
Comoros	..	..	33.9	34.1	38.2	41.2	28.5	27.2	25.0	22.4	..	..	25.8
Congo, People's Republic of the	5.4	4.1	4.3	5.2	4.5	3.3	6.0	6.6	4.0	3.6	8.0	4.4	5.1
Cote d'Ivoire	2.0	1.5	1.8	2.3	1.9	1.8	2.0	2.4	4.3	4.5	2.0	1.9	3.3
Djibouti	..	..	..	..	31.1	24.1	31.7	28.3	23.5	18.7	..	..	25.5
Equatorial Guinea	..	..	..	..	..	19.0	20.7	35.7	33.4	33.7	..	..	30.9
Ethiopia	5.2	5.7	4.5	7.0	7.5	15.0	12.1	11.7	17.1	12.3	4.5	7.5	13.3
Gabon	1.3	1.1	1.7	1.9	2.2	1.7	2.3	2.4	3.3	3.8	1.6	1.6	2.9
Gambia, The	23.2	32.2	22.4	20.4	32.6	29.0	68.3	53.8	38.6	42.1	12.9	26.6	50.7
Ghana	4.3	3.4	3.5	2.7	4.9	4.5	6.5	7.3	9.1	10.5	3.4	3.9	8.4
Guinea	..	..	..	..	..	..	8.7	10.1	10.8	12.7	..	..	10.6
Guinea-Bissau	56.2	42.2	39.1	39.2	39.6	36.6	56.3	64.8	64.0	60.3	31.6	42.2	61.3
Kenya	5.5	6.6	7.5	6.7	6.6	7.1	6.3	7.2	9.5	11.6	4.5	6.7	8.6
Lesotho	25.6	27.8	27.3	30.6	32.7	38.4	32.3	30.1	25.3	28.3	20.5	30.4	29.0
Liberia	8.8	9.9	9.7	11.1	12.2	8.3	8.9	6.9	..	..	4.6	10.0	7.9
Madagascar	5.7	6.5	6.9	5.2	5.2	6.6	9.7	12.5	12.5	13.1	3.3	6.0	11.9
Malawi	11.6	11.1	10.3	9.5	13.1	10.0	16.8	23.7	27.4	25.1	10.7	10.9	23.3
Mali	16.4	16.9	17.1	19.9	30.3	35.9	24.4	19.3	22.0	22.7	13.3	22.7	22.1
Mauritania	24.8	28.6	24.9	22.3	24.1	29.2	26.7	19.5	18.9	24.3	30.6	25.7	22.3
Mauritius	2.9	5.1	4.4	3.7	3.4	2.6	3.8	3.5	2.9	2.8	3.3	3.7	3.3
Mozambique	7.0	6.3	8.5	9.3	10.2	8.8	10.2	44.7	71.3	59.2	..	8.3	46.3
Namibia	0.0	0.0	0.0	0.0	0.0	0.5	1.1	1.0	1.2	3.1	..	0.1	1.6
Niger	6.7	8.9	13.1	9.8	11.0	21.1	16.5	16.3	15.9	14.5	10.0	11.8	15.8
Nigeria	0.0	0.0	0.0	0.1	0.0	0.0	0.1	0.3	0.4	1.2	0.1	0.0	0.5
Rwanda	13.4	11.6	10.7	9.9	10.4	10.6	10.8	11.3	10.8	10.8	13.8	11.1	10.9
Sao Tome & Principe	8.8	21.9	27.4	33.2	34.4	34.8	19.2	31.0	48.9	71.9	15.8	26.8	42.7
Senegal	8.7	16.0	11.0	13.0	15.8	11.4	15.1	13.9	11.4	14.0	8.2	12.7	13.6
Seychelles	14.6	10.9	12.2	10.7	10.0	13.1	13.7	9.8	7.2	6.7	17.2	11.9	9.3
Sierra Leone	8.2	5.1	6.1	4.4	5.6	5.0	6.1	12.3	8.9	10.5	4.0	5.7	9.5
Somalia	71.8	53.5	59.6	46.7	44.4	40.4	55.1	57.3	41.6	38.5	28.9	52.8	48.1
Sudan	9.2	8.0	9.4	12.7	7.1	11.0	6.8	5.5	10.1	6.5	5.7	9.6	7.2
Swaziland	9.2	6.4	5.5	6.4	6.4	7.0	7.5	8.2	6.5	5.0	8.8	6.8	6.8
Tanzania	13.2	11.9	10.9	9.4	9.6	7.1	13.9	25.6	29.7	32.6	10.5	10.3	25.5
Togo	8.0	6.6	9.4	14.6	15.3	15.1	16.7	10.1	14.6	13.7	9.3	11.5	13.8
Uganda	9.0	10.9	7.1	7.0	6.9	8.5	5.8	7.6	8.9	12.7	..	8.2	8.8
Zaire	3.0	3.1	2.6	2.9	4.0	4.5	5.5	8.2	6.5	7.3	2.2	3.3	6.9
Zambia	8.2	5.8	8.2	6.5	8.8	14.6	27.9	20.7	13.2	9.0	5.0	8.7	17.7
Zimbabwe	3.1	3.3	3.2	3.3	5.8	5.4	4.5	5.5	4.6	4.5	0.2	4.0	4.8
NORTH AFRICA	**2.1**	**2.2**	**2.1**	**1.7**	**1.9**	**2.1**	**1.7**	**1.8**	**1.8**	**1.8**	**4.1**	**2.0**	**1.8**
Algeria	0.4	0.4	0.3	0.2	0.2	0.3	0.3	0.3	0.3	0.3	0.7	0.3	0.3
Egypt, Arab Republic of	6.1	5.5	5.6	5.2	5.9	5.2	4.8	5.0	5.0	4.7	14.9	5.6	4.9
Libya	0.0	0.0	0.0	0.0	0.0	0.0	0.1	0.0	0.0	0.0	0.0	0.0	0.0
Morocco	4.8	6.8	5.0	2.9	2.8	6.1	2.4	2.4	2.2	2.0	3.2	4.7	2.2
Tunisia	2.7	2.8	2.6	2.5	2.2	2.0	2.5	2.8	3.1	2.4	4.4	2.5	2.7
ALL AFRICA	**3.0**	**3.1**	**3.1**	**2.9**	**3.1**	**3.4**	**4.1**	**4.8**	**5.4**	**5.4**	**3.5**	**3.1**	**4.9**
South Africa	..	..	..	..	..	..	..	..	..	..	..	..	..

12–6. Net ODA from DAC donors as a share of recipient GDP

	Percentage of GDP										Average		
	1980	1981	1982	1983	1984	1985	1986	1987	1988	1989	75–80	80–85	86–MR
SUB-SAHARAN AFRICA	2.1	2.2	2.2	2.2	2.4	2.7	3.9	4.9	5.6	5.5	1.8	2.3	5.0
excluding Nigeria	4.2	4.4	4.4	4.7	5.2	5.9	6.0	6.7	7.9	7.6	3.3	4.8	7.1
Angola	..	..	0.8	0.9	1.0	1.0	1.7	1.5	1.5	1.1	..	..	1.5
Benin	3.1	4.3	3.9	4.2	4.1	4.6	5.4	4.9	5.8	9.0	4.7	4.0	6.3
Botswana	9.4	7.5	9.6	7.7	5.7	5.7	7.0	8.5	6.2	4.8	11.9	7.6	6.6
Burkina Faso	8.8	10.0	9.4	9.0	9.4	8.5	8.6	7.8	7.9	8.0	7.3	9.2	8.1
Burundi	6.5	6.7	7.4	6.4	7.1	6.7	7.4	7.7	7.7	8.1	5.8	6.8	7.7
Cameroon	2.3	1.6	2.0	1.4	1.9	1.5	1.6	1.4	1.9	2.7	2.9	1.8	1.9
Cape Verde	27.3	26.0	30.4	32.6	29.7	29.5	40.0	26.7	22.5	17.2	17.1	29.3	26.6
Central African Republic	9.4	10.5	9.2	9.8	10.7	8.7	8.6	10.4	9.7	9.2	6.5	9.7	9.5
Chad	2.8	5.1	6.0	8.8	9.1	13.1	13.6	14.7	13.9	12.6	7.0	7.5	13.7
Comoros	..	..	12.3	13.5	16.9	15.6	12.7	16.6	16.7	15.9	..	..	15.5
Congo, People's Republic of the	3.2	2.1	2.8	2.6	3.1	2.2	5.5	5.7	3.5	3.3	4.9	2.7	4.5
Cote d'Ivoire	1.4	1.1	1.4	2.1	1.7	1.6	1.5	2.1	2.2	2.8	1.5	1.5	2.2
Djibouti	..	..	..	..	14.7	13.7	17.8	15.9	18.0	15.8	..	..	16.9
Equatorial Guinea	..	..	..	..	..	7.6	10.0	18.1	18.3	15.7	..	..	15.5
Ethiopia	2.2	1.8	1.7	1.9	3.9	8.7	7.6	5.8	9.8	6.3	2.1	3.4	7.4
Gabon	1.1	0.9	1.6	1.7	1.9	1.4	1.7	2.1	3.1	3.4	1.2	1.4	2.6
Gambia, The	7.0	9.1	11.0	10.3	19.7	18.0	39.8	27.3	25.7	25.4	5.8	12.5	29.6
Ghana	2.4	2.1	1.6	1.5	2.2	2.1	2.1	2.6	4.5	6.7	2.1	2.0	4.0
Guinea	..	..	..	..	..	..	4.8	5.7	6.6	7.0	..	..	6.0
Guinea-Bissau	32.5	26.8	20.2	19.7	22.0	15.4	32.3	28.8	30.9	31.6	19.8	22.8	30.9
Kenya	3.8	5.3	5.2	5.7	4.8	5.4	5.3	5.6	7.2	7.4	3.6	5.0	6.4
Lesotho	17.3	15.8	15.6	17.4	20.4	19.8	19.3	16.3	15.6	14.5	12.0	17.7	16.4
Liberia	5.4	7.9	7.6	8.3	9.8	5.9	6.4	4.5	..	..	2.4	7.5	5.4
Madagascar	2.2	2.6	4.5	3.3	3.3	3.5	5.4	7.1	8.7	7.1	1.6	3.2	7.1
Malawi	6.1	6.6	5.5	4.6	4.3	4.7	7.2	14.4	13.6	11.4	7.2	5.3	11.6
Mali	8.0	9.7	7.8	9.0	21.1	23.7	13.3	11.7	13.4	15.0	6.7	13.2	13.4
Mauritania	7.5	8.9	8.2	9.1	9.5	14.0	12.5	10.4	11.4	15.9	4.7	9.6	12.6
Mauritius	2.2	4.2	2.8	2.3	2.3	2.1	3.3	2.7	2.2	2.4	1.8	2.6	2.6
Mozambique	4.8	4.8	6.6	7.0	7.5	6.4	7.7	36.7	58.3	42.1	..	6.2	36.2
Namibia	0.0	0.0	0.0	0.0	0.0	0.2	0.5	0.9	0.9	1.9	..	0.0	1.0
Niger	4.1	5.6	6.3	6.0	7.0	14.3	9.9	9.9	10.4	9.8	5.9	7.2	10.0
Nigeria	0.0	0.0	0.0	0.0	0.0	0.0	0.1	0.2	0.3	1.0	0.1	0.0	0.4
Rwanda	8.3	7.8	7.0	6.3	6.0	6.0	6.4	6.4	5.9	6.0	8.7	6.9	6.2
Sao Tome & Principe	2.8	6.1	10.7	9.7	12.3	8.3	10.7	7.8	16.2	24.1	3.6	8.3	14.7
Senegal	6.0	8.6	7.3	8.6	10.5	7.6	8.4	7.8	7.4	11.6	4.8	8.1	8.8
Seychelles	12.3	8.8	9.9	9.3	8.9	7.2	9.9	7.6	6.3	5.1	16.0	9.4	7.2
Sierra Leone	5.1	2.8	4.2	2.4	2.1	2.3	3.6	7.9	4.6	7.5	1.8	3.1	5.9
Somalia	23.1	20.0	18.3	20.6	24.5	18.7	38.2	39.3	29.9	24.4	5.5	20.9	33.0
Sudan	4.0	3.7	4.6	5.8	3.5	6.3	3.4	2.7	5.4	3.7	1.3	4.6	3.8
Swaziland	6.0	4.1	3.7	3.9	3.8	5.0	5.3	5.4	3.8	1.9	5.9	4.4	4.1
Tanzania	10.2	8.2	7.7	6.8	7.0	5.4	10.5	20.8	23.7	24.3	8.2	7.5	19.8
Togo	4.6	3.8	6.1	6.3	7.4	7.1	8.8	6.9	9.4	8.1	5.7	5.9	8.3
Uganda	3.3	6.3	2.8	2.2	2.0	2.0	2.3	2.4	4.6	5.0	..	3.1	3.6
Zaire	2.2	2.2	1.8	1.8	2.7	2.9	3.7	4.4	4.5	4.9	1.5	2.3	4.4
Zambia	6.0	4.5	4.9	5.4	6.6	9.5	20.8	16.5	11.1	7.2	4.2	6.1	13.9
Zimbabwe	2.1	2.1	2.1	3.0	4.8	4.9	3.8	4.9	3.9	3.9	0.2	3.2	4.1
NORTH AFRICA	1.3	1.3	1.4	1.3	1.7	1.6	1.5	1.5	1.6	1.5	1.5	1.4	1.5
Algeria	0.3	0.3	0.3	0.2	0.2	0.2	0.2	0.2	0.2	0.2	0.5	0.3	0.2
Egypt, Arab Republic of	5.2	4.7	4.8	4.4	5.4	4.8	4.4	4.4	4.6	4.2	4.2	4.9	4.4
Libya	0.0	0.0	0.0	0.0	0.0	0.0	0.0	0.0	0.0	0.0	0.0	0.0	0.0
Morocco	1.0	1.4	1.5	1.4	1.9	2.5	1.7	1.9	1.8	1.7	1.5	1.6	1.8
Tunisia	1.8	1.9	1.8	1.9	1.7	1.5	1.7	2.1	2.3	1.7	3.1	1.8	2.0
ALL AFRICA	1.8	1.8	1.9	1.9	2.1	2.2	2.8	3.2	3.7	3.7	1.7	2.0	3.4
South Africa	..	..	..	..	..	..	..	..	..	..	..	..	..

12–7. Net ODA from multilateral donors as a share of recipient GDP

	Percentage of GDP										Average		
	1980	1981	1982	1983	1984	1985	1986	1987	1988	1989	75–80	80–85	86–MR
SUB-SAHARAN AFRICA	1.1	1.2	1.1	1.1	1.3	1.5	2.1	2.6	2.7	3.0	1.0	1.2	2.6
excluding Nigeria	2.4	2.5	2.4	2.5	3.0	3.3	3.4	3.7	4.1	4.3	1.9	2.7	3.9
Angola	..	..	0.4	0.6	0.6	0.5	0.7	0.5	0.7	0.7	..	..	0.7
Benin	4.6	3.4	3.8	4.4	4.0	4.3	4.7	3.8	4.2	7.2	4.0	4.1	5.0
Botswana	2.5	2.1	1.4	2.1	2.4	3.3	1.8	2.2	1.2	1.7	3.2	2.3	1.7
Burkina Faso	3.6	3.7	4.0	3.9	4.2	5.0	4.8	3.1	2.8	2.8	4.0	4.1	3.4
Burundi	5.9	5.6	4.5	5.9	5.9	5.1	7.4	9.1	9.4	9.8	4.9	5.5	8.9
Cameroon	0.9	0.8	0.8	0.3	0.3	0.4	0.4	0.3	0.4	1.5	1.4	0.6	0.6
Cape Verde	16.5	10.1	7.5	10.3	17.6	19.7	16.5	10.2	9.9	9.0	11.1	13.6	11.4
Central African Republic	4.2	4.1	2.6	4.3	7.1	6.0	5.1	5.6	7.9	8.8	3.8	4.7	6.8
Chad	2.1	4.6	4.4	7.4	8.6	11.7	8.3	9.6	11.2	11.3	4.8	6.5	10.1
Comoros	..	..	12.6	14.9	17.1	21.8	14.3	10.6	8.3	6.4	..	..	9.9
Congo, People's Republic of the	1.3	1.3	1.2	1.3	0.9	1.2	0.6	0.9	0.5	0.4	2.5	1.2	0.6
Cote d'Ivoire	0.6	0.4	0.5	0.2	0.2	0.2	0.5	0.3	2.1	1.6	0.6	0.3	1.1
Djibouti	..	..	..	..	6.1	6.8	5.9	6.0	4.6	2.6	..	..	4.8
Equatorial Guinea	..	..	..	..	..	11.4	10.6	17.6	15.1	17.8	..	..	15.3
Ethiopia	2.9	3.5	2.8	3.6	3.6	6.0	4.6	6.0	7.2	6.0	2.3	3.8	6.0
Gabon	0.2	0.1	0.1	0.2	0.2	0.3	0.2	0.2	0.3	0.4	0.2	0.2	0.3
Gambia, The	13.2	13.1	9.7	9.7	12.5	10.4	28.9	26.5	13.8	17.3	5.5	11.4	21.6
Ghana	1.3	1.0	1.8	1.3	2.8	2.5	4.3	4.9	4.3	3.8	1.1	1.8	4.3
Guinea	..	..	..	..	..	..	3.6	3.9	3.6	5.0	..	..	4.0
Guinea-Bissau	22.4	15.3	16.1	15.8	16.0	19.3	21.1	32.8	29.2	27.3	9.3	17.5	27.6
Kenya	1.6	1.2	2.3	1.0	1.4	1.4	0.9	1.6	2.3	4.2	0.9	1.5	2.2
Lesotho	8.3	11.1	10.6	11.5	10.3	16.1	11.8	12.7	9.0	13.2	8.5	11.3	11.7
Liberia	2.6	1.8	2.0	2.8	2.4	2.4	2.6	2.3	..	..	1.9	2.3	2.5
Madagascar	2.3	2.4	2.3	2.1	2.2	3.3	4.3	5.6	3.8	6.0	1.6	2.4	4.9
Malawi	5.5	4.5	4.8	4.9	8.8	5.3	9.6	9.3	13.8	13.7	3.5	5.6	11.6
Mali	6.3	6.6	6.0	8.0	8.3	9.6	8.4	7.2	8.3	7.6	5.5	7.5	7.9
Mauritania	5.1	6.7	6.5	7.3	7.8	6.8	6.7	7.8	7.9	8.8	8.5	6.7	7.8
Mauritius	0.7	0.8	1.4	1.2	0.8	0.4	0.5	0.7	0.5	0.5	1.5	0.9	0.5
Mozambique	1.4	1.4	1.7	2.2	2.6	2.3	2.3	7.8	12.7	16.9	..	1.9	9.9
Namibia	0.0	0.0	0.0	0.0	0.0	0.3	0.6	0.1	0.3	1.2	..	0.0	0.5
Niger	2.5	2.3	2.2	2.8	3.6	6.7	6.3	6.0	5.3	4.6	3.5	3.3	5.6
Nigeria	0.0	0.0	0.0	0.0	0.0	0.0	0.0	0.1	0.1	0.1	0.0	0.0	0.1
Rwanda	4.9	3.8	3.7	3.5	3.9	4.2	4.2	4.7	4.8	4.5	4.6	4.0	4.5
Sao Tome & Principe	6.0	15.8	16.7	23.6	22.1	26.5	8.4	23.3	32.7	47.8	12.1	18.5	28.1
Senegal	2.6	5.2	3.1	2.5	2.7	2.3	5.8	5.5	3.6	2.2	3.2	3.1	4.3
Seychelles	2.3	1.3	2.1	1.3	1.1	5.1	3.1	1.9	0.8	1.6	0.9	2.2	1.9
Sierra Leone	2.7	2.2	2.0	2.0	2.3	2.7	2.1	3.8	3.5	3.0	2.0	2.3	3.1
Somalia	27.6	26.9	20.7	20.7	19.0	17.6	18.0	17.8	11.3	14.0	8.7	22.1	15.3
Sudan	2.8	2.8	2.8	2.2	2.2	2.6	2.1	1.5	3.6	2.5	1.5	2.6	2.4
Swaziland	3.2	2.3	1.9	2.5	2.6	2.0	2.1	2.8	2.7	3.0	3.0	2.4	2.7
Tanzania	2.5	2.9	3.0	2.4	2.4	1.5	3.3	4.7	5.9	8.2	2.2	2.4	5.5
Togo	3.4	2.7	2.8	7.9	7.6	6.8	7.1	3.0	5.3	5.7	3.5	5.2	5.3
Uganda	5.5	4.6	4.2	4.5	5.0	6.5	3.4	5.2	4.3	6.8	..	5.1	4.9
Zaire	0.7	0.8	0.7	1.1	1.3	1.6	1.9	3.8	2.0	2.3	0.6	1.0	2.5
Zambia	1.6	1.3	1.4	1.0	2.1	5.0	6.9	4.0	1.9	1.8	0.8	2.1	3.7
Zimbabwe	0.9	1.0	0.4	0.4	1.0	0.6	0.7	0.5	0.7	0.7	0.0	0.7	0.7
NORTH AFRICA	0.2	0.3	0.3	0.3	0.2	0.2	0.1	0.2	0.2	0.3	0.8	0.2	0.2
Algeria	0.0	0.0	0.0	0.0	0.0	0.0	0.0	0.0	0.0	0.1	0.1	0.0	0.0
Egypt, Arab Republic of	0.9	0.9	0.9	0.9	0.5	0.4	0.3	0.4	0.4	0.5	3.6	0.7	0.4
Libya	0.0	0.0	0.0	0.0	0.0	0.0	0.0	0.0	0.0	0.0	0.0	0.0	0.0
Morocco	0.4	0.4	0.4	0.6	0.2	0.5	0.2	0.2	0.3	0.3	0.3	0.4	0.2
Tunisia	0.3	0.4	0.3	0.5	0.4	0.4	0.4	0.5	0.8	0.6	0.5	0.4	0.6
ALL AFRICA	0.8	0.8	0.8	0.8	0.8	0.9	1.2	1.4	1.6	1.7	0.9	0.8	1.5
South Africa	..	..	..	..	..	..	..	..	..	..	..	..	..

12–8. Net ODA from all donors as a share of recipient GDI

	Percentage of GDI										Average		
	1980	*1981*	*1982*	*1983*	*1984*	*1985*	*1986*	*1987*	*1988*	*1989*	*75–80*	*80–85*	*86–MR*
SUB-SAHARAN AFRICA	17.5	17.8	21.9	27.6	37.3	37.9	42.7	51.8	56.6	58.4	14.7	26.7	52.4
excluding Nigeria	38.6	42.6	45.0	56.0	63.1	69.0	67.3	71.4	76.2	76.2	30.9	52.4	72.8
Angola	..	..	..	..	..	..	..	..	..	..	..	..	..
Benin	42.4	40.3	22.8	76.0	109.3	102.0	76.8	68.2	77.4	182.1	40.1	65.5	101.1
Botswana	29.0	21.9	26.6	36.6	36.8	31.0	48.9	169.0	72.7	26.7	38.3	30.3	79.3
Burkina Faso	68.2	81.0	63.4	62.7	85.5	53.3	61.0	56.3	48.6	47.6	48.0	69.0	53.4
Burundi	91.8	73.7	86.4	56.6	78.0	89.3	133.9	78.9	115.3	108.0	101.4	79.3	109.0
Cameroon	18.8	9.6	11.7	6.7	11.2	7.8	6.8	7.1	14.3	22.9	22.0	11.0	12.7
Cape Verde	108.2	79.6	73.7	88.2	109.7	112.0	125.3	84.5	79.1	62.4	87.7	95.2	87.8
Central African Republic	198.7	167.2	179.7	119.3	144.7	102.3	114.6	122.7	154.5	160.4	91.4	152.0	138.0
Chad	..	..	..	529.8	328.0	304.8	240.4	198.3	320.5	266.4	..	..	256.4
Comoros	..	..	..	117.4	83.4	139.3	120.8	117.0	156.8	161.2	..	..	138.9
Congo, People's Republic of the	15.1	8.4	7.2	13.4	14.7	10.8	20.2	33.5	21.5	22.8	27.3	11.6	24.5
Cote d'Ivoire	7.1	5.7	7.8	11.2	17.8	14.2	17.9	20.0	29.6	52.3	7.9	10.6	29.9
Djibouti	..	..	..	..	109.2	101.4	196.4	151.7	151.1	101.3	..	..	150.1
Equatorial Guinea	..	..	..	..	..	204.3	163.6	147.7	159.5	158.0	..	..	157.2
Ethiopia	51.4	55.0	38.2	62.7	61.0	107.0	95.5	80.3	111.2	92.4	49.5	62.6	94.8
Gabon	4.6	3.1	4.9	5.3	6.4	4.5	5.1	8.6	10.3	14.9	3.3	4.8	9.7
Gambia, The	88.5	131.1	108.4	118.0	169.9	182.9	335.4	291.5	213.9	191.5	69.5	133.1	258.1
Ghana	76.6	75.2	103.5	72.1	71.1	47.1	69.2	70.4	83.5	77.8	41.8	74.3	75.2
Guinea	..	..	..	..	..	..	55.9	57.4	55.2	68.9	..	..	59.4
Guinea-Bissau	190.2	163.9	138.5	173.2	132.2	114.5	231.8	194.7	186.9	169.5	161.6	152.1	195.7
Kenya	18.7	23.7	34.5	32.1	32.0	27.5	28.9	29.5	38.0	47.2	20.2	28.1	35.9
Lesotho	60.4	64.8	54.9	91.3	78.6	76.8	71.2	67.0	54.8	51.6	76.9	71.1	61.1
Liberia	32.1	60.5	68.0	93.9	119.0	95.2	92.3	..	..	..	14.7	78.1	..
Madagascar	38.0	56.8	80.8	62.4	60.5	76.7	107.4	123.9	93.7	96.5	34.7	62.5	105.4
Malawi	46.7	62.9	48.0	41.8	101.8	53.6	137.1	154.0	146.3	124.0	35.5	59.1	140.3
Mali	96.6	96.4	97.3	136.5	199.0	183.6	106.5	83.6	84.0	82.3	82.5	134.9	89.1
Mauritania	68.6	68.2	52.8	125.5	96.1	120.3	116.1	95.2	106.9	165.4	90.8	88.6	120.9
Mauritius	14.1	20.1	24.3	21.4	15.5	11.2	17.5	14.0	9.4	9.1	11.1	17.8	12.5
Mozambique	37.1	30.9	43.8	93.0	96.2	128.3	105.2	185.9	213.3	166.9	..	71.5	167.8
Namibia	0.0	0.0	0.0	0.0	0.0	3.6	8.7	6.2	5.9	18.7	..	0.6	9.9
Niger	18.3	43.9	71.9	76.8	346.3	165.9	163.2	176.5	145.1	152.8	57.4	120.5	159.4
Nigeria	0.2	0.2	0.3	0.5	0.6	0.5	1.3	2.5	3.3	9.3	0.4	0.4	4.1
Rwanda	82.8	87.3	60.1	73.3	65.6	61.0	68.3	72.7	69.0	69.0	97.9	71.7	69.8
Sao Tome & Principe	25.8	46.6	55.0	112.8	72.0	94.1	132.5	180.5	173.7	260.4	68.0	67.7	186.8
Senegal	57.1	135.2	97.9	109.5	134.7	116.6	137.1	119.1	91.4	130.1	49.8	108.5	119.4
Seychelles	38.1	33.5	37.9	50.5	46.3	57.9	59.9	52.5	36.3	33.9	..	44.0	45.7
Sierra Leone	50.8	26.5	45.9	31.1	43.9	50.3	54.3	118.1	77.2	92.2	31.2	41.4	85.4
Somalia	169.3	194.2	203.7	208.4	183.5	135.7	218.7	172.0	174.3	127.2	120.1	182.5	173.0
Sudan	61.3	55.7	41.4	79.4	51.7	243.1	53.2	53.5	100.8	71.3	36.1	88.8	69.7
Swaziland	22.6	20.5	17.2	18.3	20.3	23.5	33.6	53.8	39.1	..	28.4	20.4	42.2
Tanzania	57.4	57.5	51.9	69.0	62.6	44.9	71.4	113.4	150.2	132.2	43.6	57.2	116.8
Togo	26.5	21.7	35.8	66.0	72.2	52.6	69.3	49.8	72.4	64.0	25.0	45.8	63.9
Uganda	148.4	180.8	90.2	76.7	77.8	86.2	46.4	59.3	87.6	128.5	..	110.0	80.4
Zaire	29.8	29.9	30.7	30.6	37.9	36.1	41.9	57.8	45.0	50.0	14.8	32.5	48.7
Zambia	35.2	29.9	48.8	47.5	59.9	97.9	117.2	149.2	115.8	90.4	24.5	53.2	118.1
Zimbabwe	16.3	14.3	14.9	21.1	30.8	25.9	23.2	28.6	23.5	21.8	1.4	20.5	24.3
NORTH AFRICA	7.2	6.9	6.5	5.5	7.5	8.6	7.1	8.6	8.3	7.8	12.1	7.0	7.9
Algeria	1.1	1.0	0.8	0.5	0.7	0.9	0.8	1.1	1.1	1.0	1.4	0.8	1.0
Egypt, Arab Republic of	22.0	18.7	18.7	18.1	21.3	19.4	20.2	27.7	20.5	19.9	48.1	19.7	22.1
Libya	0.2	0.1	0.1	0.1	..	..	..	..	..	..	0.2	..	..
Morocco	19.7	26.0	17.8	11.9	10.9	24.4	10.4	11.3	10.3	8.4	11.7	18.4	10.1
Tunisia	9.0	8.8	8.1	8.6	6.9	7.4	10.7	13.8	16.1	10.4	14.7	8.1	12.8
ALL AFRICA	12.6	12.5	13.6	14.4	18.9	20.4	21.7	26.7	29.5	29.7	13.4	15.4	26.9
South Africa	..	..	..	..	..	..	..	..	..	..	..	..	..

12–9. Net ODA from DAC donors as a share of recipient GDI

				Percentage of GDI							Average		
	1980	1981	1982	1983	1984	1985	1986	1987	1988	1989	75–80	80–85	86–MR
SUB-SAHARAN AFRICA	10.3	10.6	12.9	16.5	22.9	23.2	26.7	33.1	37.5	37.7	8.3	16.1	33.7
excluding Nigeria	22.5	25.2	26.3	33.2	38.2	41.9	41.4	44.8	49.8	48.4	17.3	31.2	46.1
Angola	..	..	..	..	..	..	..	..	..	..		..	..
Benin	16.7	22.2	11.5	36.4	55.8	50.9	40.3	38.1	44.6	100.9	21.5	32.3	56.0
Botswana	22.8	17.1	21.8	26.3	23.3	19.0	39.2	134.8	60.4	20.0	30.1	21.7	63.6
Burkina Faso	48.6	59.1	43.8	43.7	55.4	33.0	37.6	39.2	35.7	35.1	31.0	47.3	36.9
Burundi	46.7	39.2	51.2	28.0	38.7	48.2	63.9	34.0	51.1	48.7	55.1	42.0	49.4
Cameroon	12.1	6.5	8.5	5.7	9.3	6.2	5.3	6.0	12.1	14.6	14.2	8.1	9.5
Cape Verde	65.3	57.3	57.4	66.8	67.4	65.5	87.3	60.2	54.1	40.6	46.9	63.3	60.6
Central African Republic	134.5	119.9	138.0	83.0	87.0	60.4	70.2	76.0	84.5	82.6	56.3	103.8	78.3
Chad	..	..	..	285.5	167.7	161.0	149.0	119.7	177.1	140.8	..	..	146.7
Comoros	..	..	..	46.3	36.9	52.7	54.0	71.4	104.5	114.3		..	86.0
Congo, People's Republic of the	9.1	4.4	4.6	6.8	10.1	7.2	18.5	29.0	18.6	20.3	16.6	7.0	21.6
Cote d'Ivoire	5.1	4.2	5.8	10.1	15.9	12.6	13.2	17.5	15.3	33.0	5.7	8.9	19.7
Djibouti	..	..	..	..	51.7	57.5	110.1	85.4	115.9	85.7	..	..	99.3
Equatorial Guinea	..	..	..	..	..	81.2	78.8	74.7	87.5	73.7	..	..	78.7
Ethiopia	22.2	17.1	14.7	17.2	31.4	62.3	59.6	39.6	64.2	47.1	22.9	27.5	52.6
Gabon	4.1	2.6	4.6	4.8	5.7	3.8	3.8	7.4	9.6	13.6	2.5	4.2	8.6
Gambia, The	26.6	37.2	53.5	59.7	102.4	114.0	195.7	147.8	142.4	115.6	33.0	65.6	150.4
Ghana	42.8	45.2	48.0	39.8	31.4	22.2	22.5	24.7	41.5	49.3	24.1	38.2	34.5
Guinea	..	..	..	..	..	..	31.2	32.1	33.7	37.9	..	..	33.7
Guinea-Bissau	110.0	104.2	71.6	86.9	73.2	48.1	132.9	86.6	90.3	88.9	99.0	82.3	99.7
Kenya	13.0	19.1	23.7	27.2	22.9	20.7	24.3	22.9	28.7	30.1	16.2	21.1	26.5
Lesotho	40.7	36.8	31.4	51.9	49.0	39.7	42.6	36.3	33.8	26.4	43.8	41.6	34.8
Liberia	19.7	48.2	53.2	70.1	96.0	67.5	65.6	..	..	..	7.6	59.1	..
Madagascar	15.0	22.7	53.2	39.8	38.5	40.6	59.9	69.9	65.8	52.5	16.1	35.0	62.0
Malawi	24.6	37.5	25.7	20.1	33.2	25.1	58.6	93.3	72.5	56.4	24.0	27.7	70.2
Mali	47.4	55.7	44.5	61.6	138.7	121.5	58.3	50.8	51.1	54.4	41.8	78.2	53.6
Mauritania	20.8	21.3	17.4	51.4	37.7	57.8	54.3	51.0	64.3	108.7	14.5	34.4	69.6
Mauritius	10.7	16.5	15.7	12.9	10.6	8.8	14.9	10.7	7.1	7.7	6.2	12.5	10.1
Mozambique	25.2	23.7	33.9	70.7	70.6	92.6	79.7	152.7	174.6	118.7	..	52.8	131.4
Namibia	0.0	0.0	0.0	0.0	0.0	1.7	3.6	5.9	4.5	11.4	..	0.3	6.4
Niger	11.3	27.8	34.5	47.0	219.3	112.4	97.7	107.4	94.5	102.7	34.0	75.4	100.6
Nigeria	0.1	0.1	0.1	0.3	0.3	0.2	0.9	1.8	2.6	8.4	0.3	0.2	3.4
Rwanda	51.5	58.3	39.5	46.3	38.2	34.5	40.0	40.9	37.5	38.6	61.6	44.7	39.3
Sao Tome & Principe	8.1	13.0	21.5	32.8	25.7	22.4	74.4	45.1	57.4	87.3	13.9	20.6	66.1
Senegal	39.5	72.9	64.9	72.1	90.0	77.7	76.3	66.6	59.1	107.3	29.2	69.5	77.3
Seychelles	32.1	26.9	30.5	44.1	41.2	31.6	43.5	40.8	31.3	25.8	..	34.4	35.3
Sierra Leone	31.7	14.8	31.1	16.7	16.2	23.0	32.0	75.4	39.5	65.8	14.1	22.3	53.2
Somalia	54.4	72.4	62.4	92.1	101.2	62.7	151.4	118.1	125.3	80.6	22.4	74.2	118.8
Sudan	26.7	26.0	20.0	36.2	25.6	139.2	26.3	26.3	53.6	41.1	8.5	45.6	36.8
Swaziland	14.7	13.2	11.4	11.2	11.9	16.9	24.0	35.2	22.9	..	18.4	13.2	27.4
Tanzania	44.3	39.6	36.7	49.6	45.8	34.1	53.6	92.1	119.7	98.3	34.1	41.7	90.9
Togo	15.2	12.7	23.4	28.7	34.8	26.4	36.4	34.1	46.6	37.8	14.8	23.2	38.7
Uganda	55.2	104.7	35.8	24.4	22.5	20.1	18.2	18.4	45.3	50.3	..	43.8	33.0
Zaire	22.1	21.0	22.1	18.8	25.4	23.3	27.7	31.2	31.3	33.9	10.3	22.1	31.0
Zambia	25.9	23.1	29.0	39.1	45.2	63.5	87.3	119.1	98.0	72.1	20.1	37.6	94.1
Zimbabwe	11.1	9.2	9.8	18.7	25.2	23.3	19.7	25.7	20.1	18.6	1.4	16.2	21.0
NORTH AFRICA	4.4	4.1	4.4	4.2	6.6	6.7	6.0	7.1	7.2	6.7	4.3	5.1	6.8
Algeria	0.7	0.9	0.8	0.5	0.6	0.7	0.6	0.7	0.7	0.6	1.2	0.7	0.6
Egypt, Arab Republic of	18.8	16.0	16.1	15.4	19.6	18.2	18.4	24.6	19.1	17.9	13.5	17.3	20.0
Libya	0.1	0.0	0.0	0.0	..	..	..	..	..	..	0.1	..	..
Morocco	4.1	5.2	5.3	5.7	7.7	9.9	7.5	8.9	8.6	7.2	5.4	6.3	8.0
Tunisia	6.1	5.9	5.8	6.5	5.5	5.5	7.1	10.1	12.0	7.7	10.3	5.9	9.2
ALL AFRICA	7.5	7.4	8.4	9.2	12.8	13.3	14.5	18.0	20.5	20.1	6.5	9.8	18.3
South Africa	..	..	..	..	..	..	..	..	..	..	..	..	..

12–10. Net ODA from multilateral donors as a share of recipient GDI

	Percentage of GDI										Average		
	1980	1981	1982	1983	1984	1985	1986	1987	1988	1989	75–80	80–85	86–MR
SUB-SAHARAN AFRICA	5.6	5.8	6.6	8.4	12.2	12.6	14.2	17.1	18.2	20.3	4.7	8.5	17.4
excluding Nigeria	12.5	13.8	13.7	17.2	21.2	23.1	22.9	24.3	25.0	27.2	9.9	16.9	24.9
Angola	..	..	..	..	..	..	..	..	..	..	..	..	..
Benin	24.8	17.4	11.2	37.8	53.8	48.1	35.0	29.8	32.3	81.2	18.3	32.2	44.6
Botswana	6.2	4.7	3.2	7.2	9.9	11.0	10.2	34.4	11.9	7.0	8.2	7.0	15.9
Burkina Faso	19.7	21.9	18.5	18.8	24.6	19.3	21.1	15.7	12.5	12.4	16.9	20.5	15.4
Burundi	42.2	33.2	31.0	25.8	31.9	37.0	63.8	40.1	62.6	58.6	45.3	33.5	56.3
Cameroon	5.0	3.1	3.3	1.3	1.4	1.5	1.4	1.1	2.4	8.2	6.7	2.6	3.3
Cape Verde	39.5	22.3	14.3	21.0	40.1	43.6	36.1	23.1	23.8	21.3	38.4	30.1	26.1
Central African Republic	60.5	47.3	39.3	35.9	57.5	41.6	41.7	40.9	68.2	78.3	33.0	47.0	57.3
Chad	..	..	..	242.6	159.4	143.8	91.4	78.5	143.4	125.6	..	..	109.7
Comoros				51.3	37.4	73.9	60.5	45.6	52.1	46.2	..	..	51.1
Congo, People's Republic of the	3.6	2.7	2.1	3.3	3.0	3.8	1.9	4.5	2.9	2.4	8.6	3.1	2.9
Cote d'Ivoire	2.0	1.5	2.0	1.1	1.9	1.6	4.7	2.6	14.3	19.3	2.2	1.7	10.2
Djibouti	..	..	..	..	21.4	28.5	36.7	32.4	29.6	14.1	..	..	28.2
Equatorial Guinea	..	..	..	..	..	123.1	84.1	72.6	72.0	83.6	..	..	78.1
Ethiopia	29.2	33.8	23.5	32.5	29.5	43.2	36.1	40.9	47.2	45.3	25.4	31.9	42.4
Gabon	0.5	0.3	0.3	0.5	0.5	0.7	0.4	0.7	0.9	1.4	0.5	0.5	0.9
Gambia, The	50.3	53.5	46.9	55.8	64.9	66.0	142.1	143.4	76.7	78.5	29.3	56.2	110.2
Ghana	23.7	22.6	53.3	35.3	41.2	26.3	46.1	46.6	39.6	28.2	14.6	33.7	40.1
Guinea	..	..	..	..	..	..	23.3	22.0	18.7	27.4	..	..	22.9
Guinea-Bissau	75.7	59.5	56.9	69.6	53.4	60.4	87.1	98.6	85.2	76.8	48.1	62.6	86.9
Kenya	5.6	4.4	10.4	4.7	6.6	5.5	4.3	6.4	9.2	17.1	4.0	6.2	9.2
Lesotho	19.6	25.9	21.3	34.3	24.7	32.2	26.1	28.3	19.5	24.0	33.0	26.3	24.5
Liberia	9.3	11.0	14.0	23.7	23.0	27.7	26.7	..	..	..	6.2	18.1	..
Madagascar	15.1	20.7	26.6	25.0	25.3	38.1	48.1	54.9	28.4	44.7	17.5	25.1	44.0
Malawi	22.1	25.4	22.3	21.7	68.6	28.5	78.3	60.5	73.8	67.5	11.5	31.4	70.0
Mali	37.4	37.7	34.3	54.7	54.5	49.2	36.7	31.1	31.8	27.5	33.9	44.6	31.8
Mauritania	14.1	16.1	13.8	41.1	31.2	27.9	29.3	37.9	44.6	59.8	26.7	24.0	42.9
Mauritius	3.4	3.3	7.8	7.1	3.6	1.7	2.1	2.6	1.8	1.5	5.0	4.5	2.0
Mozambique	7.5	7.1	8.6	21.7	24.5	32.9	23.8	32.3	37.9	47.5	..	17.1	35.4
Namibia	0.0	0.0	0.0	0.0	0.0	1.9	5.1	0.3	1.4	7.3	..	0.3	3.5
Niger	6.8	11.5	12.2	21.9	111.7	52.5	62.7	64.8	48.3	48.8	20.1	36.1	56.1
Nigeria	0.1	0.1	0.1	0.2	0.3	0.2	0.4	0.7	0.6	1.0	0.1	0.2	0.7
Rwanda	30.6	28.6	29.0	26.1	25.0	24.5	26.2	30.0	30.7	28.6	33.1	25.9	28.9
Sao Tome & Principe	17.7	33.6	33.4	80.0	46.3	71.7	58.2	135.4	116.3	173.1	54.1	47.1	120.7
Senegal	17.2	43.9	27.3	21.1	23.3	23.9	52.7	46.9	28.4	20.5	19.9	26.1	37.1
Seychelles	6.0	4.0	6.5	6.1	5.2	22.4	13.5	10.2	4.2	8.1	..	8.4	9.0
Sierra Leone	16.7	11.6	14.7	14.3	17.8	27.0	18.6	36.1	30.0	26.1	16.3	17.0	27.7
Somalia	65.0	97.6	70.6	92.5	78.7	59.0	71.3	53.5	47.4	46.4	36.0	77.2	54.6
Sudan	18.9	19.6	12.1	13.7	16.3	57.6	16.1	14.8	35.8	27.8	9.3	23.0	23.6
Swaziland	7.9	7.3	5.8	7.0	8.4	6.6	9.6	18.5	16.1	..	10.1	7.2	14.7
Tanzania	10.8	14.2	14.2	17.4	15.7	9.6	16.9	20.9	30.0	33.3	9.2	13.6	25.3
Togo	11.3	8.8	10.7	35.6	36.1	23.8	29.7	14.7	26.4	26.5	9.7	21.0	24.3
Uganda	91.3	75.9	53.7	49.9	56.5	66.1	27.5	40.1	42.3	68.2	..	65.6	44.5
Zaire	7.4	7.7	8.1	11.8	12.5	12.8	14.2	26.6	13.7	16.1	4.4	10.0	17.7
Zambia	6.8	6.5	8.1	7.3	14.4	33.7	29.1	29.0	17.1	17.7	4.0	12.8	23.2
Zimbabwe	4.7	4.5	2.1	2.3	5.5	2.8	3.7	2.7	3.7	3.3	0.0	3.6	3.4
NORTH AFRICA	0.8	0.8	0.8	1.0	0.7	0.8	0.5	0.7	0.9	1.1	2.4	0.8	0.8
Algeria	0.1	0.1	0.1	0.1	0.1	0.1	0.1	0.1	0.1	0.3	0.2	0.1	0.2
Egypt, Arab Republic of	3.1	3.0	2.9	3.1	2.0	1.5	1.1	2.0	1.6	2.2	11.7	2.6	1.7
Libya	0.1	0.1	0.1	0.0	..	..	..	..	..	..	0.1	..	..
Morocco	1.4	1.6	1.4	2.6	1.0	2.0	1.1	0.9	1.2	1.2	1.1	1.7	1.1
Tunisia	1.0	1.3	1.1	1.5	1.1	1.6	1.8	2.3	3.9	2.7	1.7	1.3	2.7
ALL AFRICA	3.3	3.4	3.5	4.0	5.1	5.5	6.1	7.6	8.5	9.4	3.6	4.1	7.9
South Africa	..	..	..	..	..	..	..	..	..	..	..	..	..

303

12–11. Net ODA per capita from all donors

	U.S. dollars (current prices and exchange rates)										Average		
	1980	1981	1982	1983	1984	1985	1986	1987	1988	1989	75–80	80–85	86–MR
SUB-SAHARAN AFRICA	20	20	20	18	19	20	24	27	29	29	13	20	27
excluding Nigeria	27	26	26	24	24	27	32	35	39	37	16	26	36
Angola	7	8	7	9	11	10	15	15	17	15	5	9	15
Benin	26	23	22	23	20	24	33	32	36	54	19	23	39
Botswana	118	104	104	104	99	90	92	136	128	131	77	103	122
Burkina Faso	30	30	29	24	25	25	35	34	35	32	20	27	34
Burundi	29	29	29	32	31	30	39	40	37	37	16	30	38
Cameroon	30	22	23	13	19	16	21	20	25	41	22	21	27
Cape Verde	222	173	183	193	199	218	332	258	247	207	91	198	261
Central African Republic	48	43	37	37	44	39	51	63	68	65	26	41	62
Chad	8	13	14	20	23	36	32	38	49	44	20	19	41
Comoros	131	137	111	103	108	121	113	129	118	97	58	119	114
Congo, People's Republic of the	56	48	53	60	52	36	55	73	41	40	47	51	52
Cote d' Ivoire	26	15	15	17	13	13	18	24	39	35	17	16	29
Djibouti	243	208	183	199	299	233	311	278	238	184	172	228	253
Equatorial Guinea	27	29	40	30	40	46	57	109	108	102	4	35	94
Ethiopia	6	6	5	8	9	16	14	14	20	15	4	8	16
Gabon	69	52	71	69	79	61	77	78	98	121	58	67	94
Gambia, The	86	103	70	60	74	67	131	125	100	109	38	77	116
Ghana	18	13	12	9	18	16	28	28	34	38	11	14	32
Guinea	20	23	19	14	25	24	34	41	48	63	8	21	46
Guinea-Bissau	73	80	77	76	63	65	79	116	105	106	51	72	102
Kenya	24	26	27	21	21	22	22	26	36	41	14	23	31
Lesotho	70	75	65	74	67	61	55	66	64	74	34	69	65
Liberia	52	56	54	57	63	41	43	33	27	24	24	54	32
Madagascar	26	26	26	19	16	19	31	30	28	29	11	22	29
Malawi	23	22	19	17	23	16	27	36	46	49	16	20	39
Mali	41	34	31	30	45	51	49	47	53	55	23	39	51
Mauritania	114	134	115	107	104	121	127	100	99	127	116	116	113
Mauritius	34	59	48	40	35	28	54	62	56	55	31	41	57
Mozambique	14	12	16	16	19	22	30	45	60	50	7	16	46
Namibia	0	0	0	0	0	4	10	10	13	34	0	1	17
Niger	31	34	43	28	25	46	45	50	51	40	28	35	47
Nigeria	0	0	0	1	0	0	1	1	1	3	1	0	1
Rwanda	30	29	27	26	28	30	33	38	38	34	23	28	36
Sao Tome & Principe	42	61	97	117	112	111	112	156	199	276	50	90	186
Senegal	47	70	49	53	59	46	86	95	81	90	35	54	88
Seychelles	358	280	302	262	253	317	406	346	293	280	223	295	331
Sierra Leone	28	18	24	19	17	18	23	18	26	25	10	21	23
Somalia	93	78	94	68	67	66	92	101	73	69	40	77	84
Sudan	33	32	37	46	29	51	42	39	39	31	21	38	38
Swaziland	89	63	47	54	46	39	50	64	52	39	59	56	51
Tanzania	37	38	35	30	27	23	31	39	42	39	23	32	38
Togo	35	24	28	40	37	37	55	39	59	52	30	34	51
Uganda	9	10	10	10	11	12	13	18	22	24	3	11	19
Zaire	16	15	13	11	11	11	14	19	17	19	11	13	17
Zambia	56	40	52	35	37	49	66	59	63	50	27	45	60
Zimbabwe	23	29	29	27	37	28	26	33	29	28	1	29	29
NORTH AFRICA	31	30	28	23	25	29	24	25	23	22	35	27	24
Algeria	9	9	7	5	6	8	7	9	7	6	8	7	8
Egypt, Arab Republic of	34	31	33	33	40	39	36	36	31	31	55	35	33
Libya	5	3	4	2	1	1	3	2	1	2	3	3	2
Morocco	46	52	38	19	16	36	18	19	20	19	21	35	19
Tunisia	36	37	31	30	25	22	30	36	41	30	40	30	34
ALL AFRICA	22	22	21	19	20	22	24	26	28	27	17	21	26
South Africa	..	..	..	..	..	..	..	..	..	..	..	..	..

12–12. Net ODA per capita from DAC donors

	U.S. dollars (current prices and exchange rates)										Average		
	1980	1981	1982	1983	1984	1985	1986	1987	1988	1989	75–80	80–85	86–MR
SUB-SAHARAN AFRICA	12	12	11	11	11	12	15	17	19	19	7.2	11.7	17.5
excluding Nigeria	15	15	15	14	15	17	20	22	25	23	9.0	15.2	22.6
Angola	5	5	5	6	7	7	10	11	11	9	2.2	5.6	10.3
Benin	10	13	11	11	10	12	17	18	21	30	10.1	11.1	21.5
Botswana	93	82	85	75	63	55	74	109	106	98	59.9	75.4	96.8
Burkina Faso	22	22	20	17	16	16	22	24	24	24	12.6	18.8	23.6
Burundi	15	15	17	16	15	16	18	17	16	17	8.4	15.8	17.2
Cameroon	20	15	17	11	16	12	17	17	21	26	14.3	15.2	20.2
Cape Verde	134	125	142	146	123	127	231	184	169	135	54.8	132.8	179.9
Central African Republic	32	31	28	26	26	23	31	39	37	34	15.8	27.8	35.3
Chad	5	7	8	11	12	19	20	23	27	23	11.4	10.1	23.2
Comoros	41	52	40	41	48	46	50	79	78	69	23.4	44.6	69.1
Congo, People's Republic of the	34	25	34	30	36	24	50	63	36	36	28.6	30.6	46.3
Cote d'Ivoire	19	11	12	15	12	11	13	21	20	22	12.1	13.2	19.0
Djibouti	106	117	138	125	142	132	174	156	183	156	108.4	126.7	167.3
Equatorial Guinea	4	12	14	11	21	18	27	55	59	48	0.1	13.4	47.4
Ethiopia	2	2	2	2	4	10	9	7	12	8	1.9	3.8	8.7
Gabon	61	43	66	62	70	52	58	67	91	110	44.6	59.0	81.5
Gambia, The	26	29	35	30	45	41	76	63	66	66	17.0	34.3	68.0
Ghana	10	8	6	5	8	8	9	10	17	24	6.6	7.4	15.0
Guinea	7	7	6	6	9	12	19	23	30	34	1.8	7.1	26.4
Guinea-Bissau	42	51	40	38	35	27	45	52	51	56	32.1	38.8	50.9
Kenya	17	21	19	18	15	16	18	20	27	26	11.1	17.6	22.9
Lesotho	47	43	37	42	42	31	33	36	40	38	20.4	40.4	36.6
Liberia	32	44	43	43	50	29	30	22	20	16	12.2	40.2	22.0
Madagascar	10	10	17	12	10	10	17	17	20	16	5.1	11.8	17.4
Malawi	12	13	10	8	7	7	11	22	23	22	10.5	9.7	19.6
Mali	20	20	14	14	31	34	27	29	33	37	11.5	22.1	31.1
Mauritania	35	42	38	44	41	58	59	54	60	83	17.8	42.8	64.0
Mauritius	26	48	31	24	24	22	46	48	43	47	17.6	29.2	45.9
Mozambique	9	9	13	12	14	16	23	37	49	36	5.3	12.2	36.0
Namibia	0	0	0	0	0	2	4	10	10	21	0.0	0.3	11.2
Niger	19	21	21	17	16	31	27	31	33	27	16.5	21.0	29.5
Nigeria	0	0	0	0	0	0	0	0	1	3	0.5	0.2	1.1
Rwanda	19	19	18	17	16	17	20	21	21	19	14.4	17.6	20.1
Sao Tome & Principe	13	17	38	34	40	26	63	39	66	93	11.8	28.1	65.0
Senegal	33	38	32	35	40	31	48	53	53	74	20.4	34.7	57.0
Seychelles	302	225	243	228	225	173	294	269	253	213	206.0	232.7	257.1
Sierra Leone	17	10	16	10	6	8	14	11	13	18	4.6	11.4	14.1
Somalia	30	29	29	30	37	30	64	70	53	44	7.5	30.8	57.5
Sudan	14	15	18	21	14	29	21	19	21	18	4.9	18.6	19.6
Swaziland	58	41	31	33	27	28	36	42	31	15	39.5	36.1	30.8
Tanzania	29	26	25	21	20	17	23	32	34	29	18.0	23.1	29.5
Togo	20	14	18	17	18	18	29	26	38	31	18.3	17.5	31.0
Uganda	3	6	4	3	3	3	5	6	12	9	0.7	3.8	7.9
Zaire	12	10	9	7	7	7	9	10	12	13	8.0	8.7	11.1
Zambia	41	31	31	28	28	32	49	47	54	40	22.8	31.8	47.5
Zimbabwe	16	19	19	24	30	25	22	29	25	24	1.2	22.1	25.1
NORTH AFRICA	19	18	19	17	22	22	20	21	20	18	13.1	19.5	20.0
Algeria	6	8	7	4	5	6	5	6	5	4	6.6	6.1	5.0
Egypt, Arab Republic of	29	26	29	28	36	36	33	32	29	28	16.4	30.8	30.4
Libya	3	1	1	1	1	1	2	1	0	2	1.3	1.1	1.2
Morocco	10	11	11	9	12	14	13	15	17	16	9.1	11.1	15.1
Tunisia	25	25	22	23	20	17	20	26	30	22	28.1	21.8	24.6
ALL AFRICA	13	13	13	12	13	14	16	18	19	19	8.3	13.2	17.9
South Africa	..	..	..	..	..	..	..	..	..	..	..	..	..

12–13. Net ODA per capita from multilateral donors

	U.S. dollars (current prices and exchange rates)										Average		
	1980	1981	1982	1983	1984	1985	1986	1987	1988	1989	75–80	80–85	86–MR
SUB-SAHARAN AFRICA	6	6	6	6	6	7	8	9	9	10	4.0	6.2	9.0
excluding Nigeria	9	8	8	7	8	9	11	12	13	13	5.1	8.2	12.2
Angola	2	3	2	3	4	4	4	4	5	6	2.3	3.1	4.8
Benin	15	10	11	11	10	11	15	14	15	24	8.4	11.3	17.1
Botswana	25	23	12	21	27	32	19	28	21	34	16.9	23.2	25.5
Burkina Faso	9	8	8	7	7	9	12	9	9	8	6.9	8.2	9.7
Burundi	13	13	11	14	13	13	18	21	20	20	7.3	12.7	19.8
Cameroon	8	7	7	3	2	3	4	3	4	15	6.6	5.0	6.5
Cape Verde	81	49	35	46	73	85	95	71	75	71	34.1	61.4	77.9
Central African Republic	15	12	8	11	17	16	19	21	30	32	9.3	13.2	25.4
Chad	3	6	5	9	11	17	12	15	22	21	7.7	8.8	17.4
Comoros	40	48	41	45	48	64	57	50	39	28	26.3	47.9	43.4
Congo, People's Republic of the	13	15	15	15	11	13	5	10	6	4	14.9	13.7	6.2
Cote d'Ivoire	7	4	4	2	1	1	5	3	19	13	4.4	3.2	9.9
Djibouti	28	47	39	39	59	65	58	59	47	26	10.5	46.3	47.4
Equatorial Guinea	24	17	25	19	19	28	29	54	49	54	3.4	22.0	46.4
Ethiopia	3	4	3	4	4	7	5	7	9	7	2.1	4.2	7.1
Gabon	8	5	4	7	6	10	6	7	8	12	7.1	6.6	8.1
Gambia, The	49	42	30	28	28	24	55	61	36	45	16.4	33.6	49.3
Ghana	6	4	6	5	10	9	19	18	16	14	3.7	6.6	16.8
Guinea	13	11	8	9	11	11	14	16	16	25	4.9	10.4	17.8
Guinea-Bissau	29	29	32	30	26	34	30	59	48	48	15.1	30.0	46.1
Kenya	7	5	8	3	4	4	3	6	9	15	2.9	5.3	8.1
Lesotho	23	30	25	28	21	26	20	28	23	35	13.7	25.4	26.4
Liberia	15	10	11	14	12	12	12	11	7	8	10.2	12.5	9.7
Madagascar	10	10	9	8	7	9	14	13	8	13	5.1	8.7	12.2
Malawi	11	9	9	9	15	8	15	14	23	26	5.3	10.2	19.8
Mali	16	13	11	12	12	14	17	17	20	18	9.4	13.0	18.3
Mauritania	23	32	30	35	34	28	32	40	41	46	32.6	30.3	39.8
Mauritius	8	10	15	13	8	4	6	11	11	9	13.9	9.9	9.5
Mozambique	3	3	3	4	5	6	7	8	11	14	2.1	3.8	9.9
Namibia	0	0	0	0	0	2	6	1	3	13	0.0	0.4	5.7
Niger	12	9	7	8	8	15	17	19	17	13	9.8	9.8	16.4
Nigeria	0	0	0	0	0	0	0	0	0	0	0.2	0.2	0.2
Rwanda	11	9	9	9	11	12	13	16	17	14	7.8	10.3	14.8
Sao Tome & Principe	29	44	59	83	72	85	49	117	133	183	38.0	61.9	120.8
Senegal	14	23	14	10	10	9	33	37	25	14	14.2	13.4	27.5
Seychelles	57	33	52	32	28	123	91	67	34	67	13.3	54.1	65.0
Sierra Leone	9	8	8	9	7	10	8	5	10	7	5.0	8.3	7.7
Somalia	36	39	32	30	29	29	30	32	20	25	12.5	32.4	26.7
Sudan	10	11	11	8	9	12	13	11	14	12	5.4	10.2	12.3
Swaziland	31	22	16	21	19	11	14	22	21	24	19.9	20.0	20.3
Tanzania	7	9	10	8	7	5	7	7	8	10	4.9	7.5	8.2
Togo	15	10	8	21	19	17	24	11	21	22	11.2	15.0	19.5
Uganda	6	4	6	6	8	10	8	12	11	13	1.3	6.7	10.9
Zaire	4	4	3	4	3	4	5	9	5	6	3.4	3.8	6.2
Zambia	11	9	9	5	9	17	16	11	9	10	4.4	9.8	11.8
Zimbabwe	7	9	4	3	7	3	4	3	5	4	0.0	5.4	4.0
NORTH AFRICA	4	4	4	4	2	3	2	2	3	3	7.3	3.3	2.4
Algeria	1	1	0	1	0	1	1	1	1	2	0.9	0.7	1.2
Egypt, Arab Republic of	5	5	5	6	4	3	2	3	2	3	13.6	4.5	2.6
Libya	2	3	3	1	1	1	1	1	1	1	1.8	1.7	0.8
Morocco	3	3	3	4	1	3	2	2	2	3	2.0	3.0	2.1
Tunisia	4	5	4	5	4	5	5	6	10	8	4.3	4.6	7.2
ALL AFRICA	6	6	5	5	5	6	7	7	8	9	4.7	5.6	7.8
South Africa	..	..	..	..	..	..	..	..	..	..	..	..	..

Technical Notes

ODA is defined here to include flows to developing countries by official agencies, including state and local governments, or by their executive agencies. The main objective of these flows is to promote economic development and welfare in developing countries. They are concessional in character and contain a grant element of at least 25 percent (based on a standard 10 percent discount rate). Net ODA disbursements equal gross ODA disbursements less principal repayments (amortization) of previous ODA loans.

ODA includes both grants (inflows of unrequited transfers from official sources) for current and capital expenditures and disbursements of concessional loans. However, because of different sources and definitions of data, the ODA flows shown in this chapter will not necessarily equal those that could be calculated by adding net disbursements of official concessional long-term loans (Table 6-1 less Table 6-4) and net official transfers (Table 5-6). For example, one of the reasons for differences is that the flows shown here include "off-shore" disbursements of grants, primarily for technical cooperation, which are generally excluded from transfers as defined in the balance of payments (Table 5-6). Other reasons include possible differences in the timing of disbursements and other reporting errors.

The data on net ODA disbursements — gross disbursements of ODA less repayments of principal on earlier concessional loans — are taken from the most recent version of OECD, *Geographical Distribution of Financial Flows to Developing Countries* and from the annual reports by the DAC chairman on *Development Cooperation*. The DAC bilateral data are based on submissions by DAC member countries to the DAC secretariat. The multilateral data are compiled from published reports of multilateral agencies, supplemented by additional information received by the DAC

secretariat directly from the agencies. Data for the Organization of Petroleum Exporting Countries (OPEC) are based on survey replies to the DAC secretariat from their respective ministries of finance. The data for Council for Mutual Economic Assistance (CMEA) countries and China are retrieved from secondary sources, supplemented with DAC secretariat estimates. Financial flow data for OPEC and CMEA countries and China have been classified by the DAC secretariat as far as possible according to DAC norms and definitions. The tables include only those flows for which the recipient is specified in creditor reports, except Table 12-5, donor's ODA performance in Sub-Saharan Africa, which includes flows for which creditors have not specified recipients (for example, aid for subregional programs).

Table 12-1. Net ODA from all donors

This represents the total for the following categories of donors.

Table 12-2. Net ODA from DAC donors

This table includes net ODA from Australia, Austria, Belgium, Canada, Denmark, Finland, France, the former Germany, Italy, Japan, the Netherlands, Norway, Sweden, Switzerland, the United Kingdom, and the United States. (Ireland and New Zealand have been excluded in this compilation because their ODA to Africa is negligible.)

Table 12-3. Net ODA from non-DAC bilateral donors

This is net ODA from OPEC countries, CMEA countries, and China. OPEC countries are Algeria,

Iran, Iraq, Kuwait, Libya, Nigeria, Qatar, Saudi Arabia, the United Arab Emirates (UAE), and Venezuela. (For 1987-89 data, the DAC secretariat has redefined the OPEC group to include only Arab donors [Kuwait, Qatar, Saudi Arabia, and UAE]. The data in these tables reflect this definition for 1987-89 but not for earlier years.) CMEA countries are Bulgaria, Czechoslovakia, the former German Democratic Republic, Hungary, Poland, Romania, and the former USSR.

Table. 12-4. Net ODA from multilateral donors

This includes net ODA most notably from the African Development Fund, the European Development Fund for the Commission of the European Communities, the International Development Association (IDA), the International Fund for Agricultural Development (IFAD), Arab/OPEC-financed multilateral agencies, and UN programs and agencies. The UN programs and agencies include mainly the UN regular program of Technical Assistance (UNTA), the UN Development Programme (UNDP), the UN High Commissioner for Refugees (UNHCR), the UN Children's Fund (UNICEF), and the World Food Programme (WFP). Arab/OPEC-financed multilateral agencies include the Arab Bank for Economic Development in Africa (BADEA), the Arab Fund for Economic and Social Development (AFESD), the Islamic Development Bank, the OPEC Fund for International Development, the Arab Authority for Agricultural Investment and Development, the Arab Fund for Technical Assistance to African and Arab Countries, and the Islamic Solidarity Fund. ODA flows from the IMF Trust Fund and Structural Adjustment Facility are not included.

The growth rates of net ODA disbursements for individual donors and donor groups to African countries are least-squares estimates of deflated series. These growth rates are a measure of the change in the volume of aid flows from donors to recipients. Donor country GNP deflators are used to deflate each donor's aid flows. The GNP deflators for DAC countries are taken from the 1988 DAC chairman's report.

These deflators are used to estimate the volume of flows in constant prices and exchange rates of donor countries, thereby indicating the real resource transfer from individual donors. The deflators take account of domestic price changes and include the effect of exchange rate changes between the U.S. dollar and the national currencies of other donors.

Exchange rate changes depress the dollar equivalent of financial flows when the dollar appreciates and inflate them when the dollar depreciates. This "valuation effect" was especially substantial in 1986 and 1987, when the dollar depreciation raised the value of aid flows in U.S. dollar equivalent by 18.6 and 11 percent, respectively.

Alternatively, other price deflators could also be used to estimate the volume of aid flows in terms of the real resource transfer to recipient countries. One such deflator is the import price index for recipients. The ODA flows from multilateral agencies and non-DAC donors are deflated by the average import price deflator for Sub-Saharan countries, which indicates the volume of imports the multilateral aid can finance.

Tables 12-5, 12-6 and 12-7. Net ODA from all donors, from DAC donors and from multilateral donors as a share of recipient GDP

These tables show the relative importance of these aid flows to recipients' economies. Data for GDP (at purchaser values) from Table 2-18 reflect current prices and exchange rates; for a given level of aid flows, devaluation of a recipient's currency may inflate the ratios shown in the table. Thus, trends for a given country and comparisons across countries that have implemented different exchange rate policies should be interpreted carefully.

Tables 12-8, 12-9 and 12-10. Net ODA from all donors, from DAC donors and from multilateral donors as a share of recipient GDI

These tables highlight the relative importance of the indicated aid flows in maintaining and increasing investment in these economies. Data for GDI are based on Table 2-8 and the same caveats mentioned above apply to their interpretation. Furthermore, aid flows do not exclusively finance investment (for example, food aid finances consumption), and the share of ODA going to investment varies across countries.

Tables 12-11, 12-12 and 12-13. Net ODA per capita from all donors, from DAC donors and from multilateral donors

These tables are based on mid-year population estimates that may be slightly different from those shown in Table 1-2 because the latter may contain updated data. These ratios offer some indication of the importance of aid flows in sustaining per capita income and consumption levels (shown in Tables 2-17 and 2-18, respectively), although comparisons must be done carefully because exchange rate changes, the actual rise of ODA flows, and other factors vary across countries and over time.

Part II

Social and Environmental Data

13

Social Indicators

This chapter provides indicators in the areas of demography, health, education, and gender issues in development. The indicators that are included can be useful in evaluating and monitoring the social impact of development progress, aid flows, and structural adjustment policies.

The chapter presents such indicators as dependency ratio, urbanization, crude death rate, life expectancy at birth, infant mortality rate, child mortality rate, immunization rates for children, maternal death rate, average caloric intake, and number of population per physician. These indicators, among others, give some picture of the physical well-being of the people. In the same vein, such indicators as literacy rate among adults, school enrollment ratios by gender, pupil-teacher ratio, school drop-out rate, and repetition rate give some picture of the progress being made in education and training. Social indicators refer to phenomena that are inherently more qualitative than macroeconomic variables and thus need to be interpreted cautiously. Further caution is called for due to the particular limitations of the data. One of these limitations is the paucity — or even nonexistence — of data on certain indicators in many of the countries covered. This is especially true of indicators dealing with gender issues in development. Many countries have no data showing the gender breakdown of several social indicators.

Even when data are available, comparison among countries is limited due to varied practices in data gathering and reporting. Often the countries report survey data that cover different proportions of the nation. Sometimes surveys are limited to just the urban areas to cover only the largest cities or the capital city alone. This is especially true of the health indicators. Such indicators as immunization rates for children under one year of age, percentage of births attended by health personnel, infant mortality rate, child mortality rate, and maternal death rate are often based on surveys of a handful of hospitals in the urban areas.

Another source of limitation is the definition of terms, which may differ from country to country. Some countries, for example, consider an institution as a "private school" only if it receives no form of financial support from the government, while others classify as "private" all schools not run by the government, whether or not they receive financial support from the government. In like manner, some countries include personnel other than doctors and trained nurses in the term "medical personnel."

Cultural norms may also affect the reported data. This is especially true for gender issues. In some, it is assumed that no woman can be the head of any household that also contains an adult male. In population censuses therefore, enumerators and respondents simply take some such assumptions for granted, reporting a male rather than a female as head of the household or family (See United Nations, *The World's Women, 1970-90).* This distorts the true picture of the percentage of households headed by women.

This chapter includes performance of students at international, rather than national, examinations to eliminate the influences of such factors as curriculum differences, and the policy of passing a predetermined percentage of candidates practised in some countries. Nonetheless, caution is still needed in making comparisons among countries. Candidates for international examinations usually are not representative of the entire student population of a country. Countries with substantial proportions of low-income students taking a test tend to score lower than others. Also, the more students take the test, the lower will be the average

score. Further, where only a few selected schools are authorized to supervise an international examination, as for the Baccalaureate, access will be denied pupils in schools not authorized, thus reducing the representativeness of the student population.

Except for Table 13-21, the figures in this chapter are given as "around" the years shown. Thus, for exemple, 1980 should be understood to mean "around 1980," and 1985 "around 1985." All group summaries are population-weighted averages. When a country lacks data for a period, it is eliminated before the group summary is calculated. This ensures that the same countries are used to represent a given group for all the periods shown. If data are missing for more than one-third of the countries, group summaries are not computed for the affected indicator.

13-1. Age and gender structure of the population

	Females as percentage of total population			Age groups as percentage of total population								
				1980			1985			1989		
	1980	1985	1989	0-14	15-64	65+	0-14	15-64	65+	0-14	15-64	65+
SUB-SAHARAN AFRICA	50.6	50.5	50.5	44.2	51.8	2.8	44.5	52.5	2.9	44.9	52.2	2.9
excluding Nigeria	50.6	50.5	50.5	43.4	52.0	2.9	44.3	52.6	3.0	44.7	52.3	3.0
Angola	50.9	50.8	50.7	42.5	54.5	3.1	43.3	53.6	3.1	42.8	54.0	3.2
Benin	50.9	50.9	50.8	45.9	51.0	3.0	45.0	52.0	3.0	45.7	51.4	2.9
Botswana	52.9	52.5	52.2	45.4	49.3	5.3	46.3	49.8	4.0	45.9	50.5	3.6
Burkina Faso	50.5	50.5	50.5	43.9	53.3	2.8	42.9	53.9	3.3	43.7	53.1	3.2
Burundi	51.4	51.2	51.0	42.4	54.2	3.4	42.8	53.8	3.4	44.6	52.4	3.0
Cameroon	50.9	50.7	50.7	40.5	55.5	4.0	43.8	52.1	4.1	45.1	51.0	3.9
Cape Verde	54.1	53.5	52.9	45.9	47.3	6.4	42.4	52.2	5.4	43.4	52.2	4.4
Central African Republic	51.8	51.6	51.3	40.9	55.2	4.0	41.6	56.1	2.3	40.7	56.4	2.9
Chad	50.8	50.7	50.7	40.6	55.7	3.7	39.6	56.8	3.6	40.2	56.1	3.7
Comoros	50.5	50.5	50.4	44.2	52.9	2.9	45.4	52.0	2.6	46.1	51.3	2.6
Congo, People's Republic of	50.8	50.7	50.6	42.1	54.5	3.4	42.8	53.1	4.1	43.4	52.6	4.0
Cote d' Ivoire	49.3	49.3	49.3	48.3	49.4	2.3	46.8	50.9	2.3	46.7	50.9	2.4
Djibouti	49.2	49.4	49.6	43.9	53.9	2.2	43.4	54.2	2.3	42.4	55.2	2.4
Equatorial Guinea	51.0	50.9	50.9	39.7	56.1	4.3	36.9	58.7	4.4	37.6	58.0	4.4
Ethiopia	50.2	50.2	50.4	42.9	54.3	2.7	43.4	53.6	3.0	44.7	52.4	2.9
Gabon	50.9	50.9	50.7	29.5	64.4	6.1	34.2	60.6	5.2	37.0	58.0	5.0
Gambia, The	50.7	50.7	50.7	42.6	54.4	3.0	40.7	56.9	2.3	41.8	55.5	2.6
Ghana	50.4	50.4	50.4	44.9	52.4	2.8	44.7	52.4	3.0	45.2	51.8	2.9
Guinea	50.6	50.6	50.6	0.0	0.0	0.0	44.9	52.4	2.7	44.6	52.7	2.7
Guinea-Bissau	51.6	51.4	51.3	37.8	57.7	4.4	41.8	54.6	3.6	41.9	54.7	3.4
Kenya	50.0	50.0	50.0	48.1	48.4	3.5	48.6	48.2	3.2	48.6	48.5	3.0
Lesotho	51.9	51.9	51.9	40.4	55.9	3.7	41.2	55.1	3.8	41.5	54.7	3.8
Liberia	49.4	49.3	49.5	43.5	53.3	3.2	42.9	53.3	3.8	43.2	53.5	3.3
Madagascar	50.7	50.6	50.5	42.5	54.4	3.1	44.7	51.9	3.3	44.8	51.9	3.3
Malawi	51.4	51.1	50.8	44.8	52.8	2.4	44.2	53.2	2.6	44.8	52.6	2.6
Mali	51.9	51.6	51.4	44.8	52.4	2.8	44.8	51.7	3.6	44.9	51.8	3.3
Mauritania	50.7	50.6	50.6	42.5	54.4	3.1	42.2	54.4	3.3	42.7	53.8	3.4
Mauritius	50.7	50.6	50.6	32.9	64.0	3.1	31.4	64.0	4.6	29.0	65.7	5.3
Mozambique	50.8	50.7	50.7	41.9	54.9	3.2	42.2	54.5	3.3	42.3	54.4	3.3
Namibia	50.4	50.3	50.2	57.1	40.4	2.5	43.3	53.2	3.5	43.8	52.9	3.3
Niger	50.5	50.5	50.4	44.1	52.0	3.9	44.3	53.1	2.6	45.4	52.0	2.6
Nigeria	50.6	50.5	50.4	46.7	50.9	2.5	45.1	52.3	2.6	45.5	51.8	2.6
Rwanda	50.6	50.6	50.6	47.3	50.3	2.5	47.4	50.2	2.4	46.5	51.0	2.5
Sao Tome & Principe	50.0	50.0	50.0	0.0	0.0	0.0	39.4	54.8	5.8	39.6	55.3	5.2
Senegal	50.5	50.5	50.5	40.8	56.1	3.1	44.9	52.1	2.9	45.1	52.2	2.8
Seychelles	..	..	..	..	..	..	33.8	58.5	7.7	33.4	59.1	7.5
Sierra Leone	51.0	50.9	50.9	42.0	54.8	3.2	41.1	55.9	3.1	41.7	55.1	3.2
Somalia	52.5	52.5	52.3	42.0	55.0	3.0	43.8	53.2	3.0	44.2	52.8	3.0
Sudan	49.9	49.8	49.8	44.7	52.6	2.7	43.6	53.5	2.9	43.5	53.6	2.9
Swaziland	50.9	50.8	50.6	44.4	52.6	3.0	46.6	50.8	2.6	46.6	51.0	2.4
Tanzania	50.8	50.7	50.6	44.7	52.8	2.5	44.9	51.9	3.2	45.1	51.8	3.1
Togo	50.7	50.6	50.6	42.8	54.0	3.3	45.0	51.8	3.3	45.9	50.9	3.2
Uganda	50.5	50.5	50.4	46.4	51.1	2.6	46.2	51.2	2.6	46.7	50.8	2.5
Zaire	50.8	50.7	50.5	44.3	53.1	2.6	44.5	52.9	2.6	44.4	53.0	2.7
Zambia	51.1	50.9	50.7	47.7	49.8	2.5	46.7	50.9	2.4	47.2	50.4	2.4
Zimbabwe	50.4	50.4	50.4	46.2	51.1	2.7	45.3	52.1	2.6	44.7	52.8	2.5
NORTH AFRICA	49.6	49.5	49.5	40.4	55.5	4.1	40.1	56.0	3.9	39.6	56.5	3.9
Algeria	50.4	50.2	50.0	44.8	51.1	4.1	44.4	51.5	4.1	42.7	53.5	3.8
Egypt, Arab Republic of	49.3	49.3	49.2	37.5	58.3	4.3	38.0	58.1	4.0	38.1	57.7	4.2
Libya	47.1	47.3	47.6	44.2	53.4	2.4	44.1	53.5	2.4	44.3	53.2	2.5
Morocco	49.9	50.0	49.9	41.8	54.0	4.2	40.3	55.6	4.0	39.8	56.5	3.7
Tunisia	49.3	49.4	49.4	40.0	56.1	3.9	38.1	58.0	3.9	37.0	58.9	4.1
ALL AFRICA	50.4	50.3	50.3	43.4	52.5	3.0	43.7	53.2	3.1	43.9	53.0	3.1
South Africa	50.2	50.3	50.3	38.6	57.4	4.0	36.2	59.6	4.2	36.5	59.4	4.1

Note: Some age groups may not add up to 100 due to rounding up error.

13–2. Poverty

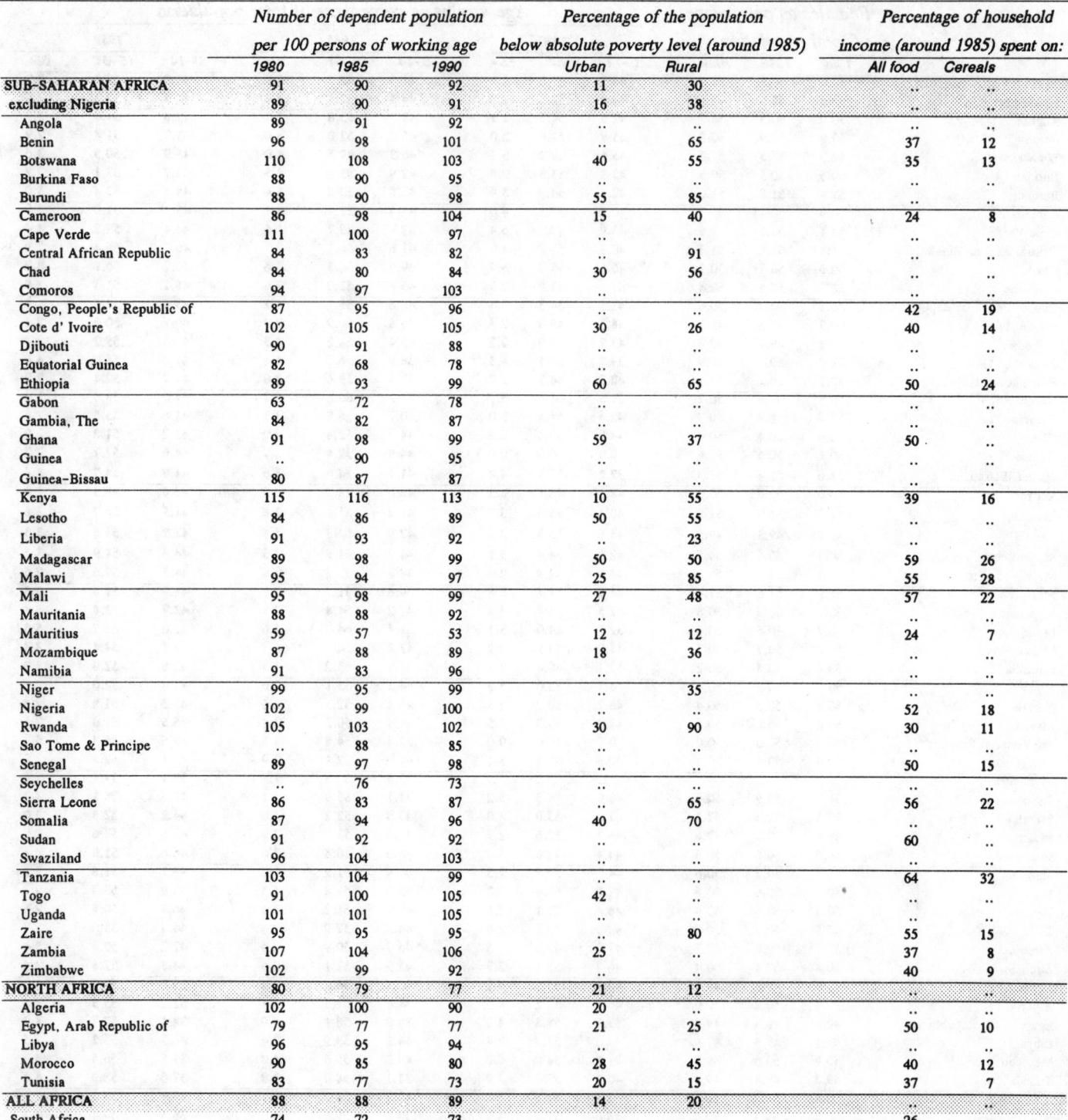

	Number of dependent population per 100 persons of working age			Percentage of the population below absolute poverty level (around 1985)		Percentage of household income (around 1985) spent on:	
	1980	1985	1990	Urban	Rural	All food	Cereals
SUB-SAHARAN AFRICA	91	90	92	11	30	..	..
excluding Nigeria	89	90	91	16	38	..	..
Angola	89	91	92	..	..	..	..
Benin	96	98	101		65	37	12
Botswana	110	108	103	40	55	35	13
Burkina Faso	88	90	95	..	..	..	..
Burundi	88	90	98	55	85	..	..
Cameroon	86	98	104	15	40	24	8
Cape Verde	111	100	97	..	..	..	..
Central African Republic	84	83	82	..	91	..	..
Chad	84	80	84	30	56	..	..
Comoros	94	97	103	..	..	..	..
Congo, People's Republic of	87	95	96	..	..	42	19
Cote d' Ivoire	102	105	105	30	26	40	14
Djibouti	90	91	88	..	..	..	..
Equatorial Guinea	82	68	78	..	..	..	..
Ethiopia	89	93	99	60	65	50	24
Gabon	63	72	78	..	..	..	..
Gambia, The	84	82	87	..	..	..	..
Ghana	91	98	99	59	37	50	..
Guinea	..	90	95	..	..	..	..
Guinea-Bissau	80	87	87	..	..	..	..
Kenya	115	116	113	10	55	39	16
Lesotho	84	86	89	50	55	..	..
Liberia	91	93	92	..	23	..	..
Madagascar	89	98	99	50	50	59	26
Malawi	95	94	97	25	85	55	28
Mali	95	98	99	27	48	57	22
Mauritania	88	88	92	..	..	..	..
Mauritius	59	57	53	12	12	24	7
Mozambique	87	88	89	18	36	..	..
Namibia	91	83	96	..	..	..	..
Niger	99	95	99	..	35	..	..
Nigeria	102	99	100	..	..	52	18
Rwanda	105	103	102	30	90	30	11
Sao Tome & Principe	..	88	85	..	..	..	..
Senegal	89	97	98	..	..	50	15
Seychelles	..	76	73	..	..	..	..
Sierra Leone	86	83	87	..	65	56	22
Somalia	87	94	96	40	70	..	..
Sudan	91	92	92	..	..	60	..
Swaziland	96	104	103	..	..	..	..
Tanzania	103	104	99	..	..	64	32
Togo	91	100	105	42	..	..	..
Uganda	101	101	105	..	..	..	..
Zaire	95	95	95	..	80	55	15
Zambia	107	104	106	25	..	37	8
Zimbabwe	102	99	92	..	..	40	9
NORTH AFRICA	80	79	77	21	12	..	..
Algeria	102	100	90	20	..	..	..
Egypt, Arab Republic of	79	77	77	21	25	50	10
Libya	96	95	94	..	..	..	..
Morocco	90	85	80	28	45	40	12
Tunisia	83	77	73	20	15	37	7
ALL AFRICA	88	88	89	14	20	..	..
South Africa	74	72	73	..	..	26	..

13-3. Urbanization

	Total population (millions)			Average annual percentage growth of total population			Urban population as percentage of total population			Average annual percentage growth of urban population		
	1980	1985	1990	75–80	80–85	86–90	1980	1985	1990	75–80	80–85	86–90
SUB-SAHARAN AFRICA	352.8	409.7	479.8	2.8	3.1	3.2	22.2	25.5	29.1	6.0	6.0	5.7
excluding Nigeria	270.4	313.3	366.1	2.9	3.0	3.2	20.7	23.8	27.2	6.2	5.9	5.7
Angola	7.5	8.6	9.7	3.5	2.5	2.8	21.0	24.5	28.3	7.1	5.7	5.4
Benin	3.4	3.9	4.6	2.7	3.1	3.2	28.2	35.2	42.0	7.7	5.1	4.8
Botswana	0.9	1.0	1.2	3.6	3.5	3.2	15.3	19.2	23.6	8.6	9.9	8.7
Burkina Faso	6.8	7.7	8.8	2.3	2.5	2.7	7.0	7.9	9.0	4.5	5.0	5.1
Burundi	4.0	4.6	5.3	2.0	2.7	3.1	4.1	5.6	7.3	8.4	5.4	5.3
Cameroon	8.4	9.9	11.6	3.2	3.2	3.3	34.7	42.4	49.4	6.7	6.0	5.6
Cape Verde	0.3	0.3	0.4	0.6	2.4	2.8	23.4	25.7	28.0	2.4	4.5	4.7
Central African Republic	2.3	2.6	3.0	2.7	2.7	2.8	38.2	42.4	46.6	5.0	4.8	4.6
Chad	4.4	4.9	5.5	2.1	2.3	2.5	20.8	27.0	33.3	7.1	6.5	5.8
Comoros	0.3	0.4	0.5	2.1	3.5	3.8	23.2	25.2	27.6	4.0	5.3	5.5
Congo, People's Republic of	1.6	1.9	2.2	3.4	3.5	3.3	37.3	39.5	42.2	4.6	4.8	4.4
Cote d'Ivoire	7.9	9.5	11.7	4.0	3.9	4.3	37.1	42.0	46.6	7.5	3.8	5.6
Djibouti	0.3	0.3	0.4	4.8	3.1	3.9	73.7	77.7	80.7	6.3	4.2	4.6
Equatorial Guinea	0.3	0.4	0.4	1.7	1.8	2.3	53.7	59.7	64.5	2.0	2.0	2.9
Ethiopia	36.7	42.1	49.5	2.7	2.8	3.4	10.5	11.6	12.9	4.8	4.9	5.4
Gabon	0.8	1.0	1.1	4.5	4.6	2.6	35.8	40.9	45.7	7.9	7.4	4.7
Gambia, The	0.6	0.7	0.8	3.5	3.4	3.2	18.1	20.1	22.5	5.4	5.8	5.5
Ghana	10.5	12.2	14.4	1.6	3.3	3.3	30.7	31.5	33.0	2.2	3.8	4.1
Guinea	4.4	4.9	5.6	1.4	2.3	2.8	19.1	22.2	25.6	4.7	5.4	5.5
Guinea-Bissau	0.8	0.9	1.0	5.6	1.8	2.1	23.8	27.1	30.8	6.8	3.4	3.9
Kenya	16.0	19.5	23.5	3.9	4.0	3.8	16.1	19.7	23.6	8.7	8.3	7.1
Lesotho	1.3	1.5	1.7	2.6	2.7	2.8	13.6	16.7	20.3	7.5	7.0	6.4
Liberia	1.8	2.1	2.5	3.1	3.2	3.1	34.9	39.5	44.0	6.1	6.0	5.6
Madagascar	8.5	9.7	11.3	2.8	2.8	3.1	18.9	21.8	25.0	5.5	5.5	6.4
Malawi	5.9	7.0	8.2	3.0	3.4	3.4	9.7	12.0	14.8	6.6	6.2	5.8
Mali	6.4	7.2	8.2	2.2	2.3	2.8	17.3	18.0	19.2	3.6	3.1	4.0
Mauritania	1.5	1.7	1.9	2.5	2.2	2.7	26.9	34.6	42.1	10.4	8.0	6.5
Mauritius	0.9	1.0	1.1	1.8	1.1	1.0	42.9	42.2	42.3	1.6	0.4	0.6
Mozambique	11.8	13.4	15.3	2.7	2.6	2.8	13.1	19.4	26.8	12.0	11.0	8.7
Namibia	1.3	1.5	1.7	2.7	3.1	3.2	45.2	51.3	57.0	4.8	5.1	5.1
Niger	5.3	6.3	7.4	3.2	3.6	3.1	13.2	16.2	19.5	7.9	7.9	6.5
Nigeria	82.4	96.4	113.8	2.4	3.3	3.3	27.1	31.0	35.2	5.5	6.1	5.7
Rwanda	5.0	5.9	6.9	3.3	3.4	3.1	5.0	6.2	7.7	8.1	8.0	7.0
Sao Tome & Principe	0.1	0.1	0.1	1.6	2.7	2.9	32.7	37.6	42.3	4.9	5.8	5.1
Senegal	5.4	6.2	7.2	2.9	2.9	3.1	34.9	36.4	38.4	3.3	3.8	4.1
Seychelles	0.1	0.1	0.1	1.4	0.6	0.9	42.8	51.8	59.3	6.8	4.6	3.3
Sierra Leone	3.2	3.6	4.0	2.2	2.3	2.5	21.5	24.2	27.2	5.3	5.3	4.9
Somalia	4.6	5.2	6.1	2.6	2.9	3.2	30.2	34.1	38.1	5.1	5.3	5.3
Sudan	18.6	21.3	24.5	3.0	2.7	2.8	19.7	20.6	22.0	3.9	3.7	4.1
Swaziland	0.5	0.6	0.8	3.2	3.3	3.5	19.8	26.3	33.1	10.8	9.3	7.8
Tanzania	17.5	20.5	23.8	3.3	3.2	3.0	16.5	24.4	32.8	14.5	11.6	8.5
Togo	2.5	2.9	3.5	2.4	3.3	3.7	18.8	22.1	25.7	6.1	6.7	6.5
Uganda	12.3	14.2	16.8	2.6	3.0	3.4	8.7	9.4	10.4	3.6	4.7	5.3
Zaire	25.5	29.5	34.5	2.9	3.0	3.2	34.2	36.6	39.5	4.2	4.4	4.6
Zambia	5.5	6.5	7.8	3.0	3.7	3.8	42.8	49.5	55.6	5.8	6.2	5.8
Zimbabwe	6.8	8.1	9.6	2.8	3.7	3.1	21.9	24.6	27.6	5.4	6.2	5.2
NORTH AFRICA	86.0	98.7	112.3	2.6	2.8	2.4	44.2	46.4	49.1	3.7	3.7	3.9
Algeria	18.1	21.2	24.4	3.1	3.2	2.7	41.2	42.6	44.7	4.7	5.1	4.5
Egypt, Arab Republic of	39.9	45.3	51.0	2.4	2.6	2.2	44.7	46.5	48.8	2.5	2.7	3.5
Libya	2.9	3.6	4.4	4.4	4.5	3.6	56.6	64.5	70.2	8.6	7.2	5.4
Morocco	18.9	21.5	24.5	2.3	2.6	2.5	41.3	44.8	48.5	4.1	4.3	4.1
Tunisia	6.2	7.1	8.0	2.6	2.6	2.4	52.2	53.0	54.3	4.5	2.9	2.9
ALL AFRICA	438.8	508.4	592.1	2.8	3.0	3.1	26.5	29.6	32.9	5.6	5.5	5.3
South Africa	27.7	30.8	35.0	2.3	2.2	2.6	53.2	55.9	58.5	3.2	3.5	3.7

13-4. Components of population change

	Total fertility rate			Crude birth rate			Crude death rate			Net migration as percentage of total population		
	1980	1985	1989	1980	1985	1989	1980	1985	1989	1980	1985	1989
SUB-SAHARAN AFRICA	6.8	6.8	6.6	48	48	47	18	17	15	..	..	..
excluding Nigeria	6.7	6.7	6.6	48	48	47	19	17	15	..	..	..
Angola	6.4	6.4	6.5	47	47	47	23	21	19	4.5	-0.1	0.0
Benin	6.5	6.5	6.3	49	48	46	19	17	15	..	-0.1	-0.1
Botswana	6.7	5.9	4.7	48	42	35	14	9	6	..	-0.6	0.0
Burkina Faso	6.5	6.5	6.5	47	47	47	21	19	18	-1.4	-0.6	-1.0
Burundi	6.5	6.7	6.8	47	47	48	20	17	15	..	-0.3	-0.3
Cameroon	6.5	6.5	6.5	47	46	44	15	14	12	..	0.0	0.0
Cape Verde	6.5	5.9	5.4	39	35	43	8	8	8	-2.7	-1.5	-2.9
Central African Republic	5.5	5.6	5.8	41	42	42	17	16	15	..	0.0	0.0
Chad	5.9	5.9	6.0	44	44	44	22	20	19	..	0.0	0.0
Comoros	7.0	7.0	6.8	49	50	48	16	14	12	..	0.0	0.0
Congo, People's Republic of	6.0	6.3	6.6	46	47	47	16	15	15	..	0.0	0.0
Cote d'Ivoire	7.4	7.4	7.3	51	51	49	16	15	14	3.7	3.2	2.4
Djibouti	6.6	6.6	6.6	48	47	45	20	18	17	7.7	11.2	4.1
Equatorial Guinea	5.0	5.3	5.5	40	41	41	22	20	19	..	8.6	0.0
Ethiopia	6.9	7.5	7.5	47	51	51	20	20	18	..	-0.7	-0.4
Gabon	4.5	5.1	5.8	33	39	42	18	16	15	..	0.0	0.0
Gambia, The	6.5	6.5	6.5	49	49	47	24	22	20	3.5	0.0	1.7
Ghana	6.5	6.4	6.2	45	46	44	15	14	13	-4.9	-0.1	0.0
Guinea	6.1	6.4	6.5	47	48	48	24	22	21	..	-0.4	0.2
Guinea-Bissau	6.0	6.0	6.0	46	46	45	27	26	24	13.8	-0.6	-0.5
Kenya	8.0	7.4	6.6	53	50	45	14	12	10	..	0.0	0.0
Lesotho	5.8	5.8	5.6	41	41	40	15	14	12	..	-0.6	-0.6
Liberia	6.5	6.5	6.3	45	45	44	16	16	14	0.8	0.2	..
Madagascar	6.5	6.5	6.5	45	46	46	17	16	15	..	0.0	0.0
Malawi	7.6	7.6	7.6	54	54	54	22	20	19	..	-0.4	-0.3
Mali	6.6	6.9	7.0	49	50	50	22	20	19	-2.3	-1.7	-1.7
Mauritania	6.5	6.7	6.8	47	48	48	21	20	19	..	-1.7	-1.5
Mauritius	2.7	2.2	1.9	24	19	17	7	7	6	-0.6	-2.0	-0.9
Mozambique	6.4	6.3	6.4	46	45	46	20	18	17	..	0.0	0.0
Namibia	6.1	6.1	5.9	45	44	42	14	13	11	..	0.0	0.0
Niger	7.1	7.1	7.1	51	52	51	23	21	20	..	0.0	0.0
Nigeria	6.9	6.8	6.6	50	49	47	18	16	15	..	0.0	0.0
Rwanda	8.2	8.3	8.3	52	50	54	20	18	17	..	-0.2	-0.1
Sao Tome & Principe	..	5.3	5.1	39	37	35	10	10	9	..	0.0	0.0
Senegal	6.6	6.6	6.5	46	45	45	20	18	16	..	0.8	0.7
Seychelles	3.8	3.2	2.8	29	27	24	7	7	7	..	-3.0	-4.3
Sierra Leone	6.5	6.5	6.5	49	48	47	26	24	22	..	0.0	0.0
Somalia	6.8	6.8	6.8	50	49	48	21	20	18	..	1.3	0.4
Sudan	6.6	6.5	6.3	46	45	44	18	16	15	..	0.0	-0.2
Swaziland	6.5	6.5	6.3	47	47	45	15	13	12	..	0.0	0.0
Tanzania	6.8	6.7	6.6	50	48	48	20	18	17	..	0.0	0.0
Togo	6.8	6.8	6.6	51	51	48	17	15	14	..	0.0	0.0
Uganda	7.3	7.3	7.3	50	51	51	19	18	16	-0.4	-0.3	-0.3
Zaire	6.1	6.1	6.0	45	45	44	16	15	14	..	0.0	0.0
Zambia	6.8	6.8	6.7	49	50	49	16	14	12	-0.5	0.1	0.0
Zimbabwe	6.8	5.9	4.9	49	43	37	13	10	7	..	-0.3	0.0
NORTH AFRICA	5.6	5.0	4.5	39	36	33	12	10	9	..	..	..
Algeria	6.7	5.8	5.1	44	38	36	12	9	8	..	..	..
Egypt, Arab Republic of	5.1	4.6	4.1	39	35	31	13	11	10	..	..	..
Libya	7.3	7.0	6.6	46	45	43	12	10	8	..	..	..
Morocco	5.6	5.1	4.7	38	36	36	12	10	9	..	..	..
Tunisia	5.2	4.5	3.8	35	32	30	9	8	7	..	..	..
ALL AFRICA	6.5	6.4	6.2	47	46	44	17	16	14	..	..	..
South Africa	4.9	4.6	4.2	34	35	33	11	11	9	..	0.1	0.1

Note: Minus sign indicates population outflow.

13–5. Survival prospects

	Life expectancy at birth (years)			Infant mortality (per thousand)			Mortality of children under 5 years (per thousand)			Maternal mortality (per 100,000 live births)
	1980	1985	1990	1980	1985	1990	1980	1985	1990	1985
SUB-SAHARAN AFRICA	47	49	51	127	118	107	212	178	159	561
excluding Nigeria	47	48	51	131	121	110	217	179	162	475
Angola	41	43	46	153	142	129	260	232	209	1680
Benin	47	49	51	124	118	111	176	169	155	300
Botswana	60	66	68	63	45	37	110	53	43	250
Burkina Faso	44	46	48	154	142	133	266	205	193	810
Burundi	45	47	50	114	86	68	225	118	98	..
Cameroon	53	55	57	106	98	88	176	134	118	300
Cape Verde	62	65	67	59	47	40	..	56	47	134
Central African Republic	47	49	51	117	108	98	244	171	152	600
Chad	42	44	47	147	136	125	254	223	201	960
Comoros	51	53	55	113	103	92	..	142	124	..
Congo, People's Republic of	50	52	54	124	121	113	132	185	165	900
Cote d'Ivoire	49	52	53	109	100	91	167	157	140	..
Djibouti	44	46	49	136	126	115	..	205	183	129
Equatorial Guinea	43	45	47	142	131	120	..	214	193	..
Ethiopia	43	45	48	155	146	131	260	204	186	500
Gabon	48	51	53	116	107	96	194	169	149	..
Gambia, The	40	42	44	159	147	136	..	242	221	2000
Ghana	52	53	55	100	93	84	166	145	129	1000
Guinea	40	42	43	161	150	138	275	235	219	..
Guinea-Bissau	37	39	40	168	156	145	..	245	227	1070
Kenya	55	57	59	83	75	66	133	113	96	170
Lesotho	52	55	57	116	104	93	162	144	127	510
Liberia	51	52	54	159	146	135	245	196	174	..
Madagascar	50	50	51	138	124	116	216	176	164	240
Malawi	44	46	48	169	155	146	299	250	235	100
Mali	44	46	48	184	173	166	325	228	220	250
Mauritania	43	45	47	142	131	121	249	214	196	..
Mauritius	66	68	70	32	25	20	42	28	23	100
Mozambique	45	47	49	156	146	135	268	210	194	300
Namibia	53	55	58	120	110	99	202	138	121	479
Niger	42	44	46	150	139	128	259	228	207	420
Nigeria	48	50	52	118	109	98	198	173	152	800
Rwanda	46	48	49	135	126	116	231	205	188	210
Sao Tome & Principe	..	64	66	83	77	69	..	63	47	..
Senegal	45	47	48	103	91	80	232	127	110	600
Seychelles	..	69	71	..	19	17	..	22	21	..
Sierra Leone	38	40	42	171	159	146	300	260	239	450
Somalia	44	46	48	145	136	126	247	223	204	1100
Sudan	47	49	51	123	112	102	210	179	160	660
Swaziland	52	54	57	133	122	112	..	155	140	..
Tanzania	47	48	50	122	117	110	202	153	138	340
Togo	49	52	54	110	98	88	184	153	134	370
Uganda	46	47	49	113	107	96	187	169	149	300
Zaire	49	51	53	111	102	91	163	160	140	110
Zambia	50	52	54	90	83	74	146	127	109	150
Zimbabwe	55	60	64	82	63	42	116	77	50	480
NORTH AFRICA	57	60	62	108	84	65	157	105	86	265
Algeria	59	63	65	98	80	67	147	98	80	130
Egypt, Arab Republic of	56	58	60	124	91	66	172	116	94	320
Libya	57	60	62	101	88	74	150	104	84	80
Morocco	57	60	62	99	81	67	153	101	86	300
Tunisia	62	65	67	72	55	44	103	65	51	310
ALL AFRICA	49	51	53	123	111	98	200	162	144	498
South Africa	57	59	62	88	76	65	120	100	82	83

13-6. Immunization and ORT use

	Percentage of children (0-1 years) immunized against												ORT use among the under fives (percent)
	Tuberculosis			DPT			Polio			Measles			
	1980	1985	1989	1980	1985	1989	1980	1985	1989	1980	1985	1989	1987
SUB-SAHARAN AFRICA	29	37	68	22	26	42	19	29	43	33	30	45	19
excluding Nigeria	32	43	66	21	26	42	16	31	43	22	35	50	19
Angola	47	30	32	9	19	11	7	13	13	17	44	56	12
Benin	37	30	50	20	20	26	45	20	30	6	21	30	26
Botswana	91	68	99	70	68	78	45	67	75	63	69	74	46
Burkina Faso	16	33	73	2	9	32	2	9	26	23	40	57	15
Burundi	65	65	66	38	36	60	6	29	55	30	42	47	30
Cameroon	8	68	77	5	68	33	5	64	31	16	43	29	22
Cape Verde	..	76	99	..	60	78	0	46	77	..	65	71	9
Central African Republic	26	59	53	12	24	28	12	24	28	12	30	36	15
Chad	..	15	38	..	3	12	..	3	14	..	7	33	2
Comoros	..	56	51	..	31	50	..	32	49	..	18	49	18
Congo, People's Republic of	92	80	88	42	59	71	42	59	71	49	52	73	2
Cote d'Ivoire	..	16	52	42	43	28	34	11	32	28	31	30	4
Djibouti	..	58	79	..	30	71	..	30	71	..	27	91	22
Equatorial Guinea	..	30	65	..	3	6	..	12	20	..	12	44	21
Ethiopia	10	11	29	6	16	16	7	6	16	7	12	15	23
Gabon	..	50	79	..	14	48	..	44	48	..	58	57	7
Gambia, The	99	92	97	80	77	75	53	62	69	71	75	82	3
Ghana	9	11	56	7	23	38	7	18	39	15	83	59	36
Guinea	..	43	82	..	16	38	..	15	39	..	35	60	1
Guinea-Bissau	4	10	31	..	2	9	..	2	9	15	30	18	1
Kenya	..	75	87	..	72	73	..	57	74	..	65	63	26
Lesotho	81	87	90	56	65	77	54	66	73	49	63	79	68
Liberia	87	47	62	39	43	22	26	42	28	99	44	47	9
Madagascar	13	13	62	35	35	32	3	3	33	..	0	27	2
Malawi	86	80	90	58	48	69	28	42	63	49	46	64	42
Mali	19	13	64	18	2	14	0	2	14	10	13	42	3
Mauritania	57	74	79	18	21	28	18	21	28	45	59	45	2
Mauritius	89	87	88	87	88	87	87	91	87	34	67	74	4
Mozambique	46	56	49	56	32	36	32	32	36	32	46	42	14
Namibia	..	..	..	..	..	..	..	..	..	..	..	..	..
Niger	28	28	39	6	4	12	6	4	16	19	22	24	24
Nigeria	23	25	72	24	25	41	24	25	42	55	20	36	20
Rwanda	51	73	91	17	44	79	15	50	79	42	45	71	24
Sao Tome & Principe	95	76	..	42	28	71	48	28	69	25	22	64	46
Senegal	22	56	81	34	37	59	34	37	64	22	38	61	9
Seychelles	67	99	..	13	98	96	16	98	96	29	98	92	..
Sierra Leone	36	45	73	13	9	25	7	12	38	36	21	38	31
Somalia	6	31	33	9	22	25	8	22	25	9	30	33	12
Sudan	2	14	67	1	9	53	1	9	53	1	20	57	25
Swaziland	59	95	22	30	79	75	22	60	72	30	51	47	..
Tanzania	..	53	94	58	46	78	56	46	77	55	58	93	14
Togo	44	55	87	9	11	49	9	11	55	47	11	50	19
Uganda	18	18	77	9	8	40	8	8	41	22	22	48	5
Zaire	34	51	59	18	16	37	18	66	41	20	22	44	10
Zambia	72	83	92	44	46	75	77	46	81	21	55	80	59
Zimbabwe	64	76	86	39	55	77	38	63	81	56	59	75	26
NORTH AFRICA	62	68	83	60	50	76	54	55	76	40	66	72	57
Algeria	59	83	95	33	30	65	30	32	65	17	45	58	16
Egypt, Arab Republic of	72	53	80	84	57	87	72	67	87	65	84	84	83
Libya	55	77	92	55	..	52	55	62	52	57	50	52	10
Morocco	45	78	78	43	46	61	45	46	61	..	42	58	44
Tunisia	65	88	85	36	80	91	37	80	91	65	84	83	50
ALL AFRICA	37	44	72	31	32	50	27	35	51	34	39	52	28
South Africa	..	..	..	..	..	..	..	..	..	..	..	..	..

Notes: ORT = Oral rehydration therapy; DPT = diphtheria, pertussis (whooping cough), and tetanus.

13–7. Child malnutrition

	Percentage of mothers breast-feeding (around 1985) for			Percentage of infants with low birth weight (1985)	Percentage of children (around 1985) suffering from		
	3 months	6 months	12 months		Underweight (under 5 years)	Wasting (12–23 months)	Stunting (24–59 months)
SUB-SAHARAN AFRICA	..	..	..	..	..	..	..
excluding Nigeria	..	..	..	..	..	..	..
Angola	..	..	..	17	..	..	..
Benin	90	90	76	8	..	14	..
Botswana	96	93	73	8	15	19	51
Burkina Faso	98	98	97	..	..	..	..
Burundi	..	95	90	9	38	10	60
Cameroon	92	90	77	13	17	2	43
Cape Verde	..	..	..	..	..	..	..
Central African Republic	..	..	..	15	..	..	..
Chad	..	..	..	..	..	..	..
Comoros	..	..	..	..	..	..	..
Congo, People's Republic of the	100	98	90	16	24	13	33
Cote d'Ivoire	87	84	78	14	12	4	10
Djibouti	..	..	..	..	..	..	..
Equatorial Guinea	..	..	..	..	..	..	..
Ethiopia	..	97	95	..	38	19	43
Gabon	..	..	..	..	..	..	..
Gambia, The	..	..	..	..	..	..	..
Ghana	91	90	72	17	27	28	31
Guinea	100	90	85	..	..	..	..
Guinea-Bissau	..	..	..	..	..	..	..
Kenya	86	82	67	15	..	10	42
Lesotho	..	87	..	11	16	7	23
Liberia	96	92	70	..	20	7	38
Madagascar	..	..	..	..	33	18	41
Malawi	..	..	96	20	24	8	61
Mali	91	..	82	17	31	16	34
Mauritania	91	86	67	11	31	24	37
Mauritius	79	55	40	9	24	16	22
Mozambique	99	96	..	20	57	..	..
Namibia	..	..	..	..	..	..	..
Niger	65	30	15	15	49	23	38
Nigeria	98	80	60	20	..	21	..
Rwanda	97	97	74	17	28	23	45
Sao Tome & Principe	..	..	..	..	..	..	..
Senegal	94	94	82	11	22	8	28
Seychelles	..	..	..	..	..	..	..
Sierra Leone	99	98	92	17	23	26	46
Somalia	92	78	54	..	..	..	..
Sudan	91	86	72	..	41	13	..
Swaziland	..	..	..	..	..	..	..
Tanzania	100	90	70	14	48	17	..
Togo	99	90	58	20	25	10	37
Uganda	85	70	20	..	7	3	32
Zaire	100	100	86	13	28	11	40
Zambia	..	..	93	14	28	12	41
Zimbabwe	98	96	84	15	12	1	29
NORTH AFRICA	..	..	..	..	..	..	..
Algeria	..	..	..	9	10	4	14
Egypt, Arab Republic of	90	87	81	5	17	3	34
Libya	..	..	..	..	..	..	..
Morocco	87	81	70	..	16	6	34
Tunisia	95	92	71	8	21	3	45
ALL AFRICA	..	..	..	..	..	..	..
South Africa	..	..	..	12	..	..	..

13-8. Average daily caloric intake

	Kilocalories per capita			Average		
	1980	1985	1988	75–79	80–85	86–MR
SUB-SAHARAN AFRICA	2,107	2,040	2,007	2,059	2,054	2,027
excluding Nigeria	2,063	2,017	1,997	2,032	2,026	2,010
Angola	2,100	1,819	1,725	2,008	1,938	1,742
Benin	2,005	2,132	2,145	2,079	2,064	2,115
Botswana	2,122	2,208	2,269	2,079	2,168	2,251
Burkina Faso	1,790	1,887	2,061	1,772	1,782	2,002
Burundi	2,288	2,337	2,253	2,373	2,310	2,320
Cameroon	2,179	2,145	2,161	2,206	2,131	2,142
Cape Verde	2,433	2,476	2,436	2,242	2,440	2,500
Central African Republic	2,028	1,803	1,980	2,093	1,919	1,965
Chad	1,762	1,741	1,852	1,779	1,595	1,821
Comoros	2,068	2,092	2,046	2,029	2,099	2,059
Congo, People's Republic of	2,409	2,530	2,512	2,310	2,455	2,519
Cote d'Ivoire	2,498	2,482	2,365	2,342	2,489	2,405
Djibouti	..	..	..	..	..	..
Equatorial Guinea	..	..	..	..	..	..
Ethiopia	1,777	1,550	1,658	1,600	1,681	1,684
Gabon	2,243	2,384	2,396	2,247	2,292	2,398
Gambia, The	2,009	2,307	2,360	1,995	2,143	2,339
Ghana	1,909	2,122	2,209	2,036	1,943	2,167
Guinea	1,992	1,984	2,042	2,065	2,017	2,007
Guinea-Bissau	1,797	2,065	2,690	1,756	1,940	2,437
Kenya	2,145	2,175	1,973	2,169	2,112	2,016
Lesotho	2,360	2,269	2,307	2,208	2,286	2,275
Liberia	2,319	2,326	2,270	2,292	2,314	2,344
Madagascar	2,397	2,300	2,101	2,414	2,356	2,174
Malawi	2,197	2,194	2,009	2,301	2,197	2,057
Mali	1,695	1,985	2,181	1,735	1,805	2,114
Mauritania	1,963	2,292	2,528	1,816	2,070	2,465
Mauritius	2,676	2,714	2,679	2,602	2,702	2,690
Mozambique	1,797	1,614	1,632	1,777	1,705	1,604
Namibia	1,842	1,818	1,889	1,894	1,842	1,862
Niger	2,236	2,270	2,340	2,083	2,261	2,321
Nigeria	2,250	2,114	2,039	2,148	2,147	2,083
Rwanda	1,986	1,950	1,786	1,977	1,987	1,817
Sao Tome & Principe	2,258	2,343	2,657	2,083	2,289	2,529
Senegal	2,373	2,298	1,989	2,278	2,327	2,162
Seychelles	2,125	2,179	2,146	2,096	2,146	2,117
Sierra Leone	2,027	1,851	1,806	2,021	1,941	1,813
Somalia	1,796	1,752	1,736	1,494	1,794	1,781
Sudan	2,304	2,084	1,996	2,183	2,104	1,981
Swaziland	2,428	2,468	2,548	2,452	2,495	2,554
Tanzania	2,244	2,229	2,151	2,184	2,209	2,186
Togo	2,151	2,188	2,133	1,985	2,140	2,110
Uganda	2,098	2,081	2,013	2,175	2,157	2,034
Zaire	2,068	2,076	2,034	2,163	2,065	2,079
Zambia	2,174	2,094	2,026	2,233	2,122	2,028
Zimbabwe	2,132	2,127	2,232	2,115	2,146	2,193
NORTH AFRICA	2,781	2,928	3,011	2,593	2,862	2,992
Algeria	2,563	2,577	2,726	2,262	2,548	2,699
Egypt, Arab Republic of	2,900	3,152	3,213	2,682	3,058	3,196
Libya	3,379	3,416	3,384	3,308	3,409	3,393
Morocco	2,676	2,757	2,820	2,612	2,704	2,808
Tunisia	2,695	2,814	2,964	2,602	2,742	2,911
ALL AFRICA	2,239	2,212	2,200	2,164	2,211	2,213
South Africa	2,849	2,890	3,035	2,837	2,889	2,963

13–9. Access to safe water

	Percentage of population with access to safe water								
	1980			1985			1988		
	Total	Urban	Rural	Total	Urban	Rural	Total	Urban	Rural
SUB-SAHARAN AFRICA	..	..	..	..	..	..	..	..	..
excluding Nigeria	..	..	..	..	..	..	..	..	..
Angola	23	85	10	28	90	12	30	87	15
Benin	21	26	15	..	..	..	52	80	34
Botswana	..	..	..	60	98	47	54	84	46
Burkina Faso	27	27	31	..	..	..	67	43	69
Burundi	20	..	20	24	90	22	26	98	21
Cameroon	..	..	..	26	..	..	33	43	24
Cape Verde	52	100	21	..	..	..	69	83	50
Central African Republic	16	..	5	16	37	5	..	13	..
Chad	..	..	..	26	27	30	..	..	..
Comoros	..	..	..	28	53	20	..	..	..
Congo, People's Republic of	21	36	3	20	42	3	21	42	7
Cote d'Ivoire	20	30	10	..	..	..	19	30	10
Djibouti	51	50	20	..	..	..	44	80	40
Equatorial Guinea	..	..	..	..	47	..	..	43	..
Ethiopia	..	..	..	4	..	42	16	69	9
Gabon	..	75	34	..	..	..	92	..	..
Gambia, The	15	85	..	45	100	33	60	97	50
Ghana	52	71	33	..	..	..	56	93	39
Guinea	20	69	2	..	..	..	19	41	12
Guinea-Bissau	10	18	8	..	..	..	21	17	22
Kenya	26	85	15	27	61	21	30	61	21
Lesotho	14	37	11	..	..	..	36	65	30
Liberia	12	..	16	34	50	16	55	100	23
Madagascar	22	80	7	21	73	9	32	81	17
Malawi	41	77	37	51	66	49	56	97	50
Mali	7	37	1	14	48	8	17	46	10
Mauritania	80	80	85	..	..	..	..	73	..
Mauritius	99	100	98	..	..	..	100	100	100
Mozambique	9	82	2	13	50	7	16	38	9
Namibia	..	..	..	..	..	..	..	..	..
Niger	34	41	32	33	41	34	47	35	49
Nigeria	39	60	30	..	..	..	46	100	20
Rwanda	56	48	55	..	..	..	50	79	48
Sao Tome & Principe	..	..	..	82	95	50	..	..	..
Senegal	44	77	25	44	69	27	53	79	38
Seychelles	..	..	..	79	..	..	83	..	95
Sierra Leone	16	50	2	22	61	6	25	68	7
Somalia	34	60	20	31	65	21	34	58	22
Sudan	22	100	31	48	..	31	21	60	10
Swaziland	..	..	..	38	75	35	34	100	7
Tanzania	..	..	..	46	88	39	56	90	42
Togo	42	70	31	34	68	26	55	99	41
Uganda	4	45	..	16	90	7	20	37	18
Zaire	..	..	..	20	43	5	33	52	21
Zambia	48	65	32	..	..	..	59	76	41
Zimbabwe	..	..	..	52	100	10	..	..	32
NORTH AFRICA	..	..	..	..	..	..	..	..	..
Algeria	77	100	70	90	100	80	68	85	55
Egypt, Arab Republic of	80	88	64	..	..	..	73	92	56
Libya	98	100	90	98	100	90	97	100	90
Morocco	..	..	..	35	63	15	60	100	25
Tunisia	64	100	17	58	86	27	68	100	31
ALL AFRICA	..	..	..	..	..	..	..	..	..
South Africa	..	..	..	..	..	..	..	..	..

13–10. Access to health services

	Percentage of population with access to health services								
	1980			1985			1988		
	Total	Urban	Rural	Total	Urban	Rural	Total	Urban	Rural
SUB-SAHARAN AFRICA	..	..	..	..	..	..	..	..	..
excluding Nigeria	..	..	..	..	..	..	..	..	..
Angola	..	..	..	40	..	..	18	..	..
Benin	49	51	48	48	51	48	49	51	48
Botswana	..	..	..	31	90	30	61	90	30
Burkina Faso	..	..	..	100	..	..	..	..	..
Burundi	..	..	..	32	61	11	45	..	..
Cameroon	..	..	..	..	..	..	30	..	..
Cape Verde	..	..	..	..	..	..	82	..	..
Central African Republic	..	..	..	38	43	20	65	78	17
Chad	..	..	..	..	..	..	..	..	..
Comoros	..	..	..	43	..	..	46	..	..
Congo, People's Republic of	..	..	..	..	..	..	..	..	..
Cote d'Ivoire	..	..	..	64	92	45	60	92	45
Djibouti	..	..	..	13	..	..	47	100	40
Equatorial Guinea	..	..	..	..	..	..	..	..	..
Ethiopia	..	..	..	..	..	..	..	..	..
Gabon	..	..	..	50	..	..	80	40	20
Gambia, The	..	..	..	39	50	39	30	50	30
Ghana	..	..	..	60	..	..	56	..	..
Guinea	..	..	..	80	..	..	80	..	..
Guinea-Bissau	..	..	..	15	..	..	15	46	10
Kenya	30	..	..	30	..	..	30	..	..
Lesotho	..	..	..	30	100	30	39	100	30
Liberia	..	..	..	..	..	..	..	..	..
Madagascar	..	..	..	40	100	30	41	99	30
Malawi	27	60	25	..	..	..	27	60	25
Mali	..	..	..	..	..	..	80	100	69
Mauritania	..	..	..	..	..	..	40	..	..
Mauritius	..	..	..	..	..	..	..	..	..
Mozambique	27	50	15	..	..	..	27	50	15
Namibia	..	..	..	52	100	40	51	90	40
Niger	76	99	72	..	..	..	..	..	..
Nigeria	..	..	..	61	25	..	61	..	..
Rwanda	61	90	57	61	90	57	61	90	57
Sao Tome & Principe	..	..	..	20	60	17	26	40	17
Senegal	75	100	50	75	..	..	75	100	50
Seychelles	89	100	85	88	100	85	89	100	85
Sierra Leone	30	61	11	..	..	..	30	61	11
Somalia	..	..	..	98	100	..	100	100	100
Sudan	..	..	..	99	..	..	100	..	..
Swaziland	..	..	..	..	..	..	..	..	..
Tanzania	..	..	..	71	100	62	71	100	62
Togo	30	..	..	30	..	..	30	..	..
Uganda	..	..	..	41	44	39	41	44	39
Zaire	..	..	..	..	..	..	83	97	70
Zambia	90	..	..	80	..	..	90	..	..
Zimbabwe	..	..	..	40	75	30	40	75	30
NORTH AFRICA	..	..	..	..	..	..	..	..	..
Algeria	..	..	..	90	100	80	88	100	80
Egypt, Arab Republic of	..	..	..	..	..	..	..	..	..
Libya	..	..	..	..	..	..	..	..	..
Morocco	..	..	..	52	93	24	70	100	50
Tunisia	..	..	..	90	100	80	90	100	80
ALL AFRICA	..	..	..	..	..	..	..	..	..
South Africa	..	..	..	..	..	..	..	..	..

13–11. Health care

	Population per physician			Population per nursing personnel			Percentage of births attended by trained health personnel
	1980	1985	1989	1980	1985	1989	1985
SUB-SAHARAN AFRICA	..	..	..	..	..	..	..
excluding Nigeria	..	..	..	..	..	..	..
Angola	..	17,786	..	..	1,015	..	15
Benin	16,985	..	..	1,907	..	..	45
Botswana	7,765	..	..	700	..	..	77
Burkina Faso	55,269	..	80,642	3,073	..	1,682	30
Burundi	..	21,120	21,035	..	3,035	4,382	21
Cameroon	..	..	..	..	..	..	..
Cape Verde	5,667	..	..	690	..	..	..
Central African Republic	23,174	..	..	1,994	..	..	66
Chad	..	..	38,358	..	..	3,395	24
Comoros	..	12,290	..	..	2,268	..	..
Congo, People's Republic of	8,324	..	..	587	..	..	..
Cote d'Ivoire	..	..	..	..	..	..	20
Djibouti	4,486	4,183	..	1,000	506	..	..
Equatorial Guinea	..	..	..	..	..	..	..
Ethiopia	88,088	78,772	..	4,996	5,391	..	14
Gabon	2,561	..	..	272	..	..	92
Gambia, The	..	11,688	..	..	..	..	58
Ghana	..	14,894	20,463	622	..	1,669	40
Guinea	45,470	..	..	5,058	..	..	25
Guinea-Bissau	7,491	7,262	..	1,130	1,129	..	73
Kenya	10,123	10,045	10,202	988	..	..	28
Lesotho	..	18,615	..	..	..	..	40
Liberia	9,459	..	..	2,960	..	..	87
Madagascar	9,892	9,780	..	1,721	..	..	62
Malawi	53,305	11,339	..	3,007	..	..	45
Mali	25,728	25,392	23,505	2,301	..	..	27
Mauritania	..	11,901	..	..	1,182	..	20
Mauritius	1,870	1,899	..	602	..	..	85
Mozambique	38,074	..	..	5,122	..	..	28
Namibia	..	..	..	..	..	..	28
Niger	..	39,669	..	..	458	..	47
Nigeria	10,543	..	..	1,297	..	..	40
Rwanda	31,923	..	74,880	10,329	..	4,298	22
Sao Tome & Principe	2,466	..	..	565	..	..	..
Senegal	12,690	..	..	1,932	2,031	..	50
Seychelles	..	2,173	..	..	..	..	..
Sierra Leone	18,177	13,618	..	1,980	1,089	..	25
Somalia	16,547	16,080	..	1,956	1,530	..	2
Sudan	9,416	10,189	..	1,441	1,258	..	20
Swaziland	..	..	..	742	..	..	..
Tanzania	..	25,040	24,983	..	7,772	5,487	60
Togo	19,817	8,703	..	1,422	1,236	..	15
Uganda	21,273	..	..	1,996	..	..	45
Zaire	..	..	12,940	..	..	1,797	..
Zambia	10,406	7,154	..	1,660	..	..	69
Zimbabwe	6,595	6,698	7,214	960	1,000	1,002	69
NORTH AFRICA	..	..	..	..	..	..	..
Algeria	..	2,338	2,330	..	331	316	15
Egypt, Arab Republic of	836	..	767	762	..	..	47
Libya	681	..	..	355	..	..	76
Morocco	18,602	..	4,763	900	..	1,053	29
Tunisia	3,668	..	2,155	956	..	367	68
ALL AFRICA	..	..	..	..	..	..	..
South Africa	..	..	..	..	..	..	..

13–12. Illiteracy rate

	Percentage of the population 15 years of age and above that is illiterate								
	1980			**1985**			**1989**		
	Total	Male	Female	Total	Male	Female	Total	Male	Female
SUB-SAHARAN AFRICA	..	..	..	56	45	68	..	..	..
excluding Nigeria	..	..	..	56	45	68	..	..	..
Angola	..	..	..	64	50	77	58	44	72
Benin	72	60	83	81	74	88	77	68	84
Botswana	..	..	..	30	19	40	26	16	35
Burkina Faso	..	..	..	86	77	94	82	72	91
Burundi	73	61	85	58	47	68	50	39	60
Cameroon	..	..	..	52	39	64	46	34	57
Cape Verde	..	..	..	53	39	61	34	..	..
Central African Republic	67	52	81	69	55	81	62	48	75
Chad	..	..	..	77	66	88	70	58	82
Comoros	..	..	..	..	..	..	..	..	..
Congo, People's Republic of the	..	..	..	48	34	62	43	30	56
Cote d'Ivoire	65	55	76	51	38	66	46	33	60
Djibouti	..	..	..	..	..	..	..	..	..
Equatorial Guinea	63	..	..	55	41	69	50	36	63
Ethiopia	..	..	..	..	..	..	..	..	..
Gabon	..	..	..	44	30	57	39	27	52
Gambia, The	80	71	88	80	70	90	73	61	84
Ghana	..	..	..	47	36	58	40	30	49
Guinea	..	..	..	83	75	92	76	65	87
Guinea-Bissau	81	75	87	70	57	82	64	50	76
Kenya	53	40	65	35	23	47	31	20	42
Lesotho	..	..	..	26	38	16	..	..	..
Liberia	..	..	..	68	57	79	61	50	71
Madagascar	..	..	..	23	14	32	20	12	27
Malawi	..	..	..	59	48	69	..	..	..
Mali	..	..	..	77	69	85	68	59	76
Mauritania	..	..	..	73	60	84	66	53	79
Mauritius	21	14	28	17	11	23	..	..	..
Mozambique	67	56	77	72	61	84	67	55	79
Namibia	..	..	..	28	26	29	..	..	..
Niger	90	86	94	79	68	89	72	60	83
Nigeria	66	54	77	57	45	69	49	38	61
Rwanda	50	39	61	55	41	68	50	36	63
Sao Tome & Principe	..	..	..	..	..	..	..	..	..
Senegal	..	..	..	68	55	81	62	48	75
Seychelles	..	..	..	..	..	..	..	..	..
Sierra Leone	..	..	..	87	79	94	79	69	89
Somalia	94	89	97	83	73	91	76	64	86
Sudan	..	..	..	76	61	90	73	57	88
Swaziland	..	..	..	32	30	34	..	..	..
Tanzania	..	..	..	..	..	..	..	..	..
Togo	..	..	..	62	49	75	57	44	69
Uganda	48	35	60	57	43	71	52	38	65
Zaire	46	26	63	34	21	47	28	16	39
Zambia	..	..	..	33	23	41	27	19	35
Zimbabwe	31	24	39	38	30	45	33	26	40
NORTH AFRICA	..	..	..	53	39	67	..	..	..
Algeria	..	..	..	51	37	65	43	30	55
Egypt, Arab Republic of	..	..	..	55	40	71	52	37	66
Libya	..	..	..	33	19	50	36	25	50
Morocco	..	..	..	58	46	71	51	39	62
Tunisia	54	39	68	42	32	53	35	26	44
ALL AFRICA	..	..	..	56	43	68	..	..	..
South Africa	..	..	..	..	..	..	..	..	..

13–13. Primary school gross enrollment ratio

	Total			Males			Females		
	1980	1985	1988	1980	1985	1988	1980	1985	1988
SUB-SAHARAN AFRICA	70	68	65	82	72	71	62	60	57
excluding Nigeria	70	68	65	82	72	71	62	60	57
Angola	158	93	..	158	..	..	137	..	..
Benin	64	65	63	88	87	83	40	43	43
Botswana	92	108	116	84	103	114	100	112	119
Burkina Faso	18	29	31	23	36	41	14	21	24
Burundi	29	53	70	35	61	..	22	44	..
Cameroon	104	108	111	113	117	119	94	98	102
Cape Verde	112	109	109	115	112	114	108	106	106
Central African Republic	71	77	67	93	94	83	51	59	51
Chad	..	43	51	..	63	73	..	24	29
Comoros	95	87	80	110	100	89	79	75	71
Congo, People s Republic of the	..	..	..	..	..	..	..	..	..
Cote d'Ivoire	74	70	..	89	82	..	59	58	..
Djibouti	..	43	46	..	..	..	..	35	39
Equatorial Guinea	84	..	..	..	..	..	..	..	..
Ethiopia	35	34	36	45	40	44	25	27	28
Gabon	..	..	..	..	..	..	..	..	..
Gambia, The	51	68	61	67	84	76	35	52	47
Ghana	80	76	73	89	85	81	71	63	66
Guinea	31	30	30	42	42	42	21	19	19
Guinea-Bissau	67	60	53	94	81	69	41	39	37
Kenya	115	98	93	120	101	95	110	96	91
Lesotho	103	113	112	85	101	101	120	125	123
Liberia	49	40	..	63	51	..	34	28	..
Madagascar	143	118	97	146	122	99	139	114	95
Malawi	60	62	72	72	70	79	48	53	65
Mali	27	23	23	34	29	29	19	17	17
Mauritania	37	49	52	47	60	61	26	39	43
Mauritius	108	105	105	108	105	104	108	106	105
Mozambique	75	86	68	115	97	76	84	75	59
Namibia	..	..	..	..	..	..	..	..	..
Niger	27	28	30	35	36	38	19	20	21
Nigeria	97	81	62	110	..	76	84	..	48
Rwanda	63	63	64	66	64	69	60	61	66
Sao Tome & Principe	..	..	138	..	..	..	..	..	..
Senegal	46	57	59	55	69	70	36	46	49
Seychelles	..	..	..	..	..	..	..	..	..
Sierra Leone	52	61	53	61	73	65	43	50	40
Somalia	27	15	..	35	20	..	19	10	..
Sudan	50	50	..	59	58	..	41	41	..
Swaziland	103	107	105	104	108	105	102	105	104
Tanzania	93	72	66	100	73	67	86	71	66
Togo	71	95	101	151	118	124	93	73	78
Uganda	50	70	77	56	..	66	43	63	50
Zaire	94	88	76	109	106	86	79	70	65
Zambia	90	99	..	98	106	..	82	93	..
Zimbabwe	85	135	128	..	140	130	..	131	126
NORTH AFRICA	84	88	88	97	99	98	69	77	77
Algeria	95	93	96	108	103	105	81	82	87
Egypt, Arab Republic of	78	87	90	90	96	100	65	78	79
Libya	..	..	..	..	..	..	..	..	..
Morocco	78	78	67	96	94	80	59	60	53
Tunisia	103	116	116	118	126	121	88	106	105
ALL AFRICA	74	74	72	86	80	79	64	65	63
South Africa	..	..	..	..	..	..	..	..	..

13–14. Pupil progression and efficiency indicator

	Percentage of cohort reaching final grade of primary school		Percentage of final grade pupils (primary school) progressing to first grade of secondary education(a)	Percentage of grade 1 enrollment not completing primary school
	1980	1989(b)	1980	1985
SUB-SAHARAN AFRICA	..	..	..	..
excluding Nigeria	..	..	..	..
Angola	..	24	50	..
Benin	56	36	40	64
Botswana	90	89	31	11
Burkina Faso	70	68	22	26
Burundi	94	87	8	13
Cameroon	67	70	26	33
Cape Verde	..	39	..	..
Central African Republic	47	56	36	83
Chad	29	78	19	83
Comoros	..	31	..	..
Congo, People's Republic of the	68	71	73	25
Cote d'Ivoire	89	73	30	32
Djibouti	..	88	..	..
Equatorial Guinea	..	..	..	..
Ethiopia	50	50	93	59
Gabon	56	44	27	41
Gambia, The	92	96	44	..
Ghana	74	..	..	..
Guinea	41	43	69	30
Guinea-Bissau	15	19	68	..
Kenya	61	51	35	38
Lesotho	38	52	45	48
Liberia	..	..	63	..
Madagascar	..	..	..	70
Malawi	32	31	7	67
Mali	40	40	42	61
Mauritania	80	78	39	8
Mauritius	..	98	54	4
Mozambique	21	34	40	61
Namibia	..	..	..	..
Niger	79	75	35	25
Nigeria	..	..	..	37
Rwanda	41	46	4	51
Sao Tome & Principe	..	77	..	..
Senegal	84	85	29	17
Seychelles	..	91	..	..
Sierra Leone	48	..	73	..
Somalia	..	..	50	67
Sudan	..	76	53	39
Swaziland	63	62	68	..
Tanzania	76	71	8	24
Togo	26	52	31	41
Uganda	76	..	13	24
Zaire	..	60	71	40
Zambia	83	80	21	9
Zimbabwe	..	74	74	26
NORTH AFRICA	..	..	..	..
Algeria	..	91	..	10
Egypt, Arab Republic of	..	95	..	36
Libya	..	..	..	18
Morocco	..	67	..	31
Tunisia	..	..	..	23
ALL AFRICA	..	..	..	..
South Africa	..	..	..	..

Note: (a) "Secondary" refers to secondary general education.
(b) Data are for cohort starting around 1985.

13–15. Primary school repetition rate

	Number of repeaters per 100 pupils enrolled								
	Total			Males			Females		
	1980	1985	1988	1980	1985	1988	1980	1985	1988
SUB-SAHARAN AFRICA	..	..	..	..	..	..	..	..	..
excluding Nigeria	..	..	..	..	..	..	..	..	..
Angola	29	..	..	..	..	..	..	..	..
Benin	20	27	26	19	26	26	22	28	27
Botswana	3	6	5	..	6	5	..	6	5
Burkina Faso	17	15	17	16	16	17	18	15	17
Burundi	30	18	..	30	18	..	30	18	..
Cameroon	30	29	29	31	30	30	30	29	28
Cape Verde	29	28	..	..	29	30	26	29	26	22
Central African Republic	35	29	34	33	31	34	37	29	34
Chad	..	24	32	..	23	31	..	30	35
Comoros	25	33	..	..	33	..	..	33	..
Congo, People's Republic of the	26	30	35	27	31	36	25	29	34
Cote d'Ivoire	20	28	..	20	28	..	20	28	..
Djibouti	..	13	10	..	..	..	..	..	..
Equatorial Guinea	..	..	..	..	..	..	..	..	..
Ethiopia	12	10	0	11	9	10	14	11	13
Gabon	35	32	31	36	29	13	34	35	31
Gambia, The	13	17	18	13	18	19	13	16	16
Ghana	2	..	..	2	..	..	2	..	..
Guinea	22	27	22	..	25	20	..	31	26
Guinea–Bissau	29	41	42	29	40	41	30	42	43
Kenya	13	..	..	13	..	..	13	..	..
Lesotho	21	23	..	22	26	25	20	21	21
Liberia	..	..	..	..	..	..	..	..	..
Madagascar	..	..	35	..	..	37	..	..	33
Malawi	17	18	21	17	19	22	17	17	20
Mali	30	30	30	30	28	30	30	29	30
Mauritania	14	18	..	12	17	18	17	20	21
Mauritius	..	6	8	..	6	8	..	6	8
Mozambique	29	24	25	27	24	24	31	24	26
Namibia	..	..	..	..	..	..	..	..	..
Niger	14	15	..	14	15	..	14	15	..
Nigeria	..	..	..	..	..	..	..	..	..
Rwanda	6	12	..	6	12	10	6	12	10
Sao Tome & Principe	30	48	35	..	..	35	..	..	35
Senegal	16	16	15	16	15	15	16	17	15
Seychelles	0	0	0	0	0	0	0	0	0
Sierra Leone	..	..	..	..	..	..	..	..	..
Somalia	..	..	..	..	..	..	..	..	..
Sudan	0	0	0	0	0	0	0	0	0
Swaziland	11	14	15	13	16	17	9	12	13
Tanzania	1	1	5	1	1	5	1	1	5
Togo	37	35	31	35	34	30	38	36	32
Uganda	..	14	..	..	14	..	..	14	..
Zaire	19	0	..	19	..	..	19	..	..
Zambia	2	2	..	2	2	..	2	2	..
Zimbabwe	0	..	..	..	..	..	0	1	..
NORTH AFRICA	..	..	..	..	..	..	..	..	..
Algeria	12	8	7	13	10	9	11	6	5
Egypt, Arab Republic of	8	2	..	7	5	..	9	1	..
Libya	9	..	..	10	..	..	8	..	..
Morocco	30	20	15	30	21	16	28	18	14
Tunisia	21	20	21	22	21	22	19	19	20
ALL AFRICA	..	..	..	..	..	..	..	..	..
South Africa	..	..	..	..	..	..	..	..	..

Notes: In Sudan and Seychelles, a policy of automatic promotion is practiced at the primary level of education. Tanzanian figures refer to mainland only.

13-16. Enrollment in private schools

	Pupils enrolled in private schools as percentage of total number of pupils enrolled					
	Primary			Secondary		
	1980	1985	1989	1980	1985	1989
SUB-SAHARAN AFRICA	10.5	9.9	..	..	..	..
excluding Nigeria	10.5	9.9	..	..	..	..
Angola	0.0	..	..	..	..	..
Benin	3.4	0.0	3.7	..	..	..
Botswana	4.7	5.6	6.7	26.7	37.5	65.9
Burkina Faso	8.4	8.7	9.1	50.9	48.5	..
Burundi	4.3	1.2	..	51.0	..	..
Cameroon	36.3	33.8	..	47.5	..	..
Cape Verde	0.0	0.0	0.0	..	..	..
Central African Republic	0.0	0.0	0.0	..	..	..
Chad	..	5.5	..	0.9	..	..
Comoros	0.0	0.0	..	..	..	..
Congo, People's Republic of the	0.0	0.0	0.0	47.0	..	..
Cote d'Ivoire	14.0	11.2	..	28.8	29.3	..
Djibouti	9.0	9.9	11.1	3.9	3.1	17.8
Equatorial Guinea	..	..	..	..	..	..
Ethiopia	15.6	11.0	10.7	..	..	..
Gabon	39.0	33.4	..	0.0	..	..
Gambia, The	15.1	18.1	..	7.2	..	..
Ghana	..	..	6.3	33.8	..	..
Guinea	0.0	0.0	2.9	..	..	..
Guinea-Bissau	..	0.0	0.0	0.0	..	..
Kenya	..	..	..	41.0	..	..
Lesotho	98.4	..	..	89.9	88.7	..
Liberia	40.0	33.4	..	46.5	..	..
Madagascar	12.7	13.2	16.7	44.2	..	..
Malawi	6.8	5.5	..	12.4	14.3	..
Mali	4.2	4.2	4.2	1.4	..	..
Mauritania	..	0.1	..	8.3	..	..
Mauritius	25.9	23.2	24.3	30.1	78.4	..
Mozambique	0.0	0.0	..	0.0	..	..
Namibia	..	..	..	0.0	..	..
Niger	3.0	2.7	2.8	..	..	..
Nigeria	..	..	..	43.9	..	..
Rwanda	..	0.6	..	15.5	..	..
Sao Tome & Principe	0.0	0.0	..	37.0	..	..
Senegal	11.0	8.8	8.9	..	..	..
Seychelles	0.0	0.0	1.3	..	..	..
Sierra Leone	..	..	..	30.1	..	..
Somalia	0.0	0.0	..	..	..	..
Sudan	2.5	2.3	..	..	44.1	..
Swaziland	79.8	80.1	80.5	..	..	..
Tanzania	0.2	0.3	0.2	..	49.1	59.2
Togo	23.3	23.4	23.8	10.2	11.6	..
Uganda	..	..	..	12.0	..	..
Zaire	..	4.0	..	..	..	..
Zambia	0.6	0.3	0.7	0.0	..	..
Zimbabwe	83.5	87.6	87.4	40.6	..	..
NORTH AFRICA	3.0	3.0	..	..	..	..
Algeria	0.0	0.0	0.0	..	..	..
Egypt, Arab Republic of	5.0	4.8	5.9	..	..	..
Libya	0.0	0.0	..	..	..	..
Morocco	3.0	3.4	3.6	..	..	..
Tunisia	0.9	0.4	0.5	..	..	..
ALL AFRICA	8.3	7.8	..	..	..	..
South Africa	..	..	..	..	..	..

Note: In Lesotho, Zimbabwe, Zambia, Kenya, and Malawi, "private" does not include government-assisted schools.

13–17. Number of school teachers

	Primary						Secondary					
	Total teaching staff			Percentage females			Total teaching staff			Percentage females		
	1980	1985	1988	1980	1985	1988	1980	1985	1988	1980	1985	1988
SUB-SAHARAN AFRICA	1,068,449	..	..	..	..	..	..	..	..	..	..	..
excluding Nigeria	698,813	..	..	..	..	..	..	..	..	..	..	..
Angola	40,027	..	..	..	..	..	..	..	..	..	..	..
Benin	7,994	13,452	13,821	23	24	25	..	3,657		..	..	..
Botswana	5,316	6,980	8,104	72	78	78	1,137	1,675	2,573	37	40	39
Burkina Faso	3,700	6,091	6,359	20	25	26	1,451	..	..	..	..	..
Burundi	4,805	6,866	..	47	47	..	1,269	1,849	..	20	21	..
Cameroon	26,763	33,598	36,548	20	27	29	8,926	11,096	17,032	20	22	21
Cape Verde	1,436	1,493	1,892	..	61	60	184	247	268	..	49	47
Central African Republic	4,130	4,718	4,226	25	25	25	724	922	1,052	16	9	..
Chad	..	4,779	..	..	4	..	..	..	..	..	..	..
Comoros	1,292	1,901	1,777	7	21	..	449	..	..	20	..	..
Congo, People's Republic of the	7,186	7,745	7,429	25	30	33	5,117	6,322	6,697	..	..	..
Cote d'Ivoire	26,460	33,500	..	15	..	..	..	..	..	..	..	..
Djibouti	419	514	592	..	..	..	278	306	320	..	..	..
Equatorial Guinea	647	..	..	..	..	..	..	..	..	..	..	..
Ethiopia	33,322	50,922	65,993	22	26	23	..	..	..	..	..	..
Gabon	3,441	4,008	4,229	27	35	37	1,587	2,074	2,271	24	22	19
Gambia, The	1,808	2,979	2,604	34	36	32	620	..	..	25	..	..
Ghana	47,921	64,795	60,567	42	40	39	31,636	37,290	53,514	21	26	23
Guinea	7,165	7,605	7,239	14	19	20	5,109	4,642	..	..	7	..
Guinea-Bissau	3,257	3,103	3,065	24	23	22	462	764	..	21	13	..
Kenya	102,489	138,374	155,694	..	34	36	17,081	23,055	26,025	..	36	30
Lesotho	5,097	5,663	5,880	75	77	77	1,299	1,897	2,074	..	..	..
Liberia	9,099	..	..	23	..	..	..	..	..	..	..	..
Madagascar	39,474	42,462	37,894	..	..	53	..	..	16,176	..	..	..
Malawi	12,540	15,440	..	32	33	..	878	1,192	..	..	..	..
Mali	6,862	8,593	8,124	20	22	22	..	..	..	..	..	..
Mauritania	2,183	2,785	3,166	9	15	17	..	1,687	1,915	..	..	..
Mauritius	6,379	6,450	6,203	43	43	44	..	..	..	..	..	..
Mozambique	17,030	20,286	..	22	22	..	3,388	4,688	..	22	21	..
Namibia	..	..	..	..	..	..	..	..	..	..	..	..
Niger	5,518	7,383	7,859	30	33	33	1,284	..	2,035	21	..	13
Nigeria	369,636	292,821	..	33	..	..	81,492	..	..	20	..	..
Rwanda	11,912	14,896	16,975	38	44	47	1,454	3,120	3,616	16	9	9
Sao Tome & Principe	588	546	616	..	59	59	..	..	..	..	..	..
Senegal	9,175	12,559	11,985	24	27	27	4,302	..	4,515	..	..	15
Seychelles	658	652	702	80	85	..	127	364	309	37	29	42
Sierra Leone	9,528	..	..	..	..	..	..	..	..	..	..	..
Somalia	8,122	10,338	..	29	45	..	2,089	2,786	..	7	11	..
Sudan	43,451	50,089	..	31	44	..	18,831	23,035	..	..	33	..
Swaziland	3,278	4,107	4,665	79	80	80	..	..	..	..	..	..
Tanzania	81,153	92,586	95,503	37	39	39	3,837	5,267	6,678	28	24	24
Togo	9,193	10,049	10,217	21	20	21	..	4,351	4,374	..	12	12
Uganda	38,422	61,424	75,561	30	31	..	3,833	8,252	15,437	19	..	..
Zaire	..	113,468	..	..	..	..	..	49,153	..	..	..	..
Zambia	21,455	27,302	..	40	43	..	4,882	..	..	..	..	..
Zimbabwe	28,118	56,067	57,566	38	43	..	3,782	19,507	17,796	..	29	..
NORTH AFRICA	350,730	484,232	..	..	..	..	..	..	..	..	..	..
Algeria	88,481	125,034	139,917	37	40	40	41,137	84,676	..	..	..	37
Egypt, Arab Republic of	141,375	194,929	235,586	47	48	49	121,999	187,580	..	31	35	37
Libya	36,591	41,515	..	47	..	..	24,323	35,825	..	24	..	..
Morocco	56,908	81,867	83,787	30	33	34	36,526	64,079	..	26	28	..
Tunisia	27,375	40,887	44,208	29	38	42	14,328	25,245	29,762	29	31	32
ALL AFRICA	1,419,179	..	..	..	..	..	..	..	..	..	..	..
South Africa	160,286	..	..	..	..	..	..	..	..	..	..	..

Note: Figures include both part–time and full–time teachers.

13–18. Pupil–teacher ratio

	Primary			Secondary		
	1980	1985	1988	1980	1985	1988
SUB-SAHARAN AFRICA	47	42	..	..	..	..
excluding Nigeria	47	42	..	..	..	..
Angola	32	..	..	28	32	32
Benin	48	33	35	28	33	34
Botswana	32	32	32	14	21	25
Burkina Faso	55	58	65	89	77	48
Burundi	37	56	..	..	41	..
Cameroon	52	51	51	38	23	..
Cape Verde	40	39	33	32	..	..
Central African Republic	60	66	70	29	32	36
Chad	..	71	..	..	..	..
Comoros	46	35	..	30	..	..
Congo, People's Republic of	54	61	66	33	..	..
Cote d'Ivoire	39	36	..	18	20	19
Djibouti	40	49	49	18	17	20
Equatorial Guinea	..	..	..	23	21	17
Ethiopia	64	48	43	28	25	..
Gabon	45	46	46	26	23	..
Gambia, The	24	23	28	12	11	..
Ghana	30	24	24	27	21	22
Guinea	36	36	40	23	22	23
Guinea-Bissau	23	25	25	48	..	..
Kenya	38	34	33	..	..	24
Lesotho	48	55	56	22	23	21
Liberia	16	..	..	..	12	14
Madagascar	38	40	41	34	26	23
Malawi	65	61	..	49	45	..
Mali	42	34	38	..	..	..
Mauritania	42	51	50	33	20	20
Mauritius	20	22	23	20	28	..
Mozambique	69	62	..	..	..	..
Namibia	..	..	..	18	19	20
Niger	42	37	41	..	37	34
Nigeria	37	..	..	35	30	27
Rwanda	59	56	57	..	..	..
Sao Tome & Principe	28	30	29	33	21	..
Senegal	46	47	54	22	26	..
Seychelles	22	22	21	..	..	..
Sierra Leone	..	..	..	25	22	20
Somalia	34	19	..	33	24	29
Sudan	34	35	..	27	26	20
Swaziland	34	34	33	..	..	..
Tanzania	42	34	33	18	16	18
Togo	55	46	52	24	21	24
Uganda	35	30	..	..	..	..
Zaire	..	37	..	..	..	..
Zambia	49	49	..	25	28	22
Zimbabwe	44	40	..	39	46	36
NORTH AFRICA	36	30	29	20	..	..
Algeria	35	28	28	24	21	19
Egypt, Arab Republic of	35	32	30	18	..	..
Libya	18	..	..	10	..	..
Morocco	38	28	26	22	18	..
Tunisia	39	32	30	13	15	16
ALL AFRICA	44	39	..	..	..	..
South Africa	..	..	..	..	..	..

Note: Figures include both part-time and full-time teachers.

13-19. Secondary school gross enrollment ratio

	Total			Males			Females		
	1980	1985	1988	1980	1985	1988	1980	1985	1988
SUB-SAHARAN AFRICA	13	15	..	16	18	..	9	10	..
excluding Nigeria	10	13	..	13	17	..	7	10	..
Angola	19	..	..	..	..	..	..	..	..
Benin	16	17	..	25	25	..	9	10	..
Botswana	21	30	33	20	29	32	22	31	33
Burkina Faso	3	5	6	4	6	8	2	3	4
Burundi	3	4	..	4	5	..	2	3	..
Cameroon	19	24	27	24	29	33	13	18	21
Cape Verde	8	13	16	9	14	16	7	11	15
Central African Republic	14	16	11	21	24	17	7	8	6
Chad	..	6	6	..	11	10	..	2	2
Comoros	23	31	..	31	37	..	16	24	..
Congo, People's Republic of the	..	..	..	..	..	..	..	..	..
Cote d'Ivoire	18	19	19	26	27	26	11	11	12
Djibouti	..	13	15	..	16	18	..	10	12
Equatorial Guinea	..	..	..	..	..	..	..	..	..
Ethiopia	9	13	15	11	16	17	6	11	12
Gabon	..	..	..	..	..	..	..	..	..
Gambia, The	11	17	16	16	24	23	7	10	10
Ghana	41	40	39	51	49	47	31	31	30
Guinea	14	10	9	21	15	13	8	5	4
Guinea-Bissau	6	7	6	10	..	..	2	3	3
Kenya	20	21	23	23	26	27	16	16	19
Lesotho	17	23	25	14	19	20	20	27	30
Liberia	23	..	..	33	..	..	13	..	..
Madagascar	..	..	19	..	40	20	..	..	19
Malawi	3	4	4	5	6	6	2	2	3
Mali	9	7	6	13	9	9	5	4	4
Mauritania	11	15	16	18	23	23	4	8	10
Mauritius	48	51	53	50	53	53	47	49	53
Mozambique	5	7	5	8	10	7	3	4	4
Namibia	..	..	..	..	..	..	..	..	..
Niger	5	6	7	7	8	9	3	3	4
Nigeria	19	18	16	24	22	19	13	10	7
Rwanda	3	6	6	4	7	7	3	5	5
Sao Tome & Principe	..	..	..	..	..	..	..	..	..
Senegal	11	14	16	15	18	21	7	9	10
Seychelles	..	..	..	..	..	..	..	..	..
Sierra Leone	14	16	18	20	26	..	8	..	..
Somalia	10	10	..	15	13	..	5	7	..
Sudan	16	20	..	20	23	..	12	17	..
Swaziland	38	42	44	39	43	45	37	42	43
Tanzania	3	3	4	4	4	5	2	2	3
Togo	34	21	24	..	33	36	..	10	12
Uganda	5	10	8	7	..	..	3	8	..
Zaire	34	23	22	49	..	..	18	14	..
Zambia	16	17	..	22	23	..	11	13	..
Zimbabwe	8	41	51	..	50	60	..	33	42
NORTH AFRICA	41	53	58	50	62	67	31	44	49
Algeria	33	51	62	40	59	71	26	43	53
Egypt, Arab Republic of	54	65	69	65	77	79	41	54	58
Libya	..	..	..	..	..	..	..	..	..
Morocco	25	34	36	32	40	43	19	27	30
Tunisia	27	39	44	34	46	50	20	32	38
ALL AFRICA	19	23	23	24	28	27	14	18	17
South Africa	..	..	..	..	..	..	..	..	..

13–20. Secondary school repetition rate

	Number of repeaters per 100 pupils enrolled								
	Total			Males			Females		
	1980	1985	1988	1980	1985	1988	1980	1985	1988
SUB-SAHARAN AFRICA	..	..	..	..	..	..	..	..	..
excluding Nigeria	..	..	..	..	..	..	..	..	..
Angola	..	..	..	..	..	..	..	..	..
Benin	9	31	..	8	..	..	12	..	..
Botswana	..	1	0	..	0	..	..	2	0
Burkina Faso	14	14	19	..	..	..	..	..	..
Burundi	10	12	12	9	11	..	12	14	13
Cameroon	19	19	19	18	18	19	20	20	19
Cape Verde	23	19	18	21	20	18	25	18	18
Central African Republic	25	20	21	24	20	20	29	20	24
Chad	..	..	23	..	..	19	..	..	21
Comoros	11	23	33	12	..	..	10	..	34
Congo, People's Republic of the	33	42	..	33	41	..	33	44	..
Cote d'Ivoire	12	19	..	11	18	19	15	22	20
Djibouti	..	13	9	..	..	..	..	..	..
Equatorial Guinea	..	..	..	..	..	..	..	..	..
Ethiopia	..	11	13	..	8	10	..	15	17
Gabon	22	24	25	..	25	..	..	23	..
Gambia, The	2	2	..	2	2	..	2	2	..
Ghana	..	..	..	..	..	..	..	..	..
Guinea	46	43	25	..	43	25	..	44	25
Guinea-Bissau	16	31	20	14	28	18	23	35	22
Kenya	..	..	..	..	..	..	..	..	..
Lesotho	..	6	6	..	6	6	..	6	6
Liberia	..	..	..	..	..	..	..	..	..
Madagascar	..	20	18	..	..	18	..	20	18
Malawi	..	..	2	..	..	2	..	..	2
Mali	35	30	33	..	..	32	..	..	35
Mauritania	8	13	17	7	..	..	10	..	18
Mauritius	10	15	13	10	..	..	10	..	..
Mozambique	21	20	44	19	19	42	25	22	48
Namibia	..	..	..	..	..	..	..	..	..
Niger	7	19	20	7	..	..	8	..	20
Nigeria	..	..	..	..	..	..	..	..	..
Rwanda	5	4	4	..	4	..	..	3	..
Sao Tome & Principe	..	..	..	..	..	..	..	..	..
Senegal	14	17	16	..	..	..	..	..	13
Seychelles	0	0	0	0	0	0	0	0	0
Sierra Leone	..	..	..	..	..	..	..	..	..
Somalia	..	..	..	..	..	..	..	..	..
Sudan	..	..	..	..	..	..	..	..	..
Swaziland	4	7	10	3	7	10	5	7	10
Tanzania	..	..	..	..	..	..	..	..	..
Togo	31	31	35	30	31	26	34	30	39
Uganda	..	..	..	..	..	..	..	..	..
Zaire	10	..	..	7	..	..	8	..	..
Zambia	1	2	..	..	..	..	..	..	..
Zimbabwe	..	0	..	..	..	..	..	0	..
NORTH AFRICA	..	..	..	..	..	..	..	..	..
Algeria	9	7	13	14	..	..	7	7	11
Egypt, Arab Republic of	17	..	..	19	..	..	14	..	..
Libya	15	..	..	16	..	..	13	..	..
Morocco	15	16	17	15	16	17	15	16	17
Tunisia	11	17	18	12	18	18	10	16	16
ALL AFRICA	..	..	..	..	..	..	..	..	..
South Africa	..	..	..	..	..	..	..	..	..

Note: In Seychelles, a policy of automatic promotion is practiced at the secondary level of education.

13–21. Performance on international examinations

Percentage of test–takers that passed the indicated examination

	Cambridge overseas school certificate			Baccalaureate (general)			London (and Cambridge) GCE "O" level		
	1980	1985	1990	1980	1985	1990	1980	1985	1990
SUB-SAHARAN AFRICA	..	..	..	..	..	..	..	..	..
excluding Nigeria	..	..	..	..	..	..	..	..	..
Angola	..	..	..	..	..	..	..	..	..
Benin	..	..	..	..	..	..	..	..	..
Botswana	59	83	70	..	..	..	..	67	78
Burkina Faso	..	..	..	37	36	28	..	..	..
Burundi	..	..	..	..	..	..	..	..	..
Cameroon	..	..	..	29	36	32	27	31	29
Cape Verde	..	..	..	..	..	..	..	..	..
Central African Republic	..	..	..	27	11	..	..	..	..
Chad	..	..	..	..	..	..	..	..	..
Comoros	..	..	..	..	..	..	..	..	..
Congo, People's Republic of the	..	..	..	..	..	..	..	..	..
Cote d'Ivoire	..	..	..	38	56	..	..	..	..
Djibouti	..	..	..	..	53	68	..	..	..
Equatorial Guinea	..	..	..	..	..	..	..	..	..
Ethiopia	..	..	..	..	83	80	..	..	..
Gabon	..	..	..	..	..	..	..	..	..
Gambia, The	..	..	..	..	..	..	..	..	..
Ghana	..	..	..	..	..	..	..	..	..
Guinea	..	..	..	..	..	..	..	..	..
Guinea-Bissau	..	..	..	..	..	..	..	..	..
Kenya	..	..	0	..	80	91	68	..	90
Lesotho	27	31	27	..	..	68	56	80	75
Liberia	..	..	..	..	..	..	..	..	..
Madagascar	..	..	..	..	..	..	..	..	..
Malawi	81	96	52	..	..	..	..	67	56
Mali	..	..	..	..	30	..	..	..	..
Mauritania	..	..	..	..	..	..	..	..	..
Mauritius	44	65	62	..	..	..	72	93	90
Mozambique	..	..	..	..	..	..	..	..	94
Namibia	..	..	21	..	..	..	..	..	73
Niger	..	..	..	..	..	..	..	..	..
Nigeria	..	..	33	..	..	..	..	72	80
Rwanda	..	..	..	..	..	..	..	..	..
Sao Tome & Principe	..	..	..	..	..	..	..	..	..
Senegal	..	..	..	..	..	..	..	..	..
Seychelles	..	..	45	..	..	..	..	92	94
Sierra Leone	..	..	..	..	..	..	..	..	..
Somalia	..	..	..	..	..	..	..	..	..
Sudan	..	..	..	..	..	..	..	..	84
Swaziland	36	48	54	..	..	70	84	64	79
Tanzania	..	..	..	..	69	93	..	..	..
Togo	..	..	..	24	22	..	..	..	..
Uganda	..	..	..	..	..	..	..	..	..
Zaire	..	..	..	..	..	..	..	..	..
Zambia	62	62	..	..	..	..	45	36	39
Zimbabwe	84	..	..	..	..	..	100	88	92
NORTH AFRICA	..	..	..	..	..	..	..	..	..
Algeria	..	..	..	..	..	..	..	..	..
Egypt, Arab Republic of	..	..	..	..	..	..	..	82	85
Libya	..	..	..	..	..	..	..	..	..
Morocco	..	..	..	..	..	..	..	..	67
Tunisia	..	..	..	..	..	..	..	..	..
ALL AFRICA	..	..	..	..	..	..	..	..	..
South Africa	..	..	100	..	..	..	..	..	100

Note: Cambridge school certificate data include only candidates gaining full certificate. GCE data include candidates passing at least one of the subjects sat for.

13–22. Household and economic participation of women

	Percentage of households headed by women, 1980	Percentage of unpaid female family workers 1985	Percentage of women in occupational group, 1980				
			Agricultural workers	Professional, technical	Adminisrative, managerial	Clerical, sales, services	Production, transport, laborers
SUB-SAHARAN AFRICA	..	..	..	..	..	..	..
excluding Nigeria	..	..	..	..	..	..	..
Angola	..	..	..	..	..	..	..
Benin	..	..	..	..	..	..	..
Botswana	45	57	51	61	36	66	23
Burkina Faso	5	..	..	..	..	..	..
Burundi	..	73	..	..	..	..	..
Cameroon	14	68	45	14	6	21	8
Cape Verde	..	..	..	..	..	..	..
Central African Republic	..	..	..	..	..	..	..
Chad	..	..	..	..	..	..	..
Comoros	..	..	..	..	..	..	..
Congo, People's Republic of the	21	..	..	..	..	..	..
Cote d'Ivoire	5	..	..	..	..	..	..
Djibouti	..	..	..	..	..	..	..
Equatorial Guinea	..	..	..	..	..	..	..
Ethiopia	12	..	..	..	..	..	..
Gabon	..	..	..	..	..	..	..
Gambia, The	..	..	..	..	..	..	..
Ghana	27	63	42	23	5	67	35
Guinea	..	..	..	..	..	..	..
Guinea-Bissau	..	..	..	..	..	..	..
Kenya	..	..	..	..	..	..	..
Lesotho	..	52	..	..	..	..	..
Liberia	15	..	..	..	..	..	..
Madagascar	15	..	..	..	..	..	..
Malawi	29	50	..	..	..	..	..
Mali	15	30	..	..	..	..	..
Mauritania	..	..	..	..	..	..	..
Mauritius	19	..	23	37	6	32	6
Mozambique	..	..	..	..	..	..	..
Namibia	..	..	..	..	..	..	..
Niger	..	..	..	..	..	..	..
Nigeria	..	42	..	..	..	..	..
Rwanda	25	70	..	..	..	..	..
Sao Tome & Principe	..	54	..	..	..	..	..
Senegal	..	..	..	..	..	..	..
Seychelles	..	60	30	58	17	63	10
Sierra Leone	..	..	..	..	..	..	..
Somalia	..	..	..	..	..	..	..
Sudan	..	..	..	..	..	..	..
Swaziland	..	..	..	..	..	..	..
Tanzania	..	..	..	..	..	..	..
Togo	..	54	..	..	..	..	..
Uganda	..	..	..	..	..	..	..
Zaire	..	..	..	..	..	..	..
Zambia	28	72	12	21	11	14	..
Zimbabwe	..	..	..	..	..	..	..
NORTH AFRICA	..	..	..	..	..	..	..
Algeria	..	2	2	21	6	10	4
Egypt, Arab Republic of	..	41	17	30	16	20	8
Libya	..	..	12	19	1	7	1
Morocco	17	31	11	15	23	..	16
Tunisia	10	77	20	14	21	18	22
ALL AFRICA	..	..	..	..	..	..	..
South Africa	22	..	29	46	4	56	7

Technical Notes

The sources for the data in the tables on population include the United Nations' publications: Demographic Yearbook, — various issues, World Demographique Estimates and Projections, 1950-2025, World Population Prospects, 1990, Statistics on Children in UNICEF — Assisted Countries, April 1989"; the ECA's publication, Demographic Guide for Africa; World Bank's data file, "World Development Reports", "African Regional Population Projections 1990-91," as well as various country reports. Sources for the data on health include various issues of the World Health Organization's (WHO) publications: The State of The World Children, World Health Statistics Annual, World Health Statistics Qurterly; the ECA (Economic Commission for Africa); and UNDP's "Human Development Report, 1990." Data on education are from various publications of the United Nations Educational, Scientific and Cultural Organization (Unesco), reports of conferences of ministers of education and those responsible for economic planning in African member states of the Unesco, the World Bank data file, as well as various country specific reports.

Table 13-1. Age and gender structure of the population

Age and gender structure of the population is the distribution of the total population according to age and gender. Only the female composition of the population is presented, as the male composition can easily be figured as residuals. Figures relate to mid-year populations as estimated from the latest censuses.

Table 13-2. Poverty

This table presents data that relate to the incidence and extent of poverty. Three indicators are given, including the age dependency ratio for the country as a whole, the percentage of the population below absolute poverty level according to urban-rural parts of the country, and the percentage of household income spent on all food, and separately, on cereals.

Age dependency ratio is defined as the ratio of the population considered to be dependent (under 15 and over 64 years) to the working age population (15-64). We have shown the number of dependent population per 100 persons of working age. Absolute poverty level is defined as the country-specific income level below which adequate standards of nutrition, shelter, and personal amenities cannot be assured.

While the data on absolute poverty are for years around 1985 due to sketchy reporting this is not always the case. For Algeria, data are for 1977, for Burundi they are for 1978, Cameroon is 1979, Chad is 1976, and Mali is 1975, and Sudan is also 1975.

Table 13-3. Urbanization

This table presents the number of persons living in urban areas as a percentage of the total population. Average annual percentage growth rates are shown separately for urban population and the total population. Growth rates are calculated using the least-square method. Group summaries for growth rate are weighted by the countries' absolute populations. The urban population percentages are based on the number of persons living in areas defined as "urban" according to national definitions of this concept. Since national definitions differ cross-country comparisons should be made with caution.

Table 13-4. Components of population change

Here, we present four determinants of population change: total fertility rate, crude birth rate, crude death rate, and net migration. Crude death rate is the number of deaths per 1,000 population in a given year. Crude birth rate is the number of births per 1,000 population in a given year. Total fertility rate is the average number of children that would be born alive to a woman during her lifetime, if she were to bear children at each age in accordance with prevailing age-specific fertility rates. Migrants are taken to be individuals who have resided for at least a year in countries other than their previous residence. An exception is made for refugees living in officially designated camps; they continue to be counted in their country of origin regardless of period of residence.

Table 13-5. Survival prospects

This table shows four health related indicators: life expectancy at birth, infant mortality rate, child mortality rate, and maternal mortality rate.

Life expectancy at birth is the number of years a newborn infant would live if prevailing patterns of mortality at the time of its birth were to stay the same throughout its life. Infant mortality rate is the number of deaths of infants under one year of age per 1,000 live births in a given year. Child mortality rate is the number of deaths of children under 5 years of age per 1,000 live births in a given year. Maternal mortality rate is the annual number of deaths of women from pregnancy-related causes per 100,000 live births.

Table 13-6. Immunization and ORT use

This is the percentage of children under one year of age immunized against tuberculosis, DPT, polio, and measles. It also gives the ORT use rate among children under five years of age. DPT refers to diphtheria, pertussis (whooping cough), and tetanus. ORT use is the percentage of all cases of diarrhea in children under five years of age treated with oral rehydration salts or an appropriate household solution.

Table 13-7. Child malnutrition

Data reported on this table gives the percentage of children and babies suffering from nutrition-related problems of low birth weight, underweight, wasting, and stunting. Figures are also given on the extent of breast-feeding among nursing mothers.

Low birth weight refers to babies born weighing less than 2,500 grams. Underweight refers to children, under the age of five weighing two standard deviations below the median weight-for-age of the reference population. Wasting refers to children between 12 and 23 months weighing two standard deviations below the median weight-for-height of the reference population. Stunting refers to children between 24 to 59 months standing two standard deviations below the median height-for-age of the reference population.

Table 13-8. Average daily caloric intake

Table 13-8 shows the per capita intake of calories. The figures here may be different from the per capita supply of calories as intake is supply net of waste.

Table. 13-9. Access to safe water

This table refers to the percentage of the population with reasonable access to safe water supply which includes treated surface waters or untreated but uncontaminated water such as that from springs, sanitary wells, and protected boreholes. In an urban area this may be a public fountain or standpost located not more than 200 meters away. In rural areas it implies that members of the household do not have to spend a disproportionate part of the day fetching water.

Data are presented separately for total, urban and rural population.

Table 13-10. Access to health services

Here, access to health services refers to the percentage of the population that can reach appropriate local health services by the local means of transport in no more than one hour.

Data are presented separately for total, urban and rural population.

Table 13-11. Health care

Indicators presented here are population per physician, population per nursing personnel, and the percentage of births attended by trained health personnel.

The figure for physicians includes, in addition to the total number of registered practitioners in the country, medical assistants whose medical training is less than that of qualified physicians, but who nevertheless dispense similar medical services, including simple surgical operations. The definition of recognized medical practitioners differs among countries. Nursing persons include graduate, practical, assistant, and auxiliary nurses, as well as paraprofessional personnel such as health workers, first-aid workers, and traditional birth attendants. Inclusion of auxiliary and paraprofessional personnel provides a more realistic estimate of available nursing and health care overall. "Births attended" refers to births attended by physicians, nurses, midwives, trained primary health care workers or trained traditional birth attendants.

Table 13-12. Illitercy rate

This is the percentage of illiterate adults to the total adult population aged 15 years and over. Literacy is defined as the ability to read and write. A person who can, with understanding, both read and write a short, simple statement about his everyday life is literate. Persons who can can read but not write are included with illiterates. Figures are shown separately for males, females, and both genders combined.

Tables 13-13. Primary school gross enrollment ratio

This is the total number of pupils enrolled at the primary level of education, regardless of age, expressed as a percentage of the population corresponding to the official school age of primary education in a given country. Data are given separately for males, females, and both genders combined. Figures shown may be more than 100 percent since total enrollment includes pupils above and pupils below the primary school age, as well as repeaters.

Tables 13-14. Pupil progression and efficiency indicator

This table provides three education indicators. "Percentage of cohort reaching final grade of primary school", otherwise known as survival rate to final grade of first level education, shows the percentage of children starting primary school who eventually attain the final grade. The estimate is based on the Reconstructed Cohort Method which uses data on enrollment and repeaters for two consecutive years. "Percentage of final grade enrollment progressing to first grade of secondary general education" indicates the proportion of pupils enrolled in the final grade of primary school who enroll in the first grade of secondary school in the following year. The rate is derived by subtracting the number of repeaters in grade one of secondary education in year t from the total enrollment in year t+1 and dividing this by the enrollment in the final grade of primary school in year t. "Percentage of grade 1 enrollment not completing primary school", also called dropout rate, is the proportion of children entering the first grade of primary school who do not successfully complete that level of education in due course.

Table 13-15. Primary school repetition rate

This is the number of students still enrolled in the grade that they attended the previous year expressed as a percentage of the total enrollment in that level of school.

Figures are shown separately for males, females and both genders combined. For Sudan and Seychelles, the 0 percent of repeaters is due to the fact that these countries practice a policy of automatic promotion at the primary level of education.

Table 13-16. Enrollment in private primary schools

This shows the number of students enrolled in private schools expressed as a percentage of total number of students enrolled in both public and private schools. Figures are shown separately for primary schools, and secondary schools. "Private school", as defined by the UNESCO, is one "not operated by a public authority whether or not it receives financial support from such authorities".

Comparability may be affected in situation where some countries limit the term "private schools" to non-aided schools. This is the case of the data reported here for Zambia, Kenya, and Malawi. In Lesotho, while the government pays the teachers most of the schools are run by religious organizations. This account for the very high percentage of private school enrollment reported here. Similarly in Zimbabwe, the government pays the teachers while most of the schools are run by local groups.

Table 13-17. Number of school teachers

Teachers in both public and private schools are covered in this table. Data refer to both full-time and part-time teachers excluding other instructional personnel without teaching functions. Figures are here shown separately for primary and secondary schools. "Percentage females" means the number of female teachers expressed as a percentage of total teaching staff.

Table 13-18. Pupil/teacher ratio

This ratio gives the average number of pupils per teacher. Figures are given separately for primary and secondary schools. As teaching staff includes, both full- time and part-time teachers, comparability of this ratio inter-country may be affected as the proportion of part-time teachers varies greatly from one country to another.

Table 13-19. Secondary school gross enrollment ratio

This is the secondary school equivalent of the data presented on table 13-13, and it gives the total number of students enrolled at the secondary level of education, regardless of age, expressed as a percentage of the population corresponding to the official school age of secondary education. Data are presented separately for males, females, and both gender combined.

The term "second level, general" refers to education in secondary schools that provide general or specialised instruction based upon at least four years previous instruction at the first or primary level, and which do not specifically aim at preparimg the pupils directly for a given trade or occupation. Such schools may be called high schools, middle schools, lyceums etc., and offer courses of study whose completion is a minimum condition for admission into universities. In some countries, some of such schools provide both academic and vocational training. These *composite* secondary schools are considered as equivqlent to the academic type of secondary school and are thus classified as *second level, general*.

Table 13-20. Secondary school repetition rates

This table gives the number of students still enrolled in the grade that they attended the previous year expressed as a percentage of the total enrollment in secondary schools. Figures are shown separately for males, females, and both genders combined. In Seychelles, the 0 percent repetition rate is due to a policy of automatic promotion practiced at the secondary level of education.

Table 13-21. Performance on international examinations

This table provides average test scores for three international examinations are reported on. These are the Cambridge overseas school certificate examination, conducted by the University of Cambridge; the Baccalaureate conducted by the International Baccalaureate Organization, and the General Certificate of Education (GCE "O" level) conducted by the Universities of London and Cambridge. All these examinations are accepted for admission into universities.

The figures show the number of candidates that passed, expressed as a percentage of all candidates that sat for a given examination. In the case of GCE "O" level examination, data include all candidates passing at least one of the subjects sat for. For the Cambridge and Baccalaureate examinations only candidates gaining full certificate are included in the number that passed.

Care should be exercised in interpreting very high or very low percentages of passes due to the varying sizes of the total number of candidates used as denominators. For instance, in 1990, only two candidates sat for the cambridge overseas school certificate examination in Kenya and both of them failed yieldindg a 0 percent pass rate. On the other hand, only one person sat for the same examination the same year in South Africa and the candidate passed yielding a 100 percent pass rate.

For the GCE "O" level examinations, figures reported for Kenya, Sudan, Zambia, Nigeria, and Egypt refer to the examinations conducted by the University of London. For the rest of the countries, "O" level data are for the examinations conducted by the University of Cambridge.

Table 13-22. Household and economic participation of women

This table Presents some indicators on gender issues in development. Sources include the UN publications: "The World's Women 1970-1990, Trends and Statistics", and "Compendium, of Statistics and Indicators on the Situation of Women, 1986"; the joint publication of the ILO and the UN Research and Training Institute for the Advancement of Women (INSTRAW): "Women in Economic Activity: A Global Statistical Survey (1950-2000)"; as well as, "Women of the World" (a publication of the United States Department of Commerce).

"Households headed by women" refer to families in which a woman is acknowledged as the head by the other members.

"Unpaid family workers" are persons working in their family business without receiving salary or wages. The occupational statistics are based on the revised International Standard Classification of Occupations (ISCO) issued by ILO in 1968.

14

Environmental Indicators

This chapter includes data on natural resources, their use by sector, and the trends in their use. The first seven tables comprise information on natural endowments, including land area and uses, forest resources, roundwood production and consumption, and water resources, with special emphasis on freshwater withdrawal. Tables 14-8 through 14-14 consist of data on total commercial energy consumption and its components. Table 14-15 sheds light on the extent and the scope of greenhouse gas discharges.

Until the early 1970s, environmental issues were primarily regarded as rich country concerns, and emphasis was placed on water and air pollution, acid rain, and greenhouse gas emissions. Since the publication of the Club of Rome's *The Limit to Growth* in 1972, however, issues of natural resource depletion and degradation have received considerable attention in assessing environmental factors and their impacts on the development prospects of developing nations. At the national level, environmental concerns revolve around population expansion, desertification, deforestation, and the by-products of energy consumption.

Environmental destruction is not, however, confined by geographic borders. For instance, global warming, said to be caused by greenhouse gas emissions, has become a major global environmental concern. The issue of the greenhouse effect may be subject to controversy at the theoretical level and difficult to prove at the practical level. The fact that industrial wastes generated in one country cross frontiers and cause environmental damage to other nations is, however, widely acknowledged. Common interests, therefore, compel the international community to jointly work toward a common goal of preserving the environment.

Increasing emphasis on the linkages between the environment and development, both at the national and international levels, is reflected in the growing number of scientific and analytical studies. Challenging the hegemony of the SNA national income accounting convention, numerous scholarly endeavors are under way to internalize environmental consequences in national income calculations. The argument is made that the SNA methodology overstates national income levels for two reasons. First, it does not account for both the direct and indirect costs of drawing down natural resources. Second, it counts expenditure on resources for environmental protection activities as income. The changes both in methodology and emphasis have created an urgent demand for physical data. The information in this chapter aims to meet this growing demand, notwithstanding the limitations in data coverage and reliability.

The rate of deforestation is of particular concern because the cost of deforestation goes far beyond the loses of forest products such as timber and fuelwood. There are equally significant indirect costs including soil erosion; the substitution of animal and agricultural residues for cooking, which would otherwise be used for fertilizer; and climate changes. Deforestation is caused by factors including increased demand for settlement area, cultivation, woodfuel, or a combination thereof. The information in this chapter provides an empirical framework for assessing policy alternatives in reversing the trend in natural resource depletion.

Data on roundwood production and consumption are important in monitoring the causes of deforestation. In addition, since roundwood is a primary source of energy in developing nations, data on roundwood consumption proves essential in analyzing air pollution. For instance, for 1985-1987, Africa used close to 88 percent of its roundwood production for fuel and charcoal production, while approximately 12 percent of the roundwood production went to industrial uses. To put these figures in perspective, the corresponding figures for Europe are 16 and 84 percent, respectively (World Resources Institute 1990-91).

Information on fresh water resources available and on the extent and the methods of their uses can provide a partial basis for analyzing Africa's agricultural performance, its potential hydroelectric power, and its populations' health conditions. Almost all Sub-Saharan African countries use a very small fraction of their internal renewable water resources. For instance, Ethiopia, a nation that has suffered from repeated draughts, uses only 2 percent of its water resources. The major problem rests in the uneven geographic distribution of water resources with respect to population density and the state of freshwater drawing technology. The quality of water is as important as the quantity of water available. Water-related disease accounts for 80 percent of all sicknesses and for 90 percent of the 15 million deaths in developing countries each year (Myers 1989).

Data on energy use consist of information on energy consumption and on related environmental consequences. Biomass fuel, comprising woodfuel and animal and agricultural residues, accounts for 40 to 90 percent of total energy used in Sub-Saharan Africa (Armitage and Schramm 1989).

The data on net addition to greenhouse heating effect (Table 14-15) provide information on the global climate warming that is caused by a change in chemical composition of the atmosphere due to the emission of industrial and agricultural greenhouse gases. The table highlights data that provide a continental perspective of potential environmental damage associated with fossil fuel consumption, deforestation, and other industrial activities as well as each country's contribution to the problem.

The data in this chapter have serious limitations. For instance, with respect to deforestation, most publications still use national deforestation rates based on data published in the early 1980s by the FAO. Similarly, the data on energy consumption are extrapolated from general consumption trends. Because definitions of terms differ, data obtained from other sources may not match with the figures provided here. For instance, FAO classifies forest and woodlands or other lands as wilderness. World Resources Institute, however, defines wilderness as lands with no prospect for development, such as roads and settlement.

14-1. Land use: agriculture

	Land area (000 ha) 1988	Arable land (000 ha)			Land under permanent crops (000 ha)			Permanent pasture (000 ha)		
		1980	1985	1988	1980	1985	1988	1980	1985	1988
SUB-SAHARAN AFRICA	2,051,072	122,582	125,825	128,193	14,117	14,525	14,675	577,953	577,661	583,343
excluding Nigeria	1,959,995	94,732	97,275	99,393	11,582	11,990	12,140	557,053	556,701	562,353
Angola	124,670	2,950	2,950	3,050	550	550	550	29,000	29,000	29,000
Benin	11,062	1,350	1,390	1,410	445	448	450	442	442	442
Botswana	56,673	1,360	1,360	1,380	..	..	..	44,000	44,000	44,000
Burkina Faso	27,380	2,772	3,022	3,551	13	13	13	10,000	10,000	10,000
Burundi	2,565	1,110	1,120	1,120	195	205	214	910	910	912
Cameroon	46,540	5,910	5,910	5,930	1,020	1,055	1,068	8,300	8,300	8,300
Cape Verde	403	38	38	38	2	2	2	25	25	25
Central African Republic	62,298	1,870	1,900	1,920	75	83	86	3,000	3,000	3,000
Chad	125,920	3,145	3,150	3,200	5	5	5	45,000	45,000	45,000
Comoros	223	75	76	77	16	21	22	15	15	15
Congo, People's Republic of the	34,150	655	655	144	14	22	24	10,000	10,000	10,000
Cote d'Ivoire	31,800	1,955	2,380	2,420	1,140	1,200	1,240	3,000	3,000	3,000
Djibouti	2,318	..	..	..	..	..	..	200	200	200
Equatorial Guinea	2,805	130	130	130	100	100	100	104	104	104
Ethiopia	110,100	13,150	13,200	13,200	730	730	730	45,400	45,150	45,000
Gabon	25,767	290	290	290	162	162	162	4,700	4,700	4,700
Gambia, The	1,000	156	165	175	..	..	..	90	90	90
Ghana	23,002	1,090	1,120	1,150	1,670	1,700	1,720	3,470	3,420	3,390
Guinea	24,586	1,500	1,500	1,500	70	76	82	3,000	3,000	3,000
Guinea-Bissau	2,812	255	290	300	30	30	35	1,080	1,080	1,080
Kenya	56,697	1,790	1,880	1,930	480	490	495	3,760	3,740	3,730
Lesotho	3,035	292	300	320	..	..	..	2,000	2,000	2,000
Liberia	9,632	126	126	128	245	245	245	240	240	240
Madagascar	58,154	2,510	2,530	2,560	490	510	518	34,000	34,000	34,000
Malawi	9,408	2,300	2,350	2,360	20	26	27	1,840	1,840	1,840
Mali	122,019	2,047	2,070	2,090	3	3	3	30,000	30,000	30,000
Mauritania	102,522	192	192	196	3	3	3	39,250	39,250	39,250
Mauritius	185	100	100	100	7	7	6	7	7	7
Mozambique	78,409	2,850	2,860	2,870	230	230	230	44,000	44,000	44,000
Namibia	82,329	655	660	660	2	2	2	52,906	52,906	52,906
Niger	126,670	3,552	3,530	3,600	..	..	..	9,668	9,250	9,270
Nigeria	91,077	27,850	28,550	28,800	2,535	2,535	2,535	20,900	20,960	20,990
Rwanda	2,495	760	820	830	255	287	290	470	420	395
Sao Tome & Principe	96	1	2	2	35	35	35	1	1	1
Senegal	19,253	5,220	5,220	5,220	5	5	6	5,700	5,700	5,700
Seychelles	27	1	1	1	4	5	5	..	..	..
Sierra Leone	7,162	1,620	1,635	1,655	146	146	146	2,204	2,204	2,204
Somalia	62,734	897	911	1,022	16	16	17	28,850	28,850	28,850
Sudan	237,600	12,360	12,420	12,450	57	58	58	56,000	56,000	56,000
Swaziland	1,720	185	160	160	4	4	4	1,102	1,120	1,175
Tanzania	88,604	4,110	4,130	4,160	1,050	1,060	1,080	35,000	35,000	35,000
Togo	5,439	1,355	1,358	1,370	65	69	69	200	200	200
Uganda	19,955	4,080	4,900	5,000	1,600	1,700	1,705	5,000	5,000	5,000
Zaire	226,760	5,764	6,000	7,250	550	600	600	9,221	9,221	15,031
Zambia	74,072	5,100	5,180	5,230	8	8	8	35,000	35,000	35,000
Zimbabwe	38,667	2,465	2,650	2,720	74	84	90	4,856	4,856	4,856
NORTH AFRICA	474,294	19,348	19,973	20,321	2,945	2,992	3,010	73,151	68,770	67,650
Algeria	238,174	6,875	6,910	6,970	634	601	570	36,321	31,540	30,400
Egypt, Arab Republic of	99,545	2,286	2,320	2,410	159	166	173	..	..	..
Libya	175,954	1,753	1,787	1,800	327	340	345	13,000	13,300	13,300
Morocco	44,630	7,530	7,878	8,250	474	526	570	20,900	20,900	20,900
Tunisia	15,536	3,190	3,398	3,301	1,510	1,525	1,525	2,930	3,030	3,050
ALL AFRICA	2,525,366	141,930	145,798	148,514	17,062	17,517	17,685	651,104	646,431	650,993
South Africa	122,104	12,440	12,355	12,360	814	814	814	81,420	81,378	81,378

14–2. Land use: forest and other

	Forest and woodland (000 ha)			Other land (000 ha)			Protected area (000 ha)	Wilderness area (000 ha)
	1980	*1985*	*1988*	*1980*	*1985*	*1988*	*1989*	*1989*
SUB-SAHARAN AFRICA	664,289	649,316	623,944	737,970	750,035	751,030	123,508	..
excluding Nigeria	647,906	634,416	622,544	714,561	725,903	726,278	122,548	..
Angola	53,760	53,310	53,040	38,410	38,860	39,030	890	27,050
Benin	3,970	3,720	3,570	4,855	5,062	5,190	844	1,209
Botswana	962	962	962	10,351	10,351	10,331	10,025	31,255
Burkina Faso	7,200	6,900	6,720	7,395	7,445	7,095	739	750
Burundi	62	64	65	288	266	254	0	..
Cameroon	25,640	25,090	24,760	5,670	6,185	6,472	1,702	1,320
Cape Verde	1	1	1	337	337	337	0	..
Central African Republic	35,895	35,850	35,820	21,458	21,465	21,472	3,904	20,917
Chad	13,532	13,130	12,890	64,238	64,635	64,825	114	61,254
Comoros	35	35	35	82	76	74	0	* ..
Congo, People's Republic of the	21,360	21,260	21,200	2,121	2,213	2,782	1,353	11,837
Cote d'Ivoire	9,880	7,380	5,880	15,825	17,840	19,260	1,958	4,268
Djibouti	6	6	6	2,112	2,112	2,112	10	..
Equatorial Guinea	1,295	1,295	1,295	1,176	1,176	1,176	0	..
Ethiopia	28,132	27,600	23,700	22,688	23,420	23,870	6,873	19,716
Gabon	20,000	20,000	20,000	615	615	615	1,753	7,333
Gambia, The	216	186	168	538	559	567	0	..
Ghana	8,770	8,420	8,210	8,002	8,342	8,532	1,175	..
Guinea	10,650	10,160	9,652	9,366	9,850	10,343	13	..
Guinea–Bissau	1,070	1,070	1,070	377	342	327	0	..
Kenya	3,860	3,710	3,620	46,807	46,877	47,194	3,095	11,221
Lesotho	..	..	..	743	735	715	7	2,133
Liberia	2,103	2,103	2,103	6,918	6,918	6,916	131	1,420
Madagascar	15,860	15,060	14,580	5,294	6,054	6,496	1,031	691
Malawi	5,074	4,520	4,190	174	672	991	1,067	781
Mali	8,800	8,600	8,480	81,169	81,346	81,446	876	58,814
Mauritania	15,000	15,000	15,000	48,077	48,077	48,073	1,483	71,370
Mauritius	58	58	57	13	13	15	4	..
Mozambique	15,689	15,090	14,730	15,640	16,229	16,358	0	6,130
Namibia	18,420	18,420	18,420	10,346	10,341	10,341	..	..
Niger	2,900	2,600	2,420	110,550	111,290	111,380	1,654	65,633
Nigeria	16,383	14,900	1,400	23,409	24,132	24,752	960	1,526
Rwanda	520	505	497	490	463	483	262	..
Sao Tome & Principe	..	..	..	59	58	58	..	..
Senegal	6,000	5,942	5,930	2,328	2,386	2,397	2,177	1,586
Seychelles	5	5	5	17	16	16	..	..
Sierra Leone	2,113	2,090	2,070	1,079	1,087	1,087	101	..
Somalia	9,160	8,900	8,750	23,811	24,057	24,095	..	10,460
Sudan	48,940	47,390	46,460	120,243	121,732	122,632	8,116	79,377
Swaziland	103	104	108	326	332	273	39,545	..
Tanzania	43,260	42,665	42,305	5,184	5,749	6,059	11,913	7,053
Togo	1,700	1,450	1,300	2,119	2,362	2,500	463	..
Uganda	6,060	5,810	5,660	3,215	2,545	2,590	1,332	530
Zaire	177,610	175,960	174,970	33,615	34,979	28,909	8,827	11,763
Zambia	29,890	29,390	29,090	4,074	4,494	4,744	6,359	15,075
Zimbabwe	19,930	19,930	19,930	11,342	11,147	11,071	2,760	..
NORTH AFRICA	10,755	10,822	11,174	465,195	468,796	469,101	1,680	..
Algeria	4,384	4,384	4,699	189,960	194,739	195,535	497	140,424
Egypt, Arab Republic of	31	31	31	97,069	97,028	96,931	685	42,540
Libya	600	650	680	160,274	159,877	159,829	155	65,497
Morocco	5,200	5,200	5,200	10,526	10,126	9,710	298	..
Tunisia	540	557	564	7,366	7,026	7,096	45	1,901
ALL AFRICA	675,044	660,138	635,118	141,930	145,798	148,514	17,517	..
South Africa	4,150	4,515	4,515	23,280	23,042	23,037	5,802	..

14–3. Forest resources

	Extent of forest and woodland (000 hectares) 1980s			Average annual deforestation (000 hectares) 1980s			Average annual reforestation (000 hectares) 1980s	Protected closed forest (000 hectares) 1980s
	Closed forest	Open forest	Total forest	Closed forest	Open forest	Total forest		
SUB-SAHARAN AFRICA	216,134	462,334	678,468	1,440	2,406	3,846	..	..
excluding Nigeria	210,184	453,534	663,718	1,140	2,306	3,446	..	..
Angola	2,900	50,700	53,600	44	50	94	3	..
Benin	47	3,820	3,867	1	66	67	0	..
Botswana	0	32,560	32,560	0	20	20	..	0
Burkina Faso	271	4,464	4,735	3	77	80	2	..
Burundi	27	14	41	1	0	1	3	9
Cameroon	16,500	6,800	23,300	100	90	190	1	..
Cape Verde	..	..	..	..	..	..	1	..
Central African Republic	3,590	32,300	35,890	5	50	55	0	0
Chad	500	13,000	13,500	80	80	160	..	0
Comoros	16	0	16	1	0	1	..	..
Congo, People's Republic of the	21,340	0	21,340	22	0	22	..	130
Cote d'Ivoire	4,458	5,376	9,834	290	220	510	6	648
Djibouti	2	68	70	..	..	..	..	..
Equatorial Guinea	1,295	0	1,295	3	0	3	..	0
Ethiopia	4,350	22,800	27,150	8	80	88	10	..
Gabon	20,500	75	20,575	15	0	15	1	..
Gambia, The	65	150	215	2	3	5	0	..
Ghana	1,718	6,975	8,693	22	50	72	2	397
Guinea	2,050	8,600	10,650	36	50	86	0	0
Guinea-Bissau	660	1,445	2,105	17	40	57	0	..
Kenya	1,105	1,255	2,360	19	20	39	10	405
Lesotho	..	..	..	..	..	..	1	..
Liberia	2,000	40	2,040	46	0	46	2	..
Madagascar	10,300	2,900	13,200	150	6	156	12	930
Malawi	186	4,085	4,271	0	150	150	1	146
Mali	500	6,750	7,250	0	36	36	1	..
Mauritania	29	525	554	1	13	14	0	..
Mauritius	3	0	3	0	0	0	0	..
Mozambique	935	14,500	15,435	10	110	120	4	25
Namibia	..	..	..	..	..	..	..	..
Niger	100	2,450	2,550	3	65	68	..	..
Nigeria	5,950	8,800	14,750	300	100	400	32	..
Rwanda	120	110	230	3	2	5	3	11
Sao Tome & Principe	..	..	..	..	..	..	..	..
Senegal	220	10,825	11,045	0	50	50	3	63
Seychelles	..	..	..	..	..	..	..	..
Sierra Leone	740	1,315	2,055	6	0	6	0	..
Somalia	1,540	7,510	9,050	4	10	14	1	..
Sudan	650	47,000	47,650	4	500	504	13	..
Swaziland	4	70	74	..	..	0	5	..
Tanzania	1,440	40,600	42,040	10	120	130	9	410
Togo	304	1,380	1,684	2	10	12	0	..
Uganda	765	5,250	6,015	10	40	50	2	45
Zaire	105,750	71,840	177,590	182	188	370	0	5,690
Zambia	3,010	26,500	29,510	40	30	70	2	220
Zimbabwe	200	19,620	19,820	0	80	80	4	..
NORTH AFRICA	..	..	..	..	..	..	..	..
Algeria	1,518	249	1,767	..	..	..	66	8
Egypt, Arab Republic of	..	..	..	..	..	..	2	..
Libya	134	56	190	..	..	..	39	..
Morocco	1,533	1,703	3,236	..	..	..	16	7
Tunisia	186	111	297	..	..	..	4	..
ALL AFRICA	216,134	462,334	678,468	1,440	2,406	3,846	..	..
South Africa	300	..	300	..	..	..	..	..

14-4. Roundwood production: total

	Thousands of cubic meters										Average annual percentage growth		
	1980	*1981*	*1982*	*1983*	*1984*	*1985*	*1986*	*1987*	*1988*	*1989*	*75–80*	*80–85*	*86–MR*
SUB-SAHARAN AFRICA	361,413	371,893	383,101	395,038	407,256	418,300	430,599	443,405	456,424	468,787	3.3	3.0	2.9
excluding Nigeria	279,938	286,687	295,882	305,682	314,920	322,844	332,140	341,807	351,543	360,489	3.0	3.0	2.8
Angola	4,331	4,399	4,522	4,655	4,813	4,890	5,000	5,125	5,258	5,402	1.6	2.6	2.6
Benin	3,802	3,914	4,030	4,150	4,273	4,399	4,537	4,690	4,845	5,000	2.8	3.0	3.3
Botswana	960	995	1,033	1,071	1,110	1,149	1,189	1,232	1,276	1,321	3.6	3.7	3.6
Burkina Faso	6,768	6,936	7,104	7,285	7,472	7,665	7,870	8,076	8,298	8,526	4.9	2.5	2.7
Burundi	3,155	3,228	3,310	3,409	3,520	3,634	3,747	3,857	3,966	4,083	1.8	2.9	2.9
Cameroon	10,167	10,485	10,733	11,050	11,453	11,887	12,149	12,422	12,574	12,850	3.7	3.1	1.8
Cape Verde	..	..	..	..	..	..	..	..	..	..	..	..	..
Central African Republic	3,009	3,088	3,113	3,147	3,338	3,417	3,417	3,443	3,449	3,455	2.0	2.5	0.3
Chad	3,179	3,253	3,328	3,404	3,482	3,566	3,653	3,740	3,834	3,936	2.1	2.3	2.5
Comoros	..	..	..	..	..	..	..	..	..	..	..	..	..
Congo, People's Republic of the	2,193	2,176	2,190	2,238	2,347	2,380	2,581	2,841	3,216	3,300	4.5	1.9	9.0
Cote d'Ivoire	12,139	11,664	12,032	12,352	12,562	12,294	12,377	12,341	12,813	13,243	3.4	0.9	2.4
Djibouti	..	..	..	..	..	..	..	..	..	..	..	..	..
Equatorial Guinea	445	489	532	557	548	607	607	607	607	607	0.5	5.7	0.0
Ethiopia	33,564	34,286	35,200	35,838	36,347	36,804	37,422	38,098	38,839	39,640	2.5	1.9	1.9
Gabon	3,113	2,984	3,058	3,305	3,565	3,540	3,531	3,537	3,618	3,700	-3.5	3.6	1.6
Gambia, The	904	928	705	807	880	886	892	904	910	922	3.2	-0.4	1.1
Ghana	12,932	13,371	14,326	16,208	16,414	16,540	16,584	16,825	17,025	17,169	2.6	5.8	1.2
Guinea	3,801	3,883	3,788	4,058	4,150	4,249	4,348	4,452	4,559	4,669	2.1	2.4	2.4
Guinea-Bissau	550	552	554	555	557	559	561	563	565	567	1.9	0.3	0.4
Kenya	24,799	25,620	26,642	27,774	29,002	30,200	31,459	32,786	34,183	35,650	2.6	4.1	4.3
Lesotho	463	475	488	502	516	532	547	563	579	596	2.4	2.8	2.9
Liberia	4,837	4,295	4,386	4,063	4,185	4,442	5,286	5,627	5,889	5,960	8.5	-1.6	4.1
Madagascar	6,137	6,301	6,471	6,646	6,827	7,014	7,213	7,420	7,635	7,856	4.2	2.7	2.9
Malawi	5,808	5,972	6,124	6,298	6,477	6,688	6,905	7,132	7,374	7,621	3.5	2.8	3.3
Mali	4,262	4,369	4,488	4,610	4,752	4,903	5,052	5,202	5,358	5,516	2.3	2.8	3.0
Mauritania	10	10	10	10	10	10	11	12	12	12	1.5	0.0	2.6
Mauritius	42	37	33	30	15	17	24	32	34	31	0.8	-19.3	8.2
Mozambique	13,245	13,698	14,443	14,792	15,011	15,216	15,591	15,973	16,002	16,027	5.6	2.9	0.8
Namibia	..	..	..	..	..	..	..	..	..	..	..	..	..
Niger	3,404	3,500	3,600	3,703	3,811	3,920	4,036	4,158	4,285	4,418	2.6	2.9	3.1
Nigeria	81,475	85,206	87,219	89,356	92,336	95,456	98,459	101,598	104,881	108,298	4.2	3.1	3.2
Rwanda	4,796	4,973	5,157	5,266	5,634	5,842	5,842	5,842	5,842	5,842	-1.4	4.0	0.0
Sao Tome & Principe	8	6	2	6	6	6	7	8	9	9	6.9	-1.0	9.1
Senegal	3,675	3,674	3,700	3,989	4,073	4,002	4,090	4,183	4,283	4,391	4.0	2.3	2.4
Seychelles	..	..	..	..	..	..	..	..	..	..	..	..	..
Sierra Leone	2,473	2,528	2,561	2,617	2,682	2,745	2,805	2,870	2,938	3,014	-20.2	2.1	2.4
Somalia	5,101	5,340	5,558	5,756	5,934	6,089	6,306	6,526	6,758	6,986	11.3	3.6	3.5
Sudan	16,927	17,468	18,023	18,593	19,181	19,763	20,364	20,972	21,581	22,199	3.1	3.2	2.9
Swaziland	2,154	2,223	2,223	2,223	2,223	2,223	2,223	2,223	2,223	2,223	-4.5	0.5	0.0
Tanzania	23,468	24,263	25,159	26,122	27,166	28,244	29,492	30,840	31,955	33,103	8.2	3.8	3.9
Togo	662	681	701	721	743	765	790	815	840	866	2.4	2.9	3.1
Uganda	10,600	10,945	11,298	11,669	12,066	12,499	12,943	13,402	13,873	14,365	3.2	3.3	3.5
Zaire	26,824	27,668	28,606	29,497	30,361	31,268	32,164	33,178	34,239	35,348	3.3	3.1	3.2
Zambia	8,866	9,211	9,563	9,955	10,353	10,820	11,259	11,718	12,167	12,204	2.7	4.0	2.8
Zimbabwe	6,365	6,799	7,089	6,752	7,061	7,170	7,266	7,572	7,832	7,862	4.9	1.9	2.7
NORTH AFRICA	8,135	8,255	8,479	8,887	9,216	9,575	9,622	9,849	9,861	10,327	3.3	3.5	2.2
Algeria	1,621	1,671	1,721	1,773	1,826	1,883	1,941	2,003	2,065	2,131	3.1	3.0	3.2
Egypt, Arab Republic of	1,781	1,831	1,881	1,933	1,985	2,040	2,096	2,154	2,211	2,266	2.7	2.7	2.6
Libya	628	630	631	633	634	636	637	639	640	642	4.0	0.2	0.3
Morocco	1,586	1,537	1,601	1,845	1,973	2,164	2,018	2,046	1,866	2,111	4.6	7.2	0.4
Tunisia	2,519	2,586	2,645	2,703	2,799	2,852	2,930	3,007	3,079	3,178	2.8	2.5	2.7
ALL AFRICA	369,548	380,148	391,581	403,925	416,472	427,875	440,221	453,254	466,285	479,114	3.3	2.2	1.6
South Africa	18,968	19,524	19,475	20,584	19,022	19,022	18,643	19,015	19,361	19,361	1.9	0.0	1.3

14–5. Roundwood production: for industrial use

| | Thousands of cubic meters | | | | | | | | | | Average annual percentage growth | | |
	1980	1981	1982	1983	1984	1985	1986	1987	1988	1989	75–80	80–85	86–MR
SUB-SAHARAN AFRICA	38,366	38,587	38,268	38,407	39,617	40,071	40,448	41,278	42,373	42,981	3.8	0.9	2.1
excluding Nigeria	31,006	30,080	30,384	31,082	32,060	32,202	32,580	33,410	34,505	35,113	2.2	1.2	2.6
Angola	890	850	869	905	980	990	1,003	1,023	1,044	1,067	-3.9	2.9	2.1
Benin	199	204	209	215	219	222	229	247	254	262	2.5	2.3	4.4
Botswana	59	61	64	66	68	71	73	76	79	82	3.8	3.7	4.0
Burkina Faso	310	317	325	333	339	347	356	365	375	385	5.1	2.3	2.7
Burundi	35	36	37	38	45	44	45	47	48	49	2.0	5.4	2.8
Cameroon	2,194	2,296	2,320	2,406	2,570	2,758	2,771	2,792	2,689	2,708	8.0	4.4	-1.1
Cape Verde	..	..	..	..	..	..	..	..	..	..	..	..	..
Central African Republic	524	541	500	467	478	492	427	388	394	400	0.8	-2.1	-1.8
Chad	450	460	470	481	493	504	517	529	542	556	2.0	2.3	2.5
Comoros	..	..	..	..	..	..	..	..	..	..	..	..	..
Congo, People's Republic of the	800	747	724	727	805	796	945	1,159	1,488	1,524	8.7	0.6	18.3
Cote d'Ivoire	5,369	4,606	4,677	4,683	4,567	3,961	3,694	3,290	3,382	3,413	2.5	-4.3	-2.1
Djibouti	..	..	..	..	..	..	..	..	..	..	..	..	..
Equatorial Guinea	24	60	94	110	101	160	160	160	160	160	-15.3	37.7	0.0
Ethiopia	1,465	1,497	1,765	1,813	1,795	1,785	1,775	1,765	1,756	1,756	2.2	4.6	-0.4
Gabon	1,347	1,142	1,135	1,303	1,484	1,382	1,295	1,222	1,222	1,222	-0.8	3.1	-1.7
Gambia, The	10	10	19	21	21	21	21	21	21	21	0.0	18.3	0.0
Ghana	981	931	791	955	984	1,081	1,101	1,101	1,101	1,101	-11.8	2.4	0.0
Guinea	557	565	394	584	593	604	614	625	636	647	1.5	2.7	1.8
Guinea-Bissau	128	130	132	133	135	137	139	141	143	145	3.5	1.3	1.4
Kenya	1,397	1,272	1,301	1,383	1,514	1,559	1,606	1,655	1,713	1,766	9.1	3.3	3.2
Lesotho	..	..	..	..	..	..	..	..	..	..	..	..	..
Liberia	859	569	506	469	447	544	678	953	1,155	1,160	7.5	-8.4	19.8
Madagascar	807	807	807	807	807	807	807	807	807	807	16.6	0.0	0.0
Malawi	366	360	334	315	300	310	318	327	337	346	5.0	-4.0	2.9
Mali	273	278	283	292	299	307	319	331	343	353	1.9	2.4	3.4
Mauritania	4	4	4	4	4	4	4	5	5	5	0.0	0.0	6.9
Mauritius	18	13	9	8	3	5	7	12	13	15	-0.3	-28.5	24.5
Mozambique	939	1,030	931	922	941	946	948	951	980	1,005	-0.2	-0.7	2.1
Namibia	..	..	..	..	..	..	..	..	..	..	..	..	..
Niger	210	216	222	228	235	242	249	256	264	272	2.7	2.9	3.0
Nigeria	7,360	8,507	7,884	7,325	7,557	7,869	7,868	7,868	7,868	7,868	13.3	-0.3	0.0
Rwanda	276	286	297	214	232	240	240	240	240	240	41.2	-4.6	0.0
Sao Tome & Principe	8	6	2	6	6	6	7	8	9	9	6.9	-1.0	9.1
Senegal	483	497	511	524	536	546	559	573	588	605	4.3	2.5	2.7
Seychelles	..	..	..	..	..	..	..	..	..	..	..	..	..
Sierra Leone	158	161	140	140	140	143	140	140	140	140	5.2	-2.6	0.0
Somalia	73	75	77	79	80	82	84	86	88	90	6.4	2.3	2.3
Sudan	1,600	1,650	1,702	1,754	1,808	1,862	1,918	1,974	2,030	2,087	2.6	3.1	2.9
Swaziland	1,611	1,663	1,663	1,663	1,663	1,663	1,663	1,663	1,663	1,663	-6.5	0.5	0.0
Tanzania	1,187	1,168	1,205	1,253	1,330	1,386	1,612	1,910	1,943	1,989	3.8	3.5	6.7
Togo	143	147	151	155	159	163	168	173	178	183	2.1	2.7	2.9
Uganda	1,399	1,438	1,483	1,529	1,579	1,633	1,688	1,746	1,796	1,858	2.7	3.1	3.2
Zaire	2,180	2,210	2,326	2,398	2,454	2,574	2,571	2,641	2,714	2,791	3.2	3.4	2.8
Zambia	462	474	488	502	518	535	551	576	602	639	1.9	3.0	5.0
Zimbabwe	1,211	1,303	1,418	1,198	1,328	1,289	1,278	1,433	1,563	1,593	7.1	0.6	7.8
NORTH AFRICA	961	1,003	1,044	1,113	1,258	1,424	1,273	1,299	1,112	1,378	3.0	8.1	0.8
Algeria	200	206	211	217	223	230	236	243	250	257	2.7	2.8	2.9
Egypt, Arab Republic of	83	85	87	90	92	95	97	100	103	105	2.8	2.7	2.7
Libya	92	94	95	97	98	100	101	103	104	106	22.2	1.6	1.6
Morocco	471	502	542	607	714	884	717	724	523	747	0.1	13.2	-2.0
Tunisia	115	116	109	102	131	115	122	129	132	163	7.1	0.8	9.2
ALL AFRICA	39,327	39,590	39,312	39,521	40,874	41,495	41,721	42,577	43,485	44,359	3.8	-2.7	-5.1
South Africa	11,782	12,482	12,373	13,524	11,944	11,944	11,565	11,937	12,283	12,283	2.7	0.1	2.1

14-6. Roundwood production: for fuel and charcoal

	Thousands of cubic meters										Average annual percentage growth		
	1980	1981	1982	1983	1984	1985	1986	1987	1988	1989	75-80	80-85	86-MR
SUB-SAHARAN AFRICA	323,048	333,306	344,833	356,631	367,639	378,229	390,151	402,127	414,051	425,806	3.2	3.2	3.0
excluding Nigeria	248,933	256,607	265,498	274,600	282,860	290,642	299,560	308,397	317,038	325,376	3.2	3.2	2.8
Angola	3,441	3,549	3,653	3,750	3,833	3,900	3,997	4,102	4,214	4,335	3.4	2.6	2.7
Benin	3,603	3,710	3,821	3,935	4,054	4,177	4,308	4,443	4,591	4,738	2.8	3.0	3.2
Botswana	901	934	969	1,005	1,042	1,078	1,116	1,156	1,197	1,239	3.6	3.7	3.5
Burkina Faso	6,458	6,619	6,779	6,952	7,133	7,318	7,514	7,711	7,923	8,141	4.9	2.5	2.7
Burundi	3,120	3,192	3,273	3,371	3,475	3,590	3,702	3,810	3,918	4,034	1.8	2.9	2.9
Cameroon	7,973	8,189	8,413	8,644	8,883	9,129	9,378	9,630	9,885	10,142	2.6	2.7	2.6
Cape Verde	..	..	..	..	..	..	..	..	..	..	..	..	..
Central African Republic	2,485	2,547	2,613	2,680	2,860	2,925	2,990	3,055	3,055	3,055	2.3	3.5	0.6
Chad	2,729	2,793	2,858	2,923	2,989	3,062	3,136	3,211	3,292	3,380	2.1	2.3	2.5
Comoros	..	..	..	..	..	..	..	..	..	..	..	..	..
Congo, People's Republic of the	1,393	1,429	1,466	1,511	1,542	1,584	1,636	1,682	1,728	1,776	2.6	2.6	2.8
Cote d'Ivoire	6,770	7,058	7,355	7,669	7,995	8,333	8,683	9,051	9,431	9,830	4.3	4.2	4.2
Djibouti	..	..	..	..	..	..	..	..	..	..	..	..	..
Equatorial Guinea	421	429	438	447	447	447	447	447	447	447	1.8	1.3	0.0
Ethiopia	32,099	32,789	33,435	34,025	34,552	35,019	35,647	36,333	37,083	37,884	2.5	1.8	2.1
Gabon	1,766	1,842	1,923	2,002	2,081	2,158	2,236	2,315	2,396	2,478	-5.2	4.1	3.5
Gambia, The	894	918	686	786	859	865	871	883	889	901	3.2	-0.6	1.1
Ghana	11,951	12,440	13,535	15,253	15,430	15,459	15,483	15,724	15,924	16,068	4.9	6.0	1.2
Guinea	3,244	3,318	3,394	3,474	3,557	3,645	3,734	3,827	3,923	4,022	2.2	2.4	2.5
Guinea-Bissau	422	422	422	422	422	422	422	422	422	422	1.5	0.0	0.0
Kenya	23,402	24,348	25,341	26,391	27,488	28,641	29,853	31,131	32,470	33,884	2.3	4.1	4.3
Lesotho	463	475	488	502	516	532	547	563	579	596	2.4	2.8	2.9
Liberia	3,978	3,726	3,880	3,594	3,738	3,898	4,608	4,674	4,734	4,800	8.7	-0.5	1.4
Madagascar	5,330	5,494	5,664	5,839	6,020	6,207	6,406	6,613	6,828	7,049	2.9	3.1	3.2
Malawi	5,442	5,612	5,790	5,983	6,177	6,378	6,587	6,805	7,037	7,275	3.4	3.2	3.4
Mali	3,989	4,091	4,205	4,318	4,453	4,596	4,733	4,871	5,015	5,163	2.4	2.9	2.9
Mauritania	6	6	6	6	6	6	7	7	7	7	2.6	0.0	0.0
Mauritius	24	24	24	22	12	12	17	21	21	17	1.6	-14.9	-0.7
Mozambique	12,306	12,668	13,512	13,870	14,070	14,270	14,643	15,022	15,022	15,022	6.1	3.1	0.8
Namibia	..	..	..	..	..	..	..	..	..	..	..	..	..
Niger	3,194	3,284	3,378	3,475	3,576	3,678	3,787	3,902	4,021	4,146	2.6	2.9	3.1
Nigeria	74,115	76,699	79,335	82,031	84,779	87,587	90,591	93,730	97,013	100,430	3.6	3.4	3.5
Rwanda	4,520	4,687	4,860	5,052	5,402	5,602	5,602	5,602	5,602	5,602	-2.5	4.5	0.0
Sao Tome & Principe	..	..	..	..	..	..	..	..	..	..	..	..	..
Senegal	3,192	3,177	3,189	3,465	3,537	3,456	3,531	3,610	3,695	3,786	4.0	2.3	2.4
Seychelles	..	..	..	..	..	..	..	..	..	..	..	..	..
Sierra Leone	2,315	2,367	2,421	2,477	2,542	2,602	2,665	2,730	2,798	2,874	-21.1	2.4	2.5
Somalia	5,028	5,265	5,481	5,677	5,854	6,007	6,222	6,440	6,670	6,896	11.4	3.6	3.5
Sudan	15,327	15,818	16,321	16,839	17,373	17,901	18,446	18,998	19,551	20,112	3.1	3.2	2.9
Swaziland	543	560	560	560	560	560	560	560	560	560	3.0	0.4	0.0
Tanzania	22,281	23,095	23,954	24,869	25,836	26,858	27,880	28,930	30,012	31,114	8.5	3.8	3.7
Togo	519	534	550	566	584	602	622	642	662	683	2.5	3.0	3.2
Uganda	9,201	9,507	9,815	10,140	10,487	10,866	11,255	11,656	12,077	12,507	3.3	3.4	3.6
Zaire	24,644	25,458	26,280	27,099	27,907	28,694	29,593	30,537	31,525	32,557	3.4	3.1	3.2
Zambia	8,404	8,737	9,075	9,453	9,835	10,285	10,708	11,142	11,565	11,565	2.8	4.1	2.7
Zimbabwe	5,154	5,496	5,672	5,554	5,733	5,881	5,988	6,140	6,269	6,269	4.4	2.2	1.6
NORTH AFRICA	7,174	7,252	7,435	7,774	7,959	8,151	8,349	8,550	8,749	8,950	3.3	2.8	2.3
Algeria	1,421	1,465	1,510	1,556	1,603	1,653	1,705	1,760	1,815	1,874	3.1	3.1	3.2
Egypt, Arab Republic of	1,698	1,746	1,794	1,843	1,893	1,945	1,999	2,054	2,108	2,161	2.7	2.7	2.6
Libya	536	536	536	536	536	536	536	536	536	536	2.0	0.0	0.0
Morocco	1,115	1,035	1,059	1,238	1,259	1,280	1,301	1,322	1,343	1,364	7.0	4.2	1.6
Tunisia	2,404	2,470	2,536	2,601	2,668	2,737	2,808	2,878	2,947	3,015	2.6	2.6	2.4
ALL AFRICA	330,222	340,558	352,268	364,405	375,598	386,380	398,499	410,677	422,800	434,755	3.2	2.9	2.4
South Africa	7,186	7,042	7,102	7,060	7,078	7,078	7,078	7,078	7,078	7,078	0.7	-0.2	0.0

14-7. Freshwater withdrawal

	Annual internal renewable water resources (cubic km.)(1990)	Year of data	Annual withdrawal Total (cubic km.)	Percentage of water resources	Per capita (cubic meters)	Sectoral withdrawal percentage of total Domestic	Industry	Agriculture
SUB-SAHARAN AFRICA	3,713.38		..	..	..	..	..	..
excluding Nigeria	3,452.38		..	..	..	..	..	..
Angola	158.00 a	1987	0.48	0.30	52.00	14.00	10.00	76.00
Benin	26.00	1987	0.11	0.42	26.00	28.00	14.00	58.00
Botswana	1.00	1990	0.09	9.00	100.00	5.00	10.00	85.00
Burkina Faso	28.00 a	1987	0.15	0.54	18.00	28.00	5.00	67.00
Burundi	3.60 a	1987	0.10	2.78	20.00	36.00	0.00	64.00
Cameroon	208.00	1987	0.40	0.20	37.00	46.00	19.00	35.00
Cape Verde	0.20	1972	0.04	20.00	146.00	9.00	2.00	89.00
Central African Republic	141.00 a	1987	0.07	0.05	25.00	21.00	5.00	74.00
Chad	38.40 a	1987	0.18	0.47	34.00	16.00	2.00	82.00
Comoros	1.02 a	1987	0.01	0.98	24.00	48.00	5.00	47.00
Congo, People's Republic of the	181.00 a	1987	0.04	0.00	19.00	62.00	27.00	11.00
Cote d'Ivoire	74.00	1987	0.71	0.96	66.00	22.00	11.00	67.00
Djibouti	0.30	1973	0.01	3.33	47.00	28.00	21.00	51.00
Equatorial Guinea	30.00 a	1987	0.01	0.03	26.00	81.00	13.00	6.00
Ethiopia	110.00	1987	2.21	2.01	48.00	11.00	3.00	86.00
Gabon	164.00 a	1987	0.06	0.00	57.00	72.00	22.00	6.00
Gambia, The	3.00	1982	0.02	0.67	29.00	7.00	2.00	91.00
Ghana	53.00	1970	0.30	0.57	35.00	35.00	13.00	52.00
Guinea	226.00 a	1987	0.74	0.33	141.00	10.00	3.00	87.00
Guinea-Bissau	31.00 a	1987	0.01	0.03	11.00	31.00	6.00	63.00
Kenya	14.80	1987	1.09	7.36	50.00	27.00	11.00	62.00
Lesotho	4.00 a	1987	0.05	1.25	31.00	22.00	22.00	56.00
Liberia	232.00	1987	0.13	0.06	56.00	27.00	13.00	60.00
Madagascar	40.00	1984	16.30	40.75	1,680.00	1.00	0.00	99.00
Malawi	9.00 a	1987	0.16	1.78	21.00	34.00	17.00	49.00
Mali	62.00 a	1987	1.36	2.19	175.00	2.00	1.00	97.00
Mauritania	0.40	1978	0.73	182.50	493.00	12.00	4.00	84.00
Mauritius	2.20	1974	0.36	16.36	414.00	16.00	7.00	77.00
Mozambique	58.00 a	1987	0.76	1.31	52.00	24.00	10.00	66.00
Namibia	9.00	1987	0.14	1.56	87.00	6.00	12.00	82.00
Niger	14.00 a	1987	0.29	2.07	41.00	21.00	5.00	74.00
Nigeria	261.00 a	1987	3.63	1.20	34.00	31.00	15.00	54.00
Rwanda	6.30 a	1987	0.15	2.38	23.00	24.00	8.00	68.00
Sao Tome & Principe	..	1987	..	..	..	78.00	9.00	13.00
Senegal	23.20 a	1987	1.36	5.86	200.00	5.00	3.00	92.00
Seychelles	..	1987	..	..	..	58.00	7.00	35.00
Sierra Leone	160.00 a	1987	0.37	0.23	96.00	7.00	4.00	89.00
Somalia	11.50	1987	0.81	7.04	142.00	3.00	0.00	97.00
Sudan	30.00	1977	18.60	62.00	1,059.00	1.00	0.00	99.00
Swaziland	6.96 a	1987	0.29	4.10	408.00	5.00	2.00	93.00
Tanzania	76.00 a	1970	0.48	0.63	36.00	21.00	5.00	74.00
Togo	11.50	1987	0.09	0.78	28.00	62.00	13.00	25.00
Uganda	66.00 a	1970	0.20	0.30	20.00	32.00	8.00	60.00
Zaire	1,019.00 a	1987	0.70	0.07	22.00	58.00	25.00	17.00
Zambia	96.00 a	1970	0.36	0.38	87.00	63.00	11.00	26.00
Zimbabwe	23.00 a	1987	1.22	5.30	136.00	14.00	7.00	79.00
NORTH AFRICA	55.15		..	..	..	..	..	..
Algeria	18.90	1980	3.00	15.87	161.00	22.00	4.00	74.00
Egypt, Arab Republic of	1.80	1985	56.40	3,133.33	1,213.00	7.00	5.00	88.00
Libya	0.70	1985	2.62	374.29	262.00	15.00	10.00	75.00
Morocco	30.00	1985	11.00	36.67	499.00	6.00	3.00	91.00
Tunisia	3.75	1985	2.30	61.33	317.00	13.00	7.00	80.00
ALL AFRICA	3,768.53		..	..	..	..	..	..
South Africa	50.00	1970	9.20	18.40	410.00	16.00	17.00	67.00

Note: Estimated by the Institute of Geography, Moscow, former U.S.S.R.

14-8. Energy consumption: total

	Kilotons of oil equivalent										Average annual percentage growth		
	1980	1981	1982	1983	1984	1985	1986	1987	1988	1989	75-80	80-85	86-MR
SUB-SAHARAN AFRICA	120,200	125,982	139,440	143,678	147,027	149,911	148,148	153,301	159,360	161,869	7.4	4.4	6.4
excluding Nigeria	94,846	96,063	106,210	109,476	112,215	114,411	115,069	119,180	122,988	124,336	6.3	5.5	6.9
Angola	1,518	1,531	1,557	1,602	1,608	1,653	1,570	1,533	1,574	1,618	10.0	1.7	1.2
Benin	942	972	1,016	1,037	1,055	1,082	1,144	1,178	1,217	1,258	3.4	2.8	3.2
Botswana	2,388	2,433	2,520	2,615	2,695	2,802	2,885	2,993	3,133	3,256	3.6	3.3	4.2
Burkina Faso	1,633	1,678	1,717	1,762	1,800	1,843	1,899	1,956	2,013	2,070	6.3	2.4	2.9
Burundi	770	797	812	840	878	900	920	954	974	1,009	2.7	3.2	3.0
Cameroon	2,508	2,426	4,560	4,720	5,149	5,218	4,220	4,212	4,232	4,387	7.1	18.5	1.2
Cape Verde	34	34	40	36	35	31	20	26	24	26	..	..	..
Central African Republic	645	657	674	694	734	749	757	805	795	806	4.0	3.2	1.8
Chad	705	720	735	749	767	784	800	817	836	855	3.3	2.1	2.2
Comoros	12	12	12	12	12	12	15	16	17	17	..	..	..
Congo, People's Republic of the	418	429	448	465	468	487	915	911	923	961	4.1	3.1	1.6
Cote d'Ivoire	7,066	7,304	7,325	7,792	7,913	8,040	8,362	8,703	8,985	9,228	8.7	2.7	3.3
Djibouti	64	49	68	66	65	67	110	115	122	107	..	..	..
Equatorial Guinea	115	122	126	127	129	130	129	133	137	140	3.5	2.3	2.6
Ethiopia	8,086	8,213	8,386	8,511	8,559	8,697	8,922	9,265	9,428	9,626	3.7	1.4	2.5
Gabon	1,004	1,085	1,399	1,357	1,431	1,439	1,361	1,413	1,464	1,568	6.6	7.7	4.7
Gambia, The	261	266	214	236	257	258	257	266	270	271	6.8	-0.2	1.7
Ghana	3,704	3,864	4,192	4,376	4,300	4,449	4,768	4,718	4,846	4,849	7.6	3.7	0.8
Guinea	1,045	1,060	1,086	1,109	1,126	1,149	1,205	1,223	1,255	1,281	6.0	1.9	2.1
Guinea-Bissau	128	127	123	123	124	126	148	148	154	147	4.2	-0.4	0.3
Kenya	7,059	7,187	7,201	7,504	7,664	7,868	8,190	8,862	9,098	9,644	5.5	2.2	5.3
Lesotho	108	111	114	117	120	124	127	131	135	139	2.4	2.8	2.9
Liberia	1,444	1,380	1,443	1,372	1,404	1,447	1,324	1,349	1,388	1,386	12.7	0.0	1.7
Madagascar	1,666	1,691	1,577	1,554	1,674	1,724	1,882	1,976	2,037	1,959	5.1	0.4	1.5
Malawi	1,493	1,512	1,560	1,604	1,640	1,666	1,750	1,788	1,893	1,951	5.2	2.4	3.9
Mali	1,069	1,085	1,123	1,175	1,203	1,222	1,239	1,278	1,318	1,356	4.2	3.0	3.1
Mauritania	197	196	207	208	206	207	154	1,038	978	989	84.8	1.2	73.6
Mauritius	3,491	3,565	3,699	3,746	3,801	3,903	3,959	4,021	4,253	3,918	53.8	2.2	0.2
Mozambique	3,844	3,622	4,012	4,121	4,173	4,204	3,761	3,850	3,863	3,871	8.3	2.6	0.9
Namibia	..	..	..	..	..	..	..	..	..	..	..	..	..
Niger	921	932	983	1,007	1,043	1,069	1,079	1,107	1,141	1,172	5.9	3.2	2.8
Nigeria	25,354	29,920	33,231	34,202	34,812	35,500	33,079	34,121	36,371	37,532	10.9	6.4	4.5
Rwanda	1,120	1,154	1,258	1,318	1,400	1,449	1,438	1,441	1,448	1,448	-1.5	5.6	0.3
Sao Tome & Principe	11	11	12	12	12	12	20	20	22	12	..	..	..
Senegal	1,527	1,520	1,588	1,497	1,576	1,557	1,608	1,502	1,539	1,856	11.0	0.4	4.7
Seychelles	10,111	9,864	15,188	15,484	15,870	16,001	14,639	14,743	15,780	15,431	..	..	..
Sierra Leone	732	764	730	765	757	791	821	844	862	885	-15.9	1.2	2.5
Somalia	1,485	1,538	1,641	1,691	1,736	1,766	1,713	1,791	1,848	1,900	14.9	3.7	3.5
Sudan	4,710	4,834	4,972	5,026	5,180	5,253	5,421	5,589	5,764	5,746	5.7	2.2	2.1
Swaziland	1,562	1,446	1,676	1,997	2,080	2,109	2,641	2,776	2,604	2,272	3.0	8.2	-5.0
Tanzania	5,827	5,986	6,209	6,420	6,655	6,887	7,133	7,392	7,650	7,909	9.2	3.5	3.5
Togo	269	365	240	239	263	240	295	307	318	325	16.0	-4.3	3.4
Uganda	2,388	2,433	2,520	2,615	2,695	2,802	2,885	2,993	3,133	3,256	3.3	3.3	4.2
Zaire	7,066	7,304	7,325	7,792	7,913	8,040	8,362	8,703	8,985	9,228	6.0	2.7	3.3
Zambia	3,491	3,565	3,699	3,746	3,801	3,903	3,959	4,021	4,253	3,918	8.8	2.2	0.2
Zimbabwe	210	217	226	234	243	251	260	269	279	289	19.3	3.7	3.5
NORTH AFRICA	50,950	48,694	41,145	49,941	51,294	52,989	59,665	61,641	63,161	68,598	63.5	1.6	4.5
Algeria	22,826	19,600	8,254	14,039	11,639	12,043	17,413	17,726	16,538	16,671	87.4	-11.4	-2.0
Egypt, Arab Republic of	15,510	15,824	18,230	18,885	21,245	22,175	23,748	24,506	25,183	27,595	62.4	8.0	4.9
Libya	4,390	4,669	6,234	7,817	8,914	9,048	8,045	8,822	10,239	12,429	69.6	18.0	15.6
Morocco	4,855	5,061	4,904	5,219	5,198	5,317	6,178	6,227	6,638	7,169	51.5	1.7	5.2
Tunisia	3,369	3,540	3,525	3,981	4,298	4,406	4,282	4,360	4,562	4,734	31.1	6.0	3.5
ALL AFRICA	171,149	174,676	180,586	193,619	198,321	202,900	207,813	214,942	222,520	230,466	14.1	4.5	5.8
South Africa	61,307	64,723	69,056	73,459	79,301	81,573	102,789	104,273	105,250	102,622	55.0	6.2	0.0

14–9. Energy consumption: solid fuel

	Kilotons of oil equivalent										Average annual percentage growth		
	1980	1981	1982	1983	1984	1985	1986	1987	1988	1989	75–80	80–85	86–MR
SUB-SAHARAN AFRICA	..	..	..	..	..	..	..	..	..	..	..	..	..
excluding Nigeria	..	..	..	..	..	..	..	..	..	..	..	..	..
Angola	..	..	..	..	..	..	..	..	..	..	..	..	..
Benin	..	..	..	..	..	..	..	..	..	..	..	..	..
Botswana	..	..	..	..	..	..	..	..	..	..	..	..	..
Burkina Faso	0	0	0	0	0	0	0	0	0	0	..	..	..
Burundi	1	2	4	5	5	3	7	9	6	7	..	27.4	-4.0
Cameroon	0	1	1	1	1	1	1	1	1	1	..	..	..
Cape Verde	0	0	0	0	0	0	0	0	0	0	..	..	..
Central African Republic	..	..	..	..	..	..	..	..	..	..	..	..	..
Chad	0	0	0	0	0	0	0	0	0	0	..	..	..
Comoros	..	..	..	..	..	..	..	..	..	..	..	..	..
Congo, People's Republic of the	..	..	..	..	..	..	..	..	..	..	..	..	..
Cote d'Ivoire	..	..	..	..	..	..	..	..	..	..	..	..	..
Djibouti	..	..	..	..	..	..	..	..	..	..	..	..	..
Equatorial Guinea	..	..	..	..	..	..	..	..	..	..	..	..	..
Ethiopia	0	0	0	0	0	0	0	0	0	0	..	..	..
Gabon	..	..	..	..	..	..	..	..	..	..	..	..	..
Gambia, The	..	..	..	..	..	..	..	..	..	..	..	..	..
Ghana	1	1	1	1	1	1	2	3	3	3	-35.6	0.0	12.9
Guinea	..	..	..	..	..	..	..	..	..	..	..	..	..
Guinea-Bissau	..	..	..	..	..	..	..	..	..	..	..	..	..
Kenya	12	62	23	64	83	61	86	92	114	132	-46.0	33.2	16.2
Lesotho	..	..	..	..	..	..	..	..	..	..	..	..	..
Liberia	..	..	..	..	..	..	..	..	..	..	..	..	..
Madagascar	21	21	17	21	8	10	16	12	17	13	38.0	-16.7	-2.7
Malawi	51	34	43	34	27	20	28	26	66	66	-8.1	-14.8	42.0
Mali	..	..	..	..	..	..	..	..	..	..	..	..	..
Mauritania	4	4	5	5	5	5	5	6	6	6	4.6	5.2	5.6
Mauritius	1	1	1	10	17	19	46	38	38	75	..	107.4	15.8
Mozambique	172	206	294	294	308	294	66	63	65	64	0.8	11.7	-0.6
Namibia	..	..	..	..	..	..	..	..	..	..	..	..	..
Niger							..	..	..	..	..	..	..
Nigeria	126	119	42	40	38	38	111	107	103	98	-10.8	-23.7	-4.0
Rwanda	..	..	..	..	..	..	..	..	..	..	..	..	..
Sao Tome & Principe	..	..	..	..	..	..	..	..	..	..	..	..	..
Senegal	..	..	..	..	..	..	..	..	..	..	..	..	..
Seychelles	..	..	..	..	..	..	..	..	..	..	..	..	..
Sierra Leone	0	0	0	0	0	0	0	0	0	0	..	..	..
Somalia	..	..	..	..	..	..	..	..	..	..	..	..	..
Sudan	0	0	0	0	0	0	0	0	0	0	..	..	..
Swaziland	..	..	..	..	..	..	..	..	..	..	..	..	..
Tanzania	1	1	1	1	1	1	5	4	4	4	-19.7	0.0	-6.5
Togo	0	0	0	0	0	0	0	0	0	0	..	..	..
Uganda	..	..	..	..	..	..	..	..	..	..	..	..	..
Zaire	199	200	218	220	219	225	316	319	321	330	22.3	2.6	1.4
Zambia	336	293	356	267	301	301	461	386	521	330	-14.2	-2.1	-6.8
Zimbabwe	2,065	1,798	1,610	1,548	1,525	1,558	4,090	4,900	5,052	5,130	7.0	-5.4	7.4
NORTH AFRICA	1,437	2,154	1,976	2,210	2,505	2,678	3,670	4,006	4,023	4,210	..	-12.3	-18.4
Algeria	417	636	521	831	1,060	1,132	1,027	1,118	1,112	1,125	45.3	22.1	2.7
Egypt, Arab Republic of	471	752	849	595	667	729	1,042	1,087	1,095	1,095	-36.7	4.3	1.6
Libya	1	1	1	1	1	1	2	2	2	2	..	0.0	0.0
Morocco	456	651	556	715	707	750	1,514	1,704	1,698	1,860	-0.7	8.9	6.3
Tunisia	92	114	49	68	70	66	85	95	116	128	10.2	-7.7	15.3
ALL AFRICA	..	..	..	..	..	..	..	..	..	..	..	..	..
South Africa	48,184	52,350	56,938	60,262	66,500	68,669	90,216	91,665	92,581	89,975	13.3	7.5	0.0

14–10. Energy consumption: liquid fuel

	Kilotons of oil equivalent										Average annual percentage growth		
	1980	*1981*	*1982*	*1983*	*1984*	*1985*	*1986*	*1987*	*1988*	*1989*	*75–80*	*80–85*	*86–MR*
SUB-SAHARAN AFRICA	20,436	20,024	25,094	25,461	25,656	25,606	23,999	25,629	26,807	26,664	10.7	5.5	3.9
excluding Nigeria	13,496	13,093	15,355	15,825	16,076	15,967	15,378	16,876	16,821	16,822	1.4	4.5	3.1
Angola	554	530	521	523	493	523	405	320	332	337	-12.1	-1.4	-5.0
Benin	95	99	112	105	103	102	129	129	134	140	-14.9	1.2	2.9
Botswana	..	..	..	..	..	..	..	..	..	..			
Burkina Faso	129	137	138	143	139	139	150	161	168	174	30.2	1.3	5.1
Burundi	39	48	33	38	51	48	43	49	46	52	33.3	4.0	5.3
Cameroon	545	386	2,424	2,559	2,897	2,908	1,831	1,757	1,713	1,798	25.2	51.2	-0.8
Cape Verde	34	34	40	36	35	31	20	26	24	26	14.5	..	..
Central African Republic	61	59	60	64	62	62	55	87	77	88	26.7	0.8	14.0
Chad	70	70	69	68	71	71	70	69	69	68	6.3	0.3	-0.9
Comoros	12	12	12	12	12	12	15	16	17	17	-0.8	..	..
Congo, People's Republic of the	86	86	90	91	87	95	498	480	481	506	-4.8	1.6	0.5
Cote d'Ivoire	857	739	983	1,164	1,270	1,310	1,719	1,822	1,659	1,317	-15.0	11.8	-8.5
Djibouti	64	49	68	66	65	67	110	115	122	107	12.1	..	..
Equatorial Guinea	17	22	24	23	25	26	25	29	33	36	-7.1	7.3	12.3
Ethiopia	571	537	550	534	459	487	566	748	736	748	28.2	-3.6	8.6
Gabon	424	485	738	678	733	727	644	656	664	675	-3.4	11.6	1.5
Gambia, The	53	52	54	53	57	57	55	61	63	62	25.5	1.8	4.0
Ghana	546	565	659	638	573	614	806	676	746	714	-14.1	1.7	-2.6
Guinea	283	280	289	293	291	293	322	317	327	329	4.0	0.9	1.0
Guinea-Bissau	30	29	25	25	26	28	50	50	56	49	0.6	-1.9	0.8
Kenya	1,481	1,322	1,130	1,129	1,013	945	956	1,310	1,185	1,372	8.6	-8.3	10.3
Lesotho	..	..	..	..	..	..	..	..	..	..	..	..	..
Liberia	493	487	510	506	505	510	224	233	258	241	6.2	0.8	3.3
Madagascar	394	380	221	152	243	248	351	400	404	277	-2.6	-10.9	-6.8
Malawi	141	137	133	138	134	119	144	129	140	142	9.3	-2.5	0.3
Mali	136	128	135	158	154	140	128	129	136	139	12.6	2.5	3.1
Mauritania	192	191	201	202	200	201	148	1,031	970	981	10.3	1.1	75.5
Mauritius	189	188	165	186	185	183	224	275	268	266	1.7	-0.3	4.9
Mozambique	466	394	490	503	492	490	256	259	268	277	7.8	2.7	2.7
Namibia	..	..	..	..	..	..	..	..	..	..	..	..	..
Niger	171	161	186	187	185	188	184	183	190	191	24.3	2.6	1.5
Nigeria	6,940	6,931	9,739	9,636	9,580	9,639	8,620	8,754	9,986	9,843	43.3	7.7	5.4
Rwanda	50	46	112	127	126	128	118	120	127	127	23.2	25.1	2.6
Sao Tome & Principe	11	11	11	11	11	11	20	20	22	11	37.1	..	..
Senegal	784	780	845	690	752	752	785	662	679	975	1.6	-1.5	7.0
Seychelles	34	33	29	32	32	27	42	50	42	45	39.8	..	..
Sierra Leone	193	213	166	188	165	185	200	208	210	215	-0.7	-2.4	2.4
Somalia	314	312	365	369	373	367	264	292	294	294	43.0	3.9	3.3
Sudan	*1,099*	1,109	1,127	1,061	1,090	1,040	1,080	1,121	1,166	1,017	-0.9	-1.1	-1.4
Swaziland	..	..	..	..	..	..	..	..	..	..	..	..	..
Tanzania	592	560	580	575	585	579	583	599	605	606	-3.6	0.0	1.3
Togo	132	225	94	88	114	81	130	135	142	143	18.7	-12.2	3.5
Uganda	218	182	208	217	216	219	228	241	278	294	-18.4	1.7	9.5
Zaire	770	801	616	890	824	758	720	838	882	874	8.1	1.1	6.5
Zambia	684	728	643	688	635	607	427	443	453	446	4.6	-2.6	1.5
Zimbabwe	482	486	499	615	593	589	656	630	635	645	-15.1	5.3	-0.4
NORTH AFRICA	34,458	34,861	29,761	32,500	35,134	35,383	35,627	36,757	37,121	40,859	34.9	0.7	4.3
Algeria	12,235	11,973	3,861	4,763	5,649	5,686	6,546	6,541	6,659	6,829	56.5	-15.5	1.5
Egypt, Arab Republic of	12,389	12,406	14,081	14,920	16,636	16,740	17,652	18,382	18,545	19,454	21.7	7.2	3.0
Libya	3,560	4,088	5,433	5,880	6,060	6,253	4,377	5,376	4,672	6,886	36.2	12.4	13.0
Morocco	3,949	3,972	3,978	4,095	4,088	4,155	4,227	4,066	4,485	4,834	30.1	1.1	5.1
Tunisia	2,325	2,422	2,408	2,842	2,701	2,549	2,824	2,392	2,760	2,857	27.8	2.8	1.8
ALL AFRICA	54,894	54,885	54,855	57,961	60,790	60,989	59,625	62,386	63,928	67,524	24.3	0.0	-1.0
South Africa	10,420	10,372	10,189	11,071	10,727	10,832	10,810	10,787	10,803	10,823	-3.7	1.1	0.1

14–11. Energy consumption: natural gas

	Kilotons of oil equivalent										Average annual percentage growth		
	1980	1981	1982	1983	1984	1985	1986	1987	1988	1989	75–80	80–85	86–MR
SUB-SAHARAN AFRICA	..	..	..	..	..	..	..	..	..	..	..	..	..
excluding Nigeria	..	..	..	..	..	..	..	..	..	..	..	..	..
Angola	70	82	84	96	107	107	120	143	145	155	6.4	9.1	8.3
Benin	..	..	..	..	..	..	..	..	..	..	..	..	..
Botswana	..	..	..	..	..	..	..	..	..	..	..	..	..
Burkina Faso	..	..	..	..	..	..	..	..	..	..	..	..	..
Burundi	..	..	..	..	..	..	..	..	..	..	..	..	..
Cameroon	..	..	..	..	..	..	..	..	..	..			
Cape Verde	..	..	..	..	..	..	..	..	..	..	..	..	..
Central African Republic	..	..	..	..	..	..	..	..	..	..	..	..	..
Chad	..	..	..	..	..	..	..	..	..	..	..	..	..
Comoros	..	..	..	..	..	..	..	..	..	..	..	..	..
Congo, People's Republic of the	0	2	0	0	0	0	2	2	2	2	..	0.0	0.0
Cote d'Ivoire	..	..	..	..	..	..	..	..	..	..	..	..	..
Djibouti	..	..	..	..	..	..	..	..	..	..	..	..	..
Equatorial Guinea	..	..	..	..	..	..	..	..	..	..	..	..	..
Ethiopia	..	..	..	..	..	..	..	..	..	..	..	..	..
Gabon	139	141	191	191	191	187	138	160	184	258	-21.1	7.1	22.4
Gambia, The	..	..	..	..	..	..	..	..	..	..	..	..	..
Ghana	..	..	..	..	..	..	..	..	..	..	..	..	..
Guinea	..	..	..	..	..	..	..	..	..	..	..	..	..
Guinea-Bissau	..	..	..	..	..	..	..	..	..	..	..	..	..
Kenya	..	..	..	..	..	..	..	..	..	..	..	..	..
Lesotho	..	..	..	..	..	..	..	..	..	..	..	..	..
Liberia	..	..	..	..	..	..	..	..	..	..	..	..	..
Madagascar	..	..	..	..	..	..	..	..	..	..	..	..	..
Malawi	..	..	..	..	..	..	..	..	..	..	..	..	..
Mali	..	..	..	..	..	..	..	..	..	..	..	..	..
Mauritania	..	..	..	..	..	..	..	..	..	..	..	..	..
Mauritius	..	..	..	..	..	..	..	..	..	..	..	..	..
Mozambique	..	..	..	..	..	..	..	..	..	..	..	..	..
Namibia	..	..	..	..	..	..	..	..	..	..	..	..	..
Niger	..	..	..	..	..	..	..	..	..	..	..	..	..
Nigeria	732	4693	4777	5255	5281	5255	3071	3252	3510	4024	14.9	34.2	9.3
Rwanda	1	1	1	1	1	1	1	1	1	1	0.0	0.0	0.0
Sao Tome & Principe	..	..	..	..	..	..	..	..	..	..	..	..	..
Senegal	..	..	..	..	..	..	..	..	..	..	..	..	..
Seychelles	..	..	..	..	..	..	..	..	..	..	..	..	..
Sierra Leone	..	..	..	..	..	..	..	..	..	..	..	..	..
Somalia	..	..	..	..	..	..	..	..	..	..	..	..	..
Sudan	..	..	..	..	..	..	..	..	..	..	..	..	..
Swaziland	..	..	..	..	..	..	..	..	..	..	..	..	..
Tanzania	..	..	..	..	..	..	..	..	..	..	..	..	..
Togo	..	..	..	..	..	..	..	..	..	..	..	..	..
Uganda	..	..	..	..	..	..	..	..	..	..	..	..	..
Zaire	..	..	..	..	..	..	..	..	..	..	..	..	..
Zambia	..	..	..	..	..	..	..	..	..	..	..	..	..
Zimbabwe	..	..	..	..	..	..	..	..	..	..	..	..	..
NORTH AFRICA	12421	9022	6684	12453	10809	12010	17658	18255	19363	20777	64.8	2.9	-5.1
Algeria	9822	6628	3481	8064	4506	4777	9422	9618	8334	8263	48.8	-10.6	-5.2
Egypt, Arab Republic of	1443	1443	1981	2038	2597	3340	3901	4043	4528	5993	347.0	18.7	15.0
Libya	704	455	675	1811	2728	2669	3541	3319	5441	5416	..	45.1	19.4
Morocco	62	69	73	78	78	79	80	80	62	59	-6.3	4.8	-11.1
Tunisia	390	427	474	462	900	1145	714	1194	999	1046	26.6	24.2	10.2
ALL AFRICA	..	..	..	..	..	..	..	..	..	..	..	..	..
South Africa	..	..	..	..	..	..	..	..	..	..	..	..	..

14–12. Energy consumption: primary electricity

	Kilotons of oil equivalent										Average annual percentage growth		
	1980	1981	1982	1983	1984	1985	1986	1987	1988	1989	75–80	80–85	86–MR
SUB-SAHARAN AFRICA	3,215	3,127	3,203	2,928	2,882	3,090	4,584	4,414	4,524	4,385	15.5	3.2	3.0
excluding Nigeria	2,918	2,811	3,005	2,759	2,711	2,918	4,326	4,155	4,265	4,126	14.5	3.2	2.8
Benin	8	9	14	16	8	7	13	15	15	15	35.5	3.0	3.2
Burkina Faso	..	..	..	..	..	..	..	..	..	..	..	2.5	2.7
Burundi	3	4	13	12	13	13	8	9	10	10	17.6	2.9	2.9
Cape Verde	..	..	..	..	..	..	..	..	..	..	..	..	..
Central African Republic	5	5	6	6	6	6	6	6	6	6	9.3	3.5	0.6
Chad	..	..	..	..	..	..	..	..	..	..	..	2.3	2.5
Comoros	..	..	..	..	..	..	..	..	..	..	..	..	..
Djibouti	..	..	..	..	..	..	..	..	..	..	..	..	..
Equatorial Guinea	0	0	0	0	0	0	0	0	0	0	0.0	1.3	0.0
Ethiopia	40	41	50	54	54	55	55	56	56	56	14.7	1.8	2.1
Gambia, The	..	..	..	..	..	..	..	..	..	..	..	-0.6	1.1
Ghana	374	401	380	185	133	234	355	378	389	390	11.1	6.0	1.2
Guinea	7	7	7	7	7	7	14	15	15	15	0.0	2.4	2.5
Guinea-Bissau	0	0	0	0	0	0	0	0	0	0	0.0	0.0	0.0
Kenya	116	133	147	165	167	192	196	210	237	250	20.9	4.1	4.3
Lesotho	..	..	..	..	..	..	..	..	..	..	..	2.8	2.9
Liberia	25	25	29	29	29	29	27	27	28	27	-1.6	-0.5	1.4
Madagascar	10	11	20	21	21	21	23	24	26	27	-15.0	3.1	3.2
Malawi	34	34	36	39	41	42	44	48	49	49	20.2	3.2	3.4
Mali	4	4	9	11	12	12	8	15	15	15	12.2	2.9	2.9
Mauritania	..	..	..	..	..	..	..	..	..	..	..	0.0	0.0
Mozambique	340	72	81	94	97	97	29	30	32	32	156.9	3.1	0.8
Namibia	..	..	..	..	..	..	..	..	..	..	..	..	..
Niger	6	6	10	11	25	25	13	15	15	16	17.6	2.9	3.1
Rwanda	16	16	13	14	15	15	15	15	16	16	15.2	4.5	0.0
Sao Tome & Principe	0	0	1	1	1	1	1	1	1	1	..	..	..
Senegal	..	..	..	..	..	..	..	..	..	..	..	2.3	2.4
Sierra Leone	..	..	..	..	..	..	..	..	..	..	..	2.4	2.5
Somalia	..	..	..	..	..	..	..	..	..	..	..	3.6	3.5
Sudan	42	42	44	44	44	44	45	44	45	45	25.6	3.2	2.9
Tanzania	45	47	50	53	53	53	53	52	52	53	9.3	3.8	3.7
Togo	16	16	18	19	13	19	20	22	22	23	43.5	3.0	3.2
Uganda	27	37	26	37	37	53	36	38	42	50	-14.5	3.4	3.6
Zaire	358	375	371	372	371	375	436	434	441	442	3.3	3.1	3.2
Zambia	514	509	587	590	575	600	577	598	585	448	4.1	4.1	2.7
Botswana	..	..	..	..	..	..	..	..	..	..	..	3.7	3.5
Cote d'Ivoire	114	148	150	93	89	117	102	90	106	108	123.8	4.2	4.2
Mauritius	7	5	8	3	6	10	10	12	8	9	14.4	-14.9	-0.7
Seychelles	..	..	..	..	..	..	..	..	..	..	..	..	..
Swaziland	..	..	..	..	..	..	..	..	..	..	..	0.4	0.0
Zimbabwe	570	601	620	583	554	549	529	331	344	345	10.5	2.2	1.6
Angola	93	93	101	110	115	115	115	115	115	116	7.5	2.6	2.7
Cameroon	106	132	176	147	182	183	205	211	216	226	0.0	2.7	2.6
Congo, People's Republic of the	8	8	17	22	22	23	34	36	38	39	3.1	2.6	2.8
Gabon	30	30	22	22	22	22	58	58	58	58	46.5	4.1	3.5
Nigeria	297	316	198	169	171	172	180	181	181	181	25.9	3.4	3.5
NORTH AFRICA	963	968	993	968	993	1,020	1,096	904	882	954	15.1	2.8	2.3
Algeria	21	22	39	19	51	63	20	38	11	18	-7.1	3.1	3.2
Egypt, Arab Republic of	812	816	901	903	904	913	687	515	524	550	15.3	2.7	2.6
Libya	..	..	..	..	..	..	..	..	..	..	..	0.0	0.0
Morocco	128	128	50	43	32	35	54	69	80	99	20.4	4.2	1.6
Tunisia	2	2	3	3	6	9	5	9	1	0	-7.8	2.6	2.4
ALL AFRICA	16,744	15,822	16,168	15,111	14,931	15,844	22,198	20,933	21,440	20,988	18.3	3.2	2.9
South Africa	1,030	361	275	482	426	424	115	173	218	176	185.8	-0.2	0.0

14–13. Energy consumption: fuelwood

	Kilotons of oil equivalent										Average annual percentage growth		
	1980	1981	1982	1983	1984	1985	1986	1987	1988	1989	75–80	80–85	86–MR
SUB-SAHARAN AFRICA	75,227	77,616	80,300	83,048	85,611	88,077	90,853	93,642	96,419	99,156	3.2	3.2	-33.5
excluding Nigeria	57,968	59,755	61,826	63,945	65,869	67,681	69,758	71,816	73,828	75,769	3.2	-16.2	-33.6
Angola	801	826	851	873	893	908	931	955	981	1,009	3.4	2.6	2.7
Benin	839	864	890	916	944	973	1,003	1,035	1,069	1,103	2.8	3.0	3.2
Botswana	210	217	226	234	243	251	260	269	279	289	3.6	3.7	3.5
Burkina Faso	1,504	1,541	1,579	1,619	1,661	1,704	1,750	1,796	1,845	1,896	4.9	2.5	2.7
Burundi	727	743	762	785	809	836	862	887	912	939	1.8	2.9	2.9
Cameroon	1,857	1,907	1,959	2,013	2,069	2,126	2,184	2,243	2,302	2,362	2.6	2.7	2.6
Cape Verde	..	..	..	..	..	..	..	..	..	..	..	..	..
Central African Republic	579	593	608	624	666	681	696	711	711	711	2.3	3.5	0.6
Chad	635	650	666	681	696	713	730	748	767	787	2.1	2.3	2.5
Comoros	..	..	..	..	..	..	..	..	..	..	..	..	..
Congo, People's Republic of the	324	333	341	352	359	369	381	392	402	414	2.6	2.6	2.8
Cote d'Ivoire	1,577	1,644	1,713	1,786	1,862	1,940	2,022	2,108	2,196	2,289	4.3	4.2	4.2
Djibouti	..	..	..	..	..	..	..	..	..	..	..	..	..
Equatorial Guinea	98	100	102	104	104	104	104	104	104	104	1.8	1.3	0.0
Ethiopia	7,475	7,635	7,786	7,923	8,046	8,155	8,301	8,461	8,635	8,822	2.5	1.8	2.1
Gabon	411	429	448	466	485	503	521	539	558	577	-5.2	4.1	3.5
Gambia, The	208	214	160	183	200	201	203	206	207	210	3.2	-0.6	1.1
Ghana	2,783	2,897	3,152	3,552	3,593	3,600	3,605	3,662	3,708	3,742	4.9	6.0	1.2
Guinea	755	773	790	809	828	849	870	891	914	937	2.2	2.4	2.5
Guinea-Bissau	98	98	98	98	98	98	98	98	98	98	1.5	0.0	0.0
Kenya	5,450	5,670	5,901	6,146	6,401	6,670	6,952	7,249	7,561	7,890	2.3	4.1	4.3
Lesotho	108	111	114	117	120	124	127	131	135	139	2.4	2.8	2.9
Liberia	926	868	904	837	870	908	1,073	1,088	1,102	1,118	8.7	-0.5	1.4
Madagascar	1,241	1,279	1,319	1,360	1,402	1,445	1,492	1,540	1,590	1,641	2.9	3.1	3.2
Malawi	1,267	1,307	1,348	1,393	1,438	1,485	1,534	1,585	1,639	1,694	3.4	3.2	3.4
Mali	929	953	979	1,006	1,037	1,070	1,102	1,134	1,168	1,202	2.4	2.9	2.9
Mauritania	1	1	1	1	1	1	2	2	2	2	2.6	0.0	0.0
Mauritius	6	6	6	5	3	3	4	5	5	4	1.6	-14.9	-0.7
Mozambique	2,866	2,950	3,147	3,230	3,276	3,323	3,410	3,498	3,498	3,498	6.1	3.1	0.8
Namibia	..	..	..	..	..	..	..	..	..	..	..	..	..
Niger	744	765	787	809	833	856	882	909	936	965	2.6	2.9	3.1
Nigeria	17,259	17,861	18,475	19,102	19,742	20,396	21,096	21,827	22,591	23,387	3.6	3.4	3.5
Rwanda	1,053	1,091	1,132	1,176	1,258	1,305	1,305	1,305	1,305	1,305	-2.5	4.5	0.0
Sao Tome & Principe	..	..	..	..	..	..	..	..	..	..	..	..	..
Senegal	743	740	743	807	824	805	822	841	860	882	4.0	2.3	2.4
Seychelles	..	..	..	..	..	..	..	..	..	..	..	..	..
Sierra Leone	539	551	564	577	592	606	621	636	652	669	-21.1	2.4	2.5
Somalia	1,171	1,226	1,276	1,322	1,363	1,399	1,449	1,500	1,553	1,606	11.4	3.6	3.5
Sudan	3,569	3,683	3,801	3,921	4,046	4,169	4,295	4,424	4,553	4,683	3.1	3.2	2.9
Swaziland	126	130	130	130	130	130	130	130	130	130	3.0	0.4	0.0
Tanzania	5,189	5,378	5,578	5,791	6,016	6,254	6,492	6,737	6,989	7,245	8.5	3.8	3.7
Togo	121	124	128	132	136	140	145	150	154	159	2.5	3.0	3.2
Uganda	2,143	2,214	2,286	2,361	2,442	2,530	2,621	2,714	2,812	2,912	3.3	3.4	3.6
Zaire	5,739	5,928	6,120	6,310	6,499	6,682	6,891	7,111	7,341	7,581	3.4	3.1	3.2
Zambia	1,957	2,035	2,113	2,201	2,290	2,395	2,494	2,595	2,693	2,693	2.8	4.1	2.7
Zimbabwe	1,200	1,280	1,321	1,293	1,335	1,369	1,394	1,430	1,460	1,460	4.4	2.2	1.6
NORTH AFRICA	1,671	1,689	1,731	1,810	1,853	1,898	1,944	1,991	2,037	2,084	3.3	-16.5	-33.9
Algeria	331	341	352	362	373	385	397	410	423	436	3.1	3.1	3.2
Egypt, Arab Republic of	395	407	418	429	441	453	466	478	491	503	2.7	2.7	2.6
Libya	125	125	125	125	125	125	125	125	125	125	2.0	0.0	0.0
Morocco	260	241	247	288	293	298	303	308	313	318	7.0	4.2	1.6
Tunisia	560	575	591	606	621	637	654	670	686	702	2.6	2.6	2.4
ALL AFRICA	78,571	80,945	83,686	86,502	89,113	91,623	94,446	97,281	100,104	102,888	3.2	-16.2	-33.5
South Africa	1,673	1,640	1,654	1,644	1,648	1,648	1,648	1,648	1,648	1,648	0.7	-0.2	0.0

14-14. Energy consumption: thermal electricity

	Kilotons of oil equivalent										Average annual percentage growth		
	1980	*1981*	*1982*	*1983*	*1984*	*1985*	*1986*	*1987*	*1988*	*1989*	*75–80*	*80–85*	*86–MR*
SUB-SAHARAN AFRICA	48,249	47,097	50,307	48,652	48,588	50,568	38,450	39,443	40,020	39,041	14.8	0.8	0.6
excluding Nigeria	41,410	39,897	41,858	39,959	39,759	41,708	31,614	32,587	33,149	32,163	11.8	-0.1	0.7
Angola	1,500	1,500	1,600	1,740	1,790	1,790	1,252	1,259	1,266	1,273	7.3	4.4	0.6
Benin	105	115	171	187	95	90	108	121	122	124	31.9	-3.5	4.2
Botswana	..	..	..	..	..	..	..	..	..	..	..	..	..
Burkina Faso	113	115	107	110	115	115	86	87	90	91	41.3	0.3	1.9
Burundi	40	47	152	142	147	152	62	76	82	82	20.1	33.2	9.4
Cameroon	1,340	1,655	2,147	1,804	2,230	2,237	1,710	1,766	1,806	1,887	1.4	9.8	3.2
Cape Verde	9	9	19	21	25	26	20	22	24	24	4.8	27.4	8.2
Central African Republic	64	65	70	71	74	75	66	64	65	64	9.0	3.5	-0.5
Chad	64	65	65	65	65	65	36	36	36	36	5.8	0.2	0.8
Comoros	10	10	10	10	10	10	10	10	10	11	38.8	0.0	4.1
Congo, People's Republic of the	157	165	226	260	260	264	279	300	308	320	15.5	12.4	4.5
Cote d'Ivoire	1,743	1,903	1,950	1,966	1,644	1,785	1,459	1,587	1,615	1,640	29.7	-0.9	3.8
Djibouti	105	110	126	147	148	150	120	124	122	122	17.3	8.4	0.5
Equatorial Guinea	26	26	14	15	15	15	11	12	12	12	5.9	-11.6	1.8
Ethiopia	675	677	763	819	816	831	564	566	570	573	0.7	4.9	0.5
Gabon	450	450	530	535	539	540	606	610	613	613	26.1	4.3	0.4
Gambia, The	40	40	40	40	42	42	40	43	48	44	18.4	1.1	4.2
Ghana	4,492	4,793	4,460	2,189	1,588	2,766	2,943	3,127	3,214	3,222	11.2	-16.8	3.0
Guinea	500	498	498	499	499	500	348	350	358	362	-0.2	0.0	1.4
Guinea-Bissau	14	13	13	13	14	14	10	10	10	10	-5.2	0.6	2.8
Kenya	1,805	1,909	2,112	2,407	2,468	2,707	1,932	1,962	2,066	2,107	18.3	8.7	3.2
Lesotho	..	..	..	..	..	..	..	..	..	..	..	..	..
Liberia	900	1,100	891	887	897	904	573	577	583	580	2.7	-1.7	0.5
Madagascar	415	425	432	450	452	449	350	352	371	393	10.4	1.8	4.1
Malawi	432	426	445	485	509	513	369	403	408	410	19.9	4.3	3.3
Mali	110	110	129	150	164	164	143	147	147	148	7.6	10.0	1.0
Mauritania	102	102	103	103	102	103	77	84	85	86	3.5	0.1	3.5
Mauritius	438	441	452	501	510	521	370	412	447	448	13.1	4.1	6.8
Mozambique	4,471	1,299	1,349	1,500	1,540	1,540	497	541	559	566	102.2	-12.6	4.4
Namibia	..	..	..	..	..	..	..	..	..	..	..	..	..
Niger	134	135	269	175	339	338	219	234	239	243	7.6	22.0	3.4
Nigeria	6,839	7,200	8,449	8,693	8,829	8,860	6,836	6,857	6,871	6,878	41.1	5.7	0.2
Rwanda	193	193	155	165	173	174	122	130	133	136	16.2	-2.2	3.5
Sao Tome & Principe	11	11	11	11	15	15	10	10	10	10	16.0	7.3	2.1
Senegal	559	599	675	677	695	696	441	465	421	441	14.9	4.5	-1.0
Seychelles	50	51	53	56	56	62	46	54	58	59	31.4	4.1	8.7
Sierra Leone	235	235	270	277	280	278	74	110	117	141	8.0	4.1	22.1
Somalia	75	75	75	92	140	145	177	178	180	180	16.6	16.6	0.7
Sudan	*1,000*	1,000	1,010	1,010	1,032	1,037	736	738	742	742	17.1	0.8	0.3
Swaziland	..	..	..	..	..	..	..	..	..	..	..	..	..
Tanzania	710	715	834	867	870	875	617	611	615	619	3.6	4.9	0.2
Togo	252	254	230	255	260	247	185	208	215	217	34.8	0.2	5.3
Uganda	335	447	313	440	441	621	294	310	343	407	-13.9	10.2	11.3
Zaire	4,295	4,490	4,469	4,460	4,448	4,500	3,652	3,639	3,694	3,699	2.8	0.6	0.5
Zambia	6,172	6,120	6,878	6,891	6,726	7,010	4,718	4,894	4,791	3,680	2.9	2.7	-7.4
Zimbabwe	7,269	7,504	7,742	7,467	7,526	7,342	6,285	6,359	6,555	6,566	7.5	0.1	1.6
NORTH AFRICA	38,540	39,657	47,252	50,364	52,155	54,721	51,109	53,171	56,151	59,066	32.4	7.8	5.0
Algeria	7,123	7,170	9,370	10,198	11,253	12,360	9,066	9,628	10,431	10,706	33.1	12.7	6.0
Egypt, Arab Republic of	18,520	18,590	22,576	22,800	22,870	23,220	24,685	24,105	24,762	25,804	28.6	5.2	1.6
Libya	4,833	5,600	6,000	7,150	7,270	8,170	9,287	10,909	11,189	12,587	53.5	10.8	9.8
Morocco	5,267	5,277	6,132	6,664	6,877	6,950	4,969	5,202	6,178	6,333	27.2	6.7	9.4
Tunisia	2,797	3,020	3,174	3,552	3,885	4,021	3,103	3,327	3,591	3,636	38.7	8.0	5.7
ALL AFRICA	86,789	86,754	97,559	99,016	100,743	105,289	89,354	92,395	95,946	98,335	21.6	4.2	3.3
South Africa	105,306	100,667	111,028	113,984	122,723	122,587	100,785	104,335	109,099	113,174	16.7	4.0	4.0

14–15. Net additions to the greenhouse heating effect

	Carbon dioxide emissions (000 mt carbon)			Methane emissions	1986 CFC Use	Net total atmospheric increase (000 mt carbon)
	Fossil fuels and cement (1987)	Annual land use change	Net annual atmospheric increase	Equivalent carbon dioxide heating effect (000 mt carbon)	Equivalent carbon dioxide heating effect (000 mt carbon)	
SUB-SAHARAN AFRICA	16,261	167,714	184,883	31,033	..	224,400
excluding Nigeria	9,461	142,714	152,883	27,933	..	171,400
Angola	540	2,400	2,900	470	..	3,400
Benin	61	1,100	1,100	160	..	1,300
Botswana	190	310	490	370	..	860
Burkina Faso	54	1,800	1,900	470	..	2,400
Burundi	20	-1	19	120	..	140
Cameroon	720	15,000	16,000	580	..	16,000
Cape Verde	4	..	4	5	..	9
Central African Republic	31	1,500	1,600	210	..	1,800
Chad	24	1,800	1,900	590	..	2,400
Comoros	6	..	6	31	..	37
Congo, People's Republic of the	210	1,400	1,600	26	..	1,600
Cote d'Ivoire	630	43,000	44,000	550	..	47,000
Djibouti	31	..	31	32	..	64
Equatorial Guinea	8	110	120	4	..	120
Ethiopia	320	3,400	3,700	4,000	..	7,800
Gabon	600	780	1,400	12	..	1,400
Gambia, The	22	85	110	53	..	160
Ghana	360	3,300	3,600	300	2,400	6,300
Guinea	110	3,800	3,900	890	..	4,800
Guinea–Bissau	14	1,300	1,300	200	..	1,500
Kenya	610	680	1,300	1,800	..	3,100
Lesotho	..	..	..	120	..	..
Liberia	81	3,300	3,400	180	410	4,000
Madagascar	100	10,000	10,000	2,600	..	13,000
Malawi	58	6,800	6,900	350	..	7,300
Mali	46	910	960	1,100	..	2,100
Mauritania	380	..	380	430	..	810
Mauritius	140	..	140	15	..	160
Mozambique	140	3,000	3,200	380	..	3,600
Namibia	..	..	..	..	..	..
Niger	89	700	790	720	..	1,500
Nigeria	6,800	25,000	32,000	3,100	18,000	53,000
Rwanda	43	130	170	140	..	310
Sao Tome & Principe	..	..	..	..	..	..
Senegal	270	1,300	1,500	400	1,200	3,100
Seychelles	..	..	..	..	..	..
Sierra Leone	66	430	500	290	..	790
Somalia	110	430	550	1,900	..	2,400
Sudan	390	12,000	12,000	3,300	..	15,000
Swaziland	53	..	53	78	..	130
Tanzania	250	2,100	2,300	2,300	..	4,600
Togo	54	300	360	87	..	440
Uganda	86	950	1,000	780	..	1,800
Zaire	420	15,000	16,000	790	..	16,000
Zambia	320	1,800	2,100	340	..	2,500
Zimbabwe	1,800	1,800	3,600	760	1,500	5,900
NORTH AFRICA	24,400		24,400	17,510	..	52,800
Algeria	8,400	..	8,400	12,000	4,100	25,000
Egypt, Arab Republic of	9,000	..	9,000	3,100	5,100	17,000
Libya	3,200	..	3,200	1,300	..	4,500
Morocco	2,400	..	2,400	860	..	3,300
Tunisia	1,400	..	1,400	250	1,300	3,000
ALL AFRICA	40,661	167,714	209,283	48,543	..	277,200
South Africa	34,000	..	34,000	7,800	5,800	47,000

Technical Notes

Data on land area and uses, forest resources, roundwood production and consumption, water resources, and greenhouse gas discharges are from *World Resources 1990-91* or from World Resources Institute's unpublished data base. World Resource Institute draws the data from the FAO, to which member countries submit a detailed account of natural resources in reply to questionnaires. Definitions are also from *World Resources (1990-91)*. The definitions for arable land, land under permanent crops, and other land are taken from the *World Bank Statistical Manual (1983)*.

Data on energy consumption is from United Nation's *Yearbook of World Energy Statistics*. The data are compiled primarily from annual questionnaires distributed by the United Nations Statistical Office and supplemented by official national statistical publications. Where official data are not available or are inconsistent, estimates are made by the statistical office.

Table 14-1. Land use: agriculture

This table includes data on land area, size of arable land, land under permanent crops, and permanent pasture. Land area shows the size of the country less the area of major inland water bodies. Arable land includes land under temporary crops, temporary meadows for mowing or pasture, land under market and kitchen gardens, and land temporarily fallow or lying idle. Land under permanent crops refers to land cultivated with crops that occupy the land for long periods and need not be replaced after each harvest, such as coffee, cocoa, and fruit trees. Permanent pasture indicates the size of the area covered both by natural and cultivated crops used primarily for grazing.

Table 14-2. Land use: forest and other

This comprises forest and woodland, other land, protected area, and wilderness area. Forest and woodland pertains to land area covered by either natural or planted trees and areas that are logged over but are planned for reforestation. Other land represents land area that is uncultivated and grassland that is not used as forage. Protected area represents areas set up explicitly for wildlife conservation. Wilderness area includes lands with no prospect for immediate development such as settlements. Wilderness is not included in calculating land area because often times forest and woodland and other land are classified under wilderness.

Table 14-3. Forest resources

Provides data on the extent of forest and woodland, average annual deforestation, average annual reforestation, and protected closed forest. The extent of forest and woodland comprises area covered by naturally grown woody vegetation in which trees predominate. Closed forest pertains to land that is predominantly covered by trees, while open forest refers to land covered by trees and grassland with at least 10 percent of the land covered by trees. Average annual deforestation refers to the permanent destruction of forest resources. Average annual reforestation depicts rates of forest resources planting. Regeneration of old trees is not included.

Table 14-4. Roundwood production: total

Total roundwood production is harvesting and processing of woods in the rough for fuel and charcoal, and industrial uses.

Table 14-5. Roundwood production: for industrial use

This refers to all roundwood products other than woodfuel and charcoal. Common products include sawlogs, veneer logs, and pulpwood.

Table 14-6. Roundwood production: for fuel and charcoal

This contains information on all rough wood harvested and used for cooking, heating, and power production. Roundwood used for charcoal production is also included.

Table 14-7. Freshwater withdrawal

This table provides information on water resources and their use by sector. The primary sources of fresh water include internal renewable resources and annual river flows from other countries. Annual internal renewable water resources refers to the average annual accumulation of rivers and aquifers generated from endogenous precipitation. Per capita annual withdrawal is derived by dividing total annual withdrawal figures by the appropriate year's population data.

Notably, North African countries rely primarily on river flows from other countries to meet their needs. For instance, Egypt's annual withdrawal for the year 1985 is 56.4 cubic kilometers while its annual internal renewable water resource is only 1.8 cubic kilometers — hence the figure 3,133.3 for annual withdrawal percentage of water resource.

Table 14-8. Energy consumption: total

Total commercial energy consumption, including energy generated from primary electricity, solid, liquid, gaseous, and fuelwood fuels is reported on this table. Energy consumption data are provided in kilotons of oil equivalent (ktoe) or kilotons of coal equivalent (ktce). Original national production data reported in other units are converted to oil equivalent on the bases of the heat energy that may be obtained from each of them under ideal conditions.

Some energy is lost to the environment in the process of converting heat energy to mechanical energy. Different publications use different conversion factors to account for the loss of energy during the conversion process; hence the differences in the data reported. For instance, the United Nations converts electricity on the basis of the heat energy produced under ideal conditions, that is, at the coal equivalency of 0.123 metric tons per 1,000 kilowatt hours. The Economic Analysis and Projection (now International Economics) Department of the World Bank, however, computes the coal equivalency of electricity at 3.1 times the UN conversion factor to approximate the average conditions of electricity generation.

Table 14-9. Energy consumption: solid fuel

This represents data on the energy derived from bituminous coal, lignite, peat, and oil shale burned directly. Lignite is a form of coal with a low degree of coalification, which has retained the anatomical structure of the vegetable matter from which it was formed. Peat refers to solid fuel formed from the partial decomposition of dead vegetation under conditions of high humidity and limited air access. Oil shale is a sedimentary rock containing a high proportion of organic matter (kerogen), which can be converted to crude oil or gas by heating. In general less than half of African countries consume energy from solid fuel.

Table 14-10. Energy consumption: liquid fuel

Table 14-10 provides data on the energy consumption of crude petroleum and natural gas liquids. Crude petroleum refers to mineral oil consisting of a mixture of hydrocarbons of natural origin and of variable specific gravity and viscosity, including crude mineral oils extracted from bituminous minerals. Natural gas liquids constitute liquid or liquified hydrocarbon produced in the manufacture, purification and stabilization of natural gas.

Table 14-11. Energy consumption: natural gas

Presents information on the consumption of natural gas and other petroleum gases. Natural gas is a mix of hydrocarbon compounds and small quantities of nonhydrocarbons existing in the gaseous phase or in solution with oil in natural underground reservoirs.

Table 14-12. Energy consumption: primary electricity

Comprises electricity generated from nuclear, geothermal, and hydroelectric power. The data show gross production by a generation station before auxiliaries and transformer losses within the station are deducted.

Table 14-13. Energy consumption: fuelwood

This table show the conversion of fuelwood (solid volume, 0.333 TCE/m³), which is based on the average 20-30 percent moisture content. The UN's production data include the volumetric equivalent of charcoal, using a factor of 6 to convert from a weight basis. Unesco (1987) uses fuelwood (10^3 m³) = 9.768 terajoules/metric tons.

Table 14-14. Energy consumption: thermal electricity

This refers to electricity generated from thermal sources. Since the production of thermal electricity uses other fuels, to avoid double counting, it is not included in total energy consumption. Because of an energy loss in the process of conversion, a thermal efficiency of 34 percent is used in converting electricity into oil equivalences.

Table 14-15. Net additions to the greenhouse heating effect

Presents the three most important greenhouse gases: carbon dioxide, methane, and chlorofluorocarbon (CFC).

Conversion factors for common energy units

Kilo = 10^3
Mega = 10^6
Giga = 10^9
Tera = 10^{12}
Peta = 10^{15}

1 gigawatt hour = 3.6 X 10^{12} joules
1 gigawatt hour = 0.086 kilo tons of oil equivalent (ktoe)
1 ktoe = 0.7 kilo tons of coal equivalent (ktce)
1 petajoul (10^{15} joules) = 0.0009478 Quads (10^{15} British termal units).
1 petajoul (10^{15} joules) = 163,400 "UN standard" barrels of oil.
7.3 barrels of oil = 1 metric tone
1 kcal/kg = 0.555 BTU/lb

1 Jule = 0.2388 calories. One calorie provides the amount of energy that will raise the temperature of one gram of water from 14.5 to 15.5 degrees celsius at a constant pressure of one atmosphere.

1 British termal unit (BTU)= the heat required to raise the temperature of one pound of water by one degree fahrenheit.

References

Armitage, Jane, and Gunter Schramm. 1989. "Managing the Supply and Demand for Fuelwood in Africa." In Gunter Schramm and Jeremy Warford, eds., *Environmental Management and Economic Development*. Baltimore, Md.: Johns Hopkins University Press.

Candoy-Sekse, Rebecca. 1988. *Techniques of Privatization of State-Owned Enterprises. Volume III. Inventory of Country Experience and Reference Materials*. World Bank Technical Paper 90. Washington, D.C.

Development Assistance Committee (DAC). 1988. *Development Cooperation*. Chairman's report. Paris.

Food and Agriculture Organization (FAO). 1987. *Agrostat Code Book*. Rome.

—. annual. *Food and Agriculture Organization Production Yearbook*. Rome.

—. annual. *Fertilizer Yearbook*. Rome.

—. annual. *Food Aid in Figures*. Rome.

—. annual. *Trade Yearbook*. Rome.

—. annual. *Yearbook of Forest Products*. Rome.

Galal, Ahmed. 1990. "Public Enterprise Reform: A Challenge for the World Bank. PRE Working Paper 407. World Bank, Country Economics Department, Washington D.C. Processed.

—. 1991. *Public Enterprise Reform: Lessons from the Past and Issues for the Future*. World Bank Discussion Paper 119. Washington, D.C.: World Bank.

Heller, Peter S., and Alan A. Tait. 1983. *Government Employment and Pay: Some International Comparisons*. IMF Occasional Paper 24. Washington, D.C.

Hemming, Richard, and Ali M. Mansoor. 1988. Privatization and Public Enterprises. IMF. Occasional Paper 56.

International Labour Organization (ILO). annual. *Yearbook of Labor Statistics*. Geneva.

—. 1987. *World Labour Report*. Oxford University Press. Oxford.

International Labour Organization and the United Nations Research and Training Institute for the Advancement of Women (INSTRAW). 1990. *Women in Economic Activity: A Global Statistical Survey (1950–2000)*. Geneva.

International Monetary Fund (IMF) 1977. *Balance of Payments Manual, Fourth Edition*. Washington, D.C.

—. 1986. *Manual on Government Finance Statistics*. Washington, D.C.

—. annual. *Balance of Payments Yearbook*. Washington, D.C.

—. annual. *Government Finance Statistics. Yearbook*. Washington, D.C.

—. monthly. *International Financial Statistics*. Washington, D.C.

Jager, William, and Charles Humphreys. 1988. "The Effect of Policy Reforms on Agricultural Incentives in Sub–Saharan Africa." *American Journal of Agricultural Economics* 70 (5): 1036–43.

McCarthy, F. Desmond ed. 1990. *Problems of Developing Countries in the 1990s. Volume I, General Topics*. World Bank Discussion Paper 97. Washington, D.C.

Metallgesellschaft AG. annual. *Metallstatistik*. Frankfurt am Main.

Myers, Norman. 1989. "The Environmental Basis of Sustainable Development." In Gunter Schramm and Jeremy Warford, eds., *Environmental Management and Economic Development*. Baltimore, Md.: Johns Hopkins University Press.

Nair, Govindan, and Anastosios Filppides. 1988. "How Much Do State–Owned Enterprises Contribute to Public Sector Deficits in Developing Countries?" PPR Working Paper 45, World Bank, Development Economics Vice Presidency, Washington, D.C. Processed.

Numbering, Barbara. 1990. "Public Sector Management Issues in Structural Adjustment Lending." PRE Working Paper 217. World Bank, Country Economics Department, Washington D.C. Processed.

Ogbu, Michael, and Mark Gallagher. 1991. "On Public Expenditure and Delivery of Education in Sub–Saharan Africa." *Comparative Education Review 35* (2).

Organisation for Economic Co–operation and Development (OECD). 1983–88. *Geographical Distribution of Financial Flows to Developing Countries*. Paris.

Swanson, Daniel, and Teferra Wolde–Semait. 1989. *Africa's Public Enterprise Sector and Evidence of Reforms*. World Bank Technical Paper 95. Washington, D.C.

Republic of South Africa. 1990a. *South Africa Statistics*. Pretoria: Government Printer.

–. 1990b. *South Africa Labour Statistics*. Pretoria: Government Printer.

United Nations. 1989. *Compendium of Statistics and Indicators on the Situation of Women*. Department of International Economic and Social Affairs. New York.

–. annual. *Yearbook. G., International Trade Statistics*. New York.

United Nations Children's Fund (UNICEF). annual. *The State of the World's Children*. New York.

United Nations Department of International Economic and Social Affairs. Various years. *Population and Vital Statistics Report*. New York.

United Nations Development Programme. *Human Development Report 1990*. New York.

United Nations Development Programme and the World Bank. 1989. *African Economic and Financial Data*. Washington, D.C.

United Nations Statistical Office. 1975. "United Nations Standard International Trade Classification," revision 2 (SITC, rev. 2). *Statistical Papers*, Series M. no. 32, rev 2. New York.

United Nations Educational, Scientific and Cultural Organization (UNESCO). 1982. *Conferences of Ministers of Education and Those Responsible for Economic Planning in African Member States*. Paris

–. 1986. *Regional Bulletin of Education Statistics BREDA - STAT*. Regional Office for Education in Africa. Paris.

–. 1989. *Trends and Projections of Enrollment by Level of Education and by Age, 1960-2025 (as assessed in 1989.)* Division of Statistics on Education. Paris.

–. 1990a. *Basic Education and Literacy: World Statistical Indicators*. Paris.

–. 1990b. *Compendium of Statistics on Illiteracy: 1990 Edition. Division of Statistics on Education*. Paris.

–. annual. *Statistical Yearbook*. Paris.

United States, Department of Commerce. 1984. *Women of the World: Sub-Saharan Africa*. Washington, D.C.

–. 1985. Women of the World: *Near East and North Africa*. Washington, D.C.

World Bank. 1988. *Education in Sub-Saharan Africa: Policies for Adjustment, Revitaization, and Expansion*. Washington, D.C.

–. 1990. *The World Bank and the Environment: First Annual Report, Fiscal 1990*. Washington, D.C.

–. 1991a. *World Development Report 1991*. New York: Oxford University Press.

–. 1991b. *World Population Projections, 1989-90 Edition*. Washington, D.C.

–. annual. *Commodity Trade Price Trends*. Washington, D.C.

—. annual. *Social Indicators of Development*. Washington, D.C.

—. annual. *Trends in Developing Economies*. Washington, D.C.

—. annual. *World Bank Atlas*. Washington,

—. annual. *World Debt Tables*. Washington, D.C.

—. annual. *World Tables*. Washington, D.C.

World Resources Institute. 1990-91. *World Resources*. Washington, D.C.

World Bureau of Metal Statistics Monthly. *World Metal Statistics*. London.

World Health Organization. annual. *World Health Statistics Annual*. Geneva.

—. various issues. *World Health Statistics Quarterly*. Geneva.

Distributors of World Bank Publications

ARGENTINA
Carlos Hirsch, SRL
Galeria Guemes
Florida 165, 4th Floor-Ofc. 453/465
1333 Buenos Aires

AUSTRALIA, PAPUA NEW GUINEA,
FIJI, SOLOMON ISLANDS,
VANUATU, AND WESTERN SAMOA
D.A. Books & Journals
648 Whitehorse Road
Mitcham 3132
Victoria

AUSTRIA
Gerold and Co.
Graben 31
A-1011 Wien

BAHRAIN
Bahrain Research and Consultancy
  Associates Ltd.
Esterad Building No. 42
Diplomatic Area
P.O. Box 2750
Manama Town 317

BANGLADESH
Micro Industries Development
  Assistance Society (MIDAS)
House 5, Road 16
Dhanmondi R/Area
Dhaka 1209

  Branch offices:
  156, Nur Ahmed Sarak
  Chittagong 4000

  76, K.D.A. Avenue
  Kulna

BELGIUM
Jean De Lannoy
Av. du Roi 202
1060 Brussels

CANADA
Le Diffuseur
C.P. 85, 1501B rue Ampère
Boucherville, Québec
J4B 5E6

CHINA
China Financial & Economic
  Publishing House
8, Da Fo Si Dong Jie
Beijing

COLOMBIA
Infoenlace Ltda.
Apartado Aereo 34270
Bogota D.E.

COTE D'IVOIRE
Centre d'Edition et de Diffusion
  Africaines (CEDA)
04 B.P. 541
Abidjan 04 Plateau

CYPRUS
MEMRB Information Services
P.O. Box 2098
Nicosia

DENMARK
SamfundsLitteratur
Rosenoerns Allé 11
DK-1970 Frederiksberg C

DOMINICAN REPUBLIC
Editora Taller, C. por A.
Restauración e Isabel la Católica 309
Apartado Postal 2190
Santo Domingo

EGYPT, ARAB REPUBLIC OF
Al Ahram
Al Galaa Street
Cairo

The Middle East Observer
41, Sherif Street
Cairo

EL SALVADOR
Fusades
Avenida Manuel Enrique Araujo #3530
Edificio SISA, 1er. Piso
San Salvador

FINLAND
Akateeminen Kirjakauppa
P.O. Box 128
Helsinki 10
SF-00101

FRANCE
World Bank Publications
66, avenue d'Iéna
75116 Paris

GERMANY
UNO-Verlag
Poppelsdorfer Allee 55
D-5300 Bonn 1

GREECE
KEME
24, Ippodamou Street Platia Plastiras
Athens-11635

GUATEMALA
Librerias Piedra Santa
5a. Calle 7-55
Zona 1
Guatemala City

HONG KONG, MACAO
Asia 2000 Ltd.
48-48 Wyndham Street
Winning Centre
2nd Floor
Central Hong Kong

INDIA
Allied Publishers Private Ltd.
751 Mount Road
Madras - 600 002

  Branch offices:
  15 J.N. Heredia Marg
  Ballard Estate
  Bombay - 400 038

  13/14 Asaf Ali Road
  New Delhi - 110 002

  17 Chittaranjan Avenue
  Calcutta - 700 072

  Jayadeva Hostel Building
  5th Main Road Gandhinagar
  Bangalore - 560 009

  3-5-1129 Kachiguda Cross Road
  Hyderabad - 500 027

  Prarthana Flats, 2nd Floor
  Near Thakore Baug, Navrangpura
  Ahmedabad - 380 009

  Patiala House
  16-A Ashok Marg
  Lucknow - 226 001

INDONESIA
Pt. Indira Limited
Jl. Sam Ratulangi 37
P.O. Box 181
Jakarta Pusat

ISRAEL
Yozmot Literature Ltd.
P.O. Box 56055
Tel Aviv 61560
Israel

ITALY
Licosa Commissionaria Sansoni SPA
Via Duca Di Calabria, 1/1
Casella Postale 552
50125 Florence

JAPAN
Eastern Book Service
37-3, Hongo 3-Chome, Bunkyo-ku 113
Tokyo

KENYA
Africa Book Service (E.A.) Ltd.
P.O. Box 45245
Nairobi

KOREA, REPUBLIC OF
Pan Korea Book Corporation
P.O. Box 101, Kwangwhamun
Seoul

KUWAIT
MEMRB Information Services
P.O. Box 5465

MALAYSIA
University of Malaya Cooperative
  Bookshop, Limited
P.O. Box 1127, Jalan Pantai Baru
Kuala Lumpur

MEXICO
INFOTEC
Apartado Postal 22-860
14060 Tlalpan, Mexico D.F.

MOROCCO
Société d'Etudes Marketing Marocaine
12 rue Mozart, Bd. d'Anfa
Casablanca

NETHERLANDS
De Lindeboom/InOr-Publikaties
P.O. Box 202
7480 AE Haaksbergen

NEW ZEALAND
Hills Library and Information Service
Private Bag
New Market
Auckland

NIGERIA
University Press Limited
Three Crowns Building Jericho
Private Mail Bag 5095
Ibadan

NORWAY
Narvesen Information Center
Book Department
P.O. Box 6125 Etterstad
N-0602 Oslo 6

OMAN
MEMRB Information Services
P.O. Box 1613, Seeb Airport
Muscat

PAKISTAN
Mirza Book Agency
65, Shahrah-e-Quaid-e-Azam
P.O. Box No. 729
Lahore 3

PERU
Editorial Desarrollo SA
Apartado 3824
Lima

PHILIPPINES
International Book Center
Fifth Floor, Filipinas Life Building
Ayala Avenue, Makati
Metro Manila

PORTUGAL
Livraria Portugal
Rua Do Carmo 70-74
1200 Lisbon

SAUDI ARABIA, QATAR
Jarir Book Store
P.O. Box 3196
Riyadh 11471

MEMRB Information Services
  Branch offices:
  Al Alsa Street
  Al Dahna Center
  First Floor
  P.O. Box 7188
  Riyadh

  Haji Abdullah Alireza Building
  King Khaled Street
  P.O. Box 3969
  Damman

  33, Mohammed Hassan Awad Street
  P.O. Box 5978
  Jeddah

SINGAPORE, TAIWAN,
MYANMAR,BRUNEI
Information Publications
  Private, Ltd.

02-06 1st Fl., Pei-Fu Industrial
  Bldg.
24 New Industrial Road
Singapore 1953

SOUTH AFRICA, BOTSWANA
For single titles:
Oxford University Press
  Southern Africa
P.O. Box 1141
Cape Town 8000

For subscription orders:
International Subscription Service
P.O. Box 41095
Craighall
Johannesburg 2024

SPAIN
Mundi-Prensa Libros, S.A.
Castello 37
28001 Madrid

Librería Internacional AEDOS
Consell de Cent, 391
08009 Barcelona

SRI LANKA AND THE MALDIVES
Lake House Bookshop
P.O. Box 244
100, Sir Chittampalam A.
  Gardiner Mawatha
Colombo 2

SWEDEN
For single titles:
Fritzes Fackboksforetaget
Regeringsgatan 12, Box 16356
S-103 27 Stockholm

For subscription orders:
Wennergren-Williams AB
Box 30004
S-104 25 Stockholm

SWITZERLAND
For single titles:
Librairie Payot
6, rue Grenus
Case postale 381
CH 1211 Geneva 11

For subscription orders:
Librairie Payot
Service des Abonnements
Case postale 3312
CH 1002 Lausanne

TANZANIA
Oxford University Press
P.O. Box 5299
Dar es Salaam

THAILAND
Central Department Store
306 Silom Road
Bangkok

TRINIDAD & TOBAGO, ANTIGUA
BARBUDA, BARBADOS,
DOMINICA, GRENADA, GUYANA,
JAMAICA, MONTSERRAT, ST.
KITTS & NEVIS, ST. LUCIA,
ST. VINCENT & GRENADINES
Systematics Studies Unit
#9 Watts Street
Curepe
Trinidad, West Indies

UNITED ARAB EMIRATES
MEMRB Gulf Co.
P.O. Box 6097
Sharjah

UNITED KINGDOM
Microinfo Ltd.
P.O. Box 3
Alton, Hampshire GU34 2PG
England

VENEZUELA
Libreria del Este
Aptdo. 60.337
Caracas 1060-A